Revised Second Edition

Masterplots

1,801 Plot Stories and Critical Evaluations
of the World's Finest Literature

Revised Second Edition

Volume 11
Spo – Und
6241 – 6868

Edited by
FRANK N. MAGILL

Story Editor, Revised Edition
DAYTON KOHLER

Consulting Editor, Revised Second Edition
LAURENCE W. MAZZENO

SALEM PRESS
Pasadena, California   Englewood Cliffs, New Jersey

96-284

Editor in Chief: Dawn P. Dawson

Consulting Editor: Laurence W. Mazzeno	*Managing Editor:* Christina J. Moose
Project Editors: Eric Howard	*Research Supervisor:* Jeffry Jensen
Juliane Brand	*Research:* Irene McDermott
Acquisitions Editor: Mark Rehn	*Proofreading Supervisor:* Yasmine A. Cordoba
Production Editor: Cynthia Breslin Beres	*Layout:* William Zimmerman

Library of Congress Cataloging-in-Publication Data
Masterplots / edited by Frank N. Magill; consulting editor, Laurence W. Mazzeno. — Rev. 2nd ed.
    p.   cm.
Expanded and updated version of the 1976 rev. ed.
Includes bibliographical references and indexes.
1. Literature—Stories, plots, etc. 2. Literature—History and criticism. I. Magill, Frank Northen, 1907-   . II. Mazzeno, Laurence W.
PN44.M33   1996
809—dc20   96-23382
ISBN 0-89356-084-7 (set)   CIP
ISBN 0-89356-093-6 (volume 9)

Revised Second Edition
First Printing

LIST OF TITLES IN VOLUME 11

page

The Sport of the Gods—*Paul Laurence Dunbar* 6241
Spring Awakening—*Frank Wedekind* 6245
The Spy—*James Fenimore Cooper* 6250
The Star of Seville—*Unknown* 6256
Steppenwolf—*Hermann Hesse* 6261
Steps—*Jerzy Nikodem Kosinski* 6266
Steps to the Temple—*Richard Crashaw* 6270
The Stones of Venice—*John Ruskin* 6274
The Story of an African Farm—*Olive Schreiner* 6278
The Story of Burnt Njal—*Unknown* 6283
The Story of Gösta Berling—*Selma Lagerlöf* 6287
The Strange Case of Dr. Jekyll and Mr. Hyde—*Robert Louis Stevenson* 6291
Strange Interlude—*Eugene O'Neill* 6294
Strange Stories from a Chinese Studio—*P'u Sung-ling* 6298
The Stranger—*Albert Camus* 6301
Stranger in a Strange Land—*Robert A. Heinlein* 6305
Street Scene—*Elmer Rice* 6309
A Streetcar Named Desire—*Tennessee Williams* 6313
Studs Lonigan—*James T. Farrell* 6318
A Study in Scarlet—*Arthur Conan Doyle* 6323
A Study of History—*Arnold Toynbee* 6328
The Subjection of Women—*John Stuart Mill* 6331
Suddenly Last Summer—*Tennessee Williams* 6335
Sula—*Toni Morrison* 6339
Summa Theologica—*Saint Thomas Aquinas* 6343
The Sun Also Rises—*Ernest Hemingway* 6346
The Sunken Bell—*Gerhart Hauptmann* 6351
The Sunlight Dialogues—*John Gardner* 6355
The Suppliants—*Aeschylus* 6359
The Suppliants—*Euripides* 6363
The Surrounded—*D'Arcy McNickle* 6367
Swallow Barn—*John Pendleton Kennedy* 6371
The Swiss Family Robinson—*Johann David Wyss* and
    Johann Rudolf Wyss 6375
Sybil—*Benjamin Disraeli* 6379

	page
Tala—*Gabriela Mistral*	6383
A Tale of a Tub—*Jonathan Swift*	6387
The Tale of Genji—*Murasaki Shikibu*	6391
A Tale of Two Cities—*Charles Dickens*	6395
Tales of Ise—*Unknown*	6399
Tales of Soldiers and Civilians—*Ambrose Bierce*	6403
Tales of Uncle Remus—*Joel Chandler Harris*	6406
The Talisman—*Sir Walter Scott*	6409
Talley Family Saga—*Lanford Wilson*	6414
Tamar—*Robinson Jeffers*	6418
Tamburlaine the Great—*Christopher Marlowe*	6422
The Taming of the Shrew—*William Shakespeare*	6427
Tarr—*Wyndham Lewis*	6431
Tartuffe—*Molière*	6435
The Task—*William Cowper*	6439
A Taste of Honey—*Shelagh Delaney*	6442
The Tempest—*William Shakespeare*	6446
The Temple—*George Herbert*	6451
The Temple of the Golden Pavilion—*Yukio Mishima*	6455
The Temptation of Saint Anthony—*Gustave Flaubert*	6459
The Tenant of Wildfell Hall—*Anne Brontë*	6464
Tender Is the Night—*F. Scott Fitzgerald*	6468
Tess of the D'Urbervilles—*Thomas Hardy*	6472
Tevye the Dairyman—*Sholom Aleichem*	6476
Thanatopsis—*William Cullen Bryant*	6480
The Thebaid—*Statius*	6483
Their Eyes Were Watching God—*Zora Neale Hurston*	6487
Thérèse—*François Mauriac*	6491
Thérèse Raquin—*Émile Zola*	6496
These Jaundiced Loves—*Tristan Corbière*	6500
Thesmophoriazusae—*Aristophanes*	6504
The Thin Man—*Dashiell Hammett*	6508
Things Fall Apart—*Chinua Achebe*	6512
The Thirty-nine Steps—*John Buchan*	6516
Three Lives—*Gertrude Stein*	6520
The Three Musketeers—*Alexandre Dumas*, père	6524
The Three Sisters—*Anton Chekhov*	6530
Three Soldiers—*John Dos Passos*	6535
The Threepenny Opera—*Bertolt Brecht*	6539
Through the Looking-Glass—*Lewis Carroll*	6543
Thus Spake Zarathustra—*Friedrich Wilhelm Nietzsche*	6548
Thyestes—*Seneca*	6551

LIST OF TITLES IN VOLUME 11

                                                                    page

Tiger at the Gates—*Jean Giraudoux* 6555
The Time Machine—*H. G. Wells* 6559
The Time of Your Life—*William Saroyan* 6563
Timon of Athens—*William Shakespeare* 6567
The Tin Drum—*Günter Grass* 6571
'Tis Pity She's a Whore—*John Ford* 6575
The Titan—*Theodore Dreiser* 6579
Titus Andronicus—*William Shakespeare* 6584
To His Coy Mistress—*Andrew Marvell* 6590
To Kill a Mockingbird—*Harper Lee* 6593
To the Lighthouse—*Virginia Woolf* 6597
To Urania—*Joseph Brodsky* 6602
Tobacco Road—*Erskine Caldwell* 6606
The Toilers of the Sea—*Victor Hugo* 6609
Tom Brown's School Days—*Thomas Hughes* 6613
Tom Jones—*Henry Fielding* 6617
Tono-Bungay—*H. G. Wells* 6623
Top Girls—*Caryl Churchill* 6628
Torch Song Trilogy—*Harvey Fierstein* 6632
Tortilla Flat—*John Steinbeck* 6636
The Tower—*William Butler Yeats* 6640
The Tower of London—*William Harrison Ainsworth* 6643
The Town—*William Faulkner* 6648
The Tragedy of Tragedies—*Henry Fielding* 6653
The Tragic Muse—*Henry James* 6657
The Tragic Sense of Life in Men and in Peoples—
    Miguel de Unamuno y Jugo 6662
The Travels of Lao Ts'an—*Liu Ê* 6665
The Travels of Marco Polo—*Marco Polo* 6669
Treasure Island—*Robert Louis Stevenson* 6675
A Tree Grows in Brooklyn—*Betty Smith* 6681
The Tree of Man—*Patrick White* 6685
The Tree of the Folkungs—*Verner von Heidenstam* 6689
The Trial—*Franz Kafka* 6693
The Trickster of Seville—*Tirso de Molina* 6697
Tristan and Isolde—*Gottfried von Strassburg* 6701
Tristia—*Osip Mandelstam* 6705
Tristram—*Edwin Arlington Robinson* 6709
The Triumph of Death—*Gabriele D'Annunzio* 6713
Troilus and Cressida—*William Shakespeare* 6717
Troilus and Criseyde—*Geoffrey Chaucer* 6722
The Trojan Women—*Euripides* 6726

MASTERPLOTS

	page
Tropic of Cancer—*Henry Miller*	*6730*
Tropic of Capricorn—*Henry Miller*	*6733*
Trout Fishing in America—*Richard Brautigan*	6737
A True History—*Lucian*	6741
The Truth Suspected—*Juan Ruiz de Alarcón*	6745
Tung-chou lieh-kuo chih—*Fêng Mêng-lung*	6749
The Turn of the Screw—*Henry James*	6753
Twelfth Night—*William Shakespeare*	6758
The Twelve—*Aleksandr Blok*	6763
Twenty Thousand Leagues Under the Sea—*Jules Verne*	6767
Two Essays on Analytical Psychology—*Carl Gustav Jung*	6771
The Two Gentlemen of Verona—*William Shakespeare*	6774
The Two Noble Kinsmen—*William Shakespeare* and *John Fletcher*	6778
The Two Towers—*J. R. R. Tolkien*	6781
Two Treatises of Government—*John Locke*	6786
Two Women—*Alberto Moravia*	6790
Two Years Before the Mast—*Richard Henry Dana, Jr.*	6794
Typee—*Herman Melville*	6799
Ulysses—*James Joyce*	6803
The Unbearable Bassington—*Saki*	6808
The Unbearable Lightness of Being—*Milan Kundera*	6812
Uncle Silas—*Joseph Sheridan Le Fanu*	6816
Uncle Tom's Cabin—*Harriet Beecher Stowe*	6822
Uncle Vanya—*Anton Chekhov*	6826
Under Fire—*Henri Barbusse*	6831
Under Milk Wood—*Dylan Thomas*	6835
Under the Greenwood Tree—*Thomas Hardy*	6839
Under the Volcano—*Malcolm Lowry*	6843
Under the Yoke—*Ivan Vazov*	6848
Under Two Flags—*Ouida*	6852
Under Western Eyes—*Joseph Conrad*	6857
The Underdogs—*Mariano Azuela*	6861
Undine—*Friedrich de La Motte Fouqué*	6865

Revised Second Edition

THE SPORT OF THE GODS

Type of work: Novel
Author: Paul Laurence Dunbar (1872-1906)
Type of plot: Naturalism
Time of plot: Late nineteenth century
Locale: A town in the southern United States and New York City
First published: serial, 1901; book, 1902

Principal characters:
BERRY HAMILTON, an African American servant
FANNIE, his wife
JOE, his son
KITTY, his daughter
MAURICE OAKLEY, his employer
FRANK, his employer's half brother
HATTIE STERLING, an African American performer

The Story:

After the Civil War, Maurice Oakley, a Southern businessman, had been able to quickly recover his fortune; he had been able to do this because of his prudence. He was generous to his African American servant, Berry Hamilton, and Oakley was more than generous in supporting his younger half brother Frank, who was studying art in Paris.

On the last night of one of Frank's brief visits home, a jolly going-away party was held; the party was spoiled for the brothers when Frank discovered that the $986 for his trip had been stolen; he had left the money in his room. Maurice said that the crime did not embarrass him financially—he would resupply Frank with funds—but he was hurt by the fact that a friend or employee would steal from his house. Suspicion fell on Berry, who was the only person other than Frank who had been alone in the room. When it was discovered that on the day after the theft, Berry had deposited a large sum in the bank, Maurice and the police felt that the case against Berry was proved. Although Berry's years of loyal service made his stealing very out of character, the servant received a ten-year prison sentence.

For the town's whites, Berry's alleged criminal behavior confirmed their belief in the natural depravity of blacks. Ironically, the town's African Americans were almost as prejudiced against Berry as the whites were. His son, Joe, was fired from his barbershop job, and no one would hire him because of the family disgrace. For the same reason, no fellow African American would rent rooms to Berry's wife, Fannie, when she needed quarters.

The family made the momentous decision to relocate to New York City. Although Fannie feared that her children might succumb to the temptations of urban life, the family had to start anew in order to survive.

Her fears proved all too justified. Joe was the first to fall. As a first-class barber in a whites-only establishment down South, he had listened enviously as the town's young blades had recounted their high-living exploits. In New York, he found that even African Americans could aspire to this type of aristocratic dissipation. Becoming friends with the sporting character William Thomas, Joe was quickly initiated into the wild goings-on in cabarets, gambling dens, and cheap saloons. He met and fell for the aging, hardened showgirl Hattie Sterling, who, charmed by his youth and, particularly, by the good money he was making as a barber, became his mistress.

Meanwhile, Fannie and her daughter Kitty maintained their respectability by working in a factory. Their humdrum life was shattered, however, when Minty, a hometown acquaintance, arrived and spread the story of Berry's imprisonment. As a result of the scandal, Fannie and Kitty lost their apartment and jobs. Lacking other economic prospects, Kitty auditioned as a vaudeville singer. Once hired, she soon followed her brother into blind devotion to the sensations of the moment.

Concurrently, at the Oakley mansion, an equally somber story was unfolding. Maurice received a revelatory letter from his brother. Frank confessed that the money had never been stolen; instead, he had gambled it away and had been ashamed to admit it. Stunned by this admission, Maurice became a changed man. Rather than damage his family honor, he refused to divulge the secret, thereby leaving Berry in prison. Growing almost psychotically fearful of exposure, he kept the letter in a hidden pocket at his breast; he changed from an affable man-about-town into a reclusive misanthrope.

Five years passed. The New York Hamiltons had gone further down the road to ruin. The despairing Fannie had been talked into marrying a racetrack character, Gibson, who had convinced her that her first marriage was void. Now, however, Berry's fortunes, at least, changed for the better. A white newspaper reporter, Skaggs, was interested in Joe's story of how his father had been railroaded into jail. His curiosity piqued, Skaggs traveled to the Hamiltons' hometown. Posing as a friend of Frank, he tricked the half-mad Maurice into handing him the letter, which he then published in his New York newspaper. Public outcry over this miscarriage of justice forced Berry's pardon, and the paper sponsored his trip to New York.

While these events were going on, Joe was being driven to despair by Hattie's repeated rejections; he strangled her. Kitty was so estranged from her family that she paid no attention to Joe's murder trial. When Berry reached his wife's home he found her married to another man and his children jailed or out of touch.

Berry had nothing left but one desire: to kill the man who had taken his wife. For a second time, though, fortune smiled. When Berry had worked up the courage to confront Gibson, he discovered the man's house in mourning. Gibson had been killed in a brawl, and Fannie was ready to go back to Berry.

The couple returned to the cottage on the Oakley place; they were welcomed back by Maurice's repentant wife. Maurice himself had gone insane, and the couple could occasionally hear his ravings as they lived their simple life.

Critical Evaluation:

Readers of Paul Laurence Dunbar's first three novels, which were light, sentimental potboilers, were surprised by the vehemence and darkness of his last one, *The Sport of the Gods.* Dunbar had already proven himself as one of the first African American writers of the period to break into polite letters. His facile magazine verse showed him the equal of his fashionable peers. In his last novel, however, under the threat of death from the tuberculosis that would eventually kill him, he turned from his popular vein to compose a work of naturalism.

Naturalism was a literary movement that began in the United States in the 1890's. Naturalism is a child of realism, but it differs from its parent in some points of content and attitude. American realism emphasizes everyday situations, whereas naturalism focuses on the out-of-the-ordinary, such as portraits of killers, prostitutes, and showgirls. Whereas the psychology and sociology that form the background of realist fiction is a reworked and clarified common sense, naturalism tends to draw on "scientific" doctrines, such as those concerning genetic inheritance, for its conceptual framework. As a consequence, whereas realism, like common sense, posits human beings with free will and shows its characters fighting and often overcoming obstacles, naturalism stresses the inexorability of scientific laws and gives all the power to the obstacles. Naturalism's characters fell prey to forces that they cannot effectively combat.

Although Dunbar differed in a few respects from other naturalists, he shared their interest in seamy subjects (as indicated by his fascination with drunks and chiselers) and their belief in the overwhelming strength of circumstances.

A typical naturalist way of stressing the power that events and milieu exert on personality was to depict an innocent being sucked down by the whirlpools of vice in a big city. In Theodore Dreiser's *Sister Carrie* (1900), for example, the heroine, after moving from a small town to Chicago, is so dazzled by department store displays that she quickly drops her factory jobs and her morals so that she can indulge her taste for splendor; she becomes a well-off salesman's mistress. Dunbar gives a male version of this story. As is usual in naturalism, it is a lover, in this case, Hattie Sterling, who starts the protagonist on a downward spiral. Joe sinks from degradation to degradation until he ends as an unrepentant murderer.

Dunbar's refusal to abide by strictly naturalist tenets is seen, however, in his use of a background conceptual network. As his novel's title indicates, the author blames his characters' misfortunes on a mischievous fate, rather than on the effect of a powerfully stimulating environment on weak personalities. Dunbar indicates this feeling in many explicit statements, such as "One might find it in him to feel sorry for this small-souled, warped being," Joe, "for he was so evidently the jest of Fate." Although such invocation of supernatural entities hardly fits in with the prosaic tone dominating much naturalism, in Dunbar's text, it does work well to tie together his mixed discourse in which fantastic coincidences of one genre meet the gritty actualities of another. Dunbar's fate can mediate between these worlds because, while fate is held accountable for unusual events (such as Berry's unlucky depositing of his savings on the day after the robbery), such accidents result in effects (such as the imprisonment of an African American on flimsy evidence) that were in keeping with the everyday realities of the time.

In fact, what is special about Dunbar is that he pioneered in describing the important but unexplored post-Civil War migration of African Americans from the country to the cities. Although the novel is marred by moralizing and by Dunbar's inclusion of trite, melodramatic elements, it is valuable as a groundbreaker in its portrayal of the kind of uprooting that would take place more often later in the century and that would be redescribed in such major novels as Ralph Ellison's *Invisible Man* (1952). Moreover, in many of its city passages, Dunbar's book rises to creative heights in the depiction of human interaction. In Hattie's first meeting with Joe, for example, great skill is displayed in simultaneously picturing the charm and the implicit threat in her response to his overtures. At such places, Dunbar moves beyond professional facility to achieve a refined and moving execution.

James Feast

Bibliography:
Brawley, Benjamin. *Paul Laurence Dunbar: Poet of His People*. Port Washington, N.Y.: Kennikat Press, 1967. Recommends Dunbar's verse over his prose. In this biography, Brawley speaks penetratingly about how *The Sport of the Gods*' emotional roots are to be found in Dunbar's feelings after the breakup of his marriage.
Cunningham, Virginia. *Paul Laurence Dunbar and His Song*. New York: Dodd, Mead, 1947.

Sees *The Sport of the Gods* as the culmination of Dunbar's career-long move away from melodrama toward a more realistic approach, an approach only imperfectly realized in this book.

Lawson, Victor. *Dunbar Critically Examined*. Washington, D.C.: Associated Publishers, 1941. This critical study is valuable in showing how the generally insipid magazine writing of the time actually descended from better models earlier in the century. Dunbar's novel is viewed as an attempt at throwing off the shackles of stiflingly weak but widely accepted conventions.

Martin, Jay, and Gossie H. Hudson, eds. *The Paul Laurence Dunbar Reader*. New York: Dodd, Mead, 1975. The editors argue persuasively in the introduction that, unlike earlier African American writers, Dunbar, although he worked largely within the confines of polite, white literature, was able in dialect poetry and in *The Sport of the Gods* to partly remove himself from these influences to draw strength from the black community.

Revell, Peter. *Paul Laurence Dunbar*. Boston: Twayne, 1979. The author looks at *The Sport of the Gods* as a milestone because, although its execution is weak, it breaks new ground in portraying undocumented areas of African American life.

SPRING AWAKENING
A Children's Tragedy

Type of work: Drama
Author: Frank Wedekind (1864-1918)
Type of plot: Psychological
Time of plot: Late nineteenth century
Locale: Germany
First published: Frühlings Erwachen, 1891 (English translation, 1909); first performed, 1906

Principal characters:
    MELCHIOR GABOR, an intelligent high-school boy
    MORITZ STIEFEL, his friend
    WENDLA BERGMANN, a schoolgirl, aged fourteen
    MRS. BERGMANN, her mother
    MR. AND MRS. GABOR, Melchior's parents
    MARTHA and
    THEA, schoolgirls
    ILSE, a young prostitute and model
    RENTIER STIEFEL, Moritz' father
    THE MASKED MAN

The Story:

Wendla placed in the closet the long, grown-up dress that her mother had just completed, protesting that she did not see why next year would not be soon enough to put on such a penitential garment. Mrs. Bergmann acquiesced with motherly affection to her daughter's wish to continue wearing, for the present, the freer, familiar clothes of childhood, remarking at the same time on the fact that Wendla had retained her childhood grace without a trace of the gawkiness usual to her age. Mrs. Bergmann was not without misgivings, even while she cherished that appearance of innocence and grace, and she expressed her uneasiness in various equivocating substitutes for her real fears.

Melchior Gabor, Moritz Stiefel, and their classmates ended their games to attend to their homework. Moritz and Melchior, walking home in the spring night, discussed the meaningless-ness of the exam system and the sexual phenomena of adolescence that they were beginning to experience. For Moritz, the mysterious sexual pressures were a great burden, partly because they hindered his already desperate attempts to meet the demands of school and parents. Although he was a poor student and excessively timid, he possessed an acute sensitivity that was unrecognized by all but Melchior, who was his closest friend and, unlike Moritz, an extremely promising student. The ease with which Melchior dealt with his schoolwork left him time not only for metaphysical speculation but also for a scholarly acquisition of the facts of reproduction, which he now offered to impart. Moritz accepted Melchior's offer on the condition that the facts be in written form and slipped into his books, where he could come upon them as if by chance.

On a blustery spring day not long afterward, Wendla, Thea, and Martha also exchanged confidences on the subjects of parental tyranny, love, marriage, and children. The talk turned to boys of their own age and to the peculiar behavior they sometimes exhibited. Wendla disclosed that Melchior had once told her he believed in nothing. Mention of the spring floods reminded them that Melchior had come near drowning in one of the swollen streams but had been saved by his ability as a swimmer.

Moritz illicitly entered the staff common room (repository of all records), driven by the need to know whether he was to be promoted. When he reappeared, dazed by his own boldness but relieved by the knowledge of a provisional remove, he was taunted by the other boys for having said that he would have shot himself if he had not been promoted.

Melchior and Wendla met by chance in the woods, where Wendla had gone to gather woodruff for her mother and had stopped to daydream by a brook. Melchior persuaded her to sit down and asked if she enjoyed going among the poor to take them food and money, errands on which her mother often sent her. Wendla's answer, that it gave her pleasure, began an argument on the reality of virtue and selflessness.

Wendla also confessed that she daydreamed of being a poor beggar child, beaten by a cruel father, although she herself had never been beaten. She picked a switch and begged Melchior to strike her, to show her how such punishment felt. The boy at first refused; then, as she persisted in her request, he threw the stick aside and pummeled her with his fists before he ran away into the wood, crying in anguish.

Moritz found himself again on the verge of school failure. While reading Johann Wolfgang Goethe's *Faust* (1790) with Melchior, he related his grandmother's story of the headless queen, a tale that had haunted him while he studied. It told of a beautiful queen born without a head who was one day conquered by a king who happened to be provided with two heads that argued constantly. The court wizard gave one to the queen, on whom it proved very becoming, and the two were married with great joy, the heads now being on the best of terms. Melchior's mother entered with tea and words of encouragement for Moritz. Noticing the *Faust*, she wondered if they ought to be reading it, saying elliptically that she preferred to place her trust in Melchior rather than in pedagogical principles. Realizing that she was thinking of the Gretchen episode, they became annoyed, Melchior because everyone insisted on acting as if the world turned on nothing but obscenities, Moritz because he had begun to fear that it actually did. He had received Melchior's essay on sex, which affected him like a series of dim recollections. He was disposed to exalt the satisfaction experienced by the woman and to regard that of the man as insipid.

Meanwhile, Wendla persistently interrogated her mother on the subject of her sister's latest baby. She mocked her mother's silly fairy tales by pretending to see a ridiculous vision outside the window. At Wendla's insistence, Mrs. Bergmann was forced to begin telling her daughter how babies come about, but she managed to evade the issue by saying that the things required were marriage and a capacity for love that Wendla was too young to comprehend. A short time later, Wendla went looking for Melchior and, swayed by his intensity and his tortured insistence that there is no such thing as love, she remained with him in the hayloft, where she conceived a child.

Moritz finally reached the end of his resources and, at the brink of suicide over the realization that he was about to fail, wrote to Mrs. Gabor for a loan that would enable him to leave home. She considered it her duty to refuse and appealed to his common sense and better nature. At dusk, in a parting soliloquy pervaded by his unfailing wry humor mixed with self-pity, he concluded that life was not his responsibility. The headless queen beckoned. Life was a matter of taste. His only regret was in not having known sexual fulfillment, the most human experience of all. When Ilse, a young model with an insatiable appetite for life, appeared to tempt him with tales of her warm, carefree, animal existence, he wavered but then rejected the opportunity she offered.

Moritz's suicide precipitated an investigation by the school officials. Melchior, charged with indecency on the basis of the notes on sex discovered among Moritz's books, became the scapegoat.

At the funeral service, the adults condemned Moritz for his crime against humanity and God. Rentier Stiefel comforted himself by repeating that he had never cared for the boy from a child; he was no son of his. With consummate coarseness, the pastor urged that he seek comfort in the arms of his wife. While the reaction of the schoolboys at the funeral was largely one of curiosity as to the exact manner of the suicide, Martha and Ilse brought a profusion of flowers to the grave. Ilse had discovered the suicide pistol and concealed it.

Mrs. Gabor indignantly opposed her husband's decision to send Melchior to the reformatory. She defied anyone to perceive moral corruption in what the boy had written, but she was unable to stand up to the discovery that Melchior was responsible for Wendla's pregnancy. After undergoing various treatments concocted by Dr. Von Brausepulver and mother Schmidt for inducing abortion, Wendla died. After her death, Melchior, hounded by society and by his own self-contempt, managed to return to look at her grave. As he wandered enviously among the graves, he encountered Moritz Stiefel, with his head under his arm, who attempted to persuade Melchior to join him in his life among the dead, which he pictured as a fabulous if grotesque freedom. While Melchior hesitated, a masked man appeared to take Moritz to task for his attempt, his lack of a head, and his general crumbling condition. He accused Moritz of charlatanism and asked Melchior to submit himself to his care. Melchior, contending that he could not entrust himself to a masked unknown, interrogated the man regarding his moral position. Moritz admitted that he had been boasting and urged Melchior to accompany the gentleman, who was, in any event, alive. The two living beings withdrew together while Moritz returned to warm himself with putrefaction.

Critical Evaluation:

Frank Wedekind's *The Awakening of Spring*, subtitled *A Children's Tragedy*, was his first major work and the one that made him famous—and infamous. Many regarded the play as pornographic; riots broke out at performances and it was subjected to repeated censorship. Yet the work avoids the explicit and obscene, and later generations have come to see it as a powerful creation shaped out of inner experience.

The world of anxiety in which students live and suffer was familiar to Wedekind from his own school years. Yet he shaped the work not as a documentary but as a bizarre fantasy charged with irony. The adults, especially the teachers and the pastor, are grotesque parodies. Even their names resemble the sort of mocking epithets students might invent. Scenes such as that in which Melchior is interrogated by the faculty, or that of Moritz's funeral, are bitter parodies of the cruelty inflicted upon children by adults as that cruelty is perceived by the children.

Indeed, Wedekind places all the lyricism and humanity in the play in the world of the young, perhaps for the first time on the German stage giving expression to the experience of this age group. Using naturalist techniques, Wedekind accurately captured the speech patterns and behavior of young people, while yet lifting them beyond the level of mere naturalism. That the play is allied more with the symbolist school is evident from the fantasy of the final scenes, the temptation of Melchior by Moritz, and his rescue by the "masked man." Wedekind dedicated the play to this mysterious figure, who clearly represents the life force, perhaps within Melchior himself, which enables him to reject death and return to the world of the living, grotesque though it may be, to experience the fullness of life, of which Moritz, by his suicide, has robbed himself.

Many have considered Wedekind a precurser of German literary expressionism, and Bertolt Brecht considered him to be one of the principal influences on his own political and experimental plays. *Spring Awakening* cannot be considered an example of pure expressionism, but Wedekind does anticipate expressionism in his concern with authority and rebellion, his portrayal of youthful experimentation, his virtually plotless method of storytelling (particularly in scenes that are sprung on the audience unprepared, as for example the homosexual love scene and the masturbation scene), and his use of the ambiguous Masked Man (the original role of which was played by Wedekind himself). In portraying the adult world, Wedekind projects the children's subjective and innocent interpretations of the world of experience on to the authority figures.

As the adults in *Spring Awakening* clearly show, bourgeois society was incapable of accepting sexuality as natural. Wendla's mother, by constructing motherhood as a secret world, prepares the way for her daughter's downfall. Almost all the tragic events that happen to the children are the result of adult interference. The schoolteachers refuse to consider Melchior's humanity when they indict him for describing reproduction, for they cannot accept their own sexual, in other words human, side. When the Masked Man appears, he offers a kind of salvation for Melchior from conventional society. As long as the Melchiors of the world—in Wedekind's world, he is the hero—survive, there is a glimmer of hope that the human instinct can be explored and celebrated.

Ironically, organized religion cannot cope with human nature because it has constructed a false set of ideals that are unattainable. With the approval of the Church, Moritz's father condemns his son to an eternity in hell and takes no responsibility for having driven him to his death. Moritz, who is modeled on one of Wedekind's friends, can no longer face the pressures of trying to conform to adult expectations. Rather than teach the children what they need to know, adults fill children's heads with trivial details and the history of dead cultures. Rather than teach children to think for themselves as Frau Gabor, the most redeemable of the adult characters, has taught Melchior, the adults fear questions and resent children when they do not conform.

Wedekind's indictment of the adult world is reflected in his language. When the children speak, they often do so in lofty, lyrical, highly subjective language, whereas the adults use the rhetoric of avoidance and noncommunication. When the teachers speak, their words are full of the language of oppression, power, and control over the imagination and the emotions.

The greatest victims of adult oppression in the play are Moritz and Wendla, both of whom die as a direct result of adult intervention (Moritz from suicide and Wendla from a botched abortion). Adults' unwillingness to accept their own humanity, as well as the humanity of children, often brings about such devastating results. The Masked Man represents an affirmation of life and offers the only possibility for hope. By rejecting social definitions of morality (which he and Melchior claim are nothing more than social constructs) and by refusing to give in to society's narrow definitions of normality and reality, Melchior illustrates Wedekind's youthful optimism. To reform society the individual must risk life and social rejection.

"Critical Evaluation" revised by D. Dean Shackelford

Bibliography:
Boa, Elizabeth. *The Sexual Circus: Wedekind's Theatre of Subversion.* New York: Basil Black-
    well, 1987. Excellent exploration of Wedekind's primary and subversive purpose in attack-
    ing bourgeois authoritarianism and speaking out for the rights of the individual. Useful

interpretation of *Spring Awakening* as a critique of social roles and an examination of moral authority. Extensive bibliography.

Bond-Pable, Elizabeth. Introduction to *Spring Awakening*. Translated by Edward Bond. London: Methuen, 1980. Gives a brief biographical introduction to Wedekind's life and career, and points out central themes in the play. The volume also includes Edward Bond's "A Note on the Play," in which he concludes that the play is about "the misuse of authority" and shows the effects of the state on the individual.

Del Caro, Adrian. "The Beast, the Bad, and the Body: Moral Entanglement in Wedekind's *Frühlings Erwachen*." *Colloquia-Germanica* 24, no. 1 (1991): 1-12. Focuses on the influence of Georg Büchner and Friedrich Nietzsche and the difficulty of integrating morality, humanity, and nature. Wedekind criticized society's attempts to expunge the natural from human existence.

Gittleman, Sol. *Frank Wedekind*. New York: Twayne, 1969. A somewhat dated but still useful general introduction to Wedekind's life and work. Analyzes *Spring Awakening*, focusing on the tragic effects of society's failure to teach children about their instincts. Concludes that the play blends tragedy, absurdism, allegory, surrealism, and morality.

Jelavich, Peter. "Wedekind's *Spring Awakening*: The Path to Expressionist Drama." In *Passion and Rebellion: The Expressionist Heritage*, edited by Stephen Eric Bronner and Douglas Kellner. New York: Universe Books, 1983. An excellent analysis of the play's central themes, as well as the connections between Wedekind, expressionism, and Brecht.

Shaw, Leroy R. "Frank Wedekind's *Spring Awakening*." In *Alogical Modern Drama*, edited by Kenneth S. White. Amsterdam: Rodopi, 1982. A good general analysis of the play. Calling it a critique of rationalism, Shaw suggests the play is an alogical and amoral indictment of bourgeois Christianity.

THE SPY
A Tale of the Neutral Ground

Type of work: Novel
Author: James Fenimore Cooper (1789-1851)
Type of plot: Historical
Time of plot: Late eighteenth and early nineteenth centuries
Locale: New York State
First published: 1821

> *Principal characters:*
> HARVEY BIRCH, a peddler
> MR. HARPER, General George Washington
> MR. WHARTON, a Loyalist sympathizer
> FRANCES and
> SARAH, his daughters
> HENRY, his son
> MAJOR PEYTON DUNWOODIE, an American officer
> CAPTAIN LAWTON, another American officer
> COLONEL WELLMERE, a British officer

The Story:

At the beginning of the revolutionary war, Harvey Birch, a peddler, became a spy for the American side. Because of the extremely secret nature of Birch's work, few Americans were aware of his true mission. As a matter of fact, they suspected that he was a British spy. At the time, Westchester County in New York was considered common ground for both the rebels and the Loyalists, and the inhabitants of the county pretended to possess a neutrality they did not feel. This was the case of Mr. Wharton, a British sympathizer, who at the outbreak of hostilities had retired to his country estate with his two daughters, Sarah and Frances, and their aunt, Miss Jeanette Peyton.

One evening, as a storm was approaching, a horseman rode up to the Wharton house, The Locusts. He was a tall man of powerful frame, military in his bearing but plain in his dress. After being let into the house by the Whartons' servant, Caesar Thompson, the traveler introduced himself as Mr. Harper and asked for shelter from the storm. Mr. Wharton courteously granted the traveler's request, and the two men were soon engaged in conversation concerning the progress of the war. Mr. Wharton expressed his views cautiously in order to determine Mr. Harper's sentiments, but the stranger remained uncommunicative in his replies.

The conversation between the two men was interrupted by the arrival of Henry Wharton, Mr. Wharton's son and a captain in the British army. The young man wore a disguise in order to cross the American lines safely, but Mr. Harper recognized him. Later, Harvey Birch, the peddler believed by all to be a Loyalist spy, came to the Wharton home bringing supplies and news of the war. During Birch's visit, Caesar remarked to his master that he had heard voices in Mr. Harper's room.

With the return of fair weather, Mr. Harper said good-bye to his host. Before he departed, he promised to help Henry Wharton, if the latter ever needed help, in return for Mr. Wharton's hospitality. Shortly after Mr. Harper left, the Wharton home was surrounded by a troop of Virginia cavalry looking for a man answering Mr. Harper's description. When the American soldiers entered Mr. Wharton's house, they discovered Henry. Captain Lawton, in command of the troop, saw through Henry's disguise. The captain was certain that Henry was a spy because he knew that Birch had recently been visiting the Whartons. Not certain what to do, Captain Lawton consulted his superior, Major Peyton Dunwoodie, who was interested not only in Henry Wharton but also in Henry's sister, Frances. She pleaded with her lover for Henry's release, but, when Henry was found to have a pass signed by General Washington, Major Dunwoodie thought that the case warranted Henry's arrest.

Further investigation into the matter by Major Dunwoodie was halted by a report that British troops were in the neighborhood. The major rushed to his command. In the confusion, Henry escaped. He reported to his superior, Colonel Wellmere, leader of the advancing British troops, who professed to be in love with Sarah Wharton. When Henry advised the colonel to be wary of Major Dunwoodie and his Americans, Wellmere scorned the advice and determined to force a fight with the rebels. In the brief engagement that followed, the British were routed, and Captain Lawton succeeded in recapturing Henry, who was returned under guard to his father's home. Colonel Wellmere, also taken prisoner, was slightly wounded in the action.

Birch was watching Major Dunwoodie's success from a distant hill when he was sighted by Captain Lawton. In the pursuit, Lawton overtook Birch, but he fell from his horse and found himself at the peddler's mercy. Birch, however, spared Lawton's life, and for that act of magnanimity, the captain would not allow his men to overtake the peddler.

A price was put on Birch's head. One night, his house was ransacked and burned by a band of lawless men called Skinners. They then delivered Birch to Captain Lawton and claimed their reward. Major Dunwoodie, who was also present when the peddler was brought in, accused him of treason. Although Birch possessed a paper which would have cleared him of the charge, he swallowed it rather than betray the confidence of his secret employer. Birch was put in jail, but that night he escaped in the guise of a washerwoman who visited his cell. The next morning, on the outskirts of the American camp, he confronted Major Dunwoodie again. With a gun pointed at the officer, to prevent recapture, the peddler warned him to be on guard against danger to the Whartons. Major Dunwoodie was alarmed by the thought of danger threatening Frances Wharton. He was also disturbed because he felt that he could never win Frances if her brother were executed as a spy. Major Dunwoodie's troubles were magnified when, after assuring Frances that he would try to get General Washington's help for her brother, she turned from him coldly because she believed that he was in love with Isabella Singleton, the sister of an American officer who was recuperating at The Locusts from injuries sustained in the battle.

Meanwhile, Sarah Wharton had accepted Colonel Wellmere's proposal of marriage, and the date for the wedding had been set. Major Dunwoodie and Captain Lawton were among the guests during the truce arranged for the exchange and the wedding. The ceremony was suddenly interrupted, however, by the appearance of Birch. Sarah fainted when Birch told the colonel that his wife, Mrs. Wellmere, had crossed the ocean to find him. Captain Lawton challenged Colonel Wellmere to a duel. The Englishman missed his mark, but Captain Lawton was prevented from killing his adversary when the Skinners overpowered him. Colonel Wellmere fled the scene, and Captain Lawton was able to escape his enemies only after a fierce struggle.

The Skinners then burned Mr. Wharton's house. Captain Lawton returned to the scene with troops he had met on the road, and, after routing the Skinners, he rescued Frances from the blazing house. Birch rescued Sarah, and, again, Captain Lawton permitted the peddler to escape. A bullet fired at Captain Lawton from the darkness struck Isabella Singleton. On her deathbed, she confessed that Major Dunwoodie thought of her only as a friend.

At his trial, Henry Wharton admitted that he had used a disguise in order to pass through the

American lines, but he insisted that he had done so only in order to visit his family, especially his aged father. Major Dunwoodie himself vouched for Henry's character. Frances, however, ruined her brother's chances for acquittal when she admitted that Henry had had dealings with Birch. Henry was found guilty and sentenced to be hanged on the following day. Major Dunwoodie made an appeal to General Washington for the life of his friend but was unsuccessful, for the commander-in-chief was not at his headquarters.

Soon afterward a tall, gaunt man in clerical dress appeared and announced himself as a minister from a nearby village who had come to offer spiritual comfort to the condemned man. Admitted to Henry's cell, he revealed himself as Harvey Birch. He helped Henry to disguise himself as Caesar Thompson, the faithful servant of the Whartons, and led the young officer past the unsuspecting sentinel. Frances, hearing of the escape, thought that her brother and the peddler would probably hide in a nearby cabin. Stealing away, she set out to join them, but she found the cabin occupied by Mr. Harper. Recalling his promise to help her brother, she told him the whole story. He reassured her that all would be well and told her to return to headquarters to await Major Dunwoodie.

Orders from General Washington arrived in time to relieve Major Dunwoodie of the necessity of finding Henry. Several days later, Birch saw him safely aboard a British man-of-war in New York harbor. Frances and Major Dunwoodie decided to be married immediately. Within a short time, however, their bliss was tempered by the news that Captain Lawton had fallen in battle with the British.

Some time later, Birch appeared at the headquarters of the American army in a New Jersey town. There he had a long interview with a grave and noble man whom the Whartons would have recognized as Mr. Harper; he was also known as General Washington. During their talk, the General attempted to reward his faithful spy by giving him money. The peddler refused to accept payment for his services to his country, but he did welcome a letter of approbation from his commander-in-chief. It was agreed that the peddler's real mission as an American spy should remain a secret that only they would share.

Thirty-two years later, in the War of 1812, a gaunt old peddler appeared on the Canadian border and carried word of British troop movements to the American lines. There he met Captain Wharton Dunwoodie, the son of Major Peyton Dunwoodie and his wife Frances. To him, the peddler acknowledged his earlier acquaintanceship with the young officer's parents. A few days later, during a battle, the old peddler threw away his pack and rushed into the fight with a musket seized from a fallen soldier. After the battle, Captain Dunwoodie found the old man's body and on his person a letter, signed by George Washington, which revealed Harvey Birch, not as a despicable spy, but as a loyal, heroic, and long-suffering patriot.

Critical Evaluation:

Judged by contemporary standards, *The Spy: A Tale of the Neutral Ground* is still a satisfactory historical novel. As James Fenimore Cooper remarked in the introduction to his novel, however, his purpose in *The Spy* is frankly patriotic. If one bears this fact in mind, one can see that Peyton Dunwoodie is supposed to represent the ideal American soldier and officer; Frances Wharton, the ideal of American womanhood; and Washington, the ideal father of his country, combining Roman strength and vigor with American humanity and humility. This understanding will help the reader to appreciate Cooper's point of view. The great historical novelist of the early nineteenth century was an intensely nationalistic individual who, conscious of the past achievements and potentialities of his country, eagerly looked forward to the development of a great nation.

The Spy is an important novel both in Cooper's career and in the history of American literature. For Cooper, *The Spy* represented a first success in a literary career which was to include thirty-three fictional works as well as a number of other writings over a period of thirty-one years. *The Spy*, however, also signifies the establishment of an independent American literature, a literature based on American life, American characters, and set in an American landscape. It is significant, then, that the novel which declared "independence" from European, and especially English, literature should take for its subject the American War of Independence.

In his preface to *The Spy*, Cooper showed that he was acutely conscious of being an American writer and of writing about American subjects. Still, there is no doubt that he was influenced by the major currents in literature written abroad, and, though in his preface Cooper offers a tongue-in-cheek apology for not including castles and nobles as Sir Walter Scott had done in his works, it is certain that Scott influenced Cooper in *The Spy* and in his later career as well. Scott was a great pioneer in the art of the historical novel, and *The Spy* shows that Cooper learned much from Scott.

An important aspect of the historical novel is authenticity of historical types, characters who live in a specific historical period and in a particular place. One of the key differences between an authentic historical novel and a contemporary novel in a historical setting is characterization. Though one may argue that people are, in a sense, the same everywhere and at all times, it is apparent that the differences cannot be overlooked if one is mainly interested in accurately portraying a specific era. Thus, to capture a particular place at a particular time, the novelist must do more than merely dress his contemporaries in the clothing of days past. He must have a grasp of those human features and aspects which a historical period typically requires of men and women.

The Spy is full of historically typical men. The spy himself is a courageous and ingenious man able not only to affect the times in which he lives but also permitted (and encouraged) by those times to display such qualities. Thus, another difference between an ordinary novel in a historical setting and a historical novel as such is that the characters help fashion history as they are fashioned by it. Set during the American Revolutionary War, fought on political as well as military grounds, involving civilians to a great extent and always posing the problem of divided loyalties, Cooper's choice of a spy is especially effective. The spy is not only a soldier in a war, he must have a grasp of politics (and theater) as well.

Cooper discovered another advantage in the use of a spy as a central character. This advantage is connected to the subtitle of the novel, *A Tale of the Neutral Ground*. Effective historical novels tend to focus on periods in which significant conflicts occur. Such conflicts as the American Revolution not only provide good dramatic material for the novelist but also offer later readers an insight into their own condition, since significant conflicts in the past have shaped their lives.

There is, however, an artistic problem in portraying such conflicts. To give a full picture of the clash of forces, an author must describe both sides in the fight (in Cooper's case, both the British and the Americans). Describing only one side tends to rob the novel of drama—but how is the novelist to show both and, at the same time, focus these forces on a single, central character?

Scott solved this problem by using figures of secondary historical interest as his primary focus of dramatic action. These secondary figures are able to move from one side to another as negotiators, go-betweens, and messengers. This movement back and forth allows scope for the novelist to show both sides of the conflict in a specific, concrete fashion.

Cooper has done this in *The Spy*. Instead of choosing Washington himself as a central character, Cooper has chosen a spy, a man able (and required) to move from one side to the other and yet a man who remains in the thick of the dramatic action. The "Neutral Ground," the space between opposing forces that Birch must cross and recross in his missions, the seam between the opponents, also reflects the need for an effective historical novel to move from one side to the other.

Other aspects of the historical novel are also significant. Besides the presence of other, minor "type" characters (the doctor, the housekeeper, the servant), there are the details of the warfare—the names, dates, places, and historical facts—that Cooper made a conscious effort to use; *The Spy* reflects a degree of historical accuracy and fidelity to the facts which, despite moments of highly imaginative drama and humor, lend an air of reality to the action of the book as a whole.

Additionally, Cooper expends much print and dialogue on the arguments for and against the American Revolution. The revolutionaries argue with the counterrevolutionaries. Because he is able to show both sides dramatically, in real life, Cooper is able to describe the intellectual and political conflict of the era. In this way, Cooper avoids the trap of turning a historical novel into a mere adventure story; for in the course of history, and certainly in the course of the revolutionary war, the battle of ideas deeply influences the physical battles. If Cooper is less successful in showing how arguments change individuals, he is still able to give a richer sense of the times and of the war than if he had concentrated entirely on physical action and adventure.

There are obvious weaknesses in Cooper's work. Cooper was, apart from being an opinionated man, one who shared many of the prejudices and preconceptions of his day. These views naturally affected the quality of his work. One problem, for example, was that he seemed unable to characterize certain types of people in much depth. His attitude toward women and African Americans specifically is condescending. As a result, his portrayal of these figures is frequently superficial. Cooper also has a tendency to use a rather heavy-handed ironic tone. In *The Spy*, Cooper follows a long tradition in English literature by making his comic characters members of the lower class. One senses that the class characteristics of those below him were humorous to Cooper. Corresponding to this general characterization of the lower orders (not true in every case, to be sure) is a general deference to those of higher rank.

Thus, in fully evaluating *The Spy* as literature, the reader is drawn to a central contradiction. On the one hand, Cooper clearly supports the American side of the revolutionary war and agrees with the arguments for independence, especially those arguments based on equality. In Cooper's mind, people are equal before God. At the same time, Cooper himself is a creature of his own time and upbringing. For him, though people may be equal under God, they are by no means equal to one another.

The conflict between ideals and reality is an old one in the United States, and it is no surprise that Cooper, declaring himself an authentic American novelist, should exhibit that conflict. Thus, *The Spy* is an informative historical novel both because it reflects a basic conflict in the history of a nation and because, as a work of art, it contains a basic conflict in human nature.

"Critical Evaluation" by Howard Lee Hertz

Bibliography:
Clark, Robert, ed. *James Fenimore Cooper: New Critical Essays*. Totowa, N.J.: Barnes & Noble Books, 1985. Superior scholarship offered with insight and solid critical analysis. Excellent source for the beginner and for the serious student.

Crawford, T. Hugh. "Cooper's *Spy* and the Theatre of Honor." *American Literature* 63 (September, 1991): 405-419. An interesting and controversial gaze into the character and motivations of Harvey Birch, Cooper's protagonist.

Darnell, Donald. *James Fenimore Cooper: Novelist of Manners*. Newark: University of Delaware Press, c. 1993. A recent close analysis presenting manners as Cooper's method of introducing his views on society, humor, and social mores. Chapter three is especially insightful concerning *The Spy*.

Fields, Wayne, ed. *James Fenimore Cooper: A Collection of Critical Essays*. Englewood Cliffs, N.J.: Prentice-Hall, c. 1979. This useful volume offers lengthy biographical, historical, and critical studies of Cooper as the representative American author. The volume is particularly well edited.

Long, Robert Emmet. *James Fenimore Cooper*. New York: Continuum Books, 1990. This lively text offers a colorful introduction to Cooper the man and insightful comparisons to his contemporaries. Chapter 2 provides a concise summary of *The Spy*.

Ringe, Donald. *James Fenimore Cooper*. New York: Twayne, 1962. The book contains an excellent chronology, bibliography, and cogent biographical sketch. *The Spy* is referenced in Cooper's canon.

Spiller, Robert E., and Philip C. Blackburn. *A Descriptive Bibliography of the Writings of James Fenimore Cooper*. New York: B. Franklin, 1968. This is an outstanding and essential tool for a study of Cooper.

THE STAR OF SEVILLE

Type of work: Drama
Author: Unknown (but sometimes attributed to Lope de Vega Carpio)
Type of plot: Tragedy
Time of plot: Thirteenth century
Locale: Seville
First produced: La estrella de Sevilla, c. 1617 (English translation, 1837)

> *Principal characters:*
> KING SANCHO IV, THE BRAVE
> ESTRELLA TABERA, the Star of Seville
> DON BUSTOS TABERA, her brother
> DON ARIAS, the king's confidant
> DON PEDRO DE GUZMÁN and
> DON FARFÁN DE RIVIERA, alcaldes of Seville
> DON SANCHO ORTIZ, a nobleman of Seville
> CLARINDO, Don Sancho's servant

The Story:

Sancho IV, King of Castile, was delighted with his welcome to Seville, and he was especially charmed by a black-haired beauty seen on a balcony. The alcaldes of the city identified her as Estrella Tabera, the Star of Seville. King Sancho whispered orders to his confidant, Arias, telling him to arrange for the monarch to visit her the next evening. He also sent for her brother, Don Bustos Tabera, in the hope of winning his agreement to the royal suit.

When he offered Don Bustos Tabera the command of the military post at Archidona, already sought by two veteran soldiers, the nobleman amazed the king by refusing the honor and by accepting with obvious reluctance other friendly gestures; his excuse was that he did not deserve them. At home, Don Bustos found his sister and Don Sancho Ortiz planning their marriage. Before long the disguised king appeared, but Don Bustos, pleading a house in disorder and foreseeing the possibility of a scandal, did not invite him in. However, Arias did succeed in entering the house. When he revealed his errand, Estrella indignantly refused his request that she be kind to the king. He had better luck when he tried to bribe Matilde, the maid, who promised to admit the king to the house after dark.

That night, after the king had been admitted, Don Bustos returned home unexpectedly and found the monarch there. Pretending not to believe that the intruder was the king, since a noble and just ruler would not stoop to dishonor, Don Bustos insulted him as a masquerader. The angry king, with no legal way to get his revenge for the insults he had endured, sent for Don Sancho Ortiz and offered to arrange the young nobleman's marriage to anyone he should choose, in return for ridding the king of an enemy. Don Sancho was given a paper on which was written the name of the man he was supposed to kill.

In the meantime Don Bustos, having forced Matilde to confess her treachery, hanged her from the king's balcony. Then he instructed Estrella to arrange for her marriage to Don Sancho at once, and the woman sent her lover a message informing him of the plan and asking him to come to her. The two notes posed for Don Sancho a conflict between duty and inclination. He loved Estrella, but he had sworn to serve the king faithfully; and so, when he met Don Bustos, he picked a quarrel with his sweetheart's brother and killed him in a duel. Afterward he stubbornly refused to give any explanation of his deed and was taken, under arrest, to the Triana prison.

Estrella, awaiting the arrival of Don Sancho, received instead the body of her dead brother. When she learned the name of his murderer, she decided to go at once to the king to demand vengeance. Before her arrival at the palace, the king had already been assured that Don Sancho was loyally keeping silent about the king's part in the death of the don. Since justice would be expected, however, the king was forced to order the beheading of Don Sancho. To Arias he marveled at the honor and dignity of the citizens of Seville.

When Estrella appeared, the king delegated to her the power to pass sentence on the murderer of her brother and sent her, with his ring, to the Triana prison. Alone, he soliloquized on the tragic results of his unbridled passion. Meanwhile, in the prison, loyal Clarindo was trying to amuse Don Sancho, who seemed to be out of his mind. The alcaldes could not understand his ravings or his refusal to explain his crime. He kept telling them that he had acted as a king, and that it was the duty of someone else to confess. As they were about to order his execution, Estrella appeared, veiled. By now her love had conquered her anger, and she ordered the release of the prisoner.

At the palace, Arias kept insisting that Don Sancho deserved to be saved. On the other hand, if the king were to confess, his action might cost him his throne. At last he sent Arias to smooth things over, and in private he urged each alcalde to spare Don Sancho's life. They, however, considered a pardon incompatible with their concepts of honor and royal dignity, and in spite of both Estrella and the king they ordered Don Sancho's execution.

With such examples of honor confronting him, the king was moved by his own conscience to confess that he had instigated the assassination. Since a king could do no wrong, he was unpunished, and Don Sancho was set free. Don Sancho and Estrella refused to obey the king's order that they marry. The blood of Estrella's slain brother separated them forever.

Critical Evaluation:

With the reasoning that *The Star of Seville* is an excellent play and that Lope de Vega Carpio was an excellent playwright, people have believed for centuries that he wrote it; but scholars have recently taken a closer look at the two extant versions and have begun to doubt his authorship. The play is unlike dramas that Vega Carpio is known to have written. Whoever the author may have been, he produced a masterpiece of the Golden Age.

The Star of Seville is frequently cited as the best example of the Spanish honor play, a form popular during that country's Golden Age of drama and related to similar productions in France and England during the sixteenth and seventeenth centuries. It is no surprise that *The Star of Seville* was long thought to be the work of Vega Carpio, since that popular and prolific playwright wrote a number of dramas characteristic of the genre. The interest in grand themes and in characters whose actions could determine the fate of a city, a kingdom, or an empire seems to have gripped audiences throughout Europe.

No audience or reader of *The Star of Seville* can appreciate the play without a sound understanding of the importance of honor in sixteenth and seventeenth century Spain. The term "honor" had both a private and public meaning, and Don Sancho's predicament is a perfect example of the problems that arise from the demands of private and public honor. Honor regulated all social relationships: those between king and subject, between superior and inferior, between friend and friend, and between family members. It lay at the root of all personal transactions, and established a foundation for social interactions. Upholding one's honor took precedence over personal satisfaction and over other commitments one might make. Such an attitude may seem extreme to succeeding generations, but it served as the informing principle of the society depicted in *The Star of Seville*.

Similarly, for the first audiences who viewed this play, the king remained a figure of paramount importance in their lives, and people believed in the special privileges of monarchs, who, when acting as head of the state, were not subject to the laws that governed ordinary individuals. That idea, coupled with the belief that the sovereign was protected by God and enjoyed special favors from God, made it possible for Sancho the Brave to act with impunity. The assumption was that the king would always act in accord with the dictates of honor. When he did not, the potential for chaos hovered over society and served as the breeding ground for tragedy. Such is the situation that the author of *The Star of Seville* dramatizes in his play.

The admirable male characters in the play, Bustos Tabera and Sancho Ortiz, believe in honor as a quality inherent in the individual and earned through deeds. Not surprisingly, their adherence to this demanding code of behavior leads them into conflict with the king, who has a very different sense of how his subjects should behave. Hence, when Bustos is offered a key military appointment by Sancho, he refuses because he is not worthy, making it impossible for the king to use the commission as a bribe for Bustos' cooperation in seducing Estrella. Sancho is forced to use other means to gain his evil end. Similarly, Sancho is quick to agree to be the king's emissary in eliminating the purported traitor; he never questions the king's motives, and even though he is distraught at having to kill the brother of his betrothed, he carries out his promise rather than stain his honor. The king refuses to come to Sancho's aid when the citizens of Seville demand his execution, so he nearly loses his life for a deed he committed as a matter of honor.

King Sancho and his confidant Don Arias possess a different notion of honor. For the king, the blind allegiance of his subjects to this code of behavior permits him to use them for his personal pleasure. Don Arias, ever present with words of advice, urges Sancho on in his plot to satisfy his passion for Estrella by taking advantage of the high-minded notions of men such as Bustos and Sancho. One of the great ironies of the drama is that the king makes glib promises, often in writing, to a number of people who fail to benefit from them because the king is unwilling to admit his evildoing when these individuals face punishment and death. For the king, as it is for William Shakespeare's Falstaff, honor is but a word.

In *The Star of Seville*, the concept of honor is saved by the citizenry in Seville, who force the king to admit publicly his role in the murder of Bustos, thereby halting the execution of Sancho. Through the heroic stance of the mayor and city elders, who defy the king's efforts to bribe them to set Sancho free, the king is made to act in accordance with the principles that should govern the behavior of rulers and admit his role in the murder. It is not clear that the king is actually changed by his actions, but at least Sancho is spared and the citizenry reassured that social justice is still possible in their city.

Modern audiences will have difficulty with the portrait of women in *The Star of Seville*. Estrella is little more than an object to be bargained for. She enters into the action of the play only rarely, most notably in the scene in which she pardons Sancho for killing her brother. As a symbol of constancy and an object for evoking sympathy, she is well drawn. She remains, however, little more than an appendage to the central moral action, which involves the male figures only.

At the time of the play's writing, Spain was the most powerful nation on earth. The country, despite its power, was still under the influence of medieval superstitions and customs. The Spanish Inquisition had purged the land of heretics and infidels. Silver was pouring into the king's coffers. The war with the Moors was still fresh in the memory of the people. Duels were fought every day and sometimes several were fought in one day. *The Star of Seville* is a reflection of the ethical and moral concerns of the time. Abstractions such as honor and corruption presented themselves to the people of the time with an immediacy like that of the play.

The theme of fatalism is also central to the play. The thinking of the time was, in comparison to modern times, very religious. It was widely accepted that God is supreme and the ultimate reality. God allows evil and mischance to enter one's life, but nothing is hopeless because God is the rewarder of the faithful. Miraculous and accidental events govern their lives and circumstances. Given this condition, one must be resigned to fate. In *The Star of Seville*, stars are an important metaphor for fate.

The Star of Seville dramatically portrays the intervention of the stars. Throughout the drama the stars are referred to many times. Estrella (her name means "star") denies their influence in her life as long as it appears to be going in the direction that she desires. As soon as her wishes are thwarted, by the killing of her brother by her lover, she gives vent to her grief and declares that her star is on the decline. Estrella, known as the Star of Seville, is so beautiful and bright that her influence is enough to change the lives of all the men who love or desire her—her brother, her lover, and even the king.

The king further portrays, with the help of Tabera, the belief that ultimately all things are in the hand of God. Monarchs are appointed by God and are accountable only to God. The duty and responsibility of any loyal subject is to obey the king. One of the king's men reminds him that the staves of his office point to God and signify the King's accountability to God, but if the staves are bent, they point to humanity. Herein lies the king's dilemma: He cannot be true to God and achieve his heart's desire.

In the character of Don Sancho Ortiz the audience sees the terrible consequences of loyalty and obedience to the king. Sancho knows he must kill his friend or disobey his monarch. He struggles with his conscience until he finally rationalizes that the king is accountable to God alone and he, Don Sancho Ortiz, is accountable to the king. In this way he resolves the conflict and does the king's bidding.

The people of Seville believe they are like pawns in a giant chess game with outside forces moving them to and fro—without malice or forethought—wreaking havoc in their lives. There are several scenes in which a morbid humor is displayed, notably in the third act, in which the disguised king tries to break into the Taberas' house and is caught. Another humorous scene occurs when Don Sancho and Clarindo debate upon "the other world" where all professions are represented except lawyers. Don Sancho asks why and is told it is because they would bring lawsuits if they were there. He then says, "If there are no lawsuits . . . hell's not so bad."

"Critical Evaluation" by V. Addington
Updated by Laurence W. Mazzeno

Bibliography:
Bergmann, Emilie. "Reading and Writing in the *Comedia*." In *The Golden Age Comedia: Text, Theory, and Performance*, edited by Charles Ganelon and Howard Manning. West Lafayette, Ind.: Purdue University Press, 1994. Discusses the ways that reading and writing define women's roles in the play; compares the treatment of women in *The Star of Seville* with that given them in another contemporary drama.
Fitzmaurice-Kelly, James. *A New History of Spanish Literature*. New York: Oxford University Press, 1926. Classifies the play as the best of the heroic dramas of the Golden Age. Briefly comments on the controversy over authorship.

Oriel, Charles. *Writing and Inscription in Golden Age Drama.* West Lafayette, Ind.: Purdue University Press, 1992. A chapter on *The Star of Seville* focuses on the written texts (letters and such) that appear in the play and explores their function in illuminating the code of honor.

Thomas, Henry. Introduction to *The Star of Seville*. New York: Oxford University Press, 1950. Calls the work one of the greatest plays of the Golden Age of Spanish drama. Analyzes the development of the king, Sancho, and Busto, whose varying understanding of the concept of honor lies at the heart of the drama.

Ziomek, Henryk. *A History of Spanish Golden Age Drama.* Lexington: University Press of Kentucky, 1984. Briefly sketches the dramatic conflict of the play, discusses the theme of loyalty, and comments on historical parallels.

STEPPENWOLF

Type of work: Novel
Author: Hermann Hesse (1877-1962)
Type of plot: Psychological
Time of plot: 1920's
Locale: Germany
First published: Der Steppenwolf, 1927 (English translation, 1929)

Principal characters:
>HARRY HALLER, the steppenwolf
>HERMINE, a friend
>PABLO, a saxophonist
>MARIA, a demimondaine

The Story:

The aunt, who kept a spotless bourgeois house, was attracted to Harry Haller, the new lodger who had rented her attic, but her nephew's suspicions were aroused when the lodger asked them not to report his domicile to the police. Haller explained that he had a repugnance for official contacts. His room was always in disorder; cigar ends and ashes, wine and brandy, pictures and books littered the apartment.

Haller was about fifty years old, sometimes in poor health and addicted to painkillers. He arose very late and became active only at night. He was invariably polite but remote. Once the nephew found him sitting on the stairs near a landing. Haller explained that the landing, which smelled of wax and turpentine and was decorated with washed plants, seemed to him the epitome of bourgeois order. Occasionally a pretty girl came to see Haller for brief visits, but her final visit ended in a bitter quarrel.

One day, Haller disappeared, after meticulously paying his accounts. He left behind a manuscript, written during his stay, which told the story of a steppenwolf. The nephew, sure that Haller was not dead, made the account public.

Haller had suffered a series of blows. His wife had become mad and had chased him from the house. His profession was closed to him. Living a solitary life, he had become a divided personality, one part of him a neat, calm bourgeois, the other, a wolf from the steppes. When he acted politely and genteelly, the world mocked his respectability. When he snarled and withdrew from society, he shocked his bourgeois self. He seemed to be a true steppenwolf.

On a solitary night ramble, he thought he saw an electric sign over a Gothic door in an old wall. The words, which he could barely discern, told of a magic show only for madmen. A little later, he saw a peddler with a similar sign. From a hawker he bought a treatise on the steppenwolf and read it avidly.

The treatise explained the popular concept of a steppenwolf, a creature that was half wolf and half human being as a result of mischance or spell. This was an oversimplified concept, however, for everyone was actually composed not of two but of many selves. The great bulk of the populace was held to one self through the rigid patterns of the sheeplike bourgeoisie; only a few individuals, ostensibly complying, were not really part of the pattern. They acted like the lone wolf and were the leaders in all fields.

Meditating on this philosophy, Haller understood his own nature a little more clearly, but it was difficult to think of himself as containing many selves.

An old acquaintance, a professor, met him and insisted on inviting him to dinner. The occasion was not a happy one. The professor and his wife were naïvely jingoistic and approved a vicious newspaper attack on a writer who had advanced the opinion that perhaps the Germans shared the guilt for World War I. The professor did not realize that the writer was his guest. Haller, for his part, ridiculed a pompous painting of Goethe that turned out to be greatly prized by the professor's wife.

Feeling the wolf in him gain ascendancy, Haller dropped in at the Black Eagle Tavern, where merriment reigned. At the bar, he encountered a young girl whom he thought sympathetic. He told her his long tale of woe, including about the professor's dinner and his mad wife, Erica, whom he saw only every few months and with whom he quarreled. The girl, who refused to give her name, good-naturedly ridiculed his preoccupation with Mozart and Indian myths when he did not even know how to dance. She seemed almost motherly in her concern for him; when he confessed he was afraid to go back to his lodging, she sent him upstairs to sleep. Before they parted, Haller made a dinner date with her.

At their next meeting, the girl, who said that her name was Hermine, set out to change Haller. She would help him for friendship's sake, so that in the end Haller would love her enough to kill her. Haller himself had thought of death; in fact, he was seriously contemplating committing suicide on his fiftieth birthday. Perhaps that was why he did not think Hermine's plan strange.

Hermine began her campaign. First she took him shopping for a gramophone, whereupon he took dancing lessons in his cluttered room. Although he was stiff, he learned the steps of the foxtrot. Then she took him to a tavern to dance. At her urging, he asked the most beautiful girl there, Maria, to be his partner. To his amazement, she accepted, and they danced well together. Hermine complimented him on his progress.

Late one night, as Haller returned quietly to his bedroom, he found Maria in his bed. Thinking he was too old for her, Haller hesitated; Maria was so sympathetic, however, that he lost his reluctance. He met Maria frequently in another room he rented nearby. Haller was grateful to Hermine, who had arranged it all. She kept track of his progress in love. After some time Haller realized that only through a lesbian relation could Hermine have known Maria's technique so well.

Another new acquaintance was Pablo, a gentle, accommodating saxophonist. He agreed readily with Haller's criticisms of modern jazz and with his preference for Mozart. Nevertheless, Pablo felt that music was not something to criticize; it was something for listeners and dancers to enjoy. Part of Pablo's great popularity came from his ability to provide drugs for jaded profligates. One night, Pablo invited Haller and Maria to his room and proposed a love episode for three. Haller refused abruptly, but Maria would have liked to accept.

On several occasions, Hermine hinted that she was more unhappy than Haller. He was learning other sides of life, but she knew only a life of pleasure and the senses. She was hoping that Haller would come to love her, because at the coming masquerade ball she would give her last command.

At the ball, Hermine was dressed as a man, reminding Haller of his friend Hermann. They danced with many different women. When Hermine finally changed into women's clothes, Haller knew that he loved her. After the ball, Pablo took them up to his Magic Theater. In a hall of mirrors, Haller saw his many selves; in the various booths, he lived his many lives. In one booth, he killed automobile drivers recklessly. In another, he met all the girls he had ever loved. Toward the end, he was Mozart, a laughing, reckless Mozart who played Handel on a radio.

The whirling came to an end. In the last booth, he saw Hermine and Pablo naked on a rug. They were asleep, sated with love. Haller stabbed Hermine. In the court, Mozart was his friend and comforted him when the judges sentenced him to eternal life; he was to be laughed out of court. Mozart turned into Pablo, who picked up Hermine's body, shrank it to figurine size, and put it in his pocket.

Critical Evaluation:

Hermann Hesse, one of the most influential German writers of the twentieth century, traveled widely and lived for a time in Italy and India. Following his journey to the Orient, he settled in Switzerland, where he spent the remainder of his life. He began writing at the turn of the century and published short stories, essays, and poems as well as several novels. In 1946, he was awarded the Nobel Prize in Literature.

Hesse himself called *Steppenwolf*, which fell in the middle of his literary career, his most misunderstood novel. The work is complex and confusing because it is never clear whether the narrator, Harry Haller, is sane or not. There is ample evidence to indicate that Haller is schizophrenic, but to dismiss his account as the vision of a madman is to ignore the basic conflict of the novel. The safe, middle-class reaction that sees Haller as mad is precisely the type of reaction that Hesse and Haller find most despicable. As Hesse has said: "You cannot be a vagabond and an artist and at the same time a respectable, healthy, bourgeois person. You want the ecstasy so you have to take the hangover." Hesse's attitude is basically Romantic, and this work is a Romantic statement.

The most dangerous way of misreading the novel is to see Haller/Steppenwolf as a hero. He sees himself that way, but by the final scene it is clear that Haller is a failure. Despite the temptation to interpret the character of the steppenwolf as that of the intellectual outsider at war with the middle class, Haller, when put to the final test in the Magic Theater, suddenly finds himself responding with the middle-class values he hates. Faced with Hermine's hallucination while she is in Pablo's arms, Haller reacts like any bourgeois husband and stabs, or believes he stabs, the unfaithful lover. With that, it becomes clear that he has not learned how to laugh and thus that he has not become one of the Immortals, the original purpose of his quest. He tells the reader: "One day I would be a better hand at the game. One day I would learn how to laugh." Haller himself is aware of his failure.

Mirrors have an important function throughout the novel. The doubling effect of a mirror is indicative of the split that Haller sees in himself. The act of doubling abounds: Streetlights reflect on wet pavement; Haller sees himself in Hermine's eyes; Hermine herself is a double at the ball, appearing first in the costume of a male and then in that of a female. As a male, she reminds Haller of a high-school male friend. Mirrors in the novel range from Hermine's pocket mirror to Pablo's magic hall of mirrors, and the reader is reminded of the standard magician's reply: "It was done with mirrors." Pablo is the magician who shows Haller that magic is the creative will of the imagination. Human beings are not singular or even double; each is filled with infinite possibilities, all of which can be realized if people will only open themselves to the experience.

The novel is a definition of the moral and intellectual condition of Western culture in the early twentieth century, more particularly of Germany in the 1920's. The setting is a large, modern city filled with electric lights, signs, bars, movies, music, and impersonal streets. The culture depicted is essentially humorless, just as Harry Haller lacks humor. Throughout the novel, Haller and the reader are told that they must learn to laugh, that is, to laugh at themselves and their condition. They must achieve detachment. When readers first see Haller, he is taking himself far too seriously. At the age of forty-eight, he had promised himself the dramatic gesture of suicide at fifty.

The novel falls into three general sections: the introduction of Harry Haller, the education of

Harry Haller, the test of Harry Haller. The introduction itself is divided into three parts. There is the burgher's view of Haller; Haller's own view of himself as a split personality, both middle class and steppenwolf; and the view represented by the treatise. Whereas the burgher's view is superficial and Haller's view is subjective, the treatise is the objective observation of a higher intelligence. Haller sees only the conflict between his steppenwolf character and the middle class, but the treatise distinguishes three types of individuals: saints, middle class, and sinners. The burgher must resist the temptation to either extreme. It is with this burgher mentality that Haller is at odds. The treatise points out that this is the wrong battle. Haller is pulled in all three directions: He wants to be burgher yet hates it; he enjoys the role of steppenwolf yet loathes it; and he desires to be an immortal but does not have the humor to achieve that level. The introduction gives an exposition, development, and a recapitulation, the same structure as that of sonata allegro form in music.

Music is central to much of Hesse's writing. He himself played the violin, and his first wife was a gifted pianist. In *Gertrude* (1910), Hesse tells the story of a composer; in *Journey to the East* (1932), he writes of a violinist; and in *Glass Bead Game* (1943), there is a pianist and a musical theorist. In *Steppenwolf*, too, music plays an important role. Pablo is a jazz musician, and the music of Mozart epitomizes the level of the immortal. Music becomes the synthesis of opposites, harmony within dissonance. Music, for Hesse, is the ideal abstract statement of harmony: It is written, heard, and felt. Moreover, it is timeless or outside of time at a level that language can never achieve.

During the middle section of the novel—the education of Harry Haller—the narrator, on the verge of mental collapse, discovers his initiator to self-understanding to be a strange young girl named Hermine. Under her tutelage, Haller must first learn to dance; that is, to experience the sensual side of his nature without disgust. Following the direction of Hermine and her friends, Maria and Pablo, Haller is forced to realize that the self has infinite possibilities. By experiencing the sensual, Haller is following the downward path to wisdom and sainthood. The trip is essentially a mystical one, and Haller experiences what so many mystics before him have discovered. Many of the Christian saints were first profligates who rose from sinner to saint. Other mystics, such as Walt Whitman, relate that salvation is through indulgence of the flesh, not through denial of it. As T. S. Eliot was to discover in the *Four Quartets* (1943), the way down and the way up are one and the same. In learning to dance, Haller learns to divest himself of his ego. On his way to the intuitive mystic vision that all Romantics eventually achieve, he experiences dance, drink, music, sex, and drugs. Haller is flawed, however. Like the quester in Eliot's *The Waste Land* (1922), Haller, when put to the final test, fails.

In Pablo's Magic Theater, Haller, on a hallucinatory drug trip, experiences the recapitulation of the first two sections of the novel and sees his personality in all of its aspects. Pablo tells him: "I help you make your own world visible, that's all." From the Magic Mirror spring two versions of himself, one of which goes off with Pablo implying the latent homosexual side of Haller that Sigmund Freud insisted exists in all men. During The Great Automobile Hunt, Haller, the pacifist, learns that he loves to kill. All things contain their opposites. In his third vision—The Marvels of Steppenwolf Training—Haller sees a surrealistic presentation of the main metaphor of the novel that reappears from the introduction. It is with the final vision of Hermine being unfaithful to him that he is unable to cope. In the hallucination, he stabs her, but Pablo cannot take it seriously, just as Haller cannot laugh at it. Because Haller cannot let his ego dissolve, he cannot join the universal flow of things.

"Critical Evaluation" by Michael S. Reynolds

Bibliography:

Boulby, Mark. "*The Steppenwolf.*" In *Hermann Hesse: His Mind and Art*. Ithaca, N.Y.: Cornell University Press, 1967. Compares the structure and motifs of *Steppenwolf* with those of Hesse's other novels. Discusses how depersonalization becomes an essential element in the solution of Harry Haller's dilemma.

Casebeer, Edwin F. "*Steppenwolf:* Siddhartha Today." In *Hermann Hesse*. New York: Warner Paperback Library, 1972. A Jungian interpretation of *Steppenwolf*. Sees Hermine as the anima and Pablo/Mozart as the Self of Harry Haller, especially in the Magic Theater dream world that the Self creates to discover its real nature.

Field, George Wallis. "*Der Steppenwolf:* Crisis and Recovery." In *Hermann Hesse*. Boston: Twayne, 1970. Traces the autobiographical element and the development of the humor theme from Hesse's earlier works into *Steppenwolf*. Discusses the themes of sexuality, cultural criticism, music, and the transcendence of reality.

Freedman, Ralph. "Person and Persona: The Magic Mirrors of *Steppenwolf.*" In *Hesse: A Collection of Critical Essays*, edited by Theodore Ziolkowski. Englewood Cliffs, N.J.: Prentice-Hall, 1973. Posits that Hesse created protagonists as images and distortions of himself to reflect the interplay between self-in-life (person) and self-in-art (persona). Discusses how Jungian psychoanalysis fashioned many of the artistic strategies in *Steppenwolf*.

Ziolkowski, Theodore. "*The Steppenwolf:* A Sonata in Prose." In *The Novels of Hermann Hesse: A Study in Theme and Structure*. Princeton, N.J.: Princeton University Press, 1965. Focuses on the technical problems of the novel's structure and explains how Hesse used musical sonata form to shape *Steppenwolf*.

96-284

STEPS

Type of work: Novel
Author: Jerzy Nikodem Kosinski (1933-1991)
Type of plot: Existentialism
Time of plot: Indeterminate
Locale: Indeterminate
First published: 1968

> *Principal characters:*
> THE NARRATOR, the protagonist
> A WOMAN, his wife or mistress
> THE READER, a participant

The Story:

The novel's main character, the narrator, was a young man who traveled from place to place experiencing life in its rawest form. In a small village, he showed his credit cards to an orphan girl who washed and mended his clothes and told her that she would never need money again if she would come with him. She followed him to the city to find a better life for herself and traded sex with him for money. The situation was reversed when he found himself in a strange city without money and had to trade sex for food.

As a ski instructor in an area close to a tubercular sanatorium, he made love to a woman patient through mirrors, never touching. An encounter with a woman at a zoo led to the pick-up of another woman, who turned out to be a male transvestite. The waiter at a train station arranged for him to attend a show where a woman and a large unidentified animal copulated while observers placed bets as to the depth of penetration.

In a grouping of anecdotes about the army, two civilians were killed by a sniper, a group of soccer players disappeared when they drove across the artillery practice field, and soldiers played a macho gambling game for entertainment. Punishment for a man who cheated in that game was to have his organ crushed to a pulp between rocks.

The narrator remembers events that occurred during World War II but were not army experiences. As a boy, he was boarded out with farmers who mistreated him. He revenged himself by enticing their children to swallow concealed fishhooks and broken glass which killed them. A cemetery caretaker he knew had been a boxer before being put into a concentration camp; his captors let him survive so that he could entertain them by fighting with professionals, but the rules were such that no one wanted to fight with him.

When the narrator was a student at the university, he heard about a scientist who at a Communist Party reception pinned gold condoms on every guest instead of medals. At one time the narrator was banished to an agricultural settlement where he met a circus contortionist who could do sexy things with her body. As editor of the university newspaper, he was assisted by a girl who took pictures of herself nude. He stole some of the pictures and showed them to people. When the girl died a natural death, everyone assumed that she had committed suicide in shame because he had displayed lewd pictures of her.

Among the narrator's stories about sexual force being used against women were descriptions of a gang rape in a city park; of farmers in a village who kept a woman enslaved in a cage high up in a barn so that men who wanted to use her had to lower the cage with a rope; and of a friend whom he enlisted to help him have sex with a woman who had spurned him.

6266

The narrator tells of senseless killings. Butterflies in a jar were killed slowly by exhausting their supply of oxygen with burning matches. Empty beer bottles murdered a factory watchman. An innocent bystander was beheaded in a "book-knock-off" driving game, in which cars drove close to parked cars that had books attached to them.

When the narrator left his original country, he wore a silvery Siberian wolf coat that was totally unsuitable for his new life. Unemployed and broke, he got a job chipping paint and rust from a ship, but his fur coat became stiff and heavy with paint and at night the fumes nauseated him. He was fired from the painting job and had to park cars in a parking lot. He got into a protection racket that victimized his fellow immigrants. From there he went into truck driving.

As he tried to adjust to his new city, he saw black people living in poor areas where there was no future, but he envied them their freedom. He wished that he could make his own skin dark so that he would not be seen at night. Then he could kill the rich, destroy the city, and put bent nails on highways to crash cars. That might destroy his dream of having material things, and it might drive away the image of what he had been so that he could live in peace with no fear of failure. He played at being a deaf-mute for a while before flying to another country to join a revolution. There, he found himself forced to behead a man with a knife.

Without warning, the narrator left a woman with whom he had been living. After the hotel clerk delivered a message from the narrator that he would not return, she dove deep into the ocean. On the seaweed covering the ocean floor was a moving shadow cast there by a tiny rotten leaf that was floating slowly on the surface above.

Critical Evaluation:

Winner of the National Book Award in 1969, *Steps* is experimental fiction belonging to the "new wave" school led by the French author Alain Robbe-Grillet. Events dominate and readers must participate in the action if they are to find meaning. Its unusual, brilliant tone and technique sets the work apart from other fiction of its time.

In 1967, Jerzy Kosinski received a Guggenheim Fellowship to write the novel. His purpose, as he explained it, was to discover the self through incidents that were symbolic of the world. He said that the book's characters and their relationships existed in a fissure of time between past and present.

Place-names are not given. Poland may be the setting for some of the incidents, America that for others. The author lived in both places. There is no unifying plot, no order to time. Characters are like stick figures, stripped to their bare bones. They have no personality and are nameless. Only women are allowed admirable traits.

The narrator is a man trying to discover who he is in a world he considers hostile. Having come from a Communist country where human beings are externally controlled, he is surprised to find that there are collective forces in the new country that prevent the self from being free. Both society and religion exert control over people.

Much of Kosinski's writing is autobiographical. He spews the horrors he encountered in Poland out onto his pages in graphic form, colored dramatically by his vivid imagination. The jobs held by his narrator are jobs that Kosinski, too, held at various times.

An outgrowth of his first novel, *The Painted Bird* (1965), in which he was a child, *Steps* shows the author as a young man. The incidents seem disconnected, like a mirror that has been broken and the fragments scattered. If the protagonist could only find the pieces and put them together again, perhaps he could look into the reflective surface and see himself clearly. His self is shattered like the narrative, and the chaotic society in which he lives seems shattered as well. A former photographer, Kosinski records each event in visual detail as a camera would see it.

He uses sight to achieve neutrality. The book is almost totally without emotion.

The significance of the title is elusive. Steps should go somewhere, but these steps seem only to travel between experiences. Some readers see the steps as a moral descent into hell, but it is certain that the author hoped that the steps would be his narrator's progression toward self-discovery.

As in other novels of its time, disease is used to symbolize the sick modern world. The disease used in *Steps* is tuberculosis, which is introduced when a ski instructor gets involved with a woman in a European sanatorium. Many of the book's incidents are about people consumed by their desires. In one story an octopus consumes itself. The narrator preys on and consumes women.

Interspersed with thirty-five anecdotes in the past tense are fifteen italicized dialogues with a woman told in the present tense. Most of them concern personal feelings about sexual subjects: circumcision, menstruation, fellatio, jealousy, infidelity, and prostitution. *Steps* is strongly sexual, and these dialogues take place during or after sex. The narrator tells the woman two stories. One is about an architect who designed funeral parlors and concentration camps, the latter because certain humans, like rats, had to be exterminated. In the second, he reminisces about a student at his university who spent time in lavatory cubicles that he called his temples. When he got into trouble over a political mistake, he killed himself in one of the "temples."

Reality and fantasy are so entwined that it is hard to distinguish one from the other. Every awful thing that humans can do to each other seems to have been included. As Kosinski said of his protagonist, "To him the most meaningful and fulfilling gesture is negative."

The theme of the book may be that brutality and violence are so destructive that they make life meaningless. Kosinski believes that human beings are no freer in a free society than they are in a politically controlled society. Told in the first person except for the last incident, which is in the third person, the novel's sentences are short. There is an anticollectivist bias and a detached, objective viewpoint. Dispassionate acceptance of crude, degrading acts in an uncaring world gives tremendous power to the narrative. Kosinski preferred *Steps* to all his other writings. It has been translated into twenty-six languages, and in 1970 it won the National Institute of Arts and Letters Award for Literature.

Distinguished by a commanding structure, poetic prose, and, despite its portrayal of depravity, an underlying morality, the work has been called existential. Its epigraph from the *Bhagavad Gita* (c. fifth century B.C.E.) indicates that the author hoped for peace and happiness to be restored to human life. That cannot occur if manipulative sex and brutal violence are the sum total of an individual's experience. The stark reality of this powerful novel is an admonition to modern society that bizarre relationships and fragmented experiences are capable of destroying the self.

Josephine Raburn

Bibliography:
Cahill, David. "Jerzy Kosinski: Retreat from Violence." *Twentieth Century Literature* 18, no. 2 (April, 1972): 121-132. Discusses Kosinski's belief that incessant violence can destroy the power of humans to create a moral society and describes *Steps* as the author's plea that people turn away from that violence.
Coale, Samuel. "The Quest for the Elusive Self: The Fiction of Jerzy Kosinski." *Critique: Studies in Modern Fiction* 14, no. 3 (1973): 25-37. Discusses the use in *Steps* of detailed, concrete impressions to simulate external reality. Compares the radical and secular art, with

which Konsinski tries to depict the human struggle toward personal identity in the modern world, with techniques used by Franz Kafka.

Howe, Irving. "From the Other Side of the Moon." *Harper's* 238, no. 1426 (March, 1969): 102-105. A detailed critical review that concludes that *Steps* is the hallucinatory self-displacement of a man looking too closely at his own experience.

Kauffman, Stanley. "Out of the Fires." *New Republic* 159, no. 17 (October 26, 1968): 22, 41. A critical review that considers the incidents of *Steps* as unified visions, subtly conceived as proof that the past is very much a part of the present.

Lupak, Barbara. *Plays of Passion, Games of Chance: Jerzy Kosinski and His Fiction.* Bristol, Ind.: Wyndham Hall Press, 1988. Examines all of Kosinski's work, including *Steps.* Includes a discussion of the ways in which the author's life affected his work and points out how his novels differ from other twentieth century novels.

STEPS TO THE TEMPLE

Type of work: Poetry
Author: Richard Crashaw (c. 1612-1649)
First published: 1646

The 1646 edition of Richard Crashaw's *Steps to the Temple*, apparently edited by the anonymous author of the preface, also included a section of secular poems called "The Delights of the Muses," equivalent to another volume. The 1648 edition contained revisions of some of the originals and many new poems, including "The Flaming Heart," a famous poem about Saint Teresa of Ávila in Spain and her mystical religious ecstasy. This discussion will focus on the sacred poems composing the first edition.

The central, unifying metaphor of the title was based on a collection of poems called *The Temple* (1633) by Welsh poet George Herbert. Crashaw's modification of Herbert's title invites comparison between the two poets; indeed, Crashaw included in his volume a poem called "On Mr George Herbert's Book entitled 'The Temple of Sacred Poems.'" In this poem, Crashaw posed as a donor of Herbert's book to a lovely, pious woman. The poem tells the lady reader that she will, by reading the lines, kindle in herself the fire that lies in the words of the meditational poems. Unlocking the secrets of the poems will be like finding an angel and grasping its wings. This angel will transport the perceptive reader daily to heaven, where she can become acquainted with the glories that await her among the gentle souls residing there.

The simple eighteen-line poem, written in rhymed iambic tetrameter couplets, ends with a strange act of appropriation: Crashaw says that the poems in the book, as he gives them to the lady, actually belong to him rather than to Herbert, under whose name they appear. This paradox combines many of the tensions that appear throughout the poetry of Crashaw's entire career. It merges the heavenly and the inspirational with the earthly and the physical. His earthly admiration of the lady, a kind of love, finds its high fulfillment in his homage to her spirit and his attempt to help it strive toward ultimate bliss. The paradox also allows Crashaw to place himself in a tradition of meditative poetry and to choose his own literary precursor.

Even though the subject matter of Herbert's and Crashaw's poems was similar, the two were well distinguished in their styles. Herbert's faith was filled with daily drama and grounded in concrete, mundane experience. In a tone of intimacy, he spoke directly and honestly with his God, trying to discover God's will. Crashaw's poetry, at the other extreme, was lofty, elevated, and elaborate in diction and situation.

Some of the difference may stem from religious influence. Although both had been associated with Little Gidding, a High Church Anglican place of retreat, Herbert had been famous as a country minister, having taken orders in the Church of England in 1630. Crashaw, while raised by a staunch Protestant father, was drawn to the ritual, color, and tradition of Roman Catholicism and converted, probably by 1645, after also having taken orders in the Church of England seven years earlier (1638). During his stays in Paris and Rome, after having left Cambridge shortly before it was visited by Cromwellian anti-Royalist forces, Crashaw also became influenced by a continental and anti-Reformationist strain of thought and art. The qualities of Roman Catholic meaning and matter in his poetry and his tie to continental style mark Crashaw's poetry as unique in England during this period.

The anonymous writer of the preface to the sacred poems of Crashaw indicates that they are the document of an extraordinary man. The title is apt, this writer maintains, because Crashaw lived his life literally and metaphorically on the steps to the temple. The poems are presented as a key to Crashaw's own holy life and as a link whereby the reader might achieve a similar intensity of religious devotion. Crashaw was to lead the reader up the steps to the temple; his poems were to participate in the spirit of scripture. They were to be as inspiring in their turn as the Psalms and other meditational matters that they translated or emulated.

Although Crashaw's style was unique, he also synthesized many of the poetic trends of the seventeenth century. At various times he was master equally of the plain style, the classical imitation, and the metaphysical mode, which he inherited from poets like John Donne. Crashaw, like the metaphysical poets, employed the poem as a form of creation; within its lines, paradoxes, or mutually exclusive realities, could be proven to be true. However, Crashaw exhibited little of the cynicism of his predecessors; his poems often strove for a mystical transformation, of unity with God through the medium of the poem. As vehicles of meditative transformation, the poems drew from a tradition of contemplation of a sacred image for inspiration.

This guise of imagistic contemplation had several effects. First, Crashaw's poems did not resist flowery and extended description as a way of achieving the sensory intensity of the image. Because Crashaw seemed to have a propensity for using the physical details of the body's experience of holiness, these poems became packed with tears, blood, wounds, milk, water, and wine. This exuberance of detail led some to term Crashaw's poetry baroque, ornate, rococo, and excessive. Because it was possible to discover actual paintings and sculptures upon which certain of his poems could have been based, critics also began to use the vocabulary of the plastic arts to describe Crashaw's poetic artistry. His imagistic intensity led many to compare his poetry to painting, sculpture, and music and label it with terms by which these arts are categorized, such as "mannerist." Crashaw's complexity has been contextualized richly in the light of the artistic movements of his time.

Steps to the Temple begins with a translation of a portion of a long poem by Neapolitan Giambattista Marino called "Sospetto d'Herode" ("The Suspicion of Herod"). In Crashaw's translation, this poem appears to be a hybrid of Dante Alighieri's inferno (from the early Renaissance in Italy) and John Milton's *Paradise Lost* (1667). In Crashaw's poem, Satan, knowing that the birth of Christ will conquer Death, sends Alecto, one of the classical Furies, to stir Herod Antipas, ruler of Galilee, into a frenzy in order to vex if not to hinder the birth of Jesus under his jurisdiction. The eight-line narrative stanzas are in iambic pentameter with an *ababababcc* rhyme scheme.

Most notable about this translation is the vivid picture painted of Satan. Stanza after stanza visualizes his situation, while Crashaw enlivens his portrait with an interior monologue. We glimpse the actual psychological and cognitive processes of the Devil. Snakes, flames, horns, chains, red eyes, black nostrils, blue lips, spacious dark wings, groans, stench, gnashing of teeth, lashing of tail—these physical properties set the scene for his mental pondering of God's planned benevolent pattern of history and Lucifer's ultimately insignificant role as a character in that plan.

Lucifer was cast in semiheroic terms, as one who exhibited an individualistic will to strive and to dare. He felt himself to be in painful conflict with God, a regent of a rival kingdom. His thoughts stimulated him to act against the impending birth of Christ for he felt he would lose even the pale prize he earned after his rebellion in heaven, the rule over his own nether world, for Christ would render Death an impermanent state through his capacity to save and redeem the souls of humanity. The translation of book 1 of this poem ends with a stunning irony, that the power of Christ is cloaked in humility, in the modesty of the human form, and with the homage of rude stable beasts.

Other translations in the collection include the famous twenty-third psalm, which begins with the words, "The Lord is my Shepherd." Crashaw recasts this song as rhymed iambic tetrameter couplets filled with rich sensory images. He animates the pastoral landscape by personifying spring and death and by having the elements of the natural scene partake of human qualities and actions, such as weeping, sweating, and breathing. By the end of the poem, Crashaw has turned dying into an act of loving. Rather than a goal of simply to "dwell in the house of the Lord forever," the speaker in this translation would merge with Death as with a lover, after sating on balm and nectar specifically rather than the more traditional image of the brimming cup.

Psalm 137 is also translated, and the collection has a long section of epigrams based on scripture and on events in the life of Christ. These epigrams range from two-lined rhymed couplets in iambic pentameter to a twenty-six-line sequence of rhymed iambic tetrameter couplets, Crashaw's preferred meter, meditating on Matthew 22:46.

The best and most famous poem among the epigrams is "On the Wounds of Our Crucified Lord." This poem is typical of Crashaw, simultaneously metaphysical and baroque. The metaphysical element consists of the elaborate conceit (or metaphorical "concept"), evidenced by the many levels on which the wounds of Christ are interpreted as eyes or mouths, resulting in an impossible transformational truth: "This foot hath got a mouth and lips, . . . [and]/ To pay thy tears, an eye that weeps." By the end of the poem, the worshiper who weeps pearly, watery tears for the suffering of Christ is repaid by Christ with reciprocal tears from the wounded foot, tears of saving blood called ruby drops. The baroque quality of this poem is its almost unsavory, excessive dwelling on the physicality of the conceit. That the metaphor is unusual and far-fetched is metaphysical, but that it is extended beyond all predictable limits is baroque.

"On a Treatise of Charity" is a poem that tries to reclaim the original state of the true religion. It is, in fact, addressed to religion personified as a beautiful maiden. The poet entreats the maiden to brush away the dust of human perception that has dimmed and altered her true beauty and to take her place as queen served by the handmaiden Charity (used in the sense of the Latin root, *caritas*, or love). The middle of the poem changes abruptly in tone, becoming a call to action and transforming the poem into a treatise considering the relative merits of the primacy of individual faith, as the Protestant Reformation proposed, as opposed to the Catholic and Anglican stress on the primacy of good works, bolstered by faith. Archbishop Laud led the latter faction, advocating both love and social works, to animate charity by redeeming "virtue to action." Crashaw ends this poem with an atypically sarcastic comment, that the definition of a Protestant is simply a person who hates the Pope. This movement toward a return to Catholic ways marks the biographical path of Crashaw's life and testifies to his poetry as indeed the literary and spiritual document of an extraordinary Englishman.

Sandra K. Fischer

Bibliography:

Bertonasco, Marc F. *Crashaw and the Baroque*. Tuscaloosa: University of Alabama Press, 1971. Considers meditative exercises and the baroque style. Includes a helpful biblio-graphical essay surveying twentieth century criticism.

Parrish, Paul A. *Richard Crashaw*. Boston: Twayne, 1980. The classic beginning reference point for a critical approach to Crashaw. Surveys historical and cultural context and Crash-aw's life, gives close readings of his poems, and includes a thorough bibliography.

Roberts, Lorraine M. "Crashaw's Sacred Voice: 'A Commerce of Contrary Powers.'" In *New*

Perspectives on the Life and Art of Richard Crashaw, edited by John R. Roberts. Columbia: University of Missouri Press, 1990. Argues that the sacred poems are not personal or mystical, rather that Crashaw creates an objectified voice that can witness artistic renderings of religious events and enter them by a typological connectiveness.

Roberts, Lorraine M., and John R. Roberts. "Crashavian Criticism: A Brief Interpretive History." In *New Perspectives on the Life and Art of Richard Crashaw*, edited by John R. Roberts. Columbia: University of Missouri Press, 1990. A valuable outline and evaluation of criticism of Crashaw's work, beginning in the seventeenth century. Types of criticism are helpfully grouped together.

Young, R. V., Jr. "Crashaw and Biblical Poetics." In *New Perspectives on the Life and Art of Richard Crashaw*, edited by John R. Roberts. Columbia: University of Missouri Press, 1990. Examines Protestant poetics in Crashaw's poetry, concluding that the poet becomes an imitator of God, inscribing the holy word in and through the saving blood of Christ.

THE STONES OF VENICE

Type of work: Criticism
Author: John Ruskin (1819-1900)
First published: 1851-1853

The Stones of Venice has been called not only a great work of scholarship but also a great work of art. It is not merely a catalog of architectural accomplishments; it is a work of cultural history and a commentary on human character. For John Ruskin, the relationship between a nation's buildings and its morality were inseparable, and his three-volume treatise on the edifices of Venice ranges widely to tell the story of the city he sees as the midpoint, both literally and figuratively, between the cultures of East and West. In *The Stones of Venice*, Ruskin praises the accomplishments not only of the great leaders of Venice, but also of the countless numbers of common workers who toiled with skill, patience, and reverence on the great Gothic structures of medieval Europe.

For Ruskin, the polish of the Renaissance was anathema. The exquisite finish of Renaissance architecture values perfection in a limited sphere, and slavish copying of idealized form counts more than attempts to re-create human emotions in art. By contrast, the workers who constructed Gothic buildings were given greater freedom to express themselves. Although their work may appear rougher, even unfinished, it is the consequence of each person's struggle to make something unique; the value of the work lies in the effort of the worker, not in the perfection of the work itself. In Ruskin's view, Renaissance artisans built to please other men and gain glory for themselves, but Gothic workers built to celebrate life and praise God. Small wonder that, for Ruskin, the persistence of Renaissance values indicated a decline in moral stature for humankind.

Ruskin stands with his contemporary, the architect A. W. Pugin, as one of the premier exponents of the Gothic movement of the time. His influence on Victorian sensibility should not be underestimated. In addition to supporting the movement that led to the construction of a number of nineteenth century buildings in the Gothic style, his writings on the Gothic, particularly his celebration of Gothic qualities in *The Stones of Venice* and his praise of painters and sculptors of the medieval and early Renaissance periods, had a significant impact on a younger generation of artists who eventually dubbed themselves Pre-Raphaelites. Poets and painters such as Dante Gabriel Rossetti, William Holman Hunt, and William Morris found Ruskin's works inspirational. Additionally, the tenets of architecture expressed so gracefully and in such detail in *The Stones of Venice* were among the first to make an impression on the most important architect of the twentieth century, Frank Lloyd Wright. *The Stones of Venice* was the first book on architecture that Wright read, and its influence can be seen not only in his designs but, more important, in his constant assertion of the value of architecture in reflecting the aspirations of a society.

In the three volumes of *The Stones of Venice*, John Ruskin traces the development, apex, and decline of three architectural expressions: Byzantine, Gothic, and Renaissance. Ruskin relates their growth and deterioration to the rise and fall of the Venetian state. He shows that the virtue and piety that marked Venice at its flourishing found expression in Gothic architecture and that as this faith declined, Venice's corruption was expressed in Renaissance architecture. The architecture expressed not only the morality of the state but also the morality of the individual architect and common workmen who designed the buildings and did the labor. Ruskin believed that the artistic expression of any nation is clear and direct evidence of its moral and spiritual condition; thus when Ruskin states that since the fading of the Gothic tradition there has been no architectural growth in all of Europe, he is also commenting on the spiritual poverty of his own time.

In the first volume, *The Foundations*, he traces the history of Venice. For nine hundred years the Venetians had struggled to bring power and order out of anarchy. They succeeded in doing so largely because they possessed a childlike religious spirit that dignified even their business transactions and brought them peace, energy, and, whenever necessary, heroes. The geographical location of the city and the nature of its maritime activities were crucial. In Venice, the three pre-eminent architectures of the world—Roman, Lombardic, and Arabian, each expressing a different religious view—flourished separately and blended into one another. For this reason Ruskin calls the Ducal Palace the central building of the world.

According to Ruskin, in order to appreciate or judge any architecture, one must first establish canons of judgment. To do so, one must understand the basic requirements and structure of any building. When speaking of buildings, parts of buildings, or decorations, Ruskin consistently uses words such as moral, immoral, virtuous, and corrupt, terms that normally are applied to people or actions. His descriptions are such that he makes buildings come alive, as indeed they were to him, visible manifestations of the souls of their builders. As a result he speaks of the three virtues required of a building as being: to act well, or do properly what was intended; to speak well, that is, record fact, feelings, history; to look well, present a pleasing appearance. He feels that the second virtue is an individual matter, depending on the character of the observer and his or her mood, but that the first and third are matters which can be weighed and judged according to a known standard. People should admire in architectural construction an admirable human intelligence whose work may be imperfect, but whose feelings are deep and true and honest and show delight in God's work. He then describes brilliantly the construction of the parts of a building—foundation, wall veil, cornice, roof, and apertures—and explains with great clarity not only how a part is constructed, but, more important, why. The why involves not only logical, practical considerations, but geographical, moral, and spiritual ones as well; all these observations testify to the wide scope of Ruskin's perception and historical sense. After describing the practical construction of a building, he considers the decoration. To judge decoration, one must determine the rightness of the material in terms of function and treatment and its placement with regard to the whole. Ornament should not take for its subject human work, such as figures taken from agriculture, sailing, or manufacture, for that is too self-centered. Ornament should express delight in God's work; thus, architects may use the abstract lines in nature, moving from the lower to the higher through the whole range of systematized inorganic and organic forms: earth, water, fire, air, animal organisms, and humanity. An ornament should be so fitted to its place and service that if it were lifted out and placed elsewhere, it would not be satisfactory or complete. The architect must govern the ornament and so design it that workmen will be able to accomplish the architect's intention. It is the architect's duty not to try to improve upon nature but to explain it and express his own soul.

In the second volume, *Sea-Stories*, Ruskin describes the Byzantine period and the Gothic, and he concludes with a careful, elaborate detailing of the Ducal Palace. He describes three churches, Torcello, Murano, and St. Marks. Torcello lies to the northeast of Venice, in the marshes. It was an early church built by people fleeing their pillaged homeland. Thus it was built in haste but with effective simplicity, expressive, Ruskin feels, of the great faith they placed in God. It admits an unusual amount of sun and light for such a building, a psychological need, Ruskin points out, in a people fleeing the darkness of oppression. The pulpit is built with simplicity but is sturdy and functional, and Ruskin ponders the effect of the pulpit on congregations. Such a pulpit inspires confidence, whereas many modern pulpits distract the congregations by being too ornate or raising fears that the entire structure will presently collapse.

Murano, built in the tenth century, furnishes a particularly fine study in proportion and the use of color. The apse is heptagonal on the outside and constructed with mathematical precision. Inside, the placement of the shafts with respect to one another, to the nave and the aisles, reflects subtle, true harmony.

St. Marks was constructed in the Byzantine style during the eleventh century and underwent Gothic additions during the fourteenth century. Its peculiarity is adroit incrustation, brick covered with precious materials. This practice saved materials, expense, and weight, and it required that cutting must be shallow, so that the ornamentation had to be done with care and simplicity rather than with crude force. Also, shallow design permitted delicate shading of color. Beauty, Ruskin thought, is a legitimate offering to God, and the entirety of St. Marks, with its rich colors, mosaics, paintings, and inscriptions, is one great book of Common Prayer, a poor person's Bible. Color is one of God's most divine gifts and one that the most thoughtful value highly; thus, Venice was most colorful during the time of its early, earnest religion. Ruskin says that no style of architecture can be exclusively ecclesiastical. Wherever Christian church architecture has been good and lovely, it has been the perfect development of the common dwelling house architecture of the period. A style fit for a church, he felt, is no less fit for a dwelling, and no form was ever brought to perfection where it was not used for both purposes. Once St. Marks has been judged as a work of art, it must be judged for its fitness as a place of worship. If a church is too beautiful, it will divert the attention of intelligent persons from religion to admiration. Thus, Ruskin believed that effective religious art lies between barbarous idol-fashioning on one side and magnificent craftsmanship on the other.

Ruskin lists six moral elements of the Gothic style: savageness or rudeness, love of nature, love of change, disturbed imagination, obstinacy, and generosity. Gothic is the most rational of forms in that it can fit itself to all services; it is also restless, unquiet, tender, and reverent. Its most striking outward feature is the pointed arch. The Ducal Palace, originally Byzantine, was superseded by Gothic, begun in 1301, and later united with Renaissance in 1423, the year in which Venice and its architecture began to decline.

In the third volume, *The Fall*, Ruskin discusses the moral nature of the Central Renaissance, which is corrupt, its two main immoral elements being pride and infidelity. It is a cold, inhuman form. It is highly trained and erudite and meant only for the act of worship, not, as was the Gothic, for humanity or for the praise of God. Ruskin stresses again forcefully his belief that a fault in feeling induces a fault in style. It was a self-centered, pleasure-seeking, and hypocritical age in that it named one god but dreamed about pagan gods, meanwhile dreading none.

Ruskin deplored machinelike work. He thought one should never encourage the production of anything in which invention has no major share. Imitation or copying should be done only for the sake of preservation. He believed that a truly religious painter or architect would more often than not be rude and simple. The work of such an artist, Ruskin argues, should not be scorned for lack of perfection; the demand for perfection implies a complete misunderstanding of the ends of art. No one, says Ruskin, ever stops until one has reached a point of failure, and so imperfection is essential; it is a sign of life, of change and progress. One of the chief elements of power in all good architecture is the acceptance of rude and uncultivated energy in the workers. Ruskin believed that many people possess, even unsuspected by themselves, talent that is wasted from lack of use. Ruskin hoped, through the work of common people, for a rebirth of true and expressive art throughout Europe.

Updated by Laurence W. Mazzeno

Bibliography:

Cate, George Allan. *John Ruskin: A Reference Guide, A Selective Guide to Significant and Representative Works About Him.* Boston: G. K. Hall, 1988. Surveys Ruskin's literary career and responses to his work. Bibliography covers the years 1843 to 1987, with detailed annotations.

Conner, Patrick. *Savage Ruskin.* Detroit: Wayne State University Press, 1979. Examines Ruskin's art criticism, its nature and significance, its flaws and virtues. Analysis of *The Stones of Venice* concludes that the second volume of the work is Ruskin's masterpiece. Helpful bibliography listing pertinent texts from the eighteenth century to the 1970's.

Kirchhoff, Frederick. *John Ruskin.* Boston: Twayne, 1984. Detailed analysis of *The Stones of Venice.* Selected bibliography with brief annotations.

Rosenberg, John D. *The Darkening Glass: A Portrait of Ruskin's Genius.* New York: Columbia University Press, 1961. An influential text that gives considerable attention to defining the character of *The Stones of Venice* and its thesis.

_____. *The Genius of John Ruskin: Selections from His Writings.* New York: George Braziller, 1963. Arranges a number of Ruskin's works under headings such as "Art" and "Society," discussing *The Stones of Venice* under "Architecture." The introduction to each section illustrates how each work relates to the others and to the development of Ruskin's thought. Selected bibliography.

THE STORY OF AN AFRICAN FARM

Type of work: Novel
Author: Olive Schreiner (1855-1920)
Type of plot: Social realism
Time of plot: 1880's
Locale: South Africa
First published: 1883

Principal characters:
>TANT' SANNIE, a Boer farm woman
>LYNDALL, her stepdaughter
>EM, Lyndall's cousin
>WALDO, the son of a German overseer
>BONAPARTE BLENKINS, a hypocrite
>GREGORY ROSE, a young Englishman

The Story:

Shortly before the Englishman had died, he had married Tant' Sannie, so that there would be someone to take care of his farm and his motherless daughter, Lyndall. Tant' Sannie, a heavy, slow, and simple Boer woman, took over the farm and the care of Lyndall and her cousin, Em. Most of the hard work was done by an old German, who lived with his young son in a small house nearby. The boy, Waldo, watched over the sheep and helped his father take charge of the black natives who did the heaviest work.

The farm lay in a dreary flat plain of red sand that was sparsely dotted with pale bushes. The sun always glittered in a blinding way on the zinc roofs of the buildings and on the stone walls of the enclosures for the animals. Life was monotonous and deadly. Tant' Sannie sat in the farmhouse drinking coffee; the children played in a halfhearted way; young Waldo did his chores, and the German went about seeing that things were as they should be.

Tant' Sannie had been asked by the Englishman to see that the two girls were educated, but she, believing only in the Bible, paid no attention to their demands for books. The two girls and Waldo found some old histories and studied them when they could. Lyndall learned rapidly, for she was a quick, serious girl, fascinated especially by the story of Napoleon. Em was more quiet and reserved. Waldo was the strangest of the three. His father was deeply devout, with an innocent faith in the goodness of man and the mercy of God. He had filled the boy's head with frightening and overpowering ideas.

One day a visitor came to the farm and asked for a night's lodging. He introduced himself as Bonaparte Blenkins. Tant' Sannie would have nothing to do with him, because he was English-speaking. The old German interceded for the visitor, however, and finally won Tant' Sannie's grudging permission for him to spend the night. The German could not bear to pass up an opportunity to practice Christian charity.

Blenkins soon won the German over completely with his fantastic tales of adventure and travel, and he even conquered Tant' Sannie by the wonderful way he read and preached the service on Sunday. The children, however, were not fooled. Lyndall knew that the man was lying when he talked and that his religion was all hypocrisy. Nevertheless, Blenkins was soon installed on the farm as tutor to the children. After a few days, Lyndall walked out of class and refused to return.

Blenkins slowly gained Tant' Sannie's esteem, until he felt that it was safe to try to get rid of the German and take over his job. With a trumped-up charge, he accused the overseer to his mistress and stood by happily as the old German was ordered off the farm. Shocked the more deeply because of the support he had given Blenkins, the German went to his house to pack up and leave. It was not in his nature to argue or fight for his rights; what God sent must be accepted. In his grief he died that night.

Bonaparte Blenkins took over the farm. Like his namesake, he loved power and took advantage of his new position. He ordered Waldo about, beat him, and destroyed the model for a sheep-shearing machine the boy had made. None of these matters made any impression on Tant' Sannie. She thought that Blenkins had a wonderful sense of humor, and daily he grew more and more valuable to her. She hoped some day to be his wife.

A visit by one of Tant' Sannie's nieces disillusioned her. The niece was young, only a little overweight, and wealthy. One day Tant' Sannie climbed up to the loft to see if everything there was neat, and she let her maid take the ladder away. While she was there, Blenkins came into the room below with the niece and began to make love to her. Furious at Blenkins' deception, Tant' Sannie dropped a barrel of salt meat on his head, almost knocking him out, and drenching him with pickle water. His stay on the farm was over.

When the children grew up, Lyndall had her way about going to the city to work and study. Waldo began to doubt the God he had so terribly feared in his childhood, and Em grew to attractive, if not beautiful, womanhood. Tant' Sannie rented part of the farm to a young Englishman named Gregory Rose, who soon fell in love with Em. It was the first time anyone had paid much attention to the girl, and she was enraptured at the prospect of marriage. Tant' Sannie thought she herself might as well marry again, and she sent out word to the surrounding farms that she was looking for a husband.

Waldo eagerly awaited Lyndall's return from the city. He wanted to know what she had discovered about the world and to tell her of his own problems. He had learned wood carving. One day, while he was watching the sheep, a stranger had approached to talk with him. After looking at one of Waldo's carvings, the traveler told the boy a story of a man who searched for truth but found merely a creed until, just before his death, he caught a glimpse of his goal. The meeting was short but unforgettable. Waldo wanted to go out into the world, to find the man again, to learn more about the search for truth.

When Lyndall returned, she was a different person. Waldo found that he could not talk with her as he had before. She had learned the problems a woman faces in the world, and she refused to be held down by the laws and restrictions which bound her. Neither Em nor Gregory Rose, her fiancé, could understand Lyndall. Gregory disliked her at first, but he became more attracted to her as time passed. At Tant' Sannie's wedding feast, for she had found a widower who wanted to marry again, Em discovered that she did not really love Gregory, and she asked him to forget the plans they had made.

When Lyndall asked him to marry her—just to give her his name—Gregory consented. It was a long time before he discovered the reason. Lyndall had made a friend in the city, a man who wanted her to marry him, but she could not stand the idea of being tied down by legal marriage. She wanted freedom, not bondage. She felt that if she could threaten her lover with marriage to another man, she could get what she wanted from him. Her plan worked. When he received a letter telling of her plans, he set out at once to see her. Lyndall met her friend secretly at the farm and went away to live with him, but not as his wife.

Since Waldo, too, had gone off to seek his way in the world, the farm was quiet for a time. Gregory did not know what to do about Lyndall's disappearance. The longer she was away, the more he felt he loved her. At last he started out to learn what had become of her. As Gregory tracked Lyndall from town to town, he learned the story of a slowly fading love between the two people he was following. In time he found Lyndall, lying sick in a hotel room, deserted by her lover. She had had a child, but it had died shortly after birth. Seeing her so weak and sick, Gregory wanted to be near her, to care for her. Dressed as a woman, he was hired as Lyndall's nurse. When she died, he took her body back to the farm for burial.

One night Em was startled by a knock on the door. Waldo had returned. He had traveled much but had learned little. Once he had seen the stranger who had talked to him so wonderfully about truth, but the man, not recognizing him, had turned away. The first thing Waldo did was to sit down and begin a letter to Lyndall. When Em learned what he was doing, she told him that Lyndall was dead.

Gregory still thought of Lyndall and kept as his greatest treasure the one letter he had received from her, a letter which advised him to marry Em. In time, he asked Em again to be his wife, and she accepted. Waldo knew that Em felt she would have only half a husband, but he also knew that she had never learned to hope for much, as he and Lyndall had. Waldo kept one of Lyndall's dancing shoes in his blouse. He spent much of his time wandering about the farm watching the insects and looking at the flowers. He wanted to be like them, to die, to sleep in the same earth with Lyndall. One day, lying in the warm sunshine, he died.

Critical Evaluation:

The Story of an African Farm is one of the first postcolonial novels in English. Schreiner's South African setting is not just an exotic local-color background. It is inextricable from the novel's significance. Olive Schreiner explores the transplantation of European culture and ideals to a new landscape. In chronicling the personal, spiritual, and intellectual evolution of Lyndall and Waldo from childhood to adulthood, she explores the effect this transplantation has on individuals who, though of European background, have never known Europe itself.

Schreiner has been criticized for seeming to depict a depopulated landscape, for effacing the presence of native Africans from the lands colonized by English and Boers. Yet Schreiner, who concerns herself explicitly with issues of racism and colonization in later works such as "Trooper Peter Halket of Mashonaland" even in *The Story of an African Farm* makes clear how foreign, how estranged from the land, the European colonizers feel themselves to be.

Lyndall is perhaps the most beloved character in all of South African literature. Many generations of women, in South Africa and elsewhere, have been named Lyndall after Schreiner's heroine. Although Lyndall derives much of her character and outlook from the environment— Tant' Sannie's ostrich farm in which she spends her youth—her sensibility is always roving; it strives to go outside the bounds of locality and circumstance in which it is constrained. As opposed to the more domesticated Em, Lyndall finds the straitjacketing effects of Victorian definitions of womanhood exacerbated by the cultural impoverishment of her colonial setting. Lyndall knows that the lover she takes is unworthy of her, but she can think of no other option to escape her situation. There is a vast gulf between the level of Lyndall's personal aspirations and the practical steps she can take to fulfill them. That she is never able to return the love of the two men who truly love her, Waldo and Gregory Rose, is an indication of the unfulfilled quality of Lyndall's life. For all her energy and ambition, her character is not able to take root in African soil, to establish itself as a spirit and a presence capable of taking on the dominating circumstances of life in that place and time.

Waldo, weak and sensitive, is in a way even more vulnerable than Lyndall, lacking her drive and willpower. Yet he has an outlet unavailable to the young girl, his penchant for speculating and philosophizing. Untalented in any aspect of life but the mental one, Waldo is nonetheless a rare soul, somebody whose mixture of simple belief in God and complex intellectual musings would make him unusual in any setting, but especially that of colonial South Africa. The peak of Waldo's introspection is achieved when he encounters the stranger who tells the story of the man who searches for truth. The feather that is the only material vestige of this search becomes Waldo's symbol. The feather does not represent the truth itself, but rather the small specimen of art or experience that is left when the search for truth inevitably fails to achieve its goal. The feather, however, is enough for the man in the stranger's story, and, inferentially, for Waldo. Art, as represented by Waldo's carvings, has the power to express an otherwise elusive truth.

Despite Waldo's mental strength, he is too weak in character to withstand the devastating blow of Lyndall's early death. The understated scene at the end of the book in which Waldo dies as the chickens go on living in their instinctual way (a death-scene so understated that readers often do not immediately understand what has happened) shows that without the spark of Lyndall to animate him, Waldo recedes and yields to the land, not able to sustain the mental and physical energy necessary to keep himself alive. Lyndall's other oddly passive male admirer, Gregory Rose, is similarly lost without Lyndall and unable to help her, despite the enormity of his admiration for her. Gregory's willingness to dress up as a woman in order to comfort Lyndall after her tragic childbirth indicates his willingness to discard Victorian gender stereotypes and to respect the vigor of Lyndall's self-assertion. In casting an androgynous haze over his sexual identity, however, the act implies that Gregory is not strong enough to be the kind of man Lyndall needs as her soulmate.

The other characters in the book are largely foils to the tragically doomed ambition and spirit of Lyndall and Waldo. The spiritual differences between the two main characters and figures such as Tant' Sannie and Em are so vast as to make the situation almost ridiculous. That Tant' Sannie and Em should both be hoodwinked by an opportunistic buffoon such as Bonaparte Blenkins even as Waldo is working out his own inner destiny is almost pathetically incongruous. Yet Tant' Sannie and Em do provide a loving and supportive environment for the youngsters to grow up in. In addition, Em's marriage to Gregroy at the end of the book is a signal that, despite the deaths of the two main characters, life in the farm will go on and that Lyndall and Waldo will not be forgotten.

In *The Story of an African Farm*, Schreiner combines the philosophical inclinations of a novelist such as George Eliot with the concern about practical issues of women's self-definition raised by novelists of the 1890's such as George Egerton, Mona Caird, and Mary Cholmondeley. Schreiner's book is not, however, only a Victorian woman's novel; it is an exploration of the colonial experience. Without Schreiner, later South African novelists such as Pauline Smith, Sarah Gertrude Millin, and Nadine Gordimer would have lacked a crucial precedent and reference point for their work. Schreiner explores social and cultural issues that are still resonant. That she does this while writing a novel of striking originality and imagination is a tribute to her power as a novelist.

"Critical Evaluation" by Margaret Boe Birns

Bibliography:
Berkman, Joyce Avrech. *The Healing Imagination of Olive Schreiner: Beyond South African Colonialism.* Amherst: University of Massachusetts Press, 1989. Stresses Schreiner's humanistic and progressive sociological views and discusses how they are represented in her fiction.

Chrisman, Laura. "Empire, Race, and Feminism at the *fin de siècle*: The Works of George Egerton and Olive Schreiner." In *Cultural Politics at the fin de siècle*, edited by Sally Ledger and Scott McCracken. Cambridge, England: Cambridge University Press, 1995. Examines Schreiner's work in the light of the new woman movement of the 1890's and its contribution concerning gender and imperialism.

First, Ruth, with Ann Scott. *Olive Schreiner*. London: André Deutsch, 1980. Authoritative chronicle of Schreiner's life and times, co-written by an African National Congress activist, explores the relationship of Schreiner's life to the history of her troubled nation.

Monsman, Gerald. *Olive Schreiner's Fiction: Landscape and Power*. New Brunswick, N.J.: Rutgers University Press, 1991. Examines Schreiner's art in aesthetic terms, stressing her sensitivity to nature and her philosophical ambitions. Especially useful for interpreting Waldo's aesthetic evolution and the development of Lyndall's character.

Van Wyk Smith, Malvern, and Don MacLennan, eds. *Olive Schreiner and After: Essays on Southern African Literature in Honour of Guy Butler*. Cape Town, South Africa: D. Philip, 1983. Situates Schreiner in the tradition of white South African writing in English that she was crucial in founding.

THE STORY OF BURNT NJAL

Type of work: Fiction
Author: Unknown
Type of plot: Adventure
Time of plot: Tenth century
Locale: Iceland
First transcribed: Njáls Saga, thirteenth century (English translation, 1861)

Principal characters:
NJAL, a man of law
BERGTHORA, his wife
GUNNAR, Njal's friend
HALLGERDA, Gunnar's wife
FLOSI, Njal's enemy

The Story:

Harold Grayfell ruled in Norway. Hrut Heriolfsson had come out of Iceland to claim an inheritance, and he sat on the high seat of Gunnhilda, the king's mother. He was handsome and strong. He found favor with the king as well, so that he claimed his inheritance and got a great store of rich goods while sea roving. Then he sailed back to Iceland, but not before Gunnhilda put a spell on him that he might never have pleasure living with the woman he had set his heart on.

Soon after, Hrut married Unna, Fiddle Mord's daughter. Things did not go smoothly between Hrut and Unna, and she soon left him. When Mord asked at the Thing for her goods to be returned, Hrut offered to fight him instead. Mord refused and got great shame by his suit.

Hrut's brother Hauskuld had a fair daughter, Hallgerda, but she was hard-hearted. She married Thorwald Oswifsson, and he was killed by Thiostolf, her foster father. Then she married Glum, son of Olof the Hall, and he was murdered. She then sent Thiostolf to Hrut to tell of Glum's death, and Hrut struck him dead. Fiddle Mord died, and Unna ran through her goods. Then she asked her kinsman Gunnar Hamondsson to get back her goods from Hrut. Gunnar was the best skilled in arms of all men. His brother's name was Kolskegg.

Njal was Gunnar's friend. They swore nothing should come between them. Njal was so great a lawyer that his match was not to be found. Bergthora was his wife.

Gunnar asked Njal how to get Unna's goods, and Njal advised him to trick Hrut into summoning himself to the Thing where the suit would be tried. There Gunnar challenged Hrut to single combat, but Hauskuld made Hrut pay the money. There was much ill feeling.

Gunnar and Kolskegg went sea roving and came back with many goods. They rode to the Thing, and there Gunnar saw Hallgerda and asked for her. Njal foretold ill from this but went to the wedding.

At the wedding Thrain Sigfusson put away his shrewish wife and asked for Thorgerda, Hallgerda's daughter. So there were two weddings.

Each year Gunnar and Njal had feasts for friendship's sake. Njal had it the year Bergthora insulted Hallgerda and Hallgerda asked Gunnar to avenge her. Gunnar refused and took her home. Then Hallgerda had Bergthora's thrall killed. Gunnar paid atonement to Njal. Bergthora retaliated, and Njal paid for that death. The women urged their men on until Njal's sons were involved, but Gunnar and Njal kept their friendship.

When Otkell Skarfsson tricked Gunnar into buying a deceitful thrall, Hallgerda sent him to burn Otkell's storehouse. Gunnar offered atonement but refused Otkell friendship. Then Otkell gave Gunnar a hurt, and Gunnar killed Otkell. This was the beginning of Gunnar's slayings. Njal warned him not to kill more than one man in the same stock or he would get his death.

Then Starkad, son of Bork the Waxy-toothed Blade, challenged Gunnar to a horse fight. Thorgeir Otkellsson was hurt and wanted to be revenged against Gunnar. Starkad, his son Thorgeir, and Thorgeir Otkellsson tried to ambush Gunnar, and Thorgeir Otkellsson was killed. This was the second man slain in the same stock. Thorgeir Starkadsson swore vengeance. At the Thing the atonement was that Gunnar and Kolskegg were to go away within three years or be slain by the kinsmen of those they had killed.

They made plans to go abroad, but as they rode away, Gunnar's horse threw him with his face turned toward home. When he decided not to go, Kolskegg went alone. Gunnar was outlawed. Njal warned him that Geir the Priest was getting up a band to slay him, and Gunnar asked Njal to see after his son Hogni.

When Geir the Priest and his men came to Gunnar's house, they killed his hound Sam. Sam howled loudly before he died, so that Gunnar was prepared. Gunnar put up a long fight and killed two men and wounded sixteen before his enemies pulled the roof off his house to get at him.

They built a cairn over Gunnar. Skarphedinn Njalsson and Hogni Gunnarsson saw the cairn open, and Gunnar with a merry face sang a song before the cairn closed again. Then Skarphedinn and Hogni killed Starkad and Thorgeir Starkadsson and avenged Gunnar.

Njal's sons then went abroad, and wrongs piled up between them and Thrain Sigfusson in the Orkneys. Kari Solmundsson was with them. When they came back, Skarphedinn killed Thrain. Kettle of the Mark was Thrain's brother but Njal's son-in-law, and so Kettle and Njal made atonement. Njal took Hauskuld Thrainsson as his foster son. Kari asked for and got Njal's daughter Helge to wife. Then Flosi Thordsson became involved in the feud. He was tall and bold.

There was a change of rulers in Norway. Olaf Tryggvisson made a change of faith and sent Thangbrand to Iceland to preach Christianity. He did that by challenging any man who spoke against the new faith. At the Thing, Thorgeir of Lightwater challenged the men for the new law, and they all made pledges. Then Njal went to Flosi to ask his daughter Hildigunna for his foster son Hauskuld. She said she would not be wedded unless they would get Hauskuld a priesthood.

Njal tried to get a priesthood for Hauskuld, but no one would sell his. At the Thing that summer, when no one could get his suit settled, Njal said it would be wiser to have a Fifth Court to take over those suits that could not be finished in the Quarter Courts. Skapti Thorodsson then brought the Fifth Court into law. Njal begged a new priesthood for Hauskuld, and Hildigunna and Hauskuld were married.

Soon after Lyting, Thrain's sister's husband, took offense at Hauskuld, Njal's baseborn son, and killed him. Rodny, Hauskuld's mother laid it upon Skarphedinn to avenge that death. Skarphedinn and his brothers went after Lyting and his brothers. When Njal's foster son Hauskuld made atonement for the slaying, Aumund, Hauskuld Njalsson's baseborn and blind son, came to Lyting at the Thing and demanded his share. Lyting refused. When Aumund came to the door, he turned short around, and his eyes were opened. Then he ran straight to Lyting and killed him with an ax. Aumund turned to go out again, and his eyes were sealed. Njal made the atonement.

Mord Valgardsson planned to talebear before Njal's sons so that they would kill Hauskuld the Priest. A coolness sprang up between Njal's sons and Hauskuld. Finally, Mord with them,

Njal's sons slew Hauskuld. Njal said the next deaths would be his and those of his wife and sons.

Hauskuld's death brought his father-in-law Flosi Thordsson much grief and wrath. He gathered together a great band. Skarphedinn sought help, and they all went to the Thing. There the atonement fell through. Flosi gathered his men for an attack with fire and sword on Njal's sons.

Njal gathered all of his sons in the house, and Flosi's band tried to master them with weapons. When the attackers had got great many wounded, Flosi took fire and made great piles before the doors. He called the women out, and Helgi Njalsson tried to escape with them but was killed. Bergthora stayed indoors with Njal and Kari's son Thord. The three lay down on the bed with an ox hide over them. Then the fires burned hot and timbers began to fall. Kari ran along the crossbeams and beat his way out with a burning bench. He was hidden by the smoke as he ran away. Skarphedinn tried to follow but was pinned to the wall, and Grimm fell dead in the fire. After Flosi's men were sure Skarphedinn was dead, they heard him sing a song. When men came to find them, Njal and Thord and Bergthora were not burned, but the ox hide was shriveled.

Flosi dreamed that many men would die. Kari set about getting his men together. They all went to the Thing. All who wished to avenge the burning shouted their war cries. Many men were killed before an atonement was reached. Since Kari would not have that atonement cover the burning, there was another award for that. The payment covered all but Thord Karisson. Flosi and his men were to go abroad.

Thorgeir Craggeir, a kinsman, went along with Kari. They came upon some of Flosi's men and killed them. Then Flosi made an atonement with Thorgeir, so that Kari would be left alone. Kari said he would take it ill if Thorgeir did not make his peace. He agreed that the burning was avenged but not his son's death. Then Kari went to the Orkneys and killed more men who had sailed out of Iceland until he had slain fifteen. His wife died while he was sea roving.

Then Kari and Flosi made separate pilgrimages south for absolution. When they came home, Kari went straight to Flosi's house. Flosi sprang up and kissed Kari. Then they were fully atoned, and Flosi gave to Kari his brother's daughter Hildigunna. They dwelt there a long time.

Critical Evaluation:

Icelanders defined sagas as the telling over and over of great ancestral feuds and battles; the sagas were often told during long winter nights. The distinction between fact and fiction was not made. Actually, the saga form had a more lofty purpose: to maintain pride in family history and to tell the stories of the ancestral heroic age and of the introduction of Christianity to Iceland. The king's sagas and the family sagas were the most popular. *The Story of Burnt Njal* (also known as *Burnt Njál*) is of the latter form. Some scholars argued up until the 1920's that the work was originally two distinct sagas, Gunnar's saga and Njal's saga. Presently it is considered to be the work of one author because of the cohesion of stylistic form and thematic structure. The saga is differentiated from the epic in that the former is prose. Otherwise there are great similarities with the Njal and Homer's epics. The use of battle scenes, festivals, and games are prevalent in both and delight the reader in their pageantry.

The Story of Burnt Njal is of the late classical period in Icelandic literary history. The romanticism and chivalry are not evident in the more skeletal earlier sagas. Njal's role of hero is that of a more ordinary man than known in the Greek epics. His initial naïveté over the deteriorating social situation and the misunderstood peace offering to Flosi conspire to cause Njal's death. He is a victim of fate and of the old code of honor, exemplified throughout the saga in his wife Bergthora. Foreshadowings in this saga are effected by employing dreams and portents, a much different literary device than the modern technique of suspense. In *The Story of Burnt Njal*, the reader is usually aware of the events to transpire. The purpose of the saga and epic forms was to retell and remind the listeners of history and myth, not, as with the moderns, to compose something completely new.

Although this Icelandic saga contains an elaborate plot and subplot structure, an abundance of characters often mentioned briefly then forgotten, and a recalling of events and names foreign and relatively unknown to modern readers, the saga provides insight into the oral tradition and codes of a past society.

The Thing, the Icelandic assembly or parliament, was the supreme lawgiver. The Thing was established in 930 C.E. and served the Old Icelandic Commonwealth while it lasted, which was until 1262. The problem of the system and the crucial concern for the characters of the saga are that, even after being judged as correct in an audience at the Thing, those who sought justice had to carry out justice for themselves.

One of the fundamental issues relating to the execution of justice was the interplay between the heathen code of killing and revenge and the Christian idea of forgiveness. Christianity was introduced into Iceland in 1000. It is recalled in the saga by Thangbrand's journey to Iceland, which initiated that land's adoption of Christianity as the national religion. The intertwining of codes and religions again comes into play with the juxtaposition of pagan magic and Christian miracles. Ironically, often the miracles were performed not to provide healing but to carry out pagan vengeance. Kari and Flosi journey to Rome to obtain forgiveness for the bloodshed caused by their animosity, yet the reason this hostility began involved the heathen code of honor. Thus, the saga involves not only the continuous decisions of the Thing and their often tragic aftermath but also the inception of a new religion and code of order. The narrator of this saga maintained an objective eye. Very little moralizing or psychological probing of actions is evident. The characters, six hundred in all with twenty-five main actors, are developed through their actions, a behavioristic approach, rather than by their thoughts or reflections.

The Story of Burnt Njal follows three main stories: first, the downfall of Gunnar; second, the burning of Njal and his sons; and third, the exacting revenge required by Kari. The middle section for which the saga was named is the climax and turning point of the story. All events lead toward it, and it involves all the preceding arguments and attempted honorable reconciliations. It also reflects the breakdown of the lawmaking by the Thing into jealousy and seeming dishonor; the battle is fought essentially because of the misunderstood intentions of Njal's gift. The saga then leads away from the burning and death of Njal toward atonement at the Thing as all parties meet to arrange a settlement. Finally the saga ends on a Christian note: Forgiveness is sought from the Church, and reconciliation is effected between the enemies.

"Critical Evaluation" by Gayle Steck

Bibliography:
Schach, Paul. *The Icelandic Saga*. Translated and with an introduction by Paul Schach. Lincoln: University of Nebraska Press, 1962. The chapter "Several Individual Sagas" contains a discussion of *The Story of Burnt Njal*.
Tucker, John. *Sagas of the Icelanders: A Book of Essays*. New York: Garland, 1989. Three different essays, on pages 272 to 322, discuss *The Story of Burnt Njal* in detail. An excellent reference for further research.

THE STORY OF GÖSTA BERLING

Type of work: Novel
Author: Selma Lagerlöf (1858-1940)
Type of plot: Picaresque
Time of plot: Early nineteenth century
Locale: Sweden
First published: Gösta Berlings Saga, 1891 (English translation, 1898)

Principal characters:
GÖSTA BERLING, a former minister
THE COUNTESS ELIZABETH, Gösta's wife
MARGARETA SAMZELIUS, the wife of a major
MARIANNE SINCLAIR, a woman in love with Gösta
CHRISTIAN BERGH, Gösta's crony

The Story:

Gösta Berling stood in the pulpit on what for him was a critical Sunday. The congregation had complained of his conduct to the bishop, who had thereupon come to investigate his ministry. Gösta drank far too much and too often. With his crony, Christian Bergh, he had begun to spend more and more time in tavern taprooms, and brandy had become a necessity for him.

That morning, he preached his sermon as if inspired. At the end of the service, the bishop stood up and asked for complaints against the minister, but no one said a word. In his heart, Gösta felt love for his flock. As he sat up that night, thinking of the wonder that had happened, Bergh came to his window to assure him that the bishop would never trouble him again. With the intention of helping his drinking crony, Bergh had driven the bishop and his attendant priests in his carriage, taking them on a wild ride, up and down hill and over plowed fields at top speed. Drawing up at their destination, he had warned the bishop not to bother Gösta again. As a result, Gösta was dismissed from the church.

He became a beggar. In the winter he had only rags on his feet. He met the twelve-year-old daughter of the wicked clergyman of Bro. Neglected by her father, she was hauling a heavy sled with a sack of meal for her own food. Gösta took hold of the rope with her. When she left him in charge of the sled, he promptly bartered both sled and meal for brandy.

Awaking from a drunken sleep, Gösta saw Margareta Samzelius, the major's wife, looking at him with compassion. Margareta, strong and rough, ruled Ekeby and six estates. She had been betrothed to a young man named Altringer, but her parents did not allow her to wait five years for Altringer to make his fortune, instead forcing her to marry Major Samzelius. When Altringer had come back rich and famous, Margareta became his mistress. At his death, he had left his lands ostensibly to the major, but in reality to Margareta.

After great urging, Gösta became a pensioner, one of the group of merry wastrels who existed handsomely on Margareta's bounty. On Christmas Eve, the pensioners had a grand party, at which there was much to drink. Sintram, who was so evil that he thought himself the chosen of Satan, came in dressed as the devil. He said he was going to renew his pact with Margareta. The half-drunk pensioners thought uneasily of Margareta's great wealth and power. Surely something supernatural had helped her. It was said that she held her power by sacrificing the soul of one pensioner to the devil each year.

In a frightening bit of nonsense, the pensioners made a pact with the devil; no one of their number was to die that year. Once in charge of Ekeby and the six estates, the pensioners agreed to conduct themselves as masters in a manner pleasing to Satan himself.

The next day, when the grouse was being passed at the Christmas feast, Bergh said they were just crows, and he threw them one by one against the wall. When Margareta ordered him out of the house, Bergh in revenge accused her of having been Altringer's mistress with the compliance of her husband. Margareta proudly confessed the truth of what he said. Then, to save his honor, the major disowned his wife. All the pensioners, who owed her so much, turned their faces when she asked for help. Margareta left her home to become a beggar.

That year, the pensioners were in charge at Ekeby. The major, indifferent to the estates, returned to his own farm. Gösta learned that Anna Stjarnhök, the rich and beautiful belle of the district, had broken her engagement to a timid man named Ferdinand to become engaged to a rich old man with a bald head.

Determined to bring Anna back to Ferdinand, Gösta harried her so much at a ball that she slapped his face. That slap revealed that Anna really loved Gösta. Forgetting his duty to Ferdinand, Gösta set out with Anna for Ekeby. On the way, however, their sleigh was followed by wolves, and they were forced to stop at Ferdinand's home for protection. Thus Gösta involuntarily brought Anna back to Ferdinand and was saved from committing a sin. Ferdinand soon died, however, and Anna went through a marriage ceremony with his corpse. Ever after she concealed her love for Gösta.

At a ball at Ekeby, Gösta and Marianne Sinclair took part in a tableau that presented them as lovers. Marianne, succumbing to Gösta's charm, kissed him after the tableau. Later, at the gaming table, Gösta won all the money Marianne's father had; then, in jest, Gösta won his consent to a betrothal with Marianne. When the father discovered that Gösta, a drunkard and an unfrocked minister, was in earnest, he was furious with his daughter.

After the ball, the pensioners found Marianne locked out by her father and half-frozen. Supposedly asleep in the guest room at Ekeby that night, the girl had heard Margareta, full of wrath against her pensioners, plan a riot to drive the wastrels out. Marianne ran to a bear hunter, enlisted his aid, and succeeded in breaking up the riot.

Marianne contracted smallpox on her errand, and the scars greatly marred her beauty. Not wishing Gösta to see her, she returned to her father. Gösta, thinking she had jilted him and too proud to go after her, soon forgot her.

At the age of twenty, Countess Elizabeth Dohna was a carefree, sympathetic young woman married to a stupid husband. At a dance, Gösta asked her for a polka. She refused because she had heard that Gösta had caused the death of Ebba, her husband's sister, who had died in sorrow after hearing the story of Gösta's life. Angry at her refusal, Gösta and his friends abducted the countess and took her home. There the stupid husband sided with Gösta. The poor girl led a miserable life. When she finally ran away to live as a peasant, the count had the marriage annulled. After she was legally a single woman again, she bore a child. Not wishing to have an unnamed baby, she asked Gösta to marry her. Gösta, awed and grateful, accepted, for he loved her.

Helped by his wife, Gösta turned over a new leaf, and all the pensioners followed his lead. Ekeby rang with the smith's hammer; walls and docks were repaired. When Margareta came back after the death of the major, she reentered Ekeby as mistress of a prosperous estate. Gösta and his wife retired to a modest cottage where Gösta earned his living as a carpenter and helped those who were in trouble; the countess served the sick. So Gösta became, after many years, a good man.

Critical Evaluation:

Selma Lagerlöf was born into a once prosperous Varmland family that, like most families in the district, had fallen on bad times. Although circumstances were straitened and the fear of poverty was a constant presence, memories of better times in the recent past were still vivid and carefully preserved as part of the family lore that Lagerlöf absorbed in anecdotes as she was growing up. In many ways, *The Story of Gösta Berling* reflects this background. The novel's characters and scenes, drawn from rural Swedish life, are reminiscent of Anton Chekhov's treatment of similar material dealing with life in rural Russia. The loss of ancestral estates, for example, strongly affects the plot development in *The Story of Gösta Berling* as it does in Chekhov's *The Cherry Orchard* (1904), just as upper-middle-class decadence seems to direct the course of events both in Lagerlöf's novel and in Chekhov's *The Three Sisters* (1901). Other parallels can be drawn with Lagerlöf's depiction of the deterioration of a comfortable way of life and the generous hospitality that accompanied it. So, too, does the psychology of fear—suspicion of being exploited when the security of property is lost—find Chekhovian echoes. These factors most particularly shape Lagerlöf's portrayal of the pensioners in her novel.

The Story of Gösta Berling was Lagerlöf's first and most famous novel, but it is not unique in her output, for which she won a Nobel Prize in Literature in 1909—the first woman and the first Swede to be so honored. Her later novels and tales, including *The Miracles of Antichrist* (1897), *Jerusalem* (1901-1902), and *The Wonderful Adventures of Nils* (1906-1907), especially—also show the same concerns with the failure of the social system, the plight of the peasant, the corruption of people in positions of authority, and the eternal verities of folk wisdom. The latter aspect of Lagerlöf's novels is one of her strongest and most unusual points. The folkloric qualities, expressed through supernatural elements and a great sensitivity toward nature, combine romanticism with shrewd sociopolitical insight. In *The Story of Gösta Berling* Lagerlöf's powerful imagination creates a happily reckless amalgam of unlikely, even contradictory, attitudes.

Despite apparently disparate elements in the novel, Gösta himself is the unifying force, even though in some respects he is not a credible protagonist. Lagerlöf, who seems unaware of his imperfections, observed a number of conventional taboos—mostly dealing with sex, religion, and politics—that obscured the realities of life around her and blocked her ability to deal creatively with such matters in her novels. As a result, Lagerlöf overlooked contradictions in the substantive development of her novel in pursuing situations she wanted to see occur or that she was trained, by her background, to expect. The novel must therefore be accepted on its own unconventional terms.

In Lagerlöf's time, conventional terms meant the naturalism of Émile Zola and August Strindberg. Lagerlöf chose instead to follow the timeless old truths of ancient tales and archetypal myths. Such utter indifference to contemporaneity made Lagerlöf an anomaly, but the compelling power of her art elevated her work to a level that gained her a position of respect in the literary world. Without bowing to literary fashion, she wrote a first novel that has ever since captured the attention of readers. In this work, Lagerlöf commanded a theme that is of enduring interest: Can one have fun and still be good? This question is as pertinent today as it was in the 1890's when *The Story of Gösta Berling* was first published.

Ultimately, the question confronts the sanctions of social opinion, and the definitions of "fun" and "good." To Gösta, fun was drinking and wenching. His contemporary counterpart would hardly dispute such a value system. In 1836, Nathaniel Hawthorne's *The Minister's Black Veil* exposed a previously unexplored aspect of clerical activity. Henrik Ibsen's *Brand* (1866) similarly revealed the contradictions of a clergyman caught between duty and inclination.

Lagerlöf's *The Story of Gösta Berling* in 1894 came midstream in these treatments of religious crises, which continued in such later works as Sinclair Lewis' *Elmer Gantry* (1927). Lagerlöf probed this clerical dilemma, part of the larger theme of ethical responsibility, with extraordinary sensitivity and insight.

The Story of Gösta Berling is a novel that combines elements of realism to suit the fashion of the time when it was written (the characterization of Gösta Berling is here exemplary) with elements of fantasy that suited Lagerlöf's own predilection for deferring to ancient custom and observance of traditional ways. Lagerlöf was not aware of contradictions between these two ways of viewing reality, and her novel demonstrates the level of her artistic accomplishment and of her psychological grasp of human interaction.

"Critical Evaluation" by Joanne G. Kashdan

Bibliography:
Edström, Vivi. *Selma Lagerlöf*. Translated by Barbara Lide. Boston: Twayne, 1984. An accessible study by a recognized authority on Lagerlöf. Contains an overview of Lagerlöf's biography and separate chapters on her most important works, including *The Story of Gösta Berling*. Edström discusses the form of the novel, its elements of historical reality and folklore, and its place in Swedish literary history.
Gustafson, Alrik. *A History of Swedish Literature*. Minneapolis, University of Minnesota Press, 1961. In this overview of the literature of Sweden from the beginning to the post-war era, Gustafson places Lagerlöf's works in historical context and discusses the place of the novel within her own oeuvre.
_____. *Six Scandinavian Novelists*. Princeton, N.J.: Princeton University Press, 1940. A comprehensive overview of Lagerlöf's work, including a discussion of *The Story of Gösta Berling*.
Olson-Buckner, Elsa. *The Epic Tradition in Gösta Berling's Saga*. New York: Theo Gaus, 1978. In an extended analysis, Olson-Buckner points out the many points of contact between *The Story of Gösta Berling* and the conventional epic. Also notes that there are structural similarities to the traditional heroic saga.
Wivel, Henrik. *Selma Lagerlöf: Her Works of Life*. Minneapolis: The Center for Nordic Studies, University of Minnesota, 1991. Contains a brief discussion of the idea of love as it is presented throughout Lagerlöf's works, including *The Story of Gösta Berling*.

THE STRANGE CASE OF DR. JEKYLL AND MR. HYDE

Type of work: Novella
Author: Robert Louis Stevenson (1850-1894)
Type of plot: Gothic
Time of plot: Nineteenth century
Locale: London
First published: 1886

> *Principal characters:*
> DR. HENRY JEKYLL, a London physician
> MR. UTTERSON, the counselor for Dr. Jekyll
> POOLE, Dr. Jekyll's manservant
> DR. HASTIE LANYON, Dr. Jekyll's close friend

The Story:

Mr. Richard Enfield, and his cousin, Mr. Utterson, a lawyer, were strolling according to their usual Sunday custom when they came upon an empty building on a familiar street. Mr. Enfield told that some time previously he had seen an ill-tempered man knock down and trample on a small child at the doorway of the deserted building. He and other indignant bystanders had forced the stranger, who gave his name as Hyde, to pay a sum of money for the child's welfare. Enfield remembered Hyde with deep loathing.

Utterson had reasons to be interested in Hyde. When he returned to his apartment, he reread the strange will of Dr. Henry Jekyll. The will stipulated that in the event of Dr. Jekyll's death all of his wealth should go to a man named Edward Hyde. Utterson sought out Hyde, the man whom Enfield had described, to discover if he were the same person who had been named heir to Dr. Jekyll's fortune. Hyde was suspicious of Utterson's interest and, becoming enraged, closed his door to Utterson. When the lawyer questioned his client, Dr. Jekyll refused to discuss the matter but merely insisted that in the event of his death the will be executed. Utterson believed that Hyde must be an extortioner who was getting possession of Dr. Jekyll's money and would eventually murder the doctor.

About a year later, Hyde was wanted for the senseless murder of a kindly old gentleman, Sir Danvers Carew. Dr. Jekyll presented the lawyer and the police with a letter signed by Hyde, in which the murderer declared his intention of making good his escape and never returning to England. The letter ended with Hyde's apology to Dr. Jekyll for having abused his friendship.

About this time, Dr. Lanyon, who had been for years a great friend of Dr. Jekyll, became ill and died. A letter addressed to Utterson was found among his papers. Opening it, Utterson discovered an inner envelope also sealed and bearing the directive that it was not to be opened until after Dr. Jekyll's death. Utterson suspected that this, too, was somehow connected with the evil Hyde, but he could in no way fathom the mystery.

One Sunday, Enfield and Utterson were walking again in the street where Enfield had seen Hyde abusing the child. They now realized that the deserted building provided a side entrance to an additional wing in the house of Dr. Jekyll that was used as a laboratory. Looking up, they saw Dr. Jekyll sitting at a window, looking disconsolate. Then his expression seemed to change, and his face took on a grimace of horror or pain. Suddenly, he closed the window. Utterson and Enfield walked on, too overcome by what they had seen to be able to speak.

Not long afterward, Utterson was sitting by his fireside when Dr. Jekyll's manservant, Poole, sought entrance. He related that for the past week something strange had been going on in Dr. Jekyll's laboratory. The doctor himself had not appeared. Instead, he had ordered his meals to be sent in and had written curious notes demanding that Poole go to all the chemical houses in London in search of a mysterious drug. Poole was convinced that his master had been slain and that the murderer, masquerading as Dr. Jekyll, was still hiding in the laboratory.

Utterson and Poole returned to Dr. Jekyll's house and broke into his laboratory with an ax. They entered and discovered that the man in the laboratory had killed himself by draining a vial of poison just as they had broken the lock. The man was Edward Hyde.

They searched in vain for the doctor's body, convinced that it must be somewhere, since there was a note from him to Utterson dated that day. In the note, Dr. Jekyll said he was planning to disappear, and he urged Utterson to read the note that Dr. Lanyon had left at the time of his death. An enclosure contained Henry Jekyll's confession.

Utterson returned to his office to read the letters. The letter of Dr. Lanyon described an occasion when Dr. Jekyll had sent Poole to Dr. Lanyon with a request that the doctor search for a particular drug in Dr. Jekyll's laboratory and give it to Hyde, who had come to claim the drug. Then, in Dr. Lanyon's presence, Hyde had taken the drug and been transformed into Dr. Jekyll. The shock of this transformation had caused Dr. Lanyon's decline in health, which led to his death.

Dr. Jekyll's own account of the horrible affair was more detailed. He had begun early in life to live a double life. Publicly, he had been genteel and circumspect; privately, however, he had practiced strange vices without restraint. Becoming obsessed with the idea that people had two personalities, he had reasoned that men were capable of having two physical beings as well. Finally, he had compounded a mixture that transformed his body into the physical representation of his evil self. He became Hyde. In that disguise, he was free to haunt the lonely, narrow corners of London and to perform the darkest acts without fear of recognition.

Dr. Jekyll did everything he could to protect himself in his disguise. He cautioned his servants to let Hyde in at any hour, he took an apartment for Hyde, and he made out his will in Hyde's favor. His life proceeded safely enough until he awoke one morning in the shape of Edward Hyde and realized that his evil self had appeared even without the drug. Frightened, he determined to cast off the nature of Hyde. He sought out better companions and tried to occupy his mind with other things. He had not been strong enough, however, and had finally permitted himself to assume the shape of Hyde again. On that occasion Hyde, full of an overpowering lust to do evil, murdered Sir Danvers Carew.

After that, Dr. Jekyll renewed his effort to abandon the nature of Hyde, but one day, walking in the park, he suddenly changed into Hyde. On that occasion, he had sought out his friend Dr. Lanyon to go to his laboratory to obtain the drug that would change him back to the personality of the doctor. Dr. Lanyon had watched the transformation with horror. From that day on, the nature of Hyde asserted itself repeatedly. When his supply of chemicals had been exhausted and could not be replenished, Dr. Jekyll, as Hyde, shut himself up in his laboratory and experimented with one drug after another. Finally, in despair, as Utterson now realized, he had killed himself.

Critical Evaluation:

The gothic novel enjoyed its heyday in England in the eighteenth century. Robert Louis Stevenson's *The Strange Case of Dr. Jekyll and Mr. Hyde* was a late example of the highly popular genre, but it became one of the best-known tales of its kind. The novella has predilections for the far and remote, the marvelous and abnormal. It is an escape from reality, emphasizing intuition over reason and impulse over rationality. Like most Romantic novels, it values impulsive, childlike, savage, or peasant behavior as uncorrupted by civilized ways. It is transcendental, grotesque, and bizarre while maintaining a sensitive approach to nature, beauty, and women. It is philosophically anti-intellectual but notable for being remote, simple, and focusing on the supernatural.

The central feature of *The Strange Case of Dr. Jekyll and Mr. Hyde* is its theme of duality. Two personalities—opposite and antagonistic—mesh within one body, a psychological insight that was remarkably prescient for its time. Dr. Jekyll, an essentially good man, was fascinated with the idea of evil and pursued the idea until he had developed a drug that would alter his conscious state from that of one person to another. After taking the drug, he could split off one half of his personality to produce his evil self, the violent Mr. Hyde. The schizophrenia persisted until the "bad" Mr. Hyde overcame "good" Dr. Jekyll to become the dominant personality of the two, at which time it became apparent that Mr. Hyde—and by extension Dr. Jekyll—would have to be annihilated.

The process of transformation was alchemic and tainted with witchcraft. This touch of the occult, a distinct gothic feature, rescued the novel from the banal and elevated it to the realm of genuine horror. Alchemy, witchcraft, and the occult were to earlier ages what technology, especially the computer, became in the second half of the twentieth century: a threat to the status quo and comfortable assumptions. The occult and technology are usually similarly treated with awe and apprehension. *The Strange Case of Dr. Jekyll and Mr. Hyde* fascinates readers for just those qualities of verisimilitude, fear, and hostility. It is with his masterful language and characterization that Stevenson evokes reader identification with his protagonist, which accounts for the powerful impact of the tale.

Bibliography:
Eigner, Edwin M. *Robert Louis Stevenson and Romantic Tradition*. Princeton, N.J.: Princeton University Press, 1966. Relates *The Strange Case of Dr. Jekyll and Mr. Hyde* to the tradition of the nineteenth century prose romance. As evidence, Eigner considers the novella's narrative structure, the theme of pursuit, and the struggle of the hero against self.
Geduld, Harry M., ed. *The Definitive "Dr. Jekyll and Mr. Hyde" Companion*. New York: Garland, 1983. An anthology offering a wide spectrum of approaches from commentary to parodies and sequels. Appendices list the main editions; recordings; staged, filmed, and televised versions; and published and unpublished adaptions.
Jefford, Andrew. "Dr. Jekyll and Professor Nabokov: Reading a Reading." In *Robert Louis Stevenson*, edited by Andrew Noble. Totowa, N.J.: Barnes & Noble Books, 1983. Evaluates the main points of writer and teacher Vladimir Nabokov's eccentric reading of the work. Provides a brief summary of Nabokov's lecture.
Maixner, Paul, ed. "The Strange Case of Dr. Jekyll and Mr. Hyde." In *Robert Louis Stevenson: The Critical Heritage*. Boston: Routledge & Kegan Paul, 1981. This selection of opinions from Stevenson's contemporaries, while often superficial and out of date, is of historical interest. Includes a rejoinder by Stevenson to his critics.
Swearingen, Roger G. *The Prose Writings of Robert Louis Stevenson: A Guide*. Hamden, Conn.: Archon Books, 1980. Supplies details regarding publication and Stevenson's sources of inspiration. Draws on letters, memoirs, and interviews to discuss the circumstances surrounding the writing of the work.

STRANGE INTERLUDE

Type of work: Drama
Author: Eugene O'Neill (1888-1953)
Type of plot: Psychological realism
Time of plot: Early twentieth century
Locale: New England and New York
First performed: 1928; first published, 1928

> *Principal characters:*
> NINA LEEDS, a neurotic woman
> PROFESSOR HENRY LEEDS, her father
> SAM EVANS, her husband
> MRS. AMOS EVANS, his mother
> GORDON EVANS, Nina's son
> EDMUND DARRELL, a doctor, Nina's lover
> CHARLES MARSDEN, a novelist
> MADELINE ARNOLD, in love with Gordon

The Story:

If Nina Leeds had married her first love, Gordon Shaw, her whole life might have been different. Gordon went off to the war in France, however, and when his plane burst into flames and crashed near Sedan, he left Nina with nothing to show for her life.

Before leaving, Gordon had urged Nina to marry him, but her father had objected. Now Gordon was dead, and Nina had not even the memory of one night alone with him. Instead, she had indiscriminate affairs with one soldier after another, those who like Gordon were going out to die, because she thought she could give to others what Gordon had been denied. When promiscuity failed to ease her sorrow, she returned to her father's house an embittered and lonely woman. She was particularly bitter toward her father, a professor in the university, for she suspected that her father's jealousy and irrational desire to keep her with him had led to his opposing her marriage with Gordon.

Nina had an admirer in Charles Marsden, the novelist, an old friend of her father. Marsden had known Nina since she was a little girl, and he had often thought of marrying her. Since, however, he was attached to his aging mother, who did not entirely approve of Nina, he had never proposed. Her half-serious, half-mocking fondness for him annoyed him, for it was a reminder of his own failure to come to grips with life.

Nina had an admirer of quite a different nature in Edmund Darrell, an ambitious young physician who had taken an interest in Nina's case when she was a nurse in the hospital of which he was a staff member. Although he found her attractive, Darrell had no intention of endangering his career by getting involved with a neurotic woman. Nevertheless, he realized that she needed help, and he concluded that a husband and a child would be the logical solution for her difficulties. His choice was Sam Evans, scion of a well-to-do family, who was in love with Nina.

When Nina's father died, she turned almost automatically to Marsden as a kind of surrogate. Marsden, taking his cue from Darrell, suggested Evans as a possible husband, and Nina drowsily assented. Sam Evans married Nina realizing that she was not in love with him, but he lived in the hope that a child would bring them closer together. About seven months after she came to live on the Evans homestead in northern New York State, Nina found herself pregnant, but when she confided her condition to her mother-in-law, Mrs. Evans found it necessary to reveal what she had kept hidden even from her own son: Sam's aunt, hopelessly insane, lived on the top floor of the old house, and Sam's grandmother and her father before her had both died in an asylum. Overwhelmed by the situation in which she found herself, Nina could think of no way out except to abort her child through an operation and to leave Sam. Mrs. Evans protested, pointing out that Sam needed her, that he needed the confidence a child would give him, even if this child were not his own.

While Nina was still pondering the situation, she encountered Darrell, who had just returned from Europe, and told him about her marriage and the child. She and Darrell at last decided that it would be best for Nina to have another child, of which Darrell would be the father. Sam Evans was delighted when he learned that his wife was to have a child. Unfortunately, Nina and Darrell were unable to proceed as rationally as they had planned. Nina fell in love with Darrell, and he, despite the risk to his career, could not tear himself away from her.

Fatherhood made a startling change in Sam Evans. The old look of self-conscious inferiority disappeared from his face, to be replaced by a look of determination and confidence. Nina also changed. She became noticeably older, but her face wore an expression of peace and calm that had never been there before. Marsden, however, changed most of all. His mother had died and he had aged. His hair was almost pure white.

When Darrell returned from Europe, ostensibly because of his father's death but actually because he could no longer stay away from the woman he loved, Nina for the first time in her life felt complete, surrounded as she was by her men—her spiritual father, her husband, her lover, and her son.

The next eleven years brought yet more changes into these linked lives. Darrell and Marsden had backed Sam Evans in one of his enterprises, and all had become wealthy men. Darrell had long ago given up his career in medicine. Marsden, on the other hand, had taken to writing genteel novels about dear old ladies and devilish bachelors, stories completely unrelated to real life.

Young Gordon Evans had no use for his real father, whom he called Uncle Ned, and with whom he quarreled on the slightest provocation. He identified himself completely with his mother's stories of Gordon Shaw, built up by Nina into a hero in the boy's imagination.

As time went by, Darrell managed to break the stranglehold Nina had on his soul, devoting himself as assiduously to biology as he had formerly done to medicine. He became his own firm self again, impervious to all of Nina's wiles. Nina's neurotic tendencies increased, however, and she possessively opposed Gordon's marriage to Madeline, a girl of good family; she even went so far as to consider informing Madeline of the strain of insanity in the Evans family. She grew to hate Sam Evans and at times actively wished for his death, a wish that was fulfilled when Sam suffered a stroke while witnessing Gordon's victory over the Navy crew.

After Sam Evans' death, Gordon somehow could not rid himself of the feeling that his mother had never loved his father, and he remembered a time in his boyhood when he had seen his Uncle Ned kiss his mother. He had repressed this memory, but it reemerged one day when Gordon slapped Darrell across the face during an argument. Gordon instantly regretted his act and apologized, and the matter ended without his realization that Sam Evans was not his real father.

In the end, Nina was really alone. She had finally given her consent to her son's marriage to Madeline. Her own marriage to Darrell at this late date was out of the question because there were too many regretful memories between them. Nina was left alone with Marsden, who had waited patiently all these years until she turned to him at last like a daughter.

Critical Evaluation:

Strange Interlude, though a very long drama, was enormously successful. The curtain went up on its nine acts at 5:30 P.M.; the evening included a supper break after the fifth act, and the final curtain did not fall until after 11:00 P.M. There were two touring companies and a London production for the play, which brought Eugene O'Neill his third Pulitzer Prize. In book form, the play became a best-seller. Later there was a motion picture (starring Norma Shearer), and, in the midst of posthumous revival of interest in the playwright, a restaging of the play in 1963.

While its psychology came to seem somewhat dated, the play appeared fresh, experimental, and exciting in the 1920's. Its major dramatic departure, the soliloquies (in themselves scarcely new to the theater), are as long as the regular surface dialogue. The action freezes when they are delivered. The technique is a way of dramatizing the fact that below the surface of our lives there are fears, drives, and obsessions that rarely see the light of day. The technique also enables O'Neill to present one of his favorite themes, that of identity conflict or division, a theme evident in many of his plays, including *The Emperor Jones* (1920), *The Hairy Ape* (1922), *All God's Chillun Got Wings* (1924), *The Great God Brown* (1926), *Days Without End* (1934), and *A Touch of the Poet* (1958). At times, as in *The Great God Brown*, O'Neill employed masks to suggest sharp conflict between our public and our private images. In *Days Without End*, he divides his hero literally in two, employing two actors to present the two sides of his hero. Sometimes, as in *Days Without End*, O'Neill sought to heal the divisions, but elsewhere, as in *A Touch of the Poet*, he presents them as tragic facts of life.

The technique also suggests another favorite theme of O'Neill—that of the past reaching into and controlling the present. As the characters deliver their soliloquies, they seem to live not only in the moment but in their remembered pasts as well. Thick heaps of time surround and control them. Past and future are always present. This theme is also present in other O'Neill plays such as *The Emperor Jones*, *Mourning Becomes Electra* (1931), and *Long Day's Journey into Night* (1956). O'Neill occasionally suggests the possibility of redemption from the past, as in *Anna Christie* (1921) and *The Fountain* (1925), but finds it increasingly difficult to do so, and his last plays are his most pessimistic.

As a character Nina Leeds suggests a figure who appears in other plays, the woman who is at once wife, mother, and lover. Nina resembles Cybele of *The Great God Brown* and Josie Hogan of *A Moon for the Misbegotten* (1947). She is the archetypal woman; she is daughter, adolescent hero worshiper, wife, mistress, and possessive mother. Each part of her being seeks expression and, frequently, gets in the way of the others, leading to much of the play's bitter torment. Yet while the feminine drives are located in one person, Nina finds it necessary to satisfy these urges with different men, which leads to conflict and bitterness. Nina summarizes the conflicting drives of the play when she speaks of "God the Mother," an image of the life force, as opposed to God the Father, who is hard, arbitrary, moral.

Conflict and ambivalence appear at the very beginning of the play. Nina's hero worship is vested in the aviator Gordon Shaw who, as a youthful ideal, appropriately does not appear. He is dead when the curtain rises. As daughter, Nina lives with the genteel, withdrawn history professor Henry Leeds. Nina's father and her hero have already been in conflict, the professor in his jealousy having seen to it that Gordon went off to war without marrying Nina. The result is that, feeling cheated and guilty, Nina retreats into nymphomania. Her father moves through a series of emotions: fear of what Nina will do, contempt for himself, resignation. A third character who appears in Act I, Charles Marsden, who suffers from a mother fixation, loathes sex but feels alternately drawn to and repelled by Nina. O'Neill early establishes him as Nina's father substitute. Thus both hero and (in the guise of Charlie) father accompany Nina through the play.

Having reacted from hero-worship to cynical depravity, Nina reacts again, exhibiting another necessary facet of woman's being: She seeks solace in a conventional family life with yet another man, Sam Evans. Pregnant, and briefly happy in her role as would-be mother, Nina reacts against her role as wife when she discovers that she cannot have her baby. Thus it is that she calls on Edmund Darrell, who makes her happy again and supplies her with a son but discovers that his relations with Nina interfere with his career. Each of the men in the play has his own problems and urges and needs, but each is drawn into Nina's orbit as she seeks to fulfill herself.

At the end of part 1, Nina has her son, her husband, and her father-substitute, but loses her lover. Only at the beginning of part 2, and then briefly, is Nina fully in control of all her men, which gives her a momentary sense of wholeness. Quickly enough, the splintering, fragmentation, and tension resume. Ultimately, there is no escape for Nina except in the loss of her drives, yet these drives are her life. As she moves from stage to stage of her existence, nothing really changes for Nina, and nothing really changes in life—O'Neill insists—except those who play the roles. Nina finally discovers herself in her father's position, playing the possessive parent just as her father had. After Sam dies, Edmund leaves, and Gordon flies off with his fiancée, Nina returns to her father in the guise of Charlie, who can provide her with a sexless, passionless haven.

"Critical Evaluation" by Max Halperen

Bibliography:

Alexander, Doris. *Eugene O'Neill's Creative Struggle: The Decisive Decade, 1924-1933.* University Park: Pennsylvania State University Press, 1992. Attempts to trace the creation of the plays to probable sources. Sees O'Neill's writing of plays as opportunities "to confront and solve" problems in his own life. Asserts that *Strange Interlude* evolved from O'Neill's attempt to confront the family "lie" about his mother's drug problem and inadequacies as well as his growing disillusionment with his second wife.

Bogard, Travis. *Contour in Time: The Plays of Eugene O'Neill.* Rev. ed. New York: Oxford University Press, 1988. Recognizes O'Neill's plays as efforts of self-understanding. Attempts to analyze the plays in relationship to events in O'Neill's life. Excellent commentary on *Strange Interlude* and its psychological, mythical, and autobiographical elements, especially in relation to gender conflicts and attractions.

Carpenter, Frederic I. *Eugene O'Neill.* Rev. ed. Boston: Twayne, 1979. An effective, short introduction to O'Neill's life and plays, emphasizing the tragic dimension of the dramas. Sees *Strange Interlude* as a twentieth century morality play that lacks O'Neill's usual high tragic vision. Emphasizes why the play has been successful in spite of weaknesses.

Greene, James J. *Eugene O'Neill's "Strange Interlude": A Critical Commentary.* New York: Monarch Press, 1980. A brief introduction to the plot, characterization, themes, staging, strengths, and weaknesses of the play.

Sheaffer, Louis. *O'Neill: Son and Artist.* Boston: Little, Brown, 1973. Authoritative biography of O'Neill, which emphasizes the personal and autobiographical details that helped to create *Strange Interlude.* Gives special attention to the psychological and theatrical elements in this experimental drama.

STRANGE STORIES FROM A CHINESE STUDIO

Type of work: Short fiction
Author: P'u Sung-ling (1640-1715)
First published: Liao-chai chih-i, 1766 (English translation, 1880)

Despite the rationalist tradition of Confucianism, the Chinese people before the republican era were no less superstitious and credulous than were Europeans during the Middle Ages. Supernatural tales are still cultivated in Taiwan, though less extensively or seriously than they were from the mid-seventeenth to the early twentieth centuries under the Manchu dynasty, when a great number of such collections were published and enjoyed by a wide audience. Of these collections, *Strange Stories from a Chinese Studio* is the recognized classic, superior to the rest for its style, learned allusions, wonderful mixture of humanity with the preposterous, and inventiveness. Although P'u Sung-ling claimed in his preface that he did nothing more than copy down what he had heard and edit contributions from his friends, quite a number of the stories were his creations, judging from the sophistication of sentiment and the neatness of plot. These stories, mostly supernatural in theme, rich in poetic symbolism, and deep in psychological insight, are a unique achievement in Chinese literature as studies of the feminine mind clothed in vivid imagination.

The preponderant supernatural element in these stories is far from naïve: The human nature revealed here is what is known rather to a wise scholar or a passionate lover than to an innocent blessed with sense of wonder but little experience. Like the fairy tales of Western civilization, the stories are governed by their own logic. Supernatural intervention is common, and men associate freely with spirits. Causes are followed by effects, but not in the same manner as in the natural or everyday human world. Spirits, demons, and human beings are all under the control of the law of causation, or just retribution; good deeds or evil bring forth rewards or punishments. Therefore the author believed that his stories, in spite of their weirdness, absurdity, or even, in certain cases, obscenity, had a moral purpose.

Of the 431 pieces collected here, some are short bits of curious information. The account of a chorus composed of frogs, for example, runs to no more than two lines in the original. Another account, in three lines, concerns a show with a cast of mice that performed, under masks, a puppet-like drama. Some longer ones, about a page in length, have greater human interest. In "Mr. Chu, the Considerate Husband," an old man, revived after he had been thought dead, had his old spouse lie down by his side, whereupon they died together. In "The Tiger of Chao-ch'eng," a tiger, after killing a man, allowed himself to be arrested, confessed his crime to the court, and agreed to serve as a son to the destitute and lonesome old mother. He constantly brought dead animals and other valuables to her door, and he would sometimes come to her house to keep her company. After her death, he was present at the funeral. When the human mourners were all frightened off, he roared terribly to give vent to his grief.

Short and comparatively artless pieces like these can be found in other collections of a similar nature. The fame of this book rests principally on the longer tales, which the author narrates with admirable delicacy and poignancy. None is truly tragic, for one essential condition of tragedy—a belief that death is final and irrevocable—is missing here, as in many other Chinese stories. P'u Sung-ling, apparently like his readers, did not even take death seriously; in these tales, a dead woman (most of the stories are remembered for their heroines rather than their heroes), can always in one way or another recover life or assume an animate shape. A man will feel hardly any scruple about making love to a female ghost, especially when she is young and beautiful. Moreover, the ghostly heorines are often learned, their ghostly occupations often the composition of poetry, works of great self-pity and chilliness, and they prefer a poetical, handsome young man as a lover. The poetical qualities seem to be important, too, for in one story ("The Young Gentleman Who Couldn't Spell") the ghost spurns a very good-looking young man only because he is stupid. It may be supposed that a ghost can only be loved spiritually, but in this book love means sexual love. When a man and a ghost sleep in the same bed, he may suffer from exposure to the ghostly air, but he can be cured with proper medical treatment. In one story the ghost absorbs so much vitality from her lover that she feels that life has come back to her, and she bids him reopen her grave. The coffin is decayed, but the corpse looks lifelike and feels warm. After he takes her body home, the first words she utters after her resuscitation are: "Aren't they like a dream—these ten odd years buried there!"

A great number of stories are about spirits—the spirits of rocks, trees, flowers, frogs, snakes, fish, birds, and various mammals. The most notable is that of the fox. A fox spirit can be vicious in the popular legends, but here he, or she, is almost invariably witty, charming, highly sophisticated, and possessed of human qualities as well as magical powers. A female fox in human shape may be only plain, as in the case of the Dowdy Fox of "The Marriage Lottery," but that was because the man she chose was a simple peasant who, according to her, deserved neither wealth nor a beautiful mistress. Or the fox may be middle-aged and "modestly good-looking," like the celebrated Heng-niang, who lectures on the art of feminine charm and helps a disfavored wife to win back her husband's love. Most foxes, however, are young girls of unearthly beauty who have the power to cast spells but are also capable of wifely virtues and undying love. In one story, "Miss Lien-hsiang," the fox saves her human lover from the deadly influence of a female ghost. Then the rivals, both exceedingly beautiful, are reconciled, and each assumes a reincarnated form and marries the lucky man.

Indeed, few Chinese writers understood the woman's heart so fully and profoundly as did P'u Sung-ling who, no less than the storytellers of the Western world, was fascinated by the mystery of woman. Instead of being stiff, pale paragons of virtue or unattractive harlots, the women in this book shine with brilliance and charm. They choose their lovers freely, yet leave them when they see that they must part. Since the liberty they took was morally censurable and hardly conceivable as a theme of literature, P'u Sung-ling solved his problem by adopting the form of the supernatural tale, thus winning praise for his fancy and style. Later readers, however, recognize the author's ghosts and his spirits of foxes or other animals as realistic portraits of the eternal woman.

There are about twenty female characters in this book who will long be remembered as among the best creations of Chinese literature. Altogether, these tales present a full gallery of portraits of women, whether human, superhuman, or subhuman; women in various moods and situations, women as lovers and wives, women with all their passion, tenderness, flirtation, perseverance, and devotion. The popularity of the tales in *Strange Stories from a Chinese Studio* has been as much the result of their strangeness as their appeal to common humanity. The author, as a product of his age, may have intended to be simply entertaining or didactic, or both, but his genius allowed him to probe psychological depths that were often beyond the imagination of other storytellers.

Bibliography:

Buber, Martin. *Chinese Tales*. Translated by Alex Page. Atlantic Highlands, N.J.: Humanities Press International, 1991. A critical introduction to translations of several of the tales provides biographical information and discusses the composition of the stories and the psychological significance of the ghosts.

Ch'en, Shou-Yi. "Ch'ing Fiction." In *Chinese Literature: A Historical Introduction*. New York: Ronald Press, 1961. Describes P'u Sung-ling's fascination with the unusual. Claims he was a master of his craft in his command over the classical Chinese language and in the way he handled characterization and description.

Ma, Y. W., and J. S. M. Lau, eds. *Traditional Chinese Stories: Themes and Variations*. New York: Columbia University Press, 1978. Translations of six stories from P'u Sung-ling's collection, along with brief critical commentary on each that places them in the context of Chinese tales about similar themes. Includes an excellent summary of the writer's literary achievement.

Plaks, Andres. "Towards a Critical Theory of Chinese Narrative." In *Chinese Narrative: Critical and Theoretical Essays*, edited by Author. Princeton, N.J.: Princeton University Press, 1977. Uses *Strange Studies from a Chinese Studio* as an example of a collection of tales written in elevated language that nevertheless conveys intensely personal emotions.

Zeitlin, Judith T. *Historian of the Strange: Pu Songling and the Chinese Classical Tale*. Stanford, Calif.: Stanford University Press, 1993. Places the writer's works in the context of Chinese narratives dealing with fantasy and the strange. Traces the critical history of his work and provides detailed analyses of selected tales dealing with obsession, the obfuscation of boundaries between male and female, and the significance of dreams.

THE STRANGER

Type of work: Novel
Author: Albert Camus (1913-1960)
Type of plot: Existentialism
Time of plot: Late 1930's to early 1940's
Locale: Algeria
First published: L'Étranger, 1942 (English translation, 1946)

        Principal characters:
           MEURSAULT, an office worker
           MARIE CARDONA, his girlfriend
           RAYMOND SINTES, his friend and neighbor, a pimp
           SALAMANO, another neighbor, an old man

The Story:

When Meursault was notified of his mother's death, he left immediately for Marengo, where she had been living in The Home for Aged Persons. He was taken to the room where her coffin had been placed and casually declined the doorkeeper's offer to unscrew the lid so he could look at her. Meursault spent the night there, drinking coffee, smoking, and chatting with the doorkeeper. The next day, a Friday, he attended the funeral and left immediately afterward to return to Algiers.

Saturday morning, Meursault went for a swim and ran into Marie Cardona, a girl who had formerly worked in his office. He invited her to a movie and later took her to bed.

Meursault spent Sunday lounging on the balcony of his flat, smoking and watching people on the street below. The next day, returning home from work, Meursault came upon Raymond Sintes, a young man who lived on the same floor. Raymond, who called himself a warehouseman but was reputed to be a pimp, had just been in a fight with the brother of a Moorish girl he had been seeing. Believing that the girl was cheating on him, he had beaten her up, and her brother had accosted him, seeking revenge. Raymond asked Meursault to draft a letter to entice the girl back so he could humiliate her, and Meursault agreed to help.

One afternoon, Meursault was in his room with Marie when they heard Raymond beating the girl again. A policeman was summoned. Later, Raymond asked Meursault to testify to his own knowledge that the girl had been false to Raymond. Again, Meursault agreed to help, and he and Raymond went out to a café. Upon returning, they encountered another neighbor, an old man named Salamano, whose dog had run off. Although he had abused the animal mercilessly, he was weeping and fearful of what would become of him without his longtime companion.

That Sunday, Meursault and Marie accompanied Raymond to the beach, where they encountered two Arabs who had been following Raymond for some time. A fight broke out, and Raymond was cut before the Arabs slipped away. Later, with his wounds patched, Raymond went walking and came upon the Arabs again. This time, Raymond pulled a gun, but Meursault, who had followed, offered to hold it to ensure a fair fight. Almost immediately, however, the Arabs vanished.

Raymond went back to the bungalow, but Meursault—Raymond's pistol still in his pocket—stayed out in the blazing afternoon sunlight and soon came upon the Arab who had stabbed Raymond. Meursault stepped forward and, seeing the flash of a knife blade in a blur of light and heat, pulled the trigger. He pumped four more bullets into the Arab's inert body.

Meursault was arrested and questioned by the examining magistrate for the next eleven months, usually with a court-appointed lawyer present. The questions focused on two things: his apparent callousness at his mother's funeral and the fact that he had hesitated after his first shot and then fired four more times. At one point, the magistrate displayed a small silver crucifix and asked Meursault whether he believed in God. When Meursault replied matter-of-factly that he did not, the magistrate was visibly upset.

Meursault was held in prison, where he was visited by Marie, who held out hope for his acquittal. He soon became accustomed to prison life, although small privations occasionally upset him, most of all, the fact that he was not allowed to smoke. He began to sleep sixteen to eighteen hours a day. Soon, six months had passed, and he had begun talking to himself without realizing it.

In June, his trial began. One of the first witnesses called, the warden of the Home for Aged Persons in Marengo, testified that Meursault's mother had complained about her son's conduct toward her and that on the day of the funeral Meursault had neither cried nor lingered by the grave. The doorkeeper was called to testify that Meursault had not wanted to view his mother's body. When Marie took the stand, the prosecutor maneuvered her into admitting that her affair with Meursault began the day after his mother's funeral and that they had first gone to the movies to see a comedy. When Raymond attempted to exonerate his friend, he was exposed as a criminal and a pimp.

After a trial that seemed almost to exclude him from its proceedings, Meursault was pronounced guilty and sentenced to death by decapitation. Meursault refused repeatedly to see the chaplain, but one day the chaplain entered the cell without his permission and tried to talk to him about God. Meursault was patient at first, but then, becoming bored and annoyed, lashed out, cursing him and pointing out that all his supposed certainty amounted to nothing in the end. Hearing the commotion, the guards rushed in to rescue the priest, leaving Meursault to drop off to sleep, exhausted.

When he woke, he found himself awash in a strange feeling of peace and resignation, devoid of hope and accepting of what he described as "the benign indifference of the universe." He was content to await his execution and, in fact, hoped that it would be witnessed by a large crowd of spectators cursing him.

Critical Evaluation:

A French author born in Algeria just before the outbreak of World War I, Albert Camus saw the history of his times as a history of "murder, injustice, and violence." He lost his father in the Battle of the Marne, grew up in the shadow of a world war, and participated in the next as a member of the French resistance movement.

Athletic and intellectually gifted, Camus played football while attending the University of Algiers, where he studied philosophy and the Greek classics, planning to become a teacher. In 1937, however, at the age of twenty-four, he was stricken with tuberculosis, which led to four years of enforced inactivity while he recuperated. During this period, he began to write and to formulate the philosophy that would underlie his novels, plays, and essays. In 1957, Camus was awarded the Nobel Prize in Literature.

As much a philosopher as a creative writer, Camus is closely associated with the atheistic branch of existentialism, a philosophy emphasizing humanity's consciousness of its mortality and its consequent need to find meaning in a universe that seems indifferent and inhospitable to such a quest. Camus believes that there is no god, hence that life has no purpose. Things— human beings, plants, animals—simply live and die as part of a natural process that has no transcendent meaning or value. Human beings are distinguished from plants and animals only by virtue of the fact that they are conscious of their own mortality. Alone among all living things, human beings know that they must die. This awareness pushes them to seek explanations, to try to find meaning in what is essentially meaningless. Camus and other thinkers describe this situation as "the absurd." Human beings—seekers of meaning in a meaningless universe—live in a condition of absurdity.

Meursault, in *The Stranger*, is not at first a seeker of meaning, nor is he particularly aware of his own mortality. He simply sleepwalks through life, as many do, ignoring the inevitability of death and the implications of mortality. Camus argues that most human beings live in this condition for as long as they can, going about their daily routines like automatons, refusing to think, seeking solace in simple physical and material pleasures. Yet most are doomed to be awakened to their condition when something—the death of a loved one, perhaps, or a serious illness as in his own case—disturbs their routine.

For Meursault, the event that forces him out of his complacency is the killing of the Arab—not the murder itself, a meaningless event brought about by a natural response to the sun and danger, but its aftermath. When society condemns him, Meursault realizes that he is not being condemned for taking a human life but for refusing to accept the illusions society promotes to protect itself from having to acknowledge the absurdity of the human condition. In effect, Meursault is condemned to death for failing to weep at his mother's funeral.

After he is condemned, Meursault could fall back on the illusions proffered by society through its priests and clergymen—hucksters and shills, as Camus thought of them. To do so would have been intellectually dishonest. In fact, the novel's real turning point occurs when the priest visits Meursault in his cell. Here, for the first time, Meursault shows passion, revolting against the priest's effort to impose on him the platitudes and false certainties of religion. Meursault chooses, instead, to accept his condition; he refuses to deny the reality of his impending death. In doing so, he discovers the one tie that links him to all other beings: death. Once death, or the inevitable cessation of existence, is recognized as the single inescapable condition of existence, life, however meaningless it might ultimately be, becomes valuable. Yet whatever value life has must be imposed on it; people must engage it actively. Ironically, Meursault learns this too late.

The Stranger is a deeply disturbing novel. From its famous dispassionate opening—"Mother died today. Or maybe, yesterday; I can't be sure."—to its conclusion, where Meursault expresses the hope that on the day of his execution he will be greeted by "a huge crowd of spectators," all hurling at him "howls of execration," the novel challenges assumptions about life and literature. Just when it appears that Meursault could be dismissed as a callous egoist, he reveals complexities of emotion common to all; he merely refuses to pretend to feelings he does not possess. When Meursault becomes enmeshed in the legal system, Camus shows how society is more concerned with appearances than with any meaningful concept of justice. When Meursault, instead of repenting and seeking solace in some transcendent reality, refuses to acknowledge the possibility of anything beyond the immediate facts of his situation, the heroism of his attitude is made clear.

Camus' style in this novel is disturbingly flat and objective, an anomaly for a first-person narrative. It has often been suggested that Camus was influenced by Ernest Hemingway in this respect. With this curiously flat style, Camus suggests that in an absurd universe all things have equal value. Nothing in the entire universe is intrinsically more meaningful than anything else.

Ron Carter

Bibliography:

Bree, Germaine, ed. *Camus: A Collection of Critical Essays*. Englewood Cliffs, N.J.: Prentice-Hall, 1962. An early collection of essays by outstanding critics. Includes a translation of Jean-Paul Sartre's influential "Explication of *The Stranger*."

Ellison, David R. *Understanding Albert Camus*. Columbia: University of South Carolina Press, 1990. An overview of the development of Camus' themes and writing style. Focuses on Camus as a literary man whose works embody a consistent philosophical outlook. Especially useful for first-time readers of Camus.

King, Adele, ed. *L'Étranger: Fifty Years On*. New York: St. Martin's Press, 1992. Twenty original essays by leading Camus scholars. Offers a variety of viewpoints and provides a valuable companion to a study of the novel.

McCarthy, Patrick. *Albert Camus: The Stranger*. Cambridge, England: Cambridge University Press, 1988. Analyzes the strengths and weaknesses of the novel. McCarthy is especially good on the novel's political aspects and on how Camus manages to transform an unsympathetic protagonist into an Everyman.

Rhein, Phillip H. *Albert Camus*. Rev. ed. Boston: Twayne, 1989. Relates *The Stranger* to the whole of Camus' philosophy and focuses on the novel as a reflection of that philosophy. Provides an enlightening companion volume to Ellison's *Understanding Albert Camus*.

STRANGER IN A STRANGE LAND

Type of work: Novel
Author: Robert A. Heinlein (1907-1988)
Type of plot: Science fiction
Time of plot: Early twenty-first century
Locale: Bethesda, Maryland; the Poconos; and Las Vegas
First published: 1961

> *Principal characters:*
> VALENTINE MICHAEL SMITH, a human raised by Martians
> JUBAL E. HARSHAW, a lawyer who befriends Smith
> ANNE,
> DORCAS, and
> MIRIAM, Harshaw's secretaries
> GILLIAN BOARDMAN, a nurse who helps Smith "escape" government
>   control
> BEN CAXTON, journalist who supports Smith's cause
> JOSEPH E. DOUGLAS, Secretary General of Earth's world government

The Story:

Valentine Michael Smith was the first human born on Mars, son of two members of the first Earth expedition to the red planet. His mother died in childbirth, and his father soon after; Smith was raised by Martians. Culturally he was a Martian.

When a second expedition arrived on Mars a generation later, they found Smith fully grown and brought him back to Earth. There, he presented a dilemma to the authorities: Through his human parents he inherited vast wealth, but without human cultural understanding he was not competent to control it. Further, under a legal oddity known as the Larkin Decision, he could be construed as the legal "owner" of the entire planet Mars. To Joseph E. Douglas, the Secretary General of Earth's global government, the World Federation of States, Smith posed a potential threat. This potential caused Smith to be isolated—a kind of prisoner—under various ruses, the first being medical, at Bethesda Medical Center.

Ben Caxton, a gadfly journalist opposed to Douglas' administration, accused Douglas of limiting the freedom of the man from Mars, and attempted to help Smith "escape" government custody. When Caxton's girlfriend, Gillian Boardman, a nurse at Bethesda, stumbled on Smith's heavily guarded hospital room, she effected the "escape" by disguising Smith as a nurse and taking him out of the hospital. Unwittingly, she had assured Smith's compliance with her slightest request by offering him water—on Mars the equivalent of swearing a lifetime bond with the sharer in the ritual. In Smith's eyes, she and he were "water brothers."

Gillian took Smith to Ben's apartment, but Federation authorities had already nabbed Ben, and they closed in on her and Smith. Yet despite their numbers and heavy weapons, Smith easily overcame their force with Martian methods—he caused the Federation goons to disappear. Frightened, Gillian fled with Smith to the Poconos retreat of Jubal Harshaw, a famed attorney, physician, and popular author with a reputation for standing up against powerful bullies if the cause appealed to him.

Intrigued by Smith, as well as by Gillian's bravery and innocence, Jubal undertook their defense, both legal and practical, forcing Douglas to acknowledge Smith's legal claim to be the official representative of Mars to the Federation. It later turned out that such a turn of events had been in fact the intention of the Martians; Smith was to be their envoy to Earth. Yet "freeing" Smith from Douglas still left him in an ambiguous position. Smith still was a stranger in a strange land (Exodus 2:22). Harshaw set about educating Smith—or Mike as he became known—on being human. Harshaw urged members of his household not to teach Mike their own cultural prejudices.

In the bosom of Harshaw's artificial family, Mike discovered a "nest" like the ones he had known on Mars. Harshaw, whose first name means "father of many," was a father figure to the three women who acted as his secretaries and housekeepers (Anne, Dorcas, and Miriam; their last names are purposely omitted) and the two men who kept his estate in repair (Larry and Duke). When Gillian and Mike joined the household, everyone in it shared water with Mike, making them water brothers with the man from Mars. Mike learned about being human while Jubal and his surrogate children learned about Mike's Martian-trained powers. He could cause things to disappear. He had complete and conscious control of his body; he could levitate; he could exit his body at will; he could read minds.

Mike's water brothers discovered the nature of these feats by learning the Martian language. The first difficulty was the Martian verb *grok*, which Mike used often without translating. Its etymological meaning appeared to be "to drink," but metaphorically it held a rich variety of meaning: to understand, to contemplate, to cherish, to love, to become one with a thing (or person). The metaphysical nature of Mike's teaching (although to the Martians physical and metaphysical are one) led Mike's water brothers to view it as religion. The religious aspect was heightened by Mike's discovery of a recently developed Earth religion, the Fosterite church, which shared some elements of Martian beliefs—primarily the idea of "discorporation" rather than death: The initiated choose the moment of their translation into heaven.

Mike's contact with the Fosterites proved damaging. When he met with the head of the Fosterite church, Archbishop Digby, Mike "grokked a wrongness" about the religious leader, and caused him to disappear. This act, as well as the humans' inability to follow the moral codes that Mike's teaching entailed, made him a marked man, eventually the Antichrist to the Fosterites. Either the Fosterites or organized crime, who had been angered by the encroachment of Mike's Las Vegas temple on their territory, burned his temple to the ground. Finally, although Mike could have escaped his fate, they beat him to death on the streets of Philadelphia, while the police turned the other way. This was not the end of Mike, however; having discorporated, he was free to continue his work of educating humans.

Critical Evaluation:

The appearance of *Stranger in a Strange Land* in 1961 marked a turning point in Robert A. Heinlein's science fiction career. Heinlein has been one of the most popular American science fiction writers since he began writing in 1939, yet few readers were aware how much he had fought against editors whose concepts of literary decorum Heinlein considered outmoded, puritanical, or just plain wrong. The conflict had come to a head with Heinlein's 1959 novel *Starship Troopers*, which many readers considered too militaristic. Heinlein's editor at Scribner's had rejected it. Heinlein sold it to Putnam's instead, and in 1960 it won the Hugo Award, the highest honor given by the World Science Fiction Convention. The controversy did not diminish Heinlein's popularity; in 1961 he was the guest of honor at the convention, and the following year *Stranger in a Strange Land* won for Heinlein another Hugo.

The novel broke several taboos in discussing religion and sexuality, topics usually shunned in science fiction. Looking at human culture from an alien point of view—a staple in science fiction—Heinlein gives the impression that human moral codes are not absolute. While Putnam published *Stranger in a Strange Land* as it had *Starship Troopers*, Heinlein still encountered editorial opposition. Heinlein's sexual references were never explicit, but many of them were toned down even more, and other matters were changed to calm the editor's qualms—an offhand reference to a Professor Kennedy, for example, was changed to "Professor Tiergarten"; the book appeared during the Kennedy Administration. Equally significant was the extensive editing for brevity. Heinlein submitted a typescript of some 220,000 words; Putnam published the novel at 160,087 words. Heinlein's original version did not appear until after the author's death.

Before its publication, Heinlein told his literary agent that *Stranger in a Strange Land* is "*not* science fiction by any stretch of the imagination." He intended it to be social satire, the expeditions to Mars being merely a framing device for the story. While it is true that there is less hard science in the book than in most Heinlein novels, one minor bit of engineering is noteworthy: In the beginning of the novel Heinlein describes a waterbed exactly as it would appear commercially a decade later. The patent holder of the waterbed admits that he got the idea from Heinlein's novel. If readers extend the meaning of "science" into the social sciences, there are many tidbits of scientific speculation in the book. The idea of a "fair witness," a professional trained to observe dispassionately and objectively, and whose testimony is admissible in a trial, is one such. Another is the study of mass psychology as seen in the building of Mike's "religion." Ultimately, Heinlein is right: *Stranger in a Strange Land* is more valuable for its philosophical than its scientific speculation.

This novel's success as a cult classic is largely a result of misunderstanding its message. Readers saw Mike (and sometimes Heinlein himself) as a guru of a futuristic metaphysic, rather than the antithesis of all gurus. The Martian phrase, translated as "thou art god," which some fans mistook as a deification of the individual, was intended by Heinlein, according to a letter to his agent, as an existentialist refusal to resort to any concept of god to escape moral responsibility. The cultic co-opting of the novel and its catchword, *grok*, by the counterculture of 1960's America led to an untrue yet widely believed story that mass murderer Charles Manson used it as a model for his own cult family. Life imitates art.

Critics have been kind to this novel, even when they fault Heinlein's work as a whole, but they have consistently brought two charges against it: First, that it is really two (or three) novels imperfectly joined, and second, that the major characters are not fully developed. The second criticism is related to a feminist charge that the female characters are sexual wish fulfillments rather than real women. The first charge has some merit, although if the pieces of *Stranger in a Strange Land* do not fit together well, it is not for lack of plotting, as Heinlein insisted that this was the only novel he ever outlined beforehand. His letters from the time the book was first conceived (1949) until its publication bear this out. The second charge is a matter of judgment that readers may decide for themselves.

John R. Holmes

Bibliography:

Franklin, H. Bruce. *Robert A. Heinlein: America as Science Fiction*. New York: Oxford University Press, 1980. This general treatment of Heinlein's fiction is more an attack on Heinlein's belief system, as well as America in general, than literary criticism. Its section on *Stranger in a Strange Land* suggests that the novel is adversely affected by a tacit Calvinism.

Heinlein, Robert A. *Grumbles from the Grave*. Edited by Virginia Heinlein. New York:

Ballantine, 1990. This posthumously published selection of Heinlein's letters mentions *Stranger in a Strange Land* throughout. Chapter 14 contains letters about the novel itself, chapter 15 about reactions to the novel.

Panshin, Alexei. *Heinlein in Dimension*. Chicago: Advent, 1968. Critiques Heinlein's work in terms of craftsmanship, though most of it boils down to a complaint that Heinlein did not write his stories the way Panshin would have. Five pages are devoted to *Stranger in a Strange Land*.

Plank, Robert. "Omnipotent Cannibals in *Stranger in a Strange Land*." In *Robert A. Heinlein*, edited by J. D. Olander and M. H. Greenburg. New York: Taplinger, 1978. This psychoanalytical study of Heinlein's novel examines the implications of the philosophy presented in the book, which Plank sees as Utopian fantasy.

Slusser, George Edgar. *Robert A. Heinlein: Stranger in His Own Land*. San Bernardino, Calif.: Borgo Press, 1976. Touches on all of Heinlein's fiction, and the middle third deals exclusively with *Stranger in a Strange Land*.

STREET SCENE

Type of work: Drama
Author: Elmer Rice (Elmer Leopold Reizenstein, 1892-1967)
Type of plot: Social realism
Time of plot: 1929
Locale: New York
First performed: 1929; first published, 1929

> *Principal characters:*
> ROSE MAURRANT, a twenty-year-old woman
> ANNA, her mother
> FRANK, her father
> SAM KAPLAN, a frustrated young intellectual
> ABE, his father
> SHIRLEY, his sister
> HARRY EASTER, a fairly prosperous real estate agent

The Story:

It was a hot June evening in New York, and in front of an old brownstone walk-up apartment in a mean quarter of the city, residents were discussing the weather and the affairs of the day. Anna Maurrant and her lover, Sankey, a collector for the milk company, were the subjects of the gossip of a small group of residents. They were shocked at Anna's behavior—after all, she had a grown daughter. One neighbor reported that Sankey had already been there twice this week while Anna's husband and their daughter, Rose, were away.

The gossip ceased with the appearance of Anna and the arrival of her husband. Frank Maurrant was irritated that Rose was not yet at home and that her whereabouts was a mystery. He told Anna that he would have to be out of town the next day; as a stagehand, he was working on a show that was opening outside New York. After the Maurrants had left, the janitor of the building quietly predicted that Frank would someday kill Sankey.

A short time later, Sam Kaplan appeared. The arguments and trivial talk that passed between the occupants of the tenement bored him. A twenty-year-old college student, he was depressed over his current situation. He felt trapped by his environment, although Abe, his father, seemed content with life in the tenement, reading his newspapers, criticizing the government, longing for a social revolution, and arguing politics with anyone interested. Sam would be happy to leave the tenement atmosphere at the first opportunity.

After the street cleared, Rose Maurrant finally arrived, escorted by Harry Easter, manager of the real estate office where she worked. Easter wanted to set Rose up in an apartment and take her away from her twenty-five-dollar-a-week job, but Rose refused his offer. Easter was married, in the first place, and she was not really very fond of him. Besides, she realized that there would be strings attached to his proposal. Easter left at the arrival of Frank Maurrant, who lectured his daughter on her late hours. Maurrant, ironically enough, spoke up for family happiness, security, and proper behavior. Sam came out and sympathized with Rose, who knew of her mother's situation. Sam felt that neither of them belonged in this sordid atmosphere. He was even more crushed when he tried unsuccessfully to defend Rose from an amorous taxi driver who passed by; the incident added to his bitterness, which Rose tried in vain to allay. Rose left Sam sitting despondently on the curb.

Bustling tenement life went on as usual the next morning. In the middle of the hubbub, Sam's sister Shirley warned him to spend more time on his studies and less with Rose. Later, she asked Rose to avoid Sam. Since he was going to be a lawyer, Shirley felt he should not be distracted from his studies. Rose pleaded innocence to the charge of taking Sam's mind from his work. They possibly were slightly drawn to each other, Rose did admit.

Sam's entrance led to another conversation with Rose concerning life and death. Although Rose, unlike Sam, admitted there was joy to be found in life, certainly it was not to be found in their environment. They talked of running away; it was clear that Sam was interested in Rose romantically. Rose, however, was simply interested in getting away from her surroundings.

Although Frank Maurrant had left his wife with a less-than-subtle hint that he knew what was going on in his absence, soon after his departure Anna incautiously informed Sankey that no one was at home, Rose having left for a funeral. After a few minutes, Frank reappeared, dashed inside, and killed both his wife and her lover. He emerged, torn and bloody, and escaped. Rose arrived in time to see her mother being carried through the crowd on a stretcher.

Later that afternoon, the tabloids contained full accounts of the bloody murders. Everyone in the neighborhood was talking about the killings and speculating on the whereabouts of Frank Maurrant, who was still at large. Rose, returning from a grim shopping trip, declined sincere offers of help from Easter and others. She simply did not wish to feel obligated to anyone; she and her twelve-year-old brother would soon be leaving New York. For the present, they were moving away from the tenement immediately.

An excited crowd surged down the street, heralding the appearance of two policemen and a battered Frank Maurrant. Frank tearfully cried that he was out of his head when he committed murder. He had tried to be a good father, but this was just the way things turned out. Rose and Sam Kaplan eventually found themselves alone in the street. Sam, renewing his plea that he and Rose go away together, spoke of their belonging to each other. Rose, however, felt that people should never belong to anyone. If her mother had not depended on someone else for what she should have had inside her, Rose said, the tragedy might have been averted.

She tenderly explained that loving and belonging were different emotions; a person should believe in himself or herself. She told Sam that perhaps something would work out for them when they were older and wiser. After Sam had gone into the house, a sympathetic Shirley appeared to say good-bye before Rose left for what she hoped would be a new and better life. As she was leaving, a shabby-looking couple had spotted the vacancy notice on the building and were ringing for the janitor. From the wreath on the door, they decided that someone had died; it was probably the reason why the apartment was being vacated.

Critical Evaluation:

Among the important U.S. dramatists of the 1920's and early 1930's, Elmer Rice was probably second only to Eugene O'Neill in the scope of his vision and the range of his theatrical experimentation. Although he had achieved some early recognition with his courtroom drama *On Trial* (1914), it was *The Adding Machine* (1923), a wildly expressionistic episodic fantasy about a harried average man, Mr. Zero, who is trapped in an eternity of meaningless, machine-like activities, that earned Rice recognition as one of the most important dramatists in the United States. Then, having written one of the best nonrealistic plays of his time, Rice realized his greatest commercial and critical success with *Street Scene*, one of the most starkly realistic plays ever put on the U.S. stage.

In spite of their radically differing theatrical styles, *On Trial* and *Street Scene* are about the same thing: the dehumanizing effect of modern, urban, industrial society on the human spirit.

In *Street Scene*, however, Rice dramatizes his thesis by showing average people in situations of painful personal suffering, instead of abstract characters in symbolic settings, which makes the latter play more powerful.

Street Scene is the forerunner of the social drama of the 1930's. Before this time, what social drama the United States had produced criticized only indirectly. In *Street Scene*, however, as soon as the curtain rises, before any plot is set in motion, the audience sees and feels the crowding, ugliness, noise, heat, and general agitation that constantly surrounds these urban dwellers. Such an environment is certain to bring out the worst in people; their necessary proximity guarantees conflict and violence. The situation is bad enough for the unimaginative, who are less aware of alternatives to the stifling quality of their condition, but for the more sensitive soul, who is conscious of being dehumanized, the life is doubly painful. *Street Scene* is a play about individuals who, rebelling in the most limited ways against their plight, unleash the fury that exists beneath the surface of the oppressive status quo.

The story begins with a scene of everyday life in front of the teeming tenement. This close mix of the various racial and social types quickly establishes the general atmosphere of tension, bitterness, and petty viciousness. From this agitated surface, Rice skillfully and naturally draws out one major story and a number of minor ones. The primary plot line concerns Frank Maurrant's violent attack on his wife, Anna, and her lover, Sankey. Paralleled to this is the bittersweet love affair between Maurrant's daughter, Rose, and Sam Kaplan, a sensitive, young Jewish neighbor. The Maurrant family story is counterpointed against several other action lines and character studies, such as the birth of the Buchanan baby, the eviction of the Hildebrands, Harry Easter's attempt to seduce Rose, old man Kaplan's Marxist rhetoric, and Mae Jones's open promiscuity. It is all powerfully punctuated by the constant intrusions of the neighbors who, out of boredom and petty vindictiveness, meddle whenever they can.

Although the tenement inhabitants are confined by their economic circumstances, they are even more thoroughly imprisoned by their own distorted social, racial, and religious beliefs and assumptions. All the characters retain their ethnic prejudices and cling to notions of social superiority. The worst family in the building is the most "purely American," the Joneses, with their bullying taxi-driver son, Vincent, their whorish daughter, Mae, and their most vicious of gossips, Mrs. Jones.

Maurrant is driven to murder his wife from a combination of half-understood frustration and residual Puritan moralism. It is clear that the Maurrants had once been happy together, but time, circumstance, and Frank's distorted concept of the husband's role have combined to destroy their closeness. Anna Maurrant takes Sankey as a lover because she feels lost and in need of a kind word. After the killings, Maurrant admits that he cannot understand what it was that drove him to murder.

Rose understands and, because she does, she is the pivotal figure in the play. The romance with Sam is never really serious, because he is a bright child and she is already a mature woman. Rose alone affirms life and sees the possibility of living it meaningfully as an autonomous human being. The only answer, Rice seems to say, is to insist on one's humanity in the face of all the pressures that modern civilization can bring against it.

Bibliography:
Durham, Frank. *Elmer Rice.* New York: Twayne, 1970. Discusses the long career of Elmer Rice as a microcosm of the history of dramatic writing in the United States. Centers on Rice's employment of types and techniques as an accommodation of the changing tastes and artistic demands of the theater.

Gould, Jean. "Elmer Rice." In *Modern American Playwrights*. New York: Dodd, Mead, 1966. Focuses on Rice's background in law and its incorporation in his plots. Considers his experiments with form as efforts to find a new method of dramaturgy. Asserts that both *The Adding Machine* and *Street Scene* are indictments of overmechanization.

Hogan, Robert. *The Independence of Elmer Rice*. Carbondale: Southern Illinois University Press, 1965. Laments the "unhealthy" effects of the theater as a commercial vehicle on all playwrights, especially Rice. Assesses Rice's achievements in relation to other playwrights and within the limitations of the theater itself.

Krutch, Joseph Wood. *The American Drama Since 1918*. New York: George Braziller, 1957. Classic survey of trends in U.S. drama from 1918 to 1956. Believes the dignifying of human beings in *Street Scene* is the antithesis of *The Adding Machine*, which posits people as ciphers victimized by the machine age.

Rabkin, Gerald. "Elmer Rice and the Seriousness of Drama." In *Drama and Commitment: Politics in the American Theatre of the Thirties*. Bloomington: Indiana University Press, 1964. Evaluates *Street Scene*, *The Adding Machine*, and *The Subway* as indications of the prevailing fear that mechanistic civilization dehumanizes people. Argues that *Street Scene*, although despairing of modern life, is optimistic.

A STREETCAR NAMED DESIRE

Type of work: Drama
Author: Tennessee Williams (Thomas Lanier Williams, 1911-1983)
Type of plot: Tragedy
Time of plot: 1940's
Locale: New Orleans, Louisiana
First performed: 1947; first published, 1947

> *Principal characters:*
> BLANCHE DuBois, a neurotic young woman in her late twenties
> STELLA KOWALSKI, her younger sister
> STANLEY, Stella's husband
> STEVE HUBBELL,
> HAROLD MITCHELL (MITCH), and
> PABLO GONZALES, Stanley's poker-playing friends
> EUNICE HUBBELL, Steve's wife

The Story:

Two streetcars, one named Desire, the other Cemeteries, brought Blanche DuBois on a spring afternoon to the Elysian Fields address of her sister Stella, whom she had not seen since Stella's marriage to Stanley Kowalski. Blanche, dressed in a fluttering white garden party outfit, jarred with the shabbiness and menace of the neighborhood from her first appearance. The proprietress of the building admitted her to the Kowalski apartment a few minutes before Stella's return. One of Blanche's weaknesses became immediately apparent when, after a successful search for Stanley's whiskey, she drank a half-glass of it neat.

When Stella returned, Blanche made only a token effort to hide her dismay at her sister's new surroundings. Stella was happy with her wild man and regarded Blanche's criticisms with good-humored tolerance. Blanche turned on Stella and defended herself against a fancied accusation that she had allowed Belle Reve, the family mansion, to be lost. When Stanley entered some time later, he greeted Blanche brusquely. When he mentioned her dead husband, Blanche became first confused and shaken, then ill. Later, while Blanche was in the bath, Stanley and Stella were free to discuss the implications of her sudden visit. Stella asked him not to tell Blanche that she was going to have a baby. Stanley, who was suspicious over the loss of Belle Reve and imagined himself cheated of property, tore open Blanche's trunk looking for papers. Blanche entered and, using a pretext to get Stella out of the house, presented him with legal papers detailing the forfeiture of all the DuBois property. Blanche demonstrated a bewildering variety of moods in this scene, flirting with Stanley, discussing the legal transactions with calm irony, and becoming abruptly hysterical when Stanley picked up old love letters written by her dead husband. Her reaction to the news of Stella's pregnancy was reverent wonderment.

It was Stanley's poker night with three cronies, one of whom, Mitch, was a large, sentimental man who lived with his mother. Stella and Blanche entered after an evening in the French Quarter that they extended to two-thirty in the morning to keep out of the way of the poker game. They crossed into the bedroom, separated only by portieres from the living room, and met Mitch leaving the bathroom. Blanche looked after him with some interest as he returned to the game. She began undressing in a shaft of light through the portieres that she knew would expose her to the men in the next room. She donned a robe in time for Mitch's next trip to the bathroom. Out of the game, he stopped to talk to Blanche, and during their conversation she adopted an air of primness and innocence. Not wanting Mitch to see how old she really was, she asked him to cover the naked light bulb with a little Chinese lantern she had bought in the French Quarter. They danced briefly to some music from the radio, but when the radio distracted the poker players, Stanley became violent and threw the radio out of the window, which set off displays of temper that involved everyone in the house. Blanche and Stella fled to the upstairs apartment, leaving the men to deal with an outraged Stanley. When Stanley discovered that he was alone, he bellowed up the stairway like a lost animal until Stella came down to him.

The next morning Blanche persisted in regarding as desperate a situation that Stella had long since accepted as normal. Blanche recollected an old admirer, Shep Huntleigh, who she thought might rescue them. When Stella defended Stanley, Blanche retaliated with a long speech describing Stanley as a Stone Age man. Because the noise of his entry was covered by the sound of a train, Stanley heard the entire speech. To keep them from realizing that he had overheard, he left and entered again. Stella ran into his arms.

Several weeks later, well into the humid Louisiana summer, Blanche was hoping for a proposal of marriage from Mitch, whom she had been dating. One day, Stanley, who had been making investigations into Blanche's conduct in Laurel, Mississippi, tormented Blanche with hints of what he had found out. After he left, a young man came to the door to collect for the newspaper. Blanche made tentative advances to him and before he left, she kissed him very gently on the lips.

Later that evening, Blanche and Mitch returned from a date. He stayed on for a talk in which Blanche told him she was hardly able to put up with Stanley's boorishness any longer. Mitch almost ended the conversation by asking Blanche how old she was. His mother wanted to know. Blanche diverted his attention from her age by telling him about her husband, whom she had married when they were both very young. One evening, she had discovered her husband in a homosexual act with an older man. Later, while they danced to the Varsouviana at a casino outside town, she had confronted him with her knowledge. Rushing outside, the young man had shot himself. Somehow, the mood of this speech prompted the long-awaited proposal from Mitch. Blanche was incoherent with gratitude and relief.

On Blanche's birthday, in the autumn, Stella prepared a birthday dinner, which Stanley spoiled as effectively as he could. He told Stella that Blanche had been a prostitute at a disreputable hotel in Laurel, a hotel she was asked to leave, and that she had lost her high school job because of an affair with a seventeen-year-old student. At first Stella refused to believe Stanley, then she defended Blanche's behavior as a reaction to a tragic marriage. Stanley had given the same information to Mitch, who did not appear for the birthday dinner. Stanley climaxed the scene by smashing the dinner dishes on the floor and giving Blanche his birthday present, a bus ticket back to Laurel. At this point, Stella revealed that she was in labor, and Stanley took her to the hospital.

Much later that same evening, Mitch came to the Kowalski apartment in an ugly mood. He repeated to Blanche the lurid details of her past that he had learned from Stanley. She admitted them angrily and volunteered even worse episodes. In the street outside the house, an old Mexican woman sold her flowers for the dead. Even though Mitch no longer wanted to marry Blanche, he began a clumsy sexual assault on her that she repelled by screaming, illogically, that the building was on fire.

With the help of Stanley's liquor, Blanche retreated into the safety of madness. By the time Stanley returned from the hospital, she had decked herself fantastically in scraps of old finery from her trunk. Stanley raped her, their struggle underlined by jazz music from a neighboring bar and by a fight between a drunk and a prostitute in the street outside.

In the final scene, another poker game was in progress when Blanche was taken to an asylum. Stella could not accept her sister's claim that Stanley had raped her, for to do so would mean the end of her marriage. To persuade Blanche to leave quietly, Stella told her that Shep Huntleigh had come for her. When Blanche saw the attendants, she was frightened at first, but then quickly responded to their kindness. Mitch raged at Stanley and had to be pulled off him by the other men. Stanley comforted Stella's weeping, and the neighborhood returned to normal, its values undisturbed.

Critical Evaluation:

Tennessee Williams was a prolific writer who published short stories, poems, essays, two novels, an autobiography, and dozens of plays. It is for his plays that he is most widely known. The most successful of these, in both commercial and critical terms, are *The Glass Menagerie* (1944), *A Streetcar Named Desire* (1947), *Cat on a Hot Tin Roof* (1955), and *The Night of the Iguana* (1961). All four received New York Drama Critics Circle awards, and both *A Streetcar Named Desire* and *Cat on a Hot Tin Roof* won Pulitzer prizes. Although Williams received less critical acclaim in his later years, he is regarded as one of the foremost American playwrights of the twentieth century.

Williams claimed that for him writing was therapy. He was always open about his troubled family background: his father's drunken violence, the unhappy marriage of his parents, his own mental breakdown, and the insanity of his beloved sister, who as a young woman was institutionalized for the rest of her life. Nor did Williams hide his homosexuality or his own alcohol and drug abuse. Although he denied that his writing was autobiographical, elements from his life appear frequently in his work.

In *A Streetcar Named Desire*, Williams shows the reality of people's lives, an enduring concern of his throughout his writing career. He wrote this play believing he was about to die, so he wrote about what he felt needed to be said. When it was first presented, the play was considered shocking because of its frank presentation of sexual issues.

Williams did not rely on realism alone to portray reality. In *A Streetcar Named Desire* as in other plays, he effectively uses dramatic devices to convey and enrich meanings. Most of the action of the play takes place in the Kowalskis' apartment, but there is also action in the street. This action—the Mexican woman with "flores para los muertos" and the struggle of the drunk and the prostitute—provide not only local color but also a commentary on the main action. When Blanche first arrives at the apartment, a screeching cat is heard, a minor bit of stage business that helps create a sense of Blanche's tension. The background music, too, is carefully contrived. The "Blue Piano" and the "Varsouviana" fade in and out according to what is going on in the minds of the characters, particularly Blanche. Blanche's rape is accompanied by "hot trumpet and drums."

The use of literary devices also underlines the meanings of the play. There are a number of significant names. Blanche DuBois, white woods, as Blanche herself points out "like an orchard in spring," is clearly ironic. The family plantation was Belle Reve, a "beautiful dream" now gone. The Elysian Fields address of Stella and Stanley is an ironic comment on the unheavenly reality of the place, and Blanche arrives there by means of two streetcars, Cemeteries and Desire, which foreshadow the recurring images of death and desire throughout the play.

It is death and desire that have brought Blanche to this low point in her life. She never recovered from the devastating death of her young husband, indirectly caused by the nature of his sexual desires. The deaths of her relatives have been instrumental in reducing her to poverty, as have the desires, the costly "epic fornications" of her forebears. Her own promiscuous sexual desire has destroyed her reputation and her professional career. The rape by Stanley, which he claims is the culmination of a perverse desire they have felt for each other all along, is the act that finally pushes her into insanity.

Just as Belle Reve is a relic of the plantation system that was the cornerstone of the civilization of the old South, so is Blanche an anachronistic leftover from that culture. She is a Southern belle, born to privilege and meant to be beautiful and refined, to read poetry, to flirt, and ultimately to marry and reproduce. Blanche is born too late in the history of her family and in the history of the South to inherit this legacy: The money is gone; the values are disintegrating. She hangs on to what vestiges of gentility she can, but this serves only to alienate rather than to shield her. Tender and delicate, like the moth she resembles, Blanche is unable to survive in the harsh reality of modern society.

There is more to the character of Blanche than merely the role of pathetic victim. She, too, has been active in her destruction. As she confesses to Mitch, she was not blameless in her husband's suicide, for her cruel remark seems to have pushed him to it. "I have always depended on the kindness of strangers," she remarks pathetically to the doctor who leads her away, and perhaps it is a search for "kindness," some warmth of human response, that has led to her gross, self-destructive sexual promiscuity. Despite recognizing her own undeniable flaws, she makes very little attempt to disguise her contempt for those she feels are inferior to her in refinement, and she is willing to use Mitch and Stanley to provide for her. She is also cruel to Stella, the one remaining person who loves her, in criticizing Stella's husband and her way of life.

If Blanche represents defunct Southern values, Stanley represents the new, urban modernity, which pays little heed to the past. If Belle Reve is not going to mean a financial inheritance, Stanley is no longer interested in Belle Reve. Williams' stage directions indicate that Stanley's virile, aggressive brand of masculinity is to be admired. Yet Stanley, like Blanche, is an ambiguous character. His cruel intolerance of Blanche can be seen as justifiable response to her lies, hypocrisy, and mockery, but his nasty streak of violence against his wife appalls even his friends. His rape of Blanche is a horrifying and destructive act, as well as a cruel betrayal of Stella. Ultimately, however, Stanley prevails. He has gotten rid of Blanche, who has lost everything, and as we see in the closing lines of the play, he is able to soothe Stella's grief, and their life goes on.

"Critical Evaluation" by Susan Henthorne

Bibliography:
Falk, Signi. *Tennessee Williams*. 2d ed. Boston: Twayne, 1978. An introduction to both the fiction and drama. Places Williams in the Southern tradition and examines his early exploratory work. Provides a good general overview with a focus on recurring character types. Includes a chronology of publication and production of works and a useful critical bibliography.

Hayman, Ronald. *Tennessee Williams: Everyone Else Is an Audience*. New Haven, Conn.: Yale University Press, 1993. Biographical study that examines how Williams used events from his life and characters he knew, including himself, as source material for his drama.

Miller, Jordan Y., ed. *Twentieth Century Interpretations of "A Streetcar Named Desire."* Englewood Cliffs, N.J.: Prentice-Hall, 1971. Excellent collection of twenty essays and reviews divided into two sections that treat the play as commercial theater and as dramatic literature. Provides views from a variety of critics and includes a notebook of the director of the original production.

Thompson, Judith J. *Tennessee Williams' Plays: Memory, Myth, and Symbol*. New York: Peter Lang, 1987. Examines eight plays in considerable detail, including *A Streetcar Named Desire*, in terms of recurring archetypal characters and patterns of action. Interesting analysis of tragic, romantic, and comic images.

Weales, Gerald. *American Drama Since World War II*. New York: Harcourt, Brace and World, 1962. Places Williams' work in the context of his time and questions the world and the values that Williams depicts as those of his characters, which often represent marginalized "fugitive types."

STUDS LONIGAN
A Trilogy

Type of work: Novel
Author: James T. Farrell (1904-1979)
Type of plot: Naturalism
Time of plot: June, 1916-August, 1931
Locale: Chicago, Illinois
First published: 1935: *Young Lonigan: A Boyhood in Chicago Streets*, 1932; *The Young Manhood of Studs Lonigan*, 1934; *Judgment Day*, 1935

> *Principal characters:*
> STUDS LONIGAN, a street tough
> PATRICK LONIGAN, his father, a contractor
> MARY LONIGAN, his mother, a pious housewife
> MARTIN,
> FRANCES, and
> LORETTA, Studs's siblings
> LUCY SCANLAN, a neighborhood girl
> HELEN SHIRES, a tomboy
> WEARY REILLEY, the neighborhood bully
> PHIL ROLFE, the husband of Frances
> CATHERINE BANAHAN, Studs's fiancée
> DANNY O'NEILL, a bright neighborhood youngster

The Story:

William "Studs" Lonigan, nearly fifteen years old, had just graduated from St. Patrick's Grammar School, "the old dump," and was surreptitiously puffing a cigarette in the bathroom as he contemplated his future as son, Catholic, and American. His proud parents were satisfied with raising all of their children within the Catholic religion; they confidently counted on the Church and its unquestioned authority to provide all the guidance the family would need. At a service attached to the graduation ceremony, they heard the parish priest describe very graphically the omnipresence of sin in society as well as the daily temptations of Satan's attempts to recruit adherents to unholy causes. At a party afterward, Studs and his crowd played kissing games. That night, talking over the evening's activities with his sister, Studs began to have evil thoughts and to experience sinful feelings. He feared the imminent punishment of God; before dropping off to sleep, the youngster nervously prayed and wondered about contrition.

With only the ease of summer stretching before him, Studs aimlessly roamed neighborhood streets and vaguely dreamed of performing feats of heroism. He played soccer with tomboy Helen Shires but really longed to impress Lucy Scanlan, who he hoped might witness his prowess. Studs and Helen talked about spying on a nearby "can-house," where unmentionable activities were presumed to occur. A truculent Weary Reilley joined their ball game but played too aggressively, deliberately trying to hurt Helen, cursing at them all the while. Studs and Weary fought, and an enthusiastic crowd soon gathered to encourage the vicious battle. In standing up to the notorious Weary, the feared local bully, Studs became a hero and established his reputation as a "tough." In days following, when he walked the streets, Studs Lonigan heard even the adults speaking his name; he was a celebrity. Life was promising.

Studs attracted the company of old-time street fighters and, from one of them named Old Man O'Brien, heard vigorous expressions of neighborhood prejudice, particularly that blacks and Jews were ruining the city. Studs unquestioningly accepted this view and accompanied other hoodlums on expeditions to beat and brutalize such racial and religious interlopers. When Studs's father mildly reprimanded him for staying out late, the youngster reacted with anger and ignored any attempted discipline. Studs fantasized about a relationship with Lucy. Reflecting on the purity of Catholic girls, he spent one euphoric afternoon in Lucy's company, sitting on a tree limb while they sang and chatted about the future. Studs felt that moment to be a turning point in his life. As the summer progressed, however, he often walked the streets and parks alone. Disrespectful of adult playground supervisors, Studs bullied youngsters and, after starting a fight at a baseball game, was invited by witnesses to join an older, tougher group of associates.

Studs now openly smoked and chewed tobacco. He began to drink. He stood on the street corner and joined fellow loafers in ethnic slurs, racial jokes, and sex talk that he did not quite understand. Studs Lonigan regarded the poolroom as home, derided school as irrelevant, and cynically wisecracked at ordinary people going about their daily business. Studs's worried father tried to instigate a man-to-man talk but the weak attempt failed. Studs lost his virginity when he joined a "gangshag." He felt he was a man. The ending of the summer was a violently formative experience for Studs. He dreamed of some amorphous, unplanned future. He felt free but uneasy.

One year later Studs Lonigan, truant and school dropout, pondered about enlisting for war service, but he and his friends were rejected. He thought much about death even as he listened to the continued, dreary conversations of his daily associates at Charley Bathcellar's Pool Room concerning the futility of working for a living, the uselessness of education, and the joys of alcohol and sex. Angered at his son's pointless life, Patrick Lonigan put his son to work for him as a house painter. Still, the young man's self-destructive behavior continued. Studs was a confirmed drunk, frequently having to be carried home by his friends. He was caught with the promiscuous Elizabeth Burns and horsewhipped by the girl's enraged father. As weeks and months passed, Studs Lonigan's pattern for living remained unchanged. He went from poolroom to saloon, drank and fought, and heard and ignored sidewalk discussions of venereal disease. A frightened Studs finally examined his conscience and went to confession after having a premonition of death. He vowed to change his ways but never did; the course of his life was irretrievably set. His character hardened. Studs and his friends deliberately crippled "Jewboy" Schwartz in a game of football that ended with a riot broken up by police. He then disgraced his family with his public drunkenness on Christmas Eve, his all-night carousing precipitating an emotional family crisis on Christmas Day. Studs plunged downward.

As the months progressed, the twenty-three-year-old Studs experienced a spasm of virtue. Joining the Young Men's Christian Association (YMCA), he attended respectable dances and dreamed of heroic exploits. Yet, he continued to drink, fought at dances, and battled at crap games. Tenuously and unrealistically, he continued hoping for a relationship with Lucy. Studs escorted her to a dance but turned the evening into a disaster when he brutally tried to force sex on the astonished young woman. Studs moved on, righteously regarding himself as strong and denigrating as weak those who followed moral rules.

One evening in the park, Studs boxed a young opponent and was soundly beaten. The old physical Studs appeared to be diminishing, but, after the bout, he and his cronies heckled social reformers and other serious political speakers at the Bug Club. Studs then got drunk on Jamaica ginger and collapsed. Not even a powerful hell-fire sermon from heated missionary Father

Shannon could deflect Studs from his path. He attended a vile and decadent New Year's Eve party at which Weary Reilley was arrested for rape. The next morning, a semiconscious Studs Lonigan was found lying in the gutter, his body soiled with vomit. He had been robbed for eight dollars.

As time progressed, Lonigan's gang started disappearing into death, illness, or jail. Weakened physically, Studs wondered what he might have done with his life. He became engaged to Catherine Banahan, a plain but stable religious young woman, and he resolved once more to change. America, however, was in the beginnings of the Great Depression, and Studs had invested his meager savings in stocks that failed. His view of life now thoroughly pessimistic, Studs blamed the state of things on foreigners and international bankers and felt that only a leader like Italy's Fascist dictator Benito Mussolini could save the reeling country. Studs Lonigan visited the home of his sister Frances, married to Phil Rolfe, whom Studs had always regarded as unimportant. He was jealous of their apparent happiness and comfort while he, sickly and unemployed, had to walk the streets in search of a job, his father's business having gone bankrupt. Studs witnessed many scenes of the Depression: people in panic over the closing of banks, down-and-outers begging for work, and radicals talking revolution. Studs regarded communists as misguided people without moral values. A disillusioned Studs fought with his upstart brother Martin, who was intent on following a street-tough path. A vanquished Studs realize how far he had slipped, and when he presented himself as candidate for the Order of Christopher, he was maligned as "runt" and "shrimp."

During the seemingly endless days, Studs wandered the city half heartedly. When he tried to play sandlot baseball, he was physically inadequate and was ridiculed by the younger men. He escorted Catherine to the beach, to movies, and to dance marathons. After they quarreled over his selfish, thoughtless manners, however, Studs went to a betting parlor, won six dollars, and paid a distraught woman for sex, as she tried desperately to recoup the food money she had lost. The following day Studs, mistakenly feeling he had made a conquest and desiring another ego-building encounter, returned to the woman's apartment. The irate woman, shocked to see him, insulted his manhood, verbally flayed his character, and threatened to call the police. The disconsolate Studs made up with Catherine and recklessly seduced her. Not long thereafter, when Catherine told him of her probable pregnancy, Studs suggested that she have an abortion but finally acquiesced to a wedding. At the beach, however, Studs suffered a heart attack and fainted in the water. His health continued to decline.

Studs interviewed for several jobs; each revealed his shortcomings. He continued his careless behaviors of drinking and smoking. During one particularly chilly, rainy day, Studs sat in wet clothing through a burlesque show. He arrived home desperately ill. When his condition worsened, a terrified Catherine appealed to Mrs. Lonigan for a bedside wedding to give her unborn child a name, but Studs's mother reviled the young woman, blaming her for Studs's present deteriorated condition. Studs Lonigan died as his mother fell into hysterics and his brother and his father got drunk.

Critical Evaluation:

Studs Lonigan is a sociological case study in fiction, a stern indictment of society awash in empty cultural institutions, and a chronicle of the failed American Dream amid a fractured urban landscape. It charts, in often brutal episodes, the life and premature death of a once promising middle-class Irish Catholic American, a product of parochial education, of a devout home, and of the city streets. The action is discontinuous, with episodes sometimes moving only minutes forward but on occasion leaping ahead years. Nevertheless, the gloomy tread of inevitability stalks every page of the degenerate journey made by James T. Farrell's archetypal protagonist.

The failed authority symbols of church, home, and school dominate Studs Lonigan's landscape. Despite the principles articulated before the young man, there never evolves within him an ethical purpose or moral center. His response to life focuses on the ephemeral fame that underscores his street identity. Studs's models become the fast-talking, luridly fascinating poolroom hacks; his poetry becomes the accessible braggadocio of the saloon. Education is for "goofs" like Danny O'Neill, whose later commitment to radical social values would testify to his humanism; civilized behavior is for the weak. Cynically, Studs concludes that everything is "crap"; a bleak nihilism comes to shroud his every attitude, even the fearful moments of halfhearted reform. His life reflects a compendium of failure. Studs Lonigan's imminent death is foreshadowed by the demise of the institutions that fail to reach him and that leave a spiritual vacuum in his life, unable to deflect him from the path of self-destruction.

Indoctrinated early into the streetwise brotherhood of sadism and self-indulgence, Studs remains surrounded by an urban ambience whose very physical environment reeks of threat and violence: decrepit poolrooms, sleazy bars, greasy diners, ominous brothels, and menacing parks. The milieu about him crushes his early romantic yearnings and his potential for fulfilling heroic plans. Corrupted into an ethos of brutality and ignorance, Studs succumbs to the crude clichés of the street and the sensual lures to his libido dominate his maturing days. In the safe haven of an escapist movie theater where he had once identified with the luminous hero, Studs now sympathizes with the plight of the gangster; he feels unaccountably sad when the villain is killed. Studs Lonigan, in fact, knows right from wrong; the powerful forces about him, however, easily control his will.

The theme of isolation runs through the trilogy, for "Lonewolf" Lonigan develops a psychological system for separating from his essential self and observing his own behaviors as a seemingly objective judge. He recriminates, rationalizes, and condones the behavior of Studs Lonigan, a person standing against the world, superior to those people and institutions that have victimized him. Studs walks alone. Even with his antisocial cronies accompanying him on immoral activities, he maintains his own counsel with himself. Taking part in violent episodes, he remains alone in feelings of fear and guilt. Ironically, he never comes to belong anywhere, an embodiment of the alienated, the outsider. He is alone and awash in his own filth, lying in the gutter on New Year's Day, another vivid foreshadowing of decline. From page one of this trilogy, Studs Lonigan's fundamental estrangement from church, family, school, and self takes its toll. He is on his inexorable journey to an early grave.

A number of urban venues aid in mirroring the deterioration and degeneration of Studs Lonigan: the burlesque theater, the betting parlor, the park bench, and the dance marathon. His life filled with illusion and prejudice, Studs has no beliefs, and his solitary wanderings only serve to intensify the bigotry of his feelings. Hating himself, he nevertheless goes to the burlesque show, associating with a clientele he regards as inferior and depraved. He considers himself above the desperate patrons in the bookie-joint, for he is Studs Lonigan, brother-in-law of Phil Rolfe, one of the operators. In the park he mindlessly threatens an intelligent Communist, who, Studs reasons, must oppose God and family. The dance marathon, however, epitomizes the meaningless fox-trot of death that Studs Lonigan has joined. Like the sick and tired dancers who barely move their feet to stay alive in the tawdry dance competition, hoping for a few dollars, Studs too is engaged in a marathon of sorts, his own *danse macabre*. Without reflective thought he, too, is moving his feet out of instinct; he, too, is governed by capricious laws; he, too, is without essential hope but carries vague expectations. Around and around the dancers and Studs Lonigan move, surrounded by decrepitude and dissonance. To the end, Studs maintains a totally unrealistic assessment of himself, his prospects, and his talent. With his death he leaves "the old dump" of a world just as he left St. Patrick's Grammar School a decade and a half earlier.

Abe C. Ravitz

Bibliography:
Beach, Joseph Warren. *American Fiction, 1920-1940*. New York: Macmillan, 1941. Farrell's fiction examined in the context of his contemporaries. Sections dealing with themes in *Studs Lonigan* include "James T. Farrell: Tragedy of the Poolroom Loafer" and "JTF: The Plight of the Children."
Branch, Edgar M. *James T. Farrell*. New York: Twayne, 1971. A sound assessment of Farrell's achievement as well as a perceptive interpretation of his aesthetic philosophy. Two separate chapters deal with *Studs Lonigan* specifically.
Frohock, William M. *The Novel of Violence in America, 1920-1950*. Dallas: Southern Methodist University Press, 1958. In a section entitled "James T. Farrell: The Precise Content," there is an analysis of the novelist's "documentary" style of writing that is much in evidence in the trilogy.
Walcutt, Charles C. *American Literary Naturalism: A Divided Stream*. Minneapolis: University of Minnesota Press, 1956. An analytical account of naturalistic literary theory and Farrell's "aspects of telling the whole truth."
Wald, Alan M. *James T. Farrell: The Revolutionary Socialist Years*. New York: New York University Press, 1978. A thorough historical account of Farrell's intellectual roots and evolving political stance. Important for an understanding of the sociopolitical underpinnings of the trilogy.

A STUDY IN SCARLET

Type of work: Novel
Author: Arthur Conan Doyle (1859-1930)
Type of plot: Detective and mystery
Time of plot: Nineteenth century
Locale: London
First published: 1887

Principal characters:
SHERLOCK HOLMES, the detective
DR. JOHN WATSON, his friend
JEFFERSON HOPE, an American
TOBIAS GREGSON and
LESTRADE, detectives from Scotland Yard

The Story:

To many, the Afghan wars brought fame and promotion, but to John H. Watson, M.D., they brought only misfortune. He was wounded by a Jezail bullet, succumbed to enteritis during his convalescence, and after months of suffering was sent home with a pension of eleven shillings and sixpence a day. At first, Watson lived in a hotel, but his pension scarcely covered his bills. By chance, he met an old friend, Stamford, to whom he confided his difficulties. Stamford told him of an amateur scientist, Sherlock Holmes, who had rooms at 221B Baker Street and was looking for someone to share them. Stamford did warn him that Holmes pursued unorthodox studies—one day, Stamford had found him beating a cadaver to see if bruises could be produced after death—and that he had a queer habit of making deductions from trifling details. Watson grew curious about Holmes and arranged to have Stamford introduce them. Soon after that first meeting, Watson went to share Holmes's rooms on Baker Street.

Watson never went out and consequently spent much time studying his new friend. He found Holmes an amazingly contradictory man, one who knew nothing at all of literature, philosophy, or astronomy but had a profound knowledge of chemistry, anatomy, and sensational crime stories. He also played the violin. From time to time, Holmes had visitors, but Watson never knew why they came.

One day at breakfast, Watson learned a good deal more about his friend. Holmes showed him a letter from Tobias Gregson, a Scotland Yard investigator, who was asking him for help in a case of murder. A gentleman identified by his visiting cards as Enoch J. Drebber, Cleveland, Ohio, U.S.A., had been found murdered in a deserted house in Lauriston Gardens. Holmes then explained that he was a consulting detective and that Scotland Yard asked for his help whenever an unusual case came up that was outside police jurisdiction or too difficult.

Holmes and Watson took a cab to Lauriston Gardens to look into the affair. Holmes spent a long time outside in the road and in the yard. Watson was impatient at the delay, but Holmes examined everything carefully. Inside the house, Gregson and another detective from Scotland Yard, Lestrade, greeted them and pointed out the body of Drebber, which was surrounded by spatters of blood. Holmes went over the body painstakingly.

As the orderlies were carrying out the corpse, a woman's wedding ring fell to the floor. The Scotland Yard men were sure a woman was involved, and Lestrade was triumphant when he found the word "Rache" printed in letters of blood on the wall. As Holmes left the room, he announced his findings to the detectives. The murderer was more than six feet in height and florid. He wore square-toed boots, smoked a Trichinopoly cigar, had long nails on his right hand, and had driven up to the house in a four-wheeler drawn by a horse with a new shoe on his off forefoot. Further, the murder was done by poison, and "Rache" was not an abbreviation for Rachel but rather the German word meaning revenge.

Holmes had read the story from the cigar ashes, the tracks, the height of the writing, and the scratches made during the writing on the wall. From the fact that the blood on the floor came from a nosebleed, for example, he had deduced that the murderer had ruddy coloring. After uncovering these initial clues, however, Holmes was baffled for a time. When he advertised the wedding ring as lost, an old woman came to claim it, who eluded him when he tried to follow her. At that point, he realized that he was dealing with a clever opponent.

The murdered man's trail led to his secretary, Stangerson. Gregson was sure that if he found Stangerson, he would have the murderer. When, however, Stangerson was found dead in his hotel room, stabbed through the heart, the case began to seem impenetrable. Gregson and Lestrade came to Holmes one night, and the three detectives and Watson went over the difficulties. Holmes was tying up a trunk preparatory to sending it away. He called a cab to deliver it. When the bell rang, he asked the driver to come up to help with the ropes. As the man bent down, Holmes deftly slipped handcuffs over his wrists. The driver was a large, vigorous man who fought as if possessed, but the four men subdued him. With a theatrical flourish, Holmes introduced him as Jefferson Hope, the murderer of Drebber and Stangerson.

Hope calmed down and told the men he had nothing to fear. He asked Watson to feel his pulse, and Watson, who immediately detected an aneurism, agreed that Hope had not long to live. Indeed, Hope never came to trial, for he died in less than a week, but before that he recounted his strange story.

On the great alkali plain in Utah, a man named John Ferrier and his little daughter Lucy had been the only survivors of a wagon train. The two were providentially picked up by Mormons, who, under the leadership of Brigham Young, were on their way to a new settlement in the wilderness. Ferrier had to agree to adopt the Mormon faith in return for being rescued, and he prospered and became a rich man; Lucy grew up to be a beautiful woman. Although he was a Mormon, Ferrier refused to take wives, and he made a vow that Lucy should never marry a Mormon. When a traveler named Jefferson Hope stopped at their house on his way to the silver mines, an attraction developed between him and Lucy. After Hope left, the Mormon elders decreed that before thirty days should elapse, Lucy must choose a husband. She was given the choice between two men, Drebber or Stangerson, who already had several wives. Ferrier sent word to Hope, who returned on the thirtieth day, and that night Hope, Ferrier, and Lucy stole out of the Mormon village and rode away toward the mountains.

Once he judged that they were far enough away, Hope left Ferrier and Lucy in camp while he went hunting. On his return, he found that Ferrier had been murdered and that Lucy was gone. Hope hid near the Mormon village in the hope of rescuing Lucy, but he was thwarted by the strong, watchful Latter-day Saints. Lucy was married off to Drebber, but survived only one month. While the women watched at night over her coffin, Hope stormed in, kissed his dead love, and took the wedding ring from her finger. Then he vanished.

Shortly afterward, both Drebber and Stangerson renounced Mormonism and moved to Cleveland. They were wealthy, but they were also afraid, for they knew that Hope was pursuing them. They fled to Russia and Germany and finally ended up in London. Hope followed them from place to place. To survive in London, and in order to follow his prey conveniently, he took a job as cabdriver. When Drebber engaged him one night when he was drunk, Hope drove him to the deserted house in Lauriston Gardens. After showing Drebber the wedding ring, he took a small box from his pocket containing two pills, one harmless and one deadly. He forced Drebber to choose one and swallow it and put the other in his own mouth. Hope felt that Lucy's spirit had guided the choice when it was Drebber who died. On impulse, Hope had scribbled "Rache" on the wall with the blood that had gushed from his nose in his excitement. Later, Hope found Stangerson in his hotel room and offered him the same fatal choice. Stangerson had attacked him, and Hope had killed him with a knife. He refused to give the name of the old woman who had appeared to claim the ring. On the day he was to appear in court, Hope died from the bursting of his aneurism, but his work was done and Lucy had been avenged.

Critical Evaluation:

A Study in Scarlet was Arthur Conan Doyle's first full-length detective novel. His short stories had already earned him some success and recognition, but with this effort he hoped to attract the attention of critics as well as the general reading public. Doyle longed to write serious historical fiction, in which he intended to chronicle the deeds of the men and women who had made England great, but he believed that he must first establish himself as a respected and popular author. *A Study in Scarlet* met with several rejections from publishers, however, before Doyle finally managed to sell it in 1886 for the modest sum of twenty-five pounds. When the book appeared the following year as part of *Beeton's Christmas Annual*, most of the London critics completely ignored it, but it soon became very popular in the United States. Encouraged by his American publisher to write another full-length Holmes adventure, Doyle revived his detective for *The Sign of Four* in 1890, which was a success on both sides of the Atlantic. The reception of this novel stimulated renewed interest in *A Study in Scarlet*, which thereupon appeared in several separate editions and assured the author's fame and the immortality of the world's first consulting detective. (*Beeton's Christmas Annual* for 1887 has become one of the rarest and most collectible works of modern fiction.)

A Study in Scarlet provides the reader with a great deal of vital information about Sherlock Holmes and Dr. John Watson, and while it lacks the polish and style of Doyle's later detective novel, *The Hound of the Baskervilles* (1902), it remains one of the most popular adventures in the canon. The greatest weakness of the novel lies in Doyle's failure completely to integrate the tragic tale of Lucy Ferrier and Jefferson Hope into the narrative of the dual murder. In later stories, Doyle became a master of integrative devices, but in *A Study in Scarlet* the reader's concentration is immediately diverted by two equally fascinating tales joined together by only the flimsiest of connections.

To students of detective fiction, *A Study in Scarlet* is valuable because it presents the details of the meeting of Dr. Watson and Sherlock Holmes. In the opening pages of the novel, Doyle uses the occasion of a mutual acquaintance introducing them to each other to delineate the personalities of his two characters. Although he added a wealth of subtle details in later stories, Holmes and Watson remain fixed in readers' minds from the moment they read of the world's first consulting detective rushing up to the bemused physician with the prophetic cry "I've found it! I've found it!"

In *A Study in Scarlet*, Doyle demonstrated his ability to create a believable atmosphere through the subtle use of detail. From a careful reading of the adventures of Holmes and Watson, a serious student of Victorian culture is able to re-create the England of the last quarter of the nineteenth century. Doyle's portrait of London in all its varied aspects is particularly vivid. He did not try to create a fictional landscape or make merely random references to suggest a particular locale but incorporated his setting into each tale as an integral part of the story line—the setting itself becomes a character. Doyle is equally adept at using the events of everyday life to give his characters credibility and to create a degree of verisimilitude often missing in popular fiction. For Doyle's contemporaries, Holmes and Watson soon ceased to be the creations of a skilled novelist and became instead living human beings. Their daily routine seemed so real, their reactions to the world about them so natural, that they assumed an existence independent of their creator. In time, even Doyle became aware of this remarkable metamorphosis, though he did not always find it gratifying.

A Study in Scarlet is, above all else, an absorbing tale, particularly the portion that deals with solving the double murder. Doyle is a master of detective fiction without equal. He does not conceal information from his readers, and every clue is presented and examined in detail, yet the reader sleuth finds the solving of each crime as difficult as do the two professionals from Scotland Yard. Doyle's final solutions seem so logical and reasonable that the reader experiences the conflicting emotions of relief and frustration, while at the same time longing for one more chance to best Mr. Sherlock Holmes at his own game.

That portion of *A Study in Scarlet* that deals with the early Mormon settlement in Utah is weaker because it is based more on myth and nescience than on fact and because Doyle brings into his narrative all the popular contemporary prejudices against Latter-day Saints. Yet he accords to Jefferson Hope an honor he reserved only for those among his characters who commit crimes for noble motives: His untimely death saves Hope from an earthly tribunal.

While Holmes, Watson, Gregson, and Lestrade, who begin their long evolution here, are already rounded, full-dimensional characters, the other figures in the tale—Drebber, Stangerson, Lucy, and John Ferrier—often appear one-dimensional, familiar players in the pulp fiction of the time. Only Jefferson Hope reveals greater depth of personality, but his literary life is of course cut short by an aortic aneurism. In his later stories, Doyle would form even his minor characters with much greater and more subtle skill, another trait that set his work apart from traditional detective fiction.

Through his master detective, Doyle portrays the understanding of the criminal mind as a matter of scientific principles that may easily be comprehended but not easily mastered. Although Holmes is an enigmatic figure, given to unorthodox and unaccountable behavior, he is at heart a rationalist and enamored, like any enlightened nineteenth century scientist, by the idea that there is no such thing as a mystery; there are only puzzles that anyone devoted to fact can solve. Hence, his famous exclamation: "It's elementary, my dear Watson!" For Holmes, human evil and passion are not without reason and motive; they are, therefore, rational and deducible. The world is only mysterious and uncontrollable to those who will not see. Sherlock Holmes, offspring of nineteenth century enlightenment and the scientific revolution, is among the brightest—and perhaps the last—offspring of that age.

"Critical Evaluation" by Clifton W. Potter, Jr.

Bibliography:
Carr, John Dickson. *The Life of Sir Arthur Conan Doyle.* New York: Harper, 1949. Considered the definitive biography of Doyle because it is based on a thorough study of Doyle's private papers by one of the masters of the mystery novel.
Doyle, Arthur Conan. *The Annotated Sherlock Holmes.* Edited by William S. Baring-Gould. 2 vols. 2d ed. New York: Clarkson N. Potter, 1967. A store of valuable information on Victorian England compiled by one of the leading Holmes scholars. The bibliography includes references to a number of articles from *The Baker Street Journal*, the official

publication of the Baker Street Irregulars, an organization dedicated to the study of the cases of Mr. Sherlock Holmes.

_____. *Memories and Adventures*. Boston: Little, Brown, 1924. Leaves many matters untouched and questions unanswered but provides valuable insights into the life of the author toward the end of his career.

Jaffe, Jacqueline A. *Arthur Conan Doyle*. Boston: Twayne, 1987. Part of Twayne's English Authors Series, this is an excellent brief introduction to Doyle's life and in particular to his works. Two chapters, "The Beginnings of a Modern Hero: Sherlock Holmes" and "The Return of Holmes," deal with Doyle's detective fiction. Includes a short but useful bibliography.

A STUDY OF HISTORY

Type of work: History
Author: Arnold Toynbee (1889-1975)
First published: 1934-1961, twelve volumes

Not every work that is monumental because of its size is monumental in character. Arnold J. Toynbee's *A Study of History*, a twelve-volume work, compels the continuing critical attention of historians, philosophers, and other students of civilizations rising and falling over time. Despite its scope, this book is not superficial; despite its author's ambition—to account for the death of civilizations—it shows no sign of a confusion between modesty and unoriginality: considered as a theory, it is daring and illuminating.

Is it, however, true? Most readers hesitate to enter upon a multi-volume pilgrimage if the only reward is acquaintance with a scholar's laborious fancies. In the sense in which Toynbee is a philosopher of history, a philosopher of history is someone, generally a historian, who tries to make sense out of the mass of events presumed to have occurred. Proceeding from records and signs, or what are thought to be records and signs, a story of the presumed past is constructed: That is history. The story is then surveyed in an attempt to find its theme, the moral of the tale: The account of these reflections is this person's study of history.

Such a study may be true, or it may not. To be true, such a study practically requires a historian who is a genius, something of a seer, and levelheaded. Such a person might discover or create an explanation of history that shows that the fortunes and accidents of history are fortunes and accidents only relative to people's ignorance. Considered in such a light, history is inevitable. Given the demands of an accurate study of history, it is more likely that, strictly speaking, a given study of history is false—that at best it approximates the truth and makes some sense to people who share something of the author's perspective. In any case, the truth of such a study is unimportant.

Not the truth of the theory, but its plausibility is what counts; not its conformity to undiscoverable facts, but its organizing power in the face of evidence. Even if a reader rejects a study of history because of its failure to make sense out of the evidence, it is still possible that the work will have had the value of showing a creative mind's response to a historical problem. That Toynbee's study has this latter value is beyond question. To some, his theory is plausible; to others, it is as clearly false; but to all, it is exciting and worthy of respect.

Toynbee's study of history led him to present and defend the thesis that "societies," not nations, are the proper concern of the historian. According to Tonybee, civilized societies—civilizations—arise in response to challenging conditions; the civilizations grow in response to further challenges; they break down, that is, cease to respond creatively, because of some idolization of the past; and finally, they disintegrate. The civilization then becomes a dominant minority, an internal proletariat (in the society, but not of it), and an external proletariat (formerly, but no longer, of the society) as a result of the failure to respond in such a way as to meet a challenge that is repeatedly presented.

The answer to the central question, "Why do civilizations die?" is that they die as a result of an inability to determine themselves creatively. The failure of self-determination results, if petrifaction does not set in instead, in a schism of the society that is paralleled by a schism in the soul of the member of the society.

The thesis and each point in its defense is illustrated historically in Toynbee's work. One of the values of the work comes from its ability to charm the reader into a reexamination and reappraisal of the content of history. It also introduces readers to many historical findings with which they may not have been acquainted previously.

Dispassionately considered at some distance from the wealth of historical material that gives the thesis great persuasive force, Toynbee's central claim is perhaps not as remarkable as it may seem to be while one is reading *A Study of History*. It may be that in his use of the term "civilization," Toynbee has employed a criterion by reference to which he dismisses certain societies as primitive. The analysis reveals what his use of the term "civilization" indicates: societies that grew not from favorable, but from unfavorable and challenging conditions.

Similarly, it might be argued that his account of disintegration is a question-begging truism, handsomely disguised. Civilizations decline before they fall; they fall because they fall apart; and they fall apart because they can no longer hang together creatively.

The value of the study, however, is not a function of the remarkableness of the claim. Perhaps for the first time, a historian has shown civilizations, to a considerable extent, as they are: not as living organisms, not as accidents, not as the fruits of fortune—but as societies, achieving their characters as civilizations from the mode and quality of their responses to challenges, and falling apart when, either because of the absence of challenge or because of the presence of challenges too strong to be met, the society and the individuals composing it divide into irreconcilable parts. If what Toynbee presents is a truism, at least he has had the wit to see it as a truth and the historical knowledge to make it respectable. Furthermore, he has imagination and spiritual courage.

It takes spiritual courage to argue, as Toynbee does, that history is "a vision of God's creation on the move," and that the historian finds six dimensions—the three of space, then time, life, and the Spirit. He also appraises the chances that humans have in Western civilization to pursue their "true" end: glorifying God. He argues that the laws of nature do not control all of peoples' actions, but that, within limits, humans are free; perfect freedom, he adds, is to be under the law of God. Finally, he conducts a "survey of saviours" and concludes that only Jesus has made good his claim to be the son of God.

These beliefs are not unpopular; indeed, they are shared by millions. What is odd, and therefore demanding of courage, is the expression of these beliefs in a study of history, not merely as token reminders of the faith of people in Western civilization, but as necessary to both the understanding and the existence of Western civilization itself. Although it may seem strange and unhistorical to explain history by a declaration of religious faith, it is possible, even for the unbeliever, to appreciate the historical point of Toynbee's declaration of religious faith. First, as Toynbee shows, Western civilization is, for the most part, a Christian civilization. Second, if Toynbee is right in arguing that civilizations rise and grow as they make creative responses and break down and disintegrate as they fail to determine themselves, then to be born and to grow through an exercise of the proper spirit is the special business of any individual or civilization that values life and the special quality of life that creative activity provides. It is certainly excusable for a Christian scholar to make these points in Christian terms.

A particular benefit of Toynbee's spiritual approach to historical problems is his analysis of "schism in the soul" in a disintegrating society. In a growing society, people are creative or mimetic; that is, they are leaders or imitators. In a disintegrating society, however, there is an increasing tendency to substitute for creativity and mimesis, either passively or actively. For example, instead of being creative, people might be inclined either to live with abandon, to follow their impulses (the passive substitute), or to live with self-control, keeping their passions in check (the active substitute). Truancy (desertion) and martyrdom (action above and beyond the call of duty) are considered to be the passive and active substitutes, respectively, for mimesis. Toynbee also considers "the sense of drift" and the "sense of sin" as alternative substitutes for the feeling of creative advance that accompanies the growth of a civilization. His discussion of other spiritual attitudes and characteristics is intelligent and illuminating.

Toynbee refuses to be either pessimistic or optimistic about the possibility of the survival of Western civilization. Of the twenty-eight civilizations that Toynbee finds in history, only Western civilization is not clearly disintegrating or already dead. Toynbee sees some signs of breakdown in the West, but believes they are not conclusive. He considers that the extreme destructiveness of the atomic bomb, together with the continued effort of the Christian spirit, might finally bring about a world order that will allow Western civilization to continue to grow.

Bibliography:
Mason, Henry. *Toynbee's Approach to World Politics.* Tulane Studies in Political Science vol. 5. New Orleans: Tulane University Press, 1958. Critical analysis of Toynbee's political theories, including both positive and negative evaluations of Toynbee's methodology. Surveys his study of international affairs. Appendix covers general reception and specific criticisms of *A Study of History.*
Samuel, Maurice. *The Professor and the Fossil: Some Observations on Arnold J. Toynbee's "A Study of History."* New York: Alfred A. Knopf, 1956. Evaluates *A Study of History* and concludes that much of the work is meaningless, many of Toynbee's historical facts are inaccurate, and purposeful omissions create a distorted picture.
Singer, C. Gregg. *Toynbee.* Grand Rapids, Mich.: Baker Book House, 1965. Presents background material that helps in understanding *A Study of History.* Discusses assumptions that Toynbee followed but did not always make clear. Analyzes problems in establishing patterns for the rise and fall of major civilizations.
Tomlin, E. W. F., ed. Introduction to *Arnold Toynbee: A Selection from His Works.* Oxford, England: Oxford University Press, 1978. Defines and clarifies key phrases used repeatedly in *A Study of History.* Each selection includes the editor's description of it, its background, and the major principles it contains.
Urban, G. R. *Toynbee on Toynbee: A Conversation Between Arnold J. Toynbee and G. R. Urban.* New York: Oxford University Press, 1974. Transcribed radio discussions with Toynbee. Discusses Toynbee's personal theories that became key principles in *A Study of History*; covers the problem of selecting historical evidence.

THE SUBJECTION OF WOMEN

Type of work: Philosophy
Author: John Stuart Mill (1806-1873)
First published: 1869

Written in 1860-1861, *The Subjection of Women* first appeared as a pamphlet in 1869, shortly after John Stuart Mill finished a three-year term as a member of Parliament. While member of Parliament, Mill presented a petition for women's suffrage (1866) and sponsored the Married Women's Property Bill (1868). After losing his seat in Parliament in the 1868 election, Mill revised his early draft of the essay and published it. Mill's primary activity in Parliament was aimed at women's enfranchisement—their right to vote—and *The Subjection of Women* makes clear Mill's liberal feminism and his commitment to sexual equality.

The Subjection of Women is divided into four chapters, each chapter presenting and support-ing an aspect of Mill's argument. In chapter 1, Mill states his general aim explicitly. He challenges the common notion that women are by nature unequal to men. He explains that "the legal subordination of one sex to the other is wrong in itself, and one of the chief hindrances to human improvement," and the systematic subordination of women by men "ought to be replaced by a principle of perfect equality, admitting no power or privilege on the one side, nor disability on the other." Mill acknowledges that his views fly in the face of accepted views and practices, but he counters by pointing out the historical foundations of subjection, that is, the conversion of "mere physical fact into a legal right." The subjection of women, then, is based on a premodern law of force, not on the modern use of reason. Since no other system has been tried, the present system of subjugation of the weaker female sex to the stronger male sex rests upon unproven theory, says Mill. Mill hopes to pave the way for a new system of equality, based on theory, as no practice of sexual equality has as yet been allowed.

Using an analogy that angered many of his readers, Mill compares women's subordination to men to that of the slave to his master and speaks of a kind of domestic slavery to the family. Unlike the slave, however, the woman's master wants not only her labor, but also her senti-ments, and he conspires to bind nature and education to accomplish his desire for the loving, submissive, domestic slave over whom he, as husband, has absolute control. The relationship between men and women is merely the customary relationship, and whatever is customary appears natural. To those with power over others, their domination appears natural, perhaps even good, and appears owing to the nature of the dominated. Women's true natures cannot be verified, however, for they are repressed in some areas and unnaturally stimulated in others, according to Mill. Furthermore, women have seldom been allowed to testify to their own natures; rather they have been described by the men who exercise power over them. Since women have never been allowed to develop naturally without the repression, stimulation, or guidance of men, a system of subordination founded on women's "natural" sensitivity and lack of more "masculine" qualities is not inherently more valid than any other system based on theory alone.

In chapter 2, Mill attacks the position of women in the marriage contract, which he sees as a kind of legal bondage. All property and any income derived from it belonged to the husband, even if the wife had brought the property to the marriage. Additionally, only the father had legal rights over his children. A woman who left her husband could take nothing with her, not even the children she had borne. Any action she might take must have her husband's tacit approval. Indeed, Mill sees the bondage of marriage as a more profound slavery than slavery itself, not because a woman might be treated as badly as any slave—though he does not neglect the physical power the husband has over his wife and the potential for domestic violence—but because "hardly any slave . . . is a slave at all hours and all minutes." A wife and mother, on the other hand, is available at all times to all people. No activity she does is considered important enough to protect her from being interrupted to meet the needs of others.

Mill argues for a marriage contract based on equality before the law and the division of powers in the home. And though in chapter 3 he makes the case for women's admission to all "functions and occupations" held by men, he does not call for a division of duties within the home. Rather, he claims that just as a man chooses a profession, a woman who marries is choosing the management of the household and the raising of the children. The latter view is seen by many feminist readers and critics as a weakness in Mill's liberal feminism, but it is not surprising that he should hold that view in the Victorian period. Mill nonetheless states that the "*power* of earning is essential to the dignity of a woman."

As Mill argues for women's freedom to enter all the professions and jobs monopolized by men. He boldly attacks male self-interest, which uses women's so-called disabilities to maintain subordination in domestic life. Most men cannot tolerate the notion of living with an equal, says Mill.

One of the functions women should exercise, he argues, is the vote, and there is no justification for excluding women, who, as a principle of self-protection, have as much right as men to choose who is to govern them. In *The Subjection of Women* and in an earlier essay, "Enfranchisement of Women" (1851), Mill notes the new freedoms of the modern world, where an accident of birth no longer determines individual destiny. With the new freedoms of industry, of conscience, of the press, and of action and political liberty, men should not subject half of the race to restrictions that men are no longer required to tolerate. It is only women who still suffer from that "relic of an old world of thought and practice," presuppositions based on a simple accident of birth.

As for the mental differences said to exist between men and women, Mill attributes these to the differences in their education and circumstances, rather than to their natures. Women are trained away from, and men are trained for, certain occupations and functions. What women have done, they have proven they can do, and their capabilities for other pursuits are unknown because they are untried. Women have not been allowed entrance into most occupations; hence, there is no evidence that they cannot be as accomplished in these forbidden offices as they have been in those offices they have exercised. Mill uses royalty as an example of women's capabilities when allowed to develop. Queen Elizabeth fulfilled well the duties of the highest office in the land. Had she not inherited the throne, she would not have been permitted even the least important of political duties.

Mill attacks the male notion of women's nervous susceptibility, seeing it as the overflow of unused energies and often the result of conscious or unconscious cultivation, as exemplified by the popularity and then the unpopularity of fainting spells. He counters the biological argument that because women are smaller than men and thus have smaller brains, they have inferior intellectual powers, and points out that stereotypes of women differ from one culture to another. Women are seen as voluptuous in one country, fickle in another, and cold in yet another. In regard to the lack of cultural artifacts produced by women, Mill claims that women have had insufficient time to practice those vocations that lead to such productions. Women have been trained away from what men have been trained for. Women have been trained for the social obligations of house and family and have been discouraged from creating books, art, and the like.

Mill closes chapter 3 with a strong statement: "Women cannot be expected to devote themselves to the emancipation of women, until men in considerable number are prepared to join them in the undertaking." From a practical perspective, a married woman could be legally stopped from engaging in any activity of which her husband disapproves. In chapter 4, Mill explains why an end to the subordination of women would benefit even the privileged men most likely to resist it.

He posits two questions: What good would come from the proposed changes in customs and institutions? Would humanity be better off if women were free? He argues that the inequality of marriage—the only actual bondage known to law since the abolition of slavery—contradicts all the principles of the modern world. He also claims that it is damaging to boys to grow up believing that they are superior to half the human race merely because they are male, rather than through any merits of their own. If such sexual preference were eliminated, children would, "for the first time in man's existence on earth, be trained in the way [they] should go," as members of a just society.

A second benefit of giving women the free use of their faculties and free choice of employment is the advantage gained by doubling the available brain trust for the advancement of humanity. By subjugating women, society is wasting half its resources. Relations between men and women would also be much improved if women were allowed to develop their faculties. Women's influence would extend beyond the boundaries of the domestic, and men and women would be better companions to one another.

And lastly, the most direct benefit from an end to the subordination of women would be the "unspeakable gain in private happiness to the liberated half of the species," allowing them a life of rational freedom. Mill sees freedom as the third necessity of life, after food and clothing. Withholding from women freedoms that are available to men is a "positive evil," says Mill, and "leaves the species less rich." Mill knows that societal change can occur after the opinions of society change. By his arguments in *The Subjection of Women* he hopes to encourage exactly that.

The Subjection of Women remains Mill's least studied work, but it has not lost its relevance with the passage of time. In his discussion of women's true nature, Mill anticipates the "nature versus nurture" debates that have continued to the present. It is true that women have the vote, they can own property, and legal conditions have changed. Women have entered many of the occupations once closed to them and exercise many of the functions once the purview of men only, but Mill's goal of sexual equality has yet to be completely realized. *The Subjection of Women* contains many arguments of practical use for today's feminists and other believers in individual freedom.

Linda Ledford-Miller

Bibliography:
August, Eugene R. "John Stuart Mill." In *Concise Dictionary of British Literary Biography.* Vol. 4. Detroit: Gale Research, 1991. An overview of the life and works of Mill, placing him in the context of the intellectual history of the Victorian period; a good, brief introduction to Mill.

Himmelfarb, Gertrude. *On Liberty and Liberalism.* New York: Alfred A. Knopf, 1974. A much-cited examination of Mill's most famous work, *On Liberty*; chapter 7 discusses his essays on women as examples of the political philosophy expressed in *On Liberty*.

Lonoff, Sue. "Cultivated Feminism: Mill and *The Subjection of Women*." In *Philological*

Quarterly 65, no. 1 (Winter, 1986): 79-102. Describes Mill as an apostle of liberal feminism rather than its prophet. A lucid examination of the rhetorical structure of his essay.

Okin, Susan Moller. *Women in Western Political Thought*. Princeton, N.J.: Princeton University Press, 1979. Examines traditional philosophical views on women expressed in Plato, Aristotle, and Rousseau. Part 4 focuses on Mill, the only one of the major liberal political philosophers to include women in the application of principles of liberalism.

Tulloch, Gail. *Mill and Sexual Equality*. Boulder, Colo.: Lynne Rienner Publishers, 1989. The only work with *The Subjection of Women* as its central theme. Examines in detail the essay and Mill's arguments for reconstructed marriage. Traces the development of Mill's liberal feminism and its relationship to the themes of his major works.

SUDDENLY LAST SUMMER

Type of work: Drama
Author: Tennessee Williams (Thomas Lanier Williams, 1911-1983)
Type of plot: Psychological realism
Time of plot: 1936
Locale: New Orleans, Louisiana
First published: 1958

> *Principal characters:*
> MRS. VIOLET VENABLE, an eccentric matriarch
> DR. CUKROWICZ, a young, handsome psychiatrist
> CATHARINE HOLLY, Mrs. Venable's niece
> MISS FOXHILL, Mrs. Venable's secretary/companion
> MRS. HOLLY, Catharine's mother
> GEORGE HOLLY, Catharine's brother
> SISTER FELICITY, a nun at St. Mary's Institution

The Story:

Mrs. Venable summoned Dr. Cukrowicz to her mansion in New Orleans' Garden District. He came as a result of his interest in an enormous endowment from the Sebastian Venable Memorial Foundation. Mrs. Venable and Cukrowicz strolled through the exotic garden that had been the realm of Mrs. Venable's late son, Sebastian. Mrs. Venable and Cukrowicz discussed Sebastian's occupation, which she insisted was Sebastian's life because "a poet's life is his work and his work is his life." She showed the doctor one of Sebastian's poems from his collection, *Poems of Summer*. She explained that her son had written only one poem a year and to write the poem took nine months. The rest of the year Mrs. Venable and Sebastian traveled to exotic locales.

Mrs. Venable recalled one specific summer that she and Sebastian had spent in the Encantadas, where they watched sea turtle eggs hatch. As the newly hatched turtles scurried to the sea, most were devoured by birds. Cukrowicz wondered why Sebastian was fascinated by this savage display of nature. Mrs. Venable explained it was Sebastian's search for God. The doctor asked Mrs. Venable to show her a picture of Sebastian. The photographs demonstrated how Sebastian retained his youthful beauty for twenty years.

Miss Foxhill interrupted the discussion to announce the arrival of George Holly and his mother. Mrs. Venable told Miss Foxhill to keep the Hollys upstairs. Mrs. Venable resumed her talk with the doctor, who asked her about Sebastian's personal, private life. Mrs. Venable explained that her son, while chased, had been chaste. She insisted that he had been celibate. She explained that during their travels, they were always spoken of as a couple. Mrs. Venable explained that the previous summer Sebastian had traveled with his cousin, Catharine. During the trip to Cabeza de Lobo, Sebastian died. Catharine had a terrible reaction to Sebastian's death and was institutionalized at St. Mary's. Mrs. Venable explained to Cukrowicz that Catharine "babbles," vandalizing the memory of Sebastian. To stop Catharine's rantings and ravings, Mrs. Venable wanted the doctor to perform a lobotomy on Catharine; insulin shock and electric shock therapies had not silenced her.

When Miss Foxhill announced that Catharine had arrived, Mrs. Venable refused, at first, to face her. The doctor went alone to see Catharine. He noticed Catharine with Sister Felicity standing behind her. Catharine lit a cigarette. Sister Felicity insisted that Catharine extinguish the cigarette, which she did in the palm of the nun's hand. Catharine recalled how Sebastian was "famished for blonds." She related to the nun how Sebastian talked about people as if they were items on a menu. Catharine told the nun that Sebastian lived on pills and salads. Mrs. Holly and her son, George, greeted Catharine. George revealed that Sebastian had bequeathed him and Catharine fifty thousand dollars each. Mother and son insisted that Catharine never tell the story of what happened to Sebastian in Cabeza de Lobo again. Catharine insisted the story was true and refused their request.

Mrs. Venable joined the scene. Cukrowicz also made his presence known. Catharine knew that the doctor was from Lion's View, a sanatorium where lobotomies were performed. When Mrs. Venable accused Catharine of taking Sebastian away from her, Catharine tried to explain why she had accompanied Sebastian on his summer tour. Mrs. Venable interrupted Catharine's explanation, denying that she had suffered a stroke and insisting that Sebastian wanted Catharine to accompany him because of a scandal Catharine had made over a married man at a Mardi Gras ball.

Cukrowicz asked to be left alone with Catharine. He questioned her about her feelings about Sebastian. She admitted that she loved her cousin, but in a "motherly way." When the doctor asked her what she wanted to save Sebastian from, she said from completing a terrible image of himself. Catharine told the doctor the story of the scandal she caused at the Mardi Gras ball. Catharine's date was too drunk to drive her home. She went for a taxi, but a man took her by the arm and offered to drive her home. The man took her to Duelling Oaks. Catharine knew the man's intentions, but he decided against a liaison since his wife was pregnant. At home, Catharine remembered she had left Mrs. Venable's mink stole at the ballroom. She went back and assaulted the man. Sebastian intervened and invited her to join him on his summer tour. Telling the story agitated Catharine and Cukrowicz gave her an injection to calm her. After she had been sedated, she forced a kiss on the doctor.

The entire family gathered on the terrace and Cukrowicz coaxed an agitated Catharine to tell her story while Mrs. Venable tried to deny the truth and preserve the myth she held of Sebastian. After Mrs. Venable promised to keep quiet, Catharine told of an afternoon she and Sebastian spent at Cabeza de Lobo on a private beach cordoned off from a public beach by a barbed-wire fence. Catharine said she went for a swim in a white bathing suit that turned transparent when wet. She realized she was procuring young men for Sebastian, as his mother had before her.

The following afternoons, the crowd of homeless, hungry young men at the public beach grew, waiting for Sebastian to toss them money. Sebastian grew ill at the public display and insisted that he and Catharine go north. Before they had a chance to leave, a large band of the young men formed and made loud, percussive music on crude tin instruments. The band pursued Sebastian through the streets of Cabeza de Lobo, catching him, stripping him, and cannibalizing him. To silence Catharine, Mrs. Venable ordered the doctor to take Catharine to Lion's View and "cut this hideous story from her brain." Cukrowicz suggested that the Hollys consider that Catharine's story could be true.

Critical Evaluation:

A critical and popular success, Tennessee Williams was the most important playwright to emerge onto the American theatrical scene after World War II. Graduated from the University of Iowa in 1938, Williams was granted a Rockefeller Fellowship to write *Battle of Angels* (1940). *The Glass Menagerie* (1944) won the New York Drama Critics Circle Award for the 1945 season. He won Pulitzer Prizes for *A Streetcar Named Desire* (1947) and *Cat on a Hot Tin Roof* (1955). His plays are both regional and naturalistic with vivid, highly individual characters—debauched and debased—in drama that has an air of fantasy about it. Exotic settings and strange, often perverse personalities populate Williams' plays. Those in *Suddenly Last Summer* are excellent examples.

The play deals with homosexuality, while never using the word. Since Sebastian Venable is dead when the play begins, he is defined only by what other characters say about him. Their statements about the dead poet tend to polarize into two extremes; between these two disparate views lies the truth. It is the dead poet's homosexuality and how it affects his reputation—both when he is alive and when he is dead—that is the crux of the play. Sebastian Venable seems both an exploitative outsider and an alienated victim.

The play weaves an interesting set of variations of the theme of exposure for the homosexual in society. At the time the play was written, homosexuality, while no longer "the love that dare not speak its name," was not a subject that was openly discussed. Sebastian, both the man and poet, chose to distance himself from public recognition, in an endeavor to conceal his homosexuality from society. When Cukrowicz asks to see a photograph of Sebastian, Mrs. Venable produces two of Sebastian in disguise. For twenty years, Sebastian Venable presented a disguised face to society. This public persona is carefully guarded by Mrs. Venable, who denies the true nature of her son's sexual identity even after his death. Catharine's accusation that Mrs. Venable procured for her son during his life is counterbalanced by Mrs. Venable's actions as his self-appointed protector after his death.

Sebastian used his mother as his procurer to deny his homosexuality to the society in which they lived and traveled. The summer that Sebastian chose to travel with Catharine, he broke his mother's bond. That summer Sebastian also broke the ties that bound him to tradition, youth, and the closet: "suddenly, last summer, he wasn't young any more, and we went to Cabeza de Lobo, and he suddenly switched from the evenings to the beach." With his mother, Sebastian traveled under the cover of the night, using his mother's forceful personality to seduce his prey. With his cousin, Sebastian operates in the light of day, painfully aware that his youth is slipping away. He uses his cousin's youth and beauty to attract ever-more-youthful prey. Soon, Sebastian no longer needs Catharine; money replaces her youth and beauty to attract his prey.

Sebastian's cannibalization is foreshadowed during his trip to the Encantadas. The turtles' rush to the sea to avoid the carnivorous birds overhead demonstrates the power of an untamed primal urge, not unlike the crowd's homophobic reaction in Cabeza de Lobo, an emotion that sweeps the frenzied mass into a primal act of cannibalism. Sebastian is just as powerless among the crowd as the turtles are among the carnivorous birds. In the Encantadas, Williams also tries to discern the role of God in the life of a homosexual. Sebastian looks for God, possibly to make some sense of a world that forced him to deny his sexual identity. He finds a savage, uncaring God. Sebastian's anger at what he finds forces him to consider his place in a society where God makes no provision for homosexuals.

Sebastian is powerless in New Orleans society. As a homosexual, he must suppress his sexual identity. When he finally chooses to go public, he does it outside New Orleans and becomes an object for public consumption. Because he chooses to make those he desires into objects who can be bought, Sebastian becomes an exploiter in a society where he is an outsider. The young men who seek out Sebastian become representatives of their society as a whole. Their social anxiety—or homophobia—results in their consuming Sebastian in a ritual act of destroying him whom they adored. Sebastian then becomes the victim. Sebastian is an exploitative outsider and an alienated victim, a character Williams deftly uses to articulate the ambiguous nature of the homosexual's role in society.

Thomas D. Petitjean, Jr.

Bibliography:

Bloom, Harold. *Tennessee Williams*. New York: Chelsea House, 1987. A collection of essays that gives the reader a sense of how *Suddenly Last Summer* fits into the scope of Williams' oeuvre.

Bruhm, Steven. "Blackmailed by Sex: Tennessee Williams and the Economics of Desire." *Modern Drama* 34, no. 4 (December, 1991): 528-537. Argues that Sebastian is in a system of power relations that he cannot control. For critics of the play, the incident in the Encantadas foreshadows Sebastian's death at Cabeza de Lobo.

Clum, John M. "Something Cloudy, Something Clear': Homophobic Discourse in Tennessee Williams." *South Atlantic Quarterly* 88, no.1 (Winter, 1989): 161-179. Notes that *Suddenly Last Summer* weaves an interesting set of variations on the theme of exposure of the artist as homosexual. Sebastian's carnivorous sense of life is linked with homosexuality.

Debusscher, Gilbert. "Minting Their Separate Wills: Tennessee Williams and Hart Crane." *Modern Drama* 26, no. 4 (December, 1983): 455-476. Examines the influence of Hart Crane on Tennessee Williams and the writing of *Suddenly Last Summer*.

Spoto, Donald. *The Kindness of Strangers: The Life of Tennessee Williams*. Boston: Little, Brown, 1985. An accessible, accurate biography of Tennessee Williams that discusses Williams' homosexuality and its influence on his life and works.

SULA

Type of work: Novel
Author: Toni Morrison (1931-   )
Type of plot: Psychological realism
Time of plot: 1919-1965
Locale: Medallion, Ohio
First published: 1973

>   *Principal characters:*
>   SULA PEACE, the daughter of Hannah Peace
>   NEL WRIGHT, the daughter of Helene Wright
>   EVA PEACE, Sula's grandmother
>   HELENE WRIGHT, Nel's mother
>   HANNAH PEACE, the daughter of Eva Peace
>   SHADRACK, a World War I Veteran

The Story:

The Bottom, the black community of Medallion, Ohio, originated in the time of slavery. Through trickery, an enslaved black man accepted a portion of higher land from his master in exchange for completing "some very difficult chores." The black man had been told by his master that the land was nearer heaven and of better quality, but it was actually less desirable and subject to erosion.

In 1919, Shadrack, an African American World War I veteran and Medallion resident, was recuperating in a military hospital; he was suffering from psychological trauma. After his discharge from the hospital, he was arrested by the police but eventually released. Following the new year in 1920, Shadrack, carrying a cowbell and a hangman's noose, walked through Medallion informing the residents that he offered them their "only chance to kill themselves." With this act, he began National Suicide Day.

Helene Wright, another Medallion resident, was born in New Orleans to Rochelle, a "Creole whore." Helene, who was reared by her grandmother, Cecile Sabat, married Wiley Wright, the grandnephew of Cecile, and was brought north to Medallion. A civic-minded woman, Helene reared her daughter, Nel, in a protective manner. When Helene's grandmother became ill, Helene journeyed with Nel to New Orleans. They experienced segregation on their journey, and in New Orleans Nel met her grandmother, Rochelle.

After Nel and her mother returned to Medallion, Nel seemed to have achieved a "new found me-ness." At this time, Nel met Sula Peace, who loved the orderly "oppressive neatness" of the Wright household. In contrast, Sula's home, headed by Eva Peace, was a "woolly house, where a pot of something was always cooking on the stove."

In 1921, the household of Eva Peace included her children, Hannah and Plum, Hannah's daughter Sula, and various "strays" such as the Deweys, three children given the same name by Eva. Eva, who had been deserted by her husband BoyBoy after five years of marriage, was rumored to have lost her leg by intentionally allowing a train to run over it so that she could collect money.

Both of Eva's children died in tragic ways. Plum, a World War I veteran, returned in 1919 addicted to heroin. Eva sacrificed Plum by burning him to death. Hannah, a sexually liberated woman and threat to the "good" women of the town, was burned to death accidentally when she tried to light the yard on fire. Eva attempted to save her daughter, whose death was witnessed silently by Sula.

In 1922, Sula and Nel, both about twelve years of age, shared a friendship which was "as intense as it was sudden." On one occasion, when they were harassed by four white boys, Sula demonstrated her resolve to fight by cutting off the tip of her own finger. Nel and Sula also shared the secret of Chicken Little's accidental drowning. While playing, Sula had tossed the young boy into the river.

In 1927, Nel married Jude Greene, a tenor in Mount Zion's Men's Quartet. Nel's marriage affected her friendship with Sula, who left Medallion. She returned in 1937 "accompanied by a plague of robins." While away from Medallion, Sula attended college and traveled to big cities. After her return, Sula was defiant and disrespectful to Eva. Sula also contributed to the breakup of Nel's marriage by having an affair with Jude.

In 1939, Sula placed Eva in Sunnydale home for the elderly. Consequently, the African American community considered Sula to be bewitched. Sula's sexual activities, her sleeping with white men and the husbands of African American women, contributed to her pariah status. At age twenty-nine, Sula met Ajax—Albert Jacks—a man thirty-eight years of age, whose mother was a conjure woman. Sula became emotionally attached to Ajax through their "genuine conversations." After Ajax deserted Sula, she realized that she had not really known him.

In 1940, Sula, who had become seriously ill, was visited by Nel. They recounted the past and Nel blamed Sula for having slept with Jude. In 1941, Sula's death was "the best news folks up in the Bottom had had since the promise of work at the tunnel." The building of a home for the African American aged was another sign of the community's revitalization. However, this hope was countered by ominous signs such as the ice storm that ruined crops, beginning a "dislocation" that Shadrack had prophesied. Shadrack and residents from Carpenter's Road marched to the tunnel, where their protest ended with an accidental cave-in.

In 1965, integration occurred in downtown Medallion. The land in the hills, which became more expensive, was used for building television towers, and a golf course was proposed. The hills were left to "the poor, the old, the stubborn—and the rich white folks."

When Nel visited Eva at the home for the elderly, Eva accused Nel of having killed Chicken Little. Eva told Nel that Plum, though dead, had revealed the truth about Chicken Little's drowning. Eva's revelations upset Nel, especially when Eva said that Nel and Sula were the same, stating, "never was no difference between you."

After Nel left Eva, Nel began to remember Chicken Little's death and Sula's burial. While Nel reflected, she was passed on the road by Shadrack, who was a "little shaggier, a little older" and "still energetically mad." Recollecting the past, Nel whispered to Sula as if Sula were present. Nel affirmed their childhood friendship and cried "loud and long."

Critical Evaluation:

Toni Morrison is one of the most significant novelists of the postmodern period. Her novels have consistently explored the African American experience, using historical, social, and psychological themes to focus especially on the experiences of women. Beginning with *The Bluest Eye* (1970), Morrison has published six novels. *Song of Solomon* (1977) won for her the National Book Critics' Circle Award. Morrison's work as an editor at Random House led to the publication of *The Black Book* (1974). *Beloved* (1987) was awarded the Pulitzer Prize in fiction in 1988, and *Playing in the Dark: Whiteness and the Literary Imagination* (1992), a critical work, was a national best-seller. Morrison received the 1993 Nobel Prize in Literature.

Morrison's novels combine psychological realism, social critique, symbolism, and the mythopoetic, resulting in a style similar to Magical Realism. Although her works are not limited to social protest, Morrison is concerned with racial themes frequently encountered in African American literature. Her novels reflect the workings of communities, the dilemmas faced by these families, and the problems encountered in their relationships. She has also addressed historical issues such as nineteenth century slavery. Her fiction celebrates survival and defines black identity as multifaceted. Influenced by William Faulkner and Ralph Ellison, she uses vernacular and poetic prose to create a stylistic balance between narrative perspective and dialogue.

In *Sula*, her second novel, Morrison creates an African American community in a fictional town which, like Lorain, Ohio, the author's hometown, borders Lake Erie. Morrison's concern for history and social context are evident in *Sula*. Her critique of nineteenth century slavery is strongly implied in the ironic naming of "The Bottom." By using chronological sequences, Morrison suggests how the lives of her characters relate to broader societal transitions from World War I to the desegregation and urban renewal of the 1960's. Economic disparity caused by segregation—an indirect cause of the failure of relationships—is one of the underlying central themes in the novel.

Sula, however, is not primarily concerned with the social conflict between the white and African American communities of Medallion. It mostly concerns the way African American communities both include and exclude those members who have violated community mores or who have become dislocated in ways which cause them to live on the moral or social margins. The novel presents characters each of whom signifies an adaptation to this community, which is divided by class. Sula and Nel are reflections not only of sisterhood but also of two African American families. The Wright and Peace households, one middle-class and nuclear, the other folk-centered and extended, are two reflections of the African American community. In tracing the relationship of Nel and Sula through adulthood, Morrison shows how sisterhood can be affected by the differing routes taken by African American women. Nel's pursuit of the traditional ideal—marriage and family—contrasts with the sexually liberated path chosen by Sula. Sula, although of the folk culture, eventually moves beyond it when she leaves Medallion.

Other characters show problematic adjustments to social-historical conditions and family dislocation. Shadrack represents the returning African American World War I veteran whose National Suicide Day is an ironic comment on the life chances of African Americans in 1920. Shadrack, however, becomes an accepted "eccentric" character, who, in many respects, defines the political direction of the community in protest and collective action. Eva Peace represents the folk tradition and the continuity of African American matriarchy, which seeks to protect and maintain a family faced with the absence of the father.

One of the most important themes is African American female sexuality. Hannah and Sula are both portrayed as sexually liberated. Because of Sula's relationship with men, she is viewed as an outcast by the community. Despite Sula's sexual freedom, she also searches for genuine love with Ajax. The theme of desertion, a pattern in Morrison's fiction, is developed in *Sula*. Eva is deserted by BoyBoy, Nel by Jude, and Sula by Ajax. Though injured by desertion, Morrison's women survive and shape identities which are not dependent on relationships with men.

Morrison's Magical Realism is formed by a variety of elements. Natural phenomena, such as the plague of robins and the ice storm, are used as parallels to the action. Morrison employs folkloric elements in the portrayal of Ajax's mother as a conjure woman and in the notion of Sula as bewitched. The significance of dreams, Eva's claim of having been in communication with her dead son Plum, and Nel's attempt to communicate with Sula's spirit are other examples of the magical dimension of the novel.

The literary style of the novel is achieved through vernacular expression and symbolism. African American vernacular gives authentic voice to Eva, Nel, and Sula. The conversation between Sula and Nel, when Nel visits Sula on her deathbed, is a reconstruction of verbal devices used by African American women. The symbolism of fire is used when Eva burns Plum and when Hannah is mysteriously destroyed by fire. Shadrack's name implies the biblical furnace and invulnerability to destruction by fire.

As Morrison's second novel, *Sula* confirmed her reputation as a gifted writer destined for both national and international acclaim. The novel remains influential because Morrison provides a spectrum of African American women and challenges romanticized portrayals of relationships. Ultimately, the novel does not present sisterhood as an alternative to relationships between men and women but questions that which hinders emotional bonding.

Joseph McLaren

Bibliography:
Baker, Houston A. "When Lindbergh Sleeps with Bessie Smith: The Writing of Place in *Sula*." In *Toni Morrison: Critical Perspectives Past and Present*, edited by Henry Louis Gates, Jr., and K. A. Appiah. New York: Amistad, 1993. This article addresses Morrison's naming strategies, the significance of characters, and communal place. Comparisons are made to Richard Wright, Jean Toomer, and Zora Neale Hurston.

Bell, Roseann P. Review of *Sula*, by Toni Morrison. In *Critical Essays on Toni Morrison*, edited by Nellie Y. McKay. Boston: G. K. Hall, 1988. This review focuses primarily on Eva Peace as a nonstereotypical African American matriarch and relates the novel to the Black Aesthetic.

Blackburn, Sarah. Review of *Sula*, by Toni Morrison. *The New York Times Book Review*, December 30, 1973, 3. Primarily positive, this review summarizes the novel and praises Morrison's stylistic abilities. Morrison is faulted, however, for provincialism.

McDowell, Deborah E. "'The Self and the Other': Reading Toni Morrison's *Sula* and the Black Female Text." In *Modern Critical Views: Toni Morrison*, edited by Harold Bloom. New York: Chelsea House, 1990. This article explores the complex process of reading *Sula*, a book that goes beyond simple opposites of good and evil. Sula and Nel are interpreted as dual parts of a single self.

Samuels, Wilfred D., and Clenora Hudson-Weems. *Toni Morrison*. Boston: Twayne, 1990. This critical study is devoted to Morrison's novels up to *Beloved*. The chapter on *Sula*, "Experimental Lives: Meaning and Self in *Sula*," focuses on the outcast theme used in the portrayal of Sula and Shadrack; the development of men and women characters is addressed.

SUMMA THEOLOGICA

Type of work: Philosophy
Author: Saint Thomas Aquinas (1224 or 1225-1274)
First transcribed: c. 1265-1273 (English translation, 1911-1921)

This towering edifice of thought, often called simply the *Summa*, stands as a bulwark against the forces of doubt and skepticism that invaded the Western world during the late Middle Ages, toward the close of which Saint Thomas created this great summation of philosophical and theological knowledge. In it two of the mightiest forces in the realm of human thought meet: Hellenism and Christianity. It was their first real encounter.

Simply stated, what Saint Thomas did was collect and synthesize the philosophical knowledge and thinking of previous eras and apply them to Christian theology. This was an immensely ambitious task, and the wonder is that Saint Thomas did so well with it. Though unfinished, because of the divine doctor's sudden death from illness, the *Summa* unites, or at least joins elements of thought from, the Greek, Arabian, and Asian traditions in a highly detailed fashion. Saint Thomas thus became a historian of philosophy; but he was a critical historian, carefully weighing and evaluating each premise and conclusion.

The largest part of this previous thought is, as might be expected, that of the Greeks. Saint Thomas is usually given the credit for having reinterpreted the philosophy of Aristotle on a Christian basis. This statement is, however, something of an oversimplification, for the reading of Aristotle and other great Greek thinkers, including Plato, was a very special one. Saint Thomas was himself a magnificent philosopher, and the *Summa* is unquestionably his book. What he did, in essence, was to organize the thought of Aristotle along Christian lines, to apply it to the problems and principles of religion. For example, some philosophers had interpreted Aristotle's *Physics* (fourth century B.C.E.) as a denial of Creation; Saint Thomas saw it as merely falling short of this fundamental concept.

The *Summa* is an exceedingly long work, running into several volumes, a necessary length in order to accomplish the goal of applying Scholasticism, the prevailing philosophical influence in the thirteenth century, to religion. In doing so, Saint Thomas gave credit for ideas and lines of thought to many earlier thinkers, and he found the seeds of much thirteenth century belief in the works of previous philosophers. His work, then, is in the nature of a summary of past thinking on the highest subjects and a setting forth of the essential principles of Christian theology as he was able to formulate them from this past material and from his own conviction and thinking.

There are three main divisions of the *Summa*: the first dealing with God and the divine nature of the creation of humanity and the universe; the second, often called the Moral Philosophy of Saint Thomas, treating humanity and the goal of human life and the ways of reaching that goal; the third devoted to Christ and his role as Savior. Within this general framework virtually every possible subject pertaining to theology is discussed: good and evil, pleasure, knowledge, duty, property. The list is almost endless.

The method of attacking these questions is the Socratic one. A basic question is asked and the negative side of it is enforced by a fictitious opponent; then Saint Thomas undertakes to resolve the problem and explain the positive side of the contrived argument. This method, besides making for more interesting reading, tends to create an atmosphere giving fairer treatment to opposing beliefs.

The opening of the *Summa* presents a good example. In it, Saint Thomas poses the question of "Whether, Besides the Philosophical Sciences, Any Further Doctrine Is Required?" How fundamental is the divine doctor's approach can easily be seen: At the beginning of his book, he wishes first to convince the reader of the necessity for sacred doctrine. Following the question there are listed two chief objections to the writing of sacred doctrine; then Saint Thomas explains the need for it and refutes each objection in turn. This tightly organized discussion is maintained throughout; in a book that is so closely reasoned it is essential.

Part of the reason for this clear organization was the fact that the *Summa* was not primarily intended for learned divines. Instead, it was written for people whom Saint Thomas called beginners, the common people in search of the truth. Also, such an intention probably had much to do with the style of the writing. Although the *Summa* is extremely long, it is praised for its economy of language, with no wasted words, no useless introduction of extraneous points of logic, and no pursuit of attenuated lines of reasoning past the point of common sense. The work is encyclopedic, not tedious.

Although much of what Saint Thomas has written in the *Summa* has long been accepted doctrine in the Roman Catholic church, there is for the contemporary reader considerable material that may seem remarkably up to date, for, theology aside, this book is pivotal in the history of Western philosophy. Possibly most interesting to the modern reader will be not the ethical elements, which are fairly familiar and do not seem to mark such a sharp break with earlier Greek views, but the metaphysical and epistemological aspects of the treatise. Two particularly important issues are raised by Saint Thomas in these areas, and both are in opposition to Greek thought, especially that of Plato.

The first of these concerns the very nature of reality, which is the main point of inquiry in metaphysics. While Plato saw reality as made up of essences, largely perceived as abstractions in the mind (here the "way of knowing," the central question of epistemology, enters in), Saint Thomas maintained that the basic statement was that something had being; that is, it had existence. This is the basis for an argument that has raged ever since among philosophers: Which is the supreme reality, essence or existence? Which is the more fundamental statement, what it is or that it is?

In his defense of the latter statement. Saint Thomas propounded principles that might be called Thomistic existentialism. Certainly the conflict created in the *Summa* over this question in the thirteenth century was of vital importance. Equally so was Saint Thomas' disagreement with the Platonic belief that a person is really two separate things, a soul and a body. To Saint Thomas a person was a composite, a unity composed of soul and body, both essential to one's nature.

This conflict connects with Saint Thomas' convictions about the "way of knowing" that is basic to his epistemology. Since reality is fundamentally existence rather than essence, in order to know this reality one must have a body—one must be able to perceive reality through the senses. Certainly Saint Thomas' statements in this area would meet with much warmer approval by most readers today than would the Greek notions concerning reality as essences, known only by abstractions in the mind. The practicality of the Thomistic viewpoint makes it appeal to scientifically minded modern thinkers.

In building this great philosophical and theological structure, Saint Thomas dealt with three of the most pressing problems in the thinking of the thirteenth century—the nature of being, of humanity, and of knowledge—and these three subjects parallel the divisions of philosophy as it is generally studied today: metaphysics, ethics, and epistemology. In approaching this skillful and subtle blending of theology and philosophy, the reader must be willing to do what nearly every philosophical writer demands: The reader must be agreeable to accepting certain general premises or principles. Without these, few philosophers can operate, and Saint Thomas is no exception. He assumes certain beliefs in his reader (the prevailing beliefs toward the close of the Middle Ages) concerning theology and religion. Granting these convictions, the reader will find in the *Summa* well-documented (quotations are frequent) and carefully reasoned statements on both sides of every issue involved in the Christian doctrine.

This work, which death ended as Saint Thomas was working on the article about the sacrament of Penance, has been widely translated into most modern languages and continues to be assiduously studied by all who wish to grasp the moment when, in the opinion of many, modern Christian theology began.

Bibliography:

Chenu, M. D. *A Guide to the Study of Thomas Aquinas.* Chicago: University of Chicago Press, 1964. An in-depth study. Part 1 discusses Aquinas' literary forms and his procedures of documentation and construction of the *Summa Theologica.*

D'Arcy, M. C. *St. Thomas Aquinas.* Westminster, Md.: Newman Press, 1953. Presents a good overview of Aquinas' thought on the first principle of knowledge, the nature of reality, and the existence of God. One of the most important books on Aquinas.

Gilson, Étienne. *The Christian Philosophy of St. Thomas Aquinas.* Translated by L. K. Shook. London: Victor Gollancz, 1957. Landmark study by one of the leading Thomists of the twentieth century. Presents Aquinas as precursor to modern existentialism.

Kreeft, Peter. *A Summa of the "Summa."* San Francisco: Ignatius Press, 1990. Contains essential passages from the *Summa Theologica* selected and translated by Kreeft. The extensive footnotes are lucid and generally helpful. A good starting place.

McInerny, Ralph. *A First Glance at St. Thomas Aquinas: A Handbook for Peeping Thomists.* Notre Dame, Ind.: University of Notre Dame Press, 1990. Despite the "first glance" of the title, this study is useful for both beginning and more advanced readers of Aquinas. Discusses the relationship of Aquinas' thought to that of other philosophers, particularly Aristotle and Plato.

THE SUN ALSO RISES

Type of work: Novel
Author: Ernest Hemingway (1899-1961)
Type of plot: Social realism
Time of plot: 1920's
Locale: Paris and Pamplona, Spain
First published: 1926

Principal characters:
JAKE BARNES, an American newspaperman
LADY BRETT ASHLEY, one of the lost generation
ROBERT COHN, a young writer
MICHAEL "MIKE" CAMPBELL, Brett's fiancé
BILL GORTON, Jake's friend
PEDRO ROMERO, a Spanish bullfighter

The Story:

Jake Barnes knew Robert Cohn in Paris shortly after World War I. Somehow Jake always thought Cohn typical of the place and the time. Cohn, the son of wealthy Jewish parents, had once been the middleweight boxing champion of Princeton, and he never wanted anyone to forget that fact. After leaving college, he had married and lived unhappily with his wife until she ran off with another man. Then, he met some writers in California and decided to start a little, arty review. He also met Frances Clyne, who became his mistress. When Jake knew Cohn, he and Frances were living unhappily in Paris, where Cohn was writing his first novel. Cohn wrote and boxed and played tennis, and he was always careful not to mix his friendships. A man named Braddocks was his literary friend. Jake Barnes was his tennis friend.

Jake Barnes was an American newspaperman who had fought with the Italians during the war. His own private tragedy was a war wound that had emasculated him so that he could never marry Lady Brett Ashley, a young English war widow with whom he was in love. So as not to think too much about himself, Jake spent a lot of time listening to the troubles of his friends and drinking heavily. When he grew tired of Paris, he went on fishing trips to the Basque country or to Spain for the bullfights.

One night, feeling lonely, Jake asked Georgette, a prostitute, to join him in a drink at the Café Napolitain. They dined on the Left Bank, where Jake met a party of his friends, including Robert Cohn and Frances Clyne. Later, Brett Ashley came in with a group of young men. Cohn was attracted to her, and Frances was jealous. Brett refused to dance with Cohn, however, saying that she had a date with Jake in Montmartre. Leaving a fifty-franc note with the café proprietor for Georgette, Jake left in a taxi with Brett for a ride to the Parc Montsouris. They talked for a time about themselves without mentioning Jake's injury, though they both thought of it. At last, Brett asked Jake to drive her back to the Café Select.

The next day, Cohn cornered Jake and asked him about Brett. Later, after drinking with Harvey Stone, another expatriate, on the terrace of the Café Select, Jake met Cohn and Frances, who announced that her lover was dismissing her by sending her off to London. She abused and taunted Cohn while he sat quietly without replying. Jake was embarrassed. The same day, he received a telegram from his old friend Bill Gorton, announcing his arrival on the *France*.

Brett went on a trip to San Sebastian with Robert Cohn; she thought the excursion would be good for him.

Jake and Bill Gorton had planned to go to Spain for the trout fishing and the bullfights at Pamplona. Michael Campbell, an Englishman whom Brett was to marry, had also arrived in Paris. He and Brett arranged to join Jake and Bill at Pamplona. Because Cohn had gone to San Sebastian with Brett and because she was now staying with Mike Campbell, everyone felt that it would be awkward if Cohn accompanied Jake and Bill on their trip. Nevertheless, he decided to join them at Bayonne. The agreement was that Jake and Bill would first go trout fishing at Burguete in the mountains. Later, the whole party would meet at the Montoya Hotel in Pamplona for the fiesta.

When Jake and Bill arrived in Bayonne, they found Cohn awaiting them. Hiring a car, they drove on to Pamplona. Montoya, the proprietor of the hotel, was an old friend of Jake because he recognized Jake as a true aficionado of bullfights. The next morning, Bill and Jake left by bus for Burguete, both riding atop the ancient vehicle with several bottles of wine, amid an assortment of Basque passengers. At Burguete, they enjoyed good fishing in the company of an Englishman named Wilson-Harris.

Once back in Pamplona, the whole party gathered for the festival of San Fermín. The first night they went to see the bulls come in and the men let the savage animals out of the cages one at a time. Much wine made Mike Campbell loquacious and he harped on the fact that Cohn had joined the group knowing he was not wanted. At noon on Sunday, the fiesta exploded. The carnival continued for seven days. Dances, parades, religious processions, the bullfights, and much wine furnished the excitement of that hectic week. Also staying at the Montoya Hotel was Pedro Romero, a bullfighter about twenty years old, who was extremely handsome. At the fights, Romero acquitted himself well, and Brett fell in love with him, as she admitted to Jake with embarrassment. Brett and the young man met at the hotel, and Romero soon became interested in her.

Besides the bullfights, the main diversion of the group was drunken progress from one drinking spot to another. While they were in the Café Suizo, Jake told Cohn that Brett had gone with the bullfighter to his room. Cohn swung at both Mike and Jake and knocked them down. After the fight, Cohn apologized, crying all the while. He could not understand how Brett could go off with him to San Sebastian one week and then treat him like a stranger the next time they met. He planned to leave Pamplona the next morning.

The next morning, Jake learned that after the fight Cohn had gone to Pedro Romero's room and, when he found Brett and the bullfighter there together, had beaten Romero badly. In spite of his swollen face and battered body, Romero performed beautifully in the ring that day, dispatching a bull that had recently killed another torero. That night, after the fights, Brett left Pamplona with Romero. Jake got very drunk.

As the fiesta ended, the party dispersed. Bill Gorton went back to Paris and Mike Campbell to Saint Jean de Luz. Jake was in San Sebastian when he received a wire from Brett asking him to come to the Hotel Montana in Madrid. Taking the express, Jake met her the next day. Brett was alone. She had sent Pedro Romero away, she said, because she thought she was not good for him. Then, without funds, she had sent for Jake. She had decided to go back to Mike, she told Jake, because the Englishman was her own sort.

After dinner, Jake and Brett rode around in a taxi, seeing the sights of Madrid. This, Jake reflected wryly, was one of the few ways they could ever be alone together—in bars and cafés and taxis. Both knew the ride was as purposeless as the war-wrecked world in which they lived, as aimless as the drifting generation to which they belonged.

Critical Evaluation:

Upon its publication in 1926, Ernest Hemingway's *The Sun Also Rises* was instantly recognized as one of the important American novels of the post-World War I period. This was in part the result of the fact that sophisticated readers identified current expatriate celebrities among the book's characters. As most of these personages faded into obscurity, however, this aspect of the novel soon lost its appeal. A more important reason for the book's success is that it perfectly captured the mood and style of the American artistic and intellectual exiles who drank, loved, and searched for meaning on the Paris Left Bank in the aftermath of that first world struggle.

The principal theme of *The Sun Also Rises* is indicated by two epigraphs. Gertrude Stein's "you are all a lost generation" encapsulates the ambiguous and pointless lives of Hemingway's exiles as they aimlessly wander about the Continent, drinking, making love, and traveling from place to place and party to party. The quote from Ecclesiastes, which gives the novel its title, implies a larger frame of reference, a sense of permanence, order, and value. If the activities of the characters seem to arise out of Stein's quotation, their search for new meanings to replace the old ones—or at least to enable them to deal with that loss—demonstrates their desire to connect with the biblical idea.

Early in the novel the hero, Jake Barnes, declines to kiss Georgette, a prostitute, on the grounds that he is "sick." "Everybody's sick. I'm sick too," she responds. This sickness motif is opposed in another early conversation Jake has, this one with Count Mippipopolous, a most vivid minor character, who tells him "that is the secret. You must get to know the values." The search for values and the willingness to pay the price, first to acquire them and then to live by them, are what separates some of Hemingway's exiles from simple, pointless hedonism. At the center of this search for values is the Hemingway hero, Jake Barnes. As in all of Hemingway's important fictions, *The Sun Also Rises* is a novel of education—of learning to live with the conditions faced.

Jake's problem is complicated by his war injury, for, having been emasculated, Jake's "affair" with Lady Brett Ashley takes on a comical aspect, as he himself freely admits. Hemingway, however, has a very serious intention. Jake's wound is a metaphor for the condition of the entire expatriate group. They have all been damaged in some fundamental way by the war—physically, morally, psychologically, or economically—and their aimless existence can be traced back to it. The real symbolic importance of Jake's wound is that while it has deprived him of the capacity to perform sexually, it has not rid him of the desire. The people in *The Sun Also Rises* fervently want meaning and fulfillment, but they lack the ability and means to find it.

The heroes in Hemingway's major works learn values in two ways: through their own actions and by contact with other characters who already know them. These exemplars understand the values either, like Count Mippipopolous, from long, hard experience or, like the bullfighter, Pedro Romero, intuitively and automatically. Those characters never articulate their values, however, they only embody them in action. Indeed, once talked about, they become, in the Hemingway lexicon, spoiled. Jake's education can be most clearly seen in his relationship to Robert Cohn, Pedro Romero, and Lady Brett Ashley.

Critics have speculated on why Hemingway begins the novel with a long discussion of Robert Cohn, a relatively minor character. Clearly, Cohn embodies the old, false, romantic values that Hemingway is reacting against. While it is hard to define precisely what the important values are, it is easy to say what they are not.

In the beginning, Jake feels that Cohn is "nice and awful," but tolerates and pities him as a case of "arrested development." By the end of the book, he thoroughly hates him. Cohn's flaws include a false sense of superiority—reinforced by his pugilistic skills—and a romantic attitude toward himself and his activities that distorts his relationship with everyone around him. To reinforce this false romanticism, Cohn alters reality to suit his preconceptions. Falling in love with Brett, he refuses to see her realistically but idealizes her. When she spends a weekend with him, because she thinks it would be good for him, he treats it as a great affair and demands the rights of a serious lover, striking out at all the other men who approach her. Cohn's false perception of reality and his self-romanticization underscore his chief fault, the cardinal sin in Hemingway's view: Cohn refuses to "pay his bill."

Cohn's romantic self-image is finally destroyed by the bullfighter Pedro Romero. Affronted that Brett has been taken from him, Cohn forces the young man into a prolonged fistfight. Although totally outmanned as a boxer, Romero refuses to give in to Cohn and after absorbing considerable punishment, he rallies to defeat and humiliates his opponent by sheer will, courage, and endurance. His romantic bubble deflated, Cohn bursts into tears and fades from the novel.

It is appropriate that Cohn's false values be exposed by Pedro Romero, because his example is also central to the educations of Jake and Brett. As an instinctively great bullfighter, Romero embodies the values in action and especially in the bullring. In a world bereft of religious certainties, Hemingway saw the bullfighter's performance as an aesthetic ceremony that substituted for obsolete religious ritual. Without transcendental meanings, human dignity must come from the manner in which individuals face their certain destiny; the bullfighter, who repeatedly does so by choice, was, for Hemingway, the supreme modern hero, providing he performed with skill, precision, style, and without falsity (that is, making it look harder or more dangerous than it really is). Shortly before the bullfight, Jake's group watches the local citizenry run with the bulls down the main street of the town. They see one man gored to death from behind. The following day, that same bull is presented to Romero, and he kills it perfectly by standing directly in front of it as he drives home his sword. This obvious symbolism states in a single image the most important of all the values, the need to confront reality directly and honestly.

It is not only Pedro's example that helps to educate Jake but also Jake's involvement in the Brett-Romero affair. His role as intermediary is the result of his would-be romance with her. They have long been in love and deeply frustrated by Jake's funny-sad war injury. Yet, despite the impossibility of a meaningful relationship, Jake can neither accept Brett as a friend nor cut himself off from her, although he knows that such a procedure would be the wisest course of action. She can only be a temptress to him, and she is quite accurate when she refers to herself as Circe.

The only time Jake feels whole and happy is when he and Bill Gorton take a fishing trip at Bayonne. There, in a world without women, they fish with skill and precision, drink wine (naturally chilled in the stream) instead of whiskey, relate to the hearty exuberance of the Basque peasantry, and feel serene in the rhythms of nature. Once they return to town and Jake meets Brett at San Sebastian, his serenity is destroyed.

Jake puts his group up at a hotel owned by Montoya, an old friend and the most honored bullfighting patron. Montoya is an admirer and accepts Jake as someone who truly understands and appreciates bullfighting, not only with his intellect but with his whole being. Montoya even trusts Jake to the point of asking advice about the handling of this newest, potentially greatest young bullfighter, Pedro Romero. When Jake presents Brett to Pedro, fully understanding the implications of his act, he violates Montoya's trust. Through his frustrated love for Brett, Pedro is exposed to her corrupting influence. When Jake realizes his own weakness and recognizes that it has cost him his aficionado status, he is left a sadder, wiser Hemingway hero.

Pedro is not destroyed because Brett sends him away before she can do any damage. More than simple altruism is involved in her decision. Life with Pedro held the possibility of wholeness for her—as it held the possibility of dissipation for him. By sending him away rather than risk damaging him, she relinquishes her last chance for health and happiness.

It is unclear whether or not Jake's insights and Brett's final moral act give meaning to the lives of these exiles. During their Bayonne fishing trip, Jake's friend Bill Gorton sings a song about "pity and irony," and that seems to be the overall tone of the book, and especially of the ending: pity for the personal anguish and aimless searching of these people, but ironic detachment toward characters whose lives and situations are, at best, at least as comical as they are tragic.

"Critical Evaluation" by Keith Neilson

Bibliography:
Aldridge, John W. *"The Sun Also Rises:* Sixty Years Later." *Sewanee Review* 94, no. 2 (Spring, 1986): 337-345. Abundant criticism on Hemingway's most analyzed novel may overpower rather than enlighten nonspecialist readers. Aldridge, however, succeeds in blending accessibility and scholarship. Discussion of Hemingway's meticulous language usage, based on the strong presence of things unsaid, is particularly interesting.
Bloom, Harold, ed. *Ernest Hemingway's "The Sun Also Rises."* New York: Chelsea House, 1987. Contains ten essays that Bloom considers to represent the most helpful criticism published on the novel. Authors include Hemingway scholars such as Carlos Baker (Hemingway's prime biographer), Scott Donaldson, and Linda Wagner-Martin.
The Hemingway Review 6, no. 1 (Fall, 1986): 2-111. This special issue celebrates the sixtieth anniversary of *The Sun Also Rises*. The nine articles deal with topics as diverse as the original manuscript, Hemingway's presentation of women and war, the moral axis of the novel, and the word "sun" as title and metaphor.
Reynolds, Michael S. *"The Sun Also Rises": A Novel of the Twenties*. Boston: Twayne, 1988. An excellent overall reference accessible to the general reader. Reynolds discusses the novel's importance and critical reception and considers it from analytic, structural, historical, and thematic perspectives.
Wagner-Martin, Linda, ed. *New Essays on "The Sun Also Rises."* Cambridge, England: Cambridge University Press, 1987. Designed as a critical guide for students of American history and culture, this volume of five commissioned essays is thought-provoking yet accessible to nonspecialist readers.

THE SUNKEN BELL

Type of work: Drama
Author: Gerhart Hauptmann (1862-1946)
Type of plot: Fantasy
Time of plot: Indeterminate
Locale: A mountain, a valley, and the paths between
First performed: 1896; first published, 1896 as *Die versunkene Glocke* (English translation, 1898)

Principal characters:
> HEINRICH, a bell-founder
> MAGDA, his wife
> THEIR CHILDREN
> RAUTENDELEIN, an elfin mountain sprite
> OLD WITTIKIN, her grandmother, a sorceress
> THE NICKELMANN, an elemental water spirit
> THE VICAR,
> THE SCHOOLMASTER, and
> THE BARBER, representatives of the world

The Story:

In a mountain forest glade Rautendelein, a beautiful elf-child, sat singing and combing her long, golden hair while calling to a water spirit, the Nickelmann. She made fun of the croaking froglike monster who came out of a nearby well. Into that setting skipped a faun who seemed enamored of the lovely sprite and who invited her to be his love. She refused, as if this were not her destiny. When she left, the wood and water sprites discussed the intrusion of man in their hallowed realms, the sprites having that day forced off the road and into a valley lake a bell meant for a mountaintop church. The bell-founder appeared, quite exhausted and badly injured from his fall. He collapsed before the cottage of Wittikin, a witch whom mortals in the region greatly feared. Her granddaughter, Rautendelein, strangely drawn to the thirty-year-old Heinrich, made him a bed of straw and gave him milk to drink.

Heinrich was also drawn to this beautiful creature whose speech was song and who made him glad to leave the mundane life below. He had tried to match the musical note of her voice in his supreme creation, the bell in the lake. He called her his sweet fantasy and the glade his real home. He begged for a dying kiss. Wittikin told the child all mortals die while they, the mountain folk, Thor's children, must go about their immortal business.

When voices interrupted a merry troll dance, Rautendelein feared she would lose this strange man. A wood sprite answered the rescue party, which consisted of a clergyman, a teacher, and a barber—envoys of the outer world of spirit, mind, and body. The Vicar, spirit-weak, could not go on, though the Barber urged them all to leave the bewitched area and the Schoolmaster declared such an attitude mere superstition. Frightened, each addressed Wittikin, who in turn ridiculed their master-worker and his trade as well as their respective callings, for she and her kind hated clanging bells and all human enterprise. The villagers carried Heinrich away as a group of elves and sprites danced furiously. Rautendelein also danced, though she told the Nickelmann her spirit was not in it. They examined in wonder a tear from her eye, a globe of human pain. Thor flashed out and mocked her with raindrops. The Nickelmann warned her not to live with this half-man who belonged partly in their world, but she turned to the world of men.

In the meantime, the bad news had reached the bell-maker's home. Magda, Heinrich's wife, told a neighbor what labor the task had cost her husband and then went off to meet her husband's body, terribly disconcerted by the pallbearer appearance of the rescuers. Heinrich revived and, speaking as one already dead to his anxious wife, begged her pardon for hurts done. He renounced his great work as a misshapen thing providentially destroyed—a work for the valley rather than for the mountaintops. Saying that he now wanted no part of this world of flesh, he refused all aid and became unconscious. The Vicar would not seek aid from Wittikin; but Rautendelein, thought to be deaf-mute Anna from the wayside inn nearby, breathed life into the body while the villagers sought other help. Heinrich, recovering, recognized her as nature, essential life, beauty; he would go with her onto the mountain. He declared to the returning Magda that he would live, though he was unaware of her joyful embrace.

Heinrich's presence in the mountains irritated all the supernatural folk. Taking up quarters in an abandoned glassworks, he mined ore, cut trees, and worst of all, made Rautendelein his bride. The Nickelmann was jealous, though the wood sprite said she would never love a water spirit, at least not as long as Wittikin remained the bell-founder's friend. When these creatures teased Rautendelein about her earthly lover, she replied that their accursed race could by his industry and strength become renewed.

The Vicar, now dressed in mountain costume and determined on his course, interrupted this argument. He accused the sprite of bewitching and holding Heinrich without his consent. This charge she denied. At that moment the master craftsman appeared. Misled by flattery, Heinrich declared by occult signs that he was a new man, and he drank to the Vicar's health while explaining his exuberant yet fundamental new life.

The bell-founder's vision was a chime of the finest metals which would ring by itself, through God's will and for no earthly church. The Vicar, denouncing this ecstasy, recounted Heinrich's earthly obligations to the Church and especially to his bereaved wife and children. He said it would be better if Heinrich were dead than to see him sustained by supernatural and sacrilegious beliefs. When Heinrich defended Rautendelein and his new life, the minister declared that both the people and God would crush him, that the arrow of rue would pierce though not kill him. This arrow could not pierce him any more than his great bell could ever toll again, Heinrich declared.

Some time later Heinrich, desperately working his forge, drove his dwarf helpers to exhaustion in an attempt to create his beatific vision, to mold the ideal. As one dwarf whispered in his ear, another angrily shattered the piece on which they worked so furiously; it was imperfect. Heinrich gave them a holiday and declared all could go to the devil and he would garden, eat, drink, sleep, and die. Exhausted, he dreamed that the Nickelmann ridiculed his mortality, his weakness, and his uncompleted works. He thought his old bell longed to ring out, though choked with blood and sunk so deep. He awoke in terror and called Rautendelein for comfort; she responded by calling him her God and caressing him into illusions of immortality.

Incompleteness and imperfection goaded him still, however, and he struck out pridefully for work. He was warned not only by her but by the spirit of the wood, the faun of sensuality, and by distant voices which cried out from below. Though he thought himself triumphant, a half-remembered tolling unsettled him as the phantom forms of his two children brought him a pitcher of Magda's tears and the news that her dead hand rang the sunken bell. Heinrich renounced Rautendelein and tore himself from her.

At midnight, near the well, the weary Rautendelein met her fate as the bride of the Nickelmann and sank into the water. Wood and water spirits discussed the matter, and the former prophesied that a manchild would soon fill a watery cradle. Meanwhile, defiant Heinrich called out for his loved one, ready to throw a stone at parson, barber, teacher, or sexton. Wittikin barred his way and pointed to a flaming, incomplete cathedral-castle. Determined to go on and yet exhausted, he drank from the well before he attempted to reach the flaming ruins. A beloved voice sang a good-bye, although the sound was only half remembered.

Wittikin comforted Heinrich in his final minutes, told him he was a hardy one, and granted him a boon. He drank first a goblet of the white wine of life, which he drained to the last drop. Then he drank a second of red, of the questing spirit. Just then Rautendelein appeared, although urged back into the well by the Nickelmann. Heinrich called for the final goblet of yellow wine, which was brought by Rautendelein. This he felt was all aspiration, sun wine poured into his veins by the evanescent one. Only in death did the master bell-founder, embraced and kissed by his great love, hear the chimes of the sun break through the night of life into the dawn of eternity.

Critical Evaluation:

This play is the most autobiographical and poetic of all the great Silesian playwright's efforts. It is about the problem of the artist against the world, the creative spirit against reality. The problem of living while maintaining standards of idealism is Gerhart Hauptmann's own very real problem, one that Hauptmann himself did not solve. *The Sunken Bell* is a tale of two worlds that briefly overlap by virtue of a doomed love affair. The English subtitle "A Fairy Play" gives a misleading impression to modern readers because the elves and elementals that populate traditional German *Märchen* (folktales) and the *Kunstmärchen* (art-folktales) of German Romanticism are very different from the gentle and benign insect-winged fairies of English art and fiction. In Teutonic mythology the world of nature-spirits was a dangerous place whose beauty and wildness were treacherous. Like the wood-sprite in the play, who lures the vicar, the schoolmaster, and the barber deeper into the woods by calling for help in Heinrich's voice, the population of the other world takes a mischievous delight in confusing human beings and in leading them to destruction.

The Sunken Bell's plot is reminiscent of a famous *Kunstmärchen*, Friedrich Heinrich Karl de la Motte Fouqué's *Undine* (1811), in which a water-sprite marries a young knight against the wishes of her own folk, who are swift to take their revenge when he proves unable to remain faithful to her. Hauptmann's play complicates this plot. Heinrich is no handsome young man free to plight his troth; he is a mature man who already has a loving wife and two children. Nor is Rautendelein's attachment to him a matter of spontaneous sympathy; she has a fervent desire to escape the claims of her own kind, embodied in the lascivious ambitions of the ugly Nickelmann. Heinrich's failure to make good his alliance with Rautendelein does not arise from lack of faith but from the fact that his ambition to make a bigger and better bell than any which has ever been made before—a bell fit for the mountaintops—destroys his mental composure.

The mountains have symbolic roles in *The Sunken Bell*. On the one hand they are wilderness regions, untamed by human culture, where the supernatural still holds sway. On the other hand, they are the heights of human aspiration and ambition. Heinrich's first bell, which falls into the lake and is lost when the wood-sprite causes the cart transporting it to lose its wheel, is a church bell. The sprites and the witch have cause to hate such bells, whose peals announce the faith that seeks to banish sprites and witches from the world.

Heinrich's conclusion—that the sunken bell was, after all, only a bell for the valleys and that a better bell might be built by one who had the means and the inspiration—is blasphemous. It is recognized as such by the angry vicar, but it is not the vicar's arguments that break Heinrich's resolve. Heinrich's breakdown is contrived by the jealous Nickelmann, who cunningly causes the bell to be rung underwater, so that its tolling might echo in Heinrich's overtaxed brain. Its sounding is not so much the knell of doom as the ominous clamor of his conscience, bringing forth a vision of his two children carrying a bucket of his wife's tears.

Heinrich's reasons for renouncing Rautendelein are far better than the reasons Fouqué's knight has for renouncing Undine, and they are reasons of which a committed Christian would approve. His death might be regarded by the vicar as the salvation of an imperilled soul, but this is not Hauptmann's opinion. There is ample evidence within *The Sunken Bell* to prove this point, but if more were needed it would only be necessary to consult Hauptmann's novel *The Heretic of Soana* (1918), in which a priest is converted to a doctrine of nature-worship that is pagan and poetic. Such a faith embodies everything that Rautendelein stands for.

Rautendelein's role in the play resembles the role played by hundreds of literary femmes fatales who lure good men away from the demands of duty with promises of erotic ecstasy. There is also more to her than that. Under her spell, Heinrich becomes twice the man he was before; far from abandoning himself to erotic bliss, he throws himself into his work more extravagantly than ever. She has no intention of distracting him from his labors, but instead uses her magic to support them in every possible way, providing wealth, raw materials, and laborers. The final tragedy is as much hers as his. It is arguable that her loss is the greater, in that it will be eternal. He, after all, was always bound to die.

Hauptmann was by no means the only writer to think that humankind would lose something precious if it were to put away forever the kind of enchantments associated with folklore, and to regret that the church was committed to the annihilation of belief in sprites, fairies, and the like. Nor was he the only one to clothe such regret in the form of an adult fairy tale. What is exceptional about *The Sunken Bell* is that through the character of Rautendelein, Hauptmann looks at the question from the side of the spirits, insisting that there is something in human beings whose absence leaves the world of spirits direly impoverished. Humans do things and make things, something that the spirits, in their immortality, often forget to do. When Heinrich finally dies, hearing the song of the sun's "bells," Rautendelein must, tragically, return to the Nickelmann. This represents, in a sense, the triumph of nonsense over sense and of idleness over accomplishment.

"Critical Evaluation" by Brian Stableford

Bibliography:
Garten, Hugh F. *Gerhart Hauptmann.* New Haven, Conn.: Yale University Press, 1954. A useful general introduction to the writer and his work.
McInnes, E. O. H. "The 'Active' Hero in Gerhart Hauptmann's Dramas." In *Hauptmann: Centenary Lectures,* edited by K. G. Knight and F. Norman. London: University of London's Institute of Germanic Studies, 1964. A relevant essay in a collection that mostly deals with later works.
Maurer, Warren R. *Gerhart Hauptmann.* Boston: Twayne, 1982. A study with emphasis on the works; *The Sunken Bell* is discussed in chapter 6, "Folklore and Symbolism."
_____. "Hauptmann's '*Die versunkene Glocke*' and Ibsen's '*Auf den Höhen.*'" *Monatshefte* 52 (1960): 189-193. A comparison of the two works.
Reichart, Walter A. "Gerhart Hauptmann's Dramas on the American Stage." *Maske und Kothurn* 8 (1962): 223-232. About the staging of Hauptmann's plays in the United States.

THE SUNLIGHT DIALOGUES

Type of work: Novel
Author: John Gardner (1933-1982)
Type of plot: Psychological realism
Time of plot: Mid-1960's
Locale: Batavia, New York
First published: 1972

Principal characters:
>FRED CLUMLY, the aging chief of police of Batavia, New York
>TAGGART HODGE or THE SUNLIGHT MAN, a former lawyer and insane
>>magician
>WILL HODGE, SR., Taggart's older brother and an attorney in Batavia,
>>New York
>MILLIE JEWEL HODGE, Will Hodge's former wife
>LUKE HODGE, Will and Millie's son
>NICK SLATER, a young American Indian, companion of Taggart Hodge

The Story:

A scarfaced, bearded, and semi-deranged man was arrested in Batavia, New York, for writing the word "love" in the street in large, white letters. Refusing to identify himself, ironically he came to be known as the Sunlight Man, due to his cynical diatribes against, among other targets, the American legal system, Western capitalism, and the Judeo-Christian tradition. After befuddling Police Chief Clumly with his magic tricks, he easily escaped from jail, but he soon returned to free Nick Slater, a young Indian in jail for vehicular homicide. While escaping, Nick killed one of Chief Clumly's deputies. An intense, prolonged manhunt began. Soon afterward, Nick murdered Mrs. Palazzo, the landlady of Will Hodge, Sr., when she surprised Nick and the Sunlight Man, in hiding at Will's home. Nick and the Sunlight Man then fled to the farm of Luke Hodge, one of Will's sons and the Sunlight Man's nephew. While there, the Sunlight Man engaged in a bizarre series of arranged meetings and "dialogues" with Chief Clumly; the Sunlight Man teased Clumly with displays of magical prowess (stealing Clumly's gun and mysteriously appearing and disappearing) and lecturing Clumly about the disparity between human law and universal principles (the former scorned by the Sunlight Man as he alleged obedience to the latter). These secret meetings did no t remain so long, and the resultant publicity subjected Clumly to criticism both for meeting with the Sunlight Man and for failing to capture him. The publicity also made Will Hodge and the other Hodge family members aware of the fact that the Sunlight Man was really Taggart, who had been disbarred sixteen years earlier and who had left New York after the disbarment and after having been hideously burned when his mentally ill wife set fire to their home.

The family members did not reveal the Sunlight Man's identity; they realized that Taggart had returned to Batavia because his wife was now institutionalized there. The family members' conversation revealed that Taggart had left years ago in order to accompany Taggart's wife as he and her brothers sought treatment for her at various mental institutions around the country; there was no alleviation of her steadily increasing illness. Two family members could not reveal Taggart's identity because Taggart kept Luke Hodge and Millie Hodge, Luke's mother and

Will's former wife, bound and gagged at Luke's farm while Taggart constructed his magical devices and met with, tantalized, and lectured Chief Clumly. After several days, a neighbor, Mr. Hardesty, came to visit, but when he recognized Taggart as the now-notorious Sunlight Man, Nick Slater also killed Mr. Hardesty, again without Taggart's approval—but also without his condemnation.

In the intervals between meetings with the Sunlight Man, Chief Clumly finally learned that his tormentor was Taggart Hodge. Clumly traced the movements of the wife, Kathleen Paxton, from hospital to hospital, and he discovered that a man fitting the Sunlight Man's description had always accompanied her. Clumly then visited Kathleen, finding her virtually comatose, and at his next meeting with the Sunlight Man, Chief Clumly revealed his knowledge. He then managed to disarm Taggart, but due to Taggart's eloquent arguments and due to sympathy with the tragic circumstances which had made Taggart almost insane, Clumly allowed Taggart to escape, despite the fact that Taggart was an accessory to several murders. Such continued failure to apprehend the Sunlight Man, despite known meetings with him, along with general neglect of his other duties in his absorption with Taggart, caused Chief Clumly to be fired by Batavia's mayor. Clumly was still convinced that Taggart deserved better than the fate the American criminal justice system would impose on him. Taggart's philosophical arguments had affected Clumly and had made Clumly more humane.

Meanwhile, Taggart Hodge had remembered, despite his semi-deranged condition, why he had come back to Batavia and what he had done just prior to writing "love" in the street. After his years of travel, as he attempted to help his deranged wife in defiance of her domineering and vicious father, her father had found them and had taken Kathleen back to Batavia and had had her given shock treatment. That treatment had destroyed what remained of her consciousness. Taggart also remembered that he had learned that Mr. Paxton had Taggart's sons killed after the fire at Taggart's home. Taggart also recalled that he had strangled Kathleen's father the evening before his deranged, ironic street-writing. Aware now of his need to escape from New York before his killing of Mr. Paxton became known (and, in fact, Clumly already suspected), Taggart enlisted Luke as a getaway driver. Luke had recognized his uncle, however, and being semi-suicidal, anyway, due to the effect his parents' troubled marriage had had upon him, Luke decided to drive his truck off a bridge and kill himself and Taggart, thereby preserving the Hodge family from the infamy of public awareness of Taggart's identity. A premonition caused Taggart and Nick Slater to jump from the truck prior to the wreck, however, and they escaped death. The knowledge that he had indirectly caused his nephew's death deeply affected Taggart, however, and he returned to Batavia in order to surrender. Unable to resist one more trick against the police, however, Taggart stole Officer Figlow's gun and hid it in a desk drawer. Figlow found the gun and, terrified at seeing the Sunlight Man and not realizing the Sunlight Man's peaceful intent, Figlow grabbed the gun and killed Taggart. All that remained was for Clumly to deliver the speech to the Dairyman's League that he had long been planning; he made the speech an eloquent, impassioned eulogy and defense of the Sunlight Man and a plea for a more concerned and enlightened American system of criminal justice.

Critical Evaluation:

Widely regarded as John Gardner's most ambitious and important novel, *The Sunlight Dialogues* operates on a very inclusive thematic level. The holistic nature of that inquiry is clarified in the prologue, in which the old, unnamed Judge, analogous to God, says, "I made that man [Chief Clumly]. I created him, you might say. I created them all." He assumes that "nothing in the world is universal any more; there is neither wisdom nor stability, and faithfulness is dead." The Judge also states his opinion that entropy (the general trend of the universe toward death and disorder) explains all those people he once knew who have since disappeared. These beliefs provide the framework for the fundamental question explored in the tragic destruction of Taggart Hodge and in the destruction indirectly wrought by him via Nick Slater. The question: In an existential universe (one lacking absolute realities or truths) in which stupidity, instability, and unfaithfulness abound, what can combat entropy? Gardner's answer is provided through the change in Chief Clumly; the change is due to his interaction with the Sunlight Man, and the change is most clearly stated in Clumly's speech to the Dairyman's League at the novel's end.

At the beginning of *The Sunlight Dialogues,* Clumly is a letter-of-the-law, inflexible automaton, "'a man of principle,' people said, which was to say as inflexible as a chunk of steel, with a heart so cold that if you touched it you'd stick as your fingers stick to iron at twenty below zero." Also, as the Sunlight Man has realized through his wife's insanity and his sons' murder, "It's sorrow that changes a man. But there was no sorrow in the life of the chief of police. That was his crime. There was only order, lifted against the world like rusty chickenwire to keep out a herd of cows." Taggart himself, in his semi-insane state after the tragedies in his family, becomes the "herd of cows," the disorder of an entropic universe, that Clumly must struggle with; the police chief immediately senses this. Clumly reports that "the old feeling came over him again, the absolute, irrational certainty that the bearded man was the sum total of all Clumly had been fighting all his life." Clumly's fight has not been highly successful, however, as crime is rampant in Batavia, and he is a virtual laughingstock on the verge of being fired. It is only when Clumly meets with and has four "dialogues" with the Sunlight Man that Clumly begins to understand the ambiguities of the diverse, disordered world that he has refused to previously acknowledge (except to try to imprison as much of it as possible). Clumly's increasing awareness, via the "dialogues," of the inadequacies of Western capitalism, the American criminal justice system, and the Judeo-Christian tradition, makes him incapable of the larger injustice of arresting the Sunlight Man and costs him his job as police chief. Ironically, however, this awareness makes him a saner, wiser human being, a humanist and a moralist who finally possesses Gardner's answer to the question of how to counteract the entropic tendency of the world. After Taggart is killed by mistake, epitomizing the stupidity, instability, and unfaithfulness that characterize twentieth century existence, Chief Clumly combats the entropy in his speech. His answer is to bemoan "the injustice of it!" (Taggart's death), to note that laws benefit "all of *us,* anyway" (his law-abiding and financially secure audience), and to warn that "the danger is, it (a society of law) can get cold. Turn ice." He further notes, "Ladies and gentlemen, we mustn't let that happen, I feel. I feel we must all be vigilant against growing indifference to people less fortunate." The repetition of "I feel" and the emphasis upon caring about others less fortunate show that Clumly's (and Gardner's) answer to death and disorder is moral and emotional empathy, tempered by an awareness of the complexities and inherent ambiguities of modern life. This latter awareness is illustrated in Clumly's comment that "we may be wrong about the whole thing . . . the whole kaboodle. If we could look at ourselves from the eyes of history—" (Taggart Hodge has helped him to do just that). Clumly then concludes with the human empathy emphasis of the Judeo-Christian tradition, not its law-and-order, hierarchial dimension emphasis, when he states that, "Blessed are the meek, by which I mean all of us, including the Sunlight Man. . . . God be kind to all Good Samaritans and also bad ones. For of such is the Kingdom of Heaven." Clumly embodys Gardner's inclusive theme, his response to an entropic universe is to look around beyond laws to justice; to look beyond self-interest to concern for others; to look beyond logic to feeling; to look beyond simplistic certainty to informed relativity; and to look beyond hierarchial divisiveness to holistic acceptance. Although entropy may ultimately prevail, the importance of Gardner's *The Sunlight Dialogues* is its illustrating the fact that the only effective response is indeed, love written large in the streets of the world.

John L. Grigsby

Bibliography:

Cowart, David. *Arches and Light: The Fiction of John Gardner*. Carbondale: Southern Illinois University Press, 1983. Interprets *The Sunlight Dialogues* as centered on the human struggle against universal entropy. Includes helpful genre analysis and perceptive analogizing to Sir Thomas Malory, Dante Alighieri, and Homer.

Morris, Gregory L. "A Babylonian in Batavia: Mesopotamian Literature and Lore in *The Sunlight Dialogues*." In *John Gardner: Critical Perspectives*, edited by Robert A. Morace and Kathryn VanSpanckeren. Carbondale: Southern Illinois University Press, 1982. A thorough explanation of the Mesopotamian history, lore, and cultural tradition underlying the four "dialogues" between the Sunlight Man and Chief Clumly; the four dialogues are the controlling structures of *The Sunlight Dialogues*.

_____. *A World of Order and Light: The Fiction of John Gardner*. Athens: University of Georgia Press, 1984. Astute analysis of *The Sunlight Dialogues* as "the artistic and intellectual center" of all Gardner's fiction; Gardner explains his "governing metaphysical system" in *The Sunlight Dialogues*. Analyzes the complex, multilayered structure of Gardner's most challenging novel, *The Sunlight Dialogues*.

Payne, Alison. "Clown, Monster, Magician: The Purpose of Lunacy in John Gardner's Fiction." In *Thor's Hammer: Essays on John Gardner*, edited by Jeff Henderson, et al. Conway: University of Central Arkansas Press, 1985. A perceptive study of insanity in several Gardner novels. Includes detailed analysis of the symbolic divergence of the emotional idealism of the Sunlight Man and the rational practicality of Chief Clumly in *The Sunlight Dialogues*.

Winther, Per. *The Art of John Gardner: Instruction and Exploration*. Albany: State University of New York Press, 1992. Discusses Gardner's literary theory and his fiction and provides insight into the philosophical bases of important characters in *The Sunlight Dialogues*. Includes helpful discussion of Gardner's collage technique.

THE SUPPLIANTS

Type of work: Drama
Author: Aeschylus (525/524-456/455 B.C.E.)
Type of plot: Tragedy
Time of plot: Mythical age
Locale: Argos
First performed: Hiketides, 463 B.C.E.? (English translation, 1777)

>   *Principal characters:*
>   DANAÜS, an Egyptian of Greek descent
>   HIS FIFTY MAIDEN DAUGHTERS
>   PELASGUS, the king of Argos
>   THE FIFTY SONS OF AEGYPTUS
>   BROTHER OF DANAÜS

The Story:

Danaüs and his fifty maiden daughters fled from Egypt after Danaüs' brother, Aegyptus, had decided that his fifty sons should take their cousins to wife. The fugitives finally reached the shores of Argos, the land of their illustrious ancestress Io, a mortal who had been loved by Zeus. Holding olive branches wrapped in wool before an Argive altar, the maidens sought Zeus' protection of their purity. Their supplications to the father of the gods included the wish that the sons of Aegyptus might meet disaster at sea between Egypt and Argos. In fear of being forced to marry Aegyptus' sons, the maidens also invoked the wretched Procne, who had been given in marriage to the perfidious Tereus and had taken the life of her child, Itylus, out of hatred for her husband. They repeated their supplication to Zeus to protect them from forced love, and they invoked Artemis, the goddess of chastity, to be favorable to them. They declared that they would end their lives themselves before submitting to the sons of Aegyptus. They went on to invoke not only Zeus but Apollo as well, who had himself once been an exile. They prayed to Poseidon, god of the sea, and to Hermes, the messenger of the gods. Danaüs recalled that the gods were merciless to those who indulged in lustful pleasures.

Danaüs, observing that someone approached, cautioned his daughters to stay near the altar and to conduct themselves with modesty. A man, followed by servants and warriors, entered the sacred area. Seeing that the maidens wore Oriental clothing and that suppliant wands had been placed on the altar, he asked whence Danaüs and the young women had come. Questioned in turn, he disclosed that he was Pelasgus, the king of Argos. One of the maidens then told him that they were of Argive stock, descendants of Io, the Argive woman who had given birth to a son by Zeus. Pelasgus interrupted to remark that the maidens appeared to be North Africans and to resemble the Amazons rather than Grecians.

The maiden resumed her tale, recounting that when Hera, the wife of Zeus, saw that Zeus loved the mortal Io, she transformed Io into a heifer and placed her under the guard of Argus, the many-eyed god. Hera also created a gadfly to sting Io into a miserable, wandering existence on earth. Io's wanderings took her to Memphis, Egypt, where by mystical union with Zeus—the touch of his hand—she gave birth to a son. She named him Epaphus, from the nature of his birth. Epaphus had a daughter, Libya, after whom a great stretch of North Africa was named. Libya had a son, Belus, who fathered two sons, Danaüs—the father of fifty daughters, whom the king beheld before his very eyes—and Aegyptus, the father of fifty sons.

Pelasgus, satisfied that they were of Argive stock, asked why they had left Egypt. The maiden explained that they had fled because they were threatened with forced marriage to their cousins; it was not so much that they hated their cousins as that they wanted their husbands to love them. Pelasgus, observing that in the most advantageous marriages there was no aspect of love, was not sure he could support the maidens in their cause. The maidens pointed to the wand-decked shrine and asked Pelasgus to heed the sign.

All the sisters pleaded for assistance from Pelasgus, who feared that his meddling in the affair might bring war to Argos. Apprehensive, yet anxious to help, he insisted that he would have to consult his people. The suppliants answered that he was an absolute ruler and could, if he so desired, make his own decisions. They warned him to beware of the wrath of Zeus, the god who took pity on humans in distress and was merciless with those who refused to assist others. Still Pelasgus insisted on consulting his people, for he feared to bring disaster to Argos. Even after searching deeply in his soul for an answer, he declared that the problem was one with which he alone could not cope, that to resolve it would involve frightful sacrifices to the gods.

In despair, the maidens proposed that Pelasgus use their girdles to hang them to the statues in the sacred area. Deeply disturbed, Pelasgus suggested that Danaüs gather up all of the wands and, in hopes of eliciting general Argive sympathy for the maidens, place them on altars in the city of Argos itself. Once he was assured of safe passage into the city, Danaüs accepted the suggestion and departed with the wands. When Pelasgus directed the maidens to an unhallowed area of the sacred ground, they asked how they were to be protected there from their cousins. Pelasgus, advising them to pray to the Argive gods, returned to Argos to consult with his people.

Left alone, the maidens resumed their earnest prayers and invocations to Zeus. They again recalled Zeus' love for their ancestress and appealed to him—who was after all responsible for their being—to save them from the lust of Aegyptus' sons.

Danaüs returned to report that to a man the Argives would defend any refugees from seizure. Pelasgus had reminded the Argives that if they failed to assist and to offer sanctuary to suppliants, Zeus would send a man-eating monster to the city. The maidens sang their gratitude to the people of Argos and invoked the gods to look auspiciously upon the land.

Danaüs, standing on an elevated place in the sacred ground, saw the sons of Aegyptus approaching the shore in their ships. He calmed his frightened daughters by reminding them of the Argives' promise, but when he wished to leave them to summon help, they begged him to stay with them. He pointed out that it would take Aegyptus' sons some time to make proper anchorage and that there was plenty of time for him to seek aid.

After Danaüs had gone, the maidens, overcome with apprehension at the approach of their cousins, spoke of the death they preferred to the enforced love that appeared to be imminent. As they cried in anguish to Zeus, a messenger came to them from the ships and, treating them with brutality, ordered them to the ships. While he sneered at their frantic appeals to the Greek gods, Pelasgus came upon the scene of violence and demanded of the messenger his business. The Egyptian answered that he had come to take what belonged to him and that only force, not any fear of the Greek gods, could prevent his taking the maidens back to Egypt. Pelasgus declared that the sons of Aegyptus would have to fight to claim their captives. When the messenger asked his name, Pelasgus retorted that his name did not matter; what did matter was that the women would not be taken from Argos by force.

The messenger returned to the ships, and Pelasgus invited the maidens to take shelter with the friendly people of Argos. The maidens first sought the approval of their father, Danaüs, who advised them to treasure their chastity before their lives and gave them permission to go. Rejoicing, the daughters of Danaüs sang reverently and thankfully to Artemis, goddess of chastity. They also invoked Aphrodite, goddess of love, who they were sure would help in guiding them to marriages blessed by true love.

Critical Evaluation:

Aeschylus' *The Suppliants* brilliantly depicts strong passions and moral greatness. The play is nevertheless very difficult to interpret. For one thing, *The Suppliants* was part of a trilogy dealing with the fate of the daughters of Danaüs; the sequel plays are lost except for a few fragments. Most Greek tragedies were in the form of a trilogy, in which the related mythical stories presented in the first play were developed to a conclusion in the third. In this trilogy, the Danaids were probably central actors in all three plays. Consequently evaluation of the one surviving play is problematic. A second difficulty to interpretation is the high proportion of lyric poetry contained in the drama: nearly half of the preserved play is choral lyrics that allude to complex myths. This beautiful and allusive poetry is unusual in a drama, and yet interpretation of these mythical references is crucial to understanding the subtler themes of the work. A third challenge to appreciating *The Suppliants* is its lack of action, which is sparse even when compared with other extant Greek tragedies. As it stands, the plot seems to turn on Pelasgus' agonizing decision whether or not to protect the maidens who had come to him for refuge. This focus on the king of Argos rather than on the fate of the maidens may not be what Aeschylus actually intended as the focus of the trilogy. Each of these major difficulties must be considered in evaluating Aeschylus' art in *The Suppliants*.

It is virtually certain that *The Suppliants* was the first play of a trilogy, of which *The Egyptians* and *The Danaids* were the second and third parts. Aeschylus wrote the only extant Greek trilogy, *The Oresteia* (458 B.C.E.). From his practice in that work and the myth as it is known from other sources, the probable development of the Danaid trilogy can be tentatively reconstructed. It is possible that even before *The Egyptians* opens, the war between Argos and the sons of Aegyptus is over, with Pelasgus dead and Argos utterly defeated. The maidens are forced to return to Egypt, are married, and all but one murder their husbands on the wedding night. Only Hypermestra refused out of love to kill her new husband. As in *The Oresteia*, a trial probably ensued: A fragment of *The Danaids* suggests that Hypermestra is tried for disobedience in not killing her husband. Yet Aphrodite intervenes and defends her by citing the invincible power of love. If this reconstruction is correct, the courageous vow of Pelasgus to protect the maidens turns out to have been futile. The resistance of the Danaids to marriage, a prominent theme in *The Suppliants*, leads to an act for which, according to some versions of the myth, they are eternally punished in Hades by being compelled to carry water in leaky urns. The resolution in the third play may affirm the same power of matrimony and sexual union that the maidens so passionately reject in the opening play. Clearly, any first impressions of *The Suppliants* must be qualified by reference to the story as it unfolded in the complete trilogy.

In the extant play, the audience is confronted by a dense work full of allusive choral lyrics that are intended to elaborate on the plight of the Danaids. This unusual reliance on lyric once led scholars to assume that *The Suppliants* was a very early play, written perhaps as early as c. 490 B.C.E., when the dramatic possibilities of dialogue and plot were still unexplored. Subsequently, a spectacular papyrus discovery confirmed that the play was in fact first performed in the 460's, near the close of Aeschylus' career. For whatever reason, the dramatist chose to portray the situation of the Danaids, a "protagonist" in the form of fifty maidens, primarily through lyric song rather than through dramatic confrontation and dialogue. The choral songs often dwell on the story of Io, who was loved by Zeus and persecuted by Hera. Her experience of pursuit and exile is obviously a parallel to the plight of the Danaids. Yet not only the Danaids but also the Argives and the sons of Aegyptus trace their origins back to Io. The maidens express revulsion at the idea of forced marriage to their cousins, but while their resistance to marriage may seem to suggest an assertion of women's rights, this may be an anachronistic interpretation. It is likely that Aeschylus intended the maidens to express a more common fear of the time, that of leaving childhood and accepting the role of wife and mother.

Pelasgus is undoubtedly the most interesting character in the play. He is faced with a tragic choice, either to protect the suppliants and risk war with Egypt or to return them and incur the wrath of Zeus. Some have seen his decision to champion the Danaids' cause as a mark of weakness, since it is precipitated by their threat to commit suicide on the altar of the gods. Yet Aeschylus skillfully depicts a leader who is at once reluctant to endanger his people and afraid not to do what is right. Rather than himself deciding an issue with such far-reaching implications for his country, he submits his proposal to a vote of the people, who unanimously approve the plan to protect the suppliants. This detail is surely a nod to the evolution of mature Athenian democracy in the 460's, even though the action is translated to Argos in mythical times. Although their decision leads to a war that Argos loses, the Argive resolve to defend the suppliants presents a noble contrast to the use of force by the brutal Egyptians.

The Suppliants is an intense, lyrical depiction of the helpless refugees who find defenders willing to act selflessly and to take risks for what is right. A pious Greek king and his subjects take upon themselves the problems of unjustly persecuted barbarians. With its brief acknowledgment of democracy as the only proper way for a community to decide such important matters, even if the decision should have tragic consequences, the play also represents a fascinating fusion of literature and history.

"Critical Evaluation" by John M. Lawless

Bibliography:
Aeschylus. *The Suppliants*. Translated by Peter Burian. Princeton, N.J.: Princeton University Press, 1991. The best modern translation of the play. Also provides a sound introduction to the themes and imagery of the play and includes brief notes explaining references in the translation.
Beck, Robert Holmes. *Aeschylus: Playwright Educator*. The Hague: Martinus Nijhoff, 1975. Chapter 7 examines *The Suppliants* and its themes in the context of the supposed trilogy to which it belonged. Beck places particular emphasis on the moral message that the playwright may have intended with the drama.
Garvie, A. F. *Aeschylus' "Supplices": Play and Trilogy*. Cambridge, England: Cambridge University Press, 1969. The standard work on the style, structure, and meaning of the play. Garvie tends to be cautious in his speculation about the content of the lost plays and their possible relevance for interpretation of *The Suppliants*.
Spatz, Lois. *Aeschylus*. Boston: Twayne, 1982. An excellent and accessible general work on the art of Aeschylus. Chapter 4 on *The Suppliants* is especially rewarding for discussion of possible political ideas in the drama and of various themes in the choral odes.
Winnington-Ingram, R. P. *Studies in Aeschylus*. Cambridge, England: Cambridge University Press, 1983. A sober and intelligent survey of Aeschylean drama that repays consultation. Chapter 4 on "The Danaid Trilogy" is concerned mainly with the speculative reconstruction of the trilogy and its value for interpreting the drama. This work updates earlier work on the Danaid trilogy.

THE SUPPLIANTS

Type of work: Drama
Author: Euripides (c. 485-406 B.C.E.)
Type of plot: Tragedy
Time of plot: Antiquity
Locale: Eleusis, not far from Athens
First performed: Hiketides, c. 423 B.C.E. (English translation, 1781)

Principal characters:
THESEUS, King of Athens
AETHRA, his mother
ADRASTUS, King of Argos
EVADNE, Capaneus' wife
IPHIS, her father
CHILDREN OF THE SLAIN CHIEFTAINS
THE GODDESS ATHENA
HERALD OF CREON
CHORUS OF ARGIVE MOTHERS

The Story:

Adrastus, the Argive king who had led the disastrous war of the Seven against Thebes and had alone escaped with his life, brought the mothers and the children of the slain chieftains to Athens, the most democratic and hospitable city of Greece. There they gathered at the temple of Demeter at Eleusis, and when Aethra, the mother of Theseus, came to pray, they formed a ring of supplication about her, begging for help in recovering the dead bodies of their sons for burial according to the prescribed rites. The anguish of the mothers so moved Aethra that she sent at once for her own son.

The powerful young king closely cross-examined the defeated old ruler and refused to help after discovering that Adrastus had foolishly married off his daughters to quarrelsome exiles, Tydeus and Polynices, and had engaged in war against Thebes despite the advice of the prophet Amphiaraus. Aethra, however, discreetly reminded her son that, although his logic was sound as far as it went, he was nevertheless obligated by honor and the religious customs of Attica to go to the aid of all who sought proper burial and funeral rites for the dead. Theseus, recognizing the wisdom and humanity of her counsel, departed to seek a vote of the Athenian assembly on the matter.

Upon his return, Theseus announced that, with the support of the assembly, he was ready to send two messages to Creon, king of Thebes. The first was a polite request for permission to bury the dead. If this one were to be refused, the second was a warning that his armies were on their way. He was interrupted by the arrival of an insolent herald from Creon who demanded in the name of his despot that Adrastus be driven from Athens. The herald added that courageous wisdom called for peace. Theseus, although detesting war, felt obligated by the ancient laws of the gods to bury the dead, by force of arms if necessary. After a heated exchange of words, the Theban herald withdrew, and Theseus prepared for battle. He rejected Adrastus' offer of aid, for he was unwilling to blend his fortunes with those of a king who had brought upon himself the wrath of the gods. As Theseus marched off with his troops, the chorus chanted fear of the fickleness of heaven and prayed for deliverance.

Soon a messenger brought news of Theseus' victory, describing how the Athenians arrived at the Theban gates, expressed an intent to avoid war if they were permitted to bury the Argive chieftains but finally found it necessary to fight the Thebans. Theseus, refusing to enter the gates and sack the city, had personally gathered together the dead bodies and washed their wounds. Adrastus, deeply moved, lamented that the Thebans had not learned the lesson of compromise from his own experience and wished that he, too, had died with his fellow warriors.

When the bodies were brought to Athens, Adrastus delivered a eulogy over each (Capaneus, Eteocles, Hippomedon, Parthenopaeus, Tydeus, and Polynices) before they were prepared for cremation on the funeral pyre. Suddenly Evadne, widow of Capaneus, appeared on a rock overhanging the burning pyre, determined to be with Capaneus in death as she had in life. Her aged father, Iphis, pleaded with her in vain. Dressed in festive garments, she leaped into the fire. As the children of the cremated warriors carried away the ashes in funeral urns, the grief-stricken Iphis withdrew to the dark interior of his house to die.

Marching in a funeral procession, the children (thereafter known as the Epigoni) chanted an oath with the chorus to avenge their fathers. Theseus extracted from them a promise that they and all their children would always remember the kindness they had received from Athens and honor the city of democracy. Before the children could carry off the ashes of their fathers, however, the goddess Athena appeared in midair and called upon Theseus not to permit the ashes to be returned to Argos. Instead, after appropriate animal sacrifices, they must be delivered to the safekeeping of the oracle at Delphi. Then, turning to the children, Athena prophesied that when they reached adulthood they would successfully sack the city of Thebes and avenge the slaughter of their fathers.

Critical Evaluation:

Euripides' *The Suppliants* explores the themes of grief, the inhumanity of war, the proper democratic model for government, justice, and civic duty. *The Suppliants* is less effective than Euripides' other antiwar play, *The Trojan Women* (415 B.C.E.), because of a weaker blend of emotional and political themes and a weaker dramatic structure. The detached episodes within the play do not allow for complex developments within the characters of Theseus and Adrastus. Moreover, Theseus' climactic victory over Creon's army occurs very early in the play. *The Suppliants* ends without a true catharsis or a denouement that is emotionally satisfying. However, the play is blessed with eloquent speeches by Theseus and by the chorus of the wives of the seven slain chieftains who plead for the retrieval of the bodies of the dead soldiers.

The Suppliants is more political and didactic in nature than other Greek plays dealing with themes of supplication such as Aeschylus' *The Libation Bearers* (458 B.C.E.), Sophocles' *Antigone* (441 B.C.E.), and Euripides' *Trojan Women*. Euripides in *The Suppliants* is motivated to show how the Athenians might avenge the loss of the Peloponnesian War against the Spartan confederacy.

The idea of supplication as practiced by the Greeks was to make humble petitions and prayers to the gods by pouring liquids, usually wine, over the graves of the dead. The chorus of Argive mothers cannot perform this sacred ritual without the corpses of their seven sons Capaneus, Eteocles, Hippomedon, Parthenopaeus, Tydeus, and Polynices. However, that Theseus needs to be persuaded on the grounds of justice and civic duty into helping the Argive women retrieve the seven warriors does not allow for much character complexity or emotional subtlety. Aethra, Theseus' mother, at first distressed by the women's wailing and lamentation at the temple of Demeter, requests Theseus to either drive the suppliants from the land or free them from their grief by fighting Creon and stealing the bodies. "To mourn the dead/ brings honor to those who live," the women plead to Theseus. The intense mourning and funeral marching unsettles Theseus in part because the women are foreigners, not Athenians. Theseus initially resists Adrastus' request to help by pointing out that Adrastus went to Thebes to please Tydeus and Polynices—suitors of two of his daughters—while ignoring a prophecy of doom. Theseus answers that Adrastus got what he deserved when be became confused by the squabbling of Tydeus and Polynices, two young warriors hungry for power.

Only when the goddess Athena appears *deus ex machina* at the end is Theseus moved to act. Preservation of the laws is what holds Greece together, and the gods would be slighted if the traditional laws were not obeyed. Motivated by Athena's wishes and his own desire to win glory for Athens, Theseus finally agrees to do it. Theseus really wishes to prove democracy (the politics of Athens) better than oligarchy (the politics of Thebes) and demonstrate Greek justice in action. Theseus' sense of politics and civic duty fails to match the emotional intensity of the "inhumanity of war" pleas of the Argive women, unlike Achilles' fully developed personal and political rage against Agamemnon and Hector in Homer's *Iliad* (c. 800 B.C.E.).

The appearance of Creon's herald allows Theseus to pontificate on his political motive for attacking Thebes: Citizens of Athens are free and democratic while Creon tyrannizes Thebes with his absolute rule. Theseus' speech explains that Athens is ruled by people who share equally in governmental affairs, reigning in succession without yielding power to the rich. Creon's herald counters that Thebans do not need persuasive political rhetoric to make decisions and that the poor are incapable of attending to public matters. Theseus believes that absolute monarchy is bad and that Athenian rule is the law preserving equality and freedom. While one is aware that Athenian democracy in practice excluded many people, the discussion is intriguing on theoretical grounds, even though it provides insufficient motivation to invade Thebes.

Theseus bridges the gap between politics and personality by making the abandonment of the Argive dead into a justice issue, saying that all Greeks are hurt by devaluation of the dead. Theseus is driven by his desire to obey an ancient law when he had earlier wanted only to be rid of the inconvenience of wailing mothers. To honor justice, Theseus begins his war against Creon.

Similarly, Adrastus' burial catalog of the seven chieftains after Theseus' victory lacks emotional impact because the audience has never encountered these characters except through other plays and legends. The audience cannot empathize with the Argive women, never having known the slain warriors. Adrastus and Theseus remain undeveloped as protagonists; they do not learn from their suffering. Evadne's desires to release herself from suffering and to join her husband Capaneus on the funeral pyre are surprising only because of inadequate exposition. Again, the audience does not really know Evadne or Capaneus apart from secondhand descriptions from other characters, so Evadne's suicide produces no cathartic release or visceral identification with suffering.

That the children of the seven chieftans are commanded by Athena to grow and extract revenge against the murder of their fathers runs counter to the main purpose of the play as a statement against the cruelty of war. Thus even with Theseus' rhetorically ornamented speech about the superiority of Athenian government and justice, the goddess Athena says the sons are lion cubs and "true-born sackers of cities," disregarding Theseus' justifications for the battle. Of course, the gods always possess the power to override any mortal desire to advance justice. Blessed with Euripidean political eloquence and the passion of suffering wrought through war, *The Suppliants* is an imperfect creation, but an intriguing one.

"Critical Evaluation" by Jonathan L. Thorndike

Bibliography:

Conacher, D. J. *Euridipean Drama: Myth, Theme, and Structure.* Toronto: University of Toronto Press, 1967. Argues against the prevailing belief that Euripides destroyed Greek drama. Maintains that, while he never accepted myth as the basis for tragedy, Euripides continually created new dramatic structures to suit new perceptions of human tragedy.

Grube, G. M. A. "Euripides and the Gods." In *Euripides: A Collection of Critical Essays,* edited by Erich Segal. Englewood Cliffs, N.J.: Prentice-Hall, 1968. Argues that the divine framework is still an important aspect of Euripides' drama, though he used a different concept of the gods than other dramatists did.

Halleran, Michael R. *Stagecraft in Euripides.* Totowa, N.J.: Barnes & Noble Books, 1985. Examines specific aspects of Euripides' technique such as stage actions, entrances, surprises, exits, and lyrics. Euripides changed the basic structural pattern of Greek drama in many of his plays.

Harsh, Philip Whaley. *A Handbook of Classical Drama.* Stanford, Calif.: Stanford University Press, 1944. A classic survey of the range of Greek and Roman drama, arguing for the greatness of the achievement and for its influence on modern literature. Skillful thematic reading of *The Suppliants* and the Euripidean plays leading up to it.

Zuntz, G. *The Political Plays of Euripides.* Oxford, England: Manchester University Press, 1955. Foundational study of political ideas in *The Suppliants* and other political dramas. Zuntz explains that the play greatly impressed Euripides' contemporaries and does not deserve the low status assigned to it by modern critics.

THE SURROUNDED

Type of work: Novel
Author: D'Arcy McNickle (1904-1977)
Type of plot: Social realism
Time of plot: Early twentieth century
Locale: Flathead Indian Reservation in Montana
First published: 1936

Principal characters:
    ARCHILDE LEON, a young man of mixed race
    LOUIS LEON, his brother
    CATHARINE LEON, his Native American mother
    MAX LEON, his Spanish father
    MIKE and
    NARCISSE, his nephews
    DAVE QUIGLEY, the sheriff

The Story:

Archilde Leon, who had been making his living as a musician in Portland, returned to his family's ranch in Montana for a visit. His father, Max, lived in the big house with Archilde's sister, Agnes, and her two sons, Mike and Narcisse, while his mother, Catharine, the daughter of a Salish chief and one of the most pious women on the reservation, lived in a cabin on the property and maintained a fairly traditional Indian lifestyle. Upon his return, Archilde discovered that his brother, Louis, had stolen some horses and was hiding in the nearby mountains. Catharine celebrated Archilde's return by inviting several Indians, including the highly respected Modeste, an old Salish chief, over for feasting and storytelling. Max, on the other hand, was worried about Archilde. Of all of his sons, Archilde was the one he had hoped would be able to take over the farm. Max was frustrated to discover that Archilde would rather go back to Portland and play the fiddle than stay in Montana and work the land. Max shared his concern with his confidant, the elderly priest Father Grepilloux, who offered to help Archilde with his music if he would stay and work.

To Max's surprise and delight, Archilde helped with the harvest that fall and spent time with the priests, practicing his music. These times reminded Archilde of his childhood days at the Indian boarding school. He remembered one day in particular when the clouds formed a cross in the sky, and everyone knelt down before the "sign." Archilde, however, did not kneel; instead, he chose to identify with a bird he saw fly across the sky, unaware of any other "sign." During the fall harvest, Archilde's nephews, Mike and Narcisse, were rounded up and sent to the priests' school against their wishes.

Catharine decided that she wanted to go deer hunting, and Archilde went with her. While they were in the mountains, they encountered, first, Dave Quigley, the sheriff who was hunting for Louis, and then Louis himself. The three—Catharine, Archilde, and Louis—continued with their hunting until they were stopped by a game warden for hunting doe out of season. Louis' nervous fidgeting alarmed the warden, who shot and killed Louis. When the warden got off his horse to examine Louis' body, Catharine killed him with an ax. Archilde, stunned by these events, helped his mother bury the game warden's body and take Louis' body home, where they told people they had found him dead in the mountains.

Given the suspicious circumstances, Archilde was detained at the Government Indian Agency for some time. When he was finally released, he discovered that Max had become ill at Father Grepilloux' funeral. Not long after Archilde and his father reconciled, Max died. Archilde decided to stay on and tend his father's land, and a series of changes followed. Catharine moved back into the house, and Mike and Narcisse returned from the Indian school. Mike, however, was changed; he suffered emotionally as a result of the abusive treatment he had received at the school.

At the annual Fourth of July dance, Modeste arranged to have Mike assist him. Mike danced with the other Indians and seemed healed by the experience. Catharine, in a meeting of tribal elders, announced that she wanted to renounce her baptism. She had been dreaming that she had died and went to the white people's heaven, where they told her to be happy, but she could not be happy because there were no Indians there; she was sent to the Indians' heaven, but the Indians would not let her enter because she had been baptized. She had been upset, not only by guilt at murdering the game warden but also by the loss of her son Louis, and she had not been able to gain peace through confession to the priests. She asked the tribe to allow her to be whipped, according to the ancient custom, in order to pay for the wrongs she had done. Archilde enjoyed the afternoon Indian dancing, but in the evening he went into town carousing with Elise, Modeste's raucous granddaughter. Eventually, the two were thrown out of the white people's dance hall.

Afraid to return to school and in an effort to keep alive what they had learned at the dance, Narcisse and Mike went into the hills to live. The relationship between Archilde and Elise developed as they spent the remainder of the summer together; nonetheless, Archilde planned to leave after the fall harvest. His leaving was postponed again, however, when his mother had a stroke.

Archilde, unaware of Catharine's total return to traditional belief, sent for both a doctor and a priest. She refused the priest and asked for Modeste instead. Before he left to bring Modeste, the priest informed Archilde that Catharine had confessed to him the game warden's murder, and the priest prodded Archilde to call in the sheriff. Archilde went to the Indian commissioner and told him the story, promising to return after his mother's death. As soon as Catharine died, however, Elise, Archilde, Mike, and Narcisse disappeared. Elise led the others into the mountains, traveling a roundabout path to a place where she thought they would be safe. One night, however, the sheriff, Dave Quigley, who had been hunting them, walked into their camp. Elise very calmly offered him a cup of coffee and, going over to him, threw the hot coffee in his face and shot him, killing him instantly. In the confusion, Mike and Narcisse escaped. Elise and Archilde did not escape, however; the Indian commissioner and the tribal policeman had been waiting in the bushes and stepped forward to arrest them.

Critical Evaluation:

D'Arcy McNickle was born on the Flathead Indian Reservation in Montana and was a member of the Confederated Salish and Kootenai tribes. As a child, he was sent to the federal Indian boarding school, where he was punished if he spoke an Indian language rather than English. He spent four years at the University of Montana and went on to study in Europe, both at Oxford and at the University of Grenoble. He was an anthropologist, historian, and scholar; an administrator in the Bureau of Indian Affairs, he founded the Newberry Library Center for the History of the American Indian in Chicago, which now bears his name. *The Surrounded* was his first work of fiction and is still the most readily available. It received some critical acclaim when it was first published and has become increasingly popular since it was reprinted in the 1970's.

The Surrounded has strong autobiographical overtones. The novel focuses on Archilde, through whom the readers see the identity conflicts that trouble the racially mixed hero. Archilde is caught between the white and the Indian cultures, neither of which is unambiguously good or bad, making his position even more difficult.

One of the ways that the novel emphasizes this cultural conflict is by describing many characters and events as opposing pairs. Catharine LaLoup Leon and Max Leon, for example, each present to Archilde some of the positive aspects of Indian and white culture, respectively. The Indian dancing on the Fourth of July, full of ancient meaning and beauty, is contrasted with the white people's meaningless dance in a dark, bare hall.

The novel expresses particular concern for the decline of Native American culture. McNickle describes in great detail the transformation of Mike and Narcisse as the older women prepare them for the dance, emphasizing the beauty of traditional culture. McNickle applies his expertise as an anthropologist to the detailed explanation of all the old dances, stressing each dance's particular meaning. This is contrasted with the scene at the Fourth of July dance, where white people come to laugh disrespectfully at the old men as they move slowly through the only dances that they are still allowed to do.

In addition, *The Surrounded* presents an interesting view of nature. Archilde goes into the wilderness to be alone, and nature is generally seen as an ally to the Indians, who can live in mountain caves and hunt for their food if they so choose. The scene in which Archilde sees the cloud-cross in the sky and ignores it because the bird ignores it, stresses the preeminence of nature. Archilde remembers this experience and teaches this same lesson to Mike and Narcisse: If the birds are not frightened by signs and demons, they should not be either. Nature is seen as a better source of encouragement and truth than are the priests.

An interesting aspect of the novel is the presence of two especially strong female characters. Elise is reckless and determined to get what she wants. She can ride and hunt as well as any man. She takes the initiative, not only in her relationship with Archilde but also in their escape into the mountains. She, like Catharine, is not afraid to kill when Archilde is threatened. Catharine is held in high regard, not only among the Indians but also among the whites (which is one reason that Max married her in the first place). Even in her advanced age, she hunts for herself. Her death is described as a triumphant moment. She dies unafraid, surrounded by her Indian family and friends.

The plot structure of *The Surrounded* demonstrates a certain circularity and reflects the work's thematic concern for Archilde's identity. Archilde left the reservation, trying to put some distance between himself and his people. When he returns, it is only for a short and final visit. Yet, he continues to stay as he becomes increasingly entangled in events on the reservation. The apparent inaction—staying—is actually the action that helps him determine his identity as an Indian. He does not succeed in going to Portland to be a fiddler or even in running his father's farm. Archilde succeeds in finding his identity at those times when he feels most connected to his tribal heritage: at the dance and at his mother's death. His identity comes, not from breaking away and succeeding in isolation, but from living in his proper context, with his people and his land.

Kelly C. Walter

Bibliography:
Bevis, William. "Native American Novels: Homing In." In *Recovering the Word: Essays on Native American Literature*, edited by Brian Swann and Arnold Krupat. Berkeley: University

of California Press, 1982. A very helpful introduction to Native American narrative struc-tures. Discusses *The Surrounded* in the context of other recent Native American novels.

Oaks, Priscilla. "The First Generation of Native American Novelists." *MELUS (Multi-Ethnic Literature of the United States)* 5 (1978): 57-65. Surveys several Native American novels of the 1930's, and discusses McNickle in that context.

Parker, Dorothy R. *Singing an Indian Song: A Biography of D'Arcy McNickle.* Lincoln: Uni-versity of Nebraska Press, 1992. A very thorough biography, including photographs as well as some literary discussion. Useful in light of the highly autobiographical nature of *The Surrounded.*

Purdy, John Lloyd. *Word Ways: The Novels of D'Arcy McNickle.* Tucson: University of Arizona Press, 1990. Takes an especially anthropological point of view and includes, in an appendix, several Salish oral stories which are a useful supplement to *The Surrounded.*

Ruppert, James. *D'Arcy McNickle.* Boise, Idaho: Boise State University Press, 1962. Provides biographical information and discusses McNickle's novels as well as his ethnographic writings.

Wiget, Andrew. *Native American Literature.* Boston: Twayne, 1985. One of the most readily available general histories of Native American writing by a reputable scholar. Includes some discussion of McNickle.

SWALLOW BARN
Or, A Sojourn in the Old Dominion

Type of work: Novel
Author: John Pendleton Kennedy (1795-1870)
Type of plot: Social realism
Time of plot: Early nineteenth century
Locale: Virginia
First published: 1832

Principal characters:
> MARK LITTLETON, the narrator
> NED HAZARD, his cousin
> FRANK MERIWETHER, Ned's brother-in-law
> MR. ISAAC TRACY, a gentleman farmer
> BEL TRACY, his daughter
> HARVEY RIGGS, a Tracy kinsman

The Story:

After receiving many invitations from his cousin Ned Hazard, Mark Littleton at last felt that he could no longer put off a visit to Virginia. He left his mother and sisters in New York and began his journey south. At Swallow Barn, his cousin's home, Mark met or renewed acquaintance with a great many relatives and friends. Ned Hazard's sister had married Frank Meriwether, who was now the head of the family. The estate had been left to Ned. It had been heavily encumbered, and Frank had paid off the heaviest debts and put the plantation on a paying basis. The house was filled with Meriwether and Hazard relatives, all permanent guests. Some performed small functions as a pretense of paying their own way, but their tasks were no more than token duties kindly thought up for them so that they would feel useful.

Mark found life in Virginia restful and pleasant, for there was an unhurried rhythm about Swallow Barn that appealed to him. The plantation was filled with slaves and freed blacks who were fiercely loyal to Frank, a good master. Indeed, everyone loved Frank for his thoughtfulness and generosity. Mark's special favorite, however, was his cousin Ned Hazard. The two young men were inseparable companions. Ned was a man of excellent spirits, always indulging in pranks and jokes. Swallow Barn would one day revert to him, but he was content to let Frank use it as his own, wanting only to have a good time without the need of responsibilities. Ned took Mark on several excursions around the countryside and introduced him to local beauties of nature.

While Ned and Mark walked through the woods one day, they indulged in one of their favorite pastimes by singing their loudest, each trying to outdo the other. In one verse, Ned called out the name of Bel Tracy. He was deeply chagrined when that lady, having ridden up unnoticed, answered him. Bel Tracy was the daughter of old Isaac Tracy, master of the neighboring estate, The Brakes. Ned's confusion at being discovered by Bel made Mark think that his cousin felt more than friendship for her. She teased him gently about his boisterous use of her name, leaving Ned stammering in confusion. Bel was accompanied by her sister and Harvey Riggs, a Tracy kinsman. Harvey joined in the teasing, but Mark saw at once that it was good-natured teasing and that Harvey felt great friendship for Ned.

The two parties went back to Swallow Barn, where Harvey delivered a letter from Mr. Tracy to Frank Meriwether. The subject matter was of long standing, and it afforded Frank some amusement. For many years, Mr. Tracy had imagined himself in possession of one hundred acres of marshlands separating The Brakes from Swallow Barn. Every court in Virginia had denied his claim, but the old gentleman was adamant. Frank would long since have given him the land, for it was worthless, but he knew the old gentleman would be lost without the affair, which provided him with mental activity as he plotted ways to get possession of the land. In his letter, Mr. Tracy suggested that he and Frank let their lawyers go over the matter again, the two disputants to abide by the legal decision. Frank planned to ask his lawyer to arrange matters so that Mr. Tracy would win the suit after what looked like a difficult legal maneuver.

Old Mr. Tracy was a detriment to Ned, even though Ned loved the old gentleman. He was a gentleman of the old school, dignified and sober; Ned, on the other hand, could not repress his merry spirits. Bel, however, had absorbed some of her father's dignity and was usually not very receptive to Ned's foolishness. The poor young man tried hard to change, but his disposition was almost as firm as Mr. Tracy's.

After Ned had admitted to Mark that he loved Bel, the two friends mapped out a campaign to win her heart to Ned's cause. Their plans were temporarily postponed, however, by the arrival of the lawyers who would decide the disputed land claim. The legal gentlemen afforded the young men much entertainment, one being a dandy known throughout Virginia. He was pursued by two of the maiden relatives, each of whom pretended to be pursued by him. When the dandy learned of their intentions, he finished his business and departed as quickly as possible. The settling of the suit gave everyone but old Mr. Tracy a lot of amusement. Ned was serious about the whole matter, so he lost more ground in his suit when he unwittingly made light of the affair. It took a great deal of clever legal terminology to fool the old man, but at last he was awarded the land and convinced that justice had been done.

Sometimes Ned, Mark, and the others found entertainment in listening to the tales of goblins and ghosts told by old slaves on the plantation. The two families frequently gave large dinner parties, when the whole community would be invited to come and spend the day. Mark, thinking he would find it hard ever to return to New York and his own family, hoped to stay long enough to help Ned in his courtship of Bel. At one of the parties, Ned had a little wine and became more boisterous than ever, causing Bel to lose the esteem she had gradually been developing for him. He gained her good will once more by finding her pet falcon which had flown away, but later he lost her affection by engaging in a fistfight with a town bully. Harvey Riggs, joining Mark in attempts to help Ned with his suit, told Bel that Ned had fought the bully because the ruffian had cast slurs on her father. Pity at last entered Bel's heart, and she treated her suitor with more favor.

Mark at last left Virginia and went home to New York. Some months later, he learned that Ned had been successful; Bel had married him on New Year's Day. Ned wrote, too, that it was as Frank had feared. Old Mr. Tracy was sorry the land suit was settled and wished to open it again. Without the pending suit, he felt like a man who had lost an old and faithful friend.

Critical Evaluation:

Although John Pendleton Kennedy states definitely that *Swallow Barn* is not a novel, it is usually listed as such because of the continuous theme running through it. In reality the book is a series of sketches or dramatic episodes concerned with plantation life and manners in Virginia during the early eighteenth century, sketches held together by a continuity of characters and events. *Swallow Barn*, the first work of popular fiction to be set in Virginia, was the forerunner of a large number of novels dealing with the historic background of that state.

Had Kennedy approached literature as a profession rather than an avocation, he might have become one of America's most important nineteenth century writers; but he felt his first obligation was to his career, initially as a lawyer in Baltimore, where his second marriage allied him firmly to the business community, and, subsequently, in the face of growing political and sectional unrest, as a man of public affairs, serving terms in the Maryland House of Delegates, the United States House of Representatives, and as the secretary of the Navy. In between legal, business, and political commitments, he managed to write three very different novels: *Swallow Barn*; *Horse-Shoe Robinson* (1835), a historical novel about the Revolutionary War in South Carolina; and *Rob of the Bowl* (1838), a "Cavalier Romance" of Colonial Maryland. In addition, he wrote numerous essays, satires, and miscellaneous writings.

For all his lightness of touch, Kennedy had very serious motives in the writing of all of his literary efforts, especially in *Swallow Barn*. Having become progressively alarmed by the growing national tension and disunity, Kennedy hoped that this realistic, yet sympathetic portrait of Southern society might foster harmony by stimulating understanding.

In its own time, *Swallow Barn* was highly praised for its realism, but Kennedy's vision of Virginia seems romanticized; indeed, the book's primary interest for a modern reader lies in the fact that it was the novel in which the myth of the old plantation South was first fictionalized. This atmosphere of serenity and pastoral elegance, described with affectionate, gentle, and humorous irony, is based on a fixed, secure society without major social or political problems. In *Swallow Barn*, the most serious issue revolves around how to give away one hundred worthless acres in a manner that will not hurt the recipient's feelings. This uncomplicated vision of things was not, as Kennedy freely admitted, an unbiased one. The author carefully keeps the conflicts in the background—but he also makes sure they are there.

The primary conflict was the issue of slavery. The slaves at Swallow Barn and The Brakes conform to the plantation myth stereotype; they are well-treated, contented, amusing, and affectionate. At the same time, Kennedy acknowledges the basic injustice of the system. Far from being a Southern apologist, he was a mild abolitionist, considering slavery to be both immoral and inefficient. He remained a Unionist throughout the Civil War. As a Southerner living in the midst of the situation, however, he saw and felt the complexity of the issue, and probably expressed his own sentiments through Frank Meriwether, who stated that it is wrong to keep slaves, but that it would be equally wrong to "whelm them in greater evils than their present bondage." To his own personal sorrow, Kennedy lived to see the worst of his expectations realized.

Bibliography:
Bohner, Charles H. "Virginia Revisited." In *John Pendleton Kennedy: Gentleman from Baltimore*. Baltimore: The Johns Hopkins University Press, 1961. Discussion of Washington Irving's influence upon this collection of sketches, which accurately portray early nineteenth century domestic life in Virginia. The Southern plantation romance began with *Swallow Barn*, but Kennedy's partial detachment from Virginia society allowed objectivity and irony.
Gwathmey, Edward M. *John Pendleton Kennedy*. Nashville: Thomas Nelson, 1931. Evaluation of Kennedy's strengths—descriptions, close observation of human nature, thoroughly grounded philosophical conclusions, and a wholesome view of life. Argues that Kennedy inaccurately records slave dialect but succeeds as a pioneer in regional fiction, presenting one of the earliest and most accurate portrayals of Virginia plantation life.
Hubbell, Jay B., ed. Introduction to *Swallow Barn: Or, A Sojourn in the Old Dominion*, by John Pendleton Kennedy. New York: Harcourt Brace Jovanovich, 1929. Discusses *Swallow Barn*

in its historical context—a transition period in which Virginia society was disordered by the American Revolution but not yet frightened by Nat Turner's slave insurrection.

Ridgely, Joseph Vincent. *John Pendleton Kennedy*. New York: Twayne, 1966. A chapter on *Swallow Barn* discusses its structure and style, including excerpts from nineteenth century reviews. Although true to Virginia life, *Swallow Barn* employs stock devices and literary sources. Kennedy's growing ambivalence toward the South precluded the possibility of a sequel.

Tomlinson, David O. "John Pendleton Kennedy." In *Fifty Southern Writers Before 1900: A Bio-Bibliographical Sourcebook*, edited by Robert Bain and Joseph M. Flora. Westport, Conn.: Greenwood Press, 1987. Discusses major themes and surveys criticism. Argues that Kennedy was a nationalist who feared disunion and combined his intended satire with affection for his characters and dismay at some Virginia social customs.

THE SWISS FAMILY ROBINSON

Type of work: Novel
Author: Johann David Wyss (1743-1818) and Johann Rudolf Wyss (1782-1830)
Type of plot: Adventure
Time of plot: Late eighteenth century
Locale: An island near New Guinea
First published: Der Schweizerische Robinson, 1812-1827 (English translation, 1814, 1818, 1820)

Principal characters:
MR. ROBINSON, a shipwrecked Swiss gentleman
MRS. ROBINSON, his wife
FRITZ,
ERNEST,
JACK, and
FRANCIS, their sons
EMILY MONTROSE, a shipwrecked English girl

The Story:

Of all the passengers and crew on board the ship, only the Robinson family was saved when the vessel broke apart on a reef and the crew and other passengers jumped into lifeboats without waiting for the little family to join them. As the ship tossed about, the father prayed that God would spare them. There was plenty of food on board, and after they had eaten the boys went to sleep, leaving the father and the mother to guard them.

In the morning their first concern was to get to the island they could see beyond the reef. With much effort, they constructed a vessel out of tubs. After they had filled the tubs with food and ammunition and all other articles of value they could safely carry, they rowed toward the island. Two dogs from the ship swam beside them, and the boys were glad they would have pets when they reached their new home.

Their first task on reaching the island was to erect a tent of sailcloth they had brought from the ship. They gathered moss and dried it so that they would have some protection from the ground when they slept. They were able to find a lobster and to shoot some game and thus to add fresh food to their supplies. Since they had no utensils for eating, they used shells for spoons, all dipping out of the iron kettle which they had brought from the ship. They had released some geese and pigeons while they were still on the ship and had brought two hens and two cocks with them. The father knew that they must prepare for a long time on the island, and his thoughts were as much on provisions for the future as for their immediate wants.

The father and Fritz, the oldest son, spent the next day exploring the island. They found gourds from which they would make dishes and spoons, and many edible fruits and roots. Coconuts, growing in abundance, provided a treat for the mother and the younger boys. Fritz captured a small monkey, which he took back for a pet. The younger boys were enchanted with the mischievous little animal.

The Robinsons spent the next few days securing themselves against hunger and danger from wild animals. The father and Fritz made several trips to the ship in their efforts to bring ashore everything that they could possibly use. The domesticated animals on the ship were towed back to the island. There was also a great store of firearms and ammunition, hammocks for sleeping, carpenter's tools, lumber, cooking utensils, silverware, and dishes.

While the father and Fritz were salvaging these supplies, the mother and the younger boys were working on the shore, sowing seeds, examining the contents of the kegs which floated to shore, and in every way possible making the tent a more livable home. The mother and boys also explored the island to find a spot for a more permanent home. When the father and Fritz could join them, the whole family helped to construct a tree house which would give them protection from wild animals that they feared might dwell on the island.

Through the following weeks, each day brought a new adventure of some kind. There were encounters with wild birds and terrifying animals. Ernest, the second son, had studied nature with great interest before their ill-fated voyage, and he identified many of the animals and birds. They found some food that they considered luxuries—sugarcane, honey, potatoes, and spices. They fenced in a secluded area for their cattle so that they might have a constant supply of milk and fresh meat. Several new dwellings were constructed to provide homes on all sides of the island. The father found a tree that contained long threads, and after he had constructed a loom, the mother was able to weave cloth for new clothing. Jack and Francis, the younger boys, contributed to the welfare of the family by helping their mother to care for the animals and thresh the grain grown from seeds brought from the ship.

Many times the little band found their labor destroyed by uncontrollable forces. Goats ate the bark off young fruit trees they had planted; monkeys robbed their food stores frequently; and jackals and serpents killed some of their pets. Nevertheless, the family was not too discouraged, for they knew that they had been very fortunate to be saved on an island that provided food and shelter in such abundance.

About a year later they discovered a cave, which became a home and a storage place for their supplies. The cave protected them from the rains, and their supplies were safe from intruders. They spent many enjoyable evenings reading books they salvaged from the ship. The father and mother had found a way to make candles from the sap of a native tree. Altogether, their lives were agreeable and happy, and each morning and evening they thanked God for his goodness.

Ten years passed. The boys had become young men, and Fritz often sailed long distances in the canoe he had constructed. One day he captured a wounded albatross and found attached to it a note, written in English, asking someone to help an English girl who was in a cave near a volcano. The father and Fritz decided that Fritz must try to find her without telling the rest of the family of the note or the proposed search. Fritz, successful in his search, found a girl, Emily Montrose, who had also been shipwrecked as she was sailing from India to her home in England. The members of the Robinson family accepted Emily as a daughter and a sister who was able to help the mother in her duties and give the boys much joy with her stories of life in India. Her own mother was dead. Emily had lived in India with her father, an army officer, who had sailed back to England on a different ship. She knew he would be worried about her, but there was no way for her to communicate with him.

One morning, a few months later, the castaways were astonished to hear the sound of three cannon shots. Not knowing whether the sound came from a friendly ship or from a pirate vessel, they loaded their small boat with firearms and sailed out to investigate. There they found an English ship that had been driven off course by a storm. It was impossible for this ship to take Emily back to England, but the captain promised to notify her father and to send a ship back for her. A captain, his wife, and two children, who were on board, were so enchanted with the island that they asked to be allowed to stay. It seemed as if a little colony would grow there.

Six months later the ship sent by Emily's father arrived. Fritz and Francis had a great longing to see their homeland again, and since they were now mature young men, their mother and father allowed them to return with Emily. Before he left, Fritz told his father that he loved Emily and intended to ask her father's permission to propose marriage to her. The Robinsons, who loved Emily dearly, gave their blessing to their son.

The father had prepared a manuscript relating their adventures and gave it to Fritz before the boy sailed, in the hope that their story might be of interest to the rest of the world. The father and mother wanted to spend their remaining days on the island. Now that their island was known, commerce would begin and a colony could grow there. The father prayed that the little colony would increase in prosperity and piety and would continue to deserve and receive the blessings of the merciful God who had cared for them all so tenderly in the past.

Critical Evaluation:

The Swiss Family Robinson has remained extraordinarily popular. In its various translations, editions, adaptations, and shortened versions, it has continued to delight a child audience, despite the fact that it has never been highly regarded as a work of literature. This delight is carried principally by the work's adventure, beginning with the exciting shipwreck and removal to the island, and continuing through the exploration of the island, the establishment of the two children-pleasing homes in a treehouse and in a cave, and the battles with boa constrictors and lions, among other beasts.

The delight is perpetuated as various characters go out to explore and generally come upon some astonishing and unexpected adventure. In addition, the ingenuity of the family, both in the face of these adventures and the desperate situation in which they find themselves, forms much of the satisfaction of the novel. Do wild animals threaten? Build a tree house. Is the vine ladder too unsteady? Build a staircase within the trunk of the hollowed tree. Is the treehouse unsuitable for the rainy season? Discover a vast cave with the added bonus of an unlimited source of rock salt. The pattern of a problem followed by an ingenious solution forms much of the novel.

A second thing is suggested by the many versions of *The Swiss Family Robinson*: There is a discomfort with the text. This seems to have been felt by its authors, for an early French translator was allowed to change the ending and add some of her own episodes. Since its first publication, the text has been so added to and altered that it is difficult to speak of a definitive text.

The problem is that much of what occurs on the island is simply ludicrous. The island seems to be blessed with animals from all over the globe, ripped out of their natural habitats and placed on the island for the benefit of the Robinson family. Tigers, found only in Asia, romp with kangaroos, found only in Australia. Elephants sport with walruses, while on the shores flamingoes trot beside penguins. Though the father claims he is no naturalist, he can identify and name the properties—as well as give the Latin name—of every plant and animal they come across, and there are plenty. On the novel's island animals have young although they seem to have no mate; dogs can change instincts in the flick of an eye, one moment tearing a monkey apart, the next allowing its young to ride its back; and albatrosses can act as carrier pigeons. These problems and the coincidence that concludes the book make the story difficult to accept.

There are other difficulties. Much of the book is heavily didactic and pious; it seems that the father cannot speak without reference to a moral aphorism. This is not so true with the boys. While it is perfectly natural for real piety to play a role in the life of a religious family, the pious lines that flow from the father quickly become formulaic. From a literary standpoint there are more difficulties. The dialogue is stilted and unnatural, so that even an attack by a tiger is told in cold and dispassionate prose. The characters show little change or growth, this despite ten years on the island. They never change in their relationships to one another, nor do the boys ever seem to mature. The narrative pace is halting and jerky; it is usually the case that no one scene or adventure develops beyond itself. One wishes for a single narrative thread, fully developed.

It may be argued, however, that the episodic nature of the book and its halting pace are intended to simulate a journal form. In fact, the father sends the manuscript back to Europe with Fritz to be published as a journal of their time on the island. The didactic and pious passages, it might be further argued, are to underscore the principal point of the book: that people are to lead industrious and productive lives, living in harmony with one another (particularly families) and with God. The Robinsons set about establishing a peaceable kingdom. In short, New Switzerland becomes a kind of Eden, where all needs are provided for, where all live in harmony, and where there is enough difficulty and danger to make life interesting. Certainly this last element dominates thematically.

A modern reader may be troubled in more ways than one by the book's manner of presenting its theme. One may ask if the island, so rich in natural resources, could be so conveniently free of a native population. A modern reader may also be put off by the slaughter of animals— a walrus (visiting, perhaps, from colder climes) is killed so that its head can adorn a canoe, and a platypus killed because it is such an oddity. There is a strong implication that the industrious and devout family is deservedly rewarded with not only provisions but also a security and harmony. This security and harmony lead the parents to decide to stay on the island for the rest of their lives. This is not to say that they despise Europe—Fritz and Franz go back to make their way, their trunks filled with pearls and spices to start them out in the world of commerce—but they certainly see the island as a kind of utopia, and they see no need to go searching for what they have already found.

Still, the story of a family struggling to survive on a deserted island continues to capture the imaginations of readers. There continues to be a place in children's literature for a story about a loving and pious family working together in harmony in order to bring about a good life for themselves.

"Critical Evaluation" by Gary D. Schmidt

Bibliography:
Bashore, J. Robert. "Daniel Defoe." In *Writers for Children: Critical Studies of Major Authors Since the Seventeenth Century*, edited by Jane Bingham. New York: Charles Scribner's Sons, 1987. A comparison of *The Swiss Family Robinson* to *Robinson Crusoe* (1719), examining the enduring appeal of each to a young readership.
Fisher, Margery. *Who's Who in Children's Books*. New York: Holt, Rinehart and Winston, 1975. In a short entry, Fisher argues that rather than being simply a series of loosely connected episodes, the novel is a depiction of a natural and accustomed piety within a family context.
Glaenzer, Richard Butler. "The Swiss Family Robinson." *Bookman* 34 (1911): 139-142. Focusing on the causes for the enduring appeal of this story, Glaenzer argues that the Wysses made the novel enjoyable despite a serious purpose: to instruct his children. He did this through emphasizing a good-natured rivalry among four young boys, thus dealing with the serious business of life in an engaging way.
Loxley, Diana. *Problematic Shores: The Literature of Islands*. London: Macmillan, 1992. A study of the nineteenth century successors to Defoe, looking at the connections between children's books and imperialism, as well as the depiction of childhood innocence by means of empty islands.

SYBIL
Or, The Two Nations

Type of work: Novel
Author: Benjamin Disraeli (1804-1881)
Type of plot: Political realism
Time of plot: 1837-1843
Locale: London and the north of England
First published: 1845

Principal characters:
SYBIL GERARD, a young woman
CHARLES EGREMONT, younger brother to Lord Marney, a member of
    Parliament
LORD MARNEY, a wealthy landowner
LADY DELORAINE, his mother
WALTER GERARD, Sybil's father, a Chartist leader
STEPHEN MORLEY, a Chartist and editor
BAPTIST HATTON, an antiquarian
"BISHOP" HATTON, his brother, a locksmith
DEVILSDUST, one of the people of Mowbray
MICK RADLEY "DANDY MICK," his friend
JOHN TROTMAN "CHAFFING JACK," an innkeeper
LORD DE MOWBRAY, supposed lord of Mowbray Castle
MR. ST. LYS, vicar of Mowbray
MR. TRAFFORD, a manufacturer, Gerard's employer
URSULA TRAFFORD, Lady Superior of Mowbray Convent, sister to
    Trafford and mentor to Sybil

The Story:

In the spring of 1837, the Reform Bill had been passed five years before, and the king, William IV, was dying. A new election was called as the youthful Queen Victoria ascended the throne. One of the new Conservative Party members of Parliament was Charles Egremont, younger brother of Lord Marney. Their mother, Lady Marney, had set up her son's election and helped to defray some expenses. Egremont asked his brother to defray the rest.

While visiting the ruins of Marney Abbey, Egremont met two unusual men, Walter Gerard and Stephen Morley, and heard Gerard's daughter, Sybil, sing. Although only brief, the meeting made a deep impression on him. Egremont, with other family members, then went to visit Mowbray Castle, the home of the de Mowbrays. Lord Marney wanted his brother to marry Lady Joan, heiress to the rich estates, thus solving Egremont's financial problems. Egremont hardly noticed her.

The castle stood just outside Mowbray, a large manufacturing town in the north of England. The wretched life and amusements of the working people contrasted with the high life of the castle. The only link was Mr. St. Lys, the reforming vicar of Mowbray, himself the younger son of aristocracy.

Egremont had become interested in the political views of Gerard and Morley, who lived just outside Mowbray, and he wished to see the real living conditions of the people. Visiting Warner, an impoverished handloom weaver, with St. Lys, Egremont met Sybil, who regularly engaged in acts of charity out of Mowbray Convent.

On the Marneys' return home, the two brothers had a terrible argument about expenses and Marney's wife. Egremont walked out and, Parliament being in recess, rented a cottage near Gerard and took on the alias of Mr. Franklin, so that he could more easily hold lengthy discussions with Gerard, Morley, and Sybil. He also visited a nearby model factory run by the Traffords who, like the Gerards, were Roman Catholics. Morley's and Gerard's views were widely different even though both were active Chartists (a working-class movement for political reform). They were both also interested in pursuing certain claims to the Mowbray estates, and were seeking a Mr. Baptist Hatton, an antiquarian, whose previous research had unearthed some evidence that the Gerards were the rightful owners. Morley discovered Hatton's brother in a lawless manufacturing area called Wodgate.

Egremont was then recalled to London by his mother's remarriage to Lord Deloraine. Parliament sat but remained deadlocked. The Chartists marched to London to present their petition to Parliament and to hold an alternative assembly. Gerard had been elected a delegate with Morley, and brought Sybil with him to the capital. Various chance meetings took place: Morley discovered Baptist Hatton, now grown wealthy, but who was willing to take up Gerard's claims again. Morley and Gerard called on Egremont and recognized him as Franklin. Egremont also met Sybil on a separate encounter. The recognition of Egremont put a distance between him and his former friends, as did his disagreement with their political views. Even so, Egremont declared his love for Sybil. She rejected him, declaring that the difference in class was unbridgeable and citing her desire to be a nun.

The Charter was finally presented to Parliament but was met with little interest or debate. Some disillusioned Chartists rioted in Birmingham, and the government determined to clamp down. Egremont learned of the dangers to the Chartist leaders still left in London and warned Sybil, and she her father, but too late. Both were arrested. Egremont obtained her release, but her father was eventually sent to prison at York for eighteen months. Morley had declared his love for Sybil. Even Baptist Hatton saw Sybil as a future wife, especially if the Gerard claims were substantiated. The vital evidence for this was locked up in Mowbray Castle, it was discovered.

An economic depression followed. Factories closed or put their workers on short-time. In Lancashire there were widespread strikes. In Mowbray, two of the activists, Devilsdust and Dandy Mick, had joined trades unions and helped plan a national strike. In nearby Wodgate, "Bishop" Hatton was converted to Chartism and immediately began a crusade, marching on Mowbray with his workers. The Mowbray people joined them, closing down the factories, including Trafford's, though only after a confrontation in which Gerard, now released from prison, acted as mediator.

Hatton and Morley were at the scene, and through Devilsdust and Dandy Mick, directed the mob's attention to Mowbray Castle. While it was being attacked, Lord Marney's yeomanry, setting out to quell the mob, met Gerard leading a quiet demonstration. Marney acted in a high-handed manner; Gerard was killed, and in the ensuing melee, Marney also. Another group of yeomanry, led by Egremont, retook Mowbray Castle, though not before the vital documents had been seized. Although Morley was also killed, Mick took the documents to the nearby convent to be given to Sybil. She, meanwhile, having previously gone to the castle, helped save its inhabitants before being trapped by the rioters. Egremont dashed in to save her.

In a final scene, Egremont, now Lord Marney, married Sybil, whose claim to the Mowbray estates had been proved. Devilsdust and Dandy Mick had been set up in business and were about to prosper.

Critical Evaluation:

Sybil: Or, The Two Nations has been described as "one of few examples of the truly political novel," and is certainly one of the few novels to be written by a future British prime minister. It was written at a crucial time for both political debate over the social condition of a newly industrialized Britain, and for the development of the English novel. Benjamin Disraeli believed that fiction could be used as a means of transmitting political ideas; in doing this, he extended the limits of the novel form, creating a new genre of social comment and finding new ways to document social conditions.

At the time of writing, Disraeli represented a reform element within the British Conservative Party, dubbed "young England" (a reference perhaps to the novel's closing remark: "It is the past alone that can explain the present, and it is youth that alone can mould the remedial future.") In the novel, Disraeli depicts a Parliament marked out by interparty bickering, pettiness, personal ambition, and lack of leadership. Its most serious failure is the failure to respond to Chartism, a popular movement to reform the democratic system of the country. With the accession of a young queen, Disraeli hoped that new parliamentarians would arise and put forward reforming legislation to avert the most serious consequences of a disunited country and an oppressive economic system.

Sybil: Or, The Two Nations is, in many ways, a deeply reactionary novel. It constantly returns to the Middle Ages for its social models, creating a medieval sense of race and of class (monarchy, aristocracy of various degrees, the church, and the people). Its plea to a revitalized aristocracy to take up its leadership role reflects a doctrine of social paternalism. This doctrine is also to be found in other contemporary writers, such as Thomas Carlyle (*Chartism*, 1840) and Arthur Helps (*Claims of Labour*, 1844), and even, to an extent, in Charles Dickens. Mr. St. Lys and Mr. Trafford are clear examples of such paternalism. Egremont's political awakening stands in contrast to the political views of his brother, who represents the decayed old order. His death and the burning of Mowbray Castle symbolize the end of the old order.

Disraeli does reveal serious ambivalence. His depiction of the aristocracy, one of the best literary features of the book, and a skill derived from his earlier "silver fork" novels, suggests strongly the unreformable nature of the aristocracy, whose position rests largely, it would seem, on past social pretension, fraud, and intrigue. Baptist Hatton's efforts to restore the Gerards is seen as typically amoral. A similar ambivalence marks Disraeli's attitude to Roman Catholicism. Coming from a Jewish background, he rejects Catholic claims to authority, since they fail to recognize the priority of the Old Testament in the fabric of Christianity as "fulfilled Judaism." On the other hand, his reactionary medievalism sees the medieval Catholic church with its care for the people as ideal Christian practice, contrasted with the present Church of England, which has become merely a part of the political system and moribund structures. Sybil's Catholicism is never criticized, though her desire to become a nun is.

The novel, dealing largely with political ideas, also depicts current events (for example, the presentation of the Charter to Parliament), and the social conditions prevalent in both town and country in the North. Degrading living and working conditions make for a degraded populace, whether such populace is controlled by capitalists (as in Mowbray) or by free association (as in Wodgate). Disraeli considers Morley's radicalism, and the trades unions, dangerous, because they rely on leadership from the people, a leadership the people are incapable of giving, and because the radicalism is secular and denies the past. In many ways, Disraeli's opinions are prophetic.

As a novelist, Disraeli makes heavy demands on his reader. Not only is his style high-flown, balanced, and antithetical, but his plot is also often melodramatic, episodic, and loose, full of subplots that go nowhere. The reader also has to support long passages of authorial comment on British history and institutions, most of which are out of reach for modern readers. Even as a historical documentary, there are gaping omissions; for example, there is no discussion on the Factory Acts or the Labor laws. The Reform Bill is treated superficially; liberal and radical views are given short shrift. Despite its shortcomings, the novel really was, in itself, a historical event, and the author's political commitment to a united society provides a dynamic that engages the reader's intellectual attention.

David Barratt

Bibliography:
Braun, Thom. *Disraeli the Novelist*. Winchester, Mass.: Allen & Unwin, 1981. Concentrates on Disraeli's career as a novelist rather than as a politician. It seeks to reconstruct his life through his novels and to show his development as a novelist. Chapter 5 particularly relates *Sybil: Or, The Two Nations* to the political events in Disraeli's life.
Cazamian, Louis. *The Social Novel in England, 1830-1850*. Translated by Martin Fido. Boston: Routledge and Kegan Paul, 1973. Cazamian's book is the classic study of the subject. *Sybil: Or, The Two Nations* is fully treated along with Disraeli's other two social novels. Bibliography and index.
Gallagher, Catherine. *The Industrial Reformation of English Fiction: Social Discourse and Narrative Form, 1832-1867*. Chicago: University of Chicago Press, 1985. Surveys the whole field of the industrial novel, with an excellent introductory discussion of "The Condition of England" question. Chapter 8 deals extensively with *Sybil: Or, The Two Nations*. Notes, bibliography, index.
Ridley, Jane. *The Young Disraeli, 1804-1846*. London: Sinclair-Stevenson, 1995. A recent biography, and one of the most objective. It draws extensively from letters and papers, and demonstrates clearly that although Egremont may represent Disraeli's political views, in no way does he represent Disraeli's actual life.
Schwarz, Daniel R. *Disraeli's Fiction*. New York: Barnes & Noble Books, 1979. Seeks to establish Disraeli's skill and importance as a novelist, and that writing fiction actually helped form Disraeli's character.

TALA

Type of work: Poetry
Author: Gabriela Mistral (Lucila Godoy Alcayaga, 1889-1957)
First published: 1938

For fear of losing her job as a schoolteacher in provincial Chile, Lucila Godoy Alcayaga used the pseudonym Gabriela Mistral. Her writings include poetry, stories, criticism—political and literary—and numerous prose pieces, many of them political enough to have attracted unwelcome fame. Never having had children of her own, she made an international reputation early in her career with elegant poems about children and motherhood. As a teacher, she devoted a significant portion of her life to young students, who included, informally, a teenager named Ricardo Reyes, who would receive, as she did, a Nobel Prize in Literature. His pen-name was Pablo Neruda.

Tala was the third of four collections that Mistral published in her lifetime. *Tala* means "felling," as in the felling of trees; the title has also been translated as *Devastation*. The modest volume's proceeds went to the benefit of orphans displaced by the Spanish Civil War. This gesture was typical of Mistral, particularly so considering how strongly her poetry speaks to the nurturing of children. At the same time, her work was by turns emotional, visionary, and possessed by a sensuality that in part may account for her desire to separate her life as a poet from her life as a teacher.

By the time *Tala* was published, Mistral had seen much more of the world as a diplomat and education consultant than she had when her first book appeared in 1922. Mistral's deep interests in children and the mystic qualities of nature remain a key element of her third collection, but the intensity of anguish that distinguished much of her previous work gives way, in *Tala*, to a more controlled sense of observation. This is not to suggest any lack of maturity in her early work, only that with *Tala*, the reader encounters an older, widely traveled poet who has come to more comfortable terms with the tragic events of life. There is an undeniable emotional drive to these poems, but the reader will find a noticeably heightened sense of the poet's journalistic eye. The collection conveys a sense of the somewhat ethereal atmosphere of life on the South American landscape. In "Riches," Mistral writes:

> I have an abiding bliss
> and a lost fortune,
> one like a rose,
> the other like a thorn.

There is a touch of autobiography here, pointing to the devastating loss she suffered as a young woman in love with a man who committed suicide. Mistral's poems often deal with her grief over Romelio Ureta's death. Here, the poet's grief is merely implied, offered more as the memory of an emotion than the emotion itself. The poet has attained the necessary distance from the tragedy to be able to apply her art to it in new ways. Earlier poems on the subject deal with recent wounds, the poet now looks at old scars. All likelihood seems to have been that Ureta and Mistral would have married and had the family the poet longed for all of her life. Mistral never did marry, creating for herself a surrogate family in every community she joined as a teacher or diplomat.

"Riches" is a brief, imagistic lyric that considers the inadvertent exchange, as it were, of the conventional family she had anticipated for the unconventional one she found. There is surely pain in this poem, but it is pain in retrospect:

> I am rich with purple and with melancholy.
> Oh, how beloved is the rose,
> and what a lover, the thorn!

The direct statement of her grief in Mistral's earlier work is here given over to sensory image.

"Grace" is an example of the type of work for which Mistral earned "visionary" as one of the many honorable adjectives commonly ascribed to her work. Once again, the poem's primary vehicle of expression is the image. The speaker's acute awareness of the senses seeks the reader's appeal on an affective level rather than an intellectual one. Sensory experience is made palpable; the poet shares a deceptively simple epiphany, without explanation or analysis. The reader is led to feel the poet's experience through images that appear almost surreal:

> A dappled bird,
> a bird like jasper
> went rainbow
> wild
> through the carriage
> of the air.
>
> This same early
> morning,
> the river passed by
> like a lance.
> The pure and clear
> aurora remained
> dazzling
> with the wind's perfume.

The notion of grace is taken as a natural choreography, perfect and perfectly random, following the graceful, seemingly visible turns of the passing air. The wind is akin to the river, currents of natural power and beauty to which the poet is bound yet distanced from. The speaker surveys the scene in solitude, while the rest of the village sleeps. In her small revelation, the poet is similarly distant from her community. In the moment of the poem, she is part member, part outsider of both environment and society.

Mistral undertakes a surprising description of air channeled into form as wind, which then collapses back into formlessness as it reaches the open sky. The speaker:

> remained trembling
> on uncertain ground,
> my good news
> swept away!

"The Air Flower" bears a very similar quality, although its discursive and confessional content is more extensive than that of "Grace." There is a dialogue between the poem's speaker and the subject of the title, in which the air flower makes a series of demands:

> Climb the mountain.
> I never leave the meadow.

> Cut the snow white flowers,
> the tough and tender ones;
> make them mine."

After her climb and search, the speaker returns with her quarry, to which the benignly imperious air flower seems to be blind. She calls for "only red flowers" next, and the speaker complies, searching through a landscape that is lush but steep, and makes for arduous searching. After the yellow flowers come the colorless, or "colored like sleep and dreams." This is the most difficult request of all. The colorless flowers cannot be found in the usual places, and the resourceful speaker must harvest them out of the air.

When this final request has been fulfilled, the poet returns with her blossoms of air and addresses the air flower figure as Queen. The Queen is now no longer bound to the meadow, moving past her servant as a sleepwalker. She subsequently follows the Queen through life, continually plucking blossoms from the air in her wake. Mistral herself characterized this poem as "my adventure with poetry." It is not surprising to find her view of her own pursuit of poetry to be an adventure in sensory experience. For Mistral, or at least for her poetry, all experience is tied to an undercurrent of natural force. "The Air Flower" raises this undercurrent to the surface, and as in "Grace," the unseen is given shape.

Consistent with Mistral's visual sense of the invisible is a strong sense of location, most often created without relying on the explicit naming of places or landmarks. Each of these poems exhibits this quality, as do "The Escape," "Confession," and "Things." "Things" considers what the poet left behind when she began her nomadic career some fourteen years before *Tala* was published. She considers

> the things I never had,
> along with others
> that I no longer possess.

It is difficult not to see this as a reference to the children Mistral never had, but it is just as readily possible to again feel even the most subliminal sense of the poet's distance, both emotional and geographical, from the land she loved and left behind.

Mistral's list of things includes the pastures and orchards of her childhood, ". . . happy footsteps/ now foreign," a poem she was taught at the age of seven, and "the perfume of almond trees." She recalls an encompassing scene of early memories claiming dreams as her vehicle. Her awakening is treated as a sort of death to it all, and the poem's closure comes as something of an imagistic last will and testament, in which the poet bequeaths her past to itself.

As much as Mistral loved her homeland, and as important an element as it becomes throughout her work, *Tala* includes departure from her homeland. While she may have prized Chile especially as the cradle of her psyche and imagination, she was a committed lover and keen observer of land, sea, and nature wherever she went. "Caribbean Sea" is a deeply felt song of praise for the beauty of Puerto Rico, but before the poem's conclusion, she calls the island by the name Cordelia, after King Lear's daughter. From there, the poem becomes a longing plea to this northernmost daughter of the Caribbean to save itself:

> Before my feet
> and vision fail me,
> before my skin becomes a fable,
> before my knees
> fly in the wind

The poem is footnoted with its date of composition: Philippine Independence Day.

As a U.S. resident during the Great Depression years, Mistral would have witnessed the political and economic struggles of the poor, for whom her work as a poet expresses a deep concern and sense of kinship. "Caribbean Sea" speaks directly to Puerto Rico. This rhetorical technique, called apostrophe, is a brief departure from her more common practice of describing an unnamed universal location.

It was in 1945 that the Swedish Academy awarded Mistral the Nobel Prize in Literature. She was the first South American writer to achieve this recognition. *Lagar*, the fourth and final collection of poems to appear while she was still living, would not be published for nine more years. Thus, it was on the strength of three collections and her numerous uncollected prose works that she earned this honor. The committee's citation points out the importance the slim, lyrical volume *Tala* had in affirming the value of her relatively small but eminently notable body of work.

Sadly, no complete collection of her work has yet been translated into English, and other examples of her travel-based work must be sought in their original language. The general consensus of critics is that Gabriela Mistral was the poet of mothers and children, a poet of average people, and the first of her generation and country to speak in the idiom of those who interested her most. Many countries and many generations have had their share of poets who wrote in plain language, but precious few have done so with such remarkable craft and elegance.

Jon Lavieri

Bibliography:
Bejar, Alfredo, ed. *Globe Hispanic Biographies*. Englewood Cliffs, N.J.: Globe, 1989. A collection of essay-length biographies, including one of Mistral. Not in depth, but a source for general biographical information on the poet, which is rare.
Mistral, Gabriela. *Gabriela Mistral: A Reader*. Translated by Maria Giachetti, edited by Marjorie Agosín. Fredonia, N.Y.: White Pine Press, 1993. Wide selection of poems from *Tala* in English and perhaps only selection of Mistral's prose. Twenty-eight prose pieces provide a good view of Mistral's range.
Neruda, Pablo. *Memoirs*. Translated by Hardie St. Martin. New York: Farrar, Straus and Giroux, 1977. Neruda includes a section discussing his association with Mistral as his earliest mentor. Although brief, this is perhaps one of the best places to find a portrait of Mistral during the early years of her career as a teacher.
Rosenbaum, Sidonia Carmen. *Modern Women Poets of Spanish America*. Westport, Conn.: Greenwood Press, 1978. Historical perspectives and academic criticism of four poets. One of the more detailed studies of Mistral of the few available in English.

A TALE OF A TUB

Type of work: Satire
Author: Jonathan Swift (1667-1745)
*First published: A Tale of a Tub: To Which Is Added an Account of a Battle Between the
Ancient and Modern Books in St. James's Library; and the Mechanical Operation of
the Spirit,* 1704

Principal characters:
PETER, representing the pope or the Roman Catholic church
MARTIN, representing Martin Luther, hence the Lutheran and Anglican
churches
JACK, representing John Calvin, hence the Calvinist Dissenters

The Story:
A Tale of a Tub has been called the greatest of English satires. The point is debatable, but the
work is surely a most spirited, complex, and amusing contribution to this genre. Jonathan Swift
was also to show his satirical genius in *Gulliver's Travels* (1726) and in his famous essay, "A
Modest Proposal" (1729), advocating the eating of infants.

Satire is written when an author wishes to attack something. Swift spent a lifetime attacking
the pretensions and stupidity of the world around him. His main object in *A Tale of a Tub*, he
said, was to ridicule "the numerous and gross corruptions in religion and learning." These,
readers discover, include pedantic scholars, egoistic critics, fanatic literalists in religion, and
clever theologians. Such people poison society with misapplication of their reasoning powers.

Swift wisely saw to it that his sense of outrage at the religious and scholarly varieties of
human stupidity was complemented throughout by an elevating sense of the comic. The
opening dedication to Lord Somers, for example, shows Swift in one of his contrived comic
poses. In the dedication, engagingly posing as a gullible and naïve bookseller, he satirizes the
excessive praise so prevalent in dedications of the time. The genius of the attempt is the fact
that hyperbole itself is the method he employs.

With the second of the prefatory dedications, Swift's target becomes clearer. Addressing "His
Royal Highness Prince Posterity," Swift makes a great and ironic show of ascribing great wit
and literary achievement to his age. Swift has his tongue quite firmly in cheek in this passage
and implies that the wise one seeks out virtue and value in all ages. Modernity alone has no just
claim; what is new is not necessarily the best. Swift's position, therefore, in the "Battle of the
Books" (an intellectual controversy of his time), tended to favor the ancients or the classics as
opposed to the moderns.

In the subsequent preface, Swift continues with his consummate irony to excoriate the
writers of his time. He explains his title. When seamen meet a whale, they throw out an empty
tub to divert him lest he wreck the ship. If the ship is the ship of state and the whale represents
the vast body of scurrilous and destructive writers and thinkers who "pick holes in the weak
sides of religion and government," then the tale, says Swift, shall serve as a similar decoy for
the wits of the day to attack.

On the surface, Swift's intention and meaning seem plain. He raises the perennial cry against
two swarms of pests: the egoistic poetasters who set themselves up as wits, intellects, and
critics, and the newer philosophers whose theories seem harmful to England's Christian and
constitutional way of life, as in the case of Thomas Hobbes. As a conservative, a good Anglican,
and a defender of the ancients, Swift was understandably angered, but latent in the argument,

as is often the case with sensible Swift, is his recognition that in fact there are flaws in the existing schemes of religion and government: "a great many are hollow, and dry, and empty, and noisy, and wooden." The point here is simply that Swift's satire is distinguished not only by its sharp edge but by its double edge.

Swift proceeds through his preface by calling into play parody, well-turned phrase, artful digression, and mock diffidence—all of these in preparation for the style and method of the treatise itself and all playing harmoniously in one of the world's great symphonies of irony. Eleven sections of the tale proper go before the conclusion. Part 1 is the introduction. With part 2, the tale officially begins, with "Once upon a time. . . . " The tale resumes in sections 4, 6, 8, and 11, with the intervening sections consisting of digressions that are called such. The tale proper contains Swift's satire on abuses in religion; the digressions satirize abuses in learning.

The introduction serves further to establish Swift's pose as a pedantic and prolific scholar. Ironically, he is satirizing pedantry as he laboriously extracts allegories out of simple tales.

Swift's own tale then begins; the reader has been forewarned to observe its own patterns of allegory. The characters involved are three brothers, triplets: Peter, Martin, and Jack. They represent Saint Peter (the Roman Catholic church), Martin Luther (the Church of England, founded as a consequence of the Reformation), and John Calvin (the Dissenters). On his deathbed, their father bequeathed each a simple and durable coat to be worn carefully and never altered. The coat represents the New Testament doctrines of the early Christian Church. When the three brothers decide to become men about town, they need to remodel their coats with shoulder knots, gold lace, silver fringes, and embroidery to be in fashion. Swift focuses his satire on the sophistry and abuses of logic by which clever Peter finds in the father's will a license for these alterations.

Having thus caustically attended to Roman Catholic accretions, Swift now turns to the field of learning in his first digression. This is a biting attack on modern critics, who seek out only the worst in an author and catalog his defects. Swift ironically commends these creatures of prey, pretending to find glorious historical antecedents for their kind.

Returning now, in section 4, to the tale, Swift excoriates various institutions of the Roman Catholic church: purgatory, penance, private confession, holy water, papal bulls, celibacy, relics, and more. He describes each institution with great dignity and seriousness, as Swift here takes an opportunity to blend his satire on religious excesses with his satire on pedantry. Therefore, the focus of the tale is still on Peter, who styles himself Lord Peter and claims precedence over his brothers. Brothers Martin and Jack finally rebel and obtain a copy of their father's will, which made them all equal heirs. Angry Peter forces them from the house where all have been living together. Thus, the allegory recounts the Reformation.

At this high point, nothing could be more inappropriate than a digression; and so with intent the comic Swift presents a digression. With irony, he satirizes the habit of modern writers to expatiate on their own virtues and discoveries while they ridicule the ancients.

Swift records the further adventures of Martin and Jack. Martin carefully removes the fopperies from his coat and manages to get it somewhat back to its original state. Jack, however, with too great zeal, rips off the decorations with such haste that his coat is torn to rags. He envies Martin, and so these two have a disagreement. Thus is allegorized the split between Luther and the less temperate Calvinist reformers. Martin (or the established church in England) represents Swift's ideal or norm, a middle course between Peter's ingenuity and Jack's fanaticism. Swift offers another digression "in praise of digressions." The butt of the satire is the modern writer and his habit of neglecting method, style, good grammar, and originality. Instead, he compiles his mindless writings chiefly by plagiarizing and digression.

Swift returns to the tale proper and invents a fantastic sect of "Aeolists" as he continues his satire of Jack and his followers. They were windworshipers who venerated humanity as a wind-producing machine with outlets at both ends. Swift's satire is addressed against the bombast and energy of Calvinist preachers.

Section 9 is the famous digression on madness, full of dextrous shifts in irony that have endlessly fascinated readers. Swift is continuing his jokes on the theme of wind by suggesting that madness occurs when malign vapors rise from the lower regions of the body to poison the brain. Both good and bad results derive from this distemper: wars, new philosophies, and all striking achievements of the human race. What happens is that one's fancy gets in control of one's reason, and imagination overwhelms common sense.

Swift, an imaginative writer, is not deriding the imagination but its misuse. Swift's argument is that when minute scholarship turns into pedantry, this is evil; but to be content with superficial knowledge is evil as well. Swift slices through the dilemma by cautioning against the most serious error, self-deception. Let one conduct one's life sensibly, understanding the full nature and implications of one's acts. Be neither superficial nor pedantic but intelligent, Swift recommends.

Section 10 blends heavy irony and lighthearted comedy as Swift attacks the hypocrisy and self-regard of modern writers and slyly toys with the reader. With a jab at perverse scholars such as numerologists and cabalists, he returns to his tale proper. In the tale proper, Swift lampoons fanatic, scripture-quoting Calvinists, their doctrine of predestination, their aversion to music in churches, their insistence on simplicity, and their apparent courting of persecution. In short, Jack's increasing whims and affectations make him appear more and more like Peter, much to the dismay of both.

A rambling conclusion ends the book, after Swift has successfully defended good sense in religion and learning through the process of ridiculing aberrations. If there is one chief victim of his mockery, it is one William Wotton, a scholar whose angry comments (which might have been better left unwritten) Swift gleefully added as footnotes to subsequent editions.

Occasional use of scatology and satirical excesses flaw the work in the eyes of some critics, especially Swift's contemporaries: Swift responded in the fifth edition by making certain alterations, omitting, for example, a short synoptic piece of the tale and a digression on war, both of which had followed section 9. A lengthy and angry "Apology" (or defense) also accompanied this edition. Over the years, however, critics have frequently viewed *A Tale of a Tub* as a masterpiece, a highly moral work offering an indirect recipe for the conduct of a Christian humanist.

Bibliography:

Clark, John R. *Form and Frenzy in Swift's "Tale of a Tub."* Ithaca, N.Y.: Cornell University Press, 1970. Focuses on the artistry of Swift's satire, exploring *A Tale of a Tub* as "a work of mimetic art." Argues that Swift carries out his satiric intent with great originality while staying within the tradition.

Harth, Phillip. *Swift and Anglican Rationalism. The Religious Background of "A Tale of a Tub."* Chicago: University of Chicago Press, 1961. Rejects arguments that *A Tale of a Tub* has a unity that fuses the two objects of its satire, religion and learning, in one coherent whole. Learned investigation of the religious background.

Paulson, Ronald. *Theme and Structure in Swift's "Tale of a Tub."* New Haven, Conn.: Yale University Press, 1960. Emphasizes the moral import of *A Tale of a Tub*, stressing Swift's penetrating insight into the nature of evil; pleads a case for Swift as an artist who gave *A Tale of a Tub* a "unified structure."

Smith, Frederik N. *Language and Reality in Swift's "A Tale of a Tub."* Columbus: Ohio State University Press, 1979. Finds in *A Tale of a Tub* two styles of language that coincide with two ways of knowing the world. Swift rejects the "intellectualized" approach in favor of the "experience-oriented."

Swift, Jonathan. *A Tale of a Tub and Other Works.* Edited with an introduction by Argus Rossand and David Woolley. New York: Oxford University Press, 1986. Excellent, easily available paperback edition with illuminating introduction. Bibliography, chronology of *A Tale of a Tub*, notes, glossary, and appendices.

THE TALE OF GENJI

Type of work: Novel
Author: Murasaki Shikibu (c. 978-c. 1030)
Type of plot: Romance
Time of plot: Early medieval period
Locale: Japan
First published: Genji monogatari, c. 1004 (English translation, 1925-1933)

> *Principal characters:*
> PRINCE GENJI, the talented illegitimate son of the emperor
> THE EMPEROR, Genji's father
> KIRITSUBO, Genji's mother and the emperor's concubine
> LADY KOKIDEN, the emperor's consort
> PRINCESS AOI, Genji's first wife
> UTSUSEMI and
> YUGAO, noblewomen in love with Genji
> MURASAKI, a young girl reared by Genji

The Story:

When the emperor of Japan took a beautiful gentlewoman of the bedchamber as his concubine, he greatly displeased his consort, the Lady Kokiden. The lot of the concubine, whose name was Kiritsubo, was not easy, despite the emperor's protection and love, for Kokiden's influence was very great. Kiritsubo therefore had little happiness in the birth of a son, although the child was beautiful and sturdy. Kiritsubo's son made Kokiden even more antagonistic, for she feared that her own son might lose favor in the emperor's eyes and not be made heir apparent. Because of the hardships of her life among the other women, Kiritsubo languished away until she died.

After his mother's death, the emperor placed her young child under the protection of the clan of Gen, and he gave the child the title of Prince Genji. The boy, spirited and handsome, was a popular figure at the court. Even Kokiden could not feel a great deal of ill will toward him. Genji won a secure place for himself in the emperor's eyes, and at the age of twelve he was not only elevated to a man's estate but also given in marriage to Princess Aoi, the daughter of the minister of the left, a powerful figure at court. Genji was not impressed with his bride, nor was she entirely happy with her bridegroom, for she was four years older than he.

Genji was appointed a captain of the guard, and in this capacity he spent much of his time at the emperor's palace. Indeed, he was rarely together with his bride in their apartment in her father's home, for with his good looks, accomplishments, and position, he could have any woman he wanted. His wife became very cool toward him, but Genji cared little what Princess Aoi said or did.

One of Genji's first love affairs was with a young gentlewoman named Fujitsubo, who, like his bride, was a few years older than he. His second adventure was at the home of a young courtier, Ki no Kami, who was honored to have Prince Genji at his home. Genji went into the room of a pretty young matron, Utsusemi, and took her to his own quarters. Because of Genji's rank and pleasing self, the woman did not resent this. To keep in touch with her, Genji asked that her brother be appointed a member of his train, a request that was readily granted. When Utsusemi realized that the affair could not long continue, she broke it off; Genji named her his broom tree, after a Japanese shrub that at a distance promises shade but is really only a scrawny bush.

A short time later, Genji tried to renew the affair with Utsusemi, but she was not asleep when he entered her room and ran out ahead of him. With her was another very charming young woman, however, who had failed to awaken when Utsusemi left. Genji, refusing to be irritated by Utsusemi, gently awakened the other girl, with whom he was soon on the most intimate of terms.

One day, while visiting his foster mother, Genji made the acquaintance of a young woman named Yugao, to whom he made several masked visits. She was living a rather poor existence, despite the fact that she came from a good family. Becoming tired of the clandestine meetings, Genji arranged for them to stay for a time in a deserted palace within the imperial domains. The affair ended in tragedy when during their stay Yugao was strangely afflicted and died. Only through the good offices of his retainers and friends was Genji able to avoid a disastrous scandal.

Shortly after that, Genji fell ill of an ague. For a cure, he went to a hermit in the mountains, where he found a beautiful little girl, an orphan of a good family. Seeing something of himself in little Murasaki, who was pretty and talented, Genji resolved to take her into his care. At first, Murasaki's guardians refused to listen to Genji's plans, but he convinced them that he had only the girl's best interests at heart and would not make her a concubine at too early an age. Finally, they agreed to let him shape the little girl's future, and he took her to his own palace to rear. Lest people misunderstand his motives, and for the sake of secrecy, Genji failed to disclose the identity of the girl and her age, even though his various lovers and his wife became exceedingly jealous of the mysterious stranger known to dwell with Genji.

Soon after his return to the emperor's court with Murasaki, Genji was requested to dance the "Waves of the Blue Sea" at the annual festival in the emperor's court. So well did he impress the emperor with his dancing and with his poetry that he was raised to higher rank. Had the emperor dared to do so, Genji would have been named the heir apparent. Genji's star was in the ascendant, but he was very worried, for he had made Fujitsubo, the emperor's concubine, pregnant. After the baby's birth, everyone noticed how like Genji the baby looked, but the likeness was, to Genji's relief, credited to the fact that they were both sons of the emperor. The emperor was so pleased that he made Fujitsubo his official consort after the unexpected death of Lady Kokiden.

Genji's marriage was proceeding very badly, and he and his wife drifted farther and farther apart. Finally, she became pregnant, but her condition only seemed to make her sadder. During her pregnancy, Princess Aoi's health declined, for she was consumed with hallucinations that Genji's other lovers were stealing her life from her by hatred and jealousy. As a result of her deep affliction, Princess Aoi died in childbirth, much mourned by Genji, who finally had come to appreciate and love her. A year after her death, however, when Murasaki, the girl he had reared, was of suitable age to marry, Genji took her for his wife and resolved to settle down.

Critical Evaluation:

Lady Murasaki Shikibu was the daughter of a famous provincial governor and the widow of a lieutenant in the Imperial Guard. As a lady in waiting to the Empress Akiko, she was completely familiar with Nipponese court ritual and ceremony, and her knowledge of palace life is everywhere apparent in the adventures of her nobly born hero, Prince Genji. The novel is undoubtedly the finest example of medieval Japanese storytelling, and in it one can trace the growth of Japanese literature. In the beginning, Murasaki's romance is an adolescent affair, very much in the fairy-tale tradition of the old Japanese chronicles. As it progresses, it becomes a full-blown prose romance. It resembles the medieval prose romances of western Europe in that both genres focus on the love affairs of their heroes. *The Tale of Genji*, however, reflects the qualities of Japanese culture. Here are people whose main occupation, far removed from the arts of war and chivalry, was to live well and enjoy nature and art in all forms. In place of the idealized woman, these romances present the idealized man, in whose life women play distinctly subordinate roles.

The Tale of Genji is a long, elegant, wittily ironical court romance that is in some respects a prototype of the novel. The book is in parts, consisting of the title section, "The Sacred Tree," "A Wreath of Cloud," "Blue Trousers," "The Lady of the Boat," and "The Bridge of Dreams." Although Arthur Waley's translation from the Japanese has made the work accessible to a greater audience, few Western readers generally venture beyond the first section, *The Tale of Genji*, although Shikibu's style actually improves as she proceeds; the first chapter crudely imitates the manner of old court romances, but her characterizations become richer, more complex, and the overall design of the book—depicting a moral picture of the emperor's court of her time—becomes apparent. *The Tale of Genji* is an incomparable re-creation of life in eleventh century Japan, which faithfully reproduces the smallest details of the customs, ceremonies, and manners of the aristocracy. The book is, too, an enchanting collection of interwoven stories, some erotic and all vividly recounted. Beyond that, the book is a psychologically honest examination of passion and pretense, and of the hearts of men and women.

The first section treats Genji, "the Shining One," as a child and young man, idealistic but often unwise as he learns the arts of courtship and love. It also introduces Murasaki (who is certainly not the author, unless by ironic contrast), first as Genji's child-concubine, then as his second wife. Her character is tentatively sketched here, though in later parts of the book, she learns about the romantic and political intrigues of court life, becomes sophisticated in practicing her own wiles, and finally—in the section entitled "Blue Trousers"—dies of a lingering, wasting disease. The early section, however, treats the hero and heroine as youthful, hopeful, and inexperienced, before they fully understand how to play the cynical games of love and dissembling.

In chapter 2 of *The Tale of Genji*, the author advances the main theme of her work, the romantic education of innocent lovers. The equerry of the palace, To no Chujo, regales several noblemen, including Genji, with stories about the weakness of women. He has at last discovered that "there exists no woman of whom one can say: 'Here is perfection.'" Genji's youthful experiences tend to support this observation. Just twelve years old when he is married to the sixteen-year-old Princess Aoi, he finds more amusement in amorous adventures than in matrimonial responsibilities, and he comes to care for his wife only shortly before her untimely death. He enjoys his first dalliance with Fujitsubo (whom later he makes pregnant) and thereafter sports with the easily yielding but jealous Utsusemi, with a complaisant lady who happens, conveniently, to be sleeping in Utsusemi's bed, with Yugao, and finally, with the child Murasaki. With the exception of Murasaki, all the women disappoint him. Murasaki, the most innocent and childlike of his lovers, is the only one spirited, imaginative, and beautiful enough to hold his affections.

Yet Murasaki also undergoes a romantic education. She must learn how to function in a world controlled by men without bowing too submissively to their power. When Genji brings her to the palace, he warns her: "Little girls ought to be very gentle and obedient in their ways." At this speech, the author wryly comments: "And thus her education was begun." Several years later, Genji takes sexual liberties with Murasaki, who is too innocent and confused either to oppose or enjoy his attentions. Indeed, her own innocence excites his desire. As the author explains, "It is in general the unexplored that attracts us, and Genji tended to fall most deeply in love with those who gave him least encouragement." When Genji decides to marry the girl, she has no choice in the matter; in fact, he criticizes her lack of enthusiasm for the arrangement, since she owes so much to his friendship. In the closed world of the emperor's palace, where court ladies at best play submissive parts, Murasaki shows how women must develop resources of their own—both of mind and heart—to live with dignity. By the end of *The Tale of Genji*, her heroine is already beginning to learn that lesson.

Bibliography:
Bowring, Richard. *Murasaki Shikibu: "The Tale of Genji."* New York: Cambridge University Press, 1988. This slim volume provides readable information on cultural background, including Heian politics, the author's background and her fictionalization of history, and religions that influenced the novel. Also discusses the novel's style, language, influence, and reception.
Kamens, Edward, ed. *Approaches to Teaching Murasaki Shikibu's "The Tale of Genji."* New York: Modern Language Association of America, 1993. Following a section on materials and recommended reading, six essays suggest ways of studying *The Tale of Genji*. Other authors treat problems of reading the text and compare it with other literary works.
Miner, Earl, ed. *Principles of Classical Japanese Literature.* Princeton, N.J.: Princeton University Press, 1985. Seven essays combine Japanese and North American viewpoints in discussing Japanese literature. Includes a discussion of whether *The Tale of Genji* is a collection rather than a single unified work and an examination of the work's structure and narrative.
Morris, Ivan. "Aspects of *The Tale of Genji*." In *The World of the Shining Prince: Court Life in Ancient Japan.* New York: Alfred A. Knopf, 1972. A classic treatment of various aspects of the Heian period. Chapter 10 discusses *The Tale of Genji*. Also includes valuable appendices.
Puette, William J. *Guide to "The Tale of Genji" by Murasaki Shikibu.* Rutland, Vt.: Charles E. Tuttle, 1983. Discusses essential aspects of the world of Genji, provides chapter summaries, and examines the novel's structure. Also includes an appendix with helpful maps, charts, and indexes.

A TALE OF TWO CITIES

Type of work: Novel
Author: Charles Dickens (1812-1870)
Type of plot: Historical
Time of plot: French Revolution
Locale: France and England
First published: 1859

Principal characters:
> DR. MANETTE, a former prisoner in the Bastille
> LUCIE MANETTE, his daughter
> MR. LORRY, an agent of Tellson & Co.
> CHARLES DARNAY, the Marquis St. Evrémonde
> SYDNEY CARTON, a lawyer's clerk
> MISS PROSS, a servant
> MADAME DEFARGE, a French revolutionary
> MONSIEUR DEFARGE, her husband

The Story:

The early rumblings of the French Revolution were echoing across the English Channel when, in Paris, an old man waited in an attic for his first meeting with a daughter whom he had not seen since she was a baby. With the aid of Mr. Jarvis Lorry, an agent for the Franco-British banking house of Tellson & Co., the lovely Lucie Manette had been brought to Paris to be reunited with her father, who had been imprisoned for eighteen years in the Bastille. Above the wine shop of Madame and Monsieur Defarge, Dr. Manette was kept secretly until his rescuers could take him safely back to England. Day after day, Madame Defarge sat outside her wine shop, knitting into a long scarf strange symbols that would later spell out a death list of hated aristocrats and enemies of the Revolution.

Five years later, Lucie Manette sat beside her father in the courtroom of the Old Bailey, where Charles Darnay, a teacher of languages, was on trial for treasonable activities that involved his passing between France and England on secret business. A man named John Barsad had brought charges against him. Lucie and her father had testified that they had met Darnay on the boat when they had traveled from France five years earlier. The prisoner was saved when Mr. Stryver, the prisoner's counsel, pointed across the courtroom to another man, Sydney Carton, who so resembled the prisoner that legal identification of Darnay was shaken and Mr. Stryver was able to secure an acquittal for the prisoner. Carton's relationship to Stryver was that of the jackal to the lion; the alcoholic, aimless Carton wrote the cases that Stryver pleaded in court.

Lucie and her father lived in a small tenement under the care of their maid, Miss Pross, and their kindly friend, Mr. Lorry. Jerry Cruncher, the porter at Tellson & Co., and a secret resurrectionist, was often helpful. Darnay and Carton became frequent callers in the Manette household, after the trial that had brought them together.

In France, the fury of the people grew. Monseigneur the Marquis St. Evrémonde was driving in his carriage through the countryside when he carelessly killed a child of a peasant named Gaspard. The nobleman returned to his castle to meet his nephew, Charles Darnay, who was visiting from England. Darnay's views differed from those of his uncle. Darnay knew that his family had committed grave injustices, and he had begged his uncle to make amends. Monseigneur the Marquis haughtily refused. That night, the marquis was murdered in his bed.

Darnay returned to England to seek Dr. Manette's permission to court Lucie. In order to construct a bond of complete honesty, Darnay attempted to tell the doctor his true French name, but Manette fearfully asked him to wait until the morning of his marriage before revealing it. Carton also approached Lucie with a proposal of marriage. When Lucie refused, Carton asked her always to remember that there was a man who would give his own life to keep a life she loved beside her.

In France, Madame Defarge knitted the story of the hated St. Evrémondes into her scarf. Gaspard had been hanged for the assassination of the marquis; Monseigneur's house must be destroyed. John Barsad, the spy, brought news that Lucie Manette would marry Charles Darnay, the nephew of the marquis. This news disturbed Defarge, for Dr. Manette, a former prisoner of the Bastille, held a special honor in the eyes of the Revolutionists.

Lucie and Darnay were married. Sydney Carton became a loyal friend of the family. Time passed, and tiny Lucie arrived. When the child was six years old, in the year 1789, the French people stormed the Bastille. At the Bastille, Defarge went to the cell where Dr. Manette had been a prisoner and extracted some papers hidden behind a stone in the wall.

One day, while Darnay was talking to Mr. Lorry at Tellson & Co., a letter addressed to the Marquis St. Evrémonde was placed on Mr. Lorry's desk. Darnay offered to deliver it to the proper person. When he was alone, he read the letter. It was from an old family servant who had been imprisoned by the Revolutionists. He begged the Marquis St. Evrémonde to save his life. Darnay realized that he must go to Paris. Only Dr. Manette knew of Darnay's family name, and the doctor had been sworn to secrecy.

Darnay and Mr. Lorry went to Paris, the latter to look after the French branch of Tellson & Co. Shortly after his arrival, Darnay was seized as an undesirable immigrant after Defarge had ordered his arrest. Mr. Lorry was considerably upset when Lucie and Dr. Manette suddenly arrived in Paris. Some of the doctor's friends had informed him of Darnay's arrest. The old man felt that his own imprisonment in the Bastille would win the sympathy of the Revolutionists and enable him to save his son-in-law.

After fifteen months of waiting, Darnay was brought to trial. Because he was able to prove himself innocent of harming the French people, he was freed but forbidden to leave France. A short time later, he was again arrested, denounced by Defarge and one other person whose name the officer refused to disclose.

While shopping one day in the Paris market, Miss Pross and Jerry Cruncher, who were in Paris with Lucie and Mr. Lorry, met a man who caused Miss Pross to scream in amazement and Jerry to stare in silent astonishment. The man was Solomon, Miss Pross's lost brother. Jerry remembered him as John Barsad, the man who had been a spy-witness at the Old Bailey. Carton arrived on the scene at that moment, and he was able to force Barsad to come with him to the office of Tellson & Co. for a private conference. Barsad feared detection of his duplicity, for he was now an employee of the Republican French Government. Carton and Jerry threatened to expose him as a former spy for the English government, the enemy of France. Carton made a deal with Barsad.

When Darnay was once more brought before the tribunal, Defarge testified against him and named Dr. Manette as the other accuser. Defarge produced the papers that he had found in Dr. Manette's cell in the Bastille. Therein the doctor had written the story of his arrest and imprisonment because he had learned of a secret crime committed by a St. Evrémonde against a woman of humble birth and her young brother. His account was enough to convict Darnay. Sentenced for the crimes of his ancestors, Darnay, the young St. Evrémonde, was condemned by the tribunal to the guillotine.

Sydney Carton now began to visit the Defarge wine shop, where he learned that Madame Defarge was the sister of the woman ruined by St. Evrémonde years before. With the help of the false Barsad, he gained admittance to the prison where Darnay had been taken. There he drugged the prisoner and, still aided by the cowed Barsad, had him carried from the cell, himself remaining behind. The resemblance between the two would allow him to pass as Darnay and prevent discovery of the aristocrat's escape.

Madame Defarge went to the lodgings of Lucie and Dr. Manette to denounce them. Only Miss Pross was there; the others, including Darnay, were already on their way to safety. To keep Madame Defarge from learning of their escape, Miss Pross struggled with the furious woman when she demanded admittance to Lucie's apartment. Madame Defarge was killed when her pistol went off. Miss Pross was deaf for the rest of her life. Lucie and Darnay returned safely to England. Sydney Carton died at the guillotine, having given his own life for the happiness of those he loved.

Critical Evaluation:

The central paradox of *A Tale of Two Cities* rests in the fact that its action involves the most important political event of modern European history—and perhaps of its entire history—the French Revolution, while the values of the novel are ultimately antipolitical. Politics and history, neither of which Charles Dickens renders with great faithfulness, loom as a necessity from which his characters must flee to save their souls. Throughout the novel, Dickens reminds his readers that all acts, whether magnanimous or petty, shrink to nothing when viewed in a cosmic context. Indeed, for him, the goal of politics, the finding of a just community, is an absurd one in this world. To paraphrase Sydney Carton's famous last speech: It is a far better thing to die and join such a community in heaven—the existence of which Dickens cannot with certainty assert—than to engage with society. *A Tale of Two Cities* demonstrates that Dickens' political will, wan in his previous novels, has finally been exhausted.

In this regard and in one of the first substantial essays dealing with Dickens' art and thought, published a year before *A Tale of Two Cities* was completed, Walter Bagehot said: "Mr. Dickens has not infrequently spoken, and what is worse, he has taught a great number of parrot-like imitators to speak, in what really is, if they knew it, a tone of objection to the necessary constitution of human society." Dickens' strength, Bagehot agreed, appeared in the quality of his moral cry, his protest against the injustices of society; yet, as he said, the novelist never indicated how these inequalities might be removed.

By the time of *A Tale of Two Cities*, distinguished by its outrage against the tyranny of both the governors and the governed, Dickens clearly indicates that society cannot be made to progress or even be substantially ameliorated. For him, the great grasp for freedom by the French people, for example, goes finally unsung, drowned out by the terrible cacophony of the guillotine. To Dickens' unwillingness to accept the "necessary constitution of human society," then, must be added his refusal to understand and accept the necessarily slow and painful processes of history.

In his early comic and satiric novels, such as *Pickwick Papers* (1836-1837), *Nicholas Nickleby* (1838-1839), and *Oliver Twist* (1837-1839), Dickens' simple stance of protest carried with it a zestful anger that was both invigorating and liberating; but as he grew more serious in his artistic intent, beginning with *Dombey and Son*, completed in 1848, and continuing through *David Copperfield* (1849-1850), *Bleak House* (1852-1853), *Hard Times* (1854), and *Little Dorrit* (1855-1857), for many readers his masterpiece, he lost his sense of the efficacy of the human will to deal with the complexities of a modern, industrial society. His gradual loss of faith was accompanied by a diminishing moral energy; his imagination seemed unable to create viable and pertinent responses to a civilization increasingly encroaching on individual freedom. Particularly in *Little Dorrit*, the novel published immediately before *A Tale of Two Cities*, readers are stunned as well as enervated by the hopelessness of the conclusion.

There is a significant scene in *A Tale of Two Cities* that appears at the conclusion of book 1 and is relevant to Dickens' social despair. After Dr. Manette has been saved from the Bastille and is on the way from Paris to London, his rescuer, Mr. Jarvis Lorry, asks him, "I hope you care to be recalled to life?" Dr. Manette answers, "I can't say." In some ways, the question is never answered by the doctor, for at the novel's conclusion his mind clouds permanently from the effects of his sufferings. If to be "recalled to life" means to be called back into civilization and history, then the novel implies that the doctor's answer is "No." The quality of life in society is actually no better, Dickens seems to claim, than perpetual imprisonment in the Bastille, and humans are caught up in an undertow of events that leaves them helpless; their imagination, intelligence, and will are useless when pitted against politics.

Indeed, the novelist goes further than this in his view of the ineptitude of human beings. If they consent to join in the machinations of society, Dickens asserts, they must inevitably expect to be corrupted. It is a tragic view, unrelieved by a belief in human dignity, or in the human ability to attain nobility through exertion of will. The readers of *A Tale of Two Cities*, left with Dickens' vision of unmitigated tragedy, remain unconsoled in their own existence, which is inextricably bound up with the demands of history and politics.

The consolation that Dickens does offer takes the form of a vague promise of supernatural communion and a picture of human fellowship and love. The fellowship, composed of Dr. and Lucie Manette, Charles Darnay and Sydney Carton, and the minor characters of Mr. Lorry, Miss Pross, and Jerry Cruncher, provides a sanctuary within the confines of history. There affection, trust, and sacrifice stand opposed to the hate, treachery, and tyranny of the world.

"Critical Evaluation" by David L. Kubal

Bibliography:

Beckwith, Charles E., ed. *Twentieth Century Interpretations of "A Tale of Two Cities."* Englewood Cliffs, N.J.: Prentice-Hall, 1972. A collection of scholarly critical essays followed by commentaries on the novel by such literary figures as George Bernard Shaw and George Orwell.

Dickens, Charles. *A Tale of Two Cities*. Oxford, England: Oxford University Press, 1988. Contains a useful chronology of the French Revolution, as well as information on the history of the novel.

Glancy, Ruth. *"A Tale of Two Cities": An Annotated Bibliography*. New York: Garland Publishing, 1993. An invaluable tool for both the student and the scholar. The references to the novel are arranged under the general headings of text and studies.

_____. *"A Tale of Two Cities": Dickens's Revolutionary Novel*. Boston: Twayne, 1991. this in-depth study places the novel in its historical and literary context and provides a careful analysis of the plot.

Kaplan, Fred. *Dickens: A Biography*. New York: William Morrow, 1988. Scholarly and well-written. It is particularly valuable in addressing Dickens' personal identification with the characters of Sydney Carton and Charles Darnay.

Nelson, Harland S. *Charles Dickens*. Boston: Twayne, 1981. An excellent introduction to Dickens' life and works.

TALES OF ISE

Type of work: Short fiction
Author: Unknown, attributed to Ariwara no Narihira (825-880)
Type of plot: Love
Time of plot: Ninth century
Locale: Japan
First published: Ise monogatari, tenth century, based on *Narihira kashū*, ninth century
  (English translation, 1968)

Principal characters:
THE NARRATOR, a man who loves love
HIS WIFE, the daughter of Aritsune
VARIOUS WOMEN

The Story:

Not too many years after the capital has been moved from Nara to Kyoto, in 794, there lived a man who loved love. Shortly after his maturity rite (which at that time was usually at the age of eleven) and when the boy had grown four and a half feet tall, the youth went falcon hunting at Kasuga in the former capital. There he happened to see two beautiful sisters and sent them a poem. The poem begins the description of the love life of this man. Later, he met and began to visit a performer in the imperial court. When their love affair became exposed, the woman was made unavailable by the simple expediency of placing her in service at court where, in 866, she became the consort of the Emperor Seiwa.

Tiring of life in the capital, the man went on a trip to eastern Japan, but he had gone no farther than the border of Ise and Owari Provinces when he became homesick and composed poems to express his nostalgia. He met an itinerant priest, saw Mount Fuji for the first time, and composed a poem. Entering the province of Musashi, at the Sumida River which runs through present-day Tokyo, he composed a celebrated poem of nostalgia concerning the oyster-catcher birds. In Musashi he also met and was attracted to various women. Later he wandered through the region to the northeast, where he made love to the local country women.

Friends since early childhood, the man and the daughter of Aritsune eventually married, but Narihira did not long remain faithful to her. Scattered through the episodes, however, are hints that cause the reader to believe that she managed to draw him back to her after each infidelity.

In another story, there was the eternal triangle involving two men and one woman, with the usual tragic results. The woman in this case waited three years for the return of a man who had left to make his fortune in the capital. Meanwhile, she was courted by a second man, who finally won her promise of marriage. The first man, returning on the wedding night, learned what had happened during his absence and left the woman with his blessing. Following him, she lost her life.

There was, in another story, a weakling son of good family and a household maid. In another, a young woman was in love but too shy to make her feelings known. She died with her love unrequited as a result. Two faithless people had an affair, each sent the other poems charging the other with faithlessness. A beloved wife had a husband who was so busy with his duties at court that she felt neglected and went with another man to the country. Eventually the husband was appointed an imperial emissary to an important shrine and there met the woman, who was by then the wife of a country official. She realized her mistake and became a nun. There was the story of an elderly woman, the mother of three sons, who was amorously starved but too diffident to say so openly, so she told her sons of her craving as something she had dreamed. The third son alone was sympathetic to his mother's plight, and he arranged for her to meet the handsome narrator.

From the earliest times it had been the custom for the emperor to appoint through divination an unmarried imperial princess to serve as the head priestess at important shrines. In the narrator's time the head priestess of the great shrine of Ise was Princess Yasuko, second daughter of Emperor Montoku. Her appointment, made in 859, lasted until 876. Sometime after her appointment, there appeared in Ise a handsome inspector in the guise of a falcon hunter. The priestess, having received word of his arrival on official matters, greeted him with special kindness; the meeting led to their falling in love with each other. For the sake of discretion she waited until nighttime before paying him a visit, and she left long before dawn. That same morning a messenger arrived from her with a poem, the gist of which was "Did you come to see me last night, or was it I who went to see you? I do not remember. Nor do I know whether it was all a dream, or was real."

The narrator replied with another poem setting a tryst for that evening, but the governor of the province gave an all-night banquet; thus the narrator's plans were thwarted. On the following day it was necessary for him to continue his tour of inspection. The lovers parted, promising each other in poems to meet again, somewhere, sometime.

So the stories of love went, ending with the poem that might be roughly translated:

> Long have I known
> That this last journey must be made,
> But little did I know
> That it might be so soon.

Critical Evaluation:

The Tales of Ise belongs to a Heian period (794-1186) genre that is referred to in Japanese as *uta monogatari* (poem tales). Most of the Japanese poetry of this period was short, usually only five lines adding up to a total of approximately thirty-one syllables. These were often occasional poems for which a headnote might clarify the subject or detail the circumstances of composition. In the poem tale, such as the *Tales of Ise*, the compiler or compilers created prose settings for the poems or for groups of poems. In some cases these settings were completely unrelated to the actual circumstances of the poems' composition. Sometimes groups of episodes might be centered around the same character or similar situations, but there was no overall unity to the narrative. Thus *Tales of Ise* is within its genre in having no narrative that may be summarized with much coherence. The narrator's presence in much of the book is the source of what unity it possesses.

The poem tale has some similarities to another genre of the period, the imperial anthology of poetry. These were anthologies commissioned by emperors and edited by the leading poets of the day. The longest section of an imperial anthology was the five books devoted to love poetry. This section describes a typical love affair from the first meeting to the inevitably unhappy ending. Thus the editor of the anthology used the selected poetry to craft a portrait of an aesthetic ideal in the courtly life of the Heian period. The *Tales of Ise* has no such organizing principle. The only link between many of the episodes is the unidentified hero, a "certain person," the "man of old," who is gallant, elegant, charming, and above all witty. The *Tales of Ise* does go much further than the anthology in anchoring its portraits of love in a realistic world populated by realistic people. In this sense the poem tale can be seen as bridging the gap between poetry and the great flourishing of the novel that would soon take place in Japan. This flowering culminated in the greatest achievement of classical Japanese literature, Lady Murasaki Shikibu's *The Tale of Genji* (c. 1004).

The exact origin or authorship of the *Tales of Ise* is unknown. Considering the lack of organizing principle, it seems likely that the *Tales of Ise* is the product of several authors over some period of time. Certain groups of episodes form short biographical sketches focusing on events in the life of Ariwara no Narihira, however, so there is speculation that these episodes may have been the original core of the work.

The fragmentary structure of the poem tale makes it nearly impossible to pinpoint any single theme in this work. However, a careful reading of the *Tales of Ise* can provide one of the clearest statements of the ideal of courtly elegance that was so important to Heian culture. For this reason this collection of subtle little vignettes was one of the most influential works in traditional Japanese literature. In spite of the lack of a theme, there is an unmistakable tone to the work.

The work shows a great sensitivity to beauty, a sensitivity that is tinged with grief over beauty's passing and the passing of time. This tone is an essential part of the aesthetics of Japanese literature in the Heian period. A good example of this sensitivity can be found in a famous episode from the *Tales of Ise* in which a young man, presumably Narihira, has been visiting a certain woman who was in service to the Empress. Suddenly the lady has been moved away. Although he knows where she is, he cannot visit her. In the early spring of the next year, when the plum trees are in bloom, the young man visits the place where he had originally met the young lady. Unable to recapture the past, he is overcome with grief and composes this poem:

> Is this not the moon?
> This spring, is it not the
> spring of old?
> Myself alone, only I
> am the same as before.

The poem suggests metaphysical interpretation in a way that is unusual for Japanese poetry of this period. The nuances are difficult to capture in translation, but the poem first asks the rhetorical question: Are not the moon and the spring different this year? They are not, but since they appear so different, perhaps it is the author who has changed. The overall impressions from the poem are of time passing, uncertainty, and subjectivity. From the context, the subject is grief over the end of a brief but intense love affair. Perhaps more than any other single poem in the work, this poem forms the clearest statement of what might be called a theme in the *Tales of Ise*.

Love is the thread that unites most of the episodes in the *Tales of Ise*, often it is the art of poetry that forms the real subject matter. Later generations looked on the *Tales of Ise* almost as a poetic guide, a "how to" manual for the elegant courtier and his lady, each pursuing their numerous affairs. Of course, since Japanese poetry is such a highly conventional verse form, often poems were only slight variations on common themes or images. In later times borrowing became formalized as poets would take two or three lines from a well-known poem and give them a new twist by adding several lines of new composition. Eventually much of the sentiment that is expressed in the poetry of the *Tales of Ise* would become nothing more than trite convention. In the *Tales of Ise*, however, there is still a sense of freshness that provides much of the charm for this pivotal work in traditional Japanese literature.

"Critical Evaluation" by Jon W. La Cure

Bibliography:

Harris, H. Jay, trans. Introduction to *The Tales of Ise*. Rutland, Vt.: Charles E. Tuttle, 1972. This translation also has a running commentary on the each episode. The introduction gives background information and summarizes the speculations about the origins and authorship of the text.

Keene, Donald. *Seeds in the Heart: Japanese Literature from Earliest Times to the Late Sixteenth Century*. New York: Henry Holt, 1993. Gives a picture of the probable circumstance of the composition of the *Tales of Ise*, the text as it is now, and other poem tales of the period.

McCullough, Helen Craig. *Tales of Ise: Lyrical Episodes from Tenth-Century Japan*. Stanford, Calif.: Stanford University Press, 1968. This complete translation of the work is scholarly and readable. There is a lengthy introduction to the *Tales of Ise* and to the poetry and poets of the early Heian period.

Okada, H. Richard. *Figures of Resistance: Language, Poetry, and Narrating in "The Tale of Genji" and Other Mid-Heian Texts*. Durham, N.C.: Duke University Press, 1991. Has a chapter devoted to the *Tales of Ise* that deals with the political and social background of the work.

Tahara, Mildred M., trans. Introduction to *Tales of Yamato: A Tenth Century Poem-Tale*. Honolulu: University Press of Hawaii, 1980. This translation of another major tenth century poem tale has a short introduction and a succinct history of Japanese literature in an appendix.

TALES OF SOLDIERS AND CIVILIANS

Type of work: Short fiction
Author: Ambrose Bierce (1842-1914?)
First published: 1891

Ambrose Bierce wrote volumes of acid, satirical prose in his long career as a journalist, and even managed to get a somewhat pretentious twelve-volume edition of his collected works published. Most of it, because of its time-bound nature, was doomed to oblivion by the time the edition appeared. The work that continues to survive is the collection of short stories titled *Tales of Soldiers and Civilians*. Bierce's literary reputation rests largely on this book.

The bland title of this collection stands in ironic contrast to the vision of life that informs the stories themselves. Indeed, Bierce seems to have striven for bland, noncommittal titles to most of his stories. Titles like "Chickamauga," "An Occurrence at Owl Creek Bridge," and "The Mocking-Bird" tell little of the macabre nature of these tales. Bierce seems to have chosen his mild titles with deliberate irony. When this volume was reprinted in 1898, it was given a more meaningful title, *In the Midst of Life*. The irony is clearer and more indicative of the true content of the book: in the midst of life is death.

Death is the sole absolute of this book, the common denominator of each story, and the final proposition in a logic of ruthless necessity. Each protagonist is part of a greater logic; each is subordinate to the plot, and each is cursed. Death is separated from life, is raised up as a separate principle antagonistic to life, and becomes an entity in its own right. Death is seen as a hostile specter, rather than a normal process of life. As such, death seeks to conquer life rather than aid it. Death then becomes an inevitable victor that "has all seasons for his own," as Bierce was fond of remarking.

Against such a powerful antagonist, the heroes become victims in a web of cruel necessity, shadow figures drawn into the Valley of the Shadow; and as such, they are depicted with sharp, relentless strokes. Bierce's heroes are essentially lonely men who derive their reality from the fear they experience. These men are cursed and driven by the logic of their curse. Their strongest motivation is fear, an all-pervasive anxiety that frequently annihilates them. The success of each story depends on its ability to arouse this same fear in the reader.

In consequence, Bierce places a great value on courage, fearlessness in the face of death. He is acute enough, however, to see that courage is not so much fearlessness as it is a greater fear overcoming a lesser fear, in most cases a fear of dishonor overcoming a fear of death. Courage, then, is the faith that one's honor is more important than one's life. Frequently the heroes Bierce admires court death with an awesome recklessness. His heroes are inevitably damned. There is no escape, no transcendence, and no salvation from the macabre situations into which they are drawn. Their dooms are inescapable facts; but the measure of their manhood is expressed in how they meet death.

Bierce's vision of life is fatalistic, but there is more to it than that. Avenging Furies hover about his stories, but they are not the same Furies that haunted Orestes. Bierce is nihilistic, but inevitably there is a macabre humor in his nihilism. The acid, satirical touch that colors the rest of Bierce's work is present here as well. Bierce's Furies are diabolical jesters, who love irony more than they love the wretched human spirit. His Furies are divine practical jokers, who drum "Dixie" and "John Brown's Body" on the human skull for laughs. One can scarcely tell whether the shriek one senses in Bierce's prose is that of humor or horror.

Bierce's grotesque wit serves as a relief from the horror of his situations. A related technique that serves the same purpose is his ironic stance, one which removes him from the petty human scene and separates him from the terror of his heroes. Bierce assumes a godlike attitude that determines the objective nature of his prose. He uses a naturalistic style that is precise in diction, spare in depiction, ironic in narration.

In effect, Bierce takes on the cruel role of the Furies in narrating his stories, and the tone of his prose is frigid, caustic, and inhuman. Yet it is precisely this emotional sterility, this godlike irony, that makes his stories so powerfully chilling. If, for example, Bierce were to sympathize with his heroes, readers would have pathos rather than terror. The very lack of an appropriate emotional response in the narration stimulates to an excessive degree the proper emotional response in the reader. The fact that Bierce himself was caustic, cruel, and sharp, demanding perfection of his fellow human beings, admirably served his limited artistic abilities and enabled him to focus his talent on evoking both terror and humor.

Tales of Soldiers and Civilians is divided into two parts, as the title suggests. There are the war stories and the mystery stories, and each type develops Bierce's vision of life in a different literary direction. The war tales anticipate Hemingway, while the civilian stories anticipate more modern horror-tale writers such as H. P. Lovecraft. Beyond a doubt, Bierce reached his artistic peak in the soldier tales. War stories provided the perfect medium for someone of his character and experience. First of all, Bierce had served in the Civil War and undoubtedly his stories draw much of their vigor from firsthand experience. His depiction of various battles and their effects has an unmistakable aura of reality. His description of war is hauntingly vivid and stands in marked contrast to the maudlin accounts given in the vast bulk of Civil War writings.

Secondly, war tales provided an acceptable outlet for his obsessions with fear, courage, and death. These leitmotifs could be presented naturally in tales of soldiers. Since war abounds in abnormal situations, Bierce could write naturally about a twin killing his twin, about a son killing his father, and about an artillery man killing his wife. In the context of their stories, these plots become necessary accidents, part of some divine causality. Thirdly, Bierce's naturalistic style was admirably suited to describing the limited vision of the soldier in war, a vision which is not permitted the luxury of feeling pity and which must avoid all contemplation. It is a vision, moreover, that must concentrate on immediate objectives and on carrying out specific orders. Finally, the army subjugates individuals to the mass. Deeds of fear and courage are the only acts by which a soldier is individualized and judged. Bierce's characters draw their reality from the way they face death. Each hero undergoes an ordeal, which means death either for him or for someone close to him, and that test determines his character. Apart from that ordeal, Bierce's characters are lifeless puppets dancing to a meretricious plot.

Bierce's war stories are his best. Nowhere else did he achieve such a perfect fusion of form and content, except perhaps in his aphorisms. In quality, the tales are superior to nearly all of the short fiction that was being written during the nineteenth century in America.

In many instances, they anticipate or rival Hemingway's stories. Actually, many points of comparison can be drawn between Bierce and Hemingway; both show obsession with fear, courage, and death; both use a crisp, ironic prose to communicate their vision; both were to find expression in stories of war; both present character tested through some ordeal; and both possess a cruel and evocative power—a power that at times gives their fiction a haunting quality as vivid as a nightmare. Bierce's war tales, particularly "Chickamauga," "An Occurrence at Owl Creek Bridge," "One Kind of Officer," and "Killed at Resaca," are first-rate for what they attempt to do.

His civilian stories, however, fall somewhat short of the high standards he achieved in his war tales. The reason for this diminished quality is that Bierce attempts to impose on his stories of civilians the same vision of life that pervades his soldier tales, and the grafting is not always successful. Pictures of war provide the perfect literary vehicle for his outlook, since war abounds in pathological situations. When he tries to impose this vision on civilian reality, however, the imperfections of plot, the implausibilities, and the grotesqueness show up much more glaringly. The trick endings come off much worse. The characters and plots never match those of the war stories. To inject a pathological fear into stories about civilians requires great skill. What Bierce succeeds in doing in the civilian stories is to extend what, at the time, was a relatively new prose genre, the short mystery tale. In this lesser genre, Bierce comes off rather well when compared with later writers who work in this vein. His stories continue to hold their own in the anthologies. Where Bierce is successful in turning his neuroses into fine artistic stories, he has few equals in suspense, evocative power, clarity, and irony.

Bibliography:

Conlogue, William. "A Haunting Memory: Ambrose Bierce and the Ravine of the Dead." *Studies in Short Fiction* 28 (Winter, 1991): 21-29. Sees ravines as symbols of death and sometimes of women's infidelity in Bierce's fiction, especially "The Affair at Coulter's Notch," "The Coup de Grace," "The Haunted Valley," and "Killed at Resaca."

Davidson, Cathy N., ed. *Critical Essays on Ambrose Bierce*. Boston: G. K. Hall, 1982. A collection of essays, including early ones by H. L. Mencken and Van Wyck Brooks.

Fatout, Paul. "Ambrose Bierce, Civil War Topographer." *American Literature* 26 (November, 1954): 391-400. Explains the uses Bierce made of his combat experiences as a topographical officer during the Civil War, in "George Thurston," "Killed at Resaca," and a few autobiographical pieces.

Knight, Melinda. "Cultural Radicalism in the American Fin de Siècle: Cynicism, Decadence and Dissent." *Connecticut Review* 14 (Spring, 1992): 65-75. Shows how Bierce and several other marginalized "aesthetes and decadents" repudiated values held by cultural and business leaders in the 1890's. Bierce attacked democracy, genteel realism, prudery, and would-be reformers.

Woodruff, Stuart C. *The Short Stories of Ambrose Bierce: A Study in Polarity*. Pittsburgh: University of Pittsburgh Press, 1964. A useful, basic introductory survey of Bierce's tales.

TALES OF UNCLE REMUS

Type of work: Short fiction
Author: Joel Chandler Harris (1848-1908)
First published: 1880-1948; anthologized as *The Complete Tales of Uncle Remus*, 1955

But for the efforts of Joel Chandler Harris, it is doubtful that many of the African American folktales he preserved would have survived, or that anyone other than folklorists would have any idea of who Brer Rabbit or any of his associates are. Bugs Bunny might not even exist.

Between 1880 and his death in August, 1908, Harris produced many "Uncle Remus" books, containing a total of 168 African American folktales: *Uncle Remus: His Songs and His Sayings* (1880) contained thirty-four tales; *Nights With Uncle Remus: Myths and Legends of the Old Plantation* (1883), sixty-nine; *Daddy Jake, the Runaway: And Short Stories Told After Dark* (1889), thirteen; *Uncle Remus and His Friends: Old Plantation Stories, Songs, and Ballads with Sketches of Negro Character* (1892), twenty-four; *Told by Uncle Remus: New Stories of the Old Plantation* (1905), sixteen; *Uncle Remus and Brer Rabbit* (1907), six; and *Uncle Remus and the Little Boy* (1910), six.

After his death, two more volumes were published: *Uncle Remus Returns* (1918), with six tales, edited by his biographer daughter-in-law, Julia Collier Harris; and *Seven Tales of Uncle Remus* (1948), edited by Thomas H. English.

The Complete Tales of Uncle Remus, edited by Richard Chase, contains all 181 of these folktales, together with the narrative frames in which they were originally presented, unbowdlerized and absent any attempt to modernize the mid-Georgia black dialect of the stories' primary raconteur, Uncle Remus, or the Gullah dialect of his friend Daddy Jack, who tells ten tales in *Nights With Uncle Remus*.

The most famous of the Uncle Remus stories is the story of Brer Rabbit and the tar-baby, told in two chapters from *Uncle Remus: His Songs and His Sayings*. In "The Wonderful Tar-Baby Story," Brer Fox fashions a small tar figure and leaves it by the side of the big road down which Brer Rabbit soon comes pacing, "lippity-clippity, clippity-lippity—dez ez sassy ez a jay-bird." When Brer Rabbit smacks the tar baby for not responding to his greeting, his paw sticks to it. Demanding to be let loose, the rabbit hits the figure three more times, getting another paw stuck each time. Then he butts it with his head, and now he is stuck in five places. Brer Fox emerges and, when he can finally stop laughing, captures the helpless Brer Rabbit.

When the story resumes, in "How Mr. Rabbit Was Too Sharp for Mr. Fox," Brer Fox first threatens to "bobbycue" Brer Rabbit, then to hang him, then to drown him. Each time, Brer Rabbit says fine, do anything you want, but please do not throw me in the briar patch. After Brer Rabbit says he would even prefer having his eye gouged out, his ears torn, and his legs cut off than to be thrown into the briar patch, the stupid fox, who "wanter hurt Brer Rabbit ez bad ez he kin," flings Brer Rabbit into the briar patch. A few minutes later, Brer Fox hears someone calling him. Looking up to the top of a hill, he sees Brer Rabbit seated on a log and combing the tar out of his fur. Brer Fox realizes he has been had, and Brer Rabbit cannot help but taunt him, hollering out, "'Bred en bawn in a brier-patch, Brer Fox—bred en bawn in a brier-patch!' en wid dat he skip out des ez lively ez a cricket in de embers."

This story is not only the most famous of the Uncle Remus stories, it is also one of the most typical. First, it is what could be termed an animal tale: The characters are sentient animals who act like human beings. There are only sixteen Uncle Remus tales in which this is not the case: from *Uncle Remus: His Songs and His Stories*, "A Plantation Witch," "Jacky-My-Lantern," and

"Why the Negro Is Black"; from *Nights With Uncle Remus*, "Spirits, Seen and Unseen" and "A Ghost Story"; from *Daddy Jake, the Runaway*, "How a Witch Was Caught," "The Little Boy and His Dogs," "The Foolish Woman," and "The Adventures of Simon and Susanna"; from *Uncle Remus and His Friends*, "Death and the Negro Man," "According to How the Drop Falls," "A Fool for Luck," "The Man and His Boots," and "How the King Recruited His Army"; from *Told by Uncle Remus*, "The Hard-Headed Woman"; and from *Uncle Remus Returns*, "Impty-Umpty and the Blacksmith."

Second, the tar-baby story belongs to the largest of the three primary groups of tales into which all Uncle Remus stories can be divided, without regard to the presence or absence of animals as main characters. It is a trickster tale, a tale in which one or more of the main characters seeks to dupe one or more others. There are more than 120 such Uncle Remus tales, of which all but four are animal tales, and all but twenty-nine have Brer Rabbit as their protagonist.

Sometimes, the consequences of the trickery are horrific, as in the following three examples. "The Awful Fate of Mr. Wolf," from *Uncle Remus: His Songs and His Stories*, is a variation on the story of "The Three Little Pigs." Brer Rabbit revenges himself on Brer Wolf by tricking him into getting into a large chest, then scalding him to death. In another story, from *Nights with Uncle Remus*, a bear cub uses trickery to get away with eating all of the alligator's children, while ostensibly taking care of them. In "Brother Bear Learns to Comb His Head," from *Seven Tales of Uncle Remus*, Brer Rabbit tricks Brer Bear into getting Miss Bear to cut off Brer Bear's head so she can comb it well.

At other times, the injury is less harsh. In "Brother Rabbit's Laughing-Place," from *Told by Uncle Remus*, Brer Rabbit sends Brer Fox into what Brer Rabbit says is his laughing place, and Brer Fox walks straight into a hornets' nest. As he struggles to escape the insects, Brer Fox protests that he does not see anything funny about the place, whereupon Brer Rabbit replies, "I said 'twas my laughin'-place, an' I'll say it ag'in. What you reckon I been doin' all dis time? Ain't you hear me laughin'?"

Sometimes, the injury is only to the dupe's pride. For example, in "The Moon in the Mill Pond," from *Nights with Uncle Remus*, Brers Rabbit and Terrapin trick Brers Bear, Fox, and Wolf into trying to seine for the moon in a mill pond, with the result that the latter three end up getting soaked and made to look foolish in front of Miss Meadows and her "gals."

The other two major kinds of stories in these collections are the myth and the supernatural tale. The myth seeks to explain the origin of something; it is sometimes called an etiological tale. There are twenty-three of these. Four tales representative of the myth are "Why the Negro Is Black," from *Uncle Remus: His Songs and His Sayings*; "Why the Alligator's Back Is Rough," from *Nights With Uncle Remus*; "Where the Harrycane Comes From," from *Uncle Remus and His Friends*; and "When Brother Rabbit Was King," from *Told by Uncle Remus*, which tells why dogs are always sniffing around.

In a supernatural tale, one of the main characters is a witch, a ghost, the devil, or some similar creature, or a magical object is used to significant effect. The sixteen supernatural tales in the Uncle Remus stories include two bargain-with-the-devil stories, "Jacky-My-Lantern" (from *Uncle Remus: His Songs and His Sayings*) and "Impty-Umpty and the Blacksmith" (from *Uncle Remus Returns*); a gruesome shape-shifter story, "How a Witch Was Caught" (from *Daddy Jake, the Runaway*); two golden-arm stories, "A Ghost Story" (from *Nights With Uncle Remus*) and "Taily-po" (from *Uncle Remus Returns*); and a chilling story about a demonic changeling, "The Baby and the Punkins" (from *Seven Tales of Uncle Remus*).

One reason the Uncle Remus tales are important is that they represent the first time anyone had seriously attempted to record the folktales of African Americans in the exact form, language, and style in which they existed. They not only inspired future folklorists to interest themselves in African American folklore, but also encouraged them to record such material as precisely as they could.

A second reason for their significance is that these tales, together with the narrative frameworks in which they are embedded, provide an insight into the psyche of blacks in the antebellum South. It should not be surprising, Harris always maintained, that a trickster rabbit is the hero of the majority of these tales. The rabbit is among the most physically helpless wild animals in the South, lacking not only fangs and claws, but also hooves and horns. Likewise, the slave was the most physically helpless person in the antebellum South, exploited almost as much by his owner as the rabbit is by the predators who rule forest and swamp. In the triumph of the prey animal over the predator, the slave could enjoy, if only vicariously, a triumph over his owner and the other predatory whites by whom he was surrounded.

This is not to say, as some have, that there is validity to the idea that Uncle Remus tells these stories in order to give a little white boy nightmares, to be Brer Rabbit to the little boy's Brer Fox. Uncle Remus says, explicitly and often, that there is a difference between the world of the "creeturs" and the world of people: Human beings have preachers and the Bible to tell them how they should behave, whereas the creatures have no idea of the difference between right and wrong. Brer Rabbit is not an allegorical embodiment of Nat Turner. Many of the stories are told, in fact, to point out to the boy that one should not try to imitate the animals in one's behavior.

The Uncle Remus stories do not present a picture of a world that Uncle Remus, or the average reader, would want to see come into being. Instead, they present readers with a world that is already far too like their own, one that human beings should work to keep from becoming realized.

Viktor R. Kemper

Bibliography:
Baer, Florence E. *Sources and Analogues of the Uncle Remus Tales*. Helsinki: Suomalainen Tiedeakatemia, 1980. Essential for cross-cultural comparison of an Uncle Remus tale with other folktales of the same type. Finds close African analogs for almost 70 percent of the Uncle Remus tales.
Bickley, R. Bruce, Jr., ed. *Critical Essays on Joel Chandler Harris*. Boston: G. K. Hall, 1981. A casebook for all of Harris' work. Eight of its eighteen scholarly articles address the Uncle Remus stories.
_____. *Joel Chandler Harris*. Boston: Twayne, 1978. Chapters 3, 4, and 7 focus on the major critical approaches to these tales. Useful notes, index, and selected bibliography.
Brookes, Stella Brewer. *Joel Chandler Harris—Folklorist*. Athens: University of Georgia Press, 1950. Chapters 3 through 7 and the appendix are especially valuable in a study of Uncle Remus tales.
Mixon, Wayne. "The Ultimate Irrelevance of Race: Joel Chandler Harris and Uncle Remus in Their Time." *Journal of Southern History* 56, no. 3 (August, 1990): 457-480. By far the most reasoned discussion of the question of whether these stories are racist.

THE TALISMAN

Type of work: Novel
Author: Sir Walter Scott (1771-1832)
Type of plot: Historical
Time of plot: Twelfth century
Locale: The Holy Land
First published: 1825

Principal characters:
RICHARD THE LION-HEARTED, the king of England
SIR KENNETH, the Knight of the Couchant Leopard
EL HAKIM SALARIN, a Muslim physician
THEODORICK OF ENGADDI, a hermit
QUEEN BERENGARIA, Richard's wife
LADY EDITH PLANTAGENET, Richard's kinswoman
CONRADE, the marquis of Montserrat
THE GRAND MASTER OF THE KNIGHTS TEMPLARS

The Story:

Sir Kenneth, the Knight of the Couchant Leopard, was one of the knights who followed King Richard the Lion-Hearted to the Holy Land during the Third Crusade. At the time, Richard was ill with a fever, and the Council of Kings and Princes had sent Kenneth on a mission to Theodorick of Engaddi, a religious hermit who acted as a go-between for both Christians and Muslims. Richard was not aware of the mission, for the other leaders in the crusade were jealous of him and his power, and they resented his high-handed methods and his conceit. In the desert, Kenneth met and fought with a Saracen, an infidel who did not know at first that Kenneth carried a pass from Saladin, the leader of the Muslims. Neither warrior was injured in the fight, and since at that time there was a truce between the Christians and the Muslims, they continued their journey together. The Saracen promised to conduct Kenneth to Theodorick's retreat.

Theodorick showed Kenneth a crypt containing a piece of the Cross. As the knight knelt by the holy relic, a group of nuns, novices, and others living at the convent came into the holy place singing and strewing flowers. One of the robed ladies, King Richard's kinswoman Lady Edith Plantagenet, several times passed him at his devotions, each time dropping a single rose by his side. Although she and Kenneth had never spoken, they loved each other. Marriage was impossible, however, because she was related to the English king and Kenneth was only a poor Scottish knight. Both his birth and his nationality formed a barrier between them, for England and Scotland were constantly at war. Edith was at the convent because she was one of the ladies attending Richard's wife, Queen Berengaria, who was on a pilgrimage to pray for the king's recovery.

Forcing himself to put Lady Edith out of his mind, Kenneth delivered his message to Theodorick, who promised to carry it to Saladin. When Kenneth returned to Richard's camp, he took a Muslim physician called El Hakim with him. This learned man had been sent by Saladin to cure Richard's fever, for although the two rulers were enemies, they respected each other's valor and honor. El Hakim used a talisman to make a potion, which cured the king and brought down his fever. Still weak but restored to health, Richard was grateful to Kenneth for bringing the physician but furious with him for acting as a messenger for the Council of Kings and Princes without his knowledge. He felt certain that the other leaders would soon withdraw from the crusade, for the Christians were greatly outnumbered by the infidels. It would be impossible for Richard to continue the war with his small band of followers.

The other leaders were growing more restless and dissatisfied. Two of them, in particular, wished to see Richard disgraced. Conrade, the marquis of Montserrat, wanted to gain a principality in Palestine for himself, and the Grand Master of the Knights Templars wanted Richard killed and out of the way. The other leaders merely wanted to give up the crusade and return to their homes. Conrade's sly hints and slurs moved the archduke of Austria to place his flag next to Richard's standard on the highest elevation in the camp. Learning of this act, Richard arose from his bed and, though still weak, tore down the flag and stamped on it. Then he ordered Kenneth to guard the English flag and to see that no one placed another flag near it.

Queen Berengaria had grown bored with life in the camp. She sent Kenneth a false message saying that Edith wanted him to come to her tent. He was bewildered by the message and torn between love for Edith and duty to King Richard. At last, overwhelmed by love, he left his trusted dog on guard and walked to Edith's tent.

There he overheard the plotters giggling over their joke. When Edith heard of the plot, she disclaimed any part in the trick and sent him at once back to his post. There he found the royal standard of England gone and his dog apparently on the verge of death. El Hakim appeared suddenly and said that he could cure the animal with his talisman. He also offered to take Kenneth to the Muslim camp to escape the king's wrath, but Kenneth refused to run away. Instead, he confessed his desertion to Richard and was instantly condemned to death. Everyone tried to save him: The queen even confessed the trick played upon him, but Richard would not be moved. Refusing to plead his own cause, Kenneth believed he deserved to die for deserting his post. He asked for a priest and made his confession. Then El Hakim asked the king for a boon in return for saving the royal life with his talisman. He was granted the favor he requested, the privilege of taking Kenneth with him. Therefore, Kenneth became an outcast from the Christian camp.

The other leaders continued their scheming to rob Richard of his power. At last, the Grand Master persuaded Conrade to join him in a plot to kill the king. They captured a dervish, a rabid Muslim member of a wild tribe of desert nomads, disguised him, and sent him, pretending to be drunk, to Richard's tent. The king's guards were lax, but one of the gifts he had been sent by Saladin, a mute Nubian slave, was extremely loyal to him. As the assassin raised his poniard to strike the king, the slave dashed him to the ground. In the scuffle, the Nubian received an arm wound from the dagger. Richard knew the knife was probably poisoned, and he sucked the slave's wound.

The grateful slave wrote a note promising that if Richard would have all the leaders pass in review he, the slave, could identify the one who had stolen the royal flag. The slave was, in reality, Kenneth in disguise. After curing his dog, El Hakim had told him that the animal undoubtedly could identify his assailant. Richard agreed to the plan. As the suspected plotters passed by, the dog attacked Conrade of Montserrat. Conrade denied his guilt, but Richard declared that his innocence could be decided only by trial of arms. The king asked Saladin to choose a neutral ground for the match and courteously invited Saladin to be present at the combat to test Conrade's innocence or guilt.

At the place of combat, where Richard and Saladin met for the first time without their battle armor, Saladin was revealed to be El Hakim. Richard confessed that he had known the slave to be Kenneth, whom he also named as the king's champion. In the fight, Conrade was seriously wounded and hastily carried away by the Grand Master of the Knights Templars, who feared that Conrade would reveal the whole plot against the king. Richard revealed to the queen and Edith that Kenneth was really David, the earl of Huntingdon and prince royal of Scotland. The king had learned his true identity from one of Kenneth's retainers. That noble knight, having vowed not to reveal himself until the Holy City had been taken, had refused to break his oath even to save his life.

The king promised to give him Edith's hand in marriage, although their betrothal belied Theodorick's earlier prophecy that Edith would marry Saladin. Abashed, the old hermit confessed that he had interpreted the signs incorrectly. His vision had been that a kinswoman of the king would marry Richard's enemy in a Christian marriage. Theodorick had thought his vision meant that Saladin would be converted and marry Edith. The true prophecy was that the king's kinswoman would marry Kenneth, a Scot and thus an enemy of the English king and that, being Christians, they would have a Christian wedding.

At a noontime repast given by Saladin in honor of his friends, Saladin killed the Grand Master of the Knights Templars because he had learned that the Grand Master, while bending over Conrade to hear his confession, had stabbed him with a dagger so that he could not confess the plot against Richard. Richard and Saladin both realized that the crusade had failed and that the Christian forces could never hope to overcome the Saracens. The two men parted friends, each honoring the other's skill and valor. A short time later, Edith and Kenneth were married, and Kenneth received the lucky talisman as a wedding gift from Saladin. Although the magic token effected some cures in Europe, it did not again have the power given it by the famous infidel.

Critical Evaluation:

The Talisman contains all the ingredients of a romantic adventure: faraway lands, love, mystery, chivalric courage, and daring. Sir Walter Scott weaves these ingredients together with his usual skill and brings the various subplots together in the final scenes. As is his custom, he makes history serve his own purposes by inventing characters and situations and blending them with real people and historical events. The result is a masterful combination of fact and fiction that makes it possible for the readers to ignore any discrepancies and simply enjoy the well-told tale.

The Talisman functions very effectively as entertainment, but it also operates on a more important level of expression. Throughout his life, Scott was committed to moral truth; he chose the historical novel as the medium for his artistic expression because that genre encompasses the facts of time as well as the truths of morality that endure the tests of time. Furthermore, he was a thoroughly eighteenth century man, concerned with the triumph of reason over passion and with proper conduct in an orderly society. These are the elements that inform *The Talisman*.

Using a particular historical period as the framework for each of his novels, Scott seeks to reveal an era or a way of life representative of that particular period and to demonstrate the relationship between past and present, thereby pointing out attitudes, conflicts, and behavior common to all human beings at all stages of history. To create the historical setting, Scott introduces a character who embodies the period or manner of life with which the novel is concerned, thus avoiding unnecessary detail. In *The Talisman*, King Richard represents the chivalric code and way of life as it was known in England during the Middle Ages. Richard also represents the excess pride and imprudence that can infect anyone, which shows that certain attitudes, weaknesses, and behavior patterns are universal to humankind. Similarly, Sir Kenneth represents the seeker of order and honor through proper conduct. Saladin, although a pagan, symbolizes the object of Sir Kenneth's quest. Clearly, Scott's approach to history relies less on facts than on general historical context. He realized that a reader required more than fact and that reality must be altered and improved to correspond with the desire for unexpected developments. Scott did not abuse history, as he has sometimes been accused of doing, but he made use of it as narrative fiction demanded.

Scott's dual purpose in *The Talisman* is at once to reveal the decadence of the chivalric code and to determine if there is intrinsic value in it. To this end, King Richard the Lion-Hearted symbolizes chivalry, its ceremony, and its power over individuals. This power has become tainted, however, as evidenced by Richard's impetuosity and prideful acts; he represents the fanaticism that blocks clear, rational thought. Honor, as represented in Richard, has become an empty ritual, arising from rashness rather than judicious thought and conduct. Moreover, the presence of such evil forces as the Grand Master and the marquis of Montserrat further demonstrates the degenerate state of the chivalric order.

To illustrate this deterioration most clearly, an antithetical figure, Saladin, is presented as a basis for comparison. He represents the rationality, fidelity, and compassion that are missing in the Crusaders' camp. Saladin does not symbolize a code, but rather the honor that evolves from the organic growth of right conduct nourished by the use of reason and common sense. The character who experiences the influences of both forces and must choose between them is Sir Kenneth, who occupies the middle ground. From the beginning, he is susceptible to the positive influence of Saladin, as is required for the young knight's structural role. Already schooled in the chivalric code and displaying the narrow vision that brings with it, Kenneth meets Saladin, disguised as Sheerkohf, in a duel and emerges victorious in might but not in honor. Afterward, Kenneth doubts the Saracen's sincerity in offering peace between them. When Saladin convinces him of the earnestness of his pledge, the "confidence of the Muslim" makes Kenneth "ashamed of his own doubts." Thereafter, Saladin's wisdom, rationality, and sense of honor affect Kenneth's development.

Saladin's impact on Sir Kenneth succeeds largely through the Saracen's many disguises. Just as King Richard's irrational interpretation of the chivalric code holds sway over the young knight principally for reasons of rank, so too Saladin's influence is an artificial imposition because of his sovereignty. It is Scott's purpose to show that reason, prudence, and moral conduct must grow organically from within the individual rather than be imposed by external forces or rituals. Scott illustrates this truth in disguising Saladin as Adonbec El Hakim, the wise paynim healer. In this role, Saladin appears as a more common individual, like Kenneth, and one who has objectively witnessed the course of events leading to the young knight's conviction and impending execution. The Saracen tries to reason with Kenneth, pointing out that it is foolish to die for a crime of which he is not entirely guilty. In any case, the knight's guilt is to some extent the result of Richard's pride, which created the precariousness of the situation in the first place. Kenneth ignores the Saracen's advice, and it is his irrational adherence to the code of honor based on ritual, not careful thought and action, that induces El Hakim to bargain with Richard and his rash pride for the young knight's life. The Saracen's wise and compassionate intervention enables him to convince Kenneth later that it is more practical to stay alive and redeem himself and his reputation by revealing the real culprit to King Richard and to the entire camp.

Shortly thereafter, when El Hakim spurs Kenneth and himself away from the attacking band of Templars in the desert, the Saracen demonstrates to Sir Kenneth that more good can be gained in living and accomplishing their positive goals than in dying foolishly at the hands of the traitorous Templars. When El Hakim becomes identified with Sheerkohf, a character with whom Kenneth can relate more closely because of their previous relationship, Kenneth begins to recognize the value of Saladin's code of honor, based more positively on reason, common sense, and prudent action. Sheerkohf convinces Kenneth that he is free to choose whatever path he wishes to follow, either to wander off aimlessly or to move forward in seeking his redemption. As Sheerkohf unfolds his plan to disguise Sir Kenneth as a mute Ethiopian slave and thus secretly to infiltrate the Crusaders' camp and reveal the real thief of England's banner, the young knight this time chooses to follow the Saracen's advice. He is beginning to absorb the value derived from reason and prudence and to appreciate the efficacy of judicious thought and self-restrained action. From this point on, the positive resolution of the conflict is inevitable.

Richard seems to learn the lessons of prudence and self-restraint, and the victorious Sir Kenneth enjoys his rewards, the announcement of his real identity and sovereignty and the hand of Lady Edith Plantagenet in marriage. The positive influence of Saladin's character becomes clear as he is identified by all concerned with his various disguises and his valuable deeds; his impact is apparent also in Kenneth's potential as a great leader, for the young knight matured largely because of Saladin's influence. As a final act in the story, the talisman—essentially the symbol of reason, order, and correct conduct—is transferred from East to West, from pagan to Christian, to carry on the magic yet curative work that it had already begun. This somewhat ironic turn reaffirms Scott's belief that human beings, regardless of origin, share a common nature throughout history and that reason and order in society, by exposing the imprudence of outdated codes like chivalry, transcend the boundaries of race, creed, nationality, and time.

"Critical Evaluation" by Larry K. Bright

Bibliography:
Hayden, John O., ed. *Scott: The Critical Heritage*. New York: Barnes & Noble Books, 1970. Information on the initial critical reception of *The Talisman*. Provides reviews ranging from 1805 to an 1883 selection written on Scott by Mark Twain.
Hillhouse, James T. *The Waverley Novels and Their Critics*. New York: Octagon Books, 1970. Provides reviews of the novels from the time of publication, as well as critical interpretations of Scott in the fifty years following his death. Most criticism of *The Talisman* is in the first section.
Johnson, Edgar. *Sir Walter Scott: The Great Unknown*. 2 vols. New York: Macmillan, 1970. A detailed, thorough discussion of Scott's biography. Provides a reading of *The Talisman* that focuses on Scott's misrepresentation of history and historical figures.
Macintosh, W. *Scott and Goethe: German Influence on the Writings of Sir Walter Scott*. Port Washington, N.Y.: Kennikat Press, 1970. Analyzes the history represented in *The Talisman*, and finds Scott to be fairly accurate and authentic in representing Germany and German culture.
Pearson, Hesketh. *Sir Walter Scott: His Life and Personality*. New York: Harper & Row, 1954. Follows the life of Scott through his many novels. Finds *The Talisman* to be one of his weaker novels. Aligns characters of the novel with people Scott may have known. Includes an extended bibliography and index.

TALLEY FAMILY SAGA

Type of work: Drama
Author: Lanford Wilson (1937-   )
Type of plot: Psychological realism
Time of plot: July 4, 1944, *Talley's Folly* and *Talley and Son*; July 4/5, 1977, *Fifth of July*
Locale: Lebanon, Missouri
First performed: Fifth of July, 1978, first published, 1978, revised, 1982; *Talley's Folly,*
    1979, first published, 1979; *Talley and Son,* 1981 (as *A Tale Told*), first published, 1986

> *Principal characters:*
> CALVIN STUART TALLEY, the family patriarch
> CHARLOTTE "LOTTIE" TALLEY, his daughter
> ELDON TALLEY, son of Calvin Talley
> NETTA TALLEY, wife of Eldon Talley
> KENNETH "BUDDY" TALLEY, SR., and
> TIMMY TALLEY, sons of Eldon and Netta
> OLIVE TALLEY, wife of Buddy
> SALLY TALLEY FRIEDMAN, daughter of Eldon and Netta
> MATT FRIEDMAN, husband of Sally Talley
> KENNETH TALLEY JR., son of Buddy and Olive
> JUNE TALLEY, daughter of Buddy and Olive
> JED JENKINS, lover of Kenneth Talley, Jr.
> JOHN and GWEN LANDIS, friends of Kenneth Jr., and June
> SHIRLEY TALLEY, daughter of June Talley and John Landis

The Story:

Talley and Son. It was sunset, July 4, 1944. The Talley family learned from a telegram delivered by Harley Campbell that Eldon Talley's youngest child, Timmy, had been killed in the Pacific in World War II. Family members argued with one another over the family fortune, the importance of war heroes, the decision whether to sell the clothing factory to the out-of-state Delaware Industries, and the difficulty of grief. The eldest Talley, Calvin, was senile, so his son, Eldon, assumed power of attorney for the family businesses, the local bank, and the factory, which he co-owned with Harley.

After Avalaine Platt, the illegitimate daughter of the family's laundry woman, accused Eldon of being her father, Calvin tricked the unsuccessful handyman Emmet Young into marrying Avalaine; he would work as head cutter at the clothing factory. When Eldon and Harley objected, Calvin said that he would not allow Young to work for him; instead, if Harley consented, the family would sell the factory to Delaware Industries and thus rid the Talley family of possible scandal. The factory would then move to Louisiana.

Although Eldon disagreed with his father and threatened to use his power to prevent losing the factory, he convinced Harley to sell him all the Campbell shares from the local bank. This enabled the Talley family to control the bank. Before this point, Eldon had hoped Timmy would return to work in the factory. Calvin and his daughter, Lottie, reminded him that neither Timmy nor his brother, Buddy, had ever truly been interested in the clothing industry. Timmy's interest in the family business was a way to obtain the love and approval of his father.

Eldon's daughter, Sally, appeared. Aunt Lottie, who had encouraged Matt Friedman to take Sally away from the Talley clan, convinced her to elope with him without telling anyone. Lottie did not inform Sally of Timmy's death until after the marriage. As the agreement between Harley and Eldon concerning the bank was finalized, Sally packed. Sally exited, but not before Eldon saw her. Ironically, although everyone in the family, except for Aunt Lottie, was anti-Semitic, Eldon allowed her to leave, telling her he hoped she was not making a mistake. The play ended with Lottie and Timmy (in his role as narrator) reflecting on the deterioration of the house—and, by implication, of the family.

Talley's Folly. At the Talley family boathouse, Matt Friedman and Sally Talley discussed their relationship, World War II, the Talley family, and each other's dreams and aspirations. Although Sally protested that she did not love Matt, it was clear that she did. Sally recognized that she was the family misfit. She worked as a nurse in an army hospital, was outspoken like her Aunt Lottie, and was fired from teaching Sunday School. She also defended Matt against the family's anti-Semitic prejudice. Her father, Eldon, and her brother, Buddy, were most suspicious of Matt's socialistic ideas, which came into direct conflict with the money-making, capitalistic patriarchs. In the past Sally was expected to wed Harley, son of the equally powerful Campbell, until she learned she was barren and thus was neither a financial nor a social asset. Matt, a bachelor in his forties, loved Sally, who was twelve years younger, and fought for her. Sally was reluctant to marry Matt because she could not bear his children; ironically, Matt did not want any children since he thought the world was much too horrible. Despite Matt and Sally's obvious differences and disagreements, the two agreed to marry.

Fifth of July. In 1977, Kenneth Jr., his sister, June, his lover, Jed Jenkins, his niece, Shirley, and his Aunt Sally reunited with June and Ken's friends, Gwen and John Landis. The Landises, Ken, and June all had attended Berkeley during the turbulent 1960's and were actively involved in antiwar protests. Hoping for a better United States, they realized the impossibility of achieving a utopian democratic society that valued the individual human being. Ken had served in Vietnam for a cause in which he did not believe—and had lost both his legs.

Ken, without the consent of his family or the devoted Jed, decided to sell the family home to John, who had become a horrible capitalist. John and Gwen planned to make the house a recording studio. A singer and a drug addict, Gwen hoped to continue her rise to the top. Ken had recently fallen down in front of a classroom of high school children and thus lost all confidence in himself. He did not want to take a position teaching English at the local high school and live on the Talley farm. Aunt Sally, whose husband, Matt, had died recently, wished to scatter his ashes into the lake. Jed, who loved and cultivated the land, scattered the ashes in his rose garden on the Talley property. Ken's decision to sell the family estate was much more difficult than expected. Ken learned that his best friends (including his former lover, John) had run away to Europe without him rather than wait until he could accompany them. He regained his self-confidence and appreciation of family ties when he learned of John's betrayal and when John accidentally knocked him down. Ken could not sell the land to one for whom honor, family, and love of nature meant nothing. Sally would live at the house with the gay couple. Ken changed his mind; he would not sell.

Ken's refusal to sell the Talley home to an outsider and Shirley's dreams for the future demonstrated that there was still hope for the Talley family. He would return to teaching—his lifelong ambition—and Shirley, by rejecting her ill-bred and corrupt father to remain with the Talley clan, might become the most famous person in Missouri history.

Critical Evaluation:

Lanford Wilson's trilogy about the Talley family traces their spiritual decline in the 1940's to their renewed hope and optimism in the late 1970's. *Talley's Folly* and *Talley and Son* take place on July 4, 1944, when the family learns that Eldon's youngest child, Timmy, has been killed. In addition, family outcast Sally agrees on that day to marry Matt Friedman, a man of Russian-Jewish descent. *Fifth of July* may be viewed as the completion of the saga.

Of the three Talley plays, *Fifth of July* and *Talley's Folly* have received the most critical attention, with *Talley's Folly* winning the Pulitzer Prize in drama in 1980. *Fifth of July*, which was first performed Off-Broadway by the Circle Repertory Company in April, 1978 and ran for 168 performances, was revised, with significant changes, and reopened on Broadway in November, 1980, for a longer run.

As does *Talley and Son*, *Talley's Folly* occurs on July 4, 1944. The plots of the two plays overlap, but *Talley's Folly* is far less plot-driven. Set at the family boathouse, *Talley's Folly* is a romantic comedy in which only two characters, Matt Friedman and Sally Talley, discuss their relationship, World War II, the Talley family, and each other's dreams and aspirations.

The events of *Talley and Son* and *Talley's Folly*, while overlapping somewhat, stress two complementary conflicts. Each is concerned with family—most particularly the role a family plays in contributing to and inhibiting the growth of individual members. *Talley and Son* demonstrates the importance of the father-son relationship, and *Talley's Folly* emphasizes the effects of family estrangement on the individual. Timmy, the narrator of the former play, represents the failure of the Talley patriarchs, Eldon and Calvin Stuart Talley, to consider family bonds as more important than money and power. The elder Talley is portrayed as a powerful and corrupt figure in the history of Lebanon; he does whatever he can to protect the family name and to maintain control. Eldon has inherited many of his traits. For example, he has fathered a child out of wedlock but is unwilling to take responsibility. None of the sons is able to relate well to his father or to become the son his father might have wished.

Sally's conflict in *Talley's Folly* concerns whether she should rebel against her patriarchal family and marry an outsider. Thus, while the title *Talley and Son* emphasizes the importance of familial male bonding, both plays stress the failure of mothers and fathers to teach their children humane values. The mother figures—Olive, Buddy's wife, Aunt Lottie, and Netta, Eldon's wife—have, like their husbands, contributed to the family's decline through their own spiritual weakness. Lottie is, however, the strongest rebel; she recognizes the flaws of her father and her brother—and the inherent problems in the capitalistic American dream—but is physically and emotionally incapable of caring for herself. Her inner strength is clear, nevertheless, when she tells Sally she will rebel vicariously through her niece's marriage. Lottie serves as a mother figure to Sally, hoping she will reject their family's corrupt values. Sally's own mother, Netta, is too neurotic to take care of herself or her family effectively, though her outbursts at Eldon show that she could, were she to allow herself, stand up against him for his extramarital affairs.

In *Fifth of July*, family plays a significant role as well, although the play advocates a broader definition of family. Aunt Sally influences and cares for Shirley, June's daughter. She becomes the clan's matriarch since Olive and Buddy have moved to California, forsaking home and the past. The ideal gay relationship between Ken and Jed may perhaps be the first in an American drama glorifying the values of family and tradition. On the one hand, *Fifth of July* critiques the American dream of capitalism, showing the flaws of the capitalists John and Gwen Landis in, for example, the harshness and vulgarity of their language and in their immoral betrayal of Ken during the Vietnam War. On the other hand, the American dream of individualism, of land, of family, and of home triumph in the historically latest Talley play.

All three plays criticize American concepts of masculinity, male-female relationships, and heroism, but *Fifth of July* most fully explores the effects of war. Although the other two Talley plays touch on antiwar sentiment (particularly evident in the cruelty and violence of Timmy's death), *Fifth of July* directly confronts the Vietnam War, the concept of American heroism, and the idealism of those who fought against the Vietnam conflict. Vietnam symbolizes for Wilson the failure of American men and women to acknowledge fundamental problems within the American psyche. As Ken and John try to convince Wes, John and Gwen's sidekick, that by definition "Heroic actions must have saving results," Wilson ironically emphasizes that for Vietnam there was no such effect—that for Ken, like so many others who fought for the United States, his sacrifice was futile. Although World War II had positive results, Vietnam failed miserably—as did the antiwar and related civil rights movements—in achieving the American Dream. The personal sacrifices of Timmy and his nephew, Ken, Jr., are underappreciated when the wars are over.

Each of the Talley plays affirms idealism while warning Americans against the effects of materialism, capitalism, and war on the American psyche. All the play's conflicts emerge from a lack of humane concern for family and for those outside the family. Like many American dramatists, Wilson fears that money and materialism lead to objectification of the human being and to denial of the most basic of American values, the worth of the individual.

D. Dean Shackelford

Bibliography:

Barnett, Gene A. *Lanford Wilson*. Boston: Twayne, 1987. Useful general interpretations of individual characters, the major themes, and other elements of the Talley plays. Bibliography.

Cooperman, Robert. "The Talley Plays and the Evolution of the American Family." In *Lanford Wilson: A Casebook*, edited by Jackson R. Bryer. New York: Garland, 1994. Excellent study of the Talley plays, emphasizing the changing social mores affecting the family. Describes Wilson's trilogy as a history of the American family. Asserts that *Fifth of July* represents the integration of traditional and modern families and thus offers hope.

Herman, William. "Down and Out in Lebanon and New York: Lanford Wilson." In *Understanding Contemporary American Drama*. Columbia: University of South Carolina Press, 1987. Offers an interpretive and biographical introduction to Wilson. Emphasizes the connections between the plays, which show Wilson's American optimism. Bibliography.

Jacobi, Martin J. "The Comic Vision of Lanford Wilson." *Studies in the Literary Imagination* 21, no. 2 (Fall, 1988): 119-134. A general but useful analysis of the comedy in several Wilson plays, including *Fifth of July* and *Talley's Folly*. Focuses primarily on how to classify the plays based on their endings.

Martine, James J. "Charlotte's Daughters: Changing Gender Roles and Family Structures in Lanford Wilson." In *Lanford Wilson: A Casebook*, edited by Jackson R. Bryer. New York: Garland, 1994. Analyzes the intersection of changing family and gender roles in the Talley plays. Sees Sally as the central figure of the Talley plays, tracing the evolution of the Talley women from Aunt Lottie to Shirley.

Williams, Philip Middleton. *A Comfortable House: Lanford Wilson, Marshall W. Mason, and the Circle Repertory Theatre*. Jefferson, N.C.: McFarland, 1993. Although focuses on the Talley plays, the primary emphasis is on the collaboration between Wilson and Mason. Useful but not heavily interpretive.

Witham, Barry B. "Images of America: Wilson, Weller, and Horovitz." *Theatre Journal* 34 (1982): 223-232. Concentrates on plays set on Independence Day, comparing Wilson's *Fifth of July* to plays by Weller and Horovitz and showing how each writer views American values.

TAMAR

Type of work: Poetry
Author: Robinson Jeffers (1887-1962)
Type of plot: Psychological
Time of plot: World War I
Locale: Carmel Coast Range, California
First published: 1924

> *Principal characters:*
> TAMAR CAULDWELL, a young woman
> LEE CAULDWELL, her brother
> DAVID CAULDWELL, her father
> JINNY CAULDWELL, David's sister
> STELLA MORELAND, the sister of David's dead wife
> WILL ANDREWS, Tamar's suitor

The Story:

Injured when his horse stumbled and fell over a sea cliff, young Lee Cauldwell was nursed back to health by his sister Tamar. Lee, who had lived a wild and dissolute life, vowed to give up his drinking and debauchery. He and Tamar became devoted to each other during his convalescence, so much so that Lee jealously warned a former suitor of his sister to stay away from her. Old David Cauldwell feared what might result from the isolation of his family. His fears were confirmed when the brother and sister, after swimming in the river, were drawn to each other.

The Cauldwell family was a peculiar group. Besides the father and the two children, it contained two old women. Aunt Jinny, an idiot sister of David Cauldwell, was cared for by Aunt Stella, the sister of David's dead wife. Through the confused mumblings of Jinny, Tamar realized that an incestuous relationship had occurred between David and his sister Helen.

A short time later, Tamar discovered that she was pregnant. Rather than admit that Lee was the father of her child, she deliberately sought out and seduced her former suitor, Will Andrews. Disgust and revulsion grew in her until she hated her two lovers and, most of all, herself. She felt that she would lose her mind unless she talked to someone.

Aunt Stella was a medium through whom the voices of the dead sometimes spoke. In desperation, Tamar appealed to her to let her speak to Helen. That evening she and Stella, with the imbecile Jinny between them, stole down to the seashore, so that they would not be discovered by the men. Stella gradually fell into a trance, and through her lips Tamar heard the voice of a man who told her that the coastline country had been the land of the Indians, where their gods used to come to them. He ordered Tamar to strip and dance so that the gods would come again. Against her will, Tamar danced to strange guttural chants from the lips of the entranced woman. After a while the chanting ceased and Tamar returned slowly to her senses. Then through the lips of Stella she heard the voice of Helen taunting her for the shameful orgy. The voice, after warning Tamar that she would lose her child, told her that a fire Tamar had earlier set in the cabin would be quenched before it fulfilled its purpose of destroying the corruption of the Cauldwell family. Then in a mournful voice Helen told Tamar of the horror of death, of her longing for life, and of her need to haunt Tamar as long as she lived, because she possessed life. On the shore, unassisted by anyone and in great pain, Tamar lost her baby.

Back in the cabin once more, Tamar could scarcely restrain the hatred she felt for her family. All pity had left her, and all love. In order to revenge herself on Helen, she tempted her old father with her beauty. Through the medium of Stella, Helen cursed Tamar and pleaded with her not to commit that ultimate folly.

Lee, who had returned to his drinking, enlisted in the army, but Tamar was determined not to let him go. She told him that the child had not been his but Will Andrews', who had visited her late at night after she had set a lighted lamp in her window as a signal. Tamar taunted Lee until he lashed her with a whip.

When Will Andrews came to the cabin that night, Tamar told him that Lee would leave the following day for the army and would like to say goodbye to him. The meeting between the two men was cool but amiable. While Lee was out of the room, Tamar showed Will her whip-lash wounds and told him that she had lost his child through outrages which both her father and Lee had perpetrated upon her. When Lee returned with his father, Will accused him of those atrocities. In turn, Lee accused Will of having attempted to set fire to their home. Tamar, who herself had been responsible, said nothing but goaded on the fight with her smiles and wordless encouragement to Will. Lee stabbed Will fatally.

Helen, through the person of Stella, tried to save old David Cauldwell from the destroying forces of hate and evil, but he refused to heed her warnings. Downstairs the idiot Jinny, alone and disturbed, was attracted by the light of a candle. She carried it to the window, where the flame set fire to the blowing curtains. Her dying shrieks attracted the attention of those upstairs.

Lee tried to run to her, but Tamar clung to him and would not let him go. Will, dying, dragged himself as far as the window. Stella rushed out into the flaming hall and perished. The old man prayed brokenly, groveling on the floor. Lee made one last effort to escape, but Tamar, glorying in the destruction of her three lovers, embraced him until the flames consumed them all.

Critical Evaluation:

Robinson Jeffers was the son of an Old Testament theologian, who gave him a classical education in Europe and in the United States. After beginning graduate studies first in medicine and then in forestry, Jeffers concluded that he wanted to become a poet, but he did not find his own voice in verse until he and his wife came to the small town of Carmel, California, at the northern end of the spectacular sweep of coast known as Big Sur, with its towering highlands, wild rivers and creeks, abundant wildlife, and crashing surf. He built a stone dwelling, Tor House, and next to it Hawk Tower, made of boulders from the shore below the house. Jeffers built the tower to please his wife, Una, who admired the towers of Ireland; he named it for his favorite animal, whose intense awareness and frightening ferocity seemed to Jeffers emblematic of life at its most intense.

Jeffers had found not only a home but also a locale for his poems. The dramatic landscape, with its tall mountains falling abruptly into the immense, boiling ocean, an arena for the struggle of animal and marine life, seemed to cry out for tragedy like all beautiful places, to paraphrase another poem by Jeffers. Directly across the mouth of the Carmel River from Tor House lies Point Lobos, its wild beauty now preserved as a state park. Here Jeffers places *Tamar* (1924), the story of the Cauldwell family; the poem is the first of many long narrative poems through which he presents his poetic themes and develops his philosophical viewpoint.

The themes of the long poems are the fatal effects of human passion, which is always egocentric and, therefore, self-destructive, not only on the people who indulge that passion, but also on those around them—usually a family. This passion is acted upon in a natural setting of beauty and power, a reminder that people are both part of nature and, therefore, driven by impulses and instincts beyond their control or understanding. They are also subject to forces outside themselves—forces which eventually defeat and destroy them. This assessment of the human condition is bleak, but the philosophical viewpoint which Jeffers has adopted is beyond that bleak position. Passion, violence, sin, and death are not just elements in people's lives; they are also elements that enable the universe to live, grow, die, and combine again to be reborn. As humans, as part of nature, people cannot escape this fate. Furthermore—and here Jeffers differs from many romantic poets—there is no point in people complaining about these elements or trying futilely to change them. People might as well "be angry at the sun for setting/ If these things anger you" (*Be Angry at the Sun*, 1941). Jeffers' position is similar to classical Stoicism. He feels that if people abandon the human perspective and think cosmically, which Jeffers calls "inhumanism," people may be at peace because they can then see the entire cycle of life as something transcendent and magnificent, fraught though it may be with violence and flux.

The Bible and the Greek tragedy are the models for Jeffers' narrative poems. Tamar Cauldwell has the same name as two Tamars in the Old Testament; one was raped by her brother (Samuel 13), and the other deceived her father-in-law into fathering her child (Genesis 38). Jeffers' character has qualities of both these literary forebears, although she has not been raped by her brother; instead, she has willingly entered into a sexual relationship , and she has seduced her father and a third lover, the last in order to cover up the cause of her pregnancy.

Tamar Cauldwell's sin is worse than those of the biblical Tamars; she chooses to be incestuous and takes not one but two other lovers. Jeffers uses human sexuality, and particularly incest, as a symbol of people's fatal self-involvement. Tamar is the first of a series of Jeffers' characters who recognize that sin and pain are not, as Fyodor Dostoevski or Friedrich Nietzsche might say, a necessity; instead, Jeffers' characters recognize that sin and pain are inevitable.

Tamar embraces, even revels in, her own excesses, but she also knows that acknowledging her guilt does not free her from the consequences of sin; she dies along with the others when the purifying fire, which wipes out the old to make way for the new, envelopes the house. The fire is accidentally set by Jinny, who thinks of a candle as a beautiful plaything; this incident emphasizes the role of chance and accident in the life of the world and the creatures in it.

Jeffers was familiar with the work of cultural anthropologists such as Francis Macdonald Cornford and Jane E. Harrison, who theorize that Greek tragedy and the myths which it dramatized grew out of fertility rituals. Jeffers was also familiar with the comparative mytho- logical work of Sir James George Frazer, whose speculations in *The Golden Bough* (1890) about the interrelatedness of world religions and myths also informed T. S. Eliot's *The Waste Land* (1922). The difference between Eliot and Jeffers is that Eliot imposed a mythic structure on an urban, modern landscape while Jeffers saw the mythic patterns growing up out of the land and the sea before him. For Jeffers, the California coast was a great stage on which the drama of existence was played out daily. *Tamar* is the most powerful work in a series of works in which he investigates the implications of this cosmic process.

"Critical Evaluation" by Jim Baird

Bibliography:
Brophy, Robert J."*Tamar.*" In *Robinson Jeffers: Myth, Ritual, and Symbol in His Narrative Poems.* Hamden, Conn.: Archon Books, 1976. Shows Robinson Jeffers' use of Greek myth and world mythology to establish his view of humankind as fated to endure pain and suffering. Contains extensive bibliography on both Jeffers and myth criticism.

_____. "*Tamar, The Cenci*, and Incest." *American Literature* 42, no. 2 (May, 1970): 241-244. Investigates the connections between Jeffers and the romantics through the incest theme as it appears in both *Tamar* and Percy Bysshe Shelley's drama, *The Cenci*.

Carpenter, Frederic I. "The Poetry of Myth: The Long Poems." In *Robinson Jeffers*. New York: Grosset & Dunlap, 1962. Analyzes all Jeffers' long narratives, with particular focus on *Tamar*. The best short introduction to Jeffers' work. Contains bibliography.

Hunt, Tim. "A Voice in Nature: Jeffers' *"Tamar" and Other Poems*. *American Literature* 61, no. 2 (May, 1989): 230-244. Reprinted in slightly different form as "The Problematic Nature of *'Tamar' and Other Poems* in *Centennial Essays for Robinson Jeffers*, ed. Robert Zaller. Newark: University of Delaware Press, 1991. Shows how Jeffers' poetic concerns are reflected in the revision of *Tamar* and the other poems in the volume in which it was first collected.

Zaller, Robert. "The Birth of the Hero." In *The Cliffs of Solitude*. Cambridge, England: Cambridge University Press, 1983. A psychological reading of the character Tamar, along with Jeffers' other major protagonists. Contains bibliography.

TAMBURLAINE THE GREAT

Type of work: Drama
Author: Christopher Marlowe (1564-1593)
Type of plot: Tragedy
Time of plot: Fourteenth century
Locale: Asia
First performed: part 1, c. 1587; part 2, 1587; first published, 1590

Principal characters:
TAMBURLAINE, the Scythian conqueror
ZENOCRATE, his wife
BAJAZETH, the emperor of the Turks
CALLAPINE, his son
MYCETES, the king of Persia
COSROE, his brother
THERIDAMAS,
TECHELLES, and
USUMCASANE, followers of Tamburlaine
ORCANES, the king of Natolia

The Story:

When Mycetes became king of Persia, his brother, Cosroe, told him openly that he was not fit for the office. Among Mycetes' greatest concerns were the raids of Tamburlaine, the Scythian shepherd who had become a bandit. Because it was rumored that this robber chief aspired to rule the East, Mycetes sent Theridamas with a thousand troops to capture Tamburlaine, and he ordered another lord named Menaphon to follow Theridamas. Cosroe sarcastically pointed out to the king that Menaphon was needed in Babylon, where the province was about to revolt against a sovereign as inferior as Mycetes. At this insult, Mycetes threatened he would be revenged against his brother.

Menaphon asked Cosroe if he were not afraid of the king's threat, but Cosroe assured the Persian lord that there was a plot afoot to make Cosroe himself emperor of Asia. He claimed that it hurt him to witness the scorn now heaped on Persia, which had formerly awed the entire world. Soon afterward, the revolt Cosroe had predicted took place. The rebellious lords offered Cosroe the crown, who set out to annex the thousand troops of Theridamas and conquer his brother Mycetes.

On a Scythian hill, Tamburlaine was holding Zenocrate, the daughter of the sultan of Egypt. He spoke grandly of kingdoms he would conquer, and Techelles and Usumcasane echoed his boasts, vowing to follow Tamburlaine to the death. The ambitious leader was in love with Zenocrate, and he promised her all the wealth and power in his kingdom. Suddenly, Mycetes' thousand horse troops attacked Tamburlaine's five hundred foot soldiers. When Theridamas accosted the Scythian, he was so impressed with his appearance and with Tamburlaine's visions of mighty kingdoms and power that the outlaw was able to persuade Theridamas to become an ally.

Cosroe prepared to send troops to join Tamburlaine and Theridamas by the river Araris and there to engage the forces of Mycetes, who was fuming with rage at the revolt. Meander, a follower of Mycetes, conceived the proposal that he who conquered Tamburlaine would be offered the province of Albania, and he who took Theridamas could have Media. Mycetes stipulated however that Cosroe be captured alive. Mycetes was convinced that the followers of the bandit Tamburlaine could be bribed to desert their leader, since he had purchased their loyalty by bribes in the first place.

When Cosroe met Tamburlaine, the Scythian boasted of his great future; Theridamas indicated to Cosroe that he believed in Tamburlaine's ability. Certain of victory, Cosroe promised Techelles and Usumcasane rewards for their deeds, and, indeed, Mycetes was defeated. After the victory, Tamburlaine then bribed Theridamas, Techelles, and Usumcasane with a promise of kingdoms of their own if they would attack Cosroe. Marveling at Tamburlaine's arrogance and daring, Cosroe prepared for battle. Cosroe was wounded in battle, and Tamburlaine, gloating over his easy conquest, proclaimed himself king of Persia.

At the court in Algiers, the kings of Fez, Morocco, and Algiers fumed at the thought that a bandit had taken Persia and was now forcing them to raise their siege of Greek Constantinople. Bajazeth, king of the Turks, dispatched a message to Tamburlaine threatening him if he dared set foot in Africa. Meanwhile the kings planned to take Greece by siege.

Zenocrate had slowly grown to admire Tamburlaine, who was now plotting the conquest of the Turkish kings. Zabina, wife of Bajazeth, sneered at Zenocrate and called her a concubine. After subduing Bajazeth, Tamburlaine made Zabina Zenocrate's attendant slave. To show his might, Tamburlaine had put Bajazeth in a cage and used it as a footstool. Bajazeth and Zabina continued however to hurl disdainful remarks and threats at him.

The next victim of the Scythian's lust for power was the sultan of Egypt, Zenocrate's father. As Tamburlaine's armies prepared to take Damascus, Zenocrate gently asked her lover to deal kindly with the city of her father, but he refused. Zenocrate grieved until Tamburlaine promised not to harm her father when Damascus fell. By now the Scythian conqueror loved Zenocrate dearly. While ordering three emissaries from Damascus to be killed, he thought of his beloved's beauty and tenderness. Zenocrate herself was torn between her conscience, which revolted against her lord's cruelty, and her love for him.

When Tamburlaine brought the sultan to Zenocrate alive, the conqueror promised to give the sultan's kingdom back to him if Zenocrate would accept the title of Queen of Egypt. She readily accepted this condition and Tamburlaine began planning the wedding.

By this time, Bajazeth and Zabina had killed themselves by dashing their heads against the bars of the cage in which Tamburlaine had imprisoned the Turkish monarch. Orcanes, the king of Natolia, who was preparing for a battle with Sigismund, the king of Hungary, learned that Tamburlaine was mustering an attack. He sent for all the Christian rulers of Europe to form an alliance against an invasion by the Scythian. The former enemies Sigismund and Orcanes the Mohammedan entered into a pact of friendship with the rulers of Buda and Bohemia.

Callapine, son of Bajazeth and a prisoner of Tamburlaine, was guarded by Almeda, whom the young prince bribed with offers of wealth and power if he would help him escape. Tamburlaine and Zenocrate by now had three sons, Calyphas, Amyras, and Celebinus. Calyphas expressed a desire to lead a peaceful life with his mother.

The treaty of the monarchs against Tamburlaine did not hold. When the Mohammedan Orcanes withdrew his troops from his campaign against the Christians, Sigismund was urged by his allies to attack Orcanes. Orcanes was trapped, for he was at the same time preparing to attack Tamburlaine. The betrayed monarch, crying for his enemies' Christ to help him defeat the traitors, prepared to defend himself. In the battle, Sigismund was killed and Orcanes emerged the victor.

Zenocrate had become ill. When she died, Tamburlaine was overcome with such grief that he would not have her buried until after his own death. Having escaped with the aid of Almeda,

Callapine returned to his father's kingdom and marshaled the allies to defeat Tamburlaine and avenge Bajazeth's death. Inconsolable in his grief for Zenocrate, Tamburlaine prepared to fight the forces of Callapine. The Scythian's sons, Amyras and Celebinus, were eager for battle, but Calyphas, who disliked bloodshed, refused to join the fighting.

After he had vanquished his Turkish enemies, Tamburlaine returned to his camp and wrathfully stabbed Calyphas, who had remained in his tent all the while. The Turkish monarchs were bridled like horses, and under Tamburlaine's whip, forced to pull his carriage. The conqueror then took Babylon, which led to terrible plunder, rape, and murder. Tamburlaine was now mad with lust and power. Only Callapine was still able to oppose him.

Finally, Tamburlaine fell ill with a mysterious malady, and his physician declared that he was dying. After crowning his son Amyras monarch of his empires, the dying conqueror sent for Zenocrate's hearse. Bidding his son to reign with power, Tamburlaine, the scourge of God, leaned over his beloved Zenocrate's coffin and died.

Critical Evaluation:

A study of driving ambition, *Tamburlaine the Great* is also notable for the dignity and beauty of Christopher Marlowe's lines. The poetry of the play is all the more remarkable for being among the first written in English blank verse. Marlowe wrote with so much original invention, that for a time many scholars believed him the author of some plays now attributed to William Shakespeare. It is safe to say that Marlowe is the best of the pre-Shakespearean playwrights.

Marlowe's turbulent life ended tragically, and perhaps characteristically, in a barroom brawl with a man named Ingram Frizer. Even though he was only twenty-nine when he died, Marlowe had managed to set a precedent for the development of English drama by leaving behind a model of Senecan dramatic form. His first production, *Tamburlaine the Great*, more a dramatic masque than a play, was a milestone of early Elizabethan drama. Certainly Shakespeare must have been influenced, especially in *Julius Caesar*, by the conjunction of "Nature," "Fortune," and "stars" in the construction of Tamburlaine's character. Above all, Marlowe made blank verse the accepted mode of Elizabethan theatrical expression, both to reflect delicate grace and to pronounce such mighty lines as, "Even as when windy exhalations/ Fighting for passage, tilt within the earth." The character Tamburlaine is shown capable of a certain tenderness because of Marlowe's poetic versatility. As the hero says to Zenocrate,

> With milk-white harts upon an ivory sled
> Thou shalt be drawn amidst the frozen pools,
> And scale the icy mountains' lofty tops,
> Which with thy beauty will be soon resolv'd.

Basing his drama on the history of Timur the Lane (1336-1406), a Mongol conqueror and descendant of Genghis Khan, Marlowe constructed his first Herculean hero who is a blood-thirsty personification of the Renaissance spirit of boldness, defiance, and determination to test the limitations of human ability. Invulnerable to all attacks but that of death, Tamburlaine moves toward his goals undaunted by considerations of destiny or accidental circumstances. He is the master of his own destiny simply because he decides to be and finds no one strong enough to deny him his ambitions. He says to Theridamas:

> Forsake thy king, and do but join with me
> And we will triumph over all the world:
> I hold the Fates bound fast in iron chains,
> And with my hand turn Fortune's wheel about.

Here is the hubris of classical Athenian tragedy, but with a difference: Tamburlaine is not struck down because of it; instead, he succeeds in everything he has time to undertake. One of the most effective moments of part 2, which is overall less compelling than part 1, is the passage in Act V when Tamburlaine says, "Give me a map; then let me see how much/ Is left for me to conquer all the world." Only physical inevitabilities bring Marlowe's hero low, although it is clear that he becomes somewhat vulnerable once he gains love and possessions and sons.

He succeeds in attaining his goals because he regards the world and every thing and every person in it as an object. It is not surprising that his mighty, rhetorical speeches are filled with references to crimson robes, meteors, jewels, vermilion tents, and gold crowns. There is, in fact, a close connection between Tamburlaine's rhetoric and his achievements. He is godlike in the sense that what he says he does; his words become deeds. It is not surprising that he regards even Zenocrate's dead body as an object "Embalm'd with cassia, ambergris, and myrrh/ Not lapp'd in lead, but in a sheet of gold." It is but another splendid, colorful object under his control to preserve or destroy. In the same vein, he uses his victims as horses to pull his chariots. Tamburlaine is the egotistic dream of the Renaissance epitomized: "Of stature tall, and straightly fashioned/ Like his desire, lift upwards and divine." In the correspondence between his appearance and his character there is a prediction of Shakespeare's Hamlet, but the difference between the two heroes—Tamburlaine does not falter in his purpose for a moment—is much more striking than any similarities.

From the very beginning, after Tamburlaine steps into the power vacuum created by Mycetes' insufficiency (which is described as the inability to use "great and thundering speech"), the play is a series of episodic atrocities, connected only by the unswerving ambition of the hero. The action of the play has as such little to recommend it by way of originality or structural genius. The hero is both the center and the continuity of the work. Cosroe calls him the model of humanity, as Shakespeare was to call his Hamlet and his Brutus. One of Tamburlaine's most sympathetic characteristics is his never waning enthusiasm—the *sprezzatura* of the Italian Renaissance:

> TAMB.: What say my other friends? Will you be kings?
> TECH.: Ay, if I could, with all my heart, my lord.
> TAMB.: Why, that's well said, Techelles, so would I.

Combined with this essential enthusiasm is Tamburlaine's expression of a typically Renaissance longing for the infinite of something, whether it be the infinite knowledge sought by Faustus, the infinite riches desired by the Jew of Malta, or Tamburlaine's insatiable thirst for power. Marlowe's prologue promises that the hero will be seen "threatening the world with high astounding terms," and all three last words have thematic significance. Tamburlaine's description of himself as "the chiefest lamp of all the earth" is the most explicit indication that he desires to join the company of the stars, that is, to escape from earth and wander among realms unknown to ordinary humans. The root of the word "astounding" is related to the intensely rhetorical nature of Tamburlaine's every speech. Indeed, his approach to stellar glory is primarily through the flamboyant energy of his language—Marlowe's "mighty line." It is no coincidence that Tamburlaine is rarely seen in action but usually in speech.

Finally, the word "terms" draws the thematic structure together and indicates the boundaries and limitations of human experience and behavior that Tamburlaine means to break through and cast aside with his speech. This explains why his victims are always so startled. He has no respect for ordinary conventions and not only does the most outlandish things to kings and generals but also slays them. Yet it is just as important to note that Tamburlaine has no divine aspirations. What he seeks to accomplish remains human: "A god is not so glorious as a king:/ I think the pleasures they enjoy in heaven/ Cannot compare with kingly joys in earth." It is for his successful extension of human terms that Tamburlaine becomes a seminal character in the development of English Renaissance drama.

"Critical Evaluation" by Kenneth John Atchity

Bibliography:

Battenhouse, Roy W. *Marlowe's Tamburlaine: A Study in Renaissance Moral Philosophy*. 1941. Reprint. Nashville, Tenn.: Vanderbilt University Press, 1964. Battenhouse contends that the play upholds traditional morality and the Christian worldview.

Friedenreich, Kenneth. *Christopher Marlowe: An Annotated Bibliography of Criticism Since 1950*. Metuchen, N.J.: Scarecrow Press, 1979. Eighty-three annotated citations to *Tamburlaine* point the reader to interpretive articles and books.

Knoll, Robert E. "Caesarism." In *Christopher Marlowe*. New York: Twayne, 1969. A good starting place for the general reader. Knoll considers the hero appealing in his diabolic aspirations.

Kocher, Paul H. *Christopher Marlowe: A Study of His Thought, Learning, and Character*. Chapel Hill: University of North Carolina Press, 1946. Argues that Marlowe's view in *Tamburlaine the Great* is highly iconoclastic and unconventional.

Levin, Harry. "The Progress of Pomp." In *The Overreacher: A Study of Christopher Marlowe*. Cambridge, Mass.: Harvard University Press, 1952. One of the most influential books on Marlowe. Presents the Marlovian hero as a rebel and explores the use of language and irony in *Tamburlaine the Great*.

Ribner, Irving, ed. *Christopher Marlowe's Tamburlaine Part One and Part Two: Text and Major Criticism*. New York: Odyssey Press, 1974. The most comprehensive book on the plays. Features an authoritative text edited and glossed by Ribner. Also reprints eleven influential essays (one from Ellis-Fermor's milestone 1927 book on Marlowe), and concludes with a useful bibliography. The final essay by Kenneth Friedenreich surveys the critical history of the plays.

THE TAMING OF THE SHREW

Type of work: Drama
Author: William Shakespeare (1564-1616)
Type of plot: Comedy
Time of plot: Sixteenth century
Locale: Padua, Italy
First performed: c. 1593-1594; first published, 1623

Principal characters:
BAPTISTA, a rich gentleman of Padua
KATHARINA, his shrewish daughter
BIANCA, another daughter
PETRUCHIO, Katharina's suitor
LUCENTIO, a student in love with Bianca
TRANIO, his servant
VINCENTIO, Lucentio's father
GREMIO and
HORTENSIO, Lucentio's rivals
A PEDANT

The Story:

As a joke, a beggar was carried, while asleep, to the house of a noble lord and there dressed in fine clothes and waited on by many servants. The beggar was told that he was a rich man who, in a demented state, had imagined himself to be a beggar, but who was now restored to his senses. The lord and his court had great sport with the poor fellow, to the extent of dressing a page as the beggar's rich and beautiful wife and presenting the supposed woman to him as his dutiful and obedient spouse. The beggar, in his stupidity, assumed his new role as though it were his own, and he and his lady settled down to watch a play prepared for their enjoyment.

Lucentio and Tranio, his servant, had journeyed to Padua so that Lucentio could study in that ancient city. Tranio persuaded his master that life was not all study and work and that he should find pleasures also in his new residence. On their arrival in the city, Lucentio and Tranio encountered Baptista and his daughters, Katharina and Bianca. These three were accompanied by Gremio and Hortensio, young gentlemen both in love with gentle Bianca. Baptista, however, would not permit his younger daughter to marry until someone should take Katharina off of his hands. Although Katharina was wealthy and beautiful, she was such a shrew that no suitor would have her. Baptista, not knowing how to control his sharp-tongued daughter, announced that Gremio or Hortensio must find a husband for Katharina before either could woo Bianca. He charged them also to find tutors for the two girls, that they might be skilled in music and poetry.

Unobserved, Lucentio and Tranio witnessed this scene. At first sight, Lucentio also fell in love with Bianca and determined to have her for himself. His first act was to change clothes with Tranio, so that the servant appeared to be the master. Lucentio then disguised himself as a tutor in order to woo Bianca without her father's knowledge.

About the same time, Petruchio came to Padua. He was a rich and noble man of Verona, come to Padua to visit his friend Hortensio and to find for himself a rich wife. Hortensio told Petruchio of his love for Bianca and of her father's decree that she could not marry until a husband had been found for Katharina. Petruchio declared that the stories told about spirited Katharina were to his liking, particularly the account of her great wealth, and he expressed a desire to meet her. Hortensio proposed that Petruchio seek Katharina's father and present his family's name and history. Hortensio, meanwhile, planned to disguise himself as a tutor and thus plead his own cause with Bianca.

The situation grew confused. Lucentio was disguised as a tutor and his servant Tranio was dressed as Lucentio. Hortensio was also disguised as a tutor. Petruchio was to ask for Katharina's hand. Also, unknown to anyone but Katharina, Bianca loved neither Gremio nor Hortensio and swore that she would never marry rather than accept one or the other as her husband.

Petruchio easily secured Baptista's permission to marry his daughter Katharina, for the poor man was only too glad to have his older daughter finally wed. Petruchio's courtship was a strange one indeed, a battle of wits, words, and wills. Petruchio was determined to bend Katharina to his will, but Katharina scorned and berated him with a vicious tongue. Nevertheless, she had to obey her father's wish and marry him, and the nuptial day was set. Then Gremio and Tranio, the latter still believed to be Lucentio, vied with each other for Baptista's permission to marry Bianca. Tranio won because he claimed more gold and vaster lands than Gremio could declare. In the meantime, Hortensio and Lucentio, both disguised as tutors, wooed Bianca.

As part of the taming process, Petruchio arrived late for his wedding, and when he did appear he wore old and tattered clothes. Even during the wedding ceremony Petruchio acted like a madman, stamping, swearing, and cuffing the priest. Immediately afterward he dragged Katharina away from the wedding feast and took her to his country home, there to continue his scheme to break her to his will. He gave her no food and no time for sleep, while always pretending that nothing was good enough for her. In fact, he all but killed her with kindness. Before he was through, Katharina agreed that the moon was the sun, that an old man was a woman.

Bianca fell in love with Lucentio, whom she thought to be her tutor. In chagrin, Hortensio threw off his disguise and he and Gremio forswore their love for any girl so fickle. Tranio, still hoping to win her for himself, found an old pedant to act the part of Vincentio, Lucentio's father. The pretended father argued his son's cause with Baptista until that lover of gold promised his daughter's hand to Lucentio as he thought, but in reality to Tranio. When Lucentio's true father appeared on the scene, he was considered an impostor and almost put in jail for his deceit. The real Lucentio and Bianca, meanwhile, had been secretly married. Returning from the church with his bride, he revealed the whole plot to Baptista and the others. At first Baptista was angry at the way in which he had been duped, but Vincentio spoke soothingly and soon cooled his rage.

Hortensio, in the meantime, had married a rich widow. To celebrate these weddings, Lucentio gave a feast for all the couples and the fathers. After the ladies had retired, the three newly married men wagered one hundred pounds each that his own wife would most quickly obey his commands. Lucentio sent first for Bianca, but she sent word that she would not come. Then Hortensio sent for his wife, but she too refused to obey his summons. Petruchio then ordered Katharina to appear, and she came instantly to do his bidding. At his request she also forced Bianca and Hortensio's wife to go to their husbands. Baptista was so delighted with his daughter's meekness and willing submission that he added another twenty thousand crowns to her dowry. Katharina told them all that a wife should live only to serve her husband and that a woman's heart and tongue ought to be as soft as her body. Petruchio had tamed the shrew forever.

Critical Evaluation:

Although it is not possible to determine the dates of composition of William Shakespeare's plays with absolute certainty, it is generally agreed that the early comedy *The Taming of the Shrew* was probably written after *The Two Gentlemen of Verona* (c. 1594-1595) and before *A Midsummer Night's Dream* (c. 1595-1596). Even at this early date, Shakespeare shows himself to be a master of plot construction. Disregarding the classical unity of action, which forbade subplots, for a more enlightened concept of unity, Shakespeare creates two distinct lines of action, each derived from a different source, and integrates them into a unified dramatic whole. A single source for the main plot of Petruchio's taming of Katharina has not been found. Misogynistic stories abounded in Shakespeare's time, stories of men exercising their "rightful" dominance over women. One in particular, a ballad entitled *A Merry Jest of a Shrewd and Curst Wife, Lapped in Morel's Skin* (printed c. 1550) tells the story of a shrewish wife who is beaten bloody by her husband and then wrapped in the salted skin of a plow horse named Morel. Like Kate, this wife has a younger sister who is the favorite of their father. If Shakespeare used this ballad as a source for the main plot of this play, it is obvious that he toned it down greatly, substituting psychological tactics for physical brutality. Nevertheless, some stage versions of *The Taming of the Shrew* have emphasized Petruchio's physical mistreatment of Katharina. The eighteenth century English actor David Garrick as Petruchio threatened Katharina with a whip. Some critics even today see in this play an unacceptable male chauvinism. One must remember that Shakespeare lived and wrote in a patriarchal world in which the father ruled the family and the husband ruled the wife. Much in this play reflects the patriarchal nature of Elizabethan society, but Katharina's strength of character may mitigate charges of male chauvinism against Shakespeare.

The source for the underplot, the wooing of Bianca by various suitors, is George Gascoigne's *Supposes* (1573). The heroine in Gascoigne's play is made pregnant by her lover, but she remains completely chaste in *The Taming of the Shrew*. Shakespeare also dispensed with the character of the bawdy Nurse of his source and modified the harsh satire that Gascoigne directed at Dr. Cleander, the pantaloon, who represents the degeneracy of "respectable" society. For this character Shakespeare substitutes Gremio, a wealthy old citizen of Padua who would marry Bianca but is thwarted by the young Lucentio. These changes are typical of Shakespeare, in whose plays sexual relationships are virtually always sanctified by marriage and in whose comedies satire is usually genial or at least counterbalanced by good humor.

The Taming of the Shrew is the only play by Shakespeare which has an "induction" or anterior section that introduces the main action. In the induction, which is set in Shakespeare's native Warwickshire, an unconscious drunken tinker is taken to the house of a lord, dressed in fine clothes, and made to think he is a lord who has been comatose for fifteen years. Convinced he is indeed a lord, Sly begins to speak in blank verse and agrees to watch a play performed by traveling players, namely *The Taming of the Shrew*. At the end of the first scene, Sly is already bored with the play and exclaims "Would 'twere done!" He is never heard from again.

This induction, which at first sight appears irrelevant, dramatizes a recurring theme in all of Shakespeare's comedies and the central theme of this play, namely the deceptiveness of appearances. Sly mistakes the opulence of his surroundings for his true reality and thinks he is a lord rather than a poor tinker of Burton-heath. In the play proper, many of the characters pose as people other than themselves and are responded to in guises not of their true nature. In the subplot, Lucentio, in order to woo Bianca, trades places with his servant Tranio and further takes on the role of Cambio, a schoolmaster hired by Gremio, to woo Bianca for himself. Hortensio, another suitor to Bianca, assumes the role of Litio, a music teacher, to gain access to her. Late in the action, a pedant is coerced to play the role of Vincentio, the father of Lucentio. When the true Vincentio appears on the scene, the disguises of the subplot are finally revealed.

In the major plot, the theme of illusion is not as literal but it is no less important. Katharina, the shrew, has played her part for so long that everyone believes she is an irritable and hateful woman. Conversely, Bianca, her sister, is universally regarded as sweet and of a mild disposition. Neither image is totally true. Bianca has to be told twice by her father to enter the house in the first scene, indicating that she is not as tractable as she is thought to be. Katharina, in her first meeting with Petruchio, does not protest when he tells her father that they will be married on Sunday. She remains silent, indicating that she has tacitly accepted him. In the final scene, the true natures of Katharina and Bianca come out for everyone to see. It is Bianca who is the disobedient wife. It is Katharina who gives a disquisition on the perfect Elizabethan wife. Whether her speech is to be taken at face value or as a statement of irony is debatable.

Petruchio has come "to wive it wealthily in Padua." He is a rip-roaring fortune hunter, who will wed any woman who is rich enough "Be she as foul as was Florentius's love/ As old as Sibyl, and as curst and shrewd/ As Socrates' Xanthippe." He is overwhelming in speech and manner and completely unintimidated by Katharina's reputation as a shrew. He annihilates her resistance by his outlandish actions. At his country house outside of Padua, he mistreats his servants unconscionably, demonstrating to Katharina the kind of behavior that she has displayed. He then deprives her of sleep, food, and drink, as one would tame a falcon. Finally, he deprives her of fine clothing. By his example, she is led to see her own unreasonable behavior. She at last decides to submit to her husband's demands rather than persist in her perverse behavior. *The Taming of the Shrew* is a perennially popular stage production that can be performed and interpreted in various ways depending on the inclinations of directors.

"Critical Evaluation" by Robert G. Blake

Bibliography:

Bloom, Harold, ed. *William Shakespeare's "The Taming of the Shrew": Modern Critical Interpretations*. New York: Chelsea House, 1988. Not for the faint-hearted, this collection of essays is useful for indicating the trends of modern scholarship regarding the play. It contains a number of essays utilizing modern critical perspectives such as feminism and deconstruction.

Greenfield, Thelma N. "The Transformation of Christopher Sly." *Philological Quarterly* 33 (1954): 34-42. Greenfield argues that the importance of the Christopher Sly framing device lies in its establishment of the juxtaposition between reality and appearance evident also through the main action of the play.

Holderness, Graham. *Shakespeare in Performance: "The Taming of the Shrew."* Manchester, England: Manchester University Press, 1989. Holderness examines four different productions of the play, including the 1966 Franco Zeffirelli movie and the 1980 television adaptation starring John Cleese. The book is valuable in that it stresses the importance of the performance of Shakespeare's works.

Huston, J. Dennis. "'To Make a Puppet': Play and Play-Making in *The Taming of the Shrew*." *Shakespeare Studies* 9 (1967): 73-88. Huston asserts that Shakespeare repeatedly shocks the audience by presenting a series of false starts (that of Christopher Sly being the first). This reflects Katharina's experience as she is tamed by Petruchio.

Wells, Stanley, ed. *The Cambridge Companion to Shakespeare Studies*. Cambridge, England: Cambridge University Press, 1986. This is where all studies of Shakespeare should begin. It includes excellent chapters introducing the poet's biography, conventions and beliefs of Elizabethan England, and reviews of scholarship in the field.

TARR

Type of work: Novel
Author: Wyndham Lewis (1882-1957)
Type of plot: Psychological realism
Time of plot: About 1910
Locale: Paris
First published: 1918

Principal characters:
 FREDERICK TARR, an English artist
 BERTHA LUNKEN, Tarr's fiancée and a German art student
 OTTO KREISLER, a German artist
 ANASTASYA VASEK, a Russian
 LOUIS SOLTYK, a Pole

The Story:

Frederick Tarr, an English artist living in Paris, was engaged to a young German woman, Bertha Lunken, a student in the Parisian art schools. Tarr disliked Germans, although he knew a great many of them in Paris. It was his theory that either one had to be very intimate with them or one had to learn how to put up with them when one was not intimate. Not wishing to have it known that he was engaged to Lunken, he was on the point of breaking with her, for he considered her a dolt. He justified his strange attitude on the grounds that all of his finer feelings had gone into his art, which left nothing over for sex. He admitted that his taste in women was deplorable.

After a conversation with a friend during which he explained his theory, Tarr went to his fiancée's apartment. He felt some remorse for his treatment of Bertha, but he had been attracted by her bourgeois-bohemian absurdities and her Germanic floridity and had unwittingly become too involved. Now, he felt, a break had to be made. He, however, had underestimated the intensity of feeling that Bertha had developed for him. The scene in the apartment, carefully decorated with sham art that Tarr loathed, was comic yet tragic. Tarr could not help feeling that he was treating Bertha shabbily, yet he was passionately convinced that marriage was not for him. Nor had he expected such floods of tears; but somehow the break was accomplished, and Tarr departed with the promise to see Bertha again after a few days.

Otto Kreisler, an impecunious German artist, lived on a small allowance grudgingly doled out by his father. He had just returned from a trip to Italy and was more than usually hard up. Four years before, Otto had made the mistake of marrying off an old sweetheart to his father. Since he refused his father's urgings that he give up art, return to Germany, and settle down into business, the monthly check, in revenge, was sent at irregular intervals. At this point, he was concerned with pawning his portmanteau as the result of failure to borrow money from an affluent compatriot, Ernst Volker. On his return from Italy, Kreisler had discovered, to his horror, that his position as the recipient of Volker's bounty had been taken by a Pole, Louis Soltyk, and that no more money could be expected. He already owed Volker fifteen hundred marks. It was the psychological effect of lack of money that, by indirect means, propelled Kreisler toward his final tragedy.

In a mood of discouragement—the check from home was late again—he went to the Café Vallet for lunch. By chance, he found himself at the same small table with an extraordinarily beautiful young woman who, after some preliminary conversation, explained that she was

Anastasya Vasek and that she had escaped to Paris from her parents' bourgeois home. Kreisler was strongly attracted to her, because to him women had always been a kind of emotional pawnshop where he could dump his sorrows. With German sentimentality, he thought of love as sorrowful. Determined to follow up that chance meeting, and despite the fact that his evening clothes were in pawn, he accepted an invitation from a member of the German colony, Fraulein Lipmann, to join her group at a dance at a club in the neighborhood. On the afternoon before the dance, he came upon Anastasya sitting with Soltyk in a cafe. Again, he decided, the Pole was interfering in his affairs.

Driven by a kind of persecution mania, Kreisler deliberately made a fiasco of the evening. On the way to the dance, he found himself walking with Bertha and somewhat behind the other members of the party. Again, their peculiar German psychologies interacted; he wished to avenge himself through her on the more affluent guests; she felt that he was suffering and that she should make a sacrifice to console him. So Kreisler kissed her roughly, and she permitted the kiss. They were seen by the other Germans, who were walking ahead. Kreisler arrived at the dance, dressed in rumpled morning clothes and still under the spell of his mania; he behaved abominably, insulted nearly every woman present, and was almost thrown out. Worse, Anastasya laughed at him, turning his admiration to hate. The next morning, when the long-awaited allowance arrived accompanied by a command to return to Germany, Kreisler replied to his father that he would kill himself in exactly one month.

Shortly afterward, Bertha received a letter from Tarr, informing her that he had heard of the episode with Kreisler and that he was leaving for London. Furthermore, the "Kreisler affair" had embroiled Bertha with her German friends. In a dreary mood, she went out to buy lunch and met Kreisler; after some conversation, she accepted his invitation to visit a café the following evening. This curious act was a defense against her friends; it was part of her theory that he was in distress, and it would contradict the story, now current, that his outrageous behavior had been the result of Anastasya's snub. Furthermore, her meeting with Kreisler would be a kind of revenge on Tarr. She succeeded in convincing herself that she was being driven into this strange friendship. Eight days later, in Kreisler's studio, he possessed her by force, and the situation that she had created became suddenly tragic. Kreisler came to her apartment, offered to shoot himself, and finally departed after swearing to be her eternal servant. With her usual sentimentality, Bertha felt uplifted, as if together they had done something noble.

Meanwhile, Tarr had merely moved to the Montmartre district, where he felt that he could work in peace. He continued to frequent his old section with its German colony so that he could keep an eye on Bertha. Inevitably, he met Anastasya, and just as inevitably, he encountered Bertha and Kreisler together. He could not resist joining this pair; their "Germanness" gave him an ironic pleasure. Kreisler was baffled by the Englishman's sudden friendship that led Tarr to join him at a café evening after evening, and he found his Teutonic solemnity not equal to the situation. Fearful of being driven mad, he threatened the Englishman with a whip, when Tarr went to his room, and then pushed him out the door.

Tarr and Anastasya had become attracted to each other. During this time, they had long conversations about life and art. A storm, however, was gathering. One evening Tarr, who had joined Kreisler and a Russian at a café, saw the German jump from his seat, rush across the room to a group of Russians and Poles, and slap Soltyk's face. That afternoon, Kreisler had met Anastasya and Soltyk; in a cold fury, he had struck Soltyk. Then he challenged the Pole to a duel. After much excited conversation, the challenge was accepted.

The duel next morning was another mixture of comedy and tragedy. The seconds were trying to effect an honorable compromise when Kreisler's mood suddenly changed: he offered to forgive Soltyk if the latter would kiss him. As he leaned forward, the enraged Pole leaped upon him; they fell to the ground, and the seconds began fighting among themselves. When the dust had settled, Soltyk's friends tried to lead him away, but they were stopped by Kreisler, who still held his pistol. A Pole struck at him; Kreisler fired and killed Soltyk. Kreisler fled. Five days later, penniless and hungry, he reached a village near the border and was put in jail. In a last display of his disordered temperament, he hanged himself in his cell. His father paid the exact sum demanded by the town for the burial.

Meanwhile in Paris, Tarr and Anastasya had rapidly become involved in an affair, and Tarr continued to see Bertha in decreasing "doses" as though he were taking medicine. As he was about to give her up, she told him that she was pregnant and that the child was Kreisler's. Out of pity, Tarr married her, but he lived with Anastasya. Two years later, Bertha divorced him to marry an eye doctor. Tarr never married Anastasya. He had three children by another woman.

Critical Evaluation:

Wyndham Lewis is probably the least-known of the great modernist authors and artists. A sometime colleague of Ezra Pound, an acquaintance of T. S. Eliot, James Joyce, and Gertrude Stein, a campaigner for innovation in the arts of painting and literature, Lewis lost fame by turning on these and other allies, who, understandably, became less than enthusiastic about promoting his reputation. His feud with the literary Sitwell family, for example, whose portraits he had painted, undoubtedly lost him many commissions. His output as painter, novelist, poet, philosopher, and controversial pamphleteer, was prodigious. His father was American, and his mother English; Lewis was born on a yacht moored in Canadian waters. He thus was a citizen of three countries. After his parents separated when he was an infant, Lewis was raised in England by his English mother. He was educated at Rugby, a famous public school, and at London's Slade School of Art. *Tarr* is his first novel.

Lewis has been called the foremost English prose stylist of his century. In *Tarr*, his skill and his rigorous aesthetic are well in evidence. His painting, of the Futuristic stamp, but which Lewis, more to name his own movement than to create a necessary distinction, termed "Vorticist," is hard-edged and done with dizzying perspective. One finds a similar technique in *Tarr*. T. S. Eliot remarked that Lewis' novel was a war of points-of-view, not only in its content, but in its form. The style of the writing alters according to which of the major characters predominates in any given chapter.

It needs to be remarked here that there are a number of texts of this novel. In 1918 alone, three different versions were published: a serialized one, an American edition, and the English edition. In 1928, Lewis issued a revision of the American version. The reprint novel that is most widely available is based on the 1918 American text and provides an exhaustive variant table. Lewis uses various devices as "distancers," so that readers are frequently reminded by these unfamiliar signs that they are reading a text, not being hypnotized into ignoring one. To the same end, Lewis loads his prose with startling words and phrases, that insist on their status as artifice. The distinction between nature and art forms the subject of several exchanges in the novel. Furthermore, Kreisler and Bertha have too much nature in them, whereas Anastasya, like Tarr, is able to separate herself.

The writing is not replete with sensuous detail. Frederick Tarr is ascetic rather than sensuous in his aesthetics, as was Lewis. Tarr, being self-invented, evinces another article of Lewis' Futurist faith, that one needs to rid oneself of the past and begin anew, to be unnatural, un-organic, to break the inertia of the species. Personality, Lewis argues, is devleoped to overcome that which is imposed by birth and environment. It is noteworthy that the tragic events in the novel are brought about by the persistence of traditions that have outlived their time—dueling, the notion that a woman is a man's possession. These events arise from the conflict of the present with the past. Lewis needs to make this historical break evident, and *Tarr* embodies this need. The reader is kept aware at all times that the novel is art. The discomfort the text can cause is a deliberate calculation on its author's part. People must wake up, the aesthetic argument underlying *Tarr* implies, and cease to function as automata of nature. To be truly human is to invent oneself, to be efficient, a modern, a machine. Kreisler, a Romantic, has much that is old-fashioned, mechanical, and inefficient in his behavior. His suicide, ironically, moves like clockwork. Old-fashioned, too, is Kreisler's vision of himself as a pawn of fate. He is the villain of the story, because he is an embodiment of much that his creator found reprehensible.

In art, however, evil is often more engaging than good, and the sections with Kreisler in them are far and away the most readable portions. This may well be part of Lewis' calculation also: The hypnotized individual is presented in hypnotic prose. There is more of Kreisler than Tarr in the book, and Lewis himself was later to remark that he should have named the book after the German.

To one way of reading, the book is an allegory. Kreisler, in his envy of the civilized, in his passionate blindness, in his march toward death and destruction, represents the Germany of 1914. Kreisler is resentful of the Frenchified culture of the Poles, fearful of the power of Russia, baffled by the detachment of the English. All these elements—the Polish, the Russian, and the English, as well as the German—formed the tragic forces of World War I. Allegorical reading alone will not neatly contain the many meanings of this difficult, stimulating, and idiosyncratic novel, which, like a mobile, can turn a different aspect toward readers each time they open the book.

"Critical Evaluation" by David Bromige

Bibliography:
Chapman, Robert. *Wyndham Lewis: Fictions and Satires*. New York: Barnes & Noble Books, 1973. Contains excellent analysis of *Tarr*, particularly regarding the relations among the principal characters. Disagrees with those critics who have said that to reject the ideas of Tarr is to reject the novel.
Jameson, Fredric. *Fables of Aggression*. Berkeley: University of California Press, 1979. A focus on libido makes for interesting writing on the topic of the nationalist allegory, which Jameson believes offers a framework in which psychic energies circulate.
Kenner, Hugh. *Wyndham Lewis*. New York: Methuen, 1954. Useful for its tracing of Lewis' earliest writings as they are transmuted in *Tarr* and of the significance of Lewis' 1928 revisions.
Materer, Timothy. *Wyndham Lewis, the Novelist*. Detroit: Wayne State University Press, 1976. Discusses the role of humor, the genesis of Frederick Tarr, and the dynamics between Tarr the "satiric commentator" and Kreisler the "tragic protagonist."
Pritchard, William H. *Wyndham Lewis*. New York: Twayne, 1968. Finds that the interest lies less in the plot than in the restlessness and self-involvement of the characters, and the stylistic differences they engender.

TARTUFFE

Type of work: Drama
Author: Molière (Jean-Baptiste Poquelin, 1622-1673)
Type of plot: Comedy
Time of plot: Seventeenth century
Locale: Paris
First performed: 1664; revision, 1667; first published, 1669 as *Tartuffe: Ou, L'Imposteur*
  (English translation, 1732)

Principal characters:
ORGON, a wealthy former officer of the King's Guard
MADAME PERNELLE, his mother
ELMIRE, his wife
DAMIS, his son
MARIANE, his daughter
VALÈRE, Mariane's lover
DORINE, Mariane's maid
CLÉANTE, Orgon's brother-in-law
TARTUFFE, a hypocrite

The Story:

Orgon's home was a happy one. He himself was married to Elmire, a woman much younger than he, who adored him. His two children by a former marriage were fond of their stepmother, and she of them. Mariane, the daughter, was engaged to be married to Valère, a very eligible young man, and Damis, the son, was in love with Valère's sister.

Then Tartuffe came to live in the household. Tartuffe was a penniless scoundrel whom the trusting Orgon had found praying in church. Taken in by his words and his pretended religious fervor, Orgon had invited the hypocrite into his home. As a consequence, the family was soon thrown into chaos. Once established, Tartuffe proceeded to change their normal, happy mode of life to a very strict one. He set up a rigid Puritan regimen for the family, and persuaded Orgon to force his daughter to break her engagement to Valère in order to marry Tartuffe. He said that she needed a pious man to lead her in a righteous life.

Valère was determined that Mariane would marry no one but himself, but unfortunately Mariane was too spineless to resist Tartuffe and her father. Confronted by her father's orders, she remained silent and remonstrated only weakly. As a result, Tartuffe was cordially hated by every member of the family, including Dorine, the saucy, outspoken servant, who did everything in her power to break the hold that the hypocrite had secured over her master. Dorine hated not only Tartuffe but also his valet, Laurent, for the servant imitated the master in everything. In fact, the only person besides Orgon who liked and approved of Tartuffe was Orgon's mother, Madame Pernelle, who was the type of Puritan who wished to withhold from others pleasures in which she herself would not indulge. Madame Pernelle highly disapproved of Elmire, maintaining that in her love for clothes and amusements she was setting her family a bad example which Tartuffe was trying to correct. Actually, Elmire was merely full of the joy of living, a fact that her mother-in-law was unable to perceive. Orgon himself was little better. When he was informed that Elmire had fallen ill, his sole concern was for the health of Tartuffe.

Tartuffe, however, was in fine health, stout and ruddy-cheeked. For his evening meal, he consumed two partridges, half a leg of mutton, and four flasks of wine. He then retired to his warm and comfortable bed and slept soundly until morning.

Tartuffe's romantic designs were not really for the daughter, Mariane, but for Elmire herself. One day, after Orgon's wife had recovered from her illness, Tartuffe appeared before her. He complimented Elmire on her beauty, and even went so far as to lay his hand on her knee. Damis, Orgon's son, observed all that went on from the cabinet where he was hidden. Furious, he determined to reveal to his father all that he had seen. Orgon refused to believe him. Wily Tartuffe had so completely captivated Orgon that he ordered Damis to apologize to Tartuffe. When his son refused, Orgon, violently angry, drove Damis from the house and disowned him. To show his confidence in Tartuffe's honesty and piety, Orgon signed a deed of trust turning his estate over to Tartuffe's management and announced his daughter's betrothal to Tartuffe.

Elmire, embittered by the behavior of this impostor in her house, resolved to unmask him. She persuaded Orgon to hide under a cloth-covered table and see and hear for himself the real Tartuffe. Then she enticed Tartuffe, disarming him with the assurance that her foolish husband would suspect nothing. Emboldened, Tartuffe poured out his heart to her, leaving no doubt as to his intention of making her his mistress. Disillusioned and outraged when Tartuffe asserted that Orgon was a complete dupe, the husband emerged from his hiding place, denounced the hypocrite, and ordered him from the house. Tartuffe defied him, reminding him that the house was now his according to Orgon's deed of trust.

Another matter made Orgon even more uneasy than the possible loss of his property. This was a casket given him by a friend, Argas, a political criminal now in exile. It contained important state secrets, the revelation of which would mean a charge of treason against Orgon and certain death for his friend. Orgon had foolishly entrusted the casket to Tartuffe, and he feared the use that villain might make of it. He informed his brother-in-law, Cléante, that he would have nothing further to do with pious men and that, in the future, he would shun them like the plague. Cléante, however, pointed out that such extreme reactions were the sign of an unbalanced mind. It was not fair to cast aspersion on religion itself simply because a treacherous vagabond was masquerading as a religious man.

The next day, Tartuffe followed through on his threat, using his legal right to Orgon's property to force Orgon and his family from their house. Madame Pernelle could not believe Tartuffe guilty of such villainy, and she reminded her son that, in this world, virtue is often misjudged and persecuted. When the sheriff's officer arrived with the notice for evacuation, however, even she believed that Tartuffe was a villain.

The crowning indignity came when Tartuffe took to the king the casket containing the state secrets. Orders were issued for Orgon's immediate arrest. Fortunately, the king recognized Tartuffe as an impostor who had committed crimes in another city. Therefore, because of Orgon's loyal service in the army, the king annulled the deed Orgon had made covering his property and returned the casket unopened.

Critical Evaluation:

The play *Tartuffe* was not published to condemn organized religion or religious people, but rather to condemn hypocrisy and to instruct audiences, through the use of humor, on the importance of moderation, common sense, and clear thinking in all areas of life. Although the play was originally condemned as an outright attack on religion and devout people, a proper reading of the play suggests just the opposite. Religion is not the problem; rather, the misuse of religion for personal gain at the expense of innocent, unsuspecting people is that about which

Molière was concerned. Ironically, rather than being condemned (as many religious zealots believed when the play was originally produced) religion is protected and promoted when works such as *Tartuffe* are written to expose impostors for who they really are and for the real danger they pose to society. Further, other legitimate institutions in society are in great danger when characters such as Tartuffe are allowed to go unchallenged in society.

The silly yet serious results of failing to act with common sense are the major emphases in the play. The playwright's creation of the play's characters and their reactions to the hypocrite, Tartuffe, serve to remind the reader of the importance of clear thinking, since there are those who will take advantage of simple thinking and blind trust. The play reinforces the golden virtue of "moderation in all things." Excess, even in the most sacred faith, leads to ridiculous conclusions and potentially catastrophic actions. The comic way the story unfolds for the audience, from seemingly harmless simple belief about religious doctrine to eventual trust in the absurd notion that Tartuffe should be in control of the family's finances and estate, is a warning for all people of all times to avoid letting others take advantage of their lives because of a lack of careful observation and scrutiny of human behavior—even when it is camouflaged in religious rhetoric. Indeed, the extreme speeches of Tartuffe should alert the audience of his suspicious motives. Orgon, unfortunately, is unable to see the absurdity in the assertions which Tartuffe places on the family. Orgon, who is a reasonable and capable man, has become so enamored with Tartuffe's manner and rhetoric that he jeopardizes his family, his wealth, his position, his self-confidence, and eventually his own faith in the value of religion for the sake of appeasing the manipulative Tartuffe. The reader is able to see the comical yet unfortunate results of Tartuffe's influence on Orgon and on his family.

The structure of the play suggests that Molière clearly understood the corporate dangers of false piety. Though some would simply dismiss such actions as unfortunate or maybe even deserved, Molière sets forth the reciprocal theme of the importance of a well-ordered soul living in a well-ordered society under the virtue of reason. In contrast to the comical yet serious unraveling of Orgon's professional and personal life at the hands of Tartuffe, is the author's implicit appeal for reason and order in personal interactions and societal institutions. The two are integrally related. When individuals such as Orgon ignore common sense and become infatuated with a charismatic figure such as Tartuffe, the results are tragic. Consider the breakdown of his relationship with his son, the mistrust between him and his wife, the eventual personal embarrassment and financial problems, all of which are directly related to Orgon's pitiful relationship with Tartuffe. The troubles, however, do not simply affect Orgon; they adversely affect everyone in Orgon's life. Thus, the reader is given a serious message for society as a whole. The dishonest intentions of one man, Tartuffe, wreak havoc on the lives of an entire family and on those with whom they interact. Yet the comic telling of the story reinforces the idea that Orgon's difficulties not only could have but should have been avoided. Tartuffe and his kind have power only when ordinary citizens willfully give up their ability to think for themselves.

In the end, the audience sees Orgon as remorseful for his foolish trust of Tartuffe; he is also angry. In his anger, he inappropriately determines that religion has been the cause of all the calamity that he and his family have undergone. The text, however, reminds the reader that the real problem is not religion, but the misuse of religion by impostors. The author, through the final speech of Cléante, reinforces the validity of the appropriate religious expression of the truly devout person.

"Critical Evaluation" by Kenneth E. Hada

Bibliography:

Bermel, Albert. *Molière's Theatrical Bounty: A New View of the Plays.* Carbondale: Southern Illinois University Press, 1990. Original interpretations of the plays, partly designed to help actors think about the characters' motivations. Discusses the possibility of a homosexual relationship between Tartuffe and Orgon; also discusses why Dorine can speak so freely to her master.

Hall, H. Gaston. *Comedy in Context: Essays on Molière.* Jackson: University Press of Mississippi, 1984. Analyzes Molière's work thematically. Especially useful in examining the historical background of religious issues, as well as social customs, in *Tartuffe.*

Lewis, D. B. Wyndham. *Molière: The Comic Mask.* New York: Coward-McCann, 1959. Discusses Molière's life and works; immerses readers in seventeenth century French society. Sees *Tartuffe* as having a fundamental flaw, Molière's lack of insight, read or feigned, into religion; as a result, Tartuffe comes across as a convincing villain, but the religious component remains confusing.

Mander, Gertrud. *Molière.* Translated by Diana Stone Peters. New York: Frederick Ungar, 1973. Includes descriptions and analyses of fourteen plays and a usefully detailed chronology of his life. Examines why Molière's contemporaries found Tartuffe so threatening and disturbing.

Walker, Hallam. *Molière.* Boston: Twayne, 1971. Examines *Tartuffe* in the context of religious controversies of the period, but also in terms of its artistic antecedents; believes Molière achieved new psychological realism and artistic complexity with this play. Sees Orgon's willingness to punish himself and his family, which Tartuffe exploits but does not create, as a central theme.

THE TASK

Type of work: Poetry
Author: William Cowper (1731-1800)
First published: 1785

The first popular poetic success of William Cowper was *The Task*, which was also his first major venture in blank verse. For the fifty-four-year-old recluse, the reception of his poem must have had a salutary effect, for he went on to become, according to his greatest champion, Robert Southey, "The most popular poet of his generation."

Cowper's place in literary history is often in dispute. He was born exactly one hundred years after John Dryden and completed his best work in the year of Samuel Johnson's death. He neither aspired to become poet laureate nor wished to be the critical arbiter of his day. In many ways, however, he was the successor of both Dryden and Johnson. Cowper's blank verse is perhaps the best between that of seventeenth century poet John Milton and William Wordsworth's work in the early nineteenth century; his criticism expresses dissatisfaction with the extreme formalism of his age and anticipates, in some measure, the nineteenth century revolt against neoclassicism. He is usually said to be a writer of this transition toward Romanticism and realism.

His first work of any magnitude, *Olney Hymns* (1779), he undertook with his evangelical friend, the Reverend John Newton, while living at Olney with the Unwin family. "Oh! for a closer walk with God" is the most beautiful of his hymns.

Although Cowper's writing of the then-fashionable couplet was not successful, his early verse was at least simple. He objected strenuously to Alexander Pope's influence, which resulted in the highly ornamented versification of that age. Several long poems in this genre, published in 1782, serve as a kind of prelude to *The Task*. "Table Talk," written in rather abstract couplets, is a dialogue concerning the political, social, moral, and literary topics of the day. Here Cowper's dislike for the artifice of the eighteenth century is quite clear, and he damns most of the literary cults with faint praise, at the same time urging a return to God and nature for inspiration. "The Progress of Error" outlines the follies of high life and living as these affect the social structure: In this work he suggests a return to Christianity for the solutions to vexing problems. "Truth" extends Cowper's religious beliefs almost as if his distant relation, the cleric John Donne, were making himself felt. Cowper's thesis in the poem is that pride is truth's greatest foe, while humility will uplift humankind. In "Expostulation," he particularly decries anti-Semitism and urges England to remove this mote from the public eye. "Hope" and "Charity" celebrate God's nature (not the human nature of the Age of Reason) as the proper study, or at least reflection, of humanity. Satirically, he contrasts humanity's ways with God's. Another poem of this early group is "Retirement," an apology for his life as a recluse, his justification for giving up a life of action for the contemplative life of the poet.

In 1783, one of Cowper's intimate friends, Lady Austen, urged him to abandon the restrictive couplet form for blank verse. Cowper tells of this happening in the "Advertisement" of *The Task*:

> A lady, fond of blank verse, demanded a poem of that kind from the author, and gave him the SOFA for a subject. He obeyed; and, having much leisure, connected another subject with it; and, pursuing the train of thought to which his situation and turn of mind led him, brought forth at length, instead of the trifle he at first intended, a serious affair—a Volume!

This volume of five thousand lines is divided into six parts: "The Sofa," "The Time-Piece," "The Garden," "The Winter Evening," "The Winter Morning Walk," and "The Winter Walk at Noon." The poem's success was immediate, launching for the middle-aged poet a career and a reputation.

The sofa that Cowper describes in the opening lines is the effete summation of humanity's efforts to indulge in comforts, a human failing the poet presents with good humor. He leaves the sofa, as he says, "for I have lov'd the rural walk" with a good companion at his side. It is immediately apparent that the poet's work is to justify humanity's ways to God: "The task of new discov'ries falls on me," he suggests as he goes abroad. The next lines indicate that he will not countenance romantic illusions of the peasant's hard life or such poetic effusion of his age that tend to overlook the sordid, cruel, or ungodly. In comparing country and town, he sets up a dichotomy that persists throughout the poem: God creates and people destroy.

In "The Time-Piece," about expediency, Cowper takes a long look at institutions, especially political. After a close examination of events now forgotten, he remarks in a memorable line, "England, with all thy faults, I love thee still." The England he loves is the nation of an earlier, more virtuous, simpler time. He examines public figures, especially ministers, and finds them wanting. He suggests that God must be in every heart, Christ in every act. The river Ouse he describes as a symbol of immortality and ease.

"The Garden" brings the poet to the eternal verities of nature and causes him to celebrate family life and domestic happiness. Within this poem is the parable of Cowper ("I was a stricken deer, that left the herd") who, wounded by society, retired to a life of religious contemplation. From this vantage point, he asks people to be humane and Christian, to eschew wars, to learn wisdom. "Who loves a garden loves a greenhouse too," is his plea to humanity to cultivate simple pleasures in a rural setting: "Health, leisure, means t' improve it, friendship, peace" are what he thinks worthwhile. He concludes with a harsh renunciation of the city.

Continuing his statement of conflicting interests, in "The Winter Evening," Cowper compares the tragic news of the world with the simple man who delivers the post, unmoved. So should one live, the poet says, interested and sympathetic but apart; nothing is pleasanter than a winter night spent with good friends in good talk, and before a good fire. Again, the town appears as the corrupter, its poison filtering down in the form of fashions spoiling the simple folk and altering the landscape. Although there are consolations in poetry, especially Milton's, rural life brings more compensations and inspiration.

"The Winter Morning Walk," a bracing though aesthetic experience, restores the poet's good humor as he observes beasts and people under winter's thrall. Cowper sees in winter a hope for immortality, for as the seeds and hibernating creatures wait out the ice, so humanity is bound in history. He next shames the greats of history as tyrants of oppression and great countries as slaveholders:

> Tis liberty alone that gives the flow'r
> Of fleeting life its lustre and perfume
> He is a freeman whom the truth makes free, and all are slaves besides.

This is the substance of his argument. He concludes with an apostrophe to godly graces and offers thanks to God.

Finally, in "The Winter Walk at Noon," the poet uses sonorous polysyllables to celebrate village bells as symbols of harmonious living—and offers also a backward glance at his own life. He describes the winter landscape in an ode to the cold, crisp season. In memorable passages, he anticipates the spring. Finally, he justifies the life of the rambler, the contemplative life of the poet who sounds the note of God's truth, whether of castigation or exaltation.

Bibliography:

Feingold, Richard. *Nature and Society: Later Eighteenth-Century Uses of the Pastoral and Georgic*. New Brunswick, N.J.: Rutgers University Press, 1978. Studies "The Task" in relation to Cowper's views on society. By viewing the poem from both pastoral and georgic perspectives, establishes that issues and conditions of contemporary life are Cowper's main concerns.

Free, William N. *William Cowper*. New York: Twayne, 1970. Comprehensive study of Cowper devotes one chapter to *The Task*. Biographical sources are cited to illustrate how Cowper's personal experiences influenced the theme, structure, tone, and metaphors of his poem. Chronology and selected bibliography.

King, James. *William Cowper: A Biography*. Durham, N.C.: Duke University Press, 1986. Cowper's poetic ambitions and literary career are the focus of this study. Good starting point for critical analysis of Cowper's poetry.

Newey, Vincent. *Cowper's Poetry: A Critical Study and Reassessment*. New York: Barnes & Noble Books, 1982. Exhaustive treatment of many of Cowper's poems, including *The Task*. Meticulous examination of Cowper's diction, tone, and syntax yields excellent interpretations of Cowper's most popular, as well as his less celebrated, poetry.

Priestman, Martin. *Cowper's "Task": Structure and Influence*. Cambridge, England: Cambridge University Press, 1983. Compares Cowper and other eighteenth century poets, illuminating the differences and similarities between Cowper and his contemporaries.

A TASTE OF HONEY

Type of work: Drama
Author: Shelagh Delaney (1939-   )
Type of plot: Psychological realism
Time of plot: 1950's
Locale: Salford, Lancashire
First performed: 1958; first published, 1959

> *Principal characters:*
> HELEN, a "semi-whore"
> JOSEPHINE (JO), her teenage daughter
> PETER, Helen's boyfriend
> THE BOY (JIMMIE), Jo's black boyfriend
> GEOFFREY (GEOFF), a homosexual art student

The Story:

Helen and her daughter Jo were moving into a comfortless apartment in a Salford slum. Jo complained about the place, but Helen said they could afford nothing better. They bickered constantly about anything from Helen's drinking and many boyfriends to the cold, their frequent moves, and Jo's determination to quit school after Christmas. Helen complained about feeling sick. In unpacking, Helen found some drawings Jo had done and thought them quite good, but Jo resented even her praise.

Peter, a brash car salesman, arrived in search of Helen, who had been avoiding him. Peter had not known before that Helen had a teenage daughter (and was thus older than he thought) but he nevertheless asked Helen to marry him. Helen seemed tempted. Jo brought coffee and continued to make sarcastic comments. While Peter told dirty jokes, Jo tried to discourage Peter from marrying Helen; he left without having received an answer. While the two women prepared for bed, Helen asked Jo what she thought about her marrying Peter. Jo considered it ridiculous.

Shortly before Christmas, Jo's boyfriend, a black sailor, walked her home from school. When he tried to kiss her, she said no, though she enjoyed it. He proposed marriage, and she agreed. He gave her a cheap ring and asked what her mother would think, especially about his race. Jo said she did not care how her mother reacted. Nevertheless, she decided to wear the ring round her neck under her clothes. Jo told him that after leaving school she would work in a bar and move out as soon as possible. They arranged to meet later.

When Jo returned home, Helen guessed that she had been seeing a boyfriend. Jo asked to be told her real birth date, who her natural father was, and when Helen's husband had thrown them out. Helen avoided answering and abruptly announced that she was going to marry again. When Peter arrived, Jo sarcastically called him Daddy and said that marrying Helen was crazy. While Helen got ready, Jo attacked Peter. She looked at photographs from his wallet, including some of other women, and derided Peter and Helen for wanting to marry. Jo was convinced that Helen and Peter would be away several days, during which time Jo, not for the first time, would be left alone. She complained about her mother's neglect, while Helen criticized her for her jealousy. Peter and Helen left, and Jo fell on the bed, crying.

Jo's boyfriend entered the apartment; thinking she might be ill, he fixed Jo some medicine. Jo told him that Helen and Peter were getting married and asked him to stay with her over

Christmas. They began necking as the lights faded. After a time, Helen returned, carrying boxes of wedding finery. Because Jo was in pajamas, Helen noticed Jo's ring and berated her for spending time with her boyfriend in the apartment. While arranging for her own wedding, she begged Jo not to ruin her life by getting married. Jo again asked about her father. Helen revealed that he had been sweet but mentally retarded; they had made love only once. Helen told Jo they would see each other after the honeymoon, and Jo wished her good luck.

In early summer, a noticeably pregnant Jo and Geoff, an art student, returned to her apartment from a fair. Geoff had been evicted from his apartment (perhaps for being homosexual), so Jo had invited him to stay with her. He, too, noticed her drawings. They discussed Jo's pregnancy, her decision against abortion, her finances, and whether to tell her mother, especially since Helen presumably now had money. Jo absolutely refused to let Helen know. Geoff sang nursery rhymes and asked about the baby's father; Jo claimed he was an African prince. Falling asleep, Jo said Geoff was like a big sister to her.

A month or two later, Geoff was still living with Jo, helping to prepare for the baby. He seemed far more nurturing than Jo, who said she hated babies. Geoff said he stayed because someone had to care for Jo. He asked her to marry him, regardless of any physical relationship, but Jo refused. She suggested that he leave and then reconsidered. Helen arrived, and Geoff asked her not to reveal that he had contacted her. Helen and Jo immediately began bickering. When Jo implied that her morals were no worse than Helen's, Helen tried to hit Jo, who fled from her. Geoff tried to intervene, but Helen chased him out. Then, somewhat calmer, she said that she had brought money to help out with the baby. Jo resentfully told Helen that the "mother-love act" was too late. Peter arrived, drunk. He insulted everyone in turn, including Helen for being old and for giving Jo "his" money. When Helen invited Jo to stay with them, Peter rejected the idea and they began to quarrel. Helen eventually left with Peter, who took back the money Helen had given Jo.

In September, Geoff was giving the apartment a thorough cleaning in preparation for the baby, which was nearly due. Jo suddenly felt frightened. When Geoff comforted her, she compared him favorably with her mother; he replied that, in some ways, Jo was just like Helen. He gave Jo a doll to practice her mothering skills, but she said the doll was the wrong color and threw it down. Then she told the truth about Jimmie. Geoff again proposed marriage; again she put him off. Helen arrived, evidently ready to move back. She criticized all Geoff's efforts, insulted him, and sent him away. Alone with Jo, she revealed that Peter had discarded her for a younger woman. When Geoff returned, Helen all but threw him out, so he left again, apparently for good. Jo awoke from a nap, calling for Geoff. She told Helen that her baby would be black. Helen was appalled and went out. Singing one of Geoff's nursery rhymes, Jo watched her go.

Critical Evaluation:

Shelagh Delaney, who wrote this play at the age of eighteen, clearly drew on aspects of her own experience to create the world of *A Taste of Honey*. Like Jo, she grew up in a gritty Lancashire town and left school at sixteen to work at various menial jobs. By identifying closely with her character Jo, Delaney was able to present an adolescent's perspective with uncanny accuracy. The incessant conflicts with her mother—with their fluid mixture of sarcasm, sensitivity, neediness, sullen rebelliousness, and longing for affection—seem especially believable. In the dialogue between Helen and Jo, Delaney reflects tensions common to most mother-daughter relationships, regardless of geography or class. The play also evokes the perpetual "now" of adolescence and the sense of drifting in the present and of being neither child nor adult. As Jo puts it, "I really am [contemporary], aren't I? I really do live at the same time as myself, don't I?" Significantly, Jo speaks of herself in question form, which accurately mirrors her uncertainty about who she is and what she wants from life.

The play's focus on life from Jo's perspective comes at a price, however, and the scenes with Helen can give the audience an uneasy sense that the author is settling old scores. Helen always appears unsympathetic, with Jo her victim. Their dialogue sounds so real that it might have been quoted verbatim from actual quarrels between Delaney and her mother, unmodified by artistic insight. The male characters fare even worse than Helen. They float, shadowlike, at the periphery of Jo's small world, fulfilling functions in the plot but having no real life of their own. The audience does not even learn the name of Jo's boyfriend until the second act, after he is long gone. Peter stands in for all the men who have cheated Jo of her mother's affection over the years, while Geoff sets a standard of good mothering that Helen (or almost any real human being) could never actually achieve. The play shows all the characters as Jo sees them, almost exclusively in terms of their relationship to her. While this self-centered worldview has resonance for the adolescent in everyone, it could be said to lack the complex insights of a more mature artist.

A Taste of Honey nevertheless represents a remarkable achievement for a young woman writing her first play in the mid-1950's, a time when "angry young men" were dominating the English theater. Following John Osborne's *Look Back In Anger* (1956), plays about working-class life became enormously popular, but hardly any were given a female perspective. In these "kitchen-sink" dramas, women were usually nurturing mother surrogates, objects of frustrated male rage, or (quite often) both. How to be a real man in the postwar, welfare-state world remained the central question for an entire generation of new playwrights. Delaney had the originality to examine the same social milieu while focusing on working-class women.

Although *A Taste of Honey* won prizes, became a hit on stage and film, and continues to be performed, Delaney's contribution has been largely overlooked or marginalized. In the context of "angry" theater, her interest in women and mothering has been treated as less relevant than issues of masculine violence. Feminist theater criticism has considered Delaney a foremother who prefigured important themes but never achieved her full promise. Some, holding Delaney's youth and inexperience against her, regard the play as a fluke and attribute its success mostly to director Joan Littlewood's modifications and insights. The failure of Delaney's only other play, *The Lion in Love* (1960), and her subsequent abandonment of the stage have confirmed these opinions. She continued, however, to write, primarily for television and film, a choice that seems reasonable given the way her work uses music and "cinematic" emotional close-ups. The high quality of the film *Dance with a Stranger* (1985) should refute charges that her early success was an accident. In these later works, Delaney retained her bitter humor, her insight into characters, especially women, and her impressive gift for pungent dialogue.

A Taste of Honey remains relevant, however, for the way in which it focuses on women's emotional struggles with motherhood and their sexuality. The similarities of Helen's and Jo's experiences (work in a bar, pregnancy and single motherhood at an early age, desertion or rejection by men, bare economic subsistence), compellingly conveys the tragic cycle of poverty, child neglect, and hopeless alienation from mainstream society, problems that certainly continued after the 1950's. The play also marks one of the earliest positive portrayals of a male homosexual character; neither a joke nor a stereotype, Geoff retains his human dignity and freely nurtures those who need him. In addressing these issues, Delaney blazed a trail for other playwrights, men and women.

Susan Wladaver-Morgan

Bibliography:

Esche, Edward J. "Shelagh Delaney's *A Taste of Honey* as Serious Text." In *The Death of the Playwright? Modern British Drama and Literary Theory*, edited by Adrian Page. New York: St. Martin's Press, 1992. Discusses the play as modern tragedy, not as an uplifting piece for high school students. Relies on a particular stage production for some of his interpretation.

Keyssar, Helene. *Feminist Theatre: An Introduction to Plays of Contemporary British and American Women*. New York: Grove Press, 1985. Discusses the importance of Joan Littlewood in Britain and of women's theatrical collectives in nurturing women playwrights; stresses continuities of feminist themes.

Taylor, John Russell. *The Angry Theatre: New British Drama*. New York: Hill and Wang, 1962. Places Delaney's work in the context of the theatrical revolution following Osborne's *Look Back in Anger*. Offers an especially interesting comparison of Delaney's original script with the workshop version produced by Joan Littlewood that formed the basis of the printed text.

Taylor, Lib. "Early Stages: Women Dramatists 1958-68." In *British and Irish Women Dramatists Since 1958*, edited by Trevor R. Griffiths and Margaret Llewellyn-Jones. Buckingham, England: Open University Press, 1993. Considers Celtic (Irish, Scottish, and Welsh) aspects of British theater. Argues that British and Irish dramatists might have written differently had their work followed, not preceded, the women's movement.

Wandor, Michelene. *Look Back in Gender: Sexuality and the Family in Postwar British Drama*. London: Methuen, 1987. Covers the same ground as Taylor but emphasizes gender roles from a feminist slant. The author is a playwright and director.

THE TEMPEST

Type of work: Drama
Author: William Shakespeare (1564-1616)
Type of plot: Fantasy
Time of plot: Fifteenth century
Locale: An island in the sea
First performed: 1611; first published, 1623

Principal characters:
PROSPERO, the rightful duke of Milan
MIRANDA, his daughter
FERDINAND, son of the king of Naples
ARIEL, a spirit, Prospero's servant
CALIBAN, Prospero's slave
ALONSO, the king of Naples
SEBASTIAN, Alonso's brother
ANTONIO, the duke of Milan, Prospero's brother
GONZALO, a philosopher, who saved the lives of Prospero and Miranda

The Story:

Alonso, the king of Naples, was returning from the wedding of his daughter to a foreign prince when his ship was overtaken by a terrible storm. In his company were Duke Antonio of Milan and other gentlemen of the court. As the gale rose in fury and it seemed certain the vessel would split and sink, the noble travelers were forced to abandon ship and trust to fortune in the open sea.

The tempest was no chance disturbance of wind and wave. It had been raised by a wise magician, Prospero, when the ship sailed close to an enchanted island on which he and his lovely daughter, Miranda, were the only human inhabitants. Theirs was a sad and curious history. Prospero was the rightful duke of Milan, but being devoted more to the study of philosophy and magic than to affairs of state, he had given much power to his ambitious brother, Antonio, who twelve years earlier had seized the dukedom with the aid of the crafty Neapolitan king. Prospero and his small daughter had been set adrift in a boat by the conspirators, and they would have perished miserably had not Gonzalo, an honest counselor, secretly stocked the frail craft with food, clothing, and some of the books Prospero valued most.

The exiles drifted at last to an island that had been the refuge of Sycorax, an evil sorceress. There Prospero found Caliban, her son, a strange, misshapen creature of brute intelligence, able only to hew wood and draw water. Also there were many good spirits of air and water who became obedient to Prospero's will when he freed them from torments to which the sorceress Sycorax had condemned them. Chief among these was Ariel, a lively sprite.

Prospero, having used his magic arts to draw the ship bearing King Alonso and Duke Antonio close to his enchanted island, ordered Ariel to bring the whole party safely ashore, singly or in scattered groups. Ferdinand, King Alonso's son, was moved by Ariel's singing to follow the sprite to Prospero's rocky cell. Miranda, who did not remember ever having seen another human face than her father's bearded one, at first sight fell deeply in love with the handsome young prince, and he with her. Prospero was pleased to see the young people so attracted to each other, but he concealed his pleasure, spoke harshly to them, and, to test Ferdinand's mettle, commanded him to perform menial tasks.

Meanwhile Alonso, Sebastian, Antonio, and Gonzalo wandered sadly along the beach, the king in despair because he believed his son drowned. Ariel, invisible in the air, played solemn music, lulling to sleep all except Sebastian and Antonio. Drawing apart, they planned to kill the king and his counselor and make Sebastian tyrant of Naples. Watchful Ariel awakened the sleepers before the plotters could act.

On another part of the island, Caliban, carrying a load of wood, met Trinculo, the king's jester, and Stephano, the royal butler, both drunk. In rude sport they offered drink to Caliban. Tipsy, the loutish monster declared he would be their slave forever.

Like master, like servant. Just as Sebastian and Antonio had plotted to murder Alonso, so Caliban, Trinculo, and Stephano schemed to kill Prospero and become rulers of the island. Stephano was to be king, Miranda his consort, and Trinculo and Caliban would be viceroys. Unseen, Ariel listened to their evil designs and reported the plan to Prospero.

Miranda had disobeyed her father's injunction on interrupting Ferdinand in his task of rolling logs and the two exchanged lovers' vows, which were overheard by the magician. Satisfied with the prince's declarations of devotion and constancy, Prospero left them to their happy company. He and Ariel went to mock Alonso and his followers by showing them a banquet that vanished before the hungry castaways could taste the rich dishes. Then Ariel, disguised as a harpy, reproached them for their conspiracy against Prospero. Convinced that Ferdinand's death was punishment for his own crime, Alonso was moved to repentance for his cruel deed.

Returning to his cave, Prospero released Ferdinand from his task. While spirits dressed as Ceres, Iris, Juno, nymphs, and reapers entertained Miranda and the prince with a pastoral masque, Prospero suddenly remembered the schemes being entertained by Caliban and the drunken servants. Told to punish the plotters, after tempting them with a display of kingly garments, Ariel and his fellow spirits, now in the shapes of fierce hunting dogs, drove the plotters howling with pain and rage through bogs and brier patches.

Convinced that the king of Naples and his false brother Antonio had repented the evil deed they had done him years before, Prospero commanded Ariel to bring them into the enchanted circle before the magician's cell. With strange, beautiful music, Ariel lured the king, Antonio, Sebastian, and Gonzalo to the cell, where they were astonished to see Prospero in the appearance and dress of the wronged duke of Milan. Prospero confirmed his identity, ordered Antonio to restore his dukedom, and severely warned Sebastian not to plot further against the king. Finally, he took the repentant Alonso into the cave, where he saw Ferdinand and Miranda playing chess. A joyful reunion followed between father and son, and the king was completely captivated by the beauty and grace of Miranda. During this scene of reconciliation and rejoicing, Ariel appeared with the master and boatswain of the wrecked ship, who reported the vessel safe and ready to continue the voyage. Ariel drove the three grotesque conspirators into the cell, where Prospero released them from their spell. Caliban was ordered to prepare food and set it before the guests, and Prospero invited his brother and the king of Naples and his entourage to spend the night in his cave.

Before he left the island, Prospero dismissed Ariel from his service, leaving that sprite free to wander as he wished. Ariel promised calm seas and auspicious winds for the voyage back to Naples and Milan, from where Prospero would journey to take possession of his lost dukedom and to witness the marriage of his daughter and Prince Ferdinand.

Critical Evaluation:

The Tempest, written toward the close of William Shakespeare's career, is a work of fantasy and courtly romance, the story of a wise old magician, his beautiful, unworldly daughter, a gallant young prince, and a cruel, scheming brother. It contains all the elements of a fairy tale in which ancient wrongs are righted and true lovers live happily ever after. The play is also one of poetic atmosphere and allegory. Beginning with a storm and peril at sea, it ends on a note of serenity and joy. None of Shakespeare's other dramas holds so much of the author's mature reflection on life itself.

Early critics of *The Tempest*, concerned with meaning, attempted to establish symbolic correlations between the characters Prospero, Ariel, Caliban, and Miranda and such qualities as imagination, fancy, brutality, and innocence. Others considered the play in terms of its spectacle and music, comparing it to the masque or *commedia dell'arte*. Most critics read into Prospero's control and direction of all the characters—which climaxes with the famous speech in which he gives up his magic wand—Shakespeare's own dramatic progress and final farewell to the stage.

In the mid-twentieth century, criticism began to explore different levels of action and meaning, focusing on such themes as illusion versus reality, freedom versus slavery, revenge versus forgiveness, time, and self-knowledge. Some suggested that the enchanted island where the shipwreck occurs is a symbol of life itself: an enclosed arena wherein are enacted a range of human passions, dreams, conflicts, and self-discoveries. Such a wide-angled perspective satisfies both the casual reader wishing to be entertained and the serious scholar examining different aspects of Shakespeare's art and philosophy.

This latter view is consonant with one of Shakespeare's principal techniques, which he employs in all of his work: the analogy between microcosm and macrocosm. This Elizabethan way of looking at things simply meant that the human world mirrored the universe. In the major tragedies, this correspondence is shown in the pattern between order and disorder, usually with violent acts (the murder of Caesar, the usurpation of the throne by Richard III, Claudius' murder of Hamlet's father, Macbeth's killing of Duncan) correlated with a sympathetic disruption of order in the world of nature. Attendant upon such human events therefore are such natural phenomena as earthquakes, strange beasts, unaccountable storms, voices from the sky, and witches.

The idea that the world is but an extension of the mind, and that the cosmic order in turn is reflected in human beings, gives validity to diverse interpretations of *The Tempest* and, as a matter of fact, encompasses many of them.

The initial storm or "tempest" invoked by Prospero, which wrecks the ship, finds analogy in Antonio's long-past usurpation of Prospero's dukedom and his setting Prospero and Miranda adrift at sea in a storm in the hope they would perish. When, years later, the court party—Alonso, Sebastian, Antonio, and Ferdinand, along with the drunken Stephano and Trinculo—is cast upon the island, its "meanderings," pitfalls, and enchantments make it a place where everyone will go through a learning process and most come to greater self-knowledge.

Illusions on this island, which include Ariel's disguises, the disappearing banquet, and the line of glittering costumes that delude Stephano, Trinculo, and Caliban, find counterparts in the characters' illusions about themselves. Antonio has come to believe he is the rightful duke; Sebastian and Antonio, deluded by ambition, plan to kill Alonso and Gonzalo and make Sebastian tyrant of Naples. The drunken trio of court jester, butler, and Caliban falsely see themselves as future conquerors and rulers of the island. Ferdinand is tricked into believing that his father has drowned and that Miranda is a goddess. Miranda, in turn, nurtured upon illusions by her father, knows little of human beings and their evil. Even Prospero must come to see he is not master of the universe and that revenge is not the answer after all. He must move to a higher reality, in which justice and mercy have greater power.

It has been noted that the island holds different meanings for different characters. Here again is an illustration of the analogy between microcosm and macrocosm. The characters with integrity see it as a beautiful place; honest Gonzalo, for example, thinks it might be a utopia. Sebastian and Antonio, however, whose outlook is soured by their villainy, characterize the island's air as perfumed by a rotten swamp. Whether a character feels a sense of freedom or of slavery is conditioned not just by Prospero's magic but by the individual's view of the island and own makeup. The loveliest descriptions of the island's beauty and enchantment come from Caliban, the half-human, who knew its offerings far better than anyone else before his enslavement by Prospero.

Perhaps in few of his other plays has Shakespeare created a closer relationship between the human and natural universes. In *The Tempest*, beauty and ugliness, good and evil, and cruelty and gentleness are matched with the external environment, and everything works toward a positive reconciliation of the best in both humans and nature. This harmony is expressed by the delightful pastoral masque Prospero stages for the young lovers, in which reapers and nymphs join in dancing, indicating the union of the natural with the supernatural. The coming marriage of Ferdinand and Miranda also foreshadows such harmony, as do the repentance and forgiveness demonstrated by the major characters.

It may be true, as Prospero states in Act V, that upon the island "no man was his own," but he also confirms that understanding has come like a "swelling tide," and he promises calm seas for the homeward journey, after which all will presumably take up the tasks and responsibilities of their respective station with improved perspective. As Prospero renounces his magic, Ariel is freed to return to the elements, and Caliban, true child of nature, is left to regain harmony with his world. Perhaps the satisfaction experienced by Shakespeare's audiences results from the harmony between humans and nature that illumines the close of the play.

"Critical Evaluation" by Muriel B. Ingham

Bibliography:
French, Marilyn. *Shakespeare's Division of Experience*. New York: Summit Books, 1981. French sees the play as Shakespeare's attempt to synthesize themes from his earlier works and finally propound a theory of justice that satisfies the hierarchical imperatives he had previously set out. An examination of gender roles plays a significant part in her attempts to explicate Shakespeare's universe. Caliban is presented as representative of colonized peoples.

Kermode, Frank. *William Shakespeare: The Final Plays*. London: Longmans, Green, 1963. Kermode sees this play as the most classically unified of Shakespeare's late works, and finds a repetition of earlier themes including "guilt and repentance, the finding of the lost, forgiveness, the renewal of the world, [and] the benevolence of unseen powers."

Lindley, David. "Music, Masque and Meaining in *The Tempest*." *The Court Masque*. Manchester, England: Manchester University Press, 1984. Lindley examines the masque as a unique Renaissance art form and uncovers the role music plays in *The Tempest* to assert and deny power.

Peterson, Douglas L. *Time, Tide, and Tempest: A Study of Shakespeare's Romances*. San Marino, Calif.: Huntington Library, 1973. Places the play in the context of Shakespeare's romance plays. Explores the themes and motifs of redemption and natural order, which elaborated on Shakespeare's earlier vision.

Smith, Hallett Darius, ed. *Twentieth Century Interpretations of "The Tempest": A Collection of Critical Essays.* Englewood Cliffs, N.J.: Prentice-Hall, 1969. Provides viewpoints and interpretations of *The Tempest* by sixteen critics, including A. C. Bradley and Northrup Frye. Includes a chronology of important dates and a bibliography.

THE TEMPLE

Type of work: Poetry
Author: George Herbert (1593-1633)
First published: 1633

Sir Richard Herbert, an aristocrat of Norman descent, died when his son George was three years old. His ten children were reared by their mother, who is known to have been a wise, witty, generous, and religious woman. John Donne said: "Her house was a court in the conversation of the best." Too frail for the family profession of soldiering, George Herbert was early guided toward the priesthood by his mother. He was not ordained until 1630, but Magdalen Herbert seems to have influenced the course of his life as much as Donne influenced his poetry. The first sonnets he wrote were addressed to her and in them he vowed to devote himself to religious poetry.

The Latin verses that Herbert wrote at Cambridge are full of classical allusion. In *The Temple*, the main body of his English verse, he eschewed all archaic references and poetic rhetoric as studiously as Donne did himself. From Donne he also learned to transmute thought into feeling so that the intellectual concept becomes the emotional experience of the poem. Like Donne's, his rhythms are colloquial; his imagery, although not often as dramatic as that of Donne, is similarly practical, concrete, and arresting.

Herbert's range was narrower than Donne's, for he wrote only religious poetry and none that was tortuous or complicated. Yet, though Herbert can be said to have a moral simplicity, he was anything but simple. Within his one central preoccupation, his thought is varied. In his last letter to Nicholas Ferrar, to whom he sent the manuscript of *The Temple*, he described his poems as "A picture of the many spiritual conflicts that have passed betwixt God and my soul, before I could subject mine to the will of Jesus my master, in whose service I have now found perfect freedom." His anguish was not at the possibility that he had lost his faith or was threatened with damnation but lest he should prove not to be a good and worthy servant to God. Herbert's greatest temptation was worldly ambition.

At Cambridge, Herbert's relaxation was music; he played the lute and wrote accompaniments to his Latin poems. This interest is evident in the vocabulary and also in the rhythm of many of his poems. Some, like his version of the twenty-third psalm, were written to be sung. In "Easter," the lute is an image for the body of Christ on the cross:

> The cross taught all wood to resound his name,
> Who bore the same.
> His stretched sinews taught all strings, what key
> Is best to celebrate this most high day.

The equation in the second stanza of the crucifixion and the lute communicates the glory and pathos of Easter. The eager invocations to the poet's own heart and lute in the first stanza are found also in the third, which carries the full implications of the previous image and reinforces it:

> Consort both heart and lute, and twist a song
> Pleasant and long:
> Or since all musick is but three parts vied,
> And multiplied;
> O let thy blessed Spirit bear a part,
> And make up our defects with his sweet art.

Ambition for worldly acclaim is as recurrent in Herbert's poetry as music. In *The Temple* he often analyzes the delights of success, and the rejection of these delights is as meaningful poetically as it was in his life. In "The Pearl," Herbert speaks of his knowledge of learning, honor, and pleasure, and he concludes each stanza with the refrain, "Yet I love thee." In the last stanza, the value of such knowledge is justified and explained: It renders his love of God significant and reasoned. "Therefore not sealed but with open eyes/ I flie to thee." This quality of quietness, certitude, and moral simplicity at the end of many of Herbert's poems gives them peculiar power. A controlled and intense late poem of rebellion contemplated, "The Collar" reflects at its close Herbert's complete humility and devotion in spite of all ambition and restlessness. The poem describes all that was lost:

> Sure there was wine,
> Before my sighs did drie it: there was corn,
> Before my tears did drown it.
> Is the yeare onely lost to me?
> Have I no bayes to crown it?
> No flowers, no garlands gay? all blasted?
> All wasted?
> Not so, my heart: but there is fruit,
> And thou hast hands.
> Recover all thy sight-bloom age
> On double pleasures: leave thy cold dispute
> Of what is fit, and not forsake thy cage. . . .

The poem is forceful, quick, and argumentative, and at the height of its fierceness the poet interrupts himself: "Methought I heard one calling, *Childe:*/ And I reply'd, *My Lord*."

Herbert's devotion to God is usually expressed with this humility and with a sensitive awareness of personal unworthiness. The ability to love is itself a gift of God. The search for a way of service is complemented by Herbert's intense consciousness of the sacrificial nature of Christ's life. In the sonnet "Redemption," the poet records a search for Christ first in heaven, then in earth's palaces, cities, and courts, and finally finds him in a rabble of thieves and murderers: ". . . there I him espied,/ Who straight, *Your suit is granted*, said, and died."

The common meeting grounds between people and their mundane activities and possessions are a great source of imagery to Herbert. His lyrics are probably his greatest poetry, and their structure, imagery, vocabulary, and rhythm all encompass one dominant idea, which, after the thought that inspired the lyric has been thoroughly explored, is finally, exactly, and directly communicated. Herbert's poems have total unity, and the impression of ease—in craftsmanship, not of feeling—is obtained by the logical and perceptive argument. Technically, this effect is most often achieved in the development of the images. In "Vertue," the clear and sensuous expression of the death of the day and a rose and of the spring that is composed of days and roses, "A box where sweets compacted lie," leads to an image of natural strength where the virtuous soul "Like season'd timber; never gives." The penultimate line, following logically from the timber image, uses a most commonplace object, coal, as a continuation of it, and reverberates with the conviction of the immortality of the soul: "But though the whole world turn to coal,/ Then chiefly lives."

In "Affliction (I)," Herbert's feeling of unworthiness is clearly related to his ill health. There is a carefully balanced argument: At first, loving God was a joyous experience, and Herbert uses the metaphor of a furnished house to express his contentment: "Thy glorious household stuff did me entwine." After the first rapture, in which there was no room for fear, sorrow and sickness overcame him. This situation was partly improved when he turned from "the way that takes the town" and won "Academic praise." Then, lest he should "too happie be" in his unhappiness, God sent him further sickness. "Thus does thy power cross-bias me." A note of rebellion sounds at the seemingly contradictory demands of God, but the poem concludes: "Ah my deare God! though I am clean forgot,/ Let me not love me, if I love thee not."

Herbert's poetry is a constant communing with God, and it presents a great variety of moods. The firm tone of "Affliction (I)" can be contrasted with the delicacy and gentleness of "Love (III)," in which the alternating long and short lines illustrate the hesitancy of a soul yearning for God's love and yet not able to grasp it because of its own inadequacies. The tenderness of love is implicit in the words "welcome," "sweetly," "smiling," and "quick-eyed love." Flat mono-syllables convey the soul's guilt in "sinne," "slacke," "marr'd," and "shame." Yet love made the eyes that call themselves unworthy, and love bore the blame for the sin; love encourages the soul until it can accept these things and the gift of love itself: "You must sit down, sayes Love, and taste my meat:/ So I did sit and eat."

Another poem in which the length of line echoes the feeling is "Easter Wings." The affected device of writing a poem in the shape of "wings"—and it was in the early editions printed vertically on the page—is in this instance effective. The first and last lines of both verses are long, and each verse has middle lines of only two words each. This arrangement conveys in reading the rise and fall of the lark's song, which is the image for the fall of man and his resurrection in Christ. "Easter Wings" is the best of the poems in which Herbert uses some trick to illustrate his meaning. Other examples are "The Altar" and "Paradise."

Donne's influence on Herbert's poetry can thus also be seen in the variety of his lyrical forms, the directness of his language, and his less learned but equally arresting imagery. In contrast to Donne's poetry, Herbert's is essentially peaceful. His poems never end on a note of desperation. His way of thinking and his sensibility, by which he perceives the nuances in an idea and the connections between varied images and then fuses these to communicate feeling, is essentially metaphysical. The quiet tone of Herbert's poetry with its power of persuasion by gentle argument is entirely original and something for which, as the "Jordan" poem tell us, he consciously strove and beautifully achieved:

> As flames do work and winde, when they ascend;
> So did I weave myself into the sense.
> But while I bustled, I might hear a friend
> Whisper, *How wide is all this long pretence!*
> There is in love a sweetness readie penn'd:
> Copie out only that, and save expense.

Herbert had great influence on other seventeenth century poets: Henry Vaughan borrowed from him extensively, and Richard Crashaw called his own first volume *The Steps to the Temple*. He was, together with the other metaphysical poets, criticized in the eighteenth century, yet Alexander Pope, although disliking his poetic method, in his *Essay on Man* appears to have been influenced by Herbert's philosophy. Samuel Coleridge restored critical favor to Herbert and consequently profoundly influenced Gerard Manley Hopkins, and the twentieth century responded with delight to all the metaphysical poets.

Bibliography:
Bloch, Chana. *Spelling the Word: George Herbert and the Bible*. Berkeley: University of

California Press, 1985. A thoroughly documented and accessible examination of Herbert's allusions, echoes, and borrowings from the Bible, as well as of his creative transformations of biblical texts.

Fish, Stanley E. "Letting Go: The Dialectic of Self in Herbert's Poetry." In *Self-Consuming Artifacts: The Experience of Seventeenth Century Literature*. Berkeley: University of California Press, 1972. A discussion of Herbert's lyrics from the point of view of a reader's response. Emphasizes their dramatic qualities and inconclusiveness. Remains one of the most controversial and provocative studies of Herbert.

Roberts, John R., ed. *Essential Articles for the Study of George Herbert's Poetry*. Hamden, Conn.: Archon Books, 1979. A useful collection of thirty-four essays representing some of the main critical and scholarly approaches to Herbert. Contains many revealing and influential discussions of such topics as Herbert's style, the structure of *The Temple*, and relevant intellectual and theological contexts for the work.

Summers, Joseph H. *George Herbert: His Religion and Art*. Cambridge, Mass.: Harvard University Press, 1954. Probably the best starting point for a comprehensive approach to Herbert. A fully integrated study of his poetry that relates it to his life, times, and religion. Fine introduction to Herbert's complex form, search for the proper language of devotion, and broad Anglican theology.

Vendler, Helen. *The Poetry of George Herbert*. Cambridge, Mass.: Harvard University Press, 1975. Close readings, some very detailed, of nearly all of Herbert's lyrics. Emphasizes Herbert's formal skill, which is often manifested in the poems in "reinventions," subtle and dramatic shifts in tone and theme.

THE TEMPLE OF THE GOLDEN PAVILION

Type of work: Novel
Author: Yukio Mishima (Kimitake Hiraoka, 1925-1970)
Type of plot: Psychological realism
Time of plot: Mid-twentieth century
Locale: Kyoto, Japan
First published: Kinkakuji, 1956 (English translation, 1959)

> *Principal characters:*
> MIZOGUCHI, a Zen Buddhist acolyte and student at the Golden Temple
> TSURUKAWA, his friend and fellow student
> KASHIWAGI, another friend and fellow student
> FATHER DOSEN, the Superior at the temple

The Story:

The son of a Zen Buddhist monk, Mizoguchi was haunted by his father's admiration of the beautiful Temple of the Golden Pavilion, but he was not himself beautiful. He was a stutterer and described himself as ugly, but he considered himself a great artist. When a naval cadet visited his middle school, he scratched the fine scabbard of his sword for no particular reason other than envy.

When he tried to confront Uiko, an attractive girl who lived nearby, she teased Mizoguchi about his stuttering, and he cursed her. A few months later she hid in a temple with her lover, a deserter from the navy, and when the military police found them, he shot her and then killed himself, but Mizoguchi was not especially disturbed by the tragedy.

When his father took him to visit the Golden Temple, Mizoguchi was disappointed and actually preferred a model of the temple to the real thing, but his ailing father's main intent was to introduce his son to the Superior, Father Dosen, who would become his teacher. Shortly after that, his father died, but Mizoguchi felt no particular grief, nor did he feel sorry for his mother, whom he knew had been unfaithful to his father. The event, which he witnessed as a boy, caused him to despise both parents and was likely the origin of his own self-loathing.

As an acolyte or student of Zen during the last year of World War II, Mizoguchi's best friend was an outgoing, likable student named Tsurukawa, but he continued to feel alienated by the beauty of the temple and drawn to a life of evil. One evening he saw a tea ceremony in which a beautiful woman used milk from her breast for a young army officer's cup, and he was stricken by the mystery of the event.

During the occupation, a drunken United States soldier insisted that Mizoguchi step on the stomach of his prostitute outside the temple. Mizoguchi found a strange pleasure in doing it, and he maliciously passed on the carton of cigarettes the soldier had given him to the Superior. After having a miscarriage, the prostitute extorted money from the Superior and later she committed suicide. Mizoguchi felt no guilt over what happened, but in fact enjoyed a certain evil pleasure.

Although the Superior knew what had happened, he sent Mizoguchi to college at Otani University, where he met the cynical, clubfooted Kashiwagi, an intellectual who detected immediately that Mizoguchi was a virgin and was afraid of women. When he tried to make love to the woman Kashiwagi provided for him, however, the image of the Golden Temple intervened and left him impotent. Upon returning from that outing, Mizoguchi learned that Tsurukawa had been killed in an accident. (Later the reader learns it was suicide.)

Kashiwagi enjoyed flower arrangement and playing the flute, but he despised literature and architecture, as they represented lasting and immutable forms of beauty. In fact, Kashiwagi preferred art forms noted for their "uselessness." One afternoon the beautiful woman who had offered her breast milk to the soldier (who had been killed in the war) turned up at Kashiwagi's apartment, but he treated her brutally. Mizoguchi followed her to her place and told her about seeing her years before, but when she offered him her breast, he saw it transformed into the Golden Temple and was again struck impotent. The eternal beauty of the temple stood between him and mortal beauty, but it also stood as a challenge to him, and after this Mizoguchi resolved to "rule" over the temple.

Increasingly Mizoguchi felt no kinship with anyone or anything but the temple, which became his focus in life. When he discovered the Superior with a geisha, he tried to blackmail him, but to no avail, and he began to do poorly in his studies. He took delight in not being understood, and when he ran off in the fall of 1948, facing the wildness of the Sea of Japan, he realized his mission in life was to burn down the Golden Temple.

At age twenty-one, in the spring of 1950, Mizoguchi had a run-in with Kashiwagi when he pressed the Father Dosen on one of Mizoguchi's IOUs, but the Superior paid it. The Superior's threat to expel Mizoguchi freed him to pursue his scheme, and Kashiwagi's malicious revelation that Tsurukawa's death was a suicide prompted by an unhappy love provided an additional incentive. Subsequently, Mizoguchi took the Superior's money and paid for a prostitute with it instead of paying off Kashiwagi. He was able to consummate the sexual relation, but it offered him no satisfaction, as he could see the beauty of the day changing before his eyes and realized that everything, including the woman, was destined to die.

Shortly after the outbreak of the Korean War, Mizoguchi bought arsenic and a knife, intending to set fire to the temple and then to commit suicide. Just before lighting the fire, Mizoguchi contemplated the beauty of the temple one last time and recognized that it was a dream of perfection that could never be completed but that always pursued the next unknown beauty. Paradoxically, then, "Nothingness was the very structure of this beauty." The beauty of the Golden Temple never ceased, and it was unsurpassed. He also recalled a Buddhist proverb: When you meet the Buddha, kill the Buddha. Mizoguchi saw that he must burn the temple "precisely because it was so futile" to do so. At the end of the novel, sitting on a hill overlooking the burning temple, Mizoguchi discarded the knife and arsenic, lit a cigarette, and told himself he wanted to live.

Critical Evaluation:

The Temple of the Golden Pavilion is based on an actual event, the destruction of the famous temple (completed in about 1398), a national treasure, by a disturbed monk in 1950. The temple was quickly rebuilt, and the awareness of that fact, at least among Japanese readers, could have a significant impact on how one interprets the novel. That is, one could argue that Mizoguchi fails in the end to destroy beauty and that in fact the temple is simply transformed. In the first three years of publication, the novel sold some 300,000 copies in Japan and became a successful play as well.

If it were not for the fact that the novel is narrated in first-person by the main character, who revels in his psychopathology, the novel might qualify as symbolic allegory. The temple is apparently a symbol of eternal and changeless beauty in an unstable and ugly world. Mizoguchi himself is the embodiment of the ugliness of the world. The constant threat of death and destruction is pervasive in the novel, which begins in the midst of World War II and ends at the start of the Korean War.

Every beautiful person or thing in the novel appears vulnerable. Every beauty is on the verge of transformation into ugliness or death or annihilation. Mizoguchi's mother seems an ugly peasant to him, and his father seems to be wasting away before he dies of a hemorrhage. The beautiful Uiko is killed by her desperate lover; the handsome and upbeat Tsurukawa, whom Mizoguchi believes to be a positive image of his own dark self, commits suicide; any beautiful act (flower arrangement or playing the flute) associated with Kashiwagi is compromised by his cruelty. Father Dosen's involvement with geisha girls demonstrates, as Mizoguchi sees it, the failure of religion or philosophy to deal effectively with the devastating impact of change and obliteration. When he destroys the temple, Mizoguchi performs an act of destruction that has an element of evil as an alternative to the artistic or godlike act of creation. Ironically, then, his burning of the temple can be seen as a great act of personal, individual heroism, and self-expression. Mizoguchi has rid himself of his obsession and regained the desire to live.

Those familiar with Yukio Mishima's biography will detect parallels between him and his nihilistic protagonist. Although he was able to avoid military service during World War II, Mishima later created a paramilitary organization. A brilliant student, Mishima was physically weak as a young man, but he later took up body-building and became a successful actor. He was fascinated with swordplay (kendo) and the Samurai code of Bushido, which emphasizes loyalty and acts of courage. Apparently homosexual, he married and had two children. His ambivalent sexuality appears in many characters, but especially in Mizoguchi. Mishima ended his life dramatically when his paramilitary Tatenokai (shield society) occupied the offices of a general of the Japanese Defense Force. At the end of his demonstration he committed suicide and had himself beheaded by one of his comrades. While suicide figures only tangentially in this novel, it could be argued that Mizoguchi's final act is self-destructive, and it certainly reflects Mishima's interest in acts of violence.

This may also be read as a philosophical novel concerned with the nature of art, and perhaps especially with its limitations. Drawn between the life of the artist and that of the soldier, to use the terms broadly, Mishima became increasingly frustrated with the limitations of the former and infatuated with the active life represented by the latter. Mizoguchi also finds himself unable to yield to art, unable to accept the flaws in the work that every artist must endure, presumably because the evidence of experience is too much for him. This novel attains the stature of tragedy, then, because like many great tragic heroes, Mizoguchi can find no resolution to the dilemma of life except destruction. Arguably, Mishima's death as a man of action, as a soldier who was also an artist haunted by beauty, was similarly tragic. Readers must decide for themselves whether Mizoguchi is worthy of their sympathies, whether he is comparable, for example, to such tragic heroes as Hamlet, Othello, and Faust, or whether his disillusioned nihilism makes him an unsympathetic antihero.

Ron McFarland

Bibliography:
Scott-Stokes, Henry. *The Life and Death of Yukio Mishima.* New York: Farrar, Straus & Giroux, 1974. This biography provides ample material for those who seek parallels between Mishima and Mizoguchi.
Starrs, Roy. *Deadly Dialectics: Sex, Violence and Nihilism in the World of Yukio Mishima.* Folkestone, England: Japan Library, 1994. Sees Mizoguchi as "rising heroically from passive to active nihilism." Sees "relief and catharsis" in the ending.
Ueda, Makoto. *Modern Japanese Writers and the Nature of Literature.* Stanford, Calif.: Stan-

ford University Press, 1976. Focuses on *The Temple of the Golden Pavilion* as a philosophical novel and on the role of novelist as psychiatrist. Makes ample use of details from Mishima's life.

Wolfe, Peter. *Yukio Mishima.* New York: Frederick Ungar, 1989. The most useful commentary in English on the novel. Considers Mizoguchi's act to be one of self-betrayal and sees *The Temple of the Golden Pavilion* as "a downbeat, negative book."

Yamanouchi, Hisaaki. *The Search for Authenticity in Modern Japanese Literature.* New York: Cambridge University Press, 1978. Argues for separation of Mishima from his protagonist, even though Mishima himself was nihilistic and often felt estranged from life.

THE TEMPTATION OF SAINT ANTHONY

Type of work: Novel
Author: Gustave Flaubert (1821-1880)
Type of plot: Historical
Time of plot: Fourth century
Locale: Egypt
First published: La Tentation de Saint Antoine, 1874 (English translation, 1895)

Principal characters:
SAINT ANTHONY
HILARION, his disciple
THE DEVIL
THE QUEEN OF SHEBA
TERTULLIAN
MONTANUS
APOLLONIUS

The Story:

Anthony had lived the life of a hermit for more than thirty years and now had come almost to the point of despair. He was extremely weary of life and with the world as he saw it from the limited point of view of his cell high in the mountains. At one time people had made pilgrimages to see him and be advised by him. These same people had furnished him with whatever money and clothing he needed; but everyone had stopped coming years before, and Anthony had begun to fear that his life was worthless. He then began to long for the money, women, and goods of this world through which he might regain some sort of recognition and pleasure.

One night Anthony's solitude became too much. He remembered his early life as a monk with its adventures and successes, and he thought of the things he might have done if he had not become a hermit. At last he decided that it was merely his own stubbornness that kept him alone in the mountains. Rather than allow himself to be guilty of such a sin, he prepared to depart but got no farther than the cleared area before his cell. Realizing that he had almost yielded to temptation, he threw himself upon the ground. Then, in order to regain his strength and courage, he read from the Acts of the Apostles and tried to think. His mind, however, kept coming back to worldly matters that still tempted him.

Anthony then began to review in his mind the things that were a credit to him in this world, the good works of his life. He praised himself for hardships he had suffered and for the things he had denied himself. Again, he began to feel sorry for himself; the desire for the money, goods, and women that had earlier been denied became unbearable. He fell into a trance. While Anthony lay on the ground, the Devil appeared, his wings spread like those of a giant bat to reveal beneath them the seven deadly sins. Anthony awoke hungry and thirsty. Taking up a scrap of bread, which was all that he could find to eat in his cave, he threw it on the ground in anger. Then there appeared before him a table laden with all manner of meat and fruit from which he might satisfy himself. As he watched, the table grew and delicacies he had never seen before appeared on it. Anthony almost indulged himself, but he realized, in time, that this also was the work of the Devil. When he kicked the table, it disappeared.

Soon afterward Anthony found on the ground a silver cup that had a gold coin at the bottom of it. When he picked up the coin, another coin appeared, and then another, until the cup filled and began to overflow. As Anthony watched, he began to dream of the power that could be his because of so much wealth. He soon saw himself as second in power only to the emperor and at the same time thought of the revenge he could take on all of his enemies. He even imagined himself as the emperor, taking precedence in Church affairs over the fathers of the Council of Nicaea. During this time, however, his bodily form had become more and more degraded until at last he saw himself as a beast. At this point, he awoke.

Anthony flogged himself furiously for indulging in such sinful dreams, but as he was doing so he became aware of the arrival of a caravan. Soon the Queen of Sheba presented herself before him with many promises of love and luxury, the only condition being that Anthony had to give up his solitary life and live with her. Although she used all of her feminine charms to lure him away, Anthony firmly resisted the temptation she offered.

After she had disappeared, Anthony noticed that a child, whom he supposed had been left behind by the caravan, was standing in the door of his cell. The child was Hilarion, a former disciple. As Anthony watched, the child grew to the height of a man and began accusing the saint of leading a sinful life. He charged that Anthony's abnegation was merely a subtle form of corruption, that his solitude simply freed him from the outbreak of his lusts, and that he only thought he held all the wisdom of the world because he was too lazy to learn anything new. When Anthony defended himself by saying that the Scriptures held all the wisdom necessary for anyone, Hilarion pointed out various contradictions in the New Testament. He then tempted Anthony by offering to lead him to a knowledge of the Unknown, the sources and secrets of life. At that point Anthony fell into another trance.

When he again became aware of his surroundings, he found himself in a large congregation that included all the great heretics of history, each propounding his own theories of God and the universe. Some suggested that God was feminine. Others were devoutly following one aspect of Christianity, such as drinking the blood of Christ, while completely ignoring all other aspects. Some were warming their naked bodies by an open fire in order to show the purity of Adam in paradise. Soon a man dressed as a Carthaginian monk leaped into the middle of the crowd, named them all for the impostors they were, and drove them away. Anthony recognized Tertullian and rushed forward to meet him. He found, instead, a woman seated alone on a bench.

The woman began to talk about Montanus, whom she believed to be the incarnation of the Holy Ghost. When Anthony suggested that he was dead, Montanus appeared before them in the form of a black man. Then followed another succession of people, each propounding a different heresy, until a woman called Marcellina suggested that she could cause Christ himself to appear if she invoked him with the aid of a silver image. When she was put to the test, however, only a python appeared. It quickly wrapped itself around Anthony, and the people began to proclaim him the Christ. At that point Anthony swooned in horror.

When he awoke, he found himself in prison with the early Christians who had been thrown to the lions, and he found himself wishing that he too could give his life to God in such a way. Then Simon appeared before him with a woman who he claimed was the embodiment of all the infamous women of history but who had now been cleansed through him. He offered Anthony the secret of his magic but disappeared at the mention of holy water. Apollonius and his disciple then appeared before Anthony and offered to describe the long road to salvation and immortality. Anthony was about to yield to their eloquence, but he drew back in horror when Apollonius began to describe his visions and his power of curing the sick and predicting the future. These proved the hardest to resist of the temptations offered thus far; it was not until Anthony clung to the cross and prayed that Apollonius and his disciple disappeared.

Nevertheless, Apollonius' taunts that Anthony's fear of the gods kept him from knowing them awakened in him a desire to see them. Hilarion then caused to appear before him the gods of all ages. When Anthony laughed at them, Hilarion pointed out that there was an element of truth in each one, which fact caused Anthony to grieve that these false religions could so easily lead one astray. He himself almost succumbed to the beauty of Olympus and the Greek gods, but he was able to repel their images by repeating the Apostles' Creed. Although Anthony had seen and learned enough of the false gods, the vision continued until he confessed to a desire to see the Devil. He hoped that his horror of Satan would rid him forever, once there was a confrontation, of such an evil. When the Devil appeared, Anthony was immediately filled with regret, but it was too late to recall his wish.

The Devil carried Anthony into space in order to show him that humankind and the world were not the center of the universe, that there were no limits to space and no purpose in its being. While the two engaged in a discussion on the nature of God, the Devil attempted to dispel all Anthony's beliefs in divine goodness, love, and infinite power. He tried to show that before understanding a God that had no limitations whatsoever, people must first understand the infinite. Spreading his wings to cover all space, the Devil showed himself to be infinite and called upon Anthony to believe in him and curse God. Only by raising his eyes in a last desperate movement of hope was the saint able to rid himself of this evil.

When Anthony next awoke, the figures of Death and Lust confronted him, each begging him to come and escape the ugliness of this world. Refusing to yield, Anthony was no longer disturbed by what had seemed the disparateness of all things. As dawn began to break, he no longer felt afraid; he enjoyed life once more. When the clouds rolled back and he saw the face of Jesus Christ in the middle of the sun, he made the sign of the Cross and resumed his prayers.

Critical Evaluation:

Gustave Flaubert began writing the first version of *The Temptation of Saint Anthony* on May 24, 1848, nine days after a communist uprising in Paris had briefly overturned the French government. He completed it on September 12, 1849, nine weeks after the French had restored Pius IX to the papal throne in spite of all Giuseppe Garibaldi had done to prevent it. He was, however, persuaded by his friends to put the book away, as something unsuitable for public consumption. He turned his attention to a much more prosaic tale of temptation, *Madame Bovary* (1857), before returning to *The Temptation of Saint Anthony* in 1856. The resulting second draft was also shelved. The version that he published in 1874 was very different, being rather more compact and much more distanced as well as having a markedly different ending.

Critics who hail Flaubert as the parent of French naturalism and *Madame Bovary* as a masterpiece of realism tend to dismiss *The Temptation of Saint Anthony* as a kind of aberration, but the posthumous publication of Flaubert's earlier writings has revealed that it was a natural culmination of that work. In "Rêve d'enfer" (a dream of hell) written in 1837, for example, an alchemist encounters Satan, who also appears briefly in the rhapsodic "La danse des morts" (the dance of death, 1838) before giving a very elaborate account of himself in the phantasmagoric drama "Smarh" (written in 1839), which almost qualifies as a preliminary sketch for *The Temptation of Saint Anthony*. The subject matter of *The Temptation of Saint Anthony* was decided when Flaubert saw Pieter Brueghel's painting on the theme in 1845. The novel is the last and best of a series, then, in which the character and power of the Devil are minutely examined. The Devil is the central character of the story; Saint Anthony is merely a convenient lens through which the Devil's works can be viewed.

Flaubert was wont to reply, when asked whether he had a model in mind for Emma Bovary, that she was himself. What he presumably meant by that was that his own imagination had been excited by romantic notions of much the same kind as those that lead her astray. As she does, he became desperate for a means of escaping from the appalling dullness of provincial life. He found his escape not so much in the various expeditions to the Orient that took him away from his mother's house as in the work of literary composition in which he immersed himself profoundly—perhaps more profoundly than any other writer. When he prepared the 1874 version of *The Temptation of Saint Anthony* for publication he was in his fifties and his triumph over temptation was secure enough so that the Devil had become a figure of abstract interest whose devices could be described and analyzed in a relatively clinical fashion. In the 1874 version the Devil is not personally present in the final section, the last illusions that he sends are chimerical, and the final ecstatic revelation climaxes with a tranquil vision of Jesus. In the earlier versions, by contrast, the Devil remains present in person after waving aside his last illusions (science and the seven deadly sins), and his laughter continues to mock Anthony's desperate prayer to the end. The final version has Anthony proclaiming "O bliss! bliss!" The earlier ones have him bewailing "Pity! Pity!" Such is the distance a man may travel between youth and maturity.

In all its versions, *The Temptation of Saint Anthony* is an allegory of self-discovery, in which religious faith is a sturdy but not invulnerable construction battered by all the doubts that intellect and imagination can raise. Flaubert differs sharply from other writers of Faustian fantasies in taking it for granted that the temptations of wealth and sex—the former represented by the cup and the coins, and the latter by the Queen of Sheba and Ennoïa (the companion of Simon Magus)—are by no means the most powerful levers which can be applied against virtue. When other writers add further lures to these two old favorites (and very few have seen the need) they tend to do so in terms of some search for more extreme sensations. Flaubert, however, is much more interested in the intellectual temptations of paganism and heresy. The bribery implicit in Simon's magic is easy enough to resist, but the mockery of Apollonius of Tyana is not, and the grandiose vision of the scientific cosmos displayed by the Devil is harder still to resist. This astonishing intellectual reach—reflected in the imaginative ambition of the melodrama—makes the work a masterpiece.

In the 1874 text, the wonders of nature, which provide the final challenge to Anthony's piety, are quickly redrawn into the perverted image of the Chimera and the Sphinx. Anthony's rejection of his tempters is represented as a victory, in stark contrast to the 1848-1849 text and the 1856 text, which rule any such victory impossible. In the earlier versions the Devil wins, not by carrying Anthony off to hell in the vulgar manner of some Gothic shocker, but by granting him the intellectual legacy of his discoveries and condemning him to live with the sound of diabolical laughter forever resounding in his ears.

It is understandable that a novel first composed during Europe's year of revolutions should have a much sharper awareness of the vulnerability of religious and political faiths than one prepared for publication in a relatively peaceful year, when stability seemed to have been restored after the horrors of the Paris Commune of 1871. The real change was, however, in the author's own attitude. He had found his own particular domestic stability and intellectual security. Whether he had achieved this state by compromise or capitulation, and whether it was a triumph or a defeat, must remain a matter of opinion. The decision as to which of the various versions of *The Temptation of Saint Anthony* to rank most highly will follow in train. Critics who prefer the sobriety of middle age to the recklessness of youth, and the safety of careful conservatism to the hazards of radicalism, inevitably agree with Flaubert's friends that the first version should have been hidden from public view, and perhaps that it should have remained hidden forever; others are free to think differently.

"Critical Evaluation" by Brian Stableford

Bibliography:
Brombert, Victor. *The Novels of Flaubert: A Study of Themes and Techniques*. Princeton, N.J.: Princeton University Press, 1966. Chapter 5 offers an account of *The Temptation of Saint Anthony*.
Donato, Eugenio. *The Script of Decadence: Essays on the Fictions of Flaubert and the Poetics of Romanticism*. New York: Oxford University Press, 1993. Chapter 4, "Gnostic Fictions," includes an elaborate discussion of the temptations offered by the heretics.
Ginsburg, Michal Peled. *Flaubert Writing*. Stanford, Calif.: Stanford University Press, 1986. Chapter 2 includes a detailed critique of *The Temptation of Saint Anthony*.
Griffin, Robert. *Rape of the Lock: Flaubert's Mythic Realism*. Lexington, Ky.: French Forum, 1988. A discussion of *The Temptation of Saint Anthony* is contained in pages 259 to 288.
Osborn, E. B. Introduction to *The First Temptation of Saint Anthony*, by Gustave Flaubert, translated by René Francis. London: Bodley Head, 1924. A stylish essay setting out in scrupulous detail the reasons why Osborn considers the earlier texts to be much superior to the 1874 version. The book reprints the revised 1856 text in full, including passages that were dropped from the 1848-1849 text.

THE TENANT OF WILDFELL HALL

Type of work: Novel
Author: Anne Brontë (1820-1849)
Type of plot: Social realism
Time of plot: Early nineteenth century
Locale: England
First published: 1848

Principal characters:

HELEN GRAHAM, in reality Helen Huntingdon, the tenant
FREDERICK LAWRENCE, her landlord
ARTHUR HUNTINGDON, her first husband
GILBERT MARKHAM, her second husband

The Story:

Gilbert Markham, a young gentleman farmer, was immediately interested when a strange tenant came to Wildfell Hall. Mrs. Graham, as her neighbors knew her, was young and beautiful, and her demand for seclusion aroused great curiosity among the local gentry. She was particularly criticized for the way in which she was caring for her small son, Arthur, whom she would not allow out of her sight. Gilbert's mother declared the child would become the worst of milksops.

On his first visit to Wildfell Hall, Gilbert learned that Mrs. Graham was a landscape painter of considerable ability and that she was concealing her whereabouts from her former friends. Her air of secrecy aroused both his curiosity and sympathy. Avoiding the attentions of Eliza Millward, the vicar's daughter, for whom he had until then shown a preference, Gilbert spent much of his time in the company of the young widow. He accompanied her and young Arthur on long walks to find scenes for Mrs. Graham to paint. His friends attempted to discourage his attentions to the tenant of Wildfell Hall. There was a rumor that she was having an affair with Frederick Lawrence, her landlord, and Lawrence himself assured Gilbert that he would fail in his attentions to Mrs. Graham. When he tried to tell her of his growing affection, Mrs. Graham insisted that Gilbert regard her simply as a friend.

After the vicar, Mr. Millward, accused the widow of improper conduct, Gilbert visited her, declared his love, and won from her a promise that she would reveal her secret to him. Later that night, however, he overheard Mrs. Graham in a mysterious discussion with her landlord that led him to suspect that the rumors about them were true. Gilbert thereupon resolved to have no more to do with her. On his next encounter with Lawrence, Gilbert struck his rival and wounded him severely.

When Gilbert met Mrs. Graham a short time later, she gave him a copy of her journal to read. The journal, beginning in 1821, told the story of Helen Graham's life for the past six years. It opened with an account of her meeting with Arthur Huntingdon, whom she had loved despite her aunt's claim that the young man was wild and wayward. Her aunt, with whom she made her home, had taken her away so that she could see no more of the objectionable Huntingdon, but by a miscalculation, the unwelcome suitor was invited to their summer home for partridge hunting. Helen Graham married Huntingdon that autumn, only to find, shortly afterward, that her husband's true character was exactly as her aunt had described. He was a drunkard, a man incapable of high principle or moral responsibility. She began to be contemptuous of him, and he responded with growing indifference toward her. Every year, Huntingdon spent several months in London, always returning weakened by dissipation. At home he held long hunting parties for his dissolute companions. Despite Helen's hopes, the birth of their son did nothing to change his way of life.

When Helen's father died, she was greatly disturbed by her husband's callous attitude toward her grief. The scenes of drunken debauchery continued in her home, and one day she discovered her husband making love to Lady Lowborough, a visitor in their house. When she demanded a separation for herself and her child, Huntingdon refused. To keep the affair from becoming known to others, Helen at last decided to stay with her husband.

Fearing that Huntingdon was corrupting their son and alienating his affections from her, Helen finally began to make her plans to escape. During that time she had to fight off a would-be lover of her own, Mr. Hargrave, who was determined to win her. She hoped to find refuge in a place where her husband could not find her and legally take her child from her. Her pride kept her from appealing to her brother or her uncle and aunt. After Huntingdon learned of her plan from reading her journal, he had her watched constantly, and he refused to let her have any money in her possession.

Her position became unendurable, however, when Huntingdon brought his mistress into the house on the pretext of providing a governess for young Arthur. Helen determined to ask her brother to let her occupy rooms in the old and now unused family home. She made her escape without money or resources, taking only her son with her.

The journal ended with Helen's arrival at Wildfell Hall. Reading this account, Gilbert realized that Frederick Lawrence was the brother mentioned several times in the diary. He at once sought out Helen to renew his suit; despite his entreaties, however, she insisted that they should not see each other again. Gilbert went to see her brother, whom he had treated so harshly at their last meeting. The reconciliation between the two men was prompt and sincere.

A short time later, the whole community learned the secret of the tenant of Wildfell Hall. Huntingdon had a fall from his horse, and his wife, learning of his serious condition, went to his house at Grassdale to look after him. Frederick Lawrence told Gilbert that Huntingdon had received her ungraciously but that she was determined to stay with him out of a sense of duty.

Despite her care, however, Huntingdon secured a bottle of wine and drank it in defiance of his doctor's orders. His indiscretion brought on a relapse that ended in his death.

Several months later, Gilbert heard that Helen's uncle had died and that she had gone to live with her aunt at Staningley. More than a year passed before he dared to go to her. He found her at Staningley, and the welcome of young Arthur was as joyous as Helen's was warm and gracious. She and Gilbert were married a short time later.

Critical Evaluation:

Begun in autumn 1846, shortly after the completion of *Agnes Grey* (1847), Anne Brontë's *The Tenant of Wildfell Hall* retains the social realism of the earlier work but adds a new complication of plot and a heightened sense of the dramatic. The chronological narrative, concentration on a single character, and subdued tone of the first novel here give way to a sophisticated structure that reveals increased complexity in themes, narrative techniques, and style.

The principal arguments in the preface to the second edition indicate the novel's two principal themes. Brontë expresses her desire "to tell the truth, for truth always conveys its own moral," and she pleads for the equality of male and female authors. Her comments correspond to her novel's themes of moral behavior and sexual equality.

The novel is closer to the Enlightenment than to Romanticism in its insistence on reason and moderation and its depiction of the evil consequences of excess. The latter is shown in the degradation of Arthur Huntingdon, who appears first as a rakish but amusing and sophisticated man of the world but rapidly sinks to debauched reveler, brutal husband, and, finally, to the desperate alcoholic whose ravings betoken fear of a god in whom he does not believe but whom he cannot dismiss. Brontë, drawing on the observation of her brother, Branwell Brontë, shows clearly that Huntingdon's collapse results from an addiction. Yet Huntingdon's addiction is exacerbated by a failure of reason. Devoid of intellectual interests, Huntingdon is characterized by a fundamental unseriousness, and the lightheartedness that initially makes him a witty entertainer eventually leads to a callous indifference to others and a readiness to turn any situation, however serious, into a jest.

Huntingdon is not the only character who acts without reason and self-control. His dissolute friends share his proclivities, the only exception being the despondent Lowborough, who finally overcomes the addictions of gambling, alcohol, and laudanum. Helen herself, ignoring all warnings and drawn by a physical attraction that she does not fully recognize but that Brontë presents unmistakably, marries impetuously, believing that she can reform Huntingdon. The young Gilbert Markham harbors irrational suspicions, which lead him to a rejection of Helen and violence against Lawrence.

Feminist issues form the second major theme. Brontë makes a forceful case for the independence and equality of women in showing that while Huntingdon declines into fatuous alcoholism, Helen matures into a reasoning, self-disciplined individual who is determined to maintain some control. When she locks her bedroom door against Huntingdon the night of their first quarrel, this anticipates her later rejection of all sexual relations with him. When she finally leaves the abusive marriage, she defies the Victorian social code that required a wife to remain with her husband whatever his behavior. In subsequently demanding a written contract awarding her custody of her son, Helen affirms the rights of mothers, which were not legally recognized until the passage of the Infants' Custody Bill in 1839.

After the separation, Helen achieves both financial and intellectual independence. Huntingdon controls her property, but she manages to support herself by her painting. Again she defies convention since, although the Victorians regarded painting as a suitable drawing room accomplishment for ladies, they reserved for men the serious pursuit of art as a profession. Helen's trials also bring her intellectual independence. Naturally spirited, she learns how to assert herself. Her quiet demeanor does not prevent her from challenging received opinions, most notably in her discussion with Mrs. Markham on the need to bring up boys and girls in the same way. In her marriage to Gilbert, the reader must suppose that Helen will not relinquish her hard-won independence but rather that theirs is an equal union. Earlier, Gilbert had told his mother that he would not expect his future wife to subordinate herself to his wishes and comforts.

Divided into three sections, the novel presents two narrative voices. The first section is told by Gilbert, now middle-aged, recounting events of his youth in letters to his friend Halford. Entering imaginatively into the mind of her male persona, Brontë shows how Gilbert develops from naïve egotism to a maturity marked by sensitivity and patience. This initial point of view introduces Helen as the impressive, mysterious stranger who arouses suspense at the same time that it establishes the character of the mature heroine.

The second section is the diary Helen gives to Gilbert, which provides an intimate depiction of her first marriage, shows her moral growth, and becomes a means of instruction for Gilbert. Thus enabled to understand Helen's real self, Gilbert learns about the possible pitfalls of marriage and so is better prepared for a different kind of union himself.

The third section reverts to Gilbert's narrative, supplemented by letters from Helen to her brother. The perspective alternates between Helen and Gilbert until the final scene, which brings the lovers together in the plot as the two voices blend in an open and harmonious dialogue.

In keeping with the novel's realistic mode and personal viewpoint, Brontë's style is plain and straightforward but enhanced by descriptions, irony, and symbols. The descriptions are imaginative and keenly observed and range from the gloom of the crumbling old hall to the delights of a spring morning. Occasional ironic humor sharpens the social satire, as in Gilbert's portrait of the Reverend Millward or Helen's account of her youthful conversations with her aunt. Symbols are used dramatically to reinforce character and theme. In Hargrave's chess game with Helen, both players recognize that his real object is her seduction: The scene suggests that Hargrave sees his relationship with her as both a contest that he is determined to win and a game in which he is not required to act responsibly. The winter rose that Helen offers to Gilbert, recalling the earlier rose she had picked for him, is in fact a proposal and an emblem of her heart, which, like the rose, has survived storms and hardships.

The Tenant of Wildfell Hall is remarkable for its outspokenness in developing its themes and treating its subject. Brontë's unflinching honesty in portraying and deromanticizing the darker side of human nature, her serious moral sense, and her confident feminism make this a remarkable mid-Victorian novel.

"Critical Evaluation" by Muriel Mellown

Bibliography:

Frawley, Maria H. "The Female Saviour in *The Tenant of Wildfell Hall." Brontë Society Transactions* 20, part 3 (1991): 133-143. Examines the novel in light of the Victorian ideology of woman as savior or angel in the house and shows that Helen both submits to and struggles against this conventional role.

Jackson, Arlene. "The Question of Credibility in Anne Brontë's *The Tenant of Wildfell Hall." English Studies* 63, no. 3 (June, 1982): 198-206. Discusses narrative techniques and explains how Brontë's point of view and plot organization reveal the novel's characters and increase their credibility.

Langland, Elizabeth. "The Voicing of Feminine Desire in Anne Brontë's *The Tenant of Wildfell Hall."* In *Gender and Discourse in Victorian Literature and Art*, edited by Antony Harrison and Beverly Taylor. DeKalb: Northern Illinois University Press, 1992. Analyzes the use of two narrators and shows how Gilbert finally adopts Helen's perspective. The narrative techniques are a means of refuting the idea of woman's redemptive spirituality and of providing a way for a woman to voice her desire.

McMaster, Juliet. " 'Imbecile Laughter' and 'Desperate Earnest' in *The Tenant of Wildfell Hall." Modern Language Quarterly* 43, no. 4 (December, 1982): 352-368. Argues that Huntingdon represents Regency dissipation and Helen Victorian seriousness, a dour earnestness that is finally mitigated by her love for Gilbert.

Thormahlen, Marianne. "The Villain of Wildfell Hall: Aspects and Prospects of Arthur Huntingdon." *Modern Language Review* 88, part 4 (October, 1993): 831-841. Places the work in its historical context and analyzes Huntingdon's character in light of contemporary theology, social developments, and science.

TENDER IS THE NIGHT

Type of work: Novel
Author: F. Scott Fitzgerald (1896-1940)
Type of plot: Social realism
Time of plot: 1920's
Locale: Europe
First published: 1934

> *Principal characters:*
> DICK DIVER, a psychologist
> NICOLE, his wife
> ROSEMARY HOYT, an actress
> TOMMY BARBAN, a professional soldier

The Story:

Rosemary Hoyt was just eighteen, dewy fresh and giving promise of beautiful maturity. In spite of her youth, she was already a famous actress, and her film *Daddy's Girl* was all the rage. She had come to the south of France with her mother for a rest after having become very ill from diving repeatedly into a Venetian canal during the shooting of her picture.

At the beach, she met Dick Diver and suddenly realized that she was in love. After she became well acquainted with the Divers, she also came to like Diver's wife, Nicole, a strikingly beautiful woman, and her two children. Rosemary's mother approved of Dick. At one of the Divers' famous parties, Rosemary told Dick outright that she loved him, but he made light of her declaration.

During the party, Mrs. McKisco saw Nicole behaving hysterically in the bathroom, and on the way home, she tried to talk about it. Tommy Barban, a war hero, made her keep silent. Resenting Tommy's interference, Mr. McKisco provoked a quarrel with him, which ended in a duel in which several shots were exchanged but no one was hurt. Rosemary was greatly moved by the occurrence.

Rosemary traveled to Paris with the Divers and went on a round of parties and tours with them. She made frequent advances to Dick, but he refused, apathetically, until one day a young college boy told of an escapade in which Rosemary had been involved. Then Dick began to desire the young girl. Although their brief love affair was confined to furtive kisses in hallways, Nicole became suspicious.

Abe North, a brawling composer, offended two blacks and involved a third. While Dick was in Rosemary's hotel room, Abe brought one of the black men to ask Dick's help in resolving the mess. When Dick took Abe to his own room, the black stayed in the corridor. The two other black men killed him and laid the body on Rosemary's bed. When the body was found, Dick carried it into the hall and took Rosemary's bedspread into his bathtub to wash it out. Seeing the bloody spread, Nicole broke down and in an attack of hysteria accused Dick of many infidelities. Her breakdown was like the one Mrs. McKisco had once witnessed.

Some years earlier, Dick had been doing research in advanced psychology in a clinic in Zurich. There he one day met a pathetic but beautiful patient, young Nicole Warren. At first merely attracted to her professionally, Dick later learned the cause of her long residence in the clinic. Nicole came from a wealthy Chicago family. When she was eleven, her mother died. After that her father became very close to her and they had an incestuous relationship, which led to Nicole's breakdown. Her father, too cowardly to kill himself as he had planned, had placed her in the clinic at Zurich. For many reasons, Dick became Nicole's tower of strength; with him she was almost normal. Finally, motivated by pity and love, Dick married her. For a time, he was able to maintain her in a healthy equilibrium, and the marriage seemed to be a success. This was aided by the fact that Nicole's family was rich, in fact, that Nicole's older sister was able to buy Dick a partnership in the clinic where he had first met Nicole.

For some time after the episode involving Rosemary, Nicole was quite calm but too withdrawn. Then a neurotic woman wrote her a letter accusing Dick of misdeeds with his women patients. The letter was untrue, but Nicole believed it and had another relapse. She left her family at a country fair and became hysterical while riding on the Ferris wheel.

At one time, Dick had shown great promise as a writer and as a psychologist. His books had become standard reference sources, and many of his colleagues considered him a genius. After Nicole's hysterical fit on the Ferris wheel, however, he no longer seemed able to do real work. One reason for this was Nicole's increasing wealth, which meant that Dick did not have to work. At the age of thirty-eight, still a handsome and engaging man, he began to drink heavily.

On several occasions, Nicole was ashamed of her husband's drunken behavior. She did her best to prevent his drinking and in so doing began to gain strength of her own. For the first time since the long stay at the clinic, she came to have an independent life apart from Dick's influence.

Dissatisfied with the life he was leading, Dick decided to go away by himself for a while. He ran into Tommy Barban, still a reckless, strong, professional soldier, who had just had a romantic escape from Russia. While still absent from his wife, Dick received word that his father had died.

Going back to America was for him a nostalgic experience. His father had been a gentle clergyman, living a narrow life; but his life had had roots, and he was buried among his ancestors. Dick had been away so long, had lived for so many years a footless, unfettered life, that he almost determined to remain in America.

On the way back to meet his family, Dick stopped in Naples. In the hotel, he met Rosemary again. She was making another motion picture, but she managed to find time to see him. No longer as innocent now, she proved an easy conquest. Dick also met Nicole's older sister in Naples.

One night, Dick drank far too much and became embroiled with a chiseling taxi driver. When he refused to pay an exorbitant fee, a fight broke out, and Dick was arrested. The police captain unfairly upheld the taxi driver. Blind with rage, Dick struck a policeman and in return was severely beaten by the Fascist carabinieri. Thinking his eye had been gouged out, Dick got word to Nicole's sister, who brought all her influence to bear on the consul to have her brother-in-law released.

Back in Zurich, Dick was busy for a time at the clinic. On a professional visit to Lausanne, he learned to his surprise that Nicole's father was there, very near death. When the dying man expressed a wish to see his daughter again, Dick sent for Nicole. Strangely enough, the weakened father still could not face his daughter. In a despairing frenzy, he escaped from the hospital and disappeared.

Dick continued to go downhill. He consistently drank too much. A patient, objecting to the liquor on his breath, created a scene. Finally, Dick was forced to surrender his partnership in the clinic. With no job, Dick wandered about restlessly. He and his wife, he realized, had less and less in common. At last, after Dick had disgraced his family many times in drunken scenes, Nicole began to welcome the attentions of Tommy Barban. She no longer needed Dick and looked forward confidently to an independent life with Tommy. After the divorce, Dick moved to America. Nicole heard of him occasionally. He moved several times to successively smaller towns, an unsuccessful general practitioner.

Critical Evaluation:

In his literary work, F. Scott Fitzgerald is a retrospective oracle. He describes an age of individuals who came on the scene and burned themselves out even before they were able to conceptualize themselves. His first published novel, *This Side of Paradise* (1920), is autobiographical and describes the early Jazz Age with its vague values of money, beauty, and a distorted sense of social propriety. His masterpiece, *The Great Gatsby*, came in 1925, and *Tender Is the Night* fictionalizes the personal and social disintegration that followed the success that *The Great Gatsby* had brought Fitzgerald.

In addition to describing the glamour, excitement, and frenetic pursuit of the good life between the two world wars, *Tender Is the Night* also contains a masterful attempt at thematic telescoping. Beyond his potentials as a fictional character, Dick Diver serves a double function in the novel: He is, on the largest scale, a mid-twentieth century American equivalent of the tragic hero, and he represents the complex disintegration of the American individual during a precarious point in history.

In many ways, Diver's fall follows Aristotle's formula for classical tragedy: He is an isolated hero upon whom an entire community of individuals depends to give necessary form to their lives, yet he has a tragic flaw, a lack of perspective and introspection. (He is once told by a classmate, "That's going to be your trouble—judgment about yourself.") He represents the individual in his role as a psychiatrist who is expected to understand human motivation. Ever since the precipitating element, Nicole's case, "drifted into his hands," he has been at the mercy of fate, and his fall is monumental, from an elevated position in life into failure and anonymity. Most significant of all, Diver has a perception of his own tragic importance. He realizes that he is losing his grip on situations, and even though he recognizes some of the possible consequences of his actions, he is not equipped psychologically to combat them.

Dick Diver, however, is not a strictly tragic figure; at most, he is the sort of tragic hero that America would allow in the 1920's, but it is in this capacity that Diver serves to describe the disintegration of the American character. Dick is not simply symbolic of an American; his character is individualized to represent what an American with his exemplary vulnerabilities could become in certain circumstances. Diver and his companions create their own mystique to avoid the realities of a world thrown into, and extracting itself from, war. Their frenetic rites and the aura in which the compatriots hide ultimately form the confusion that grows larger than Diver, unleashing itself and swallowing him. Diver and the American character at this time are incomplete; each is detrimentally eclectic and depends for support on props such as music, money, and material possessions. Incompleteness nourishes Diver's paternalistic assimilation of portions of the personalities that surround him and depend on him. His need to be needed, however, causes him to assimilate more weaknesses than strengths, and the organic process is abortive. The American character is presented as being a limited, possessive one. There is a sense of something existing beyond Diver's intellectual and emotional reach that could have proved to be his salvation. Fitzgerald emphasizes the eclectic and incomplete nature of the American during this era by interweaving elements of the romantic, the realistic, and the didactic when describing actions and motivations of his characters. The result presents a severely realistic emotional conflict that sporadically explodes several characters, including Dick Diver, into psychological chaos.

Diver also functions as the pivotal character of the plot itself. Fitzgerald relays Diver's decline quite convincingly and succeeds in providing the reader subliminally with the correct formula for observing Diver's actions and their consequences. In the first three chapters of the novel, the reader is taught, through Nicole's exemplary case, to appreciate the importance of psychological analysis, to isolate the "precipitating factor" in a character's development, and then to consider that factor's influence in subsequent actions. The reader thereupon becomes equipped to transfer these premises to his observations of Diver. Throughout the duration of the novel, Dick Diver is driven by a need to be needed, which leads him increasingly into circumstances that involve him directly and cause him almost voluntarily to allow his energy to be sapped.

Tender Is the Night is a psychological novel that is more successful than most novels of its type, partly because of Fitzgerald's handling of time. Time serves both a horizontal, linear, and a vertical purpose. In linear time, the reader has an advantage that Diver does not have. (This was not so in earlier drafts of the novel.) The reader knows that Diver grows older; knows that Rosemary matures and finds other interests; knows that Nicole eventually recovers from her illness, but these are circumstances of which Diver is ignorant. Yet time also functions vertically, making the notion of thematic telescoping possible. Diver is not cognizant of the passing of time until his plunge is in its advanced stages. As Diver gradually acknowledges time and the vast gap between his "heroic period" and his encroaching anonymity, his thematic function passes from that of the purely tragic figure to that of the national character and, finally, to that of the flawed individual Dick Diver, who learns to accept his situation.

"Critical Evaluation" by Bonnie Fraser

Bibliography:

Bruccoli, Matthew J. *The Composition of "Tender Is the Night": A Study of the Manuscripts.* Pittsburgh, Pa.: University of Pittsburgh Press, 1963. This definitive study of the text provides a comprehensive analysis of the novel's seventeen drafts. By chronicling significant changes between versions, Bruccoli offers valuable evidence of the forces that influenced Fitzgerald's creative process.

LaHood, Marvin J., ed. *"Tender Is the Night": Essays in Criticism.* Bloomington: Indiana University Press, 1969. Offers a wide variety of criticism ranging from discussions of theme, symbolism, and dialogue to psychological topics. Two of the essays discuss connections between Fitzgerald and John Keats.

Metzger, Charles R. *F. Scott Fitzgerald's Psychiatric Novel: Nicole's Case, Dick's Case.* New York: Peter Lang, 1989. An intriguing psychoanalytic study of the novel that examines Nicole's and Dick's mental symptoms, discusses the effectiveness of their treatments, and debates whether they recovered from their psychological problems.

Stern, Milton R. *Critical Essays on F. Scott Fitzgerald's "Tender Is the Night."* Boston: G. K. Hall, 1986. Provides two discussions of Fitzgerald's text, as well as critical responses to the novel in chronological order, beginning with contemporary reviews from the 1930's. Includes valuable essays by Matthew J. Bruccoli, Malcolm Cowley, and Arthur Mizener, among others.

_____. *"Tender Is the Night": The Broken Universe.* New York: Twayne, 1994. Provides literary and historical context for the novel, as well as a reading of various types of identities in the novel. Also contains a useful chronology of Fitzgerald's life.

TESS OF THE D'URBERVILLES
A Pure Woman Faithfully Presented

Type of work: Novel
Author: Thomas Hardy (1840-1928)
Type of plot: Philosophical realism
Time of plot: Late nineteenth century
Locale: England
First published: 1891

>   *Principal characters:*
>   JACK DURBEYFIELD, a poor worker
>   TESS, his daughter
>   ALEC D'URBERVILLE, her betrayer
>   ANGEL CLARE, her husband

The Story:

It was a proud day when Jack Durbeyfield learned that he was descended from the famous D'Urberville family. Durbeyfield had never done more work than was necessary to keep his family supplied with meager food and himself with beer, but from that day on, he ceased doing even that small amount of work. His wife joined him in thinking that such a high family should live better with less effort, and she persuaded their oldest daughter, Tess, to visit the Stoke-D'Urbervilles, a wealthy family who had assumed the D'Urberville name because no one else claimed it. It was her mother's hope that Tess would make a good impression on the rich D'Urbervilles and perhaps a good marriage with one of the sons.

When Tess met her supposed relatives, however, she found only a blind mother and a dapper son who made Tess uncomfortable by his improper remarks to her. The son, Alec, tricked the innocent young Tess into working as a poultry maid; he did not let her know that his mother was unaware of Tess's identity. After a short time, Tess decided to avoid Alec and look for work elsewhere to support her parents and her brothers and sisters. Alec, however, managed at last to get her alone and then raped her.

When Tess returned to her home and told her mother of her terrible experience, her mother's only worry was that Alec was not going to marry Tess. She worked in the fields, facing the slander of her associates bravely. Her trouble was made worse by the fact that Alec followed her from place to place. By traveling to different farms during the harvest season, Tess managed to elude Alec long enough to give birth to her baby without his knowledge. The baby did not live long, however, and a few months after its death, Tess went to a dairy farm far to the south to be a dairymaid.

At the dairy farm, Tess was liked and well treated. Angel Clare, a pastor's son who had rejected the ministry to study farming, was also at the farm. It was his wish to own a farm someday, and he was working on different kinds of farms so that he could learn something of the many kinds of work required of a general farmer. Although all the dairymaids were attracted to Angel, Tess interested him the most. He thought her a beautiful and innocent young maiden. Tess felt that she was wicked, however, and rejected the attentions Angel paid to her. She urged him to turn to one of the other girls for companionship. It was unthinkable that the son of a minister would marry a dairymaid, but Angel did not care much about family tradition. Despite her pleas, he continued to pay court to Tess. At last, against the wishes of his parents, Angel asked Tess to be his wife. Not only did he love her, but he also realized that a farm girl would be a help to him on his own land. Although Tess was in love with Angel by this time, the memory of her night with Alec caused her to refuse Angel again and again. At last, his insistence, coupled with the written pleas of her parents to marry someone who could help the family financially, won her over, and she agreed to marry him.

On the night before the wedding, which Tess had postponed many times because she felt unworthy, she wrote Angel a letter, revealing everything about herself and Alec. She slipped the letter under his door; she was sure that when he read it, he would renounce her forever. In the morning, however, Angel acted as tenderly as before, and Tess loved him more than ever for his forgiving nature. When she realized that Angel had not found the letter, she attempted to tell him about her past. Angel only teased her about wanting to confess, thinking that such a pure girl could have no black sins in her history. They were married without Angel's learning about Alec and her dead baby.

On their wedding night, Angel told Tess about an evening of debauchery in his own past. Tess forgave him and then told about her affair with Alec, thinking that he would forgive her as she had him; but such was not the case. Angel was at first stunned and then so hurt that he could not even speak to Tess. Finally, he told her that she was not the woman he loved, the one he had married, but a stranger with whom he could not live, at least for the present. He took her to her home and left her there. Then he went to his own home and on to Brazil, where he planned to buy a farm. At first, neither Tess nor Angel told their parents the reason for their separation. When Tess finally told her mother, the ignorant woman blamed Tess for losing her husband by confessing something he need never have known.

Angel had left Tess some money and some jewels that had been given to him by his godmother. Tess put the jewels in a bank; she spent the money on her parents. When it was gone, her family went hungry once more, for her father still thought himself too highborn to work for a living. Again, Tess went from farm to farm, performing hard labor in the fields to get enough food to keep herself and her family alive.

While she was working in the fields, she met Alec again. He had met Angel's minister father and, repenting his evil ways, had become an itinerant preacher. The sight of Tess, for whom he had always lusted, caused a lapse in his new religious fervor, and he began to pursue her once again. Frightened, Tess wrote to Angel, sending the letter to his parents to forward to him. She told Angel that she loved him and needed him and that an enemy was pursuing her. She begged him to forgive her and to return to her.

The letter took several months to reach Angel. Meanwhile, Alec was so kind to Tess and so generous to her family that she began to relent in her feelings toward him. At last, when she did not receive an answer from Angel, she wrote him a note saying that he was cruel not to forgive her and that now she would not forgive his treatment of her. Then she went to Alec again and lived with him as his wife.

It was thus that Angel found her. He had come to tell her that he had forgiven her and that he still loved her. When he found her with Alec, however, he turned away, more hurt than before.

Tess, too, was bitterly unhappy. She now hated Alec because once again he had been the cause of her husband's repudiation of her. Feeling that she could find happiness only if Alec were dead, she stabbed him as he slept. Then she ran out of the house and followed Angel, who was aimlessly walking down a road leading out of the town. When they met and Tess told him what she had done, Angel forgave her everything, even the murder of Alec, and they went on together. They were happy with each other for a few days, although Angel knew that the authorities would soon find Tess.

When the officers finally found them, Tess was asleep. Angel asked the officers to wait until she awoke. As soon as she opened her eyes, Tess saw the strangers and knew that they had come for her and that she would be hanged, but she was not unhappy. She had had a few days with the husband she truly loved, and now she was ready for her punishment. She stood up bravely and faced her captors. She was not afraid.

Critical Evaluation:

Best remembered as the chronicler of the fictional Wessex, England, Thomas Hardy is considered one of the greatest novelists of the late nineteenth century. Born and raised in a small hamlet in Dorset, Hardy moved to London as a young man and spent most of the rest of his life as an urban professional. He remained part enthralled and part troubled about his native Wessex, however, and wrote with passion about industrialization, the movement of labor to the cities (or the exile of rural people in search of a living), the destruction of agricultural economies (and the ways of life dependent on them), and social dislocation. Almost all of Hardy's best-known novels contrast the social conditions of urban and rural people. While his novels are complex and often deeply tragic, his poems often are eulogies to the rural landscapes he loved.

Tess of the D'Urbervilles was inspired by Hardy's concerns over the fragility of the English rural worker's livelihood. The novel was also shockingly honest for its day in its presentation of women's sexuality and power. Tess' unrelenting victimization, often considered the novel's most serious flaw, is, in part, Hardy's indictment of Victorian values, which laid the blame of economic deprivation on the poor, and the blame for sexual exploitation on the exploited (women). The theme of sexual exploitation is closely interwoven with the story of Wessex's decline.

Tess's troubles begin with her parent's economic condition; they are representatives of the disaffected and drunken villagers whose houses will soon fall to larger farms mass-producing crops for mass consumption. The novel is strewn with images of the Wessex countryside being gobbled up by machinery (the harvesting machine, for example, that is symbolically referred to as the "grim reaper"), rail tracks, and new farm enclosures. The uncertainty of Tess's parents' fate contributes to their irresponsibility. Since they are drunk at Rolliver's Inn, Tess embarks on a journey with the beehives to the market; this is the journey on which she falls asleep and accidentally kills the family's horse in a collision. The loss of the horse, in turn, prompts Tess to work for her family's upkeep. The events that follow, culminating in her psychological disintegration and final criminal act, are rooted in a cause that is not Tess's fault—her parents' drunken irresponsibility—and perhaps not even her parents' fault; rather, the tragic plot is set in motion by an economic set of circumstances. These economic conditions have social and psychological effects. Hardy's frankness regarding money was also denounced in his day. Tess, abandoned by her husband, returns to Alec only when she is at a loss to care for her mother and younger siblings.

This is not to say that all the mistakes and wrongs perpetrated in the novel have an economic basis. The rural-urban dislocations generated by England's economic circumstances play a large part in Tess's life. Alec D'Urberville is the city-bred, cultured, street-wise man who takes advantage of Tess. Her rape, and later seduction can be read as a metaphor for the city's ruthless exploitation of the country. Angel Clare is educated in the city, and he develops fine sensibilities that unrealistically construct Tess into an ethereal and pure being (he likens her to Demeter). The unrealistic nature of Angel Clare's expectations makes him unable to forgive her for not being a virgin. Alec and Angel both manipulate Tess: the former through sexual and economic exploitation, and the latter through myths and idealistic moral constructs. Hardy continually draws readers' attention to, and calls on readers' compassion for, his female protagonist. The men who exploit her—representative of the deeds and words, respectively, that oppress women—are brought under the readers' critical gaze. In a broad sense, the female is associated with the rural. For example, in one of the first scenes traveling students, of whom Angel Clare is one, survey and "penetrate" the countryside in which Tess dances with the village maidens. Hardy's imagery evokes conceptions of power in the act of the urban gaze focusing on the rural, doubling as Angel's gaze on Tess.

The novel ends a tragedy. Unlike the protagonists of classic tragedies, the protagonist in this tragedy bears very little of the blame for her fate. Her mistakes are at best innocence, helplessness, and an overdeveloped sense of responsibility toward her loved ones. For many critics, such helplessness makes Tess a flawed, almost unrealistic, character. In any case, her fate must be read as a symbolic representation of the social power dynamics that Hardy is criticizing. The novel is more than a simple realistic account of a fallen milkmaid.

Hardy is considered to be a realistic, naturalistic writer. His style has been described as cinematic, painterly, and pictorial because of its elaborate and meticulous renditions of landscape and architecture. Some of the ways in which readers make meaning of his narratives—for example, Tess as a symbol—do not fall into the realistic tradition, however, and Hardy's best novels may be read on many levels in addition to those of realistic or naturalistic fiction. *Tess of the D'Urbervilles* may also be read for its historical, moral, satirical, and aesthetic concerns.

"Critical Evaluation" by Bishnupriya Ghosh

Bibliography:

Casagrande, Peter J. *Tess of the D'Urbervilles: Unorthodox Beauty*. New York: Twayne, 1992. Focuses on Hardy's intertwining of beauty and ugliness, of moral and aesthetic issues. Examines Victorian attitudes toward women, Tess's "terrible beauty" and parallels between her suffering and the horse's death. Analyzes Angel as a mix of convention and newness.

Kramer, Dale, and Nancy Marck, eds. *Critical Essays on Thomas Hardy: The Novels*. Boston: G. K. Hall, 1990. Discusses Hardy's plots and rhetoric, with focus on individual novels. Good essay on Hardy's understanding of Tess as a woman, examining Victorian debates and postromantic ideas. Treats awareness of language as a shaping force.

Moore, Kevin Z. *The Descent of the Imagination: Postromantic Culture in the Later Novels of Thomas Hardy*. New York: New York University Press, 1990. Uses language and cultural dominance issues to discuss Tess's quest for beauty and freedom.

Vigar, Penelope. *The Novels of Thomas Hardy: Illusion and Reality*. London: Athlone Press, 1974. Analyzes Hardy's techniques and style. Examines *Tess of the D'Urbervilles* in terms of Hardy's notion of imaginative flights that emerge from visual effects. Analyzes the novel's structure in terms of its contrasts—Tess's purity and guilt, reality and perceptions.

Wright, Terence. *Tess of the D'Urbervilles*. Atlantic Highlands, N.J.: Humanities Press, 1987. Summarizes critical approaches to *Tess of the D'Urbervilles*: social, character, ideas, formal, and genetic. Gives overview of criticism on the novel. Synthesizes the best criticism, emphasizing importance of place, ambiguity of causes, human insignificance, and the inevitability of human tragedy, with Tess representing individual and larger tragedy.

TEVYE THE DAIRYMAN

Type of work: Short fiction
Author: Sholom Aleichem (Sholem Rabinowitz, 1859-1916)
First published: Tevye der Milkhiger, 1894-1914 (English translation, 1949, 1987)

Tevye the Dairyman is the title for a collection of eight stories published by the Yiddish writer Sholom Aleichem between 1894 and 1914. The first Tevye story appeared in the Warsaw yearbook *Der Hoyzfraynt.* A fragment titled "Vekhalaklakoys," written in 1914 and published shortly before the author's death in 1916, deals with Tevye but is generally not included in the list of the Tevye stories. The collection *Tevye's Daughters* was published in 1949; it contains the eight Tevye stories. *Tevye the Dairyman and Railroad Stories* was published in 1987. *Tevye the Dairyman* is considered by some to be a loose, episodic novel about the changes that were overwhelming Eastern European Jewish life at the beginning of the twentieth century. Tevye recounts his gradual loss of control over his family, his continued questioning of God's motives, and the appropriation of his community and livelihood by forces beyond his control. The stories are the basis for the popular stage musical *Fiddler on the Roof* (1964; the title comes not from Sholom Aleichem but from a Marc Chagall painting). While many are familiar with Tevye through the theatrical version, *Tevye the Dairyman* is of greater depth.

The stories are purportedly verbatim reportage of personal anecdotes and reflections that Tevye shares with the author in occasional meetings through the years. The tone is conversational and familiar, and Tevye often refers to the place, time, and circumstances of meeting. In an ironic twist, Tevye often pleads with Sholom Aleichem that the intimate details of his life not be published to the world.

The first story, "Tevye Strikes It Rich," is a genial tale in which a good deed reaps the humble dairyman wealth beyond imagination. Returning to his village of Kasrilevke from a round of deliveries to Boiberik, where the rich Jews from Yehupetz summer in their dachas, Tevye meets two wealthy Jewish women who engage him to drive them home. Once arrived, the women and their families thank Tevye with a generous tip and a cartload of food. He rushes home to his wife Golde and they ponder how to enjoy their newfound riches.

The story introduces many of the elements that mark the entire collection. Tevye's mode of expression is painstakingly circuitous; he constantly digresses to philosophize or quote, and in many cases misquote, Jewish scripture and wisdom. He is a master of oxymoron and paradox, as when he says, "He's only human too, don't you think, or why else would God have made him a horse?" He is also adept at hyperbole, as in "The shadows of the trees were as long as the exile of the Jews." Tevye is defined by his spiraling thought process and wry speech.

At each turn, whether dealing with the women or his horse or his wife, Tevye is endearingly skeptical and ornery. His contempt for the upper classes is evident, yet he fawns when there is money to be made; his is an odd mix of acceptance and opportunism. His thoughts never stray long from metaphysics, for Tevye is a traditional Jew, constantly searching for God's wisdom in the slightest twist of fortune. He is often more apt to curse than thank his creator, but Tevye's faith is firm. He knows that there is divine wisdom he cannot understand, and that the best he can do with his miserable lot is to accept it with a modicum of good cheer.

In the second story, "The Bubble Bursts," Tevye loses the small fortune he gained by foolishly trusting it to the speculating care of his cousin Menachem Mendl. Menachem takes a hundred rubles, promising to turn it into thousands, and then disappears. After being admonished by his wife, "Tevye . . . don't just stand there doing nothing. Think!" Tevye sets off to

Yehupetz in search of Menachem. When Tevye finally finds him, after some small adventures, he learns that his cousin has lost all the money. In the end, Tevye interprets his bad luck as a confirmation from God of his place in the great scheme of things.

The first two stories trace equal motions, one forward and one backward. In the next stories, the emotional heart of *Tevye the Dairyman* comes into focus. Tevye has seven daughters. (In some of the stories, the number is unclear. Scholars speculate that Sholom Aleichem originally intended a story about each daughter, but ultimately wrote about only five.) As a poor father of daughters, a primary concern is how Tevye will marry them into happiness and reasonable prosperity. In his culture, matches are made by matchmakers and negotiated by fathers. Tevye comes to learn that such traditions are precarious at best.

In "Modern Children," the third story, Tevye arranges a lucrative match for his oldest daughter Tsaytl with the wealthy widower butcher Layzer Wolf. Tsaytl, however, is heart-broken at the prospect, and Tevye relents, and later invents a prophetic nightmare to sway his wife Golde away from the match. Then Motl the poor tailor informs Tevye that he and Tsaytl are in love and plan to marry. While Tevye cannot conceive of a young couple making such a decision on their own, without deferring to matchmakers or parents, he ultimately gives his blessing.

This story begins the account of the unraveling of tradition and paternalism. Tevye cannot stand firm against his daughters' tears. As he is buffeted with the persistence and emotions of those around him, he debates in his mind the wisdom of the old ways and the brazenness of the new. In his humorously doubtful and self-effacing way, he searches for God's will in each moment. Tevye sees the story end well, with Tsaytl married happily to a good, although not wealthy, man.

Hodl is Tevye's second daughter, and she lends her name to the fourth story, in which the stakes are raised. Not only does Hodl choose her mate, a visiting student named Pertchik, but also she goes off with him to Siberia, where he is exiled for his revolutionary activities.

For the first time in *Tevye the Dairyman*, the tone in "Hodl" becomes pained. Tevye has always protected his wife and daughters from unpleasant truths; now, as Hodl leaves, she has secrets, confidential information, that she cannot share with him. At the train station, Tevye bids Hodl farewell and she acknowledges that they may never meet again. Having maintained a stoic front, Tevye cannot endure the heartbreak any longer:

> That did it! I couldn't keep it in a second longer. You see, just then I thought of my Hodl when I held her as a baby in my arms . . . she was just a tiny thing then . . . and I held her in these arms . . . please forgive me . . . if . . . if I . . . just like a woman . . . but I want you to know what a Hodl I have! You should see the letters that she writes me . . . she's God's own Hodl, Hodl is . . . and she's with me right here all the time . . . deep, deep down . . . there's just no way to put it into words. . . .
>
> You know what, Pani Sholom Aleichem? Let's talk about something more cheerful. Have you heard any news of the cholera in Odessa?

From this point on, humor and pain go hand in hand. Aleichem's humor is a way of understanding the developing crisis of Eastern European Jewry. He neither belabors nor belittles that crisis; rather, he attempts to convey faithfully both the farce and the tragedy that he witnesses.

In the fifth and sixth stories, "Chava" and "Shprintze," Tevye loses his next two daughters in even more devastating ways. When Chava chooses to marry a non-Jew, Tevye comes up against a wall that he cannot surmount. He declares her dead to him, and refuses any further contact. He even flees in panic when he comes upon her alone in the forest. This time, when he beseeches Sholom Aleichem, "you're not to breathe a word about this, or put any of it in your books!" Tevye is articulating the unspoken fears of a threatened people.

Then Tevye's fourth daughter, Shprintze, falls in love with the son of a rich Jewish widow. At last, Tevye believes, one of his daughters is making a brilliant match, but soon Tevye is accused of scheming to entrap the young man. The wedding is canceled, Shprintze is heartbroken, and one day Tevye arrives home to find her drowned in the river. Here, the prose becomes taut and subtle; much of the pain of Shprintze's suicide is conveyed indirectly.

In the last two stories, the unraveling of Tevye's world is complete. In "Tevye Leaves for the Land of Israel," his wife Golde has died, and his fifth daughter Beilke marries a wealthy Jew named Podhotzur. Tevye finally has a well-married daughter, but she abandons him, supporting her husband's desire to exile the aging dairyman to Israel. Beilke will not question her husband's lust for reputation, a reputation that has no room for impoverished in-laws. Always looking at the bright side, Tevye accepts his exile and is eager to return to the ancestral homeland in Palestine.

He never goes, however, because Motl the tailor dies and Tevye must look after his eldest daughter Tsaytl, and her children. In "Get Thee Out," Tevye likens himself to Abraham in the Bible, being ordered by God to leave his home. Podhotzur has lost his fortune, and he and Beilke have left for America, and now Tevye, Tsaytl, and her children are being driven from Kasrilevke. As they prepare to leave, Tsaytl reminds Tevye of the child that he so long ago banished, and he turns around to face his third daughter, Chava, whom he had pronounced dead for marrying a non-Jew. He admits, "you know as well as I do that no matter what a child may have done, when it stands there looking right through you and says 'Papa'...." Tevye ultimately leaves it to Aleichem and to the reader to intuit whether he embraces her in his arms or issues the biblical order "lekh-lekho," or "get thee out."

The reunion is the emotional conclusion of the collection, a catharsis amid social dissolution. The irony continues: Local Russians, under pressure to conduct a pogrom on their Jewish population, give their well-loved Tevye the option of breaking his own windows. The humor is fitting for a man ennobled by his humility and firm in the conviction that all the blessings and ills that visit him are the expression of God's wisdom and will.

Barry Mann

Bibliography:

Gittleman, Sol. *From Shtetl to Suburbia: The Family in Jewish Literary Imagination*. Boston: Beacon Press, 1978. Discusses Aleichem and others as pioneers of the tradition. The extended chapter on Aleichem examines the crisis of contemporary family life as conveyed through the Tevye stories.

Liptzin, Solomon. *The Flowering of Yiddish Literature*. New York: T. Yoseloff, 1963. Offers an exhaustive historical narrative of Yiddish literature from the 1860's to World War I. The chapter on Aleichem examines the historical, literary, and social values of his work.

Samuel, Maurice. *The World of Sholom Aleichem*. New York: Alfred A. Knopf, 1943. Samuel re-creates Aleichem's milieu, with explorations of Tevye's personality, landscape, philosophy, and family life. A very anecdotal volume that includes warm retellings of the Tevye stories.

Waife-Goldberg, Marie. *My Father, Sholom Aleichem*. New York: Simon & Schuster, 1968. An interesting and revealing memoir by Aleichem's daughter, full of anecdotes about Aleichem and examining the parallels between him and his fictional persona, Tevye.

Wisse, Ruth R. *The Schlemiel as Modern Hero*. Chicago: University of Chicago Press, 1971. This slim book includes a chapter on Aleichem entitled "Ironic Balance for Psychic Survival," in which Wisse discusses the uses of irony and satire and the polarization of faith and fact as reflected in Tevye's philosophical dialogues.

THANATOPSIS

Type of work: Poetry
Author: William Cullen Bryant (1794-1878)
First published: 1817

William Cullen Bryant's poem "Thanatopsis" is considered to be the best of a number of poems he wrote on the subject of death. More noteworthy, however, is the fact that this poem established his reputation as a poet. That is not to say, however, that the poet was an overnight success. The *North American Review*, the periodical in which the poem first appeared, had a small circulation. Furthermore, according to one biographer of William Cullen Bryant, the poem "Thanatopsis" had actually been submitted to the publisher by his father, and, since it was printed anonymously, one editor thought that the poem had been written by Bryant's father, Dr. Peter Bryant. Also, the American public, even the educated, were just beginning to develop an appreciation of the kind of Romanticism that the poem exhibits.

Once his reputation was established, however, Bryant was sometimes called the "American Wordsworth" because, like the British Romantic poet William Wordsworth, he excelled in creating effective descriptions of nature. Interestingly, Bryant was acknowledged as the fore-most poet in the United States even before his poems had been collected into a single volume; they had been published only singly in magazines and newspapers over a period of some fifteen years. One writer commented that Bryant had "been placed by common consent at the head of the list of American poets."

Like many of his contemporaries, Bryant did not earn a living exclusively from writing poetry. Influential in civic and political affairs, he was a lawyer and, for more than fifty years, editor of the *New York Evening Post*. That such a busy man could produce a poem judged to be of such high quality was in itself an outstanding achievement.

"Thanatopsis" filled one of the needs of Bryant's generation very well. Writing during the early days of American nationhood, when there was not yet any real sense of a national past, the very size of the young country contributing to a sense of isolation, this poem provided reflections on topics that had real relevance to the citizenry: human mortality, perceptions of death as separation, and the transience of life. Thus, the poem was sensitive to and in tune with the feelings of the times.

The poem is divided into three main sections. It has been noted that, whether Bryant was consciously aware of doing so or not, he structured the poem after the traditional rhetorical style of the "plain style" sermon that had been brought by settlers to New England during colonial days. This style provided for a three-part division that would deal with doctrine, reasons, and uses. The first section (lines 1-30) provides the philosophical background, or "doctrine," of the poem. Nature personified, that is, given human qualities—such as the ability to speak a language—is established as an authority to speak to humanity through its "still voice": "To him who in the love of nature holds/ Communion with her visible forms, she speaks/ A various language." The major problem to be resolved is that of coming to terms with the fact that everyone must eventually die. To relieve the fear that often accompanies thoughts of death, Nature can speak with a "various language." These variations include a "voice of gladness," a "smile and eloquence of beauty," and a "gentle sympathy" that is soothing and healing, offering consolation that "steals away" the fear. The "voice" in the poem then submits that when thoughts of death and burial become overwhelming, one should "go forth, under the open sky" and listen to what Nature has to say.

The "doctrine" that the poem teaches is that death means a total loss of human evidence: "Surrendering up Thine individual being, shalt thou go/ To mix forever with the elements." Some critics have criticized this passage as indicating that Bryant was not writing a Christian poem, in which a faith in immortality and a hope of being eternally with God in heaven provides consolation. Actually, some people wrote letters of gratitude to Bryant for the consolation that the poem had given them; by these people, the poem was interpreted as being a religious one.

The middle, or "reason," section of the poem (lines 31-72) becomes something of a debate, providing justification for the reason people should not view death as an isolation that forever separates. It argues against the reasons humanity would give for not wanting to face death. Not only are the dead not alone; they may actually be in more distinguished company than they have been accustomed to in life: "Thou shalt lie down/ With patriarchs of the infant world—with kings,/ The powerful of the earth—the wise, the good,/ Fair forms, and hoary seers of ages past,/ All in one mighty sepulchre." Furthermore, a return to Nature (that is, burial in the earth) means that all of the beauty of nature—the hills and vales, the "venerable woods" and "meadows green," the majestic rivers, the "complaining brooks" and even the "old ocean" itself—provide "solemn decorations" on "the great tomb of man" over which the sun never ceases to shine.

Another argument against the grave as consigning one to eternal isolation is that all the people living on the earth at a given time are but a "handful" compared to the number of the "slumbering" dead who are literally spread throughout the earth. It is just a matter of time until all will share the experience of death. Thus, death should be thought of as something of a joyful reunion with those who have gone before one.

To counter the possibilities that one may die with no one taking note of one's departure and that life may go on gaily as if one had never lived, Nature would say not to worry, for one by one, all of those still living on earth will come to the same end: "Yet all these shall leave/ Their mirth and their employments, and shall come/ And make their bed with thee." No one is exempt: Young and old alike "shall one by one be gathered" to join those who have departed earlier.

Like the Puritan sermon, the final section of the poem (lines 73-81) is analogous to the "uses" or application of the truths of the earlier sections. It "teaches" that if one is to face death without fear, one must, in life, prepare to be able to look on death at least with equanimity if not with enthusiasm. That preparation consists of taking seriously the admonition to live in such a way that, when death comes, it is not like being taken away as a prisoner in the night to some "dungeon" or "narrow house"—a coffin—and lowered into a grave, with no hope of escape. Rather, with an "unfaltering trust," one may compare going to the grave with preparing to lie down peacefully for a nap with the full expectation of having pleasant dreams.

In addition to using the Puritan sermon form innovatively, the poem, upon further analysis, reveals the use of a pattern of contrast, contradiction, and paradox in its development. For example, the intellectual and the emotional are juxtaposed to good effect. Impersonal references to details that suggest grief and loss are plentiful: "thoughts of the last bitter hour," "sad images of the stern agony, and shroud, and pall." However, there are unmistakably emotional undertones to these references.

Another example of this pattern in the poem is seen in the way the eternal, or permanent, aspect of nature is contrasted with the transient, or short-lived. The sun, the hills, the rivers, the forests, the ocean—elements that are perceived as timeless—are juxtaposed with references to the impermanence of humanity: "Earth, that nourished three, shall claim/ Thy growth, to be resolv'd to earth again." Also seen in this passage is the paradox that, even as Nature consoles with her "voice of gladness" and comes to humanity "with a mild and healing sympathy," it is "Earth, that nourished thee," who comes to "claim thy growth." Thus, the same nature that is a consoler is also seen as nature the enemy, who claims the lives of human beings. The graves of the dead, which become "one mighty sepulchre" and "the great tomb of man" that is decorated by all of the splendid beauty of nature, are also the "sad abodes of death" where "the oak shall send his roots abroad, and pierce thy mould."

Yet another paradox is that the poem is simultaneously a lesson on dying and a lesson on living. In order to learn the lesson of dying well, it is necessary to learn how to live well, and in "Thanatopsis" this involves living with such a perspective that death is seen as a natural, not a fearful, conclusion to life.

By 1825, Bryant had formulated his theory about poetry, which he shared in four "Lectures on Poetry" produced in 1825 and 1826. He believed that the "great spring of poetry" was emotion and that the source of poetic inspiration was nature. To his credit, the connections that Bryant made between "things of the moral and of the natural worlds," later known as the doctrine of analogies or correspondences, were made more than ten years before the theory would become a central tenet of American literary criticism. It is important to realize that, in its day, both the poet and this poem played a central role in the formation of the character of a national literature. Richard Henry Dana, Jr., has been credited with commenting that "no one on this side of the Atlantic is capable of writing such verses," referring to Bryant and "Thanatopsis." At that time, it was not assumed that American poetry had yet matured sufficiently to produce a poem that could so favorably be compared to the poems of well-established British poets such as William Wordsworth, to whom Bryant was, in fact, compared. Another critic of Bryant's era detected in this poem "the literature of the new nation, as distinct from colonial literature." To the large extent that this appraisal was accurate, the poem has carved for itself a permanent place in American literary history.

Victoria Price

Bibliography:
Brodwin, Stanley, and Michael D'Innocenzo. *William Cullen Bryant and His America: Centennial Conference Proceedings, 1878-1978.* New York: AMS Press, 1983. Provides a broad background against which to study "Thanatopsis." One chapter focuses on the role that Bryant and this poem play in the development of American literature. Helpful bibliography.

Brown, Charles Henry. *William Cullen Bryant.* New York: Charles Scribner's Sons, 1971. Addresses early influences on William Cullen Bryant and his concept of death. Discusses the confusion over the authorship of "Thanatopsis" and traces the evolution of the poem to its final form. Illustrations include an autograph manuscript of "Thanotopsis."

Godwin, Parke. *A Biography of William Cullen Bryant.* Vol. 1. New York: Russell and Russell, 1967. Bryant's son-in-law discusses the events that led to the publication of "Thanatopsis." Puts the writing of this and other poetry in the context of his life in general.

McLean, Albert F., Jr. *William Cullen Bryant.* New York: Twayne, 1964. While "Thanatopsis" is mentioned throughout this volume, chapter 3, "The Poem of Death," focuses on "Thanatopsis" in particular. Structure, tone, intent, and uses of language in the poem are discussed thoroughly. A chronology of Bryant's life is included.

Peckham, H. H. *Gotham Yankee: A Biography of William Cullen Bryant.* New York: Russell and Russell, 1971. Addresses Bryant's attitudes toward life and death so as to put the poem "Thanatopsis" in context. Compares this poem with other poems about death, especially Robert Blair's "The Grave."

THE THEBAID

Type of work: Poetry
Author: Statius (Publius Papinius Statius, c. 45-c. 96 C.E.)
Type of plot: Epic
Time of plot: Antiquity
Locale: Argos, Nemea, and Thebes
First transcribed: Thebais, c. 90 (English translation, 1767)

Principal characters:
OEDIPUS, the deposed king of Thebes
JOCASTA, his wife and mother
ETEOCLES,
POLYNICES,
ANTIGONE, and
ISMENE, their children
CREON, Jocasta's brother
MENOECEUS, his son
ADRASTUS, the king of Argos
ARGIA, his daughter, Polynices' wife
TYDEUS,
CAPANEUS,
AMPHIARAUS,
HIPPOMEDON, and
PARTHENOPAEUS, Argive heroes of the march against Thebes
HYPSIPYLE, the former queen of Lemnos, a slave

The Story:
    After the fall of Oedipus, Eteocles and Polynices, the two sons of Oedipus and Jocasta, were to alternate as rulers. The plan was doomed to failure because Oedipus had called down the wrath of the Furies upon his unnatural sons. The first year of the kingship falling to Eteocles, Polynices went into temporary exile in Argos. There he quarreled with Tydeus, a great warrior and hero, but King Adrastus, obeying the prompting of an oracle, settled the dispute by betrothing one of his daughters to each of the young men.
    At the end of a year, however, Eteocles refused to step aside in favor of Polynices, according to the agreement between them. Argia, the wife of Polynices, then persuaded her father to aid the prince in asserting his right to the Theban throne. Tydeus was first dispatched as an envoy to the city. Jealous of the fame of the young warrior, Eteocles set an ambush for Tydeus, who killed all of his attackers except one. The survivor, Maeon, returned to tell Eteocles what had happened and then killed himself.
    The march against Thebes began. At Nemea the army was halted by a great drought, but the Argives were saved from their distress when Hypsipyle, the one-time queen of Lemnos before the great massacre there, and reduced to a slave entrusted with the care of King Lycurgus' small son, guided them to a stream that still flowed. When a snake bit her infant charge, the Argives protected her from the king's anger and in observance of the boy's funeral instituted the Nemean games. On the arrival of the army before the walls of Thebes, Jocasta and her daughters

appeared to plead with Polynices in an effort to prevent bloodshed. The battle was joined, however, when two tigers attacked the driver of Amphiaraus' chariot; Amphiaraus himself disappeared into the underworld when the earth suddenly opened and swallowed him alive. In an engagement with the Thebans, Tydeus fell mortally wounded; he died while gnawing the skull of his foe. The Argive heroes were killed one by one, fighting valiantly but powerless against the might of the gods. Capaneus, who had rested from battle to challenge the justice of the gods, was struck by one of Jove's own thunderbolts as he attempted to scale the wall of the city. In a hand-to-hand combat, Eteocles and Polynices killed each other. Only King Adrastus survived. The war ended with the intervention of King Theseus of Athens, who had been moved by the prayers of the Argive women. Creon died at the hands of King Theseus; his son, Menoeceus, had previously listened to the words of the oracle and had thrown himself from the city wall.

Critical Evaluation:

The *Thebaid* of Statius, a retelling in epic form of *Seven Against Thebes* (467 B.C.E.) by Aeschylus, draws extensively on the general body of material dealing with the ill-fated family of Oedipus. Statius' version of the tale of the contending brothers, Eteocles and Polynices, extends to twelve books. Written over a period of twelve years, this narrative of bloody and tragic conflict is a product of the so-called Silver Age of Latin literature. Statius' epic, produced during the reign of the Emperor Domitian, represents a falling off from that of great works such as Vergil's *Aeneid* (30-19 B.C.E.), the model for this lesser and more melodramatic poem.

The *Thebaid* is usually mentioned in conjunction with Lucan's *Pharsalia* (c. 60 C.E.). Both epic works grew up under the shadow of the *Aeneid*, and both are responses to it. Lucan attempts to escape the mold, Statius to fill it. Lucan is militantly topical and innovative; Statius is unapologetically derivative. He misses few of the situations and mannerisms that have become the epic stock-in-trade—extended simile, scenes in the underworld, funeral games, catalog of forces, single combats, interference by the gods, and so on. In fact, Statius' greatest contribution to literature, for better or worse, has been to turn all that Vergil borrowed from Homer into an expected element of all future literary epics.

As a writer of verse Statius has few breathtaking passages, but considerable flexibility of language ranging from the softly pathetic to the grandly rhetorical. Statius boasts of the polishing the work received, and claims that it required twelve years of labor. This latter claim may be exaggerated, but clearly the language of the *Thebaid* has been worked over carefully.

Statius appears to have taken Aristotle's stricture against loose, episodic epics to heart. Rather than telling the whole story of Thebes, he centers on the conflict between the two sons of Oedipus, climaxing with their mutual destruction in book 11. Book 12 is an appropriate epilogue dealing with the dispute over the burial of Polynices and the Argive invaders, and ending with a general reconciliation. The frame is narrow enough for unity, but provides room for numerous digressions. One of the most conspicuous features of the epic is the dense texture of legendary and mythological allusion along with the creation of pseudomythological incidents. Such detail can seem distracting, pedantic, and artificial, but Statius generally manages to incorporate such material smoothly and economically.

The sons of Oedipus work better as a structural device than as subject matter. An epic is a large, demanding form. It is dense and ceremonious. For such a work the reader should have some stake in the material. Statius' story, written for a Roman audience, is set in Greece in a city with little historical importance to Rome. In fact, the Roman poet, Juvenal, in his first satire, includes the Thebes among the overworked and outdated themes poets too often choose. The material had already been well worked over about two millennia before, and there is nothing particularly new or involving in Statius' treatment of it. The two brothers are not sympathetic, or even particularly interesting characters traditionally, and Statius does little to make them so.

If a story's theme is not of vital interest, then at least the characters should be. By comparison, the *Odyssey* (c. 800 B.C.E.) is a compelling story, though it makes little difference to the big picture whether Odysseus makes it home or not. In the *Thebaid*, however, there is nothing like Homer's wonderful gallery of distinct and fascinating individuals. Characters in Homer may give long and formal speeches, but no two characters talk quite alike, and the language is always convincing as dialogue. Speeches in Statius are usually rhetorical set pieces, grand and melo-dramatic, but too little bound to the character and the context.

There is no truly engaging character in the *Thebaid*. The central figures, Eteocles and Polynices, are not developed in depth, and neither engages the readers' interest nor their sympathy. The character who most stands out is Tydeus, who is small and ferocious, but these two words sum up most of his character. There are few women; Oedipus' wife Jocasta has only a few scenes. The other notable female character, Hypsipyle, is little more than the standard pathetic victim.

Statius is better with the gods, although his characterization echoes Vergil's closely. The authoritarian Jupiter and the softly manipulative Venus are more memorable than any of the humans. Statius also follows Vergil's tendency to summarize rather than to dramatize as Homer does. In Vergil, however, there is always the sense of a context far vaster than whatever is happening at any one time. In the *Thebaid* the context, the fate of the faded city of Thebes, is of rather limited significance.

In following the epic pattern established by Vergil, but largely derived from Homer, Statius seems more dedicated to the epic tradition than to telling a story with its own inner dynamics. Book 5 interrupts the action for a long narrative of past events. There is a similar interruption in books 2 and 3 of the *Aeneid*, and in books 9 through 12 of the *Odyssey*. The fall of Troy and the previous adventures of Odysseus, however, are essential to the larger story; Statius' narrative of Hypsipyle is simply an unconnected interlude.

During Hypsipyle's narration a young prince left in her charge is killed by a huge snake, and book 6 is devoted to funeral games for the child. The *Iliad* (c. 800 B.C.E.) and the *Aeneid* establish funeral games as a standard epic feature. The bustle, petty quarrels, and rough humor of Homer's games seem a brilliant counterpart to the grim deaths of Patroclos and Hector, while Vergil's games for Anchises seem at least appropriate. One has to doubt the probability of such contests for the funeral of an infant, and to doubt the structural logic of devoting one whole book to the funeral of someone who never appears alive in the story.

In the late classical world and in the Renaissance, when the Vergilian epic was the supreme literary form, Statius' adherence to form, along with his rich tapestry of allusion and incident, made the *Thebaid* widely admired and influential. To the modern world, the epic has lost much of its mystique, and readers are likely to find the characterization, dialogue, and structure of the *Thebaid* less than completely satisfying.

"Critical Evaluation" by Jack Hart

Bibliography:
Butler, H. E. *Post-Augustan Poetry from Seneca to Juvenal*. Oxford, England: Clarendon Press, 1909. This standard work establishes the context and explains the intentions and aesthetic values of a literary era very alien to modern tastes and expectations.

Mendell, C. W. *Latin Poetry: The Age of Rhetoric and Satire*. Hamden, Conn.: Archon Books, 1967. Covers much of the same ground as Butler's, but may seem less remote in style and approach than the older work.

Statius. *Thebaid*. Translated by A. D. Melville. New York: Oxford University Press, 1992. This very accurate translation is written in a graceful and formal blank verse that preserves the poetic quality of the original. An introduction explains and justifies the *Thebaid* with enthusiasm.

Tillyard, E. M. W. *The English Epic and Its Background*. New York: Oxford University Press, 1954. Deals with a number of epics from the ancient world and the Renaissance. Places the *Thebaid* in the large context of a tradition extending well over two thousand years.

Vessey, David. *Statius and the "Thebaid."* Cambridge, England: Cambridge University Press, 1973. This is the largest and most comprehensive study of the *Thebaid* in recent times by an enthusiast of the poem.

THEIR EYES WERE WATCHING GOD

Type of work: Novel
Author: Zora Neale Hurston (1891-1960)
Type of plot: Bildungsroman
Time of plot: Around 1900
Locale: Florida
First published: 1937

Principal characters:
> JANIE CRAWFORD KILLICKS STARKS WOODS, the thrice-married,
>   twice-widowed protagonist
> PHEOBY WATSON, her friend
> NANNY, her grandmother
> LOGAN KILLICKS, her first husband
> JOE STARKS, her second husband
> TEA CAKE WOODS, her third husband

The Story:

Janie Starks had returned to town. One sundown, the Eatonville inhabitants watched and gossiped as Janie walked the street toward her house, dressed in overalls, with her long braid hanging down her back. Only her friend Pheoby had the kindness to greet her. Pheoby sat down to hear her friend's story.

As a little girl, Janie had assumed she was white. She lived with her grandmother and played constantly with the children of the Washburns, for whom Nanny worked. Only when a photographer took the children's picture did Janie realize that she was the black girl in the photo. Nanny was protective of her and worried when she became a teenager. To Nanny, the easiest way to protect Janie from the attentions of useless men was to marry her off young to a good one.

So Janie found herself married early to Logan Killicks, an older man with a house and land. No affection existed between them; Logan seemed to want someone to share the work. Janie could hardly stand to be around him. She complained to Nanny about his big belly, his mule-foot toenails, and the fact that he refused to wash his feet before coming to bed: "Ah'd ruther be shot wid tacks than tuh turn over in de bed and stir up de air whilst he is in dere."

One day Janie met a stranger on the road, a handsome, charming man named Joe "Jody" Starks. He was on his way to make a place for himself in a new all-black town, Eatonville. After sneaking off to meet Jody in the scrub oaks for several days and getting him to promise to marry her, Janie ran away with him.

Jody did make himself a place in the new town, becoming the mayor and opening the first store. Janie found herself the most envied woman in town, with the most important husband and the biggest house. She spent her days working in the store but soon found that life with Jody was not all wonderful. He was given to jealousy and insisted that she wear a kerchief over her beautiful long hair so that the men who came into the shop would not admire or touch it. To keep her in her place, he frequently criticized her work and refused to let her express her opinions to their acquaintances and friends who visited with them on the porch of the house in front of the store. Over the years this treatment drained the life from Janie: "She was a rut in the road. Plenty of life beneath the surface but it was kept beaten down by the wheels."

One night Joe became angry when Janie miscut a plug of tobacco. Although she knew it was better to keep silent, she talked back and he, fearing to lose face in front of his friends, struck her. From then on, Jody slept downstairs. Soon after, he became sick, but he still refused to let Janie come near him again. Even on the night of his death, when she came into his room to speak with him, he could not forgive her.

After Joe's death, Janie tended the store. Joy came back into her life with Tea Cake Woods, a young man of questionable reputation who found his way to the store one day and entertained her with checker games and his guitar. Before Jody had been dead nine months, Janie had started spending all of her time with Tea Cake, wearing colorful dresses, and showing off her hair. When Janie left town to marry Tea Cake, the town was sure she was being taken for her money. The townsfolk were wrong, though. Despite the difference in their ages—Janie was close to forty by this time—and the difference in their former lives, Janie found that her new husband loved and appreciated her. He took her to the Everglades, where they went "on de muck" picking beans. Here, Janie found herself in the center of a community of lively, happy, hardworking folk. Janie and Tea Cake's house became the center of activity after a day's work, and the main activities were making music and gambling, both of which Tea Cake did well. For the first time, Janie found happiness in a marriage.

After two good seasons, disaster came when a hurricane struck, broke the dam, and flooded the area. Most of the residents had anticipated the storm and left early enough, but Tea Cake and Janie had stayed. By the time they finally tried to make it to high ground, the dam had burst and they found themselves swimming to safety. Janie almost died in the rush of water but managed to grab a swimming cow's tail to be carried along. When a dog riding on the cow's back tried to bite Janie and force her away, Tea Cake rose up and killed the dog, but not before the dog bit him in the face. Finally, exhausted, Janie and Tea Cake reached safety.

Their relief was short-lived, however, for Tea Cake began to suffer from terrible headaches and became ill-tempered. Janie finally arranged for a doctor to see him, who informed her that the dog that had bitten him must have been rabid and that it was not too late for treatment. The doctor warned Janie to be careful around the ill man. When Tea Cake, in the midst of one of his attacks, came at Janie with a gun, she shot him in self-defense. She was brought to trial but found not guilty, and Tea Cake's death was ruled an accident. After a few weeks with Tea Cake's friends in the Everglades, she headed back to Eatonville, where her life had begun.

Critical Evaluation:

Upon its publication, *Their Eyes Were Watching God* received rather harsh judgment from such African American writers as Richard Wright and Ralph Ellison, who called the book "quaint." Above all, they criticized Zora Neale Hurston for presenting a romantic view of the African American community and for not writing in the Harlem Renaissance protest tradition. Others reviewed the book more favorably, but it was soon out of print and became forgotten.

In 1965, *Their Eyes Were Watching God* was republished, after which it began to receive a great deal of attention and to be reevaluated by many as a staple of the American literary canon. The book was lauded in particular for its calling on the black folkloric tradition, for its language, and for its female hero. Janie is light colored and beautiful, and as a child she does not even realize she is black. When she is in her forties, her neighbor, Mrs. Turner, admires her for her coffee-and-cream complexion and her luxurious hair. Yet Janie's road to self-knowledge takes her deeper into blackness. She moves from her home among white folks through two black husbands to the blackest of them all, Tea Cake, and the blackest community of all, that of the seasonal workers in the Everglades.

African American lore has been passed down not in writing but in speech. *Their Eyes Were Watching God* documents the oral tradition in two ways. The book actually describes the community passing on its lore, first on the porch of Joe Starks's store and later at the evening get-togethers at the house on the muck. In one of the most memorable and comic scenes of the book, the Eatonville inhabitants hold a ceremonious mock funeral for Matt Bonner's yellow mule, an occasion that elicits delighted participation from the entire town. A subtler device by which Hurston documents the oral tradition is in her method of narration when Janie tells her story not to the audience by the printed word but orally to her friend Pheoby. Readers get the spoken narrative, what Henry Louis Gates, Jr., called "a speakerly text."

The novel is richly packed with direct speech in poetic black dialect. Nanny, warning Janie not to give her heartache, tells her, "Put me down easy, Janie. Ah'm a cracked plate." When Janie frets to Tea Cake about being older than he, he says, " . . . don't say you'se ole. You'se uh lil girl baby all de time. God made it so you spent yo' ole age first wid somebody else, and saved up yo' young girl days to spend wid me." Even the third-person narrative is presented to the reader in Janie's dialect. After Joe Starks's death, Janie "starched and ironed her face and came set in the funeral behind her veil. . . . She sent her face to Joe's funeral, and herself went rollicking with the springtime across the world."

The richest element of the novel is Janie herself. She becomes powerful and self-reliant as she moves from being controlled by men to being self-assertive and independent. Janie is ultimately never beaten down because she learns to separate her private self from her public life until she finally gets the opportunity to combine the two. Janie provides a positive image of the black woman who is able to reject conformity and security at the same time that she controls her life on her own terms. Her choice—to trust love—invigorates her; upon her return from the muck, she tells Pheoby, "Ah been a delegate to do big 'ssociation of life. Yessuh! De Grand Lodge, de big convention of livin' is just where Ah been."

Janie's experiences reflect the difficulties of being black and female in the South in the early twentieth century. Hurston shows her both as a part of a community and as an outsider in that community by virtue of her gender and her choices. She rises above her circumstances. Saddened but not defeated at the end of her tale, Janie tells her old friend Pheoby not to judge harshly the neighbors who gossiped so cruelly upon her return to Eatonville: "Two things everybody's got tuh do fuh theyselves. They got tuh go tuh God, and they got tuh find out about livin' fuh theyselves." Janie had found out about livin', and she was at peace.

Janine Rider

Bibliography:
Awkward, Michael. *New Essays on "Their Eyes Were Watching God."* New York: Cambridge University Press, 1990. In five essays, the author presents various interpretive views of the novel.
Bloom, Harold, ed. *Modern Critical Interpretations: Zora Neale Hurston's "Their Eyes Were Watching God."* New York: Chelsea House, 1987. Collection of eight essays written between 1979 and 1987 that Bloom calls "the best" written on the novel.
_____, ed. *Zora Neale Hurston.* New York: Chelsea House, 1986. A collection of essays about Hurston and her work in the Modern Critical Views series. *Their Eyes Were Watching God* is the subject of five essays, and analysis of aspects of the novel is included throughout the volume.
Gates, Henry Louis, Jr., and K. A. Appiah, eds. *Zora Neale Hurston: Critical Perspectives Past*

and Present. New York: Amisted, 1993. Includes the original, rather harsh reviews of *Their Eyes Were Watching God*, along with positive later essays. Includes Gates's important essay, "*Their Eyes Were Watching God:* Hurston and the Speakerly Text."

Lowe, John. *Jump at the Sun: Zora Neale Hurston's Cosmic Comedy*. Chicago: University of Illinois Press, 1994. A study of humor in Hurston's work, including a fifty-page chapter on *Their Eyes Were Watching God*.

THÉRÈSE

Type of work: Novel
Author: François Mauriac (1885-1970)
Type of plot: Psychological realism
Time of plot: Twentieth century
Locale: France
First published: Thérèse Desqueyroux, 1927 (English translation, 1928)

> *Principal characters:*
> BERNARD DESQUEYROUX, a petty landowner
> THÉRÈSE DESQUEYROUX, his wife
> MARIE DESQUEYROUX, their daughter
> GEORGES FILHOT, a law student and Marie's lover
> ANNE DE LA TRAVE, Bernard's half sister
> JEAN AZÉVÉDO, a young intellectual

The Story:

In the little French town of Argelouse, where she spent the first part of her life, Thérèse Desqueyroux was known not so much for her beauty as for her charm. Her wit and independence of mind made her conspicuous in the stifling and inbred atmosphere of her native province, and she inspired in her friends and relatives as much disapproval as admiration. Left to her own devices by a father more intent on his political career than the problems of fatherhood, Thérèse had spent her girlhood in isolated brooding. Her one friend was Anne de la Trave, the half sister of Bernard Desqueyroux, whom Thérèse was later to marry.

Thérèse could remember little of her youth and the days before her marriage. For the most part, her memories were clouded over by the confusion in her own mind, consisting of her intense love of life and desire for experience joined to provincial willingness to sacrifice self to tradition. She saw her marriage to Bernard Desqueyroux as the natural culmination of a social cycle. Yet the honeymoon was not yet over before Thérèse began acutely to feel the loss to herself that her marriage represented. She discovered in Bernard all that was worst in the provincial character: a fanatical pride of family and material possessions. To a fatal degree, he lacked the insight and imagination to understand his wife. For her part, Thérèse was disgusted by the marriage.

During the honeymoon, a letter came to Bernard from his family informing him that his half sister Anne had fallen in love with a penniless young man named Jean Azévédo. To preserve the family name and honor, Bernard prevailed on Thérèse to try to help stop the affair. Thérèse returned to Argelouse and persuaded Anne to go on a trip. After Anne had gone, Thérèse met Azévédo and discovered in him that intensity and individualism she missed in her own life. Azévédo admitted that he was not really in love, and he readily agreed to write to Anne to tell her his true feelings. He and Thérèse met from time to time and were drawn to each other. When Azévédo left Argelouse, it was with the promise that he would return in a year.

After Azévédo had gone, Thérèse settled into the routine of a farmer's wife. Even the birth of a child, Marie, failed to give her life meaning, for motherhood only further intensified her frustration. Almost involuntarily, she decided to poison Bernard.

The attempted murder was quickly discovered, and Thérèse was brought to trial. At the last moment, however, a trumped-up explanation by Bernard saved her from conviction. Thérèse returned home to learn that Bernard had lied only to save the family from scandal. After telling her that divorce was impossible, he forced her, under threat of disclosing the truth, to live a life of semi-imprisonment in her bedroom. Thérèse regained her freedom, however, when Bernard allowed her to go to Paris. Alone in the city, Thérèse tried to make a new life for herself, but without success. The sense of sin she carried with her perverted all attempts to find happiness. As the years passed she retreated more and more into herself.

Fifteen years after her banishment from Argelouse, Thérèse was found living in an apartment in Paris by her daughter, Marie, now a young girl of seventeen. Marie, who explained that she had come to Paris because of a young law student from her native province, was shocked to find Thérèse in poor health and looking years older than her age. Thérèse, hoping to extirpate the sense of her own sinfulness, decided to help Marie win the love of the student, Georges Filhot. To persuade Filhot to marry Marie and to modify his parents' disapproval, Thérèse told her daughter that she would turn over to her all her own landholdings in Argelouse. The next day, Thérèse visited Filhot and invited him to dinner. At the conclusion of the evening, Marie returned to Argelouse with the promise of a final reunion with Filhot in three months.

In the next few days, it became painfully and thrillingly evident to Thérèse that Filhot was not in love with Marie but with herself. In a violently emotional scene, she confessed to the student not only her past crime but a whole series of crimes for which she believed herself guilty but which were not recognized as criminal by the law. Then she sent Filhot away. Rather than insist that he sacrifice himself to her daughter, however, she urged him to write to Marie saying that he did not love her.

A short time later, Marie returned to Paris to face her mother, who by that time was living in a confused and paranoid world in which she believed all of her acquaintances were engaged in a plot to bring her to justice for her sins, real and imaginary. Marie's anger was softened, and when she returned to Argelouse, she took the sick Thérèse with her.

In her birthplace, Thérèse slowly regained her sanity; the doctor predicted, however, that she would soon die. She was nursed during her last days by her daughter and Bernard—for whom, by this time, she felt neither pity nor disgust. During this time, Thérèse tried to put her mind in order. She awaited death with hope, seeing it as the final deliverance from self.

Critical Evaluation:

François Mauriac's literary career was launched in 1909 when he submitted his first volume of poems, "Les Mains jointes," to Maurice Barrés, who was so impressed that he predicted a glorious future for the young writer. It was, however, in the writing of novels that Mauriac's talents flourished. His first novels already dealt with those themes that preoccupied him throughout his life: the opposition between the flesh and the spirit, between sin and grace, and between godliness and godlessness. In addition to his many novels, Mauriac also wrote philosophical essays, a few biographies, and some plays. In 1952, he received the Nobel Prize in Literature. He died in 1970 at the age of eighty-five.

The story and meaning of the life of Thérèse Desqueyroux preoccupied Mauriac's mind over a long period. The book is not a novel in the conventional sense, being a series of four stories connected by the mind of the major character rather than by incident. Nevertheless, it is a powerful and dramatic revelation of the human condition and its relation to sin. Although Mauriac did at one time rebel against the religious practices of his family and did ultimately reject Jansenism, he never rejected the Catholic faith. Such is the primacy that he gives to his religious beliefs that he wished to be considered a Catholic who writes novels rather than a Catholic novelist. In Thérèse, Mauriac has caught the complex movement of guilt as it exists in everyone.

Most of Mauriac's novels take place in Bordeaux and its surrounding countryside, with Paris appearing only incidentally. The estate of the writer's grandmother, for example, becomes the home of Thérèse Desqueyroux, which he locates in a village he names Argelouse. Beyond the very important fact that he was deeply attached to his native region, the pastoral setting is featured prominently in his novels because, for Mauriac, the contrast between the physical world and the world of the spirit is more intense in the country, where nature bombards people with sensual stimuli that draw them into a preoccupation with physical things, with pleasures of the eye and ear, and ultimately with pleasures of the flesh. There the allure of physical things is much greater than in the city. In *Thérèse*, the descriptions of natural scenes are suffused with an almost erotic atmosphere.

Throughout the novel, Thérèse is strongly identified with elemental things. She thrives on the odors, colors, and shapes of nature. She yearns, in fact, to become one with nature. She says at one point that she has the pine trees in her blood. During her confrontation with Bernard, she wants to ask him to let her disappear into the night, into the forest, for she is not afraid of the trees—they know her, she and they know one another. The illusory character of this union with nature is exposed a few paragraphs later, when Bernard tells Thérèse that she will be confined in Argelouse for the rest of her life. Suddenly, the beloved pine trees become the bars of Thérèse's prison. For Mauriac, the human tragedy is that while individuals are of this world, they can never be really united with it. It is no coincidence that the key generic symbols used by Mauriac are earth, fire, and water. Whatever their immediate significance might be—and they are used in a variety of ways—the underlying sense is this dichotomy between human beings and nature.

All the characters in *Thérèse*, as in most of Mauriac's novels, are identifiable types from the social milieu of traditional provincial life. Bernard Desqueyroux, Madame de la Trave, Monsieur Larroque, Anne de la Trave, and Aunt Clara are all representative of the various shades of bourgeois aspirations, ideals, opinions, and standards. The servants have the values of their bosses. When he was criticized for making literary use of friends and acquaintances as characters, Mauriac retorted that it is impossible to create something that does not already exist.

As a young man, he had witnessed the trial of a woman accused of poisoning her husband. The image of that woman, "pale and biting her lip" (as Mauriac describes Thérèse in the prologue), was the source of inspiration for the novel. All the rest is Mauriac's invention. The real woman's motivation for murder was her desire to be with another man; Thérèse's motive is not nearly so simple. The probing analysis of motivation in the novel comes, according to Mauriac, from the uncovering of the potential for evil found in his own nature. He could say, as Gustave Flaubert did of Madame Bovary, "Thérèse Desqueyroux, c'est moi."

Influenced, like most other writers of the twentieth century, by Sigmund Freud's studies of the unconscious human processes, Mauriac's great contribution to French letters is the integration of these psychological insights with the teachings of Christianity. As a novelist writing after Marcel Proust's great probing of the inner life, Mauriac felt it was his duty to give these investigations a dimension lacking in Proust's works.

Thérèse is the study of a tormented woman's soul. Endowed with great emotional depth and intellectual curiosity, the heroine is from the beginning set apart from others. Her great affection for Anne de la Trave is, for example, tempered by Thérèse's awareness of the incongruities between them. Anne's simplicity and naïveté form a contrast to Thérèse's intelligence and subtle sensitivity. Thérèse feels superior to Anne, but this superiority is part of the reason for her alienation, and at times she almost seems to regret it.

Thérèse's marriage represents an unconscious attempt by the heroine to overcome her differentness. To be sure, the marriage is prearranged on the basis of all the proper bourgeois concerns: status, wealth, family name. Without ever questioning the marriage or examining her own feelings, she behaves according to what is expected of her and plays the role of the enamored fiancée. In retrospect, however, she realizes that she married Bernard out of a desperate hope that he would save her from a vague danger that haunts her. Although this danger is never named, it is in fact alienation itself.

During her engagement, she feels for the first time in her life that she belongs, that she is integrated into her milieu, that she fits in. She hopes that by doing what all other young women do, she will become more like them. As it turns out, however, the marriage intensifies her alienation to an unbearable degree and sets in motion a chain of events that bring about her final downfall.

As Azévédo points out in one of his conversations with Thérèse, the penalty for differentness in her society is annihilation. One either behaves as everyone else does, or one is destroyed. Thérèse's grandmother, Julie Bellade, serves as an example of this rule, for she was totally obliterated by the family in reaction to an undisclosed scandal.

There is an implication that Thérèse may be cursed by this past, a possibility of inherited evil that recurs throughout the novel, and Thérèse herself is preoccupied with the legacy of shame she will bequeath to her daughter. Mauriac's concern with the inheritance of evil can be interpreted as a holdover from his Jansenist beliefs, which emphasize predestination. Thérèse can never determine at which point her crime had its inception; it was always there. Mauriac reinforces this impression by, for example, describing Thérèse's peace at the time of her engagement as the temporary "quietness of the serpent in her bosom."

Thérèse's differentness is not in itself sinful, but it is apparently what causes her to sin. Mauriac sympathizes with her refusal to conform to the hypocrisy and mediocrity around her, but as a Christian, he can only denounce the final turn her refusal takes. If Thérèse has a basic flaw, it is her lack of self-awareness. She never consciously decides to murder Bernard; circumstances suggest it, and she slips into it. The narrator points out that Thérèse never thought anything out, never premeditated anything in her entire life. She has no positive goals, only a retrospective awareness of what she sought to escape. She never knew what she wanted, only what she did not want. The crime with which she is charged seems totally alien to her, and she cannot satisfactorily explain, even to herself or to Bernard, why she did it.

Once freed from her marriage, she attempts to give meaning to her life by engaging in a series of love affairs. That she fails should not be surprising in view of Mauriac's concept of human love: that it is destined to failure, being physical and therefore prey to time, corruption, decay. The only way to transcend one's mortality and finitude is through union with God. Thérèse is dimly aware that human love is not something upon which to base one's hope. In the farewell scene at the Café de la Paix, she considers for a moment going back to Argelouse, there to embark on the only meaningful quest, the search for God. A few moments later, however, she reaffirms her intention to look for fulfillment among men.

Thérèse's lack of awareness is compounded, if not generated, by intense self-involvement and self-indulgence. Anne's pain never evokes any sympathy, only self-pity. Thérèse is indignant that Anne, unlike herself, has been given the joy of knowing love. She always absolves herself of responsibility in shaping her own destiny. To be sure, this may be a flaw in Mauriac, not Thérèse: Jean-Paul Sartre feels that Thérèse is doomed beforehand by a flaw in her character, on the one hand, and by a divine malediction, on the other. Many other critics have denounced what they consider the lack of free will in Mauriac's characters. The line separating free will from predestination is at best nebulous in Mauriac's vision of human behavior.

Regardless of whether the novel is flawed by this predisposition, it is unquestionably a profound, moving study of a woman lost in the contradictions between her own psychology and the realities of her society.

"Critical Evaluation" by Vera Lucia de Araujo Haugse

Bibliography:

Flower, John E. *Intention and Achievement: An Essay on the Novels of François Mauriac.* Oxford, England: Clarendon Press, 1969. In his analysis of *Thérèse*, Flower links it to other novels by Mauriac with characters who seem increasingly saturnine and enigmatic. Flower contends that Thérèse is a powerful figure of alienation who stands out as an unconventional literary heroine.

Flower, John E., and Bernard C. Swift, ed. *François Mauriac: Visions and Reappraisals.* Providence, R.I.: Berg, 1991. A lucid presentation of Mauriac's fortunes. Evaluates Thérèse as an approximation of a Colette figure.

Landry, Anne G. *Represented Discourse in the Novels of François Mauriac.* New York: AMS Press, 1970. The section on *Thérèse* emphasizes the austerity of Mauriac's language and examines the dramatic flow of the novel's structure between central action and flashback.

Smith, Maxwell A. *François Mauriac.* New York: Twayne, 1970. Contains many perceptive observations about *Thérèse* based on Smith's interview with the author. Mauriac defends himself against critical reactions that are overly pessimistic about Thérèse's destiny. He insists that he has merely presented an isolated study of oppression and confinement. Smith connects *Thérèse* with Mauriac's other literary achievements.

Speaight, Robert. *François Mauriac: A Study of the Writer and the Man.* London: Chatto & Windus, 1976. An overview of Mauriac's career, which concludes that *Thérèse* is a poetic tour de force.

THÉRÈSE RAQUIN

Type of work: Novel
Author: Émile Zola (1840-1902)
Type of plot: Naturalism
Time of plot: Early 1860's
Locale: Paris, France
First published: 1867 (English translation, 1881)

Principal characters:

MADAME RAQUIN, a widow and the owner of a dry-goods shop
CAMILLE, the only son of Madame Raquin
THÉRÈSE, the niece of Madame Raquin
LAURENT, a childhood friend of Camille
MICHAUD, a retired police commissioner and the friend of Madame
    Raquin

The Story:

This dramatic story of murder and adultery took place in Paris among a small group of people from the same town in Normandy, Vernon, northwest of Paris. The group's unifying link was Madame Raquin, a widow about sixty years old, who owned a small dry-goods shop on a dark, narrow street in Paris. She had previously owned a dry-goods shop in Vernon, but, after her husband died, she sold the business and retired. At the demand of her frail, sickly, but ambitious son, Camille, then twenty-two years old and married to his cousin Thérèse, Madame Raquin was compelled to move the family to Paris. She found a tiny shop that she could afford with family living quarters above it. Madame Raquin and Thérèse ran the shop together, while Camille found employment in a railroad company office, where he hoped to rise to a high administrative post.

Thérèse was the child of Madame Raquin's brother, a French Army captain, serving in Algeria. One day, the brother, Captain Degans, appeared in Vernon and presented his sister with a two-year-old baby girl, saying that the child's mother, a native Algerian of great beauty, had died and that he was unable to care for the child himself. Captain Degans left with his sister a certificate affirming that he was the father of this child born out of wedlock and that she bore his name. Her African heritage gave Thérèse a high-strung, emotionally intense nature, but growing up in Vernon with her aunt and her cousin, she developed a self-protective mask of reserved docility. She showed little emotion but willingly did whatever was asked of her to guarantee acceptance from her aunt. Two years younger than Camille, she was raised as his sibling, and when Madame Raquin announced her hope that the two would marry, Thérèse made no objection, though she had no real affection—or even respect—for this small, delicate, insecure young man who was to become her husband.

The emotional dynamics among the Raquin threesome had to lead to trouble, even though they were, at first, isolated in Paris, living on an obscure little street seldom used except as a convenient shortcut from one lively Paris thoroughfare to another. To remedy this isolated feeling, the Raquin family began inviting company to their home every Thursday evening. Madame Raquin had run into an old acquaintance from Vernon, a retired commissioner of police named Michaud. Michaud came to the Thursday evenings, accompanied by his son and daughter-in-law. Camille invited an older man, Camille's superior at the railroad office, whose job Camille hoped one day to inherit. The Thursday evenings were mostly spent in playing dominoes, but Thérèse found the company boring and often spent much of the evening by herself in the shop downstairs.

One Thursday, Camille brought a new guest home, triumphantly declaring that this was Laurent, a schoolmate and friend of his youth in Vernon, whom he had recognized, even though Laurent had grown into a tall, robust, and darkly handsome young man. Thérèse showed immediate interest in the new Thursday guest but quickly resumed her mask of indifference before the other guests. Laurent, however, had noticed her momentary reaction. The inevitable result followed in a matter of weeks: They became lovers. The fateful drama then began to unfold.

The lovers were quickly thwarted by the lack of opportunities to meet. Laurent first came to the dry-goods shop in the middle of the day, at Thérèse's suggestion, but that proved impossible as a regular arrangement. Madame Raquin was always there, and Laurent could not regularly absent himself from work. Nor could they meet in the evenings at Laurent's place, since Thérèse had no plausible pretext for going out alone. This frustration soon tempted the lovers to consider eliminating Camille. Because Camille feared water and could not swim, Laurent devised a scheme to throw Camille out of a boat during a Sunday excursion. At a suitable moment, Laurent seized the frail Camille. To Laurent's surprise, however, Camille fought back savagely and managed to sink his teeth into Laurent's neck, leaving a horrible wound on Laurent, before being thrown into the water. Laurent then capsized the boat to make it look like an accident, and he and Thérèse were soon rescued. Laurent then shrewdly persuaded Michaud, the retired police commissioner, to report the "accident" properly and to tell Madame Raquin what had happened. As a result, no suspicions were ever raised that a murder had occurred.

After Camille was duly buried, life resumed its normal course, including the usual Thursday evenings. Laurent and Thérèse carefully regulated their public behavior to show no trace of their passion for each other and bided their time as agreed. Eventually, Michaud persuaded Madame Raquin that the best remedy for Thérèse's constant melancholy was to marry Laurent. For Michaud, this was merely a device by which he could guarantee for himself the continuation of the Thursday evenings. For Thérèse and Laurent, however, it was the opportunity they needed, and the marriage was quickly arranged.

Unhappily, the marriage solved nothing for them. To their mutual shock and dismay, Thérèse and Laurent found that they could not make love, because the "ghost" of Camille was always present and visible in the bed between them, and they could not rid themselves of his spectral presence. Their relationship became so strained that the lovers took to quarreling bitterly, each accusing the other of bad faith. To add to the horror, Madame Raquin suffered a stroke which left her paralyzed and unable to speak, but she overheard the quarrels, learned unmistakably of Camille's murder, and fervently sought the means, in her helpless state, of denouncing the culprits. She failed, but Thérèse and Laurent could tell by her demeanor that she now knew the truth. That caused the relationship between Thérèse and Laurent to become irretrievably poisoned. Each plotted the murder of the other, seeking liberation from the bond of guilt. Abruptly recognizing their own madness, the lovers tacitly agreed to a suicide pact, sharing the poison Laurent had prepared for the murder of Thérèse. As the lovers collapsed and died, Madame Raquin watched their fall with grimly avid satisfaction.

Critical Evaluation:

Thérèse Raquin, completed in 1867 when Émile Zola was only twenty-seven years old, was actually his fourth novel. The previous three novels, however, were plainly immature work, awkwardly composed and sensationalistic, written solely for money. *Thérèse Raquin*, on the other hand, embodied Zola's serious ideas about the art of the novel and was his first real critical success, not merely because it was a daring story of a wife and her lover who conspire to murder her inconvenient husband, but because it was well written, constructed with a sense of form, and filled with powerfully unforgettable scenes and images. Perhaps because, in it, Zola also succeeded so well in conveying the gritty feel of daily life among the urban poor, *Thérèse Raquin* became the first of Zola's books to attract substantial sales. That makes *Thérèse Raquin* a milestone, marking the start of Zola's distinguished career as a novelist of realism—or, as he would later call it, naturalism, the literary movement in France which Zola founded.

The significant sense of form exhibited in this novel can be seen in its unusual organization into thirty-two very short chapters, each of which advances the narrative in a terse and dramatic way. This structure imparts a feeling of rapid movement and suspense to the novel, which compels the reader's excited attention. Viewing the novel as a whole, one also recognizes a symmetrical division into three approximately equal parts, like the three acts of a play, each part ending on a note of high drama: part one, the adultery, culminating in the murder of Camille; part two, the marriage of the criminals, apparent proof that they had gotten away with their crime; part three, the horror of their haunted marriage, ending in a double suicide. By confining the plot to just a few characters and presenting their story in three relentlessly fast-paced parts leading inexorably to the fatal outcome, Zola managed to give his novel the power and inevitability of a classical tragedy. Zola also showed instinctive skill in modifying the real event which inspired his novel (in which the criminal lovers were brought to justice and executed), allowing his criminals to escape detection, only to find themselves condemned to death by their own guilty consciences and their inescapable feelings of remorse.

Zola insisted, in his preface to the second edition of *Thérèse Raquin* in 1868, that his intention was to study temperaments and not characters, showing that individuals whose temperaments are conditioned directly by their nerves and blood, rather than their intellect, will display the beast that is in every human and will invariably act according to the force of their physical drives. That is why, Zola argued, his presentation of the criminal lovers, Thérèse and Laurent, includes no moral judgment of their conduct. His purpose was simply to portray truthfully the behavior of certain human types in order to understand the physical bases of their actions. Even their remorse, Zola maintains, arises from physiological causes.

Most readers will recognize Zola's effort to emphasize the physical in *Thérèse Raquin*. Thérèse is a creature of violent passion, long suppressed by the necessity of survival but suddenly released by a chance encounter. Laurent is lazy, unambitious, and fond of sensual pleasures. Camille is a weakling and a physical coward, viewed with contempt by both Thérèse and Laurent. Nevertheless, Zola is clearly less dispassionate than he claims in this early novel. His description of the wound Camille inflicts on Laurent as a vivid, red stigma which could never heal makes it a symbolic representation of Laurent's guilt, less physical than emotional. The same is true of the several different portraits Laurent paints—in the last part of the novel—each hauntingly expressive, but each, Laurent finally recognizes, an unconscious variation on his guilty recollection of Camille's face as he had seen it in the morgue. The symbolic role of the family cat, François, is another example of Zola's indirect moralizing in spite of himself. Thérèse has a fantasy that the cat, which has witnessed her adultery, will one day tell all to the authorities, and Laurent believes that the cat is somehow possessed by the soul of Camille, which leads him to hurl the cat against a wall, killing it. Such details, which pervade the novel, mark Zola's need to show that conscience exacts a price even from the most amoral and bestial of humans. Indeed, the role, however indirect, which Zola assigned to conscience is perhaps the secret of *Thérèse Raquin*'s power as a psychological novel. The entire third part is a sustained demonstration of how much more cruelly the human conscience can punish criminals than can the law. In spite of Zola's conscious intentions, *Thérèse Raquin* is an eminently moral work of fiction.

Murray Sachs

Bibliography:
Grant, Elliott M. *Émile Zola.* New York: Twayne, 1966. A solidly researched account of Zola's life and works, including excellent pages on *Thérèse Raquin.*
Hemmings, F. W. J. *Émile Zola.* 2d ed. Oxford, England: Oxford University Press, 1966. The best critical study of Zola's literary career. The section devoted to *Thérèse Raquin* is especially insightful.
Lapp, J. C. *Zola Before the "Rougon-Macquart."* Toronto: University of Toronto Press, 1964. Offers the most detailed study of *Thérèse Raquin,* from the perspective of its place in the early development of Zola's literary career, before he became famous.
Walker, Phillip. *Zola.* London: Routledge & Kegan Paul, 1985. Well-written general study of Zola's writings, especially perceptive about Zola's use of symbols and myths.
Wilson, Angus. *Émile Zola: An Introductory Study of His Novels.* Rev. ed. London: Secker and Warburg, 1965. Readable analytical study, written by a practicing novelist.

THESE JAUNDICED LOVES

Type of work: Poetry
Author: Tristan Corbière (1845-1875)
First published: Les Amours jaunes, 1873 (English translation, 1995)

Tristan Corbière was born in Brittany in 1845 and died there thirty years later. He knew illness throughout his life, and it prevented him from completing his formal education. In a land of seafarers, he was acutely conscious of his physical debility. Corbière's exacerbated sensibility is a major part of his outstanding originality. In his poems, the image that he presents of himself is never flattering. Indeed, Corbière seems greatly to have exaggerated his unattractive appearance.

Most of Corbière's poetic production is grouped in the collection titled, in the original, *Les Amours jaunes*: literally "yellow loves" or "off-color loves." This collection, first published in 1873, went almost unnoted. The title can scarcely be fully explained, for it seems to involve a characteristic, deliberate attempt at obfuscating originality on the part of the poet. The title may seem appropriate, however, after a reading of the pieces it covers. There are in fact many poems that might be considered the product of a sickly or jaundiced view of the world.

The title of the first section of *These Jaundiced Loves*, called "That," offers little help to those seeking a thematic unity within the group. The title is also that of the first piece in the section. The poet frames a negative answer to the questions put to him about his art by his interlocutor. The dialogue is brought to a close by the poet, who says: "Art does not know me, and I don't know Art." This should not be interpreted as a declaration of ignorance on the part of an unlettered provincial. Corbière seems to have been sufficiently aware of France's nineteenth century poets to have borrowed from some—Charles Baudelaire in particular—where it suited him, and to castigate others, notably Alphonse de Lamartine and Alfred de Musset. Rather it might be useful to evoke the idea of an opposition between literature and art on the one hand, and poetry and life on the other. For what Corbière's originality causes his poetry to lose in technical value, it causes it to gain in vitality, color, relief, and strength. If Corbière's poems seem to step outside any framework of definition, so, one is tempted to add, does life.

Corbière lived for some time in Paris, and the first section of his collection contains a sonnet sequence describing the impressions made upon him by the city. The number of writers who contributed to the evolution of the myth of the capital as a tentacular city seizing and devouring its unfortunate victims is great. Corbière adds his name to this company.

A poem that is on occasion included with the eight Parisian sonnets in the first chapter is entitled "Paris at Night." Certain aspects of the poem recall the "Parisian Tableaux" in Baudelaire's *Flowers of Evil* (1857). Like Baudelaire, Corbière evokes sinister scenes and characters and frenetic activity, while sickness and death seem to hover over the poem. "Paris at Night" and others like it remain strikingly original. In the metropolis, the Breton is reminded of home, of the sea he knew well; the comparison of the city to the sea is strange, but not forced: "It's the sea,—a flat calm.—And the great tide/ With a far-off roar has withdrawn." Even where he moves from general description to closer perspectives, Corbière's sustained use of maritime imagery remains peculiarly appropriate: "The waves will soon come rumbling back in./ Can you hear the crabs scratching about in the dark?" "Paris at Night" illustrates some of the finer aspects of Corbière's technique. As is the case in many other poems, the imagery is powerful, even shocking. There is, moreover, an element of deliberate ambiguity which leaves questions in the reader's mind. Above all, the poem becomes for readers a form of adventure on which they embark with the poet; readers are involved in the discovery of a world that unfolds before them, while retaining its mystery. Whenever Corbière's name is mentioned, it seems to be linked with his use of irony. Irony generally implies the presentation of two points of view or more, the offering of landmarks, as it were, from which readers may establish proper perspective. Corbière's approaches to irony are numerous, but closely related to one another. At the most basic level, he makes considerable use of puns and plays on words. In many places, he will closely intertwine the sublime with the grossly vulgar, or the divine with the familiar. His purpose in each case seems to be to bring the lofty down to a level where it may be more easily viewed. The purposes and forms of Corbière's irony seem to be manifold in *These Jaundiced Loves*. If it is frequently corrosive and negative or even simply facetious, it is also occasionally used with serious intent to goad readers into revising their opinions, or into thinking deeply. Often the prime target of the poet's irony is himself. He will use it to prevent himself from falling into a fixed pose or attitude or identity. One example is his description of his situation in Paris: "Five-hundred-thousandth Prometheus/ Chained to the rock of painted cardboard." Corbière is equally capable of using irony to deflate the posturing of others. Often, too, it seems to take the form of a defense reaction; the poet, in the teeth of adversity, rather than give way to a hysterical lamentation, manages to raise a smile.

"These Jaundiced Loves" is also the title of a section of the poems. The unity of the section is not clear at first. The poems in it deal with love and woman, although in a somewhat bizarre and indirect fashion. It would seem unlikely that these strange pieces would ever help win over a coy mistress. This group of poems is uneven, but one or two outstanding ones are to be found, while the section does help shed light on Corbière's technique as a poet.

One of the most effective, trenchant pieces in *These Jaundiced Loves* is "A Young Man Dying." Corbière has a young poet present the question, To die or not to die? Corbière reveals in the young man an alternating appetite for and aversion to life. Corbière scathingly mocks the line of consumptive Romantic poets who seemed to spend their lives setting down their protracted death throes in writing. Avoiding the obvious, as he generally does, Corbière writes: "How many of them have I *read* die away." Corbière's refusal to identify with these poets seems doubly significant when one recalls his constant ill health and his early death.

Perhaps the most significant of the poems in this section is a long work titled "The Contumacious Poet." It is a description of a poet's taking up residence in an old ruined building, once a convent, in Brittany. The poem involves a characteristic mingling of tones humorous and nostalgic. The poet, for example, after fervently praying that his absent loved one might come to him, and even vividly imagining her to be there, hears a knock at the door of his tumbledown dwelling. He is of course disappointed when he goes to answer: "Show yourself with a dagger in your heart! . . ./ —There's a knock . . . oh! it's someone. . . . Alas! Yes, it's a rat."

The one section of *These Jaundiced Loves* in which Corbière is truly consistent in form, theme, and mood is titled "Armorica." The name refers to Brittany. It is obvious that the poet's sensibility is permeated with the atmosphere and folklore of his native province, and he communicates his feeling for it beautifully. In this section there is little of the frenetic pursuit of originality at all costs that detracts from several pieces from other sections. The first poem of "Armorica" could easily stand as one of the better short Surrealist poems of a later period. It is an irregular sonnet having as its title "Evil Landscape." It succeeds in communicating an intense impression not only of gloom but also of a spectral world from which humanity seems excluded, or in which a person would be an intruder. The starkness of the landscape, captured in Corbière's harsh alliterations, and the whole uncanny atmosphere would surely strike a receptive chord in the heart of any Celt.

"Seamen" is probably the most vitally alive, if not the most consistent, of the sections in *These Jaundiced Loves*. As the title suggests, it deals with the sea, seamen, and seaports, viewed realistically and sometimes ribaldly, from close up. The finest of these wild, undisciplined pieces is probably "Bitor the Hunchback," the tale of a deformed ship's watchman, who on his annual spree ashore heads for a brothel, eager to know love, and with money to burn. The pace of the poem is such that it seems to pick up the reader and let him or her follow hard on Bitor's heels. With Bitor, the reader sees the interior of the brothel displayed: its selection of women who are paid according to their "tonnage," the sailors of many different nationalities, for each of whom Corbière does a remarkable thumbnail sketch:

> Tall Yankees, blind-drunk as always,
> Sitting in pairs, shooting at the wall
> Their stream of tobacco-juice aiming at a target,
> Always hitting the mark.

From a joyously bawdy atmosphere, however, the mood changes to become frightening. The reader experiences the impression of mounting apprehension as he or she sees attention being turned to Bitor by all the people in the brothel. Bitor is stripped naked and tossed up and down in a blanket. He is finally badly bruised. Later, Bitor's body turns up in the harbor but the reader is left with no explanation of his death. It might be that Bitor, having known the full pleasures of the flesh, had nothing more to live for:

> What was left by the crabs now served as material
> For the jests of the public; and the street-urchins,
> Playing alongside the black water beneath the sunny sky
> Beat on his hump as you would on a drum . . .
> A burst drum . . .
> —That poor body had known love.

Paul Verlaine was one of the first writers in France to comment enthusiastically upon the originality of Tristan Corbière. Since Verlaine, other talents have pointed to the unique qualities of the Breton poet. Nonetheless, Corbière's work has attracted relatively little attention. It is perhaps worth noting that his best critics have themselves been original, creative writers. This fact seems understandable when it is realized that Corbière does not fit neatly into any real literary tradition. It may be argued, however, that Corbière belongs to an excellent tradition— one he started. Many poets have followed him.

Bibliography:
Burch, Francis F. "The Iconography of Tristan Corbière." In *International Perspectives in Comparative Literature: Essays in Honor of Charles Dedeyan*, edited by Virginia M. Shaddy. Lewiston, N.Y.: E. Mellen Press, 1991. Compares the image that Corbière presents in his pictorial self-portraits with the image that he presents in his verbal self-portrait, *These Jaundiced Loves*.

Corbière, Tristan. *The Centenary Corbière: Poems and Prose of Tristan Corbière*. Translated and with an introduction by Val Warner. Chester Springs, Pa.: Dufour, 1975. The introduction is a complete, concise appraisal of *These Jaundiced Loves* and its effect on later writers.

_____. *Selections from "Les Amours jaunes."* Translated with an introduction and notes by C. F. MacIntyre. Berkeley: University of California Press, 1954. The introduction includes a sketch of the poet's life along with short appraisals by his contemporaries and by later critics. The notes provide valuable, detailed information about each of the poems included.

_____. *These Jaundiced Loves: A Translation of Tristan Corbière's "Les Amours jaunes."* Translated by Christopher Pilling. Calstock, Cornwall: Peterloo Poets, 1995. An excellent source for study of Corbière. Translation with the original French provided.

Mitchell, Robert L. *Corbière, Mallarmé, Valéry: Preservations and Commentary.* Saratoga, Calif.: Anma Libri, 1981. Discusses *These Jaundiced Loves* in terms of the difficulty that it presents to translators. Includes extremely close analyses of ten of Corbière's poems.

_____. *Tristan Corbière.* Boston: Twayne, 1979. Mitchell places *These Jaundiced Loves* in the contexts of Corbière's life and the poetic movements of his time. Includes extremely detailed analyses of the poems. Excellent bibliography and index.

THESMOPHORIAZUSAE

Type of work: Drama
Author: Aristophanes (c. 450-c. 385 B.C.E.)
Type of plot: Satire
Time of plot: Fifth century B.C.E.
Locale: Athens
First performed: Thesmophoriazousai, 411 B.C.E. (English translation, 1837)

> *Principal characters:*
> EURIPIDES, the playwright
> MNESILOCHUS, his father-in-law
> AGATHON
> CHORUS OF THESMOPHORIAZUSAE, fertility celebrants
> LEADER OF THE CHORUS
> A SCYTHIAN ARCHER

The Story:

On the way to the house of Agathon, Euripides, the celebrated dramatist, explained to his aged but lusty father-in-law, Mnesilochus, that he was in great danger of his life. The Thesmophoriazusae were gathered at the temple of Demeter to decide on an appropriate punishment for the playwright—Euripides—who had so consistently and so bitterly insulted their sex in his plays. Agathon would surely be able to help him. At the door of Agathon's house a servant appeared and ordered the people and the winds to be quiet because his master was seized with poetical inspiration. Mnesilochus knew at once that no real help could come from such a man.

When Agathon appeared, reposing on a bed, dressed in a saffron tunic, and surrounded by feminine toilet articles, Mnesilochus insulted him roundly for his lack of manhood. As expected, Agathon refused to aid Euripides by dressing as a woman in order to mix with the fertility celebrants and plead Euripides' cause; the plan was simply too risky. Mnesilochus then offered himself and was promptly and painfully shaved, undressed, and depilated. Disguised as a woman, the old man was suddenly very reluctant to go to the temple until Euripides swore by all the gods to come to his aid if anything went wrong.

Striving to act as womanly as possible and giving his voice a feminine lilt, the old man entered the temple with a prayer to Demeter and Persephone that he would not be recognized. After certain preliminaries the women within began their deliberations concerning Euripides' fate. The First Woman, after spitting as orators do, opened with the charge that Euripides presented women in his plays as adulterous, lecherous, bibulous, treacherous, and garrulous; he caused husbands, especially old ones, to be suspicious of their wives; and he provoked them into keeping the keys to the storerooms and sealing doors upon their wives. She declared that the playwright deserved any form of death, but preferably by poison. The Second Woman explained that she, a widow with five children, had supported herself by selling religious chaplets until Euripides convinced spectators of his plays that there were no gods. Mnesilochus, unable to restrain himself upon hearing his son-in-law so defamed, agreed that Euripides had indeed committed two or three such indiscretions, but he urged the women to consider all their horrendous faults that Euripides had not attacked. Mnesilochus then proceeded to present a detailed catalog of feminine failings.

The outraged women turned upon Mnesilochus in furious wrath, but before the face-slapping could lead to hair-pulling Clisthenes arrived with the warning that a man disguised as a woman was in their midst. Unmasked, the desperate Mnesilochus seized what he thought was a woman's child and threatened to slit its throat if he were not allowed to go free. The "child," however, turned out to be a wineskin and the enraged women began to gather faggots in order to roast Mnesilochus alive.

Euripides, summoned by messages scratched on wooden idols that Mnesilochus had thrown out of the temple, entered declaiming Menelaus' lines from his play *Helen* (412 B.C.E.). Mnesilochus responded with Helen's lines, but before a rescue could be effected a magistrate accompanied by a hefty Scythian archer arrived and Euripides fled. The magistrate, after ordering Mnesilochus to be lashed to a post, left him under the guard of the Scythian. As the women began their ceremonies, Euripides, playing Echo of his drama on Perseus and Andromeda, began to echo Mnesilochus' laments as he entered the temple in the dress of Perseus. The illiterate Scythian, however, refused to believe that old Mnesilochus was really Andromeda, as Euripides insisted.

During the ceremonies the guard fell asleep. Euripides proceeded to disguise himself as a procuress. He then offered the women a proposal of peace: If they would release his father-in-law, he would no longer insult them in his plays. The women agreed, but there remained the Scythian to be outwitted. Still disguised as a procuress, Euripides offered the Scythian a good time with the little flute girl whom the barbarian eagerly purchased. While the two were away, Euripides released his father-in-law and they both escaped. His lust satisfied, the Scythian returned to find his prisoner gone; the obliging Thesmophoriazusae sent him off in hot pursuit—in the wrong direction.

Critical Evaluation:

Among the extant plays of Aristophanes, *Thesmophoriazusae* is easily the poet's best marriage of literary parody with comic farce. The actual date of production is not precisely known; the play was probably presented in 411 B.C.E., notably the same year in which *Lysistrata* was performed. Both plays deal in different ways with the tension between the sexes and depend for their comic effect on a temporary inversion of sexual roles, which were very clearly defined in classical Athens. Through the device of farcical transvestism and elaborate imitation of the elevated tragic diction of Euripidean drama, Aristophanes achieves in *Thesmophoriazusae* a masterpiece that satirizes sexual politics and literary pretension.

The play's title might be translated as "Women Celebrating the Thesmophoria," referring to an Athenian fertility festival that rigorously excluded men from its celebration. A central element of the plot, a man, disguised as a woman, trying to spy on the festival, is not entirely far-fetched. Women's festivals at Athens naturally aroused the curiosity and suspicion of the men who were obliged to support them financially but who were often excluded from participation. Few details are known about what happened at such festivities, but it is clear that they gave women a temporary autonomy and allowed them to conduct sacred fertility rites. Stories from legend and history refer to attempts made by men to infiltrate these all-female rites, often with such dire results as death or castration on discovery. Male anxiety that women secretly indulged in wine or sex or (worse yet) plotted to subvert male domination is the realistic background of the comic fantasy of *Thesmophoriazusae*.

In the play, as the women gather for the festival, they begin to debate a proposal to prosecute the tragic poet Euripides for his slanders against women. Euripides is perfectly suited to be the focus of their hatred. His reputation for misogyny, whether deserved or not, is frequently mentioned in ancient sources. The reputation seems to have arisen from a (superficial) reading of the characterization of women in his tragedies. Euripides is satirized in other surviving plays of Aristophanes, but in this play he is a principal target. Nowhere else is the criticism of his style and material more elaborate than in *Thesmophoriazusae*. In this play Aristophanes produces astonishingly close imitations of Euripides' style and diction, suggesting that he and his audience were intimately familiar with the tragedian's work. As is often the case in parody, there is a sense that Aristophanes held some grudging respect for Euripides' skill as a tragic poet.

The opening scene shows Euripides attempting to send a spy to infiltrate the meeting of the women. The transvestism is inherently comic, the stuff of farce throughout Western culture. The transvestism underscores the extraordinary separation of the sexes in ancient Athens, where women lived most of their lives apart from men, as well as the mutual ignorance that must have arisen from these circumstances. From repeated jokes that are made in the play, it appears that Athenian women were supposed to be excessively fond of drink, eager to deceive their husbands at every turn, and always ready to conspire against men, who controlled the city. These accusations represent male anxiety about the subordinate and cloistered role of women that was a fact of Athenian life. Humor at the expense of Agathon, an effeminate poet, and Clisthenes, a homosexual who is unhesitatingly welcomed by the women celebrating the festival, suggests a tension within the Athenian conception of masculinity that Aristophanes exploits for his comic purposes.

Aristophanes next presents the assembly of women, who debate the proposal to try Euripides. Such a formal meeting is, in and of itself, supposed to be comic, since Athenian women were excluded from all political life of the city. During their own private festival where no man is permitted, it is supposed that, as it were, an alternative state is created, with its own laws and customs. As Euripides' spy, Mnesilochus attempts to speak in defense of the poet but only manages to insult the women more. When he is discovered, he is seized and bound. The rest of the play involves attempts to rescue him. The humor of this remaining part of the play depends on knowledge of Euripides' work, which contains many such scenes of rescue. Aristophanes is indulging in a peculiar species of literary criticism. He parodies such plays as Euripides' *Helen* (412 B.C.E.), which had recently been presented, and implies that *Helen* is something less than a real tragedy. Scholars admit that some of Euripides' later works, such as *Helen*, are closer to what might properly be called melodrama than to traditional tragedy.

Thesmophoriazusae is different from most other surviving plays of Aristophanes in not representing riotous celebration when the protagonist finally overcomes opposition and achieves his or her goal. Through a ritual celebrating heterosexual love, this traditional element of older Greek comedy—called the marriage or *gamos*, after the Greek, because it supposedly reenacts a sacred marriage of Dionysus—usually signals closure and reconciliation at the end of an Aristophanic play. In *Thesmophoriazusae* the brief dalliance of the Scythian archer with the flute girl may have been included to substitute for this traditional motif, and there is reconciliation of a kind at the end when Euripides agrees to stop insulting the women. The parody of Euripidean schemes of rescue continues right to the end of the play. It is likely that Aristophanes' delight in his elaborate literary spoof caused him to stretch the limits that were typically imposed on the comic genre.

"Critical Evaluation" by John M. Lawless

Bibliography:
Aristophanes. *Thesmophoriazusae*. Edited and translated by Alan H. Sommerstein. Warminster, Wiltshire, England: Aris & Phillips, 1994. Provides scholarly introduction, bibliography,

Greek text, facing English translation, and commentary keyed to the translation. Sommerstein's translation supersedes most earlier versions.

Dover, K. J. *Aristophanic Comedy*. Berkeley: University of California Press, 1972. Useful and authoritative study of the plays of Aristophanes. Chapter 13 provides a synopsis of the play, a discussion of the characters, and notes on the topicality of the play. An essential starting point for study of the play.

Harriott, Rosemary M. *Aristophanes: Poet and Dramatist*. Baltimore: The Johns Hopkins University Press, 1986. The plays are discussed not in individual chapters but as each illustrates the central themes and techniques of Aristophanes' work.

Spatz, Lois. *Aristophanes*. Boston: Twayne, 1978. A reliable introduction to Aristophanes for the general reader. Chapter 7 provides a summary of the problems of the play and offers several approaches to the theme of tension between the sexes and to the role of literary parody.

Whitman, Cedric. *Aristophanes and the Comic Hero*. Cambridge, Mass.: Harvard University Press, 1964. A standard work on the characterization of the Aristophanic protagonist. Chapter 6, "The War Between the Sexes," provides excellent discussion of the issue in the play.

THE THIN MAN

Type of work: Novel
Author: Dashiell Hammett (1894-1961)
Type of plot: Detective and mystery
Time of plot: 1930's
Locale: New York
First published: 1934

> *Principal characters:*
> MIMI JORGENSEN, Clyde Wynant's former wife
> DOROTHY WYNANT, her daughter
> GILBERT WYNANT, her son
> CHRISTIAN JORGENSEN, her present husband and Wynant's
> former associate
> NICK CHARLES, a detective
> NORA CHARLES, his wife
> HERBERT MACAULAY, Wynant's attorney
> MORELLI, a gangster
> ARTHUR NUNHEIM, a former convict

The Story:

Nick Charles, a onetime detective and now a California lumberman, arrived in New York with his wife, Nora, for the Christmas holidays. He was drawn into investigating the murder of Julia Wolf, who was the secretary of Nick's old client, Clyde Wynant, a lunatic-fringe inventor whose wife had divorced him in order to marry a man named Christian Jorgensen. Wynant was reported to be out of town, working on a new project, and Herbert Macaulay, his attorney, had told police that he had not seen him since October, when Wynant had given him power of attorney.

The police suspected a number of people, including Mimi Jorgensen, her husband, a gangster named Morelli, Gil Wynant, and Clyde Wynant himself. Mimi had just returned from Europe and had gone to see Julia to get her husband's address because she needed more money to support their two children, twenty-year-old Dorothy and eighteen-year-old Gilbert; her new husband, Christian Jorgensen, had spent the large settlement Wynant had made at the time of their divorce. Mimi had arrived just in time for Julia to die in her arms.

Jorgensen had worked with Wynant several years earlier (at that time his name had been Kelterman), and he believed that Wynant had not treated him fairly. In the course of the investigation, it was discovered that Jorgensen had a wife living in Boston and that he had married Mimi only to get Wynant's money.

Morelli, the gangster, had once been fond of Julia. When he learned that Nick was on the case, Morelli went to his apartment and, just as the police arrived, shot Nick in the chest, a glancing shot that did not produce a serious wound. Nick refused to press charges because the man was apparently in enough trouble already. The police beat up Morelli but, not having a reason for holding him, released him the same day.

The members of the Wynant family did not have much love for one another. Gil was an odd young man who asked Nick about bizarre subjects such as incest and cannibalism. He was frequently found at keyholes, listening to private conversations.

The police also suspected Arthur Nunheim, who had identified Julia Wolf's body. When Nick went with a detective named Guild to see Nunheim, they found him living in an extremely untidy apartment with a big, frowzy blonde. In the presence of their callers, Nunheim and the blonde insulted each other until the woman left. Nunheim escaped from Nick through a back window, and he was reported murdered a little while later.

Macaulay reported that Wynant had made an appointment with him on the day the murder was committed but that he had failed to appear. During the course of the investigation, several people received communications from Wynant that seemed to throw suspicion on Mimi and Jorgensen. One day, there was a false report that Wynant had tried to commit suicide in Allentown, Pennsylvania.

Wynant had maintained a shop on First Avenue, which the police had examined cursorily. Nick insisted they return and tear it apart, if necessary, for he was convinced that the place held some clues. When the police thereupon noticed that one section of the cement floor was newer than the rest, they tore it up and found the bones of a dead man, a cane, clothes that apparently fit a larger man than Wynant, and a key chain with the initials D. W. Q.

Eventually, Nick accused Macaulay of murdering Wynant, Julia, and Nunheim. He believed that Macaulay and Julia had joined forces to get Wynant's money, that Wynant had gone to Macaulay's house in Scarsdale to accuse Macaulay of the plot, and that Macaulay had killed his client there. Then, Nick reasoned, Macaulay had dismembered the body and brought it back to the workshop, where he discharged the two mechanics and buried the body under new cement. The cane, the large-size clothes, and the key chain were intended to prevent identification of the body.

Macaulay, according to Nick, had renewed the lease on the shop and kept it vacant while, with a forged power of attorney and Julia's help, he began to transfer Wynant's fortune to his own accounts. Mimi's return from Europe and her search for Wynant had precipitated matters, and when Nick arrived for the Christmas holiday and agreed to help Mimi find the missing inventor, Macaulay felt he would be safer with Julia dead. He himself had written the letters that seemed to be from Wynant. Nick thought Macaulay had killed Nunheim because the former convict had been near Julia's apartment and might have heard the shots that killed her. When Nunheim had demanded hush money from Macaulay, the lawyer had murdered him to keep him permanently quiet.

So Nick outlined his case, but on that very day, Gilbert Wynant received a letter that seemed to be from his father, telling him to use an enclosed key to go to Julia's apartment and look for an important paper between the pages of a certain book. Following the instruction in the letter, Gilbert entered the apartment, where a plainclothesman struck him, handcuffed him, and took him to police headquarters. The boy showed the officials and Nick the letter he had received, but the book and paper were fictitious. When Nick took Gilbert home, he learned from Mimi that Wynant had just been there to give Mimi ten thousand dollars in bonds.

As it turned out, Macaulay, knowing the police would be in Julia's apartment, had sent the letter to Gilbert in an attempt to shift the suspicion back to Wynant. Macaulay himself had brought Wynant's bonds to Mimi, making her promise to say that Wynant had brought them and thus give credence to his own story that Wynant was in town. Nick forced Mimi to admit the truth by explaining that Macaulay now had possession of Wynant's fortune and that, if she continued to support him, she would never get more than occasional small sums, whereas if she were to stop shielding Macaulay she would get control of her former husband's entire fortune. Jorgensen had meanwhile gone back to his legal wife in Boston. When Nick finished explaining the case to Nora, she could not help feeling that the business of a detective, based as it is on so much speculation, is at best unsatisfactory.

Critical Evaluation:

Dashiell Hammett's *The Thin Man* presents a picture of sophisticated New York life at the end of the Prohibition era. The plot itself follows the pattern set by Edgar Allan Poe in *The Murders of the Rue Morgue* (1841) and by Arthur Conan Doyle in his Sherlock Holmes stories. Hammett, too, pitted an astute detective against a questioning companion and the somewhat obtuse and distrustful police, and he, too, dropped clues to give the reader a chance to solve the mystery before allowing his detective to provide the final explanation.

The Thin Man was the last and most popular of Hammett's novels. It is the most briskly paced of his books, and its intricate plot is ingenious and deceptive as well as logical and believable. The action takes place among members of New York café society during the Prohibition era, a frenzied, colorful world of money, corruption, sex, booze, and violence that Hammett portrays with accuracy and energy. The book did very well commercially, and it also spawned a radio program, a television series, and an extremely successful sequence of films in the 1930's and 1940's, starring William Powell and Myrna Loy. With the characters Nick and Nora Charles, he created one of the most distinctive detective couples in the entire genre.

They give the novel the kind of verbal wit and situational humor seen only occasionally in Hammett's earlier works. As a former detective of obvious skill and experience, Nick is adroit enough in dealing with crime solving, but he is no aggressive, hard-boiled Continental Op, Sam Spade, or Ned Beaumont. He has retired from the business to manage Nora's not inconsiderable lumber interests and—at least until his curiosity is aroused—has no desire to return to his former occupation. Nick reluctantly becomes involved because Nora coaxes and dares him. Nick is a witty, cocky, charming man who would rather party than fight, and Nora, too, loves fun. The mystery is an exciting game to her—until it gets dangerous. The best scenes in the novel are not, as in previous Hammett books, those of action and violence but those featuring witty banter and sexual byplay between Nick and Nora. Nick sums up the mood at the end of the novel: "Let's stick around for a while. This excitement has put us behind in our drinking."

Yet despite its ingenuity and charm, *The Thin Man* is one of Hammett's weaker novels and shows a clear decline in his powers. The picture of New York in the 1930's is realistic and vivid, but superficial and cliché-ridden. The plot is clever and facile but has no implications beyond that of an interesting puzzle. The character of Nick Charles, while witty and charming, is relatively shallow and frivolous, as well as morally questionable. He is content to live off of Nora's money, indulge her whims, and drift from party to party and city to city. The intense personal morality of the earlier works gives way to a kind of lazy, benevolent hedonism in which nothing is more important than a 3:00 A.M. whiskey-and-soda. The vital ethical and intellectual center of Hammett's previous works is replaced by slick, though enormously entertaining, superficiality.

Bibliography:

Dooley, Dennis. *Dashiell Hammett.* New York: Frederick Ungar, 1984. A basic survey of Hammett's work and life specifically aimed at the general reader. Chapter 9, "Time's Shadow," provides an introduction to an interpretive reading of *The Thin Man*, which Dooley finds Hammett's least successful novel.

Gregory, Sinda. *Private Investigations: The Novels of Dashiell Hammett.* Carbondale: Southern Illinois University Press, 1985. A full-length study of Hammett's five major novels. Chapter 6, "*The Thin Man*: The Detective Novel and the Comedy of Manners," argues that the novel successfully merges the genres of hard-boiled fiction and comedy of manners and constitutes a serious and artistically unified work.

Layman, Richard. *Shadow Man: The Life of Dashiell Hammett*. New York: Harcourt Brace Jovanovich, 1981. The most scholarly and reliable of the various biographies of Hammett, this is an objective, readable, and carefully researched and documented source. Provides a valuable historical and biographical context for each of the novels as well as a synopsis of the plot.

Marling, William. *Dashiell Hammett*. Boston: Twayne, 1983. A concise and well-informed introductory survey specifically aimed at the general reader. Provides a unified overview of all the novels. The brief chapter on *The Thin Man* gives a plot summary and some biographical context.

Metress, Christopher, ed. *The Critical Response to Dashiell Hammett*. Westport, Conn.: Greenwood, 1994. Includes an introduction that surveys the history of Hammett criticism; a series of excerpts from reviews, commentaries, and critical discussions of each novel; and a section dealing more generally with Hammett's work. The section on *The Thin Man* reprints a journal article on the novel by George J. Thompson.

THINGS FALL APART

Type of work: Novel
Author: Chinua Achebe (1930-   )
Type of plot: Tragedy
Time of plot: Late nineteenth century
Locale: Umuofia, an Ibo society on the lower Nile River
First published: 1958

Principal characters:
OKONKWO, warrior and leader
OBEREIKA, Okonkwo's close friend
NWOYE, Okonkwo's eldest son
IKEMEFUNA, boy held for a kinsman's crime

The Story:

Okonkwo's father was cowardly, foolish, and poor in his life, an outcast at his death. When his father died, Okonkwo, on the other hand, though still a young man, had three wives, two barns full of yams, two of his people's titles, and a reputation as the strongest wrestler and bravest warrior in the nine villages of Umuofia. Okonkwo took great pride in these accomplishments, sometimes forgetting the assistance of his personal god, or *chi*, and of the man from whom he had borrowed yams to start his own farm.

Despite his accomplishments, Okonkwo feared being seen as like his father. One of his great disappointments was his eldest son, Nwoye, who seemed to have inherited Okonkwo's father's weakness. Nwoye disliked the men's stories of war, preferring his mother's childish stories. Okonkwo, who had a quick temper, often tried to beat these behaviors out of Nwoye.

A change happened when the village leaders put under Okonkwo's care a Mbaino boy named Ikemefuna. Ikemefuna came to Okonkwo's village because the Mbainos had killed a Umuofian woman; eventually the boy was to be killed in retribution. While living in Okonkwo's compound, Ikemefuna exerted a good influence on Nwoye, and won the affection of everyone, including Okonkwo.

During Ikemefuna's stay, the village observed the sacred Week of Peace that always preceded planting season. Violence was strictly forbidden for that week. Nonetheless, Okonkwo, in a fit of anger, severely beat his youngest wife. This angered the earth goddess. As punishment Okonkwo paid a fine. He repented inwardly, but did not admit his error outwardly, and so it was said that he lacked respect for the clan gods.

Three years after Ikemefuna's arrival, the village council decided it was time for him to be killed. The oldest man in the village warned Okonkwo not to take part, because Ikemefuna was like a son to Okonkwo. Okonkwo, fearful of appearing weak, not only attended Ikemefuna's killing, but also dealt his death blow. This act disturbed Okonkwo afterward, which puzzled him, because he had only followed his people's practice. Nwoye, who had greatly loved Ikemefuna, resented his father's action bitterly. Later, Okonkwo confronted his friend Obereika, who had not taken part in the killing. Obereika only said that although the oracle said the boy had to die, it did not compel a man to take part.

Shortly, the elder who had advised Okonkwo to stay away from Ikemefuna's execution died. At his funeral rites, as the cannons and guns sounded there was a sudden silence in the dancing crowd. Okonkwo's gun had mysteriously exploded and killed the dead man's son. Guilty of another crime against the earth goddess, Okonkwo and his family were banished to his motherland for seven years. No longer could he hope to become a lord of the clan of his fathers, Okonkwo lamented. His *chi* did not affirm his plans.

While exiled, Okonkwo maintained his material wealth with the assistance of his kinsmen and Obereika. Changes were happening, chief among them the arrival of white missionaries and governing officials. After some initial confusion and severe punishment for violence against the newcomers, there came a time of peaceful coexistence. Some Umuofians were converted by the missionaries, and among them was Nwoye. He was attracted by the new religion's criticism of such Umuofian practices as killing an innocent boy like Ikemefuna and throwing newborn twins into the Evil Forest to die. Learning of Nwoye's conversion, Okonkwo beat him and banished him from the family compound.

After seven years, Okonkwo returned to his fatherland with plans for regaining his former status and for leading his people in a war against the newcomers before they destroyed Umuofia. Obereika said that by converting native people and employing them in government posts, the newcomers had already inserted a "knife" into their community. The people had already "fallen apart."

Okonkwo's opportunity to incite his people came when a native convert desecrated a Umuofian ceremony. Okonkwo rejoiced as his people took revenge by tearing down the missionaries' church building. Government officials, however, soon captured Okonkwo and the other leaders, punishing them cruelly.

Once their leaders were released, the people gathered to determine whether to respond with conciliation or with war. A Umuofian who worked for the new government arrived and ordered the meeting stopped. Angered, Okonkwo killed him, and fearful, the people disbanded. The officials who came to arrest Okonkwo were led to the place where he had hanged himself. Suicide was against the Umuofian tradition; Okonkwo was buried as an outcast.

Critical Evaluation:

Chinua Achebe was born in the colony of Niger in 1930, to Ibo parents who were Christian converts. He attended British-style schools in Nigeria, including University College, Ibadeen, and was graduated from London University in 1953.

Achebe's first novel, *Things Fall Apart*, is a classic of African literature. Among all the colonial governments in Africa, the British in Nigeria fostered first education in its territory. As a result, Nigerian writers preceded those in other areas of Africa. *Things Fall Apart* is noted as the first African novel. Achebe, a master of his craft, has also written *No Longer at Ease* (1960), *Arrow of God* (1964), *A Man of the People* (1966), and *Anthills of the Savannah* (1988). Achebe has also published poetry, short stories, and essays.

In *Things Fall Apart* and in his later novels, Achebe wanted to counter demeaning and incorrect stereotypes of his people and Eurocentric presentations of the confrontation between the Ibo of Nigeria and the British intruders. In his novels, Achebe admits, he strives for artistic excellence but also wants to give a message. Just as the oral tradition of the Ibo people served their society by sustaining its values, so the modern Ibo, writing in English, should serve Ibo society.

In *Things Fall Apart*, Achebe combined the Ibo oral tradition's narrative style with the Western world's traditional novel form. In novel form Achebe narrates an African tale in African style. The novel's narrative voice could be Achebe's or it could be the voice of a village elder. In either case, the voice is connected to the world of the novel. Though the voice is objective, it is also a part of the scene depicted.

To achieve an African voice, Achebe uses plain, short, declarative sentences. Also, through-out the novel, characters narrate or listen to traditional stories from the society's past and stories that illustrate and teach the culture's values. The novel opens with the retelling of Okonkwo's exploits in a traditional wrestling match, the ritual by which young men proved themselves worthy of a high place in their clan.

Achebe weaves Ibo proverbs into the novel's dialogue, to clarify a point, teach a lesson, and, usually, provide humor. Also, many Ibo words are used in the text without translation. Some of these can be understood by the reader through context, but others remain mysterious and create a distance between the non-Ibo reader and the Ibo world of *Things Fall Apart*. Taken together, sentence structure, Umuofian stories, proverbs, and language create a memorable colloquial narrative voice.

The novel's structure, on the other hand, is formal. There are twenty-five chapters: thirteen in book 1, six in book 2, and six in book 3. The pivotal chapter about Okonkwo's accidental shooting of a young boy and his subsequent banishment is at the book's center, in chapter 13. Achebe establishes the nature of the Umuofian society and Okonkwo's character in book 1. In book 2 tension heightens as the outsiders appear. In book 3 the conflict comes to a head when Okonkwo kills the clerk and his people retreat before the power of the new government. The novel's last page has the required unexpected yet inevitable ending. The novel is a very orderly work.

To return to character, *Things Fall Apart* presents Okonkwo as a tragic hero who struggles against internal and external forces and meets a tragic end. Obereika calls his fallen friend a "great man." The hero is a complex man with both strengths and weaknesses. At the novel's start Okonkwo's deep shame about his father's failure motivates him to become a respected man, an exemplar of all that is valued in his society. His accomplishments feed his pride and cause his rigidity. His pride, rigidity, and short temper lead to sins against the gods of his people and criticism from his *chi*. Finally, Okonkwo is banned from his fatherland for seven years and, when he returns home, kills in anger. Okonkwo then takes his own life, the greatest sin against the gods of his people. His is a tragic end.

The plot line of Okonkwo's struggle and fall reveals not only his complex character but also the strong social fabric of the Umuofian people. Like Okonkwo's character, this society is complex, having both strengths and weaknesses. Its traditions create a stable community in which each individual finds meaning. The oral storytelling and rituals for planting, harvesting, and human passage sustain an orderly society. Some of the harsher customs, such as killing the innocent Ikemefuna, exiling Okonkwo for an accidental killing, and banishing some persons to live their entire lives as outcasts, raise doubts about the ultimate wisdom of Umuofian customs. Some, like Nwoye and Obereika, question what has always been done and suggest that change is necessary. Others, like Okonkwo, stand fast in defense of the tradition. When the newcomers come with a new religion and laws, the fabric of Umuofian society is weakened.

The newcomers also have strengths and weaknesses. They offer a gentler religion and different laws. Their excessive zeal and righteousness, however, provoke the anger of the people the newcomers want to win over. Finally, the Umuofian people and the newcomers share a common weakness. Few attempt to learn each other's language, customs, or beliefs. Conflict is inevitable. The situation and characters that Achebe draws in his novel are fraught with complexity. It is this complexity, as well as Achebe's masterful writing style, that make *Things Fall Apart* a classic novel.

Francine Dempsey

Bibliography:

Carroll, David. *Chinua Achebe.* New York: Twayne, 1970. A general introduction to Achebe's first four novels.

Gikandi, Simon. *Reading Chinua Achebe: Language and Ideology in Fiction.* Portsmouth, N.H.: J. Currey, 1991. Study of the interplay of the creative process and the political situation in Achebe's five novels. Devotes a chapter to *Things Fall Apart,* analyzing writing, culture, and dominance.

Lindfors, Bernth, ed. *Approaches to Teaching "Things Fall Apart."* New York: Modern Language Association of America, 1991. Suitable for students and teachers. Contains Chinua Achebe's only essay on the novel, as well as articles of literary and cultural analysis and an excellent bibliographical essay.

Wren, Robert M. *Achebe's World: the Historical and Cultural Context of the Novels of Chinua Achebe.* Washington, D.C.: Three Continents Press, 1980. Study of the historical and cultural setting of Achebe's novels. Compares Achebe's presentation of the Ibo world with archaeological and sociological research.

THE THIRTY-NINE STEPS

Type of work: Novel
Author: John Buchan (1875-1940)
Type of plot: Spy
Time of plot: 1914
Locale: England and Scotland
First published: 1915

> *Principal characters:*
> RICHARD HANNAY, a retired mining engineer
> FRANKLIN SCUDDER, a private investigator
> SIR WALTER, a government official
> THE BLACK STONE, espionage agents

The Story:

Richard Hannay was a mining engineer who had returned to England after having made a modest fortune in South Africa. Before long, he found that he was very bored with the conversations and actions of the Englishmen he met. He had almost decided to return to South Africa when a strange series of events began.

As he was unlocking the door of his flat, he was startled by the sudden appearance of Franklin Scudder, another tenant in the building. Scudder, obviously badly frightened, begged Hannay to give him refuge in his flat. After the two men were settled comfortably, Scudder told Hannay a fantastic tale. He said that a plot to start a war between England and Germany was under way. A Greek diplomat, Karolides, the only really strong man in Europe, was scheduled to visit London on June 15. His assassination during the visit would suffice as an excuse for the declaration of war.

Scudder told Hannay that a group called The Black Stone were the agents arranging for the assassination. They knew that Scudder had learned of their plot, and they had tried several times to kill him. He had planted a body in his flat, hoping that the murderers would think the body his. He asked Hannay to let him stay with him until plans could be made to prevent the assassination.

Impressed by the sincerity with which Scudder told his story, Hannay gave him sanctuary. Soon after, he returned to his flat one day to find Scudder with a knife through his heart. Hannay knew then that The Black Stone had found Scudder and that his own life was in danger. Presumably, the police, too, would want to question Hannay.

When he saw two men strolling back and forth in front of his building, he suspected that they were part of the enemy group. By a ruse, he exchanged clothes with the milkman and left his flat, taking with him a little black book in which he had seen Scudder making notes. He was afraid to go to any government office with his fantastic story. His plan was to disappear for the three weeks remaining before June 15 and then, at the last minute, try to get someone in authority to listen to him.

He went to Scotland, thinking he might be able to hide more easily there. Because the London papers carried the story of Scudder's murder and circulated a description of Hannay, he had several narrow escapes from local Scottish police. The Black Stone had traced him as well. When an airplane, obviously on the lookout for him, flew low over the spot where he had taken refuge, he found shelter in an inn. The Black Stone found him there, too, and he was forced to flee again. In every spare moment, he studied Scudder's little black book. He deciphered the code and learned that the murder of Karolides was only a small part of the plot. The main plan was an invasion of England. Airfields were already laid out, and mines had been placed to line the shores at a given signal. The time for invasion was to be determined once The Black Stone had intercepted the French envoy who was coming to London to secure plans of the arrangement of the British fleet. Once the enemy knew where the ships were, they could lay mines in strategic positions and destroy a great portion of the fleet. The only clue Hannay could find in Scudder's book about the time and place of the enemy operation were references to thirty-nine steps and a high tide at 10:17 P.M.

By luck, Hannay met a man who had an uncle in an influential position in the government. This man believed the story and promised to write his uncle to ask him to talk to Hannay and help thwart the plot. Hannay traveled carefully, for the police and The Black Stone were still pursuing him. Once he was captured by a member of The Black Stone, but he blew up the building in which he was held and escaped. At last, he reached his friend's uncle, Sir Walter, who listened carefully to Hannay's report. At first, he was disposed to dismiss Scudder's story as that of a loyal but overly anxious young man, but when he received a call informing him that Karolides had been killed, he knew that Scudder's information was correct and he promised to take Hannay's information to the proper authorities.

Although Hannay was not to be allowed to attend the secret conference of government officials, he had the uneasy feeling that his presence there was of the utmost importance, and that only he could find out how the highly confidential information about the French envoy's visit had leaked out to the enemy. Against Sir Walter's orders, he went to the house where the officials were meeting. As he sat in the hall waiting to be admitted, one of the officials came out of the meeting room. Hannay realized that he had seen the man elsewhere, and that the man recognized him. He burst into the room and told the astonished officials that the man who had just left was an impostor.

They thought him mad, for the man was the First Lord of the Admiralty and everyone knew him well. Then they remembered that the man had scanned the drawings and figures carefully and could have memorized them. If he left the country, the whole plan of defense would be in the hands of the enemy. The only hope was to capture him.

There were hundreds of small ports where a small boat could leave England, but by checking isolated spots along the coast, Hannay found a small cove where high tide was at 10:17 P.M., and he surmised that there would be a house nearby with thirty-nine steps leading down to the cove. Accompanied by police, Hannay located just such a house, which was occupied by three Englishmen on vacation. Their actions were so natural that he doubted they could be spies. Only the presence of a fast yacht in the water close to the cove seemed suspicious, and when Hannay noticed the unconscious habit one of the vacationers had of tapping his fingers he recognized him as the enemy agent who had captured him. Hannay and the police were able to capture two of the men. The third escaped to the ship, but as it had already been boarded by English police, he also was taken.

The murder charge against Hannay had been dropped, and he was safe for the first time in many weeks. Three weeks later, war was declared between England and Germany. The war was not, however, fought on English soil, and no surprise invasion took place. Hannay enlisted in the army, but he knew that he had done his greatest service for his country even before putting on a uniform. The Black Stone was no more, and Scudder's murder had been avenged.

Critical Evaluation:

The Thirty-nine Steps is generally recognized as the first authentic spy novel. Although elements of the form are evident in earlier works—adventure tales, chase-and-capture narratives, detective stories, mystery stories, and gothic horror tales—it was John Buchan who established the patterns that became basic to the genre, which developed and flourished in the twentieth century. In an essay on Buchan, novelist Graham Greene singled out the first ingredient in his formula for what Buchan himself called the "shocker"—a formula Greene was to use with considerable success in his own spy novels: "John Buchan was the first to realize the enormous dramatic value of adventure in familiar surroundings happening to unadventurous men." The average-person-caught-in-a-web-of-intrigue formula proved to be fertile.

Buchan once stated that his own object was to write "romance where the ingredients defy the probabilities and march just inside the borders of the possible." *The Thirty-nine Steps* effectively follows that dictum. The hero, Richard Hannay, is believable and the settings are vivid and realistic, but the situations do "march" very close to the impossible.

Although not deeply characterized, Richard Hannay is colorful and convincing. He is bright, cultured, eager, and resourceful. Once his boredom and curiosity lead him to accept the challenge of strange events and become involved in an intrigue, his patriotism and optimism ensure that he commit himself totally to the cause and that he believe steadfastly in final victory. Furthermore, his experience as a mining engineer on the African veldt realistically accounts for his endurance and adroitness in evading capture, as well as his skill in exploding his way out of danger.

The settings, too, are scrupulously accurate. Buchan used locations he knew personally, and many of the sites, including the real thirty-nine steps, were important to him. Not only is Hannay's escape route geographically possible but, more important, Buchan creates a realistic atmosphere that gives the adventure immediacy.

Although the characters and settings of *The Thirty-nine Steps* are realistic, the plot moves perilously between the possible and the fantastic. The essence of the thriller is the chase, and while the hero or heroine may not begin as hunters, they soon become the hunted, frequently with both the established authorities and the villains in pursuit. Hannay is chased almost from the beginning and, despite several close calls, avoids capture by using several of the devices that became stock-in-trades of the genre: disguise (a milkman, a political speaker, a rural "road-man"), physical concealment, and plain good luck (one does not look too closely at "coincidence" in the thriller).

In *The Thirty-nine Steps*, Buchan also introduces the false rescue scene central to many intrigue novels: When the hero has apparently reached a sanctuary and is safe from his pursuers, he is suddenly thrust into an even more dangerous situation, which then leads to his most impressive escape. Hannay is rescued from the police by a kindly bald archaeologist, who turns out to be his archenemy. To get out of this perilous predicament, Hannay must demonstrate the most extreme physical courage and mental agility.

In Buchan's shockers, the hero usually clears himself with the authorities, whereupon together they defeat the conspiracy. Other thriller writers leave all the responsibility to their protagonists, but either way, it is up to the hero to direct the destruction of the villains. Hannay does so by deciphering Scudder's coded notebook (another common thriller gimmick) and exposing the criminals personally. The central motif of the thriller is that of the isolated individual who is, either by choice or by circumstance, outside the established system and pitted against an implacable and immensely powerful criminal. Often, civilization itself may be at stake.

Written during the first months of World War I, *The Thirty-nine Steps* reflects a logical world. The changes to the genre since Buchan—whether in "superman" intrigues like Ian Fleming's James Bond series or in the grimy realism of books by writers such as Eric Ambler and John le Carré—are the result of more complex and ambiguous attitudes toward the world; they are not alterations in the basic formulas first established by John Buchan in *The Thirty-nine Steps*.

Bibliography:

Cawelti, John G., and Bruce A. Rosenberg. *The Spy Story*. Chicago: University of Chicago Press, 1987. In what is probably the best overall analysis of Buchan's spy novels, the authors praise *The Thirty-nine Steps* as his most completely successful book and examine its connections to John Bunyan's *The Pilgrim's Progress* (1678).

Daniell, David. *The Interpreter's House: A Critical Assessment of John Buchan*. London: Thomas Nelson, 1975. A full-length assessment of all of Buchan's writing, both nonfiction and fiction. Focuses on the earlier, lesser-known works, but also contains a fine analysis of his spy and adventure fiction.

MacGlone, James M. "The Printed Texts of John Buchan's *The Thirty-nine Steps*, 1915-1940." *The Bibliotheck: A Scottish Journal of Bibliography and Allied Topics* 13 (1986): 9-24. MacGlone's exhaustive study of the printed texts of *The Thirty-nine Steps* traces the varying stages of the novel's development.

Panek, LeRoy L. *The Special Branch: The British Spy Novel, 1890-1980*. Bowling Green, Ohio: Bowling Green University Popular Press, 1981. Traces the origins of Buchan's spy novels to the earlier books of Edgar Wallace, E. Phillips Oppenheim, and William Le Queux and to the development of espionage fiction during the late nineteenth century.

Smith, Janet Adam. *John Buchan: A Biography*. Boston: Little, Brown, 1965. A comprehensive biography that traces the many interests of this multifaceted man. This volume is well illustrated and contains a good checklist of Buchan's works.

Winks, Robin. "John Buchan: Stalking the Wilder Game." In *The Four Adventures of Richard Hannay*, by John Buchan. Boston: David R. Godine, 1988. Attempts to dispel concerns over the racism, sexism, jingoism, and anti-Semitism that Buchan's spy novels contain. Includes a listing of libraries with holdings of Buchan's papers.

THREE LIVES

Type of work: Novellas
Author: Gertrude Stein (1874-1946)
Type of plot: Psychological realism
Time of plot: Late nineteenth and early twentieth centuries
Locale: Bridgepoint, United States
First published: 1909

Principal characters:
  ANNA FEDERNER, a servant
  MISS MATHILDA, her employer
  MISS MARY WADSMITH, Anna's former employer
  MRS. LEHNTMAN, Anna's dearest friend
  MELANCTHA HERBERT, an African American woman
  ROSE JOHNSON, Melanctha's friend
  JANE HARDEN, Melanctha's mentor
  JEFFERSON CAMPBELL, a physician Melanctha loves
  LENA MAINZ, a young German woman
  MATHILDA HAYDON, Lena's aunt
  HERMAN KREDER, the tailor Lena marries

The Story:

The Good Anna. For five years Anna Federner, a small German woman about forty, managed Miss Mathilda's full household of both women, an underservant, three regular dogs (old Baby, young Peter, and fluffy Rags), and various strays. Anna managed the household well but became flustered when her mistress spent money frivolously. Miss Mathilda, on the other hand, tried to curb Anna's lending to friends. Anna, who at seventeen had been a servant in Germany, had come to America with her mother. After her mother died, Anna moved from the Deep South to Bridgepoint (a fictional city that resembles Baltimore) where her half brother lived.

In Bridgepoint, Anna served Miss Mary Wadsmith and her orphaned niece and nephew. Anna liked working for the large, helpless woman, who let Anna manage all her affairs, but Anna did not care much for children. She preferred spoiled Edgar to obstinate Jane. One day, Jane gave Anna an order that she said came from Miss Mary. Anna angrily told Miss Mary about the incident, and her employer fainted. Jane and Anna made no more trouble.

Anna began having severe headaches. Mrs. Lehntman, a widowed friend, and Jane Wadsmith convinced her to let Dr. Shonjen operate; she improved some but was never well again.

When Jane married, Miss Mary went to live with her. Anna did not believe that she could work in a household with Jane as mistress; therefore, she began working for Dr. Shonjen. She loved working for men, who enjoyed eating and let her manage. Anna continued helping the midwife Mrs. Lehntman, who adopted a baby boy. Anna was concerned that her friend could not afford another child, but Mrs. Lehntman was resolved to keep the baby.

Anna often helped another poor family, the Drehtens, whom her sister-in-law despised. Her best friend was Mrs. Lehntman, and when that friend wanted money to start a lying-in home, Anna lent it to her, despite reservations about the venture. Anna's troubles were compounded by Mrs. Lehntman's interest in a man and her employer's marriage. Dr. Shonjen's new wife and Anna did not get along, so Anna looked for a new place. She learned of Miss Mathilda, who had recently moved to Bridgepoint. Anna was reluctant to work for a woman, but Mrs. Lehntman urged her to consult a medium, who encouraged her to take the job. Anna enjoyed working for Miss Mathilda, who let Anna manage everything and keep her dogs. However, Anna lost her friendship with Mrs. Lehntman after Mrs. Lehntman failed to pay back another loan and continued her involvement with an unscrupulous physician.

Anna continued to befriend other people and stray animals, including Mrs. Lehntman's foolish newly married daughter. She also nursed Mrs. Drehten through an operation.

Anna's life became sadder: Her old dog Baby, a gift from Mrs. Lehntman, died, and Miss Mathilda moved to another country. Anna took in boarders at Miss Mathilda's.

Anna's boarders loved her, but she charged too little to make a profit. She worked so hard that she wore herself out and died during an operation. Mrs. Drehten wrote to Miss Mathilda about Anna's death.

Melanctha. Melanctha Herbert, a young African American woman with some white blood, had recently befriended Rose Johnson, a black woman reared by white people. When Rose and Sam Johnson's baby was born, Melanctha helped her friend with the child. Rose was so lazy that when Melanctha was gone, the baby died. Melanctha did not really love her black father or her light-skinned mother. Her father once fought a man who he thought was too interested in Melanctha.

When Melanctha was quite young, she began to wander the streets talking with men. She became friends with Jane Harden, who told her much about men and the world but drank far too much. Melanctha's mother became ill, and Dr. Jefferson Campbell came. As he and Melanctha talked, she became so fond of him that she ceased to wander. They discussed his beliefs about African American people. Her mother died, her father disappeared, and she focused all her attention on Jeff Campbell.

He was uncertain about his feelings for her. As he began to love Melanctha, Jane Harden told him of Melanctha's earlier interest in men. What Jane told him made him angry, and he feared he would quarrel with Melanctha. He also doubted her love for him. Jeff Campbell's mistrust of Melanctha drove them apart. She began to love him less and surround herself with friends, including Rose Johnson.

After several break-ups and reunions with Jeff, Melanctha explained that she loved him, but not with her former passion. At that point he realized that he truly loved her. After she and Jeff ended their relationship, Melanctha casually dated white men. Jeff, now schooled in love, found that his work had improved.

Melanctha began dating Jem Richards, who, like her, loved horses. He got into trouble betting at the race track. Melanctha became more dependent on Rose and Sam Johnson, but Rose became increasingly cold toward her. Jem Richards broke up with her, leaving Melanctha quite alone in the world.

Melanctha thought about killing herself, but she did not. After an illness and brief recovery, she died.

The Gentle Lena. Lena Mainz had come from Germany with her aunt, Mrs. Haydon, to Bridgepoint, where Lena had worked for the same family for four years. Lena was gentle and found the family agreeable. Lena had been quite ill on the voyage to America but recovered upon arrival.

After Lena had worked four years, her aunt sought her a husband. She matched Lena with a tailor, Herman Kreder. Neither Lena nor Herman, however, wanted to marry. On the wedding day, Herman could not be found, so the wedding was postponed. Herman's father brought him back from his married sister's house in New York.

Lena and Herman were married and moved into his parents' house. The Kreders were sloppy, and the neat Lena adopted their ways. Mrs. Kreder scolded, but Herman took Lena's side. Lena became withdrawn.

Lena got pregnant. After her healthy baby was born, she became even more careless about her life. She had two more babies, whom Herman adored. Lena's fourth child was stillborn, and Lena died soon after. Herman happily cared for the children.

Critical Evaluation:

Gertrude Stein's *Three Lives*, a trilogy of character sketches, is remarkable for its experimental style, its lower-class characters, and its naturalistic themes.

Stein uses a deceptively simple, repetitive style, sometimes reminding the reader of a previous point. For example, in "The Good Anna," Stein writes, "Anna never liked her brother's wife." Two lines later, she writes, "Anna never liked her half brother's wife." After describing Anna's nieces, Stein writes, "our good Anna loved them not, nor their mother." The reader begins to realize that Stein means more than she says; Anna's half brother's wife does not deserve to be liked. Each repetition gets the reader closer to this truth. The repetitions also mirror the thinking of Anna, whose dislike for Mrs. Federner is constant and annoying.

Stein also eschews most punctuation, arguing that it interrupts the flow of language. The sparsity of punctuation marks makes Stein's writing read more like thought than like written ideas.

The simple language reflects the simplicity of the women whose lives Stein portrays. Anna Federner and Lena Mainz are German American servants. Melanctha Herbert is a young, relatively uneducated African American woman. The language in the first and third novellas, the ones about the servants, is less sophisticated than that of the middle piece, partly because "Melanctha" includes conversations between a physician and the young woman, who is fairly intelligent. In the second character sketch, paragraphs are longer and more fully developed. The characters use simple words and repeat their ideas, however, a hallmark of Gertrude Stein's style.

For example, Dr. Jefferson Campbell says, "You see Miss Melanctha I am a very quiet kind of fellow, and I believe in a quiet life for all the colored people." Melanctha replies, "Yes I certainly do see that very clear Dr. Campbell. . . . I see that's certainly what it is always made me not know right about you and that's certainly what it is that makes you really mean what you was always saying."

Many critics have remarked on Stein's treating lower-class characters with the same regard with which Henry James and other authors have treated upper-class characters. She illustrates the importance of the lives of servants and African Americans and makes their pains, joys, and love real to the reader. She gives their emotional and intellectual lives value.

Gertrude Stein's theme is naturalistic. No matter how hard Anna, Melanctha, and Lena try, they are defeated in their efforts by a society that does not sufficiently value them. Anna, possibly based on a woman who worked for Stein in France, is the best servant anyone can be, always trying to make her employers' lives happy and easy. In the end, her generosity is her downfall; others take advantage of her friendship, borrowing money and never paying it back, eating her good food at her boardinghouse while paying little for it, and letting her work herself to death for them. Most of them are not bad people, but Anna's goodness cannot stand up to the harsh reality of her life.

Melanctha befriends weak people, and their weakness interferes with a love that could have made her very happy. Jane Harden tells Jeff Campbell about Melanctha's youthful wanderings and interest in men, and he doubts Melanctha's love for him. His doubt destroys their love. Her sorrow and loneliness leave her vulnerable to illness and death.

Lena's gentleness destroys her. She resigns herself to being ruled by her aunt, who believes that marriage is best for all girls. Lena lets herself be married to a man who does not love her, lets herself have children, lets her husband ignore her, and finally dies bearing a fourth child. Her gentleness, like Anna's goodness, cannot stand up to a world that is not gentle.

Gertrude Stein was a well-educated, intelligent, upper-class woman who surrounded herself with artists and writers. In *Three Lives* she displays interest in and affection for people not like herself, treating them with sympathy but not pity, with respect, not condescension. Even their flaws are admirable. Her keen eye and ear and her generous heart are evident on every page.

M. Katherine Grimes

Bibliography:

Bridgman, Richard. *Gertrude Stein in Pieces.* New York: Oxford University Press, 1970. Bridgman asserts that all three women in *Three Lives* are "victimized by fate" and says that Stein is concerned more with thoughts than with actions.

Doane, Janice L. *Silence and Narrative: The Early Novels of Gertrude Stein.* Westport, Conn.: Greenwood Press, 1986. Discusses the artists who influenced Stein, explaining that Stein is not constrained by convention. Some of Doane's arguments, such as the assertion that in *Three Lives* Stein shows that marriage destroys women and uplifts men, are provocative but not always easily supported.

Hoffman, Michael J. *Gertrude Stein.* Boston: Twayne, 1976. Compares *Three Lives* with Stein's *roman à clef Things as They Are* (1950; later *Quod Erat Demonstrandum*). Hoffman provides good discussions of Stein's "wise-child" style and of the narrator of *Three Lives*.

Mellow, James R. *Charmed Circle: Gertrude Stein and Company.* New York: Praeger, 1974. Mellow's thorough treatment of Stein's literary and artistic circle includes an examination of the autobiographical undertones of *Three Lives* and circumstances of its publication.

Sutherland, Donald. *Gertrude Stein: A Biography of Her Work.* New Haven, Conn.: Yale University Press, 1951. Sutherland examines the almost scientific precision of Stein's description and style in *Three Lives*.

THE THREE MUSKETEERS

Type of work: Novel
Author: Alexandre Dumas, *père* (1802-1870)
Type of plot: Historical
Time of plot: 1626
Locale: France
First published: Les Trois Mousquetaires, 1844 (English translation, 1846)

> *Principal characters:*
> D'ARTAGNAN, a Gascon adventurer
> ATHOS,
> PORTHOS, and
> ARAMIS, the three musketeers
> CONSTANCE BONANCIEUX, the queen's seamstress
> LADY DE WINTER, Cardinal Richelieu's agent
> CARDINAL RICHELIEU, the minister of state

The Story:

In the spring of 1625, a young Gascon named D'Artagnan, on his way to Paris to join the Musketeers, proudly rode up to an inn in Meung. He was mounted on an old Bearn pony given to him by his father, along with some good advice and a letter of introduction to the captain of the Musketeers. In Meung he showed his fighting spirit by fiercely challenging to a duel a stranger who seemed to be laughing at his orange horse. Before continuing his journey to Paris, he had another encounter with the stranger, identified by a scar on his face, and the stranger's companion, a young and beautiful woman.

Athos, Porthos, and Aramis were the three best blades in the ranks of the Musketeers of the Guard, in the service of Louis XIII. D'Artagnan became a fourth member of the group within three months of his arrival in Paris. He had earned the love and respect of the other men when he challenged each in turn to a duel and then helped them drive off Cardinal Richelieu's guards, who wished to arrest them for brawling.

D'Artagnan was not made a musketeer at once; he had to serve an apprenticeship as a cadet in a lesser company of guards before being admitted to the Musketeer ranks. Athos, Porthos, and Aramis looked forward to the day when he would become their true comrade in arms, and each man took turns accompanying him when he was on guard duty. D'Artagnan was curious about his friends but could learn nothing about them. Athos looked like a nobleman. He was reserved, never mentioned women, and it was said that a great treachery had poisoned his life. Porthos was a squire of dames, bragging incessantly of his loves. Aramis, who always dressed in black, insisted that he was a musketeer only temporarily, that he was a churchman at heart and soon would enter a monastery and exchange his plumed hat for a monk's cowl.

The three musketeers had been rewarded in gold by the timid king for their bravery against the cardinal's guards but had since spent all of their money. They were trying to figure a way out of their difficulties when Bonancieux, D'Artagnan's landlord, came to D'Artagnan because he had heard that his tenant was a brave man. He said that his wife Constance, who was a seamstress to the queen and whose devotion to the queen was well-known, had been abducted. He suggested that D'Artagnan find and rescue Constance in payment for long-overdue rent and for financial compensation.

When Bonancieux described the abductor, D'Artagnan recognized him as the man he had challenged at Meung. On these two scores, the Gascon was willing to help the stricken husband, but he was even more eager when he discovered that the purpose of the abduction was to force Constance to tell what she knew of a rumored romance between the queen and the duke of Buckingham.

Constance escaped her abductors and returned to her home, where the cardinal's men again tried to seize her, only to be attacked and scattered by D'Artagnan, who had overheard the struggle. Later that evening D'Artagnan met Constance as she was hurrying along alone on the streets at a late hour. He questioned her, but she would not say where she was going. He told her that he loved her, but she gave him no encouragement. Still later that evening he encountered her again as she was leading the duke of Buckingham, in disguise, to the queen.

The queen had sent for Buckingham to beg him to leave the city, where his life was in danger. As they talked she confessed her love for him and gave him as a memento a rosewood casket containing twelve diamond studs that the king had given her. Richelieu, through his spies, learned of the gift and suggested to the king that he should give a fete and ask the queen to wear her diamond studs. The cardinal then ordered Lady de Winter, who was in London, to snip off two of the studs from Buckingham's clothing. This deed gave him a chance to strike at the king, the queen, and also Buckingham. Learning of this scheme, Constance went to D'Artagnan. D'Artagnan loved Constance, and he wanted to serve his queen, so he undertook to recover the jewels. With his three comrades he started out for London. Only D'Artagnan arrived there, for when the cardinal's agents ambushed the comrades, the three musketeers were wounded and left behind. D'Artagnan reached the duke in time to recover the studs and return to Paris with them. Richelieu's plot was foiled.

After D'Artagnan had received the thanks of the queen, he was to meet Constance that evening, but Constance was again seized and imprisoned by the cardinal's spies, one of whom was identified as the man from Meung. D'Artagnan decided that he needed the help of his three friends, and, accompanied by his servant Planchet, he went to find them. First he called at the inn where he had left Porthos and found him still there, recovering from his wounds. Later, he found Aramis talking with some doctors of theology and about to renounce the world. Athos had barricaded himself in a wine cellar. In his drunken state, Athos related a story about a friend of his, a count, who, when he was young, had married a beautiful woman and had made her the first lady in his province. Later, however, he had discovered that she was branded on the shoulder with the fleur-de-lis, the brand for a convicted criminal, and he had hanged her on a tree, leaving her for dead.

Once again the four friends were together. Then D'Artagnan, who had followed Porthos into a church, saw a beautiful woman whom he recognized as the companion of the man he had met at Meung. He followed her out of church and saw her get into her coach. Later he and his friends took the same road her coach had taken and encountered the coach by the side of the road. The lady was talking to a young man who, D'Artagnan discovered, was her brother-in-law, Lord de Winter. D'Artagnan became a friend of Lord de Winter after sparing his life in a duel; the lord introduced him to his sister-in-law. D'Artagnan fell in love with Lady de Winter, but she loved another, Monsieur de Wardes, who, unknown to her, had been killed.

D'Artagnan deceived her one night into believing she had an assignation with de Wardes. D'Artagnan presented himself to her as de Wardes that night, and she gave him a magnificent sapphire ring. When D'Artagnan showed the ring to Athos, he recognized it as the one which had belonged to his mother and which he had given to his wife. Athos began to suspect that his wife was not dead but was Lady de Winter.

D'Artagnan overheard Lady de Winter make slurring remarks about him because he had spared the life of her brother-in-law. She was Lord de Winter's heir. D'Artagnan also realized that Lady de Winter was the cardinal's spy. At his next meeting with her, D'Artagnan, as himself, confessed his duplicity to her, and she angrily struck a blow which caused him to step on her dress. The dress pulled from her shoulder, exposing the brand of the fleur-de-lis. As D'Artagnan realized the truth, Lady de Winter attacked him with a knife and screamed that she would get revenge. D'Artagnan fled to Athos.

The war between England and France was reaching a climax, and the siege of La Rochelle was of particular political importance. The four friends prepared to go to La Rochelle. Before they left, D'Artagnan was called for an interview with the cardinal. Richelieu tried to bribe D'Artagnan to enter his own guards, but D'Artagnan refused and left with the knowledge that his refusal might mean his death. In La Rochelle two young soldiers tried to kill D'Artagnan. He learned from them that they had been hired by Lady de Winter to kill him, and he also learned that she was responsible for the imprisonment of Constance.

The musketeers did not have much to do with the siege and led a carefree life. One evening they encountered two horsemen on a lonely road. One was the cardinal on his way to a nearby inn. The cardinal ordered the musketeers to go with him. Lady de Winter was at the inn, and the musketeers overheard the cardinal instruct her to go to London, where she was to tell Buckingham that unless he ended the war his affair with the queen would be exposed. If he refused, Lady de Winter was to poison him. As her reward Lady de Winter asked to have two of her enemies killed. These two were Constance, who had been conveyed to a convent by an order the queen had obtained from the king, and D'Artagnan. Richelieu then wrote out a safe-conduct for Lady de Winter.

A few minutes later, Athos, who had recognized her voice, was in Lady de Winter's room. There he revealed himself as the Count de la Fere, her husband. She was terrified, for she had thought him dead as well. Athos took the cardinal's letter of safe-conduct from her and ordered her to leave France at once under threats of exposure.

The four friends returned to the siege of La Rochelle, where they conducted themselves with such bravery that they again drew notice from the cardinal. When the cardinal spoke of them to their captain, he said that D'Artagnan was not in the service of the Musketeers. The cardinal then gave orders that D'Artagnan was to be made a musketeer, and this news, when relayed to D'Artagnan, made him very happy. The friends now wrote out a message to warn Lord de Winter against his sister-in-law and sent Planchet to deliver it. They also sent a message to a cousin of Aramis and learned from her the name of the convent in which Constance had been confined.

When Lady de Winter arrived in England, she was held a prisoner by Lord de Winter. Her pretense of religious fervor and her beauty, however, convinced her young Puritan jailer of her innocence. After she had told him a fantastic tale to the effect that her downfall had been caused by Buckingham, he helped her to escape. To avenge her, he then went to Buckingham and stabbed him. Having discovered her escape, de Winter also hurried to Buckingham but arrived too late to save his life. Before he died, a messenger from Paris brought Buckingham word from the queen of her faithful love.

Lady de Winter escaped to the convent in France where Constance was staying. There she managed to poison Constance and flee again before the four companions arrived to rescue the queen's faithful servant. Lord de Winter, also in pursuit of Lady de Winter, arrived a few minutes after they had discovered Constance. Continuing their pursuit of Lady de Winter, they overtook her and held a trial. They condemned her to die. She was executed by the public executioner of Lille, who had branded her for her crimes many years before.

On his return to La Rochelle, D'Artagnan was arrested and taken to the cardinal. The man who took him prisoner was the stranger D'Artagnan had met at Meung, identified now as the Chevalier de Rochefort. The cardinal charged D'Artagnan with treason, but D'Artagnan interrupted and named the long list of crimes of the woman who had charged him. Then he informed the cardinal of her death and produced the safe-conduct pass, signed by the cardinal, which Athos had taken from the woman. D'Artagnan told Richelieu that as bearer of the pass he should be allowed to go free. The cardinal was so pleased by the Gascon's cleverness that he could not be angry. Instead, he offered D'Artagnan a commission in the Musketeers. D'Artagnan offered it to his friends, but each refused it, insisting that he deserved the rank, an honor that great nobles often sought in vain.

La Rochelle surrendered to the French, and the faithful four disbanded. Athos returned to his estate, Porthos married a rich widow, and Aramis became an abbé. D'Artagnan became a famous soldier. He and de Rochefort, his old enemy, fought three times but finally became good friends.

Critical Evaluation:

The Three Musketeers was Alexandre Dumas' most popular novel and the one he personally considered his best. It has retained its popularity, in spite of some weaknesses. The characterization is sketchy. The dialogue, by modern, realistic standards, is often long-winded and full of preposterous declarations of adoration, fidelity, patriotism, and other noble sentiments. Dumas' dialogue shows the influence of that early genius of the historical novel, Sir Walter Scott. That *The Three Musketeers* has survived with so many generations of readers is due to Dumas' talent for describing violent action and tempestuous love affairs while maintaining suspense for nearly eight hundred pages.

An example of Dumas' craftsmanship can be seen in chapter 47, "The Council of the Musketeers." In this chapter, D'Artagnan consults with Athos, Porthos, and Aramis about how to foil the insidious schemes of Cardinal Richelieu. This could be a dull, static scene, but Dumas dramatizes it by placing his devil-may-care heroes in a bastion where they are under attack by waves of enemy soldiers. From masterful scenes such as this, professional writers of many lands have learned how to maintain suspense and avoid stretches of dreary exposition. The scene furnishes an excellent example of what American novelist Henry James meant when he advised fiction writers: "Dramatize, dramatize, dramatize!"

What made *The Three Musketeers* the best and most successful of Dumas' five or six hundred volumes was the sinister character of Cardinal Richelieu. The machinations of this seventeenth century political genius are like the mainspring in a clock that keeps the entire mechanism running. All the other characters in the book are either acting under his orders or reacting to foil a scheme he has set in motion.

The main plot running throughout *The Three Musketeers* has to do with D'Artagnan and his three friends trying to prevent Richelieu from exposing Queen Anne's love affair with the duke of Buckingham. Richelieu is like Professor Moriarty in some of the Sherlock Holmes stories of Sir Arthur Conan Doyle. Whether he is present or absent in the story, his influence can be felt. Richelieu comes to admire his resourceful, courageous opponent D'Artagnan and is forced to capitulate.

Dumas, one of the most successful writers of all time, had a strong influence over novelists for decades to come. He had a genius for plotting and understood that the most important element in a plot is a strongly motivated protagonist who will not stop until he has either achieved his goal or gone down in defeat. Richelieu is the protagonist in *The Three Musketeers* and the queen of France is his antagonist. D'Artagnan and his comrades are major characters in the novel but only minor figures in the historical context of the enormously complicated military, political, and religious conflict that embroiled most of Europe in bloodshed and destruction during the Thirty Years' War. In the novel, Richelieu is trying to undermine Queen Anne's influence over her husband King Louis XIII because she is a member of the powerful Hapsburg family, rulers of both Austria and Spain, and Richelieu's unrelenting enemies.

Dumas started his career as a dramatist and continued to write plays all his life. This valuable experience had a strong influence on his success as a novelist, because he filled his novels with dramatic scenes and impassioned dialogue. Fortunately, not all his dialogue is flowery and unrealistic: He acquired a reputation for writing whole pages of one-line verbal exchanges full of tension and information. This kind of dialogue writing is realistic and engrossing.

Dumas' action-packed plots, colorful scenes, and dramatic dialogue made his novels good candidates for motion picture adaptation. *The Three Musketeers* has been made into film repeatedly. The flamboyant costuming of the musketeers, with their enormous plumed hats, was one of the more interesting visual features that appeal to filmmakers. Another sure-fire ingredient is the many scenes in which the musketeers rode galloping thoroughbreds along dark roads infested with the cardinal's soldiers and spies. A third ingredient of audience appeal is the armed clashes that sometimes involve as many as a dozen skillful swordsmen. A fourth ingredient is the many love scenes the story provided.

Dumas knew how to please an audience; his works have taught succeeding generations. He was not the best writer of his time but probably the most popular. He was admired by writers like the great Victor Hugo, who was a far more polished and serious craftsman. Dumas earned fortunes from his writings and squandered the money on women and dissipation until his fantastic energy and inspiration ran out, and he died in poverty. He was not unlike his most famous characters, D'Artagnan, Athos, Porthos, and Aramis, who lived with gusto, fought many duels, drank a dozen bottles of wine at a sitting, and scattered gold coins to innkeepers and servants with regal liberality.

"Critical Evaluation" by Bill Delaney

Bibliography:
Hemmings, F. W. J. *Alexandre Dumas: The King of Romance*. New York: Charles Scribner's Sons, 1979. Illustrations and copious endnotes. Chapter 9, "The Novelist," discusses *The Three Musketeers* at length and describes Dumas' transition from playwright to novelist.
Maurois, Andre. *Alexandre Dumas: A Great Life in Brief*. New York: Alfred A. Knopf, 1955. Short but still authoritative and dramatic biography by the distinguished French author, dealing primarily with Dumas *père*. Several chapters discuss aspects of *The Three Musketeers*.
_____. *The Titans: A Three-Generation Biography of the Dumas*. Translated by Gerard Hopkins. New York: Harper & Row, 1957. This definitive biography of Dumas, his swashbuckling father, and his son (Dumas *fils*) was originally written in French by one of France's leading writers. A section deals with Dumas' most famous novel, *The Three Musketeers*, and its sequels.
Ross, Michael. *Alexandre Dumas*. North Pomfret, Vt.: David & Charles, 1981. One of the few books about Dumas originally written in English, this excellent biography highlights Dumas' collaboration with anonymous writers to produce his prodigious output of five to six hundred

novels, plays, travel books, and miscellaneous works. Ross discusses Dumas' colorful reputation and the truth about his character. Many references to *The Three Musketeers.* Bibliography.

Schopp, Claude. *Alexandre Dumas: Genius of Life.* Translated by A. J. Koch. New York: Franklin Watts, 1988. This biography focuses on Dumas' personal life, full of romance and adventure, with many love affairs and duels. Describes how Dumas earned and squandered fortunes and died in poverty. Many references to *The Three Musketeers.*

THE THREE SISTERS

Type of work: Drama
Author: Anton Chekhov (1860-1904)
Type of plot: Impressionistic realism
Time of plot: Nineteenth century
Locale: Russia
First performed: 1901; first published, 1901 as *Tri sestry* (revised, 1904; English translation, 1920)

> *Principal characters:*
> ANDREY PROZÒROV, a student
> NATASHA, his fiancée, later his wife
> OLGA,
> MASHA, and
> IRINA, his three sisters
> FYODOR KULIGIN, Masha's husband
> ALEXANDR VERSHININ, a battery commander
> BARON TUSENBACH, a lieutenant
> VASSILY SOLYONY, a captain
> IVAN TCHEBUTYKIN, an army doctor

The Story:

On Irina's name-day, her friends and family called to wish her happiness. It was exactly one year since the death of her father, who had been sent from Moscow eleven years before to this provincial town at the head of a brigade. Irina and her sister Olga longed to go back to Moscow, and Masha would have liked to go too, except that she had married Kuligin, whom she once thought the cleverest of men. They all pinned their hopes on their brother Andrey now, who was studying to become a professor.

An old army doctor, Tchebutykin, brought Irina a samovar because he had loved her mother. Masha's husband gave her a copy of the history of the high school in which he taught; he said he had written it having had nothing better to do. When Irina told him that he had already given her a copy for Easter, he merrily handed it over to one of the army men who was calling. Tusenbach and Solyony quarreled halfheartedly because Tusenbach and Irina had decided that what they needed for happiness was work. Tusenbach had never done anything but go to cadet school, and Irina's father had prepared his children only in languages. Both had a desire to labor hard at something.

When Vershinin, the new battery commander, came to call, he reminded the girls that he had lived on the same street with them in Moscow. He praised their town, but they said they would rather go to Moscow. They believed that they had been oppressed with an education that was useless in a dull provincial town. Vershinin thought that for every intelligent person then living, there would be many more later on, and that the whole earth would be unimaginably beautiful two or three hundred years hence. He thought it might be interesting to relive one's life to see if one could improve on the first version.

Natasha came in while they were still sitting at the dinner table. Olga criticized her dress, and the men began to tease her about an engagement. Andrey, who could not stand having her teased, followed her out of the room and begged her to marry him. She accepted.

After their marriage, Andrey lost any ambition he had ever had to become a professor; he spent much of his time gambling, trying to forget how ill-bred, rude, and selfish Natasha really was. Irina, meanwhile, had taken a job in the telegraph office, and Olga was teaching in the high school. Tired when they came home at night, they let Natasha run the house as she pleased, even to moving Irina out of her own bedroom so that Natasha and Andrey's baby could have it.

Vershinin had fallen in love with Masha, though he felt bound to his neurotic wife because of his two daughters. Kuligin realized what was going on but cheerfully hoped Masha still loved him. Tusenbach, afraid that life would always be difficult, decided to give up his commission and seek happiness in a workingman's life. Vershinin was convinced that by living, working, and struggling people can create a better life. Because his wife periodically tried to commit suicide, he looked for happiness not for himself but for his descendants.

Andrey asked Tchebutykin to prescribe for his shortness of breath, but the old doctor swore he had forgotten all the medical knowledge he had ever known. Solyony fell in love with Irina, who would have nothing to do with him. He declared that he would have no happy rivals.

One night, all gathered to have a party with mummers who were to come in. Natasha decided that the baby was not well and called off the party at the last minute. Then Protopopov, the chairman of the rural board, came by with his carriage to take Natasha riding while Andrey sat reading in his room.

A short time later, fire destroyed part of the town. Olga gave most of her clothes to those whose homes had been burned and, after the fire, invited the army people to sleep at the house. Natasha berated Olga for letting her old servant sit in her presence and finally suggested that Olga herself move out of the house. The old doctor became drunk because he had prescribed incorrectly for a woman who had died. After the fire, people wanted him to help them, but he could not. In disgust, he picked up a clock and smashed it.

Masha, more bored than before, gave up playing the piano. She was disgusted, too, because Andrey had mortgaged the house in order to give money to Natasha. Everyone but he knew that Natasha was having an affair with Protopopov, to whose rural board Andrey had recently been elected.

Irina, at twenty-four, could not find work to suit her, and she believed she was forgetting everything she had ever known. Olga persuaded her to consider marrying Tusenbach, even if he was ugly; with him Irina might get to Moscow. Masha confessed that she was in love with Vershinin and that he loved her, though he was unable to leave his children.

Andrey berated his sisters for treating his wife so badly and then confessed that he had mortgaged the house that belonged to all four of them. He had so hoped they could all be happy together. Irina heard a report that the brigade would move out of town. If that happened, they would have to go to Moscow because no one worth speaking to would be left.

On the day the first battery was to leave, the officers came to say their farewells to the sisters. Kuligin told Masha that Tusenbach and Solyony had had words because both of them were in love with her and she had promised to marry Tusenbach. Kuligin eagerly anticipated the departure of the brigade because he hoped Masha would then turn back to him. Masha was bored and spiteful. She felt that she was losing, bit by bit, whatever small happiness she had had.

Andrey wondered how he could love Natasha when he knew she was so vulgar. The old doctor claimed that he was tired of their troubles, and he advised Andrey to walk off and never look back. Yet the doctor himself, who was to be retired from the army in a year, planned to come back to live with them because he really loved them all.

Irina hoped to go off with Tusenbach. Olga intended to live at the school of which she was now headmistress. Natasha, expecting to be left in sole charge of the house, planned all sorts of changes to wipe away the memory of the sisters' having been there. Andrey wondered how his children could possibly overcome the influence of their mother's vulgarity.

Tusenbach fought a duel with Solyony, and Tchebutykin returned to tell them that Tusenbach had been killed. The sisters were left alone with their misery, each thinking that she must go on with her life merely to find out why people suffer so much in a world that had the potential to be beautiful.

Critical Evaluation:

The Three Sisters, which received its premiere in January, 1901, is the first play Anton Chekhov wrote specifically for the Moscow Art Theatre. The play was directed by co-founder Konstantin Stanislavsky, the great teacher and originator of a technique of acting, and the cast included Olga Knipper, Chekhov's future wife, in the role of Masha. Although it was not immediately successful with the critics, *The Three Sisters* has become the most frequently performed of the Chekhov canon.

Ill with tuberculosis and therefore forced to remain in the warm climate of Yalta, Chekhov instilled much of his own frustration and longing for culture and civilization into the sisters' dream of returning to Moscow. Olga, Masha, and Irina feel overwhelmed and smothered by the banality of their provincial backwater town. They had been educated for a society in which people had an appreciation of language and conversation and had perfected a graceful style of living, but that society was fast becoming obsolete. Confused and lacking resources, the sisters search for a fulfilling existence, represented by the dream of returning to Moscow. There, they believe, they could be engaged in activities commensurate with their talents, and life would be meaningful.

The Moscow existence is no more than an idealization of the past, however. Vershinin's entrance in the first act revivifies the time and environment of their Moscow girlhood, but, as a friend of the sisters' father, he is a remnant of a past time. The sisters must somehow learn to exist in the changing world of the present. That present is represented by Natasha, who comes from a new middle class and is less educated, less sensitive, and less humane. In fact, she is downright greedy and grasping, one of the few unpleasant characters that Chekhov ever created.

As the skeptical doctor Tchebutykin says, "life is ugly and petty, happiness an illusion, and the only cure for despair is work." The ideal of work, which in the eyes of Tusenbach and Irina, is the means to fulfillment and the solution to boredom, replaces the dream of Moscow. Irina's position in the telegraph office is not satisfying, however, and Tusenbach's management of the brick factory never reaches fruition. The others encounter equal disillusion: Olga's elevation to headmistress only represents more work, Masha's love relationship is doomed, and Andrey's ambitions to become a professor are fantasy. Vershinin's optimistic claim that life will be better in the future suggests a present of compromise and resignation. Throughout the play, the tension increases between the hope of fulfillment and the disappointment of reality, underscoring Chekhov's themes of the absurdity of the human condition and the futility of the quest for meaning in life.

The external action of the play concerns the Prozòrov sisters' gradual physical dispossession at the hands of Natasha. Chekhov's descriptions of the settings, the seasons of the year, and the times of day contribute to this development. Irina's pleasant name-day party of the first act occurs on the fifth of May; spring and hope are in the atmosphere, although as Olga remarks, the birches have not yet budded. It is a bright, sunny noontime, and the clock is striking twelve.

The action sprawls through the living and dining rooms. The second act occurs on a winter evening. The same setting is now darkened and constricted by the presence of Natasha and her vulgar taste. It is Shrovetide, but the carnival maskers are not permitted in the house. In the third act, Natasha has successfully even usurped more space and has consigned Olga and Irina to a small bedroom. The time is even later, between two and three in the morning, and outside a fire rages in the town.

In the fourth act, autumn has arrived, the cranes are migrating, and the leaves falling, creating a sense of farewell and resignation. Although it is noon again, Chekhov ironically contrasts the scene with the first act by setting it outside, visually conveying that the sisters have been ousted from their home by Natasha and her progeny.

Chekhov's use of sound effects is particularly notable. Seemingly insignificant by themselves, various mundane sounds echo through the play, not only creating an atmosphere but also commenting ironically on the characters and their situation. In the first production, Chekhov strenuously objected to Stanislavsky's attempts to add to the effects that had been so carefully inserted in the text. There are bells—sleighbells on Protopopov's troika, chiming bells on the clock, and the anxious alarm bell of the fire—footsteps, tappings, and musical instruments. among them, piano, violin, accordion, and a band. In the first moments of the play, Olga remembers how the band played at their father's funeral. In the final moments, the band plays more and more softly, as the brigade leaves town and the Prozòrovs' new lives begin. The clock strikes twelve as Olga speaks in the first act, Tchebutykin breaks the clock in the third act just as the dream of Moscow is shattered. Masha whistles somberly before meeting Vershinin; afterward they communicate their love through musical phrases. Tusenbach plays the piano in the first scene, and offstage Andrey plays the violin. In the last act, someone plays "The Maiden's Prayer" on the piano as the hope of Irina's marriage dies.

Some critics view the sisters as passive victims of social conditions, who lack the aggression and ingenuity necessary to realize their dreams and to better their lives. Others claim that the sisters strive to resist banality and consider that Masha's great love, Irina's decision to marry the baron, and Olga's acceptance of the headmistress position represent that active resistance.

The Three Sisters is a cleverly crafted, realistic play with neither heroes nor villains and without any startling theatrical effects (both the fire and the duel occur offstage). Chekhov has created a group of ordinary people, existing in a particular time and place, whose dreams of a better life are shared by all in any time and place.

"Critical Evaluation" by Joyce E. Henry

Bibliography:
Barricelli, Jean-Pierre, ed. *Chekhov's Great Plays: A Critical Anthology.* New York: New York University Press, 1981. An excellent collection of critical essays, of which four directly pertain to the play. One deals with the love theme, another discusses Vershinin, the third analyzes cyclical patterns and triads, and the fourth compares the women characters of the four major plays.
Clyman, Toby W., ed. *A Chekhov Companion.* Westport, Conn.: Greenwood Press, 1985. An eclectic work examining many aspects of the plays and stories. Specific essays focus on Chekhov's craftsmanship, his impact in the theater, and performance on stage and in film. Good bibliography.
Melchinger, Siegfried. *Anton Chekhov.* Translated by Edith Tarcov. New York: Frederick Ungar, 1972. A slim volume of fewer than two hundred pages with photographs and selected

bibliography. A good starting point for the student, containing biographical material, an analysis of Chekhov's craft, and discussions of individual plays and productions in Europe and America.

Troyat, Henri. *Chekhov*. Translated by Michael Henry Heim. New York: E. P. Dutton, 1986. A readable biography with rare photographs of the author. Includes an interesting description of the writing of *The Three Sisters* and the reception of the first production.

Wellek, René, and Nonna D. Wellek, eds. *Chekhov: New Perspectives*. Englewood Cliffs, N.J.: Prentice-Hall, 1984. A brief collection of eight essays with a good discussion of *The Three Sisters,* as well as a historical review of criticism, typical dramatic structure, and Chekhov's artistic development.

THREE SOLDIERS

Type of work: Novel
Author: John Dos Passos (1896-1970)
Type of plot: Social realism
Time of plot: 1917-1919
Locale: France
First published: 1921

Principal characters:
DAN FUSELLI, an American soldier from San Francisco
CHRISFIELD, an American soldier from Indiana
JOHN ANDREWS (ANDY), an American soldier from Virginia
GENEVIÈVE ROD, Andrews' friend

The Story:

Private Dan Fuselli was anxious to become Corporal Dan Fuselli. He had seen motion pictures of Huns spitting Belgian babies on their bayonets and then being chased like rabbits by heroic Yankee soldiers who were later rewarded with embraces by pretty Belgian milkmaids. He looked forward to the time when his girl, Mabe, writing from San Francisco, his hometown, would address her letters to Corporal Dan Fuselli.

Private First Class Fuselli of the Medical Corps hated the Army and everything about it, but he knew that to become a corporal he must keep clean, keep his mouth shut, obey the brass, and continually cajole the sergeant. He was infuriated one night when he went to town to see Yvonne and learned that the sergeant had taken her over. Then, when he returned to camp, he heard that the consumptive corporal was back, the one in whose absence Fuselli had been made acting corporal. Private Fuselli, however, kept his mouth shut. Someday he would be a corporal, perhaps even a sergeant, but for the time being he kept his mouth shut. Finally, after a setback doing endless kitchen police duty and following his recovery from a venereal disease, and after the Armistice, he did become Corporal Dan Fuselli; by that time, his girl had married a naval officer.

Matters worked out differently for Chrisfield. The Army was not as easygoing as life in the Indiana farm country had been. The officers shouted at the men and then made them do things that they hated, but it had to be withstood. One night, Chrisfield was so furious he pulled a knife on a sergeant named Anderson, but his friends held him back and nothing happened. In Europe, life was not much better. Occasionally, he had a talk about the stars and the fields with his educated buddy, John Andrews. Mostly, however, the war was awful.

The marches were endless, and his shoulders ached from his heavy pack. When bombardments came, the marchers scattered face down in a field. Once Chrisfield asked Andrews to speak French for him to a French girl at an inn, but nothing came of it. One day, walking alone through a wood near the front, Chrisfield found a dead German lying prone. When he kicked the body over, he saw that it had no face, only a multicolored, pulpy mass with green flies hovering around it. In the man's hand was a revolver—he was a suicide. Chrisfield ran off panting.

Chrisfield was high-strung. When he was sitting thinking, a soldier prodded him and asked him what he was dreaming about. Chrisfield punched the fellow in the nose. He and Andy hated the YMCA men who were always telling the men at the front what brutes the Huns were and urging them in the name of Old Glory to kill Germans. Chrisfield was court-martialed when he announced that he intended to kill Sergeant Anderson after the war was over. One day, he went wandering and made his way silently into the kitchen of a house near the front. Looking into the next room, he saw a man in a German uniform. He reached into his pocket, pressed the spring on the grenade he had, withdrew it, and tossed it into the room. Not long afterward he came across Anderson, now a lieutenant, seated wounded in a deserted section of the wood. Chrisfield had two more grenades in his pocket, and he threw them at the man he hated. After the armistice, the rumor that he had killed Anderson somehow leaked out. Afraid, Chrisfield went A.W.O.L. and became a refugee in France, eternally on the move.

John Andrews was a Harvard graduate and a would-be composer. An idea for a musical composition came to him as he washed the barracks' windows. He cursed the Army for slowly stamping him into its iron mold. Overseas, he saw action and was more convinced than ever that war was needless butchery. He felt happiest away from the regiment. One day, he walked away from his company in order to be alone. He was looking at little frogs in a pool when a shell burst near him. He awoke on a stretcher. For a while, the hospital was a relief from the endless orders and general mechanization of Army routine. Lying in his bed, he began to realize that he had respect for himself only when he thought of rebelling against the system, of going A.W.O.L. Soon the tedium of the hospital began to gall him. After his leg healed, he rejoined his company reluctantly, full of rebellion. The Armistice had been signed. When he heard that he could go to a French university through a school detachment being set up, he lied, secured some recommendations, and found himself in Paris.

In Paris, he met Geneviève Rod, a young Frenchwoman who admired his piano playing and his artistic tastes. She thought of artists as men who, because of their special sensitivity, should be exempt from the horrors of war. Andrews disagreed; one worker was like another; it was the whole of humanity who should be exempt. One day, he left Paris without official leave for a country trip with Geneviève. He was picked up and taken to a local office where he was beaten by the military policemen on a lieutenant's orders. He was sent to a labor battalion loading concrete for a stadium being presented by the Americans to the French. It was crushing work. Convinced that Army life was a menace to human freedom, Andrews decided to desert, for one man less in the system made it weaker by that much. One night, he leaped from a plank and swam out to a barge in the Seine.

The barge family cared for him for a few days. They sank his uniform in the river, bought him new clothes, and, as anarchists, proclaimed their solidarity with him. He went back to Paris to find Geneviève, and stayed for a while with Chrisfield and a group of other concealed deserters. Then, hearing that Geneviève was at her country place, he joined her there. At first, he did not tell her of his desertion. He lived in an inn nearby and began composing, not about the queen of Sheba, but about John Brown, liberator of slaves, using the musical ideas that had first come to him while washing the barracks' windows. When he finally confessed his plight to Geneviève, a noticeable reserve crept into her attitude toward him. Perhaps, she suggested, he should give himself up. She could not comprehend the motive for his rebellion, and left with her family to the seashore, leaving him behind.

One day he heard an American officer's voice at the door of the inn below his window. He thought of the prison sentence he must face. Too late he discovered that the landlady, who had betrayed him to the military police, had stolen his revolver. As the MP's took him away, the wind blew in through the window of his room, and the music papers on which he had been working fluttered one by one to the floor.

Critical Evaluation:

Having served in France during World War I as an ambulance driver and then as a private in the Medical Corps, Dos Passos was thoroughly conversant with the military life of an enlisted man and was able to give it a vivid and realistic portrayal. He was the first American novelist since Stephen Crane to use war as a theme for fiction, but went far beyond his predecessors in showing the immorality and brutality of the military machine, not toward the enemy but to its individual atoms, the soldiers.

The analogy with the machine is clearly seen in the six subheadings of the novel: "Making the Mould," "The Metal Cools," "Machines," "Rust," "The World Outside," and the final section, "Under the Wheels." In counterpoint to this structure are the narratives of the three soldiers who represent the diverse American experience. Fuselli, the urban ethnic who tries to get ahead by obsequiously cooperating with the machine's agents, dominates the first two sections. Chrisfield, the Indiana farm boy, is the principal figure in the third part. Andrews, the Virginia-born aristocratic aesthete, is the central figure of the final three sections. All three of the soldiers appear in each of the sections, but toward the end Fuselli is only referred to by one of the deserters as a way of the author's concluding Fuselli's narrative. Andrews increasingly becomes the dominant figure of the novel as a whole, first as the intellectual who interprets the actions that occur and finally as the personage with whom readers may identify.

Andrews' portrait is the most complex, and he is gradually revealed as first composer and aesthete, then as a music critic in civilian life, and finally as a Harvard graduate. The musical context is not always accurate and has been even disparaged as name-dropping. Thoroughly authentic, though, is Andrews' outrage at the mindless and petty indignities and harassments to which he is subjected, culminating in his beating by the military police because he failed to salute an officer and his subsequent ordeal in the labor battalion.

Although *Three Soldiers* does not incorporate the stylistic devices (such as the "Camera Eye," "Newsreel," and biographical snippets) of such later works as the *U.S.A.* trilogy (1937), his use of alternating narrative segments anticipates the later work's more complex structure. The author's use of contrast and juxtaposition to achieve an effect of irony, the dreams, and the equivalent of cinematic still images do appear, however, although in a conventional novelistic structure, in *Three Soldiers*.

Although *Three Soldiers* has often been called an anarchistic novel, ideology as such, like combat, appears in the background: The bargeman who saves and shelters Andrews after his escape from the labor battalion is an anarchist. The reader meets a similar type in Eisenstein, the older man who is drafted and is mysteriously taken away from Fuselli's company because of his subversive ideas. Yet much of Andrews' rage is aesthetic rather than ideological.

The language is straightforward, more like that of Crane than of Dos Passos' later *U.S.A.* trilogy. Snatches of popular songs are often used to capture fleeting moods. Although in the dialogue profanity is frequent, there is none of the pervasive obscenity that many subsequent writers have used to lend realism to novels of World War II and after. Some readers may be repelled by the casual use of racial and ethnic slurs, but such were common in the early years of the century, especially among the uneducated.

One common theme affects each of the three protagonists: Although each has a goal, his difficulties with the Army prevent him from achieving a sense of order in his life. Fuselli is constantly thwarted despite his compliant behavior and acceptance of the system. He finally achieves his dream of becoming a corporal, but readers are left to infer that he has achieved it at the cost of everything else. Readers last see him as one of the lowest specimens of Army life, permanent kitchen police. Chrisfield's conflict with Anderson is not really clarified for readers, but in life many conflicts that end in murder are all but impossible to clarify. The portrayal of Andrews has been considered unrealistic because of the overripe prose of his speech and of his interior monologues, but one must remember that Andrews is an aesthete of the early twentieth century.

The subordinate characters are unevenly portrayed. The two groups disdained the most by the author, the officers and the "Y men" (agents of the Young Men's Christian Association, who sought to inculcate hatred of the enemy) are referred to only by rank or occupation, very rarely by name. The love interest with Geneviève is not consummated; Andrews avoids opportunities to enhance the relationship, often by refusing to play his compositions or those of others. The central thesis is the essential mindlessness and cruelty of the mass organization as shown by the fates of the three characters who are crushed by it. Throughout his career Dos Passos displayed a fear and hatred of bureaucratic power and of its agents, whether in the anarchism of his early works, in his disillusionment with communism, and in his turning to political conservatism in his later years.

Three Soldiers had a mixed reception on its appearance. The old American literary establishment had been strongly pro-Allied and at first resented the young novelists who had served in World War I and who exposed it as a sham. Although F. Scott Fitzgerald and H. L. Mencken praised Dos Passos' novel highly, Ernest Hemingway was later to consider its dialogue false and the combat scene unconvincing. Dos Passos' first major novel will always resonate with those who have ever served in the armed forces as enlisted personnel, and its influence can be seen in a major novel of World War II, Norman Mailer's *The Naked and the Dead* (1948).

"Critical Evaluation" by R. M. Longyear

Bibliography:
Brantley, John. *The Fiction of John Dos Passos*. The Hague: Mouton, 1968. Surveys the novels chronologically, discussing the structure of *Three Soldiers* as well conceived but less successfully executed. Shows how each of the three soldiers is destroyed by the military machine.
Clark, Michael. *Dos Passos's Early Fiction*. Selinsgrove, Pa.: Susquehanna University Press, 1987. Considers Walt Whitman's poetry and William James's psychology as the main influences on this novel, and gives a psychological interpretation of the principal characters.
Cooperman, Stanley. "John Dos Passos' *Three Soldiers*." In *The First World War in Fiction*, edited by Holger Klein. London: Macmillan, 1978. Still the standard and most extensive reading of the novel, emphasizing its foreshadowing of the *U.S.A.* trilogy. The editor's excellent introductory essay provides a context for novels about the Great War.
Sanders, David. *John Dos Passos: A Comprehensive Bibliography*. New York: Garland, 1987. The brief annotations are particularly helpful, and a section is devoted to *Three Soldiers*. Especially valuable is the listing of the reviews the novel received when it first appeared.

THE THREEPENNY OPERA

Type of work: Drama
Author: Bertolt Brecht (1898-1956)
Type of plot: Social satire
Time of plot: 1837
Locale: London's Soho district
First performed: 1928; first published, 1929 as *Die Dreigroschenoper* (English translation, 1949)

> *Principal characters:*
> MACHEATH, a master criminal
> JONATHAN JEREMIAH PEACHUM, proprietor of the firm "The Beggar's Friend"
> CELIA PEACHUM, his wife
> POLLY PEACHUM, their daughter
> TIGER BROWN, the police chief of London
> LUCY BROWN, his daughter
> GINNY JENNY, the owner of a brothel
> FILCH, an aspiring beggar

The Story:

The criminal elements of London's Soho district (thieves, beggars, and harlots) plied their various occupations while the balladeer sang about crime increases in the area, because of the reappearance of master criminal Captain James MacHeath ("Mack" or "Mackie the Knife"). The song concluded as Mack strolled down the street, causing occupants to quit their businesses and draw aside.

Jonathan Jeremiah Peachum, as notorious as Mack, headed a beggar's organization that played on the sympathies of wealthier citizens. Filch, an aspiring beggar, applied to Peachum for protection and a suitable costume and paid his fee under protest. Mrs. Celia Peachum aged the costume by staining it. Polly Peachum, their daughter, was out with a man she had met a few days earlier. When Celia described the man, Peachum realized he was Mack the Knife. Celia tried to calm him, and they sang about how young love's magic soured when the novelty wore off.

Mack escorted Polly to their wedding site, an empty stable that his bumbling henchmen, formally dressed for the wedding, readied for celebration by stealing furniture and even food for the banquet. Unfortunately, the henchmen had no taste and everything was wrong, even the dirge they sang as a wedding hymn to honor the couple. A minister came to perform the ceremony, and Polly entertained everyone with a song about the revenge of the downtrodden on their social superiors. Mack's best friend, Tiger Brown, chief of the London police, appeared, and after reassuring Mack that his police record was wiped clean, the chief joined Mack in singing about being army buddies.

To her parents, Polly explained her marriage to Mack by saying that a "proper" man was not, necessarily, the "right" man. Peachum's scolding was interrupted by the beggars, but he decided to bribe Mack's harlots to turn on Mack. Polly boasted about the relationship between Tiger and Mack, but the Peachums reproached her by singing that "the world is poor and men are bad."

Polly ran to the stable and warned Mack of plans for his arrest. He agreed to leave town, provided Polly would agree to collect his share from his thieves, send the money to his banker, and then turn the thieves over to the police. She agreed, and the newly arrived thieves swore their allegiance to her. She sang of her heartbreak at losing Mack.

Celia bribed Ginny Jenny to turn in Mack, and they plotted his betrayal while singing "The Ballad of Sexual Submissiveness." Mack hid out in Jenny's brothel, where Jenny entertained him, and they sang about the days when they lived together. When the police raided the establishment, Mack attempted to escape through the window, but Celia and more police were waiting for him.

In prison, Mack refused to acknowledge Tiger's apologies for arresting him. After Tiger left, Mack attempted to bribe the jailer, singing about the "luxurious" life. Lucy Brown, Tiger's daughter, visited Mack to tell him she was pregnant with his child. When Polly arrived, Mack pretended to scorn her so that Lucy would not tell her father about her pregnancy. Polly and Lucy baited each other in "The Jealousy Duet." After Celia appeared and dragged Polly away, Mackie persuaded Lucy to help him escape. Tiger and Peachum discovered Mack's escape, and Peachum blackmailed Tiger into re-arresting him. Meanwhile, Jenny and Mack sang about how human beings live off one another.

At Peachum's establishment, while the beggars prepared to work the crowds lining the streets for queen Victoria's coronation, Jenny and her girls came by to claim their reward, but Celia refused to give it until Mack was reincarcerated. Tiger burst in and attempted to arrest everyone, but Peachum outwitted him and sent him to Sulky Tawdry's to find Mack. Peachum sang about life's futility, while Jenny sang about life's absurdities. Polly visited Lucy and they became friendly, with Lucy admitting she was not actually pregnant. Celia brought Polly news of Mack's impending execution and a widow's veil.

Back in prison, Mack sang of his despair as he tried to borrow money from his henchmen to bribe his jailer. Polly arrived, but she had no money, either. The only salvation for Mack was a queen's pardon. Tiger came with Mack's last meal. Mack paid Tiger the protection money he owed, and all of Mack's friends entered to say good-bye. There was such a crowd for his execution that no one was attending the coronation. Mack was standing on the gallows, when, at the last moment, the queen's messenger appeared with a full pardon, which also gave Mack a castle and a pension. Peachum sermonized the moral of the piece: "Life was hard, and pardons seldom came." Everyone sang a reinforcement of the moral.

Critical Evaluation:

Bertolt Brecht was one of the greatest innovators of theatrical productions and dramatic theory of the twentieth century. His approach to theater emerged from the German expressionists school, which reflected the alienation from society caused by expanding technological industrialism, as well as the discontent and disorientation that followed World War I. His first theatrical success, *The Threepenny Opera*, which received its premiere on August 28, 1928, took Berlin by storm. Jarring, jangling, irreverent, amusing, scintillating, cynical, exciting, and unnerving, the play brought international fame to Brecht.

To some extent, however, the play confirmed critics in their uneasy feelings about Brecht the creative artist: Was Bertolt Brecht a genius or a plagiarist? A joke, current in Berlin at the time, went to the heart of their uneasiness: "Who wrote it?"—"Brecht."—"All right. Who wrote it?"

The Threepenny Opera was perfect fodder for a charge of plagiarism. It was an adaptation of *The Beggar's Opera*, a 1728 ballad opera by the English playwright John Gay. Brecht's secretary had translated the first few scenes into German, but when the play was accepted for production, Brecht rushed the preparation of the script, lifting entire scenes, characters, and dialogue from the original. Rather than using the original songs and score, Brecht drew on a file of his own song lyrics and poems based on translations of the medieval French poet François Villon and the English Victorian poet-novelist Rudyard Kipling. To this mix, he added a heavy sprinkling of Bible verses. Even the most famous line from the play, "Food comes first, and then morality," originated with the German Romantic playwright Friedrich von Schiller. If Brecht escaped the accusation of plagiarism, it was because he blended the many borrowings to make a uniquely original concoction.

While *The Threepenny Opera* presented a criticism of society during the 1920's, Brecht chose to date the action at the time of Queen Victoria's coronation (1837) and to place it in London's Soho area. Berliners, who were enthralled by American gangsterism, nevertheless saw past the time and place into the references to their age. A part of Brecht's genius was that he anticipated the audience's recognition.

It was a tribute to Brecht's theatrical sense that he secured the services of the young composer Kurt Weill to provide the score for the production. Weill's music was in large part responsible for making the production the success that it became, for his compositions were as avant-garde as Brecht's lyrics and theories. Influenced by such diverse sources as a classical training and American jazz, Weill provided music that was perfect for the play: a pastiche of jazz, cabaret, operetta, and vaudeville. It was fresh, irreverent, new, and startling, and it satirized opera and traditional serious music with a jangling sound akin to a berserk hurdy-gurdy that, while it grated on the ears, excited and stimulated listeners.

Oddly enough, what made Brecht's presentational style engrossing was not stylistic consistency but the element of the anachronistic, which was subtle enough not to call attention to itself. In *The Threepenny Opera*, for example, Brecht drew on Chicago gangsters, modern music, and a Roaring Twenties atmosphere in an eighteenth century play set in nineteenth century England.

Eventually Brecht's ideas coalesced into his credo for epic theater. Even at the time of *The Threepenny Opera*, Brecht was reading Aristotle. The term epic theater was not original with Brecht; like so much of his work, it was borrowed from the German playwright and impresario Erwin Piscator, who had used the term to describe his presentational style of theater. Brecht used Piscator's term and theories and elaborated and enlarged on them.

In Aristotle's *Poetics* (c. 334-323 B.C.E.), epic and tragic poetry are contrasted. Tragic poetry was represented by the classical Greek dramas and demanded emotional involvement that reached its climax in catharsis. The epic, on the other hand, was a saga without emotional identification by the audience and was didactic in nature.

For Brecht, the social and political critic-commentator, the epic was the ideal method of communication, and he used devices in *The Threepenny Opera* that he would later incorporate into epic theater. The term most often associated with Brecht is the effect of alienation (*Verfremdungseffekt*). He believed that distancing was necessary if the spectators were to take the social message of the play to heart. To this end, Brecht developed his play in short, concise vignettes that were connected by theme rather than chronology; he interrupted the action of the play with songs that, instead of furthering the plot, reinforced the message; he used the machinery of the theater (lights, setting, the stage itself, properties, placards, slogans, signs, and later, projections) to call attention to the fact that the play was theater and not reality; and he recommended that his actors stay emotionally distant from their characters. All of these concepts can be seen in *The Threepenny Opera*. Brecht's influence on other twentieth century authors, producers, and theorists was tremendous and indelible. In many ways, Brecht was synonymous with modern theater.

H. Alan Pickrell

Bibliography:

Brecht, Bertolt. *The Threepenny Opera*. Translated by Ralph Manheim and John Willett. New York: Vintage Books, 1977. In addition to a new translation of the play, this volume contains an appendix with Brecht's extensive notations on how the play should be produced, proposed lyric changes and additional stanzas for the songs, and a letter from Kurt Weill, the composer.

Ewen, Frederic. *Bertolt Brecht: His Life, His Art, and His Times*. New York: The Citadel Press, 1967. Exhaustive examination of Brecht's total oeuvre in chronological sequence. Also examines personages and theories that influenced Brecht's work.

Hayman, Ronald. *Bertolt Brecht*. Totowa, N.J.: Barnes & Noble, 1984. Contains an excellent analysis of major themes and sources for Brecht's plays.

Morley, Michael. *Brecht: A Study*. Totowa, N.J.: Rowman and Littlefield, 1977. Contains a complete discussion of *The Threepenny Opera*. Details how the play was written and analyzes its themes.

Speirs, Ronald. *Bertolt Brecht*. New York: St. Martin's Press, 1987. Contains an analysis of Brecht's evolution as a playwright and charts the evolution of epic theater.

THROUGH THE LOOKING-GLASS
And What Alice Found There

Type of work: Novel
Author: Lewis Carroll (Charles Lutwidge Dodgson, 1832-1898)
Type of plot: Fantasy
Time of plot: Nineteenth century
Locale: The dreamworld of an imaginative child
First published: 1871

Principal characters:
ALICE, a fanciful child
DINAH, a cat
THE BLACK KITTEN
THE WHITE KITTEN
THE WHITE KING and THE WHITE QUEEN
THE RED KING and THE RED QUEEN
GNAT
TWEEDLEDUM and TWEEDLEDEE
HUMPTY DUMPTY
THE LION and THE UNICORN
THE WHITE KNIGHT and THE RED KNIGHT

The Story:

Alice was sure the whole thing was not the white kitten's fault. It must surely have been the fault of the black kitten. Dinah, the mother cat, who had been washing the white kitten's face, certainly had had nothing to do with it. The mischievous black kitten, however, had been unwinding Alice's yarn and in all ways acting naughty enough to cause the whole strange affair.

While the black kitten was curled up in Alice's lap playing with the yarn, Alice told it to pretend that the two of them could go right through the mirror and into the looking-glass house. As she talked, the glass grew misty and soft, and in a moment Alice was through the mirror and in the looking-glass room. The place was very strange; although the room looked just the same as the real room she had seen in the mirror, the clock and the fire and the other things in the room seemed to be alive. Even the chessmen (Alice loved to play chess) were alive.

When Alice picked up the White Queen and set her on the table, the White Queen screamed in terror, thinking that a volcano had shaken her about. The White King had the same fear, but he was too astonished to cry out. They did not seem to see or hear Alice, and although she wanted to stay and watch them and read the king's rather funny poetry, she felt she must look at the garden before she had to go back through the looking glass. When she started down the stairs, she seemed to float, not even once touching the steps.

In the garden, every path Alice took led her straight back to the house. She asked Tiger Lily and Rose and Violet whether there were other people in the garden, hoping they might help her find the right path. The flowers told her there was only one person, and Alice found her to be the Red Queen—but a very strange chess figure, for the Red Queen was taller than Alice herself. As Alice walked toward the Red Queen, she once more found herself back at the door of the house. Then Alice figured out that in order to get to any place in this queer land, one must walk in the opposite direction. She did so and came face-to-face with the Red Queen.

The queen took Alice to the top of a hill. There, spread out below them, was a countryside that looked like a large chessboard. Alice was delighted and said that she would love to play on this board. The Red Queen told her that they would play and that Alice could be the White Queen's pawn and that they would start on the second square. At that moment, though, the Red Queen grabbed Alice's hand and they started to run. Alice had never run so fast in her life, but although she was breathless, the things around them never changed at all. When they finally stopped running, the queen told Alice that in this land one had to run as fast as she could to stay in the same place and twice as fast as she could to get somewhere else. Then the queen showed Alice the pegs in the second square and told her how to move. At the last peg, the Red Queen disappeared, leaving Alice alone to continue the game.

Alice started to run down the hill. The next thing she knew she was on a train filled with insects and having quite an unpleasant time because she did not have a ticket. All the insects talked unkindly to her, and to add to her discomfort, the train jumped over the brook and took them all straight up in the air. When she came down, she was sitting under a tree, talking to Gnat. Gnat was as big as a chicken but very pleasant. He told her about the other insects that lived in the woods; then he too melted away, and Alice had to go on alone.

Turning a corner, she bumped into two fat little men called Tweedledum and Tweedledee, the funniest little creatures she had ever seen. Everything they said seemed to have two meanings. They recited a long poem about a walrus and a carpenter and some oysters. While they were explaining the poem to Alice, she heard a puffing noise, like the sound of a steam engine. Tweedledee told her it was the Red King snoring. Sure enough, they found him asleep. Tweedledee told Alice that the Red King was dreaming about her and that if he stopped dreaming Alice would be gone for good. Alice cried when they told her she was not real but only a part of the Red King's dream.

As she brushed her tears away, she saw Tweedledum staring in terror at something on the ground. It was an old broken rattle, over which the two foolish men got into a terrible fight—that is, they talked a terrible fight, but neither seemed very anxious to have a real battle. The Crow flew over and frightened them so that the funny men ran away into the wood. Alice ran too, and as she ran, she saw a shawl blowing about.

Looking for the owner of the shawl, Alice saw the White Queen running toward her. The White Queen was a very queer person; she lived backward and remembered things before they happened, as when she felt pain before pricking her finger. While the queen was talking, she turned into a sheep and was in a shop with Alice. It was a very curious shop; the shelves were full of things that disappeared when Alice looked at them. Sometimes the boxes went right through the ceiling. Then the sheep gave Alice some needles and told her to knit.

As she started to knit, the needles became oars, and she found herself and the sheep in a little boat rowing in a stream. The oars kept sticking in the water. The sheep explained that the crabs were catching them. Alice picked some beautiful, fragrant rushes that melted away as soon as she picked them. To her surprise, the river and boat soon vanished, and Alice and the sheep were back in the shop. She bought an egg, although in this shop two were cheaper than one, but when she started to get the egg, the egg began to grow larger and larger and more and more real, with eyes, a nose, and a mouth. Then Alice could tell as plain as day that the egg was Humpty Dumpty.

She had a queer conversation with Humpty Dumpty, a conversation filled with riddles. They took turns at choosing the topic to discuss, but even though Alice tried to be polite, most of the subjects turned into arguments. Humpty Dumpty explained to Alice what the "Jabberwocky" poem meant, the one she had seen in the White King's book. Then, while reciting another poem,

Humpty Dumpty stopped right in the middle and said that that was all. Alice thought it very queer but did not tell him so. She thought it time for her to leave, but as she walked away, there was a terrible crash that shook the whole forest.

Thousands of soldiers and horses came rushing toward her, and the riders constantly fell off of their horses. Frightened, she escaped from the wood into the open. There she found the White King, who told her that he had sent the soldiers and horses and that the loud crash she had heard was the noise of the Lion and Unicorn fighting for the crown. She went with the king to watch the fight, which was indeed a terrible one. It was silly of them to fight for the crown, since it belonged to the White King and he had no notion of giving it away. After the fight, Alice met the Unicorn and the Lion. At the king's order, she served them cake, a very strange cake that cut itself when she carried the dish around.

A great noise interrupted the party. When it stopped, Alice thought she might have dreamed the whole thing until the Red Knight came along, followed soon by a White Knight. Each claimed her as a prisoner. Alice thought the whole business silly, since neither of them could do anything except fall off his horse and climb back on again, over and over and over. At last, the Red Knight galloped off, and the White Knight told her that she would be a queen as soon as she crossed the next brook. He was supposed to lead her to the end of the wood, but she spent the whole journey helping him back on his horse each time he fell off. The trip was filled with more queer conversation, but by that time, Alice was used to strange talk from her looking-glass friends. At last, they reached the brook. The knight rode away, and Alice jumped over the brook and into the last square of the chessboard. To her delight, when she reached that square she felt something tight on her head. It was a crown, and she was a queen.

Soon she found the Red Queen and the White Queen confronting her; they were very cross because she thought she was a queen. They gave her a test for queens that she apparently passed, for before long they were calling her "Your Majesty," and inviting people to a party that she was to give. After a time, the Red Queen and the White Queen went to sleep. Alice watched them until they disappeared. Then she found herself before a doorway marked "Queen Alice." All of her new friends were there, including the queens who had just vanished. The party was the most amazing experience of all. Puddings talked, guests poured wine over their heads, and the White Queen turned into a leg of mutton. Alice was exasperated, so much so that she seized the tablecloth and jerked it and everything on it to the floor. Then she grabbed the Red Queen and shook her as she would a kitten. But what was this? It was a kitten she was shaking, the black kitten. Alice talked to Dinah and both the kittens about the adventure they had all experienced, but the silly kittens did nothing but purr.

Critical Evaluation:

It is rare for the sequel to a highly creative literary work to surpass the original. Nevertheless, such is the case with *Through the Looking-Glass, and What Alice Found There*, which followed *Alice's Adventures in Wonderland*, published seven years earlier. For most readers, the two books are so closely entwined that they are considered a unit. Although joined by a common heroine and themes, the characters in the two books are quite distinct. *Through the Looking-Glass* is perhaps more attractive to adults than to children, for this second fantasy by Lewis Carroll (the pen name for the Oxford mathematics lecturer and tutor the Reverend Charles Lutwidge Dodgson) presented an even more sophisticated puzzle about reality and logic than had the earlier story. In *Through the Looking-Glass*, there is a conscious suggestion of the cruel questions rather more delicately presented in *Alice's Adventures in Wonderland*.

The books share many characteristics: Each has twelve chapters, and both merge the fairy tale with science. Alice is seven years old in the first book and seven and a half on her second venture. A slight shift in scene turns the pleasant outdoor summer setting of *Alice's Adventures in Wonderland* into the more somber indoor winter stage of *Through the Looking-Glass*. Corresponding to the card game of the first book is chess in *Through the Looking-Glass*, another game that involves kings and queens. Within the chess-and-mirror framework of the looking-glass world, Carroll has, however, constructed an intricate symbolic plan unlike the seemingly spontaneous movement of Wonderland.

Although medieval and Renaissance sportsmen sometimes enjoyed chess that used human players on a giant field, Carroll seems to have been the first to use the idea in literature. (The science fiction of later ages often employed the technique.) In the game plan, Alice is a white pawn on a giant chessboard of life in which the rows of the board are separated by brooks and the columns by hedges. Alice never speaks to any piece who is not in a square beside her, as is appropriate for the pawn who never knows what is happening except at its spot on the board. Alice remains in the queen's field except for her last move (by which time she has become a queen) when she captures the Red Queen and shakes her into a kitten; as a result, she checkmates the Red King who has slept throughout the game. Her behavior complements the personalities assigned to the other pieces, for each assumes the qualities of the figure it represents. As in chess, the queens are the most powerful and active beings, and the kings are impotent. Erratic and stumbling, the White Knight recalls the movement of the chess knight that moves two squares in any direction, then again one square in a different direction, forming a sort of spastic "L."

Critics have noted inconsistencies in the chess game, charging that the White side makes nine consecutive moves; that the White King is placed in an unnoticed check, the queen's castle; and that the White Queen misses a chance to take the Red Knight. In a later explanatory note, however, Carroll said that the game is correct in relation to the moves, although the alternation of the sides is not strictly consistent, and that the "castling" of the queen is merely his phrase to indicate that they have entered the palace. Not interested in the game as an example of chess strategy, Carroll conceived of it as a learning experience for a child who was to "be" a pawn warring against all the other pieces controlled by an adult, an idea apparently stimulated by the chess tales Carroll had fashioned for Alice Liddell, who was learning the game. Alice, the daughter of the dean of Christ Church, Oxford, had also been the Alice whom he had placed in Wonderland.

Arising inevitably from Carroll's use of this structure has been the proposal that Alice is Everyman and that chess is Life. Like human beings who exists from birth to death only vaguely comprehending the forces directing their moves, Alice never understands her experience. Indeed, none of the pieces really assimilates the total concept of the game. Even the mobile queens do not really grasp the idea that beyond the board there is a room and people who are determining the game. People's own reality thus becomes very unreal if the individual, like the chess pieces, has such a limited perception of the total environment.

Carroll pursues still another definition of reality when Alice confronts the Red King and is told that she exists merely as part of his dreams, not as an objective being. Upsetting to Alice is the sage advice of Tweedledum and Tweedledee that if the king were to wake, Alice would vanish like the flame of a candle. The incident recalls Bishop Berkeley's empirical proposal that nothing exists except as it is perceived. Alice, like Samuel Johnson—who refuted Berkeley by painfully kicking a stone—insists that she is "real" because she cries "real" tears. When she leaves the world of the looking-glass and supposedly awakens, Carroll mischievously permits her to ask herself: Which dreamed it? His final poem apparently provides the answer in the last words: "Life, what is it but a dream?"

In examining the second structural device of the book, the mirror reversal theme (perfectly mated with chess since in that game the initial asymmetric arrangement of the pieces means that the opponents are mirror images of one another), readers find that Carroll has achieved another tour de force. The left-right reversals—including, for example, the Tweedle brothers, Alice's attempt to reach the Red Queen by walking backward, memory that occurs before the event, running to stay in the same place, and the like—are not merely mind teasers. Since then, scientists have seriously proposed the existence of antimatter that is, in effect, a mirror image of matter, just like Alice's looking-glass milk. Again readers wonder: Which is the real matter, the real milk?

Further developing this continuing paradox are Carroll's damaging attacks on ordinary understanding of language. Humpty Dumpty (like the Tweedles, the Lion, the Unicorn, and Wonderland's Jack of Hearts, a nursery rhyme character) says a person's ideas are formulated in his or her mind; to express them, he may use any word he pleases. Alice and the White Knight debate the difference between the name of the song and the song, between what the name is and what the name is called. The fawn becomes frightened of Alice only when it realizes she is a "child." In these and many more incidents, Carroll explores how language works, directly and indirectly making fun of misconceptions that on the one hand see language as part of a totally objective system of reality and on the other forget how language actually helps create that reality. His nonsense words and poems are his final jibe at so-called logical language, for they are no more and no less disorderly than ordinary table talk.

Like *Alice's Adventures in Wonderland, Through the Looking-Glass* is the sparkling achievement and incomparable vision of an alienated man who found in the world of fantasy all the delight and horror of the adult environment he was subconsciously attempting to escape.

"Critical Evaluation" by Judith Bolch

Bibliography:
Guiliano, Edward, ed. *Lewis Carroll: A Celebration.* New York: Clarkson N. Potter, 1982. A collection of fifteen essays, on the 150th anniversary of Carroll's birth. Includes one of Donald Rackin's existential readings, a surrealist reading, and an analysis of the "hair motif" in *Through the Looking-Glass.*
Kelly, Richard. *Lewis Carroll.* Rev. ed. Boston: Twayne, 1990. An excellent introduction to the works of Lewis Carroll, including a section on *Through the Looking-Glass.* Offers a broad critical study of Carroll's life and writings, with special emphasis on Carroll's mastery of nonsense.
Lennon, Florence Becker. *Victoria Through the Looking-Glass: The Life of Lewis Carroll.* London: Cassell, 1947. A lively biographical and critical study. Includes a section devoted to an analysis of *Through the Looking-Glass.*
Phillips, Robert S., ed. *Aspects of Alice: Lewis Carroll's Dreamchild as Seen Through the Critics' Looking-Glasses, 1865-1971.* New York: Vanguard Press, 1971. The largest and most important single collection of critical essays on Carroll. Analyzes Carroll as an author for adults and children.
Taylor, Alexander L. *The White Knight.* Edinburgh: Oliver & Boyd, 1952. Considers the two Alice books an adult masterpiece on the order of *Gulliver's Travels* (1726). Examines the books in the light of religious issues. Includes a discussion of the chess game in *Through the Looking-Glass.*

THUS SPAKE ZARATHUSTRA

Type of work: Philosophy
Author: Friedrich Wilhelm Nietzsche (1844-1900)
First published: Also sprach Zarathustra: Ein Buchfür Alle und Keinen, 1883-1885 (English translation, 1896)

Friedrich Nietzsche was ignored and misunderstood during his lifetime, but his ideas went on to influence a variety of disciplines, including philosophy, psychology, and literature, and eventually he came to be considered one of the greatest philosophers of all time. Trained as a classical Greek scholar, Nietzsche was a prodigy in his field and appointed associate professor at the University of Basel at the age of twenty-four. Because he suffered from poor health, particularly from problems with his vision and his digestion, Nietzsche resigned his post in 1879 and turned to writing full time. He used his training in ancient Greek culture to critique traditional philosophy, and his insights into the hidden motives behind the formation of Western morality and ethics formed the basis for much twentieth century thought. Although he never completed an organized summary of his ideas, his revolutionary approach assured him an important place in intellectual history.

In his early work, Nietzsche probed psychological phenomena and began to describe the function of the unconscious (some of this work foreshadowed his nervous breakdown in 1889, from which he never fully recovered). He analyzed humanity's hidden drives, the human desire to dominate and to be dominated—drives that he would later describe as "the will to power" and that led to the famous skeptical doctrine in which he proclaimed the death of God—as forming the core of Christian virtue.

Nietzsche's thought is best represented by his major work, *Thus Spake Zarathustra*. A long parable, full of sentimentality and satire, the work exhorts its readers to abandon their conditioning and to embrace a new mode of living: that of the *Übermensch*, or Overman, a being free from the constraints of society in general and of Christianity in particular. For Nietzsche, the Overman possessed a reason or a will that enabled them to master his passions and thus freed him to discover "truth," or what Nietzsche called "the eternal recurrence of the same."

Nietzsche declared that he chose the name Zarathustra because he was inspired by the Persian prophet, who had created the first moral vision of the world and transposed morality into the metaphysical realm so that, far from being a simple code of conduct, morality became an end in itself as both a force and a cause shaping the human universe. Consequently, Nietzsche's book *Thus Spake Zarathustra* begins with the acknowledgment of its relevance to human life. As Zarathustra abandons his mountain solitude, he proclaims that he is going to travel in the world "once again to be a man." Using metaphor, Nietzsche presents the mountain as the solitude of the soul, while the lowlands symbolize the plain inhabited by ordinary men. A similar symbolic contrast occurs with the appearance of Zarathustra's pagan attendants, or animal familiars, the serpent and the eagle. The serpent is bound to the earth while the eagle rules the sky, and Zarathustra, the bridge between the two, is the future healer of humanity's split personality, tending on the one hand toward the body and on the other toward the spirit. Zarathustra contemplates the mystery of the sun, which sets and is reborn the next morning as a new and burning god. Nietzsche thus opens his book with metaphors for rebirth and resurrection, the theme underlying the entire work. After the stultifying effect of centuries of Christianity and of the kind of dogmatic moral beliefs that had led to the Crusades and the Inquisition, Nietzsche wonders how humanity can be reborn.

Nietzsche's answer is to send his prophet Zarathustra, murderer of God, on a journey where he will preach the enlightened doctrine of daylight as a metaphor for consciousness and the limitations of human perception: "the drunken happiness of dying at midnight, that sings: the world is deep, *deeper than day had been aware*." When humanity becomes "aware," it is faced with a contradiction: How can those who have denied God find the strength to become creators themselves?

Nietzsche discusses humanity's dilemma in being forced to learn to live without God's comfort and in coming to terms with the numbing indifference of the cosmos without being paralyzed by it. To avoid destruction, members of humanity must become the *Übermensch*, they must become people capable of embracing misery with enthusiasm, even delight.

Nietzsche explores ways to reach this inner peace, which requires both perfect self-knowledge and self-transcendence. For Nietzsche, the Overman was the symbol of the robust health he himself lacked. The Overman was the individual who has learned to live without belief and without truth, yet who superhumanly accepts life as it comes to him—this individual accepts the "eternal recurrence of the same." Indeed, to embrace the prospect of repeating one's life, exactly as it occurred, day by day, complete with all of its pain and disappointment, is for Nietzsche the highest achievement and the greatest display of courage. One's personal goal, according to him, ought to be the cultivation of "perfect moments."

Having attained this existence—which is to be enjoyed if repeated endlessly—the Overman despises his former self, that weak creature who had desired that not only law and order but also his own personal morality be imposed from outside himself. Through this concept of the Overman, Nietzsche becomes the great philosophical liberator who anticipates the decline of morality in civilization by sending forth the Overman as a secular savior. Nietzsche saw that Christianity was losing its hold on the world, for with the death of God (a phenomenon Nietzsche described without necessarily welcoming it), humanity found itself exposed to itself, its own most dangerous predator. God the protector was gone, killed by science. Therefore, lest humanity destroy itself in its infancy, Nietzsche created the Overman as the model of what humanity could become if people showed courage and lived every moment as if that moment were to be repeated for all eternity.

With God dead, assassinated by skepticism and rationality, Nietzsche acknowledged that humanity, deprived of this potent ally, would, metaphysically speaking, shrink. Deprived of God and therefore of significance, humanity falls from grace and becomes not more than an animal. Yet Nietzsche does not accept humanity's decline in status simply because people lack the superstition to regard themselves as divine creations. Instead, Nietzsche counters the "shrinkage" that humanity experiences when deprived of a god by substituting the Overman, an ideal created by human beings for human beings, a thoroughly human creation that acknowledges itself as human and not divine in its origin.

The Overman, the apotheosis of the human and the apex of becoming, thus represents a kind of salvation. The eternal recurrence of salvation in turn guarantees his reappearance, and thus a kind of secular afterlife. Nietzsche sees God, then, as the ultimate form of human self-aggrandizement, as a comforting delusion, and yet he acknowledges humanity's need for something beyond itself, humanity's fundamental yearning, which, if it is not to be exploited by organized religion or unchecked nationalism, must be given an outlet. Nietzsche considers the ideal Overman humanity's only true savior.

In *Thus Spake Zarathustra*, the Overman has conquered his cloying need for God's approval. Like a child, he has learned to take care of himself, an important skill when the school bully appears. Even more important, the Overman has traveled beyond his lust for meaning outside himself, finding sufficient glory in what remains behind. Nietzsche writes, "Those who cannot bear the sentence, 'There is no salvation,' *ought* to perish!" Nietzsche argues that the old, simple, God-fearing people ought to fade into extinction like some ill-adapted hominid ancestor, making way for the *Übermensch*, bearers of the torchlight of knowledge and freedom.

Nietzsche addresses and explores the problems and pain at the heart of nineteenth and twentieth century consciousness. Raised on illusion, on exorbitant expectations and wild dreams, the mind loves life but can find no meaning in it. It despairs of ever finding fundamental purpose or of discovering the emotional riches promised in childhood. Nietzsche dares his readers to approach the abyss with him. Indeed, he subtitles *Thus Spake Zarathustra* "a book for all and none," which is a warning that only the stout of heart should approach the edge with him, for to confront the implications of the absence of God is to be utterly alone. Nietzsche writes of the end of the journey toward truth, of "the Don Juan of the Mind"—the lover of all things cursed with the inability to enjoy them—and of the final bleak candor with which the honest or "authentic" individual views existence: "And in the very end he craves for Hell . . . perhaps it too will disappoint . . . And if so, he will have to stand transfixed through all eternity, nailed to disillusion, having himself become the Guest of Stone, longing for a last supper of knowledge that he will never receive."

Nietzsche's importance lies precisely in the fact that he was finally not pessimistic. Squinting through the mist of an intellectual dark age he sparked a light and had the courage to focus on what he saw as the truth, without turning away or softening his description. Nietzsche's tool for philosophizing, as he said himself, was a hammer. Accordingly it was his driving ambition to crack open the truth, even at great personal sacrifice: "Oh grant madness, you heavenly powers! . . . I am consumed by doubts, for I have killed the Law. . . . If I am not more than the Law, then I am the most abject of all men." That he survived as long as he did, and even managed to relate the tale of his extraordinary journey off the mountaintop is Zarathustra's, and Nietzsche's, final triumph.

David Johansson

Bibliography:

Allison, David B., ed. *The New Nietzsche: Contemporary Styles of Interpretation.* 1977. Reprint. Cambridge, Mass.: MIT Press, 1985. Collection of essays that explore theological and linguistic interpretations of Nietzsche. Contributors include the noted critics Martin Heidegger and Jacques Derrida.

Bloom, Harold, ed. *Friedrich Nietzsche.* New York: Chelsea House, 1987. Collection of essays that examine Nietzsche's conception of the connection between philosophy and literature.

Camus, Albert. "Nietzsche and Nihilism." In *The Rebel: An Essay on Man in Revolt.* Translated by Anthony Bower. New York: Alfred A. Knopf, 1961. Camus, the noted French existentialist, argues that Nietzsche is a nihilist, a thinker whose conceptual rebellion constitutes the opposite of metaphysical thought.

Lampert, Laurence. *Nietzsche's Teaching: An Interpretation of "Thus Spake Zarathustra."* New Haven, Conn.: Yale University Press, 1986. An analysis of *Thus Spake Zarathustra* that reveals the eternal recurrence of the same as the central theme of Nietzsche's philosophy.

Mencken, H. L. *Friedrich Nietzsche.* 1913. New Brunswick, N.J.: Transaction Publishers, 1993. Exploration of Nietzsche's philosophy by the famous American journalist and critic.

THYESTES

Type of work: Drama
Author: Seneca (4 B.C.E.-65 C.E.)
Type of plot: Tragedy
Time of plot: Antiquity
Locale: Greece
First performed: c. 40-55 C.E. (English translation, 1581)

Principal characters:
ATREUS, the king of Argos
THYESTES, his brother
THYESTES' THREE SONS

The Story:

Megaera, one of the Furies, summoned the ghost of Tantalus to return from Hades to Argos, where Tantalus in life had been king, to watch revenge, hate, and havoc spread across that kingdom. Tantalus did not want to be reminded of the part he had played in the story of his royal house, but Megaera forced him to witness the fate of his descendants.

The grandsons of Tantalus, the sons of Pelops, whom Tantalus had sacrificed to the gods, were at war with one another. The oldest of Pelops' sons, Atreus, was the rightful ruler of Argos, but his brother, Thyestes, had seduced Atreus' wife and carried her away. With them they took the golden ram, the symbol of power held by the ruler of the kingdom. Civil war broke out, and Thyestes was defeated. After his defeat he was exiled by Atreus.

Exile was not sufficient punishment for Thyestes. The fierce hatred of Atreus, burning over his brother's crimes and his own misfortune in the loss of his wife, demanded greater revenge. A tyrant who believed that death was a comfort to his subjects, Atreus brooded over fierce and final vengeance upon his younger brother. He felt that no act of revenge could be a crime when committed against a man who had worked against him as his brother had. Moreover, he felt that he, as a king, could do as he wished; private virtues were not for rulers. When an attendant suggested that Atreus put Thyestes to the sword, Atreus said that death was only an end. He wanted Thyestes to suffer torture. The punishment Atreus finally decided on was a scheme to feed Thyestes' own children to him at a banquet.

Atreus took the first step toward accomplishing his revenge. He sent his own sons, Agamemnon and Menelaus, as emissaries of good will to Thyestes and asked the exile, through them, to return to a place of honor at his brother's side. Fearing that his sons, forewarned, might lack the discretion needed to act as friendly ambassadors, he did not tell them the part they were playing in his scheme of revenge.

Thyestes, trusting the king, returned to Argos with his three sons, including one named Tantalus, after his great-grandfather of famous memory. When he looked again at familiar landscapes, Thyestes felt a sense of foreboding. His footsteps faltered, and his sons noted his apparent unwillingness to return. The offer of peace and half the kingdom seemed to Thyestes unlike his brother's earlier hatred and fury. He felt that there had been too much hate and bloodshed between them for real peace. His sons, silencing his doubts, led him on to the court of Atreus. Atreus, seeing his brother and nephews in his power and apparently unmindful of the revenge plotted against them, was overjoyed and acted as such, concealing his hatred and welcoming them to the kingdom once again.

Atreus announced a great feast to celebrate his brother's homecoming. Then, taking the three sons of Thyestes aside, he led them to a grove behind the palace and there slew them with all the ceremony of a sacrifice to the gods. The first he stabbed in the neck, the second he decapitated, and the third he killed by a thrust through the body. The boys, knowing that appeals were useless, suffered death in silence. Atreus drew off their blood and prepared the carcasses like so much beef. The limbs he quartered and placed upon spits to roast; the bodies he hacked into small pieces and placed in pots to boil.

The fire seemed reluctant to burn as an accomplice to his deed, but Atreus stood by and acted as cook until the ghastly banquet was ready. As he cooked, the sky grew dark and an unnatural night settled across the face of the earth. The banquet prepared, Atreus felt that he was the equal of the gods themselves.

The feast began. After the banquet had progressed to the point that the guests were glutted by all they had eaten, Atreus prepared for Thyestes a drink of wine and blood drained from the bodies of Thyestes' sons.

All the while a premonition of evil hung like a cloud in the back of Thyestes' mind. Try as he would, he could not be gay and enjoy the feast, for vague terrors struck at his heart. When Atreus gave him the cup of blood and wine, he could not lift it to drink at first, and when he did try to drink the wine seemed to roll around the brim of the cup rather than pass through his lips. Filled with sudden fears, Thyestes demanded that Atreus produce his sons.

Atreus left and returned with the heads of the three sons on a platter. Thyestes, chilled with horror at the sight, asked where the bodies were. He feared that Atreus had refused them honorable burial and had left them for the dogs to eat. Atreus told Thyestes that he had eaten his own children. Then Thyestes realized why unnatural night had darkened the skies.

Still Atreus was not satisfied. He felt disappointed that he had not planned to force Thyestes to drink some of his children's blood while they were yet alive. The king bragged of what he had done and described how he himself had committed the murders and spitted the meat before the fires.

Atreus, enjoying his revenge, could never believe that the greatest weight upon Thyestes' mind was regret that he had not thought of such revenge and caused Atreus to eat of his own children.

Critical Evaluation:

The most fiendish revenge play in the history of drama, this gruesome story of a banquet at which the father partakes of his own children is a landmark in dramatic history. It is the model of many revenge plays appearing in the sixteenth and seventeenth centuries in English drama. Seneca was not the first ancient author to make use of the Thyestes legend, but his work is what most directly influenced the tragedians of the Renaissance. Versions of the story by Sophocles, Euripides, Ennius, and Accius have not survived the years; scholars do not even have enough information about the other ancient versions of the drama to compare the treatment by those authors with that of Seneca. As a result of Seneca's influence on Renaissance playwrights and of historical accident, his name is foremost in discussions of the type of play he wrote, called the revenge tragedy or the tragedy of blood.

Seneca's *Thyestes* is spectacle rather than true drama. Whereas genuine tragedy arises from character conflicts or internal divisions within character, spectacle relies on sensational events carried out by characters who exist merely for the sake of the events and who have no actual existence of their own. This is certainly the case with every character in *Thyestes*. Each exists simply to point up the horror of Atreus' revenge on his brother, Thyestes.

Another important point of difference between true drama and spectacle is their use of language. The speech of authentic tragedy approximates, in a formal way, the devices of normal conversation to reveal passions. The language of spectacle, however, being florid and highly artificial, tends toward bombast. Spectacle operates by set pieces, rhetorical essays that develop simple ideas at great length, by tedious and lush descriptive passages, and by moralizing epigrams. Seneca used all three, and the result is that his characters speak in a highly unnatural way. Instead of communicating, they attitudinize, talking largely to the audience or soliloquizing.

This characteristic of Senecan drama has led many scholars to believe that Seneca wrote his plays for private recitation rather than public performance. This idea, gives no reason for assuming they were not produced. Spectacle, rhetorical overindulgence, and horrors were a part of public entertainment under the Roman Emperors Caligula, Claudius, and Nero, who ruled during Seneca's maturity. Scholars know for a fact that his tragedies were staged in the Elizabethan period, and that they had immense influence on the dramas of Thomas Kyd, Christopher Marlowe, William Shakespeare, John Webster, and others.

Thyestes derives from Greek legend and is based upon an incident that occurred in the tragic family descended from Tantalus. Seneca's treatment of the myth has some interest in its own right, but it also serves to illuminate his own biography. He handles the figure of Thyestes rather sympathetically, making him the victim of Atreus' lunatic lust for revenge. Seneca plays down the fact that Thyestes seduced Atreus' wife, stole his symbol of power, and caused a civil war. When Thyestes appears on stage, he assumes the role of the Stoic hero, determined to bear whatever fate he has in store for him, and he frankly prefers the hardships of exile to the pomp of power that Atreus has treacherously extended to him. Exile has tempered his character. Readers may remember that Seneca underwent eight years of exile on Corsica, after being accused of an intrigue with Claudius' niece, Julia. The parallel is striking, but it extends even further. Like Thyestes, Seneca was recalled from exile with the promise of power. He was to tutor and guide Nero in the art of statesmanship. When Nero became emperor in 54 C.E., Seneca was able to exercise some control over him for the first five years of his reign, but then Nero began acting on his own, and Seneca retired from public life. *Thyestes* is Seneca's personal testament on the instability of power, and the helplessness of those who incur the wrath of an absolute and maniacal ruler. The only solution Seneca finds in this play is the same one he found in life—to bear one's misfortune with Stoic dignity. Eventually Nero ordered Seneca to commit suicide for an alleged conspiracy. Seneca met his death bravely.

Through the murky rhetoric of *Thyestes* two important themes emerge: the nature of kingship and the necessity of maintaining a Stoic endurance in the face of a murderous, disintegrating cosmos. The appearance of Tantalus and Megaera the Fury at the beginning is not accidental. Tantalus served his son, Pelops, as food for the gods, and as part of his eternal torment he must not only witness the kin murders of his descendants, he must abet them. Presumably he inspires the idea of the cannibalistic revenge in Atreus' mind, but Atreus carries it out with gloating satisfaction. Atreus is an unrelieved monster, raging with paranoid pride.

Against him Seneca sets the idea of kingship founded on morality and restraint. The aphoristic conversation between Atreus and the attendant in Act II, scene i, is a debate on whether kings should serve the people or the people should be utterly subservient to the king. In the first case morality is the main law, and in the second the will of the tyrant. The point is made that morality creates a stable kingdom, but tyranny is supremely unstable. Later, the chorus says that true kingship lies in self-control, not in wealth, power, or pomp.

Unfortunately these observations make no impression whatever on Atreus, who is intent on proving his godlike power over human life, much like the Roman emperors Seneca knew. In striving to become like a god in his pride, Atreus becomes loathsomely bestial. Seneca constantly generalizes from the concrete situation of Atreus and Thyestes to the universe. When kings are corrupt, society is corrupted, and the rot extends throughout the cosmos. Nature mirrors human conditions in Seneca: the fire hesitates to boil the children; an unnatural night falls upon the banquet. The play is full of hyperbole about the disintegrating universe, rendered in purple poetry. Against this profusion of rhetoric stand the pithy epigrams, like a Stoical element trying to bear up tightly against the frenetic declamations. The Stoic attitude can never prevail in a world full of crime, but it can enable one to endure great stress with courage. Seneca, in *Thyestes*, embodied the shame of Rome and his own valor in a style eminently suited to his subject.

"Critical Evaluation" by James Weigel, Jr.

Bibliography:
Griffin, Miriam Tamara. *Seneca: A Philosopher in Politics*. Oxford, England: Clarendon Press, 1976. Definitive study of Seneca. Evaluates the man who had so many lofty ideals and whose life was so full of less-than-lofty facts. Dramatizes the problem of public service in a corrupt state.
Henry, Denis, and Elisabeth Henry. *The Mask of Power: Seneca's Tragedies and Imperial Power*. Chicago: Bolchazy-Carducci, 1985. A study of Seneca's tragedies, placing them in their cultural context. Bibliography.
Holland, Francis. *Seneca*. London: Longmans, Green, 1920. Reprint. Freeport, N.Y.: Books for Libraries Press, 1969. For a time, this work was the only biography on Seneca available in English. Thorough, readable, and still authoritative.
Motto, Anna Lydia. *Seneca*. New York: Twayne, 1973. Clear presentation of Seneca's life and work. A good starting place.
Rosenmeyer, Thomas G. *Senecan Drama and Stoic Cosmology*. Berkeley: University of California Press, 1989. Argues that Seneca's Stoicism, as expressed in his philosophical works, must be studied in order to gain greater understanding of his plays. Bibliography.
Sutton, Dana Ferrin. *Seneca on the Stage*. Leiden, The Netherlands, E. J. Brill, 1986. Argues against the long-held idea that Seneca's tragedies were written to be read. Supports claim with its discovery of stage directions in the form of clues in the characters' speeches.

TIGER AT THE GATES

Type of work: Drama
Author: Jean Giraudoux (1882-1944)
Type of plot: Mythic
Time of plot: Trojan War era
Locale: Troy
First performed: 1935; first published, 1935 as *La Guerre de Troie n'aura pas lieu* (English translation, 1955)

Principal characters:
HECTOR, the Trojan hero and a man of goodwill, the son of Priam
ANDROMACHE, his wife
PARIS, his younger brother
HELEN, beloved of Paris
PRIAM, king of Troy
HECUBA, his wife
CASSANDRA, the daughter of Hecuba and Priam, whose predictions, always true, are never heeded
ULYSSES, the Greek ambassador
AJAX, a Greek warrior
DEMOKOS, a poet
A MATHEMATICIAN
TROJAN PATRIOTS
TROILUS, a Trojan youth

The Story:

Hector's wife, Andromache, joyfully told Cassandra, his sister, that there would be no Trojan war because Hector, as soon as he came home, would assuage the feelings of the Greek ambassador. Cassandra, true to her reputation, claimed that she knew destiny would provoke a war. She knew this not as a result of her ability to prophesy but because she always took into account the stupidity and folly of men. Since Andromache could not understand destiny in the abstract, Cassandra offered her the picture of a tiger prowling at the palace gates and waiting for the moment to enter.

Hector, home from war, was delighted to hear that Andromache would soon bear a child that she expected to be a son. Andromache feared that the child would have the father's love of battle, but Hector assured her that he and his soldiers had returned this time disabused of their former ideas of war as a glorious adventure. They were all ready for peace, and he intended to get from his father, Priam, permission to shut the gates of war permanently.

Cassandra brought the younger brother Paris to Hector to give his version of his abduction of Helen. He told Hector that he had happened to sail past Helen while she was bathing in the sea. While Menelaus was busy removing a crab from his toe, Paris had casually taken her into his ship and sailed on. He liked her because she—unlike Trojan women, who tended to cling—seemed always to be at a distance, even while in his arms. This was not the first time Hector had taken Paris away from a woman, but Paris resisted obeying Hector, promising instead to obey Priam, their father.

Cassandra realized that destiny was already lurking like a tiger because Priam would rather

6555

have given up his own daughters than let Helen leave the kingdom. Priam and all the other old men in Troy spent their days admiring Helen as she took a daily walk around Troy, to be greeted by toothless shouts whenever she appeared. To the old men Helen was a symbol; she was Beauty. Hecuba, Priam's wife, suggested that the old men would do well to find a symbol among their own Trojan women, and not a blonde one like Helen, because blonde beauty fades fast. The men, however, were intoxicated by Helen. The poet got his inspiration from her. The mathematician found that all measurements related to Helen—the weight of her footfall, the length of her arm, the range of her look. They all began to argue the justification of war for Helen's sake. Paris said he was willing to let Hector handle the situation because Paris felt humiliated to be cast as the seducer, a role that he did not want to play within his large family. He brought Helen to Hector.

While Hector spoke with her in his attempt to avoid conflict between the Greeks and the Trojans, he found that Helen was completely unpredictable. It was hard to tell whether she had any sense at all or whether she depended completely on fate to do what it would with her. She agreed to leave Troy because she could no longer see Paris plainly. She claimed also that she never had seen Menelaus plainly and supposed she had often walked over him without realizing it. She warned that she saw a battle raging, a city burning, and a figure in the dust that she recognized as Paris only by his ring. She admitted that the things she saw did not always come to pass, and she promised to leave Troy with Ulysses. Left with Cassandra, Helen begged Cassandra to make Peace appear, but could not see the figure until Peace painted herself outrageously. By that time Trojan patriots were shouting that the gods had been insulted and had struck down the temple. Peace became sick. As Hector prepared to shut the gates of war, Helen turned her blandishments on the young Troilus, who refused to kiss her. She promised him that her chance would come later. The poet, the mathematician, and others prepared for war by agreeing on a war song and by discussing the usefulness to soldiers of insulting epithets.

In spite of the opposition of the poet, the mathematician, and the others, and in spite of dire forebodings by a traveling expert on the rights of nations, Hector made an ironic Oration for the Dead and closed the gates of war just before the Greeks came ashore. Ajax was the first Greek to reach Hector. He approached in an insulting manner and struck Hector on the cheek, but Hector refused to rise to the insult. When the poet called shame on him, Hector struck the poet, who vowed revenge. Ajax, amused, admiring Hector's courage, swore he would not fight against Hector.

Hector promised Ajax and Ulysses that he would give Helen back to them. To Ulysses' questioning as to whether there had been cause for reprisals, Paris' crew told of Paris and Helen's apparent delight in each other on the trip to Troy. Ulysses sensed that war was inevitable but, talking to Hector as soldier to soldier, he regretted it, particularly since the cause of it was Helen, a woman of shallow brain, hard heart, and narrow understanding. Still trying to defy destiny, Ulysses attempted to get back to his ship. Ajax was a little slower and was caught by the mob when the poet, struck down by Hector, called for war and cried out that Ajax had mortally wounded him. The crowd killed Ajax as the gates of war opened to show Helen kissing Troilus.

Critical Evaluation:

Beginning with the production of his first play, *Siegfried*, in 1928, Jean Giraudoux dominated the French stage for the next three decades. *Tiger at the Gates*, with its witty, sparkling debate, illustrates the reason for his prominence. It presents a subject that had long been of great importance to Giraudoux, not only as a writer but also as a career diplomat: the relationship between France and Germany. In an early novel, later made into his first play, *Siegfried*, he dramatized the necessity to reconcile the German and French peoples after World War I.

Unfortunately by 1935, when Giraudoux wrote *Tiger at the Gates*, such a reconciliation seemed increasingly impossible. As does Hector, he felt that it was vital to make every effort toward peace to avoid the devastation and destruction of another war. This play, like most of his dramas, centers on one main issue: in this case, war versus peace. Despite its single-mindedness in theme, the play operates on many different levels. As he frequently did, Giraudoux turned to the classics for his plot. It is first a retelling of the *Iliad* (c. 800 B.C.E.). It is also a comment on the political situation in Europe in 1935. Finally, it is an abstract philosophical discussion about the nature of war and peace, and about those qualities in human nature that direct persons and nations to choose one or the other.

Unlike the *Iliad*, which opens in the tenth year of the Trojan War, *Tiger at the Gates* is set immediately before the war begins. The conflict in the play is not the war, but the issues that cause war. The prowar and antiwar positions are clearly and quickly drawn. On one side is Andromache and most of the female characters in the play. The women are antiwar. They would not lose their husbands and sons for the sake of Helen. Hecuba vividly describes her vision of war: "When the baboon is up in a tree with its hind end facing us, there is the face of war exactly: scarlet, scaley, glazed, framed in a clotted, filthy wig." Hector, who has just returned from war, joins their side. He has experienced the bloodshed of war. The opposing view is presented by the poet, Demokos. He finds war an inspiration. King Priam adds that only by fighting death are men truly alive; even Hector reluctantly agrees with them on this count. Demokos insists that war must be flattered and adored in order to gain its goodwill. To ensure this, he plans a war song comparing the face of war with the face of Helen. He is joined by all the old men of Troy who would sacrifice anything for another glimpse of Helen.

The play uses minimal action to develop this debate; it is primarily composed of dialogues between the representatives of war and peace. While Hecuba and Demokos may provide the most vivid definitions of war, each new dialogue brings another insight into the causes of war or the reasons for peace. In the opening scene, Andromache, who is pregnant, insists there must be peace to protect her husband and unborn child. Her faith in Hector's ability to solve the problem is countered by Cassandra's warning that Troy is too complacent; its arrogant self-confidence has antagonized fate. The crowd of Trojans is willing to accept war for national honor. If Ulysses returns Helen, swearing her virtue is intact, this will be a terrible blow to Trojan masculinity.

Ulysses, while agreeing to work for peace, presents the economic reasons why wars occur. The cunning diplomat shocks Hector when he tells him of the dangerous message Troy's golden fields and temples send to the Greeks trapped on rockier soil. When Hector insists Greece will be ashamed forever for using Helen as a pretext to take Troy's wealth, Ulysses simply responds that the Greeks will lie, denying all responsibility. Yet he is willing to try peace because Andromache's eyelashes dance like Penelope's do. Peace and the future of Troy may rest on as slender a thread as an eyelash.

Giraudoux's use of language has often been compared to impressionism in art. Although his staging may be static, his words dance. *Tiger at the Gates* is filled with brilliant images, such as Helen's description of men as being "as pleasant as soap and a sponge and water." He often makes serious points with witty epigrams. Ulysses notes that "one of the privileges of the great is to witness catastrophe from a terrace."

Giraudoux blends this wit with irony throughout the play, building toward the tragedy. The French title, *La Guerre de Troie n'aura pas lieu* (the Trojan War will not take place), provides an example. While Hector and Andromache work desperately to ensure peace, the audience and almost all of the other characters know that these two will fail. For readers familiar with the *Iliad*, many lines have extra poignancy. When Hector asks Helen to visualize the body of Paris dragged behind a chariot, this foresees Hector's death in the *Iliad*. In an ironic twist Giraudoux never planned, it also foreshadows the Nazi occupation of Paris. The final irony is that it is the peace-loving Hector himself who causes the war with one foolish act of violence. Alive, Demokos could never match Hector's influence, but in killing Demokos, Hector destroys Troy. Cassandra predicts this in the first scene. When she shouts that the tiger has arrived, Hector enters. Critics debate whether the play implies that war is inevitable. Peace, however, nearly wins in the play; Giraudoux believed that everyone must work unceasingly toward peace. In the end, Hector proves able to control everyone except himself.

"Critical Evaluation" by Mary Mahony

Bibliography:
Clurman, Harold. Introduction to *Judith, Tiger at the Gates, Duel of Angels*. Vol 1 in *Jean Giraudoux: Plays*, translated by Christopher Fry. New York: Oxford University Press, 1963. Provides clear overview of French theatrical history, placing Giraudoux as a transitional figure between classic and modern French drama. Includes discussion of Fry's translation.
Cohen, Robert. *Giraudoux: Three Faces of Destiny*. Chicago: University of Chicago Press, 1968. Examines Giraudoux's background and the intellectual system underlying his writing. Uses charts and diagrams to analyze the dialogue between war and peace, emphasizing language, imagery, and use of symbol.
Lemaitre, George. *Jean Giraudoux: The Writer and His Work*. New York: Frederick Ungar, 1971. Clear general introduction to Giraudoux. Discusses the play's portrayal of the dualism of human nature. Discusses the play's relation to Greek tragedy.
Mankin, Paul A. *Precious Irony: The Theatre of Jean Giraudoux*. The Hague: Mouton, 1971. Provides clear, precise literary explanation of the different types of irony, including examples from *Tiger at the Gates*. Presents Cassandra, Helen, and Ulysses as outsiders who function as the chorus, helping to emphasize the importance of fate.
Reilly, John R. *Jean Giraudoux*. Boston: Twayne, 1978. Divides Giraudoux's work into three periods, with *Tiger at the Gates* signaling the entrance into the final period, in which fate appears as a hostile presence and the themes of war, love, and politics predominate. Biographical details and annotated bibliography.

THE TIME MACHINE
An Invention

Type of work: Novel
Author: H. G. Wells (1866-1946)
Type of plot: Fantasy
Time of plot: Late nineteenth century
Locale: England
First published: 1895

Principal characters:
THE TIME TRAVELER
WEENA, a woman the Time Traveler meets in the future

The Story:

One evening after dinner, the Time Traveler led the discussion to the subject of the relationship of time and space. It was his theory that time was a fourth dimension and that his concept could be proved. To the astonishment of his guests, he exhibited a model of his Time Machine, and he declared that it could travel backward or forward in time. One of the guests was invited to touch a lever. To the amazement of all, the machine disappeared. The Time Traveler explained that the instrument was no longer visible because it was traveling into the past at such great speed that it was below the threshold of visibility.

The following week, the Time Traveler was not at home to greet his dinner guests when they arrived, but he had left word that they were to proceed without him. Everyone was at the table when their host came in, dirty from head to toe, limping, and with a cut on his chin. After he had changed his clothes and dined, he told his friends the story of the day's adventures.

That morning, he had taken off on his Time Machine. As he reeled through space, the days shot past him like minutes, and the rapid alternation of light and darkness had hurt the Time Traveler's eyes. Landing and falling from his machine when he braked too suddenly, he found himself on the side of a hill. In the misty light, he could see the figure of a winged sphinx on a bronze pedestal. As the sun came out, the Time Traveler saw enormous buildings on the slope. Some figures were coming toward him. One was a little man about four feet tall. Regaining his confidence, the Time Traveler waited to meet this citizen of the future.

Soon a group of these creatures gathered around the voyager. Without a common language, he and his new acquaintances had to communicate with signs. After they had examined the Time Machine, from which he had the presence of mind to remove the levers, one of them asked him if he had come from the sun.

The Time Traveler was led to one of the large buildings. There he was seated upon a cushion and given fruit to eat. Everyone was a vegetarian, since animals had become extinct. When he had eaten, he unsuccessfully tried to learn his new friends' language. These people, who called themselves the Eloi, were not able to concentrate and tired quickly.

Free to wander about, the Time Traveler climbed a hill and from the crest saw the ruins of an enormous granite structure. Looking at some of the creatures who were following him, he realized that all wore similar garb and had the same soft, rounded figures. Children could be distinguished only by their size.

The Time Traveler realized that he was seeing the sunset of humanity. In the society of the future, there was no need for strength. The world was secure and at peace. The strong of body or mind would only have felt frustrated.

As he looked about to find a place to sleep, he saw that his Time Machine had disappeared. He tried to wake the people in the building in which he had dined, but he succeeded only in frightening them. At last, he went back to the lawn and there, greatly worried over his plight, fell asleep.

The next morning, he managed to trace the path the Time Machine made to the base of the sphinx, but the bronze doors in the pedestal were closed. The Time Traveler tried to intimate to some of the Eloi that he wished to open the doors, but they answered him with looks of insult and reproach. He attempted to hammer in the doors with a stone, but he soon stopped from weariness.

Weena, a young woman he rescued from drowning, became the Time Traveler's friend and guide. On the fourth morning, while he explored one of the ruins, he saw eyes staring at him from the dark. Curious, he followed a small, apelike figure to a well-like opening. The strange figure retreated down the opening. He was convinced that this creature was also a descendant of humanity, a subterranean species that worked below ground to support the dwellers in the upper world.

Convinced that the Morlocks, as the subterranean dwellers were called, were responsible for the disappearance of his Time Machine and hoping to learn more about them, he climbed down into one of the wells. At its bottom, he discovered a tunnel that led into a cavern in which he saw a table set with a joint of meat. The Morlocks were carnivorous. He was also able to distinguish some enormous machinery.

The next day, the Time Traveler and Weena visited a green porcelain museum containing animal skeletons, books, and machinery. Since they had walked a long distance, he planned to sleep in the woods that night with Weena and to build a fire to keep the dark-loving Morlocks away. When he saw three crouching figures in the brush, however, he changed his mind and decided he and Weena would be safer on a hill beyond the forest. He started a fire to keep their enemies at a distance.

When he awoke, the fire had gone out, his matches were missing, and Weena had vanished. A fire he had started earlier was still burning, and while he slept, it had set the forest on fire. Between thirty and forty Morlocks perished in the blaze while the Time Traveler watched.

When daylight returned, the Time Traveler retraced his steps to the sphinx. He slept all day. In the evening, he prepared to ram open the doors in the pedestal with the lever he had found in the porcelain palace. He found the doors open and his machine in plain view. As a group of Morlocks sprang at him, he took off through space.

The Time Traveler had his encounter with the Morlocks and the Eloi in the year 802,701. On his next journey, he moved through millions of years toward that time when the earth would cease rotating. He landed on a deserted beach, empty except for a flying animal, which looked like a huge white butterfly, and some crablike monsters. He traveled on, finally halting thirty million years after the time he had left his laboratory. In that distant age, the sun was dying. It was bitter cold, and it began to snow. All around was deathly stillness. Horrified, the Time Traveler started back toward his present.

As he told his story that evening, his guests grew skeptical. In fact, the Time Traveler himself had to visit his laboratory to make sure his machine existed. The next day, however, all doubts ceased, for one of his friends watched him depart on his vehicle. It was this friend who wrote the story of the Time Traveler's experiences three years later. The Time Traveler had not reappeared during that time, and his friends speculated on the mishap that had made him a lost wanderer in space and time.

Critical Evaluation:

H. G. Wells's first novel, *The Time Machine*, enjoyed an instant popularity and rescued its author from obscurity and poverty. *The Time Machine* was the first of Wells's classic "scientific romances"—which, along with some of Jules Verne's "extraordinary voyages," provided the foundation of the modern genre of science fiction. Previous visions of the future had been exactly that: dreams, which were implicitly banished to the realms of mere possibility when the dreamers awoke. Wells wanted to solidify his vision of the future, to give it the status of reality, so he invented a machine capable of traveling through time.

Such a machine was thought impossible, as Wells knew perfectly well, but he also knew that its invocation would provide his story with a new kind of plausibility and narrative force. To this end, he was careful to provide a clever "explanation" of the manner of the machine's functioning, invoking the idea of duration as a fourth dimension comparable to the three dimensions of space.

Although Wells once referred to his story, in a moment of excitement, as "the new Delphic Oracle," *The Time Machine* ought not to be seen as an attempt at prophecy. In its later phases the story does try to come to grips with what Wells considered to be inevitable—the extinction of humanity when the sun runs out of fuel—but in its more interesting phase it is best construed as a warning. Wells extrapolated to a horrific extreme the division of English society into a leisured aristocracy and a mass of downtrodden workers, the lovely but effete Eloi having degenerated to the point where they become the prey of the monstrous Morlocks.

Readers can now see, after the passage of a mere hundred years, that no part of this vision will come to pass. What seemed inevitable to Wells no longer seems inevitable to readers today. Readers know that the sun gives out heat by virtue of nuclear fusion, not because it is on fire, and that it will not burn out nearly as quickly as Wells imagined. The seemingly fundamental division of society that Wells magnified in his vision of eight hundred thousand years has already been rendered not fundamental.

Readers should remember, however, that *The Time Machine*'s seeming rather old-fashioned to the contemporary reader is to some extent attributable to its own success, both as a literary landmark and as an example of how to imagine the future.

Wells's time machine became the archetype of a vast range of imaginary machines whose use has opened limitless imaginative territories. Unlike the far more modest machines employed by Verne's voyagers, which were careful extrapolations of existing vehicles, time machines, spaceships, and dimensional gateways of genre science fiction became devices that could transport characters into an infinite number of hypothetical worlds. While they did so, they stoutly maintained the pretense that these were no mere fairylands but worlds that could and actually might exist.

The fact that this was a pretense—in other words, a fiction—did not detract from the seriousness with which the best of such imaginative work could devote to the description of the hypothetical worlds. It is at least arguable that one of the most encouraging lessons learned from that serious contemplation is that the extinction of humanity need not be inevitable, even though the sun is not eternal, because the universe beyond the solar system is not inaccessible in any absolute sense.

Wells's depiction of the society of the Eloi and the Morlocks was not the unprecedented leap that his invention of a time machine was. That kind of extrapolation of the familiar to caricaturish extremes has long been a standard method of satire. *The Time Machine*, however, is not a satire; its rhetoric is not calculated to make the extreme seem absurd, but rather to make it seem tragic. The novel is science fiction instead of satire, so the argument of this parable is not simply that the divisions in society that it exaggerates are foolish or unjust, but that they possess an internal dynamic that is ominous and dangerous.

It is difficult to appreciate how difficult and how unusual it was for a nineteenth century writer to see the world as something essentially in flux, subject to constant and irresistible change. Previously, the great majority of people, and virtually all literary discourse, had seen change in terms of a lurching movement from one potentially stable state to another. Before Wells, before the scientific discoveries regarding evolution, relativity, and uncertainty, and before the popularization of ideas that follow from such discoveries, the world was seen as a place that might achieve stability. Utopian dreaming was a matter of choosing some static ideal that would obviate the need for further change. Wells's early scientific romances constitute a brilliant exploration of the vast spectrum of possibilities implicit in a world where change is constant and insistent.

If readers accept that the future is as yet unmade, and that it is unforeseeable in principle as well as in practice (or to put it another way, that God plays dice with the universe), then the real function of futuristic visions is to warn of the pitfalls which might lie before humanity. The best of such books are not those that come true, even in part, but those that help to prevent the futures they foresee. For this reason, Wells's *The Time Machine* ought not to be regarded as a dated work whose image of the future is obsolete, but as an authentic triumph of the nineteenth century imagination.

"Critical Evaluation" by Brian Stableford

Bibliography:

Bergonzi, Bernard, ed. *H. G. Wells: A Collection of Critical Essays.* Englewood Cliffs, N.J.: Prentice-Hall, 1976. Two critical essays on *The Time Machine.* One addresses the novel as myth, the other as prophecy. Readable and informative.

Costa, Richard Hauer. *H. G. Wells.* New York: Twayne, 1967. Multiple references to *The Time Machine,* with critical references. A good starting place.

Hammond, J. R. *H. G. Wells and Rebecca West.* New York: St. Martin's Press, 1991. Associates the novel with the writer's scientific understanding of the human species and with his interest in a fourth dimension. Illustrated. Bibliography.

_____. *H. G. Wells and the Modern Novel.* New York: St. Martin's Press, 1988. Finds Wells a deserving and overlooked, innovative writer. One analytical chapter calls *The Time Machine* a "watershed in the coming of modernism." Appendix, notes, bibliography, and index. Evocative, scholarly, readable.

Wells, H. G., Julian S. Huxley, and G. P. Wells. *The Science of Life.* Garden City, N.Y.: Doubleday, 1934. Describes Wells's study of science and his consequent understanding of human life.

THE TIME OF YOUR LIFE

Type of work: Drama
Author: William Saroyan (1908-1981)
Type of plot: Psychological realism
Time of plot: 1939
Locale: New York City
First performed: 1939; first published, 1939

Principal characters:
    JOE, a young loafer with money and a good heart
    TOM, his admirer, disciple, errand boy, and stooge
    KITTY DUVAL, a young woman who falls in love with Tom
    NICK, owner of Nick's Pacific Street Saloon, Restaurant and
        Entertainment Palace
    MA, Nick's mother
    ARAB, an Eastern philosopher and harmonica player
    KIT CARSON, an old Indian fighter
    MC CARTHY, an intelligent and well-read longshoreman
    KRUPP, a boyhood friend of Mc Carthy; a policeman who hates his job
    HARRY, a dancer whose efforts at comedy do not make people laugh
    WESLEY, a talented black pianist
    DUDLEY, a young man in love
    ELSIE, a nurse, the woman Dudley loves
    LORENE, an attractive woman
    MARY L., an unhappy woman of great gentility and beauty
    BLICK, the head of the vice squad in search of streetwalkers at Nick's
        restaurant

The Story:

At Nick's restaurant and saloon, a motley crew of individuals from all walks of life gathered to pass the time, converse, philosophize, seek employment, and fall in love. In the preface to his play William Saroyan describes these characters as "people you are likely to see any day in almost any part of America, certainly at least in certain kinds of American places." These colorful, odd characters all have their histories and idiosyncrasies. Joe, for example, sent Tom on errands to purchase toys—not for a child but for Kitty Duval, a woman who could not stop crying. Tom grumbled, "Aw, Joe, you're always making me do crazy things for you, and I'm the guy that gets embarrassed." When Kitty Duval, a streetwalker who formerly performed in burlesque theaters, entered the saloon, Joe bought her a bottle of champagne as if she were royalty—a gesture that made Nick exclaim, "He's crazy."

Other strange, unusual characters who entered the saloon were Dudley and Harry. Dudley constantly telephoned Elsie Mandelspiegel from the restaurant and begged her to marry him; Harry was determined to relieve the world's sorrow by becoming a famous comedian. Another newcomer who arrived on the scene was Wesley, a gifted black musician with a flair for the piano. Nick, the owner of the saloon, was dumbfounded at these eccentric people who frequented his restaurant. Joe made him stock expensive champagne in "the lousiest dive."

Kitty, a prostitute, expected to be treated like an elegant lady. Comedians and musicians begged for their debut at his obscure old honky tonk. The customers and visitors at Nick's restaurant felt a sense of belonging and experienced a sense of home. They felt security and protection from the hostile outside world. In the saloon they encountered the acceptance, friendship, generosity, and goodwill that they were deprived of by the world at large, a world that appeared mad and absurd.

The threat to Nick's restaurant and the modicum of happiness it brought to its customers came from Blick, who suspected the saloon to be a den of prostitution. Nick warned Blick that his moral earnestness for reform was doomed: "You're out to change the world from something bad to something worse." In defending his saloon, a home and a haven to a motley crew of humanity, Nick explained that, though his restaurant was "a dive in the lousiest part of town," it was also a safe haven where no one had been murdered, robbed, or cheated in five years. He referred to his honky tonk as a humble, honest place: "Well, it's not out of the world. It's on a street in the city, and people come and go. They bring whatever they've got with them and they say what they must say."

Characters who came to say what they must say included Krupp, Arab, and Mc Carthy. Krupp was disturbed by the corruption and avarice of the world, the inability of humans to enjoy the simple pleasures of life, such as taking a walk. He commented: "Here we are in this wonderful world, full of all the wonderful things—here we are—all of us, and look at us. . . . We've got everything, but we always feel lousy and dissatisfied just the same." Arab summarized his whole life as an existence of unending hard work: "Work. All my life, work." He found life inscrutable and incomprehensible, always repeating "No foundation. All the way down the line." Mc Carthy, a longshoreman, also had much to say when he came to the saloon. He believed that one has a choice to be a "heel" or a "worker," confessing "I haven't the heart to be a heel, so I'm a worker." A great reader, Mc Carthy expounded on poetry, William Shakespeare, communism, and writers. He theorized that every maniac once aspired to be a writer. Failing in their great ambition, these madmen changed their careers "by becoming important heels." Those who cannot be Shakespeare become senators or communists.

In the midst of these diverse characters with their varied backgrounds, ambitions, and philosophies, Saroyan identifies the common humanity that unites them. At the core of these individuals dwelt a simple goodness that transcended the political and economic problems of the world and the chaos of life. Tom felt the most heartfelt gratitude for Joe's kindness, expressing his appreciation for Joe's brotherly care in a time of illness: "You made me eat all that chicken soup three years ago when I was sick and hungry." Joe fondly remembered the magic of toys that cured the tearful times of his childhood; thus he urged Tom to take toys to the distressed Kitty in the hopes that they will again effect a miraculous cure. Joe also encouraged the romance of Kitty and Tom, hiring an automobile in which they rode to the ocean, where they watched the sunset and delighted in the pleasure of dancing. This time, out of the generous goodness in his heart, Joe went on an errand for Tom. Although these characters appeared and talked like ne'er-do-wells and outcasts, their kindness, friendship, and charity reflected their genuine humanity.

The customers in the saloon protected Kitty when she was pursued by Blick. When he interrogated her and learned that she was an actress who performed in burlesque theaters, Blick demanded that she mount the stage and dance for his pleasure, shouting for her to take off her clothes. Joe, Wesley, Nick, and others rose to her defense and honored her dignity. Their essential decency transformed the lowly saloon into a noble, chivalrous institution. Although Nick warned Blick and demanded, "Now get out of here," the detective was determined to make his arrest and destroy the humane world of the saloon. Suddenly, however, a shot was heard. Kit Carson, who told tall tales in the saloon (he once fought a six-footer with an iron claw for a hand), had fired the gun. The teller of tall tales who boasted about herding cattle on a bicycle stated the simple truth: "Killed a man once, in San Francisco, name of Glick or Blick or something." Kit Carson's crazy statement and wild shooting made more sense than a policeman's arrest of a lawbreaker. As Saroyan writes in the preface to the play, "Have no shame in being kindly and gentle, but if the time comes in the time of your life to kill, kill and have no regret."

Critical Evaluation:

William Saroyan announces the theme of his play in his introduction: "In the time of your life, live—so that in that wondrous time you shall not add to the misery and sorrow of the world, but shall smile to the infinite delight and mystery of it." Critics acknowledge Saroyan's appeal to the virtues of compassion and kindness as the antidote to the cruelty of the world and the problems of life. *The Time of Your Life* was such an innovative play when it first appeared that critics labeled it experimental, recognizing that it did not conform to the conventions of modern drama, specifically, the theater of ideas, as popularized by Henrik Ibsen and George Bernard Shaw. Saroyan avoids didactic polemics in his play, which was written shortly before the entry of the United States into World War II. Rather, the play evokes an atmosphere of respect for the forgotten and the unfortunate. This aspect of Saroyan's play left him vulnerable to charges of vagueness and of failure to think things through. Critics have nevertheless appreciated the well-constructed three-act play.

Some critics have objected to Saroyan's naïve sentiment and simplistic optimism about the brotherhood of man and the good will found in common humanity. They have pointed out the unlikelihood of the actual existence of a saloon that is a home for Nick the Italian, Wesley the black man, Arab, and the Assyrian Harry, among others. Other critics have praised Saroyan's play for avoiding the dramatic conventions of American theater of the time. It was refreshing as well that Saroyan was able to write a gentle, optimistic play at a time when Adolf Hitler was in ascendancy and World War II was beginning. Saroyan uses comedy to deflate the Gestapo techniques of Blick. The play's development of the camaraderie and the kinship of outsiders and of people of different racial background is more than an example of wishful thinking, it shows wisdom.

Saroyan wrote of his indebtedness to George Bernard Shaw, and many parallels have been drawn between *The Time of Your Life* and Shaw's dramas. Saroyan wrote: "Shaw . . . is the tonic of the Christian peoples of the world. He is health, wisdom, and comedy, and that's what I am too." The characters in the play who epitomize health, wisdom, and comedy are Dudley Bostwick, who overcomes the obstacles of his formal learning to realize that what he wants is a woman; the Greek American newsboy who sings "When Irish Eyes Are Smiling" to the delight of the Italian American Nick; and Krupp the policeman, whose wry commentary on human nature reveals his comic, sardonic understanding. In addition, Wesley's love of piano playing, Arab's harmonica playing, and Willie's enjoyment of the pinball machine all convey the simple exuberance of being alive, a feeling that the tragic outlook suppresses.

The Time of Your Life received the New York Drama Critics Circle Award and the Pulitzer Prize. Saroyan, however, refused the Pulitzer because he thought that moneyed interests should not influence art or corrupt the integrity of the writer's work.

Mitchell Kalpakgian

Bibliography:
Calonne, David Stephen. *William Saroyan: My Real Work Is Being.* Chapel Hill: University of North Carolina Press, 1983. A thorough account of Saroyan's life and work. Chapter 5 interprets *The Time of Your Life* as a play that views life as chaotic and miraculous and relates the play to vaudeville and to the theater of the absurd.

Floan, Howard R. *William Saroyan.* Boston: Twayne, 1966. Discusses the four main periods and genres of Saroyan's writing: short fiction, drama, the novel, and autobiography. Chapter 4 interprets the play as a microcosm of America's romanticized past and its harsh economic reality.

Foster, Edward Halsey. *William Saroyan: A Study of the Short Fiction.* New York: Twayne 1991. A valuable work that combines literary criticism of Saroyan's short fiction, autobiographical writings, and an interview with Saroyan. Includes the estimations of several critics of his place in American literature.

Hamalian, Leo, ed. *William Saroyan: The Man and the Writer Remembered.* London: Associated University Presses, 1987. A collection of essays and memoirs by critics, friends, and admirers of Saroyan. An excellent miscellany that examines topics from Saroyan's experience in an orphanage to the literary influences that shaped his art.

Lee, Lawrence, and Barry Gifford. *Saroyan: A Biography.* New York: Harper & Row, 1984. A biography of Saroyan based on many interviews with his friends, acquaintances, and family members. Provides the background and details of the film version of *The Time of Your Life.*

TIMON OF ATHENS

Type of work: Drama
Author: William Shakespeare (1564-1616)
Type of plot: Tragedy
Time of plot: Fourth century B.C.E.
Locale: Athens and the nearby seacoast
Written: c. 1607-1608; first published, 1623

Principal characters:
    TIMON, an Athenian nobleman
    FLAVIUS, his faithful steward
    APEMANTUS, his philosophical and candid friend
    ALCIBIADES, an Athenian general

The Story:

The Athens house of Timon, a wealthy lord of the city, was the scene of much coming and going. Poets, artists, artisans, merchants, politicians, and well-wishers in general sought the friendship and favors of a man whose generosity knew no bounds. While waiting to speak to Timon, a poet disclosed his vision to an artist: Timon was depicted as the darling of Dame Fortune, and his friends and acquaintances spared no effort in admiring his favored position. The vision continued; Fortune turned and Timon tumbled into penury, his friends doing nothing to comfort him.

Timon joined the crowd of suitors in his reception chamber. When a messenger reported that Ventidius, his friend, had been jailed for a debt, Timon promised to pay the debt and to support Ventidius until he became solvent again. An old man complained that one of Timon's servants had stolen the heart of his only daughter. Timon promised to match the girl's dowry with an equal sum. Then he received the poet and the painter and the jeweler graciously, accepting their shameless flattery. Apemantus, a crudely candid friend, declared broadly that these flatterers and seekers of bounty were a pack of knaves. Alcibiades, a great military leader, came with a troop of followers to dine with Timon. As all prepared to feast at Timon's bounteous table, Apemantus cursed them roundly.

A great feast was served to the accompaniment of music. Ventidius, having been freed from jail, offered to repay the money spent in his behalf, but Timon declared that friendship would not allow him to accept Ventidius' money. When Apemantus warned Timon that men would readily slay the man whose food and drink they consume, Timon expressed his gratitude at having so many friends with which to share his generosity. He wished, however, that he might be poorer so that these good friends might know the joy of sharing their largess with him. Timon's eyes filled with tears, so overcome was he by the sentiments of friendship, as a group of costumed Athenian ladies presented lavish gifts to him from men of wealth. Timon then presented rich gifts to his departing friends. Flavius, his steward, observed that his master's infinite generosity had almost emptied his coffers. Timon told Apemantus that he would give him gifts, too, if he would cease railing at these felicities of friendship.

Before long Timon was reduced to insolvency and was near beggary. A senator to whom he owed a great sum of money sent his servant to collect. Other servants of Timon's creditors also gathered in front of his house. Timon, who had never given Flavius a chance to explain that he, Timon, had no more money, asked the steward the reason for the crowd outside. When Flavius told him the truth, Timon ordered the sale of all of his lands. Flavius disclosed that his lands were already sold or mortgaged. Refusing to share Flavius' alarm, Timon declared that he now had a chance to test his friends. He directed his servants to borrow money from Lucius, Lucullus, and Sempronius; the servants were then to go to the senators and borrow more. Flavius disclosed that he had already tried without success to borrow from these sources. Timon made excuses for them, however, and suggested that the servants try Ventidius, who had recently come into a large fortune.

The servant who went to Lucullus was told that times were difficult and that Timon's friendship alone was not sufficient security for a loan. When Lucullus offered the servant a bribe to say that he had been unable to see Lucullus, the horrified servant threw down the bribe money and departed in disgust. Lucius claimed that he, needing money, had hoped to borrow from Timon. A third servant went to Sempronius. Upon learning that Lucullus, Lucius, and even Ventidius had denied Timon loans, Sempronius pretended to be hurt that Timon had not sent to him first, and he also refused.

As Timon continued to be importuned by his creditors' servants, he went out in a rage and bade them cut out of his heart what he owed their masters. Still enraged, he directed Flavius to invite all of his creditors to a feast. Alcibiades, meanwhile, plead in the senate for the remission of the death sentence on a veteran soldier who had committed murder. The senators, deaf to arguments that the man had killed in self-defense, persisted in their decision. When Alcibiades continued to plea, the senators sentenced him, on pain of death, to be banished from Athens.

At Timon's house, tables were arranged as though for a great banquet. Apologizing profusely for being unable to honor his requests for money, Timon's guests appeared at his house expecting a lavish banquet. When Timon bade them eat, however, they discovered that the covered dishes were filled only with warm water. Timon then cursed them for what they were, threw the water in their faces, and drove them out of his house.

Now a confirmed misanthrope, Timon left Athens. For the moment he focused all of his hatred on Athens and its citizens, but he predicted that his curses would eventually encompass all humanity. Flavius, meanwhile, announced to his fellow servants that their service in Timon's house had come to an end. After sharing what little money he had with his fellows, Flavius pocketed his remaining money and declared his intentions of seeking out his old master.

One day Timon, who was living in a cave near the seashore, dug for roots and discovered gold. As he was cursing the earth for producing this root of all evil, Alcibiades appeared, accompanied by his two mistresses. Timon cursed the three and told them to leave him. When Alcibiades disclosed that he was on his way to besiege Athens, Timon gave him gold and wished him every success. He also gave the two women gold, after exhorting them to infect the minds and bodies of all men with whom they came in contact. When Alcibiades and his troops marched away, Timon continued to dig roots for his dinner.

Apemantus appeared to rail at Timon for going to the opposite extreme from that which had caused his downfall. He declared that wild nature was as cruel as men, that Timon, therefore, would do well to return to Athens and flatter men who were still favored by fortune. After Apemantus left, a band of cutthroats, having heard that Timon possessed a great store of gold, went to the cave. When they told Timon that they were destitute, he threw gold at them and ordered them to practice their malign art in Athens. So bitter were Timon's words that they left him, determined to abandon all violence.

Flavius, finding the cave, wept at the pitiful state to which his master had fallen. Timon, at first rude to his faithful steward, was almost overcome by Flavius' tears. He gave Flavius gold, wished him well, and admonished him to succor only dogs.

After reports of Timon's newly found wealth reached Athens, the poet and the painter went to his cave. Timon greeted them sarcastically, praised them for their honesty, and gave them gold to use in destroying other sycophants and flatterers. Flavius returned, accompanied by two senators, who apologized for the great wrongs done to Timon and offered to lend him any amount of money he might desire. They also promised him command of the Athenian forces in the struggle against Alcibiades; Timon, however, cursed both Athens and Alcibiades. His prescription to the Athenians for ending their troubles was that they come to the shore and hang themselves on a tree near his cave. When he retreated into his cave, the senators, knowing their mission fruitless, returned to Athens.

In Athens, the senators begged Alcibiades to spare the city because its importance transcended the petty griefs of an Alcibiades or a Timon. Alcibiades agreed to spare Athens only on the condition that those who had offended Timon and him should be punished. As the city gates were opened to the besiegers, a messenger reported that Timon was dead. Alcibiades read Timon's epitaph, copied by the messenger. It reaffirmed Timon's hatred of humanity and expressed his desire that no one pause at his grave.

Critical Evaluation:

One of William Shakespeare's most neglected plays, *Timon of Athens* was probably never performed during his lifetime, and it has only rarely been performed since. The reasons for its unpopularity include its strongly bitter tone and its lack of an emotionally satisfying ending. Further, the play has many elements that are uncharacteristic of Shakespeare's work: clashing themes, irregular verse passages, confused character names, and a shallow central character. For these reasons, scholars long suspected that *Timon of Athens* was a collaborative effort. Modern scholars, however, hold that the play's problems are due to the fact that Shakespeare wrote it by himself, but never polished it because he left it unfinished. His reasons for abandoning the play are not known, but reasonable inferences may be drawn from the play's curious nature.

Timon of Athens defies easy classification. As a bleak tale about a once kind man who dies a bitter misanthrope, the play appears to be a tragedy. What leads to Timon's financial ruin and ultimate destruction is, ironically, the generosity that permits him to rise high in Athenian society. His sudden and deep fall points up the fateful vulnerability of human existence—a nearly universal theme in tragedy. Despite this tragic motif, the play has many characteristics of traditional comedy. Because of its unusual blend of tragedy and comedy, it is now regarded not only as a curious experiment, but as an important transitional phase in Shakespeare's mature writing career.

There are several reasons for regarding *Timon of Athens* as a comedy. The play's savage depiction of greed, hypocrisy, and duplicity among the Athenian nobility constitutes the kind of social satire that became a dramatic staple in seventeenth century England. The immorality of the ruling classes was itself one of Shakespeare's own favorite themes. The theme is demonstrated here in the actions of the governors of Athens, who ruin Timon by cruelly calling in his debts. When they banish Alcibiades merely for seeking clemency for a deserving veteran, they expose Athens to the threat of his sacking the city. Later, after Timon is known again to have wealth, they hypocritically try to recruit him to defend the city against Alcibiades.

The play's satire is expressed most powerfully through the voice of Timon's friend Apemantus, who frequently utters crude jokes about wealthy men and government leaders. The sheer viciousness of his remarks is in itself often comical. Even more telling, however, is the play's use of a traditional device for ending comedies: reconciliation. However, it is not Timon himself who achieves a reconciliation, but Alcibiades—who gives up his plan to sack Athens. In rejecting vengeance, Alcibiades expresses the play's ultimate theme: that mercy is more valuable than justice. This strongly positive conclusion contrasts sharply with the harshly negative manner in which Timon ends his life.

What makes this oddly ambiguous play most significant within Shakespeare's dramatic work is the timing of its composition. Hard evidence for dating the play is lacking, but Shakespeare most likely wrote it around 1606 to 1608. These years immediately followed the period in which he wrote the three dramas that have become known as his "problem plays"—*Troilus and Cressida* (c. 1601-1602), *All's Well That Ends Well* (1602-1604), and *Measure for Measure* (1604-1605). All three plays are unresolved examinations of psychological and sociological complications of life, sex, and death. *Timon of Athens* resembles them in its own ambiguities and its attention to the issues of atonement and reconciliation.

Shakespeare wrote many plays in the tradition of medieval morality plays, which combined comedy with moral lessons in order to educate audiences. The central lesson of *Timon of Athens* is that one cannot find happiness in leading a materialistic life, such as Timon lives until his downfall. While he is financially able to give great feasts and lavish expensive gifts on friends, he believes himself happy and well loved. Only after his money runs out does he realize the shallowness of his happiness. Even then, however, he still fails to recognize true friendship when it is offered by his faithful steward, Flavius. Thus, in contrast to traditional morality plays, *Timon of Athens* does not end with its hero's finding happiness by learning how to appreciate more spiritual values. Instead, Timon declines even deeper into despair and he dies miserably. The play thus begins with Timon symbolizing friendship and ends with him symbolizing misanthropy.

Whatever Shakespeare's intentions were when he began *Timon of Athens*, the play served him as an experiment in which to work out new themes. After abandoning it, he wrote the plays known as his romances: *Pericles, Prince of Tyre* (c. 1607-1608), *Cymbeline* (c. 1609-1610), *The Winter's Tale* (c. 1610-1611), and *The Tempest* (c. 1611). Like *Timon of Athens*, these plays explore such themes as exile and return, the absence of moral absolutes, and the transcendent quality of mercy.

Bibliography:
Ellis-Fermor, Una. "Timon of Athens: An Unfinished Play." *The Review of English Studies* 18, no. 71 (July, 1942): 270-283. Discusses the controversy over the authorship of the play. Concludes that it is likely Shakespeare's work alone and that it is an unfinished play.
Knight, G. Wilson. "The Pilgrimage of Hate: An Essay on Timon of Athens." In *The Wheel of Fire: Interpretations of Shakespearian Tragedy*. Rev. ed. New York: Methuen, 1949. Interprets Timon as a noble figure, abused by a harsh world. Sees the play as a great tragedy.
Nowottny, Winifred M. T. "Acts IV and V of *Timon of Athens*." *Shakespeare Quarterly* 10, no. 4 (Autumn, 1959): 493-497. Interprets the play in a religious context. Sees the substitution of secular myths for Christian ones in the play.
Nuttall, A. D. *Timon of Athens*. Hemel Hempstead, England: Harvester Wheatsheaf, 1989. Provides a stage history, an account of the critical reception to the play, and a sustained analysis.
Soellner, Rolf. *Timon of Athens*. Columbus: Ohio State University Press, 1979. Critical analysis with reference to dramatic and cultural contexts. Discusses the merits of the play.

THE TIN DRUM

Type of work: Novel
Author: Günter Grass (1927-   )
Type of plot: Social satire
Time of plot: 1899-1954
Locale: Poland and Germany
First published: Die Blechtrommel, 1959 (English translation, 1961)

Principal characters:
> OSKAR MATZERATH, the narrator and hero
> AGNES MATZERATH, his mother
> ALFRED MATZERATH, her husband
> JAN BRONSKI, Mrs. Matzerath's cousin and lover and possibly Oskar's
> father
> MR. BEBRA, a circus midget and a universal artist
> ROSWITHA RAGUNA, his associate and the most celebrated somnambulist
> in all Italy
> HERBERT TRUCZINSKI, a neighbor of the Matzeraths
> MARIA TRUCZINSKI, Herbert's youngest sister
> GREFF, a greengrocer
> LINA, his wife
> SISTER DOROTHEA KÖNGETTER, a trained nurse and a neighbor of Oskar
> in Düsseldorf
> GOTTFRIED VON VITTLAR, a man whose testimony leads to Oskar's arrest
> and later Oskar's friend

The Story:

In 1899, Oskar's Kashubian grandmother was sitting in a potato field, concealing the fugitive Joseph Koljaiczek under her wide skirts from pursuing constables. She thereby conceived Oskar's mother, Agnes. In 1923, in the free city of Danzig, Agnes Koljaiczek married Alfred Matzerath, a citizen of the German Reich, and introduced him to her Polish cousin and lover, Jan Bronski, with whom he became fast friends. When Oskar was born, he soon showed himself to be an infant whose mental development was complete at birth.

Oskar was promised a drum for his third birthday. That drum, in its many atavistic recurrences, allowed him mutely to voice his protest against the meaninglessness of a world that formulated its destructive nonsense in empty language. The drum also allowed him to re-create the history of his consciousness and to recall in the varied music of the drum the rhythms of his mind's apprehensions of the world around him. On his third birthday, Oskar, by a sheer act of will, decided to stop growing and to remain with his three-year-old body and his totally conscious mind for the rest of his life. As he later boasted, he remained from then on a precocious three-year-old in a world of adults who tower over him but are nevertheless inferior to him. While he was complete both inside and out, free from all necessity to grow, develop, and change as time passed, they continued to move toward old age and the grave.

Oskar's refusal to grow, to measure his shadow by that of older persons, or to compete for the things they desire, was the assertion of his individuality against a world that, misconstruing him, tried to force him into an alien pattern. He was pleased when he discovered his ability to shatter glass with his voice, a talent that became not only a means of destruction, the venting of his hostility and outrage, but also an art whereby he could cut a neat hole in the window of a jewelry shop, through which Bronski—upon whom he heaps the filial affection he does not feel for his actual father—could snatch an expensive necklace for his beloved Agnes.

The later period of Oskar's recorded existence was crammed with outlandish events. His mother, after witnessing a revolting scene of eels being extracted from the head of a dead horse submerged in water, perversely enforced a diet of fish on herself and died. Oskar became fascinated with the hieroglyphic scars on the massive back of his friend Herbert Truczinski, but Herbert, who worked as a Maritime Museum attendant, grew enamored of a ship's wooden figurehead called Niobe. In an attempt to make love to her, he was instead impaled to her by a double-edged ship's axe. Jan Bronski was executed after an S.S. raid on the Polish post office where he had gone with Oskar. Oskar was overwhelmed with guilt after the death of his mother and that of the man who was probably his father. In one of the most superbly preposterous seduction scenes in literature, Oskar became the lover of Herbert's youngest sister, Maria, and fathered her child. Maria then married Alfred Matzerath, and Oskar, having been as prodigious sexually as he was diminutive physically, turned to the ampler comforts of Lina Greff, whose latent homosexual husband, upon receiving a summons to appear in court on a morals charge, committed a fantastically elaborate, grotesque suicide. Oskar then joined Bebra's troupe of entertainers and became the lover of the timeless Roswitha Raguna. When the Russians invaded Danzig, Alfred Matzerath, to conceal his affiliations, swallowed the Nazi party pin that Oskar had shoved into his hand and died. Again Oskar felt responsible for the death of a parent. Before long, against his will, he began to grow and to develop a hump. His postwar life took him to West Germany, where he was at various times a black marketeer, a model, and a nightclub entertainer, and eventually to Düsseldorf, where a destiny not his own caught up with him in the guise of the accusation that he killed Sister Dorothea Köngetter, the woman in the room next to his. The testimony of Vittlar, meant to save Oskar (although Vittlar had earlier thought him guilty), damned him. Oskar submitted to being judged insane and atoning for a guilt not strictly his, because to his own sense he was guilty by implication, an emblem of the modern world even in his isolation from it.

Critical Evaluation:

Günter Grass's iconoclastic novel *The Tin Drum* shook the moral complacency of the German people and forced them to acknowledge their responsibility for the triumph of Nazism. Earlier, Grass had won minor acclaim for his poetry, but in 1959 Group 47, a German association of young artists and writers, awarded him its prepublication cash prize for *The Tin Drum*. When the novel appeared the next year, it caused the greatest uproar in the history of German literature. Translated into most major languages over the next few years, the novel won international critical acclaim. Grass himself instantly became the best-known and most controversial figure of postwar German literature.

In addition to Group 47's prepublication prize, *The Tin Drum* won three major international literary awards. In 1965, while Grass was accepting the coveted George Büchner Prize, members of a youth organization in Düsseldorf publicly burned copies of *The Tin Drum*. Despite critical acclaim and many awards, Grass and *The Tin Drum* became the target of more than forty lawsuits and innumerable denunciations in the letters-to-the editor columns of virtually every publication in Germany. People from all social strata in Germany accused Grass of pornography, blasphemy, sacrilege, slander, defamation, and other heinous crimes.

The furor over *The Tin Drum* arose from one central theme, that Grass refused to exculpate himself or any other German from guilt for the Nazi regime. In his novel, Grass identified Nazi affinities in most of the people and in all of the institutions of German society.

Critics have called Grass's account of the Nazi era wildly satirical, wickedly humorous, and morally chilling. Grass presents a German religious institution only too willing to accommodate itself to Adolf Hitler's regime. Some of his most damning barbs are directed at Grass's own Catholicism, but Protestants are not spared their share of guilt. The picture of the acclaimed German educational institution presented in *The Tin Drum* suggests that its discipline and regimentation prepared the way admirably for Hitler and his movement. In Grass's book, the German political tradition of authoritarianism and antiliberalism almost invited a Hitler to take power. Grass also showed how the Nazis capitalized on and institutionalized a widespread view of women that relegated them to a subordinate status in family relationships and the workforce. In *The Tin Drum*, all economic classes in Germany willingly sacrificed their personal freedom to gain the economic prosperity that Hitler promised and delivered. In short, Grass insists that Hitler was no accident but the logical development of German history; therefore, all the evil of the Nazi era was the direct responsibility of all Germans living at the time.

After World War II, West Germany's new economic and military partnership with the Western bloc engendered an attempt on the part of many Germans to disassociate themselves from their country's Nazi past. Many German teachers, historians, writers, and government officials argued that Hitler and his movement represented a historical anomaly, not the logical development of German history. Hitler came to power, these apologists maintained, because of a special set of circumstances: the German defeat in World War I and ensuing Treaty of Versailles; the economic dislocations in Germany during the Weimar Republic; and middle-class fear of a Communist takeover. The German nation as a whole, they concluded, should not be forced to bear the guilt for atrocities committed by a group of madmen who illegally seized control of their government.

During the period between 1945 and 1959, a body of literature in Germany and elsewhere propounded the thesis that most Germans had deplored Hitler and the Nazis. Accounts of various German resistance groups that had actively sought to overthrow Hitler appeared alongside stories of individual Germans who had helped to rescue Jews from deportation to concentration camps. German artists, writers, and scientists pointed out that many of their number had emigrated shortly after Hitler came to power. Most of those who remained insisted that they had been part of the so-called inner emigration, that though they had remained in Germany they had never cooperated with the regime and had worked in subtle ways to thwart Hitler's purposes.

Grass portrayed those Germans who had engaged in active resistance to Hitler's regime as having been opposed only to Hitler himself and not to the substance of Nazism. He also dismissed those German intellectuals engaged in the "inner emigration" as being nothing more than court jesters for Nazi propaganda minister Joseph Goebbels. Taken in total, the novel condemned all Germans and insisted that they acknowledge the moral and spiritual shortcomings of their institutions; little wonder that almost every German reader found something offensive in *The Tin Drum*.

Despite the controversy, *The Tin Drum* was widely read and discussed in Germany, especially by young people (more than half a million copies sold there during the five years following its publication). The West German government began insisting that students be taught the history of the Nazi era, which had been neglected in the immediate postwar era. In the succeeding decades, *The Tin Drum* and Grass's other novels and poetry became the foci for an entire nation in its reinterpreting its past and reexaming the moral foundations of its institutions.

After *The Tin Drum* appeared in translation in the United States in 1961, Grass was acclaimed by many critics as Germany's greatest living writer. Literary critics in France, Denmark, and many other countries went so far as to rank Grass as the world's greatest living novelist, and they praised his courage in raising such controversial issues in his own country. A few critics were perceptive enough to point out that the elements of German society that Grass satirized so scathingly—which according to him had led directly to Nazism—became present in every industrialized nation in the second half of the twentieth century. Although Grass directed his message to Germans, many of his admirers argued that all humankind must learn from his pages or suffer a resurgence of the tyranny that nearly engulfed the world before 1945.

"Critical Evaluation" by Paul Madden

Bibliography:
Hatfield, Henry. "Günter Grass: The Artist as Satirist." In *The Contemporary Novel in German: A Symposium*, edited by Robert R. Heitner. Austin: University of Texas Press, 1967. A paean of praise to Grass and *The Tin Drum*. Explains the satirical intent of many passages in the novel that are obscure to readers not intimately familiar with German history and the German language.
Hollington, Michael. *Günter Grass: The Writer in a Pluralist Society*. London: Marion Boyars, 1980. Although Hollington devotes only one chapter to *The Tin Drum*, references to the novel permeate the entire book. Hollington credits Grass with forcing Germans to look candidly at the Nazi era and with inspiring a younger generation to fight against the complacency of their elders.
Maurer, Robert. "The End of Innocence: Günter Grass' *The Tin Drum*." In *Critical Essays on Günter Grass*, edited by Patrick O'Neill. Boston: G. K. Hall, 1987. A detailed interpretation of Grass's novel but with some questionable conclusions. The major value of the article is that it delineates the many literary influences, ranging from Voltaire to Thomas Mann, that are manifest in *The Tin Drum*.
Miles, Keith. *Günter Grass*. New York: Barnes & Noble Books, 1975. Although only chapter 2 deals exclusively with *The Tin Drum*, readers will learn much about the novel and about its impact in the introduction and in the other seven chapters. Miles considers Grass to be Germany's and perhaps the world's greatest living novelist. His interpretations of and insights into *The Tin Drum* are perceptive and very useful to the reader trying to understand Grass's often cryptic prose.
Tank, Kurt Lothar. *Günter Grass*. Translated by John Conway. New York: Frederick Ungar, 1969. Contains a short biography of Grass and considerable analysis of Grass's early works, most especially *The Tin Drum*. The analysis might be difficult for readers not acquainted with German literature and the argot of literary criticism.

'TIS PITY SHE'S A WHORE

Type of work: Drama
Author: John Ford (1586-after 1639)
Type of plot: Tragedy
Time of plot: 1620's
Locale: Parma, Italy
First performed: 1629?; first published, 1633

Principal characters:
 BONAVENTURA, a friar
 SORANZO, a nobleman
 FLORIO, a citizen of Parma
 DONADO, another citizen
 GRIMALDI, a Roman gentleman
 GIOVANNI, son of Florio
 BERGETTO, nephew of Donado
 RICHARDETTO, a supposed physician
 VASQUES, servant of Soranzo
 ANNABELLA, daughter of Florio
 HIPPOLITA, wife of Richardetto
 PUTANA, tutor of Annabella

The Story:

Previously recognized as a brilliant young scholar, Giovanni confessed to his tutor, Friar Bonaventura, that his love for his own sister, Annabella, was without limit. The friar warned Giovanni of eternal damnation if he did not forget this sinful lust and exhorted his young pupil to pray. Grimaldi, a Roman gentleman, in Parma to court Annabella, fought with Vasques, the servant of Soranzo, a nobleman. Grimaldi, enraged, proclaimed that he would be revenged on Soranzo for Vasques' assault. Putana, Annabella's tutor, told the girl that she was fortunate to have Grimaldi and Soranzo wooing her; personally, the old nurse preferred Soranzo, a virile and wealthy man of twenty-three. Annabella did not care to hear of the virtues of any suitor, but she had no patience for Bergetto, a tiresome twit.

Giovanni tried prayers and fasting, but nothing alleviated his misery. It was not his lust, he felt, that led him on, but his fate. He confessed to Annabella his love for her, and she admitted that she also loved him. Their father, Florio, worried about his studious son's health, had more hope for descendants from his daughter's marriage; the father said he wanted her to marry for love rather than wealth. Florio was receptive, however, when Donado promised large amounts of money if Florio would let Donado's simple-minded nephew, Bergetto, pay court to Annabella. Giovanni and Annabella yielded to their desires and were intimate together; then they worried about being separated if she were forced to marry.

Hippolita, Soranzo's former mistress, believing she had been recently widowed, reminded Soranzo that he had promised to marry her when her husband died. In frustration and anger at being rejected, Hippolita promised to revenge herself upon Soranzo. Vasques promised to assist Hippolita in gaining her revenge. A supposed doctor, recently come to Parma, was really Hippolita's husband, Richardetto. He had come in disguise to spy on his wife. While Richardetto was suspicious of Annabella's indifference to all men, he told Grimaldi that Soranzo stood between him (Grimaldi) and Annabella's heart; together they plotted to kill Soranzo. Thus, Richardetto would have his own revenge on the man who had cuckolded him.

Giovanni confessed his relationship with his sister to the friar. The friar was greatly shocked and warned Giovanni of damnation. Giovanni tried by sophistical reasoning to prove that the love he and his sister bore for each other was not wrong. The friar replied that the only thing they could do to save themselves was to have Annabella marry. Bergetto sent a letter and jewel to Annabella, but she told Donado that she would never marry his nephew. Donado made her a gift of the jewel his nephew had sent to her, but Bergetto stubbornly decided that he would continue to woo Annabella. When Giovanni saw his sister wearing the ring originally sent by Bergetto, he was tormented with jealousy.

Florio preferred Soranzo to Annabella's other suitors, but Annabella told Soranzo that he should give up his thought of marrying her. She attempted to console him by promising that if she had to accept any of her suitors, he would be the one to win her favor. Annabella discovered that she was with child and Putana confided the news to her brother. Meanwhile, Florio had decided that his daughter had to marry Soranzo and asked the friar to help win her over. Annabella confessed her intimacy with her brother to the friar, and he eloquently warned her of hell and told her that the only way to preserve her honor was to marry Soranzo. At last, she yielded to his insistence.

At the same time, the plot between Grimaldi and Richardetto to kill Soranzo had developed. Grimaldi, mistaking Bergetto for Soranzo, stabbed him with a rapier that was coated with poison by the fake doctor. Vasques told Hippolita that her former lover, his master, was now betrothed to Annabella and that the marriage would take place in two days. Hippolita renewed her pledge to have revenge on the man she felt had betrayed her. Soon, it was revealed that it was Grimaldi who had killed Bergetto. He gave himself up to the cardinal, who granted him protection, in the name of the pope. Grimaldi explained that he had intended to kill Soranzo, not the foolish Bergetto. Donado and Florio lamented the absence of justice on earth, none came even from churchmen.

After the marriage of Annabella to Soranzo, there was a lavish banquet, but the miserable Giovanni could not hide his despair. Hippolita appeared in a masque, but believing that she would not keep her side of the bargain they had made, Vasques gave her the poisoned cup intended for his master; unknowingly, she drank it. Realizing that she had been poisoned by Vasques, Hippolita died cursing Soranzo and his new bride. Soranzo learned that Annabella was pregnant by another man; she admitted that she chose him not for love, but to protect her honor. She refused to tell him the name of her lover. In his rage he drew his sword, but was prevented from killing his young wife by the intervention of Vasques. Nevertheless, Soranzo contemplated revenge upon this woman he so recently had loved. Putana unwittingly told Vasques that Giovanni was the man who had made Annabella pregnant. She then was gagged and kidnapped—and blinded—before she could warn Annabella. Vasques told his master, Soranzo, the full truth.

Annabella, imprisoned in her room, gave the friar a letter for her brother warning him to repent and not to believe Saranzo. Meanwhile, Soranzo and Vasques plotted to have revenge upon both Annabella and Giovanni. The friar gave Annabella's letter, written in her own blood, to Giovanni. Soon after, Vasques invited Giovanni to a birthday feast that Soranzo was holding: the feast was merely a ploy to bring Soranzo's revenge to fruition. Giovanni accepted the invitation; he felt that it did not matter what he did. His fate would find him.

Soranzo paid bandits to assist him in his plot. Giovanni, Florio, the cardinal, and other citizens of Parma came to the feast. Giovanni, sent by Soranzo to fetch her, talked passionately and despairingly with Annabella in her bed chamber. Giovanni stabbed Annabella as they kissed. Giovanni entered the banquet room with Annabella's heart on his dagger. At first, the assembly was too stunned to take him seriously. Wildly, he confessed to everyone of his sin with his sister. Vasques went to Annabella's room and returned to confirm that she was, indeed, murdered. Florio fell dead at the news.

Giovanni stabbed Soranzo. Vasques and Giovanni fought, and the bandits rushed in and fought Giovanni. Soranzo, realizing that he had been mortally stabbed, died telling Vasques not to let Giovanni survive him. Giovanni soon bled to death, however, bidding death welcome.

While summoning up echoes of Thomas Kyd's *The Spanish Tragedy* (c. 1585) and William Shakespeare's *Romeo and Juliet* (c. 1594-1596), *'Tis Pity She's A Whore*, by John Ford, the last distinctive playwright in English Renaissance drama, offers new attitudes toward sex, death, and immortality. This play also provides evidence that Elizabethan and Jacobean theater had exhausted itself, even before the theaters were closed in 1642.

Critical Evaluation:

Without question, choosing incest between brother and sister was a daring choice of subject matter, one that was not ignored by other playwrights. There is incest in Cyril Tourneur's *The Revenger's Tragedy* (c. 1607) between stepmother and stepson. In John Webster's *The Duchess of Malfi* (c. 1613), there is the obsessive, incestuous love of Ferdinand, Duke of Calabria, for his twin sister, the Duchess of Malfi. There is incest between uncle and niece in Thomas Middleton's *Women Beware Women* (1621), a play directly analogous to *'Tis Pity She's a Whore*, but no where except in John Ford's play is there serious examination of the complex emotions which a love between brother and sister may involve. There is little evidence that Ford's plays were popular in his time, but *'Tis Pity She's a Whore* has been produced many times in the twentieth century.

The play does not condone a love between brother and sister. Even though it is her brother, not she, who initiates their intimacy, Annabella's reputation is sullied from the start. Lest anyone imagine otherwise, note that Ford has given her tutor the name of putana, or whore. While Annabella confesses that she loves Giovanni, she has not dared to say so, or even to think it. The friar is immediately aware that Giovanni's love is a heinous sin. Even Vasques, the Spanish servant to Soranzo, who scruples not at murder (Hippolita) or torture (Putana), who exits the play congratulating himself that he, a Spaniard, has outdone an Italian in revenge, is horrified to discover that Annabella is pregnant by her own brother: "To what height of liberty in damnation hath the devil trained our age. Her brother!" (Act IV, scene iii). Finally, the father of this brother and sister drops dead, of a heart attack, when he hears of his children's incest.

Ford's essentially nonmetaphorical dialogue can be very powerful, but too often the language of his characters, who do not have their own distinct modes of speaking, recalls other plays. Ford borrows much from William Shakespeare, for example. Ford's comic subplots are virtually pointless. Even so, Ford's characterization of the two lovers is multifaceted, and Giovanni, although he is a criminal, must be seen as a sympathetic character.

The play begins with Giovanni confessing his love for his sister to the friar. By the second scene of the first act, he is confessing his love to Annabella, to whom he lies, maintaining that the church sanctions his love. In the last scene of the play, the audience learns from Giovanni that he and his sister have now been lovers for nine months. Giovanni becomes increasingly possessive of his sister as the play progresses; Annabella's love for him remains constant. Having confessed her love to her brother, she knows she has fallen into mortal sin; she simultaneously savors her love and wants to do penance for it. Ford presents her as superior to

Putana and to Hippolita, who is guilty of adultery with Soranzo and of plotting to kill her husband. Philoitis, Richardetto's niece, a minor character, serves to remind the audience that taking refuge in a nunnery was always an option for a young woman of the time—Annabella, although less of a hypocrite than other women characters in the play, is still a sinner who has a way to escape her predicament.

Friar Bonaventura in *'Tis Pity She's a Whore* is analogous to Friar Lawrence in Shakespeare's *Romeo and Juliet*. Friar Lawrence, who should know better, secretly marries Romeo and Juliet in a marriage designed to create harmony between the feuding Capulets and Montagues. His naïveté leads to the deaths of the lovers. Friar Bonaventura is not only naïve, but also morally culpable in insisting that Annabella marry Soranzo when she is already pregnant with Giovanni's baby. This action leads only to further degradation for brother and sister. Some other elements of *'Tis Pity She's a Whore* that are also analogous to other plays could be either deliberate or accidental.

For example, there is Annabella's resemblance to Thomas Kyd's Bel-Imperia in *The Spanish Tragedy* (c. 1585-1589). Bel-Imperia's brother locks her away when she manages to write a letter in her own blood to Hieronimo, who needs to know who has killed his son. Also, Bel-Imperia was supposedly in disgrace over some early intimacy with her lover, but Don, her lover, is not her brother. When Annabella writes a letter to Giovanni in her own blood to warn him that Saranzo knows he is her lover, Giovanni is past caring whether or not anyone knows.

At no point, however, does Annabella manifest the moral and physical courage demonstrated by Bel-Imperia. Annabella is victimized by her brother, who cares less about her being beaten by Soranzo than he cares about whether or not Soranzo has been a better lover. Owned by men, Annabella is killed by her brother, as she asks forgiveness for her sins and his. Annabella's love for her brother is unfailing, but she is always aware that this love is wrong.

Giovanni, however, sees their love as in some way natural, no matter what divine law prohibits, and as decreed by Fate. Increasingly insensitive to ethical values, he welcomes death as no earlier protagonists have done. Just before he kills his sister as part of his revenge on Soranzo, Giovanni tells her that if he could believe that water burns, he might be able to believe that hell or heaven is real. As he dies, the only grace he desires is to see Annabella's face.

"Critical Evaluation" by Carol Bishop

Bibliography:
Bradbrook, M. C. *Themes and Conventions of Elizabethan Tragedy*. Cambridge, England: Cambridge University Press, 1960. Argues that Ford deals with a single subject, a personal human love, and that T. S. Eliot is quite mistaken in stating that the relationship between Giovanni and Annabella is only carnal.
Eliot, T. S. *Essays on Elizabethan Drama*. New York: Harcourt, Brace & World, 1960. Eliot asserts that the two lovers have nothing except a physical relationship. Eliot's influential criticism is often a starting point for later critics, and so needs to be read as a reference.
Ellis-Fermor, Una Mary. *The Jacobean Drama: An Interpretation*. New York: Vintage Books, 1964. Argues the importance of aristocratic virtues to Ford, including courage, chivalry, and chastity, with chastity being the greatest of those virtues. Index.
Ornstein, Robert. *The Moral Vision of Jacobean Tragedy*. Madison: University of Wisconsin Press, 1965. The chapter on Ford's plays is excellent. Argues that only the most ethically dogmatic should be offended by this play.

THE TITAN

Type of work: Novel
Author: Theodore Dreiser (1871-1945)
Type of plot: Naturalism
Time of plot: 1890's
Locale: Chicago
First published: 1914

Principal characters:
FRANK ALGERNON COWPERWOOD, a multimillionaire and financial genius
AILEEN COWPERWOOD, his mistress and then his wife
STEPHANIE PLATOW, his mistress
BERENICE FLEMING, his protégée and mistress
PETER LAUGHLIN, his business partner

The Story:

When he was released from a Pennsylvania prison in the 1870's, Frank Algernon Cowperwood was a millionaire and still young. He went to Chicago to begin a new life with his mistress, Aileen Butler, and within a short time had made friends among influential businessmen there. Divorced by his first wife, Cowperwood finally married Aileen. He prepared to increase his fortune, to become a power in the city, and to conquer its society. To this end, he sought an enterprise that would yield heavy returns on his investment quickly. In his first battle among the financial barons of Chicago, he gained control of the gas companies.

At the same time, the Cowperwoods laid siege to Chicago society, but with little success. Aileen Cowperwood was too high-spirited and lacking in the poise that was required for social success. Then Cowperwood became involved in several lawsuits, and his earlier political-economic disgrace in Philadelphia was exposed in the Chicago newspapers. After a long battle, Cowperwood was able to force the rival gas companies to buy out his franchises at a profit to himself. That deal brought social defeat to the Cowperwoods, at least temporarily, for his rivals in finance were also the social powers of Chicago at that time. Cowperwood turned once again to a mistress, but the affair ended when Aileen attempted to kill her rival.

For several years, a cable-car system of street railways claimed most of Cowperwood's time. He bought control of the horsecar company that served the north side of Chicago. Then his naturally promiscuous temperament asserted itself when he met the dark, lush Stephanie Platow. Ten years younger than his wife and interested in art, literature, and music, she was able to fill a place in his life that Aileen never could.

While involved in that affair, Cowperwood coerced the street railway company on the west side into giving its franchise to him. His enjoyment of his victory was partially spoiled by learning that Stephanie was the lover of another man. Meanwhile, financial forces were at work against Cowperwood. Two city bosses hoped to play the city politicians against Cowperwood, for without the support of the city council to aid him with franchises and grants, the financier would be helpless to merge all the street railways of the city under his control.

The first battle was fought in an election to gain possession of the Chicago city council. It was far more painful for Cowperwood to learn at this time that his wife had been unfaithful to him than to discover that he had arrayed the whole financial and social element of the city against himself. The loss of the election proved no permanent setback to Cowperwood, however, nor did his wife's infidelity. From the latter he recovered, and the former was soon undone by his opponents because they did not pave the way with favors and money when they tried to push bills through the new reform council. Even the new mayor was soon an ally of Cowperwood.

Soon afterward, Cowperwood met Berenice Fleming, the daughter of a procuress, who was being prepared in a fashionable boarding school for a career in society. Cowperwood took her and her family under his wing. He also became her lover, though with some misgivings, given the fact that Berenice was but seventeen and he was fifty-two.

At about this time, his financial rivals were trying to gain franchises for elevated lines powered by electricity. This new development meant that his own street railways had to be converted to electricity, and he had to compete for at least a share of the elevated lines to prevent ruin. The south side "L" was already a tremendous success because of the World's Fair of 1893, and the whole city was now clamoring for better transportation service. Cowperwood's opponents controlled the city's banks, which prevented those institutions from lending him funds needed to begin operations. When he attempted to secure funds in the East, Cowperwood discovered that his assets were in question. By one masterstroke, however, the financier wiped out any question of his ability and his credit; he donated three hundred thousand dollars to the local university for a telescope and observatory.

Even with unlimited credit, the problem of gaining franchises was not easy. He was determined to keep control of the Chicago transportation system, but he began to realize that neither he nor his wife would ever be accepted socially. He decided to build a mansion in New York to hold his collection of art, hoping to make that his card of entry into society.

Having obtained his franchises in Chicago, he began work on elevated lines there. Cowperwood's enemies hoped that he would overreach himself, after which they could force him out of Chicago financially as well as socially. With the collapse of the American Match Corporation, however, which was partially engineered by Cowperwood, a series of runs began on the Chicago banks controlled by his enemies. When their attempts to recall the enormous loans made to Cowperwood failed, he emerged from the affair stronger than ever.

The final battle, and the climax of Cowperwood's financial career in Chicago, was the one he waged to secure fifty-year franchises for his growing transportation system. This project was doubly difficult because of Cowperwood's latest property, the Union Loop, by which he controlled the elevated lines. This loop of elevated track, encircling the downtown business district, had to be used by all the lines in the city. The moneyed interests opposed Cowperwood because he was not with them; the newspapers opposed him because they wanted to see better and cheaper facilities. In the face of such opposition, even the most reckless of the city's aldermen feared to grant the franchises Cowperwood wanted, regardless of the money and the power he was prepared to give them. His lawyers informed Cowperwood that the state constitution prevented the city from granting such long-term franchises, even if the city council could be coerced into approving them. Cowperwood's next idea was to have a transportation commission set up by bribery in the state legislature. The bill that set up the commission included a clause extending existing franchises for a period of fifty years. The bill, passed by the legislature, was vetoed by the governor.

Meanwhile, the New York mansion had been completed, and Aileen moved in. She met with no social success, except among the bohemian set. Berenice Fleming was settled at the same time with her family in a mansion on Park Avenue. Aileen heard of Cowperwood's affair with Berenice Fleming, and when he asked her for a divorce, she tried to commit suicide but failed.

Cowperwood again tried to force his bill through the Illinois legislature, but the legislators returned it to the city council. There, as before, Cowperwood lost. The aldermen were so afraid of the people and the newspapers that they dared not grant what the financier wished, despite his huge bribes. With his hope of controlling the Chicago transportation system gone, Cowperwood sold his interests. Admitting defeat, he and Berenice went to Europe. The titan's empire had fallen.

Critical Evaluation:

The Titan is the second in Theodore Dreiser's trilogy of novels tracing the career of Frank Algernon Cowperwood, which the author had planned to call "A Trilogy of Desire." *The Financier* tells the story of Cowperwood's early successes in the financial world of Philadelphia, of the start of his extramarital affair with Aileen, and of his conviction and imprisonment for grand larceny. In the final novel, *The Stoic* (1947), Cowperwood is still portrayed as shrewdly energetic and ambitious, now living abroad after his defeat in Chicago, and amassing a large but unneeded fortune in London. Estranged from Berenice, he dies a lonely death while his overextended empire finally crumbles.

Cowperwood's character is based on that of nineteenth century Chicago financier Charles Yerkes (1837-1905). Like Dreiser's Cowperwood, Yerkes was a shrewd schemer in business who made his fortune in Philadelphia public transportation, spent a short time in prison for illegal business manipulations, and then moved to Chicago and gained control of a gas trust. Yerkes later tried to monopolize the city's transportation system through long-term franchises, and when he failed he turned to new business interests in the London Tube. According to Richard Lehan's account in *Theodore Dreiser: His World and His Novels* (1969), several even more specific incidents in *The Titan* are taken directly from Dreiser's own exhaustive research into the life of Yerkes and the activities of the Chicago business world he dominated for a time.

The Titan reflects Dreiser's absorption with the ideas of Herbert Spencer, T. H. Huxley, and other nineteenth century social Darwinists who viewed society as essentially controlled by the law of "the survival of the fittest." In Dreiser's view, it is the nature of the universe that "a balance is struck wherein the mass subdues the individual or the individual the mass." Cowperwood's struggle against Hand, Schryhart, and Arneel is one for survival in the financial jungle of Chicago big business.

For Dreiser, such a struggle is wholly amoral. There is no right or wrong because it is the nature as well as the condition of human beings to have to struggle for power and survival. Cowperwood's cause is neither more nor less just than that of his antagonists, nor are his means any less scrupulous than their own. He may be said to be more shrewd than they, or to possess more ruthlessness in certain circumstances, but for Dreiser his struggle is the elemental contest between the impulse-driven energies of the individual and those of others in his society.

The forces underlying Cowperwood's ambitions are actually larger than mere individual desires on his part. Described in the novel as "impelled by some blazing internal force," Cowperwood is driven by instincts beyond his control. Caught up in a natural struggle for survival and for power over others, he is dominated by "the drug of a personality he could not gainsay." He could no more remain satisfied with the money and success he has already attained than he could stay content with one woman. Hence, the need to conquer, to dominate and control, characterizes both Cowperwood's financial and his romantic interests. To both, he brings the same shrewd scheming and forcefulness that are needed for success.

The two major plots—Cowperwood's business life and his romantic life—alternate and mirror each other throughout the novel, and they prove to be integrally related. Cowperwood is as direct in his dealings with women as he is in his confrontations with men of business. The frankness with which he first approaches Rita Sohlberg is very similar to the blunt way he attempts to bribe Governor Swanson. In fact, many of Cowperwood's mistresses are related to the very men who, mainly as a consequence of his amorous trespassings, end up opposing him most bitterly in Chicago. His affairs with Butler's, Cochrane's, and Haguenin's daughters—like his interlude with Hand's wife—not only lessen his circle of friends but also gain him those enemies who eventually pull together to defeat him.

As the title of the novel suggests, Cowperwood is a titan among men, one striving after more and achieving greater victory because he is driven to do so by his very nature. As he had himself come to recognize, the "humdrum conventional world could not brook his daring, his insouciance, his constant desire to call a spade a spade. His genial sufficiency was a taunt and a mockery to many." Yet his is a lonely victory, a fact emphasized by his almost self-imposed alienation from the business community with which his life is so connected, and by his being socially ostracized in Chicago, despite his wealth.

In a sense, Cowperwood is as much a victim of his will to power as any of those he defeats on the stock exchange. For such men as he, power is the very means of survival; and in the world of Chicago business, power generates money, which in turn generates more power. The cycle, as much as the struggle, is endless. If a balance is ever struck between the power of the individual and that of the group, it is, Dreiser suggests, only temporary: For "without variance, how should the balance be maintained?" For Dreiser, as for Cowperwood, this is the meaning of life, a continual rebalancing, a necessary search on the part of the individual to discover a means of maintaining or acquiring his own desires against those of his society. Human beings are but a tool of their own private nature, "forever suffering the goad of a restless heart."

For men like Cowperwood, defeat is no more final or settling than triumph. If he has won anything permanent by the novel's end, it is the love of Berenice. She is part, at least, of the whole that Cowperwood has been driven to seek and attain. More than that he will never achieve or understand about life. "Thou hast lived," concludes Dreiser at the end of the novel, as if to say that the struggle and the searching are themselves the whole that human beings seek.

"Critical Evaluation" by Robert Dees

Bibliography:
Hussman, Lawrence E., Jr. *Dreiser and His Fiction: A Twentieth-Century Quest.* Philadelphia: University of Pennsylvania Press, 1983. Good discussion of Dreiser's attitudes toward women, marriage, and prostitution, as well as his belief in "the giving spirit of women." Also discusses Cowperwood's search for the ideal woman.
Lehan, Richard. *Theodore Dreiser: His World and His Novels.* Carbondale: Southern Illinois University Press, 1969. A critical study of Dreiser's novels that focuses on their genesis, evolution, pattern, and meaning. Discusses such influences on the author's imagination as family, city, work, and politics. Analyzes Cowperwood as a materialist Horatio Alger hero who appreciates beauty and art.
Lingeman, Richard. *An American Journey, 1908-1945.* Vol. 2 in *Theodore Dreiser.* New York: Putnam, 1990. Explores Dreiser's composition of *The Titan* in relation to other aspects of his life. Points out that his doing research for the book in Chicago in 1912 diverged from his previous procedure in writing *Sister Carrie* (1900) and *Jennie Gerhardt* (1911).
Mukherjee, Arun. *The Gospel of Wealth in the American Novel: The Rhetoric of Dreiser and Some of His Contemporaries.* Totowa, N.J.: Barnes & Noble Books, 1987. In the context of

the popular myth of the American dream, Mukherjee sees Cowperwood as "a representative figure, a microcosm that reflects the macrocosm of American society."

Pizer, Donald. *The Novels of Theodore Dreiser: A Critical Study.* Minneapolis: University of Minnesota Press, 1976. Discusses Dreiser's research of historical sources relating to Charles T. Yerkes for the character of Cowperwood. Chronicles his creative choices and the novel's publication history. Extensive discussion of Cowperwood's sexual life as representing Dreiser's interpretation of public morality in America.

TITUS ANDRONICUS

Type of work: Drama
Author: William Shakespeare (1564-1616)
Type of plot: Tragedy
Time of plot: Early Christian era
Locale: Rome and vicinity
First performed: 1594; first published, 1594

> *Principal characters:*
> SATURNINUS, the emperor of Rome
> BASSIANUS, his brother
> TITUS ANDRONICUS, a Roman general
> LAVINIA, his only daughter
> MARCUS, his brother, a tribune
> TAMORA, the queen of the Goths
> AARON, her lover, a Moor
> ALARBUS,
> DEMETRIUS, and
> CHIRON, her sons

The Story:

Early in the Christian era, Saturninus and Bassianus, sons of the late emperor, contended for the crown of the Roman Empire. Both men were leaders of strong factions. Another candidate, a popular one, was Titus Andronicus, a Roman famed for his victories over the barbarian Goths to the north. Marcus Andronicus, brother of Titus, stated in the forum that Titus was the popular choice to succeed the late emperor. The sons, willing to abide by the desires of the populace, dismissed their factions.

As the prominent men of the city went into the senate house, Titus made his triumphant entry into Rome. He was accompanied by his surviving sons and by a casket containing the bodies of other sons. In his train also were Tamora, the queen of the Goths; her sons, Alarbus, Demetrius, and Chiron, and her lover, Aaron, a Moor. Before the senate house, Lucius, one of Titus' sons, demanded that a Gothic prisoner be sacrificed to appease the spirits of his dead brothers in the casket. When Titus offered as sacrifice the oldest son of Tamora, the queen pleaded for mercy, reminding Titus that her sons were as precious to her as his were to him. Titus paid her no heed. Alarbus was sacrificed, and the casket was then laid in the tomb of the Andronici. At that moment Lavinia, Titus' only daughter, appeared to greet her father and brothers and to pay her respects to her fallen brothers.

Marcus came out of the senate house, greeted Titus, and informed him that he was the choice of the people for the emperorship. Titus, unwilling to take on that responsibility at his age, persuaded the people to name Saturninus emperor instead. Saturninus, in gratitude, asked for and received the hand of Lavinia to become his queen. Bassianus, however, to whom Lavinia had given her heart, seized the maid with the help of Marcus and the sons of Titus and carried her away. Titus' son Mutius, who stayed behind to cover their flight, was killed by his father.

Saturninus, who begrudged Titus his popularity with the people, disavowed all allegiance and debt to the general and planned to take Tamora as his wife. Titus, deserted by his emperor, his brother, and his sons, was deeply shaken.

Marcus and Titus' sons returned and expressed the desire to bury Mutius in the family vault. Titus at first refused, saying that Mutius had been a traitor; then he relented after his brother and his sons argued effectively for proper burial. When Bassianus appeared with Lavinia, Saturninus vowed that he would avenge the stealing of the maid who had been given him by her father. Bassianus spoke in Titus' behalf, but Titus declared that he could plead his own case before the emperor. Tamora openly advised Saturninus to be gracious to Titus, but secretly she advised him to gain Titus' friendship only because Titus was so popular in Rome. She assured Saturninus that she would destroy Titus and his family for their having sacrificed one of her own sons. Saturninus therefore pardoned the Andronici and declared his intention of marrying Tamora. Believing their differences reconciled, Titus invited Saturninus to hunt with him the next day.

Aaron, contemplating Tamora's good fortune and the imminent downfall of Saturninus and of Rome as well, came upon Chiron and Demetrius, disputing and about to draw their swords over their chances of winning the favors of Lavinia. Advising the youths to contain themselves, he told them that both could enjoy Lavinia by seizing her in the forest during the hunt, which would be attended by the lords and ladies of the court.

Later, while the hunt was under way, Aaron hid a sack of gold at the foot of a large tree in the forest. He had previously arranged to have a pit dug near the tree; this pit he covered over with undergrowth. There Tamora found him and learned that both Bassianus and Lavinia would come to grief that day. Before Aaron left Tamora, he gave her a letter with directions that the message reach the hands of Saturninus. Bassianus and Lavinia approached and, seeing that the Moor and Tamora had been together, chaffed Tamora and threatened to tell Saturninus of her dalliance in the forest. Chiron and Demetrius came upon the scene. Informed by Tamora that Bassianus and Lavinia had insulted her, they stabbed Bassianus to death. When Tamora urged them to stab Lavinia they refused, saying that they would enjoy her first. Lavinia then appealed to Tamora to remember that Titus had spared her life. Tamora, recalling how Titus had ignored her pleas to spare her son from sacrifice, was determined that her sons should have their lustful pleasure. The brothers, after throwing the body of Bassianus into the pit, dragged Lavinia away to rape her.

Meanwhile, Aaron, on the pretext that he had trapped a panther, brought two of Titus' sons, Quintus and Martius, to the pit and left them there. Martius fell into the trap, where he recognized the murdered Bassianus by a ring he wore on his finger. When Quintus tried to pull Martius out of the pit, he lost his balance and tumbled in to it. Aaron, returning with Saturninus, claimed that Titus' sons had murdered Bassianus. Tamora then gave Saturninus the letter that Aaron had given her. The letter, written ostensibly by one of the Andronici, outlined a plot to assassinate Bassianus, to bury him in a pit, and then to collect payment, which was a bag of gold hidden near the pit. When the bag of gold was found where Aaron had placed it, Saturninus was convinced of the brothers' guilt. Despite Titus' offer of his own person as security for his sons, Saturninus sentenced them to be tortured. Tamora assured Titus that she would speak to Saturninus on his behalf.

In another part of the forest, Chiron and Demetrius, their evil deed accomplished, cut off Lavinia's hands and tongue so that she would be able neither to write nor to tell of what had befallen her. Alone in the forest, Lavinia was joined at last by her uncle, Marcus, who led her to her father.

Later, in Rome, Titus recalled his years of faithful military service to the state and begged the tribunes to spare his sons, but they would not listen to him. Another son, Lucius, a great favorite with the people, attempted unsuccessfully to rescue his brothers. He was banished from the city. As Titus pleaded in vain, Marcus brought the ravished Lavinia to him. The sight of his daughter led Titus to wonder to what infinite depths of grief a man could come. Aaron announced to the grieving Andronici that Saturninus would release Martius and Quintus if one of the family would cut off his hand and send it to the court. Titus agreed to let Lucius and Marcus decide between them; when they went to get an ax, Titus directed Aaron to cut off his hand. Later, a messenger brought Titus his hand and the heads of Martius and Quintus as well. Having suffered as much as a man could suffer, Titus vowed revenge. He directed the banished Lucius to raise an invading force among the Goths.

At his home, Titus appeared to be demented. Even so, it was clear to him one day that Lavinia was trying desperately to tell him something. She indicated in Ovid's *Metamorphoses* the section in which the story of Tereus' brutal rape of Philomela was recounted. Suddenly, it occurred to Marcus that he could, by holding a staff in his teeth and between his knees, write in the sand on the floor. Lavinia took the staff thus and wrote in the sand that Chiron and Demetrius were her violators.

Titus now sent his grandson Lucius with a bundle of weapons to present to Tamora's sons. The youths did not understand the message that Titus had attached to the gift, but Aaron quickly saw that Titus knew who Lavinia's ravishers were. As the brothers admired their gift, a blast of trumpets announced the birth of a child to Tamora. A nurse entered with the newborn baby, who was black, and stated that Tamora, fearful lest Saturninus see it, had sent the child to Aaron. Chiron and Demetrius, aware of their mother's shame, insisted that the infant be killed immediately. When they offered to do the murder, Aaron, the father, defied them. As a precaution, he killed the nurse, one of three women who knew the baby's color. Then he had a fair-skinned baby, newly born, taken to Tamora before he fled to the Goths.

Titus, now reputed to be utterly demented, wrote messages to the gods, attached them to arrows, and, with Marcus and his grandson, shot the arrows into the court. He persuaded a passing farmer to deliver a letter to Saturninus. The emperor was already disturbed because the messages carried by the arrows stated Titus' grievances against the state. When Saturninus threatened to execute justice on old Titus, Tamora, feeling her revenge complete, advised him to treat the distracted old soldier gently. The farmer, meanwhile, delivered Titus' letter. Enraged by its mocking message, Saturninus commanded that Titus be brought to him to be executed.

A messenger then brought word that the Goths, led by Lucius, threatened to sack Rome. Knowing Lucius' popularity with the Romans, Saturninus was fearful. Tamora, however, confident of her ability to save the city, directed the messenger to arrange a conference with Lucius at the house of Titus.

In the camp of the Goths, Aaron and his child were brought before Lucius. Aaron's captor disclosed that he had come upon the Moor in a ruined monastery and had heard him state aloud that the baby's mother was Tamora. At Lucius' promise to preserve the life of the child, Aaron confessed to his crimes against the Andronici. Lucius decreed that the Moor must die a horrible death.

Tamora, meanwhile, believing that Titus was demented beyond all reason, disguised herself as Revenge and with her sons, also disguised, presented herself to Titus. Although Titus recognized her, she insisted that she was Revenge, his friend. Titus, for his own purposes, pretended to be taken in by the disguises; he told Rapine and Murder, Revenge's cohorts, to seek out two such as themselves and destroy them. At Tamora's bidding, Titus directed Marcus to invite Lucius to a banquet, to which Saturninus and Tamora and her sons would also come.

Titus persuaded Chiron and Demetrius to stay with him while their companion, Revenge, went to perform other duties. He then called in his kinsmen, who seized and bound the brothers.

Titus told them that he intended to kill them and feed to their mother a paste made of their bones and blood. Lavinia held a bowl between the stumps of her arms to catch their blood as Titus cut their throats.

Lucius, accompanied by a guard of Goths, came to his father's house, where he put Aaron in the charge of Marcus. Saturninus and Tamora made their appearance and were ushered to a banquet served by Titus, dressed as a cook. Titus, hearing from Saturninus that Virginius, in the legend, had done well to kill his ravished daughter, stabbed Lavinia. The startled Saturninus asked if Lavinia had been ravished and by whom. When Titus disclosed that Tamora's sons had done the evil deed, Saturninus asked to see the youths at once. Titus, declaring that Tamora was eating their remains, stabbed her. Saturninus stabbed Titus, and Lucius, in turn, stabbed Saturninus. A general fight ensued. Lucius and Marcus, with their followers, retired to a balcony to tell the people of Rome of the manifold evils wrought by Tamora, her sons, and Aaron. After the people had chosen him as their new emperor, Lucius sentenced Aaron to be buried waist deep and left to starve. He also decreed that Tamora's body be fed to wild beasts.

Critical Evaluation:

Titus Andronicus, the first of William Shakespeare's ten tragedies, was written between 1589 and 1592, probably in 1590. The young writer was eager to establish himself as a commercially successful playwright, so he resorted to the traditionally accepted form of revenge tragedy for this play. Revenge tragedy is a particularly violent form of theater and had been used by Thomas Kyd in his spectacularly successful *The Spanish Tragedy* (c. 1585). Shakespeare, no doubt, had Kyd's success in mind as he created a play of unprecedented violence. In *Titus Andronicus*, eleven of the individually named characters are murdered, eight in view of the audience, and several are horribly mutilated. Lavinia's rape and mutilation represent the acme of brutality in the Elizabethan theater, and Shakespeare was unabashedly pandering to the Elizabethan audience's taste for blood and gore in his first attempt at tragedy. It is largely because of this excessive violence that many critics, from Shakespeare's fellow dramatist Ben Jonson to twentieth century poet T. S. Eliot, have censured this play as unworthy of Shakespeare. Some critics have even denied that Shakespeare wrote the play. Such condemnation fails to recognize that it is only when *Titus Andronicus* is considered in the light of Shakespeare's mature tragedies, which are among the greatest in the English language, that it falls short of the mark. It measures up very well when it is compared with *The Spanish Tragedy* or Christopher Marlowe's *The Jew of Malta* (1589), especially in regard to the important areas of characterization, language, and theme.

Although the characters in *Titus Andronicus* are clearly not as rich and subtle as are many of those in Shakespeare's later tragedies, some of them are still quite compelling and foreshadow several of Shakespeare's mature figures. Titus Andronicus is the first of Shakespeare's great Roman warriors who falls from high status because of a fatal flaw of character or intellect. In broad outline, his tragic downfall anticipates the destructive careers of Coriolanus, Julius Caesar, and Mark Antony. Even Othello's monumental rages recall Titus' propensity for impulsive violence. Titus is an outstanding example of Aristotle's conception of the tragic protagonist as a man who is greater than the ordinary and basically good, but who suffers from a deadly defect that destroys him. Titus' terrible suffering is a harrowing dramatic experience, and his character is an altogether remarkable creation for a twenty-six-year-old dramatist.

Tamora and Aaron also deserve particular mention. Tamora is the first of a small number of Shakespeare's malevolent women, some others being Goneril and Reagan in *King Lear* (1605) and Lady Macbeth in *Macbeth* (1606). Like them, Tamora is seen in dramatic contrast to a benevolent female character, in this case Lavinia. Like the other villainesses, Tamora is crafty and manipulative, psychopathic and driven by a lust for power, but her animus against the Andronici is understandable in view of the sacrificial execution of her son Alarbus. She is perhaps ultimately less sympathetic than Lady Macbeth, who loses her mind because of her guilt, but she is clearly more human than Goneril and Reagan, who are arguably the most malignant women in all of drama. Aaron is the first of Shakespeare's Machiavellian villains, the others being Richard III in *Richard III* (c. 1592-1593), Iago in *Othello* (1604), and Edmund in *King Lear*. Like the behavior of all villains of this type, Aaron's actions are scheming, sadistic, and psychopathic. He revels in doing evil, and his catalog of his life after his capture recalls the hateful braggadocio of Ithamore in Marlowe's *The Jew of Malta*, upon whom he is partially based.

The sheer excesses of his play run the risk of disgusting the audience, even one as fond of violence as the Elizabethan audience was. The shock of Lavinia's mutilations is reduced by the language which is used to describe her. It is the language of euphemism—"what stern ungentle hands/ Hath lopped and hewed and made thy body bare/ Of her two branches" and "a crimson river of warm blood/ Like to a bubbling fountain stirred with wind/ Doth rise and fall between thy rosed lips"—and it creates a psychic distance between the fact of the violence and the audience's perception of it. References to classical myths involving physical dismemberment provide an imaginative context for the most grotesque outrages. Lavinia's rape and the removal of her tongue and hands to prevent disclosure of her persecutors recall the myth of Procne, Philomela, and Tereus, which is recorded in Ovid's *Metamorphoses* (c. 8) and which every Elizabethan would have known. The feast at which Tamora is served the baked bodies of her evil sons Chiron and Demetrius has a grim precedent in a Roman tragedy of Seneca. The language of euphemism and the language of myth buffer the shock of the most extreme episodes of violence in this play, rendering them more palatable to the audience.

Titus Andronicus is not without moral significance even though it obviously fails to achieve the catharsis of *Hamlet* (1600-1601) and *King Lear*. Revenge is shown to be unsatisfactory as a moral code of governance. Titus' obstinate sacrifice of Alarbus, a son of the captured Gothic queen Tamora, provides the motive for the subsequent outrages against his family. Avengers and victims become indistinguishable in the course of the play and are alike destroyed in the cruel and ultimately mindless bloodbath that follows Alarbus' execution. Titus, the once majestic leader, is reduced by the final act to a craftily insane murderer, not only of his enemies but also of his own daughter. Rome is in tatters until a semblance of order is restored at the end by the very Goths who were the original enemy. The play, then, is a powerful testament to the irrationality of revenge, or even of justice untempered by mercy, as a moral imperative.

"Critical Evaluation" by Robert G. Blake

Bibliography:

Bessen, Alan C. *Shakespeare in Performance: "Titus Andronicus."* Manchester, England: Manchester University Press, 1989. Dessen follows the stage history of the play, noting that the watershed performance was the highly successful 1955 production by Peter Brook, starring Laurence Olivier and Vivien Leigh. Dessen also addresses the numerous staging problems involved in a production of *Titus Andronicus*.

Bowers, Fredson T. *Elizabethan Revenge Tragedy, 1587-1642*. Princeton, N.J.: Princeton University Press, 1940. Although somewhat old, this book is still useful and enjoyable. It traces the origins of the revenge tragedy to the plays of Seneca. Bowers shows how *Titus*

Andronicus follows a pattern first formulated in English by Thomas Kyd in *The Spanish Tragedy*.

Hamilton, A. C. *"Titus Andronicus*: The Form of Shakespearean Tragedy." *Shakespeare Quarterly* 14 (1963): 201-213. Suggests that Titus' fault is in attempting to be godlike in the sacrifice of Alarbus. The rest of the play makes him increasingly human.

Rozett, Martha Tuck. *The Doctrine of Election and the Emergence of Elizabethan Tragedy*. Princeton, N.J.: Princeton University Press, 1984. Argues that the Calvinistic doctrine of predestination and election was influential upon Elizabethan tragedy.

Wells, Stanley, ed. *The Cambridge Companion to Shakespeare Studies*. Cambridge, England: Cambridge University Press, 1986. This is where all studies of Shakespeare should begin. Includes excellent chapters introducing the poet's biography, conventions and beliefs of Elizabethan England, and reviews of scholarship in the field.

TO HIS COY MISTRESS

Type of work: Poetry
Author: Andrew Marvell (1621-1678)
First published: 1681

In "To His Coy Mistress," his most famous poem, Andrew Marvell follows many of the conventions of the *carpe diem* (Latin for "seize the day") theme in poetry. This type of poem dates from ancient times and was made popular in English in the late sixteenth and early seventeenth centuries by such writers as Sir Walter Raleigh, Christopher Marlowe, and Robert Herrick. In such poems, typically, the speaker is an eager male lover lamenting the brevity of life in order to persuade his female listener to yield to his sexual advances. Thus a *carpe diem* complaint is perhaps best understood not as a love poem but as a lust poem.

Marvell adheres to this tradition in several ways, but he dispenses with the pastoral scenery and songlike lyrical quality typical of much *carpe diem* verse. Marvell cleverly invests this pagan argument (life is short and uncertain so one must partake of all the pleasures one can) with somewhat melancholy Christian allusions. His poem is more ambitious as art than the standard shepherd's lament. Marvell frames the familiar urgings of the frustrated lover within three strictly organized verse paragraphs that resemble a three-part syllogism, a formula logicians use to demonstrate the validity of an argument. The argument in the poem concerns sexual gratification. The speaker's premise in the first verse paragraph describes the rate at which he would woo the lady, given time enough to do so properly. In the second verse paragraph, the premise is the blunt fact of human mutability: Time is limited. In his conclusion, Marvell's speaker resolves these conflicts—figuratively, at least.

Marvell's poem's originality of structure has contributed to the poem's being ranked as the epitome of *carpe diem* verse. Everything contributes to the speaker's overall urgency. Marvell's clipped, tetrameter (four-beat) rhymed couplets create a hurried pace. The poem begins, for example, with two closed couplets, or couplets of a single sentence each. This clipped beginning hints at urgency. As the speaker gains confidence, he loosens this form and uses more enjambment, running lines over into the following lines more often. By the third verse paragraph, he seems hardly to pause for breath at all. The variety of allusion, metaphor, and other figures of speech give the poem an exuberance appropriate to its theme.

As if to call attention to the fleetingness of time, the speaker opens with a terse, elliptical statement, not wasting even a syllable in his wooing. "Had we but world enough, and time" saves him from having to utter the only slightly longer "If we had"; and "This coyness, lady, were no crime" similarly condenses the more customary and conversational "would be no crime." In this opening couplet, then, the speaker argues that time and distance—not his own impulsiveness or lust—are the primary enemies of love. If men and women had all eternity and all the world to devote to each other, "coyness" (her refusing his amorous suggestions) would hardly bother him. As it is, however, he deems coyness a crime against his emotions and her own—indeed, perhaps a crime against nature. He then offers examples of how, if immortal, they would pass their "long love's day." Part flattery, part display of his own inventiveness, wit, and learning, this catalog of praises follows the classical tradition of a list of charms designed to weaken the woman's resistance and make her admirer's advances more appealing.

Marvell's speaker employs a wide range of such strategems. He draws upon geography, implying that the distance between the Ganges River in India and England's Humber River is somehow equal to the distance he feels lies between them as he makes this traditional lover's complaint. From the tide of the Humber he moves to Noah's flood (near the dawn of time), and then ahead to the "conversion of the Jews," in Marvell's day a proverbial reference to the end of the world. These allusions not only emphasize the infinitely slow "rate" at which his mistress deserves to be praised, they also introduce the idea that her coyness is vaguely sacrilegious. The speaker's "vegetable love" in line eleven is botanical (hence natural), historically significant (vaster and more lasting than empires), and personal in its physical, clinging aspect.

By the end of this first verse paragraph, the speaker has achieved an almost geological perspective of love, claiming that hundreds or thousands of years, even entire ages or eras of time, would be necessary to praise adequately his prospective lover's beauty. That Marvell's ardent speaker is careful to conclude that her "heart"—her inner beauty—demands the most attention of all indicates a shrewdness hardly compatible with the inarticulate throes of sincere affection. This is a poem of persuasion, after all. The speaker aims to disarm the lady further with an even more grandiose piece of flattery: "For, lady, you deserve this state;/ Nor would I love at lower rate." This summation allows the speaker to make promises he knows he shall never be forced to keep, since, of course, the couple does not have all the world to range upon and all of time to spend.

Having professed his boundless love for her, the eager lover quickly contrasts what would be with what, unfortunately, must be: the eventual death of them both. Fittingly, this second part of the argument is the briefest, and it employs the starkest imagery of the poem. This paragraph makes reference to ashes and dust, another subtle religious echo. The first part of the poem emphasizes lasting emotion, but the second part turns grimly final before leavening these images with what might be the poem's best couplet: "The grave's a fine and private place,/ But none, I think, do there embrace."

The offhandedness of this quip is designed. It keeps the mood from becoming too somber, as if the speaker knows he runs the risk of going too far. He seems almost to be reading his mistress' expression for clues as he describes the process of bodily decay. The word "embrace" sets the final section's argument in motion.

This argument is couched in the most urgent language of the poem. The section's initial words—"Now, therefore"—provide the tone. The word "now" appears twice more in the following few lines, along with such synonymous terms as "at once." The emphasis is on the fleetingness of the present moment: "while the youthful hue/ Sits on thy skin," "while thy willing soul transpires," "let us sport us while we may." Marvell chooses metaphors and similes that make the lovers seem almost ferociously passionate. The pores of the skin burn "with instant fires." The lovers should become, he claims, like "amorous birds of prey." They shall "devour" time, roll their combined strength and sweetness "up into one ball," "tear" their pleasures with "rough strife," and so on. Time, still the enemy of their love's consummation, is defeated in the poem's final paradox, as the speaker admits that "Thus, though we cannot make our sun/ Stand still, yet we will make him run." That is, since they have not the power to stop time, they might at least control it in another way; indulging in sexual pleasures will make time seem to pass more quickly. Also making time run implies that lovers make the universe work.

Love's other enemy, distance, is overcome as well in this last section. The first two parts of the poem deal mainly in "you" and "I" constructions, but Marvell concludes the poem with no fewer than ten first-person plural pronouns emphasizing with grammatical subtlety the physical union the speaker desires from this lady. (Such pronouns occur only four times in all of the preceding thirty-two lines.) Then, too, the lovers are likened to birds of prey rather than the inert vine-and-wall relationship of section one or the union of worm and corpse in section two.

Further thematic shifts should be noted as well, such as the symbolic use of "rubies" and "marble" in paragraphs one and two, respectively. The precious, deep-red stones denote tokens of affection and befit the early catalog of praises; likewise, the more common but still impressive marble seems in keeping with the mortality theme. Then, in the last section, these find their counterpart in another element, a metal: iron, a humble enough material yet one that intimates the lovers' earthbound reality. The speaker urges their passage through the "iron gates of life," a telling contrast to the heavenly gates, the promise of which presumably forms the reason for the lady's chastity.

For years, Marvell's poem was taken to be a fairly typical instance of courtly love poetry popular among English and European poets of this era. Recently, critics have pointed to the poem's complex ambiguities as a hallmark of Marvell's work in general. One need not, however, turn this seventeenth century metaphysical poet into a mystery in order to appreciate this particular poem's unique gusto and lyrical grace. Although it employs many features of the traditional lover's complaint, "To His Coy Mistress" ranks above nearly all other *carpe diem* poems because of Marvell's keen sense of irony, reversal, and strategic order. Perhaps the sharpest irony of all rests in the poet's distinctive use of syllogistic structure. For as logically appealing as the speaker's argument may be, Andrew Marvell could very well be reminding readers that, in matters of the heart, logic holds little sway.

James Scruton

Bibliography:
Bradbrook, M. C., and M. G. Lloyd Thomas. *Andrew Marvell*. Cambridge, England: Cambridge University Press, 1940. Places "To His Coy Mistress" among Marvell's other poems of desire, with useful comparisons to the poet's mower songs and "The Definition of Love."
Brooks, Cleanth. "Andrew Marvell: Puritan Austerity with Classical Grace." In *Poetic Traditions of the English Renaissance*, edited by Maynard Mack and George deForest Lord. New Haven, Conn.: Yale University Press, 1982. Discussion of "To His Coy Mistress" and "The Garden" as companion poems offering complementary points of view.
Eliot, T. S. "Andrew Marvell." In *Selected Essays*. New ed. New York: Harcourt Brace Jovanovich, 1950. A famous piece of modern literary criticism, Eliot's essay is credited with recovering Marvell from his status as a minor metaphysical poet. Eliot examines the poem for its ironic wit and incongruous imagery.
Legouis, Pierre. *Andrew Marvell: Poet, Puritan, Patriot*. Oxford, England: Clarendon Press, 1968. Clear overview of "Marvell's most erotic poem," citing not only classical and later examples of *carpe diem* verse but also Marvell's departures in tone and persona.
Marvell, Andrew. *Andrew Marvell: A Critical Edition of the Major Works*. Edited by Frank Kermode and Keith Walker. New York: Oxford University Press, 1990. Textual and manuscript notes to the poem, explaining the sources of various images and allusions, as well as comparing specific lines to those of Marvell's contemporaries or poetic forbears.

TO KILL A MOCKINGBIRD

Type of work: Novel
Author: Harper Lee (Nelle Harper Lee, 1926-   )
Type of plot: Bildungsroman
Time of plot: Three-year span in the mid-1930's
Locale: Alabama
First published: 1960

> *Principal characters:*
> ATTICUS FINCH, a lawyer
> SCOUT (JEAN LOUISE), his daughter
> JEM (JEREMY ATTICUS), her older brother
> BOO (ARTHUR) RADLEY, a recluse

The Story:

Scout Finch, almost six years old, her brother Jem, four years older, and their little friend Dill (Charles Baker Harris), a visitor to Maycomb, Alabama, spent their summer thinking of ways to lure Boo Radley from his house. The children had never seen the recluse, but a few townspeople saw him some years ago when Boo reportedly stabbed his father in the leg with a pair of scissors, was locked up for a time, and then was returned to his family. No one in Maycomb had seen him since.

Challenged by Dill, Jem, although fearful he would be killed by Boo, who "dined on raw squirrels and any cats he could catch," ran and touched the Radley house. The children fled home and looked back to see what appeared to be an inside shutter move.

In the fall, Scout entered school and got into trouble in class because she could already read and out of class for fighting with boys. During the year, she and Jem found children's treasures in a knothole in an oak tree on the Radley place. Before they could put a thank-you note in the tree for the unknown benefactor, Nathan Radley, Boo's brother, filled the knothole with cement.

The next summer Dill returned. Rolling inside a runaway tire, Scout slammed into the Radley porch. She heard laughing inside as she recovered and ran. The three children played Boo Radley games until stopped by Jem and Scout's father, Atticus.

The last night of Dill's visit the three tried to look in a window of the Radley home. Jem raised his head to look in and the children saw a shadow coming toward them. They ran and a shotgun roared. Jem caught his pants on a wire fence and had to leave them. After Nathan Radley told the neighbors he had fired at an intruder, Jem went back for his pants and found them mended and neatly folded over the fence.

The next winter it snowed in Maycomb, and Scout and Jem made their first snowman. During the cold snap, the house of a neighbor, Miss Maudie Atkinson, burned down. Back home after shivering from the cold with the other onlookers, Scout discovered a blanket had been placed around her shoulders. The only adult in town not at the fire was Boo Radley. Jem told his father of the treasures in the tree and the mended pants, done by the strange man who never hurt them even when he had the chance.

Scout and Jem began hearing their father called a "nigger-lover" around town, because of his appointment to defend a black man, Tom Robinson. Atticus warned them to hold their heads high and not fight about it, but at Christmas Scout bloodied a boy cousin's nose for repeating the accusation.

The brother and sister received air rifles for Christmas but were cautioned by their father that to kill a mockingbird is a sin. Their friend Miss Maudie later explained that mockingbirds only make music and sing their hearts out for people.

One day a mad dog came down the street and the town's sheriff asked Atticus to shoot it. He dispatched it with one shot. The children were told their father, whom they thought of as old and feeble, was once known as "One-Shot Finch," the best shot in Maycomb County.

An old lady, Mrs. Henry Lafayette Dubose, baited Jem by calling Atticus a "nigger-lover." Enraged, Jem knocked the tops off her flowers. His father ordered Jem to read to the sick woman every afternoon for two months. After her death, Atticus told the children Mrs. Dubose, although unpleasant, was the bravest woman he ever knew; she had broken a morphine habit rather than die addicted. Real courage, the father said, is not a man with a gun in his hand. "It's when you know you're licked before you begin but you begin anyway and you see it through no matter what."

Scout and Jem went to an African American church with Cal (Calpurnia), their cook, who had raised the children since the death of their mother when Scout was two. A collection was taken for the family of Tom (Thomas) Robinson, the man Atticus was to defend. Aunt Alexandra, Atticus' proper sister, came to live with them to make a lady out of the tomboy Scout and restore proper Southern order to their home.

Before the trial, the sheriff and a group of citizens warned Atticus that death threats had been made against the defendant. Atticus stayed at the jail and, weaponless, faced a mob come to get the prisoner. Jem, Scout, and Dill arrived, and Scout kicked a man who grabbed Jem. She recognized the father of a schoolmate in the mob and embarrassed him by talking calmly about his son, until the man ordered the mob to leave. Atticus said the children made the schoolmate's father stand in his shoes for a minute and turned the animals in the mob back into humans.

At the trial, where Scout, Jem, and Dill sat in the balcony with Calpurnia's minister, Atticus demonstrated the untruth of the charges by Bob (Robert E. Lee) Ewell, a white man who lived on whiskey and welfare down by the dump, that Tom Robinson beat and raped his daughter, Mayella. A doctor had not been called to examine and treat the daughter, and the bruises on the right side of her face were caused by a left-handed man. Bob Ewell was left-handed, but Tom Robinson's left arm was withered and useless.

Atticus asked Mayella on the witness stand if her father had inflicted the abuse. She denied it, but Tom Robinson testified that the day of the alleged rape, she invited him in and kissed him. She said she had never kissed a grown man—what her father did to her did not count—so she might as well kiss a "nigger." Bob Ewell had arrived at that moment.

Jem and Scout believed that Tom Robinson would be acquitted, but he was found guilty by the all-white jury. It was the word of a white person against a black one, and Tom Robinson had made the mistake of saying he felt sorry for a white person—Mayella.

After the trial, Bob Ewell threatened Atticus in public. Tom Robinson was killed trying to escape from a prison exercise yard. He had given up hope of getting justice in the white courts, although Atticus told him they had a chance on appeal.

Near Halloween, Scout and Jem attended a school pageant. On the way home in the dark, the children were attacked. Scout was saved from a knife thrust by the wire-mesh ham costume she was wearing. Jem struggled with the man and was thrown to the ground. A fourth person appeared; there was a struggle, and Scout saw Jem being carried to their house by the stranger.

Back home Scout found that Jem had a broken arm and the "stranger" who rescued him, standing silently in a corner, was Boo Radley.

The sheriff found Bob Ewell dead where the attack occurred, with a kitchen knife stuck up under his ribs. Atticus said that he believed Jem did it and did not want it covered up. The sheriff insisted that Bob Ewell fell on his own knife, and, besides, it would be a sin to drag someone with shy ways into the limelight.

Atticus gave in and thanked Arthur Radley for his children's lives. Scout said it would be "sort of like shootin' a mockingbird" to expose their rescuer.

Scout escorted Boo home. She never saw him again. Atticus, putting her to bed, said that most people are nice, "when you finally see them."

Critical Evaluation:

Harper Lee was awarded the Pulitzer Prize in fiction in 1961 for her only novel, *To Kill a Mockingbird*, based to a large degree on her childhood experiences growing up in Monroeville, Alabama. Her father was a small-town lawyer like Atticus Finch and an old house in her neighborhood was rumored to have a reclusive owner, rather like Boo Radley. The author has stated the character of Dill was based on author Truman Capote, a childhood companion.

The voice narrating the regional story is that of Scout—Jean Louise Finch—revealing the experiences of her childhood from an adult perspective. The novel begins with a discussion of Jem's broken arm (the last event in the actual plot) and a family history of the Finches in the "tired old town" of Maycomb. Lee presents a dual vision throughout *To Kill a Mockingbird*. The two plot lines—the attempt to lure Boo Radley out and the trial of Tom Robinson—reinforce the contrasting dual themes of prejudice, ignorance, hypocrisy, and hate, opposed by courage, kindness, tolerance, calm reason—and humor.

The gradual moral awakening and growth of Scout and Jem are centered on their "education" by their father, Atticus, a man of conscience, who patiently counsels—and demonstrates—how they should walk in the other person's shoes, hold up their heads, and show restraint in the face of hate and ignorance. Atticus suggests the larger theme that the white South of the time would progress when people quit catching "Maycomb's usual disease." Those suffering from the disease are "reasonable people [who] go stark raving mad when anything involving a Negro comes up."

The novel is in part a social history of a small Southern town of the Depression period. In the novel, there is much preoccupation of white people with family trees, social class, racial matters, education (the children learn more outside the classroom than in), and superstition. Although the town (and the South) are places of tradition and ingrained habits, where the past often determines the present, the potential for progressive change resides in at least some enlightened people.

The novel is of a genre called *Bildungsroman*, or novel of maturation. In such a novel, the main character journeys through a series of adventures from innocence to experience and mature enlightenment. At the end, the character is prepared for adulthood.

In the three years covered by the novel, Scout and Jem abandon their superstitions about Boo Radley, learn to value townspeople as individuals, develop moral courage in the face of the town's hypocrisy, realize that justice should be administered without regard to race and class, and, Atticus' final lesson, learn that most people are nice when you finally come to understand them. The children have developed open minds—unprejudiced and individual.

The words "it's a sin to kill a mockingbird" echo throughout the novel. The songbird is symbolic of innocence and joy allowed to live—or threatened and destroyed. Tom Robinson and Boo Radley become its human equivalents in the novel. The editor of Maycomb's newspaper likens the killing of Tom during his escape attempt to "the senseless slaughter of songbirds," and Scout says that turning Boo over to the police for killing Bob Ewell would be "sort of like shootin' a mockingbird."

M. E. Gandy

Bibliography:
Altman, Dorothy Jewell. *Harper Lee*. Detroit: Gale Research, 1980. A concise examination of the novel's themes and symbolism. Treats the work as a regional novel with a universal message.
Erisman, Fred. "The Romantic Regionalism of Harper Lee." *Alabama Review* 26 (April, 1973): 122-136. Examines Maycomb as a microcosm of the South, having within itself the potential to move from reliance on tradition to reliance on principle and to join the larger world without loss of regional identity.
Johnson, Claudia Durst. *Understanding "To Kill a Mockingbird": A Student Casebook to Issues, Sources, and Historic Documents*. Westport, Conn.: Greenwood Press, 1994. Offers literary analysis, historical context, critical studies, and discussion of censorship issues.
Schuster, Edgar H. "Discovering Theme and Structure in the Novel." *English Journal* 52 (October, 1963): 506-511. Deals with the elements of theme and structure in *To Kill a Mockingbird*, identifying and illustrating five thematic motifs.

TO THE LIGHTHOUSE

Type of work: Novel
Author: Virginia Woolf (1882-1941)
Type of plot: Stream of consciousness
Time of plot: c. 1910-1920
Locale: The Isle of Skye in the Hebrides
First published: 1927

Principal characters:

MR. RAMSAY, a professor of philosophy
MRS. RAMSAY, his wife
JAMES, their son
CAMILLA, their daughter
MR. TANSLEY, Mr. Ramsay's guest and friend
LILY BRISCOE, an artist
MR. CARMICHAEL, a poet

The Story:

Mrs. Ramsay promised James, her six-year-old son, that if the next day were fair he would be taken on a visit to the lighthouse they could see from the window of their summer home on the Isle of Skye. James, the youngest of Mrs. Ramsay's eight children, was his mother's favorite. The father of the family was a professor of philosophy whose students often thought that he was inspiring and one of the foremost metaphysicians of the early twentieth century; but his own children, particularly the youngest, did not like him because he made sarcastic remarks.

Several guests were visiting the Ramsays at the time. There was young Mr. Tansley, Ramsay's student, who was also unpopular with the children because he seemed to delight in their discomfiture. Tansley was mildly in love with his hostess, despite her fifty years and her eight children. There was Lily Briscoe, who was painting a picture of the cottage with Mrs. Ramsay and little James seated in front of it. There was old Mr. Carmichael, a ne'er-do-well who amused the Ramsay youngsters because he had a white beard and a mustache tinged with yellow. There was also William Bankes, an aging widower, and Prue, the prettiest of the Ramsay daughters.

The afternoon went by slowly. Mrs. Ramsay went to the village to call on a sick woman. She spent several hours knitting stockings for the lighthouse keeper's child, whom they were planning to visit. Many people wondered how the Ramsays, particularly the wife, managed to be as hospitable and as charitable as they were, for they were not rich. Mr. Ramsay could not possibly make a fortune by expounding English philosophy to students or by publishing books on metaphysics.

Mr. Carmichael, pretending to read, had actually fallen asleep early after lunch. The children, except for James, who was busy cutting pictures out of a catalog, had busied themselves in a game of cricket. Mr. Ramsay and Mr. Tansley had passed the time in a pointless conversation. Miss Briscoe had only made a daub or two of paint on her canvas. For some reason, the lines of the scene refused to come clear in her painting. She then went for a walk with Mr. Bankes along the shore.

Even the dinner went by slowly. The only occasion of interest to the children, which was one of tension to their mother, came when Mr. Carmichael asked the maid for a second bowl of soup, thereby angering his host, who liked to have meals dispatched promptly. As soon as the children had finished, their mother sent the younger ones to bed. Mrs. Ramsay hoped that Mr. Bankes would marry Lily Briscoe. Lily always became seasick, so it was questionable whether she would want to accompany them in the small sailboat if they should go to the lighthouse the following day. She also thought about the fifty pounds needed to make some necessary repairs on the house.

After dinner, Mrs. Ramsay went upstairs to the nursery. James had a boar's skull that his sister detested. Whenever Camilla tried to remove it from the wall and her sight, he burst into a frenzy of screaming. Mrs. Ramsay wrapped the boar's skull in her shawl. Afterward, she went downstairs and joined her husband in the library, where they sat throughout the evening. Mrs. Ramsay knitted, while Mr. Ramsay read. Before they went to bed, it was agreed that the trip for the next day would have to be canceled. The night had turned stormy.

Night followed night. The trip to the lighthouse was never made that summer, and the Ramsays did not return to their summer home for some years. In the meantime, Mrs. Ramsay died quietly in her sleep. Her daughter Prue had been married and died in childbirth. World War I began. Andrew Ramsay enlisted and was sent to France, where he was killed by an exploding shell.

Time passed. The wallpaper in the house came loose from the walls. Books mildewed. In the kitchen, a cup was occasionally knocked down and broken by old Mrs. McNab, who came to look after the house from time to time. In the garden, the roses and the annual flowers grew wild or died.

Mr. Carmichael published a volume of poems during the war. About the time his book appeared, daffodils and violets bloomed on the Isle of Skye. Mrs. McNab looked longingly at a warm cloak left in a closet. She wished the cloak belonged to her.

At last, the war ended. Mrs. McNab received a telegram requesting that the house be put in order. For several days, the housekeeper worked, aided by two cleaning women. When the Ramsays arrived, the cottage was in order once more. Several visitors came again to share a summer at the cottage. Lily Briscoe returned for a quiet vacation. Mr. Carmichael, the successful poet, also arrived.

One morning, Lily Briscoe came down to breakfast and wondered at the quiet that greeted her. No one had been down ahead of her, although she had expected that Mr. Ramsay and the two youngest children, James and Camilla, would have eaten early and departed for the long-postponed sail to the lighthouse, to which the youngsters had not been looking forward with joyful anticipation. Very shortly, the three straggled down; all had slept past the time they had intended to arise. After a swift breakfast, they disappeared toward the shore. Lily Briscoe watched them go. She had set up her canvas with the intention of once again trying to paint her picture of the cottage.

The journey to the island where the lighthouse stood was not very pleasant, as the children had expected. They had never really liked their father; he had taken too little time to understand them. He was short and sharp when they did things that seemed foolish to him, although these actions were perfectly comprehensible to his son and daughter. James, especially, expected to be blamed caustically and pointlessly if the crossing were slow or not satisfactory in some other way, for he had been delegated to handle the sheets and the tiller of the boat.

Mr. Ramsay strode down to the beach with his offspring, each carrying a paper parcel to take to the keepers of the lighthouse. They soon set sail and pointed the prow of the sailboat toward the black and white striped pillar of the lighthouse in the hazy distance. Mr. Ramsay sat in the middle of the boat, along with an old fisherman and his son. They were to take over the boat in case of an emergency, for Mr. Ramsay had little trust in James as a reliable seaman. James himself sat in the stern, nerves tingling lest his father look up from his book and indulge in unnecessary and hateful criticism. His nervous tension, however, was needless, for within a few hours the little party reached the lighthouse, and, wonderful to relate, Mr. Ramsay sprang ashore like a youngster, smiled back at his children, and praised his son for his seamanship.

Critical Evaluation:

To the Lighthouse, Virginia Woolf's most autobiographical novel, explores two sets of inter-locking issues: perception and creativity. The stream-of-consciousness narrative forces the reader to examine and experience the complexities of individual perception and individual attempts to create coherence from the borderless flow of everyday events. As Woolf writes in her 1919 essay, "Modern Fiction": "Life is not a series of gig-lamps symmetrically arranged; life is a luminous halo, a semi-transparent envelope surrounding us from the beginning of consciousness to the end." Woolf takes her exploration of consciousness one step further by demonstrating how perception depends on sex: Men and women perceive the world differently. These contrasting perceptions of the world produce different creative urges. In the end, how-ever, creativity transcends gender boundaries.

Woolf's adult male characters, except for the poet Mr. Carmichael, are philosophers or sci-entists, analytical men. They are quantifiers of experience. Mr. Ramsay, the philosopher (who bears a resemblance to Woolf's father, Leslie Stephen) imagines that knowledge is arranged like the alphabet and that each man's intellectual worth lies in how far he can progress along that alphabet. He is frustrated because he is stalled at Q, even though he acknowledges that only one man a generation can actually reach Z. Mr. Tansley, a student of Mr. Ramsay's, finds his life in his books, his dissertation, and his acute sense of his own poverty. Mr. Bankes, the botanist, is a man who has definite opinions about properly cooking vegetables, who labels the Ramsay children with mock royal names, and who clinically examines Lily's painting. These male characters create order from life by systematizing its disparate elements and reducing them to bitter pronouncements (as Mr. Tansley does), disconnected lines of poetry (as Mr. Ramsay does), or impersonal images (as Andrew Ramsay does when he tells Lily Briscoe to picture Mr. Ramsay's work as a kitchen table).

The adult female characters, on the other hand, view life more intuitively. Mrs. Ramsay (who is based upon Woolf's mother, Julia Stephen) is celebrated for her beauty and her maternal nature. She pours herself into others, nourishing her children and her husband with her love and sympathy. What she values most in life, and what she seeks to create, is union, particularly marriage (she thinks, "they all must marry"). She also manifests her creative energies at her dinner party, where she recognizes that she must bring together the disparate people sitting at the table: "The whole of the effort of merging and flowing and creating rested on her." The artist Lily Briscoe (who perhaps represents Woolf herself) also feels creative pressures as she seeks to transform her private vision into art. Despite her own fears about the value of her work, and despite Mr. Tansley's proclamation that "Women can't write, women can't paint," Lily believes in her artistic vision and uses it to create order for herself from her puzzling, sometimes painful feelings and perceptions.

Woolf's narrative style emphasizes her definition of perception. The narrative drifts from point of view to point of view, entering various characters' minds in an apparently random succession of associations. Woolf also contrasts objective, external time with subjective, internal time. The narrative moves fluidly between past and present, memory and experience, disorienting the reader in the process.

The structure of the novel further emphasizes the contrast between external and internal time.

The first section, "The Window" occupies more than half the novel and spans a single afternoon and evening. The middle section of the novel, "Time Passes," compresses the events of ten years into twenty pages of narrative and parenthetically inserts major events into a description of the slow decay of the Ramsays' summer home. The final section, "The Lighthouse," takes approximately seventy pages to describe the events of a single morning.

Woolf uses imagery, particularly the sea and the lighthouse, to reveal the unity and individuality of human perception. The characters are drawn to the sea, often in pairs: Mr. and Mrs. Ramsay, Paul and Minta, Mr. Bankes and Lily. At such moments, the sea creates a sense of unity and constancy of vision. The same sea also represents the isolation of human beings, as when Mr. Ramsay murmurs "we perished, each alone" as he and his children journey to the lighthouse. The lighthouse unifies and isolates as well. It stands at the center of the novel, uniting the several sections. It is a focus for the family as a desired destination. The lighthouse separates them, however, through their own individual visions of it. As James thinks, "nothing was simply one thing."

In the end, it is contingent upon the artists, Mr. Carmichael and Lily Briscoe, to bring together male and female creativity, intellect and emotion, public statement and private vision. They must have, as Woolf writes in *A Room of One's Own* (1929), the clearer vision of androgynous minds, which, unimpeded by gender prejudice, are "naturally creative, incandescent and undivided." The feminized Mr. Carmichael, who sits on the edge of the domestic circle dozing and waiting for the words of his poetry to come to him, brings his deeply felt poems about Andrew Ramsay and World War I into the public sphere. Lily forges ahead with her artistic efforts despite her recognition that her paintings will end up underneath beds or in attics. As she paints, she is preoccupied with thoughts of Mr. and Mrs. Ramsay as she attempts to understand them both. Lily mocks Mrs. Ramsay's sentimentality, but she recognizes the beauty and power of the older woman's love and grieves for her loss. This grief draws Lily into sympathetic union (which she earlier refused) with the coldly intellectual Mr. Ramsay.

The final chapter brings together Mr. Ramsay and the memory of Mrs. Ramsay, as well as the male artist with the female artist, in unspoken communion. The Ramsays reach the lighthouse; Lily has her artistic vision and completes her painting; Mr. Carmichael silently pronounces a benediction on them all. The novel concludes with a moment that is a culmination and a commencement.

Judith Burdan

Bibliography:
Bassoff, Bruce. "Tables in Trees: Realism in *To the Lighthouse.*" *Studies in the Novel* 16, no. 4 (Winter, 1984): 424-434. Contends that Woolf redefines realism in her novel. Focusing on Lily Briscoe, Bassoff demonstrates how her perception is mediated by her interaction with other characters.

Daugherty, Beth Rigel. " 'There she sat': The Power of the Feminist Imagination in *To the Lighthouse.*" *Twentieth Century Literature* 37, no. 3 (Fall, 1991): 289-308. A well-argued interpretation that centers on the moment of Mrs. Ramsay's reappearance near the end of the novel. Contends that Lily's acceptance of Mrs. Ramsay as a woman, free of patriarchal influences, allows the latter to reappear in her own right.

Kelley, Alice van Buren. *"To the Lighthouse": The Marriage of Life and Art.* Boston: Twayne, 1987. A superb starting place. Provides a reading of the book, a wealth of background information, a chronology, and a discussion of critical responses.

Leaska, Mitchell A. *Virginia Woolf's Lighthouse: A Study in Critical Method.* New York: Columbia University Press, 1970. A systematic examination of Woolf's style and the multiple-point-of-view technique. Vigorously defends Woolf's method, emphasizing the importance of the reader in achieving meaning.

Matro, Thomas G. "Only Visions: Vision and Achievement in *To the Lighthouse.*" *PMLA* 99, no. 2 (March, 1984): 212-224. Sees an analogy between Lily's aesthetics and the relations between the novel's characters. Holds that the vision required for painting becomes a metaphor for the perception needed in human relationships.

TO URANIA

Type of work: Poetry
Author: Joseph Brodsky (1940-1996)
First published: Chast'rechi, 1977, and *Uraniia,* 1987 (English translation of selections, 1988)

From the time when the Soviet authorities forced Joseph Brodsky into exile on June 4, 1977, the theme of exile has dominated his poetry. Brodsky had tasted the bitterness of exile, however, even prior to his expulsion from his native land. Described by poet Anna Akhmatova as "the most gifted poet of his generation," Brodsky was charged with the crime of being a "social parasite" and was arrested in January of 1964. After a quick trial, he was sentenced to five years of hard labor in internal exile, but, thanks to pressures on the government at home and abroad, he was released in November, 1965.

After his release from the labor camp, Brodsky returned to his native city of Leningrad. Already one could see the development of the theme of exile in his poetry, for which he was awarded the Nobel Prize in Literature in 1987, along three distinct lines: an effort to convey a sense of what is sacred through images of things borrowed from everyday life, an attempt to convey in words a realm of silence that underlies all poetry, and an affirmation of a home that is forever approached but forever lies in a realm that is elsewhere. The poems in his collection *To Urania,* most of which he translated himself, exemplify these aspects of Brodsky's art.

To Urania is a collection of forty-six poems written between 1968 and 1987, including the well-known long poem *Gorbunov and Gorchakov* (1968). The title poem for the volume is its twenty-fourth poem, and it uses the metaphor of the body to express the exile of the spirit, particularly in these lines:

> And what is space anyway if not the
> body's absence at every given
> point? That's why Urania's older than sister Clio!

Urania is the muse of the heavens, while Clio is the muse of history. Urania is older because it is the longing for the heavens, which is the abode of the gods, that gives rise to history. Brodsky views history as the tale of the human effort to reach the heavens, since the heavens are the realm of the Great Elsewhere that reveals to humanity its condition of exile.

If Urania is the muse who gives rise to the poetry of exile, she does so from the beginning of Brodsky's work. Its first poem, "May 24, 1980," commemorates Brodsky's fortieth birthday, and in it he insists that, even though he has "munched the bread of exile," only gratitude will come "gushing from" his throat. While exile is a condition that may invite despair, the poet struggles to overcome that despair by writing poetry.

The next six poems—"To a Friend: In Memorium," "October Tune," "A Polar Explorer," "Lithuanian Nocturne," "Twenty Sonnets to Mary, Queen of Scots," and "North Baltic"— examine exile in terms of the separation of one human being from another. Home consists not only of familiar places but also of familiar faces, and in these poems Brodsky explores the pain of separation from loved ones. The return home that would bring exile to an end is, above all, a return to loving human relationships.

Because the poems in this collection deal with exile, many of them are set in places from all over the world. Examples include "The Berlin Wall Tune," "Dutch Mistress," "Allenby Road" (a famous road in Israel), "Polonaise: A Variation," "Cafe Trieste: San Francisco," "Near

Alexandria," "Roman Elegies," "Belfast Tune," and "In Italy." Especially noteworthy among these poems about other places is a passage from "Venetian Stanzas II," a poem about the poet's being out of place.

> I am writing these lines sitting outdoors, in winter,
> on a white iron chair, in my shirtsleeves . . .
> and the coffee grows cold. And the blinding lagoon is lapping
> at the shore as the dim pupil's bright penalty
> for its wish to arrest a landscape quite happy
> here without me.

The poet's distance from a dwelling place is here proclaimed in images of disjuncture: shirtsleeves in winter, cold coffee, and a landscape there without him. Like the eye that would arrest the landscape, the words in the poem try to capture some meaning, but both rush ahead to leave the speaker behind, outdoors in winter.

Just as some of the poems in *To Urania* are about a place that is elsewhere, so are others about a time out of joint. These include "The Fifth Anniversary," "The Hawk's Cry in Autumn," "Eclogue IV: Winter," "Eclogue V: Summer," "Letter to an Archaeologist," and "Afterword." Brodsky has described words as "almost palpable vessels of time," and these poems that deal with time often deal also with poetry itself and the words that go into it. At the end of "Eclogue IV: Winter," for example, he writes:

> That's the birth of an eclogue. Instead of the shepherd's signal,
> a lamp's flaring up. Cyrillic, while running witless
> on the pad as though to escape the captor,
> knows more of the future than the famous sybil.

What is perhaps most striking about these lines is the idea that the Cyrillic alphabet (the alphabet used in the Russian language) has a certain life of its own. According to Brodsky, language is not just a tool used by a speaker; rather, language itself speaks. In the voice of language, the voice of the muse can be heard. The task of the poet is to attend to that voice in an effort to join words to the meaning that tries to escape them. For the poet, the exile of the human being from home is the exile of meaning from words.

Another poem worth noting from among these poems about time and poetry is "The Fifth Anniversary." Its title designates the fifth anniversary of Brodsky's exile from his homeland, June 4, 1977. In it he declares that he does not know "what earth will nurse my carcass," but he ends by saying, "Scratch on, my pen: let's mark the white the way it marks us." Brodsky often uses this phrase, "the white," to designate the opposite of home. Just as one who travels through a wilderness may "mark" that landscape by building a home, so does the poet mark the white, the blank page, by constructing words. For the poet in exile, words take the place of a dwelling place. Yet marking the white with words is just what makes the white visible, making all the more visible the poet's condition of exile. The greater sense of exile, the greater the need to write; and the more the poet writes, the more deeply he is entrenched in exile.

If the blank space designated by the white represents a condition of homelessness, it also represents a condition of silence. Here Brodsky understands the task of the poet to include the transformation of silence as emptiness into silence as eloquence. Silence, he maintains, is a kind of other language, and, as a poet, he endeavors to translate silence into words. The struggle between life and death, between exile and homeland, is a struggle between word and silence. Therefore the poet, who is the bearer of signs and images in his poetry, becomes a messenger who bears more than his message can contain. He becomes the messenger of silence.

In Brodsky's poetry, the theme of silence is connected to the theme of time in that silence represents a realm of the future, which is the realm of becoming. As the poet in exile becomes the poet of exile, he is faced, if he is ever to set out for home, with the task of becoming other than who he is. Among the poems from this collection that address this issue are "Minefield Revisited," "The Bust of Tiberius," "Seaward," "Ex Voto," and "At Karel Weilink's Exhibition." In this last poem, Brodsky declares that the sign of true self-mastery lies in the ability to "not take fright at the procedure of nonbeing." With this insight, the poet discovers that he is not only in exile but is exile; not only is his home elsewhere, but he is elsewhere. Therefore, if the poet is to move homeward to that other place, then the poet must become other than who he is. And that other being who the poet must become resides in silence.

In *To Urania*, the poem that most thoroughly explores the topic of silence is the last one, *Gorbunov and Gorchakov*, which is an extended dialogue between two patients in a psychiatric hospital outside of Leningrad. This is what one of them has to say:

> Silence is the future of all days
> that roll toward speech . . .
> Indeed, the future of our words is silence . . .
> And silence is the present fate of those who
> have lived before us; it's a matchmaker
> that manages to bring all men together
> into the speaking presence of today.
> Life is but talk hurled in the face of silence.

Because Brodsky's poetry entails an examination of poetry itself, silence is often its subject matter. Like the exile that accentuates the homeland, silence calls forth the spoken part of the human being to draw him or her into a relation to another human being. Human presence is a speaking presence that harbors a non-speaking, and the human task in life is to become present as a human being before another human being. In this task, the poet is our teacher.

Poetry is the most ancient of the verbal arts. It is the medium in which humanity first seeks its voice and the place where dwelling in the world first unfolds. It continues to unfold in the poetry of Joseph Brodsky. A poet for whom language is sacred, Brodsky is attuned to the capacity of language to open up a place where a trace of the sacred may show itself. As the poems in *To Urania* indicate, however, the sacred manifests itself as something at a distance. The notion of the sacred, then, includes the idea of drawing nigh. The poet engages in an effort to join word and meaning not in the midst of the sacred, which lies in the homeland, but in a movement toward it. The poet is the one who, in his homelessness, reveals a certain homelessness within the human condition itself. This revelation is the most significant feature of Brodsky's *To Urania*, for it is the most significant to the life of the human soul.

David Patterson

Bibliography:
Bethea, David M. *Joseph Brodsky and the Creation of Exile*. Princeton, N.J.: Princeton University Press, 1994. Contains a helpful discussion of the development of Brodsky's poetry and its significance for American letters; examines the influence of other major poets on Brodsky. Chapter 6 is particularly useful for an understanding of the themes addressed in *To Urania*. Good bibliography and index.

Loseff, Lev, and Valentina Polukhina, eds. *Brodsky's Poets and Aesthetics*. New York: St. Martin's Press, 1990. A collection of essays on Brodsky's poetry; also includes Brodsky's 1987 Nobel lecture and an interview with him conducted by Bella Akhmadulina. Of special interest to students of *To Urania* are the essays by George L. Kline and Peter France. Excellent index.

Patterson, David. "Exile in the Diaspora: The Poetry of Joseph Brodsky." In *Exile: The Sense of Alienation in Modern Russian Letters*. Lexington: University Press of Kentucky, 1995. Situates the poetry and the themes from *To Urania* within the larger contexts of Brodsky's general concerns as a poet. Contains a detailed discussion of the concepts of the sacred, of silence, and of the elsewhere in Brodsky's poetry.

Polukhina, Valentina. *Joseph Brodsky: A Poet for Our Time*. Cambridge, England: Cambridge University Press, 1989. Contains insightful examinations of the notions of time and space, word and spirit, exile and silence. All of the book's six chapters discuss poems from *To Urania*, and the last three chapters include comments on the collection as a whole. Good bibliography and index.

Proffer, Carl R. "A Stop in the Madhouse: Brodsky's *Gorbunov and Gorchakov*." *Russian Literature Triquarterly* 1 (1971): 342-351. One of the first essays on Brodsky's poetry to be published (it came out before Brodsky was exiled from Russia), this one is perhaps the most thorough and most insightful examination of the longest and most significant poem in *To Urania*.

TOBACCO ROAD

Type of work: Novel
Author: Erskine Caldwell (1903-1987)
Type of plot: Naturalism
Time of plot: 1920's
Locale: Georgia
First published: 1932

> *Principal characters:*
> JEETER LESTER, a poor white man
> ADA, his wife
> DUDE, his son
> ELLIE MAY, his daughter
> PEARL, another daughter
> LOV BENSEY, Pearl's husband
> BESSIE, a backwoods evangelist

The Story:

Lov Bensey, husband of Pearl, the fifteen-year-old daughter of Jeeter Lester, felt low in his mind when he stopped by the Lester house on his way home with a bag of turnips. Pearl, he complained, refused to have anything to do with him; she would neither sleep with him nor talk to him.

The Lesters lived in a one-room shack that was falling apart. They had nothing to eat but pork rind soup. Jeeter was trying to patch an inner tube so that the Lester car, a nondescript wreck which had been refused even by the junk dealer, could be used to carry firewood to Augusta. Jeeter's harelipped daughter, Ellie May, charmed Lov away from his bag of turnips. While she and Lov were flirting in the yard in front of the shack, the other Lesters pounced upon the bag of turnips. Jeeter grabbed it and ran into the scrub woods, followed by his worthless son Dude. Jeeter ate his fill of turnips. He gave Dude several and even saved a handful for the rest of the family. They returned from the woods to find Lov gone. Sister Bessie, a woman preacher, had come for a visit. Bessie, middle-aged, and Dude, sixteen, were attracted to each other. Bessie, upon leaving, promised to return to elope with Dude.

The Lesters were starving. Jeeter had long since been unable to get credit at the local stores in order to buy seed, fertilizer, and food. His land was exhausted, and there was no chance of reclaiming it because of Jeeter's utter laziness. Jeeter and his wife Ada had had seventeen children. Twelve of them had survived, but all except Ellie May and Dude had left home.

Bessie returned and announced that God had given her permission to marry Dude, but Dude refused to listen until Bessie said that she was planning to buy a new car with some money that her late husband had left her. She and Dude went to town and bought a new Ford, the loud horn of which Dude highly approved. At the county courthouse, over the mild protestations of the clerk because of Dude's youth, Bessie got a marriage license. Back at the Lester shack, Bessie, using her authority as preacher, married herself to Dude. The newlyweds went for a ride in their new car; they returned to the tobacco road at sundown with one fender of the car completely ruined. They had run into a farm wagon on the highway and had killed an African American man whom they had left lying by the roadside.

Jeeter, anxious to get food and snuff, persuaded Bessie and Dude to take him to Augusta with a load of firewood. Their arrival in Augusta was delayed, however, by the breakdown of the car.

A gallon and a half of oil poured into the crankcase enabled them to get to the city, where Jeeter failed to sell one stick of wood. The trio sold the car's spare tire, for which they could see no use, and bought food. They mistook a brothel for a hotel; Bessie was absent from Jeeter and her young husband most of the night.

During the return trip to the tobacco road, Jeeter unloaded the wood beside the highway and set fire to it. He was about to suggest another trip in the car, but Bessie and Dude rode away before he could stop them. As the car rapidly fell apart, the warmth between Bessie and her young husband cooled. In a fight between Bessie and the Lesters over Jeeter's right to ride in the car again, Dude sided with his wife. After all, the car still ran a little.

Meanwhile, Pearl ran away from Lov; she had managed to escape after he had tied her to their bed. Jeeter advised Lov not to look for Pearl but to take Ellie May in her place. He then told Ellie May to bring back food and clothes from Lov's house. The grandmother, who had been run over by Bessie's Ford, died in the yard.

Jeeter anticipated seeding time by burning the broomsedge off his land. A wind blew the fire to the house while Jeeter and Ada were asleep. The destitute sharecroppers were burned to death on the land that Jeeter's family had once owned as prosperous farmers.

Critical Evaluation:

In *Tobacco Road*, Erskine Caldwell relied on a combination of humor and social consciousness that sometimes created confusion among critics. They wondered if they were to laugh at the impoverished and degraded characters he described or sympathize with them. They questioned whether humor was the best way to inspire social change.

Caldwell was made acquainted with the social conditions of the persons he described by his minister father. Besides helping the poor of every denomination, Ira Caldwell was also an amateur sociologist, who published his observations of the white people who lived in poverty in Georgia in *Eugenics*, a magazine concerned with the devolution of society. Entitled "The Bunglers," Ira's series of articles detailed the nearly hopeless condition of the rural poor. Erskine, who accompanied his father on his visits to impoverished households, fictionalized many of the same facts mentioned in his father's articles.

The literary movement of naturalism, which had served as a vehicle for similar subject matter in the fiction of Theodore Dreiser, Frank Norris, Jack London, and Stephen Crane, was congenial to Caldwell's purpose. Like other naturalistic works, *Tobacco Road* uses stark, realistic detail to establish its characters on the bottom of society, among its poorest and most degraded elements. Caldwell's purposes in choosing characters so remote from middle-class norms were to shock his readers out of their complacency and to call attention to the devastating effects of poverty. The details of the lives he chooses to describe are stripped of any civilized buffer. He prods his audience with Ellie's harelip, Ada's pleurisy, Grandmother's pellagra, Pearl's marriage at a young age, and Jeeter's chronic laziness resulting from malnutrition. He dramatizes a Darwinian struggle for survival over a bag of turnips; the characters are animal-like as they position themselves to steal Lov's food; equally animal-like are their sexual relations. They are controlled by the forces of hunger, sex, and tribal solidarity.

Caldwell uses the technique of fragmentation to create an impression of unremitting social chaos. Characters perform actions that are incongruous with one another. They talk at cross purposes, which dramatizes the fact that they are essentially uncivilized, motivated by their own individual desires, having no regard for others. The effect created is of a splintered society, each of its members struggling for survival in a hostile environment.

However, besides Caldwell's careful documenting of degrading and tragic social conditions, he also delights his readers with humorous accounts of his characters' antics. He achieves comedy by having those characters act and speak in a manner showing their ignorance of middle-class norms. Bessie and the Lesters virtually destroy a new automobile in one day without seeming concerned about it. In the Augusta episode, Bessie, Jeeter, and Dude are treated as country bumpkins who exit Augusta as impenetrably ignorant of the ways of the urban world as when they entered it. None realizes that he has spent the night in a brothel.

Caldwell also satirizes his characters' religious pretensions. Middle-aged Bessie is a self-styled preacher who seeks to continue her late husband's ministry by marrying, at God's command, the teenage Dude. She invokes God whenever she seeks to justify her own selfish desires. The unregenerate Jeeter, meanwhile, is pleased when Bessie chastises him for his sinfulness, for he believes that there still must be hope for him if a woman of God cares enough to criticize him. Simultaneous with his "reverence" for Bessie's religious authority is Jeeter's frank admiration of her physical presence. Caldwell's characters are unaware of the discrepancy between their spiritual desires and the trap of their animalistic sensory existence. This lack of awareness is another source of humor.

For all its degradation and bawdy humor, *Tobacco Road* approaches tragedy in its depiction of Jeeter. Despite his many flaws, his loyalty to the land stands out as a redeeming characteristic. His spirit and instincts are in harmony with the seasons, and he maintains his hope that one day he will be able to resume the planting rituals that his blood seems to call for each spring. He dies when his feeble attempt to resume his life as a farmer turns disastrous.

Although the novel's mixture of ribaldry and social protest may have puzzled critics, the novel and the play made from it enjoyed tremendous popularity with general readers whose imaginations were easily captured by them. Caldwell, who geared his books for the common reader, was gratified by the popularity of his work. He went on to write other best-selling works, such as *God's Little Acre* (1933), which made him, during the 1940's and 1950's, the most widely read writer in the world.

"Critical Evaluation" by William L. Howard

Bibliography:
Arnold, Edwin T., ed. *Erskine Caldwell Reconsidered.* Jackson: University Press of Mississippi, 1990. A series of essays about this generally underappreciated novelist dealing with both biographical and literary topics.
Cook, Sylvia Jenkins. *Erskine Caldwell and the Fiction of Poverty: The Flesh and the Spirit.* Baton Rouge: Louisiana State University Press, 1991. This study focuses on the physical and spiritual effects of poverty on Caldwell's characters. For all of their preoccupation with material reality, they aspire also to a higher purpose in life.
Devlin, James E. *Erskine Caldwell.* Boston: Twayne, 1984. An analysis of the novel's themes and techniques. Identifies Caldwell as a naturalist and the Lesters as part of a subculture. Also tries to account for the novel's seemingly contradictory combination of humor and serious social commentary.
Klevar, Harvey L. *Erskine Caldwell: A Biography.* Knoxville: University of Tennessee Press, 1993. Covers the writing of the novel, Caldwell's relationship with his publishers, and the influence of his father's study of the white Southern poor for *Eugenics* magazine.
MacDonald, Scott, ed. *Critical Essays on Erskine Caldwell.* Boston: G. K. Hall, 1981. Includes introductions that Caldwell wrote for several of his novels, including *Tobacco Road*, as well as contemporary reviews and scholarly essays.

THE TOILERS OF THE SEA

Type of work: Novel
Author: Victor Hugo (1802-1885)
Type of plot: Sentimental
Time of plot: 1820's
Locale: The Isle of Guernsey
First published: Les Travailleurs de la mer, 1866 (English translation, 1866)

Principal characters:
GILLIATT, a young recluse
MESS LETHIERRY, a shipowner and Gilliatt's friend
DÉRUCHETTE, Lethierry's niece
SIEUR CLUBIN, the captain of Lethierry's steamboat
RANTAINE, Lethierry's former partner
EBENEZER CAUDRAY, the rector and Déruchette's lover

The Story:

In the parish of St. Sampson, Gilliatt was a strange figure. He and his mother had come to the Isle of Guernsey some years before and had made their home in an old house by the shore. Nobody knew where they came from, but most people decided that they were French. When Gilliatt grew to young manhood, his mother died, and he was left alone to make his livelihood by fishing and cultivating. To the superstitious people of the town, he was a figure to be feared, for they were sure he had power to communicate with evil spirits and to cure strange ailments. The young man went his own way with seeming indifference.

One Christmas Day, Gilliatt saw a young woman tracing some letters in the snow. When he reached the spot, he discovered that the letters spelled his own name. The woman was Déruchette, the niece of Mess Lethierry and Gilliatt's supporter against the superstitious people of the parish. From that day on Gilliatt was in love with the beautiful Déruchette. Although he stood in her garden and serenaded her with his bagpipe, he lacked the courage to approach her directly. Mess Lethierry heard the music from the garden and thought that it would do the suitor, whoever he was, little good; it was to him the suitor should apply.

Gilliatt later won a race, and the prize was a Dutch sloop. Mess Lethierry thought more highly of him than ever. Lethierry was a good man who loved two things, the sea and his niece. Some time before, he had been brought to ruin by the treachery of a man he had trusted. Rantaine, his partner, had run away not only with his own share of the profits but also with Lethierry's share. In an effort to recoup his finances, Lethierry bought a steamboat, an invention the fishermen considered a work of the devil.

The *Durande*, as the ship was called, shared equal affection with Déruchette in Lethierry's heart. As captain, he engaged Sieur Clubin, a man whose honesty was the pride of the community. Despite the opposition to the steamboat, Lethierry prospered in trade with St. Malo and other points on the French coast.

Meanwhile a new rector, Ebenezer Caudray, had come to the parish. One day, while Gilliatt was fishing from his sloop, he rescued Caudray, who had climbed upon a rock exposed at low tide. The grateful rector gave him a Bible. When Caudray met Déruchette, he fell in love with her, much to Gilliatt's chagrin.

One day the *Durande* did not return from a trip to St. Malo. Lethierry was in despair, and the whole parish was in an uproar. Some days previously a group of boys had gone prowling near an old and supposedly haunted house. There they had heard men talking in Spanish, discussing payment for taking someone to South America. In St. Malo a man purchased a revolver and spoke mysteriously to various people. A short time before, a coast guardsman had been killed. Clubin, encountering Rantaine, had forced him at gunpoint to return the money stolen from Lethierry. As Rantaine left in a boat, he shouted to Clubin that he would write to Lethierry to tell him that he had given the captain the money.

While Lethierry and the townspeople waited for news of the *Durande*, that ship was in difficulty. The pilot, having discovered a flask of brandy, had gotten drunk and steered the ship off its course in the fog. The captain cursed the drunken pilot and attempted to avoid a catastrophe. Suddenly there was a crash, and the boat began to leak. The passengers took to lifeboats, but the captain remained on board. When they were gone, the captain made his way to the rocks upon which the ship had grounded. Much to his surprise and fear, he discovered that he was not where he had planned to be.

Clubin had deliberately wrecked the ship after placing the brandy where the pilot would find it. In the hope that everyone would believe he had been drowned, he planned to ground the *Durande* at a spot where he would find some smugglers hired to carry him to South America with the money taken from Rantaine. Now he realized that he had miscalculated, that he was stranded in one of the deathtraps of the sea, that he would drown.

When survivors of the wreck reached St. Sampson and told their story, Sieur Clubin became a hero. Lethierry, however, was desolate; his fortune was gone. It was not so much the vessel itself that was important—for that could be replaced—but the engine was lost, and he lacked the money to buy another. In his despair Lethierry announced that whoever should regain the engine would have Déruchette for his wife. Gilliatt stepped forward and announced that he would try to salvage the engine.

At the scene of the wreck, Gilliatt labored unceasingly against the powerful sea and bad weather. One day he swam into an underwater cave, where he was attacked by a monster that he finally managed to kill. He swam farther and in the recesses of the cavern found the remains of a man and a wallet bearing Clubin's name. The wallet contained many coins. Gilliatt pocketed it and resumed his work.

At last he succeeded in hoisting the engine. Weary and exhausted, he fell into a deep sleep. The next day, after the sun had warmed his tired body, he gained new strength. Then he discovered that part of his work had been undone by the sea. While he attempted to repair the damage, a storm came up, and all of his work seemed in vain. Finally, however, he got the engine into his boat and sailed for home.

In St. Sampson, with the arrival of Rantaine's letter, Mess Lethierry began to understand Clubin's duplicity. As time passed, Clubin's secret preparations became known, and no one any longer believed that he had gone down with the ship. Lethierry was even more dispirited than ever. One morning, as he looked out at the ocean, he saw Gilliatt's Dutch sloop with the engine aboard. Overjoyed, he sent for Gilliatt, who had slipped away to his own house. Lethierry was ready to make good his promise, with deep gratitude now that Gilliatt had returned not only the valuable engine but also the money recovered from Clubin's wallet; but Déruchette, confronting the unkempt and bedraggled Gilliatt, fainted. Gilliatt, having seen her and Caudray in the garden, knew that she secretly loved the rector.

When the shipowner, unaware of his niece's true affections, pushed the preparations for the wedding, Caudray determined to marry Déruchette without Lethierry's knowledge. The two went off to be married, only to learn that they could not have the ceremony performed without Lethierry's consent. Then Gilliatt arrived with Lethierry's consent for the wedding of Gilliatt and Déruchette. To their astonishment, Gilliatt said he would give the bride away. So Caudray and Déruchette were married.

As the newlyweds were embarking upon the *Cashmere*, which was to take them to England, Gilliatt presented Déruchette with a chest of bride's linen he had inherited from his mother. As the ship pulled out, Gilliatt went to the rock from which he had once rescued Caudray. On board, Déruchette saw that a man was sitting there, but in her happiness she gave no more thought to him. As Gilliatt watched the ship sail out of sight, the water mounted higher and higher around the rock. Soon the waves washed over it, and nothing could be seen but the sea and the sky.

Critical Evaluation:

The Toilers of the Sea represents many of the chief characteristics of French literary Romanticism. The setting, action, characterization, and style of the novel extend and exaggerate certain tendencies inherent in the Romantic worldview.

Les Misérables (1862), an earlier work by Victor Hugo, is concerned with human progress, justice, and social improvement. *The Toilers of the Sea*, on the other hand, is as much concerned with the mystical "world beyond" as with the ordinary world. It is a novel that embodies Hugo's late flowering interest in religion and the occult. Written in exile on the British-ruled Channel Islands, the novel no doubt magnified Hugo's interest in such topics, given his loneliness and isolation.

The scene of the novel is lonely and exotic, far from the ordinary experiences of men and women. Although Hugo goes to great lengths to describe the islands and surrounding ocean, picturing everything in the most particular detail—including insects, types of grasses, the everyday conditions of nature—the landscape nevertheless appears both melodramatic and supernatural. Hugo's landscape, or seascape, is overwhelming.

The action, or plot, combines typical Romantic features with these extremes. There is, first of all, an intense love story. This story is combined with considerable intrigue and mystery. Nothing is merely what it seems; everything suggests something else. These mysterious elements in the action, emphasized by Hugo at every step, are reminiscent of the devices of Edgar Allan Poe.

The scope of the action, however, especially Gilliatt's struggle for the engine and his fight against the octopus, far exceeds Poe's ambition. The will to struggle that Hugo portrays in Gilliatt is particularly notable in the light of Hugo's overall purpose: to glorify toil and the struggle against the elements and to show that this struggle is actually part of the immense human effort to master infinity. Thus Hugo's approach to human labor is decisively opposed to the realist tradition. In other words, Hugo does not record the details of work or its social meaning and function; instead, Hugo's toil is primarily metaphysical and transcendent. The character of Gilliatt, which dominates the novel, is Promethean; Gilliatt knows and understands more than others about the sea and the crafts of the sea. His energy and skill are wild and superhuman. Prometheus brings fire to humanity; Gilliatt salvages the steam engine (modern technology).

The atmosphere of the novel, however—its density and its dramatic force—is generated in Hugo's descriptions of the sea, the rocks, and the struggles of Gilliatt. Using hyperbole and antithesis, Hugo presents a powerful image of the sea in storm and at rest and of human agony and surrender.

Bibliography:

Brombert, Victor. "The Toilers of the Sea." In *Victor Hugo and the Visionary Novel*. Cambridge, Mass.: Harvard University Press, 1984. Examines the novel as Hugo's "glorification of Work," which Hugo considered an epic theme. Looks at Hugo's images as they derive from realism and from myth.

_____. "*Les Travailleurs de la mer:* Hugo's Poem of Effacement." *New Literary History* 9, no. 3 (Spring, 1978): 581-590. Argues that the novel should be treated as a prose poem because of Hugo's narrative stance. The imagery and structure are built on effacement and dissolution.

Grant, Elliott M. *The Career of Victor Hugo*. Cambridge, Mass.: Harvard University Press, 1946. Contains a brief but fascinating section on the composition of *The Toilers of the Sea*. Hugo, Grant explains, had little personal deep sea experience, but relied on encyclopedias, travel books, and his own poetic vision for his startlingly vivid images.

Grant, Richard B. "*Les Travailleurs de la mer:* Towards an Epic Synthesis." In *Victor Hugo*, edited by Harold Bloom. New York: Chelsea House, 1988. Considering the novel as an epic, Grant believes, makes it possible to see disparate elements—two-dimensional heroic characters, the encyclopedic preface, the archetypal quest—as forming a coherent whole.

Houston, John Porter. *Victor Hugo*. Boston: Twayne, 1988. A fine introductory overview of Hugo's poetry, plays, and novels. The brief section on *The Toilers of the Sea* discusses structure, theme, and prose style in the context of Hugo's later novels and poetry. The chronology, and introductory and concluding chapters, also shed light on this novel.

TOM BROWN'S SCHOOL DAYS

Type of work: Novel
Author: Thomas Hughes (1822-1896)
Type of plot: Social realism
Time of plot: Early nineteenth century
Locale: England
First published: 1857

Principal characters:
> THOMAS BROWN, a student at Rugby
> HARRY EAST, his friend
> GEORGE ARTHUR, a boy befriended by Tom Brown
> DR. ARNOLD, the headmaster of Rugby
> FLASHMAN, a bully

The Story:

Tom Brown was the son of a country squire who believed in letting his children mingle not only with their social equals but also with any children who were honorable. Before Tom left home to attend Rugby, therefore, he had the advantage of friendship with all types of boys. This training was to be of value to him when he first arrived at the famous school. When Tom alighted from the coach, he was met by Harry East, a lower-school boy who had been at Rugby for a half year. He gave Tom good advice on how to dress and how to take the hazing and bullying that every new boy must endure. The two boys became immediate friends and were to remain so throughout their years at school. From the first, Tom loved the school. He conducted himself with such bravery, both on the playing field and in dormitory scuffles, that he soon gained popularity among the other boys. One of the sixth-form boys, a leader among the students, made such an impression on Tom with his talks on sportsmanship and kindness to weaker boys that Tom for the first half-year was an almost model student. He did join in some of the mischief and was once sent to Dr. Arnold, the headmaster. By and large, however, he and East profited by the lessons they learned in classes and in games.

With the beginning of the second half-year, Tom was promoted into the lower fourth form, a large and unruly class dominated by bullies and ruffians. Formerly he had liked his masters and tried to please them; now he began to believe that they were his natural enemies, and he attempted to do everything possible to thwart them. He cribbed on his lessons and shirked many of his other duties. He and East disobeyed many rules of the school and often taunted farmers in the neighborhood by fishing in their waters or killing their fowl. All in all, Tom, East, and their friends acted in very ungentlemanly ways.

Nevertheless, Tom and East also did some good in the school, for they were basically boys of sound character. Both came from good homes and had received good early training. They finally decided that something must be done about fagging, the custom of running errands for the older boys. Each older boy was allowed two fags, but some of them made every younger lad in the school wait on them. One particular bully was Flashman. Tom and East decided to strike against Flashman's domination; they locked themselves in their room and defied his demands that they let him in. After attempting to break the door down, Flashman retreated temporarily, but he was not through with the rebels. For weeks, he caught them and tortured them at each possible chance, but they held firm and persuaded some of the other lower-school boys to join them. At last, Flashman's brutality to Tom and East and their friends so disgusted even the bully's best friends that they began to desert him. At last, his hold on the school was broken. Then Tom and East thrashed him soundly, and from that time on, Flashman never laid a hand on them. Not long afterward, Flashman was caught drunk by the headmaster and was sent away from the school.

Tom and East began to get into trouble in earnest, and the headmaster despaired of their even being allowed to stay in school. Wise Dr. Arnold, however, could see the good in the boys, good which they seemed to try hard to hide, and he arranged for them to be split up. Tom was given a new and shy young boy, George Arthur, with whom to live. Arthur was a half orphan, and Tom's better nature responded to the homesick younger boy. Arthur was to be the greatest influence to enter Tom's life during his career at Rugby. He was of slight build, but he had moral courage that made Tom ashamed. Arthur did what he thought was right, even when it meant that he must endure the taunts of his housemates. Tom could not let a younger boy appear more courageous than he, so he reverted to his own former good habits, which he had dropped because of fear of hazing. He began again to kneel in prayer morning and night, to read his Bible, and to discuss earnestly the meanings of certain passages. Indeed, as East said, although Tom was seemingly becoming a leader in the school, it was really Arthur who was leading Tom and thus the other boys. East fought the change as hard as he could, but he, too, followed Tom, and despite himself, he began to change for the better.

When fever struck the school, many of the boys were seriously ill, and Arthur was among them. One boy died. Arthur remained very weak after his illness, and his mother decided to take him out of school until he could recover his strength. Before he left, Arthur spoke to Tom about cribbing. Although Tom, believing that to fool the masters was a schoolboy's duty, scoffed at his friend's views, Arthur as usual prevailed. Tom found it hard to do his lessons honestly, but each time he would weaken, the memory of Arthur's face and voice would set him straight again. East did not completely change in this respect, but he did try harder on his own before resorting to dishonest translations.

Another result of Arthur's influence was that East took communion. He had never been confirmed, but as a result of a conversation with Tom, at which Tom put forth many of Arthur's beliefs, East talked with Dr. Arnold and received spiritual stimulation. After he began to receive communion, East rapidly changed into the good young man he had unknowingly wanted to be. So the school years passed. East finished up and went off to fight in India. Tom became the leader of the school, and he and Arthur, who had returned after his illness, made many changes in the actions and attitudes of the boys. After graduation, Tom went on to Oxford. While there, he learned of the death of his old headmaster, Dr. Arnold. He returned to his old school to mourn the man who had played such a large part in influencing his life. It was not until Dr. Arnold was gone that Tom and the others realized how much the good man had done for them. Tom's friends were scattered over the earth, but he knew that his heart would always be with them and those wonderful days at Rugby.

Critical Evaluation:

In *Tom Brown's School Days*, Thomas Hughes created what proved to be the archetypal novel of British public school (or boarding school) life. Written as his own eight-year-old son went off to Rugby School, Hughes's novel was to be an inspiration and a model of what his son might expect. Hughes had entered Rugby School in 1833, five years after Dr. Thomas Arnold had become headmaster, and many of the incidents and much of the atmosphere of the novel reflect Hughes's own years at Rugby. *Tom Brown's School Days* is not, however, merely a fictional recollection of Hughes's experiences. Hughes had a didactic purpose: He produced a moral tract of what the public schools and their students might attain.

Some of England's most prestigious public schools had their origins in the late Middle Ages. By the early nineteenth century, boarding schools had become the exclusive preserve of the sons of Britain's ruling class. Fees and tuition were charged, and although scholarships were sometimes available, the schools were extremely exclusive. The public schools were producing the next generation's government leaders, politicians, generals, admirals, and diplomats; they were the training ground for the rulers, not the ruled. The first section of *Tom Brown's School Days* has nothing to do with Rugby. Instead, it portrays Tom's early childhood and where he grew up, a rural area far removed from London and where the traditional gentry still maintained their influence. Hughes was a member of the gentry, and his choice of the common name of Brown suggests that Tom comes from that rural governing class that Hughes claimed formed the backbone of England. In this idyllic setting were young Tom's roots, and there he played with the sons of artisans and workers, people further down the social scale than the Browns. There were no boys from that lower social stratum at Rugby, however, where only the middle classes and aristocracy—the top ten percent of the population—were brought together.

Arnold's tenure at Rugby marked a milestone in the history of the public schools. If he was not the first reformer to make a significant impact upon the institution of the boarding school, he was the most prominent. The father of the poet, essayist, and critic Matthew Arnold, Thomas Arnold left an indelible mark on the nineteenth century, in part because of Hughes's *Tom Brown's School Days*. Arnold's hopes for Rugby and the Rugby portrayed in Hughes's novel were different. Arnold was committed to turning his charges into Christian gentlemen, to give them a moral grounding to shape their entire lives. Good form had to be matched, in Arnold's view, by a commitment to performing one's duties to society. Public school students would become the governing class, and their lives must be guided by Christian moral principles. Hughes would not have disagreed with the moral imperative propounded in Arnold's approach. In his novel, in what may be a reflection of Arnold's religious ideology, Hughes creates a climate that is essentially anti-intellectual. Squire Brown, musing to himself about what he wants for Tom at Rugby, notes: "I don't give a straw for Greek particles, or the digamma. . . . If he'll only turn out a brave, helpful, truth-telling Englishman, and a gentleman, and a Christian, that's all I want."

At Hughes's Rugby, games take precedence over scholarship. Tom's first introduction to Rugby is taking part in a football match, whose rules had yet to be codified into the modern sport of rugby. When the match was over, and Tom's house emerged victorious, one of the senior boys, Brooke, addressed the boys of the house and claimed that he was prouder of the house's victory than if he had won a scholarship to Oxford University's prestigious Balliol College. Tom's last activity while still a student was to captain the cricket eleven against the famous Marylebone players. Arnold, who loved and respected the intellectual life, would have opposed this overemphasis on games. As the nineteenth century went on, however, public school life more and more revolved around games. The change of focus was evident in the stories and novels of schoolboy life which multiplied in the wake of Hughes's success with *Tom Brown's School Days* and in the many new schools that emerged in the latter half of the nineteenth century. The formation of character on the sports field took precedence over the development of the intellect.

Tom Brown's School Days has never been out of print since it first appeared in 1857, and its impact upon succeeding generations has been profound not only among those who might expect to attend a school like Rugby but also among schoolboys in the middle class and in the working class. The novel's moral lessons are clear, and its events are often exciting and easily accessible even to those without roots in the public school milieu. Telling the truth, being brave and fighting fair, and doing well at games became the novel's message. Lying was breaking the code, and bullying—endemic in the schools—was condemned. Flashman, who tormented Tom and others, has become a lasting symbol of the cowardly bully. Hughes was himself a Christian gentleman who exhibited his social responsibilities in his commitment to furthering the rights and opportunities of the working class. Less than a generation after his death in 1896, it would largely be former public schoolboys who, as junior officers, died in considerable numbers leading their troops into battle during World War I. It is difficult to imagine, in the different environment of a later era, that the effect of *Tom Brown's School Days* on readers can be as influential as when it first appeared. In the late twentieth century, another British writer, George MacDonald Fraser, turned Hughes's Flashman, still the cowardly bully, into a notable success as an antihero in a series of popular novels.

"Critical Evaluation" by Eugene Larson

Bibliography:
Briggs, Asa. *Victorian People*. New York: Harper & Row, 1963. The author, an eminent British historian, discusses the notable figures, ideas, and events of the high Victorian era (1851-1867). Included is a brilliant chapter on "Thomas Hughes and the Public Schools."
Chandos, John. *Boys Together*. New Haven, Conn.: Yale University Press, 1984. In this scholarly analysis of the English public school from 1800 to 1864, Dr. Thomas Arnold plays the central role. The importance of Hughes's *Tom Brown's School Days* as popularizing Arnold's reforms at Rugby is discussed.
Mack, Edward C., and W. H. G. Armytage. *Thomas Hughes: The Life of the Author of "Tom Brown's School Days."* London: Ernest Benn, 1952. This is the standard biography of Hughes, an archetypal Victorian figure, and illustrates his many literary, political, and social endeavors. Included is an extensive discussion of *Tom Brown's School Days*.
Quigly, Isabel. *The Heirs of Tom Brown: The English School Story*. London: Chatto & Windus, 1982. Analyzes the development of the numerous stories written about England's public boarding schools, a genre that began with Hughes's *Tom Brown's School Days*.
Worth, George J. *Thomas Hughes*. Boston: Twayne, 1984. A recent analysis of Hughes the writer rather than Hughes the politician and public figure. Concentrates on *Tom Brown's School Days*.

TOM JONES

Type of work: Novel
Author: Henry Fielding (1707-1754)
Type of plot: Picaresque
Time of plot: Early eighteenth century
Locale: England
First published: The History of Tom Jones, a Foundling, 1749

Principal characters:
> TOM JONES, a foundling
> SQUIRE ALLWORTHY, his foster father
> BRIDGET, Allworthy's sister
> MASTER BLIFIL, Bridget's son
> MR. PARTRIDGE, the schoolmaster
> MR. WESTERN, an English squire
> SOPHIA WESTERN, his daughter

The Story:

Squire Allworthy lived in retirement in the country with his sister Bridget. Returning from a visit to London, he was surprised upon entering his room to find an infant lying on his bed. His discovery caused astonishment and consternation in the household. The squire was a childless widower. The next day, Miss Bridget and the squire inquired in the community to discover the baby's mother. Their suspicions were shortly fixed upon Jenny Jones, who had spent many hours in the squire's home while nursing Miss Bridget through a long illness. The worthy squire sent for the girl and in his gentle manner reprimanded her for her wicked behavior, assuring her, however, that the baby would remain in his home under the best of care. Fearing malicious gossip in the neighborhood, Squire Allworthy sent Jenny away.

Jenny Jones had been a servant in the house of a schoolmaster, Mr. Partridge, who had educated the young woman during her four years in his house. Jenny's comely face made Mrs. Partridge jealous of her. Neighborhood gossip soon convinced Mrs. Partridge that her husband was the father of Jenny's son, whereupon Squire Allworthy called the schoolmaster before him and talked to him at great length concerning morality. Mr. Partridge, deprived of his school, his income, and his wife, also left the country.

Shortly afterward, Captain Blifil won the heart of Bridget Allworthy. Eight months after their marriage, Bridget bore a son. The squire thought it would be advisable to rear the foundling and his sister's child together. The foundling had been named Jones, after his mother.

Squire Allworthy became exceedingly fond of the foundling. Captain Blifil died during his son's infancy, and Master Blifil grew up as Squire Allworthy's acknowledged heir. Otherwise, he remained on even terms with the foundling, so far as opportunities for advancement were concerned. Tom, however, was such a mischievous lad that he had only one friend among the servants, the gamekeeper, Black George, an indolent man with a large family. Mr. Thwackum and Mr. Square, who considered Tom a wicked soul, were hired to instruct the lads. Tom's many deceptions were always discovered through the combined efforts of Mr. Thwackum, Mr. Square, and Master Blifil, who disliked Tom more and more as he grew older. It had been assumed by all that Mrs. Blifil would dislike Tom, but at times she seemed to show greater affection for him than for her own son. In turn, the compassionate squire took Master Blifil to his heart and became censorious of Tom.

Mr. Western, who lived on a neighboring estate, had a daughter whom he loved more than anyone else in the world. Sophia had a tender fondness for Tom because of a deed of kindness he had performed for her when they were still children. At the age of twenty, Master Blifil had become a favorite with the young ladies, while Tom was considered a ruffian by all but Mr. Western, who admired his ability to hunt. Tom spent many evenings at the Western home, with every opportunity to see Sophia, for whom his affections were increasing daily. One afternoon, Tom had the good fortune to be nearby when Sophia's horse ran away. When Tom attempted to rescue her, he broke his arm. He was removed to Mr. Western's house, where he received medical care and remained to recover from his hurt. One day, he and Sophia had occasion to be alone in the garden, where they exchanged confessions of love.

Squire Allworthy became mortally ill. The doctor assumed that he was dying and sent for the squire's relatives. With his servants and family gathered around him, the squire announced the disposal of his wealth, giving generously to Tom. Tom was the only one satisfied with his portion; his only concern was the impending death of his foster father and benefactor. On the way home from London to see the squire, Mrs. Blifil died suddenly. When the squire was pronounced out of danger, Tom's joy was so great that he became drunk through toasting the squire's health, and he quarreled with young Blifil.

Sophia's aunt, Mrs. Western, perceived the interest her niece showed in Blifil. Wishing to conceal her affection for Tom, Sophia had given Blifil the greater part of her attention when she was with the two young men. Informed by his sister of Sophia's conduct, Mr. Western suggested to Squire Allworthy that a match be arranged between Blifil and Sophia. When Mrs. Western told the young woman of the proposed match, Sophia thought that Mrs. Western was referring to Tom, and she immediately disclosed her passion for the foundling. It was unthinkable, however, that Mr. Western, much as he liked Tom, would ever allow his daughter to marry a man without a family and a fortune, and Mrs. Western forced Sophia to receive Blifil under the threat of exposing the woman's real affection for Tom. Sophia met Tom secretly in the garden, and the two lovers vowed constancy. Mr. Western discovered them and went immediately to Squire Allworthy with his knowledge.

Aware of his advantage, Blifil told the squire that on the day he lay near death, Tom was out drinking and singing. The squire felt that he had forgiven Tom many wrongs, but this show of unconcern for the squire's health infuriated the good man. He sent for Tom, reproached him, and banished him from his house.

With the help of Black George, the gamekeeper, and Mrs. Honour, Sophia's maid, Tom and Sophia were able to exchange love letters. When Sophia was confined to her room because she refused to marry Blifil, she bribed her maid to flee with her from her father's house. Tom, setting out to seek his fortune, went to an inn with a small company of soldiers. A fight followed in which he was severely injured, and a barber was summoned to treat his wound. When Tom had told the barber his story, the man surprisingly revealed himself to be Partridge, the schoolmaster, banished years before because he was suspected of being Tom's father. When Tom was well enough to travel, the two men set out together on foot.

Before they had gone far, they heard screams of a woman in distress and came upon a woman struggling with a soldier who had beguiled her to a lonely spot. Promising to take her to a place of safety, Tom accompanied the unfortunate woman to the nearby village of Upton, where the landlady of the inn refused to receive them because of the woman's torn and disheveled clothing. When the landlady heard the true story of the woman's misfortune and had been assured that the woman was the lady of Captain Waters, a well-known officer, she relented. Mrs. Waters invited Tom to dine with her so that she could thank him properly for her rescue.

Meanwhile, a lady and her maid arrived at the inn and proceeded to their rooms. They were followed, several hours later, by an angry gentleman in pursuit of his wife. Learning from the chambermaid that there was a woman resembling his wife in the inn, he burst into Mrs. Waters' chambers, only to confront Tom Jones. At his intrusion, Mrs. Waters began to scream. Abashed, the gentleman identified himself as Mr. Fitzpatrick and retreated with apologies. Shortly after this disturbance had subsided, Sophia and Mrs. Honour arrived at the inn. When Partridge unknowingly revealed Tom's relationship with Mrs. Waters and the embarrassing situation that Mr. Fitzpatrick had disclosed, Sophia, grieved by Tom's fickleness, decided to continue on her way. Before leaving the inn, however, she had Mrs. Honour place on Tom's empty bed a muff that she knew he would recognize as hers.

Soon after setting out, Sophia overtook Mrs. Fitzpatrick, who had arrived at the inn early the previous evening and who had fled during the disturbance caused by her husband. Mrs. Fitzpatrick was Sophia's cousin, and they decided to go on to London together. In London, Sophia proceeded to the home of Lady Bellaston, who was known to her through Mrs. Western. Lady Bellaston was sympathetic with Sophia's reasons for running away.

Unable to overtake Sophia, Tom and Partridge followed her to London, where Tom took lodgings in the home of Mrs. Miller, whom Squire Allworthy patronized on his visits to the city. The landlady had two daughters, Nancy and Betty, and a lodger, Mr. Nightingale, who was obviously in love with Nancy. Tom found congenial residence with Mrs. Miller, and he became friends with Mr. Nightingale. Partridge was still with Tom in the hope of future advancement. Repeated visits to Lady Bellaston and Mrs. Fitzpatrick finally gave Tom the opportunity to meet Sophia during an intermission at a play. There, Tom was able to allay Sophia's doubts as to his love for her. During his stay with the Millers, Tom learned that Mr. Nightingale's father objected to his marrying Nancy. Through the kindness of his heart, Tom persuaded the elder Nightingale to permit the marriage, to Mrs. Miller's great delight.

Mr. Western had learned of Sophia's whereabouts from Mrs. Fitzpatrick. He came to London and took Sophia from Lady Bellaston's house to his own lodgings. When Mrs. Honour brought the news to Tom, he was in despair. Penniless, he could not hope to marry Sophia, and now his beloved was in the hands of her father once more. Then Partridge brought news that Squire Allworthy was coming to London and was bringing with him Master Blifil to marry Sophia. In his distress, Tom went to see Mrs. Fitzpatrick but encountered her jealous husband on her doorstep. In the duel that followed, Tom wounded Fitzpatrick and was carried off to jail.

There he was visited by Partridge, the friends he had made in London, and Mrs. Waters, who had been traveling with Mr. Fitzpatrick since their meeting in Upton. When Partridge and Mrs. Waters met in Tom's cell, Partridge recognized her as Jenny Jones, Tom's reputed mother. Horrified, he revealed his knowledge to everyone, including Squire Allworthy, who by that time had arrived in London with Blifil.

In Mrs. Miller's lodgings, so many people had praised Tom's goodness and kindness that Squire Allworthy had almost made up his mind to relent in his attitude toward the foundling when news of his conduct with Mrs. Waters reached his ears. Fortunately, however, the cloud was soon dispelled by Mrs. Waters herself, who assured the squire that Tom was no son of hers but the child of his sister Bridget and a student whom the squire had befriended. Tom's true father had died before his son's birth, and Bridget had concealed her shame by putting the baby on her brother's bed upon his return from a long visit to London. Later, she had paid Jenny liberally to let suspicion fall upon her former maid.

Squire Allworthy also learned that Bridget had claimed Tom as her son in a letter written before her death, a letter Blifil probably had destroyed. There was further proof that Blifil had plotted to have Tom hanged for murder. Fitzpatrick, however, had not died, and he recovered sufficiently to acknowledge himself the aggressor in the duel; Tom was released from prison.

Upon these disclosures of Blifil's villainy, Squire Allworthy dismissed Blifil and made Tom his heir. Once Tom's proper station had been revealed, Mr. Western withdrew all objections to his suit. Reunited, Tom and Sophia were married and retired to Mr. Western's estate in the country.

Critical Evaluation:

In a relatively short life span, Henry Fielding was a poet, a playwright, a journalist, a jurist, and a pioneer in the development of the modern novel. The early poetry may be disregarded, but his dramatic works gave Fielding the training that later enabled him to handle adeptly the complex plots of his novels. Although he wrote perhaps a half-dozen novels (some attributions are disputed), Fielding is best remembered for *The History of Tom Jones, a Foundling*. This novel contains a strong infusion of autobiographical elements. The character Sophia, for example, was based on Fielding's wife Charlotte, who was his one great love. They eloped in 1734 and had ten years together before she died in 1744. Squire Allworthy combined traits of a former schoolmate from Eton named George Lyttelton (to whom the novel is dedicated), and a generous benefactor of the Fielding family named James Ralph. Moreover, Fielding's origins in a career army family and his rejection of that background shaped his portrayal of various incidental military personnel in this and his other novels; he had an antiarmy bias. Fielding's feelings of revulsion against urban living are reflected in the conclusion of *Tom Jones* (and in his other novels). The happy ending consists of a retreat to the country. Published a scant five years before Fielding's death, *Tom Jones* was a runaway best-seller, going through four editions within a twelve-month period.

The structure of the novel is carefully divided into eighteen books in a fashion similar to the epic form that Fielding explicitly praised. Of those eighteen books, the first six are set on the Somersetshire estate of Squire Allworthy. Books 7 through 12 deal with events on the road to London, and the last six books describe events in London. The middle of the novel, books 9 and 10, covers the hilarious hiatus at the inn in Upton. Apparent diversions and digressions are actually intentional exercises in character exposition, and all episodes are deliberately choreographed to advance the plot—sometimes in ways not evident until later. Everything contributes to the overall organic development of the novel.

This kind of coherence was intimately connected with Fielding's concern about the craft of fiction. *Tom Jones* is one of the most carefully and meticulously written novels in the history of English literature. It is, in fact, remarkably free of inconsistencies and casual errors. Fielding saw his task as a novelist to be a "historian" of human nature and human events, and he considered himself obligated to emphasize the moral aspect of his work. More important, Fielding introduced each of his eighteen books with a chapter about the craft of prose fiction. Indeed, the entire novel is dotted with chapters on the craft of the novel and on literary criticism. The remainder of the novel applies the principles enunciated in the chapters on proper construction of prose fiction. The chapters on literature in themselves constitute a substantial work of literary criticism. Fielding amplifies these theories with his own demonstration of their application by writing a novel, *Tom Jones*, according to his own principles. So compelling a union of theory and practice renders Fielding's hypotheses virtually unassailable.

As Fielding made practical application of his theories of craftsmanship, their validity becomes readily apparent in his handling of characterization. Fielding viewed human nature ambivalently, as a combination of good and bad. Whereas the bad person has almost no hope of redemption, the fundamentally good person is somewhat tinged with bad but is nonetheless worthy for all that, according to Fielding. Therefore, the good person may occasionally be unwise (as Allworthy is) or indiscreet (as Jones often was) but still be an estimable human being, for such a person was more credible as a good person, Fielding thought, than one who is without defect. Consequently, the villain Blifil is unreconstructedly wicked, but the hero Tom Jones is essentially good, although flawed. To succeed, Jones has to improve himself—to cultivate "prudence" and "religion," as Squire Allworthy recommends. Into this dichotomy between evil and good, and villain and hero, a species of determinism creeps—possibly not a factor consciously recognized by Fielding. Blifil and Jones are born and reared in the same environment, but one is wicked and one is good. Only innate qualities could logically explain the difference. Some minor characters are not so fully psychologized; they are essentially allegorical, representing ideas (Thwackum and Square, for example). Yet overall, Fielding's command of characterization in general comprised a series of excellent portraits. These portraits, however, are never allowed to dominate the novel, for all of them are designed to contribute to the development of the story. Such a system of priorities provides insight into Fielding's aesthetic and epistemological predispositions.

Fielding subscribed to a fundamentally classical set of values, ethically and aesthetically. He saw the novel as a mirror of life, not an illumination of life. He valued craftsmanship; he assumed a position of detached objectivity; he esteemed wit; he followed the classical unity of action. His plot brings Tom Jones full circle from a favored position to disgrace back to the good graces of Squire Allworthy and Sophia. In the course of the novel, Fielding demonstrates his objectivity by commenting critically on the form of the novel. He further reveals his classical commitments by embellishing his novel with historical detail, creating a high degree of verisimilitude. His sense of humor and his sharp wit also testify to his reliance on classical ways of thought. The easygoing development of the plot additionally reveals Fielding's detachment and objectivity, and the great variety in types of characters whom he presents is another indication of his classical inclinations toward universality.

"Critical Evaluation" by Joanne G. Kashdan

Bibliography:
Dircks, Richard J. *Henry Fielding*. Boston: Twayne, 1983. Offers a detailed reading of the novel and its moral structures. Examines plot and structure, themes, realism, digressions, the sentimental tradition, and the novel's characterizations.
Irwin, Michael. *Henry Fielding: The Tentative Realist*. Oxford, England: Clarendon Press, 1967. Sees Fielding as a moralist who was intent on creating a new literature. In an analysis of the structure of *Tom Jones*, notes the didactic content of the novel's themes. Discusses the limitations of Fielding's characterizations.
Price, Martin. "The Subversion of Form." In *Henry Fielding's Tom Jones*, edited by Harold Bloom. New York: Chelsea House, 1987. Sees the joining of the naïve hero and the sophisticated narrator as a source of Fielding's humor. The result is an ironic stance that pleasantly confuses the reader's expectations.
Reilly, Patrick. *"Tom Jones": Adventure and Providence*. Boston: Twayne, 1991. Most of this book is devoted to a reading of *Tom Jones*. Examines the work's Christian comedy and its use of satire. Draws some contrasts with the work of Samuel Richardson and Jonathan Swift.

Watt, Ian. "Fielding as Novelist: *Tom Jones*." In *Henry Fielding's Tom Jones*, edited by Harold Bloom. New York: Chelsea House, 1987. Draws contrasts between *Tom Jones* and Samuel Richardson's *Clarissa*. Notes Fielding's comparatively superficial characterizations and his somewhat greater interest in plot.

TONO-BUNGAY

Type of work: Novel
Author: H. G. Wells (1866-1946)
Type of plot: Social satire
Time of plot: Late nineteenth and early twentieth centuries
Locale: England, West Africa, and Bordeaux
First published: 1909

Principal characters:
GEORGE PONDEREVO, a young scientist and the narrator
THE HONORABLE BEATRICE NORMANDY, an aristocrat
EDWARD PONDEREVO, George's uncle
SUSAN PONDEREVO, George's aunt
MARION RAMBOAT, George's wife

The Story:

George Ponderevo grew up in the shadow of Bladesover House, where his mother was the housekeeper. In that Edwardian atmosphere, the boy soon became aware of the wide distinctions between English social classes, for the neighborhood around Bladesover was England in miniature, a small world made up of the quality, the church, the village, the laborers, and the servants. Although George spent most of his time away at school, he returned to Bladesover for his vacations. During one of his vacations, he learned for the first time the class of which he was a member—the servants.

His lesson came as the result of the arrival at Bladesover House of the Honorable Beatrice Normandy, an eight-year-old child, and her snobbish young half brother, Archie Garvell. Twelve-year-old George Ponderevo fell in love with the little aristocrat that summer. Two years later, their childish romance ended abruptly when George and Archie fought each other. George was disillusioned because the Honorable Beatrice did not come to his aid. In fact, she betrayed him, abandoned him, and lied about him, picturing George as an assailant of his social betters.

When George refused flatly to apologize to Archie Garvell, he was taken to Chatham and put to work in the bakery of his mother's brother, Nicodemus Frapp. George found his uncle's family dull, cloddish, and overreligious. One night, in the room he shared with his two cousins, he told them in confidence that he did not believe in any form of revealed religion. Traitorously, his cousins reported George's blasphemy to their father. As a result, George was called upon in a church meeting to acknowledge his sins. Humiliated and angry, he ran away to his mother at Bladesover House.

Mrs. Ponderevo then took him to live with another uncle, his father's brother, Edward Ponderevo, at Wimblehurst, in Sussex. There George worked in his uncle's chemist shop (pharmacy) after school. Edward Ponderevo was a restless, dissatisfied man who wanted to expand and to make money. Aunt Susan Ponderevo was a gentle, patient woman who treated George kindly. His mother died during his years at Wimblehurst.

George's pleasant life at Wimblehurst, however, was brought suddenly to an end. By foolish investments, Edward Ponderevo lost everything of his own, including the chemist shop and also the small fund he was holding in trust for George. The Ponderevos were forced to leave Wimblehurst, but George remained behind as an apprentice with Mr. Mantell, the new owner of the shop.

At the age of nineteen, George went up to London to matriculate at the University of London for his bachelor of science degree. On the trip, his uncle, now living in London, showed him the city and first whispered to him the name of Tono-Bungay, an invention on which the older Ponderevo was working.

When George finally arrived in London to begin his studies, he was nearly twenty-two years old, and in the meantime, he had decided to accept a scholarship at the Consolidated Technical Schools at South Kensington instead of the one offered at the university. One day, he met an old schoolfellow, Ewart, an artist who exerted a broadening influence on the young man. He also met Marion Ramboat, who was later to become his wife. Under these influences, George began to neglect his studies. When he saw a billboard that advertised Tono-Bungay, he remembered the hints his uncle had thrown out several years before. A few days later, his uncle sent George a telegram in which he offered the young man a job at three hundred pounds a year.

Tono-Bungay was a patent medicine, a stimulant most inexpensive to make and only slightly injurious to the person who took it. After a week of indecision, George joined the firm. One factor that helped to sway him was the thought that Marion Ramboat might be persuaded to marry him if his income were greater. Using new and bold methods of advertising, George and his exuberant uncle made Tono-Bungay a national product. The enterprise was highly success-ful; both George and his uncle became wealthy. At last, Marion consented to marry George, but their marriage was unsuccessful. They were divorced when Marion learned that her husband had gone off for the weekend with Effie Rink, one of the secretaries in his office. After his divorce, George devoted himself to science and research, and he also became interested in flying.

In the meantime, Edward Ponderevo branched out into many enterprises, partly through the influence of the wealthy Mr. Moggs, with whom he became associated. His huge corporation, Domestic Utilities, became known as Do-Ut, and his steady advancement in wealth could be traced by the homes in which he lived. The first was the elaborate suite of rooms at the Hardingham Hotel. Next came a gaunt villa at Beckenham; next, an elaborate estate at Chiselhurst, followed by the chaste simplicity of a medieval castle, Lady Grove; and finally, the ambitious but uncompleted splendor of the great house at Crest Hill, on which three hundred workmen were at one time employed. While his uncle was buying houses, George was absorbed in his experiments with gliders and balloons, working in his special workshop with Cothope, his assistant. The Honorable Beatrice Normandy was staying near Lady Grove with Lady Osprey, her stepmother. She and George became acquainted again. After a glider accident, she nursed him back to health. Although the two fell in love, Beatrice refused to marry him.

Suddenly all of Edward Ponderevo's world of top-heavy speculation collapsed. On the verge of bankruptcy, he clutched at anything to save himself from financial ruin and the loss of his great, uncompleted project at Crest Hill.

George did his part by undertaking a voyage to Mordet Island in the brig *Maude Mary*, to secure by trickery a cargo of quap, an ore containing two new elements valuable to the Ponderevos largely because they hoped to use canadium—one of the ingredients—for making a new and better lamp filament. The long, difficult voyage to West Africa was unpleasant and unsuccessful. After the quap had been stolen and loaded on the ship, the properties of the ore were such that the ship sank in midocean. Rescued by the Portland Castle, George learned of his uncle's bankruptcy as soon as he came ashore at Plymouth.

To avoid arrest, George and his uncle decided to cross the channel at night in George's airship and escape the law by posing as tourists in France. The stratagem proved successful, and they landed about fifty miles from Bordeaux. Then Uncle Ponderevo became dangerously ill at a small inn near Bayonne, and a few days later he died, before his wife could reach his side. Back in England, George had a twelve-day love affair with Beatrice Normandy, who still refused to marry him because she said she was spoiled by the luxury of her class. George Ponderevo, by that time a severe critic of degeneration in England, became a designer of destroyers.

Critical Evaluation:

H. G. Wells's novels, as well as other literary forms, are vehicles for his social analysis and criticism. Some of his early works, such as *The Time Machine* (1895), *The Invisible Man* (1897), and *The War of the Worlds* (1898), reflect an extreme *fin de siècle* pessimism. In those works, Wells predicts nothing ahead but doom and destruction for humanity. In later writings, however, such as *A Modern Utopia* (1905), he presents at least the possibility of salvation through an elite leadership called "the Samurai." If society can produce such an elite out of the morass of democratic mediocrity, survival of the species might become possible. This elitist ideology is present in Wells's writing to the time of his death. In *Tono-Bungay*, Wells seems to take a position somewhere between the two extremes of pessimism and guarded hope with the emphasis leaning in the direction of the pessimistic. Nevertheless, elements in the character and behavior of George Ponderevo and his Aunt Susan suggest real, if qualified, signs of hope.

Tono-Bungay represents Wells at his best, using witty language and clever plotting to dramatize his dire predictions of humanity's fate. It is also his most autobiographical and intensely personal work. Although Wells denied any resemblance, his own experiences remarkably paralleled those of his hero, George Ponderevo. Like that of his protagonist in *Tono-Bungay*, Wells's father exerted little influence over his life, deferring to a domineering mother, the housekeeper of a large country estate. Wells and Ponderevo both studied science at the Consolidated Technical Schools at South Kensington but dropped out after mediocre academic careers. Both married dull, insipid women and became unfaithful husbands. In fact, the many similarities between Wells's life and Ponderevo's strongly imply that the author wrote *Tono-Bungay* as a statement of his personal beliefs.

As the children of servants, Wells and Ponderevo had opportunities to view English society from the bottom up. The descriptions of life at Bladesover House, particularly the afternoon teas over which George's mother presides, reveal its pomposity and pretension. The incident with Archie Garvell exposes the treachery and deceit of the supposed "better sort." Ponderevo's Bladesover experiences introduce an important theme that runs through the whole novel: the sham, artificiality, and superficiality of the world as Wells saw it.

The history of Tono-Bungay, the patent medicine that brought fame and fortune to Edward Ponderevo and his nephew George, serves as a metaphor for Wells's view of English society. The tonic is an instant success, rising meteorically in the commercial sky. The book contains several allusions to dramatic spurts and rapid rises. Nothing, however, sustains them; Tono-Bungay is a fraud, and the financial empire that it spawned depends upon manipulation, chicanery, and, in the end, even forgery. Its spectacular rise is followed by an equally spectacular demise: Like a rocket, it bursts into the sky, only to disintegrate and fall back to earth. The world in which Wells lived was also in a state of degeneration and disintegration.

Pervasive decay provides Wells with another theme, one that follows logically from the sudden success of a venture built upon a sham. As Edward Ponderevo's business conglomerate crumbles under the weight of its own inadequacies, the man responsible for it begins to rot away himself. Wells's account of Edward's terminal illness emphasizes its deteriorating impact. Even Beatrice Normandy is affected by the decay. Her involvement with the upper class and her role as mistress to an English nobleman have corrupted her. She finally rejects the relationship with George because she feels herself contaminated by the stench of high society. The ultimate symbol of decay is the quap, the item that, still through manipulation and fraud, was to save Edward Ponderevo and his assorted schemes. He looks on quap as a quick and total remedy for his dying empire, but instead it destroys everything it touches. It kills all life in its vicinity in Africa; it provokes George Ponderevo into killing an innocent African native; it even rots the ship carrying it back to England, causing the ship to sink to the bottom of the ocean.

Wells's criticism and accusations of degeneracy are not confined to the upper classes. In his view, all elements of English society are equally at fault. The Ramboat family, for example, represents the proletariat but does not come across as a socialist might have portrayed it. Instead, they are dull, vacuous, and inept, as decayed in their own way as the gentility of Beatrice Normandy and Archie Garvell. No group emerges from Wells's attack unscathed.

Social criticism was hardly new with Wells and *Tono-Bungay*. The uniqueness and superior quality of this novel rests not on the novelty of its format but on the skill with which Wells presents his argument in the context of an amusing story. Despite the somber message, an exuberant humor runs through the dialogue of the characters, and even their names show Wells's wit at work. Strong character development, however, is not an element of *Tono-Bungay*. The personages remain almost stereotypes of their respective classes, caricatures rather than real humans.

Only two exceptions provide relief from Wells's pessimism and criticism. One, Edward's wife Susan, lives through all of her husband's escapades without the loss of her sensible good nature or affection for George. Another very positive element appears in Ponderevo's research first with gliders and then with destroyers. "Sometimes," he says, "I call this reality Science, sometimes I call it Truth." Nevertheless, Wells fails to explain why or how Susan manages to resist the forces of illusion and decay that surrounded her, nor does he consider Ponderevo one of the "Samurai" who might save civilization through scientific research. Thus, neither exception offers an answer to the question of what might be done to provide humanity salvation from degeneration and destruction. At least Wells, through his alter ego Ponderevo, engages in a search for a solution.

"Critical Evaluation" by R. David Weber

Bibliography:
Costa, Richard Hauer. *H. G. Wells*. New York: Twayne, 1967. Includes a critical summary of the novel, seen as "heralding . . . the new [twentieth] century amidst the debris of the old." Says that *Tono-Bungay* shows H. G. Wells as both "mystic visionary" and "storyteller."

Hammond, J. R. *An H. G. Wells Companion*. New York: Barnes & Noble Books, 1979. Describes the work as "a picture of a radically unstable society and an indictment of irresponsible capitalism." Hammond's critical examination of the novel calls it Wells's "finest single achievement."

Huntington, John, ed. *Critical Essays on H. G. Wells*. Boston: G. K. Hall, 1991. Huntington's collection updates critical work on Wells, including the novel *Tono-Bungay*, and provides a useful index and a recent bibliography.

Mackenzie, Norman, and Jeanne Mackenzie. *H. G. Wells*. New York: Simon & Schuster, 1973. Discusses the autobiographical aspects of the narrator of *Tono-Bungay*, George Ponderevo, the circumstances of the writing of the novel, and its critical reception. Argues that "with *Tono-Bungay* Wells reached the peak of his career as a novelist."

West, Geoffrey. *H. G. Wells: A Sketch for a Portrait.* New York: Norton, 1930. Partly because West (pseudonym of Geoffrey H. Wells) knew Wells well, this biography is considered by some critics to be the definitive one, despite its age. West calls *Tono-Bungay* a "thought-adventure" and discusses autobiographical elements of the novel.

TOP GIRLS

Type of work: Drama
Author: Caryl Churchill (1938-   )
Type of plot: Social realism
Time of plot: Early 1980's
Locale: England
First performed: 1982; first published, 1982

Principal characters:

> MARLENE, the "top girl" who has been promoted to managing director
> of her employment agency
> JOYCE, her sister
> ANGIE, Marlene's teenage daughter, who believes that Joyce is her
> mother
> KIT, Angie's young friend
> ISABELLA BIRD, a nineteenth century Scotswoman famous for her travels
> LADY NIJO, a thirteenth century Japanese woman, first an emperor's
> courtesan, then a Buddhist nun
> DULL GRET, the subject of a Breughel painting in which she leads
> peasant women into hell to battle devils
> POPE JOAN, the legendary woman who, disguised as a man, is thought to
> have been Pope in the ninth century
> PATIENT GRISELDA, the obedient wife in Chaucer's "Clerk's Tale"

The Story:

Marlene organized a Saturday night party in a London restaurant to celebrate her promotion at the Top Girls' Employment Agency. She invited a group of women drawn from history, legend, literature, and art, who told their stories as Marlene ordered food and drink. The stories overlapped and competed with one another; the women sometimes listened, sometimes editorialized, and often talked at the same time. Isabella Bird and Lady Nijo were the earliest arrivals. Bird's story was about her problems with illness, which made her unable to deal with the life expected of a clergyman's daughter (Bird did not seem to make this connection). Her problems led to travel, a marriage proposal from mountain man Jim Nugent—"a man any woman might love but none could marry"—and a return to Scotland after her sister Hennie's death. Because of her need to atone, given Hennie's goodness and that of the doctor who cared for her through her last illness, Isabella married the doctor and devoted herself to caring for him through his long last illness. After his death and her own turning for charitable work, she experienced a return of her own nervous illness, the result of trying "very hard to cope with the ordinary drudgery of life."

Interwoven with Bird's story was Lady Nijo's account of being raised to become a courtesan of the emperor. She enjoyed the beautiful clothes and status while she was the emperor's favorite; later she took lovers and lost a daughter to one of these lovers, whose wife raised the girl to follow in Nijo's footsteps. When she lost favor with the emperor, she became a Buddhist nun and wandered the countryside.

Pope Joan entered next and told her tale, which began when as a precocious fourteen-year-old disguised as a boy she left home and traveled with a male friend who was also her lover. They studied theology together until his death. Her intelligence attracted attention, and she rose rapidly, becoming a cardinal and then pope. As pope, she discreetly took a lover and became pregnant without realizing it. When she interrupted a religious process to deliver her baby on the side of a road, she was stoned to death.

Everyone at Marlene's party was by that time quite drunk and giggling at Joan's description of the pierced chair that subsequent popes were required to sit on to prove that they were men. They were getting ready for dessert when Patient Griselda entered. Marlene told the others, "Griselda's in Boccaccio and Petrarch and Chaucer because of her extraordinary marriage," which Marlene characterized as "like a fairy story, except it starts with marrying the prince." Griselda reminded Marlene that her husband was "only a marquis." All the guests listened when Griselda told how her husband set the wedding day before telling anyone who the bride would be. Griselda, a peasant girl, was surprised when the nobleman came to ask her father for her hand. The only requirement was that if Griselda agreed to the marriage, she would have to obey her husband in everything. When the guests questioned her willingness to agree to this condition, she replied, "I'd rather obey the Marquis than a boy from the village."

Griselda recounted the things to which she was asked to agree over the years: She had to give up her six-week-old daughter to what she believed was certain death; six years later, she gave up her two-year-old son; she returned to her father twelve years after the loss of her son so that her husband could marry a young girl; she helped her husband prepare for this new marriage because only she knew "how to arrange things the way he liked them." Her reward, the "fairy tale" ending, was the restoration of her children (her daughter was the supposed new bride.) Griselda forgave her husband and stayed with him because he had "suffered so much all those years."

Griselda's tale released angry emotions in the other guests. Nijo told the story of the concubines beating the emperor in retaliation for their own beatings at the hands of his attendants during a fertility ceremony. Joan recited a thematically important passage from Lucretius on how sweet it is to observe the struggles of others from a safe remove. At this point, Dull Gret, who had said little, told the story of her march with other peasant women through the mouth of hell, where most of them fought with the devils, although some were distracted by wealth. For Gret, it was going to the source of the evil that had cost her two children. The party ended with Nijo crying, Joan vomiting, and Isabella finishing her tale of searching at the age of seventy for a "lasting chance of joy."

At the agency on Monday morning, Marlene interviewed a young woman looking for a better job. She emphasized the necessity for choosing—or appearing to choose—between career and family, as she herself had done.

In Joyce's backyard in Suffolk on the previous Sunday afternoon, Kit and Angie's play focused on Angie's attempt to intimidate the younger child. Joyce forced Angie to clean her room; Angie returned in a dress too small for her, saying she put it on to kill her mother.

Back at the agency on Monday morning, Angie showed up, to Marlene's frustration. They were interrupted by Win, the wife of the man who had expected to get Marlene's promotion, who now suggested that Marlene give up the new job. Several interviews concluded with Win talking to Angie, who had no skills. Showing no emotion, Marlene told Win, "She's not going to make it."

In Joyce's kitchen one year earlier, Angie called Marlene, who had not visited her family for six years, telling her that Joyce wanted to see her. When Marlene arrived, the sisters argued about Marlene's having abandoned her daughter, the rest of her family, and ultimately the working class from which she came. Angie, who heard some of the discussion, came to Marlene, calling her "Mum." Marlene insisted, "It's Aunty Marlene." Angie responded, "Frightening."

Critical Evaluation:

Caryl Churchill, a prolific playwright, is considered a major contemporary writer. Although she came from a rather traditional middle-class British background, her social conscience was a significant factor in her development as a playwright. In *Top Girls*, as in many of Churchill's plays, feminism and socialism are necessary and inseparable.

The structure of the play is experimental. The first scene is a fantasy influenced by Bertolt Brecht's concept of the "alienation effect" that was designed to prevent the audience from getting emotionally involved with characters. (Brecht felt such emotion would prevent the audience's developing an active concern for the problems he presented.) Churchill employs effective distancing techniques, such as the overlapping dialogue and the tales of the women guests juxtaposed with Marlene ordering a dinner more typically associated with male preferences—steak, potatoes, and plenty of liquor.

The other scenes are realistic and depict the bleak and petty world of the employment agency and of Marlene's family in Suffolk, who are unable to compete in the capitalistic world of Margaret Thatcher's England. The realistic scenes in the play are also treated experimentally, for Churchill wrenches them out of their linear time sequence. The first scene, the fantasy dinner party, actually is chronologically in the middle of the various events. Chronologically, the first scene is Marlene's visit to Joyce's home, which occurs a year before the fantasy dinner, but the scene is placed at the end of the play. The effect of this is to give the revelation that Marlene has abandoned her daughter, Angie, even greater force. The two Monday morning scenes at the employment agency are interrupted by the Sunday scene in Suffolk, which ends with Angie dressed in the too-small dress Marlene had given her—as the audience will learn in the play's final scene—one year earlier.

Churchill stated that the impetus for writing *Top Girls* came during a 1979 trip to the United States, when American feminists told her that things were going well for women here because more top executives were women. This surprised Churchill, who was used to a different kind of feminism in England, one more closely allied with socialism. This led her to explore the idea that "achieving things isn't necessarily good, it matters *what* you achieve."

In *Top Girls*, Churchill analyzes the relationship between women and work and examines possibilities of the past and present. In the first scene, the women of history and legend start by boasting of accomplishments then gradually become bitter as they realize what they have lost. The tenuous community shared by these women is based on negative aspects of experience—dead lovers, lost children, and anger at the power that others, usually male, have exercised over them.

Churchill, in this play and others, explores the meaning of feminist empowerment. She examines the dichotomy between traditional women's work, which centers on concern for and nurturing of others, and traditional men's work, which is focused on power and competition. She shows that women have been able to compete but that without concern for the powerless, winning such competitions does not constitute a feminist victory.

Churchill does not advance an answer to this problem in *Top Girls*, but she firmly rejects the notion that there has been progress by stressing the lack of women who are both successful and fulfilled. Clearly something is missing in the lives of the "top girls" as well as in the lives of those like Joyce and Angie who will not "make it."

Elsie Galbreath Haley

Bibliography:

Fitzsimmons, Linda. *File on Churchill*. London: Methuen Drama, 1989. A comprehensive listing of Churchill's plays, including unperformed ones, and selected review and comments from the playwright herself about her work. The general introduction and brief chronology are helpful. Includes a bibliography with selected play collections, essays, interviews, and secondary sources.

Kritzer, Amelia Howe. *The Plays of Caryl Churchill: Theatre of Empowerment*. New York: St. Martin's Press, 1991. Written from a feminist perspective, this book opens with an overview of theories of theatre and drama and of feminist and socialist criticism in relation to Churchill's plays. The chapter "Labour and Capital" analyzes *Top Girls*, *Fen* (1983), and *Serious Money* (1987) as characteristic of Churchill's concern about the socioeconomic effects of Margaret Thatcher's government and its conservative policies.

Marohl, Joseph. "De-Realized Women: Performance and Gender in *Top Girls*." *Modern Drama* 3 (September, 1987): 376-388. Marohl analyzes the play from the point of view of the battle between classes, emphasizing the socialist aspects more than the feminist ones.

Randall, Phyllis R., ed. *Caryl Churchill: A Casebook*. New York: Garland, 1988. A collection of essays, including one on *Top Girls* that comments on the challenge this play presents to feminists to realize that individual solutions are not successful and to confront the need to deal with the "larger contradictions created by a capitalistic patriarchy."

Thomas, Jane. "The Plays of Caryl Churchill: Essays in Refusal." In *The Death of the Playwright?*, edited by Adrian Page. New York: St. Martin's Press, 1992. This essay analyzes *Top Girls* and *Cloud Nine* (1979) in the light of Churchill's acknowledged reading of Michel Foucault's *Surveiller et punir: Naissance de la prison* (1975; *Discipline and Punish: The Birth of the Prison*, 1977).

TORCH SONG TRILOGY

Type of work: Drama
Author: Harvey Fierstein (1954-   )
Type of plot: Psychological realism
Time of plot: Mid-1970's
Locale: New York City and upstate New York
First published: 1979; first performed, 1981

> *Principal characters:*
> ARNOLD BECKOFF, a young homosexual man
> ED REISS, Arnold's lover
> LAUREL, Ed's lover
> ALAN, Arnold's lover
> DAVID, Arnold's foster son
> MRS. BECKOFF, Arnold's mother

The Story:

The International Stud. In the first of the play's three one-act segments, Arnold Beckoff, twenty-four, prepared for his performance as torch singer Virginia Hamm in a New York City nightclub. As he applied false eyelashes in his dressing room, Arnold complained about the difficulty of establishing successful romantic relationships. Disappointed with the casual nature of most male homosexual encounters, Arnold longed for a committed, domestic relationship. Arnold met Ed Reiss, a thirty-four-year-old teacher, in The International Stud bar. Arnold made clear that he was not interested in a backroom encounter, and Ed revealed that he also dated women. The men left for Arnold's apartment.

Four months later, Arnold waited for Ed to call. Arnold finally phoned Ed, who was expecting a new friend—a woman, Laurel. Arnold declared his love for Ed and accused him of preferring the woman because she would seem more acceptable to Ed's parents. Ed insisted that he loved Arnold but wanted "more" than their relationship. Three months after his break-up with Ed, Arnold accompanied his friend Murray to The International Stud. Although he protested the impersonal backroom encounters, he finally allowed Murray to talk him into venturing there, and another man had sex with him in the dark. Still not jaded, Arnold halfway expected the man to meet him outside the bar. Two months later, Ed came to Arnold's dressing room after a show. Still feeling rejected, Arnold asked Ed to leave, but Ed pleaded for Arnold's friendship. He told of a good summer with Laurel and his parents at his farm in upstate New York. Despite the fact that he and Laurel were considering commitment, Ed declared that he still loved Arnold and confessed that he sometimes thought about him during sex. Arnold decided that he loved Ed "enough" to endure the frustrations of their relationship, and the men left together.

Fugue in a Nursery. One year later, Arnold and his new lover Alan, a handsome eighteen-year-old model and former hustler, spent a few days at the farm with Ed and Laurel. Laurel was excited about the visit, but Ed was jealous of Arnold's solicitousness toward Alan. When Ed and Arnold disappeared to review their relationship, Laurel made a pass at Alan. Pressed by Ed to clarify his relationship with Alan, Arnold admitted that he still spent two or three evenings a week in The International Stud's back room. He explained that he stayed with Alan because he felt somewhat maternal toward him. Ed recalled that he had once wanted a son. The next day, while Arnold helped Laurel with the dishes, Ed seduced Alan in the barn. Arnold learned that Ed had lied to Laurel about receiving phone calls from him. He and Alan left a day early.

Ed soon telephoned to say he and Laurel were having problems and that Arnold should not cross him off his list. Visiting the city, Laurel talked with Arnold about whether she would leave Ed, and Arnold learned that Alan had had sex with Ed but not with Laurel. Despite Arnold's pessimism, Laurel and Ed became engaged, and Arnold and Alan decided to make a commitment—to raising a puppy.

Widows and Children First. Five years passed: Arnold and Alan stayed together. Alan was beaten to death by gay bashers. Arnold, partly to assuage his grief, took in a foster son, David, a fifteen-year-old gay boy, and promptly became his overbearing Jewish mother. Four days after Ed, separated from Laurel, moved in with Arnold and David, Arnold's mother herself came for a visit. Although she had been aware of Arnold's sexual orientation even before he had told her when he was thirteen, his mother clung to the hope that he would marry and have children. She arrived confused about his relationships with Ed and David, who she thought was his "friend," her euphemism for lover.

David, skipping school, arrived when Arnold was in the shower and broke the news to his foster grandmother about his status in the household. After the initial shock, Mrs. Beckoff returned David to school and spent the rest of the afternoon with him.

Despite her affection for him, she disapproved of Arnold's plans to adopt him because she feared that Arnold would develop a sexual interest in the boy. During the ensuing argument, when Arnold compared his loss of Alan to his mother's widowhood, Mrs. Beckoff became outraged. She complained that she was tired of hearing about his homosexuality and attributed her husband's decline, in part, to the strain of it. Arnold asked how she would feel if the world were predominately homosexual and she were in the minority. Confronted by Arnold's insistence that she accept his honesty or leave, Mrs. Beckoff escaped to her room.

Meanwhile, near the place where Alan had been killed, David and Ed discussed Ed's future. David, noting that Arnold lived "like an old Italian widow," encouraged Ed to resurrect the relationship. When Arnold showed up and Ed departed, David observed to Arnold that Arnold was just like Mrs. Beckoff—no more understanding about Ed's bisexuality than she was about Arnold's homosexuality.

The next morning, when Ed asked a very drunk Arnold for another chance, Arnold's bitterness about Ed's bisexuality became apparent: Ed could stay with Laurel and have a traditional family, children included. Arnold noted that, ironically, he wanted almost exactly the kind of life his mother had had. Ed said that he loved Arnold and thought that he could find the family he wanted with Arnold and David. Mrs. Beckoff, departing for the airport, interrupted, and finally noticed the black eye David had gotten in a school fight. Softened, she asked Arnold if he loved Ed, and he said yes, but not like he loved Alan. She cautioned him that, although his mourning would get easier, he would never stop missing Alan. Distracted by a song dedication David had phoned in to a radio station to remind Arnold of Alan, Arnold did not notice when his mother slipped quietly out the door.

Critical Evaluation:

Harvey Fierstein's *Torch Song Trilogy*, which won the 1983 Tony Award for best play and earned its author a Tony for best actor in his role as Arnold Beckoff, is often cited as the first play with overtly homosexual content to be popular with mainstream theater audiences. Although one of its themes is the difficulty of being homosexual in a heterosexual society, it is not essentially a problem play. The play insists that Arnold's problems are common to all relationships. Fierstein drives home the vulnerability of homosexual men through Alan's murder and David's fight, but his real interest is in the similarities—not the differences—among homosexuals, heterosexuals, and bisexuals. David says that a person's relationship with his mother involves the same difficulties whether that mother is Mrs. Beckoff or Arnold. Although Arnold's mother is initially offended when he compares his mourning to hers, her advice about coping with grief and loneliness establishes her awareness of the similarity between the relationships.

Another central theme of the play is honesty. "Honest" is the first adjective Fierstein uses to describe the characters of *The International Stud*. He wants *Widows and Children First* to be performed with "pace" and "honesty." Arnold is troubled that Ed will not acknowledge him to his parents or Laurel. As he asks himself whether he really cares if those who say, "I love you" are truthful, he concludes that his "honest" answer is yes. In *Widows and Children First*, when Arnold's mother protests that she is tired of hearing about his homosexuality, he responds that he is not flaunting his sexual orientation but just being himself. David is the play's best testament to the importance of allowing people to be themselves, having been subjected to therapists who tried to make him heterosexual.

The play advocates a traditional family atmosphere. The set for *Widows and Children First*, the most domestic of the three segments, is described by Fierstein as "the set of a conventional sit-com," and Arnold's interaction with David, from his reviewing the young man's report card to encouraging him to carry a handkerchief, is vintage television mom. The questions about relationships between lovers that *Torch Song Trilogy* examines are also quite common: What happens when one partner is much more attractive than the other? How are parents to be introduced to the lover? What happens when new lovers meet old ones? How does it feel when the lover says he will call but does not? Does the couple want to raise children? What happens if the lover dies?

Fierstein also has a knack for provoking the new perspective. When his mother complains about how often she hears about homosexuality, Arnold asks her to imagine herself, as a heterosexual, living in a world saturated with images of and norms based on homosexuality. A few pages later, David plays the same card on Arnold, attempting to show him how parents feel when their offspring violate their expectations. David asks, "What would you do if I met a girl, came home and told you I was straight?" Arnold's responses are as pat as his mother's: "If you were happy, I'd be happy." At the end of the scene, Arnold asks David to reassure him that he is not, in fact, heterosexual.

Although Fierstein's themes are ultimately conventional, his staging is often heavily stylized. This is particularly true in *Fugue in a Nursery*, the majority of which is acted by the four principles, Arnold, Alan, Ed, and Laurel, in a huge bed. As lighting focuses on one pair and then the other, Fierstein constructs a polyphony of voices all talking about the same themes. The similarities between the homosexual and heterosexual relationships are underscored by the occasional overlapping of conversations, with a person in one relationship answering a question asked by a person in the other. The trilogy's handling of impersonal sexual encounters between gay men, such as those experienced by Arnold in the back room of the bar, is obviously pre-AIDS. *The International Stud*, for example, was first performed in 1978, about five years before AIDS became a household word. Fierstein clearly sees such encounters as desperate acts; he told *Newsweek*'s Jack Kroll, "Gay liberation should not be a license to be a perpetual adolescent. If you deny yourself commitment then what can you do with your life?"

Perhaps Fierstein's greatest achievement is the character of Arnold Beckoff, a slightly overweight drag queen who is simultaneously drawn to and frightened by romance. "Beckoff,"

Fierstein has said, is a combination of "beckon" and "back off." Arnold is, in many ways, a conventional romantic heroine who, no matter how many Mr. Wrongs he finds, continues to search for Mr. Right. Described by his creator as "a kvetch of great wit and want," Arnold practices quick, sometimes biting, humor. "What's the matter?" he asks Ed, "catch your tongue in the closet door?" Playwright Marsha Norman has said that a playwright nominates characters for preservation in the public mind and then lets audiences do the voting. It seems likely that Fierstein's Arnold Beckoff will be among the elected.

Lana A. Whited

Bibliography:
Clarke, Gerald. "No One Opened Doors for Me." *Time* 119 (February 22, 1982): 70. Explains Fierstein's process in getting the play produced and the effect of the work's success on his career.
Dace, Tish. "Fierstein, Harvey (Forbes)." *Contemporary Dramatists*. 5th ed. Edited by K. A. Berney. London: St. James, 1993. Overview of Fierstein's career, with emphasis on *Torch Song Trilogy*. Discusses the play's themes and Fierstein's styles of presentation, particularly the use of fugue.
Fierstein, Harvey. "His Heart Is Young and Gay." Interview by Jack Kroll. *Newsweek* 101 (June 20, 1983): 71. Fierstein explains why his play is not homosexual propaganda. Also explores the autobiographical nature of the play and a gay reaction against it.
Oliver, Edith. "Tripleheader." *The New Yorker* 58 (February 1, 1982): 116. One of the country's foremost theater critics explains why *Torch Song Trilogy* deserves the high praise it has received. Excellent analysis of the characters.
Wiloch, Thomas. "Fierstein, Harvey." In *Gay & Lesbian Literature*, edited by Sharon Malinowski. London: St. James Press, 1994. Discusses the play's thematic and stylistic similarities with Fierstein's other prominent works including *La Cage aux folles* (1983).

TORTILLA FLAT

Type of work: Novel
Author: John Steinbeck (1902-1968)
Type of plot: Naturalism
Time of plot: The early 1920's
Locale: Tortilla Flat, the uphill section of Monterey, California
First published: 1935

> *Principal characters:*
> DANNY, the hero, a free spirit fettered by the inheritance of two houses
> PILON,
> PABLO,
> JESUS MARIA CORCORAN,
> THE PIRATE, and
> BIG JOE PORTAGEE, his friends and tenants
> MRS. MORALES,
> SWEETS RAMIREZ, and
> SEÑORA TERESINA CORTEZ, three of Danny's short-term loves

The Story:

Danny returned home from World War I to find that his grandfather had bequeathed him two houses on Tortilla Flat. The responsibility of ownership depressed Danny. A drunken spree of window breaking and the jail sentence it earned him did little to relieve his malaise. Then he ran into his friend Pilon, who moved into the larger house with him, agreeing to pay fifteen dollars a month rent. After an argument, Pilon moved into Danny's smaller house. The pair shared wine, women, and worry. Ownership plagued Danny.

The rent Pilon never intended to pay bothered him, but his troubles seemed over when he struck a deal with Pablo. Pablo agreed to move in with Pilon for fifteen dollars a month rent, money he never could or would pay.

Danny enjoyed a brief affair with his neighbor, Mrs. Morales, who owned her own house and had two hundred dollars in the bank. He wanted to give her a present but had no money. The suggestion that he cut squids for a day laborer's wages incensed him, and he demanded rent from Pilon and Pablo, who stalked away in anger. They found Jesus Maria Corcoran lying under a bush with a bottle of wine. He had recently acquired a fortune of seven dollars. Pilon and Pablo agreed to rent him space in their house for fifteen dollars a month. Masters at rationalizing self-interest into altruism, they talked Jesus Maria out of his money and bought Mrs. Morales a bottle of wine that they drank themselves.

Pilon, Pablo, and Jesus Maria fell into a drunken sleep in Danny's second house, leaving a candle lit. The house caught fire and burned to the ground. The friends escaped, dismayed that they had left a bottle of wine inside. Danny was relieved to be free of the property, and his three friends moved into the big house with him.

The Pirate lived in what had been a chicken coop with his five dogs. Each day he collected wood from the forest and sold it for a quarter. He never spent any money, so everyone wondered where he hid his savings. In one of his finest feats of logic, Pilon convinced all that finding and spending Pirate's money for him would serve the man's best interest, but try as they might, they could not discover his hiding place.

Pirate moved into Danny's house and came to trust his new friends so much that he handed his money over to Danny for safekeeping. He explained that he was saving to buy a gold candlestick for the church in honor of Saint Francis of Assisi. He believed a prayer to the saint had saved one of his dogs from death. That story ended all hopes Danny and his friends had for diverting the money to their own uses, but Pirate and his dogs were good to keep around. They begged food from the restaurants along the waterfront every day and brought it home for all to share.

Big Joe Portagee got out of jail and, learning that Danny owned a house, set off to find his friends. He joined Pilon for the traditional Saint Andrew's Eve hunt in the forest when, legend promised, buried treasure emitted a faint phosphorescent glow through the ground. Big Joe moved in with the others, stole Danny's blanket, and traded it for wine in anticipation of the fortune he expected to unearth. That night he and Pilon dug up a survey marker. They drank wine and slept on the beach. Pilon awoke first, stole Big Joe's pants as the Portagee slept, and traded the pants for wine in retaliation for Joe's theft of the blanket. Later, they stole back both the pants and the blanket.

Danny succumbed to an infatuation for Sweets Ramirez and bought her a vacuum cleaner, although Tortilla Flat was not wired for electricity. Sweets reveled in the elevated social standing the gift brought her. Danny grew listless and pale, perhaps tiring of Sweets's affections. The group of friends resolved to free him. They stole the sweeping machine and traded it for wine, probably more than a fair trade since the cleaner had no motor.

Jesus Maria rescued a Mexican corporal and his baby from the police and brought them home to Tortilla Flat. The corporal wanted his baby son to be a general someday, so he could have a better life than his father's. The baby died and the corporal returned to Mexico.

Big Joe Portagee sought shelter from the rain in the house of a woman called Tia Ignacia. Ignoring her charms, he drank her wine and fell asleep. She hit him and chased him, but he embraced her and physical closeness aroused passion. A policeman ordered the pair out of the street for fear they might get run over. Big Joe stole Pirate's money from beneath Danny's pillow and buried it by the front gate. The friends beat him, cut him, and rubbed salt in his wounds. Then they discovered the Pirate had saved enough to buy the golden candlestick. The Pirate went to church dressed in his friends' clothes to hear the priest's thanks for his gift. Reluctantly, he left his dogs at home, but they burst through the church doors to join their master. Later, Pirate felt sure the dogs actually saw a vision of Saint Francis. The friends forgave Big Joe and nursed him back to health.

Señora Teresina Cortez fed eight children on the beans she culled from the chaff after the threshers had cleared the fields. When the bean crop failed, Danny and his friends stole a variety of foods for the family, but the change in diet made the children sick. All ended well when the friends delivered four hundred pounds of beans. Teresina, pregnant again, wondered which of Danny's friends was responsible.

As Danny stepped over his sleeping tenants each night, he yearned to return to the days of his freedom, when he had slept outdoors and the weight of property was not upon him. He ran away and set about a binge of drinking, vandalism, and theft. He sold the house for twenty-five dollars, but his friends burned the transfer of ownership.

After a term in jail, Danny returned home a broken man. His friends, determined to dispel his lethargy, threw a party never equaled in Tortilla Flat, so generous was the exchange of food, wine, and love. Danny, suffused with alcohol and valor, charged out to fight some unnamed enemy. He fell to the bottom of a forty-foot gulch and died. His friends could not attend his funeral, for they had no suitable clothes. They lay in the grass to watch his burial.

Later, when his house caught fire, they made no attempt to stop the blaze (although they had learned from the previous fire to save the wine). Turning away from the smoldering ruins, they went their separate ways.

Critical Evaluation:

Turned down by nine publishers before being accepted and denounced by the Monterey Chamber of Commerce, *Tortilla Flat* earned the California Literature Gold Medal in 1936 and became one of John Steinbeck's most popular and highly acclaimed works. It was the first of his novels to look at life through the eyes of those without homes, possessions, or security, and Danny and his friends foreshadow others of their kind who appear powerfully and poignantly in such distinguished later works as *In Dubious Battle* (1936), *Of Mice and Men* (1937), and *The Grapes of Wrath* (1939).

Steinbeck wrote *Tortilla Flat* as a series of episodes with long subtitles in the style of Sir Thomas Malory's *Le Morte d'Arthur* (1485). In his preface, the author compares the escapades of Danny and his friends with the events of Arthur's Round Table: the formation of the association, the heroic deeds of its members, the passing of the almost deified king, and the subsequent dissolution of the brotherhood. The imitation is further enhanced by the use of "thee" and "thy" in the speech of the friends. Steinbeck was never a regional writer, but he was a writer of his locale, his inspiration a unique product of California, especially during the Depression years. As he was a man of place, so too are his characters. Danny and his friends exist in a deep and fundamental relationship with Tortilla Flat. It is so saturated with their spirit and melded with their consciousness that the men and their environment are as one.

Steinbeck won the Nobel Prize in Literature in 1962. Accepting the award, he said that the "writer is delegated to declare and to celebrate man's proven capacity for greatness of heart and spirit—for gallantry in defeat, for courage, compassion and love. In the endless war against weakness and despair, these are the bright rally flags of hope and of emulation." In *Tortilla Flat*, as in many other novels and stories, Steinbeck exalts the natural man, untainted by civilization, unspoiled by either conventional wisdom or conventional morality. Danny, who earns a near-god status on Tortilla Flat, is flawed not by his innate nature but by the greed, conflict, and loneliness property ownership forces upon him. He and his friends are the kinds of characters Steinbeck loves most and paints most vividly. They are human, fallible, earthy, uninhibited, irresponsible, unspoiled.

For all its irreverence, this is a deeply religious book. Through his characters, Steinbeck develops a naturalistic theology; Danny and his friends are right and good because they are as they are, without artifice and without redemption. When Steinbeck characterizes Danny as "clean of commercialism," he implies a spiritual purity akin to being washed of sin. Still, his moralizing is constrained by a gentle humor, as, for example, when he adds to the observation "the soul capable of the greatest good is also capable of the greatest evil" the offhanded qualifier "this, however, may be a matter of appearances." Ever cynical of religious conventions, he observes, "Ah, the prayers of the millions, how they must fight and destroy each other on their way to the throne of God."

Steinbeck lets his characters comment on the search for meaning in stories, perhaps reflecting his intent in relating tales from Tortilla Flat. After Pablo tells of the old man who tried to fake a suicide to win a young girl's love, only to fail and die, Pilon complains, "It is not a good story. There are too many meanings and too many lessons in it. Some of those lessons are opposite. There is no story to take into your head. It proves nothing." Pablo responds, "I like it because it hasn't any meaning you can see, and still it does seem to mean something, I can't tell what."

Faith Hickman Brynie

Bibliography:
Benson, Jackson J., ed. *The Short Novels of John Steinbeck: Critical Essays with a Checklist to Steinbeck Criticism.* Durham, N.C.: Duke University Press, 1990. A comprehensive collection of investigations into Steinbeck's characters, technique, and motivation. Complete bibliography.
Concise Dictionary of American Literary Biography, 1929-1941. Vol. 5. Detroit: Gale Research, 1989. Brief discussions of all Steinbeck's major works, set in the context of his life.
Ferrell, Keith. *John Steinbeck: The Voice of the Land.* New York: Evans, 1986. An introduction to Steinbeck's life and work written especially for secondary-school students.
Hayashi, Tetsumaro, ed. *A Study Guide to Steinbeck: A Handbook to His Major Works.* Metuchen, N.J.: The Scarecrow Press, 1974. Introduction to Steinbeck's works.
Hughes, R. S. *John Steinbeck: A Study of the Short Fiction.* New York: Macmillan, 1988. A behind-the-scenes look at the creation of Steinbeck's short fiction, including summaries of published literary criticism.

THE TOWER

Type of work: Poetry
Author: William Butler Yeats (1865-1939)
First published: 1928

The 1920's were years of professional and personal achievement for William Butler Yeats. His son, Michael, was born in 1921. He was awarded the Nobel Prize in Literature in 1923, enjoying the worldwide recognition of not only his own work but also the Irish Literary Revival. In 1922, he was appointed to the first senate in the Irish Free State and received an honorary doctorate from Trinity College. Yeats was approaching his sixties and beginning to wonder what would be the impetus for his poetry in old age since so much of it had always been love poetry. As the decade progressed, his health was failing, and he was convinced that his generation was no longer the moving force in Ireland.

The Tower reflects these conflicting forces in Yeats's life. His poetic voice and technique are at the height of their mature intensity and power, and he is excited by his developing philosophical system, yet the content and tone of many of the poems suggest that Yeats was obsessed with his own aging, angry at the violence in Ireland, and desirous of a world more conducive to art. After rereading *The Tower* shortly after its publication, he wrote to Olivia Shakspear that he "was astonished at its bitterness," yet he also recognized that "its bitterness gave the book its power."

The original edition, with a beautiful cover design by T. Sturge Moore depicting Yeats's Norman tower at Thoor Ballylee, contained twenty-one poems, including two sequences ("Meditations in Time of Civil War" and "A Man Young and Old") with their separately numbered and titled shorter poems. "The Gift of Harun Al-Rahsid" was later removed, whereas "Fragments" was added in 1933 and "The Hero, the Girl and the Fool" was cut down to "The Fool by the Roadside." Currently, *The Tower* comprises thirty-six poems in volume 1 of *The Poems* in *The Collected Works of W. B. Yeats* (1989), edited by Richard Finneran. The separately numbered and titled parts of the two sequences are listed as individual poems. Yeats added notes to six of the poems in the original edition (which are reproduced in an appendix to Finneran's edition along with many explanatory notes provided by the editor).

In his *Autobiography* (1916), Yeats had hoped that a nation could be unified by "a bundle of related images." His own bundle of images was well established, and they appear here repeatedly in images of trees, birds (especially swans), sun, moon, fish, and dancer. As usual, Maude Gonne MacBride, the woman who had been his most consistent symbol of beauty and unrequited love, is alluded to often. Moreover, his obsession with his philosophical system, expressed in *A Vision*, published in its first version in 1925, informs these poems, as it had started to do in his previous volume, *Michael Robartes and the Dancer* (1921).

Yeats's poetic prowess is evident in the range of style and poetic form in this collection. The poems range from very short epigrams to some of Yeats's longest, most obscure modernist lyrics. Concentrated, allusive, imagistically intense poems, such as "Leda and the Swan," alternate with the more discursive and conversational mood of poems such as "All Soul's Night." Like most of Yeats's poetry, the poems in this volume are written in traditional rhymed forms, ranging from many poems with six-line rhymed stanzas, to the eight-line ottava rima stanzas of "Sailing to Byzantium" and "Among School Children," to one of his rare uses of the sonnet form in "Leda and the Swan," to longer poems, such as "The Tower," with different forms juxtaposed to each other in separate sections.

The first poem, "Sailing to Byzantium," suggests that the aging poet, no longer comfortable among the fertile young in Ireland, has traveled to Byzantium—Yeats's symbol of the integration of aesthetic and practical life—to find "the singing masters of [his] soul" who will teach him to create "the artifice of eternity" in this less transient spiritual context. The volume reads as if Yeats is repeatedly retracing the steps that led him to leave for Byzantium. Three long poems follow in which Yeats continues to explore his fear of loss of creativity as well as his anger at the state of Ireland and the world. He explains some of the historical and poetic allusions in these obscure poems in his notes. After contrasting his aged body and excited imagination in section 1 of the title poem, "The Tower," and then retracing the historical and imaginative ancestry of his home in Thoor Ballylee in section 2, Yeats prepares his will in section 3, invoking images such as his fisherman and swan, as well as "memories of love." Leaving all to "upstanding men" who climb the mountain in the dawn, he will make his soul as he waits for death in peaceful indifference. The six poems that make up "Meditations in Time of Civil War" enact a contrast between the classical stasis of art and the volatile brutality of the Irish Civil War in the early 1920's. In the last poem in this sequence as well as in "Nineteen Hundred and Nineteen," he laments his growing difficulty in creating lasting art amid the violent, nightmarish, dismembering images present now as in all eras since classical Greece.

In most of the eight short poems between "Nineteen Hundred and Nineteen" and "Among School Children," Yeats creates a series of contrasts all of which pit the old against the new: winter and spring, age and youth, old and new faces, Dionysus and Christ, Eden and Lockean science. Yeats interjects "A Prayer for My Son," very different in tone and content from most of the more philosophical poems in this collection, in this part of the collection, invoking the angels to protect his infant son, Michael. Though heartfelt, the poem lacks the poetic and philosophical intensity of "A Prayer for My Daughter," written for Anne (born in 1919) and included in *Michael Robartes and the Dancer*.

"Leda and the Swan," which Yeats also included at the beginning of the "Dove and Swan" chapter in *A Vision*, uses the image of the rape of Leda by Zeus to depict the violent cataclysmic upheaval that Yeats, an occultist, believed occurred in 2000 B.C.E. This two-thousand year reversal, which happened again in 1 C.E., is the basis of the contrasting views of the classical and Christian eras as alluded to in "Two Songs from a Play." Yeats's increasing longing for a return to the art of classical Greece, which in his cyclic system also represents a forward thrust to the kind of art that would prevail again in the two-thousand-year cycle starting in 2000 C.E., is also reflected in the choruses from his adaptations of Sophocles' *Oedipus the King* and *Oedipus at Colonus*, which are included in *The Tower*.

In the book, Yeats retraces, as he has in others, his own poetic and love history in connection to the Irish struggle. "Among School Children" starts in a conversational mode with Yeats as a sixty-year-old school inspector (one of his duties as a senator) strolling among the school children and daydreaming of Maud Gonne's "Ledean body" at their age. He uses the classical allusion in a semicomic tone, admitting that her image still has the power to drive him wild while remembering that he himself had "pretty plumage once." His reverie brings him back to his own birth, and he wonders how any mother could think childbirth worth the labor if she could imagine her child at sixty. The phrase "honey of generation" in the fifth stanza, taken, as he explains in a note, from the Neoplatonist Porphry, brings Plato to mind again, and he considers the fixity of Plato's forms in contrast to changing natural bodies. At the end of this poem, as at the end of "The Tower" and "Sailing to Byzantium," he longs for a source of art that can blossom and dance without splitting and bruising nature.

He continues to focus on his past and present love relationships in the next set of poems. His more recent attractions to Iseult Gonne and to his wife are the basis of "Owen Aherne and His Dancers." He recounts his whole love history in the sequence of poems gathered under the title "A Man Young and Old." In the first edition, there were ten of these very short poems. Later, he moved the chorus entitled "From 'Oedipus at Colonus'" to the end of this sequence. "First Love," "Human Dignity," and "The Mermaid" look back from a cynical viewpoint at a lover who remembers "a heart of stone," a lack of response to his sorrow, and a lad drowning in the "cruel happiness" of a mermaid's embrace. "The Empty Cup" pictures an old man who still finds the cup "dry as bone." "His Memories," the pivotal poem (sixth of eleven in the sequence), recalls in highly allusive language that for a brief moment, "she who brought great Hector down" lay in his arms and found pleasure. This is one of Yeats's few references to the brief physical relationship he had with Maud Gonne (whom he often imaged as Helen of Troy) in the midst of a spiritual pact these two occultists had in the early years of the twentieth century. In the course of this sequence, he refers obliquely to several other women with whom he had had relationships as well. At the end, old age dominates, and he longs for the less agonized indifference of "a gay goodnight and quickly turn away."

He concludes the collection with "All Soul's Night," which he identifies in a subtitle as "Epilogue to 'A Vision.'" In this poem, as has repeatedly seemed true throughout this collection, he appears more comfortable conversing with the dead or absent of his own generation than with the young he left behind in "Sailing to Byzantium."

This attitude and focus changed drastically in his next collection, *The Winding Stair and Other Poems* (1933), where he chooses to return to a delight in the physical world. In fact, Yeats continued to produce a prolific and self-renewing output of lyric poetry without interruption until his death. As a separate collection, nevertheless, *The Tower* sounds a consistent note of concern about his own growing old and the violent state of the world. As poet, he seeks an untroubled indifference and longs for the cyclic change the next great reversal will bring, yet the intensity of the poetry undercuts any suggestion of a placid retirement from writing. *The Tower* remains one of the most intense collections in the entire body of poetry written by one of the finest lyric poets in English in the twentieth century.

Catherine Cavanaugh

Bibliography:

Adams, Hazard. *The Book of Yeats's Poems*. Tallahassee: Florida State University Press, 1990. A poem-by-poem reading that takes into consideration the order Yeats intended for the poems. Chapter 5 discusses *The Tower* as a series of returns.

Ellmann, Richard. *Yeats: The Man and the Masks*. New York: Macmillan, 1948. An excellent introductory work that melds poetic interpretation into biographical context. Brief but insightful chapter on *The Tower*.

Jeffares, A. Norman. *A New Commentary on the Poems of W. B. Yeats*. Stanford, Calif.: Stanford University Press, 1984. Indispensable companion to Yeats's poems. All proper names, place names, and autobiographical references are explicated. Prose passages included.

Unterecker, John. *A Reader's Guide to William Butler Yeats*. New York: Farrar, Straus & Giroux, 1971. A reading of the first chapter, which discusses Yeats's major themes, and the chapter on *The Tower* offers a strategy for interpreting Yeats's poems.

Yeats, William Butler. *The Autobiography of William Butler Yeats*. New York: Collier Books, 1965. Yeats's own commentary on the major influences on his life and poetry remains one of the best complements to his poetry.

THE TOWER OF LONDON

Type of work: Novel
Author: William Harrison Ainsworth (1805-1882)
Type of plot: Historical
Time of plot: Sixteenth century
Locale: England
First published: 1840

> *Principal characters:*
> DUKE OF NORTHUMBERLAND
> GUILFORD DUDLEY, Northumberland's son
> LADY JANE GREY, Dudley's wife
> CUTHBERT CHOLMONDELEY, Dudley's squire
> CICELY, Cuthbert's beloved
> LAWRENCE NIGHTGALL, the jailer
> SIMON RENARD, the Spanish ambassador
> QUEEN MARY
> PRINCESS ELIZABETH, Mary's sister
> EDWARD COURTENAY, the earl of Devonshire

The Story:

At the death of King Edward the Sixth, there were several claimants to the English throne, among them Mary, Elizabeth's older sister, and Lady Jane Grey, the wife of Lord Guilford Dudley, who was supported by her father-in-law, the duke of Northumberland. According to custom, Lady Jane was brought to the Tower of London for her coronation. There, the supporters of Mary, while pretending to be in accord with Northumberland, waited to betray Lady Jane.

Among those present was Cuthbert Cholmondeley, Dudley's squire, who, having seen a beautiful young girl in the Tower, had fallen in love with her. From inquiries among his servants, Cuthbert learned that the girl, Cicely, was the adopted daughter of Peter the pantler and Dame Potentia Trusbut, the true circumstances of her birth being unknown. The chief jailer of the Tower, Lawrence Nightgall, also loved Cicely. When Simon Renard, the Spanish ambassador, and Lord Pembroke, both Mary's supporters, conspired to assassinate Cuthbert because they knew him to be Dudley's favorite, Nightgall eagerly agreed to help them.

Nightgall told Cicely that her new lover had been taken from the Tower and that she would never see him again. Meanwhile, a prisoner in a dungeon below the Tower, Cuthbert was accosted by a strange woman who cried out that she wanted her child to be returned to her. When Nightgall visited Cuthbert, the prisoner asked his jailer about the woman, but Nightgall evaded the question by stating that the woman was mad.

At Northumberland's command, Gunnora Broase, an old woman, had administered a dose of poison to the late boy-king, Edward the Sixth. She was directed by a strange man to reveal Northumberland's part in the murder and thus to defeat his intention to place Lady Jane on the throne of England.

Simon Renard and Lord Pembroke had instigated a conflict between Lady Jane and Northumberland by convincing Lady Jane that she should not consent to make Dudley a king. Northumberland desired this distinction for his son, but Lady Jane believed that making her husband a king would cause too much dissension in the kingdom. In anger at this slight from his wife, Dudley left the Tower. Surrounded by intrigue, Lady Jane was convinced that Renard and Lord Pembroke were her friends and that Northumberland was her enemy. Lord Pembroke next persuaded Lady Jane to send Northumberland against Mary's forces, which were reportedly advancing on London. With Northumberland separated from Lady Jane, Lord Pembroke and Renard were certain that they could destroy her rule. Lady Jane was easily persuaded because she did not suspect the treachery of her two advisers.

Cuthbert Cholmondeley escaped from his dungeon. Dudley returned to his wife and his queen in time to convince her of the treachery of Lord Pembroke and Renard, whom Lady Jane ordered imprisoned. Cicely came to Dudley and Lady Jane with the tale of what had happened to Cholmondeley. Soon after the imprisonment of Lord Pembroke and Renard, Nightgall helped them to escape from the Tower. Meanwhile, Lady Jane had made Cicely a lady-in-waiting.

Gunnora Broase came to Lady Jane for an audience. The old woman declared that Northumberland had poisoned Edward and that his purpose in marrying his son to Lady Jane was to elevate Dudley to the throne; Lady Jane would then be poisoned. Meanwhile, Cuthbert had found his way from the lower dungeons, and he and Cicely were reunited. He was present when the duke of Suffolk, Lady Jane's father, urged her to avoid execution by abdicating. Dudley, however, persuaded his wife not to surrender the crown. Mary was proclaimed queen, and Lady Jane was placed in prison with Cicely and Cuthbert. Dudley was separately confined. Gunnora Broase sneaked into Lady Jane's cell and secreted her from the prison with the promise that Dudley would follow shortly, but when Northumberland disbanded his forces and acknowledged Mary as queen, Lady Jane surrendered herself and returned to her cell in the Tower.

The people acclaimed Mary when she entered London. The new queen's first act was to release all Catholic prisoners and replace them with her former enemies. When Northumberland was arrested and condemned to the scaffold, he pleaded for mercy for Lady Jane because he had been the chief proponent of her pretension to the throne. Although the Duke publicly embraced Catholicism in the mistaken belief that his life would be spared, he was executed by Mary's order. Mary put pressure upon Lady Jane and Dudley to embrace Catholicism as Northumberland had done in order to save their lives, but Lady Jane was determined to die a Protestant. Cuthbert was released from custody and returned to look for Cicely, but she was nowhere to be found. Cuthbert did find the strange madwoman again. She was lying in a cell, dead.

Edward Courtenay, the earl of Devonshire, was among the prisoners Mary had released from the Tower. The young nobleman was really in love with Elizabeth, although, covetous of Mary's throne, he pretended to love Mary. Without scruple, he was able to win Mary's promise that she would make him her husband. Renard, however, lurked menacingly in the background. When Courtenay went to Elizabeth with one last appeal of love, Mary and Renard were listening behind a curtain and overheard the conversation. In anger, Mary committed Courtenay to the Tower and confined Elizabeth to her room. On Renard's advice, Mary then affianced herself to Philip, king of Spain. Later, Mary's counselors persuaded her to release Elizabeth.

Moved by compassion for the innocent Lady Jane, Mary issued a pardon for the pretender and her husband. The couple retired to the home of Lady Jane's father, where Dudley began to organize a new plot to place his wife on the throne. Lady Jane was aware that Dudley was determined to actualize his plans. Faithful to her husband, she consented to follow him in whatever he did. Another revolt was led by Sir Thomas Wyat, a fervent anti-Catholic, supported by those who opposed an alliance between England and Spain. The rebellion was quelled, and Wyat and Dudley were captured. Lady Jane and Cuthbert surrendered themselves to Mary, and Lady Jane pleaded for the life of her husband in exchange for her surrender. The only condition on which Mary would grant Dudley's life was that Lady Jane should embrace Catholicism. When she refused, she was sentenced to death along with Dudley. Elizabeth was brought to the Tower, as Mary planned to do away with Courtenay and her sister after she had completed the destruction of Lady Jane and Dudley.

Still suffering from jealousy over Cicely's love for Cuthbert, Nightgall had held the girl in prison since the fall of Lady Jane. Meanwhile, Nightgall had been hired by the French ambassador to assassinate Renard. Renard and Nightgall met in Cuthbert's cell after the squire had been tortured, and, in the ensuing fight, Cuthbert escaped and ran to find Cicely. Renard succeeded in killing Nightgall, who lived long enough to prove Cicely's noble birth. She was the daughter of the unfortunate madwoman, Lady Grace Mountjoy. Before her execution, Lady Jane requested that Cicely and Cuthbert be allowed to marry. With strange generosity, Mary pardoned them and granted their freedom. At the scene of her execution, even the enemies of Lady Jane shuddered at the sight of so good and fair a woman about to die. On the block, she reaffirmed her Christian faith as the axe descended upon one of the most ill-fated of English monarchs.

Critical Evaluation:

The Tower of London is a historical novel in the tradition of Sir Walter Scott, yet the author's unique approach to his historical material makes the book stand apart from other novels of the genre. William Harrison Ainsworth makes the Tower itself the protagonist of the story. The author is quite explicit about this point. His goal in *The Tower of London* was to write about incidents that would illuminate every corner of the edifice, or, in his words, "Naturally introduce every relic of the old pile." Unlike a story that deals with a period in the life of a human being or with the unfolding of character development, *The Tower of London* centers on a phase in the history of a complex of buildings. If the reader is willing to accept this premise, he or she must be content to see action and character subordinate to setting and to some preconceived notions concerning plot.

The Tower not only functions as the historical backdrop for the incidents in the novel and the stage upon which the action takes place, but as the major structural device of the book. Indeed, the Tower is so thoroughly integrated with the other materials of the novel that it becomes a vital participant in the action and provides the novel's unity by acting as a focal point around which all other elements are organized. The novel has a clearly defined beginning in Lady Jane Grey Dudley's arrival at the Tower on July 10, 1553, and an equally definite end: her execution on Tower Green, February 10, 1559. In between the two events, much of the major action of the book takes place in the Tower's chapels, halls, chambers, and gateways.

The novel can be viewed as two distinct parts joined together by the Tower. During the first half of the book, Lady Jane, the queen for barely a month, is supported in her tenuous claim to the throne by her father-in-law, the duke of Northumberland, and by her husband, Lord Dudley. She is plotted against, however, by those who wish to put Mary on the throne. In the second part, Mary is queen, but she, too, is the object of conspiracies by the champions of both Elizabeth and the deposed Jane. At the novel's conclusion, Lady Jane has been beheaded, Elizabeth is in protective custody, and Mary is committed to a Spanish marriage that pleases no one. All that survives unimpaired is the Tower, having been the scene of yet one more series of events in its long history.

Although one might at first suspect that Lady Jane is the heroine of the novel since it chronicles her stay in the Tower, this is not the case. Mary Tudor and her half-sister play larger roles. Nevertheless, it is obviously the Tower itself that dominates this novel, and the book's best writing is found in the passages describing the structure. Ainsworth spaces his descriptions judiciously throughout the novel in such a way as to heighten the effect. The only apparent exception to this general descriptive practice occurs in the second book, as Ainsworth digresses for more than a dozen pages to relate an account of the Tower's history from the time of William the Conqueror down to the nineteenth century. This interruption, however, is not entirely indefensible because even the architectural history of the Tower has a decided part in creating mood, establishing motivation, and advancing action.

In turning his descriptive powers toward the people of the novel, Ainsworth generally achieves the same effectiveness that goes into his descriptions of the Tower; yet his characterizations also exhibit major flaws in technique. He describes in almost minute detail not only the physical appearance of the characters but also their dress and every aspect of the ceremonial occasions in which they participate. Although the quantity of sociohistorical research necessary for Ainsworth's descriptions of ceremonial pomp and costumery is noteworthy, the sheer detail of the descriptions tends to slow down the action of the novel in places and becomes tedious for even the most patient reader. Most readers, however, would admit that they are never left with any uncertainty concerning the appearance of the principal participants in any scene of *The Tower of London*—even regarding such minute details as the texture of the duke of Suffolk's cloak, "flowered with gold and ribanded with nets of silver."

Ainsworth's characters often tend to be mere types, such as the meritorious young man who has to make his way in the world against great odds. He is in love with a chaste maiden who is subjected to a series of threats ranging from the inconvenient to the unspeakable. These types can be seen in *The Tower of London* in the characters of Dudley's squire, Cuthbert, and his beloved, Cicely, who are the victims of imprisonment and conspiracy but escape unscathed to marry at last. A second stock character is the power-hungry schemer personified by Simon Renard, the Spanish ambassador who lurks in the background attempting to manipulate the fortunes of the other characters. His skill in plotting is seen when he effectively ruptures the relationship between Lady Jane and Northumberland by convincing her to deny Dudley the kingship as a part of a larger scheme to weaken Lady Jane's claim to the throne. A final example of Ainsworth's stock characters is the "unmotivated villain," Nightgall the jailer, who seems to perpetrate evil deeds for their own sake and who adds greatly to the misfortunes of Cuthbert and Cicely.

Ainsworth compounds his problems of characterization by use of the hackneyed device of mistaken identities. The details of Cicely's birth are unknown until the novel's conclusion, when Nightgall confirms that she is the daughter of Lady Grace Montjoy. This is at best only a slight variation of plots employed by Ainsworth in at least six of his other works. Sometimes these false identities are deliberately assumed, or, as in this novel, they stem from mysteries of parentage of which the main characters are themselves unaware. In any case, the device was overworked long before Ainsworth employed it in *The Tower of London*.

The author's treatment of the nonfictional characters is somewhat more effective because he is dealing with real people about which something is known, but he nevertheless weakens their portraits through his intrusive moral judgments of their actions. He tells the reader quite clearly what he or she is to think of the characters. The duke of Northumberland, for example, is "haughty and disdainful," while Queen Mary's "worst fault as a woman and her sole fault as a sovereign was her bigotry." No writer of his age was less reticent than Ainsworth about intruding his own personal views into his writing. These problems of characterization, however, will be overlooked by most readers in their acceptance of the premise of the novel, which is to narrate the history of the Tower.

It is true that *The Tower of London* is an unusual work and not without its flaws, but it is an effective novel in terms of its vivid and ordered chronicling of fascinating historical events. Ainsworth's appeal springs from his sense of structure and his ability to arouse in the reader a sense of being in a crowded, swarming, self-contained world where adventure and intrigue are staples of everyday life.

"Critical Evaluation" by Stephen Hanson

Bibliography:

Ellis, S. M. *William Harrison Ainsworth and His Friends*. 2 vols. London: John Lane, 1911. Although dated, this is the only complete biography of the author. Based on original correspondence and recollections, it includes a detailed discussion of the sources used for *The Tower of London*.

Fleishman, Avrom. *The English Historical Novel: Walter Scott to Virginia Woolf*. Baltimore, Md.: The Johns Hopkins University Press, 1971. This study sees Ainsworth as a mass producer of historical fiction. Fleishman judges the novel to be filled with grotesque characters, antiquarian digressions, and sentimental emotions.

Sanders, Andrew. *The Victorian Historical Novel, 1840-1880*. New York: St. Martin's Press, 1979. Sanders devotes a chapter of this comprehensive study to a harsh evaluation of *The Tower of London*. He argues that the novel is overcrowded with characters, abrupt in its transitions from scene to scene, intellectually slight, and too sensationalistic.

Sutherland, J. A. *Victorian Novelists and Publishers*. Chicago: University of Chicago Press, 1976. This is a well-written, thoughtful, and detailed examination of how business relationships between novelists and publishers affected the shape of novels in the Victorian era. Sutherland explains why *The Tower of London* was one of Ainsworth's most popular novels, although he points out its formulaic qualities.

Worth, George J. *William Harrison Ainsworth*. New York: Twayne, 1972. In this, the only book-length critical study of Ainsworth's career, Worth argues that the novel's focus on the setting (the complex of buildings that makes up the Tower of London) rather than on the plot and the characters, is a departure from Ainsworth's more typical novels. For Worth, this approach is interesting, creative, and challenging to received notions about plot.

THE TOWN

Type of work: Novel
Author: William Faulkner (1897-1962)
Type of plot: Psychological realism
Time of plot: 1909-1927
Locale: Jefferson, Yoknapatawpha County, Mississippi
First published: 1957

Principal characters:
　FLEM SNOPES, the shrewdest of the Snopes family
　EULA VARNER SNOPES, his wife
　LINDA SNOPES, their daughter
　MANFRED DE SPAIN, the mayor of Jefferson and Eula's lover
　GAVIN STEVENS, a county attorney
　V. K. RATLIFF, a salesman and friend of Gavin Stevens
　CHARLES MALLISON, Stevens' nephew
　MONTGOMERY WARD SNOPES,
　WALLSTREET PANIC SNOPES,
　BYRON SNOPES,
　MINK SNOPES,
　ECK SNOPES, and
　I. O. SNOPES, Flem's cousins

The Story:

The Snopes family, which came out of nowhere after the Civil War, had successfully completed the invasion of Frenchman's Bend. Now Flem Snopes, son of Ab Snopes, a bushwhacker, sharecropper, and horse thief, was ready for the next goal, the domination of Jefferson, county seat of Yoknapatawpha County. Flem Snopes was ruthless, shrewd, uneducated, and possessed of a fanatic belief in the power of money. The townspeople, who had seen him when he took over Frenchman's Bend and then left it under control of other family members, were wondering about Flem's next move. Among those interested were Gavin Stevens, a young lawyer educated in Heidelberg, and V. K. Ratliff, a good-natured sewing machine salesman, who made up for his lack of education with a great measure of common sense. Stevens felt a moral responsibility to defend the town against the Snopeses, and Ratliff was once the victim of Snopesism when, thinking that it contained a buried treasure, he bought worthless property from Flem for a high price. Another who became an assistant in the fight against the Snopes infiltration was Stevens' nephew, Charles Mallison, who watched the Snopes invasion from his childhood through adolescence.

Flem Snopes realized that more subtle methods for conquering Jefferson were necessary than those he had used in Frenchman's Bend. The greatest advantage for him was his marriage with Eula Varner, daughter of Will Varner, chief property owner in that community. When Eula was pregnant, impotent Flem had married her after making a profitable deal with Varner, who despised Snopes but wanted to save his daughter's honor.

In a small rented house, Flem and his wife made a modest beginning in Jefferson by operating a small restaurant of which Ratliff had been a partner before he lost his share in the

6648

business deal with Flem. Later, the restaurant was transformed into a hotel. The first hint that Flem was aiming even higher came when he was appointed superintendent of the local power plant, before the people even knew that such a position existed. As the new mayor of Jefferson, Manfred de Spain was not in favor with the town conservatives, but he had won the election in a landslide when he declared himself against an automobile ban imposed by the former mayor. Soon it became known in the town that Eula Snopes and the new mayor were lovers. No one had seen anything, but everybody seemed to know about the affair except her husband.

Shortly after the war, during which Gavin Stevens served overseas, the president of Jefferson's oldest bank was killed in an auto accident. De Spain, named president on account of the bank stock he had inherited, resigned as mayor. The election of a new president made necessary a routine check by government auditors, who uncovered the theft of a large sum of money by a defaulting clerk, Byron Snopes, who fled to Mexico. Announcement was made that the money had been replaced by the new president and that Mr. Flem Snopes had been made a vice president of the bank. Flem's appointment indicated to his opponents a new phase of Snopesism: The search for money and power was now tinted with Flem's desire for respectability. This new tactic also became apparent when he rid himself and Jefferson of some undesirable kinsmen, such as Montgomery Ward Snopes, who might have destroyed his efforts to make the name Snopes respectable. Montgomery Ward Snopes had returned from the war in France with a rich supply of pornographic pictures. A short time later, he opened a photographic studio and gave nightly slide shows for a large part of the male population of Yoknapatawpha County. Flem, not wishing to have his name associated with this shady enterprise, put bootleg whiskey in Montgomery Ward's studio to assure his arrest. When another Snopes, Mink, was jailed for murder, Flem failed to give him any assistance. There was also Eck Snopes, who did not fit into the Snopes pattern on account of his weak intelligence. Flem had no need to bring about his removal, for Eck removed himself. He had been hired to watch an oil tank. While a search was being made for a lost child, Eck, trying to make sure that the child had not climbed into his oil tank, took a lantern and went to look inside the tank. After the explosion, only Eck's metal neck brace was available for burial. Meanwhile, the child was found safe somewhere along the road.

Flem's new desire for respectability also made him forget Wallstreet Panic Snopes, who had dared to become a self-made man without his kinsman's help. Wallstreet Panic, a successful grocer, introduced the first self-service store in Jefferson. Flem also disliked the outcome of one of his family projects with I. O. Snopes, who was trained to tie mules to the railroad track in order to collect money from damage lawsuits against the railroad. When I. O. Snopes was killed during one of these operations, Flem hoped to collect the indemnity. I. O.'s stubborn wife, however, kept all the money, and Flem, in order to avoid complications, was forced to pay off the man who had supplied the mules. Flem also tried to live up to his new social standing by letting a professional decorator furnish his house.

In the meantime, Gavin Stevens, who had never been able to rid himself of the attraction Eula Snopes held for him, concentrated his reform efforts on Linda, Eula's daughter. Linda, now in high school, did not know that Flem was not her real father. The lawyer loved Linda and tried to influence her to attend a northern college far away from Snopesism. Flem, however, needing a front of outwardly solid family life for his show of respectability, was opposed to the possibility of losing his control of Linda, especially since a will existed that gave the girl a great deal of Will Varner's estate. So Flem disregarded the pleas of his daughter because he still had one more step ahead of him to achieve the position he desired in Jefferson: his scheme to replace de Spain as president of the bank. When he failed in his first attempt to ruin the bank by instigating a run on it, he decided that the time had come to use his knowledge of his wife's adultery as a weapon. Acting as if he had just learned of the eighteen-year-old affair, and armed with a declaration from Linda that she would leave her part of her inheritance to her father, he visited Will Varner. Once more, in order to save the honor of his daughter and in return for Flem's promise to destroy Linda's note about the inheritance, Varner helped Flem to get rid of de Spain, and Flem became president of the bank. Hoping Eula would run away with him, de Spain sold his bank stock, but Eula, hoping to keep her daughter from ever learning of her affairs, remained in Jefferson. She committed suicide after securing from Gavin Stevens a promise that he would marry Linda.

Flem, having reached his goal, agreed to let Linda leave Jefferson. For a short interval, the ghost of old Snopesism came back to Jefferson, when bank thief Byron Snopes sent his four half-Indian children to stay with his kinsfolk. After a series of incidents in which the children terrorized Jefferson and Frenchman's Bend, Flem himself made sure that these last reminders of primitive Snopesism were sent back to Mexico. Meanwhile, he had bought the de Spain house, and workers were busy transforming it into a mansion suitable to Flem Snopes, president of the Bank of Jefferson.

Critical Evaluation:

It was in the 1920's that William Faulkner first conceived of the Snopes saga: a clan of crude, avaricious, amoral, unfeeling, but energetic and hard-driving individuals who would move into the settled, essentially moral society of the Old South and gradually, but inevitably, usurp the old order. To Faulkner, the Snopeses were not a special Mississippi phenomenon, but a characteristic evil of the mechanized, dehumanized twentieth century which filled the void left by the collapse of the agrarian pre-Civil War South. Flem Snopes is the supreme example of the type, and the Snopes trilogy, of which *The Town* is the second part, is primarily a chronicle of his career and its implications.

Faulkner finished *The Hamlet*, the first book in the series, in 1940 (although several short stories appeared earlier), and not until 1959 did he complete the trilogy with *The Mansion*. In the intervening time, Faulkner's vision of human morality and society had become more complex and, although the original design remained intact, the quest of the Snopes Clan became more devious and complicated, and "Snopesism" took on increasingly ambiguous meanings.

At the beginning of *The Town*, Flem arrives in Jefferson fresh from his triumphs in Frenchman's Bend, but with only a wagon, a new wife, Eula Varner Snopes, and their baby daughter, Linda. The book traces his rise in short order from restaurant owner to hotel owner, to power plant supervisor, to bank vice president, and finally to bank president, church deacon, and appropriately grieving widower. The book also describes the life of his wife, Eula, her lengthy affair with Manfred de Spain, her relations to the community, and her efforts for her daughter—all of which leads her, at last, to suicide.

If Flem is the embodiment of ruthless, aggressive inhumanity and devitalized conformity, Eula is the essence of warmth, emotional involvement, sexuality, and freedom. Although their direct confrontations are muted, *The Town* is basically about the struggle between these two characters and the contrasting approaches to life that they represent. The story is told by three anti-Snopesian citizens: V. K. Ratliff, the sewing machine salesman who previously tangled with Flem in Frenchman's Bend; Gavin Stevens, Heidelberg and Harvard educated County Attorney; and Charles Mallison, Stevens' young nephew. Although they confirm the essential facts, each speaker has a separate interpretation of the events. Thus, the reader must sift through their different attitudes and conclusions to arrive at the "truth" of the book. Frequently, it is the ironical distance between the events and the characters' interpretations of them that gives the book its bite and message—as well as its humor.

Mallison, who saw the events as a child but recounts them as an adult, is probably the most detached of the narrators. Ratliff is sardonic and realistic, but his bitter experiences with the Snopeses somewhat color his accounts. Gavin Stevens is the primary narrator and chief enemy of Flem, but the reliability of his statements is jeopardized by his lengthy, emotional, somewhat confused involvements with both Eula and Linda. Stevens is a well-educated, sophisticated modern man who understands the complexities and difficulties of human relationships; but, at the same time, he is an old-fashioned Southern gentleman who clings to old attitudes and traditions. When Eula offers herself to him, it is not morality, but romanticism coupled with self-doubt that stimulates his refusal. He insists on viewing her through a romantic haze that prevents him from reacting realistically in the most critical situations. "What he was doing was simply defending forever with his blood the principle that chastity and virtue in women shall be defended whether they exist or not."

The same kinds of assumptions determine his relationship to Linda Snopes. Since he is nearly twice her age, he cannot imagine a sexual or marital arrangement between them in spite of the fact that he loves her and is encouraged by her mother. So, in the role of father protector and educator, Stevens reads poetry to Linda over sodas and feeds her dreams with college catalogs. Thus, because of his intense emotions, sense of morality, and traditional assumptions, Gavin Stevens is unable to deal either with Eula's simple sensuality or Flem Snopes's one-dimensional inhumanity.

In the final conflict between these two forces, Flem's ruthless rationality overcomes Eula's passionate free spirit. Being both physically and spiritually impotent, Flem can coldly and callously manipulate the sexual and emotional drives of others. Not only does he do so to thwart Stevens' anti-Snopes efforts, but more important to his plans, he also uses them to gain control over his primary Jefferson rival, Manfred de Spain.

Flem learns of his wife's affair with de Spain soon after his arrival in Jefferson, but he chooses to ignore it as long as it is profitable. It is even suggested that the two men work out a tacit agreement whereby Flem overlooks the affair in return for an appointment to the newly created job of power plant superintendent. De Spain's influence is later instrumental in securing Flem the vice presidency of the Sartoris Bank. After eighteen years, however, when Flem decides to make his move for the bank presidency, he suddenly becomes the outraged husband. He uses the threat of scandal to provoke Will Varner to action, to drive de Spain from the bank, to push Eula to suicide, and to coerce Stevens into unwilling complicity. Neither integrity nor sensuality can stop Snopesism.

As Flem succeeds in his drive to monetary wealth, another goal becomes predominant—respectability. He learns from de Spain that in Jefferson one can become respectable without being moral—if one has the necessary money. So Flem systematically acquires all the requisite signs of success, and they, in turn, provide him with access to respectability. Only one last obstacle remains between Flem and complete social acceptance—the other Snopeses.

Consequently, it is Flem, himself, who finally rids Jefferson of the Snopeses. Using the same callous attitude and devious strategy on his kin that he used on other victims, he eliminates all of the lesser Snopeses who might pose a threat to his new status: Mink, Byron, Montgomery Ward, I. O., and, finally, Byron's brood of wild, half-breed children, "The last and final end of Snopes out-and-out unvarnished behavior in Jefferson."

So Flem becomes respectable. Faulkner's final question to the reader is this: Has Flem's drive to social acceptance weakened and narrowed him to the point where he is vulnerable, if not to the morality of the Ratliffs, Stevenses, and Mallisons, then to the latent vengeance of Snopesism? Faulkner answers that question in *The Mansion*.

"Critical Evaluation" by Keith Neilson

Bibliography:

Kerr, Elizabeth. *William Faulkner's Gothic Domain*. Port Washington, N.Y.: Kennikat Press, 1979. Discusses Flem Snopes, Gavin Stevens, and Mink Snopes in reference to their respective roles in *The Town*. Lists and discusses interconnected themes in the trilogy. Fairly extensive bibliography.

McHaney, Thomas L. *William Faulkner: A Reference Guide*. Boston: G. K. Hall, 1976. Good index provides references and cross-references, as well as a helpful, annotated source list for research in *The Town*.

Marcus, Steven. "Snopes Revisited." In *William Faulkner: Three Decades of Criticism*, edited by Frederick J. Hoffman and Olga W. Vickery. East Lansing: Michigan State University Press, 1960. Discusses content, characterization, and criticism of *The Town*. Points out failings, but contends Faulkner wrote as he did so that the novel would represent truth, as art must. Extensive bibliography, including periodical sources.

Meriwether, James B., and Michael Millgate, eds. *Lion in the Garden: Interviews with William Faulkner, 1926-1962*. New York: Random House, 1968. Indexed and coded to specific works and characters. Provides Faulkner's own responses to specific questions about *The Town* and its chief characters. Text reports Faulkner's views on themes in his fiction.

Millgate, Michael. *The Achievement of William Faulkner*. New York: Random House, 1966. Millgate's readable, discerning text must be included in any credible bibliography of Faulkner's work. Discusses each work. Provides insight into Gavin Stevens, a central character of *The Town*. Notes and index.

THE TRAGEDY OF TRAGEDIES
Or, The Life and Death of Tom Thumb the Great

Type of work: Drama
Author: Henry Fielding (1707-1754)
Type of plot: Farce
Time of plot: Age of chivalry
Locale: King Arthur's court
First performed: 1731; first published, 1731

Principal characters:
TOM THUMB THE GREAT, a pocket-size epic hero
KING ARTHUR, Tom Thumb's liege lord
QUEEN DOLLALLOLLA, King Arthur's consort, in love with Tom
PRINCESS HUNCAMUNCA, in love with Tom and Lord Grizzle
LORD GRIZZLE, suitor for Huncamunca's hand
QUEEN GLUMDALCA, a captive giantess, in love with Tom

The Story:

According to the legends told in his lifetime, Tom Thumb's peasant father and mother were unable to have any children until Tom's father went to the magician Merlin and received from him a charm that resulted in the wife's giving birth to the valiant but diminutive Tom Thumb. When he reached manhood, Tom Thumb entered the service of King Arthur, in whose court he accomplished great deeds and earned a vast reputation. At the court, Queen Dollallolla fell in love with Tom Thumb, loving him, in fact, as much as she loved drinking, but she kept her love a secret from all. Least of all did she tell King Arthur, who was afraid of no one except his queen.

Tom Thumb's greatest achievement was his victory over the giants who dwelt in the land ruled by the amazonian Queen Glumdalca. Tom subdued ten thousand giants and then returned with the surviving foes fastened to his chariot, among them the comely Queen Glumdalca. Because of their size, all the giants except the queen, who was a foot shorter than her subjects, had to be left outside the castle walls. Queen Glumdalca was brought into the castle. As soon as he saw her, King Arthur fell in love with her.

Eager to reward Tom Thumb for his great deeds, the king promised him anything within reason. Tom at first replied that permission to serve his king was sufficient reward. When pressed, however, he asked for the hand of Princess Huncamunca, with whom he had long been in love. The queen was furious that her daughter should become the wife of the man she loved. She railed at her husband and swore that the marriage should not take place, but the king for once held his own against his virago queen and told her to be quiet. The queen, furious also at her husband, went to Lord Grizzle, a discontented courtier, to secure his aid in preventing the marriage. Lord Grizzle, who was himself in love with Princess Huncamunca, was quite willing to oblige and promised the queen that he would kill Tom Thumb. Too late, Queen Dollallolla realized that she did not want Tom killed. She hoped, instead, that King Arthur would die and that she might be free to marry Tom.

When King Arthur told Princess Huncamunca of his decision to marry her to Tom Thumb, the princess was only too happy to hear of his decision, for she had been in love with Tom for a long time. She had also been afraid that she might die an old maid and, according to old superstition, be doomed to lead apes through hell. After the king had gone, Lord Grizzle came to plead his suit with Princess Huncamunca, who told him that she loved him, too. Taking her cue from the career of the queen of the giants, who had had twenty husbands, Princess Huncamunca decided that she could love both Tom and Lord Grizzle. She promised to marry Lord Grizzle, and he went at once to secure a license for the ceremony.

Shortly after Lord Grizzle had gone on his happy errand, Tom Thumb came to the princess' apartment. Learning of her promise to Lord Grizzle, he paid no attention to it. While he was talking with the princess, Queen Glumdalca came into the room and offered herself to Tom Thumb, who, she said, would take the place of her twenty former husbands. Tom refused, saying he preferred the smaller gold coin of Princess Huncamunca to the large dross coin of the giantess. Queen Glumdalca left in a fury, but her anger abated when she discovered that the king was in love with her.

Tom Thumb hurried Princess Huncamunca off to a parson, who married them quickly and wished them at the same time a long life and many children. Lord Grizzle, returning just after the ceremony, found Princess Huncamunca married to his rival. The princess assured him that there was room in her heart for two husbands and offered to marry him as well. This did not appease Lord Grizzle, who rushed out to create a rebellion and kill Tom Thumb.

That night, the ghost of Tom Thumb's father appeared to King Arthur and warned him that Tom's life and the king's rule were both endangered by Lord Grizzle and his rebels. After the ghost's departure, the king sat meditating on what he had been told until the queen, rousing from a drunken slumber, came to see what was the matter. She was unable to set the king's mind at ease.

The next morning, Tom Thumb, in company with the giantess, went forth to subdue the rebels. On the way to the battlefield, Merlin's magic vouchsafed Tom Thumb a vision in which he saw that he was doomed to be eaten by a red cow. The vision put him in awe of death, but when Merlin then revealed that Tom would become famous through the medium of the stage, Tom was willing to die.

Lord Grizzle, who had raised an army of rebels under the banner of democracy and freedom, advanced to meet Tom Thumb and the giantess. In the bloody engagement that ensued, Lord Grizzle killed Queen Glumdalca, and Tom avenged her by killing Lord Grizzle. Once their leader was dead, the rebels dispersed. Tom cut off Lord Grizzle's head and started a victorious march to the castle.

In the castle, the king, queen, and princess awaited the news of the battle, certain that Tom Thumb would triumph and save them from the rebels. Their hopes were confirmed when a courtier ran in to tell them of Tom's success, but their happiness was short-lived, for the courtier went on to tell how, on his march back to the castle, Tom Thumb had met a large red cow that had swallowed poor Tom at a gulp.

Queen Dollallolla, outraged at the courtier for bringing news of her loved one's death, seized a sword and killed him. The courtier's mistress then killed the queen. Princess Huncamunca, anxious to avenge her mother's death, slew the courtier's mistress. Another courtier used the occasion to kill Princess Huncamunca because of a grudge he had long held against her. The princess' maid then avenged her mistress by killing Huncamunca's murderer. The king, dispensing justice, killed the maid. Then the king, with bodies lying all about him, killed himself, with the thought that his only glory was that he was the last to die.

Critical Evaluation:

Although Henry Fielding is chiefly remembered as the author of *Joseph Andrews* (1742) and *Tom Jones* (1749), he achieved his first literary success not as a novelist but as a playwright. In fact, it is fair to say that for roughly eight years between 1730 and 1737, during a particularly exciting era in the life of the London theater, Fielding was the town's single most popular and most celebrated playwright. In 1730 alone, for example, four of Fielding's plays were produced: *The Temple Beau* at the Goodman's Fields Theater, and *The Author's Farce*, *Tom Thumb*, and *Rape upon Rape*, at the Little Theatre in the Haymarket.

Two of these early plays, *The Author's Farce* and *Tom Thumb*, are farce burlesques that lampoon a variety of targets ranging from well-known London actors and playwrights to such popular dramatic genres as heroic tragedy. Both plays were initial successes, and *Tom Thumb* in particular achieved enormous popularity, running nearly forty nights over a three-month period between April 24 and June 22 to packed houses, at a time when a nine- or ten-night run was considered a success. It was with this type of dramatic satire—high-spirited, immensely entertaining theatrical "hodgepodges" featuring music, dancing, and scenes of burlesque and parody—that Fielding was to achieve his greatest popular and financial success. Unfortunately, it was also this type of satire that eventually proved to be Fielding's undoing in the theater. The satire of *The Historical Register, for the Year 1736* (performed in early 1737) proved so biting that it helped bring about the Licensing Act (on June 21, 1737) and, only a few days later, the closing of Fielding's Little Theatre in the Haymarket by order of the British prime minister, Sir Robert Walpole. The closing of Fielding's theater marked the close of his career as a playwright.

Fielding's best-known play, *The Tragedy of Tragedies*, began its theatrical life as a short "afterpiece" entitled *Tom Thumb*. In the London of Fielding's day, there were sometimes as many as six theaters open at the same time, all of them energetically competing for the theatergoer's money, and it was common practice for theater managers to attempt to vary their menus to please popular taste. On a particular evening, for example, a theater might offer a play by William Shakespeare or Ben Jonson as a mainpiece, followed by a pantomime, a brief comic farce, or even an animal act.

This first version of *The Tragedy of Tragedies* is a very general burlesque, which takes as its main target the genre of heroic tragedy. Very popular in the Restoration period, these plays tended to emphasize visual spectacle and verbal bombast at the expense of plot and character. An audience does not need prior knowledge of heroic tragedy to find Fielding's little farce amusing, although a knowledge of the ghosts at the conclusion of Thomas Otway's *Venice Preserved* (1682) would certainly add to one's appreciation of Tom Thumb's brief return as a ghost just before the multiple deaths that end the play. (Certainly the deaths themselves suggest the carnage at the conclusion of William Shakespeare's *Hamlet*, c. 1600-1601.) The many wonderful incongruities the play offers—beginning with a tragic hero compared to a "Cock-Sparrow" hopping "at the Head of an huge Flock of Turkeys"—are themselves inherently funny. The expanded version of *Tom Thumb*, first presented in March, 1731, as *The Tragedy of Tragedies*, contains most of the original play's words. It is, however, so very different from the original in so many important ways as to make it a totally new work.

Besides being nearly twice as long, *The Tragedy of Tragedies* is intended as much for readers as for theatergoers. Fielding complicated his plot through the addition of new characters and heightened conflicts, but in the published version he also added a huge array of pseudo-scholarly material: a wordy preface and a long series of footnotes, all prepared by the fictional pedant H. Scriblerus Secundus. The result is still satire, but a satire both wider in scope and more focused in its intensity.

In the new play, Fielding widens his attack on heroic tragedy; an early editor of *The Tragedy of Tragedies* counted more than forty specific plays that Fielding attacked, most of them from the late seventeenth century, the heyday of heroic tragedy. As in the original version, Fielding burlesques the pompous, inflated language typical of heroic tragedy. Within the spoken text of the play, the satiric approach is relatively simple: Removed from its ostensibly serious context and relocated into the zany world of Fielding's play, such language virtually satirizes itself. The addition of the "learned" commentary of H. Scriblerus Secundus, however, allows Fielding to expand and complicate the satire.

If there is one common thread running through Fielding's literary career, it is his hatred of pedantry and false learning. The character of H. Scriblerus Secundus, with his verbose style and vast knowledge of theatrical trivia, is itself an effectively comic caricature of the pedant, but the joke goes beyond mere caricature. By annotating one passage after another with further quotations from obscure and forgotten plays, and by missing a long series of very obvious allusions to Shakespeare ("wherefore are thou Tom Thumb" is but one particularly flagrant example), Secundus expands the attack on earlier plays, increases the satire against the kind of false, pedantic learning his own practice so vividly exemplifies, and makes an even bigger fool of himself in the process.

The Tragedy of Tragedies has often been seen as in part politically motivated, but while it is possible to see a few general political references in the play (the descriptions of King Arthur and Queen Dollallolla might, for example, suggest King George II and Queen Caroline) there is simply not enough evidence to support a reading of the play as a coherent political satire.

"Critical Evaluation" by Michael Stuprich

Bibliography:

Hume, Robert D. *Henry Fielding and the London Theatre, 1728-1737.* Oxford, England: Clarendon Press, 1988. This is the finest study of Fielding's too-often-neglected career as a playwright-manager. Hume, probably the foremost scholar in the field of Restoration and eighteenth century drama, writes lucid, entertaining prose and has marshaled a remarkably impressive array of source materials. Highly recommended.

Hunter, J. Paul. *Occasional Form: Henry Fielding and the Chains of Circumstance.* Baltimore, Md.: The Johns Hopkins University Press, 1975. Hunter, one of the foremost scholars of eighteenth century British literature, provides an excellent literary analysis of *The Tragedy of Tragedies.*

Mace, Nancy. "Fielding, Theobald, and *The Tragedy of Tragedies.*" *Philological Quarterly* 66, no. 4 (Fall, 1987): 457-472. In its published form, with a preface and extensive footnotes by the fictional H. Scriblerus Secundus, Fielding's play is a wickedly clever satire on academic learning and intellectual pretense. Mace's article examines the relationship between Fielding and Lewis Theobald, a well-known (and often satirized) pedant and a principal target of Fielding's satire.

Morrissey, L. J. "Critical Introduction." In *"Tom Thumb" and "The Tragedy of Tragedies,"* edited by L. J. Morrissey. Berkeley: University of California Press, 1970. For readers new to *The Tragedy of Tragedies,* this is probably the best place to start. Besides an excellent text of the full length play, the volume provides the earlier, afterpiece version of the play, *Tom Thumb.*

Rivero, Albert J. *The Plays of Henry Fielding: A Critical Study of His Dramatic Career.* Charlottesville: University Press of Virginia, 1989. This is the best purely literary study of Fielding's plays as a whole. The analysis of *The Tragedy of Tragedies* lacks any sense of the play's wonderful theatrical potential but is useful for its detailed study of Fielding's language.

THE TRAGIC MUSE

Type of work: Novel
Author: Henry James (1843-1916)
Type of plot: Social realism
Time of plot: 1880's
Locale: Paris and England
First published: serial, 1889-1890; book, 1890

> *Principal characters:*
> NICHOLAS "NICK" DORMER, a young politician and amateur painter
> LADY AGNES DORMER, his mother
> GRACE DORMER and
> BIDDY DORMER, his sisters
> JULIA DALLOW, their cousin
> PETER SHERRINGHAM, her brother
> GABRIEL NASH, a friend of Nicholas
> MIRIAM ROOTH, an actress
> MRS. ROOTH, her mother
> BASIL DASHWOOD, an actor

The Story:

Nicholas Dormer, a handsome young bachelor politician and amateur portrait painter, was vacationing in Paris with his formidable mother, Lady Agnes, the impoverished widow of a Liberal politician, and his two younger sisters, "spinsterish" Grace and lively, lovable Biddy. At an art exhibition, Nick met an old Oxford friend, Gabriel Nash, an aesthete and dilettante but sufficiently a gentleman to be introduced to the ladies. Another visitor in Paris was the Dormers' cousin, Julia Dallow, a rich and politically minded young widow, whose brother, Peter Sherringham, was at the British Embassy there. Nick's fondness for Julia, her devotion to his political career, Biddy's friendship with Julia and unrequited affection for Peter, and Peter and Nick's congeniality united the family group with particularly close ties. While they were together in Paris, they heard that the member of Parliament for the constituency where Julia's estate and influence lay had died suddenly. Guaranteeing her financial as well as political support, Julia wanted Nick to stand for election.

This moment of great promise and family solidarity was threatened unobtrusively by Gabriel Nash's introduction of Mrs. Rooth and Miriam. They were, respectively, the widow of limited means and vague claims to aristocratic connections in England, and her beautiful daughter, who had been brought up in a succession of Continental pensions where living is cheap, superficially cultivated, and multilingual. To promote Miriam's aspirations toward the stage, Nash had arranged an audition with a notable retired French actress whom Peter Sherringham knew through his passionate interest in the theater. Peter, also invited to the audition, persuaded Nick to join him and suggested that Nick should paint Miriam as the Tragic Muse. Although the audition was a fiasco, Peter was sufficiently intrigued to invite the Rooths to a party at his house. There Miriam recited again, met the ladies of the family, and made a bad impression on all but Biddy. Julia, disgusted both with Miriam and with what she considered the frivolousness of Nash, returned to England to organize the election campaign, and the Dormers followed soon after. Peter found himself increasingly involved with Miriam, to the extent of offering to pay for private lessons with the old French actress. At first, he assumed that his interest was in

Miriam's potential as an actress, but he eventually realized that he had been in love with her all along.

At Harsh, Julia's principal estate, where Nick had just won the election, he proposed to Julia and was accepted. To their mutual happiness there was added an undercurrent of brewing trouble in his assurance that he would give up his painting, her incomprehension of what this would mean to him, and her refusal to set their wedding date. When Nick next went to see his father's old friend and political ally, Mr. Carteret, he learned that his prospects of being the rich old bachelor's heir depended on his marriage to Julia.

Peter Sherringham, meanwhile, returning to Paris after leaving London, found that Miriam had acquired another patron, an English actor named Basil Dashwood. Peter urged her to give up her theatrical ambition for a greater role as wife of a rising diplomat, but she said that she would accept him only as the husband of an actress. In London, Nick and Julia faced similar difficulties as Julia planned to spend the Parliamentary recess on a round of strategic country-house visits, while Nick preferred to use his leisure time painting in his studio. With the wedding date set at last, they separated and Nick retired to his studio, where his first visitor was Gabriel Nash, whom Nick had not seen since their meeting in Paris. Nash told Nick that Miriam had arrived in London after her first success in Paris and wanted Nick to make good his promise to paint her as the Tragic Muse. When Nash brought her to the studio the next day, Nick was excited about her possibilities as a portrait subject. Beginning to paint immediately, he waited until later that night to write Julia about it. Julia failed to get the letter because she returned to London unexpectedly, called to surprise Nick, and was so stunned to find him with Miriam as a sitter that she left without a word and was not at home when he called that evening. When he finally saw her late at night, she broke the engagement on the grounds that his preference for the artistic life would never be compatible with her own interest in politics.

The next day, Julia left for the Continent. Stopping in Paris to see her brother and tell him what had happened, she also urged him to marry Biddy. Although he had determined to forget Miriam, Julia's account made him more eager to see Miriam than Biddy. He found a pretext for a journey to London, where he went straight to Miriam's rented villa. Not finding her at home, he then went to Nick's studio and there found Biddy alone. Discussing the break between Nick and Julia with Biddy, who was loyal to and sympathetic with both her brother and her friend, Peter failed to understand either of them; but seeing the portrait of Miriam gave him a deeper understanding of the actress' beauty and of Nick's talent. Peter gave Biddy a momentary hope by inviting her to the theater that night to see Miriam act. During the rest of his visit, he spent most of his time with the coterie of Miriam's friends who met at her house to discuss the theater.

Nick was away from London on a visit to the dying Mr. Carteret, to whom he confessed not only that the engagement was broken but also that he had just written a letter to his constituency resigning his seat in Parliament. Difficult as it was to disappoint his father's old friend, who had treated him like a son, Nick found it even harder to tell his mother, who believed that the sacrifice of his political career had betrayed his father's memory, while the dual sacrifice of Mr. Carteret's and Julia's fortunes had betrayed his sisters and herself. Only Biddy remained loyal to Nick; she spent more and more time at his studio, where she had taken up sculpture.

During Peter's prolonged stay in London, the central characters revolved around one another in a tantalizing minuet: Nick saw his devoted younger sister tortured by the knowledge that Peter, whom she loved, was in love with Miriam, and Peter was tortured by Gabriel Nash's telling him that Miriam was in love with Nick. For the third time Nash, the detached observer of life, precipitated a crisis in the lives of others. Peter tried to maintain his equilibrium by calling on Lady Agnes and accepting an invitation to dinner, but he cancelled it at the last minute when he learned that the first night of Miriam's new play had been scheduled. Her superb performance increased his passion so much that he tried again to persuade her to give up the stage to marry him, but she repeated her original terms. Defeated by her determination, Peter accepted promotion to a higher post in some remote country and withdrew.

The next year, while Miriam established herself rapidly as a success on the London stage, Nick continued to paint her, although with no interest in her except as a subject. His own artistic career was not successful, and he was worried about debts. Biddy refused a rich suitor. Julia finally came back to England accompanied by rumors of romance with a leading politician. At this depressing period, Gabriel Nash reappeared and agreed to sit for a portrait, but after only one sitting disappeared again. His encouragement of Nick's artistic bent had a lasting influence, but the complications he evoked began to disappear when he did. Julia made overtures through Biddy with the suggestion that she wanted to sit for a portrait. While Nick and Biddy were discussing this proposal, they were surprised by the arrival at the studio of Miriam and her new husband, Basil Dashwood, both excited about Miriam's opening that night as Juliet. Although the house was sold out, they managed to get a seat for Biddy as well as Nick. At the theater, they saw Peter Sherringham, who had returned from abroad in time for the first night but too late to declare again his love for Miriam, who had married three days before.

With the Tragic Muse established as a public figure, Nicholas Dormer and Peter Sherringham brought their private affairs to a swift and easy conclusion. Peter arranged for an extension of his leave in order to return to his post with Biddy as his wife. Nick painted a portrait of Julia which attracted the favorable attention of critics at a private viewing. There were also rumors that Julia's other suitor was worried about her. Whether Nick would ever achieve success in the career for which he had sacrificed heavily, as Miriam and Peter achieved it in theirs, remained a provocative question for the future.

Critical Evaluation:

Henry James is generally seen as an American novelist whose theme is innocent Americans confronting the formidable culture of Europe, sometimes to their advantage, and sometimes not. He can, however, concentrate his attention on the European scene itself. This novel is an unusual study of British characters, although it commences in Paris. It does, however, return to themes that had long interested James, and has a particular piquancy in its concern with the theater, since James, at the time the novel was published, was making a concentrated attempt to become a successful playwright, an ambition that was to prove beyond him. James knew personally what it was like to fail in the theater, and more to the point of this novel, he knew what it feels like to want desperately to succeed in an art and to be forced to face the facts not only of success but also of failure.

One of the main ideas pursued in this novel is the need to persist as the first step in the artistic life. Both Miriam Rooth and Nicholas Dormer want to be artists, one on the stage, one as a painter. James is interested in that yearning which refuses to heed advice. Miriam seems to have no real talent when she first auditions for Peter Sherringham and the old French actress, but she refuses to give up, and takes their seemingly cruel advice stoically, determined to work at her craft despite the lack of encouragement. Nicholas is, in some ways, even more courageous. Miriam has little to lose; Nicholas gives up his promising political career, the woman he loves, and the chance at a considerable fortune promised to him by Mr. Carteret if he shows himself a worthy political commodity. James is interested not only in the artistic drive that overrides all opposition, but also in what happens to the aspirant who succeeds, as Miriam does, and the person who discovers that the sacrifice has been in vain. The music of success is one thing; to face the music of failure is another, and that is Nicholas' lot.

There is much talk in the novel about the value of art and of the value of trying to be an artist. When one succeeds, as Miriam does, a further question arises in the form of how one maintains the discipline that will allow the artist to be more than a momentary phenomenon. Some of James's ideas may seem to be out of date, but the question of how one makes the best of oneself, and how to continue at a high level of endeavor, leads to what may seem a surprisingly modern confrontation. When Peter Sherringham, for all his supposed enthusiasm for the arts, suggests that Miriam could do better marrying him in order to live a life of reflected glory as he rises to social and political honor and celebrity in the world of diplomacy, readers may sense that James was ahead of his time.

The confrontation is not a simple one. It is, in part, the culmination of a battle that begins early in the novel in the relationship between Nicholas Dormer and Julia Dallow. The quarrel in their case is between the value of art versus the value of politics. This question has been, almost by chance, visited on them by Gabriel Nash, Dormer's old college friend and an avowed follower of the aesthetic life, if only as an enlightened spectator.

When the matter comes up again in the confrontation of Peter Sherringham and Miriam Rooth, it takes an ironic turn, in the first instance, since it was Peter who made it financially possible for Miriam to pursue her studies, and, more important, to appear in a theatrical production. His confidence and special knowledge of the theater makes her career initially. Afterward, however, he argues, somewhat superciliously, that theater is of less importance than the world of diplomacy, and that Miriam ought to be not only satisfied but exultant in the idea of being the wife of a distinguished ambassador, a position finer in every way than that of being a fine, even a great, actress. Oddly enough, she is not awed by his reasoning. Julia argues from a position of financial power in attempting to suppress Nicholas' artistic ambitions, and Peter is guilty of male arrogance in his argument.

There are lesser themes in the novel, which are handled with considerable care. The helplessness, for instance, of women in high society when the social status of their family is considerably higher than its income is seen in the Dormer family. The mother, the daughter, and Nicholas too are dependent upon the chance of a lucky marriage. Neither of his sisters can support themselves, and Nicholas' decision to become a painter is an act of selfishness that is understandable but harrowing to the women. The way in which they stand helpless, waiting for the good marriage or the chance benefactor to provide money, is an example of the constant theme of money that also pervades James's novels. Miriam finds herself able to make a living, but there is no such relief for the Dormer sisters unless they can make a marriage or Nicholas can make one for them. James is often defined as a novelist of the comfortable world of wealth and privilege. He was fully aware of that world's limitations and how so much of it depends on money.

James's talent for taking such themes and making drama out of them found its expression in the novel, the suitable medium for him, given his need and gift for complicated, subtle discourse. His ambitions in theater were, given this need, not surprisingly frustrated. Ideas are the major characters in a James novel; one of the gifts that James possessed was his ability to imagine human situations in which his ideas express themselves with intensity and sensitivity. The confrontation between Miriam and Peter over his proposal of marriage has a freshness and pertinence that goes far beyond the requirements of plot, and shows the way in which James recognized how constants of the male-female relationship never change, however enlightened the participants.

"Critical Evaluation" by Charles Pullen

Bibliography:

Anderson, Quentin. *The American Henry James.* New Brunswick, N.J.: Rutgers University Press, 1957. The nature of Henry James's relation to European culture has to be seen in the light of his American lineage. Devotes a chapter to *The Tragic Muse.*

Auchincloss, Louis. *Reading Henry James.* Minneapolis: University of Minnesota Press, 1970. Auchincloss, an American novelist, writes from an author's point of view, with a chapter on the novel.

Gard, Roger, ed. *Henry James: The Critical Heritage.* New York: Barnes & Noble Books, 1968. A selection of essays on various aspects of James's work, including the novel.

Leyburn, Ellen Douglas. *Strange Alloy: The Relation of Comedy to Tragedy in the Fiction of Henry James.* Chapel Hill: University of North Carolina Press, 1968. For all the seriousness of his stories, James is also continually aware of the comic side of the conduct of his characters, and some of the pleasure in reading his novels lies in how he manipulates tone sometimes so subtly that one has to pay very close attention to not fall victim to his ironies. This book will put one on close guard.

Moore, Harry T. *Henry James and His World.* New York: Thames and Hudson, 1974. A well-illustrated short study of James from childhood until his life in Europe. James's preoccupations, especially his concerns regarding class and culture, particularly European culture, may be unfamiliar to the contemporary reader; it is helpful to put his novels into the context of the world in which James lived.

THE TRAGIC SENSE OF LIFE IN MEN AND IN PEOPLES

Type of work: Philosophy
Author: Miguel de Unamuno y Jugo (1864-1936)
First published: Del sentimiento trágico de la vida en los hombres y en los pueblos, 1913
   (English translation, 1921)

One of the major original thinkers of the twentieth century, Unamuno defies clear-cut classification. His book *The Tragic Sense of Life in Men and in Peoples,* for example, is a remarkably unusual philosophical treatise because in it Unamuno passionately rejects formal logic and accepts paradox and contradiction as essential to his view of life. Even his style, a rhetoric of passion and intensity, is unlike the calm, detached style of the ordinary philosopher. This passion is a fundamental component of his thought. A Roman Catholic, Unamuno discarded the Church's view of God; a Spaniard, he denounced the Monarchy and the Falangists; a philosopher, he rejected any and all systems. His thinking reflects the movement that was to grow into "Christian Existentialism," but he preserves the Romantic duality of body and spirit and refuses to discard the mystery of the Catholic Eucharist. He is, in short, an outspoken exponent of "confusionism," the philosophical approach to the human predicament that he felt most accurately described the human experience.

Looking back to his own spiritual crisis, he begins *The Tragic Sense of Life* by stating that the only real person is the affective or feeling one, the one of flesh and bone, not the abstract creature of rationalistic philosophers. This person of flesh and blood has only one problem: the longing never to die. This problem is irrational, so all reason builds upon irrationalities. What intensifies the problem is that the individual wants to be only himself or herself. People want to prolong actual flesh-and-bone existence indefinitely. Reason tells people that this is impossible, despite their feelings. Thus people are caught in a deadlock between reason, which says that all things must die, and passion, which yearns to live forever. The deadlock is tragic because it has no solution. Unamuno says that disease is anything that disturbs unity; therefore, consciousness itself is a disease, the particular disease that causes people to find some means of self-preservation and self-perpetuation. These two "instincts"—to survive and to love—are the foundations of the individual and of society. Through love the imagination creates an ideal world in which it perpetuates itself; this is the realm of knowledge. People seek knowledge only to ascertain whether they are really going to die, because after people become conscious of themselves they do not want to die. This search for knowledge of immortality, the tragic sense of life, is the starting point of philosophy. In a stunning summation, Unamuno alters the Cartesian *cogito ergo sum* into *sum ergo cogito.*

Unamuno points out that all religions have sprung from cults of immortality and that people alone of all the animals know themselves distinct from nature. He further points out that the thirst for immortality always stifles the life that passes and never abides. The affirmation of immortality, furthermore, is based only upon the foundation of the desire for immortality. In short, there is no rational, demonstrable basis for religious faith. People cannot escape their tragic fate. Reason attacks blind faith, and faith that does not feel itself secure has to come to terms with reason, but reason and faith can never reach compromise. Each seeks nothing less than the complete destruction of the other. The only religion to bridge these contradictory states and thus bring them into any kind of harmony is Catholicism, because only Catholicism is a system of contradictions in which the greatest danger is to attempt to rationalize the paradoxical solution symbolized by the Eucharist. Rationalism in any of its forms—materialism, pragmatism, agnosticism, empiricism, pantheism, or science—cannot explain the soul. Reason deals with dead things but is unable to deal with living things that never remain the same for two moments. People, however, are prisoners of logic, without which they cannot think. Thus, people tend always to make logic subservient to the desire for immortality. This need for logic or reason is always a stumbling block of faith, always ending in skepticism, which is an anti-vitalism. Thus the longing never to die finds no consolation in reason; still, people cannot exclude reason because to do so would be to reduce themselves to an irrational animal. The only thing left is to accept both faith and reason as an association of continual struggle—faith to absorb the world into the self and to overcome time and space, reason to absorb the self into the world and perpetuate the self in love. Through this inner struggle people create God, for to believe in God is to long for His existence and to act as if He existed.

Having fully stated the problem of human existence, Unamuno turns from analysis to synthesis after carefully warning that he has no intention to construct a system. He begins with the Pauline triad, faith, hope, and charity. Love personalizes its object; in discovering the suffering in the self and in the Universe, it personalizes the Universe; that is, love creates God. Faith is the longing for the existence of God, a movement toward a practical truth that lets one live, and the creative power in the individual insofar as the individual creates God through love. Hope is love directed toward the future and growing from the disillusionment of the past; the fundamental hope is the hope for eternal life. Spirit cannot exist without matter and matter always limits spirit, so the inherent state of a person is to suffer. Charity is the impulse to liberate the self, others, and God from matter, from suffering. In the passionate longing not to die, one's instinct of living and instinct of knowing thus come into bitter conflict, all the more so because both absolute certainty (faith) and absolute doubt (reason) are denied. Spiritual love is the result of pity, the awareness of suffering in others caused by the death of carnal love; love cannot, for this reason, exist apart from suffering. The personalization of a suffering universe is the highest view of God attainable. This view is the Christian Incarnation. This view is necessarily collective and social, although originally it was the subjectivity of an individual consciousness, projected. Reason attempts to define this God created by faith, hope, and charity and in doing so attempts to kill Him.

This deadlock between faith and reason reaches its climax in the apocatastasis (the unification of all things, including sinners—even Satan—with God). The essence of religion is the problem of eternal life. People wish to possess God, not to have God possess them because people do not want to lose the ego or the awareness of self, which a complete union with God implies. What people long for is an eternal prolongation of this life; thus any hypothesis of a heaven without change or without suffering must be false because life necessarily posits change and suffering. Eternity must be unending suffering, unceasing faith, hope, and charity, but the New Testament speaks of the apocatastasis, God's coming to be all in all, and of the anacefaleosis, the gathering together of all things in Christ. Thus not only must salvation be collective, it must also be the fusion of all things into one person. This is the supreme religious sacrifice, the climax of the human tragedy. People want an eternal purgatory, however, an ascent that never reaches the climax, an eternity of hope, not of salvation.

Unamuno is not satisfied with speculations upon a mythology of the beyond; he is mainly concerned with life here and now. His system of ethics, however, is ultimately associated to his theology. Good is anything that helps one to satisfy one's longing for immortality. Bad is anything that makes one satisfied with a temporal state. The purpose of ethics is to act in such a way that each person becomes irreplaceable so that no one can fill the person's place. A good life is a vital one centered on action for others; thus the apocatastasis is the supreme rule of ethics. Such a life is symbolized for Unamuno by Don Quixote, who represents the vitalist whose faith is based on uncertainty, and by Sancho, the rationalist who doubts his own reason. In these two literary figures he sees the epitome of the tragic sense of life, the desperate, unending struggle between faith and reason.

Bibliography:
Baker, Armand F. "The God of Miguel de Unamuno." *Hispania* 74, no. 4 (December, 1991): 824-833. Draws upon *The Tragic Sense of Life in Men and in Peoples* to explicate Unamuno's theology of one deity, a "universal consciousness." Calls attention to similarities of Unamuno's work to Buddhism and to Jung's concept of the collective unconscious.
Ferrater Mora, José. *Unamuno: A Philosophy of Tragedy.* Translated by Philip Silver. Berkeley: University of California Press, 1962. An excellent introduction to Unamuno's thought. Discusses *The Tragic Sense of Life in Men and in Peoples* in detail, with attention to key themes.
Marías, Julián. *Miguel de Unamuno.* Translated by Frances M. Lopez-Morillas. Cambridge, Mass.: Harvard University Press, 1966. Discusses Unamuno's philosophy as a forerunner to existentialism. Chapter 8 makes frequent reference to *The Tragic Sense of Life in Men and in Peoples.*
Nozick, Martin. *Miguel de Unamuno.* New York: Twayne, 1971. A good introduction to Unamuno's life and works. In chapter 2 is a synopsis and critique of *The Tragic Sense of Life in Men and in Peoples.*

THE TRAVELS OF LAO TS'AN

Type of work: Novel
Author: Liu Ê (Liu T'ieh-yün, 1857-1909)
Type of plot: Social realism
Time of plot: End of the nineteenth century
Locale: Shantung Province in northeastern China
First transcribed: Lao Ts'an youji, serialized 1904-1907 (English translation, 1952; revised, 1990)

> *Principal characters:*
> LAO TS'AN, an itinerant intellectual
> SHEN TUNG-TSAO and
> HUANG JEN-JUI, decent officials
> KANG PI and
> YÜ HSIEN, incorruptible but ruthlessly ambitious officials of the hanging-judge type
> TS'UI-HUAN and
> TS'UI-HUA, young women of good family who become singsong girls after impoverishment resulting from floods
> YELLOW DRAGON, a hermit philosopher whose teachings synthesize tenets of Taoism, Buddhism, and Confucianism

The Story:

Lao Ts'an was an erudite and impoverished scholar of the late nineteenth century who used his skills in traditional Chinese medicine to earn a modest living in his native homeland of Shantung. Although he was only about thirty years old, his fame began to grow as more and more people heard about his successful treatment of Huang Jui-ho's running sores, which had long defied the ministrations of many other doctors. After Lao Ts'an adeptly cured a serious throat condition afflicting the concubine of an official named Kao, the official introduced the young man to his colleagues, including the governor of Shantung Province.

Lao Ts'an's conversation with the governor and other officials quickly turned from medicine to current events and politics. Two topics that arose during this conversation were the prosecutorial overzealousness of especially ambitious officials such as Yü Hsien and Kang Pi, who would rather err on the side of punishing many innocent citizens than in letting a single criminal go unpunished, and the ineffective policies of controlling the Yellow River's flooding. The governor was so impressed by Lao Ts'an's sensible views on these problems that he offered the young man an official post. Lao Ts'an politely declined, insisting that he preferred to offer advice in an informal capacity. Privately, Lao Ts'an realized that his fondness for frankly expressing his views on controversial topics would be difficult to maintain if he became an official. Also, he was not interested in the wealth and power, not to mention the restrictions on his independent way of life, that an official career would bring.

Through various inquiries, Lao Ts'an determined that Yü Hsien's harsh crackdown on banditry in the county of Ch'engwuhsien was resulting in the torture and execution of many innocents while not actually reducing the incidence of banditry there. Lao Ts'an thereupon managed to persuade one of Yü Hsien's well-meaning subordinates, Shen Tung-tsao, to take a personal letter from Lao Ts'an to one of his friends in the countryside who was well versed in martial arts and acquainted with many leaders of bandit gangs in the vicinity. As a favor to Lao Ts'an, his friend agreed with Shen Tung-tsao's request to move to Ch'engwuhsien and persuade the bandit gang leaders to stop preying upon the county's residents—in other words, to take their business elsewhere. The county's crime rate at once dropped, for the only bandit attacks that subsequently occurred involved isolated capers undertaken by the unskilled local criminal riff-raff. These criminal riff-raff were much easier to apprehend than members of the bandit gangs, and so the county's streets and alleys soon became among the safest in the entire province.

Lao Ts'an subsequently turned his attentions to the problem of the prosecutorial fervor of Yü Hsien and Kang Pi, which had resulted in so many wrongful convictions and executions of the innocent. Like a Chinese Sherlock Holmes, the young scholar shrewdly investigated the background of a murder case involving a respectable family in the district. At considerable risk of being arrested and tortured by Kang Pi, Lao Ts'an appeared at the latter's court to defend the wrongly accused. He was too late to save all of the family members from torture, but he did manage to uncover damning evidence against the true culprit, whom he ordered arrested and brought forth. By doing so, Lao Ts'an spared most of the wrongly accused from further torture and likely execution. The overzealous officials suffered judicial setback and a transfer to another post.

Two young women, Ts'ui-huan and Ts'ui-hua, were sold into a brothel as singsong girls after their families' impoverishment in the wake of the Yellow River's flooding. The kindly official Huang Jen-jui eventually convinced Lao Ts'an to redeem Ts'ui-huan from her brothel and take her as his lawfully betrothed concubine. Lao Ts'an subsequently returned the favor by setting up the already married Huang Jen-jui with Ts'ui-hua as his second wife. Premodern China's traditional acceptance of polygamy thus allowed this novel's loose ends to be tied together.

Critical Evaluation:

It had become a commonplace for Chinese novels of Liu Ê's day to castigate corrupt officials who would do practically anything in return for a bribe. While Liu Ê acknowledges the harm done by official malfeasance, he focuses on a less obvious but similarly grave betrayal of the public trust: that of the "honest" official who hankers after fame and promotion rather than mere profit, and whose conscience remains unruffled while imposing the most Draconian and indiscriminate crackdowns. As one of the most fascinating late nineteenth century scholarly entrepreneurs, whose achievements ranged from shrewd railway investments to the discovery of the Shang dynasty oracle bone script, Liu Ê had his share of run-ins with ruthless officials. Yuan Shih-k'ai, for example, used his influence to get the author arrested on trumped-up charges and exiled to Chinese Turkestan. There Liu Ê died, a victim of official arrogance, in 1909, a short time after completing his novel that satirized the abuse of power.

Liu Ê created a protagonist who embodied many of his own values. These included a conviction that traditional Chinese thought contained many insights that could be combined with aspects of Western thought to deal with the crises that China faced in the modern world. Just as Liu Ê admired the syncretist teachings of the T'ai-ku School, which combined the Three Teachings (Buddhism, Confucianism, and Taoism), Lao Ts'an finds the same ideas of a reclusive scholar nicknamed Yellow Dragon noteworthy. Yellow Dragon promulgates a middle way between the extremes of Europeanized Chinese revolutionaries, who want to sweep away all traditional Chinese ways, on the one hand, and backward-looking traditionalists such as the Boxers, who categorically reject all ideas from the West, on the other. Yellow Dragon argues that while the acceptance of certain Western ideas entails the rejection of negative aspects of traditional Chinese thought, China still needs to base its adaptation to global realities on the foundation of the most workable features of its traditional civilization.

As an example of a negative aspect of traditional Chinese civilization that should be rejected in favor of a Western approach, Lao Ts'an points to a friend's Chinese opium lamp. He does not do so to make the point that Chinese should not let themselves become addicted to drugs such as opium, although he quietly warns his friend of its addictive nature and refuses to smoke it whenever some is offered to him; Lao Ts'an instead marvels at the fine workmanship of the opium lamp and laments that China's lack of patent law means that excellent craftsmanship goes mostly unrewarded in China, in contrast to the situation in the West. In his view, China's technological backwardness in comparison with the West is due in considerable part to neglect of the need to reward invention and innovation.

Traditional Chinese thought also holds, in the novel, many answers to China's problems. For example, Lao Ts'an uses his knowledge of the ancient Han dynasty tracts on flood prevention to persuade key officials to discard the failed river management policy of widening the Yellow River's channel, which leads to rapid silt buildup on the riverbed, swollen riverbanks, and the subsequent bursting of dikes. He convinces the officials to adopt instead the wise approach of deepening the river channel through dredging, thereby increasing the speed of water flow and decreasing the amount of silt deposited on the river bed.

Perhaps the most striking aesthetic feature of the novel is its density of allegorical motifs. The name of the first patient Lao Ts'an cures, Huang Jui-ho, contains the two Chinese characters used for the "Yellow River," *huang* and *ho*. The sores breaking out all over his body are an allegory for the breaching of the dikes and flooding of the Yellow River valley. The successful healing of the sores is a reference to the decrease of flooding that occurs once the officials take his advice to dredge the middle of the Yellow River's channel so as to increase the speed of the water flow. Similarly, a dream Lao Ts'an has about a huge leaking sailboat on which puzzled helmsmen and a tumultuous crowd are milling about is an allegory for the state of confusion that overcame China in the last years of the Ch'ing dynasty (1644-1911). The passengers' violent rejection of Lao Ts'an's well-meant advice reflects the despair that Liu Ê sometimes felt about the possibilities of reform in China—a sadly accurate presentiment.

Philip F. Williams

Bibliography:
Dolezelova-Velingerova, Milena, ed. *The Chinese Novel at the Turn of the Century*. Toronto: University of Toronto Press, 1980. The chapter by Donald Holoch analyzes the two allegorical incidents in the novel's first chapter and claims that the remainder of the novel can be seen as a structural elaboration of these opening allegories.

Hsia, C. T. "*The Travels of Lao Ts'an*: An Exploration of Its Art and Meaning." *Tsing Hua Journal of Chinese Studies* 7, no. 2 (August, 1969). This article combines a thorough analysis of the novel's key aesthetic features with interesting historical research on the pro-Boxer-Rebellion officials who served as Liu Ê's models for Yü Hsien and Kang Pi, who run roughshod over the guilty and the innocent alike in order to garner fame as hanging judges.

Lang, D. M., and D. R. Dudley, eds. *The Penguin Companion to Classical, Oriental, and African Literature*. New York: McGraw-Hill, 1969. The section on Liu Ê emphasizes the stylistic advance represented by *The Travels of Lao Ts'an* in its highly original prose descriptions of landscape and musical performances.

Lu Hsün. *A Brief History of Chinese Fiction*. Translated by Yang Hsien-yi and Gladys Yang. Peking: Foreign Languages Press, 1976. This book's section on "novels of exposure" of the Ch'ing dynasty contains an analysis of *The Travels of Lao Ts'an*'s portrayal of the official Kang Pi, whose incorruptibility is offset by his autocratic and ruthless ways.

Shadick, Harold. Introduction to *The Travels of Lao Ts'an*, by Liu Ê. Rev. ed. New York: Columbia University Press, 1990. Includes updated introductory material. An excellent starting place.

THE TRAVELS OF MARCO POLO

Type of work: Autobiography
Author: Marco Polo (c. 1254-1324), as set down by the scribe, Rustichello
Type of plot: Adventure
Time of plot: 1260-1295
Locale: Greater Asia
First transcribed: Divisament dou monde, fourteenth century (English translation, 1579)

> *Principal characters:*
> NICOLO POLO, a Venetian merchant
> MAFFEO POLO, his brother
> MARCO POLO, Nicolo's son
> KUBLAI KHAN, the emperor of China

The Story:

Nicolo and Maffeo Polo set forth on their first trip to the East in 1260, with a cargo of merchandise for Constantinople. From there, they ventured on into the lands of the Tartar princes. Having at last reached the court of Kublai Khan, China's emperor, they managed to ingratiate themselves into his highest favor. During their stay, the khan questioned them about the Catholic faith and asked them to return to Europe and ask the pope to send missionaries to his distant land. In the year 1269, the two Polos arrived in Venice. There they learned that Pope Clement was dead, and that Nicolo Polo's wife had also died after giving birth to a son, Marco Polo.

There was a long delay in the naming of a new pope. At last, the Polos decided to return to Kublai Khan and to take young Marco with them. Scarcely had they left Italy, however, when word followed them that Gregory the Tenth had been elected in Rome. The Polos at once asked the new pope to send missionaries to Kublai Khan, and Gregory appointed two priests to accompany the merchants. Before their arrival at the khan's court, the priests turned back when confronted by strange lands and unknown dangers. Young Marco Polo remembered that the journey to the land of Kublai Khan took three and a half years.

Kublai Khan received them graciously and appointed Marco one of his attendants. In a short time, Marco Polo had learned four different languages, and he was sent by Kublai Khan on various important missions. For seventeen years, the Polos remained at the court of Kublai Khan before they expressed a desire to return to their own country with their wealth. They felt that if the great khan should die, they would be surrounded by envious princes who might harm them. The khan was unwilling to part with the Polos, but they managed to get his permission by offering to transport some barons to the East Indies. Fourteen ships were made ready for the homeward voyage. The expedition arrived at Java after about three months. Eighteen months more were required for the voyage to the territory of King Argon in the Indian seas. During the voyage, six hundred of the crew were lost as well as two of the barons. From there, the Polos took an overland route to Trebizond. En route, they learned that the great Kublai Khan was dead. The three arrived home safely in 1295, in possession of their wealth and in good health.

When the time came for him to dictate to the scribe, Rustichello, the story of his travels, Marco Polo remembered that Armenia was divided into two sections, the lesser and the greater. In Armenia Major was the mountain said to have been Mount Ararat, where Noah's ark came to rest. Near this place was a fountain of oil so great that caravans of camels hauled away the oil, which was used for an unguent as well as for heat and light.

At the boundaries of the province of Georgiania, Alexander the Great had had a gate of iron constructed. This gate, although not all of iron, was commonly said to have enclosed the Tartars between two mountains.

At Teflis was a fountain wherein hundreds of fish made their appearance from the first day of Lent until Easter Eve. During the remainder of the year, they were not to be seen. Baudas, or Baghdad, anciently known as Babylon, lay along the river that opened out upon the Sea of India. The city was one of the great cities of the world, and its ruler one of the richest men of all time. He lost his life through his unwillingness to spend a penny of his wealth for its protection. His captor locked him up in his tower, where he starved to death surrounded by gold. In that region, a Christian cobbler had caused a mountain to move and, by his miracle, converted many Arabs to Christianity.

In Irak, Marco Polo visited a monastery in which the monks wove woolen girdles said to be good for rheumatic pains. He also visited Saba, whence were said to have come the three Magi who adored Christ in Bethlehem. At Kierman, on the eastern confines of Persia, Marco saw the manufacture of steel and products in which steel was used. Much rich embroidery was also found there, as well as splendid turquoises. The Karaunas of the region had learned the diabolical art of producing darkness in order to obscure their approach to caravans they intended to rob.

At Ormus, Polo encountered a wind so hot that people exposed to it died. A whole army was once wiped out by the wind, and the inhabitants, seeking to bury the invaders, found the bodies baked so hard that they could not be moved. Bitter, undrinkable water, the tree of the sun, and the old man of the mountain were all of that region. The old man of the mountain used to administer drugs to young men to make them think they were truly in paradise. At his orders, they assassinated anyone who was not of the true faith. His followers held their own lives of little worth, convinced that they would return to Paradise upon their deaths.

On the overland route to Cathay, Marco met Nestorian Christians, as well as people who were part Christian and part Muhammadan. There he found a miraculous pillar said to remain upright without any visible means of support. In Peyn, he discovered chalcedony and jasper, as well as peculiar marriage customs. Passing over a desert, he heard strange sounds that were attributed to evil spirits but were later explained as the sounds of shifting sand dunes. At Kamul, he discovered the primitive hospitality of turning over houses and wives for the entertainment of strangers. At Chinchitalas, he discovered the use of material that would not burn; it was asbestos.

On the borders of the Gobi, the Polos gathered supplies for their trip through the desert. They passed close to the land of Prester John and heard the history of the war between Prester John and Genghis Khan. Marco saw the land of Tenduk, governed by the princes of the race of Prester John.

Kublai Khan was a great king who had rewarded generously those who had aided him in the conquest of other nations. Each noble so favored received a golden tablet inscribed by the khan for the protection of its wearer. Kublai Khan had four principal wives, plus a number of women who were given to him each year. He had some fifty sons, all of whom were appointed to high places in the empire. In the winter, the khan lived in Peking, in a magnificent palace that was eight miles square. His personal bodyguard consisted of twelve thousand horsemen.

Greatest in interest among his people were the Tibetans, who produced the scent of musk, used salt for money, and dressed in leather. Gold dust was found in their rivers, and among them were said to be sorcerers. Karazan was known for its huge serpents, or crocodiles, which the natives killed for hides and gall. This gall was a medicine for bites from mad dogs.

In Kardandan, Marco observed fathers who took over the nursing of babies. In the city of Mien, he saw two towers, one of silver and one of gold. Bengal he found rich in cotton, spikenard, galangal, ginger, sugar, and many drugs. The region also supplied many eunuchs.

For a time, Marco Polo held the government of the city of Yan-Gui upon orders of the khan. Nicolo and Maffeo Polo aided the khan in overcoming the city of Sa-Yan-Fu, the two Venetians having designed a catapult capable of hurling stones weighing as much as three hundred pounds.

Marco thought the city of Kin-sai, or Hang-chau, so beautiful that the inhabitants might imagine themselves in paradise. There were twelve thousand bridges over the canals and rivers of the city, and the houses were well-built and adorned with carved ornaments. The streets were paved with stone and brick. The people were greatly concerned with astrology. The inhabitants had provided for firefighters who kept a constant guard throughout the city. From this city, the khan received revenue of gold, salt, and sugar.

In the kingdom of Kon-cha, Marco found people who ate human flesh. He also found there a kind of chicken covered with black hair instead of feathers. He observed with much interest the manufacture of Chinese porcelain. In his travels, he saw the merchant ships of India, which were large and built in sections so that if one section sprang a leak, it could be closed off while repairs were made. On the island of Java he obtained pepper, nutmegs, spikenard, galangal, cubebs, cloves, and gold. Idolators lived there as well as cannibals. Elephants, rhinoceroses, monkeys, and vultures were in abundance. He also discovered that the natives pickled certain monkeys so that they resembled dead pygmies. These creatures were then sold as souvenirs to sailors and merchants.

In Lambri, he saw what he thought were men with tails. He also saw the sago tree, from which the natives made flour. On the island of Nocueran, he visited people living like naked beasts in trees. They possessed the red and white sandalwood, coconuts, sapanwood, and cloves. At Angaman, he saw more cannibals. In Ceylon, he found rubies, sapphires, topazes, amethysts, and garnets. The grave of Adam was believed to be on a high mountain in Ceylon.

Marco thought India the noblest and richest country in the world. Pearls were found in abundance. The kingdom of Murphili was rich in diamonds. In the province of Lac, he heard that people often lived to the age of one hundred fifty years and managed to preserve their teeth by a certain vegetable they chewed. In Kael, he found people chewing a leaf called tembul, sometimes mixed with camphor and other aromatic drugs as well as quicklime. At Cape Comorin, he found apes of such a size as to appear like men. At Malabar, he found gold brocades, silk, gauzes, gold, and silver. At Guzzerat, he discovered pirates of the worst character. In Bombay, he bought incense and horses.

Marco visited the island of Madagascar, where the inhabitants reported a bird so large it was able to seize an elephant in its talons. He thought the women of Zanzibar the ugliest in the world. The people did business in elephant teeth and tusks.

Marco recalled how Kublai Khan and his nephew, Kaidu, fought many battles for the possession of Great Turkey. More than a hundred thousand horsemen were brought to fight for each side. At first, Kaidu was victorious. Kaidu had a mannish daughter, Aigiarm, who battled with any man who wanted her for a bride. At last, she seized the man of her choice from the hosts of enemies in battle.

Marco believed that Russia was a region too cold to be pleasant. He spoke of trade in ermine, arcolini, sable, marten, fox, silver, and wax among the natives, who were included in the nation of the king of the Western Tartars. Marco Polo gave thanks to God that the travelers were able to see so much and return to tell about the marvels of many lands.

Critical Evaluation:

The story of Marco Polo's Asiatic journey is the most astounding of all travel books of Western civilization. One reason for its popularity is that Marco Polo did not mind mixing fiction and fact. Another is that he possessed in high degree a quality few travelers have ever had; he was able to see new things objectively.

The Travels of Marco Polo has been passed down in many manuscript versions, none of which is the original. Although it is nearly certain that the scribe Rustichello transcribed the original manuscript in French, extant manuscripts are in almost all of the Western European languages, the most important being those in French, Italian dialects, and Latin. None of the extant manuscripts is definitively complete; hence, much scholarly attention has been focused on speculation about what material was present in the original version and what material was interpolated by later scribes. At least an equal amount of attention has been focused upon trying to distinguish Marco Polo's observations from the embellishments of Rustichello. To some extent, Chinese historical records have been helpful in settling some of these questions. A lesser, although nevertheless vexing, problem arises in attempting to correlate Marco Polo's citation of personal names and place names with their modern-day equivalents and counterparts—a problem stemming from irregular orthography and compounded by transliteration from one alphabet to another as well as by other changes that have occurred, for example, Constantinople becoming Istanbul. The aggregate of these textual difficulties makes analysis and evaluation of Marco Polo's narrative tentative, at best.

One matter, however, is considerably less debatable than others: the place of *The Travels of Marco Polo* in literature. Marco Polo's account is, without doubt, soundly within the mainstream of medieval and Renaissance historical-travel literature. Geoffrey of Monmouth's *History of the Kings of Britain* (c. 1135-1139), Sir John Mandeville's *The Voyage and Travels of Sir John Mandeville, Knight* (c. 1356), and Richard Hakluyt's sixteenth century books on exploration, among others, join *The Travels of Marco Polo* to form the canon of this literary tradition. These and similar works share certain common features, most of which reflect the attitudes of the age: a mixture of fact and fantasy, a certain cultural ingenuousness, and a rather pervasive credulity about the supernatural. The modern reader is thus entitled to some legitimate skepticism about Marco Polo's report.

This report had the advantage of being designed for a Western readership largely ignorant about the East. Polo's overriding interest was to present the East as something interesting about which the West should learn. His motives were primarily commercial. Polo's access to information was limited by his having had contact exclusively with overlords; his judgments were based largely on mercantile and religious factors. He apparently was impervious to sociopolitical considerations, for his interest was in trade and merchandise, not in ideas. Consequently, the credibility of his eyewitness account was turned toward generating enthusiasm for finding a safe sea route to the East. Yet much of what Marco Polo had to say provides valuable insight into both Western medieval attitudes and contemporary conditions in the East.

Several significant issues are connected with these insights and attitudes, including the impact of Christianity on the East. Kublai Khan, for example, asked Nicolo and Maffeo Polo, on their earlier journey, to return with one hundred learned Christians (priests and scholars) to discuss Christianity with the wise men of the East. Yet Marco Polo recorded but two priests who came only part of the way with the Polos on their second, more important journey. Kublai Khan made other similar inquiries of Muslim scholars about Islam. One possible implication is that Kublai Khan—and thus the entire Chinese court—was not interested in evangelical Christianity and conversion to Christianity but was intellectually curious about foreign cultures and religions, Marco Polo's Christian biases notwithstanding.

Another issue revolves around Marco Polo's claim to have learned four of the languages of the Tartar nation. Probably he knew Mongol and Turkish—linguistically related languages. It is highly likely that he knew some Persian. The fourth language remains in doubt, but strong evidence suggests that he did not know Chinese. These language skills and limitations most certainly affected Polo's access to information, his perspective on his sources of information, and, as a result, his presentation of information.

Still another issue involves the spurious matter in Polo's account. He confused, for example, the locations of Alexander's barricade and the Great Wall of China with uncharacteristic geographical naïvete. He also included the Prester John legend with no empirical evidence to support it. The narrative refers to several high administrative posts that Marco Polo held under the appointment of Kublai Khan, although meticulously kept records of Chinese administrators and bureaucrats reveal no such appointments. Yet it is likely that Polo did execute some brief missions for the Khan. In addition, while Polo noted the ubiquity of rice in the diet throughout the East, he did not refer to the equally important tea, nor did he mention the well-developed art of Chinese printing—both of which could hardly have escaped his notice. Despite these inaccuracies and inconsistencies, Polo's narrative presents a generally correct picture of conditions in the East, as corroborated by other historical records.

Finally, the issue of cultural judgments reveals that Polo categorized people on the basis of religion rather than by ethnic origin or color. Polo distinguished among Jews, Christians, Muslims, and idolatrous heathens (Buddhists and Hindus, for the most part), but he had no patience for intrafaith disputes, even among Christians. As a consequence, he proved a remarkably tolerant person, a good quality for a traveler, for he made no evaluations along racial or cultural lines. Even his judgment that certain African peoples were ugly was an aesthetic pronouncement rather than a racial slur, because he did not consider them inferior. Grouping people according to their religious beliefs was a reasonably typical approach in Marco Polo's day, when religious affiliation was the crux of all matters. Cultural, racial, and ethnic considerations did not emerge as controversial questions until modern times. In this sense, Polo, like his contemporaries, may be considered, in a sense, tolerant.

These aspects of *The Travels of Marco Polo* barely scratch the surface of this remarkable literary document, an extraordinarily rewarding tale that has much to offer, not only for the historian and the student of literature but also for the thoughtful modern citizen.

"Critical Evaluation" by Joanne G. Kashdan

Bibliography:
Cordier, Henri. *The Book of Ser Marco Polo the Venetian Concerning the Kingdoms and Marvels of the East.* Translated and edited by Sir Henry Yule. 3d ed. Rev. New York: Charles Scribner's Sons, 1903. A two-volume scholarly work in the classic tradition. Extensive footnotes, drawings, engravings, maps, and photographs to illustrate each chapter of Polo's work. Comprehensive historical information and striking visual images.
_____. *Ser Marco Polo: Notes and Addenda.* London: John Murray, 1920. Corrections, clarifications, and additions to the 1903 text. Further clarification of place names and people named in *The Travels of Marco Polo.*

Komroff, Manuel. Introduction to *The Travels of Marco Polo (The Venetian)*. New York: Boni and Liveright, 1926. General introduction to the life and work of Marco Polo. Includes historical background of the period, the emperor of Asia, Kublai Khan, and how the book came to be written.

Mitchell, J. Leslie. *Earth Conquerors: The Lives and Achievements of the Great Explorers*. New York: Simon & Schuster, 1934. Chapter 3 is an overview of Marco Polo's travels and their historical context. Includes a map of his journeys and a portrait of Polo. Good general introduction for the beginning student of Polo.

Rugoff, Milton. Introduction to *The Travels of Marco Polo*. New York: The New American Library, 1961. A solid introduction to Polo's life and work. Discusses the influence of the book as the first to "pull the veil off the East."

TREASURE ISLAND

Type of work: Novel
Author: Robert Louis Stevenson (1850-1894)
Type of plot: Adventure
Time of plot: 1740's
Locale: England and the Spanish Main
First published: serial, 1881-1882; book, 1883

Principal characters:
JIM HAWKINS, the cabin boy of the *Hispaniola*
DR. LIVESEY, a physician and Jim's friend
SQUIRE TRELAWNEY, a wealthy landowner
MR. SMOLLETT, the captain of the *Hispaniola*
LONG JOHN SILVER, the leader of the mutineers
BEN GUNN, a pirate

The Story:

Young Jim Hawkins always remembered the day the strange seaman, Bill Bones, came looking for lodgings at his father's inn, the Admiral Benbow. He came plodding up to the inn door, where he stood for a time and looked around Black Hill Cove. Jim heard him singing snatches of an old sea song: "Fifteen men on the dead man's chest, Yo-ho-ho, and a bottle of rum." When he learned from Jim's father that the inn was a quiet one with little trade, he declared it was just the berth for an old seaman. From that time, the strange guest—a retired captain he called himself—kept watch on the coast and the land road by day and made himself free in the taproom of the inn at night. There he drank and sang and swore great oaths while he told fearsome tales of the Spanish Main. Bones was wary of all visiting seamen, and he paid Jim Hawkins to be on the lookout for a one-legged sailor in particular. He was so terrible in his speech and manners that Jim's father, a sick man, never had the courage to ask for more than the one reckoning Bill Bones had paid the day he came to the inn. He stayed on without ever clinking another coin into the inn's till for his meals and lodging.

The one-legged sailor never came to the inn, but another seaman named Black Dog did. The two men fought in the inn parlor, to the terror of Jim and his mother, before Captain Bones chased his visitor up the road and out of sight. He fell down in a fit when he came back to the inn. Doctor Livesey came in to attend to Jim's father and cautioned Captain Bones to contain himself and drink less.

Jim's father died soon afterward. On the day of the funeral, a deformed blind man named Pew tapped his way up to the door of the Admiral Benbow. The man forced Jim to lead him to the captain. Bill Bones was so terrified when the blind man gave him the Black Spot, the pirates' death notice, that he had a stroke and died. Jim and his mother took the keys to his sea chest from the dead man's pocket and opened it to find the money due them. As they were examining the contents, they heard the tapping of the blind man's stick on the road. Jim pocketed an oilskin packet, and he and his mother left hurriedly by the back door of the inn as a gang of men broke in to search for Captain Bones's chest. Mounted revenue officers arrived and scattered the gang. Blind Pew was trampled to death by the charging horses.

Jim gave the packet to Dr. Livesey and Squire Trelawney. The three discovered that it contained a map locating the hidden treasure of the bloody buccaneer, Captain Flint. Squire

Trelawney was intrigued and decided to outfit a ship in which to sail after the treasure. The doctor threw in his lot and invited Jim to come along as cabin boy. In Bristol, Trelawney purchased a schooner, the *Hispaniola*, and hired Long John Silver as the ship's cook. Silver promised to supply a crew. Jim went to Bristol and met Silver, who had only one leg. He was alarmed when he saw Black Dog again in the inn operated by Silver, but Silver's smooth talk quieted Jim's suspicions.

After the *Hispaniola* had sailed, Captain Smollett, hired by Squire Trelawney to command the ship, expressed his dislike of the first mate and the crew and complained that Silver had more real authority with the crew than he did. One night, Jim, having fallen into a barrel while reaching for an apple, overheard Silver discussing mutiny with members of the crew. Before Jim had a chance to reveal the plot to his friends, the island was sighted.

The prospects of treasure on the island caused the disloyal members of the crew to pay little attention to Captain Smollett's orders; even the loyal ones were hard to manage. Silver shrewdly kept his party under control. The captain wisely allowed part of the crew to go ashore; Jim smuggled himself along in order to spy on Silver and the men on the island. Ashore, Silver killed two of the crew who refused to join the mutineers. Jim, alone, met Ben Gunn, who was with Captain Flint when the treasure was buried. Gunn told Jim that he had been marooned on the island three years previously.

While Jim was ashore, Dr. Livesey went to the island and found Captain Flint's stockade. When he heard the scream of one of the men Silver murdered, he returned to the *Hispaniola*, where it was decided that the honest men would move to the fort within the stockade. Several dangerous trips in an overloaded boat completed the move. During the last trip, the mutineers aboard the ship unlimbered the ship's gun. Squire Trelawney shot one seaman from the boat. In the meantime, the gang ashore saw what was afoot and made efforts to keep Jim's friends from occupying the stockade. Squire Trelawney and his party took their posts in the fort after the enemy had been repulsed. The mutineers on the *Hispaniola* fired one shot into the stockade but did little damage.

After leaving Ben Gunn, the marooned seaman, Jim made his way to the stockade. The *Hispaniola* now flew the Jolly Roger skull and crossbones pirate flag. Carrying a flag of truce, Silver approached the stockade and offered to parley. He was admitted by the defenders and demanded the treasure chart in exchange for the safe return of Squire Trelawney's party to England. Captain Smollett would concede nothing, and Silver returned to his men in a rage. The stockade party prepared for the coming battle. A group of the pirates attacked from two sides, swarmed over the paling, and engaged the defenders in hand-to-hand combat. In the close fighting, the pirates were reduced to one man, who fled back to his gang in the jungle. The loyal party was reduced to Squire Trelawney, Dr. Livesey, Captain Smollett, and Jim.

During the lull after the battle, Jim sneaked off and borrowed Ben Gunn's homemade boat. He rowed out to the *Hispaniola* under cover of darkness and cut the schooner adrift. In trying to return to shore, he was caught offshore by coastal currents. Daylight came, and Jim could see that the Hispaniola was also aimlessly adrift. When the ship bore down upon him, he jumped to the bowsprit. Ben Gunn's little boat was smashed. Jim found himself on board alone with pirate Israel Hands, who had been wounded in a fight with another pirate. Jim took command and proceeded to beach the ship. Pursued by Hands, he climbed quickly to a crosstree just before Hands threw his knife into the mast not more than a foot below Jim as he climbed. Jim had time to prime and reload his pistols, and he shot the pirate after he had pinned the boy to the mast with another knife throw.

Jim removed the knife from his shoulder, made the ship safe by removing the sails, and returned to the stockade at night, only to find it abandoned by his friends and now in the hands of the pirates. When Silver's parrot, Captain Flint, drew attention to the boy's presence, the pirates captured him. Dissatisfied with the buccaneer's methods of gaining the treasure, Silver's men grumbled. One attempted to kill Jim, who had bragged to them of his exploits on behalf of his friends. For reasons of his own, Silver, however, took the boy's side and swore he also would take the part of Squire Trelawney. Silver's disaffected mates met Silver, gave him the Black Spot, and deposed him as their chief. The pirate leader talked his way out of his difficulty by showing them, to Jim's amazement and to their delight, Captain Flint's chart of Treasure Island.

Dr. Livesey came under a flag of truce to the stockade to administer to the wounded pirates. He learned from Jim that Silver had saved the boy's life, and Jim heard, to his mystification, that the doctor had given Captain Flint's chart to Silver. Following the directions of the chart, the pirates went to find the treasure. They approached the hiding place and heard a high voice singing the pirate chantey, "Yo-ho-ho, and a bottle of rum." The voice also spoke the last words of Captain Flint. The men were terrified until Silver recognized Ben Gunn's voice. Then the pirates found the treasure cache opened and the treasure gone. When they uncovered only a broken pick and some boards, they turned on Silver and Jim. At this moment, Jim's friends, with Ben Gunn, arrived to rescue the boy.

Early in his stay on the island Ben Gunn had discovered the treasure and carried it to his cave. After Dr. Livesey had learned all of this from Gunn, the stockade was abandoned and the useless chart given to Silver. Squire Trelawney's party moved to Gunn's safe and well-provisioned quarters. The *Hispaniola* had been floated by a tide; consequently, the group left Treasure Island, leaving on it three escaped buccaneers. They sailed to a West Indies port where, with the connivance of Ben Gunn, John Silver escaped the ship with a bag of coins. A full crew was taken on board, and the schooner sailed back to Bristol. There the treasure was divided among the survivors of the adventure.

Critical Evaluation:

Although Robert Louis Stevenson produced a large number and variety of writings during his relatively short life and was considered a serious adult author in his own day, he is largely remembered now as the writer of one gothic horror story, *The Strange Case of Dr. Jekyll and Mr. Hyde* (1886), and two boys' books, *Treasure Island* and *Kidnapped* (1886). Such a view is undoubtedly unfair and slights many valuable literary accomplishments, but the fact that these three works have endured not only as citations in literary histories but also as readable, exciting, essentially contemporary books is a tribute to their author's genius. *Treasure Island* remains Stevenson's supreme achievement of the three works. Although critics may debate its seriousness, few question its status as the purest of adventure stories. According to Stevenson, the book was born out of his fascination with a watercolor map he himself drew of an imaginary island.

When Jim Hawkins begins by stating that he is telling the story in retrospect, at the request of "Squire Trelawney, Doctor Livesey, and the rest of these gentlemen," readers are assured that all the principals survived the quest successfully, thus giving readers that security necessary in a romantic adventure intended primarily for young people. Although many exciting scenes will ensue and the heroes will face great danger on a number of occasions, readers know that they will overcome all such obstacles. Thus, the suspense centers on how they escape, not on their personal survival as such. At the same time, by denying details of either the precise time of the adventure or the exact location, Stevenson sets readers imaginatively free to enjoy the story unencumbered by the specifics of when or where.

By introducing the mysterious, threatening Bill Bones into the serene atmosphere of the Admiral Benbow Inn, Stevenson immerses readers directly into the story. The strange secret of Bones's background and nature creates the novel's initial excitement, which is then intensified by his apparent fear and subsequent encounters with Black Dog and Blind Pew. In all, the sequence that begins with Billy's arrival and ends with Pew's death serves as an overture to the adventure and sets up most of the important elements in the story, especially Captain Flint's map, which directs the group to Treasure Island, and the warnings to beware of "the seafaring man with one leg," which prepares readers for the archvillain of the tale, Long John Silver.

In the classic adventure story pattern, an ordinary individual, Jim Hawkins, living a normal, routine life, is suddenly thrust into an extraordinary and dangerous situation, which soon gets beyond the control of the individual and his cohorts. Although the hero is involuntarily pressed into danger, he nevertheless can extricate himself and return the situation to normality only through his efforts. The adventure story is, therefore, usually to some extent a "coming of age" novel, whether the hero be fourteen years old or sixty-four years old.

Near the beginning of the book, the death of Jim's father frees Jim to seek his fortune and places the responsibility upon him to find it for the sake of his widowed mother. Without a father of his own, Jim can look to the other male father-figures as substitutes. He finds two: Doctor Livesey, who represents stability, maturity, and moral responsibility, and John Silver, who suggests imagination, daring, bravado, and energy. Between these two and, more important, through his own actions, Jim finds his own adulthood along with the treasure.

Jim's education begins with the act of searching the belongings of the dead Bill Bones despite the proximity of Pew's pirate band. To accomplish this feat, however, he needs his mother's support. Once the *Hispaniola* sets sail, however, he is on his own. The next stage in his growth occurs when, crouching in the apple barrel, he overhears Silver reveal his plans to his coconspirators. Jim keeps calm, coolly informs his friends, and, with them, devises survival tactics. His initial positive, independent action takes place when they first reach the island and he goes off on his own, without a specific plan, but he is sure that he can further the cause in some undetermined way. He wanders in the woods and meets Ben Gunn, rejoins his party at the stockade, and engages in his first combat.

Next, Jim makes a second solo trip, but this time he has a definite course of action in mind; he plans to board the *Hispaniola* and cut it loose to drift with the tide, thus depriving the pirates of a refuge and an escape route. His final test in action comes onboard the boat when he encounters the evil first mate, Israel Hands. When Hands tries to manipulate him, Jim sees through the deception and, acting with considerable courage and dexterity, manages to outmaneuver the experienced pirate. Finally, faced with an enraged adversary, Jim remains calm and, with a knife sticking in his shoulder, still manages to shoot the villain.

His final test of adulthood is not physical, however, but moral. Returning to the stockade, which he still believes to be occupied by his friends, Jim is captured by the pirates. Given the opportunity a short time later to talk privately with Dr. Livesey, Jim refuses to escape: "No . . . you know right well you wouldn't do the thing yourself, neither you, nor squire, nor captain, and no more will I. Silver trusted me, I passed my word, and back I go." Therefore, Jim puts his word above his life, and consequently he signals the transition not just from boy to man but, more important to Stevenson, from boy to gentleman.

Although Jim's development is important to the novel, the most vivid and memorable element in the book remains the character of Long John Silver. All critics have noted that he is both bad and good, cruel and generous, despicable and admirable. Some have tried to fuse these elements into a single character "type," a "hero-villain," in which the good and the bad are traced back to a common source. Such an effort is probably wrong. Silver is both good and bad, and his role in the novel demands both kinds of actions. Rather than try to "explain" Silver psychologically, it is probably more profitable to analyze the ways in which Stevenson manipulates the readers' feelings toward the character.

In any pirate story, the author faces a moral and artistic dilemma. On the one hand, pirates can hardly be presented as moral exemplars or heroes; they must be criminals and cutthroats. On the other hand, they are romantically attractive and interesting characters. Enhance their attractiveness and the book becomes morally distorted; mute it and the book becomes dull.

One solution to the dilemma is to mitigate their badness by introducing an element of moral ambiguity into the characterization and behavior of some of them without denying the evil effects of their actions and then to separate the "good-bad" villains from the "bad-bad" ones. Stevenson uses this technique in *Treasure Island*. Silver is separated from his purely villainous cronies and set against the truly evil figures, Israel Hands and George Merry, with the faceless pirates remaining in the background.

Stevenson mitigates Silver's evil side with two simple strategies: He presents the ruthless, cruel aspects of Silver's character early in the novel and lets his "better" side reveal itself late in the book, and he keeps the "evil" Silver at a distance and gives readers an intimate view only of the relatively good Long John. Therefore, although readers never forget the viciousness of Long John's early words and deeds, they recede into the background as the adventure progresses.

Readers are prepared for the bad Long John Silver by the many early warnings to beware of the "one legged man." Then readers see him manipulate Squire Trelawney and even Jim in their first encounters. Therefore, readers admire his role-playing but fear the conspiratorial evil that obviously lies behind it. Silver's overt treachery is evident in the apple barrel scene, especially in his callous "vote" to kill all the nonconspirators when given the chance. Long John reaches the peak of his villainy in the killing of a sailor who refuses to join the mutiny, first stunning the sailor with his crutch and then knifing him to death.

Even these two evidences of Silver's badness, however, are seen at a distance, from inside an apple barrel and from behind a clump of trees. When Long John moves to the center of the novel and assumes an intimate relationship with Jim, his character is automatically softened, and by the time Silver and Jim become unwilling partners in survival, the pirate's image and status have considerably changed.

The early view of Silver is that he is not only evil but invincible. As he becomes less one-dimensionally evil, he becomes progressively vulnerable, and vulnerability always stimulates sympathy in a reader, regardless of the character's moral status. As the tide begins to turn against the pirates, Silver begins to lose control not only of the treasure-hunting expedition but even of his own men. This erosion of power is signaled by an increasing emphasis on his physical disability. The John Silver who must crawl on his hands and knees out of the stockade, after the failure of his "embassy," is a far cry from the Silver who can knock down an opponent with a flying crutch and then pounce on him like an animal.

Silver's glibness and adroitness in manipulating the good men of the *Hispaniola* were components of his villainy in the first parts of the book, but when Silver is threatened by a mutiny of his own men and must utilize those same talents to save himself and Jim, they become positive virtues. Although he is obviously motivated by an instinct for self-preservation, Silver does protect Jim from the others and conveys a feeling of honestly liking and wanting to help the lad.

Thus, the morally ambiguous ending of the novel is the only one artistically possible. John

Silver has not been bad enough to hang, and it is hard to imagine his vitality stifled in prison; yet if he has edged away from the villains, he hardly qualifies as a hero. He is neither punished nor greatly rewarded for his machinations and heroics but left to seek another fortune elsewhere.

"Critical Evaluation" by Keith Neilson

Bibliography:
Eigner, Edwin M. *Robert Louis Stevenson and Romantic Tradition*. Princeton, N.J.: Princeton University Press, 1966. Places Stevenson and *Treasure Island* in the Romantic tradition established in the eighteenth century and defends him from the criticism of F. R. Leavis, who did much to lower Stevenson's reputation in the mid-twentieth century.
Hellman, George S. *The True Stevenson: A Study in Clarification*. New York: Haskell House Publishers, 1972. A reprint of a 1925 study which draws upon Stevenson's letters, conversations with his contemporaries, and his wife's letters to elucidate points about the author and *Treasure Island*.
Leatham, James. *The Style of Louis Stevenson*. Folcroft, Pa.: Folcroft Press, 1970. A reprint of a 1908 study which considers Stevenson's style, vocabulary, and use of Scottish idioms. An examination of Stevenson's style and usage by a near contemporary in age and background.
McLynn, Frank. *Robert Louis Stevenson: A Biography*. London: Hutchinson, 1993. The most comprehensive biography of Stevenson up to its date of publication. Considers the impact of Stevenson's childhood and young adulthood on *Treasure Island*. Examines the sources for his story and characters and the immediate success of the work with the public.
Saposnik, Irving S. *Robert Louis Stevenson*. New York: Twayne, 1974. A good critical overview of Stevenson's work which places *Treasure Island* properly in his entire canon. Connects the character Jim Hawkins to other youthful Stevenson heroes in *Kidnapped* and *The Black Arrow* (1888). Contains a good study of the character Long John Silver.

A TREE GROWS IN BROOKLYN

Type of work: Novel
Author: Betty Smith (1896-1972)
Type of plot: Bildungsroman
Time of plot: Early twentieth century
Locale: Brooklyn, New York
First published: 1943

Principal characters:
 FRANCIE NOLAN, a Brooklyn girl
 NEELEY NOLAN, her brother
 KATIE NOLAN, her mother
 JOHNNY NOLAN, her father

The Story:

For their spending money Francie and Neeley Nolan relied on a few pennies they collected from the junk collector every Saturday. Katie, their mother, worked as a janitor in a Brooklyn tenement, and the money she and their father earned—he from his Saturday night jobs as a singing waiter—was barely enough to keep the family alive and clothed.

After their Saturday morning trips with the rags, metal, and rubber they had collected during the week, Francie would visit the library. She was methodically going through its contents in alphabetical order by reading a book each day, but on Saturdays she allowed herself the luxury of breaking the sequence. At home, sitting on the fire escape, she could look up from her book and watch her neighbors' preparations for Saturday night. A tree grew in the yard; Francie watched it from season to season during her long Saturday afternoons.

At five o'clock, when her father came home, Francie would iron his waiter's apron and then go to the dry-goods store to buy the paper collar and muslin dickey which would last him for the evening. It was her special Saturday night privilege to sleep in the front room, and there she could watch the people in the street. She got up briefly at two in the morning when her father came home and was given a share of the delicacies he had salvaged from the wedding or party at which he had served. Then, while her parents talked far into the night, Francie would fix Saturday's happenings in her mind and gradually drift off to sleep.

Johnny Nolan and Katie Rommely had met when he was nineteen and she was seventeen, and they were married four months later. In a year's time, Francie was born. Johnny, unable to bear the sight of Katie in labor, had got drunk, and when the water pipes burst at the school in which he was janitor, he was discharged. Neeley was born soon after Francie's first birthday. By that time, Johnny was drinking so heavily that Katie knew she could no longer rely on him for the family's support. In return for free rent, the Nolans moved to a house in which Katie could be janitor.

Francie was not sent to school until she was seven, and Neeley was old enough to go with her. In that way the children were able to protect each other from would-be tormentors. Seated two-at-a-desk among the other poverty-stricken children, Francie soon grew to look forward to the weekly visits of her art and music teachers. They were the sunshine of her school days.

By pretending that Francie had gone to live with relatives, Johnny was able to have her transferred to another school that Francie had seen on one of her walks. A long way from home, it was, nevertheless, an improvement over the old one. Most of the children were of American parentage and were not exploited by cruel teachers, as were those from immigrant families.

Francie noted time by holidays. Beginning the year with the Fourth of July and its firecrackers, she looked forward next to Halloween. Election Day, with its snake dances and bonfires, came soon after. Then followed Thanksgiving Day, on which the children disguised themselves with costumes and masks and begged trifles from storekeepers. Soon afterward came Christmas. The year Francie was ten and Neeley nine, they stood together on Christmas Eve while the biggest tree in the neighborhood was thrown at them. Trees unsold at that time were thrown at anyone who volunteered to stand against the impact. Bruised and scratched, Francie and her brother proudly dragged their tree home.

The week before Christmas, when Francie had just become fourteen, Johnny staggered home drunk. Two days later, he was found, huddled in a doorway, ill with pneumonia. The next day he was dead. After the funeral, Neeley was given his father's ring and Francie his shaving mug, his only keepsakes aside from his two waiter's aprons. To his wife, Johnny left a baby, due to be born the following spring.

In March, when their funds were running low, Katie cashed the children's insurance policies. The twenty-five dollars she received carried them through until the end of April. Then Mr. McGarrity, at whose saloon Johnny had done most of his drinking, came to their rescue. He hired Neeley to help prepare free lunches after school and Francie to do housework, and the money the children earned was enough to tide them over until after Katie's baby was born.

Laurie was born in May. In June, after their graduation from grade school, Francie and Neeley found their first real jobs, Neeley as errand boy for a brokerage house and Francie as a stemmer in a flower factory. Dismissed two weeks later, she became a file clerk in a clipping bureau. She was quickly advanced to the position of reader.

In the fall, there was not enough money to send both her children to high school, and Katie decided that the more reluctant Neeley should go. With the money Francie earned and with Neeley's after-school job at McGarrity's saloon, the Nolans had more comforts that Christmas than they had ever known before. The house was warm; there was enough food; and there was money for presents. Fourteen-year-old Neeley received his first pair of spats, and Francie almost froze in her new black lace lingerie when they went to church on Christmas morning.

When the clipping bureau closed with the outbreak of the war, Francie got a job as a teletype operator. By working at night, she was able to take advanced college credits in summer school that year. With the help of a fellow student, Ben Blake, she passed her chemistry and English courses. Francie was eighteen when she had her first real date, with a soldier named Lee Rhynor. The evening he was to leave to say good-bye to his parents before going overseas, Lee asked her to marry him when he returned. Francie promised to write him every day. Three days later, she received a letter from the girl he had married during his trip home.

Katie also had a letter that day. Officer McShane had long been fond of Katie. Now retired, he asked her to marry him. All the Nolans agreed to this proposal. As the time approached for the wedding, Francie resigned her job. With Katie married, she intended to go to Michigan to college, for with Ben Blake's help, she had succeeded in passing the entrance exams.

The day before Katie was to be wed, Francie put the baby in the carriage and walked down the avenue. For a time she watched the children carting their rubbish into the junk shop. She turned in her books at the library for the last time. She saw another little girl, a book in her hand, sitting on a fire escape. In her own yard, the tree had been cut down because the tenants had complained that it was in the way of their wash, but from its stump a shoot was growing.

Critical Evaluation:

A Tree Grows in Brooklyn was Betty Smith's most popular work. A playwright as well as a novelist, she later adapted *A Tree Grows in Brooklyn* for stage and screen. The novel explores the development of the protagonist, Francis Nolan. Francie is born as the twentieth century begins. Her story mirrors the times. For example, there are advances in medicine and technology (as evidenced by Aunt Sissy's abandoning of the traditional midwife for a hospital birth and Francie's learning to operate teletype machines). When World War I begins, Francie falls in love with a young soldier. These advances and events, however, serve only as a backdrop for the novel. Francie's times are not an essential element of the plot, but a backdrop for Francie's growth.

In *A Tree Grows in Brooklyn*, Smith has constructed a type of *Bildungsroman* in which the novel centers on a hero who grows to maturity and finds purpose through experiences. In short, a *Bildungsroman* is about growing up. Smith's novel contains biographical elements. Like her protagonist, she was raised in Brooklyn and struggled to obtain an education. Smith's tale chronicles Francie's development as she learns about life from her mother's family, the Rommelys. Her grandmother, an immigrant from Austria, grieved when her daughters bore daughters because she knew that to be "born a woman meant a life of humble hardship." Smith describes Francie's mother and her aunts (Evy and Sissy) as slender, frail creatures, yet Smith asserts that the women are made of "thin . . . steel."

The women are strong while often the men are weak. For example, Francie's father drinks too much and lacks strength of character. He cannot assume responsibility for himself or his family. His redeeming qualities are his singing talent and his passion for beauty. These qualities are not enough to sustain him or his family. Similarly, Francie's Aunt Evy is married to Willie Flittman, an unstable, "whimpery" man. His ill-temper creates difficulty for him and his family. Even the horse that pulls Willie's milkcart treats him with disrespect. At the close of the novel, Willie manages to "flit" away, deserting his wife and children to perform as a one-man band.

The female characters are responsible for the successful rearing of the children. Smith asserts that Johnny hailed from a family grown frail. His mother tried to keep her sons for herself. Consequently, all four Nolan boys were dead before they reached thirty-five. Unable to sustain itself, the Nolan family line collapsed. In contrast, Francie's mother Katie is confident that her son Neeley will not become a failure like his father Johnny. She relies on the contribution of her own character and nurturing to produce a stronger son than her mother-in-law Mrs. Nolan raised. Unlike Mrs. Nolan, Katie's motives are generous rather than selfish. She attempts to prepare her children for achievement. Francie's Grandmother Rommely sent her daughters to grammar school; Katie aims for high school diplomas for her children, knowing that education will provide opportunity for them to achieve a better life. The hope for future generations lies in the influence of the mothers rather than the fathers.

The theme of Smith's novel is survival. Some characters are ill-equipped to overcome poverty and hardship; others thrive. A sense of pride is required for survival and independence, but the story suggests that additional resources are needed. Strength of character and the ability to love and nurture others are critical elements for those characters who succeed. Smith seems to suggest that people cannot prosper unless they are complete emotionally and psychologically, and "love instincts" contribute to making them whole. Consequently, Mr. McShane marries Katie Nolan at the close of the novel because he needs someone to love. When Francie ponders her relationship with Ben Blake, she longs for a reciprocal relationship in which she not only needs someone but also that someone needs her.

Although generally women in the novel are better than men, women without "love instincts" are portrayed in less than complimentary roles. For example, the narrator comments that in 1908 the school system was a brutal one. Married women were not allowed to teach, leaving only those women made "neurotic by starved love instincts." In addition, the librarian at the local library is characterized as a woman who is indifferent to children. She never learns the patrons' names, never looks a child in the eye, and recommends the same book for eleven-year-old girls year after year. Even Francie's Aunt Sissy does not settle down to "normal" life until she has a family of her own to nurture.

The harsh environment of Brooklyn serves as a crucible that tests the characters. Their neighborhood is a microcosm in which Jewish shopkeepers spit and curse to protest the bargaining of the poor gentile customers. Irish, German, and Polish immigrants struggle to earn a living among the tenement dwellings. Francie loves Brooklyn, but once she crosses the bridge into New York her world enlarges. She meets a soldier going off to fight in World War I, and he breaks her heart. She learns about life from her job reading newspaper clippings, and she knows that she can never return to the small world she knew as a child. Thus, she attempts to leap from childhood to adulthood by trying to enroll in college without ever having attended high school. At the close of the novel, the family leaves Brooklyn. Francie's mother will live a prosperous life with her second husband, Officer McShane, and Francie will attend college in another state, thus expanding her sphere beyond the confines of New York. Francie makes it out of the tenement.

Smith asserts that Brooklyn is where the "Tree of Heaven" grows. The tree sprouts in empty lots, trash heaps, and tenements. When Francie leaves Brooklyn, the tree is still there flourishing—a symbol of the human spirit that continues in the face of adversity. Like Francie, the tree survives in a hostile environment. The novel ends as it began. Another eleven-year-old girl reads from the fire escape, and the young adult Francie sees herself in the girl. Smith closes the novel by emphasizing the universality of existence. Just as the scrubby tree sprouts new shoots, new generations of young girls emerge to learn of life as Francie has.

"Critical Evaluation" by Paula M. Miller

Bibliography:
Gelfant, Blanche H. "Sister to Faust: The City's 'Hungry' Woman as Heroine." In *Women Writers and the City: Essays in Feminist Literary Criticism*, edited by Susan Merrill Squier. Knoxville: University of Tennessee Press, 1984. Examines the common attributes of female protagonists such as Francie Nolan, whose physical hunger parallels her longing for knowledge and self awareness.

Ginsberg, Elaine K. "Betty Wehner Smith." In *American Women Writers: A Critical Reference Guide from Colonial Times to the Present*. Edited by Lina Mainiero. 4 vols. New York: Frederick Ungar, 1982. Gives facts about Smith's professional career and her works, including a brief assessment of *A Tree Grows in Brooklyn*.

Pearlman, Mickey. "Betty Smith." In *Biographical Dictionary of Contemporary Catholic Writing*, edited by Daniel J. Tynan. Westport, Conn.: Greenwood Press, 1989. Discusses the biographical elements of *A Tree Grows in Brooklyn* and includes background information regarding Smith's similarity to the protagonist Francie Nolan.

Prescott, Orville. "Outstanding Novels." *The Yale Review* 33, no. 1 (Autumn, 1943): 6-12. Provides an assessment of Smith's character development within the novel and examines the elements of local color or regionalism in the work.

Sullivan, Richard. "Brooklyn, Where the Tree Grew." *The New York Times Book Review*, August 22, 1948, 1. A comparison of the common elements in *A Tree Grows in Brooklyn* and Smith's later work. Focuses on related themes, settings and characters, emphasizing the superiority of the first novel.

THE TREE OF MAN

Type of work: Novel
Author: Patrick White (1912-1990)
Type of plot: Parable
Time of plot: Twentieth century
Locale: Australia
First published: 1955

Principal characters:
STAN PARKER, an Australian farmer
AMY, his wife
THELMA, their daughter
RAY, their son
MRS. O'DOWD, a neighbor

The Story:

Wanting to start a new life, young Stan Parker left the Australian bush town where he grew up and traveled to an unsettled area outside of Sydney. Both of his parents were dead, and he refused to follow in his father's footsteps as a blacksmith. Nor did he want to remain in the confining atmosphere of the town. He had inherited some property in another area, and he planned to develop the acreage into a farm. He cleared the land, planted crops, and built himself a shack.

Lonely in the wilderness, he visited some relatives in a town, and at a dance there met a simple girl named Amy. After a brief courtship, the two were married one morning, drove in a wagon across the countryside all day, and settled that evening on the primitive farm, where they remained the rest of their lives.

They both worked hard and made improvements to their property as the early years of their marriage passed. The major event to take place outside of their immediate lives was the great flood, which fortunately did not destroy their farm. Stan joined the volunteers and assisted in rescuing stranded settlers. Later Amy and her neighbor, Mrs. O'Dowd, went to town to meet their husbands after the flood waters had receded. During this period, Stan and Amy had experiences that haunted them for the rest of their lives. Stan saw an aged man suspended from a tree above the flooded land; even though the man was dead and Stan was helpless, the image continued to haunt him. Amy picked up a lost child and took him home the night after the flood. He disappeared the next morning, leaving only a bit of colored glass behind, which she saved and finally gave to her grandson.

The Parkers continued to labor, added to their house, gathered a herd of milk cows, planted and harvested crops. Other families settled nearby, a village appeared, and a wealthy Sydney family constructed a grand country house on adjoining land, naming the estate "Glastonbury." Two children were born to the Parkers: a daughter, Thelma, and a son, Ray. Amy developed a fixation on Madeleine, a visitor to Glastonbury, and believed that this elegant woman held some kind of answer to life's secrets. Later, during a raging bushfire, Stan rescued Madeleine from the burning manor house, and Amy's fantasy crumbled when she saw this idol, her hair burned away, kneeling and retching on the grass.

World War I began soon after the great fire, and Stan enlisted in the army. With Stan away, Amy depended on an old German to help her with the farmwork. The neighbors soon forced him to leave because of their hatred for all Germans.

Stan Parker returned from the battlefields of France, and once more worked his farm, while his wife carried out her domestic duties faithfully and his children grew into adults. Amy engaged in a brief sexual affair with a traveling salesman, which Stan knew about intuitively, but the infatuation passed. The son, Ray, first apprenticed to a saddle maker, left his old life behind, wandered around Australia, spent time in prison, and appeared in Sydney, where he continued his criminal ways. The daughter Thelma attended business college in Sydney, went to work in a lawyers' office, and married one of the lawyers. Through this marriage, she achieved her dream of living a sophisticated and cultured life, freed at last from the dreary farm.

Life continued for Stan and Amy on the farm. They followed a pattern of milking the cows, cooking and eating, sleeping and awakening, dreaming and longing. Amy became fatter in her old age, and Stan appeared to shrivel. The outside world encroached more and more on Stan and Amy's lives. Their daughter's marriage to the lawyer brought the Parkers in closer contact with Sydney, where for the first time in their lives they spent a week in a hotel and attended a performance of *Hamlet* (c. 1600-1601). Sydney also claimed the body of their son Ray, who took up with a prostitute, pursued petty crime, and was murdered.

The land that was unsettled in the Parker family's early years had evolved into a suburb. Developers had subdivided the farms into lots for homes, which surrounded the Parkers' old house, by this time almost entirely covered or obscured by the plants and trees Amy had planted over half a century. The awareness of mortality entered their lives, first by their son's murder, then the death from cancer of Amy's longtime friend, Mrs. O'Dowd. Finally Stan died, quickly and simply in the garden he had carved from the wilderness, with Amy at his side.

Critical Evaluation:

Without question Australia's greatest writer, Patrick White received the Nobel Prize in Literature in 1973. By that time he had published eight novels, four plays, and two collections of short stories. Four more novels and plays, along with another collection of short stories and an autobiography, followed. *The Tree of Man*, his fourth novel, holds an important place in the White canon. First, it lays the groundwork for the imaginary Sydney suburb that White called Sarsaparilla, which figures prominently in his later fiction and drama. This recurrent setting has often been compared to William Faulkner's Yoknapatawpha County. *The Tree of Man* also brought international attention to White's work, which had earlier gone largely unnoticed both in Australia and abroad. In addition, it marks the first of his books to be written after he returned to Australia, following his university years at Oxford, a stint in London as an aspiring writer, extensive travel, and military service during World War II. Of greatest significance, though, is the way this early novel irrevocably altered Australian fiction, which had previously stressed realism and avoided metaphysical speculation. White, fairly or not, once described the typical Australian novel as "the dreary dun-colored offspring of journalistic realism." This gloomy assessment of his country's fiction he set out to change—and did so.

In *The Tree of Man*, White has created a parable depicting the contemporary search for meaning. It may appear odd at first to describe the novel in this way. On a simpler level it would be better to classify it as domestic realism. It essentially unfolds the mundane story of Stan and Amy Parker, who marry, work their farm, have children, grow old, and face death. As they carve out their home in the wilderness, they experience flood, fire, dust, and flies—ironically, all of the staples of the very Australian novels White had called "dun-colored." The novel lacks conflict. It moves slowly from one event to another, the years passing almost unnoticed. The narrative fails to build to any kind of climax, and an abundance of domestic details weighs heavily.

What makes *The Tree of Man* a great novel of lasting achievement is that it is a story for all people in all places at all times. It records the history of an Australian family for three generations during the first half of the twentieth century and is quintessentially Australian, but it is finally not only Australian. In 1958, White wrote of the novel in his essay "The Prodigal Son": "I wanted to try to suggest in this book every possible aspect of life, through the lives of an ordinary man and woman. But at the same time I wanted to discover the extraordinary behind the ordinary, the mystery and poetry."

The Tree of Man presents a parable of life's greatest mystery: an individual's understanding of the divine, of God. In White's fictional world, people tend to fall into two categories, that of the doers and that of the seekers. Most often only one character acts the role of the seeker or the visionary, with those around him or her concerned more with doing and daily living than with the eternal mystery. Stan Parker is the visionary in *The Tree of Man*, even though he appears to be an ordinary man, as this passage from the novel suggests: "If a poetry sometimes almost formed in his head, or a vision of God, nobody knew, because you did not talk about such things, or, rather, you were not aware of the practice of doing so."

At times Stan's wife Amy grapples toward the extraordinary, but "She could not explain that a moment comes when you yourself must produce some tangible evidence of the mystery of life." Neither the Parker children nor any of the other characters in the novel share Stan's "vision of God," which comes to him finally in all of its glory at the moment of his death in the garden. Amy, by then a fat, rather disagreeable old woman, who neither fully appreciated nor grasped Stan's silent spiritual quest, at times even envied it, walks away from the garden and her husband's body, once more doing the practical thing by calling on those who could help her physically.

The final chapter, only two pages long, is a kind of coda to Stan's quest. His grandson, another visionary, wanders through the garden where Stan died, and pledges to put into poetry what his grandfather had known but had been unable to express. It is tempting to see the boy as White himself. In 1956, he had just set out to write a series of powerful novels, which were to make brilliant use of the actual Australian garden in such a way that far transcends the reality of the setting.

A distinguishing mark of the parable is the simplicity of its story. *The Tree of Man* possesses this quality. The metaphysical implications that stand behind every line do not intrude on the narrative itself, which offers a touching, sometimes comic, account of a family's everyday struggles over a period of fifty years. White's altogether original technique of embedding his ideas into character, narrative, and setting provides a rare, if demanding, reading experience.

Much has been said about the difficulty, at times the inaccessibility, of White's writing style, one critic even dubbing it "illiterate verbal sludge." It would be far more accurate to praise the density of the language, its near poetic qualities, and its appropriateness to the work's purpose. Just as the visionaries yearn to make their realizations known, White, with what he called "the sticks and stones" of language, attempts to express the inexpressible. The structure of the prose generates a nervous energy. This energy strives toward the revelation of the truth, "the extraordinary behind the ordinary, the mystery and poetry."

Robert L. Ross

Bibliography:

Bliss, Carolyn. "*The Tree of Man.*" In *Patrick White's Fiction.* New York: St. Martin's Press, 1986. Provides a clear analysis of the novel. Places this early novel within the White canon, which is seen as concerned with "the paradox of fortunate failure."

Colmer, John. *Patrick White*. New York: Methuen, 1984. Examines the continuity of vision in White's fiction. Discusses and places *The Tree of Man* within that context as an important early work.

Hope, A. D. "The Bunyip Stages a Comeback—*The Tree of Man*." In *Critical Essays on Patrick White*. Boston: G. K. Hall, 1990. A noted review of the novel, written in 1956 by a leading Australian poet. Praises the way White represents "a sense of the mystery of all living," but criticizes his prose style, calling it "pretentious and illiterate verbal sludge."

Kramer, Leonie. "*The Tree of Man*: An Essay in Skepticism." In *Critical Essays on Patrick White*, edited by Peter Wolfe. Boston: G. K. Hall, 1990. Traces Stan Parker's "journey towards enlightenment" by analyzing the formal structure of the novel. Argues that Stan's supposed spiritual illumination has been overestimated by critics, and sees the novel instead as expressing a skeptical "attitude towards metaphysical speculation."

Weigel, John A. *Patrick White*. Boston: Twayne, 1983. A comprehensive introduction to all aspects of White's work and life, including a well-defined discussion of *The Tree of Man*. An excellent starting point for a study of White's fiction.

THE TREE OF THE FOLKUNGS

Type of work: Novel
Author: Verner von Heidenstam (1859-1940)
Type of plot: Historical
Time of plot: Eleventh and thirteenth centuries
Locale: Sweden
First published: Folkungaträdet, 1905-1907 (English translation, 1925)

Principal characters:
> FOLKE FILBYTER, the founder of the Folkung line
> INGEMUND,
> HALLSTEN, and
> INGEVALD, his sons
> FOLKE INGEVALDSSON, his grandson
> ULF ULFSSON, a pagan udalman
> KING VALDEMAR, a descendant of Folke Filbyter
> DUKE MAGNUS, his brother
> QUEEN SOPHIA, the wife of Valdemar
> LADY JUTTA, her sister
> GISTRE HARJANSON, a minstrel
> YRSA-LILL, a goatherd
> ARCHBISHOP FULCO, the prelate of Upsala

The Story:
Folke Filbyter planted the seed from which grew the mighty Folkung tree. Returning homeward after long sea roving, he brought his ship to shore near a shield maiden's grave ground in the land of Sveas and Goths. Dwarf Jorgrimme, a Finnish sorcerer, prophesied terror would darken the land, and Thor's image would tremble.

Folke tramped inland for two nights, his sack of booty on his back. The third night he came to Jorgrimme's cave, where the sorcerer gave him drink from the horn Manegarm, treasure of the gods. Then the dwarf cut the sack so that some of the gold fell out. Discovering the leak, Folke swore he had sown the ground with riches he would also reap. There he built his mighty hall, Folketuna.

Before long Folke had land and thralls but no sons. One morning his men found Jorgrimme's daughter trapped in a wolf pit, and Folke took her home to his bed. She bore him three sons—Ingemund, Hallsten, and Ingevald—but she got no honor and crouched in the straw like the scurviest thrall. Ingevald stayed by his father's side. Ingemund and Hallsten went sea roving.

Folke, wanting a good marriage for his son, spoke for Holmdis, Ulf Ulfsson's daughter. Meanwhile old Jakob, a begging friar, preached a new faith in the region. When Ingevald tumbled the dwarfs' one-eyed god, his mother gave him sacred Manegarm, stolen from Jorgrimme's burial cairn. Folke swore blood brotherhood with the king of outlaws and got great riches. Then Holmdis proudly spurned a match with the thrall woman's son, but Ingevald carried her by force to his father's hall. There, waiting in vain for her kinsmen to rescue her, she brought one son to Folketuna before she died. After Holmdis' funeral, Folke turned away from Ingevald. Folke Ingevaldsson was his grandfather's heir.

When Jakob came again, Ingevald, hoping to save his son from the lawless life at Folketuna, gave the child to the priest. For years old Folke rode from hearth to hearth looking for his lost grandchild. Thrall and thane alike knew of the grim old man's search.

King Inge traveled through the land with his bodyguards, and wherever he stopped men either died or were baptized in the new faith. When Ulf Ulfsson spoke for the old gods, the king's earl and chief adviser, a ruthless, priest-trained young man, left him bound to perish in the forest. Ingemund and Hallsten, homeward bound, were in Ulf's hall that night and joined the king's guard.

Folke was at Upsala when the sacred grove burned and people cried out against Inge and called Blot Sven king. There Folke saw the king's earl, on his hand the star-shaped mark of the child stolen from Folketuna years before. Although the old outlaw offered his riches to help the king's need, young Folke and his uncles were proud men with little wish to have a name as unsavory as Folke Filbyter's associated with them, now that they were counted among the greatest of the king's thanes. They took the treasure he offered to advance themselves, but they seldom visited him in the bare hall where he sat in the dirty straw. At last he opened his veins and died as unwanted old men had done in ancient times.

Two hundred years later, King Holmger lay dead, with the sacred sword Grane on his grave, and Earl Birger of the Folkungs ruled in Sweden, although it was his young son Valdemar who wore the crown. Valdemar grew up weak and soft, a lover of pleasure and women. From his far ancestor, Folke Filbyter, he inherited a yeoman's love of the land and a liking for serfs and outlaws. There were many who thought that his brother, Junker Magnus, should have been king, for he was bold and cunning and the better knight. When Magnus unhorsed his brother at a great tournament at Belbo and Valdemar laughed at his tumble without shame or regret, Earl Birger was so angry with his son that he collapsed from a stroke and died soon afterward. At the division of the earl's estate, his sons quarreled over a missing drinking horn, Manegarm, an heirloom of the old days.

Valdemar's bride was Sophia, the daughter of Denmark's king. Lady Jutta was her sister. Sometimes Valdemar talked with the maid alone, and she became frightened. Valdemar also spent much time in the hut of Yrsa-lill, a woman goatherd, to whom Gistre Harjanson had carried Manegarm. The company drank from it when Valdemar went to the hut to carouse with herdsmen and outcasts. Meanwhile the land knew confusion. Peasants paid no taxes, and robbers roamed the highways. Valdemar would allow no wrongdoer to be punished.

When Jutta wished to return to Denmark, Magnus and Sir Svantepolk, a worthy knight, set out to escort her. Valdemar overtook them at the goatherd's hut, where the party had stopped to rest. After convincing Jutta that Magnus was a trickster, Valdemar accompanied her to the border, and on the way they became lovers. Sir Svantepolk, renouncing his allegiance, rode off to join Duke Magnus. Queen Sophia had Yrsa-lill thrown into a cage filled with snakes. Gistre, the minstrel, rescued her, who afterward lay speechless in the convent at Vreta.

When Jutta bore a son beyond the marches, Valdemar gave the child into the keeping of Archbishop Fulco of Upsala. Then the king threatened to take away his brother's titles. Magnus had the sword Grane brought from King Holmger's tomb and fastened it to his own belt. At Vreta, Yrsa-lill regained her speech and prophesied that whoever would get St. Eirik's banner from a man maiden's hands would rule Sweden.

Jutta, now prioress at Roskilde, went to Upsala for a holy festival honoring St. Eirik. There she found her son and saw Valdemar surrounded by his wild bodyguard. Moved by her old love, she took off her religious habit and dressed in the robes of one of the king's favorites. Together she and Valdemar stood on the balcony of the king's house while the people howled disapproval and insults. Queen Sophia ordered Jutta sent to a convent in the archbishop's keeping.

Archbishop Fulco gave St. Eirik's banner to some maidens who carried it to Duke Magnus. Afterward there was war between the brothers. Crafty, vain Magnus battled Valdemar and his army of peasants and outlaws. Valdemar, however, seemed indifferent to the outcome and sat feasting at Ramundeboda while his army was defeated at Hofva. From that time on Magnus had the crown, but the war did not end with his victory, for Valdemar fought and then fled from lost villages and provinces. At last the outlawed king had nothing left but a jeweled riding whip borrowed from Lady Luitgard, the last friend to share his misfortunes, and he gave that to Gistre and told the minstrel to go look for Yrsa-lill. Alone and unarmed, Valdemar then surrendered to his brother.

King Magnus, old and sick by that time, gave the country peace. Valdemar lived a prisoner at Nykopingshus, and Luitgard was his only company. Nevertheless, in his captivity he found such contentment that Magnus died envying him.

Critical Evaluation:

Like Sigrid Undset in Norway, Verner von Heidenstam drew inspiration from the history of his native Sweden in medieval times. *The Tree of the Folkungs* is a historical novel of imaginative freedom and dramatic vigor. There are two parts to the story. The first deals with the period at the end of the eleventh century—a barbaric, brutal age which in the North saw heathenism and Christianity in conflict. In the second half of the novel, the Folkung family, proud descendants of an ancient peasant freebooter, have pushed their way to the Swedish throne by the middle of the thirteenth century. The pageantry, heroism, humility, superstition, cruelty, and greed of the Middle Ages comes alive to the reader. The effect is not one of antiquarianism, however, for Heidenstam is interested in a living past, the growth of a culture, with its mixture of good and evil, nobility and baseness. The writer tells his story with a variety of styles and techniques, mingling myth, legend, history, saga, and fantasy. The result is a literary work of significance and tragic power. The author was awarded the Nobel Prize in Literature in 1916.

The Tree of the Folkungs is romantic with a core of realism. It presents the saga of a great family that held sway in Sweden from the close of the Viking age to the end of the thirteenth century. Written in a style reminiscent of that of ancient legends, this massive novel records the destiny of a nation. In deceptively simple, richly poetic prose, the author vividly brings to life those long-ago times. The primitive religion and lingering superstitions of the people are woven into the narrative, and the close union between these beliefs and the constant struggle of the people with the land and the forces of nature is clearly and dramatically drawn. A deep tranquillity often pervades the exquisite descriptions of the locales; a stolid force suggests throughout the book that the land and the sea are the vital elements in existence, while people come and go, transitory visitors to the scene.

The life of these ancient people is meticulously detailed, their clothes, battle gear, and homes all described with the detail of an anthropological report, yet these details never intrude into the narrative; they give the story a verisimilitude necessary for a modern reader's enjoyment. Perhaps a certain ponderous, humorless quality that exists in the writing was unavoidable, for the people Heidenstam was writing about were tough, serious individuals struggling with a world that allowed little time for gracious living or humor. The characters strongly believe in the power of fate and possess a great sense of their own destiny. This aspect of the book is both stirring and touching and provides the true emotional impetus to the narrative.

For all of their toughness, these people are essentially innocent, almost childlike. Jealousies, rivalries, hatreds, and primitive passions motivate them. Pride above all rules their lives; loss of pride is more than they can bear. The great Folke Filbyter, the founder of the clan, is memorable, almost superhuman, who weds a dwarf's daughter and lives to see his family great. Over all the family stands the lime tree and the spirit that dwells within it, watching over the family. The branches and spreading roots of the tree provide a rich symbolic framework for the novel equal to the great tree of generations begun by Folke Filbyter.

Bibliography:
Gustafson, Alrik. *Six Scandinavian Novelists.* Princeton, N.J.: Princeton University Press, 1940. A chapter on Heidenstam provides biographical information, including the origins of Heidenstam's ideas about depicting the beginnings of his nation.
Zuck, Virpi, ed. *Dictionary of Scandinavian Literature.* Westport, Conn.: Greenwood Press, 1990. Entry on Heidenstam places the poet and writer in his historical and literary contexts. Discusses Heidenstam's nationalistic enthusiasms.

THE TRIAL

Type of work: Novel
Author: Franz Kafka (1883-1924)
Type of plot: Symbolic realism
Time of plot: Twentieth century
Locale: Germany
First published: Der Prozess, 1925 (English translation, 1937)

> Principal characters:
> JOSEPH K., a bank employee
> THE ADVOCATE
> TITORELLI, a painter
> LENI, the Advocate's servant

The Story:

Perhaps someone had been telling lies about Joseph K., for one morning he was arrested. The landlady's cook always brought him his breakfast at eight o'clock, but this morning she failed to appear. Joseph looked out of the window and noticed that the old lady across the way was peering into his room. Feeling uneasy, he rang the bell. At once a man entered dressed like a tourist. He advised Joseph to stay in his room, but Joseph failed to obey. In the next room he saw another strange man reading a book. The missing breakfast was explained by the empty dishes he saw. The two strangers had eaten it.

The two strangers had come to notify Joseph that he was under arrest. They were so sure of themselves and yet so considerate that Joseph was at a loss as to the attitude he should take toward them. They tried to take his underwear, saying it was of too good quality, but when he objected, they did not press him. They refused to tell him the reason for his arrest, saying only that he would be interrogated. Finally, after Joseph had dressed according to their choices from his wardrobe, they led him to another room to be questioned by the Inspector.

To his dismay, Joseph saw that the Inspector was occupying Fräulein Bürstner's room. The Inspector gave no further hint as to the reason for the arrest, nor did he inquire into Joseph's defense. The latter at one point said that the whole matter was a mistake; but under pertinent if vague questioning, Joseph admitted that he knew little of the law. All he learned, really, was that someone in high authority had ordered his arrest.

Then Joseph was told that he could go to work as usual. His head fairly aching from bewilderment, Joseph went to the bank in a taxi. Arriving half an hour late, he worked all day long as diligently as he could. Frequently, however, he was interrupted by congratulatory callers, for this day was his thirtieth birthday. He went straight home at nine-thirty to apologize for using Fräulein Bürstner's room. She was not in, however, and he settled down to anxious waiting. At eleven-thirty she arrived, tired from an evening at the theater. In spite of her uninterested atti- tude, he told her the whole story very dramatically. At last, Fräulein Bürstner sank down exhausted on her bed. Joseph rushed to her, kissed her passionately many times, and returned to his room.

A few days later, Joseph received a brief note ordering him to appear before the court for interrogation on the following Sunday. Oddly enough, although the address was given, no time was set for the hearing. By some chance, Joseph decided to go at nine o'clock. The street was a rather mean one, and the address proved to be that of a large warehouse. Joseph did not know where to report, but after trying many doors, he finally reached the fifth floor. There, a bright-eyed washerwoman seemed to be expecting him and motioned him through her flat into a meeting hall. Joseph found the room filled with old men, most of them with long beards. They all wore badges.

When the judge asked Joseph if he were a house painter, he snappishly rejoined that he was the junior manager of a bank. Then the judge said he was an hour and ten minutes late. To this charge Joseph replied that he was present now, his appearance in court being the main thing. The crowd applauded. Encouraged, Joseph launched into a harangue damning the court, its methods, the warders who had arrested him, and the meeting time and place.

The judge seemed abashed. Then an interruption occurred. At the back of the room, a man clasped the washerwoman in his arms and screamed, all the while looking at the ceiling. Joseph dashed from the room, loudly refusing to have any more dealings with the court.

All that week Joseph awaited another summons. When none came, he decided to revisit the meeting hall. The washerwoman again met him kindly and expressed her disappointment that the court was not in session. She told him a little about the court and its methods. It seemed that the court was only a lower body which rarely interfered with the freedom of the accused people. If one were acquitted by the court, it meant little, because a higher court might rearrest one on the same charge. She seemed to know little of Joseph's particular case, although she said she knew as much as the judge. As she was speaking, a law student seized the washerwoman and carried her up the stairs.

The woman's husband kindly offered to lead Joseph up to the law offices, the inner sanctum of the court located in the attic. There Joseph found a number of people waiting for answers to petitions. Some of them had been waiting for years, and they were becoming a little anxious about their cases. The hot room under the roof made Joseph dizzy, and he had to sit down. The hostess tried to soothe him, and the director of public relations was very pleasant. Finally someone suggested that Joseph ought to leave and get some fresh air.

On his uncle's advice, Joseph hired an Advocate, an old man who stayed in bed most of the time. His servant, Leni, took a liking to Joseph and would often kiss him while he was conferring with the Advocate. Joseph liked best to dally with her in the kitchen. After some months, all the Advocate had done was to think about writing a petition. In desperation, Joseph discharged him from the case. Leni was heartbroken. She was in her nightgown entertaining another client. This man, a businessman, Leni kept locked up in a small bedroom. The Advocate warned Joseph of his high-handed behavior and pointed to the businessman as an ideal client. Disgusted, Joseph left the house.

Then Joseph went to see Titorelli, the court painter. Titorelli told him he could hope for little. He might get definitive acquittal, ostensible acquittal, or indefinite postponement. No one was ever really acquitted, but sometimes cases could be prolonged indefinitely. Joseph bought three identical paintings in return for the advice. Even the priest at the cathedral, who said he was court chaplain, offered little encouragement when consulted. He was sure that Joseph would be convicted of the crime with which he was charged. Joseph still did not know what the crime was, nor did the priest.

At last two men in frock coats and top hats came for Joseph at nine o'clock on the evening before his thirty-first birthday. Somehow they twined their arms around his and held his hands tightly. They walked with him to a quarry. There, one held his throat and the other stabbed him in the heart, turning the knife around twice.

Critical Evaluation:

The Trial is one of the most effective and most discussed works to come out of Central

Europe between World War I and World War II. Although the complex and ambiguous surface of the novel defies exact interpretation, the plight of Joseph K., consumed by guilt and condemned for a "crime" he does not understand by a "court" with which he cannot communicate, is a profound and disturbing image of humanity in the modern world. To some, the court is a symbol of the church as an imperfect bridge between the individual and God. To others, the symbolism represents rather the search of a sensitive Jew for a homeland that is always denied him. Although unfinished, *The Trial* is a powerful and provocative book.

One of the pillars upon which Franz Kafka's reputation as a major twentieth century author rests, *The Trial* was one of the works he ordered destroyed in his will. It survives only because his friend Max Brod, who possessed a manuscript of the unfinished novel, disobeyed Kafka and preserved it, along with *The Castle* (1926), *Amerika* (1913), and a host of fragments and shorter works. The salvaging of this novel from the manuscript was not an easy task, however, and controversy still exists as to the proper order of the chapters as well as over the placement and interpretation of a number of unfinished segments which are not included in the usual editions. Fortunately, both the beginning and the end of the novel are extant, and, because of the peculiar structure of the work, minor changes in the order of the sections do not really alter one's understanding of it.

The novel is structured within an exact time frame. Exactly one year elapses between the arrest of Joseph K. (the K. clearly refers to Kafka himself, though the work is hardly biographical in the usual sense), which takes place on his thirtieth birthday, and his execution, which takes place on the night before his thirty-first birthday. Moreover, the novel tells almost nothing about Joseph K.'s past; there are no memories, no flashbacks, no expository passages explaining the background. As in so many of his works, Kafka begins *The Trial* with the incursion of a totally unexpected force into an otherwise uneventful life, and the situation never again returns to normal. Kafka felt that the moment of waking was the most dangerous moment of the day, a time when one was unprotected by the structures of one's life and open to such an incursion. Joseph K., in his vulnerable state, responds to the messengers of the court; from this point, there is no turning back. Yet the court is invisible—a hierarchy in which even the lowest members are somehow beyond his grasp. There are no formal charges, no procedures, and little information to guide the defendant. Indeed, one of the most unsettling aspects of the novel is the constant uncertainty, the continual juxtaposition of alternative hypotheses, the multiple explanations for events, and the differing interpretations regarding cause and effect. The whole rational structure of the world is undermined, as perceived reality becomes the subject of detailed exegesis such as one might apply to sacred scripture. Reality itself becomes a vague concept, since the reader is denied the guiding commentary of a narrator and sees everything from Joseph's point of view. The entire work is composed of Joseph's experiences; he is present in every scene. Secondary characters appear only as they relate to him, and the reader knows no more than he does. With Joseph, the reader receives information which may be misinformation, experiences bizarre, barely credible incidents, and moves from scene to scene as if in a trance. This narrowness of the point of view becomes oppressive, but it is highly effective as a technique. The reader, in effect, becomes Joseph K.

The body of the novel consists of Joseph's attempts to approach the court through a series of "helpers." These helpers, however, offer no encouragement to his possible defense or acquittal. Since there are no charges, a defense is virtually impossible. Their advice is simply to prolong the trial, to avoid a decision, to adjust to the idea of living on trial without seeking a judgment. It is for this reason that the order of the central chapters is not crucial. Aside from Joseph's increasing exhaustion, there is no real development, merely a series of false starts, leading him no closer to a solution. Whether or not there is any development in Joseph's position before his death is open to debate, and critics have disagreed strongly. In the next to the last chapter, "In the Cathedral," Joseph is told the parable of the man who comes seeking entrance into the Law. His way is blocked by a doorkeeper, and the man's entire life is spent waiting. As he dies, he learns that this door, which he could never enter, was nevertheless meant for him alone. Typically, several possible interpretations are offered, but it is perhaps significant that the next chapter finds Joseph waiting for his executioners. Has he come to an acceptance? Does the paradox achieve meaning for him? However that may be, he does not have the strength to act, and he dies, as he thinks at the end, "like a dog."

One is left with the question of what it all means. This is perhaps the wrong question to ask, because it implies that there is a meaning which can be defined, a key to understanding which generally involves assigning some allegorical value to the court: authoritarian society, human alienation from a sense of wholeness and purpose in life, the search for God's grace. Yet it is the genius of Kafka's works that they are inexhaustible and veiled in an ultimately impenetrable mystery. They admit of many interpretations, but the more specific the definition of the meaning of the work, the more inadequate it is to encompass the full amplitude of the novel. Kafka's works are less allegorical than symbolic; their symbolism lies in the construction of an image or an experience that is analogous to a human experience that lies far deeper than any of the specific problems offered as explanations for the work's meaning. In *The Trial*, Joseph K. is confronted with the need to justify his life and to justify it at a metaphysical level deeper than any ex post facto rationalization of his actions. It is a demand he cannot meet, and yet it is inescapable because it arises from within him. He is an Everyman, but he is stripped of his religion and on trial for his life. For Kafka, the trial becomes a metaphor for life itself, and every sentence is a sentence of death.

"Critical Evaluation" by Steven C. Schaber

Bibliography:

Flores, Angel, ed. *The Kafka Problem.* New York: New Directions, 1946. An important and relatively early collection of essays, three of which deal specifically with *The Trial.*

Flores, Angel, and Homer Swander, eds. *Franz Kafka Today.* Madison: University of Wisconsin Press, 1958. Two essays treat the structure and meaning of *The Trial*, respectively; useful as a companion volume to the previous Flores collection. Includes a long bibliography.

Gray, Ronald, ed. *Kafka: A Collection of Critical Essays.* Englewood Cliffs, N.J.: Prentice-Hall, 1962. Fifteen excellent essays on general themes in Kafka, two dealing with *The Trial* in particular and several dealing with it in part. Almost all of the contributors are well-known critics. Also contains an introduction, a chronology of important dates, and a survey of recent Kafka criticism.

Rolleston, James, ed. *Twentieth Century Interpretations of "The Trial."* Englewood Cliffs, N.J.: Prentice-Hall, 1976. Ten essays with an introduction, "On Interpreting *The Trial*," offer a wide sampling of critical responses to the work's "opaqueness." Presents Kafka's relationships to psychoanalysis and other modern modes of interpretation. Extensive critical bibliography.

Tauber, Herbert. *Franz Kafka: An Interpretation of His Works.* Translated by G. Humphreys Roberts and Roger Senhouse. New Haven, Conn.: Yale University Press, 1948. Places *The Trial* in the context of literary analysis of Kafka's major works. Chapter 7 compares the book to *The Castle* in terms of both themes and execution. Should be read in conjunction with Max Brod's seminal *Biography of Franz Kafka* (1937) for interesting comparison.

THE TRICKSTER OF SEVILLE

Type of work: Drama
Author: Tirso de Molina (Gabriel Téllez, 1580?-1648)
Type of plot: Social morality
Time of plot: Seventeenth century
Locale: Naples, Italy, and Seville, Spain
First performed: c. 1630; first published, 1630 as *El burlador de Sevilla* (English translation, 1923)

Principal characters:
DON DIEGO TENORIO, a father
DON JUAN TENORIO, his son, the protagonist
CATALINÓN, Don Juan's servant
ISABELA, Duke Octavio's lover
DON PEDRO TENORIO, Don Juan's uncle
MARQUÉS DE LA MOTA, Doña Ana's lover
DON GONZALO DE ULLOA, Doña Ana's father
TISBEA, a fisherwoman
AMINTA, betrothed to Batricio

The Story:

In Naples, Italy, Don Juan Tenorio deceived Isabela by impersonating her lover, Duke Octavio, under the cover of darkness. After Isabela told Don Juan that she wanted to strike the light, he confessed to her that he was not Duke Octavio. Isabela screamed, and Don Juan was apprehended but was permitted to escape by his uncle Don Pedro Tenorio, the Spanish ambassador.

On a voyage to Spain, Don Juan became shipwrecked on the coast and was rescued by a fisherman's daughter named Tisbea. Don Juan regained consciousness in Tisbea's arms and began to conquer this woman of the lower class. He ardently declared his love, discredited arguments regarding his and her social inequality and regarding the responsibilities of a marriage vow, and finally obtained her consent to his desires by promising to marry her. Don Juan had ordered his servant, Catalinón, to prepare the mares, so that they could escape quickly after the trick. Catalinón repeatedly warned his master about the consequences of his actions with the refrain, "That is a long way off." There were also references to fire: the flames of passion and the burning of Tisbea's hut.

Upon arriving in Seville, Don Juan discovered that the king had arranged his marriage to Doña Ana, the daughter of Commander Don Gonzalo de Ulloa. Doña Ana, however, was already in love with her cousin, the Marqués de la Mota, with whom she scheduled a nightly meeting. Don Juan intercepted a letter containing the message for the Marqués de la Mota to meet Doña Ana at eleven o'clock, wearing a colored cape. The deceiver changed the hour of the meeting to midnight, traded capes with Mota, and arrived at Doña Ana's at eleven o'clock. Although this rendezvous appeared to contain the elements of a master deceit, it caused Don Juan's demise, for Doña Ana became aware of the treachery and screamed, alerting her father. The commander fought a duel with Don Juan and was killed. Don Juan departed rapidly from Doña Ana's and appeared in a small village where Aminta was going to marry Batricio, who thought that the presence of this nobleman was a bad omen for his wedding.

Batricio lamented Don Juan's prominent position at the wedding festivities. At night, when Aminta was expecting Batricio to come to her bed, Don Juan appeared. Employing the same techniques as he had previously used to deceive the fisherwoman Tisbea, he persuaded her to give in to his desires. As he had done in the past, Catalinón prepared the horses in advance. Both master and servant escaped; however, after this final deception involving Aminta, the two came to a church. Don Juan was still amused about how he had tricked the gullible peasant woman, but Catalinón disturbed him with the information that Octavio had learned the identity of Isabela's beguiler and that Don Juan was obligated to marry her. Moreover, the Marqués de la Mota was advocating Don Juan's castigation.

Don Juan and his servant approached Don Gonzalo's tomb, on which the dead commander's statue stood. The beguiler read the tomb's inscription: "Here the most loyal knight waits for the Lord to wreak vengeance upon a traitor." This inscription insulted Don Juan's honor; he proceeded to mock the statue by pulling its beard and by inviting it to supper in order for it to retaliate against him. Don Juan was so absorbed by the inscription's affront to his honor that he did not remember his sworn oath of fidelity to Aminta that led to her loss of honor. Don Juan had declared that if he failed to keep his promise to Aminta, God should kill him, by means of a dead man, for treachery and deceit.

Don Juan calmly approached the hour of his supper engagement with the stone guest. The deceiver even continued using mocking humor, by carelessly entertaining his guest with verses that combined the theme of a deceiver with that of God's justice being a long time away. In contrast to Don Juan's demeanor, the stone guest was quiet, but then he requested that Don Juan shake hands to seal his agreement to the statue's invitation for supper for the next evening. This handshake was the first time Don Juan felt intense fear, and his body dripped with a cold sweat.

The final meeting for supper took place in the chapel where the remains of the commander rested. Don Juan and the statue sat down together to a meal of scorpions and snakes, with wine made of gall and vinegar. Don Juan was the guest, so he was obliged to stay and to listen to mysterious voices that announced the theme of divine justice. Don Juan again shook hands with the statue and felt the fire that began to burn him. He wanted to confess to a priest, but God had already condemned him to the eternal fire of hell.

The king, God's representative on earth, became the dispenser of justice. He resolved the marriage problems that Don Juan had created: Octavio married Isabela, Mota married Ana, Batricio married Aminta. Tisbea, whose cold heart paralleled that of the deceiver, did not have a husband.

Critical Evaluation:

Acclaimed by many scholars as having created the first Don Juan in European literature, Tirso de Molina received the honor of accompanying the vicar-general to Santo Domingo by way of Seville. Tirso had resided in Toledo where, under the influence of Lope de Vega Carpio, the creator of the Spanish *comedia* or play, he began to compose theatrical works. Tirso, a Mercederian priest elected to several important positions in the order, prepared himself for writing plays by attending literary academies and participating in poetic competitions. Tirso showed his genius by composing more than three hundred plays—both highly animated and serious *comedias*.

The Trickster of Seville, derived from a libertine story and a Castilian ballad containing the figure of a stone guest, portrays the theological theme that God punishes blasphemy. Tirso's stylistic procedure involves varying Don Juan's multiple seductions of women, by showing the action in the middle of an episode and then modifying the setting and type of victim. The quantity of seductions provides the rapid pace of the play, which is supported by the lively dialogue of the verse form, which is varied according to the speaker. The episodic structure of repeated seductions, culminating in Don Juan's encounter with the stone guest, is unified by warnings of tragedy in previous scenes through continual allusions to the finality of death, the judgment of God, and the flames of hell. Don Gonzalo's death from his attempt to avenge his daughter's lost honor in a duel with the trickster introduces the prime unifying element of the play: the statue erected on Don Gonzalo's tomb that becomes the vehicle of Don Juan's condemnation to hell.

Another unifying factor is Don Juan's *gracioso*, or servant, who emphasizes the theme of procrastination that characterizes the deceiver. Instead of mimicking his master's ideas as a typical *gracioso* would, he cautions Don Juan not to delay his preparation for the Judgment Day. Although the fearful Catalinón underscores Don Juan's courage at the arrival of the stone guest, Catalinón assures the statue that he can trust his master's word as a gentleman, and that his dishonesty only concerns his treatment of women. The servant's posture presents an irony that shows his failure to realize that truly honorable behavior extends to dealings with both men and women.

The Spanish honor code serves to define Don Juan's character. Tirso portrays Don Juan's motivation for deceiving his four victims, of both the noble and peasant classes, and robbing them of their worth. Doña Ana, the lover of his friend, the Marqués de la Mota, attracts him because she is difficult to possess. The trickster gains access to Doña Ana and another noble woman, Isabela, by pretending to be another person. Aminta, a peasant whom he lures away from her bridegroom on the day of her marriage ceremony by assurances of wealth and social advancement, attracts Don Juan because she is an unpossessed bride. Tisbea, a fisherwoman, is the only victim who already has a passion that he does little to ignite.

The igniting of Tisbea's hut foreshadows the chapel that threatens Don Juan with hell fire. In this episode, Tirso illustrates the trickster's attitude of mockery by showing him stealing his victim's horses so that he and his servant can quickly escape. The horses, prepared for the escape in advance, symbolize two essential components of the play: speed and urgency. Since Don Juan is onstage for most of the *comedia* in order to unfold the plot, *The Trickster of Seville* contains very few pauses. The playwright's portrayal of the rapid passage of time available for his protagonist to complete his amorous conquests contrasts with the less intense manner of executing death and judgment, producing an effective dramatic tension. Don Juan's repeated declaration that he is going to enjoy his victim intensifies the irony of his assertion, "That is a long way off"; the trickster repeats his deceits under the cover of the darkness of night. The protagonist's pronouncement that these are his hours prefigures the lengthy night of his damnation.

The Trickster of Seville served as an admonition to the corrupt nobility of the seventeenth century to act in a more pious manner. Don Juan is not portrayed as a sensual lover who stays to enjoy his conquest; his friend, the Marqués de la Mota, who loves Doña Ana, manifests promiscuous behavior by frequenting the brothels of Seville. Don Juan is repeatedly warned to respect women's honor, but his refusal to obey the rules leads to his defying God in his encounter with Don Gonzalo. Tirso, therefore, furnishes a superb illustration of the seventeenth century theological concept that society is basically good, but that the individual, endowed by the Creator with the free will to choose between good and evil, often chooses to sin. Because the society's structure is established by God, it is the sinner, such as Don Juan, who makes society the victim of sin. God's representative, the king, restores honor to the victims, resolving the dramatic situation of the *comedia* in a pleasing manner.

The Trickster of Seville introduces a universal type that has been modified by French, German, and English dramatists, as well as fashioned into Mozart's famous Italian opera *Don Giovanni*. Tirso's characterization of Don Juan from a Spanish viewpoint has survived its rivals to become one of the great literary creations of all time.

"Critical Evaluation" by Linda Prewett Davis

Bibliography:
Conlon, Raymond. "The *Burlador* and the *Burlados:* A Sinister Connection." *Bulletin of the Comediantes* 42, no. 1 (Summer, 1990): 5-22. Discusses the symbolic connection between Don Juan and Duke Octavio, examining and comparing their treatment of women.
McClelland, I. L. *Tirso de Molina: Studies in Dramatic Realism.* Liverpool: Institute of Hispanic Studies, 1948. Discusses how Tirso's drama prefigures the dramatic ideals of the eighteenth century. Defines realism in the *Trickster of Seville*; gives Tirso's concept of the supernatural.
Weinstein, Leo. *The Metamorphoses of Don Juan.* Stanford, Calif.: Stanford University Press, 1959. Traces the origin of the Don Juan legend to Tirso's *The Trickster of Seville* and explains Don Juan as a practical joker. Shows how various authors have modified the original story.
Wilson, Maragret. *Spanish Drama of the Golden Age.* New York: Pergamon Press, 1969. An excellent summary of the characteristics of the new *comedia* created by Vega Carpio. Compares Tirso's *comedias* with those of Vega Carpio; chapters and 7 and 8 contain a helpful explanation of *The Trickster of Seville*.

TRISTAN AND ISOLDE

Type of work: Poetry
Author: Gottfried von Strassburg (fl. c. 1210)
Type of plot: Romance
Time of plot: Arthurian age
Locale: Northern Europe, Ireland, and England
First transcribed: Tristan und Isolde, c. 1210 (English translation, 1899)

Principal characters:
RIVALIN, a lord of Parmenie
BLANCHEFLEUR, his wife
TRISTAN, their son
RUAL THE FAITHFUL, Tristan's foster father
MARK, king of Cornwall, Tristan's uncle
ISOLDE THE FAIR, King Mark's bride, loved by Tristan
BRANGENE, Isolde's companion
ISOLDE OF THE WHITE HANDS, Tristan's bride

The Story:

Rivalin, a lord of Parmenie, tired of baiting Duke Morgan, the wicked ruler, signed a year's truce and set off for Britain where King Mark of Cornwall was establishing peace and order. Badly wounded while fighting in the defense of Cornwall, Rivalin was pitied and nursed back to health by Mark's sister Blanchefleur, whom he took back to Parmenie as his bride. Later, hearing of Rivalin's death at Duke Morgan's hand, Blanchefleur went into labor, and died during the birth of her son. Rual, Rivalin's faithful steward, and his wife reared the boy out of loyalty to their dead lord and mistress and to thwart Duke Morgan's vindictiveness. The boy was named Tristan, in keeping with the sad events preceding his birth and a prophecy of grief to come.

Tristan's education was courtly, both at home and abroad; it included music, art, literature, languages, falconry, hunting, riding, knightly prowess with sword and spear, and jousting. He used these accomplishments to great advantage throughout his short life. He was loved deeply by his foster parents, his stepbrothers, and the people of Parmenie as well.

Kidnapped by Norwegians, Tristan managed to make his way to Cornwall after an eight-day storm at sea. He immediately attached himself to King Mark's court as a hunter, later the master of the hunt. When his royal lineage was revealed, he became his uncle's knight and vassal.

Known far and wide as a doughty knight, Tristan returned to avenge his father's death by defeating and killing Duke Morgan; his lands he gave to Rual and his sons. Meanwhile, Duke Morolt of Ireland, who had exacted tribute from King Mark, demanded further payment or a fight to the death in single combat with the Cornish king. Tristan acted as King Mark's emissary to the Irish court, where his efforts to have Duke Morolt recall his demand for tribute were unsuccessful. Duke Morolt did agree, however, to let Tristan fight in King Mark's place. They met and fought in Cornwall. After wounding Tristan in the hip, Duke Morolt suggested that the young knight yield so that his sister Isolde, Queen of Ireland, could nurse him back to health. This offer was refused, and the fight waved fiercely again. Tristan finally sliced off Duke Morolt's head and hand.

Tristan, disguised as a beggar, went to Ireland to be cured. Calling himself Tantris, he ingratiated himself with Queen Isolde, who cured him of his hurt. Afterward, he became the tutor in music and languages to her daughter, Isolde the Fair. When the young Isolde learned that he was the murderer of her uncle, the queen mother forgave him and allowed him to return to Cornwall.

In Cornwall, Tristan sang the praises of the Irish princess. Because King Mark had made the young knight his heir, some jealous noblemen, hoping to have Tristan slain, suggested that he return to Ireland and bring Isolde back as King Mark's bride. On his arrival in Ireland, Tristan killed a dragon that had long ravished the kingdom. In gratitude, Queen Isolde entrusted her beautiful daughter to Tristan's care.

On the return voyage, Brangene, the faithful companion and cousin of Isolde the Fair, failed to guard carefully the love potion intended by the queen for Isolde and King Mark on their nuptial day. Tristan and the princess drank the potion and were thenceforth enslaved by love for each other. They both experienced conflicting duty and desire, turned red then white, became both depressed and exalted, and finally gave in to love. To deceive King Mark, Brangene stole into Isolde's bed so that Tristan and Isolde might meet in secret.

After some time had passed, Isolde grew apprehensive lest Brangene betray her, and she ordered her companion's death. Fortunately, the queen relented before Brangene could die, and all went on as before until the king was at last informed of Tristan's treachery. King Mark made many attempts to trap the lovers, meanwhile vacillating between trust and angry jealousy. Each time a trap was set, Tristan and Isolde proved their false innocence by some cunning ruse.

Finally, the lovers were exiled. The king invited them to return, however, when he discovered them innocently asleep in a cave, a sword between them. Although King Mark urged propriety on their return to court, Tristan and Isolde almost immediately abandoned all caution, driven as they were by the caprices of love. Knowing that the king would have them killed if they were discovered, Tristan set out from Cornwall after accepting a ring from his beloved as a token of their fidelity to each other.

During his travels, Tristan performed deeds of knightly valor in Germany, Champagne, and Normandy. In gratitude for his services in Normandy, the duke gave him his daughter Isolde, called Isolde of the White Hands to distinguish her from Isolde the Fair, as his bride. Lovesick and dejected, Tristan accepted his bride in name only—the name Isolde.

(At this point Gottfried's narrative breaks off abruptly. From his source materials and from related versions, the ending that may be constructed is that Tristan was fatally wounded by a poisoned spear and that Isolde the Fair, summoned from Cornwall, arrived after her lover had died. Shock and grief caused her death also. King Mark, learning of the love potion, forgave them and ordered the lovers buried side by side in Cornwall.)

Critical Evaluation:

Richard Wagner's opera follows the basic plot of Gottfried von Strassburg's earlier version of this famous tale. The version Wagner chose, nineteen thousand or so lines of which are attributed to Gottfried, is an excellent and extensive telling of one of the most famous love stories of all times. This metrical romance does not follow the line of chivalric romance developed by other writers, and there is no wearisome repetition of knightly deeds of valor in war and tournaments. Instead, Gottfried celebrates romantic love as being greater than chivalric love; his conception of love is more inward, at once enchanting and enthralling, bewildering and ecstatic, one that sways the soul and makes martyrs of those who have partaken of love's sacrament. The landscape against which Tristan and Isolde move often suggests an inner dream-world of mysterious compulsion.

Tristan and Isolde is unique in many ways. Although its material is courtly in nature, the poem ends tragically, rather than in the usual redemptive ending, and the sphere of reference is not specifically courtly. In his prologue, Gottfried defines his audience as those "noble hearts" who share the sufferings and joys of love, and who are willing to accept the power of love as the central value in life. All other courtly values—honor, religious faith, feudal fidelity—are subordinated to the one overriding force of passion, conceived as an external objective force and symbolized in the magic potion. Even Gottfried's conception of love departs from the courtly pattern, for rather than the usual unfulfilled longing and devoted service of the knight, love in this story is mutual, freely given, and outside the conventions of courtly society. It is a law unto itself and destructive of the social order.

The material of the legend, like that of the Arthurian sagas, may be traced back to Celtic origins, although no versions prior to the twelfth century are extant. In the late 1100's, the story took shape, and it is the French version by the Anglo-Norman poet Thomas of Brittany, or Britain (c. 1160) that provided the direct source for Gottfried—and which enables scholars to construct the probable ending of Gottfried's unfinished work. In Thomas' version, the approach is still distinctly courtly; Gottfried's departures from the norm may be attributed both to his own origin and to his time. Gottfried was most likely not a member of courtly society himself, but rather a member of the middle class of the important commercial city of Strassburg. He was wealthy and well educated—as evidenced by his extensive knowledge of theology and law—and familiar with French and German literature, as well as the Latin that was the universal language of higher education at the time. His work shows mastery of formal rhetorical devices and a knowledge of Latin literature remarkable for his time. His literary sophistication is evident in the extended discussion of German authors of his day that he inserts into the story at a point where Tristan's investiture would be discussed. It is in this literary excursus that he voices his praise of Hartmann von Aue and castigates Wolfram von Eschenbach for having an excessively difficult and erratic style.

This critical attitude toward his courtly contemporaries is reflected in his approach to the conventions of courtly romance, and helps to explain the uniqueness of his work. He is not above mocking even the rituals of the Church, as when Isolde successfully passes a trial by fire through an elaborate ruse that enables her to avoid perjury on a technicality, but destroys the intent and integrity of the trial. "Christ," Gottfried says, "is as pliable as a windblown sleeve." One must in fairness point out that by 1210, such a mockery would not be terribly shocking to the educated classes, who would regard the whole idea of trial by fire as rather archaic and superstitious.

Gottfried's discussion of love borrows heavily from the language of mystical writers, both in the prologue, where the elevating and ennobling qualities generally ascribed to courtly love take on religious significance through the use of specifically religious metaphors and in the body of the work, where, both in his imagery and in his presentation of a scale of values, Gottfried stresses the sacred and transfiguring power of love. St. Bernard of Clairvaux has been identified as a source of much of Gottfried's religious love imagery. Scholars are divided on the degree to which one should view this cult of love as an attempt to create a surrogate religion; there is no question, however, that Gottfried viewed love's claims as exerting a powerful counterforce against the social and religious conventions of the time.

The turning away from the public, external values of the courtly epics toward the inner, personal, emotional values of *Tristan and Isolde* is consistent with the wider cultural trends of the time: the new grace and sensitivity evident in the sculptures of the North Portal at Chartres, and the break with the conventions of courtly love in the later songs of Walther von der

Vogelweide, whose poems develop an ideal of love in which physical consummation replaces the state of prolonged yearning that is the subject of the poetry of the earlier phase of courtly love. The mystical qualities of this love are portrayed in the scene in the Cave of Love, which is an elaborate allegory expressing the ideal state toward which love strives. The sequence of trials and traps surrounding Tristan and Isolde, however, depicts the reality experienced by the "noble hearts" whom Gottfried is addressing in his poem when they must live in a world that does not accord to the power of love its due respect.

In this world, the lovers are far from ideal. Isolde uses her servant Brangene shamelessly, and even considers murdering her to prevent possible exposure, while Tristan, banished from the court at last, falls in love with Isolde of the White Hands, lacking the fidelity that Isolde demonstrates. How Gottfried might have resolved this dichotomy can only be guessed, but it is clear that Gottfried saw the company of "noble hearts" as forever torn between love's joy and sorrow, and accepting both as equally valid. It is precisely this quality of bitterness that separates love's votaries from the mundane world of pleasureseekers, and it is in relation to this ambivalent state that Gottfried explains the purpose of his work: Sad stories of love increase the pain of a heart that already feels love's sadness, yet the noble heart cannot help but be drawn again and again to the contemplation of love. Like the sacraments of the Church, Gottfried's work is mystical communion: "Their death is the bread of the living." In this insistence upon the centrality of love, Gottfried's romantic tragedy is both the culmination and turning point of the tradition of courtly love in Germany.

"Critical Evaluation" by Steven C. Schaber

Bibliography:

Bromwich, Rachel. "The *Tristan* of the Welsh." In *The Arthur of the Welsh: The Arthurian Legend in Medieval Welsh Literature*, edited by Rachel Bromwich, A. O. H. Jarman, and Brynley F. Roberts. Cardiff: University of Wales Press, 1991. Discusses the Celtic sources of the Tristan legend, and argues that they existed mostly in fragments until the fifteenth century.

Ferrante, Joan M. "'*Ez ist ein zunge, dunket mich*': Fiction, Deception and Self-Deception in Gottfried's *Tristan*." In *Gottfried von Strassburg and the Medieval Tristan Legend*, edited by Adrian Stevens and Roy Wisbey. Cambridge: D. S. Brewer, 1990. Masterful essay discusses how all the characters perpetrate deceits upon others. Argues that Gottfried implies that emulation of the characters would cause one to be destroyed as the characters are.

Jackson, W. T. H. "Gottfried von Strassburg." In *Arthurian Literature in the Middle Ages*, edited by R. S. Loomis. Oxford, England: Clarendon Press, 1959. Asserts Tristan's sensual love of Isolde is a reflection of the spiritual love they have for each other, and that this spirituality excuses their actions.

Jaeger, C. Stephen. *Medieval Humanism in Gottfried von Strassburg's "Tristan und Isolde."* Heidelberg, Germany: Winter, 1977. Argues that society is at fault for not being able to cope adequately with the love of Tristan and Isolde.

Rougemont, Denis de. *Love in the Western World*. Translated by Montgomery Belgion. Princeton, N.J.: Princeton University Press, 1983. Rougemont describes courtly love, in particular, the relationship in the Tristan legend. Argues that it is self-defeating and even masks a death wish.

TRISTIA

Type of work: Poetry
Author: Osip Mandelstam (1891-1938)
First published: Tristia, 1922; second edition, 1923 (English translation, 1973)

Osip Mandelstam's second collection of verses, *Tristia,* was published in 1922, under unusual and intriguing circumstances. The manuscript was taken to Berlin, and the poems were arranged by a fellow poet, Mikhail Kuzmin, who also gave it the title, after one of the best poems in the collection. Mandelstam borrowed the title itself from Ovid's work by the same name. Mandelstam was not satisfied, however, with the way the publication was handled. When he published the second edition in 1923, he changed the title to *Vtoraia kniga* (second book), and rearranged the poems. Since the collection was republished as *Tristia,* and since Mandelstam later referred to it as such, *Tristia* has now been accepted as the only legitimate title. Perhaps the reason Mandelstam accepted the title was the fact that, like Ovid, he wrote most of the *Tristia* poems on the shores of the Black Sea, and he brought the manuscript from there. Moreover, Mandelstam's life, in which he was frequently on the run, mostly as an internal exile, parallels that of Ovid. His lifelong fascination with classical antiquity also identifies him with Ovid.

Forty-five mostly untitled poems in *Tristia* were written between 1916 and 1920. The poems mark the highest achievements in the early stage of Mandelstam's poetic career, and they represent some of the best poems he wrote. There is no unifying subject in the collection, but several distinct themes can be discerned. What strikes the reader the most are the preponderant references to classical antiquity. The most obvious theme, already familiar from the first collection *Stone* (1913), is Mandelstam's homage to Rome and its civilization. The theme reflects his fascination with the Mediterranean culture and with the unity between cultures which it represents. In a poem of beautiful visual images, "Venetian Life," he uses a Renaissance painting to sing an ode to Rome, the beautiful city on the Adriatic where "jewels are heavy" and where "there is no salvation from love." A beautiful Georgian woman who had lost her cameo resembles a beautiful Roman woman ("I've lost a delicate cameo"). Persephone— the Greek goddess of the afterlife and the wife of Hades, but also used by Mandelstam as a Roman goddess—is mentioned in several poems ("I am cold," "Swallow," "As Psyche-Life goes down to the shades"). Mandelstam expresses his greatest veneration of Rome in the short poem, "Nature's the same as Rome":

> Nature's the same as Rome, was reflected in it.
> We see images of its civic might
> In the clear air, as in the sky-blue circus,
> In the forum of fields, the colonnades of groves

Mandelstam feels that nature has found its most perfect embodiment in Rome where nature and culture are one and where "stones exist in order to build."

While the references in *Kamen* are mostly to Rome, in *Tristia,* Mandelstam dwells on ancient Greece. There are references to the classical world in many poems: Phedre ("No matter how I concealed them"); "the sacred mace of Heracles" ("The Menagerie"); immortal roses of Kypris ("In Petersburg we'll meet again"); and many others. In "The Greeks planned for war," Mandelstam sees Europe as the new Hellas, and he beseeches it to save Acropolis and Piraeus.

The long poem, "The thick golden stream of honey took so long" best expresses Mandelstam's love for ancient Greece, where the proverbial golden honey flows in the streets, "the service of Bacchus is everywhere," and "the peaceful days roll by." The poet ends his apotheosis with a mournful cry:

> Golden fleece, where are you, golden fleece?
> The sea's heavy waves roared the whole way.
> Abandoning the ship, its sail worn out,
> Odysseus returned, full with space and time.

This poem, written during World War I and the Russian revolution, expresses Mandelstam's yearning for more peaceful times and sunny shores. Mandelstam identifies peace, happiness, and plenitude with ancient Greece.

The poem "Tortoise" is another apotheosis of the beauty of ancient Greece. Here "blind lyrists, like bees give us Ionic honey," "cicadas click like hammers forging out a ring," and "the honeysuckle smells, to the joy of the bees." The poem is an idyll of an arcadian landscape, yet it is an idyll different from that of the Parnassians. Mandelstam feels that the quintessential art in classical Greece was music, not visual arts—hence the metaphor of tortoise resembling the form of a lyre, an instrument. Moreover, because he wanted to use poetry to reflect the vicissitudes of his own fate—in this instance, the danger of the loss of artistic freedom—Mandelstam weaves pictorial and musical images into his own canvas of a land which he places in the Arcadia and in the islands of the Greek archipelago, the symbol of ancient Hellas.

The third frame of reference is Jewish culture and history. Though Jewish by origin, Mandelstam was drawn, first to Catholicism, then to classical antiquity; he attempted to find in them a sense of his own orientation. He not only preserved his Jewish background, but he also used his background as a bridge between the Christian and Judaean cultures—a kind of symbiosis that best reflected his own thinking and achieved the unity he desired. In "This night is beyond recall," Mandelstam re-creates the funereal atmosphere shortly after the death of his mother: "And the voices of the Israelites/ Rose above the mother./ I awoke in a cradle, shone upon/ By a black sun." This poem illustrates the poet's ability to use personal experience to transcend a fixed moment in history—in this case, the world war. The fact that the persona awakes in the cradle alone signifies the poet's danger of losing his roots altogether, without finding a new mooring. The foreboding of the potential demise of the ancient and Christian cultures is underscored by the personal tragedy of "the Israelites." Similar concerns are expressed in "The young Levite among the priests," where Levite futilely warns his older compatriots of the dangers threatening them all. At the end of the poem, however, Mandelstam sees hope: "We swaddled the Sabbath in precious linen/ With a heavy Menorah lit the night of Jerusalem." The reference to Christ corresponds to the poet's long-harbored desire for a rejuvenation of the two cultures. In "Go back to the tainted lap, Leah," Mandelstam completes his vision of unity by stating that the Hebrew, Leah, must, and will, undergo a change: "You are in love with a Jew,/ You will vanish in him, and/ God will be with you."

Finally, Mandelstam combines classical antiquity and its heir, Eastern Orthodoxy, with his Jewish roots and Catholicism in order to express his yearning for unity between all these cultures, as symbolized by a metaphor of the "eternal cathedrals" of Sofia (the East) and Peter (the West) in the final poem of the collection.

Mandelstam does not always seek refuge in antiquity; he is painfully aware of his own time and place. Even when he flees to the past, he uses these excursions to fend off the problems besetting him. Nowhere is this more evident than in "Tristia," the title poem of the book. Here, through his knowledge of classical antiquity, he foreshadows the separation from his dear ones. The poem parallels the fate of the Roman poet Ovid, who was banished for political reasons to the shores of the Black Sea, where he wrote poetry and where he died. Many of the details in Mandelstam's poem closely follow Ovid's elegy of the same title.

"Tristia" reflects the mood of a person leaving his home, his city, and, possibly, his country—an experience that was always present in the poet's mature life and that turned out to be his final destiny. Stating that he has learned the "science of parting," he gives expression to melancholy mixed with stoicism, even defiance, and he gives expression to hope mixed with latent despair, and to his tacit understanding of what life is about. In this sense, "Tristia" is one of the most essential poems in Mandelstam's works. At the time he wrote the poem, he was threatened by numerous dangers, and he had several close calls. The possibility of involuntary parting must have occurred to him often, and his thorough knowledge of classical literature enabled him, by using Ovid as a model, to give artistic expression to such thoughts and sentiments. The typically Mandelstamian formal aspects—striking images and metaphors; a mixture of lyrical and reflective passages; sporadic departures from the main train of thought; frequent interventions on the part of the poet; and the unique rhythm—all enhance the artistic qualities of "Tristia."

Other references to Mandelstam's own time and place abound. The references concern his beloved city, St. Petersburg, and the looming danger of the Bolsheviks. St. Petersburg is, for Mandelstam, the epitome of an urban society founded on spiritual values. He mentions St. Petersburg again and again, calling it Petropolis as a perfect model of a life-giving city. He is also aware of the dangers of betrayal and decay, as in the poem "At a dreadful height, a wandering fire":

> Above the black Neva, transparent Spring
> Is smashed, the wax of immortality is melting.
> O, if you, star, are Petropolis, your city,
> Your brother, Petropolis, is dying.

The source of this concern is the rise of the Bolshevik menace. In one of his most powerful poems, "The Twilight of Freedom," Mandelstam at first urges his "brothers" to glorify the twilight of freedom, which was one of the first goals and promises of the Bolsheviks. When the ship of the state is set at sea, however, the destination is ambiguous; it could lead to a new dawn or it could lead to perdition. Even though the poet urges his countrymen to have courage and try ("We will recall even in Lethe's frost,/ That our land was worth ten heavens"), and even though Mandelstam hints at Lenin taking the nation's helm, the poem has its ambiguities, beginning with the title (the Russian *sumerki*, for example, means either dawn or twilight). Written in 1918, at the beginning of the Russian revolution, the poem reflects Mandelstam's ambivalence toward the revolution.

Among other noteworthy efforts are the three poems to Olga Arbenina, a woman with whom Mandelstam was briefly in love ("I am cold," "I want to serve you," and "If I am to know how to restrain your hands"). There is also an often-cited and exquisitely crafted poem, "Solominka" (the straw), about the death of a beautiful woman in love. "Just for joy, take from my palms," in turn, is one of the most beautiful poems of the collection; in this poem, Mandelstam uses the daring metaphors of bees and honey as symbols of artistic creativity.

Tristia is one of Mandelstam's most important works, and it contains many poems of lasting value. Translations of individual poems of *Tristia* were published in various sources over the years. The first attempt at publishing most of the poems in one group was made by Bruce McClelland in *The Silver Age of Russian Culture* in 1975; in 1987, McClelland published the entire collection in a bilingual edition.

Vasa D. Mihailovich

Bibliography:
Brown, Clarence. *Mandelstam.* Cambridge, England: Cambridge University Press, 1973. The best study of Mandelstam in English. Brown stresses the artistic merits of the poems. Chapter 12 analyzes several poems of *Tristia*, and chapter 13 deals with the classical elements of the collection. Extensive notes, excellent bibliography, and index.
Broyde, Steven. *Osip Mandel'stam and His Age: A Commentary on the Themes of War and Revolution in the Poetry, 1913-1923.* Cambridge, Mass.: Harvard University Press, 1975. A book-length analysis of Mandelstam's poems about the revolution. Includes several poems from *Tristia.*
Cavanagh, Clare. *Osip Mandelstam and the Modernist Creation of Tradition.* Princeton, N.J.: Princeton University Press, 1995. A thorough study of the modernist aspects of Mandelstam's poetry based on classical traditions. Includes numerous references to *Tristia* in several chapters on specific topics. Copious notes and a detailed index.
Mandelstam, Nadezhda. *Hope Against Hope: A Memoir.* Translated by Max Hayward. New York: Atheneum, 1970. *Hope Abandoned.* Translated by Max Hayward. New York: Atheneum, 1974. A two-volume memoir by Mandelstam's widow. Relates personal circumstances guiding his life and works. Indispensable for an understanding of the poet, the genesis of many of his poems, and the efforts at preserving them from destruction.
Nilsson, Nils Ake. "Mandelstam and the Revolution." *Scando-Slavica* 19 (1973): 7-16. A succinct analysis of the poem "The Twilight of Freedom" in *Tristia.* Attempts to ascertain Mandelstam's attitude toward the Russian revolution through the obscure imagery of the poem.

TRISTRAM

Type of work: Poetry
Author: Edwin Arlington Robinson (1869-1935)
Type of plot: Arthurian romance
Time of plot: Arthurian period
Locale: England and Brittany
First published: 1927

> *Principal characters:*
> TRISTRAM, Prince of Lyonesse
> MARK, his uncle, King of Cornwall
> HOWEL, King of Brittany
> ISOLT OF THE WHITE HANDS, Howel's daughter
> ISOLT, Princess of Ireland
> GOUVERNAIL, Tristram's friend
> ANDRED, Mark's minion
> QUEEN MORGAN, the wily queen

The Story:

Isolt of the white hands was too pensive and preoccupied for a young woman. She was always looking to the north, toward England. Her father, King Howel of Brittany, loved his daughter too much to let her attitude go unquestioned. Isolt told her father she was waiting for Tristram, who some time before had made a visit to the Breton court. Fond of Isolt as an adult is fond of a child, Tristram had given her on his departure an agate for a keepsake and had promised to come back. Now Isolt was a woman of eighteen, and she waited for Tristram as a woman waits for her lover. King Howel tried to tell her that Tristram thought of her as a child, and that he probably would not return; but Isolt would not be convinced.

In Cornwall it was the wedding day of old, lecherous King Mark and the dark and beautiful Isolt of Ireland, his bride. With the wedding feast in full swing, the wine cup was often passed. Sick of the drunken merriment and sicker with inner torment, Tristram, nephew of the king, left the feast and wandered in the fresh night air. King Mark, displeased by his nephew's absence, sent Gouvernail, Tristram's preceptor and friend, to ask him to return. Tristram said only that he was sick. Then Queen Morgan came to talk to Tristram. She used all her arts and blandishments on the brooding knight, and they were cunning indeed, for Queen Morgan, much experienced in the arts of love, was more than a little attracted to Tristram. Tristram repeated stubbornly that he was sick.

Then there was a soft step on the stair, as Brangwaine came, followed a moment later by dark-caped, violet-eyed Isolt of Ireland herself. She looked at Tristram but said nothing as he took her in his arms. Memories hung about them like a cloud.

King Mark was old and unattractive, and he had wanted a young wife in his castle. Yearning for Isolt of Ireland, he had sent as emissary his gallant nephew, Tristram, to plead his cause. Tristram had to fight even to get to the Irish court. After he had slain the mighty Morhaus, Isolt's uncle, he made a bargain of state with the Irish king and took Isolt back to Cornwall in his boat. One night they were alone with only the sea and the stars to look upon them. Isolt waited in vain for Tristram to speak. If he had, she would have loved him then, and there would have been no marriage of convenience with King Mark. Bound by knightly fealty Tristram kept silent and delivered Isolt to his uncle. Now he looked at her and regretted bitterly that he had not spoken on the boat.

Andred stole behind them to spy on them. He was a faithful servitor of King Mark, but jealousy of Tristram and love for Isolt motivated him as well. Tristram saw Andred skulking in the shadow, seized him, and threw him on the rocks. When King Mark himself came out to inquire about his absent guests, he stumbled over Andred's unconscious body and stood unseen long enough to hear the passionate avowals of Tristram and Isolt. Since Tristram was his nephew, King Mark did not have him killed, but he banished Tristram forever from Cornwall on pain of burning at the stake.

The sick Tristram wandered in a fever. When he recovered, he found himself the captive of Queen Morgan in her castle. Queen Morgan eventually gave up her siege of Tristram's heart and let him go. Next Tristram went to Brittany, where a griffin, giant scourge of the Breton land, was threatening King Howel and his court. Knightly Tristram, fierce in battle although sick for love, slew the griffin. As a hero, Tristram had a secure place at King Howel's court, and there he married Isolt of the white hands. He pitied her and she loved him, although she knew of his sorrow. For two years Tristram was a faithful husband and reigning prince.

Then from the north came another ship with Gawaine aboard bringing a message from King Arthur. For his deeds Tristram was to become a Knight of the Round Table; hence his summons to Camelot. Isolt watched her husband go with quiet despair, for she feared he would not come back. She had little dread of King Mark, for Gawaine had told her in secrecy that King Mark was in prison. The Cornish king had forged the Pope's signature on a paper ordering Tristram to go fight the Saracens, and his forgery had been detected. Isolt nevertheless knew that Tristram's danger lay in Cornwall.

Guinevere, Arthur's queen, and her lover, Lancelot, plotted to bring Irish Isolt and Tristram together. Lancelot took Tristram to Joyous Guard, his trysting castle, and Guinevere brought Isolt of Ireland secretly out of Cornwall. So the lovers were together again, while King Mark was in prison. They had a happy summer together and as autumn drew near Tristram lost a little of his apprehension. Early one morning he went out on the sea while Isolt slept. When he returned, there were strangers in Joyous Guard and Isolt was gone. King Mark, released from prison, had abducted his wife and carried her off to Cornwall.

Tristram moped in silence until he had a letter from Queen Morgan. She chided him for his lovesickness and urged him to see his Isolt once more. Goaded by the wily queen, Tristram rode to Cornwall prepared to fight and die for a last look at Isolt. When he arrived at his uncle's castle, he entered easily and in surprised joy sought out Isolt. She told him that she was near death. King Mark, in pity for her wasting figure and sick heart, had given her permission to receive her lover. Isolt and Tristram, sad in their love because Isolt was to die, sat on the shore and gazed out at a still ship on the quiet ocean. While they sat thus, the jealous Andred crept up behind them and stabbed Tristram in the back. Tristram, therefore, died before the ailing Isolt. King Mark finally realized that Andred was also in love with Isolt, and he regretted that his lecherous lust for a young queen had brought sorrow and death.

Gouvernail went back to Brittany to convey the grievous news of Tristram's death to Isolt of the white hands, who divined the truth when he disembarked alone. He told her only part of Tristram's sojourn in England, only that Tristram had seen the dying Isolt of Ireland a last time with King Mark's consent, and that Andred had killed Tristram by treachery. Isolt was silent in her grief; no one could know what she was thinking, nor how much she divined of Tristram and the other Isolt. Now Isolt looked no more for a ship from England. On the white sea the white birds and the sunlight were alive. The white birds were always flying and the sunlight flashed on the sea.

Critical Evaluation:

Tristram is the most romantic of Edwin Arlington Robinson's works, in theme, poetic treatment, and philosophy. It culminates a lifetime of interest in the medieval legends surrounding King Arthur. Robinson's interest is reflected in shorter poems ("Miniver Cheevy," 1910) and other long works (*Merlin*, 1917; *Lancelot*, 1920). Although far from light reading, *Tristram* was a success with the American public, and this is only partly to be attributed to the Pulitzer Prize of 1928. Robinson wrote from a deep belief that the love of Tristram and Isolt paralleled the love of many people, even in his own time. In its elimination of some of the traditional colorful details, Robinson's treatment of the story may be considered somewhat stark, although his simpler imagery is beautiful.

The chief element in the original legend that separates the lovers from ordinary human experience was that their love springs from a supernatural potion. Prior to imbibing this potion, Tristram and Isolt were content with fulfilling their obligations: he to provide a bridge for his uncle, and she to wed a king. After drinking the brew, they cast their commitments aside. Robinson prefers to motivate the story differently, in order to bring it into the sphere of realism.

The brief journey across the sea from Ireland to Cornwall is, in an example of such a realistic touch, long enough for an attraction between two people to begin, but not enough for them to become fully conscious of it. Tristram, already pursued by Queen Morgan and adored by King Howel's daughter, was simply blasé about women finding him attractive. Isolt of Ireland was more aware of her feelings, but she was distracted by wounded pride and anxiety about her future. Once tender Isolt, with her "dark young majesty," and jaded Mark of the wet mouth and "senile claws" are placed together, the prospect of such an incompatible sexual union jolts Tristram and Isolt awake to their attraction to each other.

The experience of kicking oneself for realizing something too late, reflected in the "soul-retching waves" of the ocean, is universally human. In addition, a story has grown up around Robinson regarding his love for his sister-in-law, Emma. The facts are these: When a young man of twenty, a year out of high school, with no particular thought of settling down, Robinson met a charming young woman during a lazy summer vacation. Into this slowly evolving friendship burst Robinson's older brother, Herman, a businessman often on the road, who descended on the vacation resort and wooed and won Emma in the space of few weeks. They were married almost at once. Around the time of this wedding Robinson began a deeply pessimistic work ultimately entitled "The Night Before" (published in 1896 but excluded from his *Collected Works*). Herman's marriage was unhappy and destructive. Robinson is believed to have proposed to Emma after she was widowed (possibly reflected in his self-mocking poem, *The March of the Cameron Men*, 1932).

Regardless of whether one accepts the romanticizing of Robinson's life, the romanticism of his philosophy is fully a match for the Tristram legend. Robinson grew up in an increasingly materialistic society which seemed on the verge of explaining everything in terms of a mechanized and accidental universe. Robinson opposed this view on many fronts, guided by New England transcendentalism and other idealistic trends, including Swedenborgianism. His ultimate justification for his views was intuitive. Tristram and Isolt's love, so intense and yet, as Robinson believed, so typical rules out the possibility of a mechanistically determined universe. His Tristram argues that before human beings had ever been created, first such a love had to have been conceived. The universe was created in order to bring love about. Love is too much of a marvel to have been an accident; therefore, the universe that created it could not have been an accident. Despite the inherent tragedy of the tale, therefore, the reader comes away with a sense of optimism.

Robinson breaks into once-forbidden territory with descriptions of sexuality that are frank and poetic. The poignancy of Isolt as a tragic romantic heroine is elegantly expressed in the same vocabulary that conveys her sexual appeal: She is dark, trembling, and liquefying. The fact that she melts against Tristram, "with the sure surrender of a child," even after the years of her marriage to Mark, is a delicate indication that her feelings for Tristram are in a sense virginal. The ability of both lovers to rise above the jealousy of their rivals evolves into selflessness. This evolution of their love beyond the first romantic impulse into something complex and disciplined, is the modern, rather innovative, and not always welcomed part of Robinson's contribution to the subject.

In their philosophical colloquies, Tristram and Isolt develop Robinson's ideas of the smallness of life and death, which are two "abysmal little words" in the face of love. When Isolt is dragged by force back to Mark, Mark feels the "smallness" of death when she looks at him. Isolt is often described with irony as "small." Another word that the lovers discuss, and cut down to size, is time. Life is not years, and it is not time that fills life full.

The poem is a model of parallel construction. Episodes alternate until, at the conclusion, the original cast is reassembled. The background of the sea, a timeless symbol of human emotions, pervades the story and provides many of the secondary symbols.

"Critical Evaluation" by D. Gosselin Nakeeb

Bibliography:
Anderson, Wallace L. *Edwin Arlington Robinson: A Critical Introduction*. Boston: Houghton Mifflin, 1967. Examines Robinson's life and work. Absorbs all the preceding scholarship. Bibliography.
Carpenter, Frederick Ives. "Tristram the Transcendent." In *Appreciation of Edwin Arlington Robinson: Twenty-eight Interpretive Essays*, edited by Richard Cary. Waterville, Maine: Colby College Press, 1969. A mature and subtle interpretation of the fates and choices of Robinson's characters. Addresses the theme of time.
Davis, Charles T. "Image Patterns in the Poetry of Edwin Arlington Robinson." In *Appreciation of Edwin Arlington Robinson: Twenty-eight Interpretive Essays*, edited by Richard Cary. Waterville, Maine: Colby College Press, 1969. Guides the reader through the fully developed imagery of *Tristram* as a symbolic system.
Franchere, Hoyt C. *Edwin Arlington Robinson*. New York: Twayne, 1968. A concise and focused study of the life and work, balancing external events with the poet's internal evolution. The author's thorough research turns up interesting details not found in other general works.
Neff, Emery. *Edwin Arlington Robinson*. New York: William Sloane Associates, 1948. Lively biographical account, with emphasis on external factors in the genesis of the works. *Tristram* is discussed for its sexual frankness and modern attitude toward women.
Romig, Edna Davis. "Tilbury Town and Camelot." In *Appreciation of Edwin Arlington Robinson: Twenty-eight Interpretive Essays*, edited by Richard Cary. Waterville, Maine: Colby College Press, 1969. Brings out the beauty and poignancy of *Tristram*.

THE TRIUMPH OF DEATH

Type of work: Novel
Author: Gabriele D'Annunzio (1863-1938)
Type of plot: Psychological realism
Time of plot: Nineteenth century
Locale: Italy
First published: Il trionfo della morte, 1894 (English translation, 1896)

Principal characters:

GIORGIO AURISPA, a young Italian of wealth and family
SIGNOR AURISPA, George's materialistic father
IPPOLITA, George's mistress

The Story:

Giorgio Aurispa, a young Italian of old family and sufficient money to enjoy life without working, had fallen in love with a lovely married woman named Ippolita. She had lived with her husband only a few weeks, for she had fallen ill shortly after her marriage. When the affair with Giorgio began, she left her husband and returned to her family. Marriage was out of the question for the lovers. For religious reasons, they could not marry as long as one or the other had a living spouse.

Infatuated, both Giorgio and Ippolita often wished they could spend even more time together. On the second anniversary of their first meeting, however, an incident occurred which both regarded as an ill omen and which cast a pall over their minds. As they walked in Rome's Pincio gardens, they came to a terrace where a man had just committed suicide. Blood and a lock of blond hair were still in evidence.

The suicide of the unknown young man in the Pincio affected the lovers even more than they realized at the time. Giorgio began to feel that materialism and sensuality, fostered by his love for Ippolita, had taken too firm a hold upon him. Ippolita, on the other hand, was warned again of her own mortality and the fact that she had a tendency toward epilepsy.

Soon afterward Giorgio was called home. His father and mother did not live together, and Giorgio had known for some time that his father kept a mistress. During the visit he learned for the first time the full story of his father's conduct. His mother told him that his father had despoiled the family fortune, refused a dowry for their daughter, and lived openly with his mistress and two illegitimate children. Giorgio disliked the financial entanglements of the situation; he had inherited his own money from an uncle. When Giorgio visited his father to intercede for his family, the young man did nothing to help his mother and sister. Instead, he agreed to sign a note as surety for his father, who was trying to borrow money from a bank. Giorgio, however, was struck by the way his father had surrendered completely to a life of gross materialism.

Before he left his mother to return to Rome, Giorgio visited the apartment in the mansion where his uncle had lived. His uncle had committed suicide. The realization of his uncle's deed filled him with curiosity and melancholy, and he almost decided to kill himself with the same dueling pistol his uncle had used.

Returning to Rome, Giorgio again fell under the spell of Ippolita, even though he was now haunted by his fear of gross sensuality, the thought of suicide, and a friend's warning that Ippolita was coarse beneath her beauty and would someday find a richer lover.

In order to escape from his fears, Giorgio searched for a place where he and Ippolita could be away from the world. He thought that in a small village on the Adriatic coast they could live in peace and he could work out his emotional and psychological problems.

Their new secluded life, however, left Giorgio in even more of a quandary. There were times when he felt great happiness in being with his mistress day and night. At other times he saw in her only the embodiment of the same animal nature that was slowly but surely ensnaring him as it had ensnared his father. In order to escape, to achieve idealism, Giorgio once more considered taking his own life.

The Church offered no solution to his problem. He and Ippolita were, in their way, devout. They visited shrines, but the mobs of humanity, the beggars with their sores and ills, only repulsed the lovers. Ippolita's spell continued to work its way with Giorgio. Ippolita was proud of her power to awaken his desires, and she used this power constantly. Giorgio loved her and hated her at the same time, but he knew that he was not without blame. When their affair had begun, she was modest and almost frigid. Her husband, to whom she had been married by her family, had been brutal, and she had been ill. Giorgio, the first to stir her emotions, had helped to shape her personality.

Like all people living together, they discovered some irritating traits in each other. Giorgio was displeased with Ippolita's feet, which he regarded as too common-looking. She, on the other hand, thought he was often too morbid. Both of them tried too hard, as they readily admitted, to escape into an idealized world of pleasure.

Trying by all means to keep from antagonizing each other, they continued to make short excursions away from the village. Giorgio had a piano and music sent from Rome to their retreat. Still Giorgio found himself thinking not only of his death but of Ippolita's as well. He sometimes believed that he could escape from sensuality only through the loss of his beloved. Death was the means he knew he must take to banish her irrevocably. She, for her part, seemed to realize what was in his mind. She had dreams in which she saw him dead or taking threatening attitudes toward her. Again, in Giorgio's mind, she was the most beautiful and fascinating of women, for her power over him continued to grow. Often, when he was emotionally distressed, she could draw him from that state of mind with nothing more than a kiss.

One afternoon, while they were swimming, Giorgio had an impulse to drown Ippolita. She seemed to sense his mood and refused to go bathing with him again. One night they had a pleasant meal together. Later that evening, with great effort on his part, so strong was her physical charm at such a time, Giorgio persuaded his mistress to take a walk down to the rocky coast where fishermen were working at their nets. When they came to a one-plank bridge over which they had to walk, Ippolita grew dizzy at the sight of waves and rocks below and refused to cross. Giorgio, however, felt that he had found the time and place for his despairing deed; he swept Ippolita into his arms and plunged both of them to death on the rocks below.

Critical Evaluation:

Gabriele D'Annunzio's early work was written under the influence of French writers, particularly those associated with the Decadent movement. *The Triumph of Death* was published after *The Child of Pleasure* (1889), which had followed and analyzed the troubled inner life of a Roman nobleman in a similar fashion. *The Triumph of Death* is a more sophisticated work than its predecessor, offering a psychological analysis of greater depth, but its power comes from its relentless fascination with mortality.

The story told by the novel is essentially a long explanation of Giorgio's eventual decision to commit suicide and take Ippolita with him. Perhaps it is also a justification of that act, insofar as it might be justified, but D'Annunzio takes care to maintain a distance between himself and his subject. He describes Giorgio's impressions in minute detail, but he refrains from confirming their validity or condoning their morality. It is worth bearing in mind that D'Annunzio went on to write works of a very different nature, forsaking Decadent pessimism to the extent that he became a passionate advocate of mechanical progress, a war hero and—eventually—a supporter of Benito Mussolini; it would be a mistake to identify him too closely with his protagonist.

Giorgio's disaffection has two root causes. One is his exaggerated distaste for what he considers to be the degradation of his fellow human beings. This reaches a climax in the scenes at the shrine, where the maimed, the mad, and the miserable gather in a vast jostling crowd, competing with animalistic fervor for the privilege of begging the Virgin Mary to grant them release from their suffering. The same distaste is given more intimate expression in the savagely scathing judgment that Giorgio delivers upon his greedy and deceitful father. It is worth noting that his judgment of his whining mother, his corpulent aunt, and his enfeebled sister Cristina is no more generous. The people he cannot hate he nevertheless contrives to hold in contempt.

Giorgio frequently disguises his vituperations as attacks on vulgar materialism, but such charges only ring true when they are applied to his father and his sponging friend Exili. What really offends him is infirmity and self-delusion in all their guises. An unsympathetic reader might be tempted to draw the conclusion that Giorgio's greatest fear is that his own strength is insufficient to sustain him against the temptations of self-delusion and the consequent acceptance of weakness. If this is so, the triumph of death to which the title refers might be reckoned a meek surrender to that gnawing anxiety.

The second and more specific cause of Giorgio's morbidity is his love for Ippolita. This may seem paradoxical, in that conventional wisdom asserts that love has an unparalleled power of life-enhancement, but in Giorgio's case the magnitude of his love merely intensifies the unbearability of knowing that it cannot endure. Giorgio cannot believe, even for a moment, in the myth of eternal love. He knows, as surely as he knows anything, that passion is transient, that it is by definition something that soars to a peak and then declines. He knows, too, that the higher the peak of ecstasy is to which lovers are borne, the further they must descend thereafter; the only question to be settled is how swift the descent will be. In this context, the method of Giorgio's suicide is highly significant. Giorgio chooses the most precipitous of all possible descents.

Readers sympathetic to this kind of extreme gesture might consider that the triumph of death is at least to be credited to Giorgio rather than inflicted upon him, although this hardly seems fair to poor Ippolita, who seems utterly guiltless. Although Mario Praz reserves a conspicuous place for her in the long list of Romantic and Decadent femmes fatales, Ippolita makes no active contribution to Giorgio's unbalanced state of mind. Giorgio's abrupt closure of their affair certainly avoids the ignominy of slow decay and degradation, but the decision to take her with him serves to undermine rather than to confirm its heroic dimension. There is an early scene in the novel in which Giorgio studies the audience assembled to hear a concert organized by a famous conductor, marvelling at its odd admixture of scientists and followers of unorthodox religion: "cold explorers of life and passionate devotees of the cult of dreams." Giorgio is both of these things, and his cold exploration of his own dreams is what will not let him decorate his love or his life with illusions. When he stands witness to the imbecilic hopes and futile desires of those more wretched than himself he is filled with horror.

In the years between the publication of *The Child of Pleasure* and *The Triumph of Death* D'Annunzio had become fascinated with the philosophy of Friedrich Nietzsche, but *The*

Triumph of Death is not a Nietzschean work in any straightforward sense. Were Giorgio an authentic Nietzschean hero he would have found a way out of his impasse. The Nietzschean will to power would have given Giorgio the energy to rise above his fixation with erotic excitement and make something of himself—preferably an artist. Giorgio does, however, qualify as a Nietzschean character in that he sees through the sham of contemporary ideas and ideals. He has realized that what passes for morality is merely a form of cowardice whose ultimate results are life-denying rather than life-enhancing.

Perhaps Giorgio's philosophy is best regarded as a failed experiment, which reveals by its failure that the road to a better philosophy leads in another direction—but this does not mean that the novel that tells his story is a failure. To the contrary, the novel achieves perfect unity and a highly effective closure. The novel is brilliantly detailed and precise. In a world filled with texts that stubbornly maintain that love offers the chance of permanent life-enhancement, *The Triumph of Death* is a useful exercise in skepticism with which to balance the argument.

Brian Stableford

Bibliography:
Jullian, Philippe. *D'Annunzio*. Translated by Stephen Hardman. London: Pall Mall Press, 1972. A comprehensive study of the man and his works. *The Triumph of Death* is discussed in chapter 5.
Klopp, Charles. *Gabriele D'Annunzio*. Boston: Twayne, 1988. A compact but thorough study of the man and his works.
Praz, Mario. *The Romantic Agony*. Translated by Angus Davidson. New York: Oxford University Press, 1933. This classic study of Romanticism and Decadence makes abundant reference to D'Annunzio. Section 24 of chapter 4 considers Ippolita as a femme fatale.
Rhodes, Anthony. *The Poet as Superman: A Life of Gabriele D'Annunzio*. London: Weidenfeld & Nicolson, 1959. A biography with some critical discussion. *The Triumph of Death* is discussed.

TROILUS AND CRESSIDA

Type of work: Drama
Author: William Shakespeare (1564-1616)
Type of plot: Tragedy
Time of plot: Antiquity
Locale: Troy
First performed: 1601-1602; first published, 1609

Principal characters:
PRIAM, King of Troy
HECTOR, and
TROILUS, his sons
AGAMEMNON,
ACHILLES,
ULYSSES,
AJAX, and
DIOMEDES, Greek commanders
PANDARUS, a Trojan lord
CRESSIDA, his niece

The Story:

During the Trojan War, Troilus, younger son of Priam, King of Troy, fell in love with the lovely and unapproachable Cressida, daughter of Calchas, a Trojan priest who had gone over to the side of the Greeks. Troilus, frustrated by his unrequited love, declared to Pandarus, a Trojan lord and uncle of Cressida, that he would refrain from fighting the Greeks as long as there was such turmoil in his heart. Pandarus added to Troilus' misery by praising the incomparable beauty of Cressida; Troilus impatiently chided Pandarus, who answered that for all it mattered to him Cressida could join her father in the Greek camp.

Later, Pandarus overheard Cressida and her servant discussing Hector's anger at having received a blow in battle from Ajax, a mighty Greek warrior of Trojan blood. Pandarus extolled Troilus' virtues to Cressida, who was all but indifferent. As the two discoursed, the Trojan forces returned from the field. Pandarus praised the several Trojan warriors—Aeneas, Antenor, Hector, Paris, Helenus—as they passed by Cressida's window, all the while anticipating, for Cressida's benefit, the passing of young Troilus. When the prince passed, Pandarus was lavish in his praise, but Cressida appeared to be bored. As Pandarus left her to join Troilus, Cressida soliloquized that she was charmed, indeed, by Troilus, but that she was in no haste to reveal the state of her affections.

In the Greek camp, meanwhile, Agamemnon, commander of the Greek forces in Ilium, tried to put heart into his demoralized leaders. Old Nestor declared that the seven difficult years of the siege of Troy had been a real test of Greek stamina. It was the belief of Ulysses that the difficulties of the Greeks lay in a lack of order and discipline, not in Trojan strength. He reminded his fellow Greek leaders that the disaffection of mighty Achilles and the scurrilous clowning of Patroclus, a Greek leader, had provoked disorder in the Greek ranks. Even Ajax, usually dependable, had become fractious, and his follower, deformed Thersites, embarrassed the Greeks with his taunts.

As the Greek leaders conferred, Aeneas delivered to them a challenge from Hector, who in single combat would defend the beauty and the virtue of his lady against a Greek champion. When the leaders went their several ways to announce the challenge to Achilles and to other Greeks, Ulysses and Nestor decided that the only politic action to take, the pride of Achilles being what it was, was to arrange somehow that Ajax be chosen to fight Hector. Ajax, Achilles, and Patroclus heard of the proclamation, but tended to disregard it. Their levity caused the railing Thersites to break with them.

In Troy, meanwhile, Hector was tempted to concede to a Greek offer to end hostilities if the Trojans returned Helen to her husband, King Menelaus. Troilus chided his brother and Helenus for their momentary want of resolution. As the brothers and their father, Priam, discussed the reasons for and against continuing the war, Cassandra, prophetess and daughter of Priam, predicted that Troy would be burned to the ground by the Greeks. Hector heeded her warning, but Troilus, joined by Paris, persisted in the belief that the war, for the sake of honor, must be continued. Hector, although aware of the evil the Trojans were committing in defending Paris' indefensible theft of Helen from her husband, conceded that for reasons of honor the fighting must continue.

The Greek leaders approached Achilles, who had kept to himself since his quarrel with Agamemnon. Refusing to confer with them, Achilles retired into his tent and sent his companion, Patroclus, to make his apologies. Achilles persisted in refusing to deal with the Greek commanders, who sought in him their champion against Hector. Ulysses played on the pride of Ajax with subtle flattery and convinced this Greek of Trojan blood that he should present himself as the Greek champion in place of Achilles.

In the meantime, Pandarus had prepared the way for a tryst between Troilus and Cressida by securing the promise of Paris and Helen to make excuses for Troilus' absence. He brought the two young people together in his orchard, where the pair confessed to each other their undying love. Cressida declared that if she were ever false, then all falsehood could forever afterward be associated with her name. Pandarus witnessed these sincere avowals of faith and himself declared that if Troilus and Cressida did not remain faithful to each other, then all go-betweens would be associated with his name. These declarations having been made, Pandarus led the young people to a bedchamber in his house.

In the Greek camp, Calchas, Cressida's father, persuaded Agamemnon to exchange Antenor, a Trojan prisoner, for Cressida, whose presence he desired. Diomedes, a Greek commander, was appointed to effect the exchange. Planning to ignore Achilles, the Greek leaders passed the warrior with only the briefest recognition. When he demanded an explanation of that treatment, Ulysses told him that fame was ephemeral and that great deeds were soon forgotten. Fearful for his reputation now that Ajax had been appointed Greek champion, Achilles arranged to play host to the unarmed Hector after the contest.

Diomedes returned Antenor to Troy, and, at dawn, he was taken to Pandarus' house to escort Cressida to the Greek camp. When Troilus and Cressida learned of Diomedes' mission, Troilus appealed unsuccessfully to the Trojan leaders to allow Cressida to remain in Troy. Heartbroken, he returned to Cressida and the young couple repeated their vows in their farewells. Troilus then escorted Cressida and Diomedes, who commented on Cressida's beauty, as far as the city gates. When Diomedes and Cressida encountered the Greek leaders outside the walls, Cressida was kissed by Agamemnon, Menelaus, Nestor, Patroclus, and others. Ulysses observed that she appeared wanton.

Warriors of both sides assembled to watch Hector and Ajax fight. The two companions clashed for only a moment before Hector desisted, declaring that he could not harm Ajax, his cousin. Ajax accepted Hector's magnanimity and invited the Trojan to join, unarmed, the Greek commanders at dinner. Hector, accompanied by Troilus, was welcomed among the Greeks with many warm compliments, but Achilles, meeting Hector, rudely mentioned that part of Hector's person in which he would one day inflict a mortal wound. Stung by Achilles' pride and lack of manners, Hector declared hotly that he would destroy all of Achilles at one stroke. The result was an agreement to meet in combat the next day. Ajax managed to calm heated tempers, however, and the feasting began.

Troilus, anxious to see his beloved Cressida, asked Ulysses where he might find Calchas, and Ulysses promised to be his guide. After the banquet, they followed Diomedes to Calchas' tent, where Cressida met him and, in affectionate overtures toward Diomedes, revealed to the hidden Troilus that she had already all but forgotten him. As she gave Diomedes, as a token of her love, a sleeve that had belonged to Troilus, compunction seized her for a moment. She quickly succumbed, however, to Diomedes' charms and promised to be his at their next meeting. Diomedes left, vowing to kill in combat the Trojan whose sleeve he would be wearing on his helmet. Troilus, unable to believe that Cressida was the woman whom he loved so passionately, returned to Troy. He vowed to take the life of Diomedes.

As the new day approached, Hector was warned by Andromache, his wife, and by his sister Cassandra not to do battle that day; all portents foretold disaster. When their words proved ineffectual, King Priam tried vainly to persuade Hector to remain within the walls. During the battle, Diomedes unhorsed Troilus and sent the horse as a gift to Cressida. Despite his overthrow, Troilus continued to fight heroically. Hector appeared to be, for his part, invincible. When Patroclus was severely wounded in the action, Achilles, enraged, ordered his followers, the Myrmidons, to stand ready. As the action subsided, and Hector was unarming himself at the end of the day, the Myrmidons, at Achilles' command, closed in on brave Hector and felled him with their spears.

Troilus announced to the retiring Trojan forces that Hector had been killed by treachery and that his body, tied to the tail of Achilles' horse, was being dragged around the Phrygian plain. As he made his way to the gates, he predicted general mourning in Troy and expressed his undying hatred for the Greeks. He encountered Pandarus, whom he abruptly dismissed as a cheap panderer, a man whose name would be infamous forever.

Critical Evaluation:

In the Folio of 1623 *Troilus and Cressida* is described as a tragedy; in the Quarto it is called a history; in most structural respects it seems to be a comedy, though a very grim and bitter one. Critics have frequently classified it, with *Measure for Measure* (1604-1605) and *All's Well That Ends Well* (1602-1604), as a "problem play," perhaps as much because the play poses a problem in literary taxonomy as because it sets out to examine a problematic thesis. Probably written between *Hamlet* (1600-1601) and *Othello* (1604), during the period of the great tragedies, the play is so full of gloom and venom, so lacking in the playfulness and idealism of the earlier comedies, that critics have attributed its tone and manner either to a period of personal disillusionment in William Shakespeare's life or to his preoccupation at that time with tragic themes.

There is no external and little internal evidence for the biographical conclusion. It may be, however, that, in *Troilus and Cressida*, Shakespeare has been affected by the surrounding tragedies. It is as if he took the moral ambiguities and potential chaos of the worlds of the tragedies but ruled out the possibility of redemption and transcendence through heroic suffering. Instead, he peoples this tenuous world with blowhards, cynics, and poltroons and ruthlessly lets them muddle through for themselves. The world of *King Lear* (1605), for example, is on the brink of chaos, but at least there is the sublimity of Lear to salvage it. The world of *Troilus and Cressida* has no one to shore up its structure and challenge disintegration.

Although there were many contemporary versions of the relevant Homeric materials available to Shakespeare, it is clear that he was also familiar with the story as told by Chaucer in *Troilus and Criseyde* (c. 1382). Chaucer's world, however, was full of innocence, brilliance, and hope. If the medieval Criseyde behaves shabbily, it is only the result of feminine weakness and long importuning. If Chaucer's Troilus is naïve and a victim of courtly idealism, at least he can finally sort things out from an Olympian perspective. Shakespeare does not give his lovers, or the rest of the Greek heroes, this sympathy or opportunity but drags them through a drab and seamy degradation.

Shakespeare begins with characters traditionally honored for their nobility, but he does nothing to develop them even for a fall. He simply proceeds to betray them, to show them up, and thereby to represent the extreme precariousness of their world. The bloom of courtly love is gone as is the Christian optimism of the Middle Ages. Shakespeare seems to be reflecting not a personal situation but a late Renaissance malaise as he has his characters impotently preside at the dissolution of the revered old order.

In Chaucer, Troilus' love and woe had been instrumental in his maturation and, ultimately, in his salvation. Shakespeare's Troilus is more frankly sensual and his liaison is correspondingly sordid. He does not benefit from an ennobling passion, nor is he allowed to transcend his folly. He is not even accorded the dignity of a significant death. He fights on in pointless, imperceptive frenzy,

Cressida is also debased. She has fallen from courtly heroine to common whore. Perhaps Shakespeare borrowed her degradation from Robert Henryson's highly moralistic *Testament of Cresseid* (1532), in which the heroine sinks to prostitution. In any case, she does not have the initial austerity and later reserve which dignify the passion and fall of Chaucer's Criseyde. Her language, her every movement, suggests that she is more of a slut than a courtly heroine. Even as she enters the Greek camp, her promiscuous behavior betrays her, and her quick submission to Diomedes confirms what has been suspected all along. As if the lovers could not behave foully enough by themselves, Shakespeare provides them with Pandarus, as go-between and commentator, to further sully the relationship.

In Chaucer, the Trojan War had provided a fatalistic backdrop which enhanced the progress of the tragic love. In Shakespeare, the circumambient Homeric heroes serve only to discredit themselves and to amplify the chaos. Mark Van Doren has pointed out that, if Pandarus' role is to degrade the lovers, "the role of Thersites is to cheapen the heroes." They, however, do not need much help from their interlocutor. For example, when Ulysses gives his famous speech on order, one is more struck by the pointless bombast and strangulated rhetoric than by erudition. One is led to suspect that this world is out of touch with its ordering principles and that it is vainly trying to recapture them or to preserve their appearance with tortured language. Similarly, when Achilles delivers his set speech in Act III, it has all of the bitterness but none of the grace of Lear's corresponding speech. This Achilles is a petulant sybarite and the world is in trouble if he is its hero. The bombast, the irritability, and the inconsequentiality are all-pervasive. Agamemnon and Nestor are nothing more than windbags. When the Greeks meet to discuss plans, or the Trojans meet to discuss returning Helen, the conferences both quickly degenerate into pompous vacuity.

The moral and political disintegration is reflected in the shrill and strident language of the play. The diction, which is jawbreakingly full of inkhornisms, and the rhetorical excesses reinforce the notion that the characters are spinning out of control, no longer able to gain control of their language, no longer able to give even verbal order to their frustrations. The result is a play that can easily seem tedious. Consequently, *Troilus and Cressida* is rarely performed. It has, however, fascinated the critics. What all of this suggests is that the play is more interesting than appealing, more intriguing than satisfying, as it chronicles the demise of a world in which no one is left with the moral stature to make a last stand.

"Critical Evaluation" by Edward E. Foster

Bibliography:

Barroll, J. Leeds, ed. *Shakespeare Studies VI.* Dubuque, Iowa: William C. Brown, 1970. Part of an annual series of Shakespearean review anthologies. "The Traditions of the Troy-Story Heroes and the Problem of Satire in *Troilus and Cressida*," by Mark Sacharoff, considers the story of the play and its earlier sources in light of previous criticism.

_____, ed. *Shakespeare Studies VIII.* New York: Burt Franklin, 1975. A later volume in the above-cited series. In "Cressida and the World of the Play," by Grant L. Voth and Oliver H. Evans, the role of Cressida is considered in terms of her calculating ways, which are seen as a direct response to Troilus' temporary infatuation.

Bullough, Geoffrey, ed. *Narrative and Dramatic Sources of Shakespeare.* Vol. 6. New York: Columbia University Press, 1966. Part of a six-volume series of critical essays concerning the sources of Shakespeare's plays. *Troilus and Cressida* is discussed in a forty-page introduction, which is followed by the actual texts and translations of the sources Shakespeare would have known.

Donaldson, E. Talbot. *The Swan at the Well: Shakespeare Reading Chaucer.* New Haven, Conn.: Yale University Press, 1985. A comparison between several of Shakespeare's plays and their sources in Chaucer's poems. There are two chapters dealing with *Troilus and Cressida*, comparing the play to its literary source, Chaucer's poem *Troilus and Criseyde*.

Lloyd Evans, Gareth. *The Upstart Crow: An Introduction to Shakespeare's Plays.* London: J. M. Dent and Sons, 1982. A comprehensive discussion of the dramatic works of William Shakespeare. Although the major emphasis is on critical reviews of the plays, there are also discussions of sources as well as material on the circumstances surrounding the writing of the plays.

TROILUS AND CRISEYDE

Type of work: Poetry
Author: Geoffrey Chaucer (c. 1343-1400)
Type of plot: Love
Time of plot: Antiquity
Locale: Troy
First transcribed: c. 1382

> *Principal characters:*
> TROILUS, the young prince of Troy
> CRISEYDE, a young widow
> PANDARUS, Troilus' friend and Criseyde's uncle
> DIOMEDES, a Greek warrior

The Story:

Calchas, a Trojan prophet who divined that Troy was doomed to defeat, fled to the Greeks, leaving behind his beautiful daughter, Criseyde, a young widow. One day in April, the citizens of Troy were observing the rites of the spring festival. Among those in the temple was Troilus, a younger son of King Priam of Troy. Troilus, who had always been scornful of the Trojan swains and their lovesickness, saw Criseyde and fell deeply in love with her at first sight. Himself now sick with the love malady, Troilus invoked the god of love to have pity on him. Because he felt that he had no hope of winning Criseyde, he became the scourge of the Greeks on the battlefield.

Pandarus, Troilus friend, offered his advice and help when he learned that Troilus had lost his heart to a beautiful Trojan. When Troilus at length disclosed that his lady was the fair Criseyde, Pandarus, who was Criseyde's uncle, offered to become his mediator. He thereupon called on his niece to gossip with her. Pandarus brought up the subject of Priam's sons, and he praised the bravery of Troilus. Gradually he disclosed to Criseyde that young Troilus was dying for love of her. Criseyde suspected that the intentions of neither Troilus nor Pandarus were honorable, and she cried out in distress, but Pandarus convinced her that Troilus' love was pure. She felt herself drawn to the prince when she beheld his modesty as he rode past her house after a day of battle outside the walls of Troy. She decided, after much inner turmoil, that it would not be dishonorable to show friendship to Troilus to save the young man's life.

At the suggestion of Pandarus, Troilus wrote a letter to Criseyde, to which she responded in a restrained letter of her own. When Troilus, wishing to be with Criseyde, tired of this correspondence, Pandarus arranged a meeting by asking Deiphobus, Troilus's brother, to invite the pair to his house for dinner. After the dinner, Criseyde gave the prince permission to be in her service and to adore her.

Pandarus, eager to bring about a private meeting of the lovers, studied the stars and decided on a night that would be propitious for a tryst. He invited Criseyde to dine with him on that evening. Troilus was already hidden in his house. As the lady prepared to take her leave, it began to rain and Pandarus persuaded her to stay. Through Pandarus' wiles, the lovers were brought together. After yielding, Criseyde gave Troilus a brooch as a token of their love.

About that time a great battle was fought between the Greeks and the Trojans, and several of the Trojan leaders were captured. In an exchange of prisoners, Calchas persuaded the Greeks to ask for Criseyde in return for Antenor, a Trojan warrior. The Trojan parliament, after much debate, approved the transaction. Hector, another brother of Troilus, was unsuccessful in arguing that Criseyde should remain in Troy. Troilus was in despair.

After plans for the exchange were determined, Pandarus brought the lovers together again secretly. Criseyde, broken-hearted, told the prince that their separation would not be for long, and that she would remain faithful to him. Troilus and his party accompanied Criseyde to the place appointed for the exchange. There they met Antenor and conducted him to Troy, while Diomedes, a young Greek warrior, led Criseyde away to the Greek camp. Troilus returned to Troy to await the passing of ten days, at the end of which time Criseyde had promised she would return. Diomedes managed to seduce Criseyde by the tenth day, however, and she gave him the brooch Troilus had given her at their parting. In return, Diomedes gave her a horse he had captured from Troilus in battle.

After several weeks of anxious waiting, Troilus wrote to Criseyde. She answered him, weakly avowing her love for him and saying that she would return to Troy at the earliest opportunity. Troilus, sensing that something was amiss, grieved. One day, he saw the brooch he had given Criseyde on a piece of armor taken from Diomedes on the battlefield. Knowing that Criseyde had forsaken him for another, Troilus sought out and fought Diomedes indecisively many times. Eventually the unhappy Troilus was killed by mighty Achilles.

Critical Evaluation:

Troilus and Criseyde, the only long work completed by Geoffrey Chaucer, is based on the legend of the Trojan War. The characters, however, behave in the best tradition of the medieval romance. Chaucer, the incomparable teller of tales and the great poet, combined his two talents to create this perfectly constructed narrative poem. The effective depiction of character and its development forecasts the shrewd observations of human nature Chaucer would make in the prologue to *The Canterbury Tales* (1387-1400).

Troilus and Criseyde is a paradox of artistic creation. At once both medieval and modern, it holds vast problems of interpretation yet pleases with its wit, style, comedy, and humanity. The work cannot be dated with complete certainty, but certainly by that point in his career, Chaucer—diplomat, man of letters, public official, and onetime prisoner of war—already had a literary reputation, which the appearance of *Troilus and Criseyde* did nothing to diminish. Chaucer's contemporary reputation, in fact, probably rested with this poem at least as much as with the later and much-loved *Canterbury Tales*. It was certainly Chaucer's *Troilus and Criseyde*, more than any of the other poems, that later poets used as a source for their own works. The fifteenth century Scottish poet Robert Henryson, for example, wrote of Criseyde's ignoble end in *The Testament of Cressid* (c. 1440-c. 1500), and William Shakespeare tried his hand at the story with *Troilus and Cressida* (1601-1602).

Chaucer himself found the story in Giovanni Boccaccio's *Il filostrato* (c. 1335); possibly Chaucer was working from an intermediate source—*Le Roman de troyle et de creseida* by Beauvau. The story itself derives from the Trojan legend, but Troilus and Criseyde are such minor figures in Homer's story (and never meet there) that it is apparent that Chaucer had more in mind than the simple retelling of a classical tale.

Much of the discussion in the nineteenth and early twentieth centuries about Chaucer's purpose in writing the poem focused on the palinode, that is, the concluding section of about one hundred lines, in which the narrator repudiates the courtly love that has governed the action of the lovers for more than eight thousand lines. Subsequent criticism focused on Chaucer's attitude toward love in general, on the poem as tragedy, and on how best to read the poem.

Courtly love was a highly conventionalized, and un-Christian, tradition, dating back at least to Eleanor of Aquitane's court in twelfth century northern France. The courtly love tradition held that love was sensual, illicit, adulterous, secret, and hard to obtain. The lady, the embodiment of virtue who was yet cruel to her lover, granted him her favors only after he had suffered agonies of frustration. Troilus and Criseyde practice courtly love until Criseyde violates one of its prime tenets, loyalty. By defecting from Troilus, she destroys the spell the courtly love tradition casts upon the minds of Chaucer's audience. At the very end of the poem, all listeners are made to examine the priorities of courtly love and, on a deeper plane, devotion to human love over the love of God. The palinode at the end raises the question of how human beings should live their lives and whether they should desire and want the things of this earth, which can so easily be stripped away. Troilus clearly was the victim of the love of a weak woman, and he discovered that his fate was a tragic one. The narrator at the work's end asks the readers to avoid becoming victims of fortune by devoting themselves to God and God's love.

One of the most important aspects of the poem is the elaborate psychological development of its characters. Before Chaucer, the most advanced way of representing psychological states in literature was to abstract feelings and emotions, as well as virtues and vices, embody each in a character, and have these characters contend for possession of the individual. Never before Chaucer had the whole human being been depicted as a feeling, growing person. The tendency in earlier literature was to make the protagonist universal, as is Everyman in the morality play. The characters in Chaucer's poem are in no sense universal. While they are not particularly admirable characters, they share the same psychology with their readers, that is, show those weaknesses and strengths that are so human.

Criseyde's character depends on her situation. In the opening of the poem she is in a dangerous position, afraid of the Trojans, afraid of love, afraid of human involvement, afraid, even, of herself. Her natural inclination suggests holding back when Pandarus approaches on Troilus' behalf, but Pandarus makes a union with Troilus seem desirable, even reasonable. Troilus can protect her socially and politically, and after Pandarus approaches her complex reactions begin to develop in her: fear, resistance, questioning, need, and hope. Troilus and Criseyde are characters who live in a real world of human flaws, vices, joys, hopes, and predicaments. Chaucer's achievement in perfecting psychological realism is of the first magnitude.

Chaucer does not present a consistent view. The narrator in the first eight hundred lines of book 2—up to the point she decides to accept Troilus as her lover—is privy to Criseyde's thoughts. After that, the narrator no longer knows what she is thinking but only what she says. Chaucer seems to praise courtly love throughout much of the poem, then suddenly rejects it in conclusion. Such inconsistencies reflect the medieval aesthetic theory, which holds that art should convey truth. Since the only real truth, in this view, is the permanence of God's laws in God's realm (which is unknowable), humans, who live in their own separate, lower realm, cannot know absolute truth. What they do see is changeable and impermanent. Artists, who try to depict truth as best they can, find that their art becomes as changing and inconsistent as the world they observe. Since they cannot share in God's realm, both artists and audiences must be content with inconsistencies in art.

"Critical Evaluation" by Brian L. Mark

Bibliography:
Donaldson, E. T. *Speaking of Chaucer*. New York: W. W. Norton, 1970. In three chapters
    devoted to *Troilus and Criseyde*, Donaldson discusses the connection between Criseyde and

the masculine narrator who is described as loving Criseyde with avuncular sentimentality. Concludes that the ending of the poem reveals the instability and illusory quality of human love.

Frantzen, Allen J. *"Troilus and Criseyde": The Poem and the Frame*. New York: Twayne, 1993. Includes a chronology of Chaucer's life and works and a selected bibliography of criticism. The text covers the literary and historical context of the poem and a reading of the poem focused on internal framing devices of social and symbolic orders.

Howard, Donald R. "Troilus and Criseyde." In *Chaucer: His Life, His Works, His World*. New York: E. P. Dutton, 1987. A masterful biographical, historical, and literary study of Chaucer. Howard devotes a full chapter to *Troilus and Criseyde*, in which he focuses on Chaucer's intended audience, his transformations of Giovanni Boccaccio's *Il filostrato*, the characters of Troilus, Criseyde, and Pandarus, and the achievement of the poem. Concludes that *Troilus and Criseyde* is Chaucer's masterpiece.

Kaminsky, Alice R. *Chaucer's "Troilus and Criseyde" and the Critics*. Athens: Ohio University Press, 1980. An analytical survey of criticism on *Troilus and Criseyde* that includes chapters on the philosophy of the poem and on formalistic and psychological approaches to the poem.

Salu, Mary. *Essays on "Troilus and Criseyde."* Chaucer Studies 3. Cambridge, England: D. S. Brewer, 1982. Contains seven essays on the poem's text, lessons, realism, paganism, comedy, and use of letters.

THE TROJAN WOMEN

Type of work: Drama
Author: Euripides (c. 485-c. 406 B.C.E.)
Type of plot: Tragedy
Time of plot: Antiquity
Locale: Outside the ruined walls of Troy
First performed: Trōiades, 415 B.C.E.

Principal characters:
POSEIDON, the god of the sea and patron of Troy
PALLAS ATHENA, the goddess of wisdom
HECUBA, the queen of Troy
CASSANDRA, her daughter, a prophetess
ANDROMACHE, the wife of Hector, prince of Troy
HELEN, the queen of Sparta abducted by Paris
MENELAUS, the king of Sparta
TALTHYBIUS, the herald of the Greeks
CHORUS OF THE CAPTIVE TROJAN WOMEN

The Story:

On the second morning after the fall of Troy and the massacre of all its male inhabitants, Poseidon appeared to lament the ruins and vow vengeance against the Greeks. To his surprise, Pallas Athena, the goddess who had aided the Greeks, joined him in plotting a disastrous homeward voyage for the victors who had despoiled her temple in Troy. They withdrew as Hecuba rose from among the sleeping Trojan women to mourn the burning city and her dead sons and husband. The chorus joined her in chanting an anguished lament.

Talthybius, the herald of the Greeks, arrived to announce that Agamemnon had chosen Cassandra to be his concubine and that the other royal women of Troy had been assigned by lot—Polyxena to the tomb of Achilles, Andromache to Achilles' son Neoptolemus, and Hecuba herself to Odysseus, king of Ithaca and conceiver of the wooden horse that had led to the fall of the city. Amid the cries of the grieving women, Cassandra appeared, bearing a flaming torch in each hand. The chorus was convinced that she had gone mad as she danced and prayed to Hymen, god of marriage, that Agamemnon take her soon to Argos as his bride, for there she would cause his death and the ruin of his entire family. As for Odysseus, she foretold that he would suffer for ten more years on the seas before reaching his homeland. As Talthybius led her off, he observed that Agamemnon himself must have been mad to fall in love with the insane Cassandra.

Hecuba, broken with grief, collapsed to the ground. From the city came a Greek-drawn chariot loaded with the spoils of war and bearing Andromache and her infant son Astyanax. Cursing Helen, the cause of all their woe, Andromache called upon the dead Hector to come to her and announced enviously that Polyxena had just been killed upon the tomb of Achilles as a gift to the dead hero. Drawing upon her last remaining strength, Hecuba tried to comfort the distraught Andromache and urged that instead of mourning for Hector she win the love of Neoptolemus so that her son might grow to adulthood and perhaps redeem Troy. At this point, the reluctant herald Talthybius announced the Greeks' order that the son of so distinguished a warrior as Hector must not be permitted to reach adulthood but must be killed at once by being hurled from the battlements of Troy. As Talthybius led away Andromache and her son, a fresh lament and cursing of Helen went up from the grieving women of Troy.

Suddenly King Menelaus came striding in the sunlight with his retinue to demand that his faithless wife Helen be dragged to him by her blood-reeking hair. Hecuba pleaded with him to slay Helen at once, lest her beauty and feminine wiles soften his will, but Menelaus remained determined to take her back to Greece, where the relatives of those who died for her sake might have the pleasure of stoning her to death. Helen approached, calm and dignified. Her plea for the right to speak being supported by Hecuba, she argued that she was not responsible for the fall of Troy. The first blame must be attributed to Priam and Hecuba, who refused to kill the infant Paris as the oracle commanded; the second to Aphrodite, who bewitched her into submitting to Paris; the third to Deiphobus and the Trojan guards who prevented her from escaping to the Greeks after she had come to her senses. Goaded on by the chorus of Trojan women, Hecuba jeered at these claims, insisting that the gods would not have been so foolish as Helen would have them believe, that her own lust drove her into Paris' arms, and that she could always have escaped Troy and her own shame by way of suicide. Helen, falling to her knees, pleaded with Menelaus not to kill her. Hecuba also knelt to beg Helen's immediate death and to warn Menelaus against taking her aboard his ship. Menelaus compromised: Helen would return to Greece on another ship and there pay for her shameful life. As Menelaus led her away, the chorus wailed that Zeus had forsaken them.

Talthybius then returned, bearing the crushed body of Astyanax on Hector's shield. He told Hecuba that Andromache, as she was being led aboard Neoptolemus' ship, had begged that the infant be given proper burial. The performance of that rite was more than Hecuba could bear, and she had to be restrained by force from throwing herself into the flames of the city. As the captive women were led to the Greek ships, the great crash of Troy's collapsing walls was heard and the city was engulfed in smoke and darkness.

Critical Evaluation:

The Trojan Women is a masterpiece of pathos, as well as a timeless and chilling indictment of the brutality of war. Yet the circumstances of its composition, and the raging moral indignation behind it, all refer to an incident in the Peloponnesian War that occurred a few months before the tragedy was presented in March, 415 B.C.E. The people of Melos had tried to remain neutral in the Athenian conflict with Sparta, and Athens responded by massacring the grown males and enslaving the women and children. In *The Trojan Women* Euripides shows Troy after the men had been slaughtered, with a handful of women waiting to be taken into bondage. The parallel is clear and painful. Euripides does not stop with that. The women in their anguish have dignity, pride, and compassion, whereas their conquerors are vain, unscrupulous, and empty. Further, the conquering Greeks are shown to be headed for disaster, since the gods have turned against them. When this play was produced, Athens was preparing a large fleet to take over Sicily; an expedition that ended in calamity. The prophecies of sea disasters in the play must have made the Athenian audience squirm. Indeed, the whole tragedy seems calculated to sting the consciences of the Athenians. That they allowed it to be produced is amazing. The fact that a nonentity named Xenocles won first prize that year, defeating Euripides, is scarcely surprising.

This play concluded a trilogy of tragedies on the legend of Troy. It was preceded by *Alexandros* (another name for Paris), which dealt with the refusal of Priam and Hecuba to murder their infant Paris, who would eventually bring about the destruction of Troy. This is important, because, in *The Trojan Women*, Hecuba sees the full consequences of her choice. *Alexandros* was followed by *Palamedes*, where Odysseus exacts a dire revenge on the clever Palamedes through treachery. *The Trojan Women* merges the Trojan and Greek lines of tragedy, showing them to be complementary aspects of a central agony. This final play presents the culmination of this story of suffering. It is as bleak and agonizing a portrait of war as has ever been shown on the stage.

However, Euripides merely dramatizes a brief portion of the aftermath, about an hour or two the morning after Troy has been looted and burned and the Trojan men have been put to death. In that time, one sees enough to realize that war is the most devastating, unheroic activity that humanity has ever devised. No one wins. The Greeks in their swollen vanity have committed atrocities against both the gods and human decency, and they are about to receive their just punishment, as Poseidon, Athena, and Cassandra state. The action of the play consists of the revelation of those atrocities, one after the other, as they overwhelm the helpless old queen, Hecuba. It is primarily through Hecuba that we experience the enormity of Troy's fall. The chorus of captive women, Cassandra, Andromache, and Helen serve to balance and counterpoint Hecuba's anguish, as well as to contribute to it.

A brief time before, Hecuba was the proud queen of a great, wealthy city, and within the space of a night she has been reduced to a slave. Hecuba has witnessed her husband Priam's murder, and knows almost all of her children have been butchered. Longing for death, she experiences one dreadful thing after another. She learns that she is Odysseus' prize, the vilest Greek of all, and that her few daughters will be handed out as concubines. She sees her daughter Cassandra madly singing a marriage hymn, and she finally grasps that Cassandra, through prescience, is really singing a death song for herself and the commander of the Greeks, Agamemnon. Believing her daughter Polyxena to be alive, Hecuba learns from Andromache that the girl had her throat slit. Hecuba, trying to comfort Andromache with the prospect of Astyanax's growing to manhood, sees the little boy taken from Andromache to be executed. Menelaus arrives to drag Helen back to Greece, and Helen, who caused the whole war, calmly faces him down, oblivious of Hecuba's accusations. So Hecuba loses the satisfaction of seeing her worst enemy killed. We know that shallow, worthless Helen will go unpunished. In her final anguish, Hecuba must look upon her poor, mangled grandchild lying on the shield of her dead son, Hector. The last ounce of torment is wrung from her, and she makes an abortive suicide attempt. Hecuba's stark pathos has been drawn out to an excruciating degree.

Yet the play is not a mere shapeless depiction of human pain. Hecuba's suffering is cumulative. There is also a pattern to the appearances of the chorus, Cassandra, Andromache, and Helen. The chorus of captive women serves to generalize Hecuba's grief. If Poseidon will create future misery for the Greeks, the chorus shows the past and present pain of the Trojans on a large canvas. It places Hecuba's agony in perspective as one calamity among many. Moreover, Cassandra, Andromache, and Helen extend the portrayal of the vicitimization of the women who become the spoils of war: Cassandra, the raped virgin and crazed bride of death; Andromache, the exemplary wife and mother turned into a childless widow and handed over to the son of the man who killed her husband; and brazen Helen, the faithless wife who has the knack of getting her own way in every circumstance. The contrast among these three could not be more striking.

Euripides takes pains in *The Trojan Women* to show that the only justice in war is punitive and nihilistic. War arises from numerous individual choices and leads to disaster for everyone, the conquered and the victors alike. With Thucydides the historian, Euripides shares the view that power corrupts, promoting arrogance and criminality. His vision of the suffering caused by the war is as valid today as it was when he wrote the play, and as it must have been when Troy presumably fell.

"Critical Evaluation" by James Weigel, Jr.

Bibliography:
Conacher, D. J. *Euripidean Drama: Myth, Theme, and Structure.* Toronto: University of Toronto Press, 1967. Under "War and Its Aftermath," Conacher describes the plot in *The Trojan Women* as "a succession of unrelieved and ever deepening woe" which provides an alternating rhythm of hope and desolation. An introduction to the myth behind the play is given.

Croally, N. T. *Euripidean Polemic: "The Trojan Women" and the Function of Tragedy.* New York: Cambridge University Press, 1994. Building on Karl Marx and Michel Foucault, Croally examines the connection between the pleasure of viewing tragedy and the teaching that it conveys, specifically resulting in the questioning of received wisdom.

Euripides. *The Trojan Women.* Translated by Edith Hamilton. New York: Bantam Books, 1971. Hamilton presents the play as the greatest piece of antiwar literature ever written and explores its lack of effect on Athenians' opinions of war. The screenplay included in this volume, written by Michael Cacoyannis, provides insights into the translation of a play into film.

Gregory, Justina. *Euripides and the Instruction of the Athenians.* Ann Arbor: University of Michigan Press, 1991. Gregory examines connections between words and deeds of Andromache, Cassandra, Hecuba, and Helen, underscoring that the women had no ability to inspire action; she focuses on tragedy's political contributions in classical Athens and political elements in Euripides' works.

Scodel, Ruth. *The Trojan Trilogy of Euripides.* Göttingen, Germany: Vandenhjoeck and Ruprecht, 1980. Scodel claims that the dry, analytic rhetoric of *The Trojan Women* balances the emotional pathos. She examines relationships between *Alexandros*, *Palamedes*, *The Trojan Women*, and the satyr play *Sisyphus*.

TROPIC OF CANCER

Type of work: Novel
Author: Henry Miller (1891-1980)
Type of plot: Psychological realism
Time of plot: Late 1930's
Locale: Paris
First published: 1934

Principal characters:
NARRATOR
MONA, his wife, who never appears
VAN NORDEN, a friend
CARL, another friend

The Story:

The unnamed narrator, the "I" of the novel, was living at the Villa Borghese with his pal, Boris, during the fall of his second year in Paris. He had no money, no resources, no hopes, and yet was the happiest man alive. A year before he only thought he was an artist; now he was one. All literature had fallen from him, and the book he wrote—and that the reader is reading—was not a book; it was a libel, a slander, a defamation of character. The book was a prolonged insult, a gob of spit in the face of Art, and a kick in the pants of God. The narrator promised to sing for his readers—a bit off key perhaps, but sing nevertheless. The book would be that song.

The villa was about to be rented and the narrator had to find new lodgings; he began the narrative of the novel as he searched for another place to live in Paris and tried to survive without money. The story in the book followed his wanderings in search of work, friendship, art, and love (both emotional and carnal), as well as lodging and food. The narrator also introduced the reader to his friends: Tania, to whom he was singing in the novel; Borowski; Van Norden; his wife Mona, who never arrives from home; Boris; Moldorf, who is word-drunk; and finally Irene, who like Tania demands that he write fat letters to her. The list was endless. He prowled around Paris intoxicated by the streets, cafés, and squares—a compendium of Paris place-names and his dreams. Every day he returned to the American Express office on the Place du Opéra to see if he had received letters from home or money from Mona. He remembered his life back in the States, and the cultural baggage of his past and the freedom he felt in the present merged in his mind and his art.

He concocted a scheme to get food by writing to various acquaintances begging a meal once a week with each of them. He planned other scams. He wrote to various women and begged money from them. He scrutinized his love life and the sexual exploits of his friends. He got a job proofreading for the Paris edition of an American newspaper published for expatriates and travelers. He worked on his book, the book the reader now is reading. Mona wrote that she was coming to join him in Paris, and he worried about how his wife would react to his bohemian style of living. Would her presence retard his writing, destroy his freedom to create? He sat in cafés day after day, talking endlessly of art and writing and life.

He met Carl and Marlowe, neurasthenic American expatriates defeated by their life of exile. He discovered how stifling were the various households he visited. His sense of himself as an artist solidified amid the wanderings among his friends. He was generous to all the disadvantaged he met, offering them money when he had it, a room when one was available, and food even when he had little himself. Music enthralled him. People became the subject for his musings and the grist for his fiction. The nostalgia that dogged his memories of Mona interrupted his present pleasure with Tania. As the book developed he became the artist/hero of his own creation.

In all of his peregrinations through the netherworld of Paris, he searched for a community, one that could sustain his needs as a man and as an artist. He was constantly frustrated but never disappointed. He traveled from Paris to Dijon, a trip that was in itself unsuccessful, but he turned his effort into more material for his thoughts and for his work. At the end of the year, the novel concluded as he witnessed Fillmore's return to America, and he realized his own resiliency and survival as an artist. Walking back from the railroad station with the cash Fillmore had left for Ginette sagging in his pockets, the narrator took a cab to the Bois, past the Arc de Triomphe, to the Seine, where he got out and started walking toward the Port de Sèvres. Once again free from his entanglements, he realized that he now had enough money to return to America. He had a vision of New York in the snow, and he wondered what had happened to his wife.

A great peace settled around him as he realized that he did not want to return—not just yet, anyway. The lazy river, the soil so saturated by history that it could not be detached from its human background, gave him a golden peace that produced in him the feeling of being on the top of a high mountain. He thought about how strange humans were, so negligible at a distance; close up, so ugly and malicious. They needed to be surrounded by sufficient space, space more than time. The river flowed through him, the hills gently girdled it about; its course was fixed.

Critical Evaluation:

Tropic of Cancer is without doubt Henry Miller's most famous book. The work is also one of the most notorious novels of the twentieth century and occupies a central place in the legal battle against censorship. Banned from almost the moment it was printed in Paris in 1934, it was not legally available in the United States until Grove Press rather courageously challenged U.S. obscenity laws by openly publishing it in 1961. The book was immediately and widely condemned and suppressed. Grove Press went to court to challenge the statutes used to outlaw the book, and after a protracted and celebrated legal case the U.S. Supreme Court ruled in 1963 that the novel was not obscene. Although similar cases involving D. H. Lawrence's *Lady Chatterley's Lover* (1928) and James Joyce's *Ulysses* (1922) had been brought before the U.S. courts in celebrated attempts to overturn the country's obscenity statutes, it was the *Tropic of Cancer* litigation that finally altered the restrictions on what could be published in the United States.

Miller's first published novel is an episodic tale in fifteen loosely connected sections that reflect the author's indebtedness to, among others, Walt Whitman, another American writer who invented a personal and encyclopedic style. The novel has been called the journal of a "year" in a surreal city and an "eccentric antibook" full of ruminations, anecdotes, rhapsodies, self-promotion, caricatures, and burlesques about art and sex and culture. In any case, *Tropic of Cancer* is a book of large appetites, great ideas, and generous feelings.

Although *Tropic of Cancer* is fiction, it is nevertheless highly autobiographical. Miller has been credited with largely inventing this cross-genre, a fictional type that has become increasingly important as a literary model in contemporary writing. Miller drew heavily on his real-life experiences while living in Paris during the early years of the 1930's to provide him with the raw material for the novel. He mixes detailed examination of both individuals and locale—the environs of Paris are especially important to the flavor and structure of the novel—with a narrative commentary which encompasses a wide range of observations on art and writing. The novel deftly combines these personal reactions with objective descriptions to create a narrative of often hypnotic power.

The book's graphic sexual content and language—which Miller deliberately used to provoke offensive reactions, which raised all of the legal problems, and which attracted the greatest public attention—forms only a minor portion of the text and taken in context proves to be only one of the shocking techniques Miller employs in his assault on the literary establishment. As he states in the opening pages of the novel, he wants his writing to be a "libel, slander, defamation of character," in short a prolonged insult to Art and an attack on the conventional notions of what constitutes a novel. This insult has to do as much perhaps with the form of the writing as it does with its subject matter or its "obscene" language. The novel, which is not a novel in the usual sense of the term, is revolutionary but only partially because of its widely recognized employment of graphic sexuality.

Although much of contemporary cultural and literary criticism has positioned Miller as an important force in the development of literary modernism, modern feminists still largely have focused on the novel's and Miller's obsessive sexism. The lively debate produced by such feminist critiques has generated some provocative readings of the novel, and not all of them have been totally negative: Kate Millet, for example, defended at least some of Miller's sexual excesses in the novel. Feminist criticism has raised a number of legitimate concerns about Miller's depiction of women in his fiction—there is a persistent note of anti-Semitism in his fiction as well—which has exposed the patriarchal bias, both individual and cultural, of the novel. It is worth noting, however, that similar charges have been lodged against numerous other works of fiction of the same period. What has become clear from the debate over *Tropic of Cancer* is that the novel, more than half a century after it was published, is still controversial and is capable of stimulating debate about the nature and form of literary art. Miller's "kick in the seat of the pants" remains disturbing today and at times even enrages those who think and write about the place of literature in our culture. Miller's initial intent to upset our conventional notions of the nature of the novel and to extend the boundaries of what fiction legitimately can take for its subject matter remains viable today.

Charles L. P. Silet

Bibliography:
Hutchison, E. R. *"Tropic of Cancer" on Trial: A Case History of Censorship.* New York: Grove Press, 1968. This is the detailed history and analysis of the now infamous obscenity trial.
Martin, Jay. *Always Merry and Bright: The Life of Henry Miller.* Santa Barbara, Calif.: Capra Press, 1978. Of all the biographical reminiscences of Miller's life, this is still the most comprehensive.
Nelson, Jane. *Form and Image in the Fiction of Henry Miller.* Detroit: Wayne State University Press, 1970. In her chapter on *Tropic of Cancer*, Nelson uses a correlation between Mythology and psychology to analyze the novel.
Widmer, Kingsley. *Henry Miller.* Rev. ed. Boston: Twayne, 1990. Widmer's short biographical/critical monograph provides a good overview of both Miller's life and work.
Williams, Linda R. "Critical Warfare and Henry Miller's *Tropic of Cancer.*" In *Feminist Criticism: Theory and Practice*, edited by Susan Sellers. Toronto: University of Toronto Press, 1991. This article traces the debate over various feminist readings of the exploitative sexuality of *Tropic of Cancer.*

TROPIC OF CAPRICORN

Type of work: Novel
Author: Henry Miller (1891-1980)
Type of plot: Autobiographical
Time of plot: c. 1900-1928
Locale: Brooklyn and New York City
First published: 1939

> *Principal characters:*
> I, HENRY MILLER, the narrator
> MONA, or MARA, Miller's lover and obsessive focus
> MILLER'S WIFE
> HYMIE, a Jewish clerk at the Cosmodemonic Telegraph Company
> KRONSKI, a Jewish employee of the Cosmodemonic Telegraph Company
> O'ROURKE, a detective at the Cosmodemonic Telegraph Company
> VALESKA, a black colleague of Miller and his lover
> ROY HAMILTON, a friend of Miller
> MAXIE, an acquaintance of Miller

The Story:

Tropic of Capricorn begins with a meditation on Miller's alienation from family and homeland. His family was a group of Nordic idiots—clean, tidy, industrious, but unable to live in the present or to open the door into their souls. Nowhere on earth had he felt so degraded and humiliated as in America, which he envisioned as a cesspool of the spirit. Over the cesspool was a shrine to the spirit of work, with its chemical works, steel mills, prisons, and insane asylums. Miller wished to see it destroyed, in vengeance for unnamed crimes against him and others.

Miller commented that he had a good time as a child because he did not care about anything—a lesson learned at the age of twelve from the death of his friend. He realized that things were wrong only when one cared too much. As if to prove that he had learned not to care, he let out a loud fart beside his friend's coffin.

By the middle of the war, Miller had a wife and child and badly needed a job. In a farcical episode involving the clerk Hymie, office politics, and racism, he talked the manager of the Cosmodemonic Telegraph Company into giving him a job hiring and firing messengers. The company was inhuman, corrupt, and exploitative. After the company decreased the messengers' pay, Miller was forced to be less selective in hiring, resulting in a number of grotesque incidents involving epileptic, criminal, and delinquent messengers. In response to the poverty around him, Miller gave all his money away, in turn cadging dollars from acquaintances to buy food for himself. During Miller's time at the Cosmodemonic, he met the black woman Valeska, with whom he had a brief sexual liaison. She committed suicide.

Miller recalled an episode from his childhood in which he and his cousin Gene killed a boy in a gang fight. Miller and Gene hurried home, where Aunt Caroline, Gene's mother, gave them rye bread with butter. Miller remembers this image as particularly potent. In that house, he was never scolded; the image conveyed an angelic forgiveness, divine absolution.

Miller described his friendship with Roy Hamilton, whom he saw as a kind of mystic and prophet. Hamilton was in search of his biological father, who was either Mr. Hamilton or

Miller's friend MacGregor. Miller viewed this quest as futile; he viewed Hamilton as an emancipated man seeking to establish a biological link for which he had no need. Hamilton left having renounced both paternal candidates. The MacGregor family was distraught; Miller, in contrast, felt no need of Hamilton's presence after his departure, since Hamilton had given himself completely when he was present. Miller commented that it was his first clean, whole experience of friendship, and his last.

Miller's father fell mortally ill as a result of swearing off alcohol too quickly. He made a miraculous recovery when he made the acquaintance of a Congregationalist minister. He read the Bible and attended all the minister's services. He then learned that the minister was leaving town to go to a more advantageous position elsewhere. He tried but failed to persuade him to stay, and became bitterly disillusioned. He never laughed again, and took to sleeping and snoring his life away. Instigated by the image of Hymie's wife's diseased ovaries, Miller went to a figurative place called The Land of F**k.

One day, Miller was looking for a woman with whom he had a rendezvous. When he failed to find her, he became mad with anguish and wanted to annihilate the whole earth. Then suddenly he grew calm, light as a feather, and noticed the stars. The stars asked him who he was, to think of blowing the earth to smithereens. They had been hanging there for millions of years, and had seen it all, yet still shone peacefully every night, stilling the heart. They pointed out how in their light, even the garbage lying in the gutter looked beautiful. Miller picked up a cabbage leaf and saw it as absolutely new, a universe in itself. He broke off a piece and it was still a universe. He knew at that moment there was a woman waiting for him and that when they met, they would recognize each other immediately.

There followed a long hymn to his intense relationship with the Dark Lady, based on Miller's second wife June Smith. In the work, June became Mara or Mona. He recalled that the third time he met her she thought he was a dope fiend, the next time she called him a god, and that after that she tried to commit suicide, and then he tried, and she tried again. Nothing worked, says Miller, but it did bring them closer together, so close that they interpenetrated. Miller made the assertion that henceforth he would become hermaphroditic. In a final violent image, he asked the Dark Lady to tack her womb up on his wall, so that he could remember her.

Critical Evaluation:

Tropic of Capricorn is the first of Henry Miller's volumes of autobiographical fantasy. In spite of the title, it is not a sequel to *Tropic of Cancer*, published five years earlier. *Tropic of Capricorn* is less of an attempt at portraying reality than *Tropic of Cancer* is. *Tropic of Capricorn* is more of a free flow of fantastic and subjective associations. It contains more of the ornate, poetic prose which Miller called "dictation" or "cadenza." *Tropic of Capricorn* is a diatribe in which the outraged artist and prophet escapes into grotesque fantasy. It is an account of his alienation within the spiritual dearth of America. Miller's self-proclaimed aim in *Tropic of Capricorn* was to create a monstrous verbal skyscraper that parodied the American consciousness.

Tropic of Capricorn is subtitled *On the Ovarian Trolley*. The metaphor suggests a sexuality that is mechanistic, automatic, not within control of the individual. Certainly the novel, located in Miller's The Land of F**k, has a more than usual share of the compulsive pursuit of sex. The ovarian metaphor goes beyond this level. Early in the novel readers are introduced to Hymie's wife's diseased ovaries. Miller recounts that the image germinated a tropical growth of free associations in him. In particular he mentions that he had never done what he wanted and that out of this frustration had grown an obsessional plant in his psyche, a coral growth that, as it grew, killed all else including life itself. It made life and killed life simultaneously—much as diseased ovaries produce diseased eggs.

The obsessional plant is an image of a destructive growth strangling individual life. This theme of individual spiritual death is expanded to the cosmic level in many references to the spiritual bankruptcy of New York City. The city is described as growing like a cancer; to counterbalance this deathly growth, Miller the artist must grow like the sun. *Tropic of Capricorn* proselytizes against the dehumanizing effect of the industrialized city. Miller says that the smell of a dead horse, although almost unbearable, is preferable to the smell of burning chemicals. The sight of a dead horse with a bullet hole in its temple is better than the sight of a group of men in blue aprons with a truckload of freshly made tin.

Miller is unrivaled in his ability to sum up large truths in colloquial language. For example, he writes that music is the can opener of the soul. When he remarks on the necessity of breaking with one's friends in order to live creatively, he announces such a time as moving day for the soul.

Tropic of Capricorn has striking examples of half-serious apocalyptic rant, such as the declaration that all department stores are symbols of sickness and emptiness, and if all the significance hidden in the miscellany of Bloomingdale's were gathered together on the head of a pin, you would have left a universe in which the grand constellations would move without the slightest danger of collision.

A more serious apocalyptic treatment is saved for the Dark Lady, or Mona, or Mara, the sexually alluring yet devouring female figure whom Miller identified with his second wife, June Smith. When he meets her, he is as if baptized anew, with his real name: Gottlieb Leberecht Müller. The relationship collapses, and later, when he revisits the place where they met, he realizes that the book that he will write about her has become more important than her. The book becomes a tomb in which to bury her.

Miller surrounds the Dark Lady with paradoxical images of fullness (such as the moon, or a ship in full sail) and of death and destruction. Toward the end of the novel, he describes her in terms worthy of the Book of Revelation. She is the personification of evil, the destroyer of the soul, the maharani of the night. In the power and intensity of the sexual experience generated by her and Miller, the ovarian trolley image is taken to its furthest extreme. In the final image of the novel, he commands her to tack her womb to the wall, an act of violence and reverence simultaneously.

The novel provides many instances of iconoclastic comedy that challenge hypocrisy. Miller likes to shock, whether it is by copulating with Valeska while his wife is out having an abortion, or asking the grieving Maxie for money in the hushed silence of the funeral parlor over the coffin of their dead friend. Even readers who are appalled at Miller's cynicism cannot fail to relish the sheer theater of such occasions.

Tropic of Capricorn is a flawed work. The fragments of narrative are too slight to support Miller's endless diatribes. His time at the Cosmodemonic is poorly described. The important character Valeska disappears from the novel without comment. The characterization is almost nonexistent, since Miller is too bound up in his own egomania to observe anyone else. One notable exception to Miller's general self-obsession is the account of his father's descent into a sickness caused by too-sudden abstinence, renaissance via religion, and final disillusionment and retreat into slumber.

Despite its shortcomings, the novel makes glorious reaches into high spiritual realizations, such as the epiphany involving the stars and the cabbage leaf. The possibility of redemption shines through the grim chaos of the city. In one of his most beautiful passages, Miller says

Christ will never more come down to earth, yet he expects something terrifyingly marvelous and absurd, an invention that will bring a shattering calm and void. Not the calm and void of the death that infects urban life from the roots up, but of life such as the monks dreamed.

Claire J. Robinson

Bibliography:

Brown, J. D. *Henry Miller*. New York: Frederick Ungar, 1986. Intersperses biography with criticism. Useful for placing the works in context of the life. Bibliography includes interviews.

Hassan, Ihab. *The Literature of Silence: Henry Miller and Samuel Beckett*. New York: Alfred A. Knopf, 1967. Contains a brief but sound discussion of the themes and imagery of *Tropic of Capricorn*.

Lewis, Leon. *Henry Miller: The Major Writings*. New York: Schocken Books, 1986. The chapter on *Tropic of Capricorn* focuses on the author's relationship with June Smith. The author intelligently answers those critics who accuse Miller of misogyny and pornography.

Wickes, George, ed. *Henry Miller and the Critics*. Carbondale: Southern Illinois University Press, 1963. Contains an incisive, unforgiving, and appreciative critique of *Tropic of Capricorn*.

Widmer, Kingsley. *Henry Miller*. Boston: Twayne, 1990. The most comprehensive introduction to Miller's life and works, containing a chapter on the main themes of *Tropic of Capricorn*. Notes and bibliography.

TROUT FISHING IN AMERICA

Type of work: Novel
Author: Richard Brautigan (1935-1984)
Type of plot: Picaresque
Time of plot: Fall, 1960, through fall, 1961, with flashbacks to the 1940's
Locale: San Francisco, various trout streams in northern California and Idaho, and the recalled
cities of Tacoma, Portland, and Great Falls
First published: 1967

Principal characters:

THE NARRATOR, who is married, has a daughter, and sometimes takes
the persona of Trout Fishing in America, a symbolic non-corporeal
embodiment of the American Dream
TROUT FISHING IN AMERICA SHORTY, a legless, screaming middle-aged
wino who lives in San Francisco's North Beach area
THE KOOL-AID WINO, the narrator's childhood friend

The Story:

Trout Fishing in America begins with a description of the book's cover photograph, a picture
of Brautigan and his wife, Virginia "Ginny" Adler, in front of the statue of Benjamin Franklin
in San Francisco's Washington Square. The poor gather there around five in the afternoon to
eat sandwiches given to them by the church across the street. One of the narrator's friends
unwrapped his sandwich to find only a leaf of spinach inside.

The first time the narrator heard about trout fishing in America was from a drunken stepfather
and, as a child in Portland, Oregon, he once walked to a street corner and saw a waterfall pouring
down from a hill. The next morning, ready to go trout fishing for the first time, he returned to
find that the waterfall was only a pair of wooden stairs leading up to a house. Seventeen years
later, an actual fisherman, he tried to hitch a ride to go fishing, but no car would pick him
up—another disappointment.

Another childhood memory was The Kool-Aid Wino, a friend who, because of an injury, had
to stay home all day. Together, the narrator and the Wino bought grape Kool-Aid and ceremo-
niously made an entire gallon of it from a nickel package. Ready for a day's drinking, they
created their own Kool-Aid reality. Recipes for apple compote, pie crust, "spoonful" pudding,
and walnut catsup lead to memories of Mooresville, Indiana, the home of the John Dillinger
Museum, where a Mooresville resident once discovered a basement full of rats and, Dillinger-
like, bought a revolver to get rid of them. The narrator's memories continue to move back and
forth from early recollections to recent ones, and from urban memories to outdoor ones. In San
Francisco (a "Walden Pond for Winos"), the narrator and his friends, unemployed artists, talked
of opening a flea circus or committing themselves to a mental asylum, where it would be warm
and they would have clean clothes, hot meals, and pretty nurses. At Tom Martin Creek,
Graveyard Creek, and other fishing places, the narrator equally failed to find satisfaction,
fighting brush, poison oak, and narrow canyons to fish. Back in San Francisco, the narrator
fantasized making love in a book store to a woman whose husband owns 3,859 Rolls Royces.
Fishing in Hayman Creek, Owl Snuff Creek, and elsewhere catching great trout equally proved
to be a fantasy.

In San Francisco again, the narrator saw Trout Fishing in America Shorty, a legless, screaming middle-aged wino who trundled about in a wheelchair in the North Beach area. When not

passed out in the window of a Filipino Laundromat, Shorty wheeled through the streets shouting obscenities in fake Italian ("Tra-la-la-la-la-la-Spa-ghet-tiii!"). One day, Shorty passed out in Washington Square in front of the statue of Ben Franklin, and the narrator and a friend thought they should crate him up and ship him to American author Nelson Algren, for Shorty is like an Algren character in the books *Neon Wilderness* (1947) and *A Walk on the Wild Side* (1956). They never got around to shipping Shorty and they soon lost track of him, but Shorty should someday be buried, the narrator concluded, beside the Franklin statue, both symbols of America. The narrator fantasized another symbol of America, the Mayor of the Twentieth Century. Wearing mountains on his elbows and blue jays on his shirt collar, the Mayor was a modern Jack the Ripper, performing deeds of murder at night with a razor, a knife, and a ukelele, the latter an instrument not even Scotland Yard would suspect.

The narrator continued to fish for trout in places like Paradise Creek, Salt Creek, Spirit Prison, Duck Lake, Little Redfish Lake, but he caught very little. He was reminded of a time in Gelatao in southern Mexico when, cleaning an attic for an elderly lady, he came across a trout-fishing diary of the lady's brother. It contained a ledger calculating the number of trout he had lost over a seven-year period, over two thousand.

In another fantasy, at the Cleveland Wrecking Company, the narrator inquired about a used trout stream, plus all accessories, for sale at a bargain price. Everything is for sale: land, disassembled waterfalls, trout streams, trees and bushes, animals, birds and insects. He envisioned Leonardo da Vinci, on the payroll of the South Bend Tackle Company, inventing a new spinning lure for trout fishing called "The Last Supper." Living, like The Kool-Aid Wino, on invented reality, the narrator took up residence in a rented cabin above Mill Valley, California, and for no particular reason other than he had always wanted to, ended his trout fishing narrative with the word "mayonnaise."

Critical Evaluation:

Richard Brautigan's *Trout Fishing in America*, which appeared in 1967, is actually his first novel, written in the early 1960's. Its publication was timely: It appeared two years before the famous rock festival at Woodstock, New York, and at the height of the hippie movement. The book became a national best-seller. It is proenvironment, antiestablishment, and, simply, hip. The short chapters allow for fast reading and a lot of skipping around, and his unconventional wisdom distills much of the thinking of the Woodstock generation.

Readers after the 1960's, however, are likely to take a more critical view of the book. Brautigan's prose often slips into a primer flatness, and his messages are sometimes sophomoric and pretentious. *Trout Fishing in America* is a novel in only a very loose sense. It is a collection of random observations and experiences strung together with cute chapter titles. There is, nevertheless, a charm and folk wisdom about the book, as well as a concern with America's natural surroundings that places it in the serious mainstream of American writing, along with works such as Henry David Thoreau's *Walden: Or, Life in the Woods* (1854), Mark Twain's *Adventures of Huckleberry Finn* (1884), and Ernest's Hemingway's Nick Adams stories. Brautigan's nature descriptions are often beautiful, and his analysis of the flip side of the American Dream is quite accurate. *Trout Fishing in America* is in many ways the representative novel of Brautigan's generation, as F. Scott Fitzgerald's *The Great Gatsby* (1925) was for his generation.

The title of the novel functions in at least three different ways to unify the varied parts of the book. First, the opening chapter, "The Cover for Trout Fishing in America," not only describes the front photograph, it also suggests the author's disguise—his cover—as Trout Fishing in

America, a personification of the myth of America as a land of vast open spaces, unlimited resources, and individual opportunity. The chapter describes the statue of Benjamin Franklin in San Francisco's Washington Square; Franklin is the American prototype of the self-made man, the successful Yankee entrepreneur whose rags-to-riches life is the subject of his *Autobiography* (1791). Brautigan's book is Franklin's *Autobiography* turned upside down, a rejection of Franklin's ethic of hard work and the way to wealth. Early in the book, Brautigan recalls seeing, as a child, fishermen with three-cornered hats. The three-cornered hat, traditionally associated with the early American Puritans, reveals these fishermen as typical Americans angling for riches and success, the same kind of "fishing" that was taught to the narrator himself. On his first fishing venture, he sees that what he earlier took to be a beautiful waterfall cascading from a hill is nothing more than a wooden staircase. Like the entire notion of the American Dream, the waterfall is an illusion. In his disguise as Trout Fishing in America, therefore, the narrator presents himself as a true believer in the doctrine of hard work, success, moneymaking, and the myth of the purity of the American landscape. The events throughout the novel undermine that belief.

Second, the title also suggests that the book is about America itself, its vast lands and pure streams that offer unlimited natural riches to all citizens. The novel is a series of disenchantments, some bitter and some sweet. There are the sad dead of Graveyard Creek and the dead fish of Worsewick Hot Springs. There is the inhuman destruction of coyotes at Salt Creek that makes the narrator think of the gas chamber at San Quentin. There is Mooresville, Indiana, home of famous criminal John Dillinger, a town that still features violence, boredom, and anxiety. Most of all, there are the winos, the poor, and the homeless who wait for sandwich time at the church near Washington Square, only to find nothing but a leaf of spinach in their bread. There are bums who pick cherries for Rebel Smith and wait like vultures for her discarded half-smoked cigarettes, and the winos and impoverished artists who talk of either opening up a flea circus or committing themselves to an insane asylum for the winter, where there is television and warm beds.

Nowhere is the distance between mythology and actual American experience more evident than in Trout Fishing in America Shorty, a legless one-man riot who appears throughout the novel "in a magnificent chrome-plated steel wheelchair." Shorty is in many ways the quintessential American, a cheerful and energetic rugged individualist, a kind of Rotarian from hell. He thinks he is as good as anybody, drinks in public view, and is a militant patriot, shouting obscenities at the Italians in North Beach. He spends his days passed out in an alcoholic stupor in the front window of a Filipino laundromat, and the narrator accurately observes that Shorty should someday be buried beside the Benjamin Franklin statue in Washington Square, for Shorty is the shadow of the Franklin myth of American success.

A third way that the title functions as the controlling idea of the novel is in its evocation of the agrarian myth of the land and the great outdoors. Throughout the novel is a sense of the purity of nature, of the individualism of those isolated few who have inherited America's pioneer spirit, and the untapped primal energies that lie beneath the surface of America's eroded landscape. Brautigan's descriptions of natural wildlife and surroundings are done with a loving care that denies cynicism, and his use of American place names (Owl Snuff Creek, Tom Martin Creek, Big Redfish Lake) suggests a delight in the names that Americans attach to their rivers, lakes, and campsites. Nature is present throughout the book.

In contrast, urban life is presented as evil in the novel. Room 208 of a cheap hotel in San Francisco harbors the potential for violence and a prostitute trying to escape from her pimp. The winos and homeless of Washington Square clearly are, even in the glow of the author's sympathetic portrayal, sad, lost souls. The narrator sees his fellow urban apartment dwellers as "dead people." At the end of the book, the narrator rejects urban life and the technology and business ethic that go with it, trudging in the footsteps of Thoreau to his isolated cabin above Mill Valley.

The title, therefore, is what unifies the forty-seven short sections that compose the book, most of them no longer than a page or two. They are largely a series of reminiscences, from the narrator's childhood to the memories of the good places he has fished. Interspersed are glimpses of his present world and life with his wife and daughter. The development in the novel lies in the narrator's increasing disillusionment with the ruins of a corrupt, polluted, and destructive America. The culmination of this disillusionment is at the Cleveland Wrecking Company, one of the funniest sequences of the novel. The chapter, in which the narrator asks about a used trout stream, plus all accessories, for sale at bargain prices, is a surreal and miniaturized version of the Franklin business ethic and the modern consumer craze carried to its logical extreme. One more commodity, landscape is portioned out by friendly, affable hustlers to those with a keen eye for bargains. Waterfalls are appropriately stored in the plumbing department with toilets and urinals. The Cleveland Wrecking Company has few animals for sale because few are left. The many wild birds, the hundreds of mice, and the millions of insects that are available are the natural inheritors of the future.

At the end of the novel, Trout Fishing in America is seen for the last time, properly enough, near the Big Wood River, ten miles from Ketchum, Idaho, where Ernest Hemingway killed himself. It is Brautigan's farewell to the Hemingway code of masculine endurance and romantic pantheism. In the California bush country, the narrator takes up residence in an isolated cabin above Mill Valley, realizing that he has been angling over a sterile wasteland. He sheds his illusions, discovers his own sexual and creative powers, and creates his own world, like The Kool-Aid Wino from his childhood who "created his own Kool-Aid reality and was able to illuminate himself by it."

Kenneth Seib

Bibliography:

Chenetier, Marc. *Richard Brautigan*. London: Methuen, 1983. Introduces all of Brautigan's writing in the light of his surrealist and deconstructionist fictional theories. Sees *Trout Fishing in America* as a series of images that create a network of narrative meaning.

Foster, Edward Halsey. *Richard Brautigan*. Boston: Twayne, 1983. Good single-volume introduction to Brautigan's life and work, showing how Brautigan drew upon his experiences.

Legler, Gretchen. "Brautigan's Waters." *CEA Critic: An Official Journal of the College English Association* 54, no. 1 (Fall, 1991): 67-69. Analysis of Brautigan's treatment of nature and water in the novel.

Seib, Kenneth. "*Trout Fishing in America*: Brautigan's Funky Fishing Yarn." *Critique: Studies in Modern Fiction* 13, no. 2 (1971): 63-71. Analyzes the theme of trout fishing, showing how it functions in various ways to give the book unified form, viewpoint, and meaning.

Stull, William L. "Richard Brautigan's *Trout Fishing in America*: Notes of a Native Son." *American Literature* 56 (March, 1964): 68-80. Discusses the themes and motifs of the book, and explains many of Brautigan's allusions.

A TRUE HISTORY

Type of work: Short fiction
Author: Lucian (c. 120-after 180)
Type of plot: Satire
Time of plot: Second century
Locale: The universe
First transcribed: Alēthōn diēgēmatōn, second century (English translation, 1634)

> Principal characters:
> LUCIAN
> ENDYMION, the king of the moon
> PHAETHON, the king of the sun
> SCINTHARUS, an inhabitant of the whale's belly

The Story:

Heading westward from the Pillars of Hercules, Lucian in his sloop and with a crew of fifty finally reached the Atlantic Ocean. Filled with a thirst for adventure and an intellectual restlessness to see what was on the other side of the world, he found the first day of the voyage delightful. Then came a terrible storm that drove the ship before it for seventy-nine days. On the eightieth day, the adventurers came to a lofty wooded island and went ashore.

After resting, twenty sailors accompanied Lucian on an exploration of the island. They discovered a bronze tablet announcing that Hercules and Dionysus had been there, and they saw two huge footprints. They also discovered that the river had its source in a grapevine and contained Chian wine. Eating the fish that swam in it made them drunk.

The inhabitants of the island were women, human from the waist up, but growing on vines. Several of the crew, who became too friendly with these creatures, soon found themselves entangled in the vines and taking root. They had to be left behind. The others filled their casks with wine and water and set sail, but they ran into a whirlwind that whipped the sloop hundreds of miles into the air. A week later, the ship was thrown upon the moon, which was inhabited by men riding vultures. The king of the moon, Endymion, enlisted the service of the Greeks in his war against Phaethon and his people of the sun.

The mighty invasion force was made up of eighty thousand vulture-riding cavalry and twenty thousand troops riding birds covered with grass who had lettuce leaves for wings. This vegetarian force had armor of vegetable husks but Greek swords. Among their allies were fighters from other constellations astride monster fleas.

The army of the sun rode flying ants, gnats, and mosquitoes. Some hurled giant radishes, others wielded asparagus spears. They were nevertheless no match for the lunar troops until so many centaur reinforcements arrived that the number could not be set down for fear of creating incredulity. When the moon army was put to flight, Lucian and his friends were captured and bound with spider webs.

To bring the moon people to terms, Phaethon erected a cloud screen, and, cut off from sunlight, the moon troops soon surrendered. The terms of capitulation were inscribed on a slab of electrum. With the coming of peace, Lucian had the opportunity to explore the moon and note its wonders.

On the way home, the Greeks paused at Lamptown, which was inhabited by lanterns, and at Cloud-Cuckooland, where Lucian verified the details of Aristophanes' comedy *The Birds*

(414 B.C.E.). Finally the travelers reached the ocean again, only to have their sloop swallowed by a huge whale. In its belly, amid a clutter of wrecked ships, they found Scintharus, who was raising vegetables on an island. He had lived there for twenty-seven years, ever since leaving Cyprus.

There were many other inhabitants, all quarrelsome and unjust. Some had eel eyes and lobster faces; others were half human and half animal. Since their only weapons were fish bones, Lucian decided to attack them. The creatures were all slain in two battles in which the Greeks suffered only one casualty; the sailing master was stabbed with a mullet spine.

One day, after living in the whale for one year and eight months, the Greeks heard a loud uproar in the outside world. Peering between the whale's teeth, they watched a naval battle of giants who manned floating islands and fought with oysters and sponges.

At last, the Greeks conceived a scheme to gain their liberty. They set fire to the forest inside the whale; then, as the creature was about to suffocate, they wedged open its jaws and sailed out, with Scintharus as pilot. They did not get far, however, for a north wind froze the ocean. They found refuge in a cave they hollowed in the ice until, after a month, it occurred to them to hoist the sails and let the ship glide across the smooth ice to open water.

Sailing in a sea of milk, they took on provisions at a cheese island. They stopped at the Isle of the Blessed and watched a lawsuit between Theseus and Menelaus for the custody of Helen. While the hearing was in progress, Helen ran off with a new sweetheart, aided by some of Lucian's crew, and the tourists were deported. Lucian, however, had time to consult Homer on moot points concerning his life and writing and to catalog the famous Greeks who inhabited the isle. Also, he witnessed a prison break by the damned and watched the heroic exploits of Achilles in recapturing them.

On their voyage once again, the travelers passed a place of punishment for liars. Herodotus was there, but Lucian knew that he himself was safe because he had never written anything but the truth. The company spent a month at the Port of Dreams and also paused briefly to deliver a note to Calypso from Odysseus. Pirates attacked them several times and their ship was destroyed, but the travelers finally reached safety in a land that Lucian recognized as the continent facing his world.

Critical Evaluation:

The point of *A True History*, as Lucian explains in his preface, is to make fun of the extravagant lies put about by poets, philosophers, and historians who write about fantastic creatures and improbable events. Lucian probably had in mind such authors as Antonius Diogenes, whose *Wonders Beyond Thule* appears to have been a particularly notorious example of fictionalizing narrative. *A True History*, the author warns, is nothing of the sort; rather, everything in it is emphatically untrue. The reader, however, should enjoy it as a form of mental relaxation and because it makes fun of such earlier writers as Homer and Plato.

Lucian's narrative of a sea voyage inevitably recalls the journey of Odysseus, and, in fact, there are many allusions to Homer's epics throughout the story. In the second book, when the travelers are in the land of the dead, the narrator actually meets Homer and has the opportunity to ask him some questions. Lucian also frequently parodies philosophers. His description of the descent into the belly of the whale and the eventual reemergence into the open clearly makes fun of Plato's myth of the cave, which elaborated on ideas of knowledge and perception. Throughout *A True History*, there are references to philosophical schools and the quarrels between them. The battle between the forces of the sun and the moon, with their grotesque armies of hybrid creatures, can for example be seen as a satirical depiction of the arguments among philosophers about stars, their size and nature, their inhabitants, and their connections with the earth.

A True History is also a comment on the writing of history, a topic addressed specifically in a treatise entitled *History as It Should Be Written*, which was, however, itself a not entirely serious work. As he outlined, his prime concern was the need for the historian to be truthful and to avoid the excesses of poetry and fiction. In *A True History*, he begins in a manner that suggests he is following his own precepts and that the narrator will be a careful recorder of facts and figures. Soon, however, the narrative becomes outright fantasy, as the ship of the travelers is carried to the moon in a whirlwind. Much of the humor of the work comes from the matter-of-fact style that is maintained throughout: The narrator presents incredible details in such a way that they almost become believable. Lucian thereby proves his main point, that it is as easy to dress lies up as truth as it is difficult for the hearer to tell the difference between the two.

A True History is a work with overtones of an initiation: The god Dionysus keeps appearing throughout the story, and the first incident in the grapevine arbor has all the elements of an initiation into the Dionysian mysteries. Here, Dionysus and wine appear to represent the excesses of poetic and philosophical fictions; once the travelers have become inebriated on the wine of fantasy, they are transported to the moon, into a whale, and to the world of the dead. The narrative also parodies theories of the journey of the soul. According to popular notions, the moon was the first resting place of the soul after death. The descent into the whale is a joke on the traditional descent into the Underworld, while the visit to the land of the dead parodies stock ideas about the Isles of the Blessed.

The journey of the narrator is a search for knowledge. When, at the end of the second book, the travelers reach the "other continent" on the opposite side of the ocean, this is an allusion to Greek speculation about other lands beyond the Atlantic Ocean. Some, however, interpret that other continent as none other than the place from where the narrator started: He returns to it with all the new knowledge gained on the journey, so that it now seems like a strange place. This resembles the situation of a religious or philosophical initiate returning to the "real" world and seeing it now through different eyes.

In *A True History*, Lucian explores the intellectual landscape by blurring and challenging the oppositions and boundaries on which Greek culture was built. In his fantastic world, the male inhabitants of the moon bear children and play the role of wives for each other; men have cabbage-leaves attached to their backsides; and women are half-human, half-donkey. Lucian plays with numbers and dimensions and uses unexpected materials for certain functions, as when his ships have glass anchors and the inhabitants of the moon blow honey from their noses.

A True History partakes of many genres of writing: satire, parody, traveler's tale, romance, and initiation story. It is the first genuine work of science fiction in the Western literary tradition. While it pokes fun at various poets, historians, and philosophers, it rarely does so by name and thus ensured the work's continuing and universal appeal. It was also extremely influential for later works of satire, among them Jonathan Swift's political satire *Gulliver's Travels* (1726) and the science-fiction adventure novels of Jules Verne, which are direct descendants of Lucian's book. Perhaps most important, it was the first work to problematize the issue of truthfulness in literature, provoking many of the same questions about interpretation, authorial reliability, and the nature of fiction that came into the forefront of late twentieth century analysis of literary texts.

"Critical Evaluation" by David H. J. Larmour

Bibliography:
Baldwin, Barry. *Studies in Lucian.* Toronto: Hakkert, 1973. An evaluation of Lucian and his works by an expert scholar. Chapter 5 includes comments on Lucian's view of the writing of history. Also includes a useful bibliography.

Fredericks, S. C. "Lucian's *True History* as SF." *Science Fiction Studies* 3 (March, 1976): 49-60. Suggests that *A True History* is an early instance of science fiction writing. The landscape of Lucian's journey can be seen as an "alternative world" through which the author explores the features and problems of the real world.

Jones, C. P. *Culture and Society in Lucian.* Cambridge, Mass.: Harvard University Press, 1986. A good general study of Lucian's many works. Locates them in the social and intellectual conditions of his time, the Greco-Roman imperial age. Chapters 5 and 6 discuss *A True History* in connection with Lucian's views on truth and lies.

Robinson, Christopher. *Lucian and His Influence in Europe.* Chapel Hill: University of North Carolina Press, 1979. A thorough account of Lucian's influence on such later European writers as Henry Fielding. Offers a historical account and critical evaluation.

THE TRUTH SUSPECTED

Type of work: Drama
Author: Juan Ruiz de Alarcón (1581-1639)
Type of plot: Comedy
Time of plot: Seventeenth century
Locale: Madrid
First published: La verdad sospechosa, 1630 (English translation, 1927)

> *Principal characters:*
> DON GARCÍA, a young man given to lying
> DON BELTRÁN, his father
> TRISTÁN, his servant
> JUAN DE SOSA, a friend, in love with Jacinta
> JACINTA, niece of Don Sancho, Don Beltrán's friend
> LUCRECIA, her friend

The Story:

When Don García returned home from studies at the University of Salamanca, he learned that on the death of his brother Gabriel he had become the heir to the family estates and fortune. His father also provided him with a shrewd and cynical servant, Tristán. Don García's tutor had already reported that the young man was given to one great vice: lying. Later his discerning servant agreed. The son's habit naturally worried his father, himself a man of great honor. Though he admitted that regard for truth was uncommon at the court of Spain, he hated the vice of lying above all others, and he vowed to break his son of the habit.

During his first day in Madrid, Don García indulged in his practice after meeting two attractive women in the shopping center of the city. Taking his cue from Tristán's remark that the women of Madrid were money-mad, the young gallant told them that he was a wealthy man from the New World. Though he had been in Madrid hardly a day, he assured one of the women that he had worshiped her from afar for a year. Unfortunately, he had misunderstood the information bought from their coachman by Tristán; he thought the woman he wanted to marry was Lucrecia, but the object of his attentions was really her friend Jacinta.

More lying followed when Don García met his friend, Juan de Sosa, a young man in love with Jacinta but rejected by her uncle until he acquired a knighthood. This time, falsely claiming responsibility for a serenade and banquet the preceding night, Don García found himself challenged to a duel by Juan.

In the meantime, hoping to get his son married off before Madrid learned of his habit of lying, Don Beltrán, after giving him a lecture on the value of truth, told Don García that he had arranged for Don García's marriage to Jacinta, niece of Don Beltrán's old friend, Don Sancho. Since Don García thought it was Lucrecia whom he loved, he promptly invented a prodigious lie about his marriage to a lady of Salamanca. He declared that while visiting her one night, he had been discovered by the lady's father; to save her reputation and life, he had agreed to marry her.

Lucrecia, to help Jacinta decide which of her suitors she preferred, signed her name to a note inviting Don García to wait beneath her balcony. During his talk with the veiled ladies, his earlier story about a wife in Salamanca and his uncertainty as to which of the veiled women was the one he loved resulted in their ridicule and scorn. Rudely dismissed, he received from Tristán a lecture on the evils of lying.

More lying was necessary when Don Beltrán attempted to send for his son's wife. She could not travel, Don García told him; she was going to have a baby. Although he laughed at Tristán's warning that "one who lies needs a quick wit and a good memory," his punishment had already begun. When Lucrecia invited him to another meeting at a convent, he found himself trapped in a mesh of deceit, and the veiled ladies showed how unsuccessful had been his wooing. Tristán contributed to his unhappiness by many quotations from Latin and Greek writers. The servant also remarked that he could see no sense to his master's lies when they were so easily discovered.

Even Tristán, however, was fooled by Don García's account of his supposed duel with Juan de Sosa; actually he had placated his former friend by telling more lies. It would have been better had he silenced his challenger on the dueling field, for Juan now appeared to tell Don Beltrán that no one with the name of Don García's supposed wife lived in Salamanca. So incensed was the father that he was about to disinherit his son. Even by telling the truth, Don García could not convince him without corroboration from Tristán. The word of a servant was more trustworthy than the oath of a nobleman, the ashamed father pointed out.

When Juan's attainment of knighthood cleared away that obstruction to his suit, Don Sancho gladly arranged for the young man's marriage to Jacinta; and that lady, disillusioned and dubious of a lying suitor, was happy to agree with her uncle's decision. Don Beltrán, too, was won over, and he agreed to arrange for his son's delayed marriage. When the suitors were paired off, Don García saw his lady go to his rival. Even though the whole affair had been based on misunderstanding of identity, it was now too late to correct the mistake. Don García was honor bound to marry Lucrecia.

Tristán again underlined a moral when he assured his master that if he had told the truth instead of lying he would now be happy with Jacinta. Lucrecia, however, was also beautiful.

Critical Evaluation:

Mexican-born, Juan Ruiz de Alarcón became one of the leading dramatists of the Golden Age in Spain. The twenty-six plays now identified as his are divided into two groups. His early plays, in keeping with the romantic tradition, are marked by complicated plots. His later works are more concerned with the human qualities of his characters and less with dramatic situations. His two best plays belong to his second period. *The Walls Have Ears* (1617) attacks slander, and *The Truth Suspected* presents an excellent character study of a congenital liar. The latter play inspired Pierre Corneille's *The Liar* (1643).

While lying breaks a commandment, it is not listed among the seven deadly sins, which were central to the imagination of the Middle Ages. Lying as a sin was more fascinating to the minds of the Renaissance. Medieval moralists tended to externalize evil, visualizing it in the forms of assorted evil spirits and human actions, whereas Renaissance moralists were more eager to search for evil within, in emotions and thoughts. Medieval thinkers habitually cited Nero as representative of the worst sinner, while Iago is quite possibly the most evil man created by a Renaissance mind. Nero was guilty of such overt crimes as adultery, incest, and wanton slaughter; Iago's most destructive acts were his lies.

It is not surprising then that Alarcón should construct one of his best plays with this one vice as its cornerstone. This play deals solely and entirely with that disjunction of reality and human relationships called lying. Don García not only cannot tell the truth, but he also cannot hear it. That is to say, he does not believe the truth when he hears it, even though everyone around him does tell the truth. Lucrecia makes a vain attempt to set straight his identification of the two women, and Don Beltrán forcefully informs him of the disastrous circumstances inevitably resulting from lying, but still the young man persists almost mindlessly in distorting the truth.

Jacinta obviously was meant to be Don García's wife, for not only did he love her at first sight, with her evident approval, but she is also the one young lady of the entire city of Madrid who is chosen by Don Beltrán to become his son's bride. These two events, independent as they are, indicate by their coincidence a kind of providence at work which is subverted by Don García's affliction. In the final analysis, Don García's pathological lying is a disease that results in sterility and death.

This is a departure from the mainstream of sixteenth and seventeenth century comedy, in which societal sterility is threatened by the *senex*, an old man, usually the father of the boy or girl whose love serves as a focal point for the plot. In this play, by contrast, the threat is not a father; it is Don García's debilitating habit. Don Beltrán, far from hindering the love match, exerts himself to aid it. In *The Truth Suspected*, the social evil that needs eradication is lying.

This play departs from most comedies of the period in yet another way. Don García would seem, at first glance, to bear the full brunt of the consequences which result from his lying: He loses the young lady he loves and is forced to marry another whom he does not love. Were these the only results, it could be said that the catastrophe befalls one individual, not a society, but Don Beltrán shares heavily in the disaster. When his first and more virtuous son dies, his hopes for retention of honor in his family's future also dies. Don Beltrán is left with an heir who carries a disease fatal to honor. The young lover loses his love; the honorable older man loses his honor. The older man evidently does nothing to deserve his loss of honor. The question remains, does Don García deserve his downfall?

If this question turns, as often it does, on the motivation for his destructive lying, the question is unanswerable. Other liars lie for pleasure or for profit, but there is no such rationale behind Don García's lying. He lies when the truth would have served his purposes as well or better than his lies, as when he lies about having given the banquet and then lies again in order to extricate himself from the duel. There is no indication that he is too cowardly to fight the duel. There is only the sense that he is driven to lie.

Similarly, he lies when the truth is sure to be discovered in a matter of days. When, for example, he tells Jacinta of his Peruvian wealth, it seems to matter not at all that his true background is quite adequate to attract her attention. It is tempting to the modern reader, but probably an error, to psychoanalyze Don García. There is no rationalization provided in the play for Don García's problem. There can be no doubt that his lack of a motive for lying is a part of Alarcón's design. Alarcón isolates the central thesis of the play—the evil of lying—so as to present the phenomenon in something very near to its pure form. Certainly Alarcón's method serves to depict the fault as being even more ludicrous and damaging than it usually is in real life, thereby holding it up to ridicule and scorn.

There are minor, but telling, similarities between Don García and that other, more famous hidalgo of Spanish literature, Don Quixote. Don García shares Quixote's addiction to the beautiful lie. García is not in love with the heroic motions of ridding the earth of giants and malevolent knights, but he definitely is enamored of casting himself in the roles of traveler from a mystical land (as Peru was at this time), as silent and adoring lover-from-afar, and as giver of lavish feasts.

With both characters, the beautiful lie blinds the liar to the real world. Quixote is morally absolved by his delusion; he believes his lies. Don García is aware of his lies. Another difference between the two is that Quixote's beautiful lie has a form and an ethos of its own (outmoded though it may have been), whereas García's lies are piecemeal and extemporaneous. Quixote's lies lead to insights and revelations; García's lead only to chaos and disappointment.

"Critical Evaluation" by John J. Brugaletta

Bibliography:

Brenan, Gerald. *The Literature of the Spanish People*. Cambridge, England: Cambridge University Press, 1965. Chapter 9 establishes the importance of Lope de Vega in the development of the new comedy and discloses Alarcón's contribution to the new comedy.

Claydon, Ellen. *Juan Ruiz de Alarcón, Baroque Dramatist*. Chapel Hill, N.C.: Department of Romance Languages, University of North Carolina, 1970. Defines the *comedia* in terms of the baroque tendencies. Discusses the importance of *The Truth Suspected* in literary history.

Poesse, Walter. *Juan Ruiz de Alarcón*. New York: Twayne, 1972. Gives the English-speaking reader information about Alarcón's life and works and evaluates the technique the author used in composing his plays. Shows the marked difference between Alarcón's plays and those of his contemporaries.

Rennert, Hugo A. *The Spanish Stage in the Time of Lope de Vega*. Mineola, N.Y.: Dover, 1963. Explains the theatrical devices behind the *comedia*. A thorough discussion of the theater in Alarcón's era.

Wilson, Margaret. *Spanish Drama of the Golden Age*. New York: Pergamon Press, 1969. Traces the history of the Spanish theater to the Golden Age of the seventeenth century. Contains a superb explanation of the characteristics of the Spanish *comedia* and discusses Alarcón's contribution to the Spanish theater.

TUNG-CHOU LIEH-KUO CHIH

Type of work: Novel
Author: Fêng Mêng-lung (1574?-1645?)
Type of plot: Historical
Time of plot: 770-220 B.C.E.
Locale: China
First published: Hsin lieh-kuo chih, Ming edition, after 1627; C'ing edition, after 1644

Principal characters:
> KING YU-WANG, the last king of the Western Chou dynasty
> KING P'ING, the first king of the Eastern Chou dynasty
> DUKE HUAN OF CH'I, the first overlord
> KUAN CHUNG or KUAN I-WU, a philosopher and statesman
> DUKE WÊN OF CHIN, an overlord
> KING CHUANG OF CH'U, an overlord
> DUKE HSIAO OF CH'IN, a powerful feudal lord
> SHANG YANG or WEI YANG, a statesman and political reformer
> SU CH'IN, a diplomat
> CHANG I, a diplomat
> CHING K'O, an assassin
> SHIH HUANG-TI, "The First Emperor" of Ch'in and a tyrant

The Story:

For hundreds of years, the kings of Chou ruled China. King Yu-wang (r. 781-771 B.C.E.) had a beautiful concubine whom he loved dearly. The woman, however, always looked depressed. The king would have paid any price to make her smile. One day, he lighted the fire beacon, a signal to announce the approach of an enemy. As the feudal lords with their troops hurried to the rescue, they found the king drinking with his concubine. They were forced to lead their troops back. The concubine enjoyed the practical joke so much that for the first time she gave a hearty laugh.

The Marquis of Shen, father of the lawful queen, resented the treatment of his daughter and grandson by the king, and he allied himself with the barbarians. Together they marched on the capital. The fire beacon was again lighted, but this time no rescuing troops appeared. King Yu-wang was killed and the beautiful concubine carried away by the barbarians.

The capital was also sacked and destroyed. When the heir-apparent, P'ing-wang, was raised to the throne, he moved the government to Loyang, a city to the east. This was the beginning of the Eastern Chou dynasty (770 B.C.E.). From that time on, the royal house was weakened, and several feudal states rose to unprecedented power. The territory in the west, the present province of Shensi, was given up to the state of Ch'in, which gradually aggrandized itself as a result of the conquest of the neighboring tribes of barbarians and became the force to reunify China centuries later.

The first feudal lord to attain imperial importance was Duke Huan of Ch'i (685-643 B.C.E.), who occupied the northeast of the present province of Shangtung. His prime minister, Kuan Chung, on whom the duke relied heavily, launched a program of economic reconstruction. With his people enjoying economic prosperity at home and placing full confidence in him, the duke began a series of diplomatic moves that successfully bound various other states by treaty. He

6749

became an overlord, the leader of the feudal lords, defender of the royal house, and protector of weaker states.

The great menace to the allied states, with the king of Chou as their nominal head, was Ch'u, occupying, roughly, the present provinces of Hupeh and Hunan, a mere viscountship in the south, generally considered barbarous but grown so formidable in its military strength and vast in its territory that its rulers defied the royal house and called themselves kings. The utmost Duke Huan of Ch'i, accomplished with regard to the potential enemy in the south, though he had chased the barbarians in the northeast up to the border of Manchuria during a military campaign to help the much harassed state of Yen, was to bring about a pact of amity. The smaller states, under the pressure of circumstances, were often compelled to choose between joining the allies led by Ch'i or paying allegiance to Ch'u.

The first severe blow to Ch'u was dealt by Duke Wên of Chin, another prince who had become an overlord. Nearly a thousand chariots of war on either side, each with its allies, were engaged in a battle at a place called Ch'engp'u (632 B.C.E.) and Ch'u was defeated. This was the first great battle in Chinese history, and it is said to have saved Chinese civilization. Chin (occupying the present province of Shansi) for two centuries remained a great state in the north, but the power of the duke was usurped by his hereditary ministers until he had as little authority over his retainers as did the king of Chou over the feudal lords. The retainers fought fiercely among themselves, and the houses of Wei, Han, and Chao emerged as the victors. These three retainers were recognized as hereditary feudal lords by the king, in 403 B.C.E. In 376, they divided among them the territory of Chin.

The power and prestige of Ch'u reached its zenith under King Chuang (613-591 B.C.E.), who defeated Chin. A hundred years later two other states in the south, hitherto obscure, extended their influence to the north. The first was Wu (currently Kiangsu) whose armies in one campaign reached as far as the capital of Ch'u (506 B.C.E.) but were forced to withdraw before the intervention of Ch'in from the northwest. Although it had also defeated Ch'i, the glory of Wu soon faded; it was conquered by Yüeh (currently Chekiang) in 473; later, in 334, Yüeh was annexed by Ch'u.

After endless internal disturbance within most of the states and wars among them, seven "great powers" were left: Ch'in, Ch'u, Ch'i, Wei, Han, Chao, and Yen. The smaller and weaker states gradually became extinct, swallowed by the larger powers. The authority of the royal house was now utterly disregarded. The potentates of the great powers followed the once-detested example of Ch'u to assume kingship in the fourth century B.C.E. It was an age of the test of strength, when each state had to fight with every possible resource—military, diplomatic, material, and ideological—for survival or, with luck, supremacy.

Of the seven, Ch'in was considered geographically unassailable. Having annexed a large territory in the west, it was ready to bid for supremacy in China. Under Duke Hsiao (361-338 B.C.E.), organization of the peoples, which had been remarkable, was further strengthened by the policies of the prime minister, Shang Yang. The foundations of a totalitarian empire had been laid.

After the military strength of Ch'in had struck such terror into the other states, their main problem was how to deal with the power in the west. At one time, an alliance of six was formed to contend against Ch'in, acting upon the strategy of the diplomat Su Ch'in, who also became the chancellor of the confederation. Su's scheme, however, was obstructed by his former fellow student, Chang I, who was working for Ch'in. With crafty maneuvers, bribery, and threats, Ch'in succeeded in dividing the allies. In 317 Su Ch'in was assassinated.

The conquest of the six states by Ch'in was delayed by the efforts of the Four Statesmen of

Ch'i, Ch'u, Chao, and Wei. Able administrators and diplomats, they also gained great fame as patrons who threw open their doors to the scholars and men of ability who were wandering throughout China seeking employment. Their popularity and ability enabled their states to hold out against Ch'in while they lived; after their deaths, none was able to stop the advance of the conqueror.

Ching K'o of Yen made a heroic attempt to assassinate the man then sitting on the throne of Ch'in in 227 B.C.E. His effort failed, however, and the king of Ch'in was crowned as Shih Huang-ti, "The First Emperor," known to posterity as the builder of the Great Wall and the burner of the books, after the conquest of his six rivals in 220. The last "shadow" monarch of the Chou Dynasty died in 256.

Critical Evaluation:

Fêng Mêng-lung's *Hsin lieh-kuo chih* dates from after 1627; it is based on an earlier account by Yü Shao-yü (fl. c. 1566) titled *Lieh-kuo chih chuan*. After 1644, Fêng's version was edited slightly by Ts'ai Yuan-fang (fl. c. 1736) and given the title *Tung-chou lieh-kuo chih*; this version may be regarded as definitive. The novel contains no fictitious figures. It tells of an important time in Chinese history: from the eighth to the third centuries B.C.E. This period includes the Chou dynasty and, most significantly, China's unification under the tyrant Ch'in Shih Huang-ti. Fêng was more of a collector and editor of stories than an original fiction writer. His works were issued under various pseudonyms, and it is only through the careful investigation of modern scholars that he has been identified as the author or editor of the works now attributed to him. His prolific career was cut short by the overthrow of the Ming dynasty, which cost him his life. Fêng's novel has never been fully translated into English.

Fêng was a man of broad interests, a learned scholar, and a talented writer of prose, but he is known principally for his contributions to popular, vernacular literature as opposed to literature in classical Chinese. As a scholar, however, he was deficient enough in the writing of classical poetry that he never passed the state government examinations. He nevertheless specialized in the classic *Ch'un-ch'iu* (*Spring and Autumn Annals*) by Confucious (551-479 B.C.E.), and he published two books on the subject, which were well received by other scholars. He is best known for his three collections of vernacular short stories. He left a lasting mark on the Chinese novel.

In Chinese tradition, "history" (*shih*) and "fiction" (*hsiao-shuo*) have meanings that differ significantly from such concepts in the West. Chinese historiography developed so early (roughly the eighth century B.C.E., the time of Homer) that no trace of an epic tradition has been left. The historical consciousness was always strong. Hence very early history became one of China's most important social institutions. Numerous accounts attest to this fact. To the Chinese, therefore, "history" means a faithful representation of external reality based on an official worldview. On the other hand, "fiction" to the Chinese does not mean "falsehood" but confidential gossip that has been overheard and is not very far from the truth. In this way Chinese fiction became an outgrowth of history; it tended to derive its characters, events, locales, plots, and themes from actual history.

The earliest examples of Chinese long fiction display these historical characteristics. For example, the *San-Kuo chih yen-i* (romance of the three kingdoms), which has been ascribed to Lo Kuan-chung (fl. 1364), presents semihistorical heroes against a background of authentic history—the kingdoms of Wei, Shu, and Wu. The writing of the romance presented the author with two main problems: the balancing and harmonizing of characters and events; and the balancing and harmonizing of vernacular speech and classical Chinese prose. In this work the term "romance" means "expanded" or "heightened" and otherwise means much the same as it meant in medieval Europe—"militant," "loyal," "brave," "heroic," or "knightly." The *San-Kuo chih yen-i* may be considered a preeminent example of the Chinese military romance. Fêng's *Tung-chou lieh-kuo chih* resembles Lo's book in both character and quality. Fêng's "novel" differs little from authentic history.

Fêng himself did not hold that the worth of a story depends on whether it is completely real or completely fictive. Rather, a story's worth depends on a fair balance of the two if the story is to captivate the reader and establish credibility. Also, another measure of a story's quality and value is whether it demonstrates a good social purpose. In other words, a good story is didactic.

Fêng's romance has the surface unity of chronology and class relationship. There is no central plot that unifies the whole but a series of separate stories that take place during the Chou dynasty in China from about 788 B.C.E. to about 221 B.C.E. and the reign of the First Emperor, Chin Shih Huang-ti. The stories themselves are connected simply by being about the political and military affairs of the Chinese feudal aristocracy. These stories are told in two ways: by an impartial, unseen recorder and by the dialogue of characters. Five aspects of the stories are given prominence: the extraordinary; crimes and punishments; dramatic irony; warfare; and moral fable. The totality of the stories suggests that there is a universal moral order that tends to prevail regardless of the evil doings of humanity—betrayals, fratricides, assassinations, executions, exiles, tortures, adulteries, and warfare. The novel implies that by a decree of heaven, retribution and balance of good and evil are brought about in the long run.

"Critical Evaluation" by Richard P. Benton

Bibliography:
Fêng Mêng-lung. *Tung Chou lieh-kuo chih*. Tai-pei shih: Hua I Shu Chu, 1985. A selection of 23 chapters. In finely written Chinese script with beautiful colored illustrations.
Giles, Herbert A., trans. Excerpt from *Lieh-kuo chih chuan*, by Yü Shao-yü. In *A History of Chinese Literature*. New York: Grove Press, 1958. Useful for comparison.
Lu, Sheldon Hsiao-peng. *From Historicity to Fictionality: The Chinese Poetics of Narrative*. Stanford, Calif.: Stanford University Press, 1994. Proposes that history is the ground of narrative and ties it inevitably to time and space as well as to ideology and relativity.

THE TURN OF THE SCREW

Type of work: Novella
Author: Henry James (1843-1916)
Type of plot: Ghost
Time of plot: Mid-nineteenth century
Locale: England
First published: 1898

> *Principal characters:*
> THE GOVERNESS
> MRS. GROSE, housekeeper at Bly
> MILES and
> FLORA, the two children of the house
> MR. QUINT and
> MISS JESSEL, two apparitions

The Story:

It was a pleasant afternoon in June when the governess first arrived at the country estate at Bly, where she was to take charge of Miles, aged ten, and Flora, eight. She faced her new position with some trepidation because of the unusual circumstances of her situation. The two children were to be under her complete care, and the uncle who had engaged her had been explicit in the fact that he did not wish to be bothered with his orphaned niece and nephew. Her uneasiness disappeared, however, when she saw her charges, for Flora and Miles seemed incapable of giving the slightest trouble.

The weeks of June passed uneventfully. Then, one evening, while she was walking in the garden at twilight, the governess was startled to see a strange young man at a distance. The man looked at her in a manner that suggested a challenge and disappeared. The incident angered and distressed the young woman; she decided the man was a trespasser.

On the following Sunday evening, the young woman was startled to see the same stranger looking in at her through a window. Once again he stared piercingly at her for a few seconds and then disappeared. This time the governess realized that the man was looking for someone in particular and that perhaps he boded evil for the children in her care. A few minutes later, the governess told the housekeeper, Mrs. Grose, of the incident and described the appearance of the man. Mrs. Grose told her that it was a perfect description of Peter Quint, the valet to the governess' employer. Mr. Quint was dead.

One afternoon shortly afterward, a second apparition appeared. This time the ghost of Miss Jessel, the former governess, appeared in the garden to both the governess and the little girl, Flora. The strange part of the situation was that the little girl refused to let the governess know that she had seen the figure and knew who it was, though it was obvious that she had understood the appearance fully. The governess learned from the housekeeper that the two apparitions had been lovers while alive, though the girl had been of a very fine family and the man had been guilty of drunkenness and worse vices. For what evil purpose these two spirits wished to influence the seemingly innocent children, neither the housekeeper nor the governess could guess. The secrecy of the children about seeing the ghosts was maddening to the two women.

They both felt that the boy was continuing to see the two ghosts in private and concealed that fact, just as he had known of the illicit affair between the valet and the former governess in life and had helped them to conceal it. Yet, when in the presence of the children, the governess sometimes felt that it would be impossible for the two children to be influenced into evil.

The third time, the ghost of Quint appeared to the governess inside the house. Unable to sleep, she had sat reading late at night. Hearing someone on the stairs, she went to investigate and saw the ghost, which disappeared when faced by her unflinching gaze. Each night after that, she inspected the stairs, but she never again saw the ghost of the man. Once she glimpsed the apparition of Miss Jessel as it sat dejectedly on the lowest stair. Worse than the appearance of the ghosts was the discovery that the children had left their beds at night to wander on the lawn in communication with the spirits who were leading them to unknown evil. It became apparent to the governess that the children were not good within themselves. In their imaginations, they were living in a world populated by the evil dead restored.

In such an atmosphere, the summer wore away into autumn. In all that time, the children had given no sign of awareness of the apparitions. Knowing that her influence with the children was as tenuous as a thread which would break at the least stress, the governess did not allude to the ghosts. She herself had seen no more manifestations, but she had often felt by the children's attitude that the apparitions were close at hand. What was worse for the distressed woman was the thought that what Miles and Flora saw were things still more terrible than she imagined, visions that sprang from their association with the evil figures in the past.

One day, Miles went to her and announced his desire to go away to school. The governess realized it was only proper that he be sent to school, but she feared the results of ghostly influences once he was beyond her care. Later, opening the door of the schoolroom, she again saw the ghost of her predecessor, Miss Jessel. As the apparition faded, the governess realized that her duty was to stay with the children and combat the spirits and their deadly influence. She decided to write immediately to the children's uncle, breaking his injunction against being bothered in their behalf. That night before she wrote, she went into Miles's room and asked the boy to let her help him in his secret troubles. Suddenly a rush of cold air filled the room, as if the window had been blown open. When the governess relighted the candle blown out by the draft, the window was still closed, and the drawn curtain had not been disturbed.

The following day Flora disappeared. Mrs. Grose and the governess found her beside the garden pond. The governess, knowing she had gone there to see the ghost, asked her where Miss Jessel was. The child replied that she only wanted to be left alone. The governess could see the apparition of Miss Jessel standing on the opposite side of the pond. The governess, afraid that the evil influence had already dominated the little girl, asked the housekeeper to take the child to London, and to request the uncle's aid. In place of the lovable angelic Flora there had suddenly appeared a little child with a filthy mind and filthy speech, which she used in denouncing the governess to the housekeeper. The same afternoon, Mrs. Grose left with the child as the governess had requested.

That evening, immediately after dinner, the governess asked Miles to tell her what was on his mind before he left the dining room. When he refused, she asked him if he had stolen the letter she had written to his uncle. As she asked the question, she realized that standing outside the window, staring into the room, was the ghost of Peter Quint. She pulled the boy close to her, shielding him from any view of the ghost at the window, while he told her that he had taken the letter. He also informed her that he had already been expelled from one school because of his lewd speech and actions. Noting how close the governess was holding him, he suddenly asked if Miss Jessel were near. The governess, angry and distraught, shrieked at him that it was the ghost of Peter Quint, just outside the window. When Miles turned around, the apparition was gone. With a scream, he fell into the governess' arms. At first, she did not realize that she had lost him forever—that Miles was dead.

Critical Evaluation:

In 1908, ten years after the publication of *The Turn of the Screw* (1898) as a serial in *Collier's Weekly* (and in book form late in the same year), Henry James wrote that he considered the story "least apt to be baited by earnest criticism." His prediction was shown to be remarkably inaccurate, however, as the decades-long critical debate surrounding *The Turn of the Screw* has proven more vigorous and controversial than that surrounding any of James's other works. It seems that any critic who wishes to do so may find compelling textual evidence that the work is either a chilling, straightforward ghost story made all the more horrific by the youthful age of its menaced characters, or is a case study of a psychologically disturbed young woman in the grip of a sexually induced hallucinatory neurosis, or is an engrossing, powerful moral fable that allegorizes the intertwining of innocence and evil in the human heart, or is some combination of the above, despite the fact that the foregoing interpretations are at odds with one another.

If nothing else, then, *The Turn of the Screw* is, as James himself writes, "a piece of ingenuity . . . [and] of cold artistic calculation, an *amusette* to catch those not easily caught." The wealth of contradictory critical evaluations of the work testifies to its complexity and its artistry; the ambiguous overtones of the story readily seem to catch "those not easily caught."

For the first several years after the book's publication, most readers seemed to agree with James's appraisal of *The Turn of the Screw* as "a fairy-tale pure and simple," at least in its intent. One early critic for *The New York Times* described the work in 1898 as "a deliberate, powerful, and horribly successful study of the magic of evil," in which the characters of the two children Miles and Flora are "accursed, or all but damned, and are shown to have daily, almost hourly, communication with lost souls that formerly inhabited the bodies of a vicious governess and her paramour."

James also described the book as a "trap for the unwary," and the discussion surrounding *The Turn of the Screw* heated considerably with the publication of noted critic Edmund Wilson's essay, "The Ambiguity of Henry James" in 1934. In his essay, Wilson maintains that in the novel "almost everything from beginning to end can be read equally in either of two senses." He considers the governess an unreliable narrator, one whose perception of the events surrounding her stay at Bly is colored and distorted by her own neuroses. He writes, "the governess who is made to tell the story is a neurotic case of sex repression, and . . . the ghosts are not real ghosts but hallucinations of the governess." In taking this position, Wilson is aided by the statement made by James himself, who said that the governess has kept "crystalline" her record of "so many intense anomalies and obscurities—by which I don't of course mean her explanation of them, a different matter."

Proponents of this Freudian reading of *The Turn of the Screw* point to elements of the story that may be read as laden with sexual significance. For example, the governess herself is curiously obsessed with her employer, a handsome young man who does not appear to reciprocate the infatuation. The first appearances of the two evil ghosts, Mr. Quint and Miss Jessel, occur respectively on a tower and beside a lake, locations that could signify male and female sexuality, respectively. At the time of Miss Jessel's appearance, Flora, who is being watched by the governess, is engaged in a game involving joining together two pieces of wood, a game that could also have sexual overtones to the governess. In this interpretation of the novel as a record of sexual repression, "there is never any reason for supposing that anybody but the governess sees the ghosts," according to Wilson. "She believes that the children see them, but there is never any proof that they do."

This position is considered by many to be overly rationalistic and materialist, owing more to the philosophical and social climate at the time of the essay's publication (1934) than to elements within the novella itself. Moreover, the Freudian reading, besides being anachronistic (*The Turn of the Screw* antedates nearly all of Sigmund Freud's publications), does not convincingly explain the governess' detailed description of Quint, a man she has never seen, to Mrs. Grose, the housekeeper; nor does it explain the numerous references made by James himself to *The Turn of the Screw* as a rather conventional ghost story, even to the point of calling it "a shameless pot-boiler" and "grossly apparitional."

One of James's perennial moral themes is the relationship between innocence and experience; he often examines the idea that innocence itself may involve the provocation of evil elsewhere, and that the two are inextricably intertwined within the dual nature, both divine and demonic, of humanity. Along this line, *The Turn of the Screw* may also be interpreted as a subtle but powerful moral allegory, in which Bly becomes a type of the garden of Eden: Evil has entered this Eden with the express purpose of entrapping the souls of Miles and Flora, the archetypal male and female innocents. The governess seeks to "save" the two, and the final words of the novel ("his little heart, dispossessed, had stopped") indicate her dubious victory as the heart of Miles is freed from its "possession" by the evil Quint.

Whatever James's intentions might have been in *The Turn of the Screw*, his public statements regarding it and the textual evidence within the novella itself seem to support both sides of the argument. The modern reader must first consider this novella as a work of immense artistic skill designed to produce horror. Regardless of whether this horror originates in the supernatural or the psychological realm is of little account in assessing its final effect. In the end, all of the book's possible multiple meanings must be taken as parts of a work of art that succeeds or fails on its own terms. This remains true even though readers may not be able to make a final and definitive critical pronouncement regarding its interpretation.

"Critical Evaluation" by Craig Payne

Bibliography:
Edel, Leon, ed. *Henry James: A Collection of Critical Essays*. Englewood Cliffs, N.J.: Prentice-Hall, 1963. Covers much of James's output; ignores the early critical controversy surrounding *The Turn of the Screw* and focuses instead on explication of James's symbolic imagery and artistic techniques.

James, Henry. *The Turn of the Screw*. Edited by Robert Kimbrough. New York: W. W. Norton, 1966. An excellent collection of source materials. Covers James's background sources in his own words and presents a number of his letters regarding *The Turn of the Screw*. Presents chronologically a variety of critical reactions, from early criticism (1898-1923) through the years of the Freudian controversy (1924-1957) to more recent articles.

Tompkins, Jane P., ed. *Twentieth Century Interpretations of "The Turn of the Screw" and Other Tales: A Collection of Critical Essays*. Englewood Cliffs, N.J.: Prentice-Hall, 1970. Two essays treat *The Turn of the Screw*, placing the work in the context of James's other shorter fiction.

Wagenknecht, Edward. *The Tales of Henry James*. New York: Frederick Ungar, 1984. Thorough discussion of sources and history for *The Turn of the Screw*. Attacks Freudian readings as serious misinterpretations; presents the novel as a straightforward ghost story designed for sophisticated readers.

Willen, Gerald, ed. *A Casebook on Henry James's "The Turn of the Screw."* New York: Thomas Y. Crowell, 1960. Fifteen essays debate the Freudian readings. The essay that started the entire controversy, Edmund Wilson's "The Ambiguity of Henry James," is also included, along with an extensive postscript by the same author. Somewhat dated, but recommended for the vigor of the debate.

TWELFTH NIGHT
Or, What You Will

Type of work: Drama
Author: William Shakespeare (1564-1616)
Type of plot: Comedy
Time of plot: Sixteenth century
Locale: Illyria, a region on the east shore of the Adriatic Sea
First performed: c. 1600-1602; first published, 1623

Principal characters:
VIOLA (CESARIO), Sebastian's twin sister and Orsino's lover
OLIVIA, a wealthy countess desired by Orsino
MARIA, her maid
SEBASTIAN, Viola's twin brother and Olivia's lover
ANTONIO, Sebastian's friend, a sea captain
ORSINO, the duke of Illyria
SIR TOBY BELCH, Olivia's uncle
SIR ANDREW AGUECHEEK, Olivia's ancient suitor
MALVOLIO, Olivia's steward, a comic villain
FESTE, Olivia's jester

The Story:

Viola and Sebastian, twin brother and sister who closely resembled each other, were separated when the ship on which they were passengers was wrecked during a great storm at sea. Each thought that the other was dead and set out alone with no hope of being reunited.

The lovely and charming Viola was cast upon the shores of Illyria, where she was befriended by a kind sea captain. They decided to dress Viola in men's clothing and have her take service as a page in the household of young Duke Orsino. Dressed in man's garb, Viola called herself Cesario and became the duke's personal attendant. Impressed by the youth's good looks and pert but courtly speech, Orsino sent "him" as his envoy of love to woo the Countess Olivia, who was mourning the death of her young brother.

The wealthy Olivia lived in a splendid palace with her maid, Maria; her drunken old uncle, Sir Toby Belch; and her steward, Malvolio. Maria and Sir Toby were a happy-go-lucky pair who drank and caroused with Sir Andrew Aguecheek, an ancient nobleman who was much enamored of Olivia. In return for grog supplied by Sir Andrew, Sir Toby was supposed to press Sir Andrew's suit with Olivia. Actually, however, Sir Toby never stayed sober long enough to keep his part of the bargain. All these affairs were observed disapprovingly by Malvolio, Olivia's ambitious, narrow-minded steward, who could not tolerate jollity in those about him.

When Cesario arrived at the palace, Olivia was instantly attracted to the page—thinking her a man. She paid close attention to Orsino's message, but it was not love for Orsino that caused her to listen so carefully. When Cesario left, she sent Malvolio after her with a ring. It was a shock for Viola, who hitherto enjoyed playing the part of Cesario, to realize that Olivia had fallen in love with her in her male clothes.

Meanwhile, Maria, Sir Toby, and Sir Andrew decided to stop Malvolio's constant prying into their affairs and devised a scheme whereby Malvolio would find a note, supposedly written by Olivia, in which she confessed her secret love for him and asked him to wear garish yellow stockings tied with cross garters and to smile continually in her presence. Overjoyed to receive this note, Malvolio soon appeared in his strange dress, capering and bowing before the startled countess. Olivia decided that Malvolio had lost his wits; to the amusement of the three conspirators, she had him confined to a dark room.

As the days passed, Viola fell in love with the duke, but the latter had eyes only for Olivia, with whom he pressed his page to renew his suit. When Cesario delivered another message from Orsino to Olivia, the countess openly declared her love for the young page. Cesario insisted, however, that his heart could never belong to any woman. So obvious were Olivia's feelings for Cesario that Sir Andrew became jealous. Sir Toby and Maria insisted that Sir Andrew's only course was to fight a duel with the page. Sir Toby delivered Sir Andrew's blustering challenge, which Cesario reluctantly accepted.

While these events were unfolding, Viola's twin brother, Sebastian, was being rescued by another sea captain, named Antonio, and the two became close friends. When Sebastian decided to visit the court of Duke Orsino at Illyria, Antonio decided to accompany him, even though he feared that he might be arrested there because he had once dueled with the duke. Upon arriving in Illyria, Antonio gave Sebastian his purse for safekeeping, and the two men separated for several hours.

While wandering about the city, Antonio chanced upon the duel between Cesario and Sir Andrew. Mistaking the disguised page for her brother, Antonio immediately went to the rescue of his supposed friend. When officers arrived on the scene, one of them recognized Antonio and arrested him in the name of the duke. Thinking that Viola was Sebastian, Antonio asked her to return his purse and was surprised and hurt when she disclaimed all knowledge of the captain's money. As Antonio was dragged away, he shouted invectives at "Sebastian" for not returning his purse, thereby alerting Viola to the fact that her brother was still alive.

Meanwhile, the real Sebastian was being followed by Sir Andrew, who never dreamed that this young man was not the same Cesario with whom he had just dueled. Prodded by Sir Toby and Maria, Sir Andrew engaged Sebastian in a new duel and was promptly wounded, along with Sir Toby. Olivia then interfered and had Sebastian taken to her home, thinking that he was Cesario. After sending for a priest, she married the surprised—but not unwilling—Sebastian.

As the officers escorted Antonio past Olivia's house, Orsino—accompanied by Cesario—appeared at her gates. Orsino recognized Antonio instantly and demanded to know why the sailor had returned to Illyria—a city filled with his enemies. Antonio explained that he had rescued and befriended the duke's present companion, Sebastian, and because of his deep friendship for the lad had accompanied him to Illyria despite the danger his visit involved. Pointing to Cesario, he sorrowfully accused the person he supposed to be Sebastian of violating their friendship by not returning his purse.

The duke was protesting against Antonio's accusation when Olivia appeared and saluted Cesario as her husband. Now the duke also began to think his page ungrateful, especially since he had told Cesario to press his own suit with Olivia. Just then Sir Andrew and Sir Toby arrived, looking for a doctor because Sebastian had wounded them. Seeing Cesario, Sir Andrew began to rail at him for his violence until Olivia dismissed the two old men. The real Sebastian then appeared and apologized for having wounded the old men.

Spying Antonio, Sebastian joyfully greeted his friend. Antonio and the rest of the amazed group, unable to believe what they saw, stared from Cesario to Sebastian. After Viola revealed her true identity and explained how she and her brother became separated, she and Sebastian greeted each other warmly. Seeing that the page of whom he had grown so fond was actually a woman, Duke Orsino declared that he would marry her.

After Malvolio was summoned, the plot against him was revealed. As he stormed off, vowing revenge, the others began celebrating the impending marriages of Viola and Orsino and of Sir Toby and Maria. Only Malvolio, unhappy in the happiness of others, remained peevish and disgruntled.

Critical Evaluation:

William Shakespeare apparently wrote *Twelfth Night: Or, What You Will* to be performed on the twelfth feast day, the joyous climax of the Renaissance Christmas season; however, the feast day itself otherwise has nothing to do with the substance of the play. The play's subtitle suggests that it is a festive bagatelle to be lightly, but artfully, tossed off. Indeed, Shakespeare may have written the play earlier and revised it for the Christmas festival, for it contains many signs of revision.

The tone of *Twelfth Night* is consistently appropriate to high merriment. With nine comedies behind him when he wrote it, Shakespeare was at the height of his comic powers and in an exalted mood to which he never returned. Chronologically, the play immediately precedes Shakespeare's great tragedies and so-called problem plays. *Twelfth Night* recombines many elements and devices from earlier plays—particularly *Two Gentlemen of Verona* (c. 1594-1595) and *The Comedy of Errors* (c. 1592-1594)—into a new triumph, unsurpassed in its deft execution.

It is a brilliant irony that Shakespeare's most joyous play should be compounded out of the sadnesses of its principal characters. Yet the sadnesses are, for the most part, those mannered sadnesses that the Elizabethans savored. Orsino, for example, particularly revels in a sweet melancholy reminiscent of that which afflicted Antonio at the beginning of *The Merchant of Venice* (c. 1596-1597). Orsino's opening speech—which has often been taken overly seriously—is not a grief-stricken condemnation of love but rather owes much more to the Italian poet Petrarch. Orsino revels in the longings of love and in the bittersweet satiety of his romantic self-indulgence. He is in love with love.

On the other side of the city is the household of Olivia, which balances Orsino and his establishment. Although Olivia's sadness at her brother's death initially seems more substantial than Orsino's airy romantic fantasies, she, too, is a Renaissance melancholic who is wringing the last ounce of enjoyment out of her grief. Her plan to isolate herself for seven years of mourning is an excess, but one that provides an excellent counterbalance to Orsino's fancy; it also sets the plot in motion, since Orsino's love-longing is frustrated by Olivia's decision to be a recluse.

The point of contact between Orsino and Olivia—ferrying back and forth between the two—is Viola. As Cesario, she also is sad, but her sadness, like the rest of her behavior, is more direct and human. The sweet beauty that shines through her male disguise is elevated beyond a vulgar joke by Olivia's immediate, though circumstantially ridiculous, response to her human appeal. Viola's grief is not stylized and her love is for human beings rather than for abstractions. She seems destined to unite the two melancholy dreamers, but what the play instead accomplishes is that Viola, in her own person and in that of her alter ego, her brother, becomes part of both households. The ultimate outcome is a glorious resolution. It is, of course, immaterial to the dreamy Orsino that he gets Viola instead of Olivia—the romantic emotion is more important to him than is the specific person. Olivia, already drawn out of her seclusion by the disguised Viola, gets what is even better for her, Sebastian.

The glittering plot is reinforced by some of Shakespeare's best and most delicate dramatic poetry. Moreover, the drama is suffused with bittersweet music, and the idyllic setting in Illyria blends with language and imagery to create a most delightful atmosphere wholly appropriate to the celebration of love and the enjoyment of this world.

The one notable briar in the story's rose garden is Malvolio; however, he is easily the play's most interesting character. He is called a Puritan, but although he is not a type, he does betray the characteristics then associated with that austere Anglican sect. He is a self-important, serious-minded person with high ideals who cannot bear the thought of others being happy. As Sir Toby puts it to him, "Dost thou think because thou art virtuous, there shall be no more cakes and ale?" Malvolio suffers within a joyous world; it is against his will that he becomes part of the fun when he is duped and made to appear ridiculous. As a character, he represents a historical group, then growing in power, whose earnestness threatened to take the joy out of life (and, incidentally, to close England's theaters). Yet, Shakespeare does not indulge in a satire on Puritanism. He uses the critical powers of comedy in indirect ways.

Malvolio is ridiculous, but so are the cavaliers who surround him. The absurd Sir Andrew Aguecheek and the usually drunken Sir Toby Belch are the representatives, on the political level, of the old order that Malvolio's counterparts in the real world were soon to topple. Yet while these characters are flawed, they are certainly more engaging than the inflated Malvolio. Shakespeare does not set up the contrast as a political allegory, with right on one side and wrong on the other. Nevertheless, Malvolio is an intrusion into the otherwise idyllic world of the play. He cannot love; his desire for the hand of Olivia is grounded in an earnest will to get ahead. He cannot celebrate; he is too pious and self-involved. Nothing is left for him but to be the butt of a joke—his role in the celebration. Some critics have suggested that Malvolio is treated too harshly, but a Renaissance audience would have understood how ludicrous and indecorous it was for a man of his class to think, even for a moment, of courting Countess Olivia. His pompous and blustery language are the key to how alien he is to this festive context. When he has done his bit, Olivia casually mentions that perhaps he has been put upon, but this is the only sympathetic gesture he deserves. He is the force that threatens to destroy the celebration of all that is good and refined and joyful in Elizabethan society.

"Critical Evaluation" by Edward E. Foster

Bibliography:
Berry, Ralph. *Shakespeare's Comedies: Explorations in Form.* Princeton, N.J.: Princeton University Press, 1972. A discussion of Shakespeare's comedies in which each chapter is devoted to a specific play. In the chapter "The Messages of *Twelfth Night*," Barry discusses the deceits and illusions in the play and concludes that it calls the very nature of reality into question.
Levin, Richard A. *Love and Society in Shakespearean Comedy.* Newark: University of Delaware Press, 1985. A critical study of three of Shakespeare's romantic comedies. Two chapters deal with *Twelfth Night*: "Household Politics in Illyria" discusses the acceptance of the various characters into society, while "Feste and the Antiromantic *Twelfth Night*" focuses on the discordant elements of the play.
Lloyd Evans, Gareth. *The Upstart Crow: An Introduction to Shakespeare's Plays.* London: J. M. Dent and Sons, 1982. Focuses mainly on critical reviews of Shakespeare's plays, as well as discussing sources and historical context and background.
Muir, Kenneth, ed. *Shakespeare—The Comedies: A Collection of Critical Essays.* Englewood Cliffs, N.J.: Prentice-Hall, 1965. An anthology of essays that discuss Shakespeare's comedies from various points of view. Harold Jenkins compares *Twelfth Night* with earlier plays

by Shakespeare and others and concludes that it is the greatest of Shakespeare's romantic comedies.

Shakespeare, William. *Twelfth Night*. Edited by J. M. Lothian and T. W. Craik. London: Methuen, 1975. Includes more than eighty pages of introductory material and critical analysis, as well as the text of the play itself.

THE TWELVE

Type of work: Poetry
Author: Aleksandr Blok (1880-1921)
Type of plot: Ballad
Time of plot: 1917
Locale: Petrograd, Russia
First published: Dvenadtsat', 1918 (English translation, 1920)

> *Principal characters:*
> VANKA, a former revolutionary
> PETRUKHA (PETKA), a revolutionary
> KATYA, their girlfriend

The Story:

In a cold, snowy night a group of twelve revolutionaries was marching on a Petrograd street at the beginning of the Bolshevik revolution in Russia. A blizzard was at full strength, but it did not slow down their advance. As they were marching on in the middle of the street, several bystanders on sidewalks were looking on with fear and incomprehension etched on their faces. First, there was an old woman who was trembling fearfully, afraid of the marchers and declaring that the Bolsheviks will be the death of her and people like her. Looking at the poster made of canvas declaring "All the Power to the Constituent Assembly," she was complaining about waste because all that material could have been used to supply children with foot-clouts. A bourgeois was also standing there at the crossing, alone, with his face buried in the collar of his coat. A long-haired writer was another bystander, cursing at the traitors and lamenting the fact that Russia was dead. A fat "comrade priest" came slinking through the snow in a black and bulky cassock, with a pendent cross on his belly. A woman wrapped in a Persian fur, confiding to a companion that they had cried and cried, fell flat on her back on the slippery ice. Finally, a group of prostitutes were also at the scene plying their trade. They also looked at the canvas poster and declared that they, too, had an assembly debating how much to charge for their services. All these onlookers were horrified by the uncertainty of the future and the ferocious looks and behavior of the marching revolutionaries.

The revolutionaries paid little attention to them, however, marching on inexorably, shouting revolutionary slogans, shooting off their guns, singing rowdy revolutionary songs, killing and burning whatever stood in their way, and striking fear into bystanders. Some of them were clad in prison garb.

Vanka, a member of the revolutionary group, had run off with Katya, a girlfriend of another revolutionary, Petrukha. In the distance they still saw Vanka frolicking and dancing with Katya, a woman with a shady past. A shot was heard and they all saw Petka shooting at Vanka in a fit of jealousy. He hit Katya instead, killing her, which threw him into inconsolable despair. His comrades tried to console him, but they also chided him, saying that the times were too serious for little personal matters like that. Petka found little consolation in their comradely admonition, trying to explain plaintively to everyone who would listen how good Katya was and how much he loved her.

As the Bolsheviks marched on, they suddenly saw an apparition in the distance. At first they thought it was only a mangy mongrel and shot at it, but as they peered into the darkness they saw someone with a garland of white roses on his head, waving a red flag. They finally realized it was Jesus Christ. Immune to their bullets, he seemed to take over the leadership of the band as they continued to march into the snowy night.

Critical Evaluation:

Aleksandr Blok is considered by many critics to be the best Russian poet of the twentieth century and one of the best in all of Russian literature. He was a leading representative of the second wave of the symbolist poets around the turn of the century. His poetry was distinguished, among other things, by refined taste acquired through his aristocratic upbringing and by a pronounced spiritual content. Readers of all kinds were astounded that *The Twelve* was written by a poet of such credentials.

The Twelve is situated in Petrograd (or St. Petersburg, later renamed Leningrad, and now St. Petersburg again). Petrograd is known to have provided a spark for the revolution. There is also a reference to the Neva River, which flows through Petrograd. The behavior of the rowdy marchers resembles that of the Bolshevik revolutionaries as recorded in history. The atmosphere displayed in the poem corresponds to the tumultuous events of 1917 and throughout the revolution and subsequent civil war. Finally, Blok himself confirmed in his diaries and letters that he had the Bolshevik revolution in mind while writing *The Twelve*.

Blok was not a communist, not even a sympathizer. He supported the February revolution of 1917, during which the czar was dethroned and a democratic government was installed for the first time in Russian history. As the months wore on, however, and the assembly failed to solve the country's problems, Blok became increasingly disillusioned. When the October revolution broke out, he lent his support to it even though he was not an advocate of its ideas. As the appearance of Christ in *The Twelve* would indicate, Blok was no Bolshevik.

Blok had, however, lost faith in the ability of the government to solve the country's problems, which had worsened with the difficulties brought on by World War I. Like the prostitutes in the poem, the parliamentarians debated every issue to death. Like most Russian intellectuals, Blok hoped for a reform that would sweep away centuries of injustice, which is exactly what the October revolution promised to do. Finally, his health was deteriorating during the last years of his life, and he was going through a period of severe stress and fevers. These ailments, it turned out, contributed to his untimely death two years later. The writing of *The Twelve* was a kind of catharsis for Blok.

Most of the poem's first readers expressed confusion regarding the poem. The main reason for the negative reaction by both revolutionaries and their opponents was the inclusion of Jesus Christ. The revolutionaries saw the depiction of Christ as a leader to be a farce; they wanted to have nothing to do with religion. The opponents of revolution also rejected the connection of Christ with the communist revolution as a sacrilege. Blok insisted nevertheless that Jesus was leading the revolutionaries, drawing from an old assertion that Jesus was "the first communist." During this period in his life, Blok was also interested in the historical Christ. Blok used the poem to link the two incongruous partners. Blok himself gave contradicting explanations for his placing Christ in the poem as a revolutionary leader. Not surprised by the storm of criticism, he said that if the church were real and not merely a class of morally dull functionaries, it would have realized a long time ago that Christ is with the Bolsheviks. Blok believed that all who studied the Bible would see this "obvious" truth. Blok compounded the confusion that the poem had created by saying that sometimes he despised the "womanish phantom" of Christ. The Bolsheviks were right in being afraid of *The Twelve*, he further argued. He did not like the ending of the poem either, saying that he wished it had a different ending. The closer he looked into it, however, the more clearly he saw Christ. Some stylistic devices used by Blok in *The*

Twelve tend to confirm its religious underpinnings. Not only does the title recall the twelve apostles, the twelve cantos in the poem reinforce that reference. The question of the poem's religious connotations probably will never be solved to full satisfaction.

The Twelve excels in stylistic matters as well. A practiced symbolist, Blok employs many symbols in the poem, although he was no longer writing symbolist poems at the time of writing *The Twelve*. As mentioned, symbolism begins with the title, as well as with the first words of the poem. The "black night" symbolizes the bleak conditions in which Russia finds itself on the eve of the revolution. The "blizzard" clearly represents the revolution, and the "white snow" stands for the purifying power of the revolution. When he says, "Malice, sorrowful malice/ Bursts the heart. . . ./ Black, holy hate," Blok clearly argues that the destructive fury of the revolution is justified in avenging all the injustices done to the poor. The onlookers are also symbols. The old woman symbolizes the old people, who are by nature conservative, cautious, and fearful to lose the security they may have, even if it is but little. The bourgeois is a clear target of the communist animosity, as a representative of the class their struggle is directed against. Other classes are typified by the priest and by a rich woman. The most intriguing symbolical figure is the writer. Blok must have believed that many writers, along with other intellectuals, not only did not understand the revolution but also tried to combat it. The prostitutes serve Blok as a vehicle for ridiculing the efforts of the politicians to solve the society's problems. Ridicule is Blok's strongest weapon against the opponents of the revolution.

Further symbols are the mongrel (standing for the old world, as the poet openly says) and Jesus Christ, who represents the legitimate needs of the downtrodden for justice and love. The poet uses Christ to remind the revolutionaries not to ignore old verities in their zeal to create a new world. Furthermore, Christ and his teachings can serve as an ameliorating factor in the tendency of the revolutionaries toward brutality. It seems that Blok is reminding the twelve rowdy, murderous marchers of the healing goodness and kindness of the original twelve apostles.

There are many other stylistic qualities of the poem that, unfortunately, can be appreciated fully only in the original. The poem's musical quality, expressed in its heavy rhythm (emulating the march and other dynamic actions such as shooting), contributes to the dramatic tension of the poem. The wealth of poetic techniques and the poem's variety of prosodic structures also contribute to its power. There are also imitations of folk and factory song and popular jingles in cantos dealing with revolutionaries, along with the abundance of common speech; all are used by Blok to underscore the revolutionaries' folkish character. Blok was known as a consummate craftsman, and the artistry of *The Twelve*—the next to last poem he wrote—confirms his reputation as one of the best poets in Russian literature.

Vasa D. Mihailovich

Bibliography:

Hackel, Sergei. *The Poet and the Revolution: Aleksandr Blok's "The Twelve."* Oxford, England: Clarendon Press, 1975. One of the best analyses of the content and the form of Blok's *The Twelve*.

Kisch, Cecil H. *Alexander Blok, Prophet of Revolution*. London: Weidenfeld & Nicholson, 1960. A study of Blok's life and work, illustrated by translations from his poems and his writings.

Mochulskii, Konstantin. *Aleksandr Blok*. Detroit: Wayne State University Press, 1983. A perceptive study of Aleksandr Blok by an émigré critic of spiritual orientation, with an emphasis on Blok's relationship to the revolution.

Pyman, Avril. *The Life of Aleksandr Blok.* 2 vols. New York: Oxford University Press, 1979-1980. The most exhaustive treatment of Aleksandr Blok as a man and a writer, by a leading former Russian scholar of Russian literature. *The Twelve* is discussed from page 274 to page 305.

Vickery, Walter, ed. *Aleksandr Blok Centennial Conference.* Columbus, Ohio: Slavica, 1984. A collection of twenty-one articles about various aspects of Blok's life and works. Of special interest is "The Polyphonic Structure of Blok's *Dvenadtsat.*"

TWENTY THOUSAND LEAGUES UNDER THE SEA

Type of work: Novel
Author: Jules Verne (1828-1905)
Type of plot: Science fiction
Time of plot: 1866-1867
Locale: At sea
First published: Vingt mille lieues sous les mers, 1869-1870 (English translation, 1873)

>   *Principal characters:*
>   PROFESSOR PIERRE ARONNAX, a French scientist
>   CONSEIL, his servant
>   NED LAND, his friend and companion
>   CAPTAIN NEMO, the captain of the *Nautilus*

The Story:

In different parts of the ocean, a number of ships had sighted a mysterious monster, gleaming with light, such as no man had ever seen. After this monster had attacked and sunk several vessels, people all over the world were both amazed and alarmed. Finally an American frigate, the *Abraham Lincoln*, was fitted out to find and destroy the mysterious sea creature. Among its passengers was Pierre Aronnax, professor of natural history in the Museum of Paris, who had published his opinion that the monster was a giant narwhal. One of the crew was Ned Land, an expert harpooner. For quite a while, the ship sailed without sighting anything even remotely resembling the reported terror of the seas.

The creature was sighted at last. When an opportunity presented itself, Ned Land threw his harpoon, but the monster was uninjured, and Land realized that it was protected by a thick steel-like armor. During a pursuit in the darkness, a terrific explosion rocked the ship. Professor Aronnax, Ned Land, and Conseil found themselves floundering in the water. Aronnax fainted. Regaining consciousness, he discovered that they were aboard some sort of underwater craft. Later, two men came to greet them. The survivors from the ship spoke to them in various languages, but the men appeared not to understand. Then the captain of the vessel appeared and spoke to them in French. He revealed that his name was Nemo, that the vessel was a submarine, and that they were, in effect, prisoners who would have every liberty aboard, except on occasions when they would receive orders to retire to their cabins.

Aronnax learned that the submarine *Nautilus* had been built in a complicated manner. Parts of it had been secured from various places and secretly assembled on a desert island. Then a fire had been set to destroy all traces of the work done there. The ship manufactured its own electricity, had provisions for quantities of oxygen which allowed it to remain submerged, and was as comfortable as any home. All food came from the ocean. There was fish, but fish such as Aronnax had never before tasted. There was clothing made from some sort of sea fibers. There were cigars, not of tobacco but of a special seaweed. Captain Nemo showed them air guns which allowed him and the crew to go hunting, as well as a device that permitted the crew to walk the ocean floor.

In the Pacific, Captain Nemo invited the three survivors to a hunt in the marine forest of Crespo, where Ned Land saved Captain Nemo's life by killing a creature which was about to put an end to the captain. Later, the captain saved Land's life. In Ceylon, they watched the pearl divers in the oyster beds. There Nemo saved a native from the jaws of a shark.

Off the coast of Borneo, the three survivors decided to go ashore in the hope of bagging some land game. While they were hunting, they were attacked by natives. Although they managed to get back to the *Nautilus*, the natives remained clustered about the ship. Aronnax was alarmed, certain that the natives would board the submarine when the hatches were opened for oxygen the next morning. He took his problem to Captain Nemo, who was not at all worried. Instead he told the professor about a similar experience. Once, when the hatches were opened, natives had attempted to come aboard, but the few who touched the rails let out a shriek and retreated in terror. Ned Land touched the rail and was paralyzed with shock; the rail was electrified.

The captain announced suddenly that he would enter the Mediterranean sea. Aronnax supposed that he would have to circle the Cape of Good Hope. To his astonishment, he learned that the captain had discovered a passage under the Isthmus of Suez. The submarine entered the Mediterranean through the underwater passage.

On one occasion, the three companions were ordered to go to their cabins. Some sort of encounter occurred, and Aronnax was later called upon to treat a crew member who had been injured. When the sailor died, he was buried in a coral forest on the ocean floor. By that time, the survivors had discovered that Captain Nemo had a tremendous fortune in gold salvaged from sunken vessels. Although the captain had some mysterious hatred against society, he nevertheless used the money to benefit unfortunate people.

Ned Land grew to dislike the captain intensely. He told Aronnax that he would escape as soon as an opportunity presented itself. They thought such an opportunity had come when they rounded Spain, but their plan did not materialize. When they came close to Long Island, they thought the time for escape had come, but a sudden hurricane blew the ship off its course, toward Newfoundland.

On another occasion, the captain astonished them by heading toward the South Pole. There the ship was endangered by an iceberg, and, for several days, passengers and crew were in danger of being killed. Escaping, they headed northward. As the *Nautilus* approached the coast of Norway, it was suddenly drawn into the notorious maelstrom, the deathtrap for so many ships. Shortly before, the submarine had encountered a mysterious ship which had attacked it. The submarine succeeded in sinking the unknown vessel. Aronnax believed that in this incident there was a clue to Captain Nemo's hatred of society.

The professor never knew what actually happened after the *Nautilus* was drawn into the maelstrom. When he awoke, he and his companions were safe and sound on a Norwegian island. They also had no idea how they had reached the island. They were the only men who now knew the secrets of the ocean—if Captain Nemo and his crew had perished.

Critical Evaluation:
Twenty Thousand Leagues Under the Sea was the sixth of Jules Verne's "extraordinary voyages," published in the same year as *A Trip to the Moon* (1865). Earlier books in the series had visited a strange underworld at "the centre of the earth" and the North Pole, unreached at the time, as well as traversing Africa, Australia, and South America. After 1870, Verne began to give rather more attention to the plots of his novels, but *Twenty Thousand Leagues Under the Sea* belongs to a phase when the joys of imaginary tourism were sufficient in themselves to sustain the production of long and languorous hypothetical travelogues.

Although it is rightly regarded as a classic of science fiction, Verne invented far less than modern readers sometimes realize. The American inventor Robert Fulton had tried to interest Napoleon in his submarine boat—also called the *Nautilus*—in 1800, and Verne had had several opportunities to observe submarines being tested in the river Seine. He had certainly seen the model of Charles-Marie Brun's *Le Plongeur* that was displayed at the Paris Exhibition of 1867.

Verne's most significant innovations were the powering of the ship by electricity extracted from seawater (a technology which continues to prove elusive) and the diving suits used by Nemo and his crew (which would be fatal to users because of their lack of pressurization).

On the other hand, it is difficult for modern readers to realize how mysterious the undersea world was in Verne's day. Thanks to underwater photography and television there is now a window into that world, but Verne had none at all. The surface of the moon, which the heroes of *A Trip to the Moon* observed at close quarters, had been thoroughly mapped, at least on the side facing the Earth, but the world under the sea was entirely hidden, known only by virtue of what was cast ashore or hauled out by fishermen's nets. Verne's travelers were venturing into an unknown world for the very first time, laying its wonders bare to an audience which had few of the preconceptions that modern readers cannot help but bring to the text. His research was as conscientious as it could possibly have been, given the limitations of the available information, and he did an excellent job of weaving a memorable picture around that research. Pedants may complain that he makes seawater far more transparent than it actually is, but he did so with the best possible motives.

In its early phases, *Twenty Thousand Leagues Under the Sea* is a mystery story, and the mystery must have been effective in the early days, when readers of the book did not know that the mysterious "sea beast" pursued by the *Abraham Lincoln* was not a beast at all. To modern readers, the long opening sequence seems like a mere prelude to the real focus of interest, which is the *Nautilus* and its enigmatic captain. Nemo remains a charismatic figure, a perfect incarnation of escapist dreams. Humans are, of course, gregarious beings who cannot live well in the absence of a surrounding society, but that force of necessity inevitably creates tensions and frustrations which lend considerable power to the fantasy of "getting away from it all" and becoming entirely self-sufficient.

Nemo is a strange man, so full of vague hatreds and contempts that he is much less appealing than Ned Land or Professor Aronnax, but that does not make him any less enviable in his splendid isolation. One cannot share his misanthropy wholeheartedly, but it is precisely because it cannot be shared that one is able to understand it and to find something in it to admire. As George Bernard Shaw observed, the fact that reasonable people make every effort to fit in with their surroundings leaves the responsibilities and rewards of progress to unreasonable men. Whatever else he may be, the unreasonable Nemo is certainly a symbol of progress and of enterprise.

Progress has, unfortunately, blurred the effect of the novel's one great dramatic event: the battle with the real sea beast. The creature must have been a giant squid, as must the creature which became entangled with the French naval vessel *Alecton* in 1861, which presumably gave Verne the idea. Without the aid of modern information, however, Verne was unable to distinguish between ten-limbed squids and eight-limbed octopodes, and all his translators have hesitated over the choice of an appropriate term, most of them preferring to leave the French word *poulp* unaltered. Filmmakers have understandably made much of this episode, but suffered from similar confusions.

There is a nice irony in the fact that the desire to make a better cinematic version of *Twenty Thousand Leagues Under the Sea* was the main inspiration for the development of the first underwater camera by the Williamson brothers in 1916. The story thus became a direct inspiration to the technology which would eventually make a reality of its imaginary quest. That is the true measure of its merit and its worth.

"Critical Evaluation" by Brian Stableford

Bibliography:

Allotte de la Fuÿe, Marguerite. *Jules Verne*. Translated by Erik de Mauny. London: Staples Press, 1954. A biography of Verne by a member of his family which includes a commentary on his works, including the chapter "Nemo, Genius of the Seas."

Butor, Michel. "The Golden Age in Jules Verne." In *Inventory*. London: Cape, 1970. An excellent essay which discusses the symbolic significance of Nemo and his vessel in the context of Verne's oeuvre.

Costello, Peter. *Jules Verne: Inventor of Science Fiction*. London: Hodder and Stoughton, 1978. Chapter 8 of this critical biography deals with *Twenty Thousand Leagues Under the Sea*.

Miller, Walter James. *The Annotated Jules Verne: Twenty Thousand Leagues Under the Sea*. New York: Crowell, 1976. The first full translation of the text, elaborately annotated.

Verne, Jules. *The Complete Twenty Thousand Leagues Under the Sea: A New Translation of Jules Verne's Science Fiction Classic*. Bloomington: Indiana University Press, 1991. Emanuel J. Mickel's introduction offers a comprehensive study of the novel's background and a survey of critical analyses of Verne's work.

TWO ESSAYS ON ANALYTICAL PSYCHOLOGY

Type of work: Psychology
Author: Carl Gustav Jung (1875-1961)
First published: 1928

Two Essays on Analytical Psychology has often been called the best introduction to Carl Jung's work that the student can readily find. "The Unconscious in the Normal and Pathological Mind" and "The Relation of the Ego to the Unconscious" are 1928 revisions of essays that Jung wrote earlier. Almost all of Jung's early work was revised extensively before its appearance in the collected edition to which he devoted his last years.

The work begins, as so many of Jung's writings do, with a version of his famous criticism of Sigmund Freud and Alfred Adler. Jung, who was Freud's most famous disciple from 1909 to 1914, held differences in ideas that led to personal differences, which have been continued with rancor by their followers. One of the crucial points of disagreement was Jung's announcement that Freud's concept of the libido was too narrowly concerned with sexual energy and that Adler's definition of libido as a will to power was also too simplistic. Jung called the libido, the basic reservoir of human drives, "psychic energy." Jung, however, endorsed the cornerstone of Freud's theory, the dream analysis, calling this technique "the royal road to the unconscious." Jung would have readers rise above too exclusive a concern with sexuality or the will to power. These drives are more important to young men than they are to the complete person over a long life-span. They are partial truths, as Jung saw them, and he proposed a theory of the psyche that would transcend them.

Undoubtedly there is much to be said for Jung's criticism of Freud and Adler as being concerned too reductively with elective forces in the analysis of human motivation. As time passed, Jung turned more to mythology and folklore for keys to understanding the unconscious of his patients, while Freud always stayed within the confines of the patient's personal experience from childhood on. Moreover, no matter how positively one reacts to Jungian theory, one must acknowledge an unrelenting tendency in the Swiss psychologist to schematize. During Freud's productive career, his ideas about the unconscious and its significance changed because of the material presented him by his patients. In Jung's analysis, however, a few details from dreams led him to set up categories of psychological behavior, drawn from his extensive research into primitive religions and the mysticism of Europe and the Near East. This tendency to set up formal patterns of meaning from dream, myth, and legend have led many of Jung's critics to refuse him the name of scientist; they insist that he is a German philosopher, and a medieval one at that.

Like many makers of mystical systems, Jung insists that everything within the mind is doubled or paired. Conflict may be destructive to mental health, but it also is necessary to spiritual development. His belief is that energy results from the tension of opposites. For the young, says Jung, the conflicts are outside—with parents, with society—and here, as noted, the analysis of Freud and Adler are most valuable. The conflicts of mature people, however, are within. Many are unable to form a significant self because they are unable or unwilling to come to satisfactory terms with the threatening or "shadow" aspects of the collective unconsciousness.

This last division of the mind is another great distinction between Jungian theory and Freudian. Jung postulates a racial or collective unconsciousness, containing what he called primordial images, figures containing those qualities dramatized in the great myths of past cultures. These images of demoniac power are not inherited in themselves, but the thought patterns that produced them are. For Jung there is a personal unconsciousness such as Freud described, containing one's repressed personal emotions. The collective consciousness, however, is, according to Jung, much more obscure and more powerful, charged with potential for good and evil. Jung also formulated a distinctive dream analysis. Every interpretation of a dream that equates a dream image with a real object he calls interpretation on the objective level. He contrasts that view with his own subjective interpretation, which brings the dreamer back to the self and is synthetic rather than analytic. This is the point at which the vast store of myth and legend material come in, as Jung examines dreams in terms of the struggle for mental health and significant life. The archetype of the hero is one of the most famous he describes, and he relates how both dreams and legends are parallel in their depiction of the lonely voyage of the hero, beneath or through the sea, to a cave or castle where he must battle a monster for the treasure. The hero image is the health-giving power of the unconscious, Jung says, and the monster is the shadow side—perhaps the dark mother, the feminine image in its nihilistic phase. The treasure the hero can win is life, in the sense of mental balance, a process Jung calls individuation. For Jung, dreams are another form of the old legends; they are what they say and are not to be translated out of symbolism into psychological motivation, as they were by Freud. To analyze dreams people need to draw parallels from primitive material, because dreams come from the unconsciousness that contains remnants of human experience in all preceding epochs of evolution. These images are the dominant powers of laws and principles. Prominent in this dark reservoir of the past, besides the hero, are figures Jung called the shadows, the wise old man, the mother, the child, and the anima and the animus (images of the feminine and the masculine ideals respectively). Charged with power that is beyond good or evil, many of these images carry their own shadow or destructive charge. The wise old man in his malevolent role would appear as Satan or some other demon. The mother may be the generous, nurturing aspect of woman, or she may appear as dark chaos, the chaotic emotion into which the self can sink without a trace.

The all-important process of individuation is achieved, says Jung, by analyzing and compensating for these demoniac powers that threaten psychic stability. The process, involving suffering and action, is often depicted in dreams by rectangles and circles—enclosures of perfection that Jung termed mandalas.

Much of this analysis is like philosophy, Jung admits, but he adds that such must be, for the psyche seeks expression that will involve its whole nature, not merely correct the minor, irritating obstacles that cause neurosis. One of the essential needs of human, irrational nature is the idea of God, Jung insists. It is necessary for one's health that the image of the ideal be charged with power and projected outside oneself into religious myth. The individual needs a religious figure whose actions may be imitated and whose standards may be upheld.

Jung also describes the function of the persona, that mask the psyche creates to mediate between the desire of the unconscious and the outside world. Individuation consists of the creation of an authentic self, living in dynamic but useful tension between those two forces. If the unconsciousness rides roughshod over the persona, psychosis results. If the unconsciousness is not expressed in some useful way, however, the power from the libido can never be harnessed, and unending psychic paralysis, characterized by unceasing tension and anxiety, results. People must use this dark power, which Jung calls mana, and not be used by it.

It is interesting to observe that many literary people and humanists have become champions of Jung, but few scientists. Although Jung seems so often in his analysis merely to substitute one system of metaphor for another, rather than bring readers to any new understanding of mental process, there can be no denying that, by joining comparative mythology to psychology, Jung has had extraordinary influence upon both the reading and the writing of literary works.

Bibliography:
Barnaby, Karin, and Pellegrino D'Acierno, eds. *C. G. Jung and the Humanities: Toward a Hermeneutics of Culture*. Princeton, N.J.: Princeton University Press, 1990. The proceedings of an international conference on the significance of Jung's ideas. Includes papers and discussions on archetypes and creativity.

Jung, C. G. *Memories, Dreams, Reflections*. Edited by Aniela Jaffé and translated by Richard and Clara Winston. New York: Pantheon Books, 1963. Jung's life story, as told to his secretary. Includes a glossary of Jungian terms.

Kerr, John. *A Most Dangerous Method: The Story of Jung, Freud, and Sabina Spielrein*. New York: Alfred A. Knopf, 1993. A study of Jung's intellectual development with emphasis on his relations with Sigmund Freud and one of the first woman psychoanalysts. Discusses the early versions of *Two Essays on Analytical Psychology*.

Noll, Richard. *The Jung Cult: Origins of a Charismatic Movement*. Princeton, N.J.: Princeton University Press, 1994. A controversial study, suggesting that Jung's concept of the collective unconscious, first announced in *Two Essays on Analytical Psychology*, marked a departure from science and a turn to religion.

Stevens, Anthony. *On Jung*. New York: Penguin Books, 1991. An excellent introduction by a practicing Jungian analyst. An overview of Jung's theories of the unconscious and personality is followed by an account of Jung's life and a Jungian perspective on the different stages of development.

Wehr, Gerhard. *Jung: A Biography*. Translated by David M. Weeks. Boulder, Colo.: Shambhala, 1988. Chapter 13 discusses Jung's early papers on analytical psychology.

THE TWO GENTLEMEN OF VERONA

Type of work: Drama
Author: William Shakespeare (1564-1616)
Type of plot: Comedy
Time of plot: Sixteenth century
Locale: Italy
First performed: c. 1594-1595; first published, 1623

> *Principal characters:*
> VALENTINE and
> PROTEUS, two young gentlemen
> JULIA, the beloved of Proteus
> SILVIA, the beloved of Valentine
> THURIO, a man in love with Silvia
> THE DUKE OF MILAN, Silvia's father

The Story:

Valentine and Proteus, two longtime friends, disagreed heartily on whether, as Valentine thought, the most important thing in life was to travel and learn the wonders of the world, or whether Proteus was right in believing nothing to be more important than love. The two friends parted for a time when Valentine traveled to Milan, to seek advancement and honor in the palace of the duke. He pleaded with Proteus to join him in the venture, but Proteus was too much in love with Julia to leave her side for even a short time. Julia was a noble and pure young girl, who had had many suitors. Proteus had at last won her heart and the two were happy in their love.

Valentine journeyed to Milan, and there he learned that his friend was right about the importance of love. For Valentine met the duke's daughter, Silvia, and fell instantly in love with her. Silvia returned his love, but her father wanted her to marry Thurio, a foolish man with no personal charms but much land and gold. Valentine longed for Silvia but saw no chance of persuading her father to consent to his suit. Then he learned that Proteus, whose father was ignorant of Proteus' love affair and wished his son to educate himself by travel, was soon to arrive in Milan.

The two friends had a joyful reunion, and Valentine proudly presented his friend to Silvia. To Proteus he praised the virtue and beauty of his beloved, and when they were alone, Valentine confided to Proteus that, since Sylvia's father refused to give her to anyone but Thurio, he planned to fashion a rope ladder and steal Silvia from her room and marry her. Valentine, asking his friend to help him in his plan, was too absorbed to notice that Proteus remained strangely silent. The truth was that Proteus, at the first sight of Silvia, had forgotten his solemn vows to Julia (sealed before he left her with the exchange of rings), had forgotten too his oath of friendship with Valentine, and that he was determined to have Silvia for his own. With protestations of self-hatred for betraying his friend, Proteus told the duke of Valentine's plan to escape with Silvia from the palace. The duke, forewarned, tricked Valentine into revealing the plot and banished him from Milan on penalty of his life.

While these events were taking place, Julia, thinking that Proteus still loved her and grieving over his absence, disguised herself as a page and traveled to Milan to see her love. She was on her way to Milan when Valentine was forced to leave that city. Valentine, not knowing that his onetime friend had betrayed him, believed Proteus' promise that he would carry letters back and forth between him and Silvia.

With Valentine out of the way, Proteus proceeded to get rid of Thurio as a rival. Thurio, foolish and gullible, was an easy man to trick. One night, Proteus and Thurio went to Silvia's window to serenade her in Thurio's name, but Proteus used the occasion to sing to her and make protestations of his love for her. Julia, in the disguise of a page, stood in the shadows and heard his betrayal of her, as well as Silvia's response that she would love no one but Valentine. She also accused him of playing false with Julia, for Valentine had told her of his friend's betrothal.

Calling herself Sebastian, Julia, still in the dress of a page, became employed by Proteus to carry messages to Silvia. One day, he gave her the ring that Julia herself had given him and told her to deliver it to Silvia. When Silvia refused the ring and sent it back to Proteus, Julia loved her rival and blessed her.

Valentine, in the meantime, had been captured by outlaws, once honorable men who had been banished for petty crimes and had taken refuge in the woods near Mantua. To save his life, Valentine had joined the band and soon became their leader. A short time later, Silvia, hoping to find Valentine, escaped from the palace and, with the help of an agent, arrived at an abbey near Milan. There she was captured by the outlaws. When her father heard of her flight, he took Thurio and Proteus to the abbey to look for her. Julia followed them. Proteus, arriving on the scene first, rescued her from the outlaws before they were able to take her to their leader. Again Proteus proclaimed his love for her. When she scornfully berated him, he seized her and tried to force himself on her. Valentine, who had overheard everything, sprang upon Proteus and pulled him away from her.

Valentine was more hurt by his friend's duplicity than by anything else, but such was his forgiving nature that when Proteus confessed his guilt and his shame over his betrayal, Valentine forgave him and received him again as his friend. In proof of his friendship, he was even prepared to give up his claim on Silvia. When she heard that, Julia, still disguised, fainted. Reviving, she pretended to hand over to Silvia the ring Proteus had ordered her to deliver, but instead she offered the ring Proteus had given her when they parted in Verona. Then Julia was recognized by all, and Proteus admitted that he still loved her.

The outlaws appeared with the duke and Thurio, whom they had captured in the forest. Thurio gave up all claim to Silvia, for he thought a girl who would run off into the woods to pursue another man much too foolish for him to marry. Her father, convinced at last of Valentine's worth, gave that young man permission to marry Silvia. During the general rejoicing Valentine begged one more boon. He asked the duke to pardon the outlaws, all brave men who would serve the duke faithfully if he would return them from exile. The duke granted the boon, and the whole party made its way back to Milan. There the two happy couples intended to share their wedding day and be happy in their mutual love and friendship.

Critical Evaluation:

In *The Two Gentlemen of Verona*, William Shakespeare is learning the craft of playwriting, with plot elements, characters, and comic situations that will reappear in later plays. The work also mirrors the literary vogues of its time, particularly the popular prose romances of the day—forerunners of the later sentimental novel and the twentieth century psychological novel—that race the turbulencies of adolescence and youth. Some of Shakespeare's later comedies and his *Romeo and Juliet* (c. 1595-1596) reflect a similar concern. Himself then the father of a daughter approaching her teens, Shakespeare may have been especially sensitive to the problems of youth.

Proteus and Valentine are Italianates—young gentlemen sent abroad to acquire perfection at a foreign court. Proteus' name, a common Elizabethan label for the Italianate, further establishes that identification. Critics have made much of the geographical "inaccuracy" of Valentine's departure for Milan by boat, ignoring the fact that Shakespeare was too well read and too familiar with the geography of Europe not to know that travel from the real Verona to Milan would have had to have been by land. As in his other plays, Shakespeare uses place names for their connotations. Verona was the home of the lovers Romeo and Juliet, Milan the fashion center of Europe and the seat of the imperial court. With this Verona and this Milan he could retain the three worlds of his source, Jorge de Montemayor's prose romance *Diana* (c. 1559): the world of lovers subject to parental oversight, the sophisticated world of the court, and the green world of the forest.

In the first world, Proteus, like Felis in *Diana* and Euphues in John Lyly's romance of that name (1578-1580), goes through the wild emotional swings and naïve tentativeness of adolescence, and he submits tamely to his elders. He is in love with love and has an idealized vision of the court, where he hopes to achieve perfection.

In the second world, the world of the court, Proteus is metamorphosed by self-interest and begins to assume poses. His desire for Valentine's Silvia leads him first to disloyalty to both his friend and Julia and eventually to outright treachery. At the end, rejected by Silvia after his final pose as a knight errant who has rescued her from outlaws, Proteus tries to take Silvia by force. Even the more stable Valentine changes at court, becoming adept at exaggerated expression; perfection for him becomes a matter of rhetorical skill—"A man is no man if with his tongue he cannot win a woman"—and a proficiency in conventional formulas and flattery. In fact, as Peter Lindenbaum has pointed out, Valentine's love affair is a reaction to his court experience.

Some critics have found fault with the way the play ends in the last of these worlds, the green world. Here, outlaws are readily pardoned, Proteus is forgiven his assault on Silvia, and Valentine temporarily resigns his claim on his beloved in favor of Proteus. Though Proteus' repentance seems sudden, it is plausible because it is preceded by the shock he received when his villainy was publicly exposed and he recognized his self-deception. With this recognition, the idealized picture of perfection that the Verona youth had envisioned for himself—hearing sweet discourse, conversing with noblemen, and being in the eye of every exercise worthy of a nobleman—suddenly gives way to the truth. The court produced this villain, and "shame and guilt confound him." Proteus recognizes not only his own imperfection but that of all humankind: "were man but constant, he were perfect."

To Valentine and the duke also comes discovery. The duke discovers the true nature of his favorite, Thurio, and of the despised "peasant" Valentine, and he learns to look at Valentine with new eyes and to consider him worthy of his daughter's love. He sees the outlaws as reformed men. The corrupting influence of the court has dissolved in the healing of the green forest. Even Julia, who dreamed of idealized love at the beginning of the play and then at court learned of the flaws in her beloved Proteus, discovers that she can still love him. Valentine, though he at first reacted with rage, feels the rekindling of his old feelings of friendship. The play thus ends with the regeneration of the protagonists, a conclusion required if the play is to remain faithful to the traditional endings of the prose romances that served as sources for the play.

Shakespeare does not go into much depth in portraying the charcters in this play. In fact, some critics have suspected him of writing *The Two Gentlemen of Verona* primarily to mock the idealistic Renaissance romantic codes. It is more likely, however, that he is watching his characters with sympathetic amusement. When Valentine is smitten with Silvia and confides his feelings to Speed, Speed mocks his impassioned behavior and comments, as Silvia enters, that he is now about to witness a puppet show. Even Silvia joins in the mockery, though more gently, when she stops Valentine's exaggerated praise and Petrarchan conventions with "I guess the sequel." Proteus' sentimental gift of a little dog, "Jewel," which Launce loses and replaces with the mongrel "Crab," is transformed from a gallant gesture into farce when the dog runs under the duke's table and lifts his leg against Silvia's farthingale. Just after Proteus' tender farewell to Julia, Launce parodies lovers' partings with his dog sitting in for the loved one; when Valentine laments his banishment from Silvia, Launce mimics a lover's Petrarchan cataloging of his mistress' physical attributes.

The play also has moments of great charm. Shakespeare offers lyrical passages such as the well-known song "Who Is Silvia?," banter between charcters, and the light-hearted antics of Speed and Launce.

"Critical Evaluation" by Thomas Amherst Perry

Bibliography:

Leech, Clifford. Introduction to *The Two Gentlemen of Verona*, by William Shakespeare. London: Methuen, 1969. Concludes that the play is primarily concerned with mocking the idealistic pretensions of Renaissance codes of romantic love and friendship.

Lindenbaum, Peter. "Education in *The Two Gentlemen of Verona*." *Studies in English Literature* 15, no. 2 (Spring, 1975): 229-244. Concludes that the play is about the importance of penitence for past sins. The education of the "perfect man" envisioned at the beginning of the play takes the protagonists to the court and then to the green forest, where they will learn that they are imperfect because they are human.

Perry, Thomas A. "Proteus, Wry-Transformed Traveller." *Shakespeare Quarterly* 5, no. 1 (January, 1954): 33-40. Shows that to understand Proteus, one must first see him as a young Elizabethan Italiante in a passing phase; at the end of the play he is a chastened and regenerate youth.

Sargent, Ralph M. "Sir Thomas Elyot and the Integrity of *The Two Gentlemen of Verona*." *PMLA* 65, no. 2 (December, 1950): 1166-1180. Discusses the ways in which Proteus learns that he has violated the codes of masculine friendship and romantic love and how he is regenerated and reclaimed at the end of the play.

Stephenson, William E. "The Adolescent Dream-World of *The Two Gentlemen of Verona*." *Shakespeare Quarterly* 17, no. 2 (Spring, 1966): 165-168. Focuses on the fact that Proteus and Valentine are two very young gentlemen, sixteenth century adolescents still under parental authority. Their wild swings of emotion, naïveté, tentative behavior, tame submission to elders, and dreams and hallucinations of love are signs that they are just past the first changes of puberty. In the latter part of the play they are half-grown, and even the final denouement is a dream-action.

THE TWO NOBLE KINSMEN

Type of work: Drama
Authors: William Shakespeare (1564-1616) and John Fletcher (1579-1625)
Type of plot: Tragicomedy
Time of plot: Antiquity
Locale: Athens and Thebes
First performed: c. 1612-1613; first published, 1634

> *Principal characters:*
> THESEUS, duke of Athens
> HIPPOLYTA, his wife
> EMILIA, her younger sister
> PALAMON and
> ARCITE, nephews of Creon, king of Thebes

The Story:

During the marriage ceremony of Theseus, duke of Athens, and Hippolyta, queen of the Amazons, three widowed queens begged Theseus' aid. Creon, king of Thebes, had slain their husbands in battle and would not permit their bodies to receive decent burial. Theseus commiserated with the queens, but provided small comfort for their grief when he directed that his nuptial ceremonies be continued. The queens persisting in their pleas, Theseus conceded to the extent of ordering an expeditionary force to be readied to march against Thebes. Not to be denied, the distracted queens finally persuaded him to champion their cause. He appointed Pirithous, an Athenian nobleman, to stand in his place for the remainder of the ceremony, kissed Hippolyta farewell, and led the queens away toward Thebes.

Meanwhile, in Thebes, the cousins Palamon and Arcite, nephews of Creon, found their uncle's tyranny unbearable and stultifying, and decided to leave Thebes. No sooner had they made this decision then they learned that Thebes was threatened by Theseus. The cousins, loyal to Thebes if not to Creon, deferred their departure in order to serve their city.

When the opposing forces met, Palamon and Arcite fought with great courage, but the Athenians were victorious in the battle. Theseus, triumphant, directed the three widowed queens to bury their dead in peace. Palamon and Arcite, having been wounded and left for dead on the battlefield, were taken by the Athenians. The cousins, healed of their wounds and finding themselves in a prison in Athens, impressed their jailers with their seeming unconcern at being incarcerated. In their cell, however, they sadly bemoaned their fate to each other. Resigned to spending the rest of their lives in prison, they recalled with grief the joys of battle and the hunt, and they grieved at the thought of a future without marriage. Even so, they made some attempt to reconcile themselves to imprisonment by declaring that in their cell they had each other's excellent company and that they were insulated from the evils that beset free men.

Emilia, Hippolyta's beautiful sister, entered the prison garden. Palamon saw her and fell in love at once. When Arcite beheld her, he too fell in love. Palamon declared that Arcite must not love her, but Arcite answered that Palamon, who had called her a goddess, might love her spiritually; he, Arcite, would love her in a more earthly manner. Palamon maintained that this goddess they had beheld was his to love because he had seen her first. Arcite, in turn, insisted that he too must love her because of the propinquity of the pair. Palamon, enraged, wished for liberty and weapons so that he and Arcite might decide the issue in mortal combat.

The jailkeeper, on orders, took Arcite to Theseus. Palamon, meanwhile, was filled with despair at the thought that Arcite was now free to win Emilia. The keeper returned to report that Arcite had been sent away from Athens and that Palamon must be moved to a cell in which there were fewer windows. Palamon writhed in the knowledge that Arcite now seemed certain to win the hand of Emilia.

Arcite, banished in the country near Athens, felt no advantage over his cousin. Indeed, he envied Palamon, who he believed could see Emilia every time she visited the prison garden with her maid. Desperate, he assumed a disguise and returned to Athens to participate in athletic games in honor of Emilia's birthday. Excelling in the games, he admitted that he was of gentle birth; but Theseus did not penetrate his disguise. Theseus, admiring Arcite's athletic prowess and his modesty, designated him to be a serving-man to Emilia.

In the meantime the daughter of the jailkeeper fell in love with Palamon and effected his escape. In the forest, where the court had gone a-Maying, Arcite came upon the escaped prisoner. In spite of Palamon's harsh words to him, Arcite promised to supply his cousin with food. Two days later he brought food and drink. When he left, he promised to return the next time with armor and weapons, that the two might decide their quarrel by combat.

Arcite having returned with armor and weapons, the two youths armed themselves and fought. At the same time Theseus and his party, hunting in the forest, came upon the struggling pair. Theseus condemned them to be executed straightway, one for having defied banishment, the other for having broken out of prison. Hippolyta, Pirithous, and Emilia begged Theseus for mercy. The duke then declared that they might live if they would forget Emilia. When both refused, Theseus resolved that the youths should go free, but that in a month they must return to Athens, both accompanied by three knights of their own choice, and resolve their problem in the lists. The victor would be awarded the hand of Emilia; the loser and his companions would be executed on the spot.

A month passed. As Emilia admired likenesses of Palamon and Arcite and despaired at her inability to choose one or the other as her favorite, the cousins, with six knights, returned to Athens. Arcite and his knight-companions invoked Mars, the god of war; Palamon and his cohorts invoked Venus, the goddess of love; Emilia, in her role as a priestess of Diana, invoked the goddess of chastity to bring victory to the youth who loved her best. In the tournament that followed Arcite was the victor.

Palamon lay his head on the block in anticipation of execution, but Pirithous interrupted the beheading to announce that Arcite had been thrown and mortally trampled by a black horse that Emilia had given him. Before he died, Arcite, brought before his cousin, relinquished his claim upon Emilia to Palamon. Palamon, reconciled with his cousin, observed sorrowfully that he had lost a great love in order to gain another.

Critical Evaluation:

The Two Noble Kinsmen was a joint production of the aging Shakespeare and his protégé John Fletcher. Some specific scenes have been attributed, on the basis of stylistic traits, to each dramatist. That many scenes cannot be specifically assigned would suggest close collaboration. The main plot was taken from Giovanni Boccaccio's *Teseide* (1340-1345), which, in turn, was derived from Statius Caecilius' *Thebaid* (c. 219-166 B.C.E.). Shakespeare had already used the wedding of Theseus and Hippolyta in *A Midsummer Night's Dream* (c. 1595-1596). Chaucer had used the story of Palamon and Arcite in "The Knight's Tale." The play is marked by a sentimentality that betokens the end of the golden age of Tudor and Stuart drama.

The Two Noble Kinsmen more closely resembles the tragicomedies of Francis Beaumont and

Fletcher than it does Shakespeare's later plays, such as *Pericles* (1608), *Cymbeline* (1609), *The Winter's Tale* (1610-1611), and *The Tempest* (1611). Although the frame subplot of Theseus and Hippolyta recalls the same characters in *A Midsummer Night's Dream*, the mirthful, exuberant tone of Shakespeare's youthful comedy is replaced with one more serious, heroic, and formally stylized. For both authors, the main source of the play, as the Prologue mentions, is Chaucer's "The Knight's Tale" from *The Canterbury Tales* (1387-1400). Act I derives also from Sir Thomas North's translation of Plutarch's "Life of Theseus." The basis of both the play and Chaucer's narrative is the Thebaid of Statius, with which Shakespeare and Fletcher were probably familiar.

The major theme of the play, the tragic conflict between loyal friendship on the one hand and romantic passion on the other, is clearly but quite rigidly drawn. Palamon and Arcite, bound by noble comradeship and affection, turn at once into rivals and deadly enemies when they fall in love, nearly simultaneously and at first sight, with Emilia. Since their code is heroic, neither one compromises his claims for sole possession of the beloved. Instead of courting and winning the romantic prize, the kinsmen prepare to fight for her. Arcite, who calls upon Mars for assistance, wins the contest but loses his bride. Palamon wisely calls upon Venus to champion him. Thus, although he loses the contest he succeeds in love—which is the point of the play. When Sir William Davenant adapted *The Two Noble Kinsmen* in 1664 as *The Rivals*, he emphasized even more than did Shakespeare and Fletcher the code of heroic passion by which Palamon and Arcite live, a convention that would become exaggeratedly idealistic during the period of Cavalier drama.

In spite of its artificial conventions and sentimentality, *The Two Noble Kinsmen* is not without merit, particularly Shakespeare's limited part of the play. In Act I, for example, he introduces two themes that Fletcher fails to develop later: that of the intimate friendships between Theseus and Pirithoos and between Emilia and Flavinia. Had the theme of these parallel friendships been advanced with greater complexity and psychological insight, the play would have surely engaged the modern reader's attention as something more than a curiosity in the history of seventeenth century drama.

Bibliography:
Bertram, Paul. *Shakespeare and "The Two Noble Kinsmen."* New Brunswick, N.J.: Rutgers University Press, 1965. Discussion of the play, usually thought to be written by Shakespeare in collaboration with John Fletcher. Discussion of earlier critical works.

Donaldson, E. Talbot. *The Swan at the Well: Shakespeare Reading Chaucer.* New Haven, Conn.: Yale University Press, 1985. Compares several of Shakespeare's plays and their sources in Chaucer's poems. *"The Knight's Tale* and *The Two Noble Kinsmen"* compares Chaucer's story with Shakespeare's play.

Hillman, Richard. "Shakespeare's Romantic Innocents and the Misappropriation of the Romantic Past: The Case of *The Two Noble Kinsmen.*" In *The Tempest and After*, edited by Stanley W. Wells. Cambridge, England: Cambridge University Press, 1991. Considers the characters' responses to their notions of romance.

Muir, Kenneth. *Shakespeare's Comic Sequence.* New York: Barnes & Noble Books, 1979. The essay on *The Two Noble Kinsmen* discusses the authorship of the play. There is also critical discussion of the play.

Waith, Eugene M. "Shakespeare and Fletcher on Love and Friendship." In *Shakespeare Studies: An Annual Gathering of Research, Criticism, and Reviews*, edited by J. Leeds Barroll. New York: Burt Franklin, 1986. Explores the conflict between love and friendship in the works of Shakespeare and Fletcher.

THE TWO TOWERS

Type of work: Novel
Author: J. R. R. Tolkien (1892-1973)
Type of plot: Fantasy
Time of plot: The Third Age in a remote legendary past
Locale: Middle Earth, chiefly Rohan, Fangorn, Gondor, and Ithilien
First published: 1954

Principal characters:
> FRODO BAGGINS, the Ringbearer
> SAMWISE GAMGEE (SAM), his loyal servant
> MERIADOC BRANDYBUCK (MERRY) and
> PEREGRIN TOOK (PIPPIN), young hobbits and Frodo's cousins and friends
> GANDALF (MITHRANDIR), a wizard, returned from the depths and
>   transfigured into the White Rider
> ARAGORN, the courageous descendant of kings
> LEGOLAS, the son of the Elven-King of Mirkwood
> GIMLI, a dwarf and the friend of Legolas
> SARUMAN, a wizard, the former leader of the White Council, and now a
>   traitor greedy for power
> GOLLUM (SMÉAGOL), a loathsome, corrupted hobbit and once owner of
>   the Ring
> THÉODEN, the aged king of Rohan
> ÉOMER, his warrior nephew
> GRIMA WORMTONGUE, the minister of Théoden but a secret agent of
>   Saruman
> TREEBEARD (FANGORN), the leader of the ents, strange treelike people
> SAURON, the Dark Lord of Mordor

The Story:

Immediately after Frodo the Ringbearer and Sam set off to fulfill their quest for the destruction of the Ring of power, a band of orcs captured the two remaining hobbits, Merry and Pippin. In an attempt to defend them, Boromir of Gondor was mortally wounded. Dying, he confessed to Aragorn that he had tried to take the Ring from Frodo, who had put on the Ring and vanished to escape him. Aragorn, Legolas, and Gimli prepared Boromir's body, placed it in an elven boat, and sent it over the falls down the Great River. They followed the tracks of the orcs in an attempt to rescue Merry and Pippin. After several days, they met a company of Riders of Rohan led by Éomer, the nephew of King Théoden, who reported killing the orcs. They had not seen the hobbits but lent horses to the travelers to follow the trail.

Pippin had tempted an orc to run away with the hobbits for the Ring, which he thought they had. When a Rider killed him, they escaped in darkness and entered the mysterious forest Fangorn. There they met Treebeard, the leader of the ents, who sheltered them. After hearing their story, he called an Entmoot to decide what action the ents should take against the forces of evil. On the third day, the treelike ents reached their decision and marched on Isengard, the traitor Saruman's stronghold.

After the three hunters found hopeful signs that their friends had escaped the orcs, they entered Fangorn. There they met Gandalf, who had returned from the depths with new power as the result of his ordeal. He called Shadowfax, the great horse borrowed from Rohan's king, and the four rode toward Théoden's hall. Théoden was bent with age and greeted Gandalf inhospitably. His pale, wizened minister Wormtongue, who nourished the king's infirmities, sat at his feet and vilified Gandalf, who raised his staff; lightning flashed, and Wormtongue sprawled on the floor. Gandalf led Théoden from the shadowy hall, and the old king stood erect and returned to manhood. He announced his determination to lead his people against Saruman. To Wormtongue, whose treachery Gandalf exposed, he ordered a choice: to ride into battle against Saruman or to accept banishment. Wormtongue spat and rode away to join Saruman. Théoden left his niece Eowyn as regent. He presented Shadowfax to Gandalf, who departed on a secret mission.

The battle of Helm's Deep was fought with great odds favoring Saruman's orcs and wild hillmen. Éomer and Aragorn performed heroic deeds, and Gimli and Legolas held a contest as to who should kill more orcs. A strange forest appeared on the hills with the morning. Théoden led a gallant charge, and Gandalf returned as the White Rider, striking terror into the enemy. The orcs fled into the forest, but none came out. After the battle, Gandalf led Théoden and others to Isengard for a parley with Saruman. On the way, they saw several ents, and in the night, the strange forest strode past them. Arriving at Isengard, they found devastation. The walls were torn down, and the stronghold itself was filled with steaming water; only the ancient impregnable tower, Orthanc, remained undamaged. Seated at the ruined gates were Merry and Pippin. Merry welcomed them in the name of Treebeard and informed them that Saruman was closeted with Wormtongue in Orthanc. The hobbits told how the ents had attacked Isengard, destroyed its walls with their rootlike hands, and diverted the river waters through Saruman's underground domain. Then, to their amazement, Gandalf had arrived and asked Treebeard for help against the orcs. The walking forest had moved off toward Helm's Deep. Finally, Wormtongue had arrived. Treebeard had given him the choice of joining Saruman or waiting for Théoden and Gandalf. He had chosen Saruman.

Gandalf called Saruman to the window of Orthanc. The corrupted wizard tried to sway them with his persuasive voice. When his enchantment failed, Gandalf offered him freedom to join them against Sauron or to go to Mordor. He refused to leave Orthanc and turned away; but Gandalf called him back, cast him from the White Council, and broke his staff. As Saruman crawled away, Wormtongue flung a heavy crystal ball at Gandalf. Pippin picked it up, but Gandalf quickly retrieved it. The company left the ents to keep Saruman from escaping and rode back toward Théoden's hall. Pippin slipped the stone away from Gandalf and looked into it. His eye was drawn to the Dark Tower and, confronted by Sauron, he lost consciousness. Gandalf revived him and learned that Sauron had failed to question him about the Ring.

During these events, Frodo and Sam traveled through barren country, trailed by Gollum. They waylaid him but spared his life, and he swore by the Ring to serve Frodo loyally. From this point, he became their guide, leading them toward Mordor. During their journey, Ringwraiths sometimes passed overhead, striking terror into their hearts. As they drew nearer to Mordor, the Ring grew heavier, and Frodo felt the constant probing of Sauron's evil Eye. They entered Ithilien, a wooded land with flowing streams. Frodo and Sam were captured by men of Gondor led by Faramir, the son of Denethor and brother of Boromir, who told them they had seen Boromir's body floating in the elven boat. In a rock chamber behind a waterfall, he questioned them and learned more of their errand than they intended; he promised help and gave them provisions. He spared the life of Gollum at Frodo's entreaty, led them back to the forest, and sent them on their way.

Gollum led them toward the tower of Minas Morgul, from which an army marched out led by the chief Ringwraith, who stopped as if drawn by the power of the Ring but then marched on. Gollum slipped away. When he returned and found them asleep, a good impulse almost redeemed him, but the evil light came back into his eyes. He led them far into a climbing tunnel and deserted them. They heard a bubbling noise. Frodo held up the glass given him by Galadriel, the Elf-Queen. In its piercing light appeared Shelob, a huge spidery monster. With temporarily blinded eyes, she retreated. The end of the tunnel was blocked by her web, but Frodo cut through the cords with his elven sword, Sting, and ran outside. Sam saw that Shelob had used another exit and was pursuing Frodo. As he shouted a warning, Gollum leaped on his back. Driving Gollum off, he turned back to see Shelob winding Frodo in cords. He snatched up Sting and attacked her. As she flung her foul body on him, he held Sting so that she wounded herself. In agony, she dragged herself back to her hole, leaving a trail of slime. Finding no sign of life in Frodo, Sam decided that he must try to complete the quest alone. When he heard orc voices, he put on the Ring and vanished. The orcs discovered Frodo's body and carried it toward the tower. Sam learned from their talk that Frodo was stunned but not dead. Frodo was alive and a captive. Sam was locked outside.

Critical Evaluation:

The Two Towers is the second of the three-volume *The Lord of the Rings*, J. R. R. Tolkien's epic fantasy of war between good and evil. In Tolkien's Middle Earth, good and evil are absolutes, each a recognizable force in the shaping of character and behavior. As the power of evil wielded by the Dark Lord Sauron waxes, diverse peoples are drawn to his banner. Those who would wield the power of good to heal the wounds of Middle Earth—Gandalf, Elrond, Galadrial—find themselves besieged. *The Two Towers* traces the influence and definition of both forces as their great conflict draws once again to a climax.

The narrative of *The Two Towers* is divided into two distinct parts, each addressing the struggle in a separate way. The first portion (book 3) considers the problem in an elemental fashion, exploring the relationship between the natural world and the mechanistic inventions of human beings amid sweeping tales of war involving thousands. Book 4 is set at a far more individual level, examining the effects of good and evil on just three carefully drawn characters.

The critical event of book 3 is the meeting between the young hobbits, Pippin and Merry, and the old ent Treebeard. Newly escaped from the clutches of orcs, the hobbits have suffered a horrifying experience in what seems to be a war among the two-legged sentients who walk the earth. The military situation has become confusing; Sauron and his minions are the obvious enemy of the elves and men of the west, but Saruman the traitor has now set up in competition with both.

Treebeard helps the hobbits see the situation in a simpler and more frightening light: Both Sauron and Saruman are the enemies of nature, as are all who wantonly destroy the forests. Treebeard remembers the vast forests that once covered Middle Earth, now reduced to isolated and dangerous patches of angry trees. Sauron the destroyer had covered the world in darkness once before; even now nothing green grows in the fastness of Mordor. Given the chance, the Dark Lord would reduce the entire earth to heaps of slag and ash.

Saruman was a more immediate enemy in the eyes of Treebeard. The white wizard had once pretended a love for trees, but only mechanical artifice held true fascination for him. Isengard, Saruman's home, had once been a pleasant grove filled with living things, but now it was given over to wheels and rising smokes. All the trees were gone.

To fight evil is to fight the destruction of nature. Yet evil is a powerful seducer. Wizards, elves, and human beings had all turned their backs on the trees at one time or another. Saddest of all, even some of Treebeard's own kind had once compromised their love of nature, to the sorrow of all. The entwives, rather than sustaining the vigorous wild of the forest, had turned to gardening, ordering nature, forcing plants to grow as they saw fit. They created beautiful gardens, but war destroyed them, and the entwives disappeared. Only wild nature is vigorous enough to survive the changing whims of the peoples of the earth.

Treebeard assists the curse of men, tipping the balance in the defeat of Saruman and destroying the mechanical wizardry of Isengard. The victory destroys an evil danger to his forest while aiding the cause of the West in the great war of the ring. Yet Treebeard knows better than any that this cooperation between trees and men is temporary, and he foresees that even the free peoples will be increasingly divorced from nature in the future. The destruction of Saruman, or even Sauron, will not destroy all the evil in the world. Nature must look to its own interest as well as it can. Although the war of the ring becomes a struggle between nature and artifice on the fields of Rohan, a very different revelation of the relationship between good and evil takes place in the desolate lands east of the River Anduin. Frodo and Sam meet with Gollum, the gangrel creature nearly possessed by the great ring. What seems at first glance to be a simple confrontation between good and evil becomes something far more subtle.

All three of these hobbits have within themselves a dual capacity for good and evil. A year earlier, in the safety of his living room in the Shire, Frodo had wished Gollum dead, only to be chastised by Gandalf. To deny life is to deny the ability to act, and no one could know what any being's future acts might be. Now, stranded in the wilds on a desperate errand, Frodo finds he must turn to Gollum for help. Gollum knows the way to Mordor, and Frodo must depend on his guidance. He and Gollum complete a bargain to do good, sworn on the Ring—the greatest vessel of evil in all of Middle Earth.

Whereas Frodo is forced to compromise with evil, Gollum is torn in two. Virtually his entire identity has been swallowed by the Ring, and yet he maintains a small kernel of memory of happier times, of green fields and sunlit days. He is two beings in one: a treacherous liar consumed by evil, and an ancient and exhausted hobbit possibly capable of decency. The situation dictates that the two halves make a truce to help Frodo, each side hoping to turn the alliance to its advantage.

Sam is not an innocent bystander in the convenient alliance between Gollum and Frodo. Recognizing that the evil side of Gollum is almost certainly dominant, Sam would like nothing better than to kill the treacherous creature. He is stayed by his trust in Frodo's innate goodness, as well as by practical considerations: They do need a guide.

Each of the three hobbits has made a compromise; Frodo and Sam have done so in the service of the good quest, and Gollum has done so in the hope of somehow stealing back the Ring of evil. The two forces exist everywhere side by side; remaining pure is practically impossible. The key for each hobbit is to sacrifice the needs of the moment in order to achieve a greater goal, an ultimate triumph of one force over the other.

Within a narrative devoted to the resolution of a war and the furthering of a quest, Tolkien in *The Two Towers* developed both his definition and his concept of the function of good in its struggle with evil. Identifying evil with the enemies of wild nature, Tolkien elaborated the complexities of the ultimate choice that must be made within each individual mind.

"Critical Evaluation" by Robert Kuhn McGregor

Bibliography:

Carter, Lin. *Tolkien: A Look Behind "The Lord of the Rings."* New York: Ballantine Books, 1969. A useful general introduction to the trilogy. Contains a summary of *The Two Towers* and includes chapters discussing allegory, the inclusion in the trilogy of elements of the classical epic and fantasy, Tolkien's theory of fairy stories, the kind of names he used, and the sources on which he drew.

Ellwood, Gracia Fay. *Good News from Tolkien's Middle Earth.* Grand Rapids, Mich.: William B. Eerdmans, 1970. Discusses the "aliveness" of all things in Middle Earth and the way in which that resembles the human unconscious. Traces the blend of sacred and secular in the trilogy and evaluates Gandalf's death and return to life in *The Two Towers.*

Isaacs, Neil D., and Rose A. Zimbardo, eds. *Tolkien: New Critical Perspectives.* Lexington: University Press of Kentucky, 1981. An introduction to earlier Tolkien criticism. Includes discussions of Frodo and Aragorn as heroes, Gandalf's battle with the Balrog, and light and darkness as symbols of Galadriel and Shelob in *The Two Towers.*

Lobdell, Jared, ed. *A Tolkien Compass.* LaSalle, Ill.: Open Court, 1975. Essays on such topics as good and evil in the trilogy, as represented in *The Two Towers* by color symbolism; the corrupting force of power, represented in *The Two Towers* by Gollum; and the spiral narrative structure of *The Two Towers.*

Petty, Anne C. *One Ring to Bind Them All: Tolkien's Mythology.* Tuscaloosa: University of Alabama Press, 1979. Good introduction to Tolkien and mythology. Includes a structuralist interpretation of the trilogy and traces Frodo's development in *The Two Towers.*

TWO TREATISES OF GOVERNMENT

Type of work: Politics
Author: John Locke (1632-1704)
First published: 1690

John Locke's *Two Treatises of Government* establish the author as the intellectual father of the modern constitutional state. The political theories set forth are the foundation for later political philosophers, including Jean-Jacques Rousseau, whose *The Social Contract* (1762) influenced the beginning of the French Revolution in 1789. Before Thomas Jefferson wrote the American The Declaration of Independence in 1776, he read and absorbed Locke's *Two Treatises of Government*.

Locke lived during a time of tremendous political upheaval in England, including the Civil War (1642-1646), the beheading of King Charles I (1649), the interregnum (1649-1660), the Restoration of the Stuart monarchy (1660), and the Glorious Revolution of 1688. These events gave Locke the motivation to advocate the political changes that influenced his and future generations.

In his first treatise, Locke refuted the arguments of Sir Robert Filmer's *Patriarcha: Or, The Natural Power of Kings* (1680), which defends the established order in England. Locke's second treatise, the statement of his own political philosophy, rejects many statements in *Leviathan* (1651) by Thomas Hobbes, which advocates absolute power in the person of the king. The connection between Locke's *Two Treatises of Government* and the Glorious Revolution is also clear. Manuscripts of his work circulated in England for several years prior to 1688, helping to produce the revolution. In the preface to the published version, written in 1689 after William and Mary had been given the throne, Locke declared that his treatises "I hope are sufficient to establish the Throne of our Great Restorer, Our present King William."

The major historical impact of Locke's *Two Treatises of Government* is best defined by an analysis of the second treatise (which he subtitled "An Essay Concerning the True Original, Extent, and End of Civil Government"). The content of this essay is best summarized in five major points. The first major point is Locke's definition and discussion of political doctrine. In this point, he declares his belief that government can exist only with the consent of free people. Locke then defines the political power that the government possesses as the power to make laws for the regulation and preservation of property, to use the collective force of the people to execute the laws, and to protect the people and their property from foreign injury. This summary of the duties of government is notable for what it omits—religion, for example.

The biggest part of Locke's discussion of political doctrine is devoted to the four principles of his philosophy of state. The first principle is that there is a need for a powerful political and social organization. Locke believes that all people are born free; he also believes that the only way free people can protect themselves and their property is to form a community. The second principle is that the only legitimate claim by which a ruler can justify his or her power is by a definite agreement between the ruler and the ruled. Locke uses this contract theory to form the basis for government by consent. The next principle is that different circumstances allow for different degrees of authority being given to the government. A community in need of strong leadership can give near-absolute power to its rulers, but a stable community may severely limit its leaders' authority. In chapter 8 of his second thesis, Locke gives the example of the chiefs of Indian tribes in America, who were absolute rulers during times of war, but who exercised very little power during times of peace. The final principle in Locke's philosophy of state is that once a legitimate government is established, the people are bound to obedience. Even if the government proves unsatisfactory, they cannot claim rights not contained in the agreement.

The second major point of Locke's work expands his idea of government by consent into a social contract consisting of two parts. First is a pact of union, in which individuals surrender control over the natural rights to a community, which then acts as a unit to protect the rights of all. Second comes a compact of subjection in which each individual is subject to the will of the community, as long as the community does not violate the individual's rights. Throughout his writings, Locke discusses community by consent but never defines the exact point of origin for that community. He also writes much about the state of nature, which is what exists before the community is formed, but does not precisely describe that state.

Any discussion of Locke's theory of community must include his ideas on how consent is given and what the individual's obligation to the community is afterward. Locke states that before an individual may be bound by community action, there must be solid evidence that he or she had given consent. Direct consent can be given when, upon reaching maturity, he or she takes an oath of allegiance to the government. Tacit consent may be assumed if a person stays in a community for a long period of time without going elsewhere. This tacit consent seems unrealistic, however, because, regardless of an individual's attitude toward the government, he or she may be unable to depart for economic, political, or personal reasons. Even if he or she is able to leave, his or her choices may be so limited that he or she is no more satisfied than before. What Locke apparently means is that any individual living in a community where majority rule prevails is obligated to obey the laws of that community as long as his or her liberty and property are protected. This position establishes a sound moral basis for government, and it is considered one of Locke's major contributions to the modern constitutional state.

The third major point of Locke's second treatise is his discussion of separation of power in government, which can better be understood as a differentiation of power. Locke did not advocate three equal branches of government controlled by a system of checks and balances. Instead, he placed the basic power in the legislative branch, as he declares in chapter 11: "The first and fundamental positive Law of all Commonwealths, is the establishing of the Legislative Power; as the first and fundamental natural law . . . the preservation of the Society, and . . . is . . . sacred and unalterable in the hands where the Community have once placed it."

Legislative supremacy is to be tempered by four limitations. The first is that the legislature cannot have arbitrary power over the lives and property of the people. The legislature only has the power that is transferred to it by consent. People have arbitrary control of their own lives and property, and they have no right to take away the life and property of someone else, so these powers cannot be transferred to the legislature. The second limitation is that the legislature cannot govern by arbitrary decree. It must follow established laws that are interpreted by known and authorized judges. The third limitation is that the legislature cannot take people's property without their consent. Crucial to understanding this limitation is Locke's definition of property, given in chapter 5 of his second treatise. The concept of property consists of two elements: property inherited by all from God, and property consisting of one's body and the labor thereof. Locke combined these elements by saying that acorns and apples are given by God to all, but they become the property of those who gather and pick them. That John Locke was pleased with his definition of property is proven by a remark in a letter he wrote in 1703: "Property I have nowhere found more clearly explained than in a book entitled *Two Treatises of Government*." The fourth and last limitation that Locke placed on the legislature is that it cannot transfer its lawmaking power to any other person or organization.

In contrast to legislative supremacy is Locke's concept of executive necessity. The executive is necessary primarily to guarantee the perpetual execution of legislation. He also describes what he called federative power, by which he meant control of foreign policy. Although Locke separated the federative from the executive, he indicated that they were closely related. Conspicuous by its absence in Locke's two treatises is judicial independence, since that concept had long been a cornerstone of English constitutional tradition. He seemed to include judicial power within the realm of the executive.

The fourth major point of the *Two Treatises of Government*, discussed in chapter 13, consists of the related political principles of popular sovereignty and representative democracy. Locke assigned popular sovereignty (his definition of the term is that the people are the supreme power) to the legislature. That legislature should contain, at least in part, representatives chosen by the people for a specific period of time. When that time is over, the representatives return to their positions as subjects. Locke gave to the executive the power to issue directives regarding the election of the representatives and the assembling of the legislature.

Chapter 19, the last chapter of Locke's second thesis, covers the last major point of Locke's work: the dissolution of government. After he briefly discusses dissolution from without (external force), Locke explains and justifies how a government can be dissolved from within. He describes what is commonly called the right of revolution. One basic reason for this right is if the legislature is altered by an overreaching executive. The alteration could be by the despot's setting up arbitrary will in place of laws, preventing the legislature from assembling, or setting up a legislature of the ruler's own choosing. Revolution would be justified in such cases. It would also be justified if the community were delivered to the subjection of a foreign power. The legislature itself can provoke a justifiable revolution if it breaks its contract, by invading the property of the subjects, for example.

Locke anticipated and answered the charge that his ideas about justifiable dissolution would be foment for revolution. He first states that ill-treated people have a right to seek change. Secondly, every small problem or abuse of trust does not necessitate a revolution. Finally, Locke indicates that the threat of a revolution may prevent the abuse of power that justifies a real revolution.

John Locke's *Two Treatises of Government* contributed at least three basic principles to the modern constitutional state. First, every member of a political society should have an equal voice in governing that society. Second, the idea of social contract helped pave the way for a formal, written constitution. Third, final sovereign power should rest with the people as a whole.

Glenn L. Swygart

Bibliography:
Cook, Thomas I. *History of Political Philosophy from Plato to Burke*. Englewood Cliffs, N.J.: Prentice-Hall, 1936. Places Locke's political theories in the context of twenty-two centuries of political thought. Chapter 19 emphasizes several of Locke's concepts, including social contract and property, plus his influence.
Franklin, Julian. *John Locke and the Theory of Sovereignty*. New York: Cambridge University Press, 1978. Emphasizes Locke's role in transforming the theory of sovereignty from a limited concept to the broad principle of the eighteenth century. Includes the influence on Locke of George Lawson and his radical views concerning the dissolution of government, and reveals Locke's relationship to the English Whig Party.
Lamprecht, Sterling Power. *The Moral and Political Philosophy of John Locke*. New York:

Russell & Russell, 1962. Centers on the relationship between Locke and his predecessors and contemporaries. Goes beyond Locke's *Two Treatises of Government* to include his views on human knowledge and understanding.

Locke, John. *Two Treatises of Government.* 2d ed. Edited and with an Introduction by Peter Laslett. New York: Cambridge University Press, 1970. Accepted as the standard text for studying Locke's political theories. Contains more than one hundred pages of preliminary material, plus extensively footnoted text and an excellent bibliography.

Sabine, George. *A History of Political Theory.* 3d ed. New York: Holt, Rinehart and Winston, 1961. Covers political theory from ancient Greeks to the twentieth century. Emphasizes Locke's role in developing a theory of national state.

TWO WOMEN

Type of work: Novel
Author: Alberto Moravia (1907-1990)
Type of plot: Social realism
Time of plot: 1943-1944
Locale: Sant'Eufemia, Italy
First published: La ciociara, 1957 (English translation, 1958)

> *Principal characters:*
> CESIRA, a shopkeeper's widow from the Ciociaria hills
> ROSETTA, her daughter
> CONCETTA, a peasant woman
> VINCENZO, her husband
> ROSARIO and
> GIUSEPPE, their sons
> FILIPPO, a refugee
> MICHELE, his son
> PARIDE, a sullen peasant
> CLORINDO, a black marketeer

The Story:

Cesira was a peasant woman from the Ciociaria region southeast of Rome. The widow of a Roman shopkeeper, she had continued to run the shop after her husband's death. Selfish, shrewd, and strong-willed, Cesira had concern only for herself and her eighteen-year-old daughter, Rosetta. When the war came, she welcomed it because in wartime food becomes scarce and dear. Before long, she and Rosetta were doing a thriving black market business with the flour, eggs, hams, and potatoes they were able to get from the farmers in her home village and other country places near Rome. Sometimes she said to her daughter that she hoped the war would continue several more years, to provide the young woman with a trousseau and a dowry. When the Germans occupied Rome and Allied bombing raids began to threaten the city, she and Rosetta fled to the Ciociaria hills. At first, they planned to go to live with Cesira's parents; then they heard that the village had been evacuated, and they were forced to settle at Fondi, where they lived for a time with a slatternly woman named Concetta, her husband, Vincenzo, and their two deserter sons, Rosario and Giuseppe, who were hiding from patrols scouring the country-side for men to be sent off to work in Germany.

This refuge proved unsafe; Cesira overheard Concetta's plan to buy her loutish sons' safety by turning Rosetta over to the Fascist bravos. Mother and daughter then fled to Sant'Eufemia, a small village high in the mountain overlooking the valley. There they lived for the next nine months in circumstances of squalor, suspicion, hunger, and fear. They learned what life is like when it is reduced to its essentials of food, clothing, and sleep. At first there was plenty to eat. Filippo, a venal shopkeeper from Fondi, has his hut stuffed with food on which he and his family feasted and which he sold to his less fortunate neighbors. Paride, from whom Cesira and Rosetta rented a hut, was grasping and vicious. The wives were no better than their husbands; charity and dignity had been drained out of them. The only character worthy of respect was Michele, Filippo's son, once a student for the priesthood, who had become an embittered existentialist. His belief was that his neighbors had to lose everything before they would understand anything or be able to see themselves and their world.

Only then, as in Cesira's case, would they grow in understanding and compassion as well. As the months passed and her store of money shrank, she and Rosetta came to know something of the meaning of suffering, for their life became a struggle for survival among the brutal and vicious peasants. Some of their neighbors disappeared, taken away by the Germans. Allied bombers raided Fondi. Two English escapees appeared, were fed, and sent on their way. The daily acts of living, boredom, small excitements, and details unimportant in themselves showed the people of the area as they really were, not in peace but in wartime, when respect for law and order and the fear of God no longer existed.

The liberation, not the war, brought about the ruin of Rosetta, who was raped by a group of French Moroccan troops in a ruined church. This experience made the young woman promiscuous and caused her mother to lose all belief in decency and goodness. Rosetta took up with a flashy young black marketeer named Clorindo, Concetta's brutal son Rosario, and others of a gang of young toughs that the war had spawned. Rosetta was the second victim of the debacle; Michele had been killed by fleeing Germans. Out of these events, however, compassion, sorrow, and true understanding were reborn. Cesira discovered the evil in herself, and with a sense of renewed hope, mother and daughter returned to Rome.

Critical Evaluation:

Alberto Moravia's first novel, *The Time of Indifference* (1929), published when he was only twenty-one, preceded by several years the existential writings of Jean-Paul Sartre. Existentialism, in Sartre's words, was nothing else than an attempt to draw all the consequences of a coherent atheistic position. Existentialism declares that even if God exists, God's existence changes nothing. Existentialism, being a doctrine of action, is basically optimistic. It has frequently been found to be the opposite, however, given its severe and uncompromising bleakness. Existentialism was born of the falling away in Europe from the Christian faith. Philosophers and writers such as Albert Camus and Sartre in France, Martin Heidegger in Germany, and Moravia in Italy, in taking a hard look at the truth of existence in the twentieth century, have been dubbed pessimists. Messengers of a wicked world, they have been mistakenly called wicked themselves.

Existentialism is interested in authentic acts, acts done for their own sake, for the sake of the conscience of the doer, and not to impress others. At times, Moravia takes an extreme view, whereby the authentic can only exist as dream, fantasy, or thought; any attempt to implement the authentic is bound, he believes, to degrade it. Throughout *Two Women* Cesira, the narrator, displays differing qualities of thought. As soon as it enters the world of action, her mental life finds itself compromised. Existence is filled with contradictions; for example, Cesira is forced to depend upon the goodwill of people she loathes and despises. People justify even the most barbaric behavior with words. The double role of language is shown clearly in this book: how it is used to cover things up, even to hide the meaning of a person's deeds from the speaker, but how, from time to time, language can speak truth. Moravia is very skillful at depicting Cesira's inner life through her narration. She is the narrator; she is the primary source of information. Her judgment of a situation or person is not necessarily accurate, but is colored by her own biases. She can be admired or deplored, according to whether her thought is firsthand and forthright, or secondhand and (often) manipulative. The enjoyment of the book is chiefly the way Moravia gets in touch with truth.

Readers share Cesira's innermost registrations; with the rest of the characters, readers only know what the characters say and do in the presence of others. It is noteworthy how often their words find no grounding in reality. They speak to make others or themselves feel better (or worse), but seldom to any good purpose or, indeed, to any circumstance capable of realization. Meanwhile, the novel's most significant actions are accompanied by few, if any, words.

Moravia writes of what happens in wartime because he had firsthand experience of it, but also because something of human beings' essential nature can be glimpsed when law and order no longer prevail. Removed from the habits, goals, and insulation of peacetime, human beings find the imminence of death more difficult to ignore, while hunger and dread of the unknown drive them to uncharacteristic deeds—although Moravia might well assert that only under such circumstances are people's deeds truly characteristic. War accelerates change—desperate circumstances call for desperate measures; people are compelled to deeds that they never would have dreamed of doing in peacetime. Apparently insurmountable obstacles are circumvented on occasion by inventiveness. By the war's end, a new morality—which Cesira, for one, finds to be merely amorality—has come into being. Moravia does not say that this is good or bad, only that it is so, and that, when conditions alter drastically, people need to begin anew by acknowledging these changes, rather than by denying them and clinging mindlessly to past codes of conduct. There may be a deplorable decline in values as a result of the war, but what Rosetta and Rosario and Clorindo have to tell Cesira about this postwar world must also be considered. It may be, as Cesira says, that with peacetime many people will gradually return to time-honored standards of decency. What is certain, however, is that not everybody will, and a new strain of thinking has entered the European mind, of which World War II is at once cause and symptom, and of which *Two Women* is an early and gripping analysis.

Two Women concerns death and rebirth, and this is made evident by the importance accorded to the biblical story of Lazarus. Michele, an intellectual who is sympathetically presented, tells the story and then assures his listeners that it applies to each one of them. They are as good as dead, and, until they acknowledge this, they will stand no chance of being brought back to life—as Lazarus was raised by Christ. Only after she has contemplated and then rejected suicide (upon the advice of Michele's ghost)—only after she has dreamed herself as good as dead, and only after she and her daughter feel sorrow stir the pity that was dead in them—can these two women slowly awaken to their new, postwar existence.

This book can be chilling in its implications: Civilization is a thin veneer through which barbarism is always likely to break. But there is a relief, even a hope, in this acknowledgment, for it shows how words, so often applied to misrepresent and mislead, can occasionally be organized to embody a truth of people's condition. One leaves this novel with a chastened sense of one's ability to control one's fate, but the feeling that one has been helped to look life full in the face.

"Critical Evaluation" by David Bromige

Bibliography:
Cottrell, Jane. *Alberto Moravia*. New York: Frederick Ungar, 1974. Overall survey of the work up to that date. At times cursory, and particularly so in its proclamations about what women are and what they are not and why Rosetta and Cesira cannot be authentic depictions.
Dego, Giuliano. *Moravia*. Edinburgh, Scotland: Oliver & Boyd, 1966. Thorough study of Moravia's output that proves of use with respect to *Two Women*.
Heiney, Donald. *Three Italian Novelists*. Ann Arbor: University of Michigan Press, 1968. Studies of Cesare Pavese, Elio Vittorini, and Moravia. Focuses on the technical aspects of novel writing and the political and psychosocial aspects of the three novelists' works.

Lewis, R. W. B. "Alberto Moravia: Eros and Existence." In *The Picaresque Saint*. Philadelphia: J. B. Lippincott, 1949. Worth looking at for Lewis' analysis of Moravia's use of sexual encounters as provinggrounds of the existential.

Ross, Joan, and Donald Freed. *The Existentialism of Alberto Moravia*. Carbondale: Southern Illinois University Press, 1972. Good attempt to place Moravia's writings in relation to existentialism.

TWO YEARS BEFORE THE MAST

Type of work: Memoir
Author: Richard Henry Dana, Jr. (1815-1882)
First published: 1840

Principal personage:
RICHARD HENRY DANA, JR.

The Story:

In August, 1834, Richard Henry Dana, Jr., shipped aboard the brig *Pilgrim* out of Boston for a voyage to California as an ordinary seaman. He hoped that the journey would relieve his eye trouble and upon his return planned to reenter Harvard College. Since Dana was a greenhorn, he was forced to bunk in the steerage instead of in the forecastle with the other sailors. At first his duties were confusing, doubly so during the first two days, for he was violently seasick. He soon found his sea legs, however, and quickly learned shipboard routine: During the day, all of the sailors were kept busy cleaning and repairing the ship, and during the night they took turns standing watch.

The voyage was uneventful until October, when the *Pilgrim* passed near the mouth of the River Plate. Here Dana encountered his first real storm at sea. After that, the weather began to get cold, and the crew prepared to round Cape Horn. The seas there were high, and the crew battled snow and hail. Everyone's clothing was perpetually wet. By mid-November, the ship had rounded the Horn and was headed north.

The first mishap of the voyage occurred soon after, when a young sailor was swept overboard. A boat lowered to search for him found no trace of the lost man. In accordance with custom, the captain auctioned off the dead man's clothing. Near the end of November the brig made the island of Juan Fernandez and dropped anchor for the first time since departing from Boston. Dana was glad to see land and managed to get on shore for a short time. As soon as the ship had taken on fresh water, however, it weighed anchor and headed on for California.

Shortly after Christmas, Dana was acknowledged to be experienced enough to move into the forecastle with the other crew members. Now he was a real seaman. By the middle of January, the *Pilgrim* made her first California port at Santa Barbara. Dana learned that his work for the next year would be to load cattle hides into the ship. The sailors carried the stiff, undressed hides out through the surf on their heads and deposited them in a boat, whose crew took the hides to the ship and stowed them away.

Once the hides were on board, the *Pilgrim* took on some passengers and sailed northward to Monterey. There, Mexican customs officers inspected the cargo, after which the company agent aboard the ship set up a store to trade with the townspeople. The crew was kept busy on a shuttle service between ship and shore. Because he had some knowledge of languages, Dana became the interpreter for the *Pilgrim* and was sent ashore on errands that required a knowledge of Spanish. In this way, he became acquainted with the town and its people. He found the Spaniards to be pleasant but lazy; most of the trade was carried out by foreigners. Everyone owned horses, and they were so plentiful that the price of a fine animal was very low.

When business began to fall off, the *Pilgrim* returned to Santa Barbara to collect more cattle hides from shore. At that time, trouble began to brew aboard ship. The captain, mates, and crew were all at odds. One day, when the captain began to flog a sailor unjustly, another of the crew remonstrated, whereupon the captain flogged him too. The sailors were angry, but they had no higher power to which they could appeal, for the captain's word was law. Her hold laden with hides, the *Pilgrim* sailed for San Diego.

In San Diego, Dana got his first shore leave. After drinking for a time with the rest of the crew, he and a friend hired horses and rode to a nearby mission, where they were able to get a good Mexican meal, a welcome change from the salt beef served aboard ship.

The undressed hides were unloaded from the *Pilgrim* and placed in a large shed on the beach, where they were to be dressed and stored until a later time. Just when the ship had finished unloading and was ready to set sail, a man deserted ship. After an unsuccessful search, the brig put to sea without him.

The *Pilgrim* took on more hides at San Pedro and then continued on to Santa Barbara. It was the Lenten season, and Dana saw the celebrations ashore. The ship gathered more hides at several places and returned to San Diego. After the hides had been unloaded, the captain sent Dana and another man ashore to assist with the dressing of the hides. Then the ship sailed north on another coastal voyage.

Dana became acquainted with several Sandwich Islanders who lived on the beach and worked with him; he found them to be generous men and true friends. Some of his spare time he spent reading books and studying navigation. Each day, he had to take care of a certain number of hides, which had to be cleaned, soaked in brine, scraped, dried, beaten, and stored away.

When the ship *Alert* arrived at San Diego, Dana, anxious to be at sea again, exchanged places with a boy aboard the ship. The *Alert* belonged to the same company as the *Pilgrim* and was to take on the accumulated hides and carry them to Boston. The *Pilgrim* was not scheduled to return to Boston until later. The two vessels had exchanged captains, and Dana was under the same master as before, but because the first mate of the *Alert* was a good officer, Dana found conditions much more pleasant in his new berth.

Loading hides, the *Alert* moved up and down the coast for several months. In mid-November, 1835, she left Santa Barbara with some passengers bound for Monterey. When a terrific gale came up, however, the ship was unable to put in at Monterey and went on up the coast to San Francisco. The ship continued working up and down the coast until there were enough hides at San Diego to make a full cargo. In May, the *Alert* headed south for Cape Horn.

Rounding the Horn on the return journey was even worse than on the way out. Just when he was needed most on deck, Dana was laid low with a toothache. For days everyone had to work extra hours because of the danger from icebergs. Finally, the *Alert* got clear of the ice and ran before a strong wind around Cape Horn.

Once the ship entered the Atlantic tropics, the weather was fair except for occasional violent storms. Some of the men began to come down with the scurvy, but they were cured after the crew obtained fresh vegetables from a passing ship. On September 21, 1836, the *Alert* anchored in Boston Harbor. Hurriedly the crew performed their last duties in bringing her to the wharf. Within five minutes after the last rope had been made fast, not one of the crew was left aboard.

Critical Evaluation:

If an attack of measles had not threatened Richard Henry Dana, Jr.'s eyesight and forced his withdrawal from Harvard, America would have lost one of the most popular travel adventure books ever written, *Two Years Before the Mast*. Yet surely less arduous and unpredictable forms of convalescence were available to a well-born young Bostonian. Dana's physical condition could not have been the only reason for his shipping out as a common sailor; his decision must, to some extent, have represented important psychological and emotional needs—to have an "adventure," to "test" himself and his "manhood," to separate himself, at least temporarily, from the narrow environment and conservative religious atmosphere of his family and social class.

Immediately after returning from his voyage, while finishing his studies at Harvard and then pursuing a law degree, Dana began to record his experiences anew, largely from memory, since his brother Frank had lost the log he had kept during the voyage. When the book was published in 1840, it became, to everyone's surprise, an instant commercial success. Ten years later, following the discovery of gold in California, it enjoyed a second burst of popularity, for it was almost the only book available that dealt with the early California environment. Dana profited little from the book in a material way; discouraged in his attempts to find a publisher, he had sold all rights to the work to *Harper's Magazine* for $250.

Two Years Before the Mast probably remains popular because it combines two of the most popular motifs—those of the travel-adventure romance and the coming-of-age narrative—in a skillful, vivid manner. The genre of travel-adventure romance, which has attracted writers as diverse and talented as James Fenimore Cooper, Herman Melville, Henry David Thoreau, Mark Twain, and Ernest Hemingway, was particularly popular in the mid-nineteenth century. Such narratives vicariously fulfill at least two emotional needs of the reader: the glorification of physical hardship and an identification with the overcoming of obstacles, especially nature itself, and an escape from the confines of a narrow, dull environment to a world of sensuous experience. *Two Years Before the Mast* combines much of the former and generous hints of the latter, especially in the description of quaint customs and free lifestyle of the Californians. The secret to the depiction of such an escape vision is to make the exotic, unknown world real to the reader, and this is where Dana succeeds brilliantly.

Although *Two Years Before the Mast* is autobiographical, many readers accepted it as fiction, a tribute to Dana's storytelling abilities. His prose style is direct, concrete, and muted, lacking the rhetorical embellishment so characteristic of most mid-nineteenth century writing but frequently laced with colloquial phraseology. On the whole, the book does not depend on exciting adventures or bizarre situations but rather on careful, restrained descriptions of the seamen's everyday routines and activities, punctuated by periodic crises that Dana renders in vivid, dramatic scenes. The book capitalizes on what has always been one of the primary appeals of "realistic" writing, the intimate description of a profession or activity that seems exotic to the reader.

Moreover, *Two Years Before the Mast* is almost the only nineteenth century narrative of life at sea—Herman Melville not excepted—that does not romanticize the common sailor. Dana likes his mates but presents them as flawed, distinctive human beings, who labor at a very dangerous, difficult job in which they show courage, endurance, and tenacity.

The coming-of-age theme in *Two Years Before the Mast* is given a special twist by the fact that Dana, the initiate, is a young, relatively naïve, religiously conservative Boston aristocrat who thrusts himself into a trial among crude, uneducated, generally amoral sailors. He must not only move from youth to manhood and from innocence to experience but also from outsider to member of a subculture. Throughout the book there is, on his side, a constant tension between his aristocratic inclinations and sensibilities and his democratic convictions and the desire to identify with his cohorts; on the part of the crew, there is a resentment of Dana for his social background and intellectual pretensions coupled with an admiration for his growth and development as an efficient, hardworking seaman.

In the beginning of the book, Dana is obviously a novice, and the crew isolates him in steerage. He learns quickly, however, and gives a good account of himself in the first bad storm. He also establishes the pattern of volunteering for every difficult and dangerous job that comes up, a trait that brings him admiration from the crew, as well as a reputation for foolhardiness. When a young sailor is washed overboard, Dana confronts sudden death at sea and comes to learn the superficially joking attitude the men have toward danger and mortality. His view of the basic futility of their lives is crystallized in the summation: "A sailor's life is at best but a mixture of little good with much evil, and a little pleasure with much pain. The beautiful is linked with the revolting, the sublime with the commonplace, and the solemn with the ludicrous."

His initiation into the institutional side of sailing and the justice of the high seas comes when Captain Thompson flogs two men for trivial reasons. Young Dana had known of the captain's absolute power, but not until watching an almost demented, hysterical captain viciously flogging the men, did he realize the full meaning of the law. It was at this point that Dana committed himself to fighting for a reform of the maritime laws that allowed such flagrant and arbitrary injustice—a commitment to which he remained true all of his life.

The flogging scene leads directly to his most serious moral dilemma. Throughout the book, Dana tries to identify with the sailors, but, when threatened with a possible disruption of his own career plans, Dana invokes the family name and his place is taken by a less well situated substitute. He tries to mitigate the use of family influence by giving the substitute a handsome share of his pay, but the moral onus remains.

Two Years Before the Mast is an intelligent, exciting, sensitive story of a young man's transition to maturity, a vivid, convincing description of human beings' struggle with the elements and with themselves, an accurate account of life at sea, a colorful portrait of life in California in the early nineteenth century, and a series of colorful, dramatic vignettes. Had Dana decided to devote his life to letters, his writings might very well be today compared to those of his contemporary and friend, Herman Melville. Instead, he chose law, lecturing, and public service, where he had a moderately successful, if unspectacular, career. Although he was proud of its wide appeal, in time Dana came to consider *Two Years Before the Mast* as a boys' book and to recall his maritime adventures almost as a youthful fling. Little did Dana realize, as he stood on the bow of the *Alert* in 1836 pondering what to do with the rest of his life, that he had already lived the most important part of it.

"Critical Evaluation" by Keith Neilson

Bibliography:

Aaron, Daniel. "Two Boston Fugitives: Dana and Parkman." In *American Literature, Culture, and Ideology: Essays in Memory of Henry Nash Smith*. New York: Peter Lang, 1990. Compares *Two Years Before the Mast* and Francis Parkman's *The Oregon Trail* (1849). Though purportedly factual, both incorporate fictive devices such as psychologically motivated background descriptions and characters whose personalities affect events that are narrated suspensefully. Stresses the authors' family and vocational pressures.

Gale, Robert L. *Richard Henry Dana, Jr.* New York: Twayne, 1969. Includes an analysis of the narrative movement, structure, rhetoric, and tone of *Two Years Before the Mast*. Places it in the context of other American journey books.

Lawrence, D. H. *Studies in Classic American Literature*. New York: Seltzer, 1923. This insightful work includes a discussion of the flogging Dana observes and his response to it, his mysterious toothache, and the power of the sea and Dana's descriptions of it.

Lucid, Robert F. "The Influence of *Two Years Before the Mast* on Herman Melville." *American Literature* 31 (November, 1959): 243-256. A careful examination of the degree to which

Melville may have been influenced by Dana's narrative in composing *Redburn: His First Voyage* (1849) and *White-Jacket* (1850).

Philbrick, Thomas. *James Fenimore Cooper and the Development of American Sea Fiction.* Cambridge, Mass.: Harvard University Press, 1961. Contrasts Dana's realistically accurate depiction of life at sea with Cooper's more romantic treatment in his early sea fiction.

TYPEE

Type of work: Novel
Author: Herman Melville (1819-1891)
Type of plot: Adventure
Time of plot: Mid-nineteenth century
Locale: Marquesas Islands
First published: 1846

Principal characters:
>HERMAN MELVILLE (TOM), an American sailor
>TOBY, his friend
>MEHEVI, the chief of the Typees
>KORY-KORY, a native servant
>FAYAWAY, a native girl
>MARNOO, a native taboo man

The Story:

The whaler *Dolly* had been long at sea, and the men were discontented and restless when the captain finally gave orders to put in at Nukuheva, one of the Marquesas Islands. This was the chance for which Tom and Toby, two young sailors, had been waiting. Even though the natives of the island were known to be cannibals, Tom and Toby deserted the ship and fled inland, planning to hide until the *Dolly* sailed. They hoped to then sign aboard another ship where they would get better treatment.

Tom and Toby began their flight with only a few biscuits for food. On the first night away from the ship, Tom contracted a disease which caused his leg to swell, and he was in much pain. Nevertheless, he and Toby continued. At last, when their food was all gone, they realized that they could stay alive only by giving themselves up to one of the savage tribes that inhabited the island.

They discovered too late that the natives to whom they surrendered themselves were the Typee tribe, the most ferocious cannibals on Nukuheva. Tom and Toby were treated with respect, however, and were given food and comfortable quarters. All the natives came to see the strangers. Mehevi, the chief of the Typees, appointed Kory-Kory as personal servant to Tom. The captives went to live in the home of Tinor, Kory-Kory's mother. Mehevi had a medicine man examine Tom's swollen leg, but the native remedies had no effect on the disease.

Tom, unable to walk, spent most of his time reclining in the house while Kory-Kory attended to his needs. A beautiful young maiden, Fayaway, was also his constant companion. She, among all the Typees, seemed to understand the painful situation of the two captives. Toby convinced the Typees that he should be allowed to return to the main harbor on the island to seek medical aid for Tom. On the trail, he was attacked by hostile warriors from a neighboring tribe, and he returned to the Typees with an ugly head wound.

A few days later, Toby discovered a boat offshore. He was allowed to go down by the beach, but Tom was detained in his house. Toby promised to bring medical aid to Tom within three days, but the three days passed without the return of Toby. Tom could learn nothing from the natives; he realized that now he was the single captive of the Typees. Somewhat recovered, he was allowed to roam almost at will within the country of the Typees, but he was always accompanied by Kory-Kory, and there was no chance for escape.

As Tom's leg improved, he began to indulge in the pleasures allowed him and to observe the native life with interest. The Typees seemed to exist in a perpetual state of happiness, interrupted only by skirmishes with neighboring tribes. One of Tom's greatest pleasures was to paddle a canoe about a small lake in company with Fayaway. For the privilege of taking Fayaway with him, he had to ask special permission, since entering a canoe was ordinarily taboo for a woman.

One day a handsome stranger appeared among the Typees bearing news from other parts of the island. He was Marnoo, a taboo man, who was free to go among all the tribes without harm. When Tom learned that Marnoo knew English, he asked the native to help him escape. This Marnoo could not do for fear of arousing the anger of the Typees.

The daily life of the natives was extremely regular. Each morning they bathed and ate breakfast. After the meal, they smoked their pipes. The rest of the morning they spent sleeping, conversing, or doing odd jobs about their houses. The men often spent the afternoon in the large meetinghouse of Mehevi; there they relaxed and joked in a sort of bachelors' club. Before the evening meal, they bathed again. After the meal, the young girls entertained the rest with dancing. Everyone retired at an early hour.

Tom was present at the Feast of the Calabashes. It seemed to have some religious significance, but most of the time was spent in eating and drinking. During the two days of the festival, Tom decided that the natives did not take their religion seriously. They possessed many idols not treated with any high degree of respect. The most universal religious observance was that of tattooing; everyone was tattooed upon the face, even the women. The bodies of some of the men were completely covered with intricate designs.

Since the men outnumbered the women in the tribe, the women often had two or three husbands, but the men never had more than one wife. All in the tribe seemed happy with the various aspects of their social organization. Private property was limited to household goods; food was common property. All understood and followed the laws and customs of the tribe; there were never disputes among the Typees.

One day, a battle was fought between the Typees and a neighboring tribe. Afterward, the bodies of the dead enemies were taken to the ceremonial feasting place. For the next day or two, Tom was not allowed to leave the vicinity of his house. He suspected that the Typees were making a meal of their dead enemies. Later he discovered the remains of the meal and found that he was correct, though the Typees denied that they were cannibals.

A few days later, Marnoo again appeared among the Typees. This time he told Tom to try to escape by means of the same path by which he left. Tom was unable to leave the village, however, for Kory-Kory kept close watch on him day and night.

Not many days after Marnoo had left, the Typees excitedly announced the approach of a boat. Tom argued with the natives and finally persuaded them to let him go to the beach. He had some difficulty in getting there, since his leg had begun to swell again. At the beach, Tom found a boat from an Australian ship standing just outside the surf. Marnoo had told the Australian captain of Tom's trouble, and he had sent a boat loaded with presents to obtain Tom's release. The Typees, however, had no wish to release their captive. In desperation, Tom broke away from the guard which had been placed around him and plunged into the surf. He managed to reach the boat, and the sailors pulled away from shore. Thus ended Tom's captivity among the Typees. His only regret was in leaving the faithful Kory-Kory and the beautiful Fayaway.

Many years later Tom again met Toby and learned from him that he had intended to return to the aid of his injured friend, but he had been tricked into boarding a vessel which sailed from Nukuheva the following day. It was only long after Toby had given Tom up for lost that the two friends learned of each other's fate after their separation.

Critical Evaluation:

Herman Melville's assertion in *Moby Dick* (1851) that a whale ship was his Yale and Harvard reminds readers of how central to his development the sea adventures of his youth were and how strongly they would shape his writing. It was from the whaler *Acushnet* that Melville jumped ship in the Marquesas to spend a few weeks among the Nukuheva natives. The episode ended, sooner and less dramatically than in *Typee*, when he departed the island on another whaler, eventually to join the American warship *United States*, for a voyage back to Boston. Though the adventure had ended in actuality, it only began imaginatively for Melville when he sought to discover its meaning in the fictionalized account of his sojourn among the cannibals which he called *Typee*. Though actually a novel based upon experience, *Typee* was regarded generally as simply a travel narrative when it appeared, and the work's reputation since has had to fight against that classification. In fact, *Typee* contains more of the basic elements of Melville's later fiction than its detractors have realized, and it deserves a primary place among such other early works as *Redburn* (1849) and *White-Jacket* (1850) which give meaning to the idea of Melville's education on board the ships he sailed as a young man.

The essential facts of *Typee*, except for the time, which Melville considerably exaggerates, are true. He did jump ship in company of a friend named Toby Greene and spent a few weeks among the natives of the Typee valley, where he enjoyed a somewhat ambiguous status as a prisoner-guest. Melville did injure his leg escaping the *Acushnet* and allowed Toby to go for medical supplies. Toby failed to return, having been shanghaied by another whaler, and, after a few weeks Melville was taken off the island by a whaler in search of crewmen. The novel, however, is more than the sum of these few facts, and it cannot be done justice by a reading which regards it as no more than a slightly fictionalized autobiographical narrative. Far from simply recounting his adventures, in *Typee* Melville is examining the fundamental ambiguities in humanity and nature which would characterize his best work as the basis for the unanswerable questions his novels propose.

From its very beginning, the boys' journey into the Typee valley promises to be more than it seems. Running not only from the ship and its cruelly authoritarian master but from the world of the coast natives, which has been hopelessly corrupted by sailors, administrators, and missionaries, these adventurers make their way down a precipitous route which carries them metaphorically backward in time as it takes them beyond the reach of civilization. Eventually reaching the valley floor, the boys initially encounter Typee (which they still believe to be Happar) as a new paradise. Not only the fecundity and lushness of the rich valley but also the young lovers who are the first inhabitants encountered, point to the discovery of a South Sea Eden. This vision of innocence and beauty in the South Sea islands was, to some extent, typical of nineteenth century Romanticism with its recurrent theme of the noble savage, but Melville, even this early in his career, was no typical Romantic writer.

From the time Tom (now renamed Tommo) settles, albeit unwillingly, into life with the Typees, Melville begins to develop on him a series of symbols which point to the fundamental ambiguity that lies at the heart of the island "paradise." On the one hand, the simplicity, loyalty, and unselfconscious devotion offered by Kory-Kory, and, more particularly, the innocent love and natural sexuality of Fayaway, keep alive the vision of an Edenic garden. On the other hand, Tommo's discovery that he is in the land of the dread Typees rather than among the peaceful Happars leads to his fear of cannibalism, the most dreaded of all humanity's aberrations. Tommo's injured leg, which mysteriously grows worse as his suspicions of cannibalism near confirmation, becomes an objective correlative for his sick spirit which, cut off from the civilization it sought to escape, languishes. Tattooing also develops a symbolic value, since it would complete the initiation into the Typean world begun with the ritual name change. Once tattooed, Tommo would never again be able to return to his own world.

The essential ambiguity in *Typee* centers on the prospect of a paradise corrupted at its heart by the horror of cannibalism. In later years, Melville would assert that he could look upon a horror and be familiar with it, but this is not so of Tommo, who cannot reconcile himself to this discovery. More generally, the implications of the innate evil of *Typee* seriously challenge the view of optimistic philosophers of Melville's period who argued that the universe, and humanity, were essentially good, evil being only an appearance rather than a reality. Tommo might like to think that he, as a civilized human being, somehow transcends the essentially savage nature of humankind, but Melville will not have it so. In the escape scene, Tommo repays the hospitality of his hosts by driving the boat hook into the throat of one of his recent friends. Even as Tommo feels the horror of his violent act, readers feel the horror of Melville's world in which the savage impulse dwells even in the most civilized breast.

Though perhaps less orderly than this reading suggests, Melville's symbols are clearly present, and they serve to put his vision in a direct line of descent from that of his Calvinist forebears who endorsed the doctrine of the essential depravity of humanity. It is only because the symbols are tentative and nascent, rather than fully developed into Melville's mature symbolism, that *Typee* must be seen more as an anticipation of later Melville than as a fully realized work of art in itself. *Typee* does reveal, however, how early Melville began to develop the symbolic mode which would become the hallmark of his greatest novels, and how soon he began to discover those unsolvable questions of the nature of good and evil that would preoccupy him throughout his career.

"Critical Evaluation" by William E. Grant

Bibliography:
Anderson, Charles Roberts. *Melville in the South Seas*. New York: Columbia University Press, 1939. A still reliable account of Melville's own South Seas voyages featuring comparisons between the facts of Melville's experience and the fictions of *Moby Dick*, *Typee*, and *Omoo*.
Herbert, T. Walter. *Marquesan Encounters: Melville and the Meaning of Civilization*. Cambridge, Mass.: Harvard University Press, 1980. An examination of *Typee* alongside two other nineteenth century narratives of Americans in the South Seas in the context of how Marquesan societies were irreparably damaged by contacts with white people during this era. Provides excellent readings of the political and religious dimensions of Melville's book.
Lawrence, D. H. *Studies in Classic American Literature*. New York: Penguin Books, 1978. Lawrence was important in the re-evaluation of Melville in the 1920's. (Melville had sunk into obscurity between the end of his novelistic career in the 1850's and this rediscovery.) Lawrence has two essays on him in this book, including one on *Typee* and *Omoo*.
Leyda, Jay. *The Melville Log: A Documentary Life of Herman Melville, 1819-1891*. Vol. 1. New York: Gordian, 1951. Leyda's work is a two-volume collection of documents important to the life and career of Melville, including excerpts from letters to and from Melville and his family, reviews of his work, and snippets of Melville's novels which allude to cited biographical data.
Rogin, Michael Paul. *Subversive Genealogy: The Politics and Art of Herman Melville*. Berkeley: University of California Press, 1985. Incisive psychological and Marxist reading of Melville's life and work, arguing him as one of the leading thinkers of his age. Its reading of Melville's family's place in the historical context of the 1840's is unparalleled.

ULYSSES

Type of work: Novel
Author: James Joyce (1882-1941)
Type of plot: Epic
Time of plot: June 16, 1904
Locale: Dublin
First published: 1922

> *Principal characters:*
> STEPHEN DEDALUS, a young Irish writer and teacher
> BUCK MULLIGAN, a medical student
> LEOPOLD BLOOM, a Jewish advertising salesman
> MARION "MOLLY" TWEEDY BLOOM, his wife
> BLAZES BOYLAN, Molly's lover

The Story:

Buck Mulligan mounted the stairs of the old tower and prepared to shave himself on the morning of June 16, 1904. A moment later, Stephen Dedalus came to the stairhead and stood looking out over Dublin Bay. When Mulligan spoke of the sea glinting in the morning sunlight, Stephen had a sudden vision of his own mother; he had been called back from Paris to her deathbed a year before. He remembered how she had begged him to pray for her soul and how he, rebelling against the churchly discipline of his boyhood, had refused.

After breakfast, Stephen and Mulligan went off with Haines, a young Englishman who also lived in the old tower. Despite the Englishman's attempts to be friendly, Stephen disliked Haines, who was given to nightlong drunken sprees. Stephen felt that his own life was growing purposeless and dissolute through his association with Mulligan and other medical students. Stephen was a teacher. It was a half-day holiday at school, and the boys were restless. One of his pupils was unable to do his simple arithmetic problems, and in the boy Stephen saw for a moment an image of his own awkward youth. He was relieved when he could dismiss the class.

Later, he walked alone on the beach. He thought of literature and his student days, of his unhappiness in Dublin, his lack of money, his family sinking into poverty while his shabby genteel father made his daily round of the Dublin pubs. He saw the carcass of a dead dog rolling in the surf. Stephen remembered how a dog had frightened him in his childhood; he was, he thought wryly, not one of the Irish heroes.

Meanwhile, Leopold Bloom had crawled out of bed to prepare his wife's breakfast. He was a Jewish advertising salesman, for sixteen years the patient, uncomplaining husband of Marion Tweedy Bloom, a professional singer of mediocre talent. He was unhappy to know that she was carrying on an affair with Blazes Boylan, a sporting Irishman who was managing the concert tour that she was planning. Bloom munched his own breakfast and read a letter from his daughter Milly, who was working in a photographer's shop in Mullingar. Her letter reminded Bloom of his son Rudy, who had died when he was eleven days old. Bloom read Milly's letter again, wondering about a young student his daughter mentioned. For a moment, he was afraid that Milly might grow up to be like her mother.

Bloom set out on his morning walk. At the post office, he stopped to pick up a letter addressed to Henry Flower, Esq., a letter from a woman who signed herself Martha. Bloom, unhappy at home, was carrying on a flirtation by mail under another name. He idly wandered into a church and listened to part of the mass. Later, he joined a party of mourners on their way to the funeral of an old friend, Paddy Dignam, who had died suddenly of a stroke. During the service, Bloom watched Father Coffey. He thought again of little Rudy and of his own father, a suicide. The day's business for Bloom was a call at a newspaper office to arrange for the printing of an advertisement. While he was there, Stephen Dedalus also came to the office. The two men saw each other, but they did not speak.

Bloom left the newspaper building and walked across the O'Connell bridge. He met Mrs. Breen and gave her an account of Dignam's funeral. She told him that Mrs. Purefoy was in the maternity hospital in Holles Street. Bloom walked on, watching the sights of Dublin on a summer day. He entered Davy Byrne's pub and ordered a cheese sandwich. Later, he went to the National Library to look at some newspaper files. There Stephen, flushed with the drinks he had taken at lunch, was expounding to Buck Mulligan and some literary friends his own ingenious theory of William Shakespeare's plays and the second-best bed of Shakespeare's will. Again, Bloom and Stephen saw each other but did not speak.

Bloom went to the Ormond Hotel for a late lunch. Blazes Boylan came into the bar before he left to keep his appointment with Molly.

Late that afternoon, Bloom got into a brawl in a pub where the talk was all about the money that Blazes Boylan had won in a boxing match. Bloom escaped from the jeering crowd and walked along the Sandymount shore. In the dimming twilight, he watched young Gertie MacDowell. The moon rose. Bloom decided to stop by the hospital to ask about Mrs. Purefoy. As he walked slowly along the strand, a cuckoo clock struck nine in a priest's house that he was passing. Bloom considered that he had been cuckolded while he sat dreaming his amorous fantasies on the Dublin beach, looking at Gertie MacDowell. At the hospital, he learned that Mrs. Purefoy's baby had not yet been born. There he saw Stephen Dedalus again, drinking with Buck Mulligan and a group of medical students. Bloom was disturbed to find the son of his old friend, Simon Dedalus, in ribald, dissolute company.

Bloom went with the medical students to a nearby pub, where Stephen and Buck Mulligan began a drunken argument over the possession of the key to the old tower. When the group broke up, Stephen and one of the students went on to a brothel in the Dublin slums; Bloom followed them slowly. All were drunk by that time. Bloom had a distorted, lurid vision of his wife and Blazes Boylan together. Stephen was befuddled and thought that his dead mother suddenly appeared from the grave to ask him again to pray for her soul. Running headlong into the street, he was knocked down in a scuffle with two British soldiers. Bloom took Stephen home with him. Exhausted by his wild night, Stephen remained silent and glum while Bloom talked about art and science. Bloom had begged him to spend the night, to leave Mulligan and his wild friends and come to live with the Blooms, but Stephen refused. The bells of St. George's Church were ringing as he walked off down the silent street.

Bloom went slowly to bed. As he drifted off to sleep, he told Molly firmly that she was to get up and prepare his breakfast in the morning.

Molly Bloom lay awake thinking of Blazes Boylan. She thought of the mysteries of the human body, of people she had known, of her girlhood at the military post on Gibraltar. She considered the possibility that Stephen Dedalus might come to live with her and her husband. Stephen was a writer—young, refined, not coarse like Boylan. She heard a far, shrill train whistle. She recalled all of her past lovers, Bloom's courtship, their years together, the rose she wore in her hair the day Bloom had asked her to marry him as they stood close under a Moorish arch. Her thoughts flowed on, while her Ulysses, Bloom, the far wanderer of a Dublin day, snored in the darkness by her side.

Critical Evaluation:

On one of its many levels, *Ulysses* is an attempt at the complete recapture, so far as it is possible in fiction, of the life of a particular time and place. The scene is Dublin—its streets, homes, shops, newspaper offices, pubs, hospitals, brothels, and schools. The time is a single day in 1904. A continuation of the story of Stephen Dedalus as told in *A Portrait of the Artist as a Young Man* (1916), the novel is also a series of remarkable Homeric parallels. The incidents, characters, and scenes of a Dublin day correspond to those of the Odyssean myth. Leopold Bloom is easily recognizable as Ulysses, and Molly Bloom, his wife, as Penelope. The book is written in a variety of styles and techniques; the most important is the stream-of-consciousness method, by which James Joyce attempts to reproduce not only the sights, sounds, and smells of Dublin but also the memories, emotions, and desires of his people in the modern world. This technique, combined with multilayered wordplay, concatenated sentence structures designed to connote as well as denote, and the sheer density and richness of Joyce's allusive language, make the narrative nonlinear, and epic in its proportions. While on the surface *Ulysses* relates one day in the life of its Dubliner characters, Joyce's juxtaposition of his characters' thoughts, descriptions of place, and evocation of history make the book as true an epic as its predecessor by Homer.

Short of Joyce's other great masterwork, *Finnegans Wake* (1939), *Ulysses* is arguably the most "difficult" work in English literature—a work impossible to appreciate fully after only one reading. Approaching *Ulysses* for the first time should therefore be done somewhat aggressively. If comprehension lapses—even for pages at a time—it is better to push on. Many elements that appear early in the story make sense only after one has read much further along. Bloom's potato talisman, for example, is mentioned in the fourth episode but remains unexplained until the fifteenth. There are so many such difficulties, and of such variety, that readers sometimes feel lost. The persistent reader, however, will find that the novel is deliberately and intensely structured—Joyce later speculated that he had made it perhaps too structured. Too much or too little, the book's structure helps buoy readers voyaging into the narrative for the first time.

Although he said he did not want them published, Joyce let out two (very similar) schemas of the novel's structure. These charts indicate for each of the eighteen episodes: a title referring to the Homeric original; the time of day; a dominant color; a "technic" (the narrative style of the episode); a dominant art (history, literature, philology); an organ of the body; a dominant symbol; and miscellaneous correspondences between Homeric and Joycean characters. The charts have not been an unalloyed blessing to Joyce's readers, because the schemas are sometimes ambiguous or cryptic. Nevertheless, it is difficult to think of another major author whose critics have been so influenced, indeed dominated, by a single piece of text that is external to the work in question. The schemas are at least suggestive with regard to three of the more salient (and problematic) aspects of the book. These three are the Homeric parallels, Stephen's theory about Shakespeare and art, and the episodic structure and use of style.

Shortly after the publication of *Ulysses*, the Homeric parallel was applauded by T. S. Eliot as having "the importance of a scientific discovery." Ezra Pound thought the parallel was gratuitous, something "which any block-head could trace." The elaborate Homeric correspondence is, however, surely not, as Eliot thought, merely a backdrop to heighten "the immense panorama of futility that is the modern world." Rather, it allows readers an opportunity at faith. One may infer from the novel, if one wishes, that Bloom is a modern reincarnation of Odysseus and that, by extension, the modern age is as heroic as the ancient.

Ulysses was Joyce's favorite hero from his childhood. The quality he was to isolate as unique to the Greek hero was completeness. He observed that Ulysses had been a father, a son, a husband, a lover, a soldier who was at first a draft-dodger, and then a hawk. Although this is a rather curious ideal, it suggests what may have been Joyce's purpose. The story of Ulysses constitutes such a full representation of a given complex of attitudes and values that Joyce was able to use it as a paradigm for the structure of a modern story.

The correspondences to Homer are not consistent. Bloom and Stephen are, in only a general way, Ulysses and Telemachus. Correspondences listed on the schema indicate that in the first episode, for example, Stephen is Telemachus, but also Hamlet. In the ninth episode, Ulysses is "Jesus, Socrates, Shakespeare." Furthermore, as has been remarked, Stephen is more like a youthful aspect of Ulysses than like Telemachus, who is almost a minor character in Homer's work. There is, then, no one-to-one impersonation of Homeric characters. Rather, there is a play of functions pointing to an essential human, the abstract Ulysses who belongs not exclusively to Homer but to the entire tradition of the Ulysses theme.

The ninth episode, *Scylla and Charybdis*, contains Stephen's aesthetic theory. The action is presented as a parable of artistic creation based on Shakespeare's biography. The way the "Ulysses" of the schema functions is rather complex. The schema says that Scylla is "The Rock—Aristotle, Dogma" and Charybdis "The Whirlpool—Plato, Mysticism." "Ulysses," who must sail between these perils, is given as "Socrates, Jesus, Shakespeare." This aspect of Ulysses is manifested in Stephen's discourse; Bloom is not even immediately present. The course is the one the artist must take. It includes going between extremes of the inner and outer worlds of his personal experience. There is a struggle between the flux of everyday life and a permanent, repeated structure in the artist's self. This structure is compared to the mole that remains on Stephen's breast although all the molecules of his body have changed, and, in the parable, to a supposed psychological trauma in Shakespeare's youth that determined the structure of his plays and their themes of usurpation, humiliation, and, later, reconciliation. At the level of the individual artistic psyche, the theory recapitulates the determinism treated by the novel as historical and sociological.

As to the individual episodes, the schema names a variety of elements of style that make each unique. Joyce told friends that he intended each to be able to stand on its own. Various episodes are sometimes anthologized and read like short stories. *Circe*, episode 15, has been produced as a play many times. There is a limited narrative point of view in each episode, but it is clearly never the same. There is abundant exegetical literature for each episode, treating in detail the unity derived of its tone, style, and themes. For this overview, however, it is more important to note that the various episodic styles are part of a second structural principle in the novel.

Total autonomy and interdependence combine in the episodic structure; Stephen and Bloom, component elements of the "Ulysses" composite, partake of this combination and therefore avoid becoming mere allegorical types. They are, in fact, complete individuals. This pattern suggests the paradoxical doctrine of the Trinity, in which three complete and equal Persons have one Essence. Of the Trinity, Joyce once said that when contemplating one Person, the others slip from view. So it is with Stephen and Bloom; for that matter, any individual episode in *Ulysses* seems capable of absorbing the reader's whole attention. It is, therefore, the overview that leads the reader best through the myriad captivations of Joyce's odyssey.

"Critical Evaluation" by James Marc Hovde

Bibliography:
Benstock, Bernard, ed. *Critical Essays on James Joyce's "Ulysses."* Boston: G. K. Hall, 1989.

Contains a cross-section of criticism from the early to the more recent. Special emphasis is given to the "Nausicaa" episode.

Ellman, Richard. *James Joyce*. 2d ed. New York: Oxford University Press, 1982. Widely considered the finest literary biography of the twentieth century. Contains extensive discussion and analysis of *Ulysses*. Highly recommended.

Gilbert, Stuart. *James Joyce's "Ulysses."* New York: Vintage Books, 1955. Still highly valuable. Covers the novel chapter by chapter; discusses in useful outlines many of the schemata underlying the novel. A good starting point.

Kenner, Hugh. *"Ulysses": A Study*. Baltimore: The Johns Hopkins University Press, 1987. A substantial contribution from a preeminent literary critic; discusses the plot of the novel thoroughly. Equally useful for the beginning or the repeat reader. Bibliography, appendices.

Wilson, Edmund. *Axel's Castle: A Study in the Imaginative Literature of 1870-1930*. New York: Charles Scribner's Sons, 1931. Discusses modernist writers. The chapter on Joyce contains an excellent summary of *Ulysses*. Places Joyce's artistic and technical achievement in a historical context.

THE UNBEARABLE BASSINGTON

Type of work: Novel
Author: Saki (Hector Hugh Munro, 1870-1916)
Type of plot: Satire
Time of plot: Early 1900's
Locale: London
First published: 1912

> *Principal characters:*
> COMUS BASSINGTON, the "unbearable" Bassington
> FRANCESCA BASSINGTON, his mother
> ELAINE DE FREY, an heiress
> COURTNEY YOUGHAL, a young member of Parliament
> HENRY GREECH, Mrs. Bassington's brother

The Story:

Francesca Bassington was a successful member of London society who was able to make a little money go a long way. Her greatest interest in life was the drawing room in her small, perfect house on Blue Street. Foremost of her treasures was a famous Van der Meulen masterpiece, which hung in the paneled place of honor in that charming room. She also had a son, Comus, who presented a serious problem to his mother because of his casual attitude toward life. Francesca had come to the conclusion that there was only one solution for her son's future. He must marry a wealthy young woman. Her first choice was Emmeline Chetrof, who would eventually come into a comfortable fortune and, most important of all, would upon her marriage inherit the house in which Francesca lived.

During the time Comus was at school, Francesca wrote her son, asking him to show special kindness to Emmeline's brother Lancelot. This suggestion caused Comus to treat the child even more cruelly, and her plans for a match between Comus and Emmeline ended dismally. Two years later, when Comus was turned loose in his mother's fashionable world of Mayfair and Ascot, she persuaded her brother, Henry Greech, to secure a position for the young man as a secretary to Sir John Jull, the governor of an island in the West Indies. Not wanting to leave England, Comus sent to a newspaper an article criticizing Sir John. This scurrilous attack was written by Courtney Youghal, a young politician whom Comus knew and admired. Printed over Comus' signature, it had the desired result. Comus lost the position Sir John had promised.

At a dinner given by Lady Caroline Benaresq, Francesca Bassington first learned that her son was interested in Elaine de Frey, a wealthy young woman who resembled a painting by Leonardo da Vinci. At the same party, Francesca learned that Courtney Youghal was also interested in the young heiress.

One summer afternoon, Elaine de Frey entertained her two suitors, Comus and Courtney, at tea in her garden. Elaine, an earnest and practical young lady, had analyzed her suitors carefully; although she realized that Comus was both frivolous and undependable, she found herself falling in love with him and making excuses for his shortcomings. Courtney, a rising member of Parliament, also interested her and seemed to her practical mind a better risk than Comus. When the tea was served, Comus snatched up a silver basket containing the only bread and butter sandwiches and dashed off to feed the swans. Returning with the basket, an heirloom of the de Frey family, Comus asked permission to keep it as a souvenir of the delightful tea party.

Elaine did not wish to part with the piece of silver, but Comus made such a scene that she finally conceded to his wishes.

One fine June morning, all of London society had turned out to ride, walk, or sit in the chairs along the Row. Courtney Youghal was there discussing the theater with Lady Veula Croot. In a secluded part of the Row, Elaine and Comus had rented chairs. The two had drifted apart slightly because of small unpaid loans, which Comus had requested, and because of the affair of the silver basket. That morning, Comus again asked Elaine to lend him money—five pounds to pay a gambling debt. She promised to send him two pounds by messenger and curtly asked to be excused. He had hurt her pride and alarmed her practical sense of caution. As she was leaving the Row, she met Courtney. Over the luncheon table, they became engaged.

At an exhibition at the Rutland Galleries, Comus learned of Elaine's engagement. Elaine had intended to write Comus a gracious but final note, but instead she went to visit her cousin Suzette to break the news of her engagement. When Elaine returned home after her call, she found a letter from Comus awaiting her. In the letter, he thanked her for the loan, returned the money, and promised to return the silver basket in lieu of a wedding gift.

Francesca Bassington learned of the engagement, a blow to her elaborate plans, from the inveterate gossip, George St. Michael. She informed Comus that he must take a position in West Africa, for which Henry Greech had made arrangements. With his eyes on the Van der Meulen masterpiece, Comus asked his mother if she could not sell something. Mrs. Bassington was fiercely angry at such a suggestion and scolded him severely.

That night, lonely Comus watched the play from the stalls of the Straw Exchange Theatre. He envied Courtney and Elaine and their circle of friends. Francesca learned from St. Michael, her usual source, that Emmeline was to be married but only after a long engagement. Therefore, her beloved house on Blue Street was safe for a time. Francesca entertained at a dull dinner party in honor of her son's departure—a party to which none of Comus' friends was invited.

In the meantime, Courtney and Elaine were taking their wedding trip on the Continent. During their honeymoon, they soon discovered that neither loved the other and that the marriage was not likely to be successful. Comus Bassington had been exiled to West Africa and was bored and unhappy. Shortly before Christmas, Francesca received a cablegram saying that Comus was dangerously ill. To calm herself, she walked in the park; for the first time, she realized how selfish her love for her possessions, especially the Van der Meulen, had been. During the time she was walking, her brother brought an eminent critic to inspect the masterpiece. She returned to the house and found a cablegram announcing the death of Comus. A few minutes later, Henry Greech arrived to inform her that the Van der Meulen masterpiece was not an original but only a good copy. While his voice buzzed on and on, Francesca sat stricken among her prized pieces of silver, bronze, and porcelain—all of them as beautiful and soulless as Francesca herself.

Critical Evaluation:

The Unbearable Bassington synthesizes the attitudes, ideas, techniques, stylistic manner-isms, and narrative quirks that made Saki one of the most entertaining and provocative writers in Edwardian England. It was also his first novel and represents his most serious attempt to gain recognition as an important literary artist. The great artistic merit of *The Unbearable Bassington* suggests that, had Saki not been killed in World War I, he might well have ranked with Aldous Huxley as a satirical chronicler of the disillusioned, disintegrating British upper class in the years following the war.

The Unbearable Bassington immediately impresses the reader as a vivid, brilliant, amusing, ironical portrait of pre-World War I upper-class English society. As a member of that group,

Saki knew it intimately and, although he never seriously questioned the social and political institutions that supported it—the rigid class system, economic and social injustice, and imperialism—he saw its brittleness, shallowness, frivolity, and materialism, and he described it with a deft and bitter wit that is as provoking as it is amusing. If most of the personages are more caricature than character, they are a colorful crew, in constant motion and conflict. The dialogue is made up of a steady stream of acute observations, sharp, witty exchanges, and brilliant epigrams. The social rituals, subtle class distinctions, and special mannerisms of the group are sketched with both careful precision and ironical understatement.

There is more to *The Unbearable Bassington* than a witty description of a superficial social strata. The real importance of the novel depends on the seriousness of the action and the fates of the primary characters. Saki reveals his true feelings about not only his own social grouping but also life in general. At the center of *The Unbearable Bassington* is the tragicomic mother-son relationship of the two "unbearable" Bassingtons, Comus and Francesca.

Comus' unbearableness is mitigated by his wit, his liveliness, and his honest awareness of, and ironical attitude toward, the self-destructive streak that guarantees he will do precisely the wrong thing at exactly the wrong time to destroy any chance he may have for success or happiness. He is frustrated by his Edwardian society and alienated from it. He desperately wants to belong to it, yet he systematically botches every opportunity he has to consolidate his position in it, first in driving off Emmeline Chetrof and then, more important, in alienating himself from Elaine de Frey. It is impossible to say whether these impulsive, apparently subconscious, self-defeating actions are the result of a curious integrity or a weak perversity.

The love-hate relationship Comus feels toward his social milieu is most intensely focused in his feelings toward his mother. When Comus systematically ruins his chances for "good" marriages, does he do it to upset his mother's plans? If so, is it hostility? Or perhaps resentment at being "used" to assure her financial security? Or love—an attempt to force her to come out of her materialistic shell and behave toward him as a real mother?

The climax of the relationship comes when, after Comus has lost Elaine to Courtney Youghal, they discuss his future. He suggests they "sell something"—meaning the "Van der Meulen" painting—in order to give him the capital to go into business. She refuses and so, discouraged, Comus agrees to try West Africa, where he withers and dies.

In view of the close identification of Comus' fate with the picture, it is difficult to understand the critical objections to the final revelation that the "Van der Meulen" is, in fact, a fake. The pathos and bitterness that emerge from *The Unbearable Bassington* are due to the fact that, at the end, having chosen her material objects over her son, Francesca discovers, too late, how much she really loved and needed him and how little her possessions really matter. Thus, Henry Greech's final revelation that the picture is phoney, told to Francesca as she sits clutching the cablegram informing her of Comus' death, brings together all the book's thematic and emotional elements into a bitterly ironic and dramatically potent conclusion. Without it, the book's ending would be merely sad; with it, the finale touches the fringes of tragedy—but only the fringes.

Neither Comus nor his mother are the stuff of which real tragedy can be made. Their lives are too artificial, their preoccupations too trivial, their values too frivolous, and their flaws too venal to be taken too seriously. Nevertheless, the antiheroic view of life that has developed and flourished since Saki's time makes the poignancy and absurdity of their final situation most vivid and acceptable to the modern reader. If Saki was the chronicler of a society and world that vanished with World War I, his attitude toward that world seems especially valid for the complex, ambiguous world that succeeded it.

Bibliography:

Baring, Maurice. Introduction to *The Unbearable Bassington*, by Saki. New York: Viking, 1928. Thematic analysis of the work; calls it "an ironic tragedy on a high level." Believes Saki possessed a stoic view of life, recognizing the fragility of human relationships but resigned to struggle for the preservation of a civilized society.

Bloom, Harold, ed. *Twentieth Century British Literature*. Vol. 4. New York: Chelsea House, 1987. Collection of excerpts from reviews by eminent literary critics of the early twentieth century. Allows readers to place *The Unbearable Bassington* in the context of Saki's career, and relates it to his short stories; also comments on the quality of satire in the novel.

Gillen, Charles H. *H. H. Munro (Saki)*. New York: Twayne, 1969. General survey of the novelist's career as a historian, journalist, short-story writer, novelist, and playwright. Surveys the critical reception of *The Unbearable Bassington*; explains how the novel summarizes themes present throughout Saki's writings and discusses his handling of issues involving sexuality.

Langguth, A. J. *Saki: A Life of Hector Hugh Munro*. New York: Simon & Schuster, 1981. Well researched and well written biography integrating literary analysis with details of Saki's life. A chapter on *The Unbearable Bassington* reviews biographical genesis of the work and comments on characterization. Judges the novel a mixed success.

Spears, George James. *The Satire of Saki*. New York: Exposition Press, 1963. Demonstrates how Saki uses a number of satiric techniques in the novel to explore the "will to destruction" residing in humankind; notes how he manages to evoke sympathy for the mother in the story.

THE UNBEARABLE LIGHTNESS OF BEING

Type of work: Novel
Author: Milan Kundera (1929-   )
Type of plot: Political
Time of plot: 1960's and 1970's
Locale: Czechoslovakia and Switzerland
First published: Nesnesitelná lehkost bytí, 1984 (English translation, 1984)

> *Principal characters:*
> TOMAS, a surgeon
> TEREZA, Tomas' wife
> SABINA, an artist, Tomas' mistress
> FRANZ, a university lecturer, Sabina's lover

The Story:

Tomas was visiting a provincial town in Czechoslovakia to perform surgery when he met Tereza in a café, where she worked as a waitress. Shortly after his return to Prague, she turned up at his apartment with a heavy suitcase. They made love immediately. She came down with flu, and he was unable to throw her out for a week afterward. Even when he had installed her in an apartment of her own, he was unable to leave her. Although Tomas loved Tereza as he did no other woman, he was unable to give up seeing other women. Chief among these was the artist Sabina. Sabina resembled Tomas in her wish not to be weighed down by the heavy burden of love and in her tendency to betray those who threatened her freedom. At Tomas' request, Sabina found work for Tereza in a photographic darkroom and encouraged her to develop her talent for photography. The two women became friends, though the relationship was affected by Tereza's awareness of Sabina's continuing relationship with Tomas.

Tomas married Tereza and bought her a dog, Karenin. Both actions were partly motivated by an attempt to make amends for his womanizing. Tereza's efforts to tolerate Tomas' lifestyle were undermined by her recurrent dreams, which revealed her inability to accept his infidelities. When he saw the suffering his actions caused her, Tomas was racked by guilt, but he was unable to stop seeing other women.

Following the liberalization of Czechoslovakia under the leadership of Alexander Dubček (the Prague Spring), Soviet tanks rolled into Prague and the military occupation began. Tereza roamed the streets with her camera, capturing the horrors of the occupation on film. She gave the film to foreign visitors to smuggle out of the country and publish abroad. Tomas took up an offer of a job in Zurich, Switzerland, and moved there with Tereza. His passport was taken as he crossed the border. If he ever went back, it would be for the rest of his life.

Sabina was already living in Geneva. She became involved with Franz, a university lecturer. Franz was married to Marie-Claude, but left his wife to be with Sabina. When he turned up at Sabina's apartment, however, she was gone, leaving no forwarding address.

Tereza became worn down by Tomas' infidelities and fled back to Prague, which she dubbed the country of the weak. Tomas could not resist the pull of Tereza and followed her. Since the Czech borders were closed at that time, he knew that they could not escape again.

Tomas wrote a piece for a newspaper commenting on the guilt of the Soviet authorities which was interpreted as subversive. When he refused to sign a retraction proposed by the secret police, he had to resign from his job as a surgeon (since he was an employee of the state), and took a job as a window cleaner.

In an ironic twist, Tomas and Tereza learned that when they believed they were acting to oppose the regime, they may actually have helped it. Tereza discovered that her photographs could have been used by the secret police to identify opponents of the occupation. When Tomas was interrogated by the secret police, he lied about the appearance of the editor who commissioned his article, only to unwittingly implicate another editor who, unknown to him, resembled his made-up description.

Tomas' work as a window cleaner gave him plenty of opportunities for assignations with women. He was something of a hero to his clients, who knew that he must have refused to cooperate with the regime in order to have been hounded out of medical practice. Tereza, in an attempt to understand Tomas' appetite for extramarital sex, turned the tables on him. She had sex with a man who protected her from some abuse in the bar where she worked. When it was suggested to her that the whole scene may have been set up by the secret police as a black-mailing device, she developed a strong desire to leave Prague. She and Tomas went to live and work on a farm in the country: he as a driver, she as a cowherd. Their dog Karenin contracted cancer and died. Tereza reflected that her love for Karenin was in a sense superior to her love for Tomas, since she never asked the dog for anything in return, whereas she always wanted Tomas not to cheat on her. Tomas, however, told her that he was happy in the countryside, where he did not carry on affairs, presumably from lack of opportunity.

One day, a farmworker dislocated his shoulder and Tomas had to put it back in place. The worker, feeling happy, suggested that they drive to a nearby town to go dancing. On the way back, the truck had a flat tire. Tomas and Tereza set about changing the tire, and were accidentally crushed to death. Sabina learned of their deaths in Paris. She moved to California, where she enjoyed considerable success selling her paintings. She continued to live in avoidance of the weight of love and commitment, weight having killed Tomas and Tereza.

Critical Evaluation:

The Czech writer Milan Kundera is widely considered one of Europe's most outstanding novelists. In 1975, his books were denounced as counterrevolutionary and banned by the Czech Communist government. Partly as a result of this, he is often labeled a dissident, in spite of his conviction that his works are not political. His characters are not representatives of any ideology, but unique individuals whose viewpoints are challenged and developed by personal and social dilemmas. Kundera's works offended the Czech Communist government because they are emphatically apolitical; they insist on the primacy of the individual. Kundera's novels do not assert, but rather they pose questions and search for answers: He never knows which of his characters are right.

In line with this stance, his novels, *The Unbearable Lightness of Being* included, show the influence of writers such as Miguel de Cervantes, Franz Kafka, and Denis Diderot, in that the novels dismiss conventional novelistic structures in favor of parallel explorations of related themes, multiple standpoints represented by different characters, and integration of dreams, fantasy, and philosophical contemplation with realistic narrative. *The Unbearable Lightness of Being* was published in 1984 to great critical acclaim. This novel is notable for its bold juxtapositions: an intimate love story set against the backdrop of the Prague invasion, the subtle workings of human relationships set against larger metaphysical truths. Kundera views his characters with a sharp ironic insight balanced by immense compassion and humor. He is arguably one of the wisest observers of the pathos and paradoxes of adult love.

The novel develops a theme that had recurred in a minor way in all of Kundera's previous novels and some of his poetry: the opposition between heaviness and lightness. Tomas espouses the philosophy of lightness, which for him means the pursuit of many sexual liaisons without the burden of love and commitment. As the narrator comments, however, the heavier the burden, the more real one's life becomes; the absence of a burden makes one take leave of the earth and become as insignificant as one is free. Tomas' opposite is Tereza, who arrives with her heavy suitcase and cannot be brushed off. His commitment to lightness and consequent resistance to fidelity to Tereza is counterbalanced throughout the novel by a highly significant metaphor: Tereza seen by Tomas as an abandoned child sent downstream in a bulrush basket and washed up against his bed. The narrator repeatedly insists on the power of this metaphor over Tomas: How can he resist such an image? Tereza's fidelity to Tomas is described as the one pillar that anchors their relationship to the ground. As he becomes more closely involved with her, her grief over his womanizing weighs heavily on both of them. Tomas eventually embraces the burden of this heavy relationship, choosing to be with Tereza over a new job, a home, and freedom in Switzerland.

Sabina's devotion to lightness is more complete. She maintains lightness by betraying every expectation placed upon her: by the Communists in her youth, by those who wish her to denounce the Soviet regime; by her lover, Franz. Franz is somewhat of a parallel character with Tereza in that he favors commitment over levity. He is committed to the political ideal of the Grand March. Sabina, in contrast, had trouble with the political parades of her youth. She could never keep in step or remember the songs.

Significantly, Sabina, with her horror of being weighed down by love, by kitsch, and by heavy tombstones, is the only one of the four main characters who survives. The others are literally and metaphorically crushed to death by heavy weights: Tomas and Tereza are crushed by their truck, and Franz dies in pursuit of his earnest commitment to the Grand March, killed by a heavy blow. Tomas' and Tereza's love, and Franz's commitment, however, lend their lives significance and weight.

Related to the theme of lightness and weight is the "*Es muss sein!*" ("It must be!") motif, taken from a weighty musical phrase in a Beethoven quartet. When Tomas leaves Zurich to rejoin Tereza, he says to himself, "*Es muss sein!*" Almost immediately, a paradox strikes him: His relationship with Tereza was in fact born of a chain of laughable coincidences, such as his going to a particular town to do a surgery, and his stopping in a particular café, and so on. The narrator comments that perhaps Tomas' real "*Es muss sein!*," the overriding necessity of his existence, was his profession as a surgeon. That assumption is called into question when Tomas takes a certain joy in losing his profession and taking the job as a window cleaner. He becomes able to forget his work as soon as he goes home; he has found lightness and freedom from the vampire "*Es muss sein!*" that had sucked his blood. Finally, Tomas is left with the "*Es muss sein!*" of his womanizing. This weighty compulsion also drops away during his time with Tereza on the farm. The narrator talks of Tomas' curiosity to discover what lies beyond "*Es muss sein!*" The outcome of the novel suggests that perhaps it is death.

Kundera often uses musical structures and themes in his work, and this novel is no exception. Its structure has been called symphonic, in the sense that the first part presents the basic theme, the middle parts are explorations of the theme from the point of view of each of the characters, and the final part is the resolution of the theme. Kundera even uses musical terminology to describe the last two parts: "The Grand March" is *fortissimo* and *prestissimo*—loud, fast, and cynical in mood, with lots of events; "Karenin's Smile" is *pianissimo* and *adagio*, very soft, with few events.

Claire J. Robinson

Bibliography:

Aji, Aron, ed. *Milan Kundera and the Art of Fiction: Critical Essays.* New York: Garland, 1992. Useful collection of essays on the novels, including *The Unbearable Lightness of Being*, dealing with narrative technique and characterization.

Banerjee, Maria Nemcova. *Terminal Paradox: The Novels of Milan Kundera.* New York: Grove Weidenfeld, 1990. This philosophical and psychological analysis contains a comprehensive chapter on *The Unbearable Lightness of Being*. Well worth reading for its insights into Kundera's technique and characters.

Hruby, Peter. *Daydreams and Nightmares: Czech Communist and Ex-Communist Literature 1917-1987.* Boulder, Colo.: East European Monographs, 1990. Contains a lucid chapter on Milan Kundera's life and political and literary development. Briefly discusses individual works, including *The Unbearable Lightness of Being*.

Kundera, Milan. "An Interview with Milan Kundera." Interview by Jason Weiss. *New England Review and Bread Loaf Quarterly* 8, no. 3 (Spring, 1986): 405-410. Kundera discusses *The Unbearable Lightness of Being*, the recurrent themes in all his works, and the influence of Franz Kafka on his novels.

Review of Contemporary Fiction 9, no. 2 (Summer, 1989). Special issue devoted to Kundera and his works, including essays and an interview.

UNCLE SILAS
A Tale of Bartram-Haugh

Type of work: Novel
Author: Joseph Sheridan Le Fanu (1814-1873)
Type of plot: Gothic
Time of plot: Nineteenth century
Locale: England
First published: 1864

Principal characters:
MAUD RUTHYN, an English heiress
AUSTIN RUTHYN, her father
SILAS RUTHYN, her uncle and guardian
MILLY, Silas' daughter
DUDLEY, Silas' son
LADY MONICA KNOLLYS, Maud's cousin
DR. BRYERLY and
LORD ILBURY, trustees of the Ruthyn estate
MADAME DE LA ROUGIERRE, a governess
MEG HAWKES, a servant

The Story:

Maud Ruthyn had spent a lonely childhood in the great old house at Knowl. Her mother had died when she was very young, and her father, Austin Ruthyn, had become a recluse who seldom left the grounds of his estate. Disappointed in Parliament many years earlier, he had retired from public life to devote himself to scientific and literary studies. These had led him to Swedenborgianism, a doctrine suited to his eccentric and moral tastes. Maud knew him as a kindly but solitary and taciturn man.

For this reason, she never questioned him about her uncle Silas, her father's younger brother, who lived at Bartram-Haugh, a Derbyshire estate owned by Austin Ruthyn. His portrait as a handsome young man hung in the oak room at Knowl, but from vague hints and whispers of the servants, she knew that there was a mystery surrounding this relative whom she had never met, and that the scandal had clouded her father's life as well.

One of the few visitors at Knowl was Dr. Bryerly, a tall, ungainly man who always dressed in black and wore an untidy scratch wig. Like Maud's father, he was a Swedenborgian. The girl was greatly in awe of him, but she knew that he had her father's confidence. One day, Mr. Ruthyn showed her the key to a locked cabinet in his study. He was soon to go on a journey, he said, and after his departure she was to give the key to Dr. Bryerly.

Maud was a little past seventeen years old when her father employed a new governess, Madame de la Rougierre, a tall, masculine-looking woman with sly, smirking manners. Maud disliked her from the start. On every possible occasion, the governess questioned her charge about Mr. Ruthyn's will and business affairs; sometimes Maud thought the woman was deliberately spying on the household. One day, Madame de la Rougierre and her pupil walked to a ruined abbey near Knowl, where a strange young man accosted Maud. The girl was frightened by his coarse appearance and offensive manner, but Madame de la Rougierre ignored the incident.

Maud forgot the whole affair in her excitement over the arrival of Lady Monica Knollys, her father's cousin from Derbyshire and a brisk, sensible noblewoman. During the visit, Madame de la Rougierre pretended to be ill, and it turned out that she and Lady Monica had known each other in the past. When Lady Monica told Mr. Ruthyn that the governess was not a suitable companion for his daughter, he accused her of prejudice, and they had a terrible argument, as a result of which Lady Monica left Knowl abruptly. Before leaving, she warned Maud against Madame de la Rougierre and cautioned her always to be on guard against her. Lady Monica also told Maud that at one time her uncle Silas, whom she clearly did not like, had been suspected of murder, but that nothing had been charged. Later, Silas had become interested in religion.

A short time later, while Maud was walking with Madame de la Rougierre in the park, they saw on an unfrequented road a carriage with one woman as its only passenger. They continued on their way and met three men, among them the coarse young stranger who had approached Maud near the ruins of the abbey. All were tipsy and addressed the governess with rough familiarity. When one of the men tried to seize Maud, her screams attracted two gamekeepers. In a scuffle with the intruders, one of the gamekeepers was shot. Mr. Ruthyn and the servants tried to intercept the strangers at the park gates, but the men and their woman companion had disappeared.

Madame de la Rougierre was given notice not long afterward. One night, Maud fell asleep in her father's study. She awoke to find the governess going through his private papers. Informed of the midnight search, Mr. Ruthyn discharged the woman immediately.

When Mr. Ruthyn died suddenly of a heart attack, Maud understood at last to which journey he had been referring. She also learned that Dr. Bryerly had been her father's physician as well as his friend. With the key she gave him, the doctor unlocked the cabinet that contained Mr. Ruthyn's will. Its provisions disturbed Dr. Bryerly and filled Lady Monica with dismay. After varying bequests to relatives, friends, and servants, the remainder of Mr. Ruthyn's great estate was given to Maud, under the trusteeship of Dr. Bryerly, Lord Ilbury, Sir William Aylmer, and Mr. Penrose Cresswell. Silas Ruthyn was appointed Maud's guardian, with the stipulation that the girl was to live with him at Bartram-Haugh until her twenty-first birthday. Lady Monica immediately recalled the strange circumstances under which Mr. Charke, a turfman to whom Silas Ruthyn owed large gambling debts, had been found dead at Bartram-Haugh; only the fact that the body had been discovered in a bedroom locked from the inside had kept Silas from being charged with murder. In turn, Dr. Bryerly was disturbed by the knowledge that Silas would inherit her fortune if Maud died before her majority, and he advised that an attempt be made to have the provisions of the wardship put aside. Silas, however, refused to relinquish his guardianship. Maud, who interpreted the will as her father's wish that she vindicate her uncle's name by becoming his ward, announced that she would go to live with Silas in Derbyshire.

With her maid, Mary Quince, Maud traveled by carriage to Bartram-Haugh, where she found the house to be old and rambling; many of the rooms were closed and locked, and the grounds were wild and neglected. Although Silas welcomed his niece courteously and with many pious sentiments, it seemed to Maud that at times he was secretly laughing at her. His own rooms were furnished in great luxury. The quarters Maud shared with her cousin Milly, however, were shabby and bare. Milly was a loud, good-humored girl at whom her father had sneered because of her hoydenish manners. Maud took an immediate liking to her young relative. There was also a son, Dudley, but Milly said that her brother was seldom at home.

When Maud and her cousin went for a walk the next morning, they found the gate leading into Bartram Close locked and guarded by Meg Hawkes, the miller's rough-tongued daughter, who refused to let them pass. The girls entered the park by a seldom traveled path that Milly knew, and there they met a pleasant young gentleman who introduced himself as Mr. Carysbrook, a tenant at the nearby Grange.

Maud's only companion was Milly, and she saw very little of her uncle, who was addicted to laudanum and passed many of his days in a coma. Sometimes, the girls were summoned to sit in his room while he lay quietly in bed. One day, Dr. Bryerly appeared unexpectedly to transact some business with Silas. When the doctor questioned her, Maud replied that she was happy at Bartram-Haugh. Dr. Bryerly gave her his address in London and told her to communicate with him if the need should ever arise.

Early in December, Lady Monica Knollys opened her house at nearby Elverston and invited Maud and Milly to visit her. Among the guests at dinner was Mr. Carysbrook. Lady Monica told Maud that he was really Lord Ilbury, one of her trustees.

When Maud returned to Bartram-Haugh, she met Dudley Ruthyn, who was the same vulgar young man she had encountered twice before at Knowl. When she mentioned those meetings, Silas brushed the matter aside. He declared that the spirits of youth ran high at times, but that Dudley was a gentleman. Maud was relieved to learn that Milly disliked and feared her brother, and the girls avoided him as much as possible. When Meg Hawkes became ill, Maud brought her medicines and delicacies and won the strange girl's devotion.

Lord Ilbury called at Bartram-Haugh and expressed the hope that Maud would be allowed to visit his sister at the Grange, but Silas refused his consent. Dr. Bryerly also came and accused Silas of misusing his ward's property. Infuriated, Silas ordered him out of the house. A short time later, Milly was sent to study in a French convent. Maud missed her company, but her situation became even more unbearable when Dudley began to persecute her with proposals of marriage. Silas told her she should consider the matter seriously for a fortnight. Before that time passed, however, Dudley's unwelcome attentions abruptly ended when his secret marriage to Sarah Mangles, a barmaid, was revealed. Sarah was the woman Maud had seen in the carriage at Knowl. Silas was furious and sent Dudley and his bride away. Before his departure, Dudley offered to conduct Maud safely to Lady Monica for twenty thousand pounds. Convinced that this was another of his schemes, she refused. A few days later, she saw in the paper an announcement stating that Dudley and his wife had sailed for Melbourne.

Silas confessed to his ward that he faced final and complete ruin. To elude his creditors, he would be forced to send Maud to join Milly in France; he himself would travel by another route to join them there. Maud grew apprehensive, however, when she learned that her companion on the journey was to be Madame de la Rougierre, her former governess. Confined like a prisoner, she tried to communicate her plight to Lady Monica, but the servant she bribed to carry her letter returned the message to his master. With reproaches for her ingratitude and accusations against him, Silas told her that she was to leave for France immediately with Madame de la Rougierre; Mary Quince, the maid, would follow with him in a few days.

Guarded by her grim companion, Maud was taken to London and spent the night in an obscure hotel. The next night, they took a train to Dover, so Madame de la Rougierre informed her but when she awoke the next morning, she found herself in one of the upper chambers at Bartram-Haugh. Madame de la Rougierre said only that there had been a change in plans. Maud realized that her only hope lay in Meg Hawkes, who had unexpectedly appeared.

That night, Madame de la Rougierre drank some drugged wine intended for Maud and fell asleep on the girl's bed. Crouched in the shadows of an old press, Maud was surprised to see the window of the room swing inward and a man suspended by a rope clamber over the sill. The intruder was Dudley; the announcement of his departure for Australia had been another of

Silas' fabrications. Dazed, she saw him raise a spiked hammer and strike at the figure on the bed. When old Silas entered by the doorway and the two began to open a trunk containing the girl's jewelry, she took advantage of the noise and ran from the room. As she left the house, she encountered Tom Brice, a servant who was in love with Meg Hawkes. The man cursed his master's villainy and drove Maud to safety at Elverston.

She was so shaken by her experience that Lady Monica hurried her off to France at once, and two years passed before she learned what had happened after her flight. Silas had killed himself with an overdose of opium; Dudley had disappeared; and Madame de la Rougierre's body had been found buried in the courtyard, its whereabouts disclosed by Meg Hawkes's old father. Subsequent investigation had revealed that Maud's room was the chamber in which Charke had been found dead; the peculiar construction of the window frame explained how his murderer had been able to enter a room locked from the inside.

Eventually, Milly became the wife of a worthy clergyman. Meg Hawkes married Tom Brice and the two emigrated with money given them by Maud. Dr. Bryerly gave up his practice and undertook the management of the Ruthyn estates. Maud married Lord Ilbury and found new happiness as a wife and mother.

Critical Evaluation:

Uncle Silas is more than a sentimental, nineteenth century story of the designing uncle and the lovely heiress driven nearly insane by terror. It is a well-constructed novel, rambling in the Victorian fashion but highly effective in the mechanics of atmosphere and suspense. In fact, Joseph Sheridan Le Fanu protested against his novels being labeled as examples of the sensational school of fiction popularized by Wilkie Collins and Charles Reade. In his view, his fiction was a continuation of the type of tragic romance exemplified in *The Bride of Lammermoor* (1819) and other novels by Sir Walter Scott. The fact remains that readers have never deserted Le Fanu, and this novel represents his fiction at its best. Most notable is his handling of character and scene as they are sometimes seen in old Dutch paintings, with certain figures prominently in the foreground, others in the middle distance, and still others in the background. All are clearly visualized, however, and busy with whatever happens to be at hand. Uncle Silas and Madame de la Rougierre are creatures of terror in the foreground, but equally relevant are Dudley Ruthyn, Dr. Bryerly, Lady Monica, Milly, and Meg Hawkes, figures successively removed from the center of the action but no less necessary for the atmosphere and plot.

Uncle Silas may well represent the supreme achievement in the development of the gothic novel of terror. In the leisurely pace of its early chapters, the careful, thorough delineation of the setting and atmosphere, the ornate, sensuous prose style, the use of traditional gothic devices, and the creation of a sinister larger-than-life villain, *Uncle Silas* resembles the earlier masterpieces of "Monk" Lewis, Ann Radcliffe, and Charles Maturin. Nevertheless, the directness and simplicity of the action, the sharpness, subtlety, and psychological accuracy of the characterizations, and the carefully controlled first-person point of view all point to the sophisticated, economical modern suspense or crime novel.

The heroine of the book, Maud Ruthyn, is not particularly sympathetic; she is intellectually unimpressive, emotionally erratic, frequently snobbish, and occasionally haughty. She is, however, an excellent narrator. The reader sees everything through her eyes, and her fears become the reader's fears, but since her judgments are frequently inaccurate or incorrect, readers often see her danger and understand her mistakes long before she does. Like many gothic heroines, Maud realizes her precarious situation only after she has missed the opportunity to escape from it. It is primarily through her growing sense of desperation and panic, accompanied by a gradual, belated understanding of her plight, that Le Fanu develops the reader's own sense of impending doom.

As is often the case with gothic novels, the bad characters are more impressive than the good ones. The conspirators complement one another's particular villainies. Even the minor scoundrels, Dudley Ruthyn and "Pegtop" Hawkes, are sharply defined individually, whereas the major villains, Madame de la Rougierre and Uncle Silas, are two of the most memorable characters in the entire genre.

From the start, the governess is a dominating, grotesque, and foreboding presence. While Silas remains in the background, Madame de la Rougierre hovers over Maud, "gobbling and cackling shrilly" with her exaggerated French manners, her crude physical gestures, her effusive expressions of concern, all performed in such an overwrought and clearly hypocritical fashion that even Maud detects the conspiracy behind her actions. Her sudden reappearance in the secret room at Bartram-Haugh is one of the novel's greatest shocks.

It is, however, Silas Ruthyn who remains the novel's most vivid image. Even before Silas appears in person, Le Fanu has aroused curiosity about him through sinister hints, Austin Ruthyn's mysterious references, and Lady Monica's revelations. When Silas becomes an active character, he appears frightening and puzzling. He is associated, above all, with death. His health is precarious, and the atmosphere he projects, the objects with which he surrounds himself, the habits in which he indulges, all give off suggestions of mortality and impending doom. In him, the lines between reality and illusion and between life and death are blurred.

Yet the conspirators are not simply evil incarnate. While they have all the trappings of typical gothic villains, they are pathetic and even comic when their villainy is seen to be more the result of frustration and desperation than of outright evil. Dudley is a wastrel; he possesses good looks but neither the intellectual capacity nor the emotional stability necessary to make anything of himself. Madame de la Rougierre, despite her sinister behavior and grotesque looks, is revealed, in the end, to be weak and pitiable. She is, as Lady Monica suggests early in the book, nothing more than a crude, petty thief, mixed up in a conspiracy she only half understands and suffering from a weakness for alcohol that finally costs her her life.

Even Silas is almost as much to be pitied as condemned. A man of obvious talent and intellect, he has become dissipated and perverted by weakness of character. All of his life he has made the wrong decisions, bet on the wrong horses, and seen his efforts turn out badly. To a man as firmly committed to the idea of hereditary aristocracy as Silas, the spectacle of his son Dudley is the final disillusionment. Pressed by creditors, weakened by drug addiction, unsatisfied by his religious speculations, and painfully aware of his own worthlessness, Silas persecutes Maud as a last desperate attempt to salvage something out of his wasted life.

Bibliography:
Bowen, Elizabeth. "*Uncle Silas.*" In *Collected Impressions.* New York: Knopf, 1950. An incisive and appreciative analysis of *Uncle Silas* that places the novel on the same plane as Emily Brontë's *Wuthering Heights.*
Howes, Marjorie. "Misalliance and Anglo-Irish Tradition in Le Fanu's *Uncle Silas.*" *Nineteenth-Century Literature* 47, no. 2 (September, 1992)): 164-186. Analyzes themes of heritage and inheritance in *Uncle Silas.* Focusing on the character of Maud Ruthyn, the author develops a feminist critique of the problematic status of the Anglo-Irish. Informed and lucid use of literary theory enhances the critical discussion.
Le Fanu, Joseph. *Uncle Silas.* Edited by W. J. McCormack. Oxford, England: Oxford University Press, 1981. A scholarly edition, containing a corrected text, a Le Fanu chronology, a

bibliography, and a lengthy critical introduction that stresses connections with themes that emerged in later Irish authors such as W. B. Yeats and James Joyce. Also provides a comprehensive critical appraisal of the novel based on a sense of the central significance of deception in its formal design and complex plot.

McCormack, W. J. *Sheridan Le Fanu and Victorian Ireland*. Oxford, England: Clarendon Press, 1980. At the center of this definitive study of Le Fanu's life and times is an elaborate and sophisticated reading of *Uncle Silas*. Drawing on Le Fanu family papers and on Sheridan Le Fanu's intellectual and cultural background, this view of the novel acknowledges its place both as one of the landmark achievements of the gothic genre in English and as a revealing commentary on the mind-set of the Anglo-Irish class to which Le Fanu belonged.

Milbank, Alison. *Daughters of the House: Modes of the Gothic in Victorian Fiction*. New York: St. Martin's Press, 1992. Of the two chapters devoted to Le Fanu, one deals with *Uncle Silas* and offers an analysis of the interlinking of gothic, feminist, and Swedenborgian elements in the novel. The protagonist, Maud Ruthyn, is the focus of this critique.

UNCLE TOM'S CABIN
Or, Life Among the Lowly

Type of work: Novel
Author: Harriet Beecher Stowe (1811-1896)
Type of plot: Social realism
Time of plot: Mid-nineteenth century
Locale: Kentucky and Mississippi
First published: 1852

> *Principal characters:*
> UNCLE TOM, a slave
> EVA ST. CLARE, the daughter of a wealthy Southerner
> SIMON LEGREE, a planter
> ELIZA, a runaway slave
> TOPSY, a young slave

The Story:

Because his Kentucky plantation was encumbered by debt, Mr. Shelby made plans to sell one of his slaves to his chief creditor, a New Orleans slave dealer named Haley. The dealer shrewdly selected Uncle Tom as part payment on Mr. Shelby's debt. While they were discussing the transaction, Eliza's child, Harry, came into the room. Haley wanted to buy Harry too, but at first Shelby was unwilling to part with the child. Eliza listened to enough of the conversation to be frightened. She confided her fears to George Harris, her husband, a slave on an adjoining plantation. George, who was already bitter because his master had put him to work in the fields when he was capable of doing better work, promised that some day he would have his revenge upon his hard masters. Eliza had been brought up more indulgently by the Shelbys, and she begged him not to try anything rash.

After supper in the cabin of Uncle Tom and his wife, Aunt Chloe, the Shelby slaves gathered for a meeting. They sang songs, and young George Shelby, who had eaten his supper there, read from the Bible. In the big house, Mr. Shelby signed the papers making Uncle Tom and little Harry the property of Haley. Eliza, learning her child's fate from some remarks of Mr. Shelby to his wife, fled with her child, hoping to reach Canada and safety. Uncle Tom, hearing of the sale, resigned himself to the wisdom of Providence.

The next day, after Haley had discovered his loss, he set out to capture Eliza; however, she had a good start. Moreover, Mrs. Shelby purposely delayed the pursuit by serving a late breakfast. When her pursuers came in sight, Eliza escaped across the Ohio River by jumping from one floating ice cake to another, young Harry in her arms. Haley hired two slave-catchers, Marks and Loker, to track Eliza through Ohio. For their trouble, she was to be given to them. They set off that night.

Eliza found shelter in the home of Senator and Mrs. Bird. The senator took her to the house of a man known to aid fugitive slaves. Uncle Tom, however, was not so lucky. Haley made sure Tom would not escape by shackling his ankles before taking him to the boat bound for New Orleans. When young George Shelby heard that Tom had been sold, he followed Haley on his horse. George gave Tom a dollar as a token of his sympathy and told him that he would buy him back one day.

At the same time, George Harris began his escape. White enough to pass as a Spaniard, he appeared at a tavern as a gentleman and took a room there, hoping to find a station on the underground railway before too long. Eliza was resting at the home of Rachel and Simeon Halliday when George Harris arrived in the same Quaker settlement.

On board the boat bound for New Orleans, Uncle Tom saved the life of young Eva St. Clare, and in gratitude, Eva's father purchased the slave. Eva told Tom he would now have a happy life, for her father was kind to everyone. Augustine St. Clare was married to a woman who imagined herself sick and therefore took no interest in her daughter Eva. He had gone north to bring back his cousin, Miss Ophelia, to provide care for the neglected and delicate Eva. When they arrived at the St. Clare plantation, Tom was made head coachman.

Meanwhile, Loker and Marks were on the trail of Eliza and George. They caught up with the fugitives, and there was a fight in which George wounded Loker. Marks fled, and so the Quakers who were protecting the runaways took Loker along with them and gave him medical treatment.

Unused to lavish Southern customs, Miss Ophelia tried to understand the South. Shocked at the extravagance of St. Clare's household, she attempted to bring order out of the chaos, but she received no encouragement. Indulgent in all things, St. Clare was indifferent to the affairs of his family and his property. Uncle Tom lived an easy life in the loft over the stable. He and little Eva became close friends, with St. Clare's approval. Sometimes St. Clare had doubts regarding the morality of the institution of slavery, and, in one of these moods, he bought an odd pixielike child, named Topsy, for his prim and proper New England cousin to educate.

Eva grew more frail. Knowing that she was about to die, she asked her father to free his slaves, as he had so often promised. After Eva's death, St. Clare began to read his Bible and to make plans to free all his slaves. He gave Topsy to Miss Ophelia legally, so that the spinster might rear the child as she wished. Then, one evening, he tried to separate two quarreling men. He received a knife wound in the side and died shortly afterward. Mrs. St. Clare, however, had no intention of freeing the slaves, and she ordered that Tom be sent to the slave market.

At a public auction, he was sold to a brutal plantation owner named Simon Legree. Legree drank heavily, and his plantation house had fallen to ruin. He kept dogs for the purpose of tracking runaway slaves. At the slave quarters, Tom was given his sack of corn for the week, told to grind it himself and bake the meal into cakes for his supper. At the mill, he aided two women. In return, they baked his cakes for him. He read selections from the Bible to them.

For a few weeks, Tom quietly tried to please his harsh master. One day, he helped a sick woman by putting cotton into her basket. For this act, Legree ordered him to flog the woman. When Tom refused, his master had him flogged until he fainted. A slave named Cassy came to Tom's aid. She told Tom the story of her life with Legree and of a young daughter who had been sold years before. Then she went to Legree's apartment and tormented him. She hated her master, and she had power over him. Legree was superstitious. When she talked, letting her eyes flash over him, he felt as though she were casting an evil spell. Haunted by the secrets of his guilty past, he drank until he fell asleep. He had forgotten his fears by the next morning, however, and he knocked Tom to the ground with his fist. Meanwhile, far to the north, George and Eliza and young Harry were making their way slowly through the stations on the underground railway toward Canada.

Cassy and Emmeline, another slave, were determined to make their escape. Knowing the consequences if they should be caught, they tricked Legree into thinking they were hiding in the swamp. When Legree sent dogs and men after them, they sneaked back into the house and hid in the garret. Legree suspected that Tom knew where the women had gone and decided to beat the truth out of his slave. He had Tom beaten until the old man could neither speak nor stand. Two days later, George Shelby arrived to buy Tom back, but he came too late. Tom was dying. When George threatened to have Legree tried for murder, Legree mocked him. George struck Legree in the face and knocked him down.

Still hiding in the attic, Cassy and Emmeline pretended they were ghosts. Frightened, Legree drank harder than ever. George Shelby helped them to escape. Later, on a riverboat headed north, the two women discovered a lady named Madame de Thoux, who said she was George Harris' sister. With this disclosure, Cassy learned also that Eliza, her daughter who had been sold years before, was the Eliza who had married George and, with him and her child, had escaped safely to Canada. These relatives were reunited in Canada after many years. In Kentucky, George Shelby freed all his slaves when his father died. He said he freed them in the name of Uncle Tom.

Critical Evaluation:

In Harriet Beecher Stowe's view, slavery was an evil against which anyone professing Christianity must protest. *Uncle Tom's Cabin*, was precisely such a protest. Stowe believed that the debate over slavery often missed or minimized the essential point that the slave family was torn apart by the institution. Her own strong family orientation informs the novel throughout, even as her unconventional pursuit of a career as a professional writer gave her the means of conveying her thoughts to the wider world.

Writing this novel gave Stowe a professional outlet. Like many educated nineteenth century American women, she experienced frustration because there were few positions for women in the professions. Thus there was little opportunity for educated women to use professional voices to influence the course of American life. Like her father, husband, and brothers, Stowe felt called to preach. Denied a pulpit, she used *Uncle Tom's Cabin* as her sermon, her means of educating the world about a system that she was convinced was evil and must be stopped.

As a professional writer of the nineteenth century, Stowe knew that there was a large female reading public. Consequently, much of the novel appeals to those readers as it paints slavery as a male-devised system that women are called upon to correct. She creates several strong female characters whose common sense and strong human sympathy recoil from slavery's inhumanity. Throughout the novel, human feeling is raised above the economics of self-interest and the expediency of laws. Moreover, Stowe "feminized" the slave narrative, stressing Eliza's heroic escape from bondage with her son as well as the ingenious plan used by Cassy to free herself from Simon Legree. Prior to her novel, most accounts of slavery, such as Frederick Douglass' *Narrative of the Life of Frederick Douglass* (1845), were told from the male perspective and celebrated male courage and resourcefulness.

Uncle Tom's Cabin provides a panorama of nineteenth century American culture, which suggests that its author was a precursor of the realistic writers who dominated the literary scene after the Civil War. The novel contains innumerable characters of all types and backgrounds: slaves and slave catchers, slaveowners and Quakers, a self-pitying Southern belle and an unsympathetic New Englander, mothers and children, unprincipled politicians and slovenly cooks, the careless and the deeply caring, the sexually exploited and the sadistic, the angelic and the impish. It includes scenes along the shores of Lake Erie and in the currents of the Mississippi River, in Ohio and in Kentucky, in Arkansas and in Canada. Using a broad canvas as she did, Stowe hoped to show that slavery, far from an isolated and temporary problem, was institutionalized and nationalized and affected not only slaves and slaveowners but the entire country. Moreover, she showed that persons of all types, from the good to the evil, were caught in the power of the institution.

Uncle Tom's Cabin has been criticized on several grounds. It is said to lack form and control; its social purpose is sometimes seen as incompatible with fine aesthetic qualities. However, the moralism and didacticism were, in a sense, part of Stowe's aesthetic. That is, she did not believe that art was above morality but that it was activated by it. She did not believe in art for art's sake, but rather in the power of art to do good.

The novel's titular hero has been criticized for his willingness to submit to white men's arbitrary power and physical abuse. It is well, however, to remember Tom in the light of Stowe's Christianity. To her, his submission was not to tyranny but to Christian principle, and in that submission lay his power to change the world for the better. Stowe created Tom in the image of Jesus Christ.

"Critical Evaluation" by William L. Howard

Bibliography:

Adams, John R. *Harriet Beecher Stowe*. Updated ed. Boston: Twayne, 1989. A basic study of Stowe's writings that includes biographical information. The chapter on *Uncle Tom's Cabin* places its dual plot in the Victorian tradition and postulates that Uncle Tom's passive suffering and Eliza's rebellion are two sides of Stowe's psyche.

Crozier, Alice C. *The Novels of Harriet Beecher Stowe*. New York: Oxford University Press, 1969. Notes that Stowe was less interested in the novel as art than in the novel as history. Traces the influence of the British writers Sir Walter Scott and George Gordon, Lord Byron. Comments on the cultural context in which the novels were written, which accounts not only for the Victorian sentimentality of *Uncle Tom's Cabin* but also for a distinctively American realism that anticipates Mark Twain.

Foster, Charles H. *The Rungless Ladder: Harriet Beecher Stowe and New England Puritanism*. New York: Cooper Square, 1970. This study of Stowe's inner struggle with New England Puritanism identifies what she read and how that affected her life and writings. It shows that *Uncle Tom's Cabin* was a product of her religious thinking and personal anguish. Stowe projects herself and her own struggles, particularly her attempt to reconcile herself with the death of one of her children, onto the novel's characters.

Hedrick, Joan D. *Harriet Beecher Stowe: A Life*. New York: Oxford University Press, 1994. A good source of information about Stowe's career as a writer. Traces her writing of *Uncle Tom's Cabin* from her initial resolve, through her decision to address the sexual exploitation of female slaves, to her effort to substantiate the novel with facts collected in *A Key to Uncle Tom's Cabin*. Also mentions her work on behalf of emancipation of slaves in both America and England after publication of the novel.

Wagenknecht, Edward. *Harriet Beecher Stowe: The Known and the Unknown*. New York: Oxford University Press, 1965. A character study of Stowe, treating her as daughter, wife, and mother, as well as writer.

UNCLE VANYA

Type of work: Drama
Author: Anton Chekhov (1860-1904)
Type of plot: Impressionistic realism
Time of plot: Nineteenth century
Locale: Russia
First published: Dyadya Vanya, 1897 (English translation, 1914); first performed, 1899

> *Principal characters:*
> ALEXANDR SEREBRYAKOV, a retired professor
> YELENA ANDREYEVNA, his twenty-seven-year-old wife
> SONYA ALEXANDROVNA, his daughter by his first wife
> MARYA VOYNITSKY, the widow of a privy councillor and mother of his
>   first wife
> IVAN VOYNITSKY (UNCLE VANYA), her son
> MIHAIL ASTROV, a doctor
> MARINA, an old nurse

The Story:

Astrov, the doctor, called to attend the retired Professor Serebryakov, who had complained all night of pains in his legs. To the doctor's annoyance, the professor had left for a long walk with his wife, Yelena, and his daughter, Sonya. Astrov told the old nurse, Marina, that he was so overworked he felt a hundred years old. He also felt that, having worked with weak, discontented people for years, he had become as strange as they. Caring for nothing and no one, he wondered if people living a hundred years hence would remember men like him who had struggled to beat out the road for them.

Marina explained that the professor had completely changed the routine of the house, so that everyone waited on him and routine work was fitted in where possible. Ivan Voynitsky enviously described the fortunate life the professor had. The professor lived on the estate of his first wife, whose mother doted on his every word; he was retired now and writing as he pleased; and he had a new and beautiful young wife to cater to him. It had, however, been Ivan, Sonya's Uncle Vanya, who had blindly followed his mother's ideals and made the estate a splendidly productive place that could supply all the professor's needs. Only recently had Ivan realized how selfish the professor was. Ivan told his mother that he could no longer bear to hear of the pamphlets that had been her life for the last fifty years.

When the professor came in, he immediately excused himself to return to his writing. Yelena, apologizing to the doctor, said that her husband was well again. Both Ivan and the doctor admired her extravagantly, and the doctor invited her and Sonya to come to his estate to see his trees. A crank on the subject of trees, the doctor wanted to restore the countryside to its state before the peasants had indiscriminately cut down the forests. Yelena realized Sonya was attracted to the doctor. Yelena was bored with everything, even Ivan's love for her.

When the professor again complained of pains in his legs, he kept his wife awake for two nights. Believing that he had earned the right to be disagreeable and tyrannical at his age, and feeling that he was in a vault with stupid people who made foolish conversation, he refused to see the doctor he had summoned. He begged not to be left with Ivan, who would talk him to death. Only Marina seemed to be able to handle him; she led him away so that the others could rest.

Yelena asked Ivan to try to reconcile everyone. When Ivan declared his love to her again, she left him. Ivan realized he could have fallen in love with her ten years before and might even have married her if he had not been wrapped up in the ideal of fulfilling the professor's wishes. He felt cheated in the realization that the retired professor was a nonentity.

Ivan and the doctor continued the drinking they had started while the doctor waited to see the professor. Sonya asked them both to stop; Ivan because he was living on illusions, the doctor because she did not want him to destroy himself. She tried to tell him obliquely that she loved him, but he felt that his reactions had become blunted. He would never be able to love anyone, though Yelena might be able to turn his head.

Yelena and Sonya effected a reconciliation when Yelena explained that she had married Sonya's father in the belief that she loved him, only to find she was in love with an ideal. Having lost that illusion, she found herself very unhappy. Sonya, glad to make friends with her, was happy about everything; she had spoken at last to the doctor, even if he had not understood her.

While waiting for the hour at which the professor had asked all the family to join him, Yelena complained of being bored. Sonya suggested that she help on the estate. When Yelena declined all suggestions, Ivan told her she was too indolent to do anything. To make matters worse, her indolence was catching, for he had stopped work to follow her, as had Sonya and the doctor, who used to come once a month but now came daily. Since Yelena seemed to have mermaid blood in her veins, he said, she should let herself go for once and fall in love with a watersprite. Yelena was indignant. Ivan, as a peace offering, went to get her some autumn roses.

Sonya asked Yelena's help. She knew the doctor came to see Yelena, not even realizing Sonya was there. Yelena decided to speak to him in Sonya's behalf. When she did, he laughed at her for pretending she did not know why he came. Then he kissed her. Yelena halfheartedly held him off until she saw Ivan returning with the roses.

The professor, not content with country living but unable to live in the city on the income from the estate, suggested that they sell the estate, invest most of the money, and buy a small place in Finland with the remainder. His plan was greeted with horror, particularly by Ivan, who was driven almost mad as he felt the estate slipping away from Sonya, the work of twenty-five years undone. He explained how the estate had been bought for Sonya's mother and handed on to Sonya; how he had paid off the mortgage and made the place productive; how Sonya and he had slaved on the property by day and over books by night with only the professor in mind. Feeling cheated, he rushed away while the professor declared that he could no longer live under the same roof with Ivan. Yelena begged him to leave the place immediately, but to apologize to Ivan before they left. When the professor tried to make amends, Ivan shot at him twice, missing both times.

Marina, pleased with the arrangement, hoped that matters would settle down after the professor and his wife left. Astrov refused to go home before Ivan had given back the morphia he had taken from the doctor's bag. Ivan, saying he was a madman, begged for a way out, but the doctor laughed and said that the two of them, the only well-educated men in the district, had been swamped in the trivialities of country life and that they were both eccentric, a very normal human condition. After reconciliations all around, the professor and Yelena left, followed by Astrov. Marina rocked away with satisfaction, Ivan's mother went back to her pamphlets, and Sonya assured Ivan that they had completed their lives' work and would find rest in heaven.

Critical Evaluation:

Anton Chekhov's oeuvre opened Russian literature and world drama to the art of everyday trifles and occurrences. In exploring Russian society, Chekhov questioned the purpose of life, but he was less interested in finding an answer than in posing the right questions.

To understand Chekhov's drama, it is necessary to understand the milieu in which he wrote, the innovations that were changing Western theater practices, and the stance of the dramatist himself. Russia in the 1880's and 1890's was experiencing the erosion of rigid class distinctions that had characterized the *ancien régime*. Much of the landowning gentry was impoverished and under the necessity of selling off parcels of their large estates to the rising mercantile and industrial class. Serfdom had finally been abolished, and the enormous peasant class was faced with both displacement and new opportunities. The age of those great Russian novelists Fyodor Dostoevski and Leo Tolstoy was coming to a close, and as it did it was opening the way for a new kind of art. Throughout Western civilization, science and technology were modifying the lenses through which artists and philosophers looked at the world and humanity's place within it.

This was the age of literary realism and naturalism, and writers began to focus on the lives and problems of ordinary people. On the stage, the theater of social consciousness pioneered by Henrik Ibsen and August Strindberg gave rise to a new kind of dramaturgy and stagecraft. Chekhov took the realistic innovations of the Scandinavians one step further in creating his kind of naturalistic drama, a drama with no real beginnings or endings, and one that recognizes the complexities and continuities of life.

Chekhov, trained as a physician, was eminently suited for this kind of examination. His practice had carried him to all the levels of Russian society and intensified his objective observational powers. Initially acclaimed as a short story writer, he began to write for the theater in the early 1880's. The four plays considered his masterpieces—*The Seagull* (1896-1898), *Uncle Vanya* (1897-1899), *The Three Sisters* (1901), and *The Cherry Orchard* (1904)— emerged from the period during which Konstantin Stanislavsky and Nemirovich-Danchenko founded the Moscow Art Theatre, where Chekhov's plays first found successful productions. Chekhov did not, however, approve of the highly realistic and tragically inclined interpretations that the first productions of the Moscow Art Theatre gave to his plays. Until his death in 1904, he insisted that he had written comedies of Russian life.

Uncle Vanya, the second of Chekhov's plays produced by the Moscow Art Theatre, is a reworking of an earlier play from 1889 entitled *The Wood Demon (Leshy)*. *Uncle Vanya* eliminates many of the more romantic elements and rambling aspects of the earlier version and shifts some of the focus from the physician character (the wood demon of the 1889 play) to the new title character. Indeed, it has been argued that *Uncle Vanya* has no single protagonist, but rather four major characters, Ivan (Uncle Vanya), Dr. Astrov, Sonya, and Yelena. The critic Philip Bodinat went so far as to declare that the protagonist of the play is "the individual" as embodied by each of the four major characters in conflict with the stifling environment of provincial Russian life.

Certainly, *Uncle Vanya* depicts characters who have the potential to live fuller lives but who cannot escape from the rut of societal expectations and self-imposed restrictions. Chekhov draws these individuals sympathetically but critically. Ultimately, they are all frustrated in their attempts to embrace a more meaningful existence. They are offered the possibility of art, but this opportunity is repeatedly devalued. When Sonya pleads with Yelena to play the piano to celebrate their reconciliation, Yelena must first secure the permission of her husband, who is disturbed by the music when he is not feeling well; he refuses, and the two women must do without the music. Later, it is Yelena who is the agent obstructing the artistic impulse. She has asked to see Astrov's drawings of the forest intending to sound him out about his feelings for Sonya. He spreads them out before her and explains how they depict the destruction of the area, but when he realizes that she is bored by his passion, he whisks them out of sight.

Serebryakov, the retired professor, embodies a withered academic view of art as described in Vanya's angry outburst:

> A person lectures and writes about art for precisely twenty-five years, but he understands precisely nothing about art. For twenty-five years he's gone on chewing up and spitting out everyone else's ideas about realism, naturalism, and every other kind of nonsense. For twenty-five years he's been lecturing and writing about what intelligent people have known for a long time and what stupid people have no interest in. To put it bluntly, for twenty-five years he has been pouring from one empty pot into the next.

Vanya's anger and frustration stem from his long-held delusion that he was contributing to the world's knowledge by working to secure the means for the professor to carry on his writing.

Love, another means for rising above the mundane, is also thwarted throughout the play. Vanya's unrequited passion for Yelena is doubly painful because he realizes that he might have won her devotion had he wooed her when she was younger. Yelena confesses to Sonya that she once thought she loved her husband because of her fascination with his fame, but it was a hollow passion that could not endure. The attraction between Astrov and Yelena is thwarted by social and moral conventions, yet it also destroys any hope of Astrov's ever reciprocating Sonya's devotion.

The close of the play finds all of the characters in the same situation they had occupied before Serebryakov and Yelena descended on the estate. The one difference is that now they must live without the illusions of their hopes. Each must once again take up the stifling trifles of daily life to distract themselves from their lives of quiet desperation. Yet Chekhov has also revealed that what has transpired on stage is not the only conclusion to the dilemmas the characters face. In essence, what Chekhov has done is to throw out a challenge to the members of the audience to examine their own lives and expectations.

Jane Anderson Jones

Bibliography:
Bentley, Eric. "Craftsmanship in *Uncle Vanya*." In *Anton Chekhov's Plays*, translated and edited by Eugene K. Bristow. New York: Norton, 1977. Bentley shows that Chekhov's naturalism in *Uncle Vanya* is grounded in his mature psychological vision that life has no real endings.
Bordinat, Philip. "Dramatic Structure in Chekhov's *Uncle Vanya*." In *Chekhov's Great Plays: A Critical Anthology*, edited with an introduction by Jean-Pierre Barricelli. New York: New York University Press, 1981. Bordinat argues that *Uncle Vanya* follows classical dramatic construction if the protagonist is seen as "the individual" embodied in the four major characters. The conflict then becomes the individual's desire for happiness in the face of the provincial Russian "wasteland."
Melchinger, Siegfried. "*The Wood Demon* and *Uncle Vanya*." In *Anton Chekhov*, translated by Edith Tarcov. New York: Frederick Ungar, 1972. Melchinger analyzes how Chekhov re-worked his unsuccessful 1889 play, *The Wood Demon (Leshy)* into the groundbreaking 1897 *Uncle Vanya*. He focuses particularly on the parallel situations of Astrov and Vanya in the later play.
Peace, Richard. "*Uncle Vanya*." In *Chekhov: A Study of the Four Major Plays*. New Haven, Conn.: Yale University Press, 1983. Peace focuses on the symbolism of *Uncle Vanya* and discusses the significance in the play of tea drinking, the forest, the storm, birds and animals, and work.

Yermilov, V. "*Uncle Vanya*: The Play's Movement." In *Chekhov: A Collection of Critical Essays*, edited by Robert Louis Jackson. Englewood Cliffs, N.J.: Prentice-Hall, 1967. Discusses the use of musical and weather imagery in the play. Yermilov points out the cyclical movement of the play: The external situation at the end replicates the situation at the beginning, but internally everyone has changed.

UNDER FIRE
The Story of a Squad

Type of work: Novel
Author: Henri Barbusse (1873-1935)
Type of plot: Political
Time of plot: 1914-1915
Locale: France
First published: Le Feu: Journal d'une escouade, 1916 (English translation, 1917)

> *Principal characters:*
> VOLPATTE,
> EUDORE,
> POTERLOO, and
> JOSEPH MESNIL, French soldiers

The Story:

High up in the mountains, the rich old men had every type medical care at their sanatorium. When an obsequious servant softly told them that war had begun, they took the news in various ways. One said France must win; another thought it would be the last war.

Far down on the plain they could see specks, like ants, hurrying to and fro. Those thirty million men, in their common misery, held great power in their hands. When they became miserable enough, they would stop wars.

That morning, they came out of the dugouts to the sound of rifle fire and cannonading. They wore fantastic dress against the cold, the damp, and the mud, and all were incredibly dirty. As they stumbled out into the trenches, they reached inside their clothes to scratch their bare skins. As they walked along the trench, the oozy mud released each foot with a sticky sigh. Bertrand's squad, holding a secondary trench in the reserve line, was getting ready for another day. Lamuse, the ox man, was puffy around the eyes; he had been on fatigue duty during the night.

Three breathless fatigue men brought up the breakfast. One of the squad, Paradis, asked what was in the cans. When the mess man merely shrugged, Paradis looked in the cans and saw that there were kidney beans in oil, bully beef, pudding, and coffee.

One man explained to his neighbor the arrangement of the trenches, for he had seen a military map and had made calculations. There were more than six thousand miles of trenches on the French side and as many more on the German side. The French front was only an eighth part of the total world front. Just to think about it made one more insignificant, and it was terrible to imagine so much mud. The only possible way to look at the whole matter was to concentrate on dislodging the Germans in the opposite lines.

One man, a private, had once seen a captured Prussian colonel, who was being led along the communication trench. When the private kicked him, the officer nearly had a seizure to think that a subordinate had touched him. The squad agreed that the German officers were the real evil.

There was a disturbance just ahead; several important people were coming to visit. From their oaths and grunts it was clear that they were civilians. One of the visitors was so bold as to ask whether the coffee was good. The squad remembered the saying that a war can be won if the civilians can hold out.

When the mail came, rumors flew fast. Many were sure that their squad was soon to be sent to the Riviera for a long rest; one man had heard they were going to Egypt. The troops stopped gossiping when a company of African soldiers moved by; they concluded that an attack had been planned, for the Africans were notoriously ferocious fighters.

During a sharp attack, both of Volpatte's ears were almost severed. At the dressing station, the doctors bandaged his head. Volpatte was happy to be going to the rear, where at last he would be able to rest. After a long while, he came back to the trenches with his ears nicely sewed. When his comrades asked him about the hospital, he became so angry he could scarcely speak. Then it all came out; the hospital was swarming with malcontents, malingerers, and general shirkers. The worst were those assigned to the hospital for duty; they seemed to think they ran the whole war. The squad soothed Volpatte; let those who could, get by easily.

When the squad retired for a brief rest, they were billeted in a village where for an outrageous sum they rented a cow shed without walls. A door on boxes served as a table and a plank as a bench, but it was a wonderful experience to be above ground once more. The woman who ran the house sold them wine for twenty-two sous, although the established price was fifteen sous a bottle. Everywhere they went they heard the same story; the civilians were enduring all the hardships.

Eudore got a fourteen-day leave. His wife, a practical person, applied well in advance for a permit to go to the village of her husband's people. She ran a tiny inn with only one room, where she would have no privacy to entertain her man, whereas Eudore's people had a big house. Eudore arrived in his village after much delay with only seven days left of his furlough, but his wife was not there; her permit had not arrived. Fearing that he would miss her, he stayed with his parents and waited. Then she wrote to say that no permits were allowed for civilian travel. Eudore went to the mayor and got permission to go to his wife. It was raining very hard when he got off the train to walk the several additional miles to his home. On the way, he fell in with four poilus returning from leave. They tramped along together in the rain until they came to the inn. Eudore and his wife could not turn out the four poilus in the rain, and so all six of them spent the night on chairs in the tiny room. Early in the morning Eudore left; his furlough was over.

Fraternization with the enemy was strictly forbidden. While out looking for bodies, Poterloo took a chance and fell in with some German privates, jolly fellows who offered to go with Poterloo to a nearby Alsatian village so that he could see his wife. Poterloo put on some great boots and a Boche coat and followed his friends behind the German lines. They reached the village safely. That night, Poterloo walked twice past the house where his wife was staying with relatives. Through the lighted window, he could see his wife and her sister at dinner with a group of German noncommissioned officers. They were eating well and enjoying themselves. Poterloo carried back to the trenches a disheartening picture of his wife laughing up into the face of a German sergeant.

Of the six Mesnil brothers, four had been killed by 1915. Joseph and André were pessimistic about their own chances. On reconnaissance, one of Bertrand's squad discovered André propped upright in a shell crater. At first they were afraid to tell Joseph, but he did not seem much affected by the news. Bertrand was killed. Then Joseph was wounded in the leg and taken to the dismal dressing station, a large dugout. There were many men in the dugout, most of them resigned to death, all of them given to spiritless discussion. It was agreed that to stop war you had to kill the spirit of war. That appeared to be a difficult job. It came as a new thought to some of them that they were the masses and that the masses had the power to stop war, but it was too big a job. Many men thought only in terms of killing the enemy. It hardly mattered anyway, as nearly all of them would be dead soon. The war went on.

Critical Evaluation:

World War I was the first conflict to produce a major body of literature written by the fighting men themselves. Among the poets, novelists, and memoirists who recorded their experiences in the trenches of the Western Front, many strove to voice a protest equal to the enormities that they had suffered and witnessed. *Under Fire* is one of the earliest of these and one of the few that was written and published before the war ended, and it furnished a model for later writers. Henri Barbusse composed the book in the hospital from diaries he had written at the front in 1914-1915, and he published it in both serial and novel forms late in 1916. *Under Fire* proved an immediate success. In France, it won the prestigious Goncourt Prize, and by the end of the war it was a worldwide best-seller, having sold almost a quarter of a million copies.

The novel's critical reception was mixed. Early reviewers tended to judge it according to whether they believed that life at the front was as wretched as Barbusse depicted it to be. Some were outraged by what they felt to be seditious political views, but many critics greeted its graphic descriptions almost with relief: Here at last, they felt, was the truth about the war. At the time *Under Fire* reached the public, a time when the cost in human life continued to mount without any visible impact on the stalemate in France and Belgium, attitudes toward the war had begun to shift away from the enthusiasm and idealism of the war's first year. Those critical of the war, considered the raw immediacy of *Under Fire* to be its chief virtue; if the characters seemed less carefully drawn and the storyline less tightly constructed than in more polished literary works, this only lent it greater plausibility as a documentary.

Under Fire came to be less widely read after the late 1920's, when it was supplanted by a deluge of war writing. As of the later twentieth century, however, critics considered the novel an important milestone and a work exemplifying some of the difficulties of the protest novel, among them that of reconciling realism and prophetic vision. Although the most gripping chapters in *Under Fire* ("Of Burdens," "The Portal," "Under Fire," and "The Fatigue-Party") present a convincing picture of day-to-day survival in the trenches and of the chaos of battle, these sections are mixed with the kind of earnest political invective and dogma that can become tedious, as it does in the last chapter, "The Dawn." Barbusse had joined the army with mixed impulses; as a committed socialist and pacifist, he supported the war because he believed he would be serving the socialist cause and fighting German militarism in pursuit of a new and peaceful Europe. Yet in *Under Fire* he argued that the war must be abandoned after all, for the enemy was not Germany but the profiteers and "sword-wavers" in the rear on both sides. The collapse of the trenches into mud and water during the final bombardment described in the book effects a kind of cosmic cataclysm, a dissolution of earth, water, fire, and air into a single muddy element that apocalyptically heralds the "new heaven and new earth" glimpsed by the soldiers in the last chapter.

Here, however, the sudden transformation of his simple and unaffected comrades into the unanimous spokesmen for socialist dogma strains the reader's credulity.

Barbusse's chief interest was not in his work's qualities as fiction but as protest—to communicate the almost unspeakable facts about the experience of his fellow poilus as a corrective to the heart-cheering, idealistic accounts in the newspapers. As fiction, it could be published without interference from the official censors. Whatever its shortcomings as litera-ture, it filled an urgent need, the thirst of both civilians and soldiers for an unrestrained first-hand depiction of the front line.

Under Fire was an important influence on the war poetry of Siegfried Sassoon (1886-1967) and Wilfred Owen (1893-1918), and (perhaps partly by way of their poems) on the war prose of the late 1920's and early 1930's. Such later classics of the war as Erich Maria Remarque's

All Quiet on the Western Front (1929) and Robert Graves's *Goodbye to All That* (1929) employ a similarly episodic and graphic style but forgo the political didacticism, allowing themes to emerge from parallels among the episodes. *Under Fire* thus constitutes an important source of the enduring myth of World War I, which presents soldiers as the innocent victims of belligerent and bloodthirsty older generation of politicians, generals, and profiteers.

Barbusse's narrative strategy was influenced by naturalism, especially by novels of Émile Zola such as *Germinal* (1885) and *The Downfall* (1892). Such novels strove, with almost scientific accuracy, to document the life of the working classes yet also to show how all life is subject to natural laws, just as science produces general theories from minute observations. They urged reform by demonstrating that individual lives are determined by social and economic forces greater than the individuals. Jonathan King argues that the strengths and weaknesses of *Under Fire* cannot be appreciated without reference to the risk inherent in social realism of submerging the author's visionary purpose under the mass of detail. In *Under Fire*, it is where Barbusse abandons documentation that the writing become implausible and ineffective.

The disconnected vignettes that constitute the narrative of *Under Fire* were meant to acquire coherence from the novel's prophetic purpose; from another perspective, however, they anticipate the discontinuous, juxtaposed scenes of the great works of the 1920's. Perhaps both the strengths and weaknesses of *Under Fire* argue the impossibility of grasping the enormities of World War I, or of making coherent sense out of its wastefulness. It is as though the war had inaugurated the fragmentation that convinced such early twentieth century writers as Virginia Woolf, James Joyce, and T. S. Eliot that traditional narrative continuity was no longer appropriate.

"Critical Evaluation" by Matthew Parfitt

Bibliography:
Cruickshank, John. *Variations on Catastrophe: Some French Responses to the Great War.* New York: Oxford University Press, 1982. An informative study, chiefly concerned with the problems that the protest novel entails for authors and critics. Attempts to account for the uneasy combination of realism and political prophecy in *Under Fire*.
Field, Frank. *Three French Writers and the Great War: Studies in the Rise of Communism and Fascism.* Cambridge, England: Cambridge University Press, 1975. Pays scant attention to *Under Fire*'s literary qualities but provides extensive discussion of its place in the development of Barbusse's political commitments.
Harris, Frank. "Henri Barbusse." In *Latest Contemporary Portraits.* 1927. Reprint. New York: Johnson Reprint, 1968. An early appreciation of Barbusse, which focuses on *Under Fire*.
Jones, Tobin H. "Mythic Vision and Ironic Allusion: Barbusse's *Le Feu* and Zola's *Germinal*." *Modern Fiction Studies* 28, no. 2 (Summer, 1982): 215-228. Although occasionally overburdened with literary theory, Jones's comparison of the use of mythic patterns and social vision in the two works is illuminating.
King, Jonathan. "Henri Barbusse: *Le Feu* and the Crisis of Social Realism." In *The First World War in Fiction: A Collection of Critical Essays,* edited by Holger Klein. New York: Barnes & Noble Books, 1977. The most helpful study of *Under Fire* available in English. Places the novel in historical context, demonstrating how the literary and political movements of its time explain many of its problems and peculiarities.

UNDER MILK WOOD
A Play for Voices

Type of work: Drama
Author: Dylan Thomas (1914-1953)
Type of plot: Domestic realism
Time of plot: Indeterminate
Locale: Llaregyb, also called Llareggub, a mythical seaside village in Wales
First performed: public reading, 1953; radio play, 1954; first published, 1954; first staged, 1956

Principal characters:

CAPTAIN CAT, a blind, retired sea captain
THE REVEREND ELI JENKINS, one of God's innocents
POLLY GARTER, the village wanton
MOG EDWARDS, a draper
MYFANWY PRICE, a dressmaker and sweetshop proprietress
MR. PUGH, a schoolmaster
MRS. PUGH, his wife, a shrew
MR. WALDO, a barber, herbalist, and lecher
MRS. OGMORE-PRITCHARD, the twice-widowed owner of Bay View, a
    house for paying guests
BUTCHER BEYNON
MRS. BEYNON, his wife
GOSSAMER BEYNON, a schoolteacher
ORGAN MORGAN, a musician
CHERRY OWEN, a tippler
MRS. OWEN, his wife
WILLY NILLY, the postman
MRS. WILLY NILLY, his wife, who reads all the mail before her husband
    delivers it
SINBAD SAILORS, a young pubkeeper
MARY ANN SAILORS, his grandmother
LORD CUT-GLASS, an eccentric recluse
NOGOOD BOYO, a fisherman
OCKY MILKMAN

The Story:

Night's deep shadows lay over sleeping Llaregyb, a small, decayed seaside resort village. So a guidebook might describe the town, a place of no particular interest to the sportsman, the health-seeker, or the tourist. Under the black, moonless sky, the cobblestone streets were silent and Milk Wood was empty of lovers, the darkness disturbed only by the secret, rustling animal life. In their darkened houses the people of Llaregyb slept, their dreams filled with love or hate, desire or dismay.

Captain Cat was a retired, blind sea captain. Through his dreams echoed the voices of sailor friends lost long ago, with whom he had shared the same girl, Rosie Probert. Mog Edwards, the draper, in sleep loved Myfanwy Price more than all the cloths and weaves in the great Cloth Hall of the world. Myfanwy, secretly in love with Mog, promised in her sleep to warm his heart beside the fire so that he could wear it under his vest after he closed his shop. Mr. Waldo lay in a drunken slumber beside his unhappy, unloved wife; other women he had known passed through his dreams. Mrs. Ogmore-Pritchard gave orders to the two husbands she bossed into their graves. Inspectors flew into the dreams of Mrs. Beynon, the butcher's wife, to persecute her husband for selling the meat of cats and owls. Her daughter Gossamer, a schoolteacher, dreamed of her lover, a small, rough man with a bright bushy tail like a fox's. Sinbad Sailors hugged his pillow and imagined that he was embracing Gossamer Beynon. His grandmother dreamed of the garden of Eden. Willy Nilly, the postman, walked fourteen miles in his sleep. Polly Garter dreamed of babies.

Day broke and the people rose and went about their business. The Reverend Eli Jenkins, whose God was a God of innocence and wonder, went to his door and in the bright sunshine sang his morning service, a lyric that might have come out of Robert Herrick. Mrs. Ogmore-Pritchard, whose god was cleanliness, did not care to have boarders in her clean rooms and starched beds, their breath all over the furniture, their feet trampling her carpets. Ocky Milkman put water in the milk before he delivered it. Mr. Pugh, the schoolmaster, daydreamed of feeding his wife an arsenic and weedkiller biscuit; at breakfast he read *Lives of the Great Poisoners*, the title of his book concealed by a brown paper wrapper. Polly Garter nursed the youngest of her brood. Sinbad Sailors opened the Sailors Arms and drank a pint of beer. (The hands of the ship's clock in the bar had stood at half-past eleven for half a century, so that it was always opening time in the pub.) Mr. Cherry Owen heard how in drink he hurled sago at the wall, missed his wife and the picture of Auntie Blossom, and danced on the table. Mrs. Willy Nilly, the postman's wife, steamed open letters and read them aloud. Nogood Boyo, lying on his back among crabs' legs and tangled lines in the unbailed bottom of his dinghy looked at the sky and said that he did not know or care who might be up there looking down. Sinbad Sailors continued to dote on Gossamer Beynon. Lord Cut-Glass, in his kitchen filled with clocks, one for each of his sixty-six years, squatted to eat from a dish marked Fido. Captain Cat remembered the rowdy long ago of his youth.

Night fell and Llaregyb prepared to return to sleep. Mog Edwards and Myfanwy Price, a town's length between them, wrote to each other the daily love letters that they never mailed. Mrs. Ogmore-Pritchard sealed her house against the night airs and the damp from the sea. The Reverend Eli Jenkins recited his sunset poem, asking God to look after and bless the people of Llaregyb, a town where no one was wholly good or wholly bad. Mr. Cherry Owen went off to get drunk at the Sailors Arms; his wife had two husbands, one drunk, one sober, and she loved them both. Captain Cat, secure in his bunk, went voyaging in his dreams. In Milk Wood, where lovers stray, drunken Mr. Waldo hugged Polly Garter in the warm silence under the trees, but it was not Mr. Waldo or any of her lusty, six-foot lovers Polly was thinking of, but of Willy Weazel—little Willy Wee—who was dead and six feet underground.

Critical Evaluation:

As a human being, Dylan Thomas had many failings, but he possessed one quality that redeemed him: He was a dedicated craftsman and devoted to his art. A like claim may be made for his radio play *Under Milk Wood*, which Thomas subtitled *A Play for Voices*. Completed shortly before his death, this rich and earthy prose drama testifies to his scrupulous craftsmanship, his delight in character, his humorous apprehension of experience, and his talent for re-creating the sounds of nature. In addition, the play marks a stage in the development of his career, presenting the world without rather than a world within, for it was written at a time when Thomas seemed to be turning away from a highly personal poetry and the exploration of his own private sensibility to a wider view of society.

The work has a history stretching over more than a decade. In one of his early stories Thomas first used the invented name Llareggub, but the idea of writing a drama with this imaginary setting did not come to him, apparently, until approximately 1944. Following the suggestion that his material deserved more extended treatment, he first planned a play to be called *The Town Was Mad*, its theme the ironic contrast between individuality and innocence on the one hand, prejudice and social conformity on the other. As originally planned, the story was to deal with a government commission sent to investigate a community of eccentrics. The indignant citizens insist that a trial be held and their case heard. When the prosecution describes a town that is ideally sane, the people of the village decide that they want no part of the sane world and beg to be cut off from it as quickly as possible. Later, however, Thomas decided to let his story grow more naturally out of the personalities and everyday involvements of his people. When he died suddenly in November, 1953, three separate versions of his play existed in manuscript. The version finally decided on for presentation and publication was that accepted by his executors as the final work.

It is easy to understand the appeal that *Under Milk Wood*, holds for the radio audience and the general reader. The true quality of Dylan Thomas' verse was always more auditory than visual, so the poems which frequently look odd or complicated on the printed page often make marvelous sense when they are read aloud. Then the poet's cumulative and indirect imagery creates a tonal effect of movement between line and line. In radio presentation, in which understanding is by the ear alone, the auditory richness of Thomas' work is unhampered. The town and its people come vividly to life within the imagination of the hearer. The play relies almost entirely on the spoken word, not visual effects. Furthermore, despite its verbal sophistication, the play is democratic—rambunctious, impassioned, ribald, lyric, funny, tender.

To Thomas, Milk Wood is a place of wonder and love. To old Mary Ann Sailors, humble in her faith, it is God's garden, the proof of Eden, a heaven on earth, and her belief is that Llaregyb is the Chosen Land. To the restless, night-haunted village boys and girls it is the bridal bed of secret love. To the Reverend Eli Jenkins it is a sermon in green, wind-shaken leaves on the innocence and goodness of humanity.

No conflict develops; no problems are resolved. The material of the play is as impressive as it is simple, for the poet's chief concern was to convey a sense of the life that underlies the complicated business of living, even in commonplace lives and among people who are no better and no worse than they are in most places. *Under Milk Wood*, for all its brevity, is a play of subtly mixed effects. As an attempt to capture life at its source, it joins reality and fantasy as closely as humor and tragedy blend in the lives of the poet's characters. Dylan Thomas has in this drama presented a picture of ordinary life, but one universalized by insight and imagination. The innocence of art adds as much to his picture of life, as do the compassion and tolerance that come with experience.

Bibliography:
Holbrook, David. " 'A Place of Love': *Under Milk Wood.*" In *Dylan Thomas: A Collection of Critical Essays*, edited by C. B. Cox. Englewood Cliffs, N.J.: Prentice-Hall, 1966. Views the play as the romanticized "toy town" of Thomas' childhood. Considers the play trivial when it is contrasted with James Joyce's work.
Korg, Jacob. *Dylan Thomas*. New York: Twayne, 1965. Chapter 8 is devoted to Thomas' prose, including *Under Milk Wood*. Sees the work as lacking the substance of Thomas' poetry, but praises the play's comic vitality, its humor, and its theme of "the sacredness of human attachments."

Moynihan, William T. *The Craft and Art of Dylan Thomas*. Ithaca, N.Y.: Cornell University Press, 1966. Notes *Under Milk Wood*'s humor, its idealized characters, and its theme of the importance of asserting beauty in an imperfect world.

Rea, J. "Topographical Guide to *Under Milk Wood*." *College English* 25, no. 7 (April, 1964): 535-542. Describes a map of Milk Wood created to help students visualize the play's action, comments on the source of some place names, and includes a map of the village.

Williams, Raymond. "Dylan Thomas's Play for Voices." In *Dylan Thomas: A Collection of Critical Essays*, edited by C. B. Cox. Englewood Cliffs, N.J.: Prentice-Hall, 1966. Summarizes the play's acting history and examines Thomas' use of narrative, dialogue, and song. Compares the play to the Circe episode of James Joyce's *Ulysses* (1922).

UNDER THE GREENWOOD TREE

Type of work: Novel
Author: Thomas Hardy (1840-1928)
Type of plot: Pastoral
Time of plot: Nineteenth century
Locale: Rural England
First published: 1872

Principal characters:
REUBEN DEWY, a carrier
DICK DEWY, his son
MR. SHINER, a farmer
MR. MAYBOLD, the vicar
FANCY DAY, the schoolmistress

The Story:

On Christmas Eve, the Mellstock Choir prepared to set out on its annual caroling. In fine voice, mellowed by generous mugs of cider, the men and boys gathered at the home of Reuben Dewy. Then with their fiddles and the cello of Grandfather Dewy, they departed on their rounds. The first stop was at the schoolhouse to serenade the new schoolmistress, Fancy Day. At first, there was no indication that she had heard them; but at last, she appeared, framed, picturelike, in a window. Later, the men missed young Dick Dewy. When they found him, he was leaning against the school, staring up listlessly at the now darkened window.

At church the following morning, Fancy Day caused a stir of excitement. She was the main attraction for Dick Dewy, Farmer Shiner, and the new vicar, Mr. Maybold, but she did not endear herself to a number of other men in the congregation because she committed what they regarded almost as blasphemy. As long as anyone could remember, the male choir had provided music for the service, but the young woman, on her first day in church, led the young girls in singing along with the men. Some of the older and wiser ones foresaw trouble from a woman who was so forward.

Mr. Dewy gave his annual party on the afternoon and evening of Christmas Day. When Dick could claim Fancy for a dance, he was transported with joy; but when she danced with Farmer Shiner, a handsomer and wealthier man, Dick was downcast. When Farmer Shiner escorted the lady home, the evening was ruined for young Dick.

Using a handkerchief left behind by Fancy as his excuse, Dick found the courage to call at the schoolhouse a few days later. A very inexperienced lover, he simply returned the handkerchief, stammered a good day, and departed. It was not until spring that he made any real progress in his love affair. By that time, Dick was a wan and shadowy figure of a man. He spoke to no one of his love, but it was obvious to all but Fancy and her other two admirers that Dick was not himself.

Before Dick could declare himself, however, a delegation from the choir waited on the new vicar, Mr. Maybold. They had been made uneasy by a rumor that they were to be displaced by organ music played by Fancy Day, and they learned that the rumor was true. The vicar had brought an organ to the church because he preferred that instrument to a choir. To spare the feelings of the faithful choir members, however, he agreed to wait before deposing them. They were to have the dignity of leaving on a special day, not on an ordinary Sunday.

Dick's big day came when he was allowed to bring Fancy and some of her belongings from the home of her father. He was dismayed to find Farmer Shiner also present, but when Fancy allowed him to touch her hand at the dinner table, Dick's spirits rose perceptibly. On the ride home, he could not find the words that were in his heart; he felt, nevertheless, that he had made some progress. In the weeks that followed, rumors of her friendliness with the vicar and with Farmer Shiner drove him to desperation. One day, he wrote her a letter in which he bluntly asked whether he meant anything to her. When he received no answer from Fancy, he resolved that he would talk to her the next Sunday.

Before Sunday came, however, he had to go on an errand for the vicar's mother that took him to a neighboring town. He was preparing to leave for home again when he saw Fancy waiting for the carrier. Seizing the opportunity, Dick helped her into his cart and triumphantly carried her off. On the drive home, he finally found the courage to propose to her and was as much surprised as overjoyed to hear her acceptance.

Because they would not be able to marry for some time, they kept their betrothal a secret. Furthermore, Fancy's father had told her that he hoped she would accept Farmer Shiner for a husband. One trait of Fancy's character troubled Dick. She seemed to take undue pleasure in dressing to please others, but whenever he prepared to punish her by letting her worry about him for a change, Fancy apologized for her vanity. Unable to resist her tears, the young lover would take her back into his heart before she knew there had been a problem.

On the day he was at last to meet her father to ask for her hand, Dick prepared himself carefully. Her father told him bluntly that he was not good enough for Fancy and that she was too cultured, too well educated, and too wealthy for a plain carrier. Sadly Dick agreed, and sadly he turned toward home.

Fancy, however, was not so easily defeated. When tears failed to move her father, she resorted to the age-old trick of languishing away for love. She did not eat, at least not so that her father could notice; she merely pined and sighed. The ruse worked, and her father reluctantly found himself begging her to marry her young lover. The date was set for the coming midsummer.

On the day Fancy was installed at the organ and the choir discontinued, Dick could not attend church because he had to serve at the funeral of a friend. Fancy had put her hair in curls and in other ways dressed more lavishly than usual. Dick was sorry to see her dress so beautifully when she knew he would not be present to see her, but she put him off brusquely. On his way home that night, Dick walked through the rain to get one last glimpse of his love before he retired. She refused to lean far enough out her window to give him a kiss. Later, when she saw the vicar approaching through the rain, she greeted him warmly. The vicar, who had been enchanted with her appearance that morning and knew nothing of her betrothal to Dick, had decided to ask for her hand in marriage. Surprising even herself, Fancy accepted him.

The next morning, the vicar met Dick on the road. Dick, still thinking himself betrothed, shyly told the vicar of his coming marriage to Fancy. Shocked, the vicar kept silence, leaving Dick ignorant of Fancy's faithlessness. Then he sent a note to the young lady, telling her that she must not forsake Dick. Before it could be delivered, he received a note from Fancy, in which she wrote that she had been momentarily swayed by the prospect of a more cultured, elegant life; now she begged to withdraw her acceptance of his proposal because she had loved and still loved another.

The wedding took place that summer. It was a great celebration, marred only by the vicar's refusal to perform the ceremony. Dick was puzzled and could not think of any way in which he might have offended the vicar. After the ceremony, Dick told his bride that they would never have a secret between them; Fancy replied that they never would, beginning from that day forth.

Critical Evaluation:

Thomas Hardy's original title for his second novel was *The Mellstock Quire* and indeed, the rather slight plot deals mainly with the rustic choir members and their replacement by an organ and the new schoolteacher organist. Hardy may also have chosen the final title from William Shakespeare's *As You Like It* (c. 1599-1600) to call attention to the work as a pastoral or woodland idyll. The setting of the story has obvious similarities to the forest of Arden in Shakespeare's play, and the wedding of Dick Dewy and Fancy Day takes place at the end of the novel in Yalbury Wood under a real greenwood tree.

The book is appropriately divided into four sections: Winter, Spring, Summer, and Autumn. The characters' actions are tied to such rural activities as nutting, honey gathering, apple picking, country dances, and cider making. Even the names of the major participants in this delightful tale are evocative of nature and its varied manifestations: Dick Dewy, Fancy Day, Mr. Maybold, Farmer Shiner, Thomas Wood, and dim-witted Thomas Leaf.

Throughout the novel, Hardy painstakingly draws his background of summer mornings when "fuchsias and dahlias were laden till eleven o'clock with small drops and dashes of water" and of winter in Mellstock-Lane, where the breeze makes "fir-trees sob and moan no less distinctly than they rock" and "holly whistles as it battles with itself." The Mellstock Choir on its Christmas Eve caroling is an intrinsic part of the interlaced branches of the copse, above which stars shine frostily. Dick Dewy's passion for the new schoolteacher, Fancy Day, blooms with the delicate woodland flowers and warm sun on the grass. Hardy constantly blends the triangular love plot and story of the choir members with seasonal activities. The reader therefore sees all in terms of a benevolent nature, which envelopes, urges, and shapes the story.

Hardy gives special emphasis to the role of music in the tale, which, again, stems from Dorset's environment. The novel opens with the choir and their caroling, and the plot centers around the new organist who is to supplant the choir. Dick and Farmer Shiner sing snatches of ballads about lasses and lads "a-sheep-shearing," Hardy includes an entire hymn sung by the choir, the music and dancing at the tranter's Christmas party form almost two chapters, and at the wedding, "five country dances, two reels and three fragments of horn-pipes" carry the guests to supper time. Harmony and music, like nature, not only sketch background and inform the action but also define the characters themselves.

As in his other novels, Hardy's *Under the Greenwood Tree* shows an affectionate knowledge of the Dorset (Wessex) countryside and of rural customs, rustic speech, the peculiar humor of country dialect, and the delights of the woodland. Nature has not yet become the dire, ineluctable force it proves to be in such later novels like *Tess of the D'Urbervilles* (1891) and *Return of the Native* (1878). Unease and complications, which are certainly present even at the end of *Under the Greenwood Tree*, have not yet become tragedy, and Hardy conveys a comforting sense of a natural succession of generations consonant with seasonal change.

Bibliography:

Carpenter, Richard C. *Thomas Hardy*. New York: Twayne, 1964. Regards the Mellstock Quire as the first fully developed Wessex folk in Hardy's novels. Argues that Hardy maintains the novel's pastoral atmosphere throughout.

Gatrell, Simon. *Thomas Hardy and the Proper Study of Mankind*. Charlottesville: University Press of Virginia, 1993. Notes that *Under the Greenwood Tree* asserts an air of social harmony, though with an odd, discordant voice. Concludes that the marriage of Fancy Day and Dick Dewy symbolizes a renewal of village life.

Millgate, Michael. *Thomas Hardy: His Career as a Novelist*. New York: Random House, 1971.

Considers *Under the Greenwood Tree* to be a kind of woodland pastoral or novel of rural manners. Concludes that Hardy's novel, though an idyll, contains many elements that are less than idyllic. Reprinted in Ronald Draper, ed., *Thomas Hardy; Three Pastoral Novels: A Casebook*. London: Macmillan, 1987.

Toliver, Harold E. "The Dance Under the Greenwood Tree: Hardy's Bucolics." *Nineteenth-Century Fiction* 17, no. 1 (June, 1962): 57-68. Discusses the way in which Hardy in *Under the Greenwood Tree* examines the flaws of the old order, chief symbol of which is the Mellstock Choir. Their clumsiness and crudity, as much as their opposition of new ideas, cause the disintegration of their old ways.

Vigar, Penelope. *The Novels of Thomas Hardy: Illusion and Reality*. London: The Athlone Press, 1974. Argues that *Under the Greenwood Tree* is a light, often humorous, pastoral tale, one barely touched by extravagances of coincidence and melodrama and one that seldom strays into the realms of passion and tragedy.

UNDER THE VOLCANO

Type of work: Novel
Author: Malcolm Lowry (1909-1957)
Type of plot: Psychological realism
Time of plot: November 1, 1939
Locale: Quauhnahuac (Cuernavaca), Mexico
First published: 1947

Principal characters:
GEOFFREY FIRMIN, the British consul at Quauhnahuac
YVONNE CONSTABLE, his former wife
HUGH FIRMIN, his half brother
JACQUES LARUELLE, a French film director
DR. ARTURO DÍAZ VIGIL, Geoffrey Firmin's doctor

The Story:

On November 2, 1939, the Mexican Day of the Dead, Jacques Laruelle, a French film producer, was ready to leave Quauhnahuac, Mexico. Before leaving, Laruelle joined his friend Dr. Vigil, and the two talked about their common acquaintance, Geoffrey Firmin, former British consul to Quauhnahuac, who had been murdered exactly one year earlier.

After his visit with Dr. Vigil, Laruelle walked toward the Casino de Silva and recalled that day a year before. His recollections led Laruelle to remember the time he had spent with Geoffrey and his half brother, Hugh, at the Taskersons' home when all three were youngsters. One memory moved to another, and the story of Geoffrey and Hugh's childhood was told.

Laruelle stopped at the Cervecería XX, where he chatted with Señor Bustamente, owner of the bar and neighboring cinema. Bustamente told Laruelle that he suspected that the dead consul might have been a spy, or "spider." At the end of their conversation, Bustamente gave Laruelle the copy of Elizabethan plays that Laruelle had borrowed from Geoffrey. Laruelle had intended to create a French version of the Faustus story. As he thumbed through the book, Laruelle found a letter that Geoffrey had written to his estranged wife, Yvonne, attempting to talk her into returning to him. Geoffrey had never mailed the letter. When Laruelle left the bar, he walked up the Calle Nicaragua and remembered the day when Geoffrey Firmin was murdered and Yvonne was trampled to death by a horse.

On the morning of the 1938 Day of the Dead, Geoffrey had not slept and sat in the cantina drinking. Unexpectedly, Yvonne, the consul's former wife, appeared. She had left Quauhnahuac the year before for America, where she had secured a divorce from Geoffrey. Almost as unexpected was the return of the consul's half brother and Yvonne's lover, Hugh. Hugh had returned because he felt that he could not stay away without suffering the pains of guilt that Yvonne had suffered.

After their reunion, Geoffrey, Yvonne, and Hugh left on a trip to Tomalín. Their trip was interrupted when they stopped by the home of Jacques Laruelle. Laruelle was one of Yvonne's former lovers, and the stopover caused much distress for Geoffrey because of Yvonne and Hugh's new closeness. Geoffrey drank several tequilas. Hugh and Yvonne went to a fiesta.

When the consul awakened from his drunken sleep, he was addressed by two beings. An evil angel urged him to drink rather than think of Yvonne. At the same time, a good angel made threats about his drinking. This was the first connection between Geoffrey and the Faustus story that Laruelle had proposed. The evil angel won when Geoffrey turned to drink because he felt that he could not successfully perform his duties as a husband.

When Hugh and Yvonne returned from the fiesta, Hugh joked that perhaps his brother was a black magician. Hugh acted as a deterrent to any chances of Yvonne and Geoffrey's ever getting back together. Hugh took Yvonne for a horseback ride. On the ride, Hugh identified himself with Judas because he felt that he had betrayed his brother. When Hugh and Yvonne returned, they found Geoffrey awake, and the three continued their journey.

The trip to Tomalín was interrupted when the travelers noticed a wounded Indian. Mexican law and possible repercussions influenced the group not to make an effort to assist the wounded man. Geoffrey saw a fellow traveler rob the dying man. Geoffrey and Hugh argued about the rationality of not helping the man. None of the three travelers was decisive. Hugh and Yvonne were indecisive because of the law, and Geoffrey was indecisive because he was more concerned about finding the next cantina for a drink.

The travelers stopped and went to the Salon Ofelia for a drink. In the salon, Geoffrey's feelings erupted into a storm of violent words thrown at Yvonne and Hugh, accusing them of crimes against marriage and brotherhood. Geoffrey drank mescal, which he had earlier associated with his demise. While drinking the mescal, Geoffrey remembered a similar time when he had drunk all night and was supposed to meet a lady, Lee Maitland, who failed to arrive. To his surprise, he could not remember exactly who this lady was. Geoffrey was losing control of his perception of reality.

Geoffrey saw his doom symbolized in the nearby volcano. He showed himself to be a Faustian character by broadcasting that he loved hell and could not wait to return there. He then rushed out of the Salon Ofelia as if in pain. Yvonne and Hugh rushed after him and tried to catch up with him. Although Geoffrey had damned them for their adultery, Yvonne and Hugh knew that they had to get him back to Quauhnahuac. They took the wrong path.

As they pursued Geoffrey, Hugh and Yvonne visited several cantinas, looking for him. At each cantina they had a drink before going on. They eventually found themselves wandering around in the forest. As they wandered around, they heard a distant shot, not knowing that it was the sound of Geoffrey's execution by Mexican officials. Drunk, Yvonne tripped and fell over a log, and she was trampled by a horse that had escaped from Geoffrey. Hugh wandered through the woods singing a revolutionary song and accompanying himself on a guitar.

As he lay dying, Geoffrey imagined that he heard Jacques Laruelle and Dr. Vigil back in Quauhnahuac trying to comfort the grieving Yvonne and Hugh. When his hallucination was complete, Geoffrey screamed and died. Someone threw a dead dog into the ravine with the dead Englishman.

"The Story" by Thomas B. Frazier

Critical Evaluation:

Although *Under the Volcano* was well received on first publication, the novel did not sell well and was not reprinted for many years. Since 1958, however, it has shared in the growing appreciation of Malcolm Lowry that followed his death in 1957 and the publication of his third volume, *Hear Us O Lord from Heaven Thy Dwelling Place*, in 1961. Lowry would have appreciated the irony of late acclaim. In the first chapter of *Under the Volcano*, Jacques Laruelle receives two messages from Geoffrey Firmin, the protagonist of the novel, who died the year before. The doomed, damned, and dead Geoffrey still manages to communicate with the living, and they possibly pay more attention to his words now than they did when he was alive. The posthumous publications of Lowry serve much the same purpose; readers and critics are paying more attention to what Lowry has to say now that he is dead.

His message is summed up in one word: doom. His characters feel they cannot escape their fate; it is as if the volcano in whose shadow Geoffrey Firmin lives was also Lowry's imaginative projection of this century's crises and violence. The sense of doom is the central feature of Lowry's vision and work, and an English reviewer, noting that James Joyce in *Ulysses* (1922) and Lowry in *Under the Volcano* use one day for the action, suggests that the time of Lowry's novel is simply "Doomsday." Undoubtedly, the sense of doom, intensified by waste and exile so prevalent in Lowry's life, is a response to the mid-1930's, the time when Lowry began to write the novel. Such a sense of doom has not lost its relevance. In *Under the Volcano*, doom is presented as accident; Hugh Firmin causes the death of Geoffrey, his half brother, by leaving an incriminating cable message in the jacket he borrowed from Geoffrey; in turn, Geoffrey releases the horse that later kills Yvonne Constable, his former wife.

The novel tends to move on an allegorical level into a consideration of human destiny. This idea is important, for the novel would be a failure if it were considered only on its realistic level. The action relates very little to any moral. The qualities that tend to be presented as enduring and worthy of regard are compassion for the individual and the sense of doom that looms over the alcoholic. Geoffrey's death is not seen as a punishment for his weaknesses; it is simply the culmination of the series of tragic events that take place in the consul's soul that day—his death merely ends the series of spiritual defeats he has succumbed to during his fall.

This idea must have been unpalatable in the late 1940's and in part could account for the lack of continuing interest in Lowry. Furthermore, the difficulty of estimating the true standing of *Under the Volcano* was due to a lack of enough writing by Lowry to place the novel in a context. Readers may see that the novel is probably the center not only of Lowry's projected sequence of six novels, ending with *Hear Us O Lord from Heaven Thy Dwelling Place*, but also the center of all of his work, particularly his poetry.

Lowry's work is a continuous whole, with its central novel representing hell or the point of lowest descent. The covert references to his first novel, *Ultramarine* (1932), in the sixth chapter of *Under the Volcano* are balanced by references to Dollarton, Lowry's residence near Vancouver, in the fourth and ninth chapters. Dollarton is the setting of much of *Hear Us O Lord from Heaven Thy Dwelling Place* and of his last poems. Similarly, *Under the Volcano* is echoed in his poems, including one entitled "For *Under the Volcano*," and in his shorter fiction.

Recognition of the midway position of the Mexican novel indicates three features of Lowry's work: its painfully autobiographical sources; its unity or continuity; and its close texture and highly symbolic content, an indirect product of the first two features.

The general features of Lowry's writings are shown in four aspects of *Under the Volcano*, two of which are immediately apparent. The novel is very specifically placed in time and space; the events of the first chapter occur on November 1, 1939, exactly a year after the events of the remaining eleven chapters, which in turn are clearly timed as occurring at stated intervals throughout the eleven hours of the action. The geographical placing of the novel in Quauhnahuac, Mexico, for the first seven chapters and in nearby Tomalín and Parián for the last four affords Lowry an opportunity to use his flair for symbolism. The principal geographical feature of the area is the *barranca*, or ravine, which local legend says opened on the day of the Crucifixion. The unity of Lowry's vision, or rather possibly his single-minded view of the world, enables him to fix the novel firmly in space and time and to range rapidly over them, giving a sense of cosmic urgency to the most innocent description. For example, the first paragraph mentions the Tropic of Cancer and the Juggernaut of India. Furthermore, Lowry's delight in symbolism is evident in the apparently innocuous introduction and juxtaposition of the terms "Crucifixion," "Cancer," and "Juggernaut."

As one reads further, however, two other aspects of the novel may strike one as severe disadvantages: one is the nature of the protagonist, the other the play of allusion. Both, however, are necessary to Lowry's serious intention. The allusions are part of the web of symbols constructed of reiterated references, for example, those to a film poster advertising "Las Manos de Orlac con Peter Lorre," the Great Wheel at the fiesta (the "Maquina Infernal"), Maximilian and Carlotta, a dying turtle, shrieking fawns, a pariah dog that follows Geoffrey through the day and down into the *barranca*, the madman with the bicycle tire, and especially three signs: a fingerpost "To Parián," the inscription, to the effect that life without love is impossible, over the door of Laruelle's house, and, most important, the sign in the public garden warning that those who destroy will be evicted. At a glance, it will be seen that these are susceptible to symbolic interpretation, but Lowry uses them both in complicated sets and at crucial moments of the action to increase their power enormously. Two instances show this usage. When Yvonne meets Geoffrey again, it is the morning after the night of the Red Cross Ball, held on All Hallows Eve in the Hotel Bella Vista. The year is 1938, and the first words of the consul are the statement that a corpse will be transported by express. The time, place, occasion, and message all combine in gruesome congruity, especially if one is aware, as on a second reading, that the corpse is Geoffrey himself. In chapter 7, Geoffrey contemplates the view across the *barranca* from the top of Laruelle's house and remembers how they used to play golf together as boys, having especial difficulty with what they called "Hell Bunker" and retiring to the nineteenth hole in a pub called "The Case Is Altered." In his present changed circumstances, Geoffrey visualizes a golf shot across the *barranca* to what he terms the "Golgotha Hole," leading to his present refuge and the scene of his death, a tavern called "The Farolito" ("The Little Lighthouse") at Parián, where the fingerpost points him.

The irony of these sets of symbols is made more effective because Geoffrey Firmin knows what they presage but cannot communicate his knowledge to Yvonne, Laruelle, Hugh, or Dr. Vigil, all of whom are trying to help him escape. This lack of communication leads to what appears to be the second disadvantageous aspect of the novel, the character of the protagonist. At first sight, Geoffrey resembles the feckless drunkard of some of Lowry's short stories. The point is whether he is drinking mescal to drown his sorrows or, since he calls it the "nectar of immortality," to avoid his fate; in either case, it both enables him to recognize the signs of doom and renders him incapable of showing their meaning to others, even when he, Hugh, and Yvonne see the dying Indian.

The explanation is that Geoffrey, as British consul, is not so much a character as a type. He is deliberately isolated from his native land, from the Mexicans around him, and from Hugh, Yvonne, and the others. The reader may see him as Everyman. Within narrow limits, he exemplifies the crisis of the liberals in the 1930's when they realized that the world was heading toward violence and disorder, that liberalism could not stop the march of history.

Such was Lowry's conviction when he wrote *Under the Volcano*, and it forms part of the autobiographical base of the novel. Lowry wrote in exile, in Cuernavaca; he was divorced in 1939. The conditions of the novel's composition and its Everyman character place it in the mainstream of great modern novels. The play of symbolism is intended to raise the novel from the level of plot and action to the level of universal applicability and ritual.

Geoffrey Firmin is in a "damnable" situation: He is divorced; his consulate is closed; he cannot stop drinking. He is also damned by his own past actions: his inability to answer Yvonne's letters and the murder of German officers during an engagement. He is also doomed by the actions of those around him: the affair between Laruelle and Yvonne and the hopeless dreams of Hugh. Every stage of his progress on the Day of the Dead—his reunion with Yvonne, his visit with Laruelle, the bus ride to Tomalín, his final encounter with the secret police at Parián—is an inexorable step in the chain of circumstances that draws him to the *barranca* and his death.

If these steps are viewed as part of the elaborate ritual of preparing a victim for sacrifice, the ritual itself is an attempt to purge the awareness of disaster with the acceptance of love. The ritual fails to avert Geoffrey Firmin's fate, making *Under the Volcano* a compelling record of disaster and doom.

Bibliography:

Day, Douglas. *Malcolm Lowry: A Biography*. New York: Oxford University Press, 1973. Demonstrates how the novel is intent on making a moral statement, which is achieved by Lowry's presentation of the four major characters.

Epstein, Perle E. *The Private Labyrinth of Malcolm Lowry: "Under the Volcano" and the Cabbala*. New York: Henry Holt, 1969. Examines Lowry's use of myths and symbols for conveying the theme of *Under the Volcano*. Likens Lowry's use of Mexican folklore to the Cabbala.

Gass, William H. "In Terms of the Toenail: Fiction and the Figures of Life." In *Fiction and the Figures of Life*. New York: Alfred A. Knopf, 1970. Argues that *Under the Volcano* is a day-in-the-life story of British consul Geoffrey Firmin.

Markson, David. *Malcolm Lowry's "Volcano": Myth, Symbol, Meaning*. New York: Times Books, 1978. Probably the most thorough investigation of *Under the Volcano*. Explains Lowry's use of symbols, allusions, and themes.

Spender, Stephen. Introduction to *Under the Volcano* by Malcolm Lowry. New York: New American Library, 1971. Spender's introduction is a must for anyone reading *Under the Volcano* for the first time. Puts the novel into its context in Lowry's canon.

UNDER THE YOKE

Type of work: Novel
Author: Ivan Vazov (1850-1921)
Type of plot: Historical
Time of plot: 1875-1876
Locale: Bulgaria
First published: Pod igoto, serial, 1889-1890; book, 1893 (English translation, 1893)

> *Principal characters:*
> KRALICH, a revolutionary
> RADA, his sweetheart
> SOKOLOV, a doctor
> MARIKA, a girl

The Story:

One day Marko, a substantial family man, sat down to his evening meal. His children and his relatives were a noisy crowd, but over the din they heard an alarming noise in the yard. The women all shrieked, because they were afraid of robbers. Marko took a pistol and went to investigate. In the stable, he found an exhausted and furtive man cowering in the dark.

Ivan Kralich, the fugitive, had returned to the village of Bela Cherkva after escaping from a Turkish prison. The Turks were harsh rulers of Bulgaria, and anyone suspected of revolutionary tendencies was either killed outright or imprisoned. Nevertheless, eight years of confinement had failed to quench Kralich's spirit. Having made his getaway, he asked for sanctuary because the Turks were on his trail. Marko, a patriot who had known Kralich's family, told the fugitive to remain in hiding in his stable. As he returned to the house, however, Turkish policemen knocked at the door. They had heard the women shrieking and had come to see what the trouble was.

As soon as Marko could get rid of the Turks, he hurried back to the stable, but Kralich had disappeared. Hearing the police, he had climbed the wall and run. Unfortunately, he ran into a patrol and escaped them only after leaving his coat in the hands of the Turks. They shot at him, but the fugitive escaped into the countryside. It was raining, and at last he took refuge in a mill. As he crouched in a dark corner, the miller came in with his innocent fourteen-year-old daughter, Marika. Kralich watched unobserved as they made beds on the floor. Then two Turkish policemen knocked and forced their way into the mill. One of them was a notorious lame man who had cut off a girl's head a short while before. The miller was terror stricken when the Turks ordered him to get them some raki.

Knowing that they wanted Marika, the miller bravely refused to leave. Throwing aside all pretense, the Turks seized him and started to bind him. Kralich was moved to action when the despairing miller called to Marika for help. He took an ax and after a brief struggle killed the Turks. After Kralich and the miller had buried the bodies, the grateful miller led Kralich to a good hiding place in a nearby monastery.

While Kralich was resting, Sokolov, the village doctor, found himself in trouble. Although Sokolov was called a doctor, he had received no training and prescribed few medicines; he was regarded with suspicion by the Turks because he was a patriotic Bulgarian and because his peculiar habits included keeping a pet bear. That night, as he was playing with the bear, the Turks arrested him on a charge of treason.

What had happened was that Kralich had asked Sokolov the way to Marko's house, and the

6848

compassionate doctor had given Kralich his coat. When Kralich lost the coat during his escape from the patrol, the police recognized Sokolov's garment. In the pockets they found revolutionary documents. The arrest created a sensation in the district. Kralich, hearing of Sokolov's trouble, started to the village to clear him. Marko, however, cleverly fooled the police by substituting a harmless newspaper for the incriminating documents when the official messenger stopped for a drink in a tavern. The evidence had disappeared, so the easygoing Turkish bey released Sokolov.

Kralich changed his name and found a job teaching school. He maintained contact with the revolutionaries, however, and soon welcomed to the cause his friend Mouratliski, who had also fled from the Turks. Mouratliski, passing as an Austrian photographer, soon became a familiar figure in the village. Kralich continued to discuss the cause of liberty and won many converts. He also fell in love with Rada, a gentle orphan who taught in the girls' school.

Once the townspeople gave a play in which Kralich took a leading role. The bey, who understood no Bulgarian, was an honored guest. At the end of the play Kralich led the cast in singing patriotic and revolutionary songs. The audience was much moved. The quick-witted Bulgarian who was translating for the bey assured the Turkish official that the songs were part of the drama.

Kralich finally came under suspicion when a spy informed the Turks that the schoolmaster was working for Bulgarian independence. A detachment of police surrounded the church while the villagers were at worship, but Kralich got through the cordon by assuming a disguise. He then fled to the mountains and the woods and for months led a wandering life sheltered by patriotic Bulgars. He preached continually the need for revolution. One day, when he attended a party in a small village, Turks came and beat an old man to death. Kralich led a small group, including the giant Ivan Kill-the-Bear, out along a trail and waited in ambush. The Bulgars succeeded in killing the Turks and left their bodies to be eaten by wolves.

Meanwhile, in Bela Cherkva, Rada led an uneasy life. The village knew of her love for Kralich and twitted her on her hopeless affair after his disappearance. In particular, a student named Kandov made her life miserable by following her about. At last Kralich slipped into the village to visit her. Rada, overjoyed, was reluctant to part from him again, and Kralich invited her to go to Klissoura, a nearby village, where he was busy organizing a revolt. Soon afterward she set out, but Kandov followed her and found the house where she was staying. When Kralich appeared, he was already a little jealous because he had received an anonymous letter accusing Rada of intimacies with Kandov. As soon as he saw Kandov with her, Kralich became angry and left.

Under the fiery leadership of Kralich, the inhabitants of Klissoura prepared to revolt. On the day for the rising, the little garrison proclaimed its independence of Turkey, and the citizen soldiers, after setting their wooden cannon on the trail, prepared to battle the Turks. Bela Cherkva did not revolt as planned, however, and the whole Turkish strength was concentrated on Klissoura. The Bulgarians were quickly overwhelmed. When the victors began pillaging the town, Rada was lucky enough to get back to Bela Cherkva with the help of Ivan and his wife.

A fugitive once more, Kralich wandered hungry and cold through the Balkans. At last, he took shelter in the mill and sent the faithful Marika into town with a letter asking Sokolov to bring him clothes. Marika could not find the doctor, who had also become a fugitive, but by chance the letter fell into Rada's hands. She made up a bundle of clothing and started off to the mill.

Sokolov, meanwhile, had joined Kralich. When Rada arrived, the lovers had a brief and tearful reunion before pursuing Turks attacked the mill. Kralich and Sokolov were both armed, and for a time, they held their stronghold against the enemy. Rada was the first to be killed by gunfire. Kralich kissed her cold lips and returned to the battle. The Turks quickly closed in on the two Bulgarians when the defenders' ammunition gave out. Kralich's head was mounted on a pole and carried in triumph back to the village.

Critical Evaluation:

Under the Yoke was published after Bulgaria had won independence from Turkish rule. Translated, the novel brought to Western readers a fresh and vivid insight into the affairs of that troubled country. Although the story is tragic, the treatment of the theme is romantic in the manner of Sir Walter Scott; and through fictitious characters and events, the trials of the Bulgarians are faithfully re-created. *Under the Yoke* is a competently written political novel that glorifies Bulgarian independence through the story of a young revolutionary and his struggles. Although melodramatic and unrealistic in parts, the novel is very effective in presenting a picture of life in Bulgaria in the years of Turkish domination.

Under the Yoke reflects Ivan Vazov's keen interest in the details of the Bulgarian nationalist movement's activities. He himself had participated in the independence movement, and many of the novel's memorable scenes owe their vividness to the fact that when he wrote them Vazov was relying heavily on deeply felt personal experiences. His hometown of Sopot is the model for Bela Cherkva in the novel and was the town where he had been involved in preparations for what turned out to be an unsuccessful uprising, much like that led by Kralich in Klissoura. Unlike Bela Cherkva, however, which in the novel escapes harm by backing out of the planned rebellion, Sopot was attacked by the Turks; when Vazov returned there in 1878 after independence had been won, he found the town destroyed and his father among those murdered.

Vazov is at his best in the political scenes at the school where Kralich teaches or at the theater, and in his scenes of domestic life. The opening scene in the book, for example, in which the reader sees the Marko family at dinner and gets a vivid description of their table manners and conversation, immediately provides a realistic setting for the story. Likewise, Vazov skillfully handles the scenes at the school, with his portrayals of Rada and Kralich and their students. He shows how many of the underlying political and social problems in Bulgaria's history are crucially related to the education of the young. At the same time, on a more personal level, he weaves in the love story of Kralich and Rada. There are also weaknesses in the plot, however, such as Vazov's tendency to use action scenes, such as police searches and murders, to fill in between the much more central political scenes. These episodes occur so frequently and are over so quickly that they become almost mechanical; they seem to be tools used to hurry the narrative forward to the next key event.

The ending of *Under the Yoke* is melodramatic and bitter and reflects the author's romantic conception of revolution and his depression over the failure of the movement. It also dramatizes his basic distrust of the masses and his feelings that the common people are in some way responsible for their own oppression. It is clear, too, that the author believes that small-group terrorist acts are the only truly effective revolutionary device. In Rada's and Kralich's death scene, the author's romanticism and his cynicism about human nature can be seen simultaneously.

Bibliography:

Choice. Review of *Under the Yoke*, by Ivan Vazov. 9 (June, 1972): 514. Hails the publication in English of this important work. Praises the work of the translators and editor in making the work accessible to the English reader.

Haffner, Susanne A. Review of *Under the Yoke*, by Ivan Vazov. *Library Journal* 97 (January, 1972): 86. Describes the importance of the novel in the context of Bulgarian history. Cites some weakness in characterization and the strength of the novel's largely accurate account of a revolution.

UNDER TWO FLAGS

Type of work: Novel
Author: Ouida (Marie Louise de la Ramée, 1839-1908)
Type of plot: Sentimental
Time of plot: Mid-nineteenth century
Locale: London and environs, the Continent, and Algeria
First published: 1867

Principal characters:
> THE HONORABLE BERTIE CECIL, a young Guardsman
> BERKELEY, his younger brother
> LORD ROCKINGHAM, "THE SERAPH," Bertie's friend
> RAKE, Bertie's servant
> LADY GUINEVERE, Bertie's married lover in London
> CIGARETTE, a Frenchwoman patriot
> COLONEL CHATEAUROY, Bertie's enemy
> PRINCESS CORONA D'AMAGÜE, the Seraph's sister

The Story:

Although a fashionable member of his London set and an admirable fellow in every other respect, the Honorable Bertie Cecil, of the First Life Guards, was uncommonly low on credit. No moneylender in London would accept his note after he had mortgaged his whole inheritance. In those circumstances, he depended upon winning a race with his six-year-old horse, Forest King, and he had staked everything on the race. With good-humored generosity he nevertheless lent his younger brother, Berkeley, fifty pounds. The following day, he rode Forest King to victory over a difficult course and received the praise of his Lady Guinevere, a fashionable peeress who had worn his scarlet and white.

His father, Lord Royallieu, lived in the same mortgaged splendor that he had taught his three sons to enjoy. Lord Royallieu loved two of his sons but not Bertie, who looked too much like his dead wife's lover and, to the old viscount's detestation, carried the dead lover's name. The old man took every occasion to sneer at Bertie's extravagance; one day, he revealed his suspicions that Bertie was really the son of Alan Bertie.

Bertie was otherwise lucky in the world. Sought after by half the women in London, he carried on flirtations with many. Lady Guinevere was one of his conquests. Rake, his valet, was devoted to him. Bertie had salvaged Rake from a bad scrape in the army and had treated him with friendly decency.

Bertie was disturbed by his financial affairs, so his head groom had promised to drug Forest King for a fee. When it was learned that Forest King had been drugged before a race in Baden, his friends, far from blaming him, pretended to agree that the horse was merely ill, but Bertie felt disgraced.

Bertie's best friend, Lord Rockingham, was known to his comrades of the Guards as the Seraph. While he was attempting to discover the mystery of Forest King's condition, he received a report that Bertie Cecil had forged the Seraph's name to a note. Bertie could not deny the charge, for the note had been presented at a time when he had been dining with Lady Guinevere. Wishing to protect her name from scandal, Bertie allowed himself to be accused.

He knew that his brother had forged the note, and he hoped to protect Berkeley's name as well; consequently, he left Europe suddenly in order to escape arrest.

Accompanied by Rake, Bertie made his escape on Forest King. Rake had discovered that the groom had drugged Forest King, and he had pummeled him for it. He and his master rode to a place of safety; then Bertie ordered Rake to take Forest King to Lord Rockingham. He waited in hiding for a time, hoping Lady Guinevere would save him by telling of his whereabouts when the forged note was presented. She chose to keep silent, however, holding her reputation at greater worth than Bertie's name.

At last, by a mere throw of the dice in Algeria, Bertie decided to cast his lot with the French Foreign Legion instead of the Arab cause. The faithful Rake accompanied him. The people back in England believed Bertie dead in a French train wreck. Rockingham had Forest King; the old viscount burned Bertie's picture.

As Louis Victor, Bertie made his mark with his new companions in the Foreign Legion. They marveled at his skill with the horses, at his bravery, and at his brilliance in conversation. Bertie was a twelve-year veteran Legionnaire when he received, six months late, the news that his father had died at the age of ninety. His older brother inherited the title.

Cigarette, a woman of independent spirit and a dancer and singer for the troops, came to understand and admire Bertie. She warned him against Colonel Chateauroy, who hated Bertie because of his gallant record and popularity, and asked him never to disobey any of the Colonel's unreasonable commands. Partly because he pitied her, Bertie promised. Shortly afterward, Cigarette saved Bertie's life from some drunken Arabs. She adored him, but he was indifferent to her.

Bertie spent his spare time carving chessmen of ivory and walnut. Through this occupation, he met the lovely Princess Corona d'Amagüe, a woman who had been unhappily married to a man injured while saving her brother's life. Her husband had died soon after, and thereafter the Princess had felt responsible for his death. Bertie soon fell in love with Princess Corona.

Colonel Chateauroy made it clear that he would never permit Bertie to be promoted above the rank of corporal. Bertie learned that Rake was purposely getting himself into trouble to prevent his own promotion, for he did not wish to outrank his master.

One day, Bertie read in an old English journal that his older brother had died suddenly and that Berkeley had become Viscount Royallieu.

The regiment was ordered out. In the gory fighting that followed, Cigarette saved the day when she arrived at the head of a fresh squadron of cavalry. She found Bertie on the battlefield; he had been badly wounded. In the tent to which she had him carried, Bertie began to talk incoherently while Cigarette sat beside him. All she heard him say made her more jealous of the Princess. She also learned that Bertie was English. No French person ever hated the English more than she. At her request, Bertie was not told who had brought him back from the battlefield and cared for him during his sick ravings.

Three weeks later, Bertie was startled when the Seraph came as an English tourist to visit the Legion camp. Bertie did not wish to encounter his former friend, so he asked for and received permission to carry dispatches through hostile territory to another legion post. With faithful Rake, he rode away on a mission that meant almost certain death. Rake was killed in an Arab ambush, but Bertie delivered his dispatches safely. On his return trip, he stopped at a caravanserai and there saw his brother Berkeley, who was one of a party of tourists traveling with Princess Corona. Bertie gave no sign of recognition but spurred his horse and continued on.

Berkeley followed Bertie. When he caught up with his older brother, he revealed his fear that Bertie might claim the title. Indifferent to all except Berkeley's selfishness, Bertie asked his brother to leave Algeria at once. Shortly afterward, Bertie discovered that Princess Corona was really the younger sister of the Seraph. She also became aware of Bertie's real name and insisted that he make himself known to her brother. She begged him to claim his title, but he refused.

Cigarette went to Princess Corona, who requested her to tell Bertie that the Seraph was looking for his former friend. In another interview with Bertie, the Princess asked him to tell his story and let the world be the judge. As he left her tent, Colonel Chateauroy intercepted him and insulted the Princess. In sudden rage, Bertie struck his superior officer. Colonel Chateauroy arrested him, and Bertie was sentenced to death.

When Cigarette heard Bertie's fate, she forced Berkeley, whom she met accidentally, to acknowledge that Bertie was in reality his brother, an exile for Berkeley's crime and the true heir to the estate of Royallieu. She carried her story to a marshal of France and demanded that Bertie's honor be saved although his life was already forfeited. With a stay of execution signed by the marshal, she rode at full speed to reach the Legion camp before the hour set for Bertie's execution.

The Seraph, not Cigarette, reached Bertie first. Despite the Seraph's entreaties, Colonel Chateauroy refused to delay the time of execution. Cigarette reached the spot just as the volley was fired. With her own body, she took the bullets intended for Bertie. She died, and the marshal's order, therefore, was safely delivered. A child of the army and a soldier of France, she gave her life to save a comrade. It was a sacrifice that Bertie and Princess Corona, happily reunited, were never to forget. At the end, he was even reunited with Forest King.

Critical Evaluation:

This novel is a rollicking and absorbing, if flawed, masterpiece. It combines breathless action, preposterous situations, flashbacks, short stories, prolix and stilted dialogue, and almost interminable and often repetitious psychological analysis. It was first published serially, which may account for the regularly spaced, end-of-chapter climaxes, and for Ouida's frequent recapitulations of past events as reminders to her readers. The novel, which is about 250,000 words long, might well have been pruned.

The thirty-eight chapters of *Under Two Flags* fall into almost exactly equal thirds. Chapter 12 ends with the escape of Bertie and Rake. In chapter 24, the hero learns that his elder brother's death should give him the title of Lord Royallieu. By the end of chapter 36, which is devoted to Bertie's court-martial, readers have had sufficient foreshadowing hints to be assured that Cigarette will save the day—for his honor, his love of Princess Corona, and Cigarette's own glory. Chapters 37-38 make up a denouement and coda. Interestingly, the conclusive action of the entire novel begins in chapter 19 with the revelation that Bertie carves chessmen.

Ouida adopts an omniscient, cinematic point of view and places and moves her characters like actors and actresses. She is always telling readers about one person's actions or thoughts that other people are not privy to, sometimes by being nearby, but out of earshot. This device can become awkward, as when the Seraph is kept almost fatally unaware that Corporal Victor is actually Bertie. Related is Ouida's use of coincidence. To begin with, the appearance of Berkeley, the Seraph, and Corona in Algeria is unrealistic; even more incredible is Bertie's wandering bemused outside Corona's caravanserai, rescuing a goat from drowning, and, in the process, chancing to find Corona's broken necklace nearby—naturally, he must return it to her later. Ouida manages splendid visual effects, not only by innumerable scenic descriptions, but also by her quick, cinematic shifts to action scenes. In chapter 36 alone, there is the divisional encampment bathed in autumnal noon light; Bertie being dramatically court-martialed; Cigarette sulking in her room; a carrier pigeon flying through Cigarette's oval window with a letter; and Cigarette's fortuitous encounter with Berkeley in the crowded street.

Ouida handles time well. She intriguingly avoids dating the action of her novel, but when she briefly mentions Alexandre Dumas, *fils*, Jean Léon Gérôme, John Tenniel, and, especially, Napoleon III and Abd-el-Kader, readers can place the major African episodes in the 1850's. Ouida varies her generally chronological line by short flashbacks (for an awkward example, Bertie's escape from Baden to Marseilles, which is tardily detailed in chapter 18); protracted narrations of earlier action (the peculiar marriage of Princess Corona, whose husband's quick death makes her a rich, virgin widow, in chapter 22); Léon Ramon's joining the Foreign Legion because his girlfriend has spurned him, in chapter 23; and occasional almost Homeric lists of fellow soldiers (for example, thumbnail sketches of seven men, some with marvelous nicknames, in chapter 16). One flashback—involving Marquise, who, when insulted by his adjutant, bayoneted him to death and was executed by a firing squad (chapter 20)—is an example of Ouida's foreshadowing skill. Later, Bertie is condemned to an identical death for striking his colonel. Ouida cleverly keeps the reader in suspense by using unfulfilled foreshadowing. In one dramatic example, when Bertie learns that Forest King was drugged, he wants the culprit left to him to deal with (chapter 10); the reader eagerly awaits this scene of revenge, but in vain.

Ouida, intoxicated by words, serves them up lavishly. Her style is a unique combination of often unusual diction, syntax habitually tortured, quaint and courtly speech, snippets of French (not always translated), and spectacular figures of speech. Words such as "acquirements," "excitation," "flissa," "insouciance," "lentiscus," "rataplan," "sabretache," and "yawner," among others equally obscure, challenge the reader's attention. Ouida describes almost everything, including food both dainty and coarse, tempting drinks, opulent clothes, and stained uniforms, living quarters (boudoirs, hotel rooms, barracks, desert tents), weapons, dances, jewelry, dice and cards, and animals—especially horses, both racing and in combat. Similes and metaphors often derive from water, flowers, storms, weapons, art objects, and animals. Cigarette alone is likened to a kitten, chamois, a light-winged bird, and a menacing little leopard; in turn, she derogates Corona by repeatedly labeling her a silver pheasant. Ouida names animals so delightfully that anyone in search of a pet moniker should consult *Under Two Flags*. Readers should consider Bay Regent, Blue Ruin, Etoile Filante, Irish Roan, Pas de Charge, Wild Geranium, or Vivandière. Lady Guinevere's horse is Vivandière, whose name prefigures the advent of Cigarette, world literature's most heroic *vivandière*.

The novel is ridiculous if read with the expectation that a novel should be realistic. It contains, however, beautifully sketched natural scenery and the accoutrements of mid-nineteenth century men and women. The novel remains a very exciting book for all its sometimes wearying length, and its moral messages should be inspiring to young and old alike: unrewarded work, hiding one's good deeds, honor, loyalty, discipline, promises kept, developing endurance, and unselfish love.

Ouida reveals much of herself, as well as her times, in this rousing romance. Her father was French; her mother was English; Ouida, whose real name was Maria Louisa de la Ramée, therefore lived, in a sense, under two flags. She criticizes effete English aristocracy (especially the women) and pig-headed French militaristic colonialism alike in *Under Two Flags*, her fourth novel. As soon as it was published, she became immensely popular. The book eventually went into sixty-three editions in English. She was also controversial, being allegedly too intimate with talkative guardsmen at and after smoky dinners. She traveled restlessly; wrote forty-seven books in all; spent her considerable royalties foolishly; came to prefer her many dogs to friends; and died lonely and poverty-stricken in Italy. In *Under Two Flags* two of her most memorable generalizations concern loneliness and old age. She says that "loneliness in the midst of numbers . . . [is] the most painful of all solitude" (chapter 22), and she calls old age "nothing else but death that is *conscious*" (chapter 21). Like Cigarette, Ouida would have wished to die young, full of vigor, and surrounded by virile soldiers.

"Critical Evaluation" by Robert L. Gale

Bibliography:

Beerbohm, Max. "Ouida." In *More*. London: John Lane, 1899. The finest essay ever written on Ouida. Praises her energy, the fascination of her discursive plots, her characters, and her scenic range and store of information. Admires her love of beauty in nature and art.

Bigland, Eileen. *Ouida: The Passionate Victorian*. London: Jarrolds, 1950. Praises *Under Two Flags* as Ouida's deservedly most famous romantic extravaganza. Sees Cigarette as hauntingly vital and lovable, especially when compared to Guinevere and Corona. Admires Ouida's description of desert action.

Porch, Douglas. *The French Foreign Legion: A Complete History of the Legendary Fighting Force*. New York: HarperCollins, 1991. Discusses the maneuvers of the Emir Abd el-Kader, Arab resistance leader, against the French near Oran. In criticizing novels and movies about the Foreign Legion, approvingly quotes one commentator who calls *Under Two Flags* "giddy [and] romantic."

Smith, R. Dixon. *Ronald Colman, Gentleman of the Cinema: A Biography and Filmography*. Jefferson, N.C.: McFarland, 1991. Discusses the 1915, 1917, 1921, and 1936 film adaptations of *Under Two Flags*. Summarizes the considerably altered plot of the 1921 version.

Stirling, Monica. *The Fine and the Wicked: The Life and Times of Ouida*. New York: Coward-McCann, 1958. Includes high praise of *Under Two Flags*. Relates several elements in it to contemporary society, art, and literature, and to Ouida's personal life.

UNDER WESTERN EYES

Type of work: Novel
Author: Joseph Conrad (Jósef Teodor Konrad Nałęcz Korzeniowski, 1857-1924)
Type of plot: Psychological realism
Time of plot: Early twentieth century
Locale: St. Petersburg, Russia, and Geneva, Switzerland
First published: 1911

> *Principal characters:*
> RAZUMOV, a Russian student
> VICTOR HALDIN, a revolutionist
> NATHALIE HALDIN, his sister
> MRS. HALDIN, the mother of Victor and Nathalie
> THE ENGLISH PROFESSOR, a friend of the Haldins

The Story:

A student at the St. Petersburg University, Razumov, while not talkative or gregarious, had been generally respected by the other students. His silences were attributed to profundity of thought, and his behavior inspired confidence and good opinion. Absorbed in his studies, Razumov remained largely indifferent to the impression he made on his fellow students. He dreamed of winning scholarly honors, and he had no wish to become involved in the revolutionary activities that occupied the minds of such acquaintances as Victor Haldin, a youth in whose company he had occasionally spent some time. Razumov's mother was dead; his father, Prince K——, acknowledged his illegitimate son only to the extent of sending him money secretly, through an intermediary. As a result, the unspent feeling that Razumov was unable to direct toward parents or family found its way into other channels. He lavished much of it on his country and felt, in his loneliness, that if he were not a Russian, he would not be anything.

The pattern of Razumov's life was abruptly altered by a strange turn of circumstances. On a snowy morning in St. Petersburg, a sensational event occurred—a political terrorist assassinated a prominent government official and then escaped. An hour or two later, the unsuspecting Razumov returned to his apartment to find a visitor awaiting him. The guest was Victor Haldin. Presuming on his casual acquaintance with Razumov, Haldin had selected the latter's quarters as a place of temporary refuge. When pressed for an explanation, he confessed that he was the killer sought by the police. He asked Razumov to help him in making his escape from the city.

Razumov was dismayed and knew he could be compromised and ruined by Haldin's visit if it ever became known. He went, nevertheless, in search of a driver who might spirit Haldin away, but he found one helplessly drunk. His dismay and despair deepened; finally, Razumov decided that he could not continue to shield Haldin. In his extremity, he broke an unwritten rule by calling on Prince K—— to ask his advice and beg his protection. Prince K—— immediately contacted the authorities, and Haldin was promptly apprehended and executed. After an extended interrogation by General T—— and Councilor Mikulin, Razumov was released, but not before he had been marked down by the councilor's sharp eyes as a tool of great potential usefulness to the government.

Meanwhile, in Geneva, Haldin's mother and sister waited anxiously for news of him. When word of his execution arrived, they were grief-stricken and bewildered. Their efforts to find out the exact circumstances of his end were blocked by the mystery and vagueness that shrouded the whole affair. Nathalie, Victor Haldin's sister, was relieved when she heard that a Russian named Razumov had arrived in Geneva. According to rumors that had been circulating, this man was an escaped colleague of her brother's, a fellow conspirator and revolutionist. Surely he, better than any other, would be able to solve the puzzle of her brother's arrest and execution.

To the Haldins, Razumov proved to be an elusive and enigmatic quarry. He lost himself at once in a circle of revolutionists in exile, including the celebrated Peter Ivanovitch, the legendary Madame de S——, and the sinister Nikita. Among them, he was admired as a hero. Razumov found this role increasingly difficult to maintain, especially after he met Nathalie Haldin and fell in love with her. Razumov finally broke under the strain of maintaining his deception. Through his journal, which he sent to Nathalie Haldin, she learned his true relationship to her brother. On an impulse, he then confessed to the revolutionists the fact that he was a government spy. He was brutally beaten by Nikita, and his hearing was destroyed. Stumbling in front of a tramcar, he suffered from two broken limbs and a crushed side and was picked up by passersby and carried to a hospital.

The tragic story of Razumov might have ended there, but his will to live proved too strong. Nursed back to partial health by a motherly revolutionist, he eventually returned to his homeland. There, in the south of Russia, he shared a two-room cottage with his good Samaritan friend, the devoted Tekla. Some of the revolutionists came to regret the cruel treatment Razumov had received at their hands. Periodically, they visited his cottage to be stimulated by his intelligent and original views on politics, society, and morality.

Critical Evaluation:

Under Western Eyes was written during a time when Joseph Conrad was making great strides forward in his achievement as a writer but was not yet receiving widespread attention. When it was first released, the novel was criticized for its remote and somber subject matter, which took Conrad further away from general public reception, especially since it followed so closely on the heels of *Nostromo* (1904) and *The Secret Agent* (1907), two other books that had garnered much critical acclaim but little public reception. Since then, critical reception of the novel has developed to the point where the novel is now considered to be one of Conrad's greatest achievements.

One of Conrad's aims in writing the book was to attempt to make the Russian character comprehensible to a Western reader, whose only prior experience with Russian themes, perhaps in a cheap novel or popular magazine, might have created a stereotyped impression. The novel is a terrible indictment of Russia, suggesting that Conrad may have been moved to write about what he saw as the truth of the Russian mind-set, which differed little before and after the revolution. Critics have noted the Dostoevskian nature of the novel, but it must be noted that Conrad detested Fyodor Dostoevski, so the novel may be considered a reaction against Dostoevski rather than a tribute to him.

Appearances and their deceptive nature is an important theme in the book. Razumov's quiet and solitary nature leads his fellow students to assume that he is a deep thinker, a strong character, and politically committed, while in reality he is none of these. He is more of a blank page on which others project their hopes, desires, and emotions. Haldin comes to Razumov because of his confidence in Razumov's character. He is the first of many characters to misperceive the actual nature of Razumov's character. Haldin is also blind to the true nature of many other things. He misperceives the nature of Ziemianitch and the inhabitants of the inn where he resides. When Razumov actually goes to the inn and comes upon the people Haldin has described so glowingly, only to find them all shabby and drunk, this provides a humorous, ironic counterpoint. Even when Razumov tries to explain himself to Haldin after the betrayal has been arranged, Haldin never truly understands what Razumov is trying to tell him and goes to his death still blind to Razumov's character. He continually misinterprets Razumov's actions, emotions, and expressions as being favorable, instead of the threats to him that they actually represent.

Haldin is the victim of his own vision, which has blinded him to reality. Razumov and even Ziemianitch become victims of Haldin's ideas, as do Nathalie and her mother, who come to believe his deed not worth the sacrifice. Razumov, ironically, does come to accept that Haldin's goal—revolution—is the way of the future. He, however, cannot bring himself to adopt a cause or to lose himself in a communal effort. Razumov, unlike the revolutionists, is a man without illusions. He is condemned by his lack of illusions to remain cut off from life. Razumov even comes to embrace this isolation, since to be alone is to be free of others' misinterpretations of one's conduct and, especially, of one's words. Razumov illustrates Conrad's idea of the dangers of nonsolidarity.

Coupled with the idea of the nature of appearances, another major theme in the novel is the power of words, for destructive and for constructive purposes. For the narrator, the most striking feature of the Russian national character is its loquacity. Razumov's habit of silence sets him apart and causes his fellow students to consider him "a strong nature—and altogether trustworthy man," a man to whom Haldin unhesitatingly and wrongly entrusts his life.

In the novel, words are either incomprehensible or deliberately concealing. For example, the narrator can never quite grasp what Nathalie means when she talks of ideas, because their "enigmatical prolongations vanish somewhere beyond my reach." For the Russian, silence is dangerous—something Haldin never realizes when placing his trust in Razumov.

Razumov comes to know the awful power of words: "words . . . are the great foes of reality." "Speech has been given to us for the purpose of concealing our thoughts." Early in the novel, Razumov takes great delight in "deceiving people out of their own mouths," as he takes people's words and uses them in continuing his deception. He has been continually misinterpreted and begins to take a perverse delight in fostering this, putting it to his own use. Razumov, continually on the verge of confession, is clearly a poor candidate for a life of intrigue, which makes it strange that the astute Mikulin did not observe this. In his confrontations with the revolutionaries in Geneva, Razumov is compelled to play dangerously with lies and double meanings. He is still under the suspicion that he is being watched and judged and is seized by a spirit of perversity that, together with his hatred of lying and deception, causes him to confess, as he had earlier been driven to confess to Haldin.

Ultimately, his confession to the revolutionaries is motivated by a wish to "escape from the prison of lies." In escaping from lies, Razumov escapes from words. Razumov thinks that silence and invisibility are things to be envied: "The people that are neither seen nor heard are the lucky ones—in Russia," he tells Nathalie. What makes Haldin's crime so unforgivable to Razumov is that "he went around talking of me," thus creating the suspicion in the minds of the police and his fellow students that he had had something to do with the assassination plot.

Razumov's habit of silence is a cause of his original misunderstanding with Haldin and, much later, it is Mrs. Haldin's silence during Razumov's interview with her that is a precipitating factor in his confession to Nathalie. Razumov's silence ultimately destroys him. Ironically, his power lies in silence. His taciturnity inspires confidence. His silence also leads to the misinterpretations of his character that lead to his downfall.

"Critical Evaluation" by Craig A. Larson

Bibliography:

Hay, Eloise Knapp. *The Political Novels of Joseph Conrad*. Chicago: University of Chicago Press, 1963. Studies the variety of political thought and themes in Conrad's work. The chapter on *Under Western Eyes* calls it Conrad's "last great political novel."

Rieselbach, Helen Funk. *Conrad's Rebels: The Psychology of Revolution in the Novels from "Nostromo" to "Victory."* Ann Arbor: University of Michigan Press, 1985. Discusses the consequences of Razumov's speech and silence. Calls the novel "Conrad's most extensive treatment of the theme of betrayal—the psychological motivations behind it and its consequences."

Schwarz, Daniel R. *Conrad: "Almayer's Folly" to "Under Western Eyes."* Ithaca, N.Y.: Cornell University Press, 1980. Contains an excellent chapter on *Under Western Eyes*, focusing on the novel's "rejection of political commitment in favor of personal relationships and private commitments."

Smith, David R., ed. *Joseph Conrad's "Under Western Eyes": Beginnings, Revisions, Final Forms*. Hamden, Conn.: Archon Books, 1991. Five essays by Conrad specialists trace the development of the novel from manuscript to finished work and cover a variety of topics related to the novel.

Watts, Cedric. *A Preface to Conrad*. 2d ed. New York: Longman, 1993. A good starting point for Conrad scholarship, with general biographical and cultural background on Conrad.

THE UNDERDOGS

Type of work: Novel
Author: Mariano Azuela (1873-1952)
Type of plot: Historical
Time of plot: 1914-1915
Locale: Zacatecas, northern Mexico
First published: Los de abajo, serial, 1915; book, 1916 (English translation, 1929)

Principal characters:
DEMETRIO MACÍAS, a poor Indian of Jalisco
LUIS CERVANTES, an opportunistic journalist and political turncoat
CAMILA, a villager
LA PINTADA, "The Painted Lady," a prostitute and camp follower
WHITEY MARGARITO, a sadistic soldier

The Story:

Demetrio Macías was a peaceful Indian who knew nothing about revolutions. When, as a follower of Francisco Indalécio Madero, he was hounded by the political leader of Jalisco, he fled with his wife and child to the mountains. There, federal soldiers came upon the fugitives at breakfast and sent Demetrio fleeing. Wild and lawless, they would have raped his wife if he had not returned with a gun. Being no killer, Demetrio let them go free, only to have them come back with reinforcements and burn his fields. Demetrio then joined a band of sixty sharpshooting rebel outlaws and helped them to drive off twice that many soldiers. During the fighting, two of the rebels were killed, and Demetrio was shot in the leg.

For two weeks, the outlaws remained hidden in a native village, looked after by Indians who hated the government. Venancio, a barber-surgeon, tended Demetrio's wound. The village women used poultices of laurel and fresh pigeon blood to heal him. An attractive young woman named Camila was his nurse.

One day, the pseudointellectual Luis Cervantes blundered into the village and explained that he had deserted the government forces because his commanding officer had assigned him to menial duty. Distrusting Cervantes' glib tongue and big words, the rebels pretended to condemn him to death. One outlaw dressed in a priest's robes and pretended to hear the deserter's last confession in order to determine whether he was a spy. Accepted eventually as a revolutionist, Cervantes then urged the rebels to join the great revolutionary leaders of Mexico. Camila fell in love with him. Although she made her feelings evident, Cervantes never encouraged her, not even on the night of the outlaws' departure. The woman had never responded to Demetrio's lovemaking; he was only an Indian.

Hearing from messengers that Victoriano Huerta's *federales* had fortified the city of Zacatecas, Cervantes urged the band to hurry to join the besiegers and take part in the capture. He flattered Demetrio by telling the Indian that he was more than a common rebel, that he was a tool of destiny to win back the rights of the people.

Demetrio planned a surprise attack on one of the towns along their march, but an Indian guide betrayed the scheme, and the *federales* were prepared to resist. A friendly citizen showed the rebels a back way into the town, however, and the garrison was overwhelmed. The rebels found and stabbed the treacherous guard and killed the federal soldiers who had survived the attack.

By the time General Natera arrived in the district, Demetrio's reputation had grown so great that he was made a colonel in the revolutionary army. Failing to take Zacatecas, the rebels were forced to retreat, discarding their booty along the road. Demetrio thought of going back to Camila, until news of General Pancho Villa's coming excited the rebels and gave them fresh incentive.

During the next battle, Cervantes and Solis, an idealist, took refuge in a place where they thought they would be safe. While they discussed the significance of the revolution, a stray bullet killed Solis. Demetrio's gallant charge turned the tide of battle for Villa and won Demetrio promotion to the rank of general.

While drinking and boasting in a tavern after the battle, Demetrio met Whitey Margarito, a vicious soldier, and La Pintada, a prostitute with whom Demetrio went looking for a hotel room. Her insistence that, as a general, he should occupy a house of his own made him decide to commandeer a fine residence.

During the ransacking, Cervantes found a valuable diamond ring. The soldiers tore the pictures from books in the library and sold the ruined volumes. Whitey, joining Demetrio's forces, ran off with Cervantes' woman companion while Demetrio was arguing the matter of taking her instead of La Pintada, of whom he had tired.

Soon afterward, the rebels raided the house of Don Monico, Demetrio's landowning enemy, and burned the estate. Cervantes, having collected much loot, suggested that he and Demetrio hide it in case they were forced to leave the country. Demetrio wished to share it with the others. Still an idealist, he believed the rebel cause would triumph. Cervantes promised to get Camila for his leader; Demetrio still wanted her above all.

Cervantes went to the village and persuaded Camila to return with him. Believing that Cervantes was in love with her, she was surprised to find herself in Demetrio's bed. The next morning, La Pintada discovered Camila and offered to help her escape. Camila refused. She had found that she liked Demetrio, and she decided to stay with him and the army.

During the march against General Orozco at Jalisco, Whitey showed his cruelty when he tortured a prisoner by tightening a rope around the man's neck until his eyes bulged. Later, when kindhearted Camila persuaded Demetrio to return ten bushels of confiscated corn to a starving villager, Whitey gave the man ten lashes instead. Camila's protests at the incident won her the enmity of La Pintada, who had taken up with Whitey after Demetrio and Cervantes had discarded her. When Demetrio, siding with Camila, ordered the camp follower away, La Pintada became enraged and stabbed Camila.

When Demetrio and his men reached Aguascalientes, they found Villa and Venustiano Carranza, once allies, fighting each other. The federal forces, taking advantage of the disunity among the rebel generals, defeated Villa at Celaya. The defeat was a terrible shock to Demetrio's followers, who could not bring themselves to believe that their idol had been beaten. The rebels were forced to retreat.

Cervantes escaped safely across the border. From El Paso, he wrote to Venancio, the barber-surgeon. He said that Whitey had shot himself, and he invited Venancio to join him in Texas, where, with the barber's money, they could open a Mexican restaurant.

After Villa's defeat, Demetrio found the villagers no longer willing to help the rebels. To them, he and his followers had become outlaws once more. Somewhat discouraged, he decided to return home. He had been away two years and had seen much, but he could not answer his wife's questions when she asked him why he kept on fighting. He lacked Cervantes' glib tongue to put his true feelings into words.

Trying to pacify the landowners of the region, the government sent troops into the uplands after the outlaw band. Once more the rebels and the federal troops clashed. Outnumbered, the outlaws perished on the spot where two years before they had won their first victory. After the fighting had ended, the soldiers found the body of Demetrio Macías. His dead eyes still sighted along the barrel of his gun.

Critical Evaluation:

Mariano Azuela knew firsthand the materials of this novel, for he had served as a military doctor with Pancho Villa's Golden Boys. His vivid account of revolutionary Mexico was first published serially in a small El Paso newspaper. Almost forgotten, it was revived in 1924 and won immediate fame for its author. Pessimism marks this story of "those below"—*los de abajo*—at the beginning of the Mexican Revolution. This is no overall picture of the struggle, but a blending of excitement, cruelty, and beauty as seen through the eyes of a man practically pushed into the struggle, a soldier who fought because the enemy was in front of him. Best known of Azuela's sixteen novels, *The Underdogs* has appeared in dozens of Spanish editions and has been translated into many languages.

This favorite story about the Mexican Revolution still merits its international fame. It has literary and sociological worth. Azuela's honesty glitters in it, because he does not overly caricature the Porfirista enemy even while lampooning him. Neither does Azuela spare the hypocrisies of his own side. His characterization is true to life, and his action scenes are fast and clear. Violence, pathos, beauty, and tragedy are etched against Jalisco's night-blackened hills, so that the reader receives an indelible image of revolutionary pageantry with its women *soldaderas*, bandoliered rebels, uniformed *federales*, and greedy nouveau riche who muddy the pond of revolutionary ideals. While painting only local vignettes of a nationwide holocaust, *The Underdogs* presents both the seedy and the inspiring aspects of the entire event.

The genuine worth of this novel was not recognized until almost a decade after its publication. By the mid-1920's, however, it had been translated into various languages and was considered both a Latin American and a Mexican classic. It was written almost literally amid powder smoke, when Azuela was in despair because he saw that the revolution was drowning some injustices in blood only to spawn others as bad and as self-perpetuating. The virtue of the novel thus lies in its eyewitness impressions of intense, futile events. Azuela captured the excitement of times when bandoliered peons rode and marched off to war to the strains of the "Zacatecas March" or "La Cucaracha," when the Victorian, Bourbonic, ordered age of Porfirio Díaz was dying. Lamentably, it was being supplanted by a violently conceived but stillborn new order that was not even to attempt many of its reforms until many dismal years later.

Ranked internationally as the best novel of the Mexican Revolution, *The Underdogs* helped transform the novel (which, before 1910, had inspired few translations or fame beyond the local region that had produced each novel) into the most important literary genre of Latin America. *The Underdogs* may also be the first Latin American novel whose singular literary style was shaped by the subject matter rather than by academic tradition. For example, time is telescoped to reflect the rapidity of events, while linguistic nuances tinge different aspects of the novel, including characters, scenes, and episodes. Individual members of Demetrio's command symbolize certain features of Mexican society—one soldier is a former barber, others are peons, both poor and prosperous, and there are also prostitutes, virtuous countrywomen, a former waiter, and many other types. Although venal characters are city dwellers and never country folk, the latter are sometimes ignorant.

An elliptical style selects and spotlights a few specific characteristics of a person, a scene, or a situation so as to describe it deftly. Disjointed scenes are thus used, rather than systematic chapters, so as to strengthen the overtone of violent eruption. Selfishness wins, idealism is crucified, and the novel's true protagonist—Mexico's poor—does not march out of misery.

Although fragmented into many swift scenes, the novel is divided into three basic sections. The first section has twenty-one chapters and reflects hope; the last two sections have a total of twenty-one chapters and reflect failure. It is in the latter two portions of the novel that the filth, nastiness, lewdness, and garbage of war are best painted, when persons such as Cervantes realize that the revolutionary issues will not be decided by logic or delicacy but by brute power, as symbolized by self-made, upstart generals who care little for ideals.

Azuela uses colors and details well. The natural dialogue is regionalistic but not difficult and, although each personality uses special shades of language that subtly characterize him or her, there is a high percentage of standard Spanish.

The revolution ultimately disappeared without having helped, but having further flagellated the common people who needed help. Azuela's sympathy in *The Underdogs* is thus always with the poor, whom he neither idealizes nor attacks. For the opportunists who betrayed the revolutionary ideals, he reserves a special sarcasm.

Azuela's masterpiece became the standard novel of the revolution, which was the first significant socioeconomic upheaval in Latin America. Most other revolutionary movements of the preceding years had not sought to aid the submerged masses, the mestizo, the Indian, the laborer, the underdog in general. Following Azuela's example, many Mexican and other Latin American novelists took up the fight for reform, denouncing tyranny and championing the cause of the forgotten. Since 1916, numerous starkly realistic novels have been published throughout Latin America that defend the underdog.

William Freitas

Bibliography:
Brushwood, John S. *The Spanish American Novel: A Twentieth-Century Survey*. Austin: University of Texas Press, 1975. The second chapter of this scholarly work is dedicated to Azuela's best-known novel. Compares and contrasts it to other novels produced in 1916.

Leál, Luis. *Mariano Azuela*. New York: Twayne, 1971. A full-length biography and examination of Azuela's life and works. Asserts that Azuela's novels, especially *The Underdogs*, are the best recording of Mexico's transition from the past to the present.

Rutherford, John. *Mexican Society During the Revolution: A Literary Approach*. Oxford, England: Clarendon Press, 1971. Describes the themes, structure, characters, and social context of Azuela's novels. Discusses Azuela's portrayal of peasant revolutionaries; characters as mouthpieces for the author; and portrayals of Villistas, Indios, and intellectuals during the revolution. Extensive annotated checklist of history and criticism.

Schwartz, Kessel. *A New History of Spanish American Fiction*. Coral Gables, Fla.: University of Miami Press, 1972. A close analysis of the novels of the Mexican Revolution, with an extensive discussion of *The Underdogs*. Describes the novel as Azuela's masterpiece; asserts that Azuela has come close to writing the definitive novel of the Mexican Revolution.

Spell, Jefferson Rea. *Contemporary Spanish-American Fiction*. Chapel Hill: University of North Carolina Press, 1944. A good study of Azuela's novelistic techniques. Chapter 3, which is dedicated to Azuela as portrayer of the Mexican Revolution, contains a description of the characters, events, and methodology of *The Underdogs*.

UNDINE

Type of work: Novel
Author: Friedrich de La Motte Fouqué (1777-1843)
Type of plot: Symbolism
Time of plot: Middle Ages
Locale: Austria
First published: 1811 (English translation, 1818)

Principal characters:
UNDINE, a water spirit
SIR HULDBRAND, a knight
KÜHLEBORN, Undine's uncle
BERTALDA, Sir Huldbrand's beloved

The Story:

Near a forest in Austria there lived an old fisherman, his wife, and their foster daughter, Undine. The nearby wood was said to be inhabited by spirits who were enemies of the mortal human beings living outside the forest.

One day, the young knight Sir Huldbrand of Ringstetten was traveling through the forest when a storm broke. As he rode through the gloomy wood, he was pursued and tormented by manifestations of unearthly folk. At last he came to the edge of the forest and took refuge in the fisherman's cottage, where he was given food and shelter.

Sir Huldbrand was amazed by the beauty of young Undine, who asked him to tell the story of his adventures in the forest. The fisherman, however, forbade the telling and cautioned that it was unwise to talk of spirits at night. Undine—rebellious, mischievous, and untamed—disappeared into the night when her foster father reproved her.

The fisherman and the knight called for her to return, but their voices were lost in the noise of the wind and rain. As the storm increased, they became more worried and finally set out in search of her. It was Sir Huldbrand who found her, safe and sound in the leafy bower where she was hiding. When he returned with her to the fisherman's cottage, he told her of his adventures in the forest. The storm raged so furiously that the cottage and its four inhabitants became cut off by encircling floods.

Sir Huldbrand related how it came about that he traveled through the forest. He had fallen in love with Bertalda, a haughty lady who insisted that he prove his love and courage by a journey through the dreadful wood. At that point in his tale, Undine became jealous of the lady and bit the knight's hand. A few days later, a priest, who had lost his boat in the swirling stream, took refuge on the island. That night he married Undine and Sir Huldbrand. The marriage changed the girl completely. She became submissive, considerate, and full of affection. She had gained a soul.

After the floodwaters subsided, the couple left for the knight's home, Castle Ringstetten. On the way, they went to pay homage to the duke of the domain, and in his hall they met Bertalda. Undine took Bertalda to her bosom and announced that she had a surprise for her. Shortly before, Undine had told her husband that she really was a water spirit, and that she could live on earth only until he rejected her love; then Kühleborn, who ruled the waters, would call her back to her water home. She had lived with the fisherman and his wife since she was a child, having appeared at their cottage on the evening of the day when their own child had, apparently, been drowned.

Undine's surprise, which she arranged with the help of Kühleborn, was to reveal that Bertalda was the long-lost child of the fisherman and his wife. At first the proud lady refused to accept them as her true parents. When she demanded proof of the story, she was identified by a birthmark on her body. Bertalda's foster parents were disgusted with her and cast her off. The next day, Bertalda accosted Undine and Sir Huldbrand outside the duke's castle. Dressed as a poor fishing girl, she had been ordered to sell food to learn humility and the dignity of toil before being allowed to rejoin her real parents. Pitying her, Undine and Sir Huldbrand insisted that she live with them at Castle Ringstetten.

Life did not always go smoothly at the castle. One day, Undine, who was loved by the servants, ordered the well to be sealed. Bertalda wanted the water from it to remove her freckles, and she ordered the seal removed, but Sir Huldbrand insisted that Undine was mistress of the castle and the well remained sealed. Bertalda then decided to go to the fisherman's cottage. She went through the Black Valley, where Kühleborn, who hated her, put all sorts of difficulties in her way. She was finally rescued by Sir Huldbrand and Undine, who had followed her flight.

Later, the three started down the Danube to visit Vienna. Everything went wrong, and the sailors thought the boat was bewitched. Finally, in exasperation, Sir Huldbrand forgot Undine's advice not to remonstrate with her whenever they were close to water. He told her that he was tired of her and her spirit relatives and ordered her to return to her watery home. Although he was sorry as soon as he had spoken the words, he could not recall them; Undine had already disappeared beneath the waves.

Sir Huldbrand grieved at first, but as time passed, he thought less often of Undine. At length he and Bertalda decided to be married. The priest who had married Sir Huldbrand to Undine refused to perform the ceremony, and so they were married by another. Bertalda then commanded the workmen to remove the stone from the well that Undine had ordered sealed. All were terrified when a white figure emerged from the well. It was Undine. She went into the castle and told Sir Huldbrand that he must die.

Sir Huldbrand expired while he looked upon her face, and Undine vanished. There were some who said that she reentered the well. At the funeral, Undine joined the mourners kneeling by the grave, but by the end of the service she had disappeared. Then water sprang forth on the spot where she had knelt, and a stream appeared to flow about the knight's grave. It was Undine surrounding her lover in death.

Critical Evaluation:

Undine appeared in print the year before Jacob and Wilhelm Grimm published the first volume of their classic collection of tales drawn from local oral traditions, *Kinder- und Hausmärchen* (children's and household tales). The German Romantic movement had helped to create an intense interest in the past and the presumably obsolete beliefs preserved in folklore. Proponents of German nationalism, who supported the notion of a German nation, believed that the many small principalities and city states shared a common German heritage that was reflected and embodied in the ideas and images in Teutonic folklore. While the Grimm brothers were preserving and repackaging authentic folklore, Romantic writers like Friedrich de La Motte Fouqué set out to write *Kunstmärchen*, or "art-folktales," which would not merely capture but refine the essence of the Germanic soul.

In *Undine*, Fouqué employs one of the most frequently repeated folkloristic motifs: that of the mortal man who marries a supernatural female but loses her when he breaks some significant condition imposed on the union. In his 1891 *The Science of Fairy Tales*, Edward Hartland calls such tales "swan-maiden" stories after one of the several examples of the motif collected by the Grimm brothers. Another famous version is the story of Melusine, whose husband was forbidden to look upon her naked body on certain days—a tale that was ironically reworked by the greatest of all German Romantics, Johann Wolfgang von Goethe, in "The New Melusine" (1817). Later literary versions, written with *Undine* in mind, include Hans Christian Andersen's "The Little Mermaid" and Oscar Wilde's "The Fisherman and His Soul."

The supernatural world of Teutonic mythology is more closely connected with the world of nature than the French world of faerie, which was exported into Britain by the Norman conquest. Teutonic spirit inhabitants are "elementals" associated with the four elements of Classical belief: kobolds with the earth; sylphs with the air; salamanders with fire, and undines with water. In Austria, where Fouqué's story is set, undines were inevitably associated with the river Danube. The passage from past to future, from wilderness to civilization, is symbolically embodied in the course of the Danube as it descends from the heavily forested mountains to the agricultural plain and the great city of Vienna. This is the journey that Huldbrand, Undine, and Bertalda eventually undertake, which is beset by trouble and brings the fatal moment when Huldbrand's fit of temper allows the waters to reclaim their own. In another kind of story, this banishment of the wild past might have been a merciful release allowing Huldbrand and Bertalda to get on with their lives, safe in the ideological fortress of civilization, but in a *Kunstmärchen* the severance is fatal.

Huldbrand is the story's primary representative of civilized values—values the Romantics were more than happy to link to the chivalric code allegedly observed by the legendary knights who had secured the empire of Christendom and brought Europe out of the Dark Ages. In first abandoning Bertalda in favour of the less demanding Undine, Huldbrand yields to seduction, but not as straightforward a seduction as that featured in many folkloristic versions of the motif. Because Undine is a changeling who has already been traded for Bertalda in infancy, Huldbrand is in a sense falling in love with Bertalda as she ought to have been: poor, humble, and innocent. Unfortunately, although her marriage to Huldbrand makes Undine fully human—which means that she forsakes the values of her own kind for his—what Huldbrand ends up with is a convincing fake rather than the real thing.

When Bertalda tries to make her own journey through the Black Valley to recover her allotted place in the scheme of things, Kühleborn, the supreme spirit of the waters, puts obstacles in her way. Huldbrand and Undine come to her aid and give her the opportunity to continue pursuing her claim. While they lived in secure isolation in his castle, Huldbrand prefers Undine to Bertalda and decides in her favour in the matter of sealing the well. Once they are on the Danube, however, the balance of power is changed. It is inevitable that Huldbrand must pay the price for his confusion. Having betrayed the innocently deceptive Undine, he cannot thereafter forge a lasting union with the chastened and enlightened Bertalda. The soul that Undine acquired by virtue of their union was his, and the ghost of Undine reemerges from the well whose spring nourishes the soil of his estates to claim his life in forfeit.

On the most obvious level, *Undine* offers an allegory of the relationship between nature and humankind, in which nature can never quite be subjugated to the authority of human use because it always retains the final sanction of death. As a wholehearted Romantic, Fouqué is entirely sympathetic to Undine; it is tragic that Huldbrand is unable to be faithful to her and thus unable to secure their harmonious union. Even a wholehearted Romantic had to concede, however, that the forces of nature that produced Undine, and to whom she remains inextricably linked in spite of her temporary domestication, are not nearly as sweet as she seems to be. The story acknowledges that there is a fundamental contest between nature and humankind, one that humankind cannot ever win; the spirits that harass Huldbrand at the beginning of the story cannot prevail by storm and stress because he is a brave young knight, but they have other ways of forcing his capitulation. His bravery cannot withstand subtle seduction, his chivalric values cannot shelter him forever against attacks of bad temper, and—perhaps most important of all, for all its understatement in the text—he cannot remain forever young. In the end, nature wins because the processes of aging are irresistible.

"Critical Evaluation" by Brian Stableford

Bibliography:
Gosse, Edmund. "La Motte Fouqué: A Critical Study." In *Undine*, by Friedrich de La Motte Fouqué. London: Lawrence and Bullen, 1896. Gosse's translation is perhaps the best of several English versions; his prefatory essay discusses the sources and reception of the work.
Green, David. "Keats and La Motte Fouqué's *Undine*." *Delaware Notes* 27 (1954): 34-48. Discusses the influence of *Undine* on John Keats's *Lamia* (1820) and other poems involving supernatural women.
Hoppe, Manfred K. E. "Friedrich de La Motte Fouqué." In *Supernatural Fiction Writers: Fantasy and Horror*, edited by Everett F. Bleiler. New York: Scribner's, 1985. The essay contains an elaborate discussion of *Undine*, connecting its *femme fatale* theme to Fouqué's own experiences.
Lillyman, W. J. "Fouqué's *Undine*." *Studies in Romanticism* 10 (1971): 94-104. Provides a careful dissection of the text.
Mornin, Edward. "Some Patriotic Novels and Tales by de La Motte Fouqué." *Seminar* 11 (1975): 141-156. Places *Undine* and other works by Fouqué in the political context of German Romanticism and German nationalism.